W9-CAP-374

McGraw-Hill Machining and Metalworking Handbook

Other Books of Interest from McGraw-Hill

McGraw-Hill Machining and Metalworking Handbook

Ronald A. Walsh
Manager, Research and Development
Powercon Corporation
Severn, Maryland

McGraw-Hill, Inc.
New York San Francisco Washington, D.C. Auckland Bogotá
Caracas Lisbon London Madrid Mexico City Milan
Montreal New Delhi San Juan Singapore
Sydney Tokyo Toronto

Library of Congress Cataloging-in-Publication Data

Walsh, Ronald A.
McGraw-Hill machining and metalworking handbook / Ronald A. Walsh.
p. cm.
Includes bibliographical references.
ISBN 0-07-067958-4
1. Machining—Handbooks, manuals, etc. 2. Metal-work—Hand books,
manuals, etc. I. Title.
TJ1185.W35 1994 93-22824
671.3'5—dc20 CIP

1 2 3 4 5 6 7 8 9 0 DOC/DOC 9 9 8 7 6 5 4 3

ISBN 0-07-067958-4

The sponsoring editor for this book was Robert W. Hauserman, the editing supervisor was Paul R. Sobel, and the production supervisor was Pamela A. Pelton. It was set in Century Schoolbook by North Market Street Graphics.

Printed and bound by R. R. Donnelley & Sons Company.

This book is printed on acid-free paper.

Contents

Preface

This Handbook contains a vast array of technical data as well as many current American standards important to modern machinists, mechanical design engineers, design draftsmen, and metalworkers throughout industry. Important data from the latest ANSI, SAE, ASTM, ASME, AWS, AFBMA, NEMA, SMI, AGMA standards, and other American standard practices are included in this Handbook for your reference.

The users of this Handbook will also have the ability to review, study and apply many of the basic and specialized engineering and manufacturing disciplines encountered in the machining and metalworking industries. Students in technical teaching facilities as well as experienced mechanical designers, engineers, machinists, and machine operators will find the Handbook, "user-friendly" and indispensable.

The entire machining and metalworking industries together with the American standards have advanced and changed enormously in the past 40 years. Many new machines, processes, and materials have evolved during this 40-year interval and this new material and data are presented in an open and easy to read and understand format which the author hopes will prove valuable to the users of this Handbook throughout industry.

The implementation and application of electronic digital devices, controls, and microprocessors to metalworking machinery, have forever changed from the ways in which metalworking was done in the past. Our modern machines are smarter, faster, and more accurate, allowing higher production rates than previously possible. Previously difficult parts are now easier and faster to manufacture with closer tolerances using the various, newly developed machines, cutting tools, materials, and technologies.

Because of the widespread availability and use of the electronic hand-held calculator, many cumbersome tables such as, natural trigonometric functions and logarithms, functions of numbers, involute functions, sine bar tables, and temperature tables are not included in this modern Handbook, leaving space for new, important data.

Users of this Handbook who would like to see new data and information added to future editions are encouraged to write to the author or publisher with their requests. Your suggestions and comments are welcome; being of benefit to the entire machining and metalworking industries nationwide. The data contained in this Handbook have been developed by thousands of talented people and many industrial leaders throughout the United States over a period of many years. I wish to thank all who have contributed their talents and efforts and made the production of this Handbook possible.

Ronald A. Walsh

Introduction

Machines, machining, and metalworking practices are among the most important elements of modern technology. Almost every modern product manufactured worldwide relies on the vast array of disciplines practiced in these three major elements.

The topics and data presented in this Handbook offer the modern product design engineer, machinist, tool designer, tool maker, and general metalworker a broad base of study and basic information for the practice of their profession or trade.

The author has attempted to assemble all of those basic disciplines, data, and practices which are of prime importance to those associated with the manufacturing and metalworking industries. To be able to understand and practice the basics of the vast amount of data and principles required in these industries is beneficial to all of those associated with these industries. On-the-job training and experience, together with knowing the basics, completes the individual's skills. Specialization in the metalworking industries is, of course, required, but a firm understanding of all of the important basic aspects can only be beneficial to any individual and their company.

This Handbook provides a broad overview of the modern manufacturing and metalworking industrial practices for students in technical teaching facilities and also for the inexperienced product designer and metalworker.

Computers and CNC machine tools and other metalworking machines such as the five axis machining centers, double spindle turning and machining centers, fast wire EDM's with independent axes and RAM EDM machines have made modern metalworking faster and more accurate. Much labor has been reduced in the diemaking processes and other classifications. The conventional manual engine lathes and milling machines have been made more productive with the digital control and read-out panels. The present day 16-bit microprocessors and controllers are being gradually replaced with the new 32-bit CNC units which will allow machining times to be reduced by a factor of 2 to 5.

New cutting tool materials and tool geometries are advancing at a steady pace to improve production rates. The new cryogenic treatment of cutting tools now allows tools to remain sharp two to four times longer than was possible in the past.

The earlier technologies of water-jet cutting, laser cutting, explosive forming, plasma cutting, lost-foam casting, and EDM cutting have all improved to their present, highly efficient state of the art.

This all translates to better productivity and improved manufacturing costs and the possible improvement in the quality of the product. Improving productivity and lowering manufacturing costs does not necessarily indicate an improvement in quality. The term "quality" is being constantly debated in the industry today. Many of the authors of engineering and manufacturing papers and articles today seem to have a problem defining the word "quality," and what it means to different people. I think it would be appropriate to define quality in the broad term, "customer satisfaction and performance." The skills and knowledge of the design engineer, tool designer, die-maker, machinist, and metalworker all dictate, to a great extent, productivity and quality of a product; the satisfied or dissatisfied customer eventually determines the extent of the success of a product manufacturer. Few experienced people have difficulty in recognizing a "quality" product.

With these thoughts in mind, it is the author's and publisher's wish that this Handbook will prove useful and valuable to those users who are, or will be, associated with the metalworking industries in the United States and in developing countries, worldwide.

Acknowledgments

The author and publisher wish to express their gratitude to the following individuals and organizations, whose assistance, technical expertise, and copyright permissions made the production of this Handbook possible. The individuals are: R. Siegel, president, Powercon Corporation; Alex Feygelman, design engineer; Boris Sabintsev, product and tool-design engineer; J. Beylis, manager, manufacturing and tool-engineering; K. T. Walsh, for patience; Robert W. Hauserman and Larry S. Hager, senior editors, McGraw-Hill. The organizations are: Powercon Corporation, Severn, Maryland (manufacturers of electrical power distribution equipment) and Kennametal Inc.

The author gratefully acknowledges the permission granted by Kennametal Inc. to reproduce its technical information appearing in Kennametal's copyrighted catalogues. Further information and assistance may be obtained by writing to: P.O. Box 30700, Raleigh, NC 27622; or telephoning: (800) 248-2580 or (919) 829-5000. The KC, K, KZ, KT, KY, KD, KYON series are trademarks of Kennametal Inc., Latrobe, Pennsylvania, and are used as such herein.

The author also acknowledges these organizations: American Institute of Steel Construction (AISC); American Society of Testing and Materials, Inc. (ASTM); Society of Automotive Engineers (SAE); American National Standards Institute, Inc. (ANSI); American Iron and Steel Institute (AISI); Industrial Fasteners Institute (IFI); Spring Manufacturers Institute, Inc. (SMI); American Gear Manufacturers Association (AGMA); Anti-Friction Bearing Manufacturers Association, Inc. (AFBMA); American Society of Mechanical Engineers (ASME); IMO Industries Inc., Boston Gear Division; THE TIMKEN COMPANY; The Torrington Company; Industrial Information Headquarters, Inc.; and Ruland Co.

ABOUT THE AUTHOR

Ronald A. Walsh is director of research and development at Powercon Corporation in Severn, Maryland. He is the author of the *Electromechanical Design Handbook,* published by McGraw-Hill. An electromechanical design engineer for almost forty years, Mr. Walsh has developed high power switching devices, breakers, control systems, and other new products for the electric power distribution industry. He worked at Cape Canaveral, Florida as liaison engineer on the Titan and Gemini space vehicles and participated in the design of the Apollo aerospace vehicle. Mr. Walsh holds three U.S. patents.

Chapter

1

Modern Metalworking Machinery, Tools, and Measuring Devices

Metalworking machinery, tools, and measuring instruments have advanced considerably in the past 40 years. This chapter will show some of the new machines, tools, and instruments used throughout industry today that allow us to produce parts faster and more accurately than was possible in the past. The widespread use and implementation of microprocessors to control the actions of metalworking machinery will be evident in many of the photographs of modern equipment shown in this chapter. Photographs of other modern metalworking machinery appear throughout the *Handbook* and may be seen in the following chapters.

Common measuring instruments such as the basic micrometer, vernier caliper, depth gage, and dial indicator also have advanced in design and features. Many of these instruments are now digital and provide a direct readout, without having to read a vernier scale, making their use more positive and less prone to reading errors by the machinist or machine operator. Although this is the case, in a later subsection the method of reading scales and vernier scales found on measuring instruments will be explained.

Some of the modern metalworking machines found today in manufacturing facilities and factories nationwide include the following:

- Engine lathes
- Turning centers, automatic and computer-controlled
- Three-axis automatic milling machines, computer-controlled (machining centers)
- Bridgeport-type milling machinesπ
- Surface grinders
- Automatic screw machines
- Threading machines
- Turret lathes
- Universal milling machines (column and knee type)
- EDMs (electric discharge machines), computer-controlled
- Roll-forming machines
- Slitting machines
- Automatic stock cutoff machines
- Cylindrical grinders, center and centerless
- Automatic punch presses, computer-controlled
- Automatic hydraulic brakes
- Hydraulic shears
- Hydropresses
- Yoder hammers
- Hydraulic broaches
- Flame cutters, automatic
- Laser cutters, automatic
- Chemical milling facilities
- Stretcher benders
- Offset or joggle machines
- Structural "ironworkers"
- High-pressure water cutting machines
- Pin routers

- Vertical and horizontal boring machines
- Shapers
- Planers
- Drill presses
- Sanders
- Manual grinders, motor-operated
- Leaf brakes

1.1 Modern Metalworking Machines and Methods of Metalworking

The two most basic machines in the modern machining industry are the lathe and milling machines. Figure 1.1 shows a modern gear-driven engine lathe, and Fig. 1.2 shows an automatic three-axis computer-controlled milling machine (machining center). The milling machine is equipped to automatically change its own cut-

Figure 1.1 Geared-head engine lathe with digital control panel.

Figure 1.2 Vertical machining center with CNC controls.

Figure 1.3 Gear ratio, carriage and spindle speed controls, geared-head engine lathe.

ting tools at the computer's command, in relation to the ongoing operation being performed, as dictated by the direct numerical control (DNC) system. The modern engine lathe is equipped with a quick-change variable-ratio gear box for threading operations, as shown in Fig. 1.3. Three-jaw universal and four-jaw independent chucks are usually employed to hold the rotating stock for turning operations on the modern engine lathe. A digital readout display on the lathe shows the operator the carriage travel and cross-feed locations to three or four decimal places, thus eliminating the reading of the vernier scales on the lathe's controls. The readings are generally indicated for an *xy* axis system.

CAD/CAM (computer-aided design and computer-aided manufacturing) systems are employed throughout industry today to speed up production and balance profits. The following example is typical of operations of machinery in a modern manufacturing plant where computer-aided manufacturing is employed.

Example of CAM through DNC. Direct numerical control (DNC) is the modern method used to control the actions of machine tools by way of computers. In this system, the tool engineering or other department writes the computer program for the "host" computer, which may control more than one machine tool. After the DNC program is written into the host computer, the machine operator in the shop can call the host computer and instruct it to load the memory of the controller on the machine for manufacturing a specific part. The machine operator then instructs the controller on his or her machine to begin the machining operations.

After the part is made, the controller on the machine sends the DNC program back to the host computer, where it is checked and verified. If the machine operator changed a sequence or operating instruction, the host computer will detect the change or changes and indicate this by way of the computer monitor or readout.

In previous times, such a machine was controlled by numerical (NC) tape which was fed into the machine's controller. The pattern of holes in the NC tape provided the digital code signals required to control the operations of the machine. Tapes were cumbersome, time-consuming, and could be damaged easily by handling in the shop. This method is now ancient history, although still in existence in some manufacturing facilities. Modern machines are controlled by fast electronic digital signals coming from the memory of the machines' controller, which, in turn, was loaded by the host computer. You can see a typical machine tool controller on the right of the Enshu 550-V machining center in Fig. 1.2.

Some of the present methods of working metal include the following:

Machining-type operations

- *EDMs.* In electric discharge machines (EDMs), a moving vertical thin wire at a certain frequency voltage is used to do the actual cutting of the metal. A modern EDM is shown in Fig. 1.4. This machine is also DNC, as can be seen from its control panel. Dies of great accuracy are produced on these machines rapidly and economically. These modern machines can produce intricate dies easily that would have been difficult or impossible to produce using the old die-making methods and techniques. Dies produced on this machine can be seen in Chap. 9.
- *Laser.* A powerful laser light beam does the actual cutting of the metal, the light beam path being controlled by the axis controllers on the machine. Figure 1.5 shows a typical laser-cut metal part. This complex part was cut out in approximately 1.2

Figure 1.4 Wire EDM with CNC controls.

min. Complex thin parts whose quantity does not warrant a hard die are produced using this method.

- *Chemical milling.* Large masses of metal may be removed effectively in producing a part using the etching action of chemicals. Very thin and delicate parts also may be produced with chemical milling or etching. A tough photoresistive substance covers the parts of the metal that are not to be removed. Printed circuit board production is actually a chemical milling operation.
- *Automatic computer-controlled machining centers.* Described above.
- *High-pressure water cutting.* In this process, a very high pressure jet of water, loaded with microfine abrasives, is used to cut the material, metal, plastic, or other composition.
- *Flame cutting.* Parts may be cut automatically using the oxyacetylene flame to do the cutting on a machine with a tracer head or computer-controlled *xy* axes. Large, heavy metal parts are produced in this manner, although the outline accuracy is not great. This method has been superseded by laser cutting where metal thickness allows.
- *Forging.*
- *Casting.* See Chap. 18.
- *Extruding.*
- *Impact extruding.*

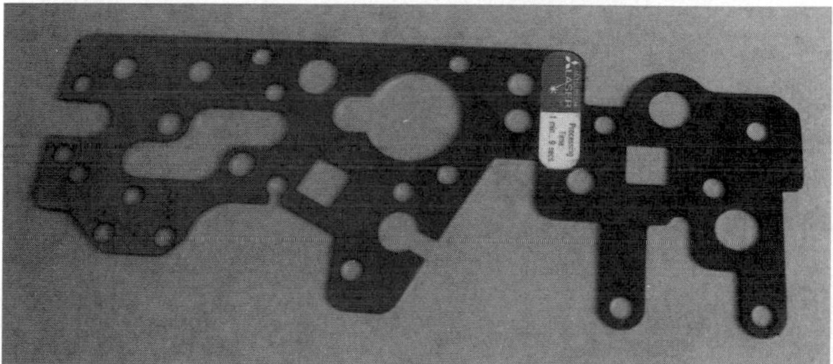

Figure 1.5 A laser-cut sheet metal part.

Sheet metal parts fabrication methods

- *Hard dies.* A die set is used to stamp out the part in flat pattern. Progressive dies also bend the part into the required shape after it is stamped in flat pattern. This is the most common, economical method devised to mass produce large quantities of parts to great accuracy.
- *Punch press.* Large sheet metal parts may be made to accurate standards using modern computer-controlled automatic multistation punch presses. Figure 1.6 shows a large Amada "Coma" machine, which is computer-controlled, very fast, and accurate. A sheet metal panel weighing over 200 lb may be rapidly indexed and punched on this machine. Programmers write the DNC programs for a machine of this type, which are then loaded into the machine's computer or controller. The machine operator starts the program and stands back to watch the machine go through the sequence of operations required to produce the finished part in flat pattern.
- *Roll forming.* Flat strips of sheet metal are fed into the roll-forming machine, where they progress through a set of sequenced

Figure 1.6 High-speed CNC multistation turret punch press.

rollers to produce a long sheet metal part of constant cross-sectional shape.

- *Hydropressing.* A sheet metal flat-pattern part is placed on a set of forming dies, being located correctly with locator pins, and is then pressed into shape by the action of the hydropress. Many aircraft sheet metal parts are produced in this manner. Lightening holes and shrink flutes are produced simultaneously with the part to control the metal along curved surfaces.
- *Hydraulic brakes.* In this machine, the flat-pattern sheet metal part is given flanges or webs to produce the finished part. The modern brakes have automatic back gages and material-handling devices to assist the operator in making the various bends and flanges required on the part. See Fig. 1.7.
- *Hydraulic shears.* The standard hydraulic shear cuts sheet metal according to the back gage set by the machine operator and his or her accuracy in placing the sheet into the machine. In order to ensure a perfect 90° squaring of the flat sheet metal blank, modern shears such as the Weideman "Optishear" are employed. See Fig. 1.8.

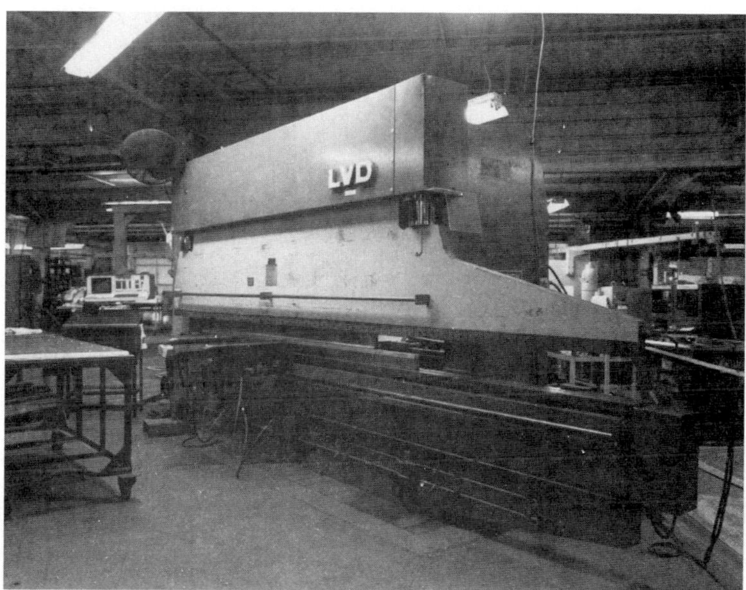

Figure 1.7 A high-tonnage press brake with digital back-gage controls.

Figure 1.8 A Weidemann squaring shear, CNC controlled.

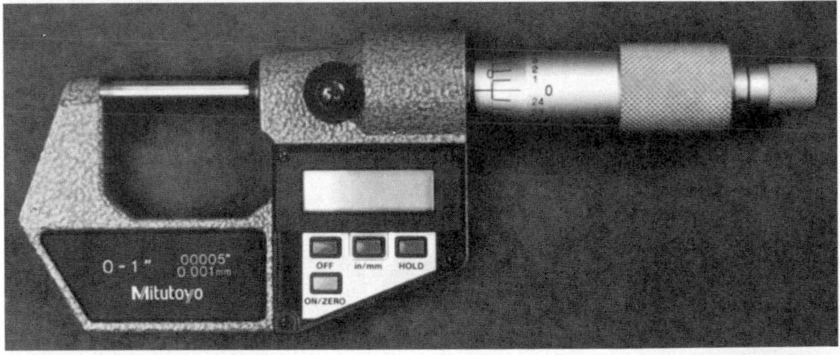

Figure 1.9 New class of LCD digital micrometer. Reading accuracy ±0.00005 in.

- *Explosive forming.* A shaped charge of explosives is placed above the flat pattern of the part, usually under water, and when detonated, the explosive force rams the metal against a die or forming block to produce the final part or subsection of a compound part.
- *Spin forming.* A flat disk of sheet metal is held and spun in a lathe-type machine while forming tools are guided along the part as it is spinning. This is similar to a swaging action on the metal. Only certain shapes of parts are possible to produce with this method.

The preceding examples are the more common methods of producing metal parts today. Specialized metal handling such as Yoder hammering is used infrequently today because this requires a great deal of hand working and operator skill.

1.2 Measuring Instruments

The most common measuring devices used in the modern machine shop are, of course, the micrometer and the vernier caliper. These instruments have gone through a gradual change over the past 40 years to keep pace with modern machinery and higher productivity.

The basic micrometer has progressed from vernier scale to mechanical number scale to the present form of digital electronic display shown in Fig. 1.9. As can be seen, the accuracy of this instrument has increased gradually to the present state shown in Fig. 1.9. The vernier caliper also has gone through this gradual change. A modern vernier caliper is shown in Fig. 1.10,

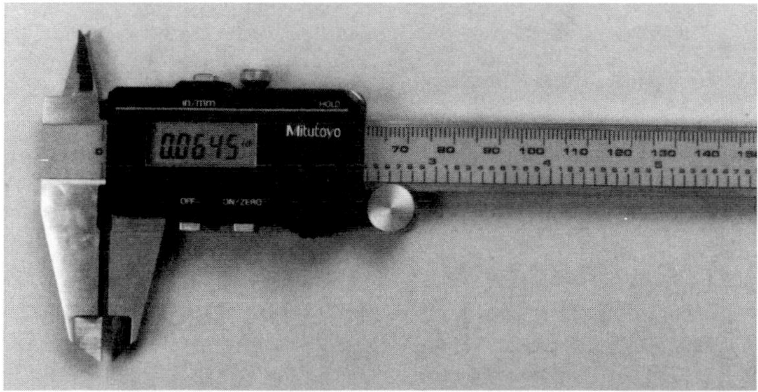

Figure 1.10 LCD digital caliper, 6-in size.

although it is no longer technically a "vernier" caliper because it has no working vernier scale. The application of digital electronics has improved these instruments a great deal, since operator reading errors due to misinterpretations in reading the vernier scale are eliminated. This translates into improved productivity.

Some of the measuring instruments used in industry today include the following:

- Digital micrometer, vernier micrometer (see Figs. 1.9 and 1.11)
- Digital caliper, vernier caliper (see Figs. 1.10 and 1.12)
- Dial indicator (see Fig. 1.13)
- Gage blocks (see Fig. 1.14)
- Sine bar (5 and 10 in) and compound sine bar for double angles
- Sine plate and compound sine plate
- Vernier protractor (see Fig. 1.15)
- "Go, no-go" gages
- Internal telescoping gages (see Fig. 1.16)
- Optical comparator
- Optical flat
- Vernier height gage
- Screw thread micrometers
- Universal surface gages
- Combination squares
- Diemakers' squares
- Steel and plastic scales (see Fig. 1.17)
- Vernier depth gage (see Fig. 1.18)
- Micrometer heads
- Hole gages
- Gear-tooth vernier calipers

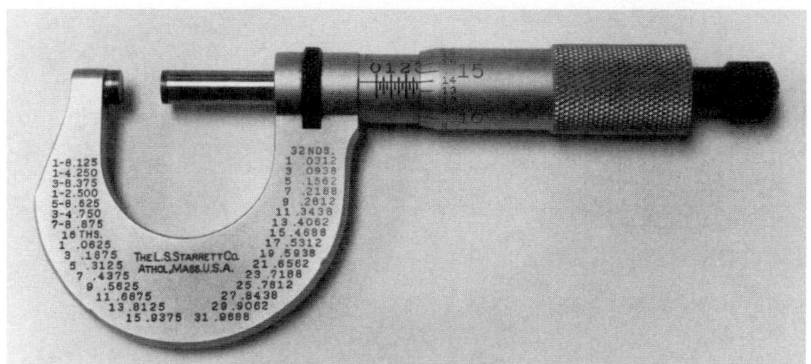

Figure 1.11 The standard "classic" 1-in micrometer, a high-quality instrument, reading to ±0.0001 in.

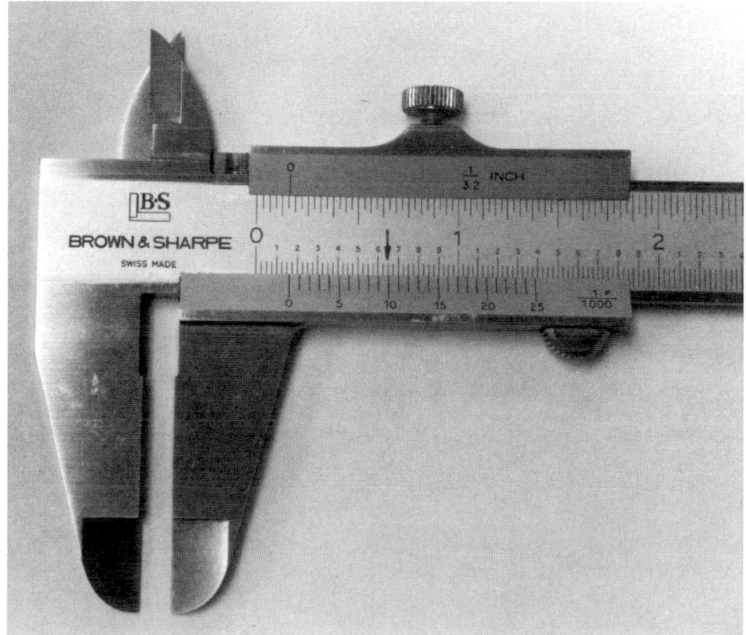

Figure 1.12 A standard "classic" vernier caliper (reading indicates 0.160 in).

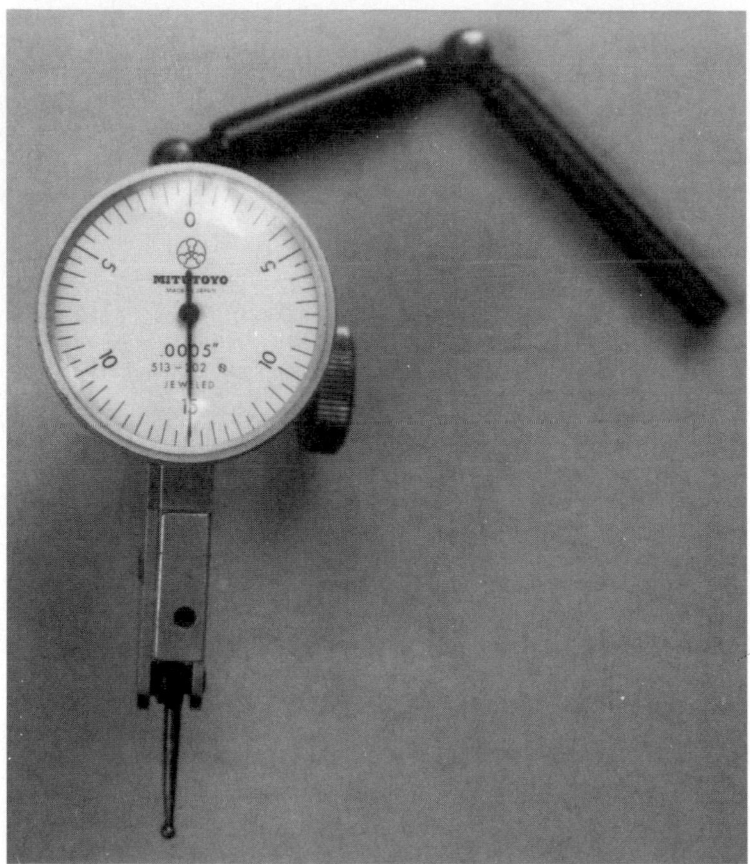

Figure 1.13 A dial indicator reading to ±0.0005-in accuracy.

1.3 Reading Scales, Dials, and Verniers

Figure 1.17 shows a machinist's scale above and an engineer's scale below. The machinist's scale is graduated in thirty-seconds and sixty-fourths of an inch and is read by merely counting the divisions in either graduation. The back of the machinist's scale is often graduated in tenths and one-hundredths of an inch. The engineer's scale is graduated in fiftieths of an inch or 0.02 ins per division. This scale is marked (*) at 1.34 in with the arrow. The bottom of the engineer's scale is divided in millimeters, and 10 mm equals 1 cm. There are 2.54 cm, or 25.4 mm, to the inch, while 1 mm equals 0.03937 in.

Figure 1.14 A set of high-quality gage blocks ("Jo-blocks").

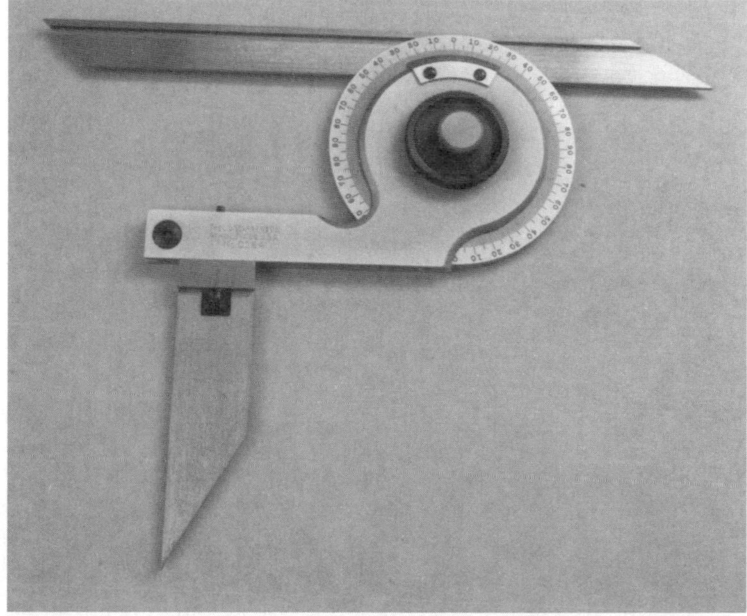

Figure 1.15 A typical vernier protractor for measuring angles to within 5 minutes.

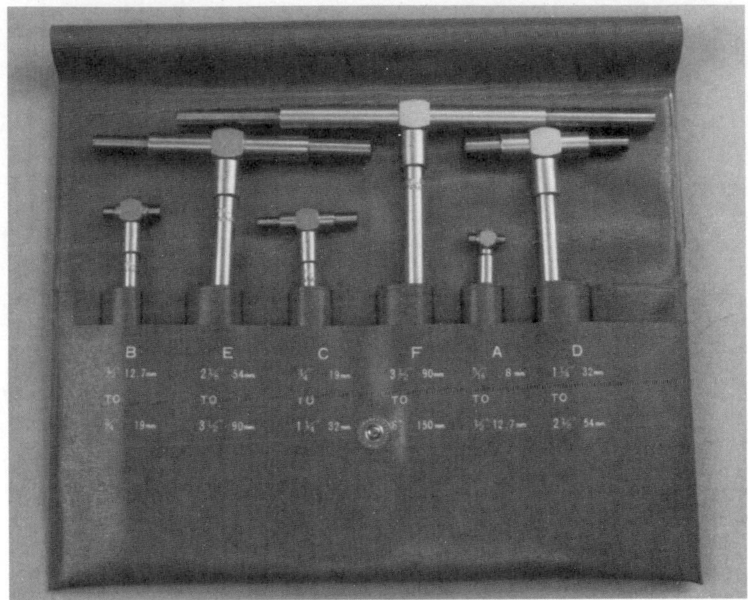

Figure 1.16 A set of inside, telescoping gages.

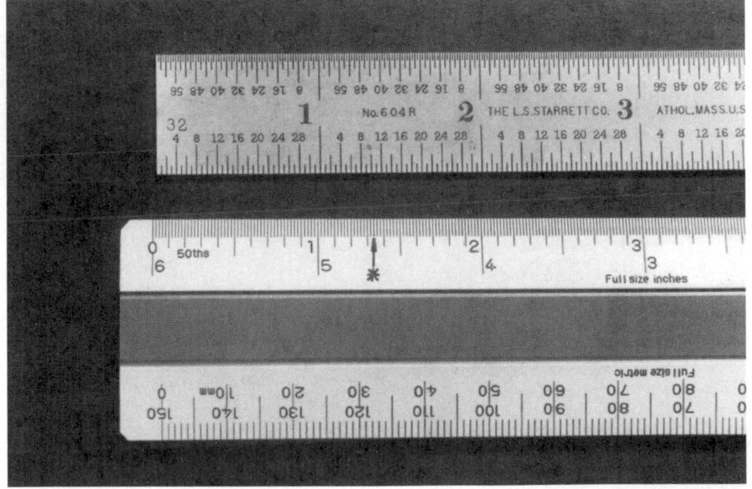

Figure 1.17 Machinist's scale (*top*), engineer's scale (*bottom*). The bottom scale is marked at 1.340 in.

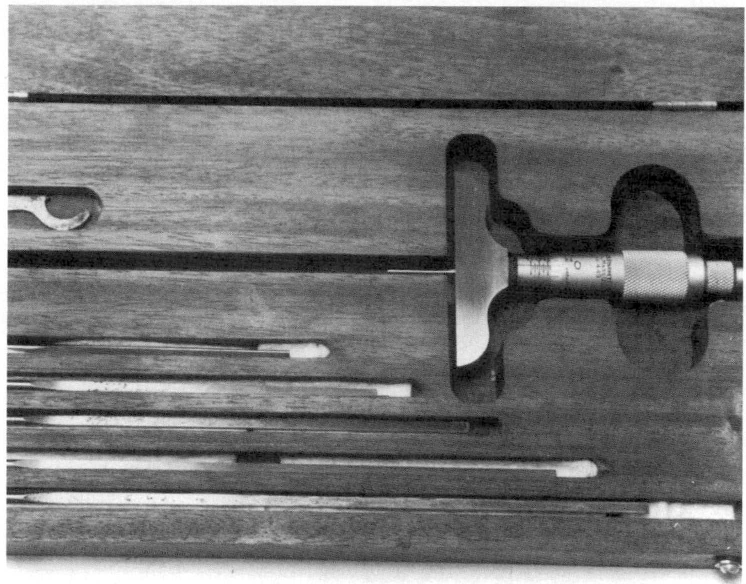

Figure 1.18 Standard micrometer depth-gage set.

The dial indicator is simple to read because its division values are given on the face of the dial (see Fig. 1.13). The dial indicator shown in Fig. 1.19 has been set to zero by turning the outer ring on the dial. When the point of this instrument is set against a lathe-mounted part and the part is rotated, the dial will indicate any eccentricity of the turned part. The small scale on this dial indicator shows the number of revolutions the needle has made to arrive at the final movement or measurement. The dial indicator may be used in any number of measuring applications where a total movement is to be measured. The term *total indicator runout* (TIR) is given on engineering drawings to control the concentricity of a cylindrical part. Thus a drawing instruction of 0.003 in TIR indicates that the part may not be out-of-round by more than 0.003 in total.

The vernier protractor is used to measure angles (see Fig. 1.15). This instrument is graduated to read in increments of 5 minutes of arc. A close-up photo of the protractor's vernier scale is shown in Fig. 1.20. The angle set on this scale is 62°45′ and is read to the left of the vernier zero position. The vernier protractor shown in Fig. 1.21 has a built-in magnifying glass and also reads to 5-minute increments of angle. Figure 1.22 explains how to properly read a vernier protractor.

Figure 1.19 A Russian-made dial indicator (0.01-mm graduations).

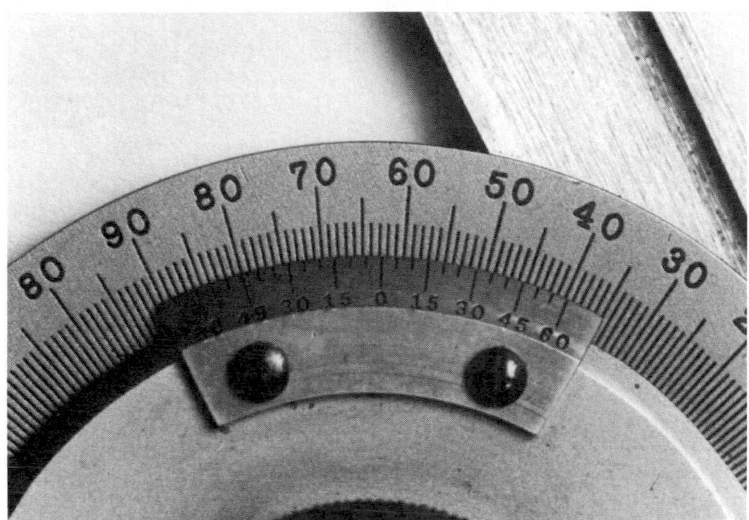

Figure 1.20 Close-up view of vernier protractor scale.

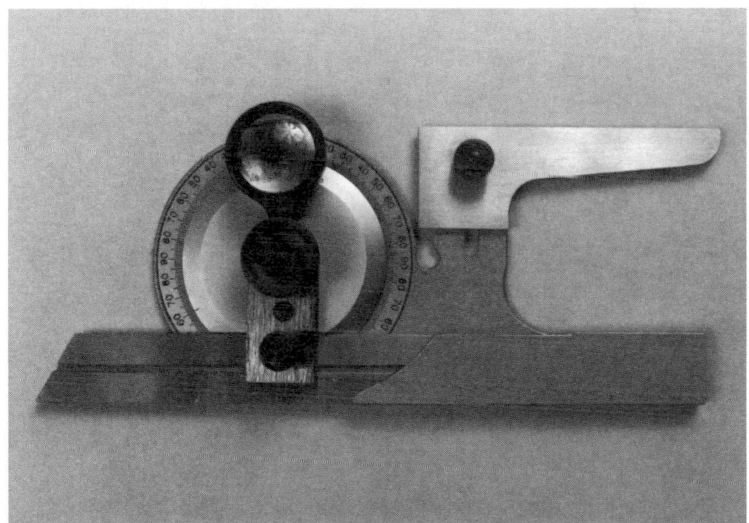

Figure 1.21 A vernier protractor with a scale magnifier.

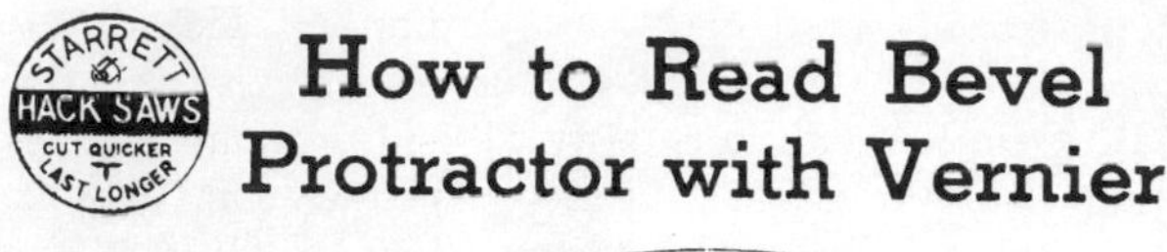

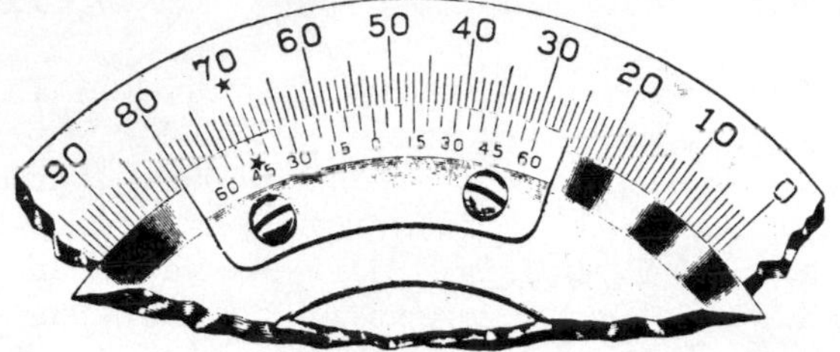

The disc of the Protractor, is graduated in degrees, and can be read to the left or to the right, from the 0 line to 90. It has clear figures each 10th space.

These figures represent degrees. The Vernier plate is graduated in such a way that 12 spaces on the plate occupy the same space as 23 spaces on the disc of the Protractor.

The difference between the width of one of the 12 spaces on the Vernier and two of the 23 spaces on the disc of the Protractor is therefore $\frac{1}{12}$ of a degree, that is to say, 5 minutes (5′).

Each space on the Vernier is $\frac{1}{12}$ of a degree, or say 5 minutes shorter than 2 spaces on the disc. The Vernier plate has clear figures each third space. These figures represent minutes.

When the 0 line of the Vernier plate coincides exactly with a graduated line on the disc of the Protractor, the reading is exact in whole degrees. When the 0 line of the Vernier plate does not coincide exactly with a graduated line of the disc of the Protractor, then find the line on the Vernier that does coincide exactly with a line on the disc of the Protractor.

This line on the Vernier indicates the number of twelfths of a degree or say 5 minutes (5′) that should be added to the reading in whole degrees.

In order to read the Protractor, note on the disc the number of whole degrees between 0 on the disc and 0 on the Vernier. Then count in the same direction the number of spaces from 0 on the Vernier to a graduated line that does coincide with a line on the disc. Multiply this number by 5 and the product will be the number of minutes that should be added to the number of whole degrees.

EXAMPLE: In the cut on this page the number of whole degrees between 0 on the disc and 0 on the Vernier is 52. The line marked 45 on the Vernier coincides with a line (70) on the disc, as is indicated by the asterisks, 9 being the number of spaces from 0 on the Vernier. By multiplying this number (9) by 5, 45 is obtained, the number of minutes that must be added to the number of whole degrees. The reading of the Protractor is, therefore, 52 degrees 45 minutes (52° 45′).

Figure 1.22 Instructions for reading vernier protractors. (*L.S. Starrett Co.*)

The vernier caliper is read in a similar manner. The vernier caliper shown in Fig. 1.12 is set to 0.160 in. Each division on the caliper scale is equal to 0.025 in, so four divisions equals 0.10 in. The vernier scale is in alignment with the caliper scale at the tenth division on the vernier, so the final reading is $0.10 + 2 \times 0.25 + 0.010 = 0.160$ in.

The vernier was invented by Pierre Vernier in 1631. The vernier consists of a small scale having a certain number of graduations which equal in combined length a different number of graduations, usually one more or one less, on a longer scale. Thus there is a small difference between a graduation on the vernier and a graduation on the scale. The readings depend on this difference between the graduations.

Utilizing the principles of the vernier, Joseph R. Brown (Brown & Sharpe) invented the vernier caliper in 1851, the first functional tool available to the machinist for measuring 0.001-in increments accurately.

Chapter

2

Mathematics for Machinists and Metalworkers

This chapter covers all the basic and special mathematical procedures of value to the modern machinist and metalworker. Geometry and plane trigonometry are of prime importance, as are the basic algebraic manipulations. Solutions to many basic and complex machining and metalworking operations would be difficult or impossible without the use of these branches of mathematics. In this chapter and other subsections of the *Handbook,* all the basic and important aspects of these branches of mathematics will be covered in detail. Examples of typical machining and metalworking problems and their solutions are presented in easy-to-understand terms in Chap. 3.

2.1 General Mathematics, Algebra, and Trigonometry

2.1.1 General mathematics and algebraic procedures

If $A/B = C/D$, then

$$A = \frac{BC}{D} \qquad B = \frac{AD}{C} \qquad C = \frac{AD}{B} \qquad \text{and} \qquad D = \frac{BC}{A}$$

Transposing an equation. We may solve for any one unknown if all other variables are known. The given equation is

$$R = \frac{Gd^4}{8ND^3}$$

An equation with five variables, shown in terms of *R*. Solving for *G:*

$$Gd^4 = R8ND^3 \qquad \text{(cross-multiplied)}$$

$$G = \frac{8RND^3}{d^4} \qquad \text{(divide both sides by } d^4\text{)}$$

Solving for *d:*

$$Gd^4 = 8RND^3$$

$$d^4 = \frac{8RND^3}{G}$$

$$d = \sqrt[4]{\frac{8RND^3}{G}}$$

Solving for *D:*

$$Gd^4 = 8RND^3$$

$$D^3 = \frac{Gd^4}{8RN}$$

$$D = \sqrt[3]{\frac{Gd^4}{8RN}}$$

Solve for *N* using the same transposition procedures shown above.

Solving a typical algebraic equation. An algebraic equation can be solved by substituting the numerical values assigned to the variables which are denoted by letters and then finding the unknown value.

Example

$$L = 2C + 1.57(D + d) + \frac{(D - d)^2}{4C} \qquad \text{(belt-length equation)}$$

If $C = 16$, $D = 5.56$, and $d = 3.12$ (the variables), solve for L (substituting the values of the variables into the equation):

$$L = 2(16) + 1.57(5.56 + 3.12) + \frac{(5.56 - 3.12)^2}{4(16)}$$

$$= 32 + 1.57(8.68) + \frac{(2.44)^2}{64}$$

$$= 32 + 13.628 + \frac{5.954}{64}$$

$$= 32 + 13.68 + 0.093$$

$$= 45.721$$

Most of the equations shown in this *Handbook* are solved in a similar manner, that is, by substituting known values for the variables in the equations and solving for the unknown quantity using standard algebraic and trigonometric rules and procedures.

Ratios and proportions. If $\frac{a}{b} = \frac{c}{d}$, then

$$\frac{a+b}{b} = \frac{c+d}{d} \qquad \frac{a-b}{b} = \frac{c-d}{d} \qquad \text{and} \qquad \frac{a-b}{a+b} = \frac{c-d}{c+d}$$

Quadratic equations. Any quadratic equation may be reduced to the form

$$ax^2 + bx + c = 0$$

The two roots, x_1 and x_2, equal

$$\frac{-b \pm \sqrt{b^2 - 4ac}}{2a}$$

When a, b, and c are real, if $b^2 - 4ac$ is positive, the roots are real and unequal. If $b^2 - 4ac$ is zero, the roots are real and equal. If $b^2 - 4ac$ is negative, the roots are imaginary and unequal.

Radicals

$$a^0 = 1$$

$$(n\sqrt{a})^n = a$$

$$n\sqrt{a^n} = a$$

$$n\sqrt{ab} = n\sqrt{a}n\sqrt{b}$$

$$n\sqrt{a/b} = n\sqrt{a} \div n\sqrt{b}$$

$$n\sqrt{a^x} - a^{x/n} \qquad \text{Hence } \sqrt[3]{7^2} = 7^{2/3}$$

$$n\sqrt{a} = a^{1/n} \qquad \text{Hence } \sqrt{3} = 3^{1/2}$$

$$a^{-n} = 1/a^n$$

Factorial. 5! is termed "5 factorial" and is equivalent to

$$5 \times 4 \times 3 \times 2 \times 1 = 120$$

$$9! = 9 \times 8 \times 7 \times 6 \times 5 \times 4 \times 3 \times 2 \times 1 = 362{,}880$$

Logarithms. The logarithm of a number N to base a is the exponent power to which a must be raised to obtain N. Thus $N = a^x$ and $x = \log_a N$. Also $\log_a 1 = 0$ and $\log_a a = 1$
Other relationships follow:

$$\log_a MN = \log_a M + \log_a N$$

$$\log_a M/N = \log_a M - \log_a N$$

$$\log_a N^k = k \log_a N$$

$$\log_a {}^n\sqrt{N} = 1/n \log_a N$$

$$\log_b a = 1/\log_a b \qquad \text{let } N = a$$

Base 10 logarithms are referred to as *common logarithms* or *Briggs logarithms,* after their inventor.

Base e logarithms (where $e = 2.71828$) are designated as *natural, hyperbolic,* or *Naperian logarithms,* the last label referring to their inventor. The base of the natural logarithm system is defined by the infinite series

$$e = 1 + \frac{1}{1} + \frac{1}{2!} + \frac{1}{3!} + \frac{1}{4!} + \frac{1}{5!} + \cdots = \lim_n \to \infty\left(1 + \frac{1}{n}\right)^n$$

If a and b are any two bases, then

$$\log_a N = (\log_a b)(\log_b N)$$

or

$$\log_b N = \frac{\log_a N}{\log_a b}$$

$$\log_{10} N = \frac{\log_e N}{2.30261} = 0.43429 \log_e N$$

$$\log_e N = \frac{\log_{10} N}{0.43429} = 2.30261 \log_{10} N$$

Simply multiply the natural log by 0.43429 (a modulus) to obtain the equivalent common log.

Similarly, multiply the common log by the modulus 2.30261 to obtain the equivalent natural log. (Accuracy is to four decimal places for both cases.)

2.1.2 Plane trigonometry

There are six trigonometric functions: sine, cosine, tangent, cotangent, secant, and cosecant. The relationship of the trigonometric functions is shown in Fig. 2.1. Trigonometric functions shown for angle A (right-angled triangle) include

$$\sin A = a/c \text{ (sine)}$$

$$\cos A = b/c \text{ (cosine)}$$

$$\tan A = a/b \text{ (tangent)}$$

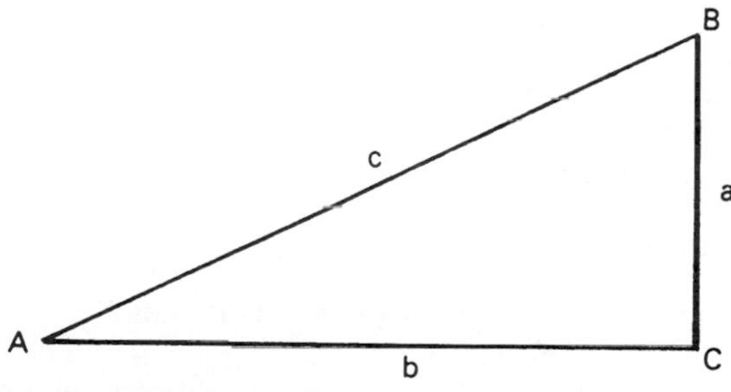

Figure 2.1 Right-angled triangle.

$$\cot A = b/a \text{ (cotangent)}$$

$$\sec A = c/b \text{ (secant)}$$

$$\csc A = c/a \text{ (cosecant)}$$

For angle B, the functions would become

$$\sin B = b/c \text{ (sine)}$$

$$\cos B = a/c \text{ (cosine)}$$

$$\tan B = b/a \text{ (tangent)}$$

$$\cot B = a/b \text{ (cotangent)}$$

$$\sec B = c/a \text{ (secant)}$$

$$\csc B = c/b \text{ (cosecant)}$$

As can be seen from the preceding, the sine of a given angle is always the side opposite the given angle divided by the hypotenuse of the triangle. The cosine is always the side adjacent to the given angle divided by the hypotenuse, and the tangent is always the side opposite the given angle divided by the side adjacent to the angle. These relationships *must* be remembered at all times when performing trigonometric operations. Also:

$$\sin A = 1/\csc A$$

$$\cos A = 1/\sec A$$

$$\tan A = 1/\cot A$$

This reflects the important fact that the cosecant, secant, and cotangent are the reciprocals of the sine, cosine, and tangent, respectively. This fact also *must* be remembered when performing trigonometric operations.

Also, in any right-angled triangle,

$$\sin x = \cos (90° - x)$$

$$\cos x = \sin (90° - x) \qquad (x \text{ is the given angle, other than } 90°)$$

$$\tan x = \cot (90° - x)$$

Equivalent expressions. The following trigonometric expressions are mathematically equivalent and may be used to advantage in solving many trigonometric problems. It is wise to try to remember as many of these expressions as possible, although they may be referred to in this chapter of the *Handbook* as required.

$$\tan x = \frac{\sin x}{\cos x}$$

$$\cot x = \frac{\cos x}{\sin x}$$

$$\sin^2 x + \cos^2 x = 1$$

$$\sin x = \pm\sqrt{1 - \cos^2 x}$$

$$\cos x = \pm\sqrt{1 - \sin^2 x}$$

$$\tan x = \pm\sqrt{\sec^2 x - 1}$$

$$\cot x = \pm\sqrt{\csc^2 x - 1}$$

$$\sec x = \pm\sqrt{\tan^2 x + 1}$$

$$\csc x = \pm\sqrt{\cot^2 + 1}$$

Note. The choice of the ± sign is determined by which quadrant the angle x is situated in (see Signs and Limits of Trigonometric Functions).

Signs and limits of the trigonometric functions. The following coordinate chart shows the sign of the function in each quadrant and its numerical limits. As an example, the sine of any angle between 0 and 90° will always be positive, and its numerical value will range between 0 and 1, while the cosine of any angle between 90 and 180° will always be negative, and its numerical value will range between 0 and 1. Each quadrant contains 90°; thus the fourth quadrant ranges between 270 and 360°.

Quadrant II	y	**Quadrant I**
(1–0) + sin		sin + (0–1)
(0–1) – cos		cos + (1–0)
(∞–0) – tan		tan + (0–∞)
(0–∞) – cot		cot + (∞–0)
(∞–1) – sec		sec + (1–∞)
(1–∞) + csc		csc + (∞–1)
x'		x
Quadrant III	0	**Quadrant IV**
(0–1) – sin		sin – (1–0)
(1–0) – cos		cos + (0–1)
(0–∞) + tan		tan – (∞–0)
(∞–0) + cot		cot – (0–∞)
(1–∞) – sec		sec + (∞–1)
(∞–1) – csc	y'	csc – (1–∞)

Trigonometric laws. The trigonometric "laws" show the relationships between the sides and angles of non-right-angle triangles or acute and obtuse triangles and allow us to calculate the unknown parts of the triangle when certain values are known. Refer to Fig. 2.2 for illustrations of the trigonometric laws that follow.

The law of sines (see Fig. 2.2)

$$\frac{a}{\sin A} = \frac{b}{\sin B} = \frac{c}{\sin C}$$

$$\frac{a}{b} = \frac{\sin A}{\sin B} \qquad \frac{b}{c} = \frac{\sin B}{\sin C} \qquad \frac{a}{c} = \frac{\sin A}{\sin C}$$

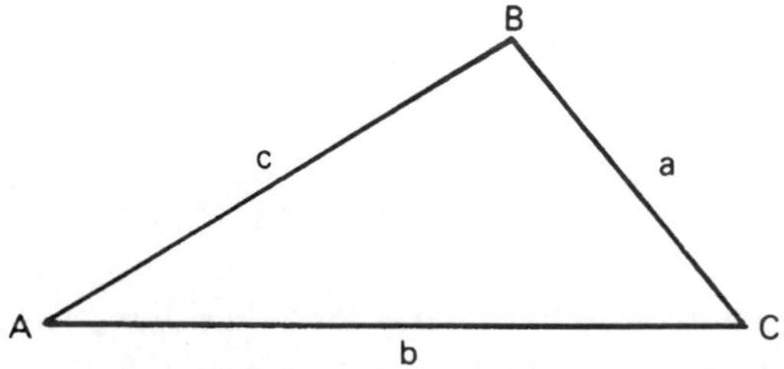

Figure 2.2 Oblique triangle.

The law of cosines (see Fig. 2.2)

$$a^2 = b^2 + c^2 - 2bc \cos A$$

$$b^2 = a^2 + c^2 - 2ac \cos B$$

$$c^2 = a^2 + b^2 - 2ab \cos C$$

The law of tangents (see Fig. 2.2)

$$\frac{a+b}{a-b} = \frac{\tan\dfrac{A+B}{2}}{\tan\dfrac{A-B}{2}}$$

With the preceding laws, the trigonometric functions for right-angled triangles, the Pythagorean theorem, and the following triangle solution chart, it will be possible to find the solution to any plane triangle problem, provided the correct parts are specified.

The Solution of Triangles

In right-angled triangles	To solve
Known: Any two sides	Use the Pythagorean theorem to solve unknown side; then use the trigonometric functions to solve the two unknown angles. The third angle is 90°.
Known: Any one side and either one angle that is not 90°	Use trigonometric functions to solve the two unknown sides. The third angle is 180°; two known angles.
Known: Three angles and no sides (*all* triangles)	Cannot be solved because there are an infinite number of triangles which satisfy three known internal angles.
Known: Three sides	Use trigonometric functions to solve the two unknown angles.

In oblique triangles	To solve
Known: Two sides and any one of two nonincluded angles	Use the law of sines to solve the second unknown angle. The third angle is 180°; sum of two known angles. Then find the other sides using the law of sines or the law of tangents.
Known: Two sides and the included angle	Use the law of cosines for one side and the law of sines for the two angles.

The Solution of Triangles (*Continued*)

In oblique triangles	To solve
Known: Two angles and any one side	Use the law of sines to solve the other sides or the law of tangents. The third angle is 180°; sum of two known angles.
Known: Three sides	Use the law of cosines to solve two of the unknown angles. The third angle is 180°; sum of two known angles.
Known: One angle and one side (non right triangle)	Cannot be solved except under certain conditions. If the triangle is equilateral or isosceles, it may be solved if the known angle is opposite the known side.

Finding heights of non-right-angled triangles. The height x shown in Figs. 2.3 and 2.4 is found from

$$x = b\,\frac{\sin A \sin C}{\sin (A + C)} = \frac{b}{\cot A + \cot C} \qquad \text{(for Fig. 2.3)}$$

$$x = b\,\frac{\sin A \sin C}{\sin (C' - A)} = \frac{b}{\cot A - \cot C'} \qquad \text{(for Fig. 2.4)}$$

Areas of triangles (see Fig. 2.5)

$$A = 1/2bh$$

The area when the three sides are known (see Fig. 2.6) (this holds true for any triangle):

$$A = \sqrt{s(s - a)(s - b)(s - c)}$$

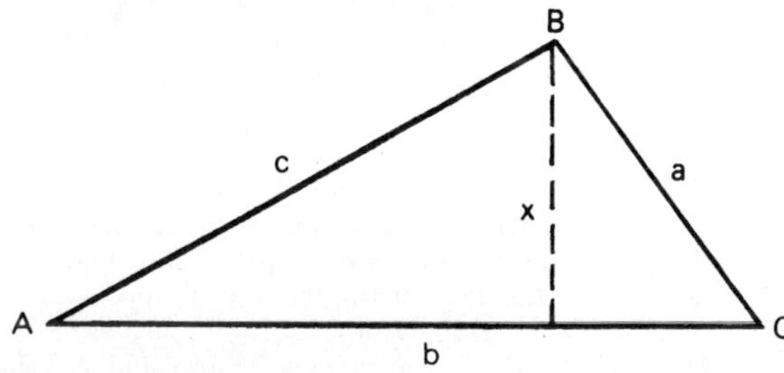

Figure 2.3 Height of triangle x.

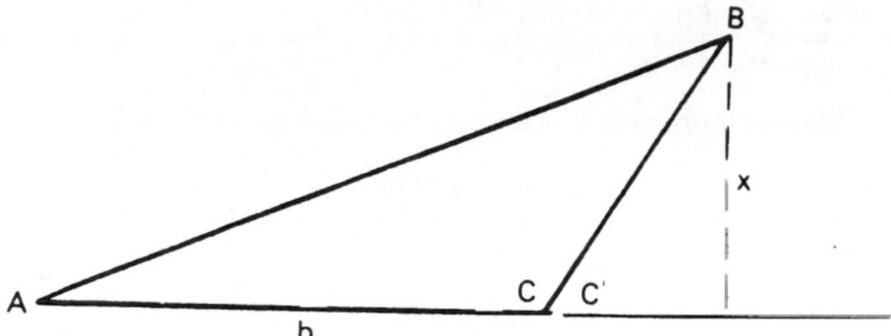

Figure 2.4 Height of triangle x.

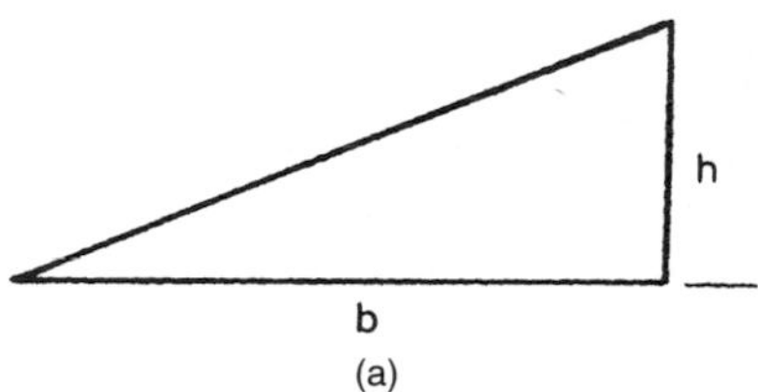

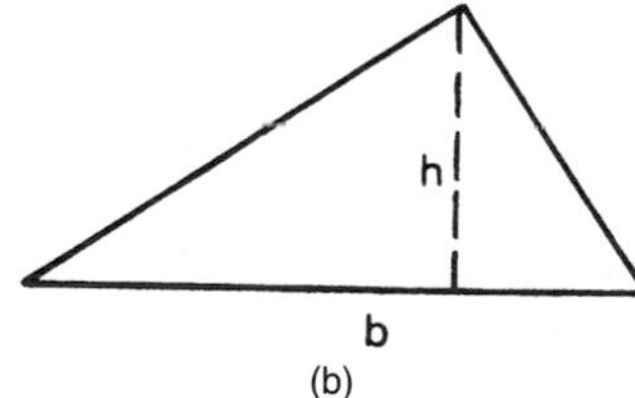

Figure 2.5 Triangles: (*a*) right triangle, (*b*) oblique triangle.

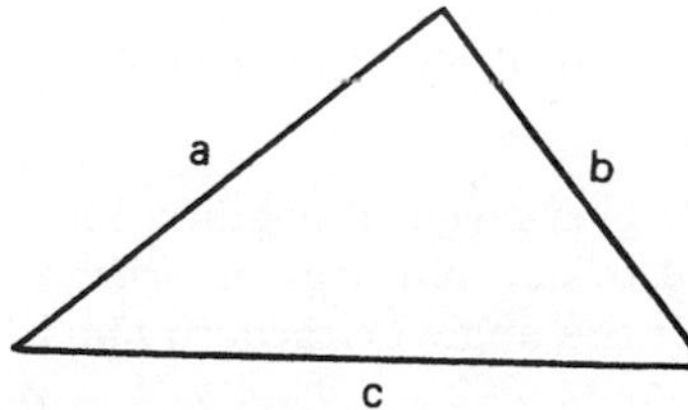

Figure 2.6 Triangle.

where $s = \dfrac{a+b+c}{2}$

The Pythagorean theorem (for right-angled triangles)

$$c^2 = a^2 + b^2$$

$$b^2 = c^2 - a^2$$

$$a^2 = c^2 - b^2$$

Note. Side c is the hypotenuse.

Practical solutions to triangles. The preceding sections concerning the basic trigonometric functions and trigonometric laws, together with the triangle solution chart, will allow you to solve all plane triangles, both their parts and areas. Whenever we solve a triangle, the question always arises, "Is the solution correct?" In the engineering office, the triangle could be drawn to scale and its angles measured, but in the shop this cannot be done with accuracy. Even when the triangle is drawn to scale, the solution can never be exact owing to the tolerances in drawing the triangle. In machining, gearing, and tool engineering problems, the triangle must be solved with great accuracy and its solution verified.

To verify or check the solution of triangles, we have the Mollweide equation, which involves all parts of the triangle. By using this classic equation, we know if the solution to any given triangle is correct or if it has been calculated correctly.

The Mollweide equation

$$\frac{a-b}{c} = \frac{\sin\left(\dfrac{A-B}{2}\right)}{\cos\left(\dfrac{C}{2}\right)}$$

Substitute the calculated values of all sides and angles into the Mollweide equation and see if the equation balances algebraically. Use of the Mollweide equation will be shown in a later section. Note that the angles must be specified in decimal degrees when using this equation.

Converting angles to decimal degrees. Angles given in degrees, minutes, and seconds must be converted to decimal degrees prior to finding the trigonometric functions of the angle on modern handheld calculators.

Procedure. Convert 26°41′26″ to decimal degrees.

Degrees = 26.000000 in decimal degrees

Minutes = 41/60 = 0.683333 in decimal parts of a degree

Seconds = 26/3600 = 0.007222 in decimal parts of a degree

The angle in decimal degrees is then

$$26.000000 + 0.683333 + 0.007222 = 26.690555°$$

Converting decimal degrees to degrees, minutes, and seconds

Procedure. Convert 56.5675 decimal degrees to degrees, minutes, and seconds.

Degrees = 56 degrees

Minutes = 0.5675 × 60 = 34.05 = 34 minutes

Seconds = 0.05 (minutes) × 60 = 3 seconds

The answer, therefore, is 56°34′3″.

Samples of solutions to triangles

Solving right-angled triangles by trigonometry. Required: Any one side and angle A or angle B (see Fig. 2.7). Solve for side a:

$$\sin A = \frac{a}{c}$$

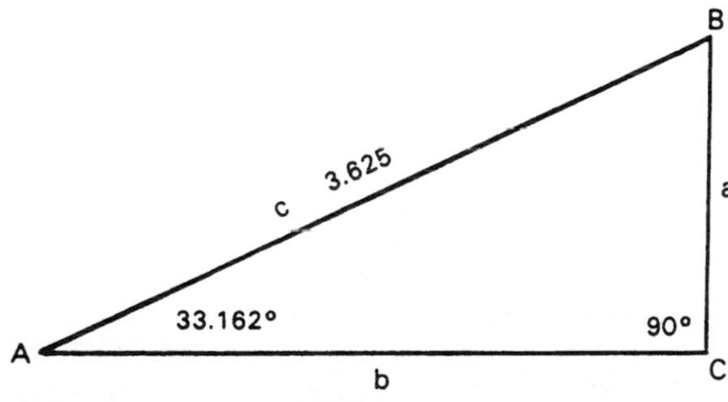

Figure 2.7 Solve the triangle.

$$\sin 33.162° = \frac{a}{3.625}$$

$$a = 3.625 \times \sin 33.162°$$

$$= 3.625 \times 0.5470$$

$$= 1.9829$$

Solve for side b:

$$\cos A = \frac{b}{c}$$

$$\cos 33.162° = \frac{b}{3.625}$$

$$b = 3.625 \times \cos 33.162°$$

$$b = 3.625 \times 0.8371$$

$$b = 3.0345$$

Then Angle $B = 180° - (\text{angle } A + 90°)$
$= 180° - 123.162°$
$= 56.838°$

We now know sides a, b, and c and angles A, B, and C.

Solving non-right-angled triangles using the trigonometric laws. Solve the triangle in Fig. 2.8. *Given:* Two angles and one side:

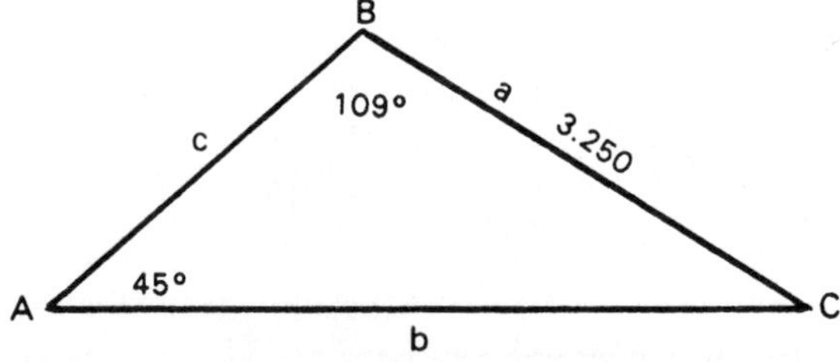

Figure 2.8 Solve the triangle.

$$A = 45°$$

$$B = 109°$$

$$a = 3.250$$

First, find angle C:

$$\text{Angle } C = 180° - (\text{angle } A + \text{angle } B)$$

$$= 180° - (45° + 109°)$$

$$= 180° - 154°$$

$$= 26°$$

Second, find side b by the law of sines:

$$\frac{a}{\sin A} = \frac{b}{\sin B}$$

$$\frac{3.250}{0.7071} = \frac{\text{b}}{0.9455}$$

Therefore, $$b = \frac{3.250 \times 0.9455}{0.7071}$$

$$= 4.3457$$

Third, find side c by the law of sines:

$$\frac{a}{\sin A} = \frac{c}{\sin C}$$

$$\frac{3.250}{0.7071} = \frac{\text{c}}{0.4384}$$

Therefore, $$c = \frac{3.250 \times 0.4384}{0.7071}$$

$$= 2.0150$$

The solution to this triangle has been calculated as $a = 3.250$, $b = 4.3457$, $c = 2.0150$, angle $A = 45°$, angle $B = 109°$, and angle $C = 26°$.

We now use the Mollweide equation to check the calculated answer by substituting the parts into the equation and checking for a balance, which signifies equality and the correct solution.

$$\frac{a-b}{c} = \frac{\sin\left(\frac{A-B}{2}\right)}{\cos\left(\frac{C}{2}\right)}$$

$$\frac{3.250-4.3457}{2.0150} = \frac{\sin\left(\frac{45-109}{2}\right)}{\cos\left(\frac{26}{2}\right)}$$

$$\frac{-1.0957}{2.0150} = \frac{\sin(-32°)}{\cos 13°}$$ (Find sin –32° and cos 13° on a calculator)

$$\frac{-1.0957}{2.0150} = \frac{-0.5299}{0.9744}$$ (Divide both sides)

$$-0.5438 = -0.5438$$ (Cross-multiplying will also show an equality)

This equality shows that the calculated solution to the triangle shown in Fig. 2.8 is correct.

Solve the triangle in Fig. 2.9. *Given:* Two sides and one angle:

$$\text{Angle } A = 16°$$

$$a = 1.562$$

$$b = 2.509$$

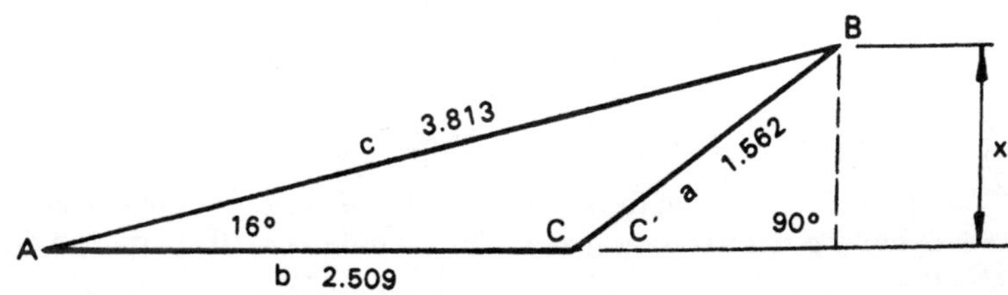

Figure 2.9 Solve the triangle.

First, find angle B from the law of sines:

$$\frac{a}{\sin A} = \frac{b}{\sin B}$$

$$\frac{1.562}{\sin 16} = \frac{2.509}{\sin B}$$

$$\frac{1.562}{0.2756} = \frac{2.509}{\sin B}$$

$$1.562 \sin B = 0.6915 \qquad \text{(by cross-multiplication)}$$

$$\sin B = \frac{0.6915}{1.562}$$

$$\sin B = 0.4427$$

$$\text{Angle B} = 26.276°$$

Second, find angle C:

$$\text{Angle } C = 180° - (\text{angle } A + \text{angle } B)$$

$$= 180° - 42.276°$$

$$= 137.724°$$

Third, find side c from the law of sines:

$$\frac{a}{\sin A} = \frac{c}{\sin C}$$

$$\frac{1.562}{0.2756} = \frac{c}{0.6727}$$

$$0.2756c = 1.0508$$

$$c = 3.813$$

We may now find the altitude or height x of this triangle (see Fig. 2.9). Refer to Fig. 2.4.

$$x = b\,\frac{\sin A \sin C}{\sin (C' - A)} \qquad \text{(where angle } C' = 180° - 137.724° = 42.276°\text{)}$$

$$= 2.509 \times \frac{0.2756 \times 0.6727}{\sin(42.276 - 16)}$$

$$= 2.509 \times \frac{0.1854}{0.4427}$$

$$= 2.509 \times 0.4188$$

$$= 1.051$$

This height x also can be found from the sine function of angle C', when side a is known, as shown below:

$$\sin C' = \frac{x}{1.562}$$

$$x = 1.562 \sin C' = 1.562 \times 0.6727 = 1.051$$

Both methods yield the same numerical solution: 1.051. Also, the preceding solution to the triangle shown in Fig. 2.9 is correct because it will balance the Mollweide equation.

Solve the triangle in Fig. 2.10. *Given:* Three sides and no angles. According to the preceding triangle solution chart, solving this triangle requires use of the law of cosines. Proceed as follows. First, solve for any angle (we will take angle C first):

$$c^2 = a^2 + b^2 - 2ab \cos C$$

$$(1.7500)^2 = (1.1875)^2 + (2.4375)^2 - 2(1.1875 \times 2.4375) \cos C$$

$$3.0625 = 1.4102 + 5.9414 - 5.7891 \cos \mathrm{C}$$

$$5.7891 \cos C = 1.4102 + 5.9414 - 3.0625$$

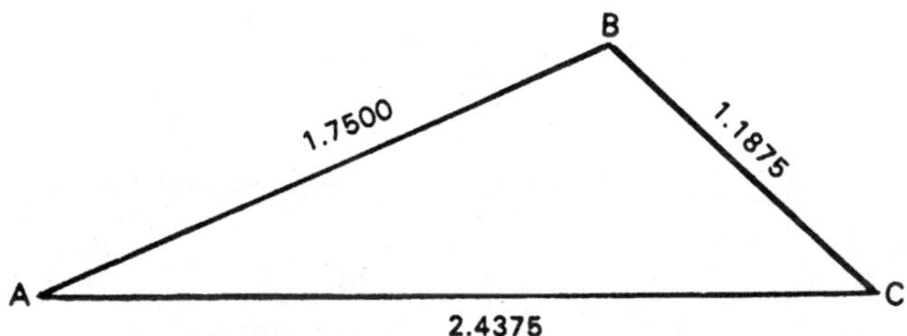

Figure 2.10 Solve the triangle.

$$\cos C = \frac{4.2891}{5.7891}$$

$$\cos C = 0.7409$$

$$\text{arc cos } C = 42.192° \qquad \text{(the angle whose cosine is 0.7409)}$$

Second, by the law of cosines, find angle B:

$$b^2 = a^2 + c^2 - 2ac \cos B$$

$$(2.4375)^2 = (1.1875)^2 + (1.7500)^2 - 2(1.1875 \times 1.7500) \cos B$$

$$5.9414 = 1.4102 + 3.0625 - 4.1563 \cos B$$

$$4.1563 \cos B = 1.4102 + 3.0625 - 5.9414$$

$$\cos B = \frac{-1.4687}{4.1563}$$

$$\cos B = -0.3534$$

$$\text{arc cos } B = 110.695° \qquad \text{(the angle whose cosine is } -0.3534\text{)}$$

Then, angle A is found from

$$\text{Angle } A = 180 - (42.192 + 110.695)$$

$$= 180 - 152.887$$

$$= 27.113°$$

The solution to the triangle shown in Fig. 2.10 is therefore a = 1.1875, b = 2.4375, c = 1.7500 (given), angle A = 27.113°, angle B = 110.695°, and angle C = 42.192° (calculated). This also may be checked using the Mollweide equation.

Proof of the Mollweide equation. From the Pythagorean theorem it is known and can be proved that any triangle with sides equal to 3 and 4 and a hypotenuse of 5 will be a perfect right-angled triangle. Multiples of the figures 3, 4, and 5 also produce perfect right-angled triangles, such as 6, 8, and 10, etc. ($c^2 = a^2 + b^2$).

If you solve the 3, 4, and 5 proportioned triangle for the internal angles and then substitute the sides and angles into the Mollweide equation, it will balance, indicating that the solution is valid mathematically.

A note on use of the Mollweide equation when checking triangles: If the Mollweide equation does not balance,

- The solution to the triangle is incorrect.
- The solution is not accurate.
- The Mollweide equation was incorrectly calculated.
- The triangle is not "closed" or the sum of the internal angles does not equal 180°.

Natural trigonometric functions. There are no tables of natural trigonometric functions or logarithms in this *Handbook.* This is due to the widespread availability of the electronic digital calculator. You may find these numerical values quicker and more accurately than any table can provide. See Sec. 3 for calculator uses and techniques applicable to machining and metalworking practices.

The natural trigonometric functions for sine, cosine, and tangent may be calculated using infinite series equations. The cotangent, secant, and cosecant functions are merely the numerical reciprocals of the tangent, cosine, and sine functions, respectively.

$$\frac{1}{\text{tangent}} = \text{cotangent}$$

$$\frac{1}{\text{cosine}} = \text{secant}$$

$$\frac{1}{\text{sine}} = \text{cosecant}$$

Calculating the natural trigonometric functions. Infinite series for the sine (angle x must be given in radians):

$$\sin x = x - \frac{x^3}{3!} + \frac{x^5}{5!} - \frac{x^7}{7!} + \frac{x^9}{9!} - \frac{x^{11}}{11!} + \cdots$$

Infinite series for the cosine (angle x must be given in radians):

$$\cos x = 1 - \frac{x^2}{2!} + \frac{x^4}{4!} - \frac{x^6}{6!} + \frac{x^8}{8!} - \frac{x^{10}}{10!} + \cdots$$

The natural tangent may now be found from from the sine and cosine using the equality

$$\tan x = \frac{\sin x}{\cos x}$$

Converting degrees to radians. To convert from degrees to radians, you must first find the degrees as decimal degrees (see previous section). If R represents radians, then

$$2\pi R = 360° \qquad \text{or} \qquad \pi R = 180°$$

From this,

$$1 \text{ radian} = \frac{180}{\pi} = 57.2957795°$$

And

$$1° = \frac{\pi}{180} = 0.0174533 \text{ radian}$$

Example. Convert 56.785° to radians.

$$56.785 \times 0.0174533 = 0.9911 \text{ radian}$$

So

$$56.785° = 0.9911 \text{ radian}$$

Example. Convert 2.0978R to decimal degrees.

$$57.2957795 \times 2.0978 = 120.0591°$$

So

$$2.0978 \text{ radians} = 120.0591°$$

2.1.3 Important mathematical constants

$\pi = 3.1415926535898$

1 radian = 57.295779513082°

1° = 0.0174532925199 radian

$2\pi R = 360°$

$\pi R = 180°$

1 radian = $180/\pi°$

$1° = \pi/180$ radians

$e = 2.718281828$ (base of natural logarithms)

2.1.4 The involute function: inv $\phi = \tan \phi - \text{arc}\ \phi$

The involute function is widely used in gear calculations (see Sec. 10). The angle ϕ for which involute tables are tabulated is the slope of the involute with respect to a radius vector R (see Fig. 2.11).

Involute geometry (see Fig. 2.11). The *involute* of a circle is defined as the curve traced by a point on a straight line which rolls without slipping on the circle. It is also described as the curve generated by a point on a nonstretching string as it is unwound from a circle. The circle is called the *base circle* of the involute. A single involute curve has two branches of opposite hand, meeting at a point on the base circle, where the radius of curvature is zero. All involutes of

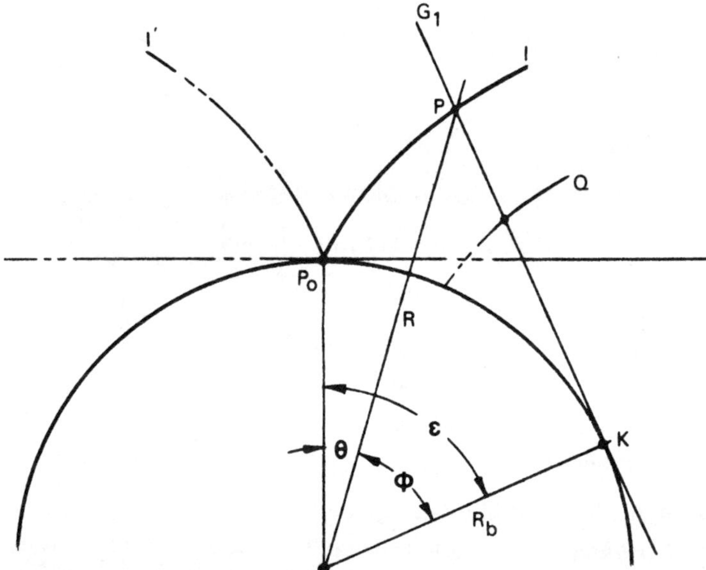

Figure 2.11 Geometry of the involute to a circle.

the same base circle are congruent and parallel, while involutes of different base circles are geometrically similar.

Figure 2.11 shows the elements of involute geometry. The generating line was originally in position G_o, tangent to the base circle at P_o. The line then rolled about the base circle through the roll angle ε to position G_1, where it is tangent to the base circle at K. The point P_o on the generating line has moved to P, generating the involute curve I. Another point on the generating line, such as Q, generates another involute curve which is congruent and parallel to curve I.

Since the generating line is always normal to the involute, the angle ϕ is the slope of the involute with respect to the radius vector R. The polar angle θ together with R constitute the coordinates of the involute curve. The parametric polar equations of the involute are

$$R = R_b \sec \phi$$

$$\widehat{\theta} = \tan \phi - \widehat{\phi}$$

The quantity $(\tan \phi - \widehat{\phi})$ is called the *involute function* of ϕ

Note. The roll angle ε in radians is equal to $\tan \phi$.

Calculating the involute function ($\text{inv}\ \phi = \tan \phi - \text{arc}\ \phi$). Find the involute function for 20.00°.

$$\text{inv}\ \phi = \tan \phi - \text{arc}\ \phi$$

where $\tan \phi =$ natural tangent of the given angle
$\text{arc}\ \phi =$ numerical value, in radians, of the given angle

Therefore,

$\text{inv}\ \phi = \tan 20° - 20°$ converted to radians
$\text{inv}\ \phi = 0.3639702 - (20 \times 0.0174533)$ **Note:** 1° = 0.0174533 radian

$\text{inv}\ \phi = 0.3639702 - 0.3490659$
$\text{inv}\ 20° = .0149043$

The involute function for 20° is 0.0149043 (accurate to 7 decimal places).

Using the procedure shown above, it becomes obvious that a table of involute functions is not required for gearing calculation procedures. It is also safer to calculate your own involute functions because handbook tables may contain typographical errors.

Plotting the involute curve (see Fig. 2.12). The x and y coordinates of the points on an involute curve may be calculated from

$$x = r \cos \theta + r\theta \sin \theta$$

$$y = r \sin \theta - r\theta \cos \theta$$

2.1.5 Summary of trigonometric procedures for triangles

There are four possible cases in the solution of oblique triangles:

Case 1. Given one side and two angles: a, A, B

Case 2. Given two sides and the angle opposite them: a, b, A or B

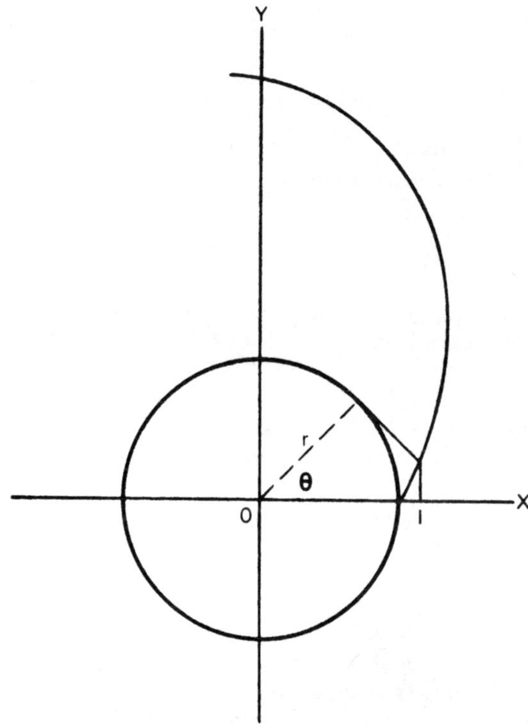

Figure 2.12 The involute curve.

Case 3. Given two sides and their included angle: a, b, C

Case 4. Given the three sides: a, b, c

All oblique (nonright angle) triangles can be solved by use of natural trigonometric functions: the law of sines, the law of cosines, and the angle formula: angle A + angle B + angle $C = 180°$. This may be done in the following manner:

Case 1. Given a, A, and B, angle C may be found from the angle formula; then sides b and c may be found by using the law of sines twice.

Case 2. Given a, b, and A, angle B may be found by the law of sines, angle C from the angle formula, and side c by the law of sines again.

Case 3. Given a, b, and C, side c may be found by the law of cosines, and angles A and B may be found by the law of sines used twice, or angle A from the law of sines and angle B from the angle formula.

Case 4: Given a, b, and c, the angles may all be found by the law of cosines or angle A may be found from the law of cosines, and angles B and C from the law of sines, or angle A from the law of cosines, angle B from the law of sines, and angle C from the angle formula.

In all cases, the solutions may be checked with the Mollweide equation.

Note. Case 2 is called the *ambiguous case,* in which there may be one solution, two solutions, or *no* solution, given a, b, and A.

- If angle $A < 90°$ and $a < b \sin A$, there is *no* solution.
- If angle $A < 90°$ and $a = b \sin A$, there is one solution—a right triangle.
- If angle $A < 90°$ and $b > a > b \sin A$, there are two solutions—oblique triangles.
- If angle $A < 90°$ and $a \geqq b$, there is one solution—an oblique triangle.
- If angle $A < 90°$ and $a \leqq b$, there is *no* solution.
- If angle $A > 90°$ and $a > b$, there is one solution—an oblique triangle.

Mollweide equation variations. There are two forms for the Mollweide equation:

$$\frac{a+b}{c} = \frac{\cos\left(\frac{A-B}{2}\right)}{\sin\left(\frac{C}{2}\right)}$$

$$\frac{a-b}{c} = \frac{\sin\left(\frac{A-B}{2}\right)}{\cos\left(\frac{C}{2}\right)}$$

Use either form for checking triangles.

The accuracy of calculated angles

Required accuracy of the angle	Significant figures required in distances
10 minutes	3
1 minute	4
10 seconds	5
1 second	6

Special half-angle formulas. In case 4 triangles where only the three sides *a, b,* and *c* are known, the sets of half-angle formulas shown below may be used to find the angles:

$$\sin\frac{A}{2} = \sqrt{\frac{(s-b)(s-c)}{bc}}$$

$$\sin\frac{B}{2} = \sqrt{\frac{(s-c)(s-a)}{ca}}$$

$$\sin\frac{C}{2} = \sqrt{\frac{(s-a)(s-b)}{ab}}$$

$$\cos\frac{A}{2} = \sqrt{\frac{s(s-a)}{bc}}$$

$$\cos\frac{B}{2} = \sqrt{\frac{s(s-b)}{ac}}$$

$$\cos\frac{C}{2} = \sqrt{\frac{s(s-c)}{ab}}$$

$$\tan\frac{A}{2} = \sqrt{\frac{(s-b)(s-c)}{s(s-a)}}$$

$$\tan\frac{B}{2} = \sqrt{\frac{(s-c)(s-a)}{s(s-b)}}$$

$$\tan\frac{C}{2} = \sqrt{\frac{(s-a)(s-b)}{s(s-c)}}$$

where $$s = \sqrt{\frac{a+b+c}{2}}$$

2.1.6 Powers-of-ten notation

Numbers written in the form 1.875×10^5 or 3.452×10^{-6} are so stated in powers-of-ten notation. Arithmetic operations on numbers which are either very large or very small are easily and conveniently processed using the powers-of-ten notation and procedures. If you will note, on the hand-held scientific calculator, this process is automatically carried out by the calculator. If the calculated answer is larger or smaller than the digital display can handle, the answer will be given in powers-of-ten notation.

This method of handling numbers is always used in scientific and engineering calculations when the values of the numbers so dictate. Engineering notation is usually given in multiples of 3, such as 1.246×10^3, 6.983×10^{-6}, etc.

How to calculate with powers-of-ten notation. Numbers with many digits may be expressed more conveniently in powers-of-ten notation, as shown below.

$$0.000001389 = 1.389 \times 10^{-6}$$

$$3{,}768{,}145 = 3.768145 \times 10^{6}$$

You are actually counting the number of places that the decimal point is shifted, either to the right or to the left. Shifting to the right produces a negative exponent, and shifting to the left produces a positive exponent.

Multiplication, division, exponents, and radicals in powers-of-ten notation are easily handled, as shown below.

$$1.246 \times 10^4 (2.573 \times 10^{-4}) = 3.206 \times 10^0 = 3.206 \qquad (\textbf{Note: } 10^0 = 1)$$

$$1.785 \times 10^7 \div (1.039 \times 10^{-4}) = (1.785/1.039) \times 10^{7-(-4)} = 1.718 \times 10^{11}$$

$$(1.447 \times 10^5)^2 = (1.447)^2 \times 10^{10} = 2.094 \times 10^{10}$$

$$\sqrt{1.391 \times 10^8} = 1.391^{1/2} \times 10^{8/2} = 1.179 \times 10^4$$

In the preceding examples, you must use the standard algebraic rules for addition, subtraction, multiplication, and division of exponents or powers of numbers. Thus,

- Exponents are algebraically added for multiplication.
- Exponents are algebraically subtracted for division.
- Exponents are algebraically multiplied for power raising.
- Exponents are algebraically divided for taking roots.

2.2 Geometric Principles

In any triangle, angle A + angle B + angle C = 180°, and angle A = 180° – (angle A + angle B), and so on (see Fig. 2.13). If three sides of one triangle are proportional to the corresponding sides of another triangle, the triangles are similar. Also, if $a{:}b{:}c = a'{:}b'{:}c'$, then angle A = angle A', angle B = angle B', angle C = angle C', and $a/a' = b/b' = c/c'$. Conversely, if the angles of one triangle are equal to the respective angles of another triangle, the triangles are similar and their sides proportional; thus if angle A = angle A', angle B = angle B', and angle C = angle C', then $a{:}b{:}c = a'{:}b'{:}c'$ and $a/a' = b/b' = c/c'$ (see Fig. 2.14).

Isosceles triangle (see Fig. 2.15). If side c = side b, then angle A = angle B.

Equilateral triangle (see Fig. 2.16). If side a = side b = side c, angles A, B, and C are equal (60°)

Right triangle (see Fig. 2.17). $c^2 = a^2 + b^2$ and $c = (a^2 + b^2)^{1/2}$ when angle C = 90°. Therefore, $a = (c^2 - b^2)^{1/2}$ and $b = (c^2 - a^2)^{1/2}$. This

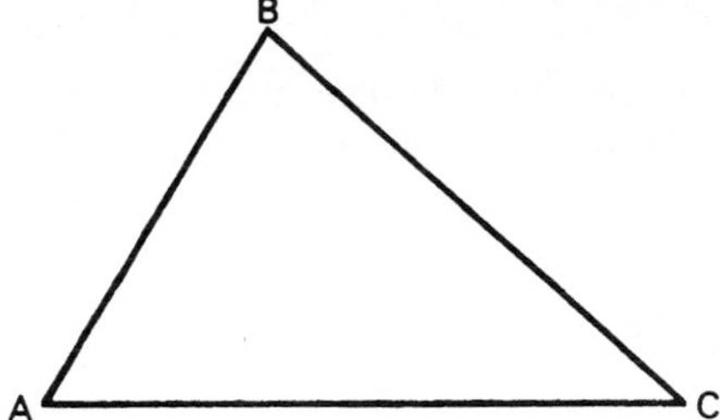

Figure 2.13 Triangle.

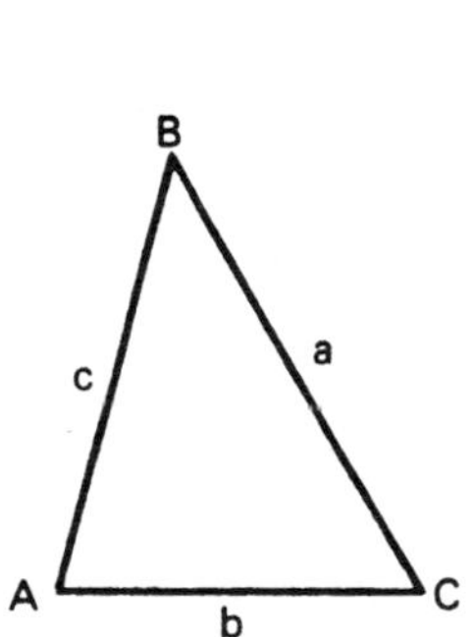

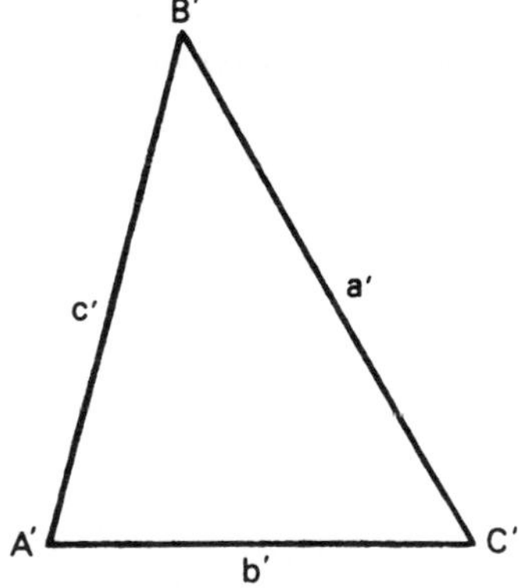

Figure 2.14 Similar triangles.

Figure 2.15 Isosceles triangle.

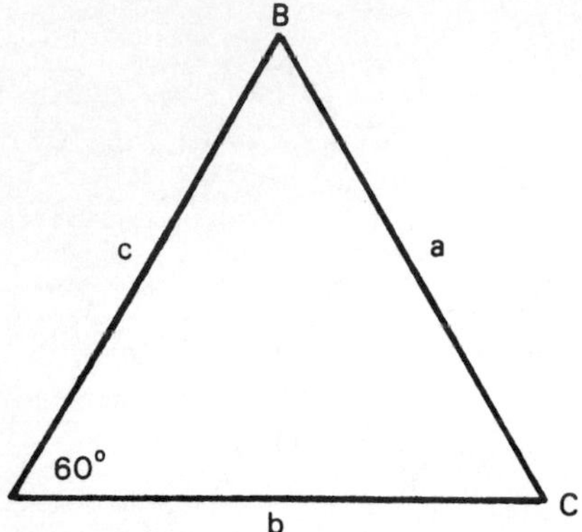

Figure 2.16 Equilateral triangle.

relationship in all right angle triangles is called the *Pythagorean theorem.*

Exterior angle of a triangle (see Fig. 2.18). Angle C = angle A + angle B.

Intersecting straight lines (see Fig. 2.19). Angle A = angle A′, and angle B = angle B′.

Two parallel lines intersected by a straight line (see Fig. 2.20). Alternate interior and exterior angles are equal: angle A = angle A'; angle B = angle B'.

Any four-sided geometric figure (see Fig. 2.21). The sum of all interior angles = 360°; angle A + angle B + angle C + angle D = 360°.

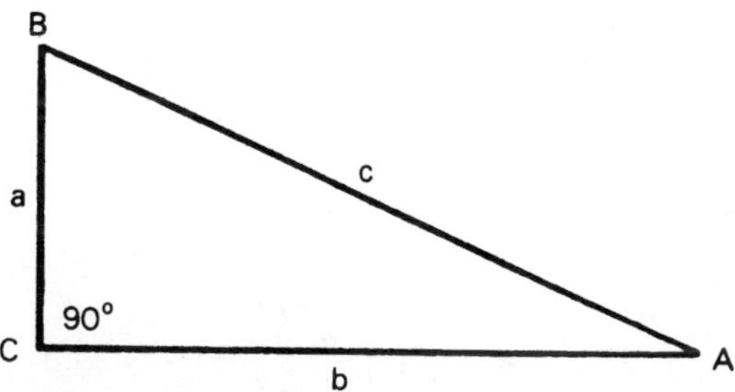

Figure 2.17 Right-angled triangle.

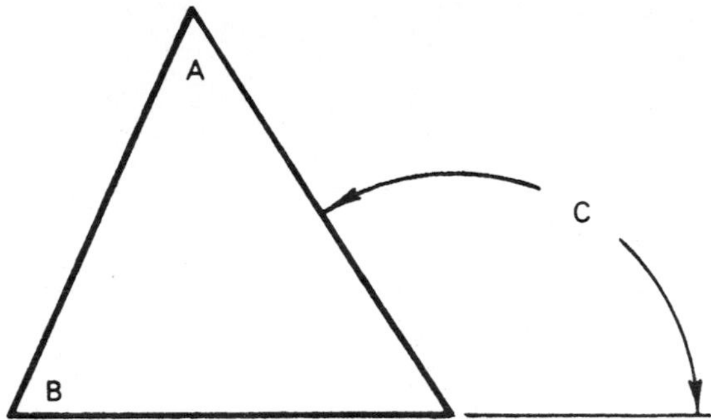

Figure 2.18 Exterior angle of a triangle.

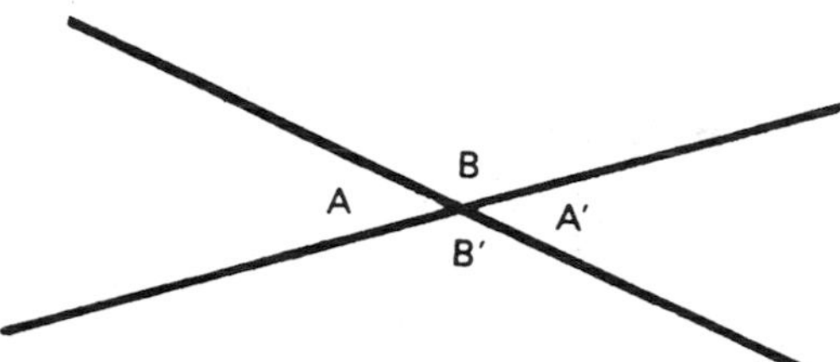

Figure 2.19 Intersecting straight lines.

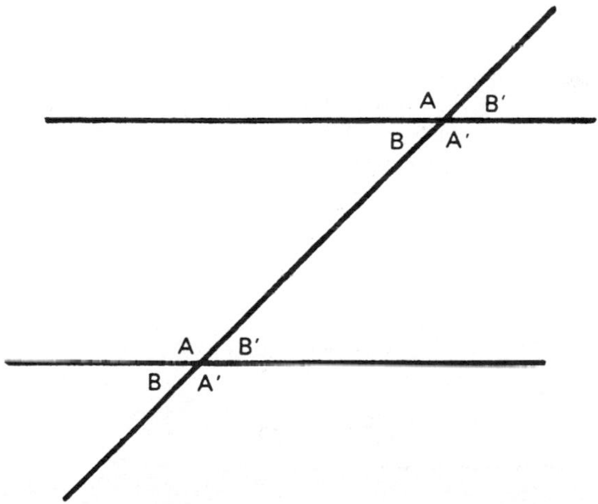

Figure 2.20 Straight line intersecting two parallel lines.

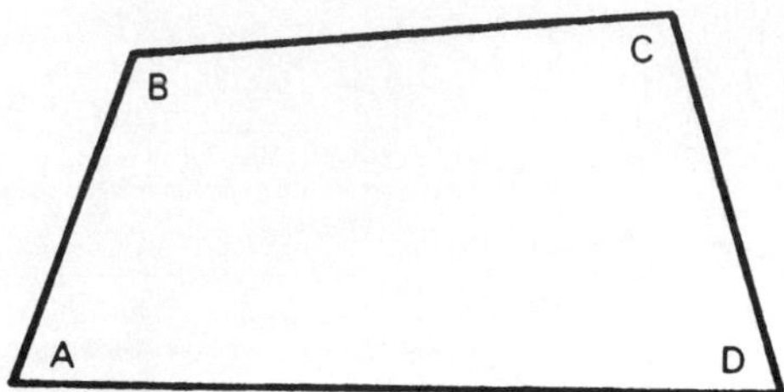

Figure 2.21 Quadrilateral (four-sided figure).

A line tangent to a point on a circle is at 90°, or normal, to a radial line drawn to the tangent point (see Fig. 2.22).

Two circles' common point of tangency is intersected by a line drawn between their centers (see Fig. 2.23).

Side $a = a'$; angle A = angle A' (see Fig. 2.24)

Angle A = ½ angle B (see Fig. 2.25)

Angle A = angle B = angle C. All perimeter angles of a chord are equal (see Fig. 2.26).

Angle B = ½ angle A (see Fig. 2.27)

$a^2 = bc$ (see Fig. 2.28)

All perimeter angles in a circle, drawn from the diameter, are 90° (see Fig. 2.29).

Arcs are proportional to internal angles (see Fig. 2.30). Angle A:angle $B = a{:}b$. Thus, if angle A = 89°, angle B = 30° and arc a = 2.15 minutes. Arc b would be calculated as

$$\frac{\text{Angle } A}{\text{Angle } B} = \frac{a}{b}$$

$$\frac{89}{30} = \frac{2.15}{b}$$

$$89b = 30 \times 2.15$$

$$= 64.5$$

$$b = 0.7247 \text{ minutes}$$

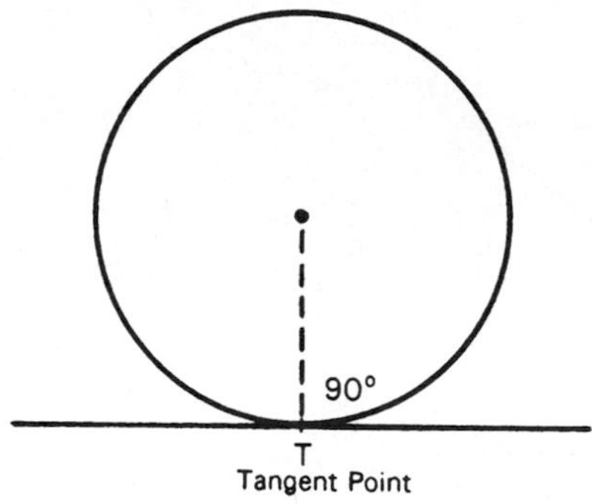

Figure 2.22 Tangent at a point on a circle.

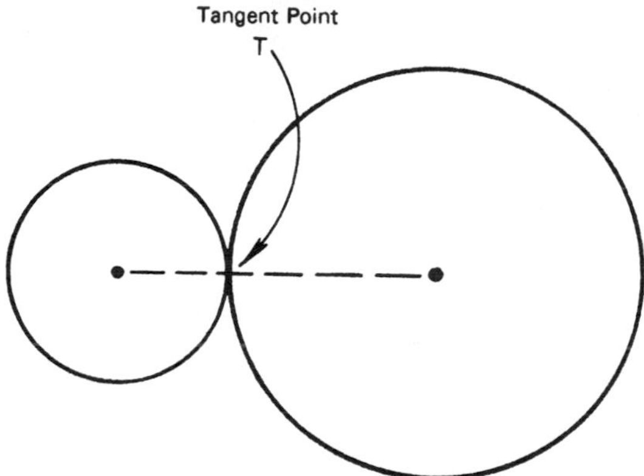

Figure 2.23 Common point of tangency.

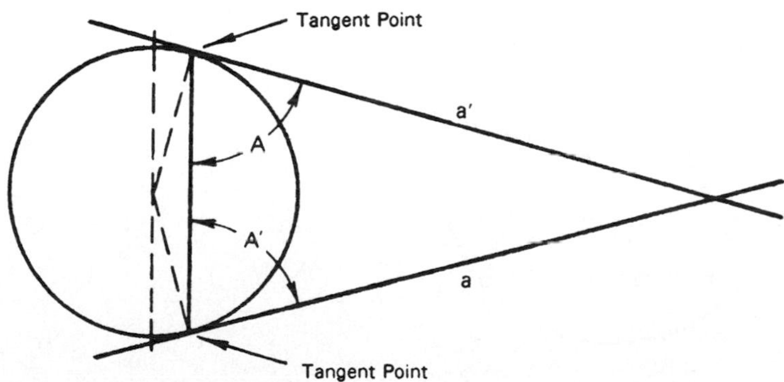

Figure 2.24 Tangents and angles.

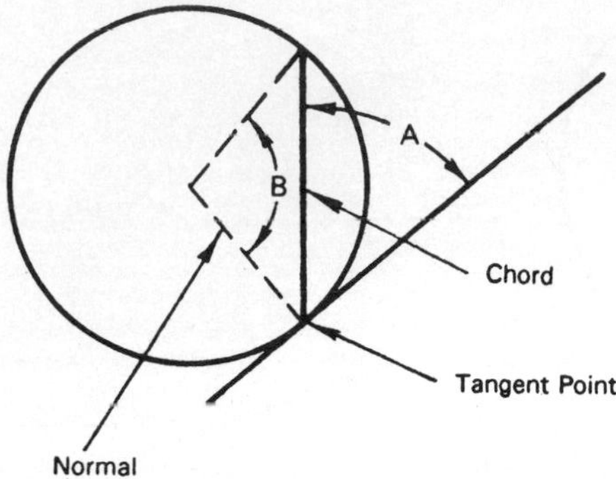

Figure 2.25 Half-angle (A).

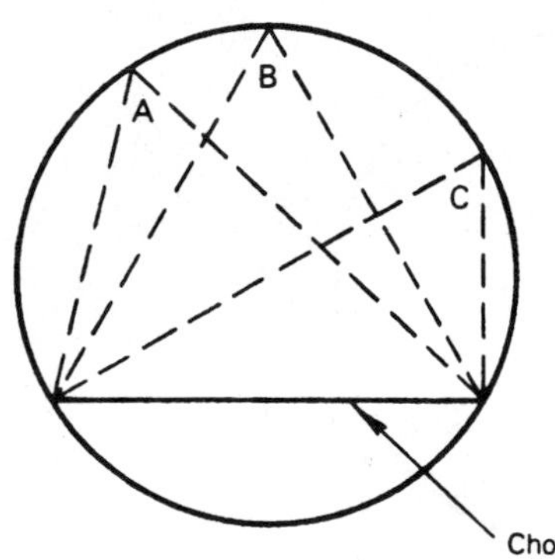

Figure 2.26 Perimeter angles of a chord.

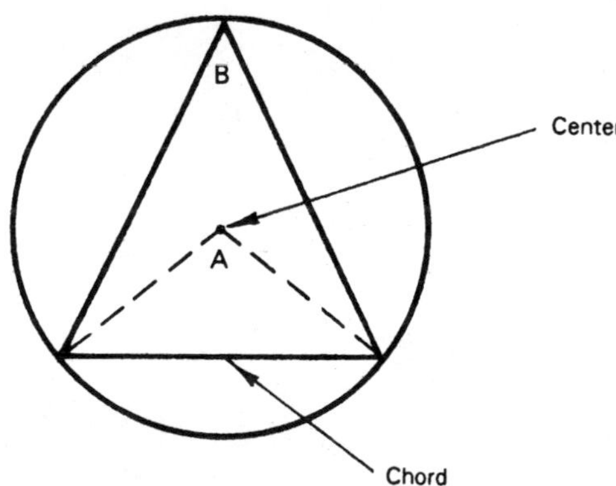

Figure 2.27 Half-angle (B).

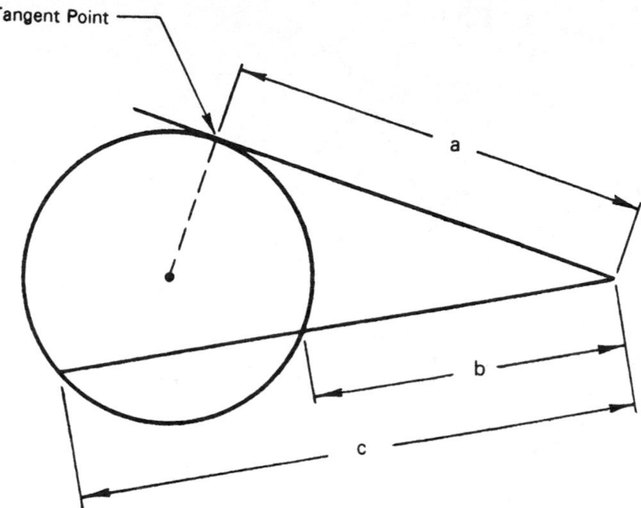

Figure 2.28 Line and circle relationship ($a^2=bc$).

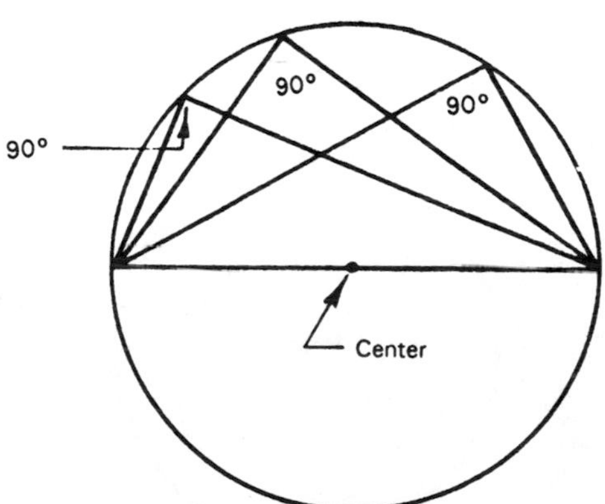

Figure 2.29 90° perimeter angles.

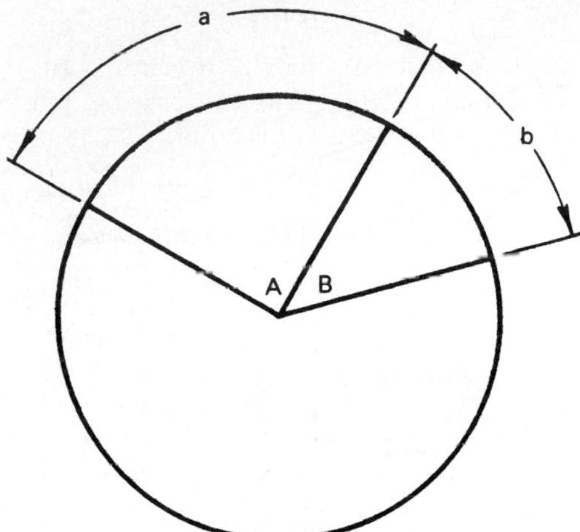

Figure 2.30 Proportional arcs and angles.

Note. The angles may be given in decimal degrees or radians, consistently.

Circumferences are proportional to their respective radii (see Fig. 2.31). $C{:}C' = r{:}R$, and areas are proportional to the squares of the respective radii.

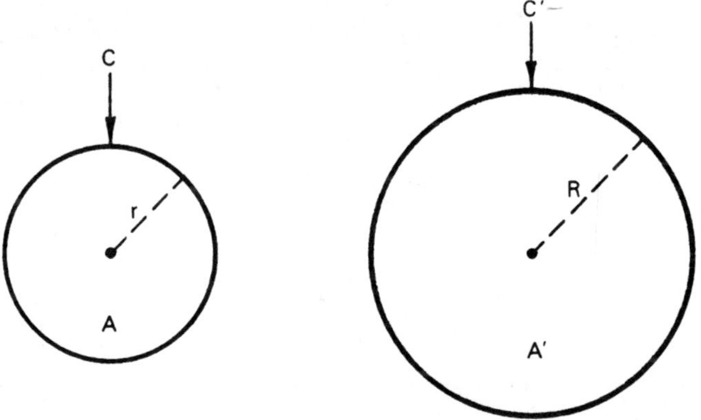

Figure 2.31 Circumference and radii proportionality.

2.3 Geometric Construction

The following figures show the methods used to perform most of the basic geometric constructions used in standard drawing practices. Many of these constructions have widespread use in the machine shop and sheet metal shop.

- *To divide any straight line into any number of equal spaces* (Fig. 2.32). To divide line *AB* into five equal spaces, draw line *AC* at any convenient angle such as angle *BAC*. With a divider or compass, mark off five equal spaces along line *AC* with a divider or compass. Now connect point 5 on line *AC* with the endpoint of line *AB*. Draw line *CB*, and parallel transfer the other points along line *AC* to intersect line *AB*, thus dividing it into five equal spaces.
- *To bisect any angle BAC* (Fig. 2.33), swing an arc from point *A* through points *d* and *e*. Swing an arc from point *d* and another equal arc from point *e*. The intersection of these two arcs will be at point *f*. Draw a line from point *A* to point *f*, forming the bisector line *AD*.
- *To divide any line into two equal parts and erect a perpendicular* (Fig. 2.34), draw an arc from point *A* that is more than half the length of line *AB*. Using the same arc length, draw another arc from point *B*. The intersection points of the two arcs meet at points *c* and *d*. Draw the perpendicular bisector line *cd*.
- *To erect a perpendicular line through any point along a line* (Fig. 2.35), from point *c* along line *AB*, mark points 1 and 2 equidistant from point *c*. Select an arc length on the compass greater

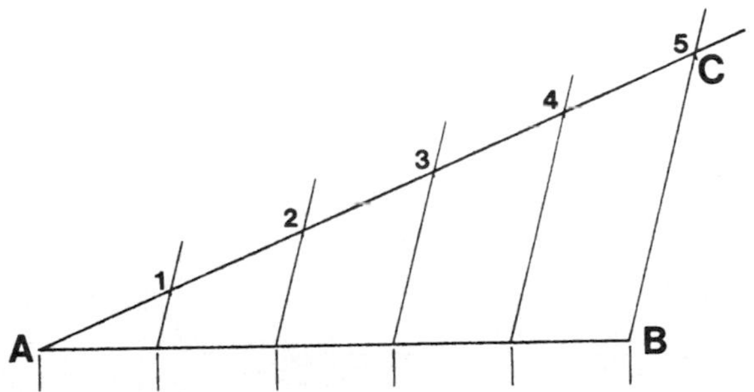

Figure 2.32 Dividing a line equally.

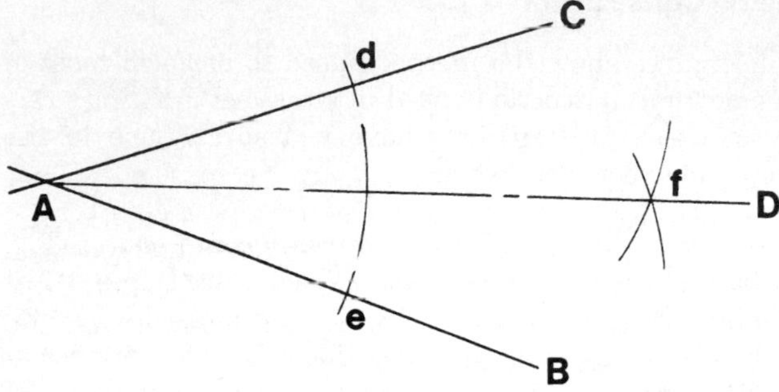

Figure 2.33 Bisecting an angle.

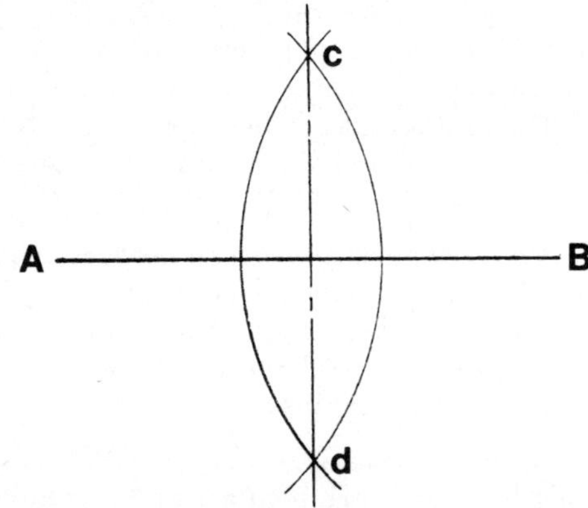

Figure 2.34 Erecting a perpendicular.

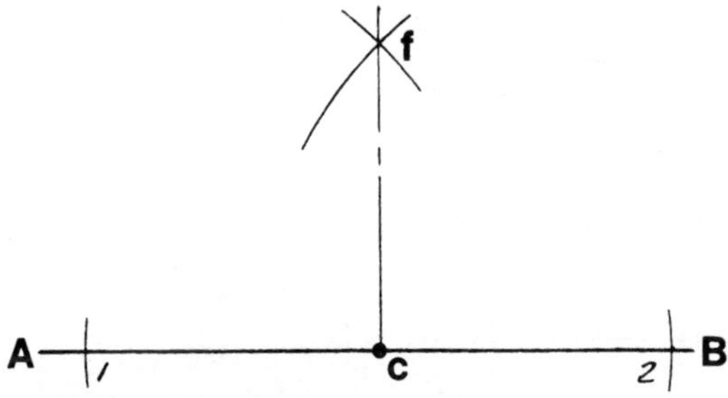

Figure 2.35 Perpendicular to a point.

than the distance from points 1 to *c* or points 2 to *c*. Swing this arc from point 1 and point 2. The intersection of the arcs is at point *f*. Draw a line from point *f* to point *c*, which is perpendicular to line *AB*.

- *To draw a perpendicular to a line AB, from a point f, a distance from it* (Fig. 2.36), with point *f* as a center, draw a circular arc intersecting line *AB* at points *c* and *d*. With points *c* and *d* as centers, draw circular arcs with radii longer than half the distance between points *c* and *d*. These arcs intersect at point *e*, and line *fe* is the required perpendicular.
- *To draw a circular arc with a given radius through two given points* (Fig. 2.37), with points *A* and *B* as centers and the set given radius, draw circular arcs intersecting at point *f*. With point *f* as a center, draw the circular arc which will intersect both points *A* and *B*.
- *To find the center of a circle or the arc of a circle* (Fig. 2.38), select three points on the perimeter of the given circle such as *A, B,* and *C*. With each of these points as a center and the same radius, describe arcs which intersect each other. Through the points of intersection, draw lines *fb* and *fd*. The intersection point of these two lines is the center of the circle or circular arc.

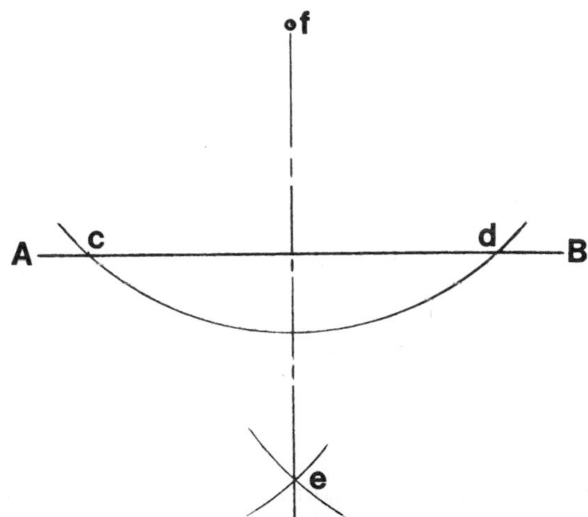

Figure 2.36 Drawing a perpendicular to a line.

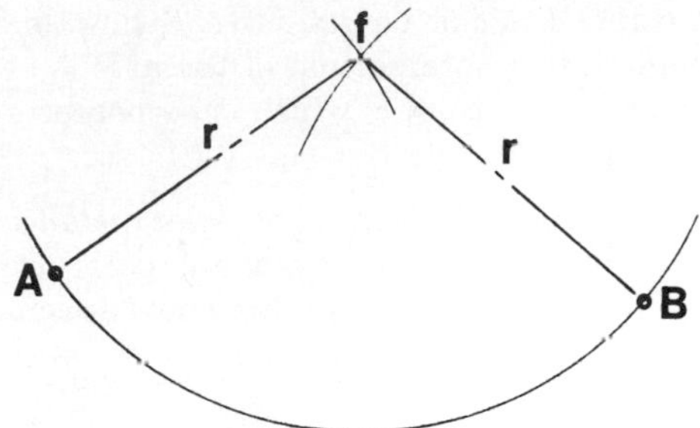

Figure 2.37 Drawing a circular arc through given points.

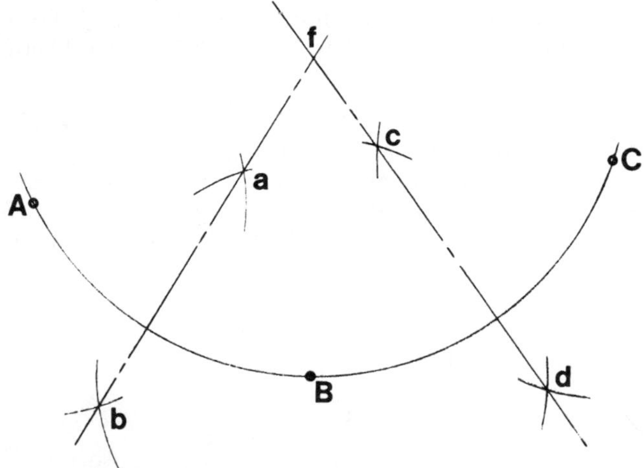

Figure 2.38 Finding the center of a circle.

- *To draw a tangent to a circle from any given point on the circumference* (Fig. 2.39), through the tangent point *f,* draw a radial line *OA.* At point *f,* draw a line *CD* at right angles to *OA.* Line *CD* is the required tangent to point *f* on the circle.
- *To draw a geometrically correct pentagon within a circle* (Fig. 2.40), draw a diameter *AB* and a radius *OC* perpendicular to it. Bisect *OB* and with this point, *d,* as center and a radius *dC,* draw arc *Ce.* With center *C* and radius *Ce,* draw arc *ef. Cf* is then a side of the pentagon. Step off distance *Cf* around the circle using a divider.

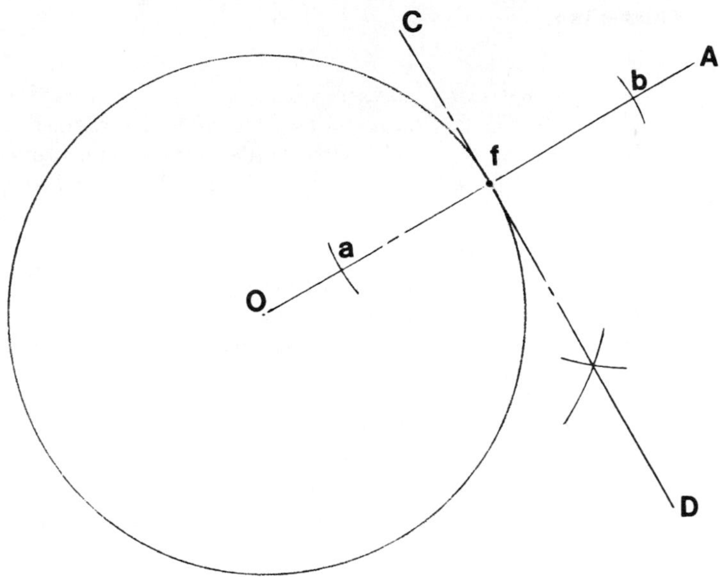

Figure 2.39 Drawing a tangent to a given point on a circle.

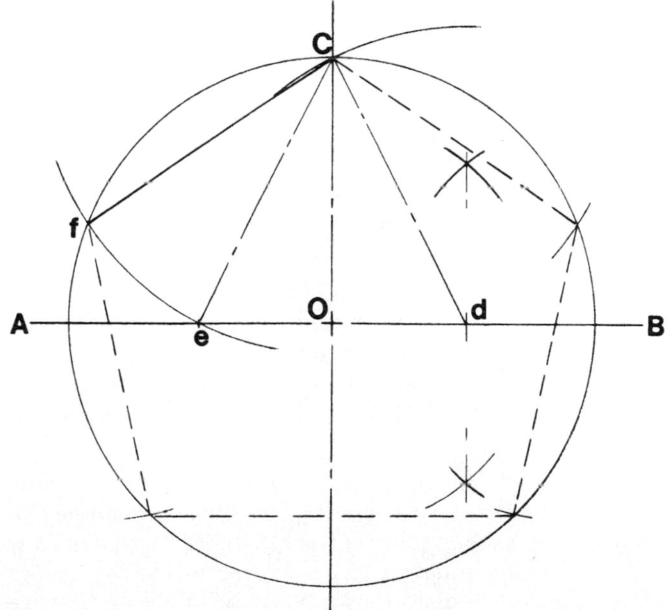

Figure 2.40 Drawing a pentagon.

- *To draw a geometrically correct hexagon given the distance across the points* (Fig. 2.41), draw a circle on *ab* with *a* diameter. With the same radius, *Of,* and with points 6 and 3 as centers, draw arcs intersecting the circle at points 1, 2, 4, and 5, and connect the points.

- *To draw a geometrically correct octagon in a square* (Fig. 2.42), draw the diagonals of the square. With the corners of the square, *b* and *d,* as centers and a radius of half the diagonal distance *Od,* draw arcs intersecting the sides of the square at points 1 through 8, and connect these points.

- *Angles of the pentagon, hexagon, and octagon* (Fig. 2.43).

- *To draw an ellipse given the major and minor axes* (Fig. 2.44). The concentric-circle method: On the two principle diameters *ef* and *cd* which intersect at point *O,* draw circles. From a number of points on the outer circle, such as *g* and *h,* draw radii *Og* and *Oh* intersecting the inner circle at points *g′* and *h′*. From *g* and *h,* draw lines parallel to *Oa,* and from *g′* and *h′*, draw lines parallel to *Od.* The intersection of the lines through *g* and *g′* and *h* and *h′* describe points on the ellipse. Each quadrant of the concentric circles may be divided into as many equal angles as required or as dictated by the size and accuracy required.

- *To draw an ellipse using the parallelogram method* (Fig. 2.45), on the axes *ab* and *cd,* construct a parallelogram. Divide *aO* into any number of equal parts, and divide *ae* into the same number of equal parts. Draw lines through points 1 through 4 from points *c* and *d.* The intersection of these lines will be points on the ellipse.

- *To draw a parabola using the parallelogram method* (Fig. 2.46), divide *Oa* and *ba* into the same number of equal parts. From the divisions on *ab,* draw lines converging at *O.* Lines drawn parallel to line *OA* and intersecting the divisions on *Oa* will intersect the lines drawn from point *O.* These intersections are points on the parabola.

- *To draw a parabola using the offset method* (Fig. 2.47), the parabola may be plotted by computing the offsets from line *O*5. These offsets vary as the square of their distance from point *O.* If *O*5 is divided into five equal parts, distance 1*e* will be $\frac{1}{25}$ distance 5*a.* Offset 2*d* will be $\frac{4}{25}$ distance 5*a;* offset 3*c* will be $\frac{9}{25}$ distance 5*a,* etc.

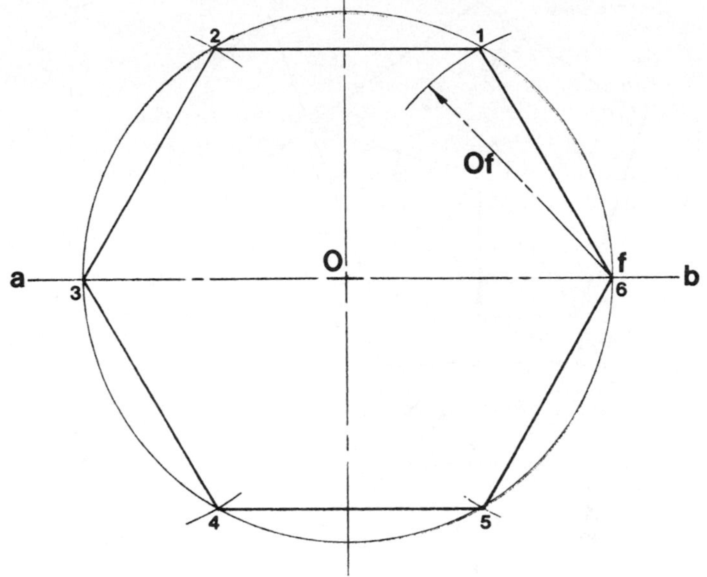

Figure 2.41 Drawing a hexagon.

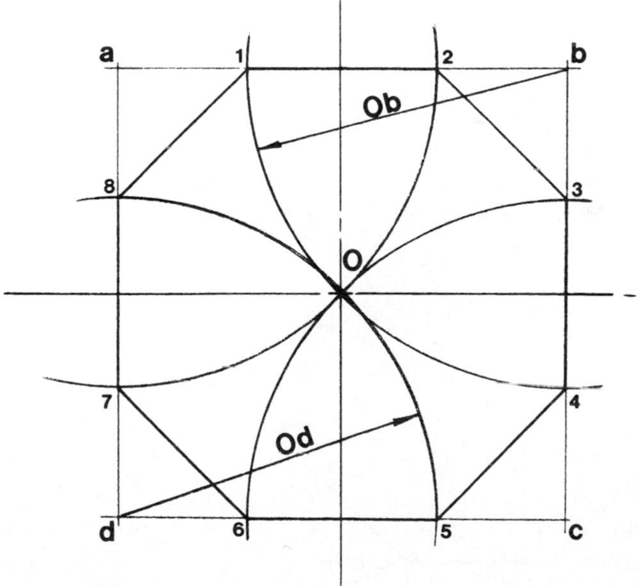

Figure 2.42 Drawing an octagon.

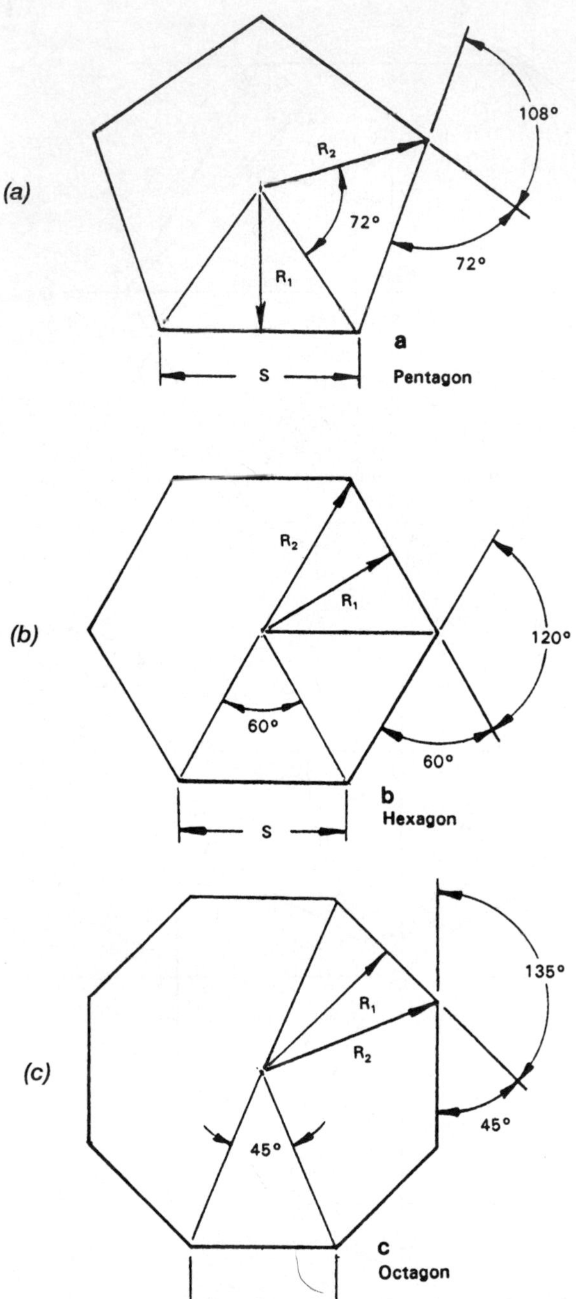

Figure 2.43 (*a*) Angles of the pentagon. (*b*) Hexagon. (*c*) Octagon.

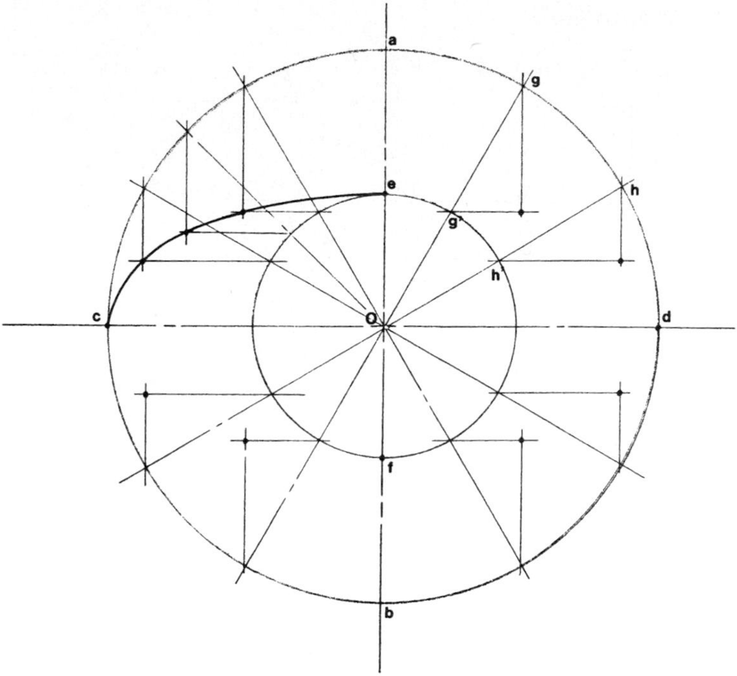

Figure 2.44 Drawing an ellipse.

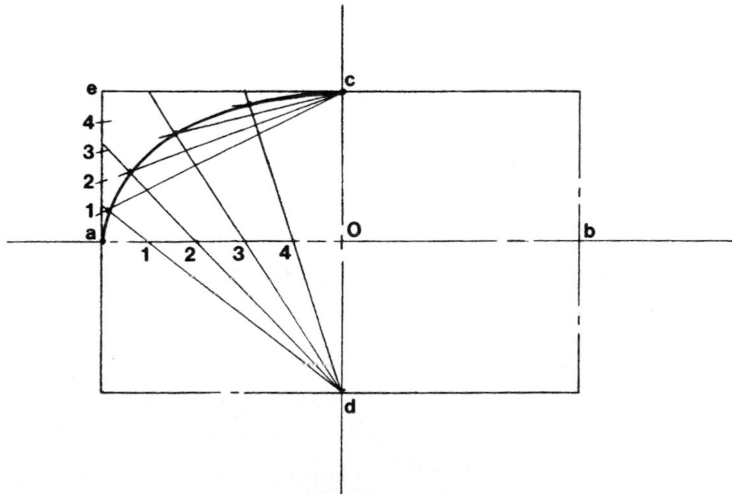

Figure 2.45 An ellipse by the parallelogram method.

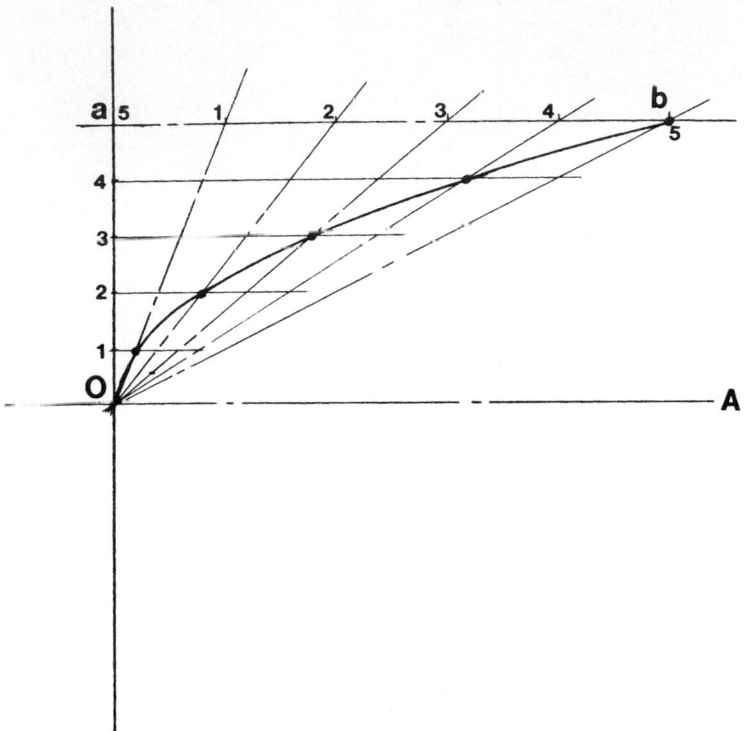

Figure 2.46 A parabola by the parallelogram method.

- *To draw a parabolic envelope* (Fig. 2.48), divide *Oa* and *Ob* into the same number of equal parts. Number the divisions from *Oa* and *Ob,* 1 through 6, etc. The intersection of points 1 and 6, 2 and 5, 3 and 4, 4 and 3, 5 and 2, and 6 and 1 will be points on the parabola. This parabola's axis is not parallel to either ordinate.
- *To draw a parabola when the focus and directorix are given* (Fig. 2.49), draw axis *Op* through point *f* and perpendicular to directorix *AB*. Through any point *k* on the axis *Op,* draw lines parallel to *AB*. With distance *kO* as a radius and *f* as a center, draw an arc intersecting the line through *k,* thus locating a point on the parabola. Repeat for *Oj, Oi,* etc.
- *To draw a helix* (Fig. 2.50), draw the two views of the cylinder and measure the lead along one of the contour elements. Divide

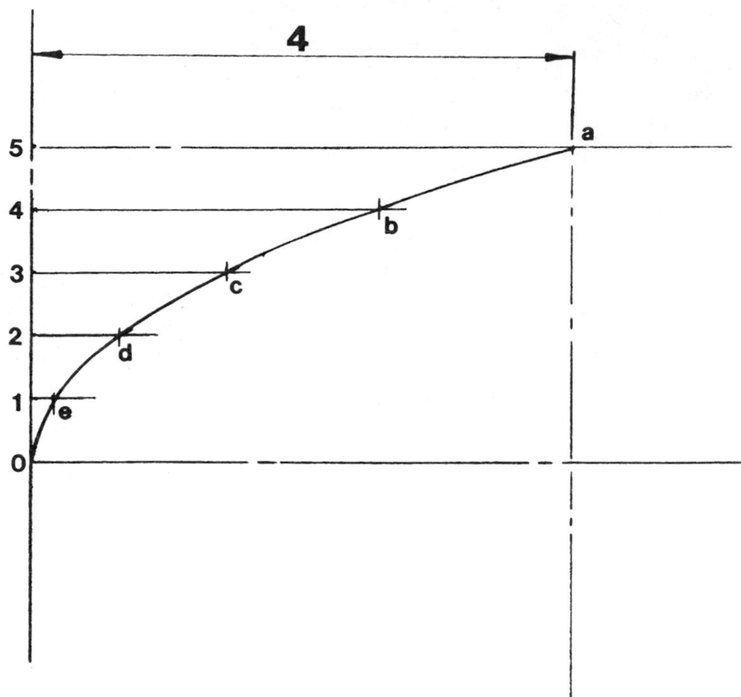

Figure 2.47 A parabola by the offset method.

the lead into a number of equal parts, say 12. Divide the circle of the front view into the same number of equal parts, say 12. Project points 1 through 12 from the top view to the stretch-out of the helix in the right view. Angle ϕ is the *helix angle,* whose tangent is equal to $L/\pi D$, where L is the lead and D is the diameter.

- *To draw the involute of a circle* (Fig. 2.51), divide the circle into a convenient number of parts, preferably equal. Draw tangents at these points. Line $a2$ is perpendicular to radial line $O2$, line $b3$ is perpendicular to radial line $O3$, etc. Lay off on these tangent lines the true lengths of the arcs from the point of tangency to the starting point, 1. For accuracy, the true lengths of the arcs may be calculated (see the section on mensuration for calculating arc lengths). The involute of the circle is the basis for the involute system of gearing. Another method for finding points mathematically on the involute is shown in Sec. 2.1.4.

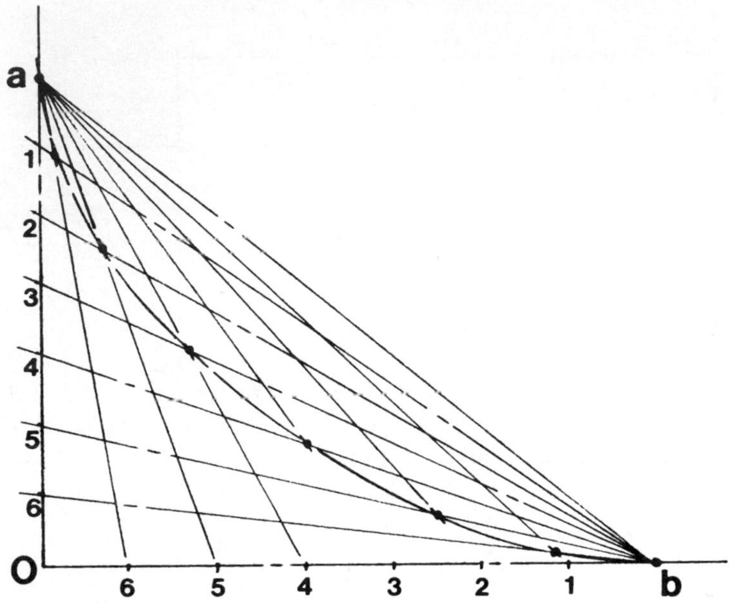

Figure 2.48 A parabolic envelope.

- *To draw the spiral of Archimedes* (Fig. 2.52), divide the circle into a number of equal parts, drawing the radii and asigning numbers to them. Divide the radius *O*8 into the same number of equal parts, numbering from the center of the circle. With *O* as a center, draw a series of concentric circles from the marked points on the radius, 1 through 8. The spiral curve is defined by the points of intersection of the radii and the concentric circles at points *a, b, c, d, e, f, g,* and *h.* Connect the points with a smooth curve. The Archimedean spiral is the curve of the heart cam, which is used to convert uniform rotary motion into uniform reciprocating motion. See the chapter on cams and cam design.

2.4 Mensuration

Mensuration is the mathematical name for calculating the areas, volumes, length of sides, and other geometric parts of standard geometric shapes such as circles, spheres, polygons, prisms, cylin-

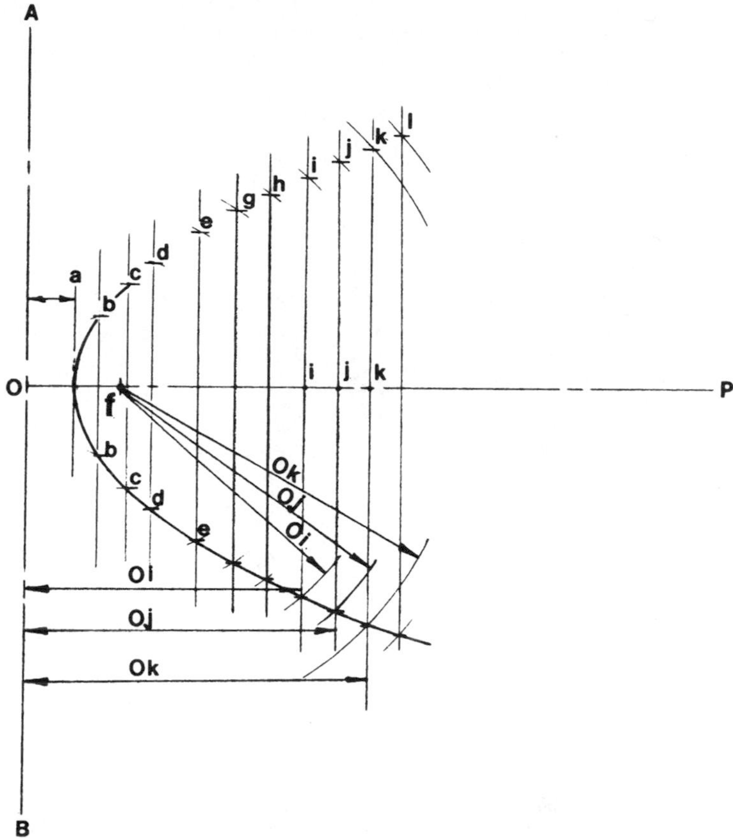

Figure 2.49 A parabolic curve.

ders, cones, etc. through the use of mathematical equations or formulas. Included here are the most frequently used and important mensuration formulas for the common geometric figures, both plane and solid.

$A = \frac{1}{2}bh$ (Fig. 2.53)

$A = \frac{1}{2}ab \sin C$ (Fig. 2.54)

Also $A = \sqrt{s(s-a)(s-b)(s-c)}$ where $s = \frac{1}{2}(a + b + c)$

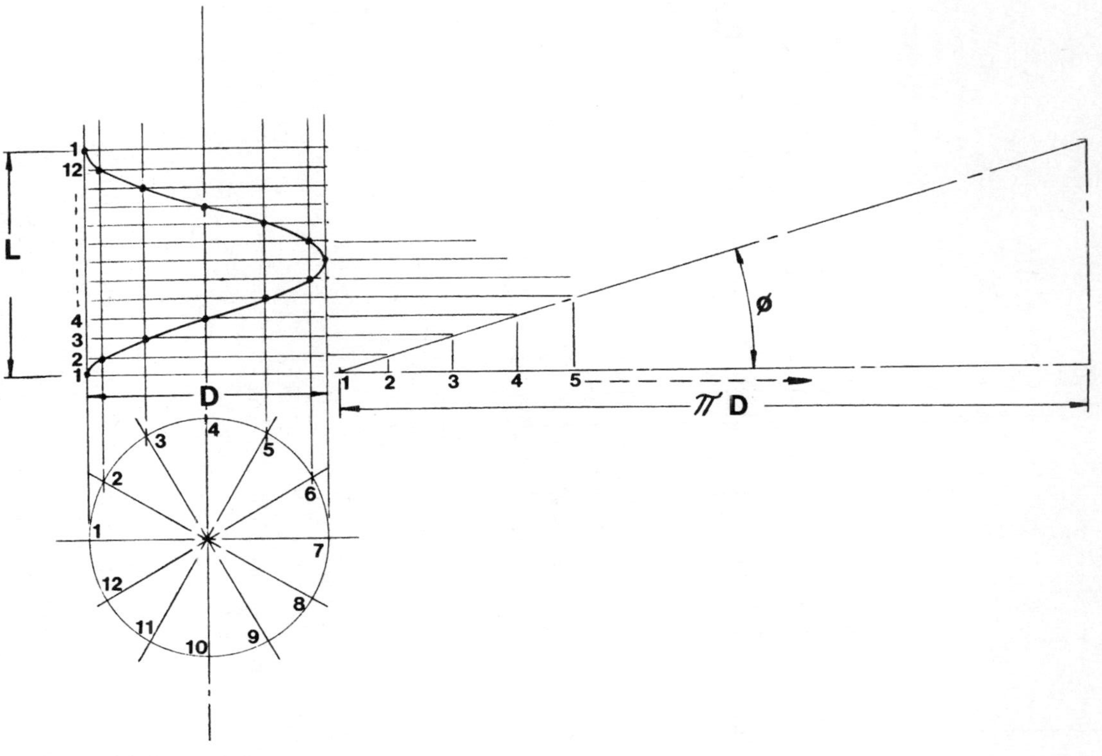

Figure 2.50 To draw a helix.

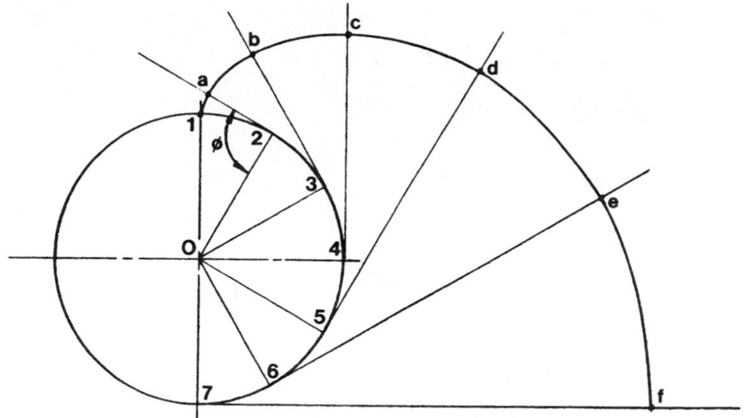

Figure 2.51 To draw the involute of the circle.

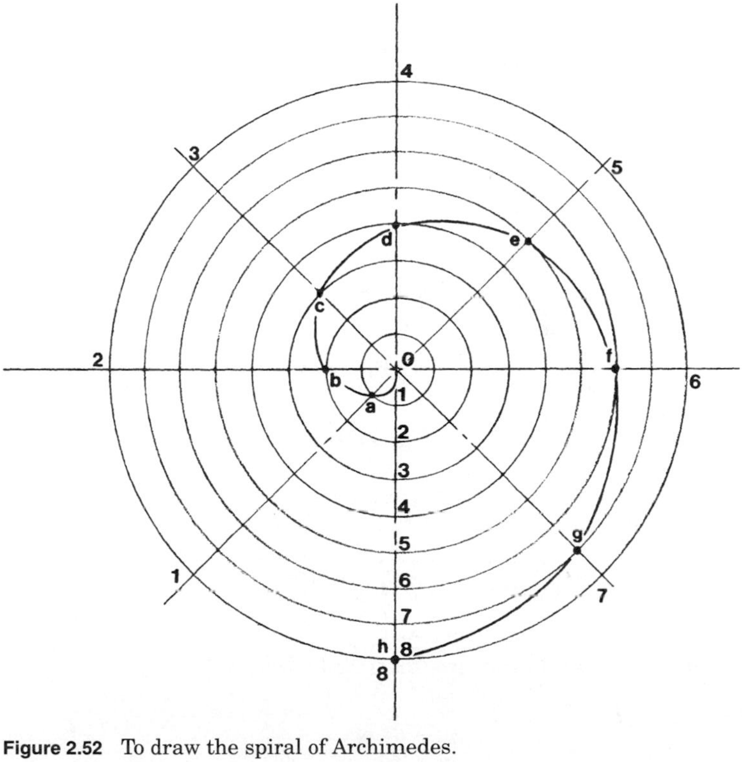

Figure 2.52 To draw the spiral of Archimedes.

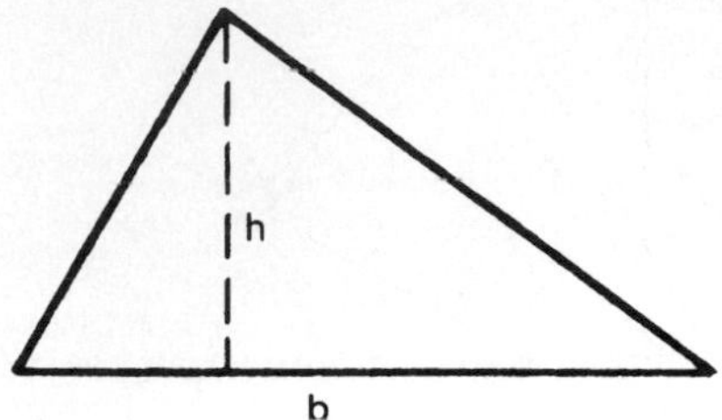

Figure 2.53 Triangle.

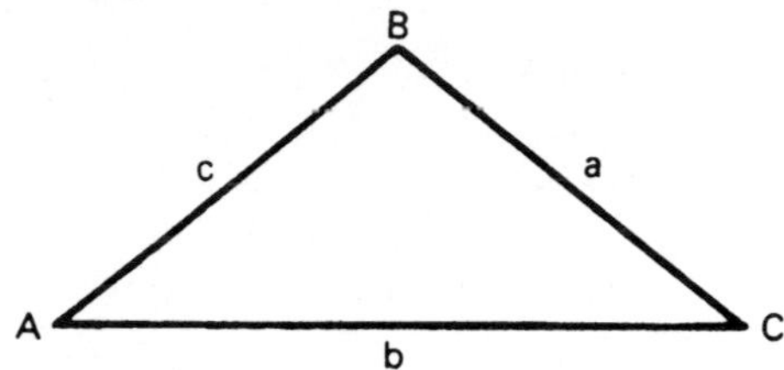

Figure 2.54 Triangle.

$A = ab$ (Fig. 2.55)

$A = bh$ (Fig. 2.56)

$A = \frac{1}{2}cd$ (Fig. 2.57)

$A = \frac{1}{2}(a + b)h$ (Fig. 2.58)

$$A = \frac{(H + h)\,a + bh + cH}{2} \qquad \text{(Fig. 2.59)}$$

$A = \frac{1}{4}nL^2 \cot (180/n)$ (Fig. 2.60)

where n = number of sides, and L = length of a side. In a polygon of n sides, each of which is L, the radius of the inscribed circle is

$$r = \frac{L}{2} \cot \frac{180}{n}$$

and the radius of the circumscribed circle is

$$r_1 = \frac{L}{2} \operatorname{cosec} \frac{180}{n}$$

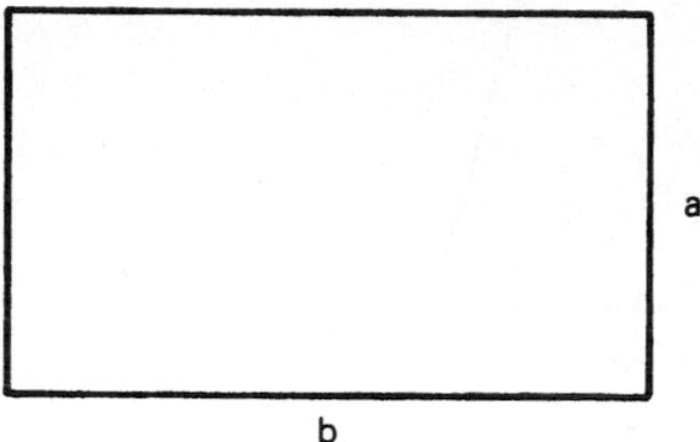

Figure 2.55 Rectangle.

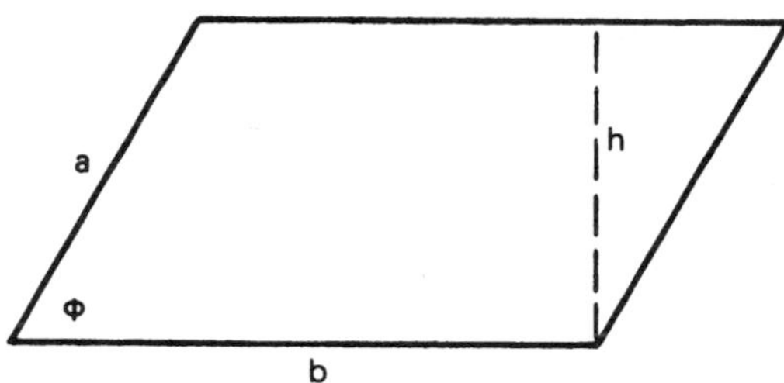

Figure 2.56 Parallelogram.

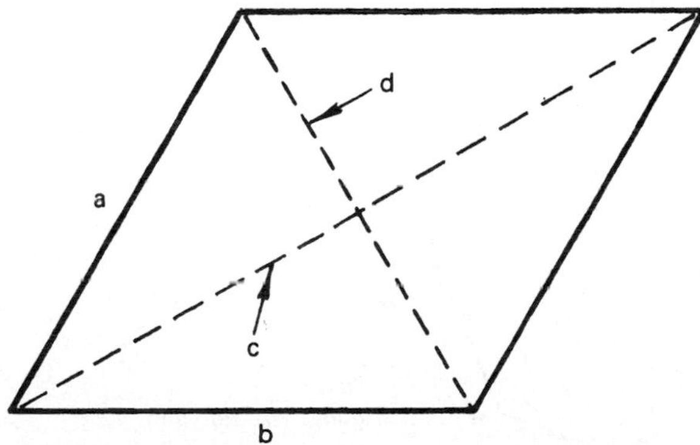

Figure 2.57 Rhombus.

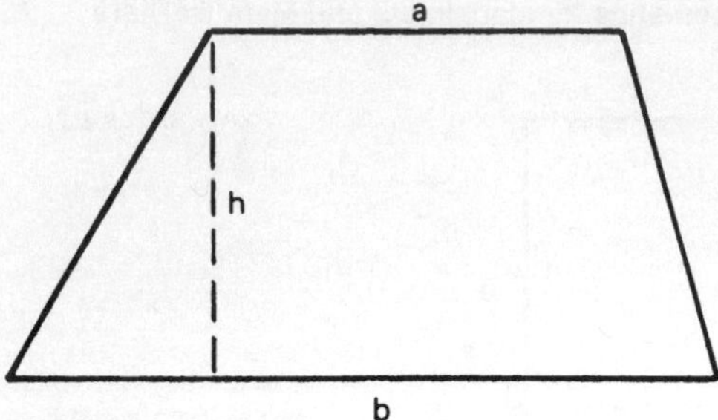

Figure 2.58 Trapezoid.

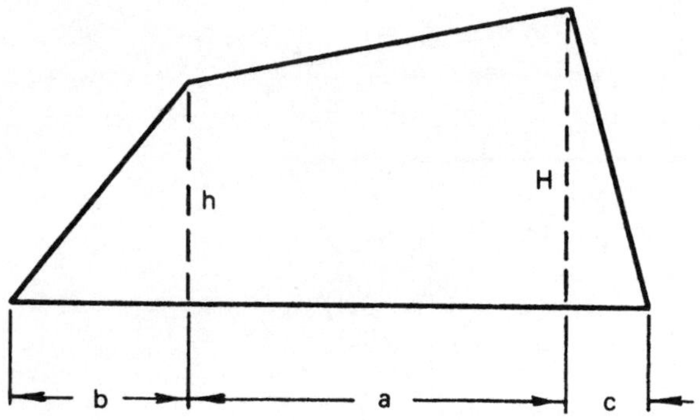

Figure 2.59 Trapezium.

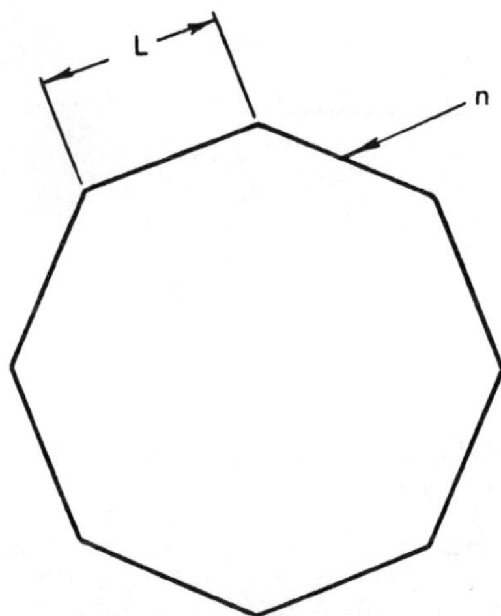

Figure 2.60 Polygon.

The radius of a circle inscribed in any triangle whose sides are *a*, *b*, and *c* is

$$r = \frac{\sqrt{s(s-a)(s-b)(s-c)}}{s} \qquad \text{(Fig. 2.61)}$$

where $s = \frac{1}{2}(a + b + c)$

The radius of the circumscribed circle is

$$R = \frac{abc}{4s(s-a)(s-b)(s-c)} \qquad \text{(Fig. 2.62)}$$

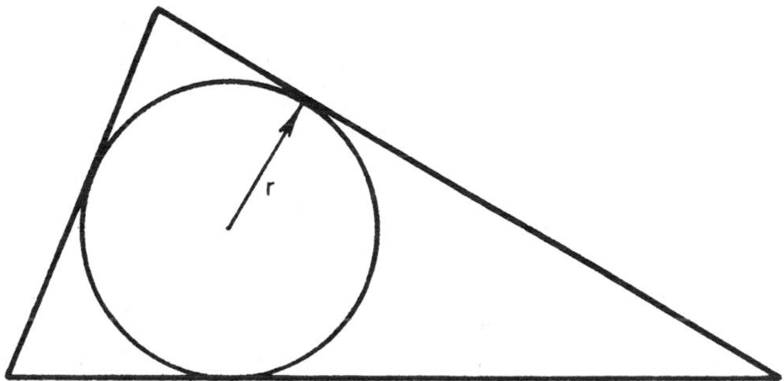

Figure 2.61 Circle inscribed in a triangle.

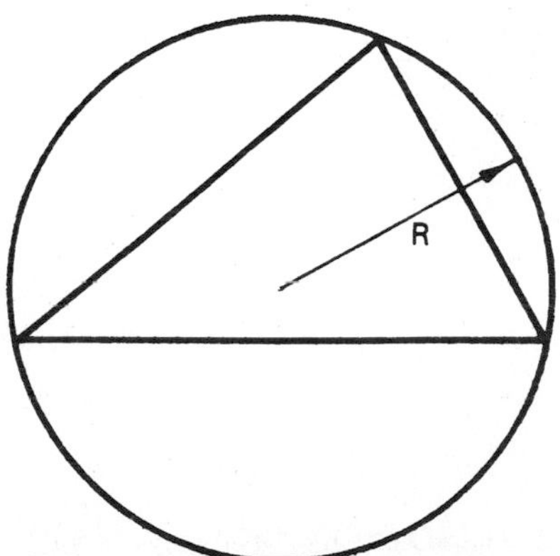

Figure 2.62 Circle circumscribed around a triangle.

Area of an inscribed polygon is

$$A = \frac{1}{2} nr^2 \sin \frac{2\pi}{n} \qquad \text{(Fig. 2.63)}$$

where r is the radius of the circumscribed circle, and n is the number of sides.

Area of a circumscribed polygon is

$$A = nR^2 \tan \frac{\pi}{n} \qquad \text{(Fig. 2.64)}$$

where R is radius of the inscribed circle, and n is the number of sides.

Circumference of a circle is

$$C = 2\pi r = \pi d \qquad \text{(Fig. 2.65)}$$

Area of a circle is

$$A = \pi r^2 = \tfrac{1}{4} \pi d^2 \qquad \text{(Fig. 2.66)}$$

Length of arc L is

$$L = \frac{\pi r \phi}{180} \qquad \text{(Fig. 2.67)}$$

when ϕ is in radians, $L = r\phi$.

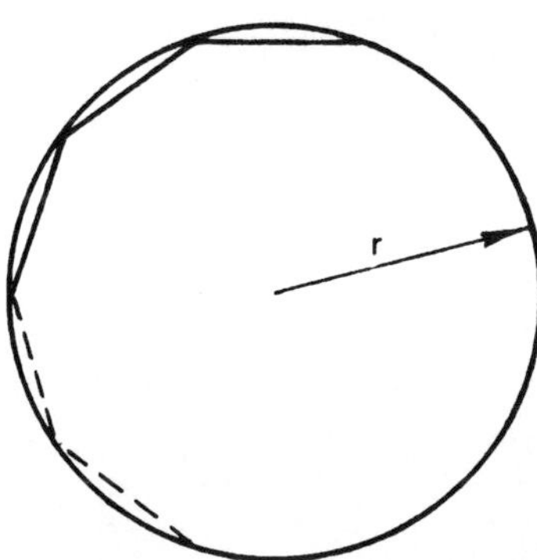

Figure 2.63 Inscribed polygon.

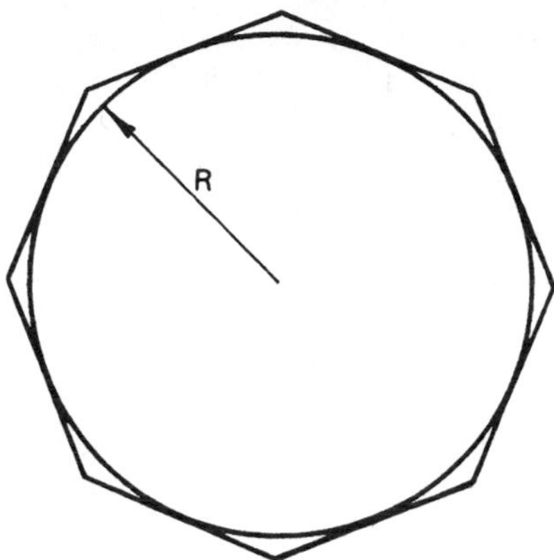

Figure 2.64 Circumscribed polygon.

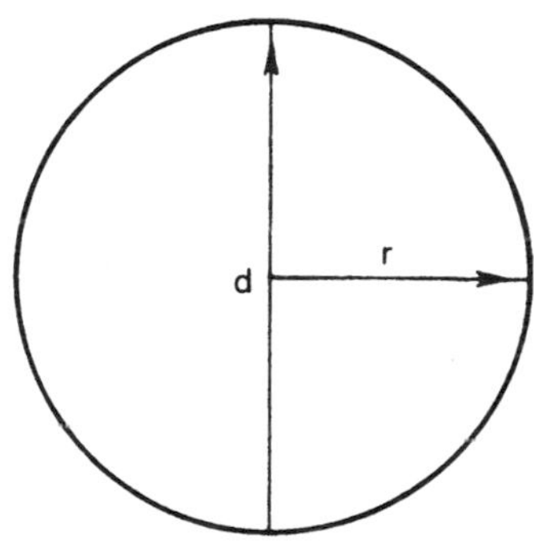

Figure 2.65 Circle.

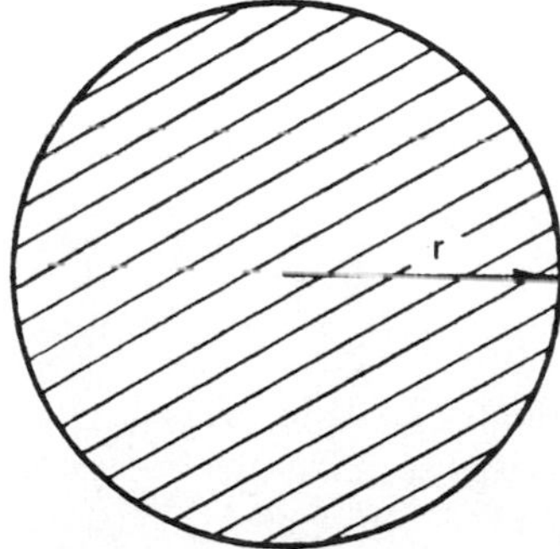

Figure 2.66 Area of a circle.

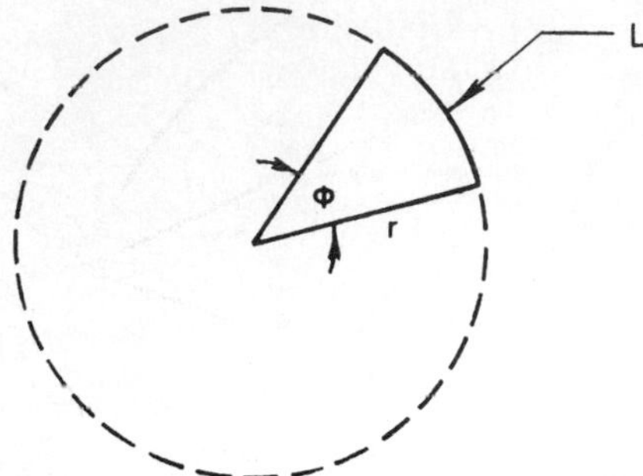

Figure 2.67 Arc length.

Length of chord AB is

$$AB = 2r \sin(\tfrac{1}{2}\phi) \qquad \text{(Fig. 2.68)}$$

Area of the sector is

$$A = \frac{\pi r^2 \phi}{360} \qquad \text{or} \qquad A = \frac{rL}{2}$$

where L is the length of the arc.

Area of a segment of a circle is

$$A = \frac{\pi r^2 \phi}{360} - \frac{r^2 \sin \phi}{2} \qquad \text{(Fig. 2.69)}$$

where $\phi = 180° - 2 \arcsin x/r$, and x = perpendicular distance, center to chord. If ϕ is in radians, $A = \tfrac{1}{2}r^2(\phi - \sin \phi)$.

Area of the ring between circles is

$$A = \pi(R + r)(R - r) \qquad \text{(Fig. 2.70)}$$

Note. The circles need not be concentric.

Circumference of an ellipse is

$$C = 2\pi \sqrt{\frac{a^2 + b^2}{2}} \qquad \text{(approximate)} \qquad \text{(Fig. 2.71)}$$

$$A = \pi ab$$

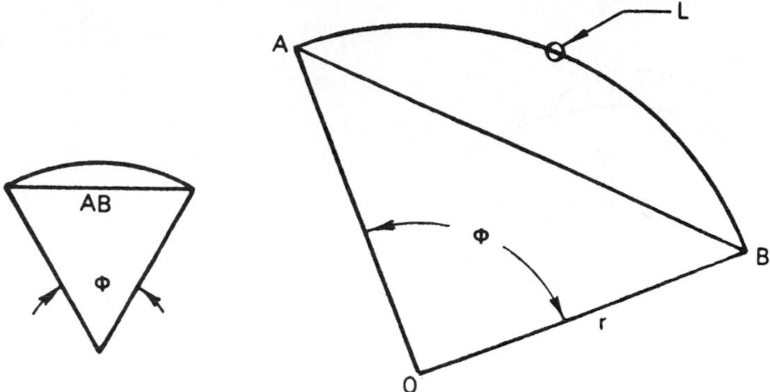

Figure 2.68 Chord.

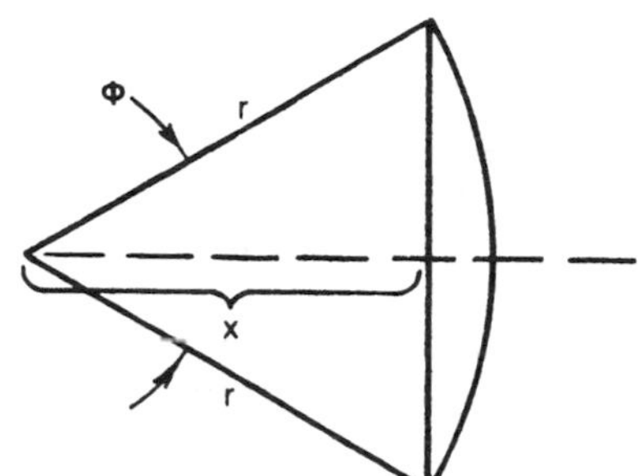

Figure 2.69 Segment.

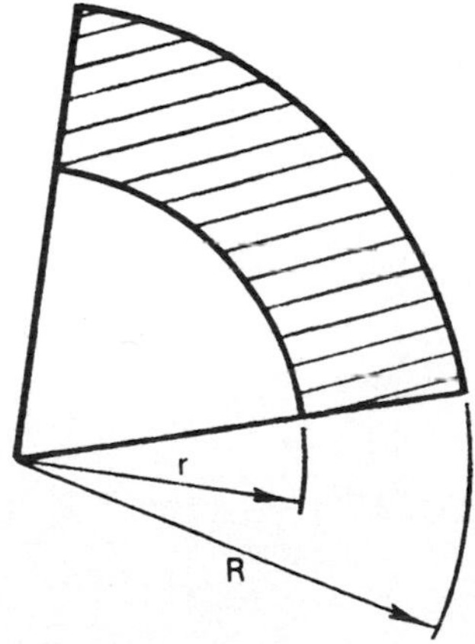

Figure 2.70 Ring between circles.

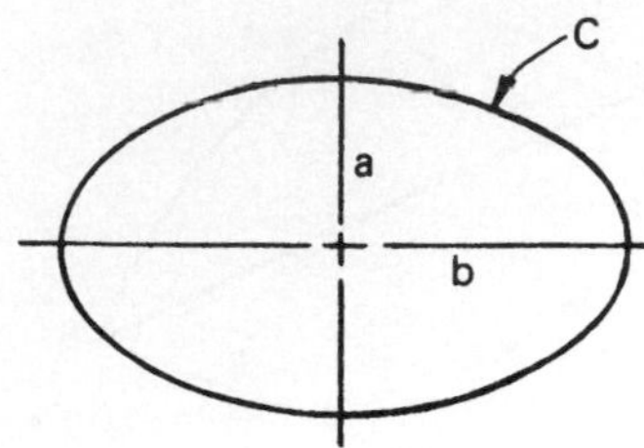

Figure 2.71 Ellipse.

Volume of a pyramid is

$$V = \tfrac{1}{3} \text{ area of base} \times h \qquad \text{(Fig. 2.72)}$$

where h = altitude.

Surfaces and volumes of polyhedra are:

	Surface	Volume
Tetrahedron	$1.73205L^2$	$0.11785L^3$
Hexahedron (cube)	$6L^2$	$1L^3$
Octahedron	$3.46410L^2$	$0.47140L^3$

Note. L = leg or edge length.

Surface and volume of a sphere are

$$S = 4\pi r^2 = \pi d^2 \qquad \text{(Fig. 2.73)}$$

$$V = \tfrac{4}{3}\,\pi r^3 = \tfrac{1}{6}\,\pi d^3$$

Surface and volume of a cylinder are

$$S = 2\pi rh \qquad \text{(Fig. 2.74)}$$

$$V = \pi r^2 h$$

Surface and volume of a cone are

$$S = \pi r\sqrt{r^2 + h^2} \qquad \text{(Fig. 2.75)}$$

$$V = (\pi/3)r^2 h$$

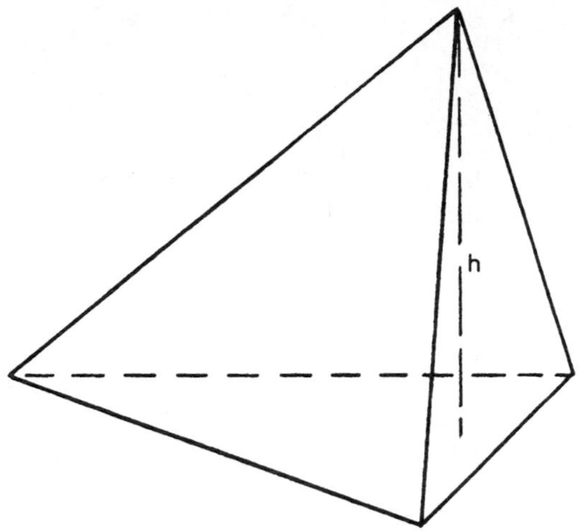

Figure 2.72 Pyramid.

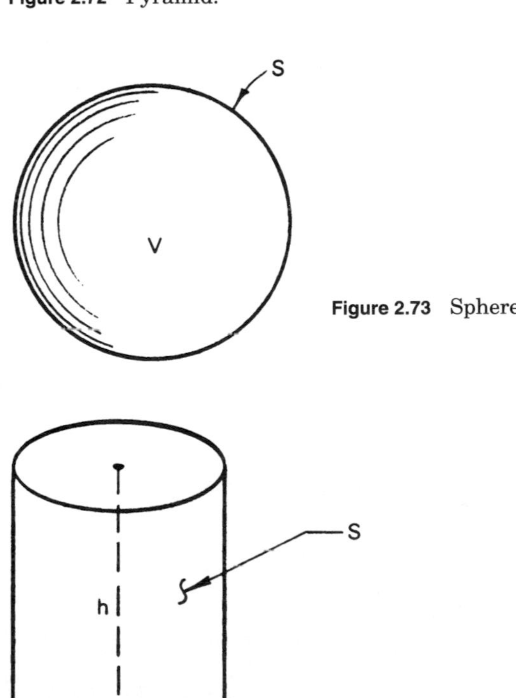

Figure 2.73 Sphere.

Figure 2.74 Cylinder.

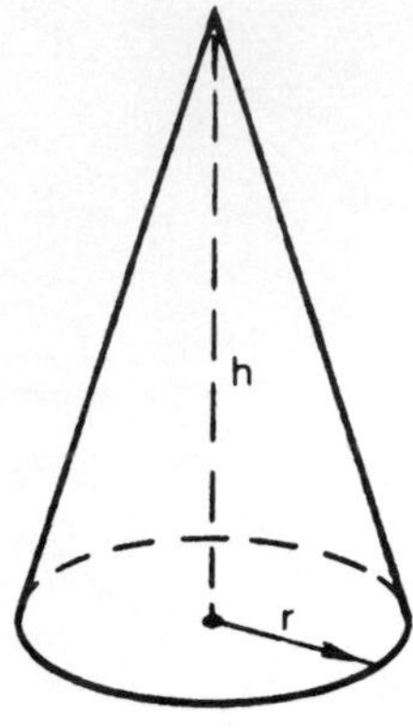

Figure 2.75 Cone.

Area and volume of curved surface of spherical segment are

$$A = 2\pi rh \qquad \text{(Fig. 2.76)}$$

$$V = (\tfrac{1}{3}\pi h^2)(3r - h)$$

When a is the radius of the base of the segment,

$$V = (\tfrac{1}{4}\pi h)(h^2 + 3a^2)$$

Surface area and volume of the frustum of a cone are

$$S = \pi(r_1 + r_2)\sqrt{h^2 + (r_1 - r_2)^2} \qquad \text{(Fig. 2.77)}$$

$$V = (h/3)\,(r_1^{\,2} + r_1 r_2 + r_2^{\,2})\pi$$

Area and volume of a truncated cylinder are

$$A = \pi r\,(h_1 + h_2) \qquad \text{(Fig. 2.78)}$$

$$V = 1.5708r^2(h_1 + h_2)$$

Area and volume of a portion of a cylinder (base edge = diameter) are

$$A = 2rh \qquad \text{(Fig. 2.79)}$$

$$V = \tfrac{2}{3}r^2h$$

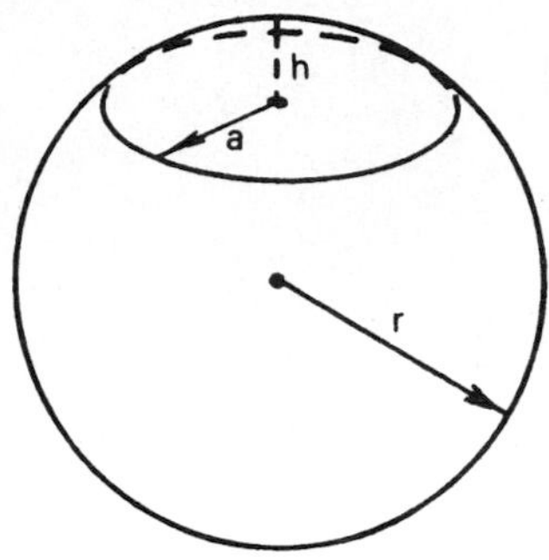

Figure 2.76 Spherical segment.

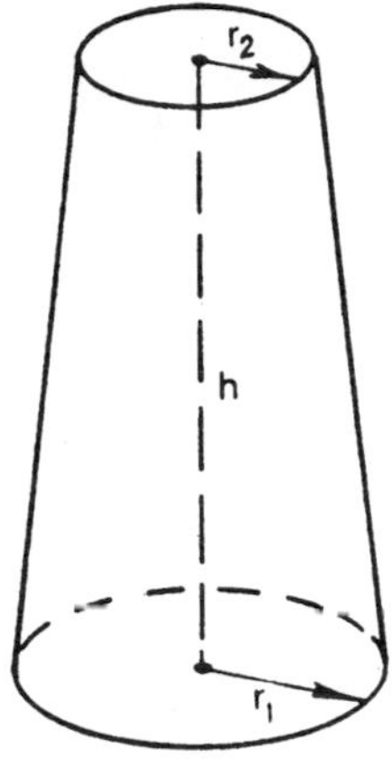

Figure 2.77 Frustum of a cone.

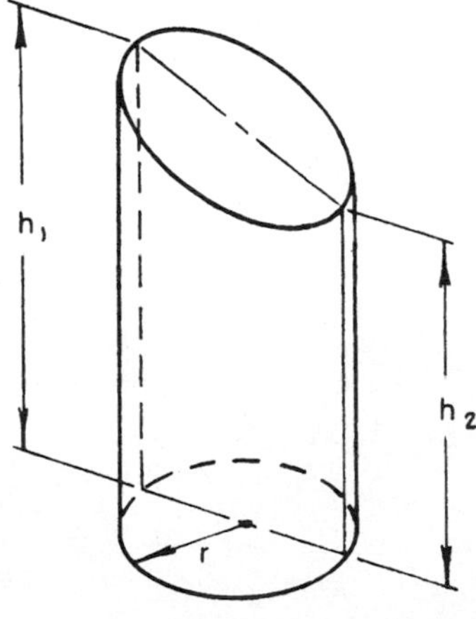

Figure 2.78 Truncated cylinder.

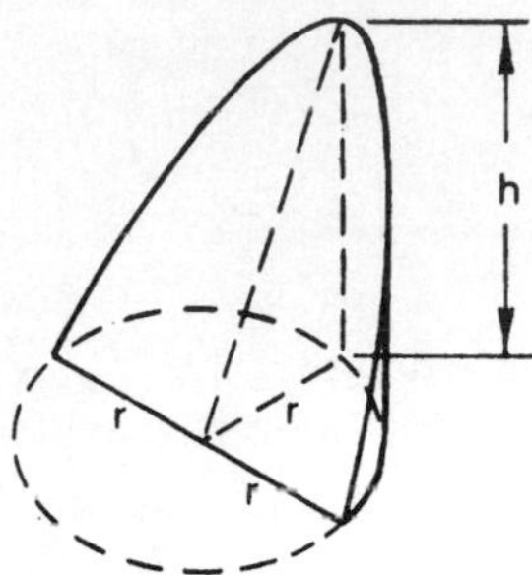

Figure 2.79 Portion of a cylinder.

Area and volume of a portion of a cylinder (special cases) are

$$A = \frac{h(ad \pm c \times \text{perimeter of base})}{r \pm c} \qquad \text{(Fig. 2.80)}$$

$$V = \frac{h(\tfrac{2}{3}a^3 \pm cA)}{r \pm c}$$

where d = diameter of base circle.

Use $+c$ when base area is larger than half the base circle; use $-c$ when base area is smaller than half the base circle.

Volume of a wedge is

$$V = \frac{(2b + c)ah}{6} \qquad \text{(Fig. 2.81)}$$

Area and volume of a spherical zone are

$$A = 2\pi rh \qquad \text{(Fig. 2.82)}$$

$$V = 0.5236h\left(\frac{3c_1^2}{4} + \frac{3c_2^2}{4} + h^2\right)$$

Area and volume of a spherical wedge are

$$A = \frac{\phi}{360}4\pi r^2 \qquad \text{(Fig. 2.83)}$$

$$V = \frac{\phi}{360} \times \frac{4\pi r^3}{3}$$

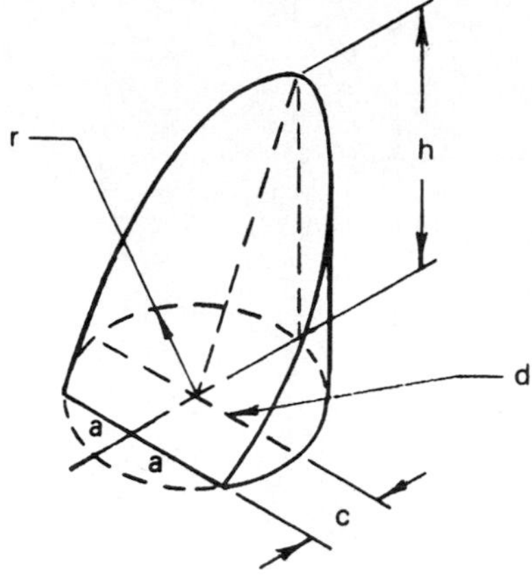

Figure 2.80 Portion of a cylinder.

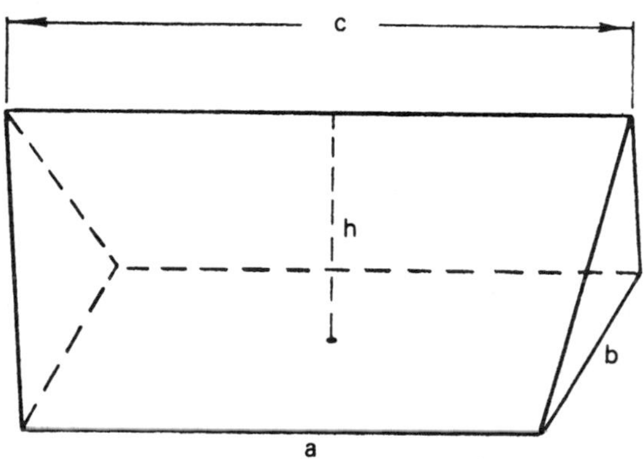

Figure 2.81 Wedge.

The volume of a paraboloid is

$$V = \frac{\pi r^2 h}{2} \qquad \text{(Fig. 2.84)}$$

Area and volume of a spherical sector are

$$A = \pi r\,(2h + c/2) \qquad \text{(total area)} \qquad \text{(Fig. 2.85)}$$

$$V = \frac{2\pi r^2 h}{3}$$

where $c = 2\sqrt{h(2r - h)}$.

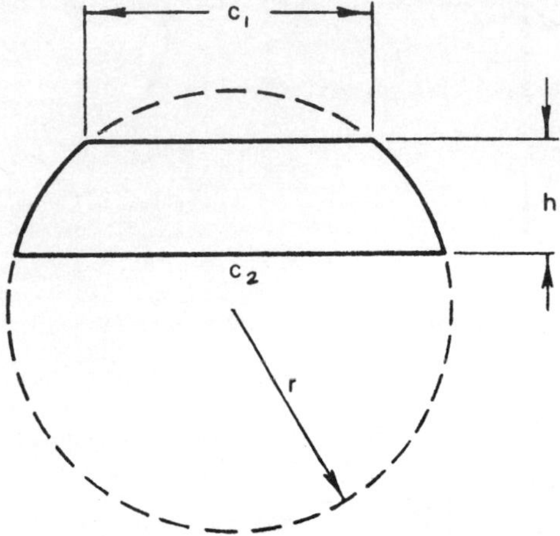

Figure 2.82 Spherical zone.

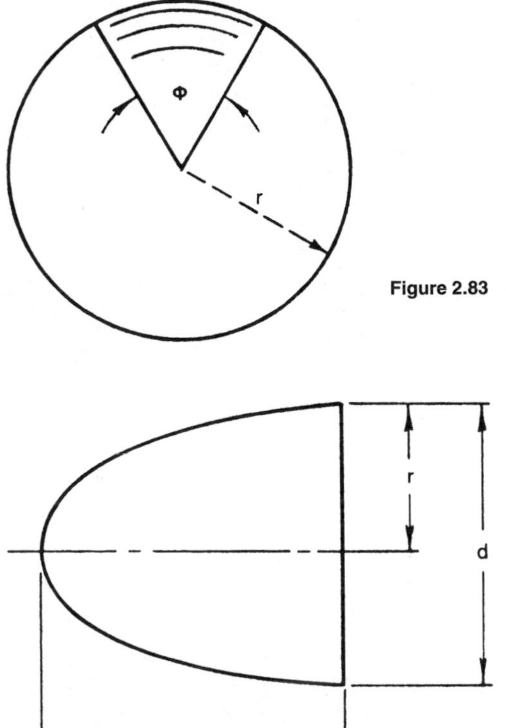

Figure 2.83 Spherical wedge.

Figure 2.84 Paraboloid.

Area and volume of a spherical segment are

$$A = 2\pi rh \qquad \text{(spherical surface)} \qquad \text{(Fig. 2.86)}$$

$$A = \pi\left(\frac{c^2}{4} + h^2\right) \qquad c = 2\sqrt{h(2r - h)} \qquad r = \frac{c^2 + 4h^2}{8h}$$

$$V = \pi h^2\left(r - \frac{h}{3}\right)$$

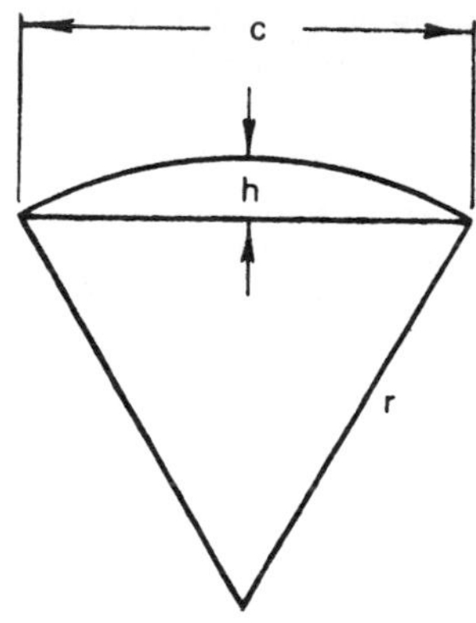

Figure 2.85 Spherical sector.

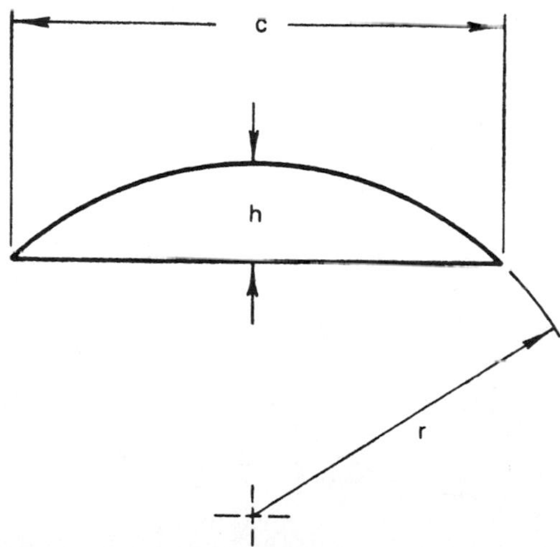

Figure 2.86 Spherical segment.

Area and volume of a torus are

$$A = 4\pi^2 cr \qquad \text{(total surface)} \qquad \text{(Figs. 2.87 and 2.88)}$$

$$V = 2\pi^2 cr^2 \qquad \text{(total volume)}$$

Properties of the circle: see Fig. 2.89.

2.5 Percentage Calculations

Percentage calculation procedures have many applications in machining, design, and metalworking problems. Although the procedures are relatively simple, it is easy to make mistakes in the manipulations of the numbers involved.

Ordinarily, 100 percent of any quantity is represented by the number 1.00, meaning the total quantity. Thus, if we take 50 percent of any quantity, or any multiple of 100 percent, it *must* be expressed as a decimal:

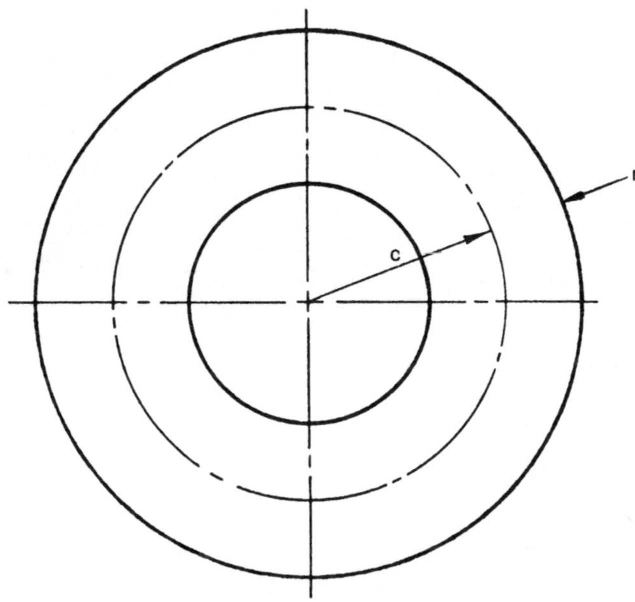

Figure 2.87 Torus.

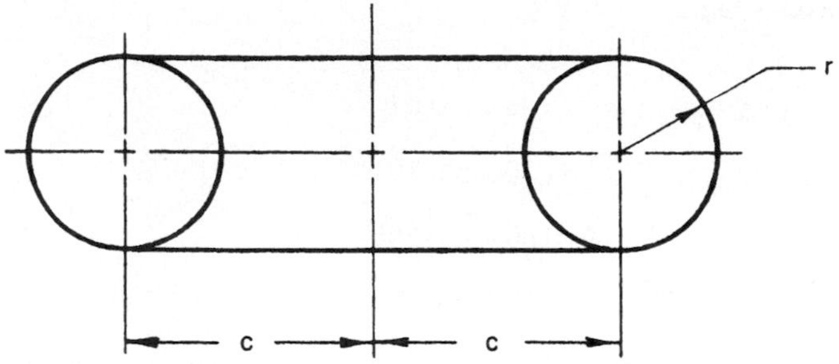

Figure 2.88 Torus.

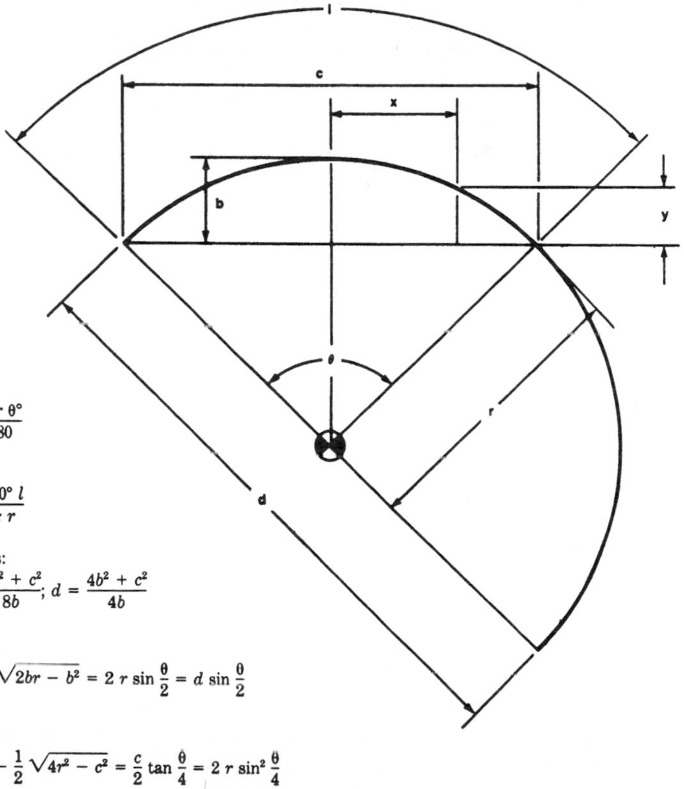

Arc:

$$l = \frac{\pi\, r\, \theta^\circ}{180}$$

Angle:

$$\theta = \frac{180^\circ\, l}{\pi\, r}$$

Radius:

$$r = \frac{4b^2 + c^2}{8b};\ d = \frac{4b^2 + c^2}{4b}$$

Chord:

$$c = 2\sqrt{2br - b^2} = 2\, r \sin\frac{\theta}{2} = d \sin\frac{\theta}{2}$$

Rise:

$$b = r - \frac{1}{2}\sqrt{4r^2 - c^2} = \frac{c}{2}\tan\frac{\theta}{4} = 2\, r \sin^2\frac{\theta}{4}$$

Rise:

$$b = r + y - \sqrt{r^2 - x^2}$$

where $y = b - r + \sqrt{r^2 - x^2}$ and $x = \sqrt{r^2 - (r + y - b)^2}$.

Figure 2.89 Properties of the circle.

$$1\% = 0.01$$

$$10\% = 0.10$$

$$65.5\% = 0.655$$

$$145\% = 1.45$$

In effect, we are dividing the percentage figure, such as 65.5 percent, by 100 to arrive at the decimal equivalent required for calculations.

Let us take a percentage of a given number:

$$45\% \text{ of } 136.5 = 0.45 \times 136.5 = 61.425$$

$$33.5\% \text{ of } 235.7 = 0.335 \times 235.7 = 78.9595$$

Let us now compare two arbitrary numbers, 33 and 52, as an illustration:

$$\frac{52 - 33}{33} = 0.5758$$

Thus the number 52 is 57.58 percent larger than the number 33. We also can say that 33 increased by 57.58 percent is equal to 52, that is, $0.5758 \times 33 + 33 = 52$. Now,

$$\frac{52 - 33}{52} = 0.3654$$

Thus the number 52 minus 36.54 percent of itself is 33. We also can say that 33 is 36.54 percent less than 52, that is, $0.3654 \times 52 = 19$ and $52 - 19 = 33$. The number 33 is what percent of 52? That is, $33/52 = 0.6346$. Therefore, 33 is 63.46 percent of 52.

Example of a practical percentage calculation. A spring is compressed to 417 lbf and later decompressed to 400 lbf, or load. The percentage pressure drop is $(417 - 400)/417 = 0.0408$, or 4.08 percent. The pressure, or load, is then increased to 515 lbf. The percentage increase over 400 lbf is therefore $(515 - 400)/515 = 0.2875$, or 28.75 percent.

Percentage problem errors are quite common, even though the calculations are simple. In most cases, if you remember that the divisor is the number of which you want the percentage, either increasing or decreasing, the simple errors can be avoided. Always "back-check" your answers using the percentages against the numbers.

2.6 Decimal Equivalents and Millimeter Chart (Fig. 2.90)

2.7 Degrees and Radians Chart (Fig. 2.91)

2.8 Factors and Prime Numbers (Table 2.1)

2.9 Mathematics Symbols and the Greek Alphabet (Tables 2.2 and 2.3)

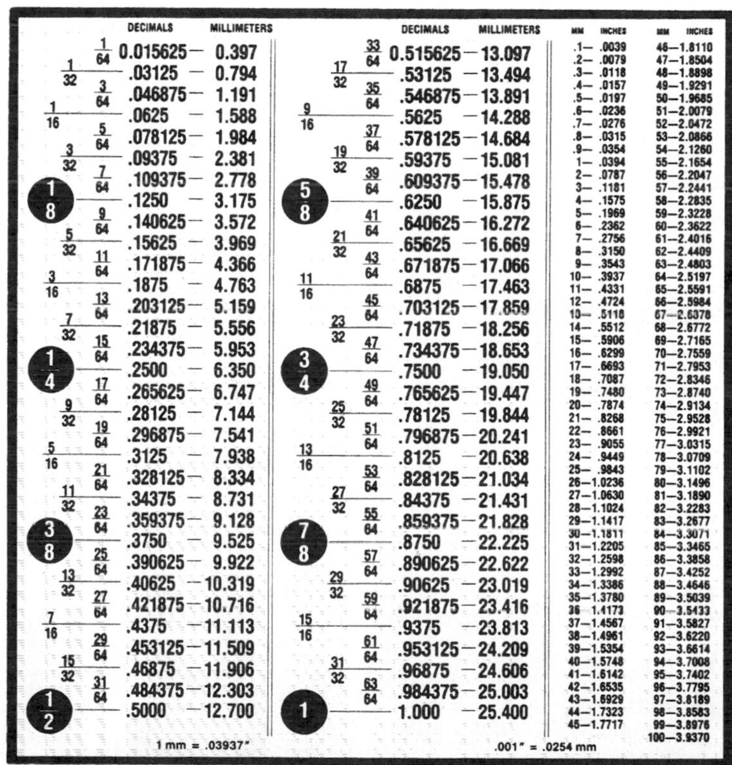

Fraction	DECIMALS	MILLIMETERS	Fraction	DECIMALS	MILLIMETERS
1/64	0.015625	0.397	33/64	0.515625	13.097
1/32	.03125	0.794	17/32	.53125	13.494
3/64	.046875	1.191	35/64	.546875	13.891
1/16	.0625	1.588	9/16	.5625	14.288
5/64	.078125	1.984	37/64	.578125	14.684
3/32	.09375	2.381	19/32	.59375	15.081
7/64	.109375	2.778	39/64	.609375	15.478
1/8	.1250	3.175	5/8	.6250	15.875
9/64	.140625	3.572	41/64	.640625	16.272
5/32	.15625	3.969	21/32	.65625	16.669
11/64	.171875	4.366	43/64	.671875	17.066
3/16	.1875	4.763	11/16	.6875	17.463
13/64	.203125	5.159	45/64	.703125	17.859
7/32	.21875	5.556	23/32	.71875	18.256
15/64	.234375	5.953	47/64	.734375	18.653
1/4	.2500	6.350	3/4	.7500	19.050
17/64	.265625	6.747	49/64	.765625	19.447
9/32	.28125	7.144	25/32	.78125	19.844
19/64	.296875	7.541	51/64	.796875	20.241
5/16	.3125	7.938	13/16	.8125	20.638
21/64	.328125	8.334	53/64	.828125	21.034
11/32	.34375	8.731	27/32	.84375	21.431
23/64	.359375	9.128	55/64	.859375	21.828
3/8	.3750	9.525	7/8	.8750	22.225
25/64	.390625	9.922	57/64	.890625	22.622
13/32	.40625	10.319	29/32	.90625	23.019
27/64	.421875	10.716	59/64	.921875	23.416
7/16	.4375	11.113	15/16	.9375	23.813
29/64	.453125	11.509	61/64	.953125	24.209
15/32	.46875	11.906	31/32	.96875	24.606
31/64	.484375	12.303	63/64	.984375	25.003
1/2	.5000	12.700	1	1.000	25.400

1 mm = .03937″ .001″ = .0254 mm

MM	INCHES	MM	INCHES
.1	.0039	46	1.8110
.2	.0079	47	1.8504
.3	.0118	48	1.8898
.4	.0157	49	1.9291
.5	.0197	50	1.9685
.6	.0236	51	2.0079
.7	.0276	52	2.0472
.8	.0315	53	2.0866
.9	.0354	54	2.1260
1	.0394	55	2.1654
2	.0787	56	2.2047
3	.1181	57	2.2441
4	.1575	58	2.2835
5	.1969	59	2.3228
6	.2362	60	2.3622
7	.2756	61	2.4016
8	.3150	62	2.4409
9	.3543	63	2.4803
10	.3937	64	2.5197
11	.4331	65	2.5591
12	.4724	66	2.5984
10	.5118	67	2.6378
14	.5512	68	2.6772
15	.5906	69	2.7165
16	.6299	70	2.7559
17	.6693	71	2.7953
18	.7087	72	2.8346
19	.7480	73	2.8740
20	.7874	74	2.9134
21	.8268	75	2.9528
22	.8661	76	2.9921
23	.9055	77	3.0315
24	.9449	78	3.0709
25	.9843	79	3.1102
26	1.0236	80	3.1496
27	1.0630	81	3.1890
28	1.1024	82	3.2283
29	1.1417	83	3.2677
30	1.1811	84	3.3071
31	1.2205	85	3.3465
32	1.2598	86	3.3858
33	1.2992	87	3.4252
34	1.3386	88	3.4646
35	1.3780	89	3.5039
36	1.4173	90	3.5433
37	1.4567	91	3.5827
38	1.4961	92	3.6220
39	1.5354	93	3.6614
40	1.5748	94	3.7008
41	1.6142	95	3.7402
42	1.6535	96	3.7795
43	1.6929	97	3.8189
44	1.7323	98	3.8583
45	1.7717	99	3.8976
		100	3.9370

Figure 2.90 Decimal equivalents and millimeters.

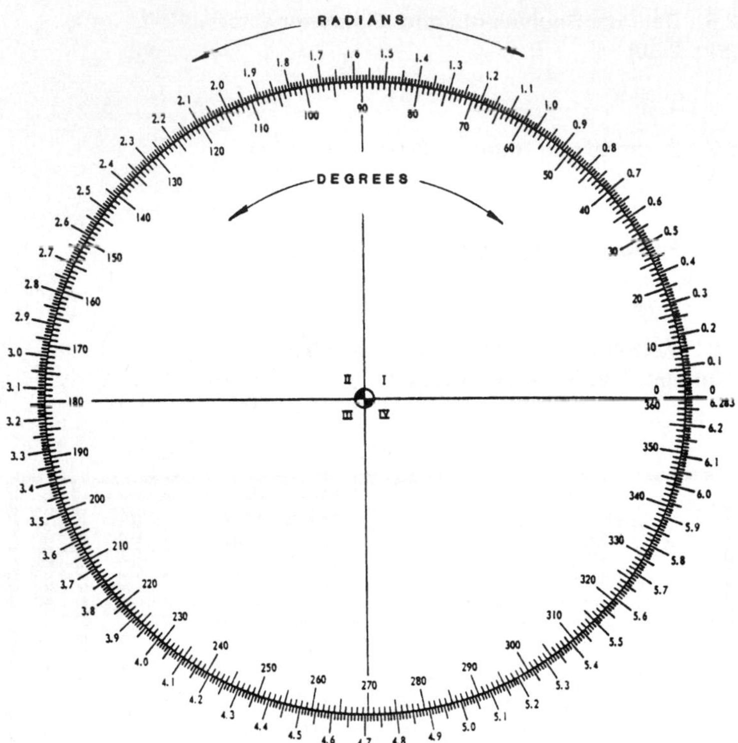

Figure 2.91 Degrees to radians conversion chart.

TABLE 2.1 Factors and Prime Numbers

n	0	1	2	3	4	5	6	7	8	9
0					2^2		$2\cdot3$		2^3	3^2
1	2.5		$2^2\cdot3$		$2\cdot7$	$3\cdot5$	2^4		$2\cdot3^2$	
2	$2^2\cdot5$	$3\cdot7$	$2\cdot11$		$2^3\cdot3$	5^2	$2\cdot13$	3^3	$2^2\cdot7$	
3	$2\cdot3\cdot5$		2^5	$3\cdot11$	$2\cdot17$	$5\cdot7$	$2^2\cdot3^2$		$2\cdot19$	3.13
4	$2^3\cdot5$		$2\cdot3\cdot7$		$2^2\cdot11$	$3^2\cdot5$	$2\cdot23$		$2^4\cdot3$	7^2
5	$2\cdot5^2$	$3\cdot17$	$2^2\cdot13$		$2\cdot3^3$	$5\cdot11$	$2^3\cdot7$	$3\cdot19$	$2\cdot29$	
6	$2^2\cdot3\cdot5$		$2\cdot31$	$3^2\cdot7$	2^6	$5\cdot13$	$2\cdot3\cdot11$		$2^2\cdot17$	$3\cdot23$
7	$2.5\cdot7$		$2^3\cdot3^2$		$2\cdot37$	$3\cdot5^2$	$2^2\cdot19$	$7\cdot11$	$2\cdot3\cdot13$	
8	$2^4\cdot5$	3^4	$2\cdot41$		$2^2\cdot3\cdot7$	$5\cdot17$	$2\cdot43$	$3\cdot29$	$2^3\cdot11$	
9	$2\cdot3^2\cdot5$	$7\cdot13$	$2^2\cdot23$	$3\cdot31$	$2\cdot47$	$5\cdot19$	$2^5\cdot3$		$2\cdot7^2$	$3^2\cdot11$
10	$2^2\cdot5^2$		$2\cdot3\cdot17$		$2^3\cdot13$	$3\cdot5\cdot7$	$2\cdot53$		$2^2\cdot3^3$	
11	$2\cdot5\cdot11$	$3\cdot37$	$2^4\cdot7$		$2\cdot3\cdot19$	$5\cdot23$	$2^2\cdot29$	$3^2\cdot13$	$2\cdot59$	$7\cdot17$
12	$2^3\cdot3\cdot5$	11^2	$2\cdot61$	$3\cdot41$	$2^2\cdot31$	5^3	$2\cdot3^2\cdot7$		2^7	$3\cdot43$
13	$2\cdot5\cdot13$		$2^2\cdot3\cdot11$	$7\cdot19$	$2\cdot67$	$3^3\cdot5$	$2^3\cdot17$		$2\cdot3\cdot23$	
14	$2^2\cdot5\cdot7$	$3\cdot47$	$2\cdot71$	$11\cdot13$	$2^4\cdot3^2$	$5\cdot29$	$2\cdot73$	$3\cdot72$	$2^2\cdot37$	
15	$2\cdot3\cdot5^2$		$2^3\cdot19$	$3^2\cdot17$	$2\cdot7\cdot11$	$5\cdot31$	$2^2\cdot3\cdot13$		$2\cdot79$	$3\cdot53$
16	$2^5\cdot5$	$7\cdot23$	$2\cdot3^4$		$2^2\cdot41$	$3\cdot5\cdot11$	$2\cdot83$		$2^3\cdot3\cdot7$	13^2
17	$2\cdot5\cdot17$	$3^2\cdot19$	$2^2\cdot43$		$2\cdot3\cdot29$	$5^2\cdot7$	$2^4\cdot11$	$3\cdot59$	$2\cdot89$	
18	$2^2\cdot3^2\cdot5$		$2\cdot7\cdot13$	$3\cdot61$	$2^3\cdot23$	$5\cdot37$	$2\cdot3\cdot31$	$11\cdot17$	$2^2\cdot47$	$3^3\cdot7$
19	$2\cdot5\cdot19$		$2^6\cdot3$		$2\cdot97$	$3\cdot5\cdot13$	$2^2\cdot7^2$		$2\cdot3^2\cdot11$	
20	$2^3\cdot5^2$	$3\cdot67$	$2\cdot101$	$7\cdot29$	$2^2\cdot3\cdot17$	$5\cdot41$	$2\cdot103$	$3^2\cdot23$	$2^4\cdot13$	$11\cdot19$
21	$2\cdot3\cdot5\cdot7$		$2^2\cdot53$	$3\cdot71$	$2\cdot107$	$5\cdot43$	$2^3\cdot3^3$	$7\cdot31$	$2\cdot109$	$3\cdot73$
22	$2^2\cdot5\cdot11$	$13\cdot17$	$2\cdot3\cdot37$		$2^5\cdot7$	$3^2\cdot5^2$	$2\cdot113$		$2^2\cdot3\cdot19$	
23	$2\cdot5\cdot23$	$3\cdot7\cdot11$	$2^3\cdot29$		$2\cdot3^2\cdot13$	$5\cdot47$	$2^2\cdot59$	$3\cdot79$	$2\cdot7\cdot17$	
24	$2^4\cdot3\cdot5$		$2\cdot11^2$	3^5	$2^2\cdot61$	$5\cdot7^2$	$2\cdot3\cdot41$	$13\cdot19$	$2^3\cdot31$	$3\cdot83$

TABLE 2.1 Factors and Prime Numbers (*Continued*)

n	0	1	2	3	4	5	6	7	8	9
25	$2\cdot5^3$		$2^2\cdot3^2\cdot7$	$11\cdot23$	$2\cdot127$	$3\cdot5\cdot17$	2^8		$2\cdot3\cdot43$	$7\cdot37$
26	$2^2\cdot5\cdot13$	$3^2\cdot29$	$2\cdot131$		$2^3\cdot3\cdot11$	$5\cdot53$	$2\cdot7\cdot19$	$3\cdot89$	$2^2\cdot67$	
27	$2\cdot3^3\cdot5$		$2^4\cdot17$	$3\cdot7\cdot13$	$2\cdot137$	$5^2\cdot11$	$2^2\cdot3\cdot23$		$2\cdot139$	$3^2\cdot31$
28	$2^3\cdot5\cdot7$		$2\cdot3\cdot47$		$2^2\cdot71$	$3\cdot5\cdot19$	$2\cdot11\cdot13$	$7\cdot41$	$2^5\cdot3^2$	17^2
29	$2\cdot5\cdot29$	$3\cdot97$	$2^2\cdot73$		$2\cdot3\cdot7^2$	$5\cdot59$	$2^3\cdot37$	$3^3\cdot11$	$2\cdot149$	$13\cdot23$
30	$2^2\cdot3\cdot5^2$	$7\cdot43$	$2\cdot151$	$3\cdot101$	$2^4\cdot19$	$5\cdot61$	$2\cdot3^2\cdot17$		$2^2\cdot7\cdot11$	$3\cdot103$
31	$2\cdot5\cdot31$		$2^3\cdot3\cdot13$		$2\cdot157$	$3^2\cdot5\cdot7$	$2^2\cdot79$		$2\cdot3\cdot53$	$11\cdot29$
32	$2^6\cdot5$	$3\cdot107$	$2\cdot7\cdot23$	$17\cdot19$	$2^2\cdot3^4$	$5^2\cdot13$	$2\cdot163$	$3\cdot109$	$2^3\cdot41$	$7\cdot47$
33	$2\cdot3\cdot5\cdot11$		$2^2\cdot83$	$3^2\cdot37$	$2\cdot167$	$5\cdot67$	$2^4\cdot3\cdot7$		$2\cdot13^2$	$3\cdot113$
34	$2^2\cdot5\cdot17$	$11\cdot31$	$2\cdot3^2\cdot19$	7^3	$2^3\cdot43$	$3\cdot5\cdot23$	$2\cdot173$		$2^2\cdot3\cdot29$	
35	$2\cdot5^2\cdot7$	$3^3\cdot13$	$2^5\cdot11$		$2\cdot3\cdot59$	$5\cdot71$	$2^2\cdot89$	$3\cdot7\cdot17$	$2\cdot179$	
36	$2^3\cdot3^2\cdot5$	19^2	$2\cdot181$	$3\cdot11^2$	$2^2\cdot7\cdot13$	$5\cdot73$	$2\cdot3\cdot61$		$2^4\cdot23$	$3^2\cdot41$
37	$2\cdot5\cdot37$	$7\cdot53$	$2^2\cdot3\cdot31$		$2\cdot11\cdot17$	$3\cdot5^3$	$2^3\cdot47$	$13\cdot29$	$2\cdot3^3\cdot7$	
38	$2^2\cdot5\cdot19$	$3\cdot127$	$2\cdot191$		$2^7\cdot3$	$5\cdot7\cdot11$	$2\cdot193$	$3^2\cdot43$	$2^2\cdot97$	
39	$2\cdot3\cdot5\cdot13$	$17\cdot23$	$2^3\cdot7^2$	$3\cdot131$	$2\cdot197$	$5\cdot79$	$2^2\cdot3^2\cdot11$		$2\cdot199$	$3\cdot7\cdot19$
40	$2^4\cdot5^2$		$2\cdot3\cdot67$	$13\cdot31$	$2^2\cdot101$	$3^4\cdot5$	$2\cdot7\cdot29$	$11\cdot37$	$2^3\cdot3\cdot17$	
41	$2\cdot5\cdot41$	$3\cdot137$	$2^2\cdot103$	$7\cdot59$	$2\cdot3^2\cdot23$	$5\cdot83$	$2^5\cdot13$	$3\cdot139$	$2\cdot11\cdot19$	
42	$2^2\cdot3\cdot5\cdot7$		$2\cdot211$	$3^2\cdot47$	$2^3\cdot53$	$5^2\cdot17$	$2\cdot3\cdot71$	$7\cdot61$	$2^2\cdot107$	$3\cdot11\cdot13$
43	$2\cdot5\cdot43$		$2^4\cdot3^3$		$2\cdot7\cdot31$	$3\cdot5\cdot29$	$2^2\cdot109$	$19\cdot23$	$2\cdot3\cdot73$	
44	$2^3\cdot5\cdot11$	$3^2\cdot7^2$	$2\cdot13\cdot17$		$2^2\cdot3\cdot37$	$5\cdot89$	$2\cdot223$	$3\cdot149$	$2^6\cdot7$	
45	$2\cdot3^2\cdot5^2$	$11\cdot41$	$2^2\cdot113$	$3\cdot151$	$2\cdot227$	$5\cdot7\cdot13$	$2^3\cdot3\cdot19$		$2\cdot229$	$3^3\cdot17$
46	$2^2\cdot5\cdot23$		$2\cdot3\cdot7\cdot11$		$2^4\cdot29$	$3\cdot5\cdot31$	$2\cdot233$		$2^2\cdot3^2\cdot13$	$7\cdot67$
47	$2\cdot5\cdot47$	$3\cdot157$	$2^3\cdot50$	$11\cdot43$	$2\cdot3\cdot79$	$5^2\cdot19$	$2^2\cdot7\cdot17$	$3^2\cdot53$	$2\cdot239$	
48	$2^5\cdot3\cdot5$	$13\cdot37$	$2\cdot241$	$3\cdot7\cdot23$	$2^2\cdot11^2$	$5\cdot97$	$2\cdot3^5$		$2^3\cdot61$	$3\cdot163$
49	$2\cdot5\cdot7^2$		$2^2\cdot3\cdot41$	$17\cdot29$	$2\cdot13\cdot19$	$3^2\cdot5\cdot11$	$2^4\cdot31$	$7\cdot71$	$2\cdot3\cdot83$	

	0	1	2	3	4	5	6	7	8	9
50	$2^2\cdot5^3$	$3\cdot167$	$2\cdot251$		$2^3\cdot3^2\cdot7$	$5\cdot101$	$2\cdot11\cdot23$	$3\cdot13^2$	$2^2\cdot127$	
51	$2\cdot3\cdot5\cdot17$	$7\cdot73$	2^9	$3^3\cdot19$	$2\cdot257$	$5\cdot103$	$2^2\cdot3\cdot43$	$11\cdot47$	$2\cdot7\cdot37$	$3\cdot173$
52	$2^3\cdot5\cdot13$		$2\cdot3^2\cdot29$		$2^2\cdot131$	$3\cdot5^2\cdot7$	$2\cdot263$	$17\cdot31$	$2^4\cdot3\cdot11$	23^2
53	$2\cdot5\cdot53$	$3^2\cdot59$	$2^2\cdot7\cdot19$	$13\cdot41$	$2\cdot3\cdot89$	$5\cdot107$	$2^3\cdot67$	$3\cdot179$	$2\cdot269$	$7^2\cdot11$
54	$2^2\cdot3^3\cdot5$		$2\cdot271$	$3\cdot181$	$2^5\cdot17$	$5\cdot109$	$2\cdot3\cdot7\cdot13$		$2^2\cdot137$	$3^2\cdot61$
55	$2\cdot5^2\cdot11$	$19\cdot29$	$2^3\cdot3\cdot23$	$7\cdot79$	$2\cdot277$	$3\cdot5\cdot37$	$2^2\cdot139$		$2\cdot3^2\cdot31$	$13\cdot43$
56	$2^4\cdot5\cdot7$	$3\cdot11\cdot17$	$2\cdot281$		$2^2\cdot3\cdot47$	$5\cdot113$	$2\cdot283$	$3^4\cdot7$	$2^3\cdot71$	
57	$2\cdot3\cdot5\cdot19$		$2^2\cdot11\cdot13$	$3\cdot191$	$2\cdot7\cdot41$	$5^2\cdot23$	$2^6\cdot3^2$		$2\cdot17^2$	$3\cdot193$
58	$2^2\cdot5\cdot29$	$7\cdot83$	$2\cdot3\cdot97$	$11\cdot53$	$2^3\cdot73$	$3^2\cdot5\cdot13$	$2\cdot293$		$2^2\cdot3\cdot7^2$	$19\cdot31$
59	$2\cdot5\cdot59$	$3\cdot197$	$2^4\cdot37$		$2\cdot3^3\cdot11$	$5\cdot7\cdot17$	$2^2\cdot149$	$3\cdot199$	$2\cdot13\cdot23$	
60	$2^3\cdot3\cdot5^2$		$2\cdot7\cdot43$	$3^2\cdot67$	$2^2\cdot151$	$5\cdot11^2$	$2\cdot3\cdot101$		$2^5\cdot19$	$3\cdot7\cdot29$
61	$2\cdot5\cdot61$	$13\cdot47$	$2^2\cdot3^2\cdot17$		$2\cdot307$	$3\cdot5\cdot41$	$2^3\cdot7\cdot11$		$2\cdot3\cdot103$	
62	$2^2\cdot5\cdot31$	$3^3\cdot23$	$2\cdot311$	$7\cdot89$	$2^4\cdot3\cdot13$	5^4	$2\cdot313$	$3\cdot11\cdot19$	$2^2\cdot157$	$17\cdot37$
63	$2\cdot3^2\cdot5\cdot7$		$2^3\cdot79$	$3\cdot211$	$2\cdot317$	$5\cdot127$	$2^2\cdot3\cdot53$	$7^2\cdot13$	$2\cdot11\cdot29$	$3^2\cdot71$
64	$2^7\cdot5$		$2\cdot3\cdot107$		$2^2\cdot7\cdot23$	$3\cdot5\cdot43$	$2\cdot17\cdot19$		$2^3\cdot3^4$	$11\cdot59$
65	$2\cdot5^2\cdot13$	$3\cdot7\cdot31$	$2^2\cdot163$		$2\cdot3\cdot109$	$5\cdot131$	$2^4\cdot41$	$3^2\cdot73$	$2\cdot7\cdot47$	
66	$2^2\cdot3\cdot5\cdot11$		$2\cdot331$	$3\cdot13\cdot17$	$2^3\cdot83$	$5\cdot7\cdot19$	$2\cdot3^2\cdot37$	$23\cdot29$	$2^2\cdot167$	$3\cdot223$
67	$2\cdot5\cdot67$	$11\cdot61$	$2^5\cdot3\cdot7$		$2\cdot337$	$3^3\cdot5^2$	$2^2\cdot13^2$		$2\cdot3\cdot113$	$7\cdot97$
68	$2^3\cdot5\cdot17$	$3\cdot227$	$2\cdot11\cdot31$		$2^2\cdot3^2\cdot19$	$5\cdot137$	$2\cdot7^3$	$3\cdot229$	$2^4\cdot43$	$13\cdot53$
69	$2\cdot3\cdot5\cdot23$		$2^2\cdot173$	$3^2\cdot7\cdot11$	$2\cdot347$	$5\cdot139$	$2^3\cdot3\cdot29$	$17\cdot41$	$2\cdot349$	$3\cdot233$
70	$2^2\cdot5^2\cdot7$		$2\cdot3^3\cdot13$	$19\cdot37$	$2^6\cdot11$	$3\cdot5\cdot47$	$2\cdot353$	$7\cdot101$	$2^2\cdot3\cdot59$	
71	$2\cdot5\cdot71$	$3^2\cdot79$	$2^3\cdot89$	$23\cdot31$	$2\cdot3\cdot7\cdot17$	$5\cdot11\cdot13$	$2^2\cdot179$	$3\cdot239$	$2\cdot359$	
72	$2^4\cdot3^2\cdot5$	$7\cdot103$	$2\cdot19^2$	$3\cdot241$	$2^2\cdot181$	$5^2\cdot29$	$2\cdot3\cdot11^2$		$2^3\cdot7\cdot13$	3^6
73	$2\cdot5\cdot73$	$17\cdot43$	$2^2\cdot3\cdot61$		$2\cdot367$	$3\cdot5\cdot7^2$	$2^5\cdot23$	$11\cdot67$	$2\cdot3^2\cdot41$	
74	$2^2\cdot5\cdot37$	$3\cdot13\cdot19$	$2\cdot7\cdot53$		$2^3\cdot3\cdot31$	$5\cdot149$	$2\cdot373$	$3^2\cdot83$	$2^2\cdot11\cdot17$	$7\cdot107$
75	$2\cdot3\cdot5^3$		$2^4\cdot47$	$3\cdot251$	$2\cdot13\cdot29$	$5\cdot151$	$2^2\cdot3^3\cdot7$		$2\cdot379$	$3\cdot11\cdot23$
76	$2^3\cdot5\cdot19$		$2\cdot3\cdot127$	$7\cdot109$	$2^2\cdot191$	$3^2\cdot5\cdot17$	$2\cdot383$	$13\cdot59$	$2^8\cdot3$	
77	$2\cdot5\cdot7\cdot11$	$3\cdot257$	$2^2\cdot193$		$2\cdot3^2\cdot43$	$5^2\cdot31$	$2^3\cdot97$	$3\cdot7\cdot37$	$2\cdot389$	$19\cdot41$

TABLE 2.1 Factors and Prime Numbers (*Continued*)

n	0	1	2	3	4	5	6	7	8	9
78	$2^2\cdot3\cdot5\cdot13$	$11\cdot71$	$2\cdot17\cdot23$	$3^3\cdot29$	$2^4\cdot7^2$	$5\cdot157$	$2\cdot3\cdot131$		$2^2\cdot197$	$3\cdot263$
79	$2\cdot5\cdot79$	$7\cdot113$	$2^3\cdot3^2\cdot11$	$13\cdot61$	$2\cdot397$	$3\cdot5\cdot53$	$2^2\cdot199$		$2\cdot3\cdot7\cdot19$	$17\cdot47$
80	$2^5\cdot5^2$	$3^2\cdot89$	$2\cdot401$	$11\cdot73$	$2^2\cdot3\cdot67$	$5\cdot7\cdot23$	$2\cdot13\cdot31$	$3\cdot269$	$2^3\cdot101$	
81	$2\cdot3^4\cdot5$		$2^2\cdot7\cdot29$	$3\cdot271$	$2\cdot11\cdot37$	$5\cdot163$	$2^4\cdot3\cdot17$	$19\cdot43$	$2\cdot409$	$3^2\cdot7\cdot13$
82	$2^2\cdot5\cdot41$		$2\cdot3\cdot137$		$2^3\cdot103$	$3\cdot5^2\cdot11$	$2\cdot7\cdot59$		$2^2\cdot3^2\cdot23$	
83	$2\cdot5\cdot83$	$3\cdot277$	$2^6\cdot13$	$7^2\cdot17$	$2\cdot3\cdot139$	$5\cdot167$	$2^2\cdot11\cdot19$	$3^3\cdot31$	$2\cdot419$	
84	$2^3\cdot3\cdot5\cdot7$	29^2	$2\cdot421$	$3\cdot281$	$2^2\cdot211$	$5\cdot13^2$	$2\cdot3^2\cdot47$	$7\cdot11^2$	$2^4\cdot53$	$3\cdot283$
85	$2\cdot5^2\cdot17$	$23\cdot37$	$2^2\cdot3\cdot71$		$2\cdot7\cdot61$	$3^2\cdot5\cdot19$	$2^3\cdot107$		$2\cdot3\cdot11\cdot13$	
86	$2^2\cdot5\cdot43$	$3\cdot7\cdot41$	$2\cdot431$		$2^5\cdot3^3$	$5\cdot173$	$2\cdot433$	$3\cdot17^2$	$2^2\cdot7\cdot31$	$11\cdot79$
87	$2\cdot3\cdot5\cdot29$	$13\cdot67$	$2^3\cdot109$	$3^2\cdot97$	$2\cdot19\cdot23$	$5^3\cdot7$	$2^2\cdot3\cdot73$		$2\cdot439$	$3\cdot293$
88	$2^4\cdot5\cdot11$		$2\cdot3^2\cdot7^2$		$2^2\cdot13\cdot17$	$3\cdot5\cdot59$	$2\cdot443$		$2^3\cdot3\cdot37$	$7\cdot127$
89	$2\cdot5\cdot89$	$3^4\cdot11$	$2^2\cdot223$	$19\cdot47$	$2\cdot3\cdot149$	$5\cdot179$	$2^7\cdot7$	$3\cdot13\cdot23$	$2\cdot449$	$29\cdot31$
90	$2^2\cdot3^2\cdot5^2$	$17\cdot53$	$2\cdot11\cdot41$	$3\cdot7\cdot43$	$2^3\cdot113$	$5\cdot181$	$2\cdot3\cdot151$		$2^2\cdot227$	$3^2\cdot101$
91	$2\cdot5\cdot7\cdot13$		$2^4\cdot3\cdot19$	$11\cdot83$	$2\cdot457$	$3\cdot5\cdot61$	$2^2\cdot229$	$7\cdot131$	$2\cdot3^3\cdot17$	
92	$2^3\cdot5\cdot23$	$3\cdot307$	$2\cdot461$	$13\cdot71$	$2^2\cdot3\cdot7\cdot11$	$5^2\cdot37$	$2\cdot463$	$3^2\cdot103$	$2^5\cdot29$	
93	$2\cdot3\cdot5\cdot31$	$7^2\cdot19$	$2^2\cdot233$	$3\cdot311$	$2\cdot467$	$5\cdot11\cdot17$	$2^3\cdot3^2\cdot13$		$2\cdot7\cdot67$	$3\cdot313$
94	$2^2\cdot5\cdot47$		$2\cdot3\cdot157$	$23\cdot41$	$2^4\cdot59$	$3^3\cdot5\cdot7$	$2\cdot11\cdot43$		$2^2\cdot3\cdot79$	$13\cdot73$
95	$2\cdot5^2\cdot19$	$3\cdot317$	$2^3\cdot7\cdot17$		$2\cdot3^2\cdot53$	$5\cdot191$	$2^2\cdot239$	$3\cdot11\cdot29$	$2\cdot479$	$7\cdot137$
96	$2^6\cdot3\cdot5$	31^2	$2\cdot13\cdot37$	$3^2\cdot107$	$2^2\cdot241$	$5\cdot193$	$2\cdot3\cdot7\cdot23$		$2^3\cdot11^2$	$3\cdot17\cdot19$
97	$2\cdot5\cdot97$		$2^2\cdot3^5$	$7\cdot139$	$2\cdot487$	$3\cdot5^2\cdot13$	$2^4\cdot61$		$2\cdot3\cdot163$	$11\cdot89$
98	$2^2\cdot5\cdot7^2$	$3^2\cdot109$	$2\cdot491$		$2^3\cdot3\cdot41$	$5\cdot197$	$2\cdot17\cdot29$	$3\cdot7\cdot47$	$2^2\cdot13\cdot19$	$23\cdot43$
99	$2\cdot3^2\cdot5\cdot11$		$2^5\cdot31$	$3\cdot331$	$2\cdot7\cdot71$	$5\cdot199$	$2^2\cdot3\cdot83$		$2\cdot499$	$3^3\cdot37$
100	$2^3\cdot5^3$	$7\cdot11\cdot13$	$2\cdot3\cdot167$	$17\cdot59$	$2^2\cdot251$	$3\cdot5\cdot67$	$2\cdot503$	$19\cdot53$	$2^4\cdot3^2\cdot7$	
101	$2\cdot5\cdot101$	$3\cdot337$	$2^2\cdot11\cdot23$		$2\cdot3\cdot13^2$	$5\cdot7\cdot29$	$2^3\cdot127$	$3^2\cdot113$	$2\cdot509$	
102	$2^2\cdot3\cdot5\cdot17$		$2\cdot7\cdot73$	$3\cdot11\cdot31$	2^{10}	$5^2\cdot41$	$2\cdot3^3\cdot19$	$13\cdot79$	$2^2\cdot257$	$3\cdot7^3$
103	$2\cdot5\cdot103$		$2^3\cdot3\cdot43$		$2\cdot11\cdot47$	$3^2\cdot5\cdot23$	$2^2\cdot7\cdot37$	$17\cdot61$	$2\cdot3\cdot173$	

104	$2^4\cdot5\cdot13$	3·347	2·521	7·149	$2^2\cdot3^2\cdot29$	5·11·11	2·523	3·349	$2^3\cdot131$	
105	$2\cdot3\cdot5^2\cdot7$		$2^2\cdot263$	$3^4\cdot13$	2·17·31	5·211	$2^5\cdot3\cdot11$	7·151	$2\cdot23^2$	3·353
106	$2^2\cdot5\cdot53$		$2\cdot3^2\cdot59$		$2^3\cdot7\cdot19$	3·5·71	2·13·41	11·97	$2^2\cdot3\cdot89$	
107	2·5·107	$3^2\cdot7\cdot17$	$2^4\cdot67$	29·37	2·3·179	$5^2\cdot43$	$2^2\cdot269$	3·359	$2\cdot7^2\cdot11$	13·83
108	$2^3\cdot3^3\cdot5$	23·47	2·541	$3\cdot19^2$	$2^2\cdot271$	5·7·31	2·3·181		$2^6\cdot17$	$3^2\cdot11^2$
109	2·5·109		$2^2\cdot3\cdot7\cdot13$		2·547	3·5·73	$2^3\cdot137$		$2\cdot3^2\cdot61$	7·157
110	$2^2\cdot5^2\cdot11$	3·367	2·19·29		$2^4\cdot3\cdot23$	5·13·17	2·7·79	$3^3\cdot41$	$2^2\cdot277$	
111	2·3·5·37	11·101	$2^3\cdot139$	3·7·53	2·557	5·223	$2^2\cdot3^2\cdot31$		2·13·43	3·373
112	$2^5\cdot5\cdot7$	19·59	2·3·11·17		$2^2\cdot281$	$3^2\cdot5^3$	2·563	$7^2\cdot23$	$2^3\cdot3\cdot47$	
113	2·5·113	3·13·29	$2^2\cdot283$	11·103	$2\cdot3^4\cdot7$	5·227	$2^4\cdot71$	3·379	2·569	17·67
114	$2^2\cdot3\cdot5\cdot19$	7·163	2·571	$3^2\cdot127$	$2^3\cdot11\cdot13$	5·229	2·3·191	31·37	$2^2\cdot7\cdot41$	3·383
115	$2\cdot5^2\cdot23$		$2^7\cdot3^2$		2·577	3·5·7·11	$2^2\cdot17^2$	13·89	2·3·193	19·61
116	$2^3\cdot5\cdot29$	$3^3\cdot43$	2·7·83		$2^2\cdot3\cdot97$	5·233	2·11·53	3·389	$2^4\cdot73$	7·167
117	$2\cdot3^2\cdot5\cdot13$		$2^2\cdot293$	3·17·23	2·587	$5^2\cdot47$	$2^3\cdot3\cdot7^2$	11·107	2·19·31	$3^2\cdot131$
118	$2^2\cdot5\cdot59$		2·3·197	$7\cdot13^2$	$2^5\cdot37$	3·5·79	2·593		$2^2\cdot3^3\cdot11$	29·41
119	2·5·7·17	3·397	$2^3\cdot149$		2·3·199	5·239	$2^2\cdot13\cdot23$	$3^2\cdot7\cdot19$	2·599	11·109
120	$2^4\cdot3\cdot5^2$		2·601	3·401	$2^2\cdot7\cdot43$	5·241	$2\cdot3^2\cdot67$	17·71	$2^3\cdot151$	3·13·31
121	$2\cdot5\cdot11^2$	7·173	$2^2\cdot3\cdot101$		2·607	$3^5\cdot5$	$2^6\cdot19$		2·3·7·29	23·53
122	$2^2\cdot5\cdot61$	3·11·37	2·13·47		$2^3\cdot3^2\cdot17$	$5^2\cdot7^2$	2·613	3·409	$2^2\cdot307$	
123	2·3·5·41		$2^4\cdot7\cdot11$	$3^2\cdot137$	2·617	5·13·19	$2^2\cdot3\cdot103$		2·619	3·7·59
124	$2^3\cdot5\cdot31$	17·73	$2\cdot3^3\cdot23$	11·113	$2^2\cdot311$	3·5·83	2·7·89	29·43	$2^5\cdot3\cdot13$	
125	$2\cdot5^4$	$3^2\cdot139$	$2^2\cdot313$	7·179	2·3·11·19	5·251	$2^3\cdot157$	3·419	2·17·37	
126	$2^2\cdot3^2\cdot5\cdot7$	13·97	2·631	3·421	$2^4\cdot79$	5·11·23	2·3·211	7·181	$2^2\cdot317$	$3^3\cdot47$
127	2·5·127	31·41	$2^3\cdot3\cdot53$	19·67	$2\cdot7^2\cdot13$	$3\cdot5^2\cdot17$	$2^2\cdot11\cdot29$		$2\cdot3^2\cdot71$	
128	$2^8\cdot5$	3·7·61	2·641		$2^2\cdot3\cdot107$	5·257	2·643	$3^2\cdot11\cdot13$	$2^3\cdot7\cdot23$	
129	2·3·5·43		$2^2\cdot17\cdot19$	3·431	2·647	5·7·37	$2^4\cdot3^4$		2·11·59	3·433
130	$2^2\cdot5^2\cdot13$		2·3·7·31		$2^3\cdot163$	$3^2\cdot5\cdot29$	2·653		$2^2\cdot3\cdot109$	7·11·17
131	2·5·131	3·19·23	$2^5\cdot41$	13·101	$2\cdot3^2\cdot73$	5·263	$2^2\cdot7\cdot47$	3·439	2·659	

TABLE 2.1 Factors and Prime Numbers (*Continued*)

n	0	1	2	3	4	5	6	7	8	9
132	$2^3\cdot3\cdot5\cdot11$		$2\cdot661$	$3^3\cdot7^2$	$2^2\cdot331$	$5^2\cdot53$	$2\cdot3\cdot13\cdot17$		$2^4\cdot83$	$3\cdot443$
133	$2\cdot5\cdot7\cdot19$	11^3	$2^2\cdot3^2\cdot37$	$31\cdot43$	$2\cdot23\cdot29$	$3\cdot5\cdot89$	$2^3\cdot167$	$7\cdot191$	$2\cdot3\cdot223$	$13\cdot103$
134	$2^2\cdot5\cdot67$	$3^2\cdot149$	$2\cdot11\cdot61$	$17\cdot79$	$2^6\cdot3\cdot7$	$5\cdot269$	$2\cdot673$	$3\cdot449$	$2^2\cdot337$	$19\cdot71$
135	$2\cdot3^3\cdot5^2$	$7\cdot193$	$2^3\cdot13^2$	$3\cdot11\cdot41$	$2\cdot677$	$5\cdot271$	$2^2\cdot3\cdot113$	$23\cdot59$	$2\cdot7\cdot97$	$3^2\cdot151$
136	$2^4\cdot5\cdot17$		$2\cdot3\cdot227$	$29\cdot47$	$2^2\cdot11\cdot31$	$3\cdot5\cdot7\cdot13$	$2\cdot683$		$2^3\cdot3^2\cdot19$	37^2
137	$2\cdot5\cdot137$	$3\cdot457$	$2^2\cdot7^3$		$2\cdot3\cdot229$	$5^3\cdot11$	$2^5\cdot43$	$3^4\cdot17$	$2\cdot13\cdot53$	$7\cdot197$
138	$2^2\cdot3\cdot5\cdot23$		$2\cdot691$	$3\cdot461$	$2^3\cdot173$	$5\cdot277$	$2\cdot3^2\cdot7\cdot11$	$19\cdot73$	$2^2\cdot347$	$3\cdot463$
139	$2\cdot5\cdot139$	$13\cdot107$	$2^4\cdot3\cdot29$	$7\cdot199$	$2\cdot17\cdot41$	$3^2\cdot5\cdot31$	$2^2\cdot349$	$11\cdot127$	$2\cdot3\cdot233$	
140	$2^3\cdot5^2\cdot7$	$3\cdot467$	$2\cdot701$	$23\cdot61$	$2^2\cdot3^3\cdot13$	$5\cdot281$	$2\cdot19\cdot37$	$3\cdot7\cdot67$	$2^7\cdot11$	
141	$2\cdot3\cdot5\cdot47$	$17\cdot83$	$2^2\cdot353$	$3^2\cdot157$	$2\cdot7\cdot101$	$5\cdot283$	$2^3\cdot3\cdot59$	$13\cdot109$	$2\cdot709$	$3\cdot11\cdot43$
142	$2^2\cdot5\cdot71$	$7^2\cdot29$	$2\cdot3^2\cdot79$		$2^4\cdot89$	$3\cdot5^2\cdot19$	$2\cdot23\cdot31$		$2^2\cdot3\cdot7\cdot17$	
143	$2\cdot5\cdot11\cdot13$	$3^3\cdot53$	$2^3\cdot179$		$2\cdot3\cdot239$	$5\cdot7\cdot41$	$2^2\cdot359$	$3\cdot479$	$2\cdot719$	
144	$2^5\cdot3^2\cdot5$	$11\cdot131$	$2\cdot7\cdot103$	$3\cdot13\cdot37$	$2^2\cdot19^2$	$5\cdot17^2$	$2\cdot3\cdot241$		$2^3\cdot181$	$3^2\cdot7\cdot23$
145	$2\cdot5^2\cdot29$		$2^2\cdot3\cdot11^2$		$2\cdot727$	$3\cdot5\cdot97$	$2^4\cdot7\cdot13$	$31\cdot47$	$2\cdot3^6$	
146	$2^2\cdot5\cdot73$	$3\cdot487$	$2\cdot17\cdot43$	$7\cdot11\cdot19$	$2^3\cdot3\cdot61$	$5\cdot293$	$2\cdot733$	$3^2\cdot163$	$2^2\cdot367$	$13\cdot113$
147	$2\cdot3\cdot5\cdot7^2$		$2^6\cdot23$	$3\cdot491$	$2\cdot11\cdot67$	$5^2\cdot59$	$2^2\cdot3^2\cdot41$	$7\cdot211$	$2\cdot739$	$3\cdot17\cdot29$
148	$2^3\cdot5\cdot37$		$2\cdot3\cdot13\cdot19$		$2^2\cdot7\cdot53$	$3^3\cdot5\cdot11$	$2\cdot743$		$2^4\cdot3\cdot31$	
149	$2\cdot5\cdot149$	$3\cdot7\cdot71$	$2^2\cdot373$		$2\cdot3^2\cdot83$	$5\cdot13\cdot23$	$2^2\cdot11\cdot17$	$3\cdot499$	$2\cdot7\cdot107$	
150	$2^2\cdot3\cdot5^3$	$19\cdot79$	$2\cdot751$	$3^2\cdot167$	$2^5\cdot47$	$5\cdot7\cdot43$	$2\cdot3\cdot251$	$11\cdot137$	$2^2\cdot13\cdot29$	$3\cdot503$
151	$2\cdot5\cdot151$		$2^3\cdot3^3\cdot7$	$17\cdot89$	$2\cdot757$	$3\cdot5\cdot101$	$2^2\cdot379$	$37\cdot41$	$2\cdot3\cdot11\cdot23$	$7^2\cdot31$
152	$2^4\cdot5\cdot19$	$3^2\cdot13^2$	$2\cdot761$		$2^2\cdot3\cdot127$	$5^2\cdot61$	$2\cdot7\cdot109$	$3\cdot509$	$2^3\cdot191$	$11\cdot139$
153	$2\cdot3^2\cdot5\cdot17$		$2^2\cdot383$	$3\cdot7\cdot73$	$2\cdot13\cdot59$	$5\cdot307$	$2^9\cdot3$	$29\cdot53$	$2\cdot769$	$3^4\cdot19$
154	$2^2\cdot5\cdot7\cdot11$	$23\cdot67$	$2\cdot3\cdot257$		$2^3\cdot193$	$3\cdot5\cdot103$	$2\cdot773$	$7\cdot13\cdot17$	$2^2\cdot3^2\cdot43$	
155	$2\cdot5^2\cdot31$	$3\cdot11\cdot47$	$2^4\cdot97$		$2\cdot3\cdot7\cdot37$	$5\cdot311$	$2^2\cdot389$	$3^2\cdot173$	$2\cdot19\cdot41$	
156	$2^3\cdot3\cdot5\cdot13$	$7\cdot223$	$2\cdot11\cdot71$	$3\cdot521$	$2^2\cdot17\cdot23$	$5\cdot313$	$2\cdot3^3\cdot29$		$2^5\cdot7^2$	$3\cdot523$
157	$2\cdot5\cdot157$		$2^2\cdot3\cdot131$	$11^2\cdot13$	$2\cdot787$	$3^2\cdot5^2\cdot7$	$2^3\cdot197$	$19\cdot83$	$2\cdot3\cdot263$	
158	$2^2\cdot5\cdot79$	$3\cdot17\cdot31$	$2\cdot7\cdot113$		$2^4\cdot3^2\cdot11$	$5\cdot317$	$2\cdot13\cdot61$	$3\cdot23^2$	$2^2\cdot397$	$7\cdot227$

159	2·3·5·53	37·43	$2^3\cdot199$	$3^3\cdot59$	2·797	5·11·29	$2^2\cdot3\cdot7\cdot19$		2·17·47	3·13·41
160	$2^6\cdot5^2$		$2\cdot3^2\cdot89$	7·229	$2^2\cdot401$	3·5·107	2·11·73		$2^3\cdot3\cdot67$	
161	2·5·7·23	$3^2\cdot179$	$2^2\cdot13\cdot31$		2·3·269	5·17·19	$2^4\cdot101$	$3\cdot7^2\cdot11$	2·809	
162	$2^2\cdot3^4\cdot5$		2·811	3·541	$2^3\cdot7\cdot29$	$5^3\cdot13$	2·3·271		$2^2\cdot11\cdot37$	$3^2\cdot181$
163	2·5·163	7·233	$2^5\cdot3\cdot17$	23·71	2·19·43	3·5·109	$2^2\cdot409$		$2\cdot3^2\cdot7\cdot13$	11·149
164	$2^3\cdot5\cdot41$	3·547	2·821	31·53	$2^2\cdot3\cdot137$	5·7·47	2·823	$3^3\cdot61$	$2^4\cdot103$	17·97
165	$2\cdot3\cdot5^2\cdot11$	13·127	$2^2\cdot7\cdot59$	3·19·29	2·827	5·331	$2^3\cdot3^2\cdot23$		2·829	3·7·79
166	$2^2\cdot5\cdot83$	11·151	2·3·277		$2^7\cdot13$	$3^2\cdot5\cdot37$	$2\cdot7^2\cdot17$		$2^2\cdot3\cdot139$	
167	2·5·167	3·557	$2^3\cdot11\cdot19$	7·239	$2\cdot3^3\cdot31$	$5^2\cdot67$	$2^2\cdot419$	3·13·43	2·839	23·73
168	$2^4\cdot3\cdot5\cdot7$	41^2	$2\cdot29^2$	$3^2\cdot11\cdot17$	$2^2\cdot421$	5·337	2·3·281	7·241	$2^3\cdot211$	3·563
169	$2\cdot5\cdot13^2$	19·89	$2^2\cdot3^2\cdot47$		$2\cdot7\cdot11^2$	3·5·113	$2^5\cdot53$		2·3·283	
170	$2^2\cdot5^2\cdot17$	$3^5\cdot7$	2·23·37	13·131	$2^3\cdot3\cdot71$	5·11·31	2·853	3·569	$2^2\cdot7\cdot61$	
171	$2\cdot3^2\cdot5\cdot19$	29·59	$2^4\cdot107$	3·571	2·857	$5\cdot7^3$	$2^2\cdot3\cdot11\cdot13$	17·101	2·859	$3^2\cdot191$
172	$2^3\cdot5\cdot43$		2·3·7·41		$2^2\cdot431$	$3\cdot5^2\cdot23$	2·863	11·157	$2^6\cdot3^3$	7·13·19
173	2·5·173	3·577	$2^2\cdot433$		$2\cdot3\cdot17^2$	5·347	$2^3\cdot7\cdot31$	$3^2\cdot193$	2·11·79	37·47
174	$2^2\cdot3\cdot5\cdot29$		2·13·67	3·7·83	$2^4\cdot109$	5·349	$2\cdot3^2\cdot97$		$2^2\cdot19\cdot23$	3·11·53
175	$2\cdot5^3\cdot7$	17·103	$2^3\cdot3\cdot73$		2·877	$3^3\cdot5\cdot13$	$2^2\cdot439$	7·251	2·3·293	
176	$2^5\cdot5\cdot11$	3·587	2·881	41·43	$2^2\cdot3^2\cdot7^2$	5·353	2·883	3·19·31	$2^3\cdot13\cdot17$	29·61
177	2·3·5·59	7·11·23	$2^2\cdot443$	$3^2\cdot197$	2·887	$5^2\cdot71$	$2^4\cdot3\cdot37$		2·7·127	3·593
178	$2^2\cdot5\cdot89$	13·137	$2\cdot3^4\cdot11$		$2^3\cdot223$	3·5·7·17	2·19·47		$2^2\cdot3\cdot149$	
179	2·5·179	$3^2\cdot199$	$2^8\cdot7$	11·163	2·3·13·23	5·359	$2^2\cdot449$	3·599	2·29·31	7·257
180	$2^3\cdot3^2\cdot5^2$		2·17·53	3·601	$2^2\cdot11\cdot41$	$5\cdot19^2$	2·3·7·43	13·139	$2^4\cdot113$	$3^3\cdot67$
181	2·5·181		$2^2\cdot3\cdot151$	$7^2\cdot37$	2·907	$3\cdot5\cdot11^2$	$2^3\cdot227$	23·79	$2\cdot3^2\cdot101$	17·107
182	$2^2\cdot5\cdot7\cdot13$	3·607	2·911		$2^5\cdot3\cdot19$	$5^2\cdot73$	2·11·83	$3^2\cdot7\cdot29$	$2^2\cdot457$	31·59
183	2·3·5·61		$2^3\cdot229$	3·13·47	2·7·131	5·367	$2^2\cdot3^3\cdot17$	11·167	2·919	3·613
184	$2^4\cdot5\cdot23$	7·263	2·3·307	19·97	$2^2\cdot461$	$3^2\cdot5\cdot41$	2·13·71		$2^3\cdot3\cdot7\cdot11$	43^2

TABLE 2.1 Factors and Prime Numbers (*Continued*)

n	0	1	2	3	4	5	6	7	8	9
185	$2\cdot5^2\cdot37$	$3\cdot617$	$2^2\cdot463$	$17\cdot109$	$2\cdot3^2\cdot103$	$5\cdot7\cdot53$	$2^6\cdot29$	$3\cdot619$	$2\cdot929$	$11\cdot13^2$
186	$2^2\cdot3\cdot5\cdot31$		$2\cdot7^2\cdot19$	$3^4\cdot23$	$2^3\cdot233$	$5\cdot373$	$2\cdot3\cdot311$		$2^2\cdot467$	$3\cdot7\cdot89$
187	$2\cdot5\cdot11\cdot17$		$2^4\cdot3^2\cdot13$		$2\cdot937$	$3\cdot5^4$	$2^2\cdot7\cdot67$		$2\cdot3\cdot313$	
188	$2^3\cdot5\cdot47$	$3^2\cdot11\cdot19$	$2\cdot941$	$7\cdot269$	$2^2\cdot3\cdot157$	$5\cdot13\cdot29$	$2\cdot23\cdot41$	$3\cdot17\cdot37$	$2^5\cdot59$	
189	$2\cdot3^3\cdot5\cdot7$	$31\cdot61$	$2^2\cdot11\cdot43$	$3\cdot631$	$2\cdot947$	$5\cdot379$	$2^3\cdot3\cdot79$	$7\cdot271$	$2\cdot13\cdot73$	$3^2\cdot211$
190	$2^2\cdot5^2\cdot19$		$2\cdot3\cdot317$	$11\cdot173$	$2^4\cdot7\cdot17$	$3\cdot5\cdot127$	$2\cdot953$		$2^2\cdot3^2\cdot53$	$23\cdot83$
191	$2\cdot5\cdot191$	$3\cdot7^2\cdot13$	$2^3\cdot239$		$2\cdot3\cdot11\cdot29$	$5\cdot383$	$2^2\cdot479$	$3^3\cdot71$	$2\cdot7\cdot137$	$19\cdot101$
192	$2^7\cdot3\cdot5$	$17\cdot113$	$2\cdot31^2$	$3\cdot641$	$2^2\cdot13\cdot37$	$5^2\cdot7\cdot11$	$2\cdot3^2\cdot107$	$41\cdot47$	$2^3\cdot241$	$3\cdot643$
193	$2\cdot5\cdot193$		$2^2\cdot3\cdot7\cdot23$		$2\cdot967$	$3^2\cdot5\cdot43$	$2^4\cdot11^2$	$13\cdot149$	$2\cdot3\cdot17\cdot19$	$7\cdot277$
194	$2^2\cdot5\cdot97$	$3\cdot647$	$2\cdot971$	$29\cdot67$	$2^3\cdot3^5$	$5\cdot389$	$2\cdot7\cdot139$	$3\cdot11\cdot59$	$2^2\cdot487$	
195	$2\cdot3\cdot5^2\cdot13$		$2^5\cdot61$	$3^2\cdot7\cdot31$	$2\cdot977$	$5\cdot17\cdot23$	$2^2\cdot3\cdot163$	$19\cdot103$	$2\cdot11\cdot89$	$3\cdot653$
196	$2^3\cdot5\cdot7^2$	$37\cdot53$	$2\cdot3^2\cdot109$	$13\cdot151$	$2^2\cdot491$	$3\cdot5\cdot131$	$2\cdot983$	$7\cdot281$	$2^4\cdot3\cdot41$	$11\cdot179$
197	$2\cdot5\cdot197$	$3^3\cdot73$	$2^2\cdot17\cdot29$		$2\cdot3\cdot7\cdot47$	$5^2\cdot79$	$2^3\cdot13\cdot19$	$3\cdot659$	$2\cdot23\cdot43$	
198	$2^2\cdot3^2\cdot5\cdot11$	$7\cdot283$	$2\cdot991$	$3\cdot661$	$2^6\cdot31$	$5\cdot397$	$2\cdot3\cdot331$		$2^2\cdot7\cdot71$	$3^2\cdot13\cdot17$
199	$2\cdot5\cdot199$	$11\cdot181$	$2^3\cdot3\cdot83$		$2\cdot997$	$3\cdot5\cdot7\cdot19$	$2^2\cdot499$		$2\cdot3^3\cdot37$	
200	$2^4\cdot5^3$	$3\cdot23\cdot29$	$2\cdot7\cdot11\cdot13$		$2^2\cdot3\cdot167$	$5\cdot401$	$2\cdot17\cdot59$	$3^2\cdot223$	$2^3\cdot251$	$7^2\cdot41$

TABLE 2.2 The Greek Alphabet

α	Α	alpha	ι	Ι	iota	ρ	Ρ	rho
β	Β	beta	κ	κ	kappa	σ	Σ	sigma
γ	Γ	gamma	λ	Λ	lambda	τ	Τ	tau
δ	Δ	delta	μ	Μ	mu	υ	Υ	upsilon
ε	Ε	epsilon	ν	Ν	nu	ϕ	Φ	phi
ζ	Ζ	zeta	φ	Ξ	xi	χ	Χ	chi
η	Η	eta	ο	Ο	omicron	ψ	Ψ	psi
θ	Θ	theta	π	Π	pi	ω	Ω	omega

TABLE 2.3 Mathematical Signs and Symbols

$+$	Plus, positive
$-$	Minus, negative
$\times$ or $\cdot$	Times, multiplied by
$\div$ or /	Divided by
$=$	Is equal to
$\equiv$	Is identical to
$\cong$	Is congruent to or approximately equal to
$\sim$	Is approximately equal to or is similar to
$<$ and $\nless$	Is less than, is not less than
$>$ and $\ngtr$	Is greater than, is not greater than
$\neq$	Is not equal to
$\pm$	Plus or minus, respectively
$\mp$	Minus or plus, respectively
α	Is proportional to
$\rightarrow$	Approaches, e.g., as $x \rightarrow 0$
$\leq, \leqq$	Less than or equal to
$\geq, \geqq$	More than or equal to
$\therefore$	Therefore
:	Is to, is proportional to
Q.E.D.	Which was to be proved, end of proof
%	Percent
#	Number
@	At
$\angle$ or $\measuredangle$	Angle
$\circ\ \prime\ \prime\prime$	Degrees, minutes, seconds
$\parallel$, //	Parallel to
$\perp$	Perpendicular to
e	Base of natural logs, 2.71828 . . .
π	Pi, 3.14159 . . .
( )	Parentheses
[ ]	Brackets
{ }	Braces
$\prime$	Prime, $f'(x)$
$\prime\prime$	Double prime, $f''(x)$
$\sqrt{\ }, \sqrt[n]{\ }$	Square root, nth root
$1/x$ or x^{-1}	Reciprocal of x
!	Factorial
∞	Infinity
Δ	Delta, increment of
∂	Curly "d," partial differentiation
Σ	Sigma, summation of terms
Π	The product of terms, product
arc	As in arcsine (the angle whose sine is)
f	Function, as $f(x)$
rms	Root mean square
$\|x\|$	Absolute value of x
i	For -1
j	Operator, equal to -1

Chapter

3

Modern Calculator Techniques for Designers, Machinists, and Metalworkers

The modern hand-held or pocket digital electronic calculator is an invaluable tool to the designer, machinist, and metalworker. Many cumbersome tables such as natural trigonometric functions, powers and roots, sine bar tables, involute functions, and logarithmic tables are not included in this *Handbook* because of the ready availability, simplicity, speed, and great accuracy of these devices.

A typical low-cost multifunction pocket calculator is shown in Fig. 3.1. This type of device will be used to illustrate the calculator methods shown in Sec. 3.1 following. Figures 3.2 and 3.3 show some of the more advanced calculators, with some having programming ability. The calculator in Fig. 3.3 has a built-in formula list wherein you may recall 128 different formulas for instant use. This machine also has the capability to allow you to enter 12 of your own formulas. In the right pocket in Fig. 3.3 is a personal formula list which the author has programmed into his machine. On this type of calculator, you are prompted for the formula variables, which you then enter. The machine then automatically calculates the correct answer in less than 1 s. With devices such as these, the problem of finding the natural sine of an angle such as 36°28′24″ is a simple matter. The angle is first converted to decimal degrees, and then that figure is entered into the machine for an almost instant and extremely accurate answer.

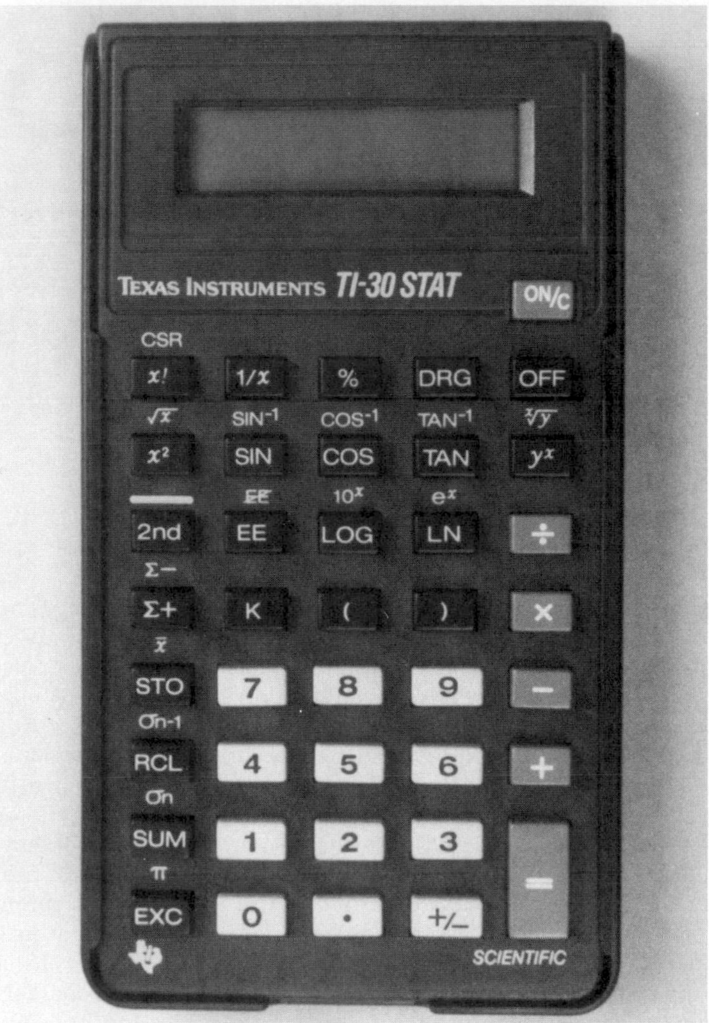

Figure 3.1 A modern low-cost pocket calculator.

Most of the newer machines also do not rely on battery power, since they have a built-in low-sensitivity solar conversion panel that converts room light into electrical energy for powering the calculator. The widespread use of these devices has increased industrial productivity considerably since their introduction in the 1970s.

Figure 3.2 Assortment of modern pocket calculators with advanced functions.

3.1 Finding Natural Trigonometric Functions

The natural trigonometric functions of *all* angles are obtained easily, with great speed and precision.

Example. Find the natural trigonometric function of sin 26°41′26″.

First, convert from degrees, minutes, and seconds to decimal degrees (see Sec. 2.1.2):

$$26°41'26'' = 26.690555°$$

Enter: 26.690555

Press: sin

Answer: 0.4491717 (the natural function)

The natural sine, cosine, and tangent of any angle may thus be found. Negative angles are found by entering the decimal degrees, changing sign to minus, and then pressing sin, cos, or tan.

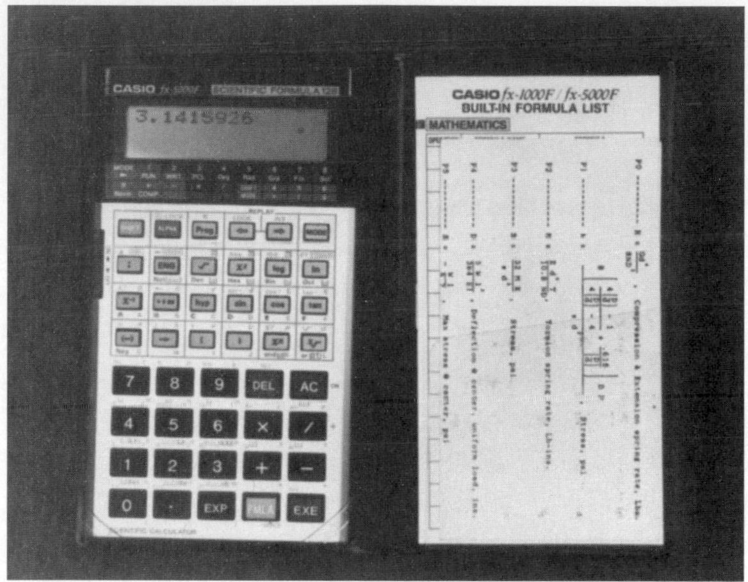

Figure 3.3 A programmable calculator with built-in equations.

3.2 Finding Common and Natural Logarithms of Numbers

The common, or Briggs, logarithm system is constructed with a base of 10 (see Sec. 2.1.1).

Example

$$10^1 = 10 \quad \text{and} \quad \log_{10} 10 = 1$$

$$10^2 = 100 \quad \text{and} \quad \log_{10} 100 = 2$$

$$10^3 = 1000 \quad \text{and} \quad \log_{10} 1000 = 3$$

Therefore, $\log_{10}$ 110.235 is found by entering the number into the calculator and pressing log:

Enter: 110.235

Press: log

Answer: 2.042319506

Since the logarithmic value is the exponent to which 10 is raised to obtain the number, we will perform this calculation:

$$10^{2.042319506} = 110.235$$

Proof

Enter: 10

Press: y^x

Enter: 2.042319506

Press: =

Answer: 110.2349999, or 110.235 to three decimal places.

The natural, or hyperbolic, logarithm of a number is found in a similar manner.

Example. Find the natural, or hyperbolic, logarithm of 110.235.

Enter: 110.235

Press: $\ln x$

Answer: 4.702614451

3.3 Powers and Roots (Exponentials)

Finding powers and roots (exponentials) of numbers is simple on the pocket calculator and renders logarithmic procedures and tables of logarithms obsolete, as well as the functions of numbers tables found in outdated handbooks.

Example. Find the square root of 3.4575.

Enter: 3.4575

Press: $\sqrt{x}$

Answer: 1.859435398

The procedure takes but a few seconds.

Example. Find $(0.0625)^4$

Enter: 0.625

Press: x^y

Enter: 4

Press: =

Answer: 1.525879×10^{-5}

Example. Find the cube root of 5.2795, or $(5.2795)^{1/3}$.

Enter: 5.2795

Press: $x\sqrt{y}$

Enter: 3

Press: =

Answer: 1.7412626

Note. Radicals written in exponential notation:

$$\sqrt[3]{5} = (5)^{1/3}$$

$$\sqrt{6} = (6)^{1/2}$$

$$\sqrt[3]{(6.245)^2} = (6.245)^{2/3}$$

3.4 Sine Bar and Sine Plate Calculations

Sine bar procedures. Referring to Fig. 3.4, find the sine bar setting height for an angle of 34°25′ using a 5-in sine bar.

$$\sin 34°25' = x/5 \qquad (34°25' = 34.416667 \text{ decimal degrees})$$

$$\sin 34.416667° = x/5$$

$$x = 5 \times 0.565207$$

$$x = 2.826 \text{ in}$$

Set the sine bar height with Jo-blocks or precision blocks to 2.826 in.

From this example it is apparent that the setting height can be found for any sine bar length simply by multiplying the length of the sine bar times the natural sine value of the required angle. The simplicity, speed, and accuracy possible for setting sine bars with the aid of the pocket calculator renders sine bar tables obsolete. No sine bar table will give you the required setting height for such an angle as 42°17′26″, but by using the calculator procedure, this becomes a routine, simple process with less chance for errors.

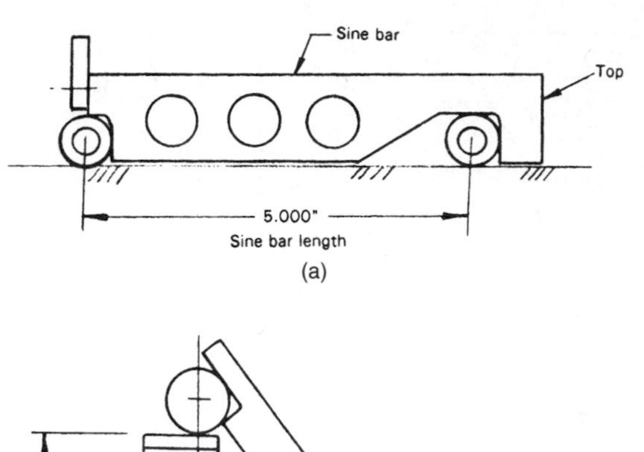

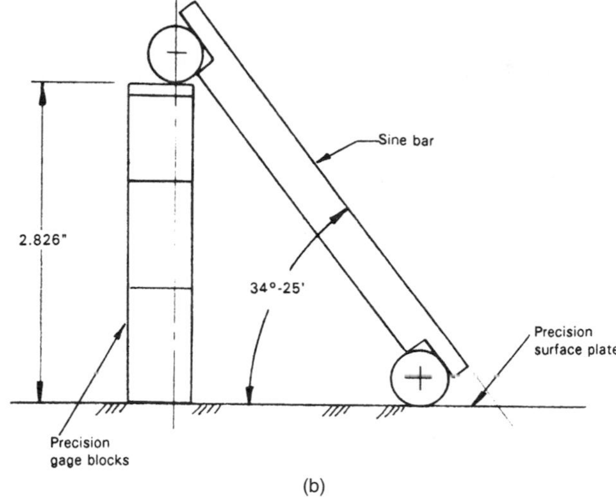

Figure 3.4 (*a*) Sine bar. (*b*) Sine bar.

Method

1. Convert the required angle to decimal degrees.
2. Find the natural sine of the required angle.
3. Multiply the natural sine of the angle by the length of the sine bar to find the bar setting height (see Fig. 3.4).

Formulas for finding angles. Refer to Fig. 3.5 when angles α and ϕ are known to find angles X, A, B, and C.

$$\tan X = \tan \alpha \cos \phi$$

$$\sin C = \cos \alpha / \cos X$$

$$\text{Angle } B = 180° - (\text{angle } A + \text{angle C})$$

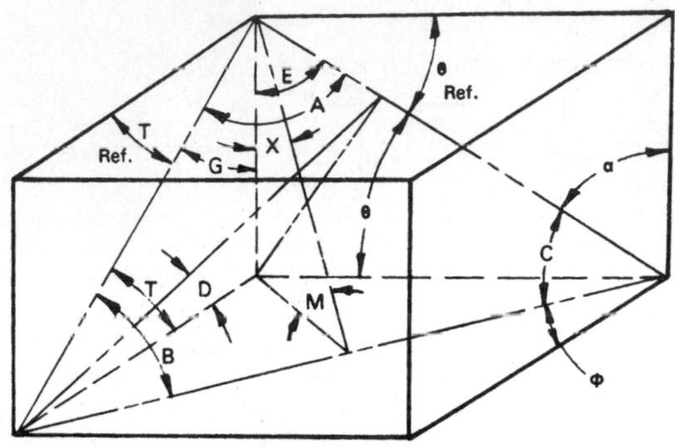

Figure 3.5 Finding the unknown angles.

$$\tan A = \frac{\sin \alpha \sin C}{\sin \phi - (\sin \alpha \cos C)}$$

$$D = \text{true angle}$$

$$\tan D = \tan \phi \sin \theta$$

$$\tan C = \frac{\sin D}{\tan \theta}$$

$$\tan M = \sqrt{(\tan \theta)^2 + (\tan T)^2}$$

$$\cos A = \cos E \cos G$$

$$\cos A = \sin \theta \sin T$$

Formulas and development for finding true and apparent angles. See Fig. 3.6*a,* where α = apparent angle, θ = true angle, and ϕ = angle of rotation.

Note. Apparent angle α is *OA* triangle projected onto plane *OB*. See also Fig. 3.6*b*.

$$\tan \theta = K/L$$

$$\tan \alpha = K/(L \cos \phi)$$

$$\tan \alpha \cos \phi = K/L$$

$$K/L = \tan \theta = \cos \phi \tan \alpha$$

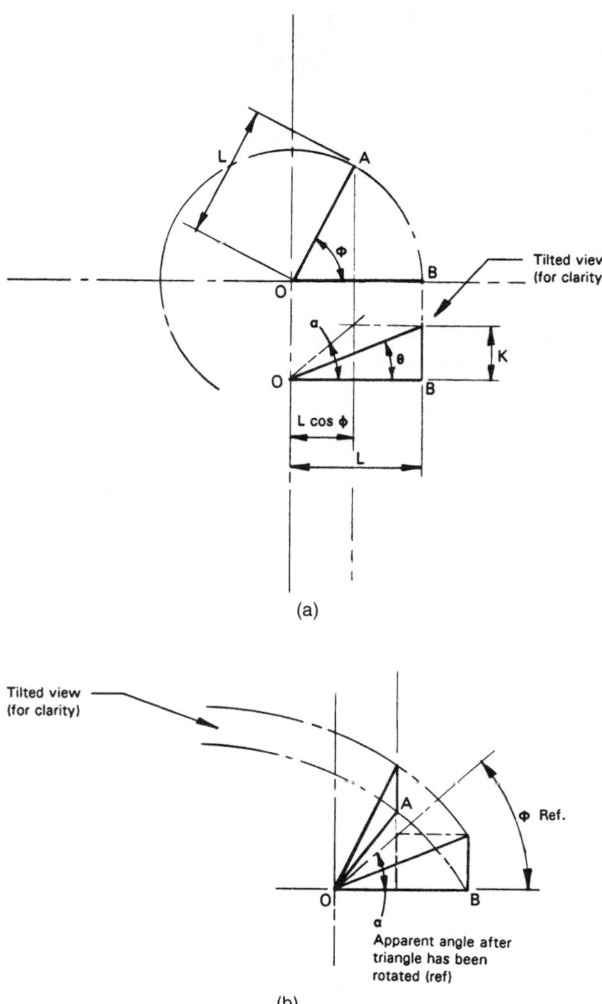

Figure 3.6 True and apparent angles.

or

$$\tan \theta = \cos \phi \tan \alpha$$

and

$$\tan \alpha = \tan \theta / \cos \phi$$

The three-dimensional relationships shown for the angles and triangles in the preceding figures and formulas are of importance and should be understood. This will help in the setting of compound sine plates when it is required to set a compound angle.

Setting compound sine plates. For setting two known angles at 90° to each other, proceed as shown in Fig. 3.7.

Example. First angle = 22.45°. Second angle = 38.58° (see Fig. 3.7). To find the amount the intermediate plate must be raised from the base plate (*X* dimension in Fig. 3.7) to obtain the desired first angle,

1. Find the natural cosine of the second angle (38.58°), and multiply this times the natural tangent of the first angle (22.45°).
2. Find the arctangent of this product, and then find the natural sine of this angle.
3. This natural sine is now multiplied by the length of the sine plate to find the *X* dimension in Fig. 3.7 to which the intermediate plate must be set.
4. Set up the Jo-blocks to equal the *X* dimension, and set in position between base plate and intermediate plate.

Example

$$\cos 38.58° = 0.781738$$

$$\tan 22.45° = 0.413192$$

$$0.781738 \times 0.413192 = 0.323008$$

$$\arctan 0.323008 = 17.900872°$$

$$\sin 17.900872° = 0.307371$$

$$0.307371 \times 10 \text{ in (for 10-in sine plate)} = 3.0737 \text{ in}$$

Therefore, set *X* dimension to 3.074 in (to three decimal places).

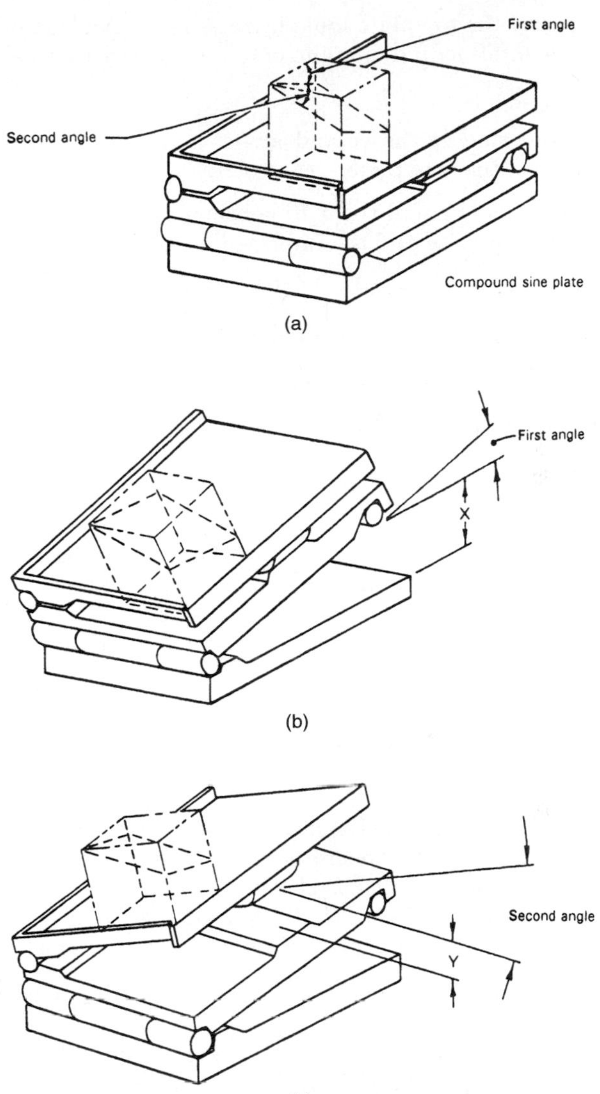

Figure 3.7 Setting angles on a sine plate.

To find the amount the top plate must be raised (Y dimension in Fig. 3.7) above the intermediate plate to obtain the desired second angle,

1. Find the natural sine of the second angle, and multiply this times the length of the sine plate.
2. Set up the Jo-blocks to equal the Y dimension, and set in position between the top plate and the intermediate plate.

Example

$$\sin 38.58° = 0.632607$$

$$0.632607 \times 10 \text{ in (for 10-in sine plate)} = 6.32607$$

Therefore, set Y dimension to 6.326 in (to three decimal places).

3.5 Involute Function Calculations

Involute functions are used in some of the equations required to perform involute gear design. These functional values of the involute curve are easily calculated with the aid of the pocket calculator. Refer to Sec. 2.1.4 for the procedure required to calculate the involute function.

3.6 Solutions to Problems in Machining and Metalworking

The following sample problems will show in detail the importance of trigonometry and basic algebraic operations as apply to machining and metalworking. By using the methods and procedures shown in Chap. 2 and this chapter of the *Handbook,* you will be able to solve many basic and complex machining and metalworking problems.

Taper (Fig. 3.8). Solve for x if y is given; solve for y if x is given; solve for d. Use the tangent function:

$$\tan A = y/x$$

$$d = D - 2y$$

where A = taper angle
D = outside diameter of rod

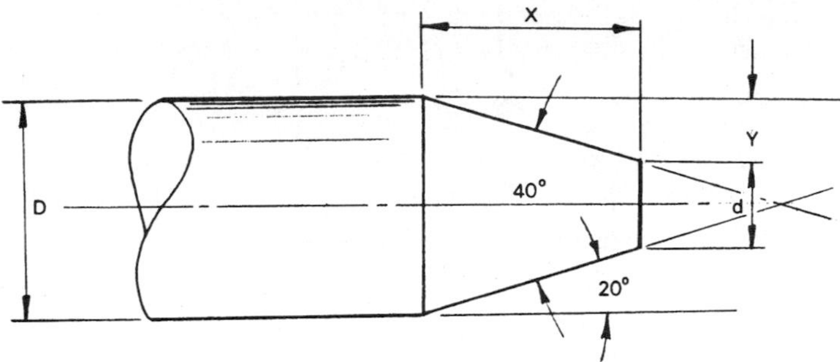

Figure 3.8 Taper.

d = diameter at end of taper
x = length of taper
y = drop of taper

Example. If the rod diameter = 0.9375 diameter, taper length = 0.875 = x, and taper angle = 20° = angle A, find y and d from

$$\tan 20^\circ = y/x$$

$$y = x \tan 20^\circ$$

$$= 0.875(0.36397)$$

$$= 0.318$$

$$d = D - 2y$$

$$= 0.9375 - 2(0.318)$$

$$= 0.9375 - 0.636$$

$$= 0.3015$$

Countersink depths (three methods for calculating)

Method 1. To find the tool travel y from the top surface of the part for a given countersink finished diameter at the part surface,

$$y = \frac{\frac{D}{2}}{\tan \frac{1}{2}A} \qquad \text{(Fig. 3.9)}$$

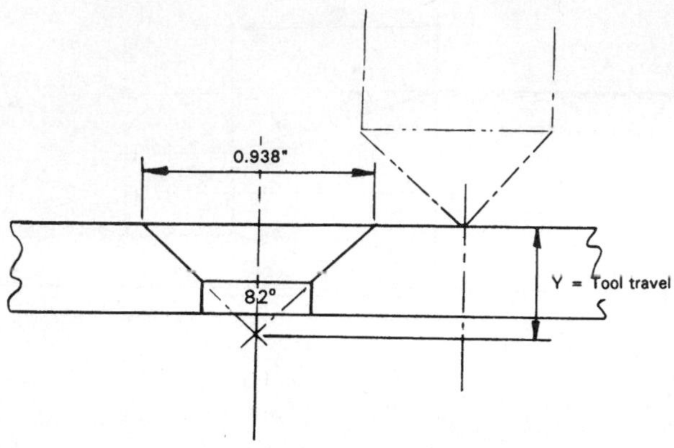

Figure 3.9 Countersink depth.

where D = finished countersink diameter
A = countersink angle
y = tool advance from surface of part

$$y = \frac{\frac{0.938}{2}}{\tan 41°} = \frac{0.469}{0.869} = 0.5397, \text{ or } 0.540$$

Method 2. To find the tool travel from the edge of the hole (Fig. 3.10) where D = finished countersink diameter, H = hole diameter, and A = ½ countersink angle, 41°,

$$\tan A = x/y$$

$$y = x/\tan A \qquad \text{or} \qquad x/(\tfrac{1}{2} \text{ countersink angle})$$

First, find x from

$$D = H + 2x$$

If $D = 0.875$ and $H = 0.500$,

$$0.875 = 0.500 + 2x$$

$$2x = 0.375$$

$$x = 0.1875$$

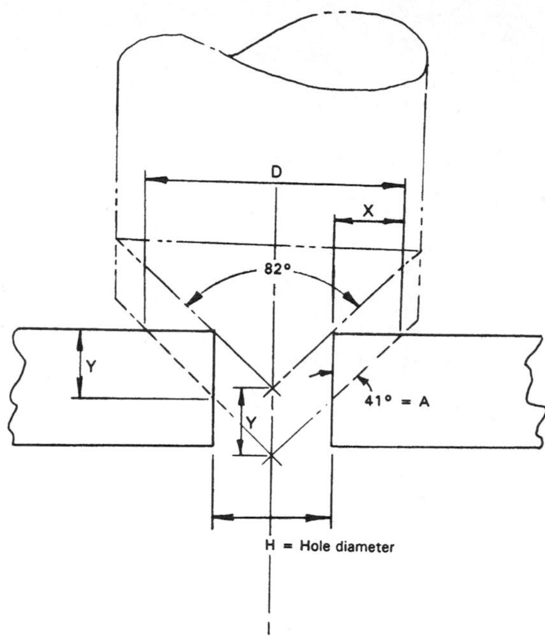

Figure 3.10 Tool travel in countersinking.

Now, solve for y, the tool advance:

$$y = x/\tan A$$

$$= 0.1875/\tan 41°$$

$$= 0.1875/0.8693$$

$$= 0.2157, \text{ or } 0.216 \text{ (tool advance from edge of hole)}$$

Method 3. To find tool travel from edge of hole (Fig. 3.11) where D = finished countersink diameter, d = hole diameter, ϕ = ½ countersink angle, and H – countersink tool advance from edge of hole,

$$H = \tfrac{1}{2}(D - d) \text{ cotan } \phi \qquad \text{or} \qquad H = \frac{D - d}{2 \tan \phi}$$

(Remember that cotan ϕ = 1/tan ϕ or tan ϕ = 1/cotan ϕ.)

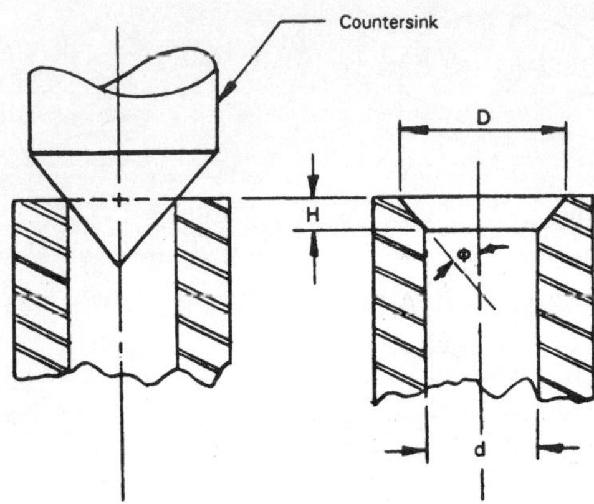

Figure 3.11 Tool travel from the edge of the hole.

Finding taper angle α. Given dimensions shown in Fig. 3.12, find angle α and length x.

First, find angle α from

$$y = \frac{1.875 - 0.500}{2} = \frac{1.375}{2} = 0.6875$$

Then solve triangle ABC for ½ angle α:

$$\tan \frac{1}{2}\alpha = \frac{0.6875}{2.175} = 0.316092$$

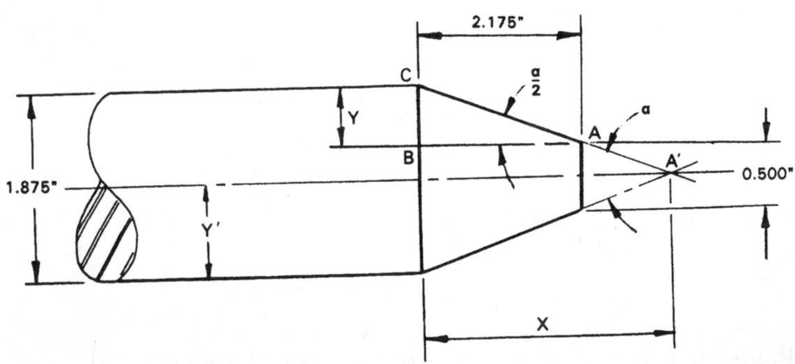

Figure 3.12 Finding taper angle (α).

$$\arctan \tfrac{1}{2}\alpha = 0.316092$$
$$\tfrac{1}{2}\alpha = 17.541326°$$
$$\alpha = 2 \times 17.541326°$$
$$\text{angle } \alpha = 35.082652°$$

Then solve triangle $A'B'C$, where $y' = 0.9375$ or ½ diameter of rod:

$$\text{Angle } C = 90° - 17.541326°$$
$$= 72.458674°$$

Now the x dimension is found from

$$\tan \frac{1}{2}\alpha = \frac{0.9375}{x}$$
$$x = \frac{0.9375}{\tan \tfrac{1}{2}\alpha}$$
$$= \frac{0.9375}{0.316092}$$
$$= 2.966 \text{ (side } A'B' \text{ or length } x)$$

Geometry of the pentagon, hexagon, and octagon. The following figures show in detail how basic trigonometry and algebra are used to formulate the solutions to these geometric figures.

The pentagon. (Fig. 3.13)

Where R = radius of circumscribed circle
R_1 = radius of inscribed circle
S = length of side

From the law of sines, we know the following relation:

$$\frac{S}{\sin 72°} = \frac{R}{\sin 54°}$$
$$S \sin 54° = R \sin 72°$$
$$S = \frac{R \sin 72}{\sin 54}$$
$$= \frac{R\,(0.9511)}{0.8090}$$
$$= 1.1756R \text{ (where } R = \text{radius of circumscribed circle)}$$

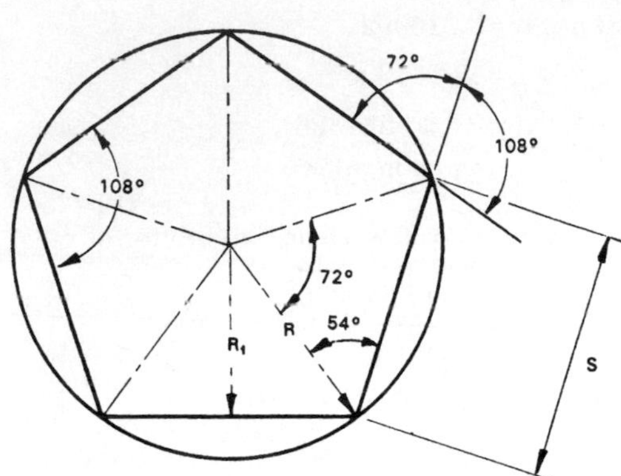

Figure 3.13 Pentagon.

Also,

$$S = \frac{R_1 \sin 72°}{\cos 36 \sin 54} \qquad (\textbf{Note:} \cos 36° = R_1/R)$$

$$= \frac{R_1(0.9511)}{(0.8090)(0.8090)}$$

$$= \frac{R_1(0.9511)}{0.6545}$$

$$= 1.4532R_1 \text{ (where } R_1 = \text{radius of inscribed circle)}$$

The area of the pentagon is thus

$$A_1 = \frac{1}{2}\left(\frac{S}{2}\right)R_1$$

$$= \frac{SR_1}{4}$$

$$= \frac{S(R \cos 36)}{4} \qquad [\textbf{Note:} (\cos 36 = R_1/R \text{ and } R_1 = R \cos 36)]$$

$$A_T = 5\left(\frac{SR_1}{4}\right)$$

$$= 1.25SR_1 \text{ (the total area of the pentagon)}$$

The hexagon (Fig. 3.14)

Where R = radius of inscribed circle
R_1 = radius of circumscribed circle
S = length of side
W = width across points

From Fig. 3.14 we know the following relation

$$\tan 30° = \frac{x}{R} \qquad \text{and} \qquad S = 2x \quad \text{or} \quad x = \frac{S}{2}$$

$$x = R \tan 30$$

Then $S = 2R \tan 30$
$= 2R(0.57735)$
$= 1.1457R$

$$\cos 30° = \frac{R}{R_1}$$

$$R = R_1 \cos 30$$

$$R_1 = \frac{R}{\cos 30}$$

$$R_1 = \frac{R}{0.86605} \qquad \text{or} \qquad R_1 = 1.15467R$$

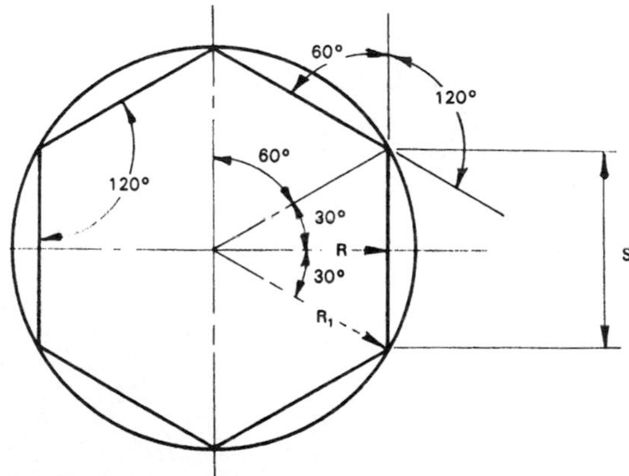

Figure 3.14 Hexagon.

and $W = 2(1.15467)R$
$= 2.30934R$ (diameter of the circumscribed circle)

Area: $A = 2.598S^2$
$= 3.464r^2$
$= 2.598R_1^{\,2}$

The octagon (Fig. 3.15)

Where R = radius of inscribed circle
R_1 = radius of circumscribed circle
S = length of side
W = width across points

From Fig. 3.15 we know the following relation

$$\tfrac{1}{2}S = R \tan 22°30'$$

$$S = 2R \tan 22°30'$$

$$S = 2R(0.414214)$$

$$S = 0.828428R$$

Also: $R = 1.20711S$

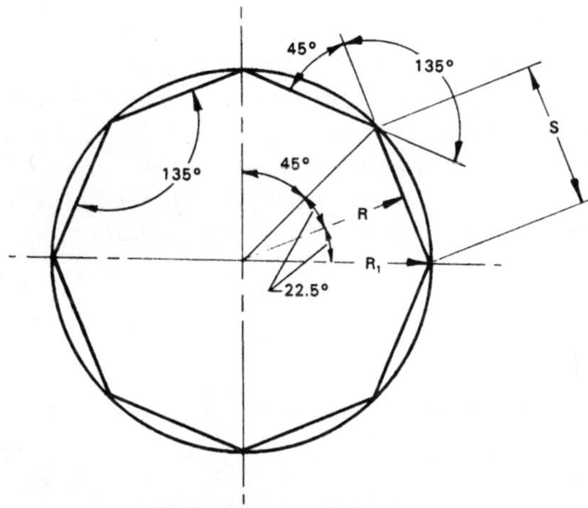

Figure 3.15 Octagon.

$$\text{Then, } \cos 22°30' = \frac{R}{R_1}$$

$$R = R_1 \cos 22°30'$$

$$R_1 = \frac{R}{\cos 22°30'}$$

$$\text{Then, } W = 2(R/\cos 22°30')$$
$$= 2.165R$$

$$\text{Area: } A = 4.828S^2$$
$$= 3.314r^2$$

In the preceding three figures of the pentagon, hexagon, and octagon, you may calculate the other relationships between S, R, and R_1 as required using the procedures shown as a guide. When one of these parts is known, the other parts may be found in relation to the given part.

Typical layout and development problems in sheet metal practice may be found in Chap. 16 of this *Handbook.*

Compound angles. A solid geometric figure consisting of several plane right triangles contains a compound angle. Each of these right triangles contains one of the angles of the compound angle, and one of these angles is called the *true angle.* The true angle of inclination of a plane to a reference plane is called the *dihedral angle.* Figure 3.16 shows a typical triangular pyramid, in which all four faces are right triangles. Most of the solids encountered in actual practice may be reduced to this type of pyramid by drawing a plane of symmetry. The unknown angle may then be calculated from any two known angles which lie in adjacent faces of the pyramid.

The trigonometric solutions for all the compound angles of Fig. 3.16 may be calculated from the following trigonometric relationships:

Solutions to Compound Angles (see Fig. 3.16)

Given	To find	Equation
α and β	γ	$\cos \gamma = \dfrac{\tan \beta}{\tan \alpha}$
α and β	δ	$\cos \delta = \dfrac{\sin \beta}{\sin \alpha}$

Given	To find	Equation
α and γ	β	$\tan\beta = \cos\gamma\tan\alpha$
α and γ	δ	$\tan\delta = \cos\alpha\tan\gamma$
α and δ	β	$\sin\beta = \sin\alpha\cos\delta$
α and δ	γ	$\tan\gamma = \dfrac{\tan\delta}{\cos\alpha}$
β and γ	α	$\tan\alpha = \dfrac{\tan\beta}{\cos\gamma}$
β and γ	δ	$\sin\delta = \cos\beta\sin\gamma$
β and δ	α	$\sin\alpha = \dfrac{\sin\beta}{\cos\delta}$
β and δ	γ	$\sin\gamma = \dfrac{\sin\delta}{\cos\beta}$
γ and δ	α	$\cos\alpha = \dfrac{\tan\delta}{\tan\gamma}$
γ and δ	β	$\cos\beta = \dfrac{\sin\delta}{\sin\gamma}$

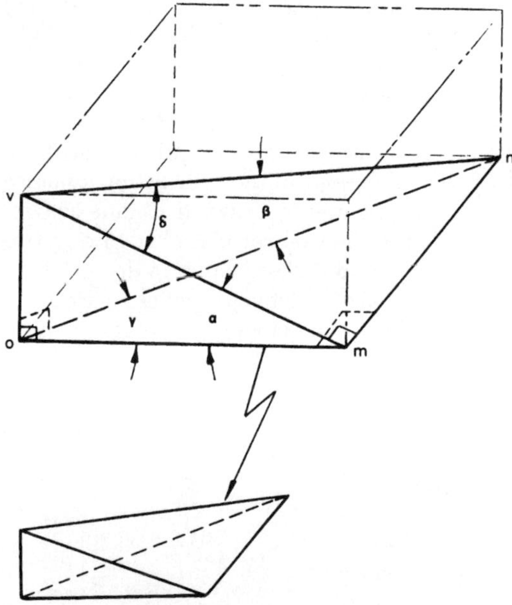

Figure 3.16 Compound angles.

Chapter

4

U.S. Customary and Metric (SI) Measures and Conversions

4.1 Conversions for Length, Pressure, Velocity, Volume, and Weight

To convert from:	to:	Multiply by:
	Length	
Centimeters	Inches	0.3937
Centimeters	Yards	0.01094
Feet	Inches	12.0
Feet	Meters	0.30481
Feet	Yards	0.333
Inches	Centimeters	2.540
Inches	Feet	0.08333
Inches	Meters	0.02540
Inches	Microns	25,400.
Inches	Millimeters	25.400
Inches	Yards	0.02778
Kilometers	Feet	3,281.
Kilometers	Miles (nautical)	0.5336
Kilometers	Miles (statute)	0.6214
Kilometers	Yards	1,094.

To convert from:	to:	Multiply by:
Meters	Feet	3.2809
Meters	Yards	1.0936
Microns	Inches	0.0000394
Microns	Meters	0.000001
Miles (statute)	Feet	5,280.
Miles (statute)	Kilometers	1.6093
Miles (statute)	Meters	1,609.34
Miles (statute)	Yards	1,760.
Miles (nautical)	Feet	6,080.2
Miles (nautical)	Kilometers	1.8520
Miles (nautical)	Meters	1,852.0
Millimcters	Inches	0.03937
Rods	Meters	5.0292
Yards	Centimeters	91.44
Yards	Feet	3.0
Yards	Inches	36.0
Yards	Meters	0.9144
	Pressure	
Dynes per cm^2	Pascals	0.1000
Grams per cm^3	Ounces per in^3	0.5780
Kilograms per cm^2	Pounds per in^2	14.223
Kilograms per cm^2	Pascals	98,066.5
Kilograms per m^2	Pascals	9.8066
Kilograms per m^2	Pounds per ft^2	0.2048
Kilograms per m^2	Pounds per yd^2	1.8433
Kilograms per m^3	Pounds per ft^3	0.06243
Ounces per in^3	Grams per cm^3	1.7300
Pounds per ft^3	Kilograms per m^3	16.019
Pounds per ft^2	Kilograms per m^2	4.8824
Pounds per ft^2	Pascals	47.880
Pounds per in^2	Kilograms per cm^2	0.0703
Pounds per in^2	Pascals	6,894.76
Pounds per yd^2	Kilograms per m^2	0.5425
	Velocity	
Feet per minute	Meters per second	0.00508
Feet per second	Meters per second	0.3048
Inches per second	Meters per second	0.0254
Kilometers	Meters per second	0.2778
Knots	Meters per second	0.5144

Miles per hour	Meters per second	0.4470
Miles per minute	Meters per second	26.8224
	Volume	
Cubic centimeters	Cubic inches	0.06102
Cubic feet	Cubic inches	1,728.0
Cubic feet	Cubic meters	0.0283
Cubic feet	Cubic yards	0.0370
Cubic feet	Gallons	7.481
Cubic feet	Liters	28.32
Cubic feet	Quarts	29.9222
Cubic inches	Cubic centimeters	16.39
Cubic inches	Cubic feet	0.0005787
Cubic inches	Cubic meters	0.00001639
Cubic inches	Liters	0.0164
Cubic inches	Gallons	0.004329
Cubic inches	Quarts	0.01732
Cubic meters	Cubic feet	35.31
Cubic meters	Cubic inches	61,023.
Cubic meters	Cubic yards	1.3087
Cubic yards	Cubic feet	27.0
Cubic yards	Cubic meters	0.7641
Gallons	Cubic feet	0.1337
Gallons	Cubic inches	231.0
Gallons	Cubic meters	0.003785
Gallons	Liters	3.785
Gallons	Quarts	4.0
Liters	Cubic feet	0.03531
Liters	Cubic inches	61.017
Liters	Gallons	0.2642
Liters	Pints	2.1133
Liters	Quarts	1.057
Liters	Cubic meters	0.0010
Pints	Cubic meters	0.004732
Pints	Liters	0.4732
Pints	Quarts	0.50
Quarts	Cubic feet	0.03342
Quarts	Cubic inches	57.75
Quarts	Cubic meters	0.0009464
Quarts	Gallons	0.25
Quarts	Liters	0.9464
Quarts	Pints	2.0

To convert from:	to:	Multiply by:
	Weight	
Grams	Kilograms	0.001
Grams	Ounces	0.03527
Grams	Pounds	0.002205
Kilograms	Ounces	35.274
Kilograms	Pounds	2.2046
Ounces	Grams	28.35
Ounces	Kilograms	0.02835
Ounces	Pounds	0.0625
Pounds	Grams	453.6
Pounds	Kilograms	0.4536
Pounds	Ounces	16.0

4.2 Standard Conversion Table: Measures are Found from the Table

Multiply:	By:	To obtain:
Acres	43,560	Square feet
Acres	4047	Square meters
Acres	1.562×10^{-3}	Square miles
Acres	4840	Square yards
Acre—feet	43,560	Cubic feet
Acre—feet	325,851	Gallons
Acre—feet	1233.49	Cubic meters
Atmospheres	76.0	Centimeters of mercury
Atmospheres	29.92	Inches of mercury
Atmospheres	33.90	Feet of water
Atmospheres	10,333	Kilograms per square meter
Atmospheres	14.70	Pounds per square inch
Atmospheres	1.058	Tons per square foot
Barrels—oil	42	Gallons—oil
Barrels—cement	376	Pounds—cement
Bags or sacks—cement	94	Pounds—cement
Board feet	$144 \text{ in}^2 \times 1 \text{ in}$	Cubic inches
British thermal units (Btu)	0.2520	Kilogram-calories
British thermal units	777.5	Foot pounds
British thermal units	3.927×10^{-4}	Horsepower-hours
British thermal units	107.5	Kilogram-meters
British thermal units	2.928×10^{-4}	Kilowatt-hours
Btu/min	12.96	Foot pounds per second

Btu/min	0.02356	Horsepower
Btu/min	0.01757	Kilowatts
Btu/min	17.57	Watts
Centares (centiares)	1	Square meters
Centigrams	0.01	Grams
Centiliters	0.01	Liters
Centimeters	0.3937	Inches
Centimeters	0.01	Meters
Centimeters	10	Millimeters
Centimeters of mercury	0.01316	Atmospheres
Centimeters of mercury	0.4461	Feet of water
Centimeters of mercury	136.0	Kilograms per square meter
Centimeters of mercury	27.85	Pounds per square foot
Centimeters of mercury	0.1934	Pounds per square inch
Centimeters per second	1.969	Feet per minute
Centimeters per second	0.03281	Feet per second
Centimeters per second	0.036	Kilometers per hour
Centimeters per second	0.6	Meters per minute
Centimeters per second	0.02237	Miles per hour
Centimeters per second	3.728×10^{-4}	Miles per minute
Centimeters per second per second	0.03281	Feet per second per second
Cubic centimeters	3.531×10^{-5}	Cubic feet
Cubic centimeters	6.102×10^{-2}	Cubic inches
Cubic centimeters	10^{-6}	Cubic meters
Cubic centimeters	1.308×10^{-6}	Cubic yards
Cubic centimeters	2.642×10^{-4}	Gallons
Cubic centimeters	10^{-3}	Liters
Cubic centimeters	2.113×10^{-3}	Pints (liq.)
Cubic centimeters	1.057×10^{-3}	Quarts (liq.)
Cubic feet	2.832×10^{4}	Cubic centimeters
Cubic feet	1728	Cubic inches
Cubic feet	0.02832	Cubic meters
Cubic feet	0.03704	Cubic yards
Cubic feet	7.48052	Gallons
Cubic feet	28.32	Liters
Cubic feet	59.84	Pints (liq.)
Cubic feet	29.92	Quarts (liq.)
Cubic feet per minute	472.0	Cubic centimeters per second
Cubic feet per minute	0.1247	Gallons per second
Cubic feet per minute	0.4720	Liters per second
Cubic feet per minute	62.43	Pounds of water per minute
Cubic feet per second	0.646317	Millions gallons per day
Cubic feet per second	448.831	Gallons per minute
Cubic inches	16.39	Cubic centimeters
Cubic inches	5.787×10^{-4}	Cubic feet

Multiply:	By:	To obtain:
Cubic inches	1.639×10^{-5}	Cubic inches
Cubic inches	2.143×10^{-5}	Cubic yards
Cubic inches	4.329×10^{-3}	Gallons
Cubic inches	1.639×10^{-2}	Liters
Cubic inches	0.03463	Pints (liq.)
Cubic inches	0.01732	Quarts (liq.)
Cubic meters	10^6	Cubic centimeters
Cubic meters	35.31	Cubic feet
Cubic meters	61.023×10^3	Cubic inches
Cubic meters	1.308	Cubic yards
Cubic meters	264.2	Gallons
Cubic meters	10^3	Liters
Cubic meters	2113	Pints (liq.)
Cubic meters	1057	Quarts (liq.)
Cubic yards	7.646×10^5	Cubic centimeters
Cubic yards	27	Cubic feet
Cubic yards	46,656	Cubic inches
Cubic yards	0.7646	Cubic meters
Cubic yards	202.0	Gallons
Cubic yards	764.6	Liters
Cubic yards	1616	Pints (liq.)
Cubic yards	807.9	Quarts (liq.)
Cubic yards per minute	0.45	Cubic feet per second
Cubic yards per minute	3.367	Gallons per second
Cubic yards per minute	12.74	Liters per second
Decigrams	0.1	Grams
Deciliters	0.1	Liters
Decimeters	0.1	Meters
Degrees (angle)	60	Minutes
Degrees (angle)	0.01745	Radians
Degrees (angle)	3600	Seconds
Degrees per second	0.01745	Radians per second
Degrees per second	0.1667	Revolutions per minute
Degrees per second	0.002778	Revolutions per second
Dekagrams	10	Grams
Dekaliters	10	Liters
Dekameters	10	Meters
Drams	27.34375	Grains
Drams	0.0625	Ounces
Drams	1.771845	Grams
Fathoms	6	Feet
Feet	30.48	Centimeters
Feet	12	Inches
Feet	0.3048	Meters
Feet	⅓	Yards
Feet of water	0.02950	Atmospheres

Feet of water	0.8826	Inches of mercury
Feet of water	304.8	Kilograms per square meter
Feet of water	62.43	Pounds per square foot
Feet of water	0.4335	Pounds per square inch
Feet per minute	0.5080	Centimeters per second
Feet per minute	0.01667	Feet per second
Feet per minute	0.01829	Kilometers per hour
Feet per minute	0.3048	Meters per minute
Feet per minute	0.01136	Miles per hour
Feet per second	30.48	Centimeters per second
Feet per second	1.097	Kilometers per hour
Feet per second	0.5921	Knots
Feet per second	18.29	Meters per minute
Feet per second	0.6818	Miles per hour
Feet per second	0.01136	Miles per minute
Feet per second per second	30.48	Centimeters per second per second
Feet per second per second	0.3048	Meters per second per second
Foot pounds	1.286×10^{-3}	British thermal units
Foot pounds	5.050×10^{-7}	Horsepower-hours
Foot pounds	3.241×10^{-4}	Kilogram-calories
Foot pounds	0.1383	Kilogram-meters
Foot pounds	3.766×10^{-7}	Kilowatt-hours
Foot pounds per minute	1.286×10^{-3}	Btu per minute
Foot pounds per minute	0.01667	Foot pounds per second
Foot pounds per minute	3.030×10^{-5}	Horsepower
Foot pounds per minute	3.241×10^{-4}	Kilogram-calories per minute
Foot pounds per minute	2.260×10^{-5}	Kilowatts
Foot pounds per second	7.717×10^{-2}	Btu per minute
Foot pounds per second	1.818×10^{-3}	Horsepower
Foot pounds per second	1.945×10^{-2}	Kilogram-calories per minute
Foot pounds per second	1.356×10^{-3}	Kilowatts
Gallons	3785	Cubic centimeters
Gallons	0.1337	Cubic feet
Gallons	231	Cubic inches
Gallons	3.785×10^{-3}	Cubic meters
Gallons	4.95×10^{-3}	Cubic yards
Gallons	3.785	Liters
Gallons	8	Pints (liq.)
Gallons	4	Quarts (liq.)
Gallons—Imperial	1.20095	U.S. gallons
Gallons—U.S.	0.83267	Imperial gallons
Gallons water	8.3453	Pounds of water
Gallons per minute	2.228×10^{-3}	Cubic feet per second

Multiply:	By:	To obtain:
Gallons per minute	0.06308	Liters per second
Gallons per minute	8.0208	Cubic feet per hour
Gallons per minute	8.0208 area (sq. ft.)	Overflow rate (ft/h)
Gallons water per minute	6.0086	Tons water per 24 hours
Grains (troy)	L	Grains (avour.)
Grains (troy)	0.06480	Grams
Grains (troy)	0.04167	Pennyweights (troy)
Grains (troy)	2.0833×10^{-3}	Ounces (troy)
Grains per U.S. gallon	17.118	Parts per million
Grains per U.S. gallon	142.86	Pounds per million gallons
Grains per Imperial gallon	14.254	Parts per million
Grams	980.7	Dynes
Grams	15.43	Grains
Grams	10^{-3}	Kilograms
Grams	10^{3}	Milligrams
Grams	0.03527	Ounces
Grams	0.03215	Ounces (troy)
Grams	2.205×10^{-3}	Pounds
Grams per centimeter	5.600×10^{-3}	Pounds per inch
Grams per cubic centimeter	62.43	Pounds per cubic foot
Grams per cubic centimeter	0.03613	Pounds per cubic inch
Grams per liter	58.417	Grains per gallon
Grams per liter	8.345	Pounds per 1000 gallons
Grams per liter	0.062427	Pounds per cubic foot
Grams per liter	1000	Parts per million
Hectares	2.471	Acres
Hectares	1.076×10^{5}	Square feet
Hectograms	100	Grams
Hectoliters	100	Liters
Hectometers	100	Meters
Hectowatts	100	Watts
Horsepower	42.44	Btu per minute
Horsepower	33,000	Foot pounds per minute
Horsepower	550	Foot pounds per second
Horsepower	1.014	Horsepower (metric)
Horsepower	10.70	Kilogram-calories per minute
Horsepower	0.7457	Kilowatts
Horsepower	745.7	Watts

Horsepower (boiler)	33,479	Btu per hour
Horsepower (boiler)	9,803	Kilowatts
Horsepower-hours	2547	British thermal units
Horsepower-hours	1.98×10^6	Foot pounds
Horsepower-hours	641.7	Kilogram-calories
Horsepower-hours	2.737×10^5	Kilogram-meters
Horsepower-hours	0.7457	Kilowatthours
Inches	2.540	Centimeters
Inches of mercury	0.03342	Atmospheres
Inches of mercury	1.133	Feet of water
Inches of mercury	345.3	Kilograms per square meter
Inches of mercury	70.73	Pounds per square foot
Inches of mercury	0.4912	Pounds per square inch
Inches of water	0.002458	Atmospheres
Inches of water	0.07355	Inches of mercury
Inches of water	25.40	Kilograms per square meter
Inches of water	0.5781	Ounces per square inch
Inches of water	5.202	Pounds per square foot
Inches of water	0.03613	Pounds per square inch
Kilograms	980,665	Dynes
Kilograms	2.205	Pounds
Kilograms	1.102×10^{-3}	Tons (short)
Kilograms	10^3	Grams
Kilograms-calories	3.968	British thermal units
Kilograms-calories	3086	Foot pounds
Kilograms-calories	1.558×10^{-3}	Horsepower-hours
Kilograms-calories	1.162×10^{-3}	Kilowatthours
Kilogram-calories per minute	51.43	Foot pounds per second
Kilogram-calories per minute	0.09351	Horsepower
Kilogram-calories per minute	0.06972	Kilowatts
Kilograms per meter	0.6720	Pounds per foot
Kilograms per square meter	9.678×10^{-5}	Atmospheres
Kilograms per square meter	3.281×10^{-3}	Feet of water
Kilograms per square meter	2.896×10^{-3}	Inches of mercury
Kilograms per square meter	0.2048	Pounds per square foot
Kilograms per square meter	1.422×10^{-3}	Pounds per square inch
Kilograms per square millimeter	10^6	Kilograms per square meter

Multiply:	By:	To obtain:
Kiloliters	10^3	Liters
Kilometers	10^5	Centimeters
Kilometers	3281	Feet
Kilometers	10^3	Meters
Kilometers	0.6214	Miles
Kilometers	1094	Yards
Kilometers per hour	27.78	Centimeters per second
Kilometers per hour	54.68	Feet per minute
Kilometers per hour	0.9113	Feet per second
Kilometers per hour	0.5396	Knots
Kilometers per hour	16.67	Meters per minute
Kilometers per hour	0.6214	Miles per hour
Kilograms per hour per second	27.78	Centimeters per second per second
Kilograms per hour per second	0.9113	Feet per second per second
Kilograms per hour per second	0.2778	Meters per second per second
Kilowatts	56.92	Btu per minute
Kilowatts	4.425×10^4	Foot pounds per minute
Kilowatts	737.6	Foot pounds per second
Kilowatts	1.341	Horsepower
Kilowatts	14.34	Kilogram-calories per minute
Kilowatts	10^3	Watts
Kilowatthours	3415	British thermal units
Kilowatthours	2.655×10^6	Foot pounds
Kilowatthours	1.341	Horsepower-hours
Kilowatthours	860.5	Kilogram-calories
Kilowatthours	3.671×10^5	Kilogram-meters
Liters	10^3	Cubic centimeters
Liters	0.03531	Cubic feet
Liters	61.02	Cubic inches
Liters	10^3	Cubic meters
Liters	1.308×10^{-3}	Cubic yards
Liters	0.2642	Gallons
Liters	2.113	Pints (liq.)
Liters	1.057	Quarts (liq.)
Liters per minute	5.886×10^{-4}	Cubic feet per second
Liters per minute	4.403×10^{-3}	Gallons per second
$\frac{\text{Lumber width (in)} \times \text{thickness (in)}}{12}$	Length (ft.)	Board feet
Meters	100	Centimeters
Meters	3.281	Feet
Meters	39.37	Inches

Meters	10^{-3}	Kilometers
Meters	10^{3}	Millimeters
Meters	1.094	Yards
Meters per minute	1.667	Centimeters per second
Meters per minute	3.281	Feet per minute
Meters per minute	0.05468	Feet per second
Meters per minute	0.06	Kilometers per hour
Meters per minute	0.03728	Miles per hour
Meters per second	196.8	Feet per minute
Meters per second	3.281	Feet per second
Meters per second	3.6	Kilometers per hour
Meters per second	0.06	Kilometers per minute
Meters per second	2.237	Miles per hour
Meters per second	0.03728	Miles per minute
Microns	10^{-6}	Meters
Miles	1.609×10^{5}	Centimeters
Miles	5280	Feet
Miles	1.609	Kilometers
Miles	1760	Yards
Miles per hour	44.70	Centimeters per second
Miles per hour	88	Feet per minute
Miles per hour	1.467	Feet per second
Miles per hour	1.609	Kilometers per hour
Miles per hour	0.8684	Knots
Miles per hour	26.82	Meters per minute
Miles per minute	2682	Centimeters per second
Miles per minute	88	Feet per second
Miles per minute	1.609	Kilometers per minute
Miles per minute	60	Miles per hour
Milliers	10^{3}	Kilograms
Milligrams	10^{-3}	Grams
Milliliters	10^{-3}	Liters
Millimeters	0.1	Centimeters
Millimeters	0.03937	Inches
Milligrams per liter	1	Parts per million
Million gallons per day	1.54723	Cubic feet per second
Miner's inches	1.5	Cubic feet per minute
Minutes (angle)	2.909×10^{-4}	Radians
Ounces	16	Drams
Ounces	437.5	Grains
Ounces	0.0625	Pounds
Ounces	28.349527	Grams
Ounces	0.9115	Ounces (troy)
Ounces	2.790×10^{-5}	Tons (long)
Ounces	2.835×10^{-5}	Tons (metric)
Ounces (troy)	480	Grains
Ounces (troy)	20	Pennyweights (troy)
Ounces (troy)	0.08333	Pounds (troy)

Multiply:	By:	To obtain:
Ounces (troy)	31.103481	Grams
Ounces (troy)	1.09714	Ounces (avoir.)
Ounces (fluid)	1.805	Cubic inches
Ounces (fluid)	0.02957	Liters
Ounces per square inch	0.0625	Pounds per square inch
Overflow rate (ft/h)	0.12468 × area (ft^2)	Gallons per minute
$\frac{1}{\text{Overflow rate (ft/h)}}$	8.0208	Square feet per gallon per minute
Parts per million	0.0584	Grains per U.S. gallon
Parts per million	0.07016	Grains per Imperial gallon
Parts per million	8.345	Pounds per million gallons
Pennyweights (troy)	24	Grains
Pennyweights (troy)	1.55517	Grams
Pennyweights (troy)	0.05	Ounces (troy)
Pennyweights (troy)	4.1667×10^{-3}	Pounds (troy)
Pounds	16	Ounces
Pounds	256	Drams
Pounds	7000	Grains
Pounds	0.0005	Tons (short)
Pounds	453.5924	Grams
Pounds	1.21528	Pounds (troy)
Pounds	14.5833	Ounces (troy)
Pounds (troy)	5760	Grains
Pounds (troy)	240	Pennyweights (troy)
Pounds (troy)	12	Ounces (troy)
Pounds (troy)	373.24177	Grams
Pounds (troy)	0.822857	Pounds (avoir.)
Pounds (troy)	13.1657	Ounces (avoir.)
Pounds (troy)	3.6735×10^{-4}	Tons (long)
Pounds (troy)	4.1143×10^{-4}	Tons (short)
Pounds (troy)	3.7324×10^{-4}	Tons (metric)
Pounds of water	0.01602	Cubic feet
Pounds of water	27.68	Cubic inches
Pounds of water	0.1198	Gallons
Pounds of water per minute	2.670×10^{-4}	Cubic feet per second
Pounds per cubic foot	0.01602	Grams per cubic centimeter
Pounds per cubic foot	16.02	Kilograms per cubic meters
Pounds per cubic foot	5.787×10^{-4}	Pounds per cubic inch
Pounds per cubic inch	27.68	Grams per cubic centimeter

Pounds per cubic inch	2.768×10^4	Kilograms per cubic meter
Pounds per cubic inch	1728	Pounds per cubic foot
Pounds per foot	1.488	Kilograms per meter
Pounds per inch	178.6	Grams per centimeter
Pounds per square foot	0.01602	Feet of water
Pounds per square foot	4.883	Kilograms per square meter
Pounds per square foot	6.945×10^{-3}	Pounds per square inch
Pounds per square inch	0.06804	Atmospheres
Pounds per square inch	2.307	Feet of water
Pounds per square inch	2.036	Inches of mercury
Pounds per square inch	703.1	Kilograms per square meter
Quadrants (angle)	90	Degrees
Quadrants (angle)	5400	Minutes
Quadrants (angle)	1.571	Radians
Quarts (dry)	67.20	Cubic inches
Quarts (liq.)	57.75	Cubic inches
Quintal, Argentine	101.28	Pounds
Quintal, Brazil	129.54	Pounds
Quintal, Castile, Peru	101.43	Pounds
Quintal, Chile	101.41	Pounds
Quintal, Mexico	101.47	Pounds
Quintal, Metric	220.46	Pounds
Quires	25	Sheets
Radians	57.30	Degrees
Radians	3438	Minutes
Radians	0.637	Quadrants
Radians per second	57.30	Degrees per second
Radians	0.1592	Revolutions per second
Radians per second	9.549	Revolutions per minute
Radians per second per second	573.0	Revolutions per minute per minute
Radians per second per second	0.1592	Revolutions per second per second
Revolutions	360	Degrees
Revolutions	4	Quadrants
Revolutions	6.283	Radians
Revolutions per minute	6	Degrees per second
Revolutions per minute	0.1047	Radians per second
Revolutions per minute	0.01667	Revolutions per second
Revolutions per minute per minute	1.745×10^{-3}	Radians per second per second
Revolutions per minute per minute	2.778×10^{-4}	Revolutions per second per second
Revolutions per second	360	Degrees per second
Revolutions per second	6.283	Radians per second

Multiply:	By:	To obtain:
Revolutions per second	60	Revolutions per minute
Revolutions per second per second	6.283	Radians per second per second
Revolutions per second per second	3600	Revolutions per minute per minute
Seconds (angle)	4.848×10^{-6}	Radians
Square centimeters	1.076×10^{-3}	Square feet
Square centimeters	0.1550	Square inches
Square centimeters	10^{-4}	Square meters
Square centimeters	100	Square millimeters
Square feet	2.296×10^{-5}	Acres
Square feet	929.0	Square centimeters
Square feet	144	Square inches
Square feet	0.09290	Square meters
Square feet	3.587×10^{-8}	Square miles
Square feet	⅑	Square yards
$\frac{1}{\text{Square feet per gallon per minute}}$	8.0208	Overflow rate (ft/h)
Square inches	6.452	Square centimeters
Square inches	6.944×10^{-3}	Square feet
Square inches	645.2	Square millimeters
Square kilometers	247.1	Acres
Square kilometers	10.76×10^{6}	Square feet
Square kilometers	10^{6}	Square meters
Square kilometers	0.3861	Square miles
Square kilometers	1.196×10^{6}	Square yards
Square meters	2.471×10^{-4}	Acres
Square meters	10.76	Square feet
Square meters	3.861×10^{-7}	Square miles
Square meters	1.196	Square yards
Square miles	640	Acres
Square miles	27.88×10^{6}	Square feet
Square miles	2.590	Square kilometers
Square miles	3.098×10^{6}	Square yards
Square millimeters	0.01	Square centimeters
Square millimeters	1.550×10^{-3}	Square inches
Square yards	2.066×10^{-4}	Acres
Square yards	9	Square feet
Square yards	0.8361	Square meters
Square yards	3.228×10^{-7}	Square miles
Temp. (°C.) + 273	1	Abs. temp. (°C.)
Temp. (°C.) + 17.78	1.8	Temp. (°F.)
Temp. (°F.) + 460	1	Abs. temp. (°F.)
Temp. (°F.) – 32	⁵⁄₉	Temp. (°C.)
Tons (long)	1016	Kilograms

Tons (long)	2240	Pounds
Tons (long)	1.12000	Tons (short)
Tons (metric)	10^3	Kilograms
Tons (metric)	2205	Pounds
Tons (short)	2000	Pounds
Tons (short)	32,000	Ounces
Tons (short)	907.18486	Kilograms
Tons (short)	2430.56	Pounds (troy)
Tons (short)	0.89287	Tons (long)
Tons (short)	29166.66	Ounces (troy)
Tons (short)	0.90718	Tons (metric)
$\frac{1}{\text{Tons dry solids per 24 hours}}$	Area (ft^2)	Square feet per ton per 24 hours
Tons of water per 24 hours	83.333	Pounds water per hour
Tons of water per 24 hours	0.16643	Gallons per minute
Tons of water per 24 hours	1.3349	Cubic feet per hour
Watts	0.05692	Btu per minute
Watts	44.26	Foot pounds per minute
Watts	0.7376	Foot pounds per second
Watts	1.341×10^{-3}	Horsepower
Watts	0.01434	Kilogram-calories per minute
Watts	10^{-3}	Kilowatts
Watthours	3.415	British thermal units
Watthours	2655	Foot pounds
Watthours	1.341×10^{-3}	Horsepower-hours
Watthours	0.8605	Kilogram-calories
Watthours	367.1	Kilogram-meters
Watthours	10^{-3}	Kilowatthours
Yards	91.44	Centimeters
Yards	3	Feet
Yards	36	Inches
Yards	0.9144	Meters

4.3 Temperature Systems and Conversions

There are four common temperature systems used in engineering and design calculations: (°F) Fahrenheit, (°C) Celsius (formerly centigrade), (K) Kelvin, and (°R) Rankine.

The conversion equation for Celsius to Fahrenheit or Fahrenheit to Celsius is

$$\frac{5}{9} = \frac{°C}{°F - 32}$$

This exact relational equation is all that you need to convert from either system. Enter the known temperature, and solve the equation for the unknown value.

Example. You wish to convert 66°C to Fahrenheit.

$$\frac{5}{9} = \frac{66}{°F - 32}$$

$$5°F - 160 = 594$$

$$°F = 150.8$$

This method is much easier than trying to remember the two equivalent equations, which are:

$$°C = \frac{5}{9}\,(°F - 32)$$

and

$$°F = \frac{9}{5}\,°C + 32$$

The other two systems, Kelvin and Rankine, are converted as described here. The Kelvin and Celsius scales are related by

$$K = 273.18 + °C$$

Thus 0°C = 273.18 K. Absolute zero is equal to –273.18°C.

Example. A temperature of –75°C = 273.18 + (–75°C) = 198.18 K. The Rankine and Fahrenheit scales are related by

$$°R = 459.69 + °F$$

Thus 0°F = 459.69°R. Absolute zero is equal to –459.69°F.

Example. A temperature of 75°F = 459.69 + (+75°F) = 534.69°R.

Chapter

5

Materials: Physical and Chemical Properties, Characteristics, and Uses

Materials, including metals, alloys, plastics, and other composite compounds are of prime importance to the mechanical designer, tool designer, machinist, and metalworker. The most important characteristics of materials to those who design and manufacture parts are the physical and chemical properties and the various uses to which the materials may be applied. This chapter discusses a great number of metals, alloys, plastics, and compounds, including elastomers. Included are composition, physical properties, hardness, heat-treatment temperatures, and other characteristics useful for design and metalworking practices.

In design and metalworking practices, sometimes a material defect or failure occurs for unknown reasons. With the information provided in this chapter and in other appropriate American Society of Testing and Materials (ASTM), Society of Automotive Engineers (SAE), American Iron and Steel Institute (AISI), and American Gear Manufacturers Association (AGMA) standards, you may decide to have the material analyzed at a metallurgical and chemical laboratory to check the properties and compositions, or you may have the material checked mechanically at your company to determine if it meets the requirements of the material standards listed herein.

When producing the engineering drawings or specifications for a particular part, the appropriate American standard material designation or military/federal specification always must be indicated on the drawings or specifications. For example, if you are preparing a drawing for a mechanical spring and you wish to use music wire in its construction, you must indicate on the drawing that the material is to meet ASTM A-228 or appropriate SAE specifications. You also may request a certified material analysis data sheet from the supplier of the material, whether it comes from a mill, a foundry, a forge or a materials processing plant. It is the responsibility of the material suppliers to provide the design engineer and purchasing departments with these analysis sheets when so directed, which is the usual procedure.

The machining chapter 7 (Sections 7.1, 7.2, and 7.3) of this *Handbook* lists the machining characteristics and machine tool cutting and drilling speeds for many common and popular steels, alloys, other metals, plastics, and compositions. In this chapter, you will also find master cross-reference tables of all current hardness scales or systems such as Rockwell, Brinell, and Vickers. With these tables, you will be able to convert the hardness numbers for all the common and currently used hardness measurement systems relative to each other.

An important characteristic of all stock mill products such as steel and alloy rod, bar, plate, and shapes is the tolerances or dimensional limits allowed during manufacturing. Tables of allowances or dimensional limits are therefore included in this chapter. A designer *cannot* design detail parts or assemblies effectively without these tolerance limits, making these tables particularly valuable in mechanical and tool design work, where dimensional limits of stock products *must* be known.

Material specifications and characteristics or properties tables throughout this and other chapters of this *Handbook* are extracted from the latest standards of the American Society of Testing and Materials (ASTM), the Society of Automotive Engineers (SAE), and the American Gear Manufacturers Association (AGMA).

There are a tremendous number of different engineering materials for which the ASTM and SAE have listings: metallic, plastic, and composite. Steels alone account for hundreds of different alloys for wrought products, castings, and forgings. Although these alloys are listed and have specifications for composition and physical properties, they may not be readily available, except as special-order "mill run" quantities. A typical example would be austenitic stainless steel sheet in light gauges, cold-rolled to three-quarters hard, spring temper. This material is listed in the various 300 series stainless steels but may only be available from stock in 301 grade, three-quarters hard, spring temper. If you require 304 grade in your design application, it may be available only in "mill run" quantities of a minimum of 500 to 2000 lb per single order.

As a general rule, during the early design stages of a particular part, alternate materials must be investigated. Due to limited availability of your chosen material, you may be forced to use another material which *is* stocked by the material vendors. When your anticipated material quantities are large, you will then have control of the material type as well as physical size and special characteristics such as finish, temper, and gauge. For example, some of the larger companies that order hundreds of tons of hot-rolled sheet steel per year may specify to the mill that they want to run light on the minus side of a particular gauge. The tolerance on hot-rolled sheet steel is such that when it is run on the minus side of the gauge limits, many thousands of pounds of steel can be saved. The same is true for wrought copper products such as bus bars and copper sheet, where the savings may be even more advantageous.

The list of steel alloys is so large that some authorities and regulating organizations have contemplated restricting the material standards to controlled listings, wherein redundant materials are eliminated. The large listings of alloys, plastics, and composites create a stocking problem for the distributors of mill products, plastics, and composite materials.

For designers, machinists, tool makers, and metalworkers employed at small to medium-sized companies, a good approach to the aforementioned materials problems is to obtain the stock materials catalogs available from the large distributors and manufacturers such as Ryerson, Vincent, Atlantic, Alcoa, Reynolds, Bethlehem Steel, U.S. Steel, Anaconda, General Electric, Dupont, Monsanto, and others. The design and fabrication data for a great number of materials are listed in this and other chapters of this *Handbook,* together with typical uses and applications for these materials.

5.1 Steels

This section lists carbon and alloy steels, as well as the stainless steels, in their wrought form; that is to say, in the hot-rolled, cold-rolled, or cold-drawn forms. The usual shapes are sheets, plates, bars or strips, rounds, hexagons, tube, pipe, and structural configurations (beams, angles, channels, tees, square and rectangular tubes, and zees). Cast irons and steels and other casting materials are listed in Chap. 18, Castings.

When carbon is added to iron in small quantities, carbon steel is produced. Besides carbon, a number of metallic elements can be added to iron to give the characteristics inherent in the various types of steels. The usual alloying elements are

- Aluminum, which controls grain size in the steel
- Boron, which improves hardenability
- Chromium, which increases response to heat treatment as well as toughness (Chromium is used in stainless steels alone or with nickel.)
- Columbium, which is used in 18-8 stainless steels and welding electrodes
- Copper, which controls atmospheric corrosion and increases yield strengths
- Lead, which greatly improves machinability
- Manganese, which imparts strength and response to heat treatment
- Molybdenum, which increases depth of hardness and toughness
- Nickel, which increases strength and toughness but is not effective in improving hardenability
- Phosphorus, which is present in all steels and increases yield strength
- Silicon, which improves tensile strength and can improve hardenability
- Sulfur, which improves machinability but is detrimental to hot-forming properties
- Tellurium, which improves machinability in leaded steels
- Titanium, which is added to 18-8 stainless steels to prevent carbide precipitation
- Tungsten, which is used in good tool steels, making a fine grain structure when used in small amounts (When used in amounts

from 17 to 20 percent, it produces a high-speed steel that retains hardness at high temperatures.)

- Vanadium, which is used to improve the shock strength of steels and retards grain growth even after hardening from high temperatures

5.1.1 Glossary of steel terms

Age hardening A process of aging that increases hardness and strength. Age hardening usually follows rapid cooling or cold working.

Annealing A process involving heat and cooling, usually applied to induce softening.

Austenite A term designating a metallurgical phase of steels, i.e., austenitic stainless steel.

Carburizing To introduce carbon while the steel is molten or while it is in the solid state by heating it in contact with carbonaceous material below its melting point.

Case hardening A process of hardening a ferrous alloy so that the "case," or surface layer, is much harder than the interior of the part. The typical case-hardening processes are carburizing and quenching, cyaniding, carbonitriding, nitriding, induction hardening, and flame hardening. Cases of Rockwell C 55 to 60 are readily obtained in medium- to high-carbon steels.

Ductility The property of a material that allows it to be drawn out of shape before fracturing by stress.

Elastic limit The maximum stress a material is capable of sustaining without a permanent set or deformation.

Fatigue The tendency for a metal to break after repeated or cyclic loadings which are below the ultimate tensile strength. Also known as *fatigue-endurance limit.*

Flame hardening A process of hardening a ferrous alloy by heating it above the transformation range by means of a flame and then by cooling as required.

Hardenability The property of a ferrous alloy that determines the depth and distribution of hardness induced by quenching.

Induction hardening A process of hardening a ferrous alloy by heating it above the transformation range by means of electrical induction and then cooling as required.

Killed steel Steel which is deoxidized with silicon or aluminum in order to reduce the oxygen content so that no reaction occurs between carbon and oxygen during solidification.

Martensite An unstable constituent in quenched steel formed without diffusion only during cooling below a certain temperature. Martensite is the hardest of the transformation products of austenite.

Nitriding A process of case hardening in which a ferrous alloy, usually of special composition, is heated in an atmosphere of ammonia or in direct contact with a nitrogenous material to produce surface hardening by absorbing nitrogen, without quenching.

Normalizing Heating a steel part of heavy section to a temperature 100°F above the critical range and then cooling in still air.

Pickeling Chemical or electrochemical removal of surface scale and oxides.

Quench hardening Heating a steel within or above the transformation range and cooling at a rate faster than the critical rate to increase the hardness substantially. Usually involves the formation of martensite.

Solution heat treatment A process in which an alloy is heated to a suitable temperature, held at this temperature long enough for certain constituents to enter into solid solution, and then cooled rapidly to hold the constituent in solution. The metal is left in a supersaturated state which is unstable and may subsequently exhibit age hardening.

Spheroidizing Any process of heating and cooling that produces a round or globular form of carbide in steels.

Strain hardening An increase in hardness and strength caused by plastic deformation at temperatures lower than the recrystallization range.

Stress relieving A process of reducing residual stresses in a metal part by heating the part to a suitable temperature and holding this temperature for a sufficient time. This process is applied to relieve stresses induced by casting, quenching, normalizing, machining, cold working (i.e., springs), or welding.

Temper A condition produced in a metal or alloy by mechanical or thermal treatment and having characteristic structure and mechanical properties. In addition to the annealed temper, conditions produced by thermal treatment are the solution heat-treated temper and the heat-treated and artificially aged temper.

Yield strength The stress at which a material exhibits a specified limited deviation from proportionality of stress to strain. In most steels, there is a proportionality between the amount of stress that produces a certain amount of strain. This phenomenon is known as *Hooke's law.* When a material passes its yield point, a lesser amount of stress produces a greater amount of strain, until the ultimate strength point is reached, where the material breaks.

5.1.2 Carbon, alloy, stainless steel, and tool and die steels: physical properties, compositions, heat treatment, and uses

Tables 5.1 through 5.40 contain the numbering system for identification of the various types of steels given in the SAE and Unified Numbering System (UNS) designations. Figure 5.1 shows properties and heat treatments for carbon, alloy, and stainless steel. Table 5.41 is an approximate equivalent hardness number table for Brinell hardness numbers for steel, with cross-reference to other hardness designation systems. Table 5.42 is an approximate equivalent hardness number table for Rockwell C hardness numbers for steel, with cross-reference to other hardness designation systems. Figure 5.2 shows a typical hardness test machine.

Typical uses for the various steels. Following is a listing of the popular and readily available steels that are usually stocked by suppliers and which have vast applications in industry. The preceding tables have shown the chemical compositions, physical properties, and heat-treatment processes for a great number of American standard steels. The following list of applications will prove useful to many designers and mechanical engineers as well as to machinists, tool engineers, tool and die makers, and other metalworkers throughout industry. The following list is not all-inclusive, but rather is indicative of the much used and readily available types of carbon, alloy, and stainless steels.

Carbon and alloy steels: Uses by SAE/AISI number

SAE/AISI 1006 through 1015 Low-carbon, high-formability, weldable. Used for sheet metal, strip, wire, and rod. Excellent drawing qualities. Low-strength applications. Sheet metal structures, body and fender work, deep drawing parts of sheet steel.

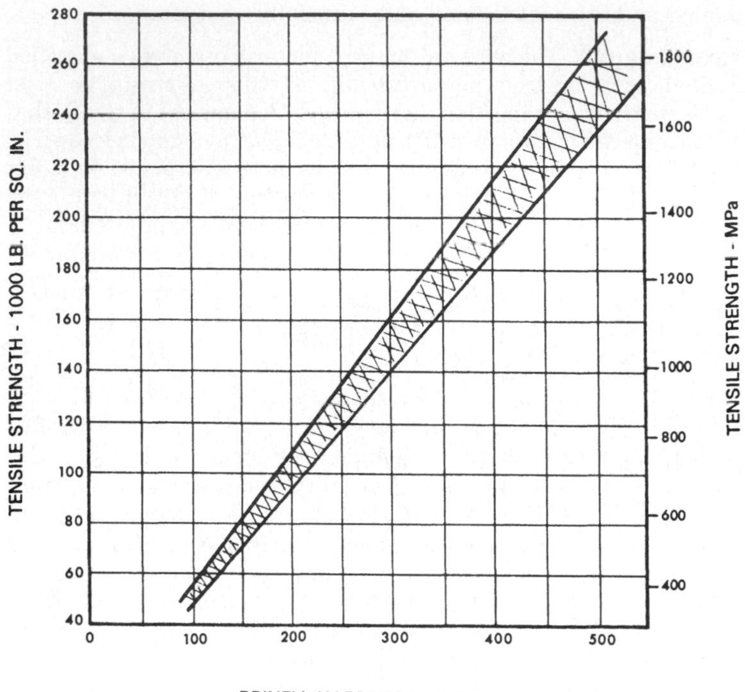

Figure 5.1 Properties and heat treatments for carbon, alloy, and stainless steel.

SAE/AISI 1016 through 1030 Increased strength over the low-carbon group. These are known as the case-hardening or carburizing grades. The higher-manganese grades machine well. The higher-carbon types are used for thicker sections where a stronger core is desired. Type 1018 is used for a great many applications, may be easily case hardened, and is readily available. Grades 1020 and 1025 are used for low-strength bolts. All these steels are readily welded.

SAE/AISI 1030 through 1052 These are the medium-carbon types of steels used where higher strength than the lower-carbon grades is required. All these steels are used for forgings. Axles and shafts are made from the 1038 to 1045 group. Widely used for machined parts, both heat-treated and non-heat-treated. Welding is possible with precautions taken during the cooling process.

(Text continued on page 224.)

Figure 5.2 A typical hardness testing machine.

TABLE 5.1 Designation System for Steels (SAE and UNS)

Numerals and digits		Type of identifying elements	Refer to SAE Standard or Information Report—JXXX for composition limits
UNS	SAE		
Carbon Steels			
G10XX0	10XX*	Nonresulfurized, manganese 1.00% maximum	403 and 1249
G11XX0	11XX	Resulfurized	403 and 1249
G12XX0	12XX	Rephosphorized and resulfurized	403
Alloy Steels			
G13XX0	13XX	Manganese steels	404 and 1249
G23XX0	23XX	Nickel steels	1249
G25XX0	25XX	Nickel steels	1249
G31XX0	31XX	Nickel-chromium steels	1249
G32XX0	32XX	Nickel-chromium steels	1249
G33XX0	33XX	Nickel-chromium steels	1249
G34XX0	34XX	Nickel-chromium steels	1249
G40XX0	40XX	Molybdenum steels	404 and 1249
G41XX0	41XX	Chromium-molybdenum steels	404 and 1249
G43XX0	43XX	Nickel-chromium-molybdenum steels	404 and 1249
G44XX0	44XX	Molybdenum steels	404 and 1249
G46XX0	46XX	Nickel-molybdenum steels	404 and 1249
G47XX0	47XX	Nickel-chromium-molybdenum steels	404
G48XX0	48XX	Nickel-molybdenum steels	404 and 1249
G50XX0	50XX	Chromium steels	404 and 1249
G51XX0	51XX	Chromium steels	404 and 1249
G50XX6	50XXX	Chromium steels	404
G51XX6	51XXX	Chromium steels	404
G52XX6	52XXX	Chromium steels	404

G61XX0	61XX	Chromium-vanadium steels	404 and 1249
G71XX0	71XXX	Tungsten-chromium steels	1249
G72XX0	72XX	Tungsten-chromium steels	1249
G81XX0	81XX	Nickel-chromium-molybdenum steels	404
G86XX0	86XX	Nickel-chromium-molybdenum steels	404 and 1249
G87XX0	87XX	Nickel-chromium-molybdenum steels	404 and 1249
G88XX0	88XX	Nickel-chromium-molybdenum steels	404
G92XX0	92XX	Silicon-manganese steels	404 and 1249
G93XX0	93XX	Nickel-chromium-molybdenum steels	404 and 1249
G94XX0	94XX	Nickel-chromium-molybdenum steels	404 and 1249
G97XX0	97XX	Nickel-chromium-molybdenum steels	1249
G98XX0	98XX	Nickel-chromium-molybdenum steels	1249
		Carbon and Alloy Steels	
GXXXX1	XXBXX	B denotes boron steels	403 and 404
GXXXX4	XXLXX	L denotes leaded steels	403 and 404
		Stainless Steels	
S2XXXX	302XX	Chromium-nickel steels	405
S3XXXX	303XX	Chromium-nickel steels	405
S4XXXX	514XX	Chromium steels	405
S5XXXX	515XX	Chromium steels	405
		Experimental Steels	
None	EX—	SAE experimental steels	1081

* SAE J403 describes UNS G 15XX0 and SAE 15XX is applicable only to semifinished products for forging, for hot-rolled and cold-finished bars, for wire rods, and for seamless tubing.

SOURCE: Reprinted with permission, copyright 1992, Society of Automotive Engineers.

TABLE 5.2 Nonresulfurized Carbon Steel Compositions Applicable to Semifinished Products for Forging, to Hot-Rolled and Cold-Finished Bars, to Wire Rods, and to Seamless Tubing: Cast or Heat Chemical Ranges and Limits

		Chemical composition limits, %*			
UNS no.	SAE/AISI no.	C	Mn	P, max	S, max
G10050	1005	0.06 Max	0.35 Max	0.040	0.050
G10060	1006	0.08 Max	0.25–0.40	0.040	0.050
G10080	1008	0.10 Max	0.30–0.50	0.040	0.050
G10100	1010	0.08–0.13	0.30–0.60	0.040	0.050
G10110	1011	0.09–0.14	0.60–0.90	0.040	0.050
G10120	1012	0.10–0.15	0.30–0.60	0.040	0.050
G10150	1015	0.13–0.18	0.30–0.60	0.040	0.050
G10160	1016	0.13–0.18	0.60–0.90	0.040	0.050
G10170	1017	0.15–0.20	0.30–0.60	0.040	0.050
G10180	1018	0.15–0.20	0.60–0.90	0.040	0.050
G10200	1020	0.18–0.23	0.30–0.60	0.040	0.050
G10210	1021	0.18–0.23	0.60–0.90	0.040	0.050
G10220	1022	0.18–0.23	0.70–1.00	0.040	0.050
G10230	1023	0.20–0.25	0.30–0.60	0.040	0.050
G10250	1025	0.22–0.28	0.30–0.60	0.040	0.050
G10260	1026	0.22–0.28	0.60–0.90	0.040	0.050
G10290	1029	0.25–0.31	0.60–0.90	0.040	0.050
G10300	1030	0.28–0.34	0.60–0.90	0.040	0.050
G10350	1035	0.32–0.38	0.60–0.90	0.040	0.050
G10380	1038	0.35–0.42	0.60–0.90	0.040	0.050
G10390	1039	0.37–0.44	0.70–1.00	0.040	0.050
G10400	1040	0.37–0.44	0.60–0.90	0.040	0.050
G10420	1042	0.40–0.47	0.60–0.90	0.040	0.050
G10430	1043	0.40–0.47	0.70–1.00	0.040	0.050
G10440	1044	0.43–0.50	0.30–0.60	0.040	0.050
G10450	1045	0.43–0.50	0.60–0.90	0.040	0.050
G10460	1046	0.43–0.50	0.70–1.00	0.040	0.050
G10490	1049	0.46–0.53	0.60–0.90	0.040	0.050
G10500	1050	0.48–0.55	0.60–0.90	0.040	0.050
G10530	1053	0.48–0.55	0.70–1.00	0.040	0.050
G10550	1055	0.50–0.60	0.60–0.90	0.040	0.050
G10590	1059	0.55–0.65	0.50–0.80	0.040	0.050
G10600	1060	0.55–0.65	0.60–0.90	0.040	0.050
G10650	1065	0.60–0.70	0.60–0.90	0.040	0.050
G10700	1070	0.65–0.75	0.60–0.90	0.040	0.050
G10740	1074	0.70–0.80	0.50–0.80	0.040	0.050
G10780	1078	0.72–0.85	0.30–0.60	0.040	0.050
G10800	1080	0.75–0.88	0.60–0.90	0.040	0.050
G10860	1086	0.80–0.93	0.30–0.50	0.040	0.050
G10900	1090	0.85–0.98	0.60–0.90	0.040	0.050
G10950	1095	0.90–1.03	0.30–0.50	0.040	0.050

NOTE: Lead—Standard carbon steels can be produced with a lead range of 0.15 to 0.35% to improve machinability. Such steels are identified by inserting the letter *L* between the second and third numerals of the grade number, for example, 10L45. The UNS designation is also modified by changing the last digit to 4 to indicate lead, for example, G10454.

TABLE 5.2 (*Continued*)

Boron—Standard killed carbon steels, which are fine grain, may be produced with a boron addition to improve hardenability. Such steels are produced to a range of 0.0005 to 0.003% boron. These steels are identified by inserting the letter *B* between the second and third numerals of the grade number, for example, 10B46. The UNS designation is also modified by changing the last digit to 1 to indicate boron, for example, G10461.

Copper—When copper is required, 0.20% minimum is generally specified.

Rods—When silicon is required, the following ranges and limits are commonly used for nonresulfurized steels: 0.10% max, 0.07 to 0.15%, 0.10 to 0.20%, 0.15 to 0.35%, 0.20 to 0.40%, and 0.30 to 0.60%.

* Certain qualities and commodities are customarily produced to lower limits of phosphorus and sulfur (see SAE J411, Table 1).

SOURCE: Reprinted with permission, copyright 1992, Society of Automotive Engineers.

TABLE 5.3 High-Manganese Carbon Steel Compositions Applicable Only to Semifinished Products for Forging, to Hot-Rolled and Cold-Finished Bars, to Wire Rods, and to Seamless Tubing: Cast or Heat Chemical Ranges and Limits

UNS no.	SAE/AISI no.	Chemical composition limits, %			
		C	M	P, max	S, max
G15130	1513	0.10–0.16	1.10–1.40	0.040	0.050
G15220	1522	0.18–0.24	1.10–1.40	0.040	0.050
G15240	1524	0.19–0.25	1.35–1.65	0.040	0.050
G15260	1526	0.22–0.29	1.10–1.40	0.040	0.050
G15270	1527	0.22–0.29	1.20–1.50	0.040	0.050
G15330	1533	0.30–0.37	1.10–1.40	0.040	0.050
G15340	1534	0.30–0.37	1.20–1.50	0.040	0.050
G15410	1541	0.36–0.44	1.35–1.65	0.040	0.050
G15440	1544	0.40–0.47	0.80–1.10	0.040	0.050
G15450	1545	0.43–0.50	0.80–1.10	0.040	0.050
G15460	1546	0.44–0.52	1.00–1.30	0.040	0.050
G15480	1548	0.44–0.52	1.10–1.40	0.040	0.050
G15520	1552	0.47–0.55	1.20–1.50	0.040	0.050
G15530	1553	0.48–0.55	0.80–1.10	0.040	0.050
G15660	1566	0.60–0.71	0.85–1.15	0.040	0.050
G15700	1570	0.65–0.75	0.80–1.10	0.040	0.050
G15800	1580	0.75–0.88	0.80–1.10	0.040	0.050
G15900	1590	0.85–0.98	0.80–1.10	0.040	0.050

NOTE: Lead—See footnote under Table 5.2.
Boron—See footnote under Table 5.2.
Phosphorus and sulfur—See footnote under Table 5.2.
Silicon—See footnote under Table 5.2.

SOURCE: Reprinted with permission, copyright 1992, Society of Automotive Engineers.

TABLE 5.4 Free-Cutting Carbon Steel Compositions Applicable to Semifinished Products for Forging, Hot-Rolled and Cold-Finished Bars, Wire Rods, and Seamless Tubing—Resulfurized Carbon Steels: Cast or Heat Chemical Ranges and Limits

		Chemical composition limits, %			
UNS no.	SAE/AISI no.	C	Mn	P, max	S
G11100	1110	0.08–0.13	0.30–0.60	0.040	0.08–0.13
G11170	1117	0.14–0.20	1.00–1.30	0.040	0.08–0.13
G11180	1118	0.14–0.20	1.30–1.60	0.040	0.08–0.13
G11230	1123	0.20–0.27	1.20–1.50	0.040	0.06–0.09
G11370	1137	0.32–0.39	1.35–1.65	0.040	0.08–0.13
G11400	1140	0.37–0.44	0.70–1.00	0.040	0.08–0.13
G11410	1141	0.37–0.45	1.35–1.65	0.040	0.08–0.13
G11440	1144	0.40–0.48	1.35–1.65	0.040	0.24–0.33
G11460	1146	0.42–0.49	0.70–1.00	0.040	0.08–0.13
G11520	1152	0.48–0.55	0.70–1.00	0.040	0.06–0.09

NOTE: Lead—See footnote under Table 5.2.
Silicon—Bars and semifinished—See footnote under Table 5.2.
Rods—When silicon is required, the following ranges and limits are commonly used:

Standard steel designations	*Silicon ranges or limits*
Up to 1110 incl.	0.10 max
1117 and over	0.10 max, 0.10–0.20 or 0.15–0.35

SOURCE: Reprinted with permission, copyright 1992, Society of Automotive Engineers.

TABLE 5.5 Free-Cutting Carbon Steel Compositions Applicable to Semifinished Products for Forging, Hot-Rolled and Cold-Finished Bars, Wire Rods, and Seamless Tubing—Rephosphorized and Resulfurized Carbon Steels: Cast or Heat Chemical Ranges and Limits

UNS no.	SAE/AISI no.	Chemical composition limits, %				
		C, max	Mn	P	S	Pb
G12120	1212	0.13	0.70–1.00	0.07–0.12	0.16–0.23	—
G12130	1213	0.13	0.70–1.00	0.07–0.12	0.24–0.33	—
G12150	1215	0.09	0.75–1.05	0.04–0.09	0.26–0.35	—
G12144	12L14	0.15	0.85–1.15	0.04–0.09	0.26–0.35	0.15–0.35

NOTE: Lead—See Footnote under Table 1.
Silicon—It is not common practice to produce the 12xx series of steels to specified limits for silicon because of its adverse effect on machinability.

SOURCE: Reprinted with permission, copyright 1992, Society of Automotive Engineers.

TABLE 5.6 M Series Carbon Steels: Cast or Heat Chemical Ranges and Limits

Grade no.	Chemical composition limits, %			
	C	Mn	P, max	S, max
M1008	0.10 max	0.25–0.60	0.04	0.05
M1010	0.07–0.14	0.25–0.60	0.04	0.05
M1012	0.09–0.16	0.25–0.60	0.04	0.05
M1015	0.12–0.19	0.25–0.60	0.04	0.05
M1017	0.14–0.21	0.25–0.60	0.04	0.05
M1020	0.17–0.24	0.25–0.60	0.04	0.05
M1023	0.19–0.27	0.25–0.60	0.04	0.05
M1025	0.20–0.30	0.25–0.60	0.04	0.05
M1031	0.26–0.36	0.25–0.60	0.04	0.05
M1044	0.40–0.50	0.25–0.60	0.04	0.05

NOTE: Merchant-quality steel bars are not produced to any specified silicon content.

SOURCE: Reprinted with permission, copyright 1992, Society of Automotive Engineers.

TABLE 5.7 Carbon Steel Compositions Applicable Only to Structural Shapes, Plates, Strip, Sheets, and Welded Tubing

		Cast or heat chemical composition limits, %			
UNS no.	SAE/AISI no.	C	Mn	P, max	S, max
G10060	1006	0.08 max	0.45 max	0.040	0.050
G10080	1008	0.10 max	0.50 max	0.040	0.050
G10090	1009	0.15 max	0.60 max	0.040	0.050
G10100	1010	0.08–0.13	0.30–0.60	0.040	0.050
G10120	1012	0.10–0.15	0.30–0.60	0.040	0.050
G10150	1015	0.12–0.18	0.30–0.60	0.040	0.050
G10160	1016	0.12–0.18	0.60–0.90	0.040	0.050
G10170	1017	0.14–0.20	0.30–0.60	0.040	0.050
G10180	1018	0.14–0.20	0.60–0.90	0.040	0.050
G10190	1019	0.14–0.20	0.70–1.00	0.040	0.050
G10200	1020	0.17–0.23	0.30–0.60	0.040	0.050
G10210	1021	0.17–0.23	0.60–0.90	0.040	0.050
G10220	1022	0.17–0.23	0.70–1.00	0.040	0.050
G10230	1023	0.19–0.25	0.30–0.60	0.040	0.050
G10250	1025	0.22–0.28	0.30–0.60	0.040	0.050
G10260	1026	0.22–0.28	0.60–0.90	0.040	0.050
G10300	1030	0.27–0.34	0.60–0.90	0.040	0.050
G10330	1033	0.29–0.36	0.70–1.00	0.040	0.050
G10350	1035	0.31–0.38	0.60–0.90	0.040	0.050
G10370	1037	0.31–0.38	0.70–1.00	0.040	0.050
G10380	1038	0.34–0.42	0.60–0.90	0.040	0.050
G10390	1039	0.36–0.44	0.70–1.00	0.040	0.050
G10400	1040	0.36–0.44	0.60–0.90	0.040	0.050
G10420	1042	0.39–0.47	0.60–0.90	0.040	0.050
G10430	1043	0.39–0.47	0.70–1.00	0.040	0.050
G10450	1045	0.42–0.50	0.60–0.90	0.040	0.050
G10460	1046	0.42–0.50	0.70–1.00	0.040	0.050
G10490	1049	0.45–0.53	0.60–0.90	0.040	0.050
G10500	1050	0.47–0.55	0.60–0.90	0.040	0.050
G10550	1055	0.52–0.60	0.60–0.90	0.040	0.050
G10600	1060	0.55–0.66	0.60–0.90	0.040	0.050
G10640	1064	0.59–0.70	0.50–0.80	0.040	0.050
G10650	1065	0.59–0.70	0.60–0.90	0.040	0.050
G10700	1070	0.65–0.76	0.60–0.90	0.040	0.050
G10740	1074	0.69–0.80	0.50–0.80	0.040	0.050
G10750	1075	0.69–0.80	0.40–0.70	0.040	0.050
G10780	1078	0.72–0.86	0.30–0.60	0.040	0.050
G10800	1080	0.74–0.88	0.60–0.90	0.040	0.050
G10840	1084	0.80–0.94	0.60–0.90	0.040	0.050
G10850	1085	0.80–0.94	0.70–1.00	0.040	0.050
G10860	1086	0.80–0.94	0.30–0.50	0.040	0.050
G10900	1090	0.84–0.98	0.60–0.90	0.040	0.050
G10950	1095	0.90–1.04	0.30–0.50	0.040	0.050

NOTE: Silicon—Where silicon is required, the following ranges and limits are commonly used:

Up to 1025, incl.	0.10 max, 0.10–0.25 or 0.15–0.35
Over 1025	0.10–0.25 or 0.15–0.35

SOURCE: Reprinted with permission, copyright 1992, Society of Automotive Engineers.

TABLE 5.8 High-Manganese Carbon Steel Compositions Applicable Only to Structural Shapes, Plates, Strip, Sheets, and Welded Tubing

UNS no.	SAE/AISI no.	Cast or heat chemical composition limits, %				Former SAE no.
		C	Mn	P, max	S, max	
G15240	1524	0.18–0.25	1.30–1.65	0.040	0.050	1024
G15270	1527	0.22–0.29	1.20–1.55	0.040	0.050	1027
G15360	1536	0.30–0.38	1.20–1.55	0.040	0.050	1036
G15410	1541	0.36–0.45	1.30–1.65	0.040	0.050	1041
G15480	1548	0.43–0.52	1.05–1.40	0.040	0.050	1048
G15520	1552	0.46–0.55	1.20–1.55	0.040	0.050	1052

SOURCE: Reprinted with permission, copyright 1992, Society of Automotive Engineers.

TABLE 5.9 Carbon Steel Cast or Heat Chemical Limits and Ranges Applicable Only to Semifinished Products for Forging, Hot-Rolled and Cold-Finished Bars, Wire Rods, and Seamless Tubing

Element	Chemical ranges and limits, %		
	When maximum of specified element	Range	Lowest max
Carbon*			0.06
	To 0.12 incl.	—	
	Over 0.12 to 0.25 incl.	0.05	
	Over 0.25 to 0.40 incl.	0.06	
	Over 0.40 to 0.55 incl.	0.07	
	Over 0.55 to 0.80 incl.	0.10	
	Over 0.80	0.13	
Manganese			0.35
	To 0.40 incl.	0.15	
	Over 0.40 to 0.50 incl.	0.20	
	Over 0.50 to 1.65 incl.	0.30	
Phosphorus			0.040
	Over 0.040 to 0.08 incl.	0.03	
	Over 0.08 to 0.13 incl.	0.05	
Sulfur			0.050
	Over 0.050 to 0.09 incl.	0.03	
	Over 0.09 to 0.15 incl.	0.05	
	Over 0.15 to 0.23 incl.	0.07	
	Over 0.23 to 0.35 incl.	0.09	
Silicon† Bars			
	To 0.15 incl.	0.08	
	Over 0.15 to 0.20 incl.	0.10	
	Over 0.20 to 0.30 incl.	0.15	
	Over 0.30 to 0.60 incl.	0.20	
Rods	When silicon is required, the following ranges and limits are commonly used: 0.10 max; 0.07–0.15, 0.10–0.20, 0.15–0.35, 0.20–0.40, or 0.30–0.60.		
Copper	When copper is required, 0.20% minimum is commonly used.		
Lead‡	When lead is required, a range of 0.15–0.35 is generally used.		

NOTE: Boron—Boron-treated fine-grain steels are produced to a range of 0.0005–0.003% boron.

* The carbon ranges shown customarily apply when the specified maximum limit for manganese does not exceed 1.10%. When the maximum manganese limit exceeds 1.10%, it is customary to add 0.01 to the carbon range shown.

† It is not common practice to produce a rephosphorized and resulfurized carbon steel to specified limits for silicon because of its adverse effect on machinability.

‡ Lead is reported only as a range of 0.15–0.35% since it is usually added to the mold or ladle stream as the steel is poured.

SOURCE: Reprinted with permission, copyright 1992, Society of Automotive Engineers.

TABLE 5.10 Carbon Steel Cast or Heat Chemical Limits and Ranges Applicable Only to Structural Shapes, Plates, Strip, Sheets, and Welded Tubing

Element	Standard chemical ranges and limits, %		
	Limit or max of specified range	Range	Lowest max
Carbon*			0.08†
	To 0.15 incl.	0.05	
	Over 0.15 to 0.30 incl.	0.06	
	Over 0.30 to 0.40 incl.	0.07	
	Over 0.40 to 0.60 incl.	0.08	
	Over 0.60 to 0.80 incl.	0.11	
	Over 0.80 to 1.35 incl.	0.14	
Manganese			0.40
	To 0.50 incl.	0.20	
	Over 0.50 to 1.15 incl.	0.30	
	Over 1.15 to 1.65 incl.	0.35	
Phosphorus			0.04
	To 0.08 incl.	0.03	
	Over 0.08 to 0.15 incl.	0.05	
Sulfur			0.05
	To 0.08 incl.	0.03	
	Over 0.08 to 0.15 incl.	0.05	
	Over 0.15 to 0.23 incl.	0.07	
	Over 0.23 to 0.33 incl.	0.10	
Silicon			0.10
	To 0.15 incl.	0.08	
	Over 0.15 to 0.30 incl.	0.15	
	Over 0.30 to 0.60 incl.	0.30	
Copper	When copper is required, 0.20 minimum is commonly specified.		

* The carbon ranges shown in the column headed "Range" apply when the specified maximum limit for manganese does not exceed 1.00%. When the maximum manganese limit exceeds 1.00%, add 0.01 to the carbon ranges shown in the table.

† 0.12 carbon maximum for structural shapes and plates.

SOURCE: Reprinted with permission, copyright 1992, Society of Automotive Engineers.

TABLE 5.11 Alloy Steel Compositions[a]

UNS no.	SAE no.	Ladle chemical composition limits, %								Corresponding AISI no.
		C	Mn	P	S	Si	Ni	Cr	Mo	V	
G13300	1330	0.28–0.33	1.60–1.90	0.035	0.040	0.15–0.35	—	—	—	—	1330
G13350	1335	0.33–0.38	1.60–1.90	0.035	0.040	0.15–0.35	—	—	—	—	1335
G13400	1340	0.38–0.43	1.60–1.90	0.035	0.040	0.15–0.35	—	—	—	—	1340
G40230	4023	0.20–0.25	0.70–0.90	0.035	0.040	0.15–0.35	—	—	0.20–0.30	—	4023
G40270	4027	0.25–0.30	0.70–0.90	0.035	0.040	0.15–0.35	—	—	0.20–0.30	—	4027
G40280	4028	0.25–0.30	0.70–0.90	0.035	0.035–0.050	0.15–0.35	—	—	0.20–0.30	—	4028
G40370	4037	0.35–0.40	0.70–0.90	0.035	0.040	0.15–0.35	—	—	0.20–0.30	—	4037
G40470	4047	0.45–0.50	0.70–0.90	0.035	0.040	0.15–0.35	—	—	0.20–0.30	—	4047
G41180	4118	0.18–0.23	0.70–0.90	0.035	0.040	0.15–0.35	—	0.40–0.60	0.08–0.15	—	4118
G41200	4120[e]	0.18–0.23	0.90–1.20	0.035	0.040	0.15–0.35	—	0.40–0.60	0.13–0.20	—	4120[e]
G41210	4121[f]	0.18–0.23	0.75–1.00	0.035	0.040	0.15–0.35	—	0.45–0.65	0.20–0.30	—	4121[f]
G41300	4130	0.28–0.33	0.40–0.60	0.035	0.040	0.15–0.35	—	0.80–1.10	0.15–0.25	—	4130
G41310	4131	0.28–0.33	0.50–0.70	0.035	0.040	0.15–0.35	—	0.90–1.20	0.15–0.25	—	4131
G41370	4137	0.35–0.40	0.70–0.90	0.035	0.040	0.15–0.35	—	0.80–1.10	0.15–0.25	—	4137
G41400	4140	0.38–0.43	0.75–1.00	0.035	0.040	0.15–0.35	—	0.80–1.10	0.15–0.25	—	4140
G41420	4142	0.40–0.45	0.75–1.00	0.035	0.040	0.15–0.35	—	0.80–1.10	0.15–0.25	—	4142
G41450	4145	0.43–0.48	0.75–1.00	0.035	0.040	0.15–0.35	—	0.80–1.10	0.15–0.25	—	4145
G41470	4147	0.45–0.50	0.75–1.00	0.035	0.040	0.15–0.35	—	0.80–1.10	0.15–0.25	—	4147
G41500	4150	0.48–0.53	0.75–1.00	0.035	0.040	0.15–0.35	—	0.80–1.10	0.15–0.25	—	4150
G43200	4320	0.17–0.22	0.45–0.65	0.035	0.040	0.15–0.35	1.65–2.00	0.40–0.60	0.20–0.30	—	4320
G43400	4340	0.38–0.43	0.60–0.80	0.035	0.040	0.15–0.35	1.65–2.00	0.70–0.90	0.20–0.30	—	4340
G43406	E4340[b]	0.38–0.43	0.65–0.85	0.025	0.025	0.15–0.35	1.65–2.00	0.70–0.90	0.20–0.30	—	E4340
G46200	4620	0.17–0.22	0.45–0.65	0.035	0.040	0.15–0.35	1.65–2.00	—	0.20–0.30	—	4620
G47150	4715[g]	0.13–0.18	0.70–0.90	0.035	0.040	0.15–0.35	0.70–1.00	0.45–0.65	0.45–0.65	—	4715[g]
G47200	4720	0.17–0.22	0.50–0.70	0.035	0.040	0.15–0.35	0.90–1.20	0.35–0.55	0.15–0.25	—	4720
G48150	4815	0.13–0.18	0.40–0.60	0.035	0.040	0.15–0.35	3.25–3.75	—	0.20–0.30	—	4815
G48200	4820	0.18–0.23	0.50–0.70	0.035	0.040	0.15–0.35	3.25–3.75	—	0.20–0.30	—	4820
G50461	50B46[c]	0.44–0.49	0.75–1.00	0.035	0.040	0.15–0.35	—	0.20–0.35	—	—	50B46

G51200	5120	0.17–0.22	0.70–0.90	0.035	0.040	0.15–0.35	—	0.70–0.90	—	—	5120
G51300	5130	0.28–0.33	0.70–0.90	0.035	0.040	0.15–0.35	—	0.80–1.10	—	—	5130
G51320	5132	0.30–0.35	0.60–0.80	0.035	0.040	0.15–0.35	—	0.75–1.00	—	—	5132
G51400	5140	0.38–0.43	0.70–0.90	0.035	0.040	0.15–0.35	—	0.70–0.90	—	—	5140
G51500	5150	0.48–0.53	0.70–0.90	0.035	0.040	0.15–0.35	—	0.70–0.90	—	—	5150
G51600	5160	0.56–0.64	0.75–1.00	0.035	0.040	0.15–0.35	—	0.70–0.90	—	—	5160
G51601	51B60[c]	0.56–0.64	0.75–1.00	0.035	0.040	0.15–0.35	—	0.70–0.90	—	—	51B60
G51986	E51100[b]	0.98–1.10	0.25–0.45	0.025	0.025	0.15–0.35	—	0.90–1.15	—	—	E51100
G52986	E52100[b]	0.98–1.10	0.25–0.45	0.025	0.025	0.15–0.35	—	1.30–1.60	—	—	E52100
G61500	6150	0.48–0.53	0.70–0.90	0.035	0.040	0.15–0.35	—	0.80–1.10	—	0.15 min	6150
G86150	8615	0.13–0.18	0.70–0.90	0.035	0.040	0.15–0.35	0.40–0.70	0.40–0.60	0.15–0.25	—	8615
G86170	8617	0.15–0.20	0.70–0.90	0.035	0.040	0.15–0.35	0.40–0.70	0.40–0.60	0.15–0.25	—	8617
G86200	8620	0.18–0.23	0.70–0.90	0.035	0.040	0.15–0.35	0.40–0.70	0.40–0.60	0.15–0.25	—	8620
G86220	8622	0.20–0.25	0.70–0.90	0.035	0.040	0.15–0.35	0.40–0.70	0.40–0.60	0.15–0.25	—	8622
G86300	8630	0.28–0.33	0.70–0.90	0.035	0.040	0.15–0.35	0.40–0.70	0.40–0.60	0.15–0.25	—	8630
G86370	8637	0.35–0.40	0.75–1.00	0.035	0.040	0.15–0.35	0.40–0.70	0.40–0.60	0.15–0.25	—	8637
G86400	8640	0.38–0.43	0.75–1.00	0.035	0.040	0.15–0.35	0.40–0.70	0.40–0.60	0.15–0.25	—	8640
G86450	8645	0.43–0.48	0.75–1.00	0.035	0.040	0.15–0.35	0.40–0.70	0.40–0.60	0.15–0.25	—	8645
G87200	8720	0.18–0.23	0.70–0.90	0.035	0.040	0.15–0.35	0.40–0.70	0.40–0.60	0.20–0.30	—	8720
G88220	8822	0.20–0.25	0.75–1.00	0.035	0.040	0.15–0.35	0.40–0.70	0.40–0.60	0.30–0.40	—	8822
G92590	9259	0.56–0.64	0.75–1.00	0.035	0.040	0.70–1.10	—	0.45–0.65	—	—	9259
G92600	9260	0.56–0.64	0.75–1.00	0.035	0.040	1.80–2.20	—	—	—	—	9260

[a] For standard variations in composition limits, see Table 4 of SAE J409. Small quantities of certain elements which are not specified or required may be found in alloy steels. These elements are to be considered as incidental and are acceptable to the following maximum amount: copper to 0.35%, nickel to 0.25%, chromium to 0.20%, and molybdenum to 0.06%.

[b] Electric furnace steel.

[c] Boron content is 0.0005–0.003%.

[d] Lead–standard carbon steels can be produced with a range of 0.015–0.35% to improve machinability. Such steels are identified by inserting the letter *L* between the second and third numerals of the grade number, for example, 10L45. The UNS designation is also modified by changing the last digit to 4 to indicate lead, for example, G10454. Lead is generally reported as a range of 0.15/0.35%.

[e] Formerly EX15.

[f] Formerly EX24.

[g] Formerly EX30.

SOURCE: Reprinted with permission, copyright 1992, Society of Automotive Engineers.

TABLE 5.12 Alloy Steel Plate Compositions (Open Hearth and Basic Oxygen)*,†,‡

UNS no.	SAE no.	Ladle chemical composition limits, %								
		C	Mn	P, max	S, max	Si§	Ni	Cr	Mo	V
G13300	1330	0.27–0.34	1.50–1.90	0.035	0.040	0.15–0.35	—	—	—	—
G13350	1335	0.32–0.39	1.50–1.90	0.035	0.040	0.15–0.35	—	—	—	—
G13400	1340	0.36–0.44	1.50–1.90	0.035	0.040	0.15–0.35	—	—	—	—
G13450	1345	0.41–0.49	1.50–1.90	0.035	0.040	0.15–0.35	—	—	—	—
G41180	4118	0.17–0.23	0.60–0.90	0.035	0.040	0.15–0.35	—	0.40–0.65	0.08–0.15	—
G41300	4130	0.27–0.34	0.35–0.60	0.035	0.040	0.15–0.35	—	0.80–1.15	0.15–0.25	—
G41350	4135	0.32–0.39	0.65–0.95	0.035	0.040	0.15–0.35	—	0.80–1.15	0.15–0.25	—
G41370	4137	0.33–0.40	0.65–0.95	0.035	0.040	0.15–0.35	—	0.80–1.15	0.15–0.25	—
G41400	4140	0.36–0.44	0.70–1.00	0.035	0.040	0.15–0.35	—	0.80–1.15	0.15–0.25	—
G41420	4142	0.38–0.46	0.70–1.00	0.035	0.040	0.15–0.35	—	0.80–1.15	0.15–0.25	—
G41450	4145	0.41–0.49	0.70–1.00	0.035	0.040	0.15–0.35	—	0.80–1.15	0.15–0.25	—
G43400	4340	0.36–0.44	0.55–0.80	0.035	0.040	0.15–0.35	1.65–2.00	0.60–0.90	0.20–0.30	—
G43406	E4340	0.37–0.44	0.60–0.85	0.025	0.025	0.15–0.35	1.65–2.00	0.65–0.90	0.20–0.30	—
G46150	4615	0.12–0.18	0.40–0.65	0.035	0.040	0.15–0.35	1.65–2.00	—	0.20–0.30	—
G46170	4617	0.15–0.21	0.40–0.65	0.035	0.040	0.15–0.35	1.65–2.00	—	0.20–0.30	—
G46200	4620	0.16–0.22	0.40–0.65	0.035	0.040	0.15–0.35	1.65–2.00	—	0.20–0.30	—
G51600	5160	0.54–0.65	0.70–1.00	0.035	0.040	0.15–0.35	—	0.60–0.90	—	—
G61500	6150	0.46–0.54	0.60–0.90	0.035	0.040	0.15–0.35	—	0.80–1.15	—	0.15 min
G86150	8615	0.12–0.18	0.60–0.90	0.035	0.040	0.15–0.35	0.40–0.070	0.35–0.60	0.15–0.25	—
G86170	8617	0.15–0.21	0.60–0.90	0.035	0.040	0.15–0.35	0.40–0.070	0.35–0.60	0.15–0.25	—
G86200	8620	0.17–0.23	0.60–0.90	0.035	0.040	0.15–0.35	0.40–0.070	0.35–0.60	0.15–0.25	—
G86220	8622	0.19–0.25	0.60–0.90	0.035	0.040	0.15–0.35	0.40–0.070	0.35–0.60	0.15–0.25	—

G86250	8625	0.22–0.29	0.60–0.90	0.035	0.040	0.15–0.35	0.40–0.070	0.35–0.60	0.15–0.25	—
G86270	8627	0.24–0.31	0.60–0.90	0.035	0.040	0.15–0.35	0.40–0.070	0.35–0.60	0.15–0.25	—
G86300	8630	0.27–0.34	0.60–0.90	0.035	0.040	0.15–0.35	0.40–0.070	0.35–0.60	0.15–0.25	—
G86370	8637	0.33–0.40	0.70–1.00	0.035	0.040	0.15–0.35	0.40–0.070	0.35–0.60	0.15–0.25	—
G86400	8640	0.36–0.44	0.70–1.00	0.035	0.040	0.15–0.35	0.40–0.070	0.35–0.60	0.15–0.25	—
G86550	8655	0.49–0.60	0.70–1.00	0.035	0.040	0.15–0.35	0.40–0.070	0.35–0.60	0.15–0.25	—
G87420	8742	0.38–0.46	0.70–1.00	0.035	0.040	0.15–0.35	0.40–0.070	0.35–0.60	0.20–0.30	—

* Small quantities of certain elements not required may be found. These elements are to be considered as incidental and are acceptable to the following maximum amounts: copper to 0.35%, nickel to 0.25%, chromium to 0.20%, and molybdenum to 0.06%

† When electric furnace steel is ordered, the carbon range is restricted 0.01%, manganese 0.05%, chromium 0.05% up to 1.25% incl. and 0.10% over 1.25%. The maximum phosphorus and sulfur is 0.025% each.

‡ Boron or lead may be added to these compositions.

§ Silicon available in ranges of 0.10–0.20%, 0.20–0.30%, and 0.35% maximum (when carbon deoxidized) when so specified by the purchaser.

TABLE 5.13 Wrought Chromium-Nickel Austenitic Steels (Not Hardenable by Thermal Treatment)

	Chemical composition limits, %									
SAE no.*	C, max	Mn, max	Si, max	P, max	S, max	Cr range	Ni range	Other elements	AISI type*	UNS
30201	0.15	5.5–7.5	1.00	0.060	0.030	16.00–18.00	3.50–5.50	N, 0.25 max	201	S20100
30202	0.15	7.5–10.0	1.00	0.060	0.030	17.00–19.00	4.00–6.00	N, 0.25 max	202	S20200
30301	0.15	2.00	1.00	0.045	0.030	16.00–18.00	6.00–8.00	—	301	S30100
30302	0.15	2.00	1.00	0.045	0.030	17.00–19.00	8.00–10.00	—	302	S30200
30302B	0.15	2.00	2.00–3.00	0.045	0.030	17.00–19.00	8.00–10.00	—	302B	S30215
30303	0.15	2.00	1.00	0.20	0.15 min	17.00–19.00	8.00–10.00	Zr or Mo, 0.60 max[‡]	303	S30300
30303 Sc	0.15	2.00	1.00	0.20	0.06	17.00–19.00	8.00–10.00	Se, 0.15 min	303 Se	S30323
30304	0.08	2.00	1.00	0.045	0.030	18.00–20.00	8.00–10.50	—	304	S30400
30304L	0.03	2.00	1.00	0.045	0.030	18.00–20.00	8.00–12.00	—	304L	S30403
30305	0.12	2.00	1.00	0.045	0.030	17.00–19.00	10.50–13.00	—	305	S30500
30308	0.08	2.00	1.00	0.045	0.030	19.00–21.00	10.00–12.00	—	308	S30800
30309	0.20	2.00	1.00	0.045	0.030	22.00–24.00	12.00–15.00	—	309	S30900
30309S	0.08	2.00	1.00	0.045	0.030	22.00–24.00	12.00–15.00	—	309S	S30908
30310	0.25	2.00	1.50	0.045	0.030	24.00–26.00	19.00–22.00	—	310	S31000
30310S	0.08	2.00	1.50	0.045	0.030	24.00–26.00	19.00–22.00	—	310S	S31008
30314	0.25	2.00	1.50–3.00	0.045	0.030	23.00–26.00	19.00–22.00	—	314	S31400
30316	0.08	2.00	1.00	0.045	0.030	16.00–18.00	10.00–14.00	Mo, 2.00–3.00	316	S31600
30316L[§]	0.03	2.00	1.00	0.045	0.030	16.00–18.00	10.00–14.00	Mo, 2.00–3.00	316L	S31603
30317	0.08	2.00	1.00	0.045	0.030	18.00–20.00	11.00–15.00	Mo, 3.00–4.00	317	S31700
30321[¶]	0.08	2.00	1.00	0.045	0.030	17.00–19.00	9.00–12.00	Ti, 5 × C min	321	S32100
30330	0.08	2.00	0.75–1.50	0.040	0.030	17.00–20.00	34.00–37.00	—	330	N08330
30347	0.08	2.00	1.00	0.045	0.030	17.00–19.00	9.00–13.00	Cb-Ta, 10 × C min	347	S34700
30348	0.08	2.00	1.00	0.045	0.030	17.00–19.00	9.00–13.00	Cb-Ta, 10 × C min; Ta, 0.0 max	348	S34800
30384	0.08	2.00	1.00	0.045	0.030	15.00–17.00	17.00–19.00	—	384	S38400
30385	0.08	2.00	1.00	0.045	0.030	11.50–13.50	14.00–16.00	—	385	S38500

* The suffixes with grade numbers denote: B—2.00–3.00 silicon range; Se—a free machining steel with selenium addition; L—extra low carbon grade; S—lower carbon grade.

[†] To minimize carbon or nitrogen pickup, 0.75–1.50 Si is recommended for high temperature application involving carbon or nitrogen atmosphere.

[‡] At producer's option; reported only when intentionally added.

[§] 10.0–15.0 Ni permitted for tubular products.

[¶] 9.0–13.0 Ni permitted for tubular products.

SOURCE: Reprinted with permission, copyright 1992, Society of Automotive Engineers.

TABLE 5.14 Wrought Stainless Martensitic Chromium Steels (Hardenable by Thermal Treatment)

SAE no.*	Chemical composition limits, %								AISI type*	UNS
	C, max	Mn, max	Si, max	P, max	S, max	Cr range	Ni range	Other elements		
51403	0.15	1.00	0.50	0.040	0.030	11.50–13.00	—	—	403	S40300
51410	0.15	1.00	1.00	0.040	0.030	11.50–13.50	—	—	410	S41000
51414	0.15	1.00	1.00	0.040	0.030	11.50–13.50	1.25–2.50	—	414	S41400
51416	0.15	1.25	1.00	0.06	0.15 min	12.00–14.00	—	Zr or Mo, 0.60 max†	416	S41600
51416 Se	0.15	1.25	1.00	0.06	0.06	12.00–14.00	—	Se, 0.15 min	416 Se	S41623
41420	Over 0.15	1.00	1.00	0.040	0.030	12.00–14.00	—	—	420	S42000
51420F	0.15 min	1.25	1.00	0.06	0.15 min	12.00–14.00	—	Mo, 0.60 max†	420F	S42020
51420F Se	0.30–0.40	1.25	1.00	0.06	0.06	12.00–14.00	—	Se, 0.15 min	—	S42023
51431	0.20	1.00	1.00	0.040	0.030	15.00–17.00	1.25–2.50	—	431	S43100
51440A	0.60–0.75	1.00	1.00	0.040	0.030	16.00–18.00	—	Mo, 0.75 max	440A	S44002
51440B	0.75–0.95	1.00	1.00	0.040	0.030	16.00–18.00	—	Mo, 0.75 max	440B	S44003
51440C	0.95–1.20	1.00	1.00	0.040	0.030	16.00–18.00	—	Mo, 0.75 max	440C	S44004
51440F	0.95–1.20	1.25	1.00	0.06	0.15 min	16.00–18.00	—	Zr or Mo, 0.75 max†	—	S44020
51440F Se	0.95–1.20	1.25	1.00	0.06	0.06	16.00–18.00	—	Se, 0.15 min	—	S44023
51501	Over 0.10	1.00	1.00	0.040	0.030	4.00–6.00	—	Mo, 0.40–0.65	501	S50100
51502	0.10	1.00	1.00	0.04	0.030	4.00–6.00	—	Mo, 0.40–0.65	502	S50200

* Suffixes A, B, and C denote differing carbon ranges for the same grade; F—a free machining steel; Se—a free machining steel with selenium addition.

† At producer's option; reported only when intentionally added.

SOURCE: Reprinted with permission, copyright 1992, Society of Automotive Engineers.

TABLE 5.15 Wrought Stainless Ferritic Chromium Steels (Not Hardenable by Thermal Treatment)

	Chemical composition limits, %									
SAE no.*	C, max	Mn, max	Si, max	P, max	S, max	Cr range	Ni range	Other elements	AISI type*	UNS
51405[†]	0.08	1.00	1.00	0.040	0.030	11.50–14.50	—	Al, 0.10–0.30	405	S40500
51409	0.08	1.00	1.00	0.045	0.045	10.50–11.75	0.50 max	Ti, 6× C or max of 0.75, Fe, rem		S40900
51429	0.12	1.00	1.00	0.040	0.030	14.00–16.00	—	—	429	S42900
51430	0.12	1.00	1.00	0.040	0.030	16.00–18.00	—	—	430	S43000
51430F	0.12	1.25	1.00	0.060	0.15 min	—	—	Mo, 0.60 max[‡]	430F	S43020
51430F Se	0.12	1.25	1.00	0.060	0.060	16.00–18.00	—	Se, 0.15 min	430F Se	S43023
51434	0.08	1.00	1.00	0.040	0.030	16.00–18.00	—	Mo, 0.75–1.25	434	S43400
51436	0.08	1.00	1.00	0.040	0.030	16.00–18.00	—	Mo, 0.75–1.25; Cb + Ta, 5 × C – 0.70	436	S43600
51439	0.07	1.00	1.00	0.040	0.030	17.00–19.00	0.50	Ti–0.20 + 4(C + N) min, 1.10 max Al–0.15 max N–0.04 max	439	S43900
51439LL	0.014	1.00	1.00	0.040	0.030	17.00–19.00	0.50	Ti–0.20 + 4(C + N) min, 1.10 max Al–0.15 max N–0.04 max	439LL	S43903
51442	0.20	1.00	1.00	0.04	0.035	18.00–23.00	—	—	—	S44200
51446	0.20	1.50	1.00	0.04	0.030	23.00–27.00	—	N, 0.25 max	446	S44600

* Suffix F—denotes a free machining steel; Se—denotes a free machining steel with selenium.
[†] Essentially nonhardenable by heat treatment.
[‡] At producer's option; reported only when intentionally added.
SOURCE: Reprinted with permission, copyright 1992, Society of Automotive Engineers.

TABLE 5.16 Wrought Stainless Steels for Special Machinability

Proprietary designation	Chemical composition limits, %								UNS
	C, max	Mn, max	Si, max	P, max	S, max	Cr range	Ni range	Other elements	
203 Ez*	0.08	5.00–6.50	1.00	0.04	0.18–0.35	16.00–18.00	5.00–6.50	Mo, 0.50 max; Cu, 1.75/2.25	S20300
303 MA*	0.15	2.00	1.00	0.05	0.11–0.16	17.00–19.00	8.00–10.00	Mo, 0.40–0.60; Al, 0.60–1.00	S30345
303 Pb*	0.15	2.00	1.00	0.04	0.12–0.25	17.00–19.00	8.00–10.00	Mo, 0.60 max; Pb, 0.12–0.30	S30360
303 Cu*	0.15	2.00	1.00	0.15	0.10 min	17.00–19.00	6.00–10.00	Se, 0.10 max; Cu, 2.50–4.00	S30330
303 Plus X*	0.15	2.50–4.50	1.00	0.20	0.15 min	17.00–19.00	7.00–10.00	Mo, 0.60 max	S30310
416 Plus X†	0.15	1.50–2.50	1.00	0.06	0.15 min	12.00–14.00	—	Mo, 0.60 max	S41610

* Not hardenable by thermal treatment.
† Hardenable by thermal treatment.
SOURCE: Reprinted with permission, copyright 1992, Society of Automotive Engineers.

TABLE 5.17 Chemical Requirements-Stainless Steels

UNS Designation[a]	Type	Composition, %									
		Carbon, max[b]	Manganese, max[b]	Phosphorus, max	Sulfur, max	Silicon, max[b]	Chromium	Nickel	Molybdenum	Nitrogen, max[b]	Other elements
		Austenitic Grades									
S 20100	201	0.15	5.50–7.50	0.060	0.030	1.00	16.00–18.00	3.50–5.50		0.25	
S 20161	—	0.15	4.00–6.00	0.040	0.040	3.00–4.00	15.00–18.00	4.00–6.00		0.08–0.20	
S 20200	202	0.15	7.50–10.00	0.060	0.030	1.00	17.00–19.00	4.00–6.00		0.25	
S 20500	205	0.12–25	14.00–15.50	0.060	0.030	1.00	16.50–18.00	1.00–1.70		0.32–0.40	
S 20910	XM-19	0.06	4.00–6.00	0.040	0.030	1.00	20.50–23.50	11.50–13.50	1.50–3.00	0.20–0.40	Cb 0.10–0.30, V 0.10–0.30
S 21800	—	0.10	7.00–9.00	0.060	0.030	3.50–4.50	16.00–18.00	8.00–9.00		0.08–0.18	
S 21900	XM-10	0.08	8.00–10.00	0.060	0.030	1.00	19.00–21.50	5.50–7.50		0.15–0.40	
S 21904	XM-11	0.04	8.00–10.00	0.060	0.030	1.00	19.00–21.50	5.50–7.50		0.15–0.40	
S 24000	XM-29	0.08	11.50–14.50	0.060	0.030	1.00	17.00–19.00	2.25–3.75		0.20–0.40	
S 24100	XM-28	0.15	11.00–14.00	0.060	0.030	1.00	16.50–19.00	0.50–2.50		0.20–0.45	
S 28200	—	0.15	17.00–19.00	0.045	0.030	1.00	17.00–19.00	. . .	0.75–1.25	0.40–0.60	Cu 0.75–1.25
S 30200	302	0.15	2.00	0.045	0.030	1.00	17.00–19.00	8.00–10.00		0.10	
S 30215	302B	0.15	2.00	0.045	0.030	2.00–3.00	17.00–19.00	8.00–10.00			—
S 30400	304	0.08	2.00	0.045	0.030	1.00	18.00–20.00	8.00–10.50		0.10	
S 30403	304L[c]	0.03	2.00	0.045	0.030	1.00	18.00–20.00	8.00–12.00		0.10	
S 30430	XM-7	0.10	2.00	0.045	0.030	1.00	17.00–19.00	8.00–10.00			Cu 3.00–4.00
S 30451	304N	0.08	2.00	0.045	0.030	1.00	18.00–20.00	8.00–10.50		0.10–0.16	
S 30452	XM-21	0.08	2.00	0.045	0.030	1.00	18.00–20.00	8.00–10.50		0.16–0.30	
S 30453	304LN	0.03	2.00	0.045	0.030	1.00	18.00–20.00	8.00–12.00		0.10–0.16	
S 30454	—	0.03	2.00	0.045	0.030	1.00	18.00–20.00	8.00–12.00		0.16–0.30	
S 30500	305	0.12	2.00	0.045	0.030	1.00	17.00–19.00	10.50–13.00			—
S 30800	308	0.08	2.00	0.045	0.030	1.00	19.00–21.00	10.00–12.00			—
S 30815	—	0.10	0.80	0.040	0.030	1.40–2.00	20.00–22.00	10.00–12.00		0.14–0.20	Ce 0.03–0.08
S 30900	309	0.20	2.00	0.045	0.030	1.00	22.00–24.00	12.00–15.00			—
S 30908	309S	0.08	2.00	0.045	0.030	1.00	22.00–24.00	12.00–15.00			—
S 30940	309Cb	0.08	2.00	0.045	0.030	1.00	22.00–24.00	12.00–16.00		0.10	Cb + Ta 10 × C min, 1.10 max

S 31000	310	0.25	2.00	0.045	0.030	1.50	24.00–26.00	19.00–22.00			—
S 31008	310S	0.08	2.00	0.045	0.030	1.50	24.00–26.00	19.00–22.00			—
S 31040	310Cb	0.08	2.00	0.045	0.030	1.50	24.00–26.00	19.00–22.00		0.10	Cb + Ta 10 × C min, 1.10 max
S 31254	—	0.020	1.00	0.030	0.010	0.80	19.50–20.50	17.50–18.50	6.00–6.50	0.18–0.22	Cu 0.50–1.00
S 31400	314	0.25	2.00	0.045	0.030	1.50–3.00	23.00–26.00	19.00–22.00			—
S 31600	316	0.08	2.00	0.045	0.030	1.00	16.00–18.00	10.00–14.00	2.00–3.00	0.10	
S 31603	316L[c]	0.03	2.00	0.045	0.030	1.00	16.00–18.00	10.00–14.00	2.00–3.00	0.10	
S 31635	316Ti	0.08	2.00	0.045	0.030	1.00	16.00–18.00	10.00–14.00	2.00–3.00	0.10	Ti 5 × (C + N) min, 0.70 max
S 31640	316Cb	0.08	2.00	0.045	0.030	1.00	16.00–18.00	10.00–14.00	2.00–3.00	0.10	Cb + Ta 10 × C min, 1.10 max
S 31651	316N	0.08	2.00	0.045	0.030	1.00	16.00–18.00	10.00–14.00	2.00–3.00	0.10–0.16	
S 31653	316LN	0.030	2.00	0.045	0.030	1.00	16.00–18.00	10.00–14.00	2.00–3.00	0.10–0.16	
S 31654	—	0.03	2.00	0.045	0.030	1.00	16.00–18.00	10.00–14.00	2.00–3.00	0.16–0.30	
S 31700	317	0.08	2.00	0.045	0.030	1.00	18.00–20.00	11.00–15.00	3.00–4.00	0.10	
S 31725	—	0.03	2.00	0.045	0.030	1.00	18.00–20.00	13.50–17.50	4.0–5.0	0.10	Cu 0.75 max
S 31726	—	0.03	2.00	0.045	0.030	1.00	17.00–20.00	13.50–17.50	4.0–5.0	0.10–0.20	Cu 0.75 max
S 32100	321	0.08	2.00	0.045	0.030	1.00	17.00–19.00	9.00–12.00			Ti 5 × (C + N) min To 0.70 max[d]
S 34700	347	0.08	2.00	0.045	0.030	1.00	17.00–19.00	9.00–13.00			Cb + Ta 10 × C min
S 34800	348	0.08	2.00	0.045	0.030	1.00	17.00–19.00	9.00–13.00			Cb + Ta 10 × C min, Ta 0.10 max, Co 0.20 max
Austenitic-Ferritic Grades											
S 31100	XM-26	0.06	1.00	0.040	0.030	1.00	25.00–27.00	6.00–7.00			Ti 0.25 max
S 31803		0.030	2.00	0.030	0.020	1.00	21.00–23.00	4.50–6.50	2.50–3.50	0.03–0.20	
Ferritic Grades											
S 40500	405	0.08	1.00	0.040	0.030	1.00	11.50–14.50	—			Al 0.10–0.30
S 42900	429	0.12	1.00	0.040	0.030	1.00	14.00–16.00	—			—
S 43000	430	0.12	1.00	0.040	0.030	1.00	16.00–18.00	—			—
S 44400	—	0.025	1.00	0.040	0.030	1.00	17.5–19.5	1.00	1.75–2.50	0.035	Ti + Cb 0.20 + 4 (C + N) min 0.80 max
S 44600	446	0.20	1.50	0.040	0.030	1.00	23.00–27.00	—		0.25	—

TABLE 5.17 Chemical Requirements-Stainless Steels (*Continued*)

UNS Designation[a]	Type	Carbon, max[b]	Manganese, max[b]	Phosphorus, max	Sulfur, max	Silicon, max[b]	Chromium	Nickel	Molybdenum	Nitrogen, max[b]	Other elements
Ferritic Grades (*Continued*)											
S 44627	XM-27[e]	0.010[f]	0.40	0.020	0.020	0.40	25.00–27.50	0.50 max	0.75–1.50	0.015[f]	Cu 0.20 max, Cb 0.05–0.20
S 44700	—	0.010	0.30	0.025	0.020	0.20	28.00–30.00	0.15 max	3.50–4.20	0.020	C + N 0.025 max, Cu 0.15 max
S 44800	—	0.010	0.30	0.025	0.020	0.20	28.00–30.00	2.00–2.50	3.50–4.20	0.020	C + N 0.25 max, Cu 0.15 max
Martensitic Grades											
S 40300	403	0.15	1.00	0.040	0.030	0.50	11.50–13.00	—			—
S 41000	410	0.15	1.00	0.040	0.030	1.00	11.50–13.50	—			—
S 41040	XM-30	0.18	1.00	0.040	0.030	1.00	11.50–13.50	—			Cb 0.05–0.30
S 41400	414	0.15	1.00	0.040	0.030	1.00	11.50–13.50	1.25–2.50			—
S 41500	[g]	0.05	0.50–1.00	0.030	0.030	0.60	11.50–14.00	3.50–5.50	0.50–1.00		
S 42000	420	Over 0.15	1.00	0.040	0.030	1.00	12.00–14.00	—			—
S 42010	—	0.15–0.30	1.00	0.040	0.030	1.00	13.50–15.00	0.35–0.85	0.40–0.85		
S 43100	431	0.20	1.00	0.040	0.030	1.00	15.00–17.00	1.25–2.50			—
S 44002	440A	0.60–0.75	1.00	0.040	0.030	1.00	16.00–18.00	—	0.75		
S 44003	440B	0.75–0.95	1.00	0.040	0.030	1.00	16.00–18.00	—	0.75		
S 44004	440C	0.95–1.20	1.00	0.040	0.030	1.00	16.00–18.00	—	0.75		
S 50400	9	0.15	0.30–0.60	0.030	0.030	0.75–1.00	8.00–10.00	—	0.90–1.10		

[a] New designations established in accordance with Practice E 527 and SAE J1086.

[b] Maximum, unless otherwise indicated.

[c] For some applications, the substitution of type 304L for type 304, or type 316L for type 316 may be undesirable because of design, fabrication, or service requirements. In such cases, the purchaser should so indicate on the order.

[d] Nitrogen content is to be reported.

[e] Nickel plus copper shall be 0.50% max.

[f] Product analysis tolerance over the maximum limit for carbon and nitrogen shall be 0.002%.

[g] Wrought version of CA 6NM.

SOURCE: Reprinted with permission, from the Annual Book of ASTM Standards, copyright 1992, American Society of Testing and Materials.

TABLE 5.18 Mechanical Requirements-Stainless Steels

Type	Condition	Finish	Diameter or thickness, in (mm)	Tensile strength, min		Yield strength,[a] min		Elongation in 2 in or 50 mm[b] min, %	Reduction of area,[c] min, %	Brinell hardness, max
				ksi	MPa	ksi	MPa			
Austenitic Grades										
201, 202	A	Hot finished or cold finished	All	75	515	40	275	40	45	—
S20161	A	Hot finished or cold finished	All	125	860	50	345	40	40	255
205	A	Hot finished or cold finished	All	100	690	60	414	40	50	—
XM-19	A	Hot finished or cold finished	All	100	690	55	380	35	55	—
XM-19	As hot rolled	Hot finished or cold finished	Up to 2 (50.8), incl	135	930	105	725	20	50	—
			Over 2 to 3 (50.8 to 76.2), incl	115	795	75	515	25	50	—
			Over 3 to 8 (76.2 to 203.2), incl	100	690	60	415	30	50	—
S21800	A	Hot finished or cold finished	All	95	655	50	345	35	55	241
XM-10, XM-11	A	Hot finished or cold finished	All	90	620	50	345	45	60	—
XM-29	A	Hot finished or cold finished	All	100	690	55	380	30	50	—
XM-28	A	Hot finished or cold finished	All	100	690	55	380	30	50	—
S 28200	A	Hot finished or cold finished	All	110	760	60	410	35	55	—
302, 302B, 304, 304LN, 305, 308, 309, 309S, 309CB, 310, 310S, 310CB, 314, 316, 316LN, 316CB, 316TI, 317, 321, 347, 348	A	Hot finished	All	75[e]	515	30[e]	205	40[g]	50	—
		Cold finished	Up to ½ (12.70) incl	90	620	45	310	30	40	—
			Over ½ (12.70)	75[e]	515	30[e]	205	30	40	—

TABLE 5.18 Mechanical Requirements-Stainless Steels (*Continued*)

Type	Condition	Finish	Diameter or thickness, in (mm)	Tensile strength, min		Yield strength,[a] min		Elongation in 2 in or 50 mm[b] min, %	Reduction of area,[c] min, %	Brinell hardness, max
				ksi	MPa	ksi	MPa			
			Austenitic Grades (*Continued*)							
304L, 316L	A	Hot finished	All	70	480	25	170	40[g]	50	—
		Cold finished	Up to ½ (12.70) incl.	90	620	45	310	30	40	—
			Over ½ (12.70)	70	480	25	170	30	40	—
304N, 316N	A	Hot finished or cold finished	All	80	550	35	240	30	—	—
202, 302, 304, 304N, 316, 316N	B	Cold finished	Up to ¾ (19.05) incl.	125	860	100	690	12	35	—
			Over ¾ (19.05) to 1 (25.40)	115	795	80	550	15	35	—
			Over 1 (25.40) to 1¼ (31.75)	105	725	65	450	20	35	—
			Over 1¼ (31.75) to 1½ (38.10)	100	690	50	345	24	45	—
			Over 1½ (38.10) to 1¾ (44.45)	95	655	45	310	28	45	—
304, 304N, 316, 316N	S	Cold finished	Up to 2 (50.8) incl	95	650	75	515	25	40	—
			Over 2 to 2½ (50.8 to 63.5) incl	90	620	65	450	30	40	—
			Over 2½ to 3 (63.5 to 76.2) incl	80	550	55	380	30	40	—
XM-21, S 30454, S 31654	A	Hot finished or cold finished	All	90	620	50	345	30	50	—
XM-21, S 30454 S 31654	B	Cold finished	Up to 1 (25.40) incl	145	1000	125	860	15	45	—
			Over 1 (25.40) to 1¼ (31.75)	135	930	115	795	16	45	—
			Over 1¼ (31.75) to 1½ (38.10)	135	895	105	725	17	45	—
			Over 1½ (38.10) to 1¾ (44.45)	125	860	100	690	18	45	—
XM-7	A	Hot finished or cold finished	All	70	480	25	170	40	50	—
S 30815	A	Hot finished or cold finished	All	87	600	45	310	40	50	—
S 31254	A	Hot finished or cold finished	All	95	650	44	300	35	50	—

S 31725	A	Hot finished or cold finished	All	75	515	30	205	40	—	—
S 31726	A	Hot finished or cold finished	All	80	550	35	240	40	—	—
			Austenitic-Ferritic Grades							
XM-26	A	Hot finished or cold finished	All	90	620	65	450	20	55	—
S 31803	A	Hot finished	All	90	620	65	448	25	—	290
		Cold finished	All	90	620	65	448	25	—	290
			Ferritic Grades							
405[f]	A	Hot finished	All	—	—	—	—	—	—	207
		Cold finished	All	—	—	—	—	—	—	217
429	A	Hot finished	All	70	480	40	275	20	45	—
		Cold finished	All	70	480	40	275	16	45	—
430	A	Hot finished or cold finished	All	60	415	30	207	20	45	—
S 44400	A	Hot finished	All	60	415	45	310	20	45	217
		Cold finished	All	60	415	45	310	16	45	217
446, XM-27	A	Hot finished	All	65	450	40	275	20	45	219
		Cold finished	All	65	450	40	275	16	45	219
S 44700	A	Hot finished	All	70	480	55	380	20	40	—
		Cold finished	All	75	520	60	415	15	30	—
S 44800	A	Hot finished	All	70	480	55	380	20	40	—
		Cold finished	All	75	520	60	415	15	30	—
			Martensitic Grades							
403, 410	A	Hot finished	All	70	480	40	275	20	45	—
		Cold finished	All	70	480	40	275	16	45	—
403, 410	T	Hot finished	All	100	690	80	550	15	45	—
		Cold finished	All	100	690	80	550	12	40	—
XM-30	T	Hot finished	All	125	860	100	690	13	45	302
		Cold finished	All	125	860	100	690	12	35	—

TABLE 5.18 Mechanical Requirements-Stainless Steels (*Continued*)

Type	Condition	Finish	Diameter or thickness, in (mm)	Tensile strength, min		Yield strength,[a] min		Elongation in 2 in or 50 mm[b] min, %	Reduction of area,[c] min, %	Brinell hardness, max
				ksi	MPa	ksi	MPa			
			Martensitic Grades (*Continued*)							
414	T	Hot finished or cold finished	All	115	790	90	620	15	45	—
403, 410	H	Hot finished	All	120	830	90	620	12	40	—
		Cold finished	All (rounds only)	120	830	90	620	12	40	—
XM-30	A	Hot finished	All	70	480	40	275	13	45	235
		Cold finished	All	70	480	40	275	12	35	—
414	A	Hot finished or cold finished	All	—	—	—	—	—	—	298
S 41500	T	Hot finished or cold finished	All	115	795	90	620	15	45	295
420	A	Hot finished	All	—	—	—	—	—	—	241
		Cold finished	All	—	—	—	—	—	—	255
S 42010	A	Hot finished or cold finished		—	—	—	—	—	—	235
		Cold finished	All	—	—	—	—	—	—	255
431	A	Hot finished or cold finished	All	—	—	—	—	—	—	285
440A, 440B, and 440C	A	Hot finished	All	—	—	—	—	—	—	269
		Cold finished	All	—	—	—	—	—	—	285
9 (S 50400)	A	Hot finished or cold finished	All	60	415	30	207	30	45	179
	T	Hot finished or cold finished	All	100	690	80	550	14	35	241

[a] Yield strength shall be determined by the 0.2% offset method in accordance with Test Methods and Definitions A 370. An alternative method of determining yield strength may be used based on a total extension under load of 0.5%.

[b] For some specific products, it may not be practicable to use a 2-in or 50-mm gage length. The use of subsize test specimens, when necessary, is permissible in accordance with Test Methods and Definitions A 370.

[c] Reduction of area does not apply on flat bars 3⁄16 in (4.76 mm) and under in thickness as this determination is not generally made in this product size.

[d] Or equivalent Rockwell hardness.

[e] For extruded shapes of all Cr-Ni grades of condition A, the yield strength shall be 25 ksi (170 MPa) min and tensile strength shall be 70 ksi (480 MPa) min.

[f] Material shall be capable of being heat treated to a maximum Brinell hardness of 250 when oil quenched from 1750°F (953°C).

[g] For shapes having section thickness of 1⁄4 in (6.5 mm) or less, 30% min. elongation is acceptable.

SOURCE: Reprinted with permission, from the Annual Book of ASTM Standards, copyright 1992, American Society of Testing and Materials.

TABLE 5.19 Response to Heat Treatment

Type[a]	Heat treatment temperature °F (°C), min	Quenchant	Hardness HRC, min
403	1750 (955)	Air	35
410	1750 (955)	Air	35
414	1750 (955)	Oil	42
420	1825 (995)	Air	50
S42010	1850 (1010)	Oil	48
431	1875 (1020)	Oil	40
440A	1875 (1020)	Air	55
440B	1875 (1020)	Oil	56
440C	1875 (1020)	Air	58

[a] Samples for testing shall be in the form of a section not exceeding ⅜ in (9.50 mm) in thickness.

SOURCE: Reprinted with permission, from the Annual Book of ASTM Standards, copyright 1992, American Society of Testing and Materials.

TABLE 5.20 Chemical Composition Requirements[a]

Type	UNS designation	Composition, %							
		Carbon, max or range	Manganese, max or range	Phosphorus, max	Sulfur, max	Silicon, max	Chromium	Nickel	Other elements
201	S20100	0.15	5.50–7.50	0.060	0.030	0.75	16.00–18.00	3.50–5.50	N 0.25 ma
202	S20200	0.15	7.50–10.00	0.060	0.030	0.75	17.00–19.00	4.00–6.00	N 0.25 max
205	S20500	0.12–0.25	14.00–15.00	0.060	0.030	0.75	16.50–18.00	1.00–1.75	N 0.32–0.40
301	S30100	0.15	2.00	0.045	0.030	0.75	16.00–18.00	6.00–8.00	
302	S30200	0.15	2.00	0.045	0.030	0.75	17.00–19.00	8.00–10.00	
304	S30400	0.08	2.00	0.045	0.030	0.75	18.00–20.00	8.00–10.50	N 0.10 ma
304L	S30403	0.030	2.00	0.045	0.030	0.75	18.00–20.00	8.00–12.00	N 0.10 ma
304N	S30451	0.08	2.00	0.045	0.030	0.75	18.00–20.00	8.00–10.50	N 0.10–0.16
304LN	S30453	0.030	2.00	0.045	0.030	0.75	18.00–20.00	8.00–10.50	N 0.10–0.15
316	S31600	0.08	2.00	0.045	0.030	0.75	16.00–18.00	10.00–14.00	Mo 2.00–3.00
316L	S31603	0.030	2.00	0.045	0.030	0.75	16.00–18.00	10.00–14.00	Mo 2.00–3.00
316N	S31651	0.08	2.00	0.045	0.030	0.75	16.00–18.00	10.00–14.00	Mo 2.00–3.00 N 0.10–0.16
(XM-11)	S21904	0.04	8.00–10.00	0.060	0.030	0.75	19.00–21.50	5.50–7.50	N 0.15–0.40
(XM-14)	S21460	0.12	14.00–16.00	0.060	0.030	0.75	17.00–19.00	5.00–6.00	N 0.35–0.50

[a] Types XM-10 and XM-19, which appeared in Specification A 412, do not appear, since XM-10 is no longer produced and XM-19 is covered in Specification A 240.

SOURCE: Reprinted with permission, from the Annual Book of ASTM Standards, copyright 1992, American Society of Testing and Materials.

TABLE 5.21 Tensile Property Requirements[a]

Annealed

Type	UNS designation	Tensile strength, min		Yield strength, min		Elongation in 2 in or 50 mm, min, %	Hardness, max	
		psi	MPa	psi	MPa		Brinell	Rockwell B
201-1[b]	S20100 Class 1	95 000	655	38 000	260	40	217	95
201-2	S20100 Class 2	95 000	655	45 000	310	40	255	100
	S20200	90 000	620	38 000	260	40	—	—
205	S20500	115 000	790	65 000	450	40	255	100
301	S30100	90 000	620	30 000	205	40	217	95
302	S30200	75 000	515	30 000	205	40	201	92
304	S30400	75 000	515	30 000	205	40	201	92
304L	S30403	70 000	485	25 000	170	40	183	88
304N	S30451	80 000	550	35 000	240	40	217	95
304LN	—	80 000	550	35 000	240	40	217	95
316	S31600	75 000	515	30 000	205	40	217	95
316L	S31603	70 000	485	25 000	170	40	217	95
316N	S31651	80 000	550	35 000	240	40	217	95
	S21904							
	Sheet, strip	100 000	690	60 000	415	40	—	—
	Plate	90 000	620	50 000	345	45	—	—
	S21460	105 000	725	55 000	380	40	—	—

1/16 Hard[c]

Type	UNS designation	Tensile strength, min		Yield strength, min		Elongation in 2 in or 50 mm, min, %		
		psi	MPa	psi	MPa	<0.015 in	≥0.015 to ≤0.030 in	>0.030 in
201	S20100 PSS[d]	95 000	655	45 000	310	40	40	40
	FB[e]	75 000	515	40 000	275	—	—	40
205	S20500	115 000	790	65 000	450	40	40	40
301	S30100	90 000	620	45 000	310	40	40	40
302	S30200 PSS	85 000	585	45 000	310	40	40	40
	FB	90 000	620	45 000	310	—	—	40
304	S30400 PSS	80 000	550	45 000	310	35	35	35
	FB	90 000	620	45 000	310	—	—	40
304L	S30403	80 000	550	45 000	310	40	40	40
304N	S30451	90 000	620	45 000	310	40	40	40
304LN	—	90 000	620	45 000	310	40	40	40
316	S31600 PSS	85 000	585	45 000	310	35	35	35
	FB	90 000	620	45 000	310	—	—	40
316L	S31603	85 000	585	45 000	310	35	35	35
316N	S31651	90 000	620	45 000	310	35	35	35

TABLE 5.21 Tensile Property Requirements[a] (*Continued*)

⅛ Hard[c]

Type	UNS designation	Tensile strength, min psi	Tensile strength, min MPa	Yield strength, min psi	Yield strength, min MPa	Elongation in 2 in or 50 mm, min, % <0.015 in	≥0.015 to ≤0.030 in	>0.030 in
201	S20100	100 000	690	55 000	380	45	45	45
205	S20500	115 000	790	65 000	450	40	40	40
301	S30100	100 000	690	55 000	380	40	40	40
302	S30200	100 000	690	55 000	380	35	35	35
304	S30400	100 000	690	55 000	380	35	35	35
304L	S30403	100 000	690	55 000	380	30	30	30
304N	S30451	100 000	690	55 000	380	37	37	37
304LN	—	100 000	690	55 000	380	33	33	33
316	S31600	100 000	690	55 000	380	30	30	30
316L	S31603	100 000	690	55 000	380	25	25	25
316N	S31651	100 000	690	55 000	380	32	32	32

¼ Hard

Type	UNS designation	Tensile strength, min psi	Tensile strength, min MPa	Yield strength, min psi	Yield strength, min MPa	Elongation in 2 in or 50 mm, min, % <0.015 in	≥0.015 to ≤0.030 in	>0.030 in
201	S20100	125 000	860	75 000	515	25	25	25
202	S20200	125 000	860	75 000	515	12	12	—
205	S20500	125 000	860	75 000	515	45	45	45
301	S30100	125 000	860	75 000	515	25	25	25
302	S30200	125 000	860	75 000	515	10	10	12
304	S30400	125 000	860	75 000	515	10	10	12
304L	S30403	125 000	860	75 000	515	8	8	10
304N	S30451	125 000	860	75 000	515	12	12	12
304LN		125 000	860	75 000	515	10	10	12
316	S31600	125 000	860	75 000	515	10	10	10
316L	S31603	125 000	860	75 000	515	8	8	8
316N	S31651	125 000	860	75 000	515	12	12	12
XM-11	S21904	130 000	895	115 000	795	15	15	—

½ Hard

Type	UNS designation	Tensile strength, min psi	Tensile strength, min MPa	Yield strength, min psi	Yield strength, min MPa	Elongation in 2 in or 50 mm, min, % <0.015 in	≥0.015 to ≤0.030 in	>0.030 in
201	S20100	150 000	1035	110 000	760	15	18	18
205	S20500	150 000	1035	110 000	760	15	18	18
301	S30100	150 000	1035	110 000	760	15	18	18

TABLE 5.21 Tensile Property Requirements[a] (*Continued*)

½ Hard

Type	UNS designation	Tensile strength, min psi	Tensile strength, min MPa	Yield strength, min psi	Yield strength, min MPa	Elongation in 2 in or 50 mm, min, % <0.015 in	≥0.015 to ≤0.030 in	>0.030 in
302	S30200	150 000	1035	110 000	760	9	10	10
304	S30400	150 000	1035	110 000	760	6	7	7
304L	S30403	150 000	1035	110 000	760	5	6	6
304N	S30451	150 000	1035	110 000	760	6	8	8
304LN	—	150 000	1035	110 000	760	6	7	7
316	S31600	150 000	1035	110 000	760	6	7	7
316L	S31603	150 000	1035	110 000	760	5	6	6
316N	S31651	150 000	1035	110 000	760	6	8	8

¾ Hard

Type	UNS designation	Tensile strength, min psi	Tensile strength, min MPa	Yield strength, min psi	Yield strength, min MPa	Elongation in 2 in or 50 mm, min, % <0.015 in	≥0.015 to ≤0.030 in	>0.030 in
201	S20100	175 000	1205	135 000	930	10	12	12
205	S20500	175 000	1205	135 000	930	15	15	15
301	S30100	175 000	1205	135 000	930	10	12	12
302	S30200	175 000	1205	135 000	930	5	6	6

Full Hard

Type	UNS designation	Tensile strength, min psi	Tensile strength, min MPa	Yield strength, min psi	Yield strength, min MPa	Elongation in 2 in or 50 mm, min, % <0.015 in	≥0.015 to ≤0.030 in	>0.030 in
201	S20100	185 000	1275	140 000	965	8	9	9
205	S20500	185 000	1275	140 000	965	10	10	10
301	S30100	185 000	1275	140 000	965	8	9	9
302	S30200	185 000	1275	140 000	965	3	4	4

[a] This specification defines minimum properties only and does not imply a range. Depending on the work hardening characteristics of the particular grade, either the yield or the tensile strength can be the controlling factor in meeting the properties. The noncontrolling factor normally will exceed considerably the specified minimum.

[b] Type 201 is generally produced with a chemical composition balanced for rich side (type 201-1) or lean side (type 201-2), austenite stability depending on the properties required for specific applications.

[c] Annealed material that naturally meets mechanical properties may be applied.

[d] PSS means plate, strip, sheet.

[e] FB means flat bar.

SOURCE: Reprinted with permission, from the Annual Book of ASTM Standards, copyright 1992, American Society of Testing and Materials.

TABLE 5.22 V-Block Bend Requirements

		Thickness ≤0.050 in		Thickness >0.050 to ≤0.1874 in	
Type	UNS designation	Included bend angle,°	Bend factor	Included bend angle,°	Bend factor
		Annealed and ⅛ Hard			
201	S20100	135	2	135	3
202	S20200	135	4	135	4
205	S20500	135	2	135	3
301	S30100	135	2	135	3
302	S30200	135	2	135	3
304	S30400	135	2	135	3
304L	S30403	135	5	135	6
304N	S30451	135	3	135	4
304LN	—	135	4	135	5
316	S31600	135	5	135	6
316L	S31603	135	6	135	7
316N	S31651	135	5	135	6
		¼ Hard			
201	S20100	135	2	135	3
205	S20500	135	2	135	3
301	S30100	135	2	135	3
302	S30200	135	2	135	3
304	S30400	135	2	135	3
304L	S30403	135	5	135	6
304N	S30451	135	3	135	4
304LN	—	135	4	135	5
316	S31600	135	5	135	6
316L	S31603	135	6	135	7
316N	S31651	135	5	135	6
		½ Hard			
201	S20100	135	4	135	4
205	S20500	135	4	135	4
301	S30100	135	4	135	4
302	S30200	135	4	135	4
304	S30400	135	4	135	4
304L	S30403	135	7	135	8
304N	S30451	135	5	135	6
304LN	—	135	6	135	7
316	S31600	135	7	135	8
316L	S31603	135	8	135	9
316N	S31651	135	7	135	8

TABLE 5.22 V-Block Bend Requirements (*Continued*)

		¾ Hard			
201	S20100	135	6	135	7
205	S20500	135	6	135	7
301	S30100	135	6	135	7
302	S30200	135	8	135	9
		Full Hard			
201	S20100	135	6	135	8
205	S20500	135	6	135	8
301	S30100	135	6	135	8
302	S30200	135	8	135	10

SOURCE: Reprinted with permission, from the Annual Book of ASTM Standards, copyright 1992, American Society of Testing and Materials.

TABLE 5.23 Estimated Mechanical Properties and Machinability Ratings of Nonresulfurized Carbon Steel Bars, Manganese 1.00% Maximum

UNS no.	SAE and/or AISI no.	Type of processing	Tensile strength, psi	Tensile strength, MPa	Estimated minimum values: Yield strength, psi	Yield strength, MPa	Elongation in 2 in, %	Reduction in area, %	Brinell hardness	Average machinability rating (cold drawn 1212 = 100%)
G10060	1006	Hot rolled	43 000	300	24 000	170	30	55	86	
		Cold drawn	48 000	330	41 000	280	20	45	95	50
G10080	1008	Hot rolled	44 000	303	24 500	170	30	55	86	
		Cold drawn	49 000	340	41 500	290	20	45	95	55
G10100	1010	Hot rolled	47 000	320	26 000	180	28	50	95	
		Cold drawn	53 000	370	44 000	300	20	40	105	55
G10120	1012	Hot rolled	48 000	330	26 500	180	28	50	95	
		Cold drawn	54 000	370	45 000	310	19	40	105	55
G10150	1015	Hot rolled	50 000	340	27 500	190	28	50	101	
		Cold drawn	56 000	390	47 000	320	18	40	111	60
G10160	1016	Hot rolled	55 000	380	30 000	210	25	50	111	
		Cold drawn	61 000	420	51 000	350	18	40	121	70
G10170	1017	Hot rolled	53 000	370	29 000	200	26	50	105	
		Cold drawn	59 000	410	49 000	340	18	40	116	65
G10180	1018	Hot rolled	58 000	400	32 000	220	25	50	116	
		Cold drawn	64 000	440	54 000	370	15	40	126	70
G10190	1019	Hot rolled	59 000	410	32 500	220	25	50	116	
		Cold drawn	66 000	460	55 000	380	15	40	131	70
G10200	1020	Hot rolled	55 000	380	30 000	210	25	50	111	
		Cold drawn	61 000	420	51 000	350	15	40	121	65
G10210	1021	Hot rolled	61 000	420	33 000	230	24	48	116	
		Cold drawn	68 000	470	57 000	390	15	40	131	70
G10220	1022	Hot rolled	62 000	430	34 000	230	23	47	151	
		Cold drawn	69 000	480	58 000	400	15	40	137	70
G10230	1023	Hot rolled	56 000	370	31 000	210	25	50	111	
		Cold drawn	62 000	430	52 500	360	15	40	121	65
G10250	1025	Hot rolled	58 000	400	32 000	220	25	50	116	
		Cold drawn	64 000	440	54 000	370	15	40	126	65

TABLE 5.23 Estimated Mechanical Properties and Machinability Ratings of Nonresulfurized Carbon Steel Bars, Manganese 1.00% Maximum (*Continued*)

UNS no.	SAE and/or AISI no.	Type of processing	Tensile strength, psi	Tensile strength, MPa	Yield strength, psi	Yield strength, MPa	Elongation in 2 in, %	Reduction in area, %	Brinell hardness	Average machinability rating (cold drawn 1212 = 100%)
			Estimated minimum values							
G10260	1026	Hot rolled	64 000	440	35 000	240	24	49	126	
		Cold drawn	71 000	490	60 000	410	15	40	143	75
G10300	1030	Hot rolled	68 000	470	37 500	260	20	42	137	
		Cold drawn	76 000	520	64 000	440	12	35	149	70
G10350	1035	Hot rolled	72 000	500	39 500	270	18	40	143	
		Cold drawn	80 000	550	67 000	460	12	35	163	65
G10370	1037	Hot rolled	74 000	510	40 500	280	18	40	143	
		Cold drawn	82 000	570	69 000	480	12	35	167	65
G10380	1038	Hot rolled	75 000	520	41 000	280	18	40	149	
		Cold drawn	83 000	570	70 000	480	12	35	163	65
G10390	1039	Hot rolled	79 000	540	43 500	300	16	40	156	
		Cold drawn	88 000	610	74 000	510	12	35	179	60
G10400	1040	Hot rolled	76 000	520	42 000	290	18	40	149	
		Cold drawn	85 000	590	71 000	490	12	35	170	60
G10420	1042	Hot rolled	80 000	550	44 000	300	16	40	163	
		Cold drawn	89 000	610	75 000	520	12	35	179	60
		NCD†	85 000	590	73 000	500	12	45	179	70
G10430	1043	Hot rolled	82 000	570	45 000	310	16	40	163	
		Cold drawn	91 000	630	77 000	530	12	35	179	60
		NCD†	87 000	600	75 000	520	12	45	179	70
G10440	1044	Hot rolled	80 000	550	44 000	300	16	40	163	
G10450	1045	Hot rolled	82 000	570	45 000	310	16	40	163	
		Cold drawn	91 000	630	77 000	530	12	35	179	55
		ACD*	85 000	590	73 000	500	12	45	170	65
G10460	1046	Hot rolled	85 000	590	47 000	320	15	40	170	
		Cold drawn	94 000	650	79 000	540	12	35	187	55
		ACD*	90 000	620	75 000	520	12	45	179	65

G10490	1049	Hot rolled	87 000	600	48 000	330	15	35	179	
		Cold drawn	97 000	670	81 500	560	10	30	197	45
		ACD*	92 000	630	77 000	530	10	40	187	55
G10500	1050	Hot rolled	90 000	620	49 500	340	15	35	179	
		Cold drawn	100 000	690	84 000	580	10	30	197	45
		ACD*	95 000	660	80 000	550	10	40	189	55
G10550	1055	Hot rolled	94 000	650	51 500	360	12	30	192	
		ACD*	96 000	660	81 000	560	10	40	197	55
G10600	1060	Hot rolled	98 000	680	54 000	370	12	30	201	
		SACD‡	90 000	620	70 000	480	10	45	183	60
G10640	1064	Hot rolled	97 000	670	53 500	370	12	30	201	
		SACD‡	89 000	610	69 000	480	10	45	183	60
G10650	1065	Hot rolled	100 000	690	55 000	380	12	30	207	
		SACD‡	92 000	630	71 000	490	10	45	187	60
G10700	1070	Hot rolled	102 000	700	56 000	390	12	30	212	
		SACD‡	93 000	640	72 000	500	10	45	192	55
G10740	1074	Hot rolled	105 000	720	58 000	400	12	30	217	
		SACD‡	94 500	650	73 000	500	10	40	192	55
G10780	1078	Hot rolled	100 000	690	55 000	380	12	30	207	
		SACD‡	94 000	650	72 500	500	10	40	192	55
G10800	1080	Hot rolled	112 000	770	61 500	420	10	25	229	
		SACD‡	98 000	680	75 000	520	10	40	192	45
G10840	1084	Hot rolled	119 000	820	65 500	450	10	25	241	
		SACD‡	100 000	690	77 000	530	10	40	192	45
G10850	1085	Hot rolled	121 000	830	66 500	460	10	25	248	
		SACD‡	100 500	690	78 000	540	10	40	192	45
G10860	1086	Hot rolled	112 000	770	61 500	420	10	25	229	
		SACD‡	97 000	670	74 000	510	10	40	192	45
G10900	1090	Hot rolled	122 000	840	67 000	460	10	25	248	
		SACD‡	101 000	700	78 000	540	10	40	197	45
G10950	1095	Hot rolled	120 000	830	66 000	460	10	25	248	
		SACD‡	99 000	680	76 000	520	10	40	197	45

* ACD represents annealed cold drawn.
† NCD represents normalized cold drawn.
‡ SACD represents spheroidized annealed cold drawn.
SOURCE: Reprinted with permission, copyright 1992, Society of Automotive Engineers.

TABLE 5.24 Estimated Mechanical Properties and Machinability Ratings of Resulfurized Carbon Steel Bars*

UNS no.	SAE and/or AISI no.	Type of processing	Tensile strength psi	Tensile strength MPa	Yield strength psi	Yield strength MPa	Elongation in 2 in, %	Reduction in area, %	Brinell hardness	Average machinability rating (cold drawn 1212 = 100%)
			Estimated minimum values							
G11080	1108	Hot rolled	50 000	340	27 500	190	30	50	101	
		Cold drawn	56 000	390	47 000	320	20	40	121	80
G11170	1117	Hot rolled	62 000	430	34 000	230	23	47	121	
		Cold drawn	69 000	480	58 000	400	15	40	137	90
G11320	1132	Hot rolled	83 000	570	45 500	310	16	40	167	
		Cold drawn	92 000	630	77 000	530	12	35	183	75
G11370	1137	Hot rolled	88 000	610	48 000	330	15	35	179	
		Cold drawn	98 000	680	82 000	570	10	30	197	70
G11400	1140	Hot rolled	79 000	540	43 500	300	16	40	156	
		Cold drawn	88 000	610	74 000	510	12	35	170	70
G11410	1141	Hot rolled	94 000	650	51 500	360	15	35	187	
		Cold drawn	105 100	720	88 000	610	10	30	212	70
G11440	1144	Hot rolled	97 000	670	53 000	370	15	35	197	
		Cold drawn	108 000	740	90 000	620	10	30	217	80
G11460	1146	Hot rolled	85 000	590	47 000	320	15	40	170	
		Cold drawn	94 000	650	80 000	550	12	35	187	70
G11510	1151	Hot rolled	92 000	630	50 500	340	15	35	187	
		Cold drawn	102 000	700	86 000	590	10	30	207	65
G12110	1211	Hot rolled	55 000	380	33 000	230	25	45	121	
		Cold drawn	75 000	520	58 000	400	10	35	163	95
G12120	1212	Hot rolled	56 000	390	33 500	230	25	45	121	
		Cold drawn	78 000	540	60 000	410	10	35	167	100
G12130	1213	Hot rolled	56 000	390	33 500	230	25	45	121	
		Cold drawn	78 000	540	60 000	410	10	35	167	135
G12144	12L14	Hot rolled	57 000	390	34 000	230	22	45	121	
		Cold drawn	78 000	540	60 000	410	10	35	163	160

* All 1100 and 1200 series steels are rated on the basis of 0.10% max. silicon or coarse grain melting practice.

SOURCE: Reprinted with permission, copyright 1992, Society of Automotive Engineers.

TABLE 5.25 Estimated Mechanical Properties and Machinability Ratings of Nonresulfurized Carbon Steel Bars, Manganese Maximum over 1.00%

			Estimated minimum values								
			Tensile strength		Yield strength					
UNS no.	SAE and/or AISI no.	Type of processing	psi	MPa	psi	MPa	Elongation in 2 in, %	Reduction in area, %	Brinell hardness	Average machinability rating (cold drawn 1212 = 100%)
G15240	1524	Hot rolled	74 000	510	41 000	280	20	42	149	
		Cold drawn	82 000	570	69 000	480	12	35	163	60
G15270	1527	Hot rolled	75 000	520	41 000	280	18	40	149	
		Cold drawn	83 000	570	70 000	480	12	35	163	65
G15360	1536	Hot rolled	83 000	570	45 500	310	16	40	163	
		Cold drawn	92 000	630	77 500	530	12	35	187	55
G15410	1541	Hot rolled	92 000	630	51 000	350	15	40	187	
		Cold drawn	102 500	710	87 000	600	10	30	207	45
		ACD*	94 000	650	80 000	550	10	45	184	60
G15480	1548	Hot rolled	96 000	660	53 000	370	14	33	197	
		Cold drawn	106 500	730	89 500	620	10	28	217	45
		ACD*	93 500	640	78 500	540	10	35	192	50
G15520	1552	Hot rolled	108 000	740	59 500	410	12	30	217	
		ACD*	98 000	680	83 000	570	10	40	193	50

* ACD represents annealed cold drawn.

SOURCE: Reprinted with permission, copyright 1992, Society of Automotive Engineers.

TABLE 5.26 Machinability of Alloy Steels

UNS no.	AISI and/or SAE no.	Machinability rating	Condition	Range of typical hardness HB	Microstructure type
G13300	1330	55	Annealed and cold drawn	179/235	A
G13350	1335	55	Annealed and cold drawn	179/235	A
G13400	1340	50	Annealed and cold drawn	183/241	A
G13450	1345	45	Annealed and cold drawn	183/241	A
G40230	4023	70	Cold drawn	156/207	C
G40240	4024	75	Cold drawn	156/207	C
G40270	4027	70	Annealed and cold drawn	167/212	A
G40280	4028	75	Annealed and cold drawn	167/212	A
G40320	4032	70	Annealed and cold drawn	174/217	A
G40370	4037	70	Annealed and cold drawn	174/217	A
G40420	4042	65	Annealed and cold drawn	179/229	A
G40470	4047	65	Annealed and cold drawn	179/229	A
G41180	4118	60	Cold drawn	170/207	C
G41300	4130	70	Annealed and cold drawn	187/229	A
G41350	4135	70	Annealed and cold drawn	187/229	A
G41370	4137	70	Annealed and cold drawn	187/229	A
G41400	4140	65	Annealed and cold drawn	187/229	A
G41420	4142	65	Annealed and cold drawn	187/229	A
G41450	4145	60	Annealed and cold drawn	187/229	A
G41470	4147	60	Annealed and cold drawn	187/235	A
G41500	4150	55	Annealed and cold drawn	187/241	A, B
G41610	4161	50	Spheroidized and cold drawn	187/241	B, A
G43200	4320	60	Annealed and cold drawn	187/229	D, B, A
G43400	4340	50	Annealed and cold drawn	187/241	B, A
G43406	E4340	50	Annealed and cold drawn	187/241	B, A
G44220	4422	65	Cold drawn	170/212	C
G44270	4427	65	Annealed and cold drawn	170/212	A

G46150	4615	65	Cold drawn	174/223	C
G46170	4617	65	Cold drawn	174/223	C
G46200	4620	65	Cold drawn	183/229	C
G46260	4626	70	Cold drawn	170/212	C
G47180	4718	60	Cold drawn	187/229	C
G47200	4720	65	Cold drawn	187/229	C
G48150	4815	50	Annealed and cold drawn	187/229	D, B
G48170	4817	50	Annealed and cold drawn	187/229	D, B
G48200	4820	50	Annealed and cold drawn	187/229	D, B
G50401	50B40	65	Annealed and cold drawn	174/223	A
G50441	50B44	65	Annealed and cold drawn	174/223	A
G50460	5046	60	Annealed and cold drawn	174/223	A
G50461	50B46	60	Annealed and cold drawn	174/223	A
G50501	50B50	55	Annealed and cold drawn	183/235	A
G50600	5060	55	Spheroidized annealed and cold drawn	170/212	B
G50601	50B60	55	Spheroidized annealed and cold drawn	170/212	B
G51150	5115	65	Cold drawn	163/201	C
G51200	5120	70	Cold drawn	163/201	C
G51300	5130	70	Annealed and cold drawn	174/212	A
G51320	5132	70	Annealed and cold drawn	174/212	A
G51350	5135	70	Annealed and cold drawn	179/217	A
G51400	5140	65	Annealed and cold drawn	179/217	A
G51470	5147	65	Annealed and cold drawn	179/229	A
G51500	5150	60	Annealed and cold drawn	183/235	A, B
G51550	5155	55	Annealed and cold drawn	183/235	A, B
G51600	5160	55	Spheroidized annealed and cold drawn	179/217	B
G51601	51B60	55	Spheroidized annealed and cold drawn	179/217	B
G50986	50100	40	Spheroidized annealed and cold drawn	183/241	B
G51986	51100	40	Spheroidized annealed and cold drawn	183/241	B
G52986	52100	40	Spheroidized annealed and cold drawn	183/241	B
G61180	6118	60	Cold drawn	179/217	C
G61500	6150	55	Annealed and cold drawn	183/241	B, A
G81150	8115	65	Cold drawn	163/202	C

TABLE 5.26 Machinability of Alloy Steels (*Continued*)

UNS no.	AISI and/or SAE no.	Machinability rating	Condition	Range of typical hardness HB	Microstructure type
G81451	81B45	65	Annealed and cold drawn	179/223	A
G86150	8615	70	Cold drawn	179/235	C
G86170	8617	70	Cold drawn	179/235	C
G86200	8620	65	Cold drawn	179/235	C
G86220	8622	65	Cold drawn	179/235	C
G86250	8625	60	Annealed and cold drawn	179/223	A
G86270	8627	60	Annealed and cold drawn	179/223	A
G86300	8630	70	Annealed and cold drawn	179/229	A
G86370	8637	65	Annealed and cold drawn	179/229	A
G86400	8640	65	Annealed and cold drawn	184/229	A
G86420	8642	65	Annealed and cold drawn	184/229	A
G86450	8645	65	Annealed and cold drawn	184/235	A
G86451	86B45	65	Annealed and cold drawn	184/235	A
G86500	8650	60	Annealed and cold drawn	187/248	A, B
G86550	8655	55	Annealed and cold drawn	187/248	A, B
G86600	8660	55	Spheroidized annealed and cold drawn	179/217	B
G87200	8720	65	Cold drawn	179/235	C
G87400	8740	65	Annealed and cold drawn	184/235	A
G88220	8822	55	Cold drawn	179/223	B
G92540	9254	45	Spheroidized annealed and cold drawn	187/241	B
G92600	9260	40	Spheroidized annealed and cold drawn	184/235	B
G93106	9310	50	Annealed and cold drawn	184/229	D
G94151	94B15	70	Cold drawn	163/202	C
G94171	94B17	70	Cold drawn	163/202	C
G94301	94B30	70	Annealed and cold drawn	170/223	A

SOURCE: Reprinted with permission, copyright 1992, Society of Automotive Engineers.

TABLE 5.27 Typical Treatments for Case Hardening Grades of Carbon Steels

UNS no.	SAE steels*	Carburizing temperature, °F	°C	Cooling medium	Reheat temperature, °F	°C	Cooling medium	Carbonitriding temperature, °F†	°C†	Cooling medium	Temper °F	°C‡
G10100	1010	—	—	—	—	—	—	1450–1650	790–900	Oil	250–400	120–205
G10150	1015	—	—	—	—	—	—	1450–1650	790–900	Oil	250–400	120–205
G10160	1016	1650–1700	900–925	Water or caustic	—	—	—	1450–1650	790–900	Oil	250–400	120–205
G10180	1018	1650–1700	900–925	Water or caustic	1450	790	Water or caustic§	1450–1650	790–900	Oil	250–400	120–205
G10200	1020	1650–1700	900–925	Water or caustic	1450	790	Water or caustic§	1450–1650	790–900	Oil	250–400	120–205
G10220	1022	1650–1700	900–925	Water or caustic	1450	790	Water or caustic§	1450–1650	790–900	Oil	250–400	120–205
G10260	1026	1650–1700	900–925	Water or caustic	1450	790	Water or caustic§	1450–1650	790–900	Oil	250–400	120–205
G10300	1030	1650–1700	900–925	Water or caustic	1450	790	Water or caustic§	1450–1650	790–900	Oil	250–400	120–205
G11170	1117	1650–1700	900–925	Water or oil	1450–1600	790–870	Water or caustic§	1450–1650	790–900	Oil	250–400	120–205
G11180	1118	1650–1700	900–925	Oil	1450–1600	790–870	Oil	—	—	—	250–400	120–205
G15130	1513	1650–1700	900–925	Oil	1450	790	Oil	—	—	—	250–400	120–205
G15220	1522	1650–1700	900–925	Oil	1450	790	Oil	—	—	—	250–400	120–205
G15240	1524	1650–1700	900–925	Oil	1450	790	Oil	—	—	—	250–400	120–205
G15260	1526	1650–1700	900–925	Oil	1450	790	Oil	—	—	—	250–400	120–205
G15270	1527	1650–1700	900–925	Oil	1450	790	Oil	—	—	—	250–400	120–205

* Generally, it is not necessary to normalize the carbon grades for fulfilling either dimensional or machinability requirements of parts made from the steel grades listed in the table although, where dimension is of vital importance, normalizing temperatures of at least 50°F above the carburizing temperatures are sometimes required.

† The higher manganese steels such as 1118 and the 1500 series are not usually carbonitrided. If carbonitriding is performed, care must be taken to limit the nitrogen content because high nitrogen will increase their tendency to retain austenite.

‡ Even where recommended tempering temperatures are shown, the temper is not mandatory on many applications. Tempering is generally employed for a partial stress relief and improves resistance to cracking from grinding operations. Higher temperatures than those shown may be employed where the hardness specification on the finished parts permits.

§ 3% sodium hydroxide.

SOURCE: Reprinted with permission, copyright 1992, Society of Automotive Engineers.

TABLE 5.28 Typical Treatments for Heat Treating Grades of Carbon Steels

UNS no.	SAE steels	Normalizing temperature, °F	°C	Annealing temperature, °F	°C	Hardening temperature, °F	°C	Quenching medium*
G10300	1030	—	—	—	—	1575–1600	855–870	Water or caustic
G10350	1035	—	—	—	—	1550–1600	840–870	Water or caustic
G10380[†]	1038[†]	—	—	—	—	1525–1575	830–855	Water or caustic
G10390[†]	1039[†]	—	—	—	—	1525–1575	830–855	Water or caustic
G10400[†]	1040[†]	—	—	—	—	1525–1575	830–855	Water or caustic
G10420	1042	—	—	—	—	1500–1550	815–845	Water or caustic
G10430[†]	1043[†]	—	—	—	—	1500–1550	815–845	Water or caustic
G10450[†]	1045[†]	—	—	—	—	1500–1550	815–845	Water or caustic
G10460[†]	1046[†]	—	—	—	—	1500–1550	815–845	Water or caustic
G10500[†]	1050[†]	1600–1700	870–925	—	—	1500–1550	815–845	Water or caustic
G10530	1053	1600–1700	870–925	—	—	1500–1550	815–845	Water or caustic
G10600	1060	1600–1700	870–925	1400–1500	760–815	1575–1625	855–885	Oil
G10740	1074	1550–1650	870–900	1400–1500	760–815	1575–1625	855–885	Oil
G10800	1080	1550–1650	845–900	1400–1500[‡]	760–815[‡]	1575–1625	855–885	Oil[§]
G10900	1090	1550–1650	845–900	1400–1500[‡]	760–815[‡]	1575–1625	855–885	Oil[§]
G10950	1095	1550–1650	845–900	1400–1500[‡]	760–815[‡]	1575–1625	855–885	Water and oil
G11370	1137	—	—	—	—	1550–1600	845–870	Oil
G11410	1141	—	—	1400–1500	760–815	1500–1550	815–845	Oil
G11440	1144	1600–1700	870–925	1400–1500	760–815	1500–1550	815–845	Oil
G11450	1145	—	—	—	—	1475–1500	800–815	Water or oil
G11460	1146	—	—	—	—	1475–1500	800–815	Water or oil
G15410	1541	1600–1700	870–925	1400–1500	760–815	1500–1550	815–845	Water or oil
G15480	1548	1600–1700	870–925	—	—	1500–1550	815–845	Oil
G15520	1552	1600–1700	870–925	—	—	1500–1550	815–845	Oil
G15660	1566	1600–1700	870–925	—	—	1575–1625	855–885	Oil

* All steels are tempered to desired hardness; however, tempering is not mandatory on many applications. Tempering is generally employed for a partial stress relief and improves resistance to cracking from grinding operations. Higher temperatures than those shown may be employed where the hardness specification on the finished parts permits.

† Commonly used on parts where induction hardening is employed. However, all steels from SAE 1030 up may have induction hardening applications.

‡ Spheroidal structures are often required for machining purposes and should be cooled very slowly or be isothermally transformed to produce the desired structure.

§ May be water or brine quenched by special techniques such as partial immersion or time quenched; otherwise they are subject to quench cracking.

SOURCE: Reprinted with permission, copyright 1992, Society of Automotive Engineers.

TABLE 5.29 Typical Heat Treatments for Carburizing Grades of Alloy Steels

UNS no.	SAE steels[a]	Pretreatments: Normalize[b]	Pretreatments: Normalize and temper[c]	Pretreatments: Cycle anneal[d]	Carburizing[e] temperature, °F	°C	Cooling method	Reheat[i] temperature, °F	°C	Quenching medium	Tempering[f] temperature, °F	°C
G40120	4012											
G40230	4023											
G40270	4027	Yes	—	—	1650–1700	900–925	Quench in oil[g]	—	—	—	250–350	120–175
G40280	4028											
G40320	4032											
G41180	4118	Yes	—	—	1650–1700	900–925	Quench in oil[g]	—	—	—	250–350	120–175
G43200	4320	Yes	—	Yes	1650–1700	900–925	Quench in oil[g]	—	—	—	250–350	120–175
					1650–1700	900–925	Cool slowly	1525–1550[h]	830–845	Oil	250–350	120–175
G44220	4422	Yes	—	Yes	1650–1700	900–925	Quench in oil[g]	—	—	—	250–350	120–175
G44270	4427											
G46200	4620	Yes	—	Yes	1650–1700	900–925	Cool slowly	1500–1550[h]	815–845	Oil	250–350	120–175
G47200	4720	Yes	—	Yes	1650–1700	900–925	Quench in oil	1500–1550[h]	815–845	Oil	250–350	120–175
G48150	4815	—	Yes	Yes	1650–1700	900–925	Quench in oil[g]	—	—	—	250–325	120–175
G48200	4820				1650–1700	900–925	Quench in oil	1475–1525[h]	800–830	Oil	250–325	120–175
G51200	5120	Yes	—	—	1650–1700	900–925	Quench in oil[g]	—	—	—	250–350	120–175
G86150	8615	Yes	—	—								
G86170	8617											
G86200	8620				1650–1700	900–925	Quench in oil[g]	—	845–870	—	250–350	120–175
G86220	8622				1650–1700	900–925	Cool slowly	1550–1600[h]	845–870	Oil	250–350	120–175
G86250	8625				1650–1700	900–925	Quench in oil	1550–1600[h]	845–870	Oil	250–350	120–175
G86270	8627	Yes	—	Yes								
G87200	8720											
G88220	8822											
G93100	9310	—	Yes	—	1600–1700	900–925	Quench in oil	1450–1525[h]	790–830	Oil	250–325	120–175
					1600–1700	900–925	Cool slowly	1450–1525[h]	790–830	Oil	250–325	120–175
G94151	94B15	Yes	—	—	1650–1700	900–925	Quench in oils	—	—	—	250–350	120–175
G94171	94B17											

[a] These steels are fine grain. Heat treatments are not necessarily correct for coarse grain.

[b] Normalizing temperature should be at least as high as the carburizing temperature followed by air cooling.

[c] After normalizing, reheat to temperature of 1100–1200°F and hold at temperature approximately 1 h per in of maximum section or 4 h minimum time.

[d] Where cycle annealing is desired, heat to at least as high as the carburizing temperature, hold for uniformity, cool rapidly to 1000–1250°F, hold 1 to 3 h, then air cool or furnace cool to obtain a structure suitable for machining and finish.

[e] It is general practice to reduce carburizing temperatures to approximately 1550°F before quenching to minimize distortion and retained austenite. For 4800 series steels, the carburizing temperature is reduced to approximately 1500°F before quenching.

[f] Tempering treatment is optional. Tempering is generally employed for partial stress relief and improved resistance to cracking from grinding operations. Temperatures higher than those shown are used in some instances where application requires.

[g] This treatment is most commonly used and generally produces a minimum of distortion.

[h] This treatment is used where the maximum grain refinement is required and/or where parts are subsequently ground on critical dimensions. A combination of good case and core properties is secured with somewhat greater distortion than is obtained by a single quench from the carburizing treatment.

[i] In this treatment the parts are slowly cooled, preferably under a protective atmosphere. They are then reheated and oil quenched. A tempering operation follows as required. This treatment is used when machining must be done between carburizing and hardening or when facilities for quenching from the carburizing cycle are not available. Distortion is at least equal to that obtained by a single quench from the carburizing cycle, as described in note e.

SOURCE: Reprinted with permission, copyright 1992, Society of Automotive Engineers.

TABLE 5.30 Typical Heat Treatments for Directly Hardenable Grades of Alloy Steels

UNS no.	SAE steels[a]	Normalizing temperature, °F	°C	Annealing[d] temperature, °F	°C	Hardening[e] temperature, °F	°C	Quenching medium[f]
G13300	1330	1600–1700[b]	870–925[b]	1550–1650	845–900	1525–1575	830–855	Water or oil
G13350 G13400	1335 1340	1600–1700[b]	870–925[b]	1550–1650	845–900	1500–1550	815–845	Oil
G40370	4037	—		1500–1575	815–855	1525–1575	830–855	Oil
G40470	4047	—		1450–1550	790–845	1500–1575	815–855	Oil
G41300	4130	1600–1700[b]	870–925[b]	1450–1550	790–845	1500–1600	815–870	Water or oil
G41370 G41400 G41420	4137 4140 4142	—		1450–1550	790–845	1550–1600	845–900	Oil
G41450 G41470 G41450	4145 4147 4140	—		1450–1550	790–845	1500–1550	815–845	Oil
G43400	4340	1600–1700[b,c]	870–925[b,c]	1450–1550	790–845	1500–1550	815–845	Oil
G50461	5046	1600–1700[b]	870–925[b]	1500–1600	815–870	1500–1550	815–845	Oil
G51300 G51320	5130 5132	1600–1700[b]	870–925[b]	1450–1550	790–845	1525–1575	830–855	Water, caustic solution, or oil
G51400	5140	1600–1700[b]	870–925[b]	1500–1600	815–870	1500–1550	815–845	Oil
G51500 G51600 G51601	5150 5160 5160	1600–1700[b]	870–925[b]	1500–1600	815–870	1475–1550	800–845	Oil
G61500	6150	—		1550–1650	845–900	1550–1625	845–885	Oil

G86300	8630	1600–1700[b]	870–925[b]	1450–1550	790–845	1525–1600	830–870	Water or oil
G86370	8637	—		1500–1600	815–870	1525–1575	830–855	Oil
G86400	8640							
G86450	8645	—		1500–1600	815–870	1500–1575	815–855	Oil
G92600	9260	—		—	—	1500–1650	815–900	Oil

[a] These steels are fine grain unless otherwise specified.

[b] These steels should be either normalized or annealed for optimum machinability.

[c] Temper at 1100–1225°F (595–665°C).

[d] The specific annealing cycle is dependent on the alloy content of the steel, the type of subsequent machining operations, and the desired surface finish.

[e] Frequently, these steels, with the exception of 4340, 50100, 51100, and 52100, are hardened and tempered to a final machinable hardness without preliminary heat treatment.

[f] All steels are tempered to desired hardness.

SOURCE: Reprinted with permission, copyright 1992, Society of Automotive Engineers.

TABLE 5.31 Typical Heat Treatments for Grades of Chromium-Nickel Austenitic Steels Not Hardenable by Thermal Treatment

SAE steels	AISI no.	Annealing temperature,* °F	°C
20201	201	1850–2050	1010–1120
20202	202	1850–2050	1010–1120
30301	301	1850–2050	1010–1120
30302	302	1850–2050	1010–1120
30303	303	1850–2050	1010–1120
30304	304	1850–2050	1010–1120
30305	305	1850–2050	1010–1120
30309	309	1900–2050	1040–1120
30310	310	1900–2100	1040–1150
30316	316	1850–2050	1010–1120
30317	317	1850–2050	1010–1120
30321	321	1750–2050	955–1120
30325	325	1800–2100	980–1150
30330	—	1950–2150	1065–1175
30347	347	1850–2050	1010–1120

* Quench to produce full austenitic structure using water or air in accordance with thickness of section. Annealing temperatures given cover process and full annealing as already established and used by industry, the lower end of the range being used for process annealing. All steels are quenched in air.

SOURCE: Reprinted with permission, copyright 1992, Society of Automotive Engineers.

TABLE 5.33 Typical Heat Treatments for Wrought Stainless Steels of Special Machinability

Proprietary designation	Subcritical annealing temperature, °F	°C	Full annealing temperature, °F	°C	Quenching medium
203-EZ	—	—	1850–2050*	1010–1120*	Water or air
303 Ma	—	—	1850–2050*	1010–1120*	Water or air
303 Cu	—	—	1850–2050*	1010–1120*	Water or air
303 Plus X	—	—	1850–2050*	1010–1120*	Water or air
416 Plus X	1300–1350†	705–730†	1550–1650‡	845–900*	—

* Quench to produce full austenitic structure using water or air in accordance with thickness of section. Annealing temperatures given cover process and full annealing as already established and used by industry, the lower end of the range being used for process annealing.

† Usually air cooled but may be furnace cooled.

‡ Cool slowly in the furnace.

SOURCE: Reprinted with permission, copyright 1992, Society of Automotive Engineers.

TABLE 5.32 Typical Heat Treatments for Stainless Chromium Steels

SAE steels	AISI no.	Subcritical annealing temperature, °F	°C	Full annealing temperature,* °F	°C	Hardening temperature, °F	°C	Quenching medium¶
51409	—	—		1625	885	—	—	Air
51410	410	1300–1350†	705–730†	1500–1650	815–900	1700–1850	925–1010	Oil or air
51414	414	1200–1250†	650–675†	—	—	1800–1900	980–1040	Oil or air
51416	416	1300–1350§	705–730†	1500–1650	815–900	1700–1850	925–1010	Oil or air
51420	420	1350–1450†	730–790†	1550–1650	845–900	1800–1900	980–1040	Oil or air
51420F*	—	1350–1450†	730–790†	1550–1650	845–900	1800–1900	980–1040	Oil or air
51430	430	1400–1500§	760–815§	—	—	—	—	—
51430F‡	—	1250–1400§	675–760§	—	—	—	—	—
51431	431	1150–1225†	620–665†	—	—	1800–1950	980–1065	Oil or air
51434	—	1400–1600§	760–870§	—	—	—	—	—
51436	—	1400–1600§	760–870§	—	—	—	—	—
51440A‡	440A	1350–1440†	730–780†	1550–1650	845–900	1850–1950	1010–1065	Oil or air
51440B‡	440B	1350–1440†	730–780†	1550–1650	845–900	1850–1950	1010–1065	Oil or air
51440C‡	440C	1350–1440†	730–780†	1550–1650	845–900	1850–1950	1010–1065	Oil or air
51440F‡	—	1350–1440†	730–780†	1550–1650	845–900	1850–1950	1010–1065	Oil or air
51442	442	1350–1500§	730–815§	—	—	—	—	—
51446	446	1450–1600§	790–870†	—	—	—	—	—
51501	501	1325–1375§	720–745§	1525–1600	830–870	1600–1700	870–925	Oil or air

* Cool slowly in furnace.
† Usually air cooled but may be furnace cooled.
‡ Suffixes A, B, and C denote three types of steel differing only in carbon content. Suffix F denotes a free machining steel.
§ Cool rapidly in air.
¶ All steels are tempered to desired hardness.
SOURCE: Reprinted with permission, copyright 1992, Society of Automotive Engineers.

TABLE 5.34 Monotonic Stress-Strain Properties of Selected Metals (Sort: Steel, A1, SAE Spec., Increasing True Fracture Strength)

SAE spec	BHn	Grain dir	Process description	Ultimate strength, ksi (MPa)	Yield strength, ksi (MPa)	True fracture strength, ksi (MPa)	%RA	True fracture ductility	Strain hard'G exponent	Strength coefficient, ksi (MPa)
A-538-A†	405	L	Sol tr & aged	220 (1517)	215 (1482)	275 (1896)	67	1.10	0.030	
A-538-B†	460	L	Sol tr & aged	270 (1862)	260 (1793)	310 (2137)	56	0.82	0.020	
A-538-C†	480	L	Sol tr & aged	290 (1999)	280 (1931)	325 (2241)	55	0.81	0.015	
AM-350†		L	HR & annealed	191 (1317)	64 (441)	298 (2055)	52	0.74		
AM-350¶	496	L	CD	276 (1903)	270 (1862)	316 (2179)	20	0.23		
Gainex¶		LT	HR sheet	77 (531)	58 (400)	117 (807)	58	0.86	0.20	
Gainex‡		L	HR sheet	74 (510)	57 (393)	118 (814)	64	1.02	0.20	
H-11	660	L	Ausformed	375 (2586)	295 (2034)	460 (3172)	33	0.40	0.120	
R-100§	236	LT	As rec plate	177 (1220)	117 (807)	214 (1475)				
R-100§	236	L	As rec plate	169 (1165)	112 (772)	236 (1627)				
RQC-100*	290	LT	HR plate	136 (938)	130 (896)	155 (1069)	43	0.56	0.06	170 (1172)
RQC-100*	290	L	HR plate	135 (931)	128 (883)	193 (1331)	67	1.02	0.06	170 (1172)
10B62	430	L	Q&T	238 (1641)	219 (1510)	258 (1779)	38	0.89	0.042	260 (1793)
1005–1009	90	LT	HR sheet	52 (359)	39 (269)	104 (717)	73	1.3	0.12	73 (503)
1005–1009	125	LT	CD sheet	68 (469)	65 (448)	108 (745)	66	1.09	0.029	78 (538)
1005–1009	125	L	CD sheet	60 (414)	58 (400)	122 (841)	64	1.02	0.049	76 (524)
1005–1009	90	L	HR sheet	50 (345)	38 (262)	123 (848)	80	1.6	0.16	77 (531)
1015	80	L	Normalized	60 (414)	33 (228)	105 (724)	68	1.14	0.26	
1020	108	L	HR plate plate	64 (441)	38 (262)	103 (710)	62	0.96	0.19	107 (738)
1040	225	L	As forged	90 (621)	50 (345)	152 (1048)	60	0.93	0.22	
1045	225	L	Q&T	105 (724)	92 (634)	178 (1227)	65	1.04	0.13	166 (1145)
1045	410	L	Q&T	210 (1448)	198 (1365)	270 (1862)	51	0.72	0.076	302 (2082)
1045	390	L	Q&T	195 (1344)	185 (1276)	270 (1862)	59	0.89	0.044	
1045	450	L	Q&T	230 (1586)	220 (1517)	305 (2103)	55	0.81	0.041	
1045	500	L	Q&T	265 (1827)	245 (1689)	330 (2275)	51	0.71	0.047	
1045	595	L	Q&T	325 (2241)	270 (1862)	395 (2723)	41	0.52	0.071	
1080 +Mn	326	L	HR plate	162 (1117)	92 (634)	181 (1248)	17	0.17		
1080 +Mn	375	L	Q&T	189 (1303)	166 (1145)	235 (1620)	31	0.37		
1080 +Mn	415	L	Q&T	206 (1420)	180 (1241)	243 (1675)	31	0.36		

1080 +Mn	505	L	Q&T	265 (1827)	235 (1620)	295 (2034)	30	0.36		
1080 +Mn	555	L	Q&T	309 (2130)	273 (1882)	339 (2337)	17	0.18		
1144	265	L	CD strain rel	135 (931)	104 (717)	168 (1158)	33	0.51		
1144	305	L	Drawn at temp	150 (1034)	148 (1020)	220 (1517)	25	0.29		
1541F	290	L	Q&T forging	138 (951)	129 (889)	185 (1276)	49	0.68	0.12	
1541F	260	L	Q&T forging	129 (889)	114 (786)	185 (1276)	60	0.93	0.13	
30304	160	L	HR & annealed	108 (745)	37 (255)	228 (1572)	74	1.37		
30304	327	L	CD	138 (951)	108 (745)	246 (1696)	69	1.16		
30310	145	L	HR & annealed	93 (641)	32 (221)	168 (1158)	64	1.01		
4130	258	L	Q&T	130 (896)	113 (779)	206 (1420)	67	1.12		
4130	365	L	Q&T	207 (1427)	197 (1358)	264 (1820)	55	0.79		
4140	310	L	Q&T drawn at temp	156 (1076)	140 (965)	221 (1524)	60	0.69		
4142	310	L	Drawn at temp	154 (1062)	152 (1048)	162 (1117)	29	0.35		
4142	335	L	Drawn at temp	181 (1248)	179 (1234)	246 (1696)	28	0.34		
4142	380	L	Q&T	205 (1413)	200 (1379)	265 (1827)	48	0.66	0.051	
4142	400	L	Q&T and deformed	225 (1551)	210 (1448)	275 (1896)	47	0.63	0.032	
4142	450	L	Q&T	255 (1758)	230 (1586)	290 (1999)	42	0.54	0.043	
4142	475	L	Q&T and deformed	295 (2034)	275 (1896)	300 (2068)	20	0.22	0.01	
4142	450	L	Q&T and deformed	280 (1931)	270 (1862)	305 (2103)	37	0.46	0.016	
4142	475	L	Q&T	280 (1931)	250 (1724)	315 (2172)	35	0.43	0.048	
4142	670	L	As quenched	355 (2448)	235 (1620)	375 (2586)	6	0.06	0.136	
4142	560	L	Q&T	325 (2241)	245 (1689)	385 (2654)	27	0.31	0.091	
4340	243	L	HR & annealed	120 (827)	92 (634)	158 (1089)	43	0.57		
4340	409	L	Q&T	213 (1469)	199 (1372)	226 (1558)	38	0.48		
4340	350	L	Q&T	180 (1241)	170 (1172)	240 (1655)	57	0.84	0.066	229 (1579)
5160	430	L	Q&T	242 (1669)	222 (1531)	280 (1931)	42	0.87	0.055	308 (2124)
52100	518	L	Sol heat Q&T	292 (2013)	279 (1924)	318 (2193)	11	0.12		
9262	260	L	Annealed	134 (924)	66 (455)	151 (1041)	14	0.16	0.22	253 (1744)
9262	280	L	Q&T	145 (1000)	114 (786)	177 (1220)	33	0.41	0.14	
9262	410	L	Q&T	227 (1565)	200 (1379)	269 (1855)	32	0.38	0.06	283 (1951)
950C	159	LT	HR plate	82 (565)	46 (317)	135 (931)	64	1.03	0.19	134 (924)
950C	150	L	HR bar	82 (565)	47 (324)	145 (1000)	69	1.19	0.21	
950X	150	L	Plate channel	64 (441)	50 (345)	109 (752)	65	1.06	0.16	98 (676)
950X	156	L	HR plate	77 (531)	48 (331)	145 (1000)	72	1.24	0.19	131 (903)
980X	225	L	Plate channel	101 (696)	82 (565)	177 (1220)	68	1.15	0.13	181 (1248)

TABLE 5.34 Monotonic Stress-Strain Properties of Selected Metals (Sort: Steel, A1, SAE Spec., Increasing True Fracture Strength) (*Continued*)

SAE spec	BHn	Grain dir	Process description	Ultimate strength, ksi (MPa)	Yield strength, ksi (MPa)	True fracture strength, ksi (MPa)	%RA	True fracture ductility	Strain hard'G exponent	Strength coefficient, ksi (MPa)
1100 AI	26	L	As received	16 (110)	14 (97)		88	2.09		
2014-T6	155	L	Sol tr & artif age	74 (510)	67 (462)	87 (600)	25	0.29		
2024-T351		L	Sol tr strn harden	68 (469)	55 (379)	81 (558)	25	0.28	0.032	66 (455)
2024-T4		L	Sol tr & RT age	69 (476)	44 (303)	92 (634)	35	0.43	0.20	117 (807)
5456-H311	95	L	Strain hardened	58 (400)	34 (234)	76 (524)	35	0.42		
7075-T6		L	Sol tr & artif age	84 (579)	68 (469)	108 (745)	33	0.41	0.113	120 (827)

* Trade name—Bethlehem Steel Corp.

† ASTM specification

‡ Trade name—Armco Steel Corp.

§ Trade name—Republic Steel Corp.

¶ Grade number—Allegheny Ludlum Steel Corp.

SOURCE: Reprinted with permission, copyright 1992, Society of Automotive Engineers.

TABLE 5.35 Cyclic Stress-Strain and Fatigue Properties of Selected Metals (Sort: Steel, Al, SAE Spec., Increasing True Fracture Strength)

SAE spec	BHn	Grain dir	Process description	Mod of elas, ksi (GPa)	Cyc yld, ksi (MPa)	Cyc strain hard'G exp	Cyc str cof, ksi (MPa)	Fat str cof, ksi (MPa)	Fat str exp	Fat duc cof	Fat duc exp
A-538-A†	405	L	Sol tr & aged	27000 (186)	150 (1034)	0.09		240 (1655)	–0.065	0.30	–0.62
A-538-B†	460	L	Sol tr & aged	27000 (186)	195 (1344)	0.075		310 (2137)	–0.071	0.80	–0.71
A-538-C†	480	L	Sol tr & aged	26000 (179)	215 (1482)	0.08		325 (2241)	–0.07	0.60	–0.75
AM-350¶		L	HR & annealed	28000 (193)	196 (1351)	0.13		406 (2799)	–0.14	0.33	–0.84
AM-350¶	496	L	CD	26000 (179)	235 (1620)	0.21		390 (2689)	–0.102	0.10	–0.42
Gainex‡		LT	HR sheet	29200 (201)	58 (400)	0.11	114 (786)	117 (807)	–0.07	0.86	–0.65
Gainex‡		L	HR sheet	29200 (201)	54 (372)	0.11	114 (786)	117 (807)	–0.071	0.86	–0.65
H-11	660	L	Ausformed	30000 (207)	340 (2344)	0.07		460 (3172)	–0.077	0.08	–0.74
R-100§	236	LT	As rec plate	28500 (197)							
R-100§	236	L	As rec plate	28000 (193)							
RQC-100*	290	LT	HR plate	30000 (207)	87 (600)	0.14	208 (1434)	180 (1241)	–0.07	0.66	–0.69
RQC-100*	290	L	HR plate	30000 (207)	87 (600)	0.14	208 (1434)	180 (1241)	–0.07	0.66	–0.69
10B62	430	L	Q&T	28000 (193)	140 (965)	0.16	309 (2130)	258 (1779)	–0.067	0.32	–0.56
1005–1009	90	LT	HR sheet	30000 (207)	35 (241)	0.12	71 (490)	84 (579)	–0.09	0.15	–0.43
1005–1009	125	LT	CD sheet	30000 (207)	41 (283)	0.11	83 (572)	75 (517)	–0.059	0.30	–0.51
1005–1009	125	L	CD sheet	29000 (200)	36 (248)	0.11	71 (490)	78 (538)	–0.073	0.11	–0.41
1005–1009	90	L	HR sheet	29000 (200)	33 (228)	0.12	67 (462)	93 (641)	–0.109	0.10	–0.39
1015	80	L	Normalized	30000 (207)	35 (241)	0.22	137 (945)	120 (827)	–0.11	0.95	–0.64
1020	108	L	HR plate plate	29500 (203)	35 (241)	0.18	112 (772)	130 (896)	–0.12	0.41	–0.51
1040	225	L	As forged	29000 (200)	56 (386)	0.18		223 (1538)	–0.14	0.61	–0.57
1045	225	L	Q&T	29000 (200)	60 (414)	0.18	195 (1344)	178 (1227)	–0.095	1.00	–0.66
1045	410	L	Q&T	29000 (200)	120 (827)	0.146	335 (2310)	270 (1862)	–0.073	0.60	–0.70
1045	390	L	Q&T	30000 (207)	110 (758)	0.17		230 (1586)	–0.074	0.45	–0.68
1045	450	L	Q&T	30000 (207)	140 (965)	0.15		260 (1793)	–0.07	0.35	–0.69
1045	500	L	Q&T	30000 (207)	185 (1276)	0.12		330 (2275)	–0.08	0.25	–0.68
1045	595	L	Q&T	30000 (207)	250 (1724)	0.13		395 (2723)	–0.081	0.07	–0.60
1080 +Mn	326	L	HR plate	30000 (207)							
1080 +Mn	375	L	Q&T	30400 (210)							
1080 +Mn	415	L	Q&T	29300 (202)							

TABLE 5.35 Cyclic Stress-Strain and Fatigue Properties of Selected Metals (Sort: Steel, Al, SAE Spec., Increasing True Fracture Strength) (*Continued*)

SAE spec	BHn	Grain dir	Process description	Mod of elas, ksi (GPa)	Cyc yld, ksi (MPa)	Cyc strain hard'G exp	Cyc str cof, ksi (MPa)	Fat str cof, ksi (MPa)	Fat str exp	Fat duc ccf	Fat duc exp
1080 +Mn	505	L	Q&T	29700 (205)							
1080 +Mn	555	L	Q&T	30400 (210)							
1144	265	L	CD strain rel	28500 (197)	80 (552)	0.15		145 (1000)	–0.08	0.32	–0.58
1144	305	L	Drawn at temp	28800 (199)	82 (565)	0.18		230 (1586)	–0.09	0.27	–0.53
1541F	290	L	Q&T forging	29900 (206)	95 (655)	0.17	255 (1758)	185 (1276)	–0.076	0.68	–0.65
1541F	260	L	Q&T forging	29900 (206)	85 (586)	0.16	235 (1620)	185 (1276)	–0.071	0.93	–0.65
30304	160	L	HR & annealed	27000 (186)	104 (717)	0.36		350 (2413)	–0.15	1.02	–0.69
30304	327	L	CD	25000 (172)	127 (876)	0.17		330 (2275)	–0.12	0.89	–0.77
30310	145	L	HR & annealed	28000 (193)	50 (345)	0.26		240 (1655)	–0.15	0.60	–0.57
4130	258	L	Q&T	32000 (221)	82 (565)	0.13		185 (1276)	–0.083	0.92	–0.63
4130	365	L	Q&T	29000 (200)	120 (827)	0.12		246 (1696)	–0.081	0.89	–0.69
4140	310	L	Q&T drawn at temp	29200 (201)	90 (621)	0.14		265 (1827)	–0.08	1.2	–0.59
4142	310	L	Drawn at temp	29000 (200)	108 (745)	0.18		210 (1448)	–0.10	0.22	–0.51
4142	335	L	Drawn at temp	28900 (199)	181 (1248)	0.14		181 (1248)	–0.08	0.06	–0.62
4142	380	L	Q&T	30000 (207)	120 (827)	0.17		265 (1827)	–0.08	0.45	–0.75
4142	400	L	Q&T and deformed	29000 (200)	130 (896)	0.16		275 (1896)	–0.09	0.50	–0.75
4142	450	L	Q&T	30000 (207)	155 (1069)	0.15		290 (1999)	–0.08	0.40	–0.73
4142	475	L	Q&T and deformed	29000 (200)	160 (1103)	0.15		300 (2068)	–0.082	0.20	–0.77
4142	450	L	Q&T and deformed	29000 (200)	155 (1069)	0.16		305 (2103)	–0.09	0.60	–0.76
4142	475	L	Q&T	30000 (207)	195 (1344)	0.13		315 (2172)	–0.081	0.09	–0.61
4142	670	L	As quenched	29000 (200)	320 (2206)	0.05		375 (2586)	–0.075		
4142	560	L	Q&T	30000 (207)	250 (1724)	0.12		385 (2654)	–0.089	0.07	–0.76
4340	243	L	HR & annealed	28000 (193)	66 (455)	0.18		174 (1200)	–0.095	0.45	–0.54
4340	409	L	Q&T	29000 (200)	120 (827)	0.15		290 (1999)	–0.091	0.48	–0.60
4340	350	L	Q&T	28000 (193)	110 (758)	0.14		240 (1655)	–0.076	0.73	–0.62
5160	430	L	Q&T	28000 (193)	145 (1000)	0.15	335 (2310)	280 (1931)	–0.071	0.40	–0.57
52100	518	L	Sol heat Q&T	30000 (207)	192 (1324)	0.16		375 (2586)	–0.09	0.18	–0.56
9262	260	L	Annealed	30000 (207)	76 (524)	0.15	200 (1379)	151 (1041)	–0.071	0.16	–0.47
9262	280	L	Q&T	28000 (193)	94 (648)	0.12	197 (1358)	177 (1220)	–0.073	0.41	–0.60
9262	410	L	Q&T	29000 (200)	152 (1048)	0.089	292 (2013)	269 (1855)	–0.057	0.38	–0.65

950C	159	LT	HR plate	29600 (204)	50 (345)	0.15		170 (1172)	–0.12	0.95	–0.61
950C	150	L	HR bar	30000 (207)	45 (310)	0.185		141 (972)	–0.11	0.85	–0.59
950X	150	L	Plate channel	30000 (207)	49 (338)	0.134	115 (793)	91 (627)	–0.075	0.35	–0.54
950X	156	L	HR plate	29500 (203)	56 (386)	0.114	134 (924)	146 (1007)	–0.10	0.85	–0.61
980X	225	L	Plate channel	28200 (194)	81 (558)	0.134	181 (1248)	153 (1055)	–0.08	0.21	–0.53
1100 AL	26	L	As received	10000 (69)	9 (62)	0.15		28 (193)	–0.106	1.8	–0.69
2014-T6	155	L	Sol tr & artif age	10000 (69)	60 (414)	0.16		123 (848)	–0.106	0.42	–0.65
2024-T351		L	Sol tr strn harden	10600 (73)	62 (427)	0.065	95 (655)	160 (1103)	–0.124	0.22	–0.59
2024-T4		L	Sol tr & RT age	10200 (70)	64 (441)	0.08		147 (1014)	–0.11	0.21	–0.52
5456-H311	95	L	Strain hardened	10000 (69)	52 (359)	0.16		105 (724)	–0.11	0.46	–0.67
7075-T6		L	Sol tr & artif age	10300 (71)	76 (524)	0.146		191 (1317)	–0.52	0.19	–0.52

* Trade name—Bethlehem Steel Corp.

† ASTM specification

‡ Trade name—Armco Steel Corp.

§ Trade name—Republic Steel Corp.

¶ Grade number—Allegheny Ludlum Steel Corp.

SOURCE: Reprinted with permission, copyright 1992, Society of Automotive Engineers.

TABLE 5.36 Fundamental Quality Description* of Carbon and Alloy Steels†

Carbon steels			Alloy steels
Semifinished for forging Forging quality Special hardenability Special internal soundness Nonmetallic inclusion requirement Special surface Carbon steel structural sections Structural quality Carbon steel plates Regular quality Structural quality Cold-drawing quality Cold-pressing quality Cold-flanging quality Forging quality Pressure vessel quality Hot-rolled carbon steel bars Merchant quality Special quality Special hardenability Special internal soundness Nonmetallic inclusion requirement Special surface Scrapless nut quality Axle shaft quality Cold-extrusion quality Cold-heading and cold-forging quality	Hot-rolled sheets Commercial quality Drawing quality Drawing quality special killed Structural quality Cold-rolled sheets Commercial quality Drawing quality Drawing quality special killed Structural quality Porcelain enameling sheets Commercial quality Drawing quality Drawing quality special killed Long-terne sheets Commercial quality Drawing quality Drawing quality special killed Structural quality Galvanized sheets Commercial quality Drawing quality Drawing quality special killed Lock forming quality Electrolytic zinc-coated sheets Commercial quality Drawing quality Drawing quality special killed Structural quality	Tin mill products Specific quality descriptions are not applicable to tin mill products. Carbon steel wire Industrial quality wire Cold-extrusion wires Heading, forging, and roll threading wires Mechanical spring wires Upholstery spring construction wires Welding wire Carbon steel flat wire Stitching wire Stapling wire Carbon steel pipe Structural tubing Line pipe Oil country tubular goods Steel specialty tubular products Pressure tubing Mechanical tubing Aircraft tubing Hot-rolled carbon steel wire rods Industrial quality Rods for manufacture of wire intended for electric welded chain Rods for heading, forging, and roll-threading wire	Alloy steel plates Drawing quality Pressure vessel quality Structural quality Aircraft physical quality Hot-rolled alloy steel bars Regular quality Aircraft quality or steel subject to magnetic particle inspection Axle shaft quality Bearing quality Cold-heading quality Special cold-heading quality Rifle barrel quality, gun quality, shell or A.P. shot quality Alloy steel wire Aircraft quality Bearing quality Special surface quality Cold-finished alloy steel bars Regular quality Aircraft quality or steel subject to magnetic particle inspection Axle shaft quality Bearing shaft quality Cold-heading quality Special cold-heading quality Rifle barrel quality, gun quality, shell or A.P. shot quality

Cold-finished carbon steel bars Standard quality Special hardenability Special internal soundness Nonmetallic inclusion requirement Special surface Cold-heading and cold-forging quality Cold-extrusion quality	Hot-rolled strip Commercial quality Drawing quality Drawing quality special killed Structural quality Cold-rolled strip Specific quality descriptions are not provided in cold-rolled strip, since this product is largely produced for specific end use. Rods for lock washer wire Rods for scrapless nut wire	Rods for upholstery spring wire Rods for welding wire	Line pipe Oil country tubular goods Steel specialty tubular goods Pressure tubing Mechanical tubing Stainless and heat-resisting pipe, pressure tubing, and mechanical tubing Aircraft tubing Pipe

* In the case of certain qualities, phosphorus and sulfur are ordinarily furnished to lower limits than the specified maximum. For details, refer to the appropriate AISI Manual.

† Detailed description of many of the categories listed in this table appear in an appropriate section of the AISI manual.

SOURCE: Reprinted with permission, copyright 1992, Society of Automotive Engineers.

TABLE 5.37 Chemical Compositions of Tool and Die Steels*

SAE steel designation	C	Mn	Si	Cr	V	W	Mo	Co
Water hardening tool steels								
W108†	0.70–0.85	—†	—†	—†	—	—	—	—
W109†	0.85–0.95	—†	—†	—†	—	—	—	—
W110†	0.95–1.10	—†	—†	—†	—	—	—	—
W112†	1.10–1.30	—†	—†	—†	—	—	—	—
W209	0.85–0.95	—†	—†	—†	0.15–0.35	—	—	—
W210	0.95–1.10	—†	—†	—†	0.15–0.35	—	—	—
W310	0.95–1.10	—†	—†	—†	0.35–0.50	—	—	—
Shock-resisting tool steels								
S1—Chromium-tungsten	0.45–0.55	0.20–0.40	0.25–0.45‡	1.25–1.75	0.15–0.30	1.00–3.00	0.40§	—
S2—Silicon-molybdenum	0.45–0.55	0.30–0.50	0.80–1.20	—	0.25§	—	0.40–0.60	—
S5—Silicon-manganese	0.50–0.60	0.60–0.90	1.80–2.20	0.30§	0.25§	—	0.30–0.50	—
Cold-work tool steels								
Oil-hardening types								
O1—Low manganese	0.85–0.95	1.00–1.30	0.20–0.40	0.40–0.60	0.20§	0.40–0.60	—	—
O2—High manganese	0.85–0.95	1.40–1.80	0.20–0.40	0.35§	0.20§	—	0.30§	—
O6—Molybdenum graphitic	1.35–1.55	0.30–1.00	0.80–1.20	—	—	—	0.20–0.30	—
Medium alloy air-hardening types								
A2—5% Chromium air hard	0.95–1.05	0.45–0.75	0.20–0.40	4.75–5.50	0.40§	—	0.90–1.40	—
High-carbon–high-chromium types								
D2—High-carbon–high-chromium (air)	1.40–1.60	0.30–0.50	0.30–0.50	11.00–13.00	0.80§	—	0.70–1.20	0.60§
D3—High-carbon–high-chromium (oil)	2.00–2.35	0.24–0.45‡	0.25–0.45	11.00–13.00	0.80§	0.75§	0.80§	—
D5—High-carbon–high-chromium (cobalt)	1.40–1.60	0.30–0.50	0.30–0.50	11.00–13.00	0.80§	—	0.70–1.20	2.50–3.50
D7—High-carbon–high-chromium–high-vanadium	2.15–2.50	0.30–0.50	0.30–0.50	11.50–13.50	3.80–4.40	—	0.70–1.20	—
Hot-work tool steels								
Chromium base types								
H11—Chromium-molybdenum-V	0.30–0.40	0.20–0.40	0.80–1.20	4.75–5.50	0.30–0.50	—	1.25–1.75	—
H12—Chromium-molybdenum-tungsten	0.30–0.40	0.20–0.40	0.80–1.20	4.75–5.50	0.10–0.50	1.00–1.70	1.25–1.75	—
H13—Chromium-molybdenum-V	0.30–0.40	0.20–0.40	0.80–1.20	4.75–5.50	0.80–1.20	—	1.25–1.75	—
Tungsten base types								
H21—Tungsten	0.30–0.40	0.20–0.40	0.15–0.30	3.00–3.75	0.30–0.50	8.75–10.00	—	—

High-speed tool steels								
Tungsten base types								
T1—Tungsten 18-4-1	0.65–0.75	0.20–0.40	0.20–0.40	3.75–4.50	0.90–1.30	17.25–18.75	—	—
T2—Tungsten 18-4-2	0.75–0.85	0.20–0.40	0.20–0.40	3.75–4.50	1.80–2.40	17.50–19.00	0.70–1.00	—
T4—Cobalt-tungsten 18-4-1-5	0.70–0.80	0.20–0.40	0.20–0.40	3.75–4.50	0.80–1.20	17.25–18.75	0.70–1.00	4.25–5.75
T5—Cobalt-tungsten 18-4-2-8	0.75–0.85	0.20–0.40	0.20–0.40	3.75–4.50	1.80–2.40	17.50–19.00	0.70–1.00	7.00–9.00
T8—Cobalt-tungsten 14-4-2-5	0.75–0.85	0.20–0.40	0.20–0.40	3.75–4.50	1.80–2.40	13.25–14.75	0.70–1.00	4.25–5.75
Molybdenum base types								
M1—Molybdenum 8-2-1	0.75–0.85	0.20–0.40	0.20–0.40	3.75–4.50	0.90–1.30	1.15–1.85	7.75–9.25	—
M2—Molybdenum-tungsten 6-6-2	0.78–0.88	0.20–0.40	0.20–0.40	3.75–4.50	1.60–2.20	5.50–6.75	4.50–5.50	—
M3—Molybdenum-tungsten 6-6-3	1.00–1.25	0.20–0.40	0.20–0.40	3.75–4.50	2.25–3.25	5.50–6.75	4.75–6.25	—
M4—Molybdenum-tungsten 6-6-4	1.25–1.40	0.20–0.40	0.20–0.40	4.00–4.75	3.90–4.50	5.25–6.50	4.50–5.50	—
Special-purpose tool steels								
Low-alloy types								
L6—Nickel-chromium[¶]	0.65–0.75	0.55–0.85[‡]	0.20–0.40	0.65–0.85	0.25[§]	—	0.25[§]	—
L7—Chromium	0.95–1.05	0.25–0.45	0.20–0.40	1.25–1.75	—	—	0.30–0.50	—

* These compositions are not intended for forging die steels.

[†] Water hardening steels listed herein are usually available in four grades or qualities as follows:

Special (grade 1)—The highest quality water hardening carbon tool steel, controlled for hardenability, chemistry held to closest limits, and subject to most rigid tests to insure maximum uniformity in performance.

Extra (grade 2)—A high quality water hardening carbon tool steel, controlled for hardenability, subject to tests to insure good service for general application.

Standard (grade 3)—A good quality water hardening carbon tool steel, not controlled for hardenability, recommended for application where some latitude with respect to uniformity is permissible.

Commercial (grade 4)—A commercial quality water hardening carbon tool steel, not controlled for hardenability, not subject to special tests.

On special and extra grades, limits on manganese, silicon, and chromium are not generally required in lieu of the following Shepherd hardenability limits:

	0.70–0.85 C and 0.85–0.95 C		0.95–1.10 C and 1.10–1.30 C	
	Hardenability, 64ths In. Penetration	Fracture Grain Size, min	Hardenability, 64ths In. Penetration	Fracture Grain Size, min
Shallow	10 max	8	8 max	9
Regular	9 to 13	8	7 to 11	9
Deep	12 min	8	10 to 16	8

On standard and commercial grades, the following limits on composition are generally required:

	Mn	Si	Cr
Standard, max.	0.35	0.35	0.15
Commercial, max.	0.35	0.35	0.20

Total of manganese, silicon, and chromium not to exceed 0.75%.

[‡] May be present in percentages other than shown.

[§] Optional element. Steels have found satisfactory application either with or without the element present.

[¶] Nickel content 1.25–1.75.

TABLE 5.38 Comparison of Tool Steels on the Basis of Properties Affecting Selection

SAE steel designation	Nondeforming properties	Safety in hardening	Depth of hardening*	Toughness	Resistance to softening effect of heat	Wear resistance	Machinability
Water-hardening tool steels							
W108	Poor	Fair	Shallow	Good†	Poor	Fair	Best
W109	Poor	Fair	Shallow	Good†	Poor	Fair	Best
W110	Poor	Fair	Shallow	Good†	Poor	Good	Best
W112	Poor	Fair	Shallow	Good†	Poor	Good	Best
W209	Poor	Fair	Shallow	Good†	Poor	Fair	Best
W210	Poor	Fair	Shallow	Good	Poor	Good	Best
W310	Poor	Fair	Shallow	Good	Poor	Good	Best
Shock-resisting tool steels							
S1—Chromium-tungsten	Fair	Good	Medium	Good	Fair	Fair	Fair
S2—Silicon-molybdenum	W Poor‡ O Fair‡	W Poor‡ O Good‡	Medium	Best	Fair	Fair	Good
S5—Silicon-manganese	W Poor‡ O Fair‡	W Poor‡ O Good‡	Medium	Best	Fair	Fair	Fair
Cold-work tool steels							
Oil-hardening types							
O1—Low manganese	Good	Good	Medium	Fair	Poor	Good	Good
O2—High manganese	Good	Good	Medium	Fair	Poor	Good	Good
O6—Molybdenum graphitic	Fair	Good	Medium	Fair	Poor	Good	Best
Medium-alloy air-hardening types							
A2—5% Chromium air hard	Best	Best	Deep	Fair	Fair	Good	Fair
High-carbon–high-chromium types							
D2—High-carbon–high-chromium (air)	Best	Best	Deep	Fair	Fair	Best	Poor
D3—High-carbon–high-chromium (oil)	Good	Good	Deep	Poor	Fair	Best	Poor
D5—High-carbon–high-chromium-cobalt	Best	Best	Deep	Fair	Fair	Best	Poor
D7—High-carbon–high-chromium–high-vanadium	Best	Best	Deep	Poor	Fair	Best	Poor

Hot-work tool steels							
Chromium base types							
H11—Chromium-molybdenum-V	Good	Good	Deep	Good	Good	Fair	Fair
H12—Chromium-molybdenum-tungsten	Good	Good	Deep	Good	Good	Fair	Fair
H13—Chromium-molybdenum-VV	Good	Good	Deep	Good	Good	Fair	Fair
Tungsten base types							
H21—Tungsten	Good	Good	Deep	Good	Good	Fair	Fair
High-speed tool steels							
Tungsten base types							
T1—Tungsten 18-4-1	Good	Good	Deep	Poor	Good	Good	Fair
T2—Tungsten 18-4-2	Good	Good	Deep	Poor	Good	Good	Fair
T4—Cobalt-tungsten 18-4-1-5	Good	Fair	Deep	Poor	Best	Good	Fair
T5—Cobalt-tungsten 18-4-2-8	Good	Fair	Deep	Poor	Best	Good	Fair
T8—Cobalt-tungsten 14-4-2-5	Good	Fair	Deep	Poor	Best	Good	Fair
Molybdenum base types							
M1—Molybdenum 8-2-1	Good	Fair	Deep	Poor	Good	Good	Fair
M2—Molybdenum-tungsten 6-6-2	Good	Fair	Deep	Poor	Good	Good	Fair
M3—Molybdenum-tungsten 6-6-3	Good	Fair	Deep	Poor	Good	Best	Fair
M4—Molybdenum-tungsten 6-6-4	Good	Fair	Deep	Poor	Good	Best	Fair
Special-purpose tool steels							
Low-alloy types							
L6—Nickel-chromium	Fair	Good	Medium	Fair	Poor	Fair	Fair
L7—Chromium	Fair	Good	Medium	Fair	Poor	Good	Fair

* These are intended to emphasize major differences between the groups of steels and do not account for the minor differences in depths of hardening that exist between steels of the same group. This is particularly true of the water-hardening W steels which are frequently furnished with varying degrees of hardenability as listed in Table 5.39.

† Toughness decreases somewhat with increasing depth of hardening.

‡ W as shown here indicates water quench. O as shown here indicates oil quench.

SOURCE: Reprinted with permission, copyright 1992, Society of Automotive Engineers.

TABLE 5.39 Approximate Comparison of Tool and Die Steels on the Basis of Some Heat-Treating Characteristics

SAE steel designation	Quench medium	Preheat temperature, °F	Hardening temperature range, °F*	Hardness after quenching, Rockwell C	Tempering temperature range, °F*	Hardness after tempering, Rockwell C	Decarburization (prevention of during heat treatment)
Water-hardening tool steel							
W108	Water	—†	1420–1450	65–67	350–525	65–56	—‡
W109	Water	—†	1420–1450	65–67	350–525	65–56	—‡
W110	Water	—†	1420–1450	65–67	350–525	65–56	—‡
W112	Water	—†	1420–1500	65–67	350–525	65–56	—‡
W209	Water	—†	1420–1500	65–67	350–525	65–56	—‡
W210	Water	—†	1420–1500	65–67	350–525	65–56	—‡
W310	Water	—†	1420–1500	65–67	350–525	65–56	—‡
Shock-resisting tool steels							
S1—Chromium-tungsten	Oil	1200–1300	1650–1800	57–59	300–1000	57–45	—§
S2—Silicon-molybdenum	Water	—†	1550–1575	60–62	300–500	60–54	—‡
	Oil	—†	1600–1625	58–60	300–500	58–54	—‡
S5—Silicon-manganese	Water	—†	1550–1600	60–62	300–650	60–54	—‡
	Oil	—†	1600–1675	58–60	300–650	58–54	—‡
Cold-work tool steels							
Oil-hardening types							
O1—Low manganese	Oil	—†	1450–1500	63–65	300–800	62–50	—‡
O2—High manganese	Oil	—†	1420–1450	63–65	375–500	62–57	—‡
O6—Molybdenum graphitic	Oil	—†	1450–1500	63–65	300–800	63–50	—‡
Medium-alloy air-hardening types							
A2—5% Chromium air hard	Air	1200–1300	1725–1775	61–63	400–700	60–57	—§
High-carbon–high-chromium types							
D2—High-carbon–high-chromium	Air	1200–1300	1800–1875	61–63	400–700	60–58	—§
D3—High-carbon–high-chromium	Oil	1200–1300	1750–1800	62–64	400–700	62–58	—§
D5—High-carbon–high-chromium-cobalt	Air	1200–1300	1800–1875	60–62	400–700	59–57	—§
D7—High-carbon–high-chromium–high-vanadium	Air	1200–1300	1850–1950	63–65	300–500 850–1000	65–63 62–58	—§

Hot-work tool steels							
Chromium base types							
H11—Chromium-molybdenum-V	Air	1450–1500	1825–1875	53–55	1000–1100	51–43	—§
H12—Chromium-molybdenum-tungsten	Oil, Air	1450–1500	1800–1900	53–55	1000–1100	51–43	—§
H13—Chromium-molybdenum-VV	Air	1400–1450	1825–1875	53–55	1000–1100	51–43	—§
Tungsten base types							
H21—Tungsten	Oil, Air	1500–1550	2100–2150	50–52	950–1150	50–47	—§
High-speed tool steels							
Tungsten base types							
T1—Tungsten 18-4-1	Oil, air, salt	1500–1550	2300–2375	63–65	1025–1100	65–63	—§
T2—Tungsten 18-4-2	Oil, air, salt	1500–1550	2300–2375	63–65	1025–1100	65–63	—§
T4—Cobalt-tungsten 18-4-1-5	Oil, air, salt	1500–1550	2300–2375	63–65	1025–1100	65–63	—§
T5—Cobalt-tungsten 18-4-2-8	Oil, air, salt	1500–1550	2300–2400	63–65	1050–1100	65–63	—§
T8—Cobalt-tungsten 14-4-2-5	Oil, air, salt	1500–1550	2300–2375	63–65	1025–1100	65–63	—§
Molybdenum base types							
M1—Molybdenum 8-2-1	Oil, air, salt	1400–1500	2150–2250	63–65	1025–1050	65–63	—§
M2—Molybdenum-tungsten 6-6-2	Oil, air, salt	1450–1500	2175–2250	63–65	1025–1075	65–63	—§
M3—Molybdenum-tungsten 6-6-3	Oil, air, salt	1450–1500	2150–2225	63–65	1025–1075	65–63	—§
M4—Molybdenum-tungsten 6-6-4	Oil, air, salt	1450–1500	2150–2225	63–65	1025–1075	65–63	—§
Special-purpose tool steels							
Low-alloy types							
L6—Nickel-chromium	Oil	—†	1500–1600	62–64	400–800	62–48	—‡
L7—Chromium	Oil	—†	1525–1550	63–65	350–500	62–60	—‡

* The purpose of these columns is to show the usual ranges of temperature employed in hardening and tempering and is not to be used as a specification.

† For large tools and tools having intricate sections, preheating at 1050 to 1200°F is recommended.

‡ Use moderately oxidizing atmosphere in furnace or a suitable neutral salt bath.

§ Use protective pack from which volatile matter has been removed, carefully balanced neutral salt bath, or atmosphere controlled furnaces. In the latter case, the furnace atmosphere should be in equilibrium with the carbon content of the steel being treated. Furnace atmosphere dew point is considered a reliable method for measuring and controlling this equilibrium.

TABLE 5.40 Forging, Normalizing, and Annealing Treatments of Tool and Die Steels

	Forging†			Normalizing‡		Annealing§			
SAE steel designation*	Heat slowly to	Start forging at	Do not forge below	Heat slowly to	Hold at	Temperature	Maximum rate of cooling, °F/h	Approximate Brinell hardness	Approximate Rockwell B
Water-hardening tool steels									
W108	1450	1800–1950	1500	1450	1500	1400–1450	75	159–202	84–94
W109	1450	1800–1950	1500	1450	1500	1375–1425	75	159–202	84–94
W110	1450	1800–1900	1500	1450	1550	1400–1450	75	159–202	84–94
W112	1450	1800–1900	1500	1450	1625	1400–1450	75	159–202	84–94
W209	1450	1800–1950	1500	1450	1500	1375–1425	75	159–202	84–94
W210	1450	1800–1900	1500	1450	1550	1400–1450	75	159–202	84–94
W310	1450	1800–1900	1500	1450	1550	1400–1450	75	159–202	84–94
Shock-resisting tool steels									
S1—Chromium-tungsten	1500	1800–2000	1600	Do not normalize		1450–1500	50	192–235	92–99
S2—Silicon-molybdenum	1500	1900–2100	1600	1500	1650	1400–1450	50	192–229	92–98
S5—Silicon-manganese	1500	1900–2050	1600	1500	1600	1400–1450	50	192–229	92–98
Cold-work tool steels									
Oil-hardening types									
O1—Low manganese	1500	1750–1900	1550	1500	1600	1425–1475	50	183–212	90–96
O2—High manganese	1500	1750–1900	1550	1500	1550	1375–1425	50	183–212	90–96
O6—Molybdenum graphitic	1500	1750–1900	1500	1500	1625	1425–1475	20	183–217	90–96
Medium-alloy air-hardening types									
A2—5% Chromium air hard	1600	1850–2000	1650	Do not normalize		1550–1600	40	202–229	94–98
High-carbon–high-chromium types									
D2—High-carbon–high-chromium (air)	1650	1850–2000	1650	Do not normalize		1600–1650	40	207–255	95–102
D3—High-carbon–high-chromium (oil)	1650	1850–2000	1650	Do not normalize		1600–1650	50	212–255	96–102
D5—High-carbon–high-chromium–cobalt	1600	1850–2000	1650	Do not normalize		1600–1650	40	207–255	95–102
D7—High-carbon–high-chromium–high-vanadium	1650	2050–2125	1800	Do not normalize		1600–1650	50	235–262	99–103

Hot-work tool steels									
Chromium base types									
H11—Chromium-molybdenum-V	1650	1950–2100	1650	Do not normalize		1550–1600	50	192–229	92–98
H12—Chromium-molybdenum-tungsten	1650	1950–2100	1650	Do not normalize		1600–1650	50	192–229	92–98
H13—Chromium-molybdenum-VV	1650	1950–2100	1650	Do not normalize		1550–1600	50	192–229	92–98
Tungsten base types									
H21—Tungsten	1600	2000–2150	1650	Do not normalize		1600–1650	50	202–235	94–99
High-speed tool steels									
Tungsten base types									
T1—Tungsten 18-4-1	1600	1950–2100	1750	Do not normalize		1600–1650	50	217–255	96–102
T2—Tungsten 18-4-2	1600	2000–2150	1750	Do not normalize		1600–1650	50	223–255	97–102
T4—Cobalt-tungsten 18-4-1-5	1600	2000–2150	1750	Do not normalize		1600–1650	50	229–255	98–102
T5—Cobalt-tungsten 18-4-2-8	1600	2000–2150	1800	Do not normalize		1600–1650	50	248–293	102–106
T8—Cobalt-tungsten 14-4-2-5	1600	2000–2150	1750	Do not normalize		1600–1650	50	229–255	98–102
Molybdenum base types									
M1—Molybdenum 8-2-1	1500	1900–2050	1700	Do not normalize		1525–1600	50	207–248	95–102
M2—Molybdenum-tungsten 6-6-2	1500	1950–2100	1700	Do not normalize		1550–1625	50	217–248	96–102
M3—Molybdenum-tungsten 6-6-3	1500	2000–2150	1700	Do not normalize		1550–1625	50	223–255	97–102
M4—Molybdenum-tungsten 6-6-4	1500	2000–2150	1700	Do not normalize		1550–1625	50	229–255	98–102
Special-purpose tool steels									
Low-alloy types									
L6—Nickel-chromium	1500	1800–2000	1600	1550	1650	1400–1450	50	183–212	90–96
L7—Chromium	1500	1800–2000	1550	1550	1650	1450–1500	50	174–212	88–96

* These tool and die steels are the same as those listed in Table 5.38 of this report.

† The temperature at which to start forging is given as a range, the higher side of which should be used for large sections and heavy or rapid reductions and the lower side for smaller sections and lighter reductions. As the alloy content of the steel increases, the time of soaking at forging temperature increases proportionately. Likewise, as the alloy content increases, it becomes more necessary to cool slowly from the forging temperature. With very high alloy steels, such as high speed or air hardening steels, this slow cooling is imperative in order to prevent cracking and to leave the steel in a semisoft condition. Either furnace cooling or burying in an insulating medium, such as lime, mica, or silocel, is satisfactory.

‡ The length of time the steel is held after being uniformly heated through at the normalizing temperature, varies from about 15 min for a small section to about 1 h for large sizes. Cooling from the normalizing temperature is done in still air. The purpose of normalizing after forging is to refine the grain structure and to produce a uniform structure throughout the forging. Normalizing should not be confused with low temperature (about 1200°F) annealing used for the relief of residual stresses resulting from heavy machining, bending, and forming.

§ The annealing temperature is given as a range, the upper limit of which should be used for large sections and the lower limit for smaller sections. The length of time the steel is held after being uniformly heated through at the annealing temperature varies from about 1 h for light sections and small furnace charges of carbon or low alloy steel to about 4 hr for heavy sections and large furnace charges of high alloy steel.

For information on the forging and heat treating of tool steels, see ASM Handbook, 1948 edition, pp. 653–655.

SOURCE: Reprinted with permission, copyright 1992, Society of Automotive Engineers.

TABLE 5.41 Approximate Equivalent Hardness Numbers* for Brinell Hardness Numbers† for Steel

	Brinell hardness No.,† 10-mm ball, 3000-kg load				Rockwell hardness No.†			Rockwell superficial hardness no. superficial Brale penetrator					
Brinell indentation dia, mm	Standard ball	Tungsten-carbide ball	Vickers hardness no.	A-scale, 60-kg load, Brale penetrator	B-scale, 100-kg load 1.6-mm ($\frac{1}{16}$-in) dia ball	C-scale, 150-kg load Brale penetrator	D-scale, 100-kg load Brale penetrator	15-N scale, 15-kg load	30-N scale, 30-kg load	45-N scale, 45-kg load	Shore scleroscope hardness no.	Tensile strength (approximate) in MPa (1000 psi)	Brinell indentation dia, mm
Col. 1	Col. 2	Col. 3	Col. 4	Col. 5	Col. 6	Col. 7	Col. 8	Col. 9	Col. 10	Col. 11	Col. 12	Col. 13	Col. 14
—	—	—	940	85.6	—	68.0	76.9	93.2	84.4	75.4	97	—	—
—	—	—	920	85.3	—	67.5	76.5	93.0	84.0	74.8	96	—	—
—	—	—	900	85.0	—	67.0	76.1	92.9	83.6	74.2	95	—	—
—	—	(767)	880	84.7	—	66.4	75.7	92.7	83.1	73.6	93	—	—
—	—	(757)	860	84.4	—	65.9	75.3	92.5	82.7	73.1	92	—	—
2.25	—	(745)	840	84.1	—	65.3	74.8	92.3	82.2	72.2	91	—	2.25
—	—	(733)	820	83.8	—	64.7	74.3	92.1	81.7	71.8	90	—	—
—	—	(722)	800	83.4	—	64.0	73.8	91.8	81.1	71.0	88	—	—
2.30	—	(712)	—	—	—	—	—	—	—	—	—	—	2.30
—	—	(710)	780	83.0	—	63.3	73.3	91.5	80.4	70.2	87	—	—
—	—	(698)	760	82.6	—	62.5	72.6	91.2	79.7	69.4	86	—	—
—	—	(684)	740	82.2	—	61.8	72.1	91.0	79.1	68.6	—	—	—
2.35	—	(682)	**737**	**82.2**	—	**61.7**	**72.0**	**91.0**	**79.0**	**68.5**	84	—	**2.35**
—	—	(670)	720	81.8	—	61.0	71.5	90.7	78.4	67.7	83	—	—
—	—	(656)	700	81.3	—	60.1	70.8	90.3	77.6	66.7	—	—	—
2.40	—	(653)	**697**	**81.2**	—	**60.0**	**70.7**	**90.2**	**77.5**	**66.5**	81	—	**2.40**
—	—	(647)	690	81.1	—	59.7	70.5	90.1	77.2	66.2	—	—	—
—	—	(638)	680	80.8	—	59.2	70.1	89.8	76.8	65.7	80	—	—
—	—	630	670	80.6	—	58.8	69.8	89.7	76.4	65.3	—	—	—
2.45	—	**627**	**667**	**80.5**	—	**58.7**	**69.7**	**89.6**	**76.3**	**65.1**	79	—	**2.45**
2.50	—	—	**677**	**80.7**	—	**59.1**	**70.0**	**89.8**	**76.8**	**65.7**	—	—	**2.50**
	—	**601**	**640**	**79.8**	—	**57.3**	**68.7**	**89.0**	**75.1**	**63.5**	77	—	

2.55	—	—	**640**	**79.8**	—	**57.3**	**68.7**	**89.0**	**75.1**	**63.5**	—	—	**2.55**
	—	**578**	**615**	**79.1**	—	**56.0**	**67.7**	**88.4**	**73.9**	**62.1**	75	—	
2.60	—	—	**607**	**78.8**	—	**55.6**	**67.4**	**88.1**	**73.5**	**61.6**	—	—	**2.60**
	—	**555**	**591**	**78.4**	—	**54.7**	**66.7**	**87.8**	**72.7**	**60.6**	73	2055 (298)	
2.65	—	—	**579**	**78.0**	—	**54.0**	**66.1**	**87.5**	**72.0**	**59.8**	—	2015 (292)	**2.65**
	—	**534**	**569**	**77.8**	—	**53.5**	**65.8**	**87.2**	**71.6**	**59.2**	71	1985 (288)	
2.70	—	—	**553**	**77.1**	—	**52.5**	**65.0**	**86.7**	**70.7**	**58.0**	—	1915 (278)	**2.70**
	—	**514**	**547**	**76.9**	—	**52.1**	**64.7**	**86.5**	**70.3**	**57.6**	70	1890 (274)	
2.75	(495)	—	**539**	**76.7**	—	**51.6**	**64.3**	**86.3**	**69.9**	**56.9**	—	1855 (269)	**2.75**
	—	—	**530**	**76.4**	—	**51.1**	**63.9**	**86.0**	**69.5**	**56.2**	—	1825 (265)	
	—	**495**	**528**	**76.3**	—	**51.0**	**63.8**	**85.9**	**69.4**	**56.1**	68	1820 (264)	
2.80	(477)	—	**516**	**75.9**	—	**50.3**	**63.2**	**85.6**	**68.7**	**55.2**	—	1780 (258)	**2.80**
	—	—	**508**	**75.6**	—	**49.6**	**62.7**	**85.3**	**68.2**	**54.5**	—	1740 (252)	
	—	**477**	**508**	**75.6**	—	**49.6**	**62.7**	**85.3**	**68.2**	**54.5**	66	1740 (252)	
2.85	(461)	—	**495**	**75.1**	—	**48.8**	**61.9**	**84.9**	**67.4**	**53.5**	—	1680 (244)	**2.85**
	—	—	**491**	**74.9**	—	**48.5**	**61.7**	**84.7**	**67.2**	**53.2**	—	1670 (242)	
	—	**461**	**491**	**74.9**	—	**48.5**	**61.7**	**84.7**	**67.2**	**53.2**	65	1670 (242)	
2.90	**444**	—	**474**	**74.3**	—	**47.2**	**61.0**	**84.1**	**66.0**	**51.7**	—	1595 (231)	**2.90**
	—	—	**472**	**74.2**	—	**47.1**	**60.8**	**84.0**	**65.8**	**51.5**	—	1585 (230)	
	—	**444**	**472**	**74.2**	—	**47.1**	**60.8**	**84.0**	**65.8**	**51.5**	63	1585 (230)	
2.95	**429**	**429**	**455**	**73.4**	—	**45.7**	**59.7**	**83.4**	**64.6**	**49.9**	61	1510 (219)	**2.95**
3.00	**415**	**415**	**440**	**72.8**	—	**44.5**	**58.8**	**82.8**	**63.5**	**48.4**	59	1460 (212)	**3.00**
3.05	**401**	**401**	**425**	**72.0**	—	**43.1**	**57.8**	**82.0**	**62.3**	**46.9**	58	1390 (202)	**3.05**
3.10	**388**	**388**	**410**	**71.4**	—	**41.8**	**56.8**	**81.4**	**61.1**	**45.3**	56	1330 (193)	**3.10**
3.15	**375**	**375**	**396**	**70.6**	—	**40.4**	**55.7**	**80.6**	**59.9**	**43.6**	54	1270 (184)	**3.15**
3.20	**363**	**363**	**383**	**70.0**	—	**39.1**	**54.6**	**80.0**	**58.7**	**42.0**	52	1220 (177)	**3.20**
3.25	**352**	**352**	**372**	**69.3**	(110.0)	**37.9**	**53.8**	**79.3**	**57.6**	**40.5**	51	1180 (171)	**3.25**
3.30	**341**	**341**	**360**	**68.7**	(109.0)	**36.6**	**52.8**	**78.6**	**56.4**	**39.1**	50	1130 (164)	**3.30**
3.35	**331**	**331**	**350**	**68.1**	(108.5)	**35.5**	**51.9**	**78.0**	**55.4**	**37.8**	48	1095 (159)	**3.35**
3.40	**321**	**321**	**339**	**67.5**	(108.0)	**34.3**	**51.0**	**77.3**	**54.3**	**36.4**	47	1060 (154)	**3.40**
3.45	**311**	**311**	**328**	**66.9**	(107.5)	**33.1**	**50.0**	**76.7**	**53.3**	**34.4**	46	1025 (149)	**3.45**
3.50	**302**	**302**	**319**	**66.3**	(107.0)	**32.1**	**49.3**	**76.1**	**52.2**	**33.8**	45	1005 (146)	**3.50**
3.55	**293**	**293**	**309**	**65.7**	(106.0)	**30.9**	**48.3**	**75.5**	**51.2**	**32.4**	43	970 (141)	**3.55**

TABLE 5.41 Approximate Equivalent Hardness Numbers* for Brinell Hardness Numbers† for Steel (*Continued*)

	Brinell hardness No.,† 10-mm ball, 3000-kg load				Rockwell hardness No.†			Rockwell superficial hardness no. superficial Brale penetrator					
Brinell indentation dia, mm	Standard ball	Tungsten-carbide ball	Vickers hardness no.	A-scale, 60-kg load, Brale penetrator	B-scale, 100-kg load 1.6-mm (1/16-in) dia ball	C-scale, 150-kg load Brale penetrator	D-scale, 100-kg load Brale penetrator	15-N scale, 15-kg load	30-N scale, 30-kg load	45-N scale, 45-kg load	Shore scleroscope hardness no.	Tensile strength (approximate) in MPa (1000 psi)	Brinell indentation dia, mm
Col. 1	Col. 2	Col. 3	Col. 4	Col. 5	Col. 6	Col. 7	Col. 8	Col. 9	Col. 10	Col. 11	Col. 12	Col. 13	Col. 14
3.60	**285**	**285**	**301**	**65.3**	(105.5)	**29.9**	**47.6**	**75.0**	**50.3**	**31.2**	—	950 (138)	**3.60**
3.65	**277**	**277**	**292**	**64.6**	(104.5)	**28.8**	**46.7**	**74.4**	**49.3**	**29.9**	41	925 (134)	**3.65**
3.70	**269**	**269**	**284**	**64.1**	(104.0)	**27.6**	**45.9**	**73.7**	**48.3**	**28.5**	40	895 (130)	**3.70**
3.75	**262**	**262**	**276**	**63.6**	(103.0)	**26.6**	**45.0**	**73.1**	**47.3**	**27.3**	39	875 (127)	**3.75**
3.80	**255**	**255**	**269**	**63.0**	(102.0)	**25.4**	**44.2**	**72.5**	**46.2**	**26.0**	38	850 (123)	**3.80**
3.85	**248**	**248**	**261**	**62.5**	(101.0)	**24.2**	**43.2**	**71.7**	**45.1**	**24.5**	37	825 (120)	**3.85**
3.90	**241**	**241**	**253**	**61.8**	100.0	**22.8**	**42.0**	**70.9**	**43.9**	**22.8**	36	800 (116)	**3.90**
3.95	**235**	**235**	**247**	**61.4**	99.0	**21.7**	**41.4**	**70.3**	**42.9**	**21.5**	35	785 (114)	**3.95**
4.00	**229**	**229**	**241**	**60.8**	98.2	**20.5**	**40.5**	**69.7**	**41.9**	**20.1**	34	765 (111)	**4.00**
4.05	223	223	234	—	97.3	(18.8)	—	—	—	—	—	—	4.05
4.10	217	217	228	—	96.4	(17.5)	—	—	—	—	33	725 (105)	4.10
4.15	212	212	222	—	95.5	(16.0)	—	—	—	—	—	705 (102)	4.15
4.20	207	207	218	—	94.6	(15.2)	—	—	—	—	32	690 (100)	4.20
4.25	201	201	212	—	93.8	(13.8)	—	—	—	—	31	675 (98)	4.25
4.30	197	197	207	—	92.8	(12.7)	—	—	—	—	30	655 (95)	4.30
4.35	192	192	202	—	91.9	(11.5)	—	—	—	—	29	640 (93)	4.35
4.40	187	187	196	—	90.7	(10.0)	—	—	—	—	—	620 (90)	4.40
4.45	183	183	192	—	90.0	(9.0)	—	—	—	—	28	615 (89)	4.45
4.50	179	179	188	—	89.0	(8.0)	—	—	—	—	27	600 (87)	4.50
4.55	174	174	182	—	87.8	(6.4)	—	—	—	—	—	585 (85)	4.55
4.60	170	170	178	—	86.8	(5.4)	—	—	—	—	26	570 (83)	4.60
4.65	167	167	175	—	86.0	(4.4)	—	—	—	—	—	560 (81)	4.65
4.70	163	163	171	—	85.0	(3.3)	—	—	—	—	25	545 (79)	4.70

4.80	156	156	163	—	82.9	(0.9)	—	—	—	—	—	525 (76)	4.80
4.90	149	149	156	—	80.8	—	—	—	—	—	23	505 (73)	4.90
5.00	143	143	150	—	78.7	—	—	—	—	—	22	490 (71)	5.00
5.10	137	137	143	—	76.4	—	—	—	—	—	21	460 (67)	5.10
5.20	131	131	137	—	74.0	—	—	—	—	—	—	450 (65)	5.20
5.30	126	126	132	—	72.0	—	—	—	—	—	20	435 (63)	5.30
5.40	121	121	127	—	69.8	—	—	—	—	—	19	415 (60)	5.40
5.50	116	116	122	—	67.6	—	—	—	—	—	18	400 (58)	5.50
5.60	111	111	117	—	65.7	—	—	—	—	—	15	385 (56)	5.60

* This table corresponds to the table in ASM Metals Handbook, 8th Edition, Vol. 1, page 1235. It has been modified to add metric equivalents for approximate tensile strength values and to indicate Brinell hardness values that are beyond the recommended range for this test.

† Values in ( ) are beyond normal range and are given for information only.

SOURCE: Reprinted with permission, copyright 1992, Society of Automotive Engineers.

TABLE 5.42 Approximate Equivalent Hardness Numbers* for Rockwell C Hardness Numbers for Steel

		Brinell hardness no., 10-mm ball, 3000-kg load†		Rockwell hardness no.†			Rockwell, superficial hardness no., superficial Brale penetrator					
Rockwell C-scale hardness no.†	Vickers hardness no.	Standard ball	Tungsten-carbide ball	A-scale, 60-kg load, Brale penetrator	B-scale, 100-kg load, 1.6-mm (1/16-in) dia ball	D-scale, 100-kg load, Brale penetrator	15-N scale, 15-kg load	30-N scale, 30-kg load	45-N scale, 45-kg load	Shore scleroscope hardness no.	Tensile strength (approximate) in MPa (1000 psi)	Rockwell C-scale hardness no.†
Col. 1	Col. 2	Col. 3	Col. 4	Col. 5	Col. 6	Col. 7	Col. 8	Col. 9	Col. 10	Col. 11	Col. 12	Col. 13
68	**940**	—	—	**85.6**	—	**76.9**	**93.2**	**84.4**	**75.4**	97	—	**68**
67	**900**	—	—	**85.0**	—	**76.1**	**92.9**	**83.6**	**74.2**	95	—	**67**
66	**865**	—	—	**84.5**	—	**75.4**	**92.5**	**82.8**	**73.3**	92	—	**66**
65	**832**	—	(739)	**83.9**	—	**74.5**	**92.2**	**81.9**	**72.0**	91	—	**65**
64	**800**	—	(722)	**83.4**	—	**73.8**	**91.8**	**81.1**	**71.0**	88	—	**64**
63	**772**	—	(705)	**82.8**	—	**73.0**	**91.4**	**80.1**	**69.9**	87	—	**63**
62	**746**	—	(688)	**82.3**	—	**72.2**	**91.1**	**79.3**	**68.8**	85	—	**62**
61	**720**	—	(670)	**81.8**	—	**71.5**	**90.7**	**78.4**	**67.7**	83	—	**61**
60	**697**	—	(654)	**81.2**	—	**70.7**	**90.2**	**77.5**	**66.6**	81	—	**60**
59	**674**	—	(634)	**80.7**	—	**69.9**	**89.8**	**76.6**	**65.5**	80	—	**59**
58	**653**	—	**615**	**80.1**	—	**69.2**	**89.3**	**75.7**	**64.3**	78	—	**58**
57	**633**	—	**595**	**79.6**	—	**68.5**	**88.9**	**74.8**	**63.2**	76	—	**57**
56	**613**	—	**577**	**79.0**	—	**67.7**	**88.3**	**73.9**	**62.0**	75	—	**56**
55	**595**	—	**560**	**78.5**	—	**66.9**	**87.9**	**73.0**	**60.9**	74	2075 (301)	**55**
54	**577**	—	**543**	**78.0**	—	**66.1**	**87.4**	**72.0**	**59.8**	72	2015 (292)	**54**
53	**560**	—	**525**	**77.4**	—	**65.4**	**86.9**	**71.2**	**58.6**	71	1950 (283)	**53**
52	**544**	(500)	**512**	**76.8**	—	**64.6**	**86.4**	**70.2**	**57.4**	69	1880 (273)	**52**
51	**528**	(487)	**496**	**76.3**	—	**63.8**	**85.9**	**69.4**	**56.1**	68	1820 (264)	**51**
50	**513**	(475)	**481**	**75.9**	—	**63.1**	**85.5**	**68.5**	**55.0**	67	1760 (255)	**50**
49	**498**	(464)	**469**	**75.2**	—	**62.1**	**85.0**	**67.6**	**53.8**	66	1695 (246)	**49**
48	**484**	**451**	**455**	**74.7**	—	**61.4**	**84.5**	**66.7**	**52.5**	64	1635 (237)	**48**
47	**471**	**442**	**443**	**74.1**	—	**60.8**	**83.9**	**65.8**	**51.4**	63	1580 (229)	**47**
46	**458**	**432**	**432**	**73.6**	—	**60.0**	**83.5**	**64.8**	**50.3**	62	1530 (222)	**46**
45	**446**	**421**	**421**	**73.1**	—	**59.2**	**83.0**	**64.0**	**49.0**	60	1480 (215)	**45**
44	**434**	**409**	**409**	**72.5**	—	**58.5**	**82.5**	**63.1**	**47.8**	58	1435 (203)	**44**

43	**423**	**400**	**400**	**72.0**	—	**57.7**	**82.0**	**62.2**	**46.7**	57	1385 (201)	**43**
42	**412**	**390**	**390**	**71.5**	—	**56.9**	**81.5**	**61.3**	**45.5**	56	1340 (194)	**42**
41	**402**	**381**	**381**	**70.9**	—	**56.2**	**80.9**	**60.4**	**44.3**	55	1295 (188)	**41**
40	**392**	**371**	**371**	**70.4**	—	**55.4**	**80.4**	**59.5**	**43.1**	54	1250 (181)	**40**
39	**382**	**362**	**362**	**69.9**	—	**54.6**	**79.9**	**58.6**	**41.9**	52	1215 (176)	**39**
38	**372**	**353**	**353**	**69.4**	—	**53.8**	**79.4**	**57.7**	**40.8**	51	1180 (171)	**38**
37	**363**	**344**	**344**	**68.9**	—	**53.1**	**78.8**	**56.8**	**39.6**	50	1160 (168)	**37**
36	**354**	**336**	**336**	**68.4**	(109.0)	**52.3**	**78.3**	**55.9**	**38.4**	49	1115 (162)	**36**
35	**345**	**327**	**327**	**67.9**	(108.5)	**51.5**	**77.7**	**55.0**	**37.2**	48	1080 (157)	**35**
34	**336**	**319**	**319**	**67.4**	(108.0)	**50.8**	**77.2**	**54.2**	**36.1**	47	1055 (153)	**34**
33	**327**	**311**	**311**	**66.8**	(107.5)	**50.0**	**76.6**	**53.3**	**34.9**	46	1025 (149)	**33**
32	**318**	**301**	**301**	**66.3**	(107.0)	**49.2**	**76.1**	**52.1**	**33.7**	44	1000 (145)	**32**
31	**310**	**294**	**294**	**65.8**	(106.0)	**48.4**	**75.6**	**51.3**	**32.5**	43	980 (142)	**31**
30	**302**	**286**	**286**	**65.3**	(105.5)	**47.7**	**75.0**	**50.4**	**31.3**	42	950 (138)	**30**
29	**294**	**279**	**279**	**64.7**	(104.5)	**47.0**	**74.5**	**49.5**	**30.1**	41	930 (135)	**29**
28	**286**	**271**	**271**	**64.3**	(104.0)	**46.1**	**73.9**	**48.6**	**28.9**	41	910 (132)	**28**
27	**279**	**264**	**264**	**63.8**	(103.0)	**45.2**	**73.3**	**47.7**	**27.8**	40	880 (128)	**27**
26	**272**	**258**	**258**	**63.3**	(102.5)	**44.6**	**72.8**	**46.8**	**26.7**	38	860 (125)	**26**
25	**266**	**253**	**253**	**62.8**	(101.5)	**43.8**	**72.2**	**45.9**	**25.5**	38	840 (122)	**25**
24	**260**	**247**	**247**	**62.4**	(101.0)	**43.1**	**71.6**	**45.0**	**24.3**	37	825 (120)	**24**
23	**254**	**243**	**243**	**62.0**	100.0	**42.1**	**71.0**	**44.0**	**23.1**	36	805 (117)	**23**
22	**248**	**237**	**237**	**61.5**	99.0	**41.6**	**70.5**	**43.2**	**22.0**	35	785 (114)	**22**
21	**243**	**231**	**231**	**61.0**	98.5	**40.9**	**69.9**	**42.3**	**20.7**	35	770 (112)	**21**
20	**238**	**226**	**226**	**60.5**	97.8	**40.1**	**69.4**	**41.5**	**19.6**	34	760 (110)	**20**
(18)	230	219	219	—	96.7	—	—	—	—	33	730 (106)	(18)
(16)	222	212	212	—	95.5	—	—	—	—	32	705 (102)	(16)
(14)	213	203	203	—	93.9	—	—	—	—	31	675 (98)	(14)
(12)	204	194	194	—	92.3	—	—	—	—	29	650 (94)	(12)
(10)	196	187	187	—	90.7	—	—	—	—	28	620 (90)	(10)
(8)	188	179	179	—	89.5	—	—	—	—	27	600 (87)	(8)
(6)	180	171	171	—	87.1	—	—	—	—	26	580 (84)	(6)
(4)	173	165	165	—	85.5	—	—	—	—	25	550 (80)	(4)
(2)	166	158	158	—	83.5	—	—	—	—	24	530 (77)	(2)
(0)	160	152	152	—	81.7	—	—	—	—	24	515 (75)	(0)

* The values in this table shown in **boldface type** correspond to the values shown in the corresponding joint SAE-ASM-ASTM Committee on Hardness Conversions as printed in ASTM E 140, Table 1.

† Values in ( ) are beyond normal range and are given for information only.

SOURCE: Reprinted with permission, copyright 1992, Society of Automotive Engineers.

SAE/AISI 1055 through 1095 These are the high-carbon grades of carbon steel. Used for flat stampings, spring wire, cutting tools, flat springs, and many other high-strength applications. These steels are usually heat treated for their particular application and provide excellent wear resistance. Not recommended for welding applications.

Specific applications

SAE/AISI 1018 Low-carbon, medium-manganese steel. Quality bar for carburized parts: gears, shafts, bolts, pins, etc.

SAE/AISI 1035 Medium-carbon, special-quality steel used for bolts, nuts, shafts, pins, etc. Can be heat treated.

SAE/AISI 1045 Medium-carbon, special-quality steel used for shafts, axles, gears, splines, etc. Can be heat treated.

SAE/AISI 12L14 Low-carbon, resulfurized, rephosphorized, and leaded steel used for screw-machine parts such as studs, nuts, and various fasteners. Can be case hardened.

SAE/AISI 1215 Similar to 12L14 and low-carbon steel used for studs, nuts, and fasteners. Can be case hardened.

SAE/AISI 12L15 Leaded version of 1215 used for screw-machine parts. Can be case hardened.

SAE/AISI 1117 Low-carbon, resulfurized, free-cutting steel used for shafts, gears, pins, nuts, etc. Can be carburized.

SAE/AISI 11L17 Leaded version of 1117 used for screw-machine parts, gears, shafts, pins, etc. Can be carburized.

SAE/AISI 1141 Medium-carbon, resulfurized, free-cutting steel used for shafts, nuts, bolts, etc. Can be hardened by heat treatment.

SAE/AISI 4140 Medium-carbon chromium-molybdenum alloy steel used for studs, nuts, bolts, gears, wrenches, shafts, etc. Can be heat treated.

SAE/AISI 41L40 Leaded version of 4140, free-machining type. Can be heat treated.

SAE/AISI 4145 Medium-carbon chromium-molybdenum steel used for studs, nuts, shafts, wrenches, gears, bolts, etc. Can be heat treated.

SAE / AISI 41L45 Leaded version of 4145, free-machining type. Can be heat treated.

SAE / AISI 4620 Low-carbon nickel-molybdenum steel used for gears, cams, pinions, and shafts. Excellent carburizing grade.

SAE / AISI 46L20 Leaded version of 4620, free-machining type. Can be carburized.

SAE / AISI 8620 Low-carbon nickel-chromium-molybdenum alloy steel used for gears, cams, shafts, and pinions. Excellent carburizing grade.

SAE / AISI 86L20 Leaded version of 8620, free-machining type. Can be carburized.

SAE / AISI 4340 Medium-carbon nickel-chromium-molybdenum alloy steel used for gears and shafting. Has high hardenability.

SAE / AISI 8642 Similar to 4340. Has high hardenability.

EF 4130 Aircraft-quality alloy steel.

EF 4140 Aircraft-quality alloy steel.

E 4340, EF 4620, EF 8740, and E 9310 All aircraft-quality alloy steels.

Rather than going into a lengthy description of all the characteristics and heat-treating properties of all the various grades of carbon and alloy steels, the preceding tables shown can be used by the engineer or designer to determine strength, ductility, hardness, and heat-treatment temperatures for each SAE/AISI and ASTM steel listed. A metallurgist should be consulted prior to making a final design choice about the various steels used in important or critical applications.

Stainless steels: Uses by AISI number

Note: The SAE numbers for stainless steels listed in the preceding tables are typically known by their three-digit numbers, such as 201, 302, 304, 440, etc. The last three digits of the listed SAE numbers are the standard industry identification numbers and are used as such in the following usage summary.

Chromium-nickel stainless steels (austenitic)

201 Low nickel, good corrosion resistance. High work-hardening rate. Excellent weldability.

202 General-purpose type equivalent to 302.

203 EZ Superior machinability. Good corrosion resistance.

216 Most corrosion resistant of all chromium-nickel-manganese stainless steels.

301 High work-hardening rate. Used in structural applications where high strength and resistance to atmospheric corrosion are required.

302 General-purpose stainless steel with good strength properties. Resistant to many corrosive conditions.

303 Free-machining type used in corrosive atmospheres, strong chemical solutions, many organic chemicals, most dyes, nitric acid, and foods.

303 Pb Leaded version of 303 used for high-volume automatic machining operations.

304 Low-carbon variation of 302. Weldable with caution. Excellent resistance to a high number of corrosive conditions and chemicals.

304 L Extra-low-carbon version of 304. Low carbon content prevents carbide precipitation during welding, which can produce cracks at the weld joints. Excellent weldability.

305 Good fabrication stainless for spinning, deep-drawing, and cold-heading operations.

309 Used in high-temperature applications. Resistant to most acids.

310 Higher alloy content improves the basic characteristics. Improved over 309 and 304 for corrosion resistance.

316 Best corrosion resistance of the standard stainless steels. Resists pitting and most chemicals. Used for paper-mill machinery parts and photographic industry parts and containers. High-temperature strength.

316 L Low-carbon version of 316 which is more easily welded without carbide precipitation.

317 Higher alloy content than 316, providing more corrosion resistance.

321 This alloy is stabilized with titanium for weldments subject to severe corrosion. Excellent corrosion resistance to a wide variety of organic and inorganic substances.

347 Stabilized with Cb and Ta for use in the carbide precipitation range of 800 to 1500°F, with no impairment to corrosion resistance.

Chromium stainless steels (ferritic)

409 Developed for automotive muffler service and used in noncritical exterior parts. Economical and easily fabricated.

430 Most widely used of the nonhardenable types of chromium stainless steel. Good mechanical properties and heat resistance. Resistant to nitric acid, sulfur gases, and many organic chemicals, including foods.

430 F Free-machining version of 430. Similar in properties to 430.

446 High resistance to corrosion and scaling at high temperatures. Excellent in sulfuric atmospheres.

Chromium stainless steels (martensitic)

403 Excellent for highly stressed parts such as turbine blades. Good resistance to water and atmospheric corrosion.

405 Variation of 410 for improved weldability. Same corrosion resistance as 403.

410 Low-cost general-purpose stainless steel that is heat treatable. Used where corrosion is not severe.

410 S Same as 410 except lower carbon range for improved weldability.

414 Modification of 410 with more nickel to improve corrosion resistance. Can be heat treated to Rockwell C25 to C43.

416 Free-machining version of 410 with corrosion resistance to food acids, basic salts, water, and most atmospheric corrosion products.

440 A, B, C, and F Series of high-carbon stainless steels. All are the same basic composition except carbon content. Can be heat treated for high strength and high hardness. These steels are corrosion resistant only in the hardened conditions. 440 F is a free-machining type used in many applications.

Low-chromium stainless steels

PH13-8Mo

15-5PH

PH15-7Mo

17-4PH
17-7PH

All these grades provide excellent corrosion resistance similar to the austenitic stainless steels and are capable of being heat treated to various high-strength conditions with minimum distortion. They are generally furnished in the annealed condition for ease of machining. They develop their high-strength properties by aging at selected temperatures. They may be provided as vacuum arc–remelted steels for more demanding applications. They are used in many high-strength, anticorrosion applications. Among other uses, 17-7PH (ASTM A313) round wire is used for helical spring applications and 17-7PH (ASTM A693) strip is used for flat spring applications. (See Chap. 13 for other stainless steel spring materials and their ASTM/AISI designations.)

Identification of stainless steels. A method for determining whether a steel is stainless steel or carbon steel is as follows:

1. Make up a 7% to 8% aqueous solution of copper sulfate ($CuSO_4$). Use the proportion of 86 g copper sulfate per liter of water. Specific gravity = 1.08 g/ml, or 11^0 Bc′.
2. Clean a small area of the metal to be tested. All grease and residue must be removed. Lightly abrade the area if necessary.
3. Apply a few drops of the copper sulfate solution to the cleaned area on the test sample.
4. If the material is regular carbon steel or iron, a metallic copper film will form where the test solution contacts the sample. Stainless steel will show *no* copper deposit.
5. Applying a small magnet to the test sample will show the difference between austenitic and ferritic stainless steels, with ferritic materials being attracted to the magnet. Austenitic

stainless steels are normally nonmagnetic, although cold-worked austenitic stainless steels will show a very weak magnetic attraction. Also, hardened chromium stainless steels are magnetic.

Tool steels: SAE designations. Refer to Tables 5.36 to 5.39 for physical and chemical properties and heat treating procedures. Also see Chap. 9, "Tooling Practices."

Steel wire for spring applications. Tables 5.43 through 5.48 establish the physical properties for spring wire materials as listed by the SAE. (See also Chap. 13, "Springs.")

TABLE 5.43 Composition and Strength of Spring Wire

Element	%, by weight
Carbon	0.60–0.75*
Manganese	0.60–0.90*
Phosphorus	0.025 max
Sulfur	0.030 max
Silicon	0.15–0.30

Wire diameter, in	Tensile strength, 10^3 psi		Hardness		Reduction of area,† min, %
	Min	Max	Min	Max	
			R45N		
0.062 to 0.092 incl	240	260	52	57	N/A‡
Over 0.092 to 0.128 incl	235	255	51	56	45
			RC		
Over 0.128 to 0.162 incl	230	250	46	51	45
Over 0.162 to 0.192 incl	225	245	45	50	45
Over 0.192 to 0.225 incl	220	240	44	49	45
Over 0.225 to 0.250 incl	215	235	44	49	45

NOTE: Examination of the tensile fracture shall not show a coarse or cuppy condition.

* Carbon and manganese may be varied from the specified ranges by agreement between the manufacturer and the purchaser, provided the mechanical properties specified are maintained.

† The 45% minimum value is for as-received wire. A 40% minimum value is acceptable for wire produced at the mill when tested immediately after tempering.

‡ N/A—Reduction of area does not apply to 0.092 and below.

SOURCE: Reprinted with permission, copyright 1992, Society of Automotive Engineers.

(Text continued on page 235.)

TABLE 5.44 Composition and Strength of Spring Wire

Element	%, by weight
Carbon	0.48–0.53
Manganese	0.70–0.90
Phosphorus	0.020 max
Sulfur	0.035 max
Silicon	0.20–0.35
Chromium	0.80–1.10
Vanadium	0.15 min

Wire diameter, in	Tensile strength, 10^3 psi		Hardness*		Reduction of area,† min, %
	Min	Max	Min	Max	
			Rockwell 15N		
0.020	300	325	88.5	89.7	N/A‡
0.031	290	315	88.0	89.3	N/A‡
0.041	280	305	87.5	88.8	N/A‡
0.054	270	295	86.9	88.3	N/A‡
			Rockwell 45N		
0.062	265	290	57.9	61.4	N/A‡
0.080	255	275	56.4	59.4	N/A‡
0.106	245	265	55.0	57.9	45
			Rockwell C		
0.135	235	255	48	51	45
0.162	225	245	47	50	40
0.192	220	240	46	49	40
0.244	210	230	45	48	40
0.283	205	225	44	47	40
0.312	203	223	43	47	40
0.375	200	220	43	46	40
0.438	195	215	42	45	40
0.500	190	210	41	45	40

NOTE: Values for intermediate sizes may be interpolated.

* Hardness ranges indicated apply to finished springs and are subject to normal variations found in standard hardness testing procedures.

† The 45% and 40% minimum values are for as-received wire. These values may be decreased by five points when tested immediately after tempering.

‡ N/A—Reduction of area does not apply to wire under 0.106 in in diameter.

SOURCE: Reprinted with permission, copyright 1992, Society of Automotive Engineers.

TABLE 5.45 Composition and Strength of Spring Wire

Element	Class 1	Class 2
Carbon, %	0.45–0.75*	0.50–0.85*
Manganese, %	0.60–1.30†	0.60–1.30†
Phosphorous, % (max)	0.040	0.040
Sulfur, % (max)	0.050	0.050
Silicon, %	0.10–0.30	0.10–0.30

Wire diameter, in	Class 1 tensile strength,‡ 10^3 psi		Class 2 tensile strength,‡ 10^3 psi	
	Minimum	Maximum	Minimum	Maximum
0.020	283	323	324	364
0.023	279	319	320	360
0.026	275	315	316	356
0.029	271	311	312	352
0.032	266	306	307	347
0.035	261	301	302	342
0.041	255	293	294	332
0.048	248	286	287	325
0.054	243	279	280	316
0.062	237	272	273	308
0.072	232	266	267	301
0.080	227	261	262	296
0.092	220	253	254	287
0.106	216	248	249	281
0.120	210	241	242	273
0.135	206	237	238	269
0.148	203	234	235	266
0.162	200	230	231	261
0.177	195	225	226	256
0.192	192	221	222	251
0.207	190	218	219	247
0.225	186	214	215	243
0.250	182	210	211	239
0.312	174	200	201	227
0.375	167	193	194	220
0.438	165	190	191	216
0.500	156	180	181	205
0.531	154	178	179	203

* Carbon in any one lot should not vary more than 0.20%.

† Manganese in any one lot should not vary more than 0.30%.

‡ The tensile strength for intermediate sizes can be interpolated. The tensile fracture shall not show a coarse or cuppy condition.

SOURCE: Reprinted with permission, copyright 1992, Society of Automotive Engineers.

TABLE 5.46 Composition and Strength of Spring Wire

Element	%, by weight
Carbon	0.51–0.59
Manganese	0.60–0.80
Phosphorus	0.035 max
Sulfur	0.040 max
Silicon	1.20–1.60
Chromium	0.60–0.80

Wire diameter, in	Tensile strength, 10^3 psi		Hardness		Reduction of area,* min, %
	Min	Max	Min	Max	
			R 15N		
0.032	300	325	88.5	90.0	†
0.041	298	323	88.5	90.0	†
0.054	292	317	88.0	89.5	†
			R 45N		
0.062	290	315	59.5	63.0	†
0.080	285	310	59.0	62.0	†
0.092	280	305	58.5	61.5	45
0.120	275	300	57.5	61.0	45
			RC		
0.135	270	295	51.5	54.0	45
0.162	265	290	51.0	53.5	40
0.177	260	285	50.5	53.0	40
0.192	260	283	50.5	53.0	40
0.218	255	278	50.0	52.5	40
0.250	250	275	50.0	52.5	40
0.312	245	270	49.0	52.0	40
0.375	240	265	48.5	51.5	40
0.438	235	260	48.0	51.0	40

NOTE: Values for intermediate sizes may be interpolated.

* The reduction of area values are for as-received wire. These values may be decreased by 5 points when tested immediately after tempering.

† Reduction of area does not apply to wire under 0.092 in in diameter.

SOURCE: Reprinted with permission, copyright 1992, Society of Automotive Engineers.

TABLE 5.47 Composition and Strength of Spring Wire

Element	%, by weight
Carbon	0.15 max
Manganese	2.00 max
Silicon	1.00 max
Phosphorus	0.045 max
Sulfur	0.030 max
Chromium	17.00–19.00
Nickel	8.00–10.00

Wire diameter, in	Tensile strength, min, ksi	Tensile strength, max, ksi
0.009 and smaller	325	355
0.010	320	350
0.011	318	348
0.012	316	346
0.013	314	344
0.014	312	342
0.015	310	340
0.016	308	338
0.017	306	336
0.018	304	334
0.019 to 0.020 incl	300	330
Over 0.020 to 0.022 incl	296	326
Over 0.022 to 0.024 incl	292	322
Over 0.024 to 0.026 incl	289	319
Over 0.026 to 0.028 incl	286	316
Over 0.028 to 0.032 incl	277	307
Over 0.032 to 0.036 incl	273	303
Over 0.036 to 0.041 incl	269	299
Over 0.041 to 0.047 incl	262	292
Over 0.047 to 0.054 incl	260	290
Over 0.054 to 0.062 incl	255	285
Over 0.062 to 0.072 incl	250	280
Over 0.072 to 0.080 incl	245	275
Over 0.080 to 0.092 incl	240	270
Over 0.092 to 0.105 incl	232	262
Over 0.105 to 0.120 incl	225	255
Over 0.120 to 0.148 incl	210	240
Over 0.148 to 0.162 incl	205	235
Over 0.162 to 0.177 incl	195	225
Over 0.177 to 0.207 incl	185	215
Over 0.207 to 0.225 incl	180	210
Over 0.225 to 0.250 incl	175	205
Over 0.250 to 0.312 incl	160	190
Over 0.312 to 0.375 incl	140	170

SOURCE: Reprinted with permission, copyright 1992, Society of Automotive Engineers.

TABLE 5.48 Composition and Strength of Spring Wire

Element	%, by weight
Carbon	0.80–1.00*
Manganese	0.20–0.60*
Phosphorus	0.025 max
Sulfur	0.030 max
Silicon	0.10–0.30

Wire diameter, in	Tensile strength,† 10^3 psi Min	Tensile strength,† 10^3 psi Max	Wire diameter, in	Tensile strength,† 10^3 psi Min	Tensile strength,† 10^3 psi Max
0.004	439	485	0.055	300	331
0.005	426	471	0.059	296	327
0.006	415	459	0.063	293	324
0.007	407	449	0.067	290	321
0.008	399	441	0.072	287	317
0.009	393	434	0.076	284	314
0.010	387	428	0.080	282	312
0.011	382	422	0.085	279	308
0.012	377	417	0.090	276	305
0.013	373	412	0.095	274	303
0.014	369	408	0.100	271	300
0.015	365	404	0.102	270	299
0.016	362	400	0.107	268	296
0.018	356	393	0.110	267	295
0.020	350	387	0.112	266	294
0.022	345	382	0.121	263	290
0.024	341	377	0.125	261	288
0.026	337	373	0.130	259	286
0.028	333	368	0.135	258	285
0.030	330	365	0.140	256	283
0.032	327	361	0.145	254	281
0.034	324	358	0.150	253	279
0.036	321	355	0.156	251	277
0.038	318	352	0.162	249	275
0.040	315	349	0.177	245	270
0.042	313	346	0.192	241	267
0.045	309	342	0.207	238	264
0.048	306	339	0.225	235	260
0.051	303	335	0.250	230	255

* Carbon and manganese may be varied from the above specified ranges by the manufacturer, by agreement with the purchaser, provided the mechanical properties specified are maintained.

† The tensile strength may be interpolated for intermediate sizes. Higher tensile strength music spring wire is available.

SOURCE: Reprinted with permission, copyright 1992, Society of Automotive Engineers.

5.2 Aluminum and Aluminum Alloys

Aluminum and its alloys are among the most used metallic materials, with countless applications and an extremely broad range of physical and chemical properties. Pure aluminum is a silvery white metal, light in weight, nontoxic, and easily cast, forged, and machined. The pure metal was first isolated in the laboratory in 1827. The method of extracting the metal by electrolysis of alumina dissolved in cryolite was discovered by Hall in 1886 in the United States. This method is still in use today and is known as the *Hall process.* Aluminum in its natural forms is the third most abundant material in the earth's crust, exceeded only by oxygen and silicon.

Aluminum alloys are mandatory in many design applications of modern technologies. Many of the modern aluminum alloys are stronger than some steels on a volume basis and weigh only 34 percent (or one-third) as much as steel. The average density of aluminum alloys is 0.098 lb/in^3 and that of steel is 0.282 lb/in^3. The electrical conductivity of aluminum is 60 percent that of an equal cross-sectional area of copper, which is the second best conductor of electric current. In order of electrical conductivity, the best four elements are silver, copper, gold, and aluminum, respectively.

Tables 5.49 through 5.57 show the chemical and physical properties of all the present aluminum alloys. Also included are the typical uses for all the wrought and cast types of aluminum alloys in use today. Figure 5.3 shows part of the SAE Standard delineating alloy and temper designation systems for aluminum.

5.3 Copper and Copper Alloys

Copper and copper alloys are also among the most important and most used metallic materials. Almost all electrical components and electrical products contain parts made of copper or one or more of its important alloys. All the electrical industries worldwide are dependent on copper and copper alloys. Many new copper alloys have been developed within the past 30 or 40 years, with beryllium-copper alloys as one of the preferred materials in many electrical applications as a replacement for the phosphor bronzes. The phosphor, silicon, and manganese bronzes have many applications where strength and current-carrying ability, combined with corrosion resistance and nonmagnetic properties, are desired. Springs with a high fatigue-endurance limit and good electrical properties are made from the beryllium-copper alloys.

(Text continued on page 245.)

1. Scope—This standard provides systems for designating wrought aluminum and wrought aluminum alloys, aluminum and aluminum alloys in the form of castings and foundry ingot, and the tempers in which aluminum and aluminum alloy wrought products and aluminum alloy castings are produced.

2. Wrought Aluminum and Aluminum Alloy Designation System (see Note 5.1)—A system of four-digit numerical designations is used to identify wrought aluminum and wrought aluminum alloys. The first digit indicates the alloy group as shown in Table 1. The last two digits identify the aluminum alloy or indicate the aluminum purity. The second digit indicates modifications of the original alloy or impurity limits.

2.1 Aluminum—In the 1xxx group for minimum aluminum purities of 99.00% and greater, the last two of the four digits in the designation indicate the minimum aluminum percentage (Note 5.2). These digits are the same as the two digits to the right of the decimal point in the minimum aluminum percentage when it is expressed to the nearest 0.01%. The second digit in the designation indicates modifications in impurity limits. If the second digit in the designation is zero, it indicates that there is no special control on individual impurities; integers 1 through 9, which are assigned consecutively as needed, indicate special control of one or more individual impurities or alloying elements.

2.2 Aluminum Alloys—In the 2xxx through 8xxx alloy groups, the last two of the four digits in the designation have no special significance but serve only to identify the different aluminum alloys in the group. The second digit in the alloy designation indicates alloy modifications (Note 5.3). If the second digit in the designation is zero, it indicates the original alloy; integers 1 through 9, which are assigned consecutively, indicate alloy modifications.

2.3 Experimental Alloys—Experimental alloys are also designated in accordance with this system, but they are indicated by the prefix X. The prefix is dropped when the alloy is no longer experimental. During development and before they are designated as experimental, new alloys are identified by serial numbers assigned by their originators. Use of the serial number is discontinued when the X number is assigned.

2.4 National Variations—National variations (Note 5.4) of wrought aluminum and wrought aluminum alloys registered by another country in accordance with this system are identified by a serial letter (Note 5) before the numerical designation.

3. Cast Aluminum and Aluminum Alloy Designation System[1] (see Note 5.1)—A system of four-digit numerical designations is used to identify aluminum and aluminum alloys in the form of castings and foundry ingot. The first digit indicates the alloy group, as shown in Table 2. The second two digits identify the aluminum alloy or indicate the

[1] The castings and ingot alloy designation system described herein is not currently in use for some SAE cast aluminum alloys. It is applicable to Aluminum Association (AA) and American National Standard Institute (ANSI), and other, specification systems. Although the chemical composition limits shown in most SAE reports conform to the limits shown for comparable castings and ingots covered in AA and ANSI publications, the designation system described herein is not currently used in SAE Standards and Information Reports.

Figure 5.3 Alloy and temper designation systems for aluminum (SAE J993). (Report of Nonferrous Metals Committee approved July 1967 and last revised September 1973. Conforms to American National Standard H35, 1-1972. Reaffirmed January 1989.) (Reprinted with permission, copyright 1992, Society of Automotive Engineers.)

TABLE 1—DESIGNATION SYSTEM FOR WROUGHT ALUMINUM AND ALUMINUM ALLOY

Composition	Alloy No.
Aluminum, 99.0% min and greater	1xxx
Aluminum alloys grouped by major alloying element[a,b,c]	
Copper	2xxx
Manganese	3xxx
Silicon	4xxx
Magnesium	5xxx
Magnesium and silicon	6xxx
Zinc	7xxx
Other element	8xxx
Unused series	9xxx

[a] For codification purposes, an alloying element is any element which is intentionally added for any purpose other than grain refinement and for which minimum and maximum limits are specified.

[b]Standard limits for alloying elements and impurities are expressed to the following places:

Less than 1/1000%	0.000X
1/1000 up to 1/100%	0.00X
1/100 up to 1/10%	
Unalloyed aluminum made by a refining process	0.0XX
Alloys and unalloyed aluminum not made by a refining process	0.0X
1/10 through ½%	0.XX
Over ½%	0.X, X.X, etc.

[c] Standard limits for alloying elements and impurities are expressed in the following sequence: silicon; iron; copper; manganese; magnesium; chromium; nickel; zinc (Note 1); titanium; other elements (each); other elements (Total); aluminum (Note 2).

Note 1—Additional specified elements having limits are inserted in alphabetical order of their chemical symbols between zinc and titanium, or are specified in footnotes.

Note 2—Aluminum is specified as minimum for unalloyed aluminum, and as a remainder for aluminum alloys.

aluminum purity. The last digit, which is separated from the others by a decimal point, indicates the product form, that is, castings or ingot. A modification of the original alloy or impurity limits is indicated by a serial letter (Note 5.6) before the numerical designation.

3.1 Aluminum Castings and Ingot—In the 1xx.x group for minimum aluminum purities of 99.00% and greater, the second two of the four digits in the designation indicate the minimum aluminum percentage (Note 5.2).

These digits are the same as the two digits to the right of the decimal point in the minimum aluminum percentage when it is expressed to the nearest 0.01%. The last digit, which is to the right of the decimal point, indicates the product form: 1xx.0 indicates castings, and 1xx.1 indicates ingot. Special control of one or more individual elements other than aluminum is indicated by a serial letter (Note 5.6) before the numerical designation.

3.2 Aluminum Alloy Castings and Ingot—In the 2xx.x through 9xx.x alloy groups, the second two of the four digits in the designation have no special significance but serve only to identify the different aluminum alloys in the group. The last digit, which is to the right of the decimal point, indicates the product form: xxx.0 indicates castings, xxx.1 indicates ingot which has chemical composition limits conforming to paragraph 3.2.1, and xxx.2 indicates ingot which has chemical com-

Figure 5.3 *(Continued)*

TABLE 2—DESIGNATION SYSTEM FOR CAST ALUMINUM AND ALUMINUM ALLOY

Composition	Alloy No.
Aluminum, 99.00% min and greater	1xx.x
Aluminum alloy group by major alloying element[a b c]	
Copper	2xx.x
Silicon, with added copper and/or magnesium	3xx.x
Silicon	4xx.x
Magnesium	5xx.x
Zinc	7xx.x
Tin	8xx.x
Other element	9xx.x
Unused series	6xx.x

[a] For codification purposes, an alloying element is any element which is intentionally added for any purpose other than grain refinement and for which minimum and maximum limits are specified.

[b] Standard limits for alloying elements and impurities are expressed to the following places:

Less than 1/1000%	0.000X
1/1000 up to 1/100%	0.00X
1/100 up to 1/10%	
Unalloyed aluminum made by a refining process	0.0XX
Alloys and unalloyed aluminum not made by a refining process	0.0X
1/10 through ½%	0.XX
Over ½%	0.X, X.X, etc.

[c] Standard limits for alloying elements and impurities are expressed in the following sequence: silicon; iron; copper; manganese; magnesium; chromium; nickel; zinc (Note 1); titanium; other elements (each); other elements (Total); aluminum (Note 2).

Note 1—Additional specified elements having limits are inserted in alphabetical order of their chemical symbols between zinc and titanium, or are specified in footnotes.

Note 2—Aluminum is specified as minimum for unalloyed aluminum, and as a remainder for aluminum alloys.

position limits that differ but fall within the limits for xxx.1 ingot. Alloy modifications (Note 5.3) are indicated by a serial letter (Note 5.9) before the numerical designation.

3.2.1 Limits for alloying elements and impurities for xxx.1 ingot are the same as for the alloy in the form of castings, except for the limits noted in Table 3.

3.3 Experimental Alloys—Experimental alloys are also designated in accordance with this system, but they are indicated by the prefix X. The prefix is dropped when the alloy is no longer experimental. During development and before they are designated as experimental, new alloys are identified by serial numbers assigned by their originators. Use of the serial number is discontinued when the X number is assigned.

4. Temper Designation System—The temper designation system is used for all forms of wrought and cast aluminum and aluminum alloys except ingot. It is based on the sequences of basic treatments used to produce the various tempers. The temper designation follows the alloy designation, the two being separated by a hyphen. Basic temper designations consist of letters. Subdivisions of the basic tempers, where required, are indicated by one or more digits following the letter. These designate specific sequences of basic treatments: but only operations recognized as significantly influencing the characteristics of the product are indicated. Should some other variation of the same sequence of ba-

Figure 5.3 *(Continued)*

TABLE 3

Element, %	For Castings	For Ingot
Iron, max	Sand and permanent mold:	
	Up thru 0.15	0.03 less than castings
	Over 0.15 thru 0.25	0.05 less than castings
	Over 0.25 thru 0.6	0.10 less than castings
	Over 0.6 thru 1.0	0.2 less than castings
	Over 1.0	0.3 less than castings
	Die	
	Up thru 1.3	0.3 less than castings
	Over 1.3	1.1 maximum
Magnesium, min	All	
	Less than 0.50	0.05 more than castings°
	0.5 and greater	0.1 more than castings°
Zinc, max	Die	
	Over 0.25 thru 0.6	0.10 less than castings
	Over 0.6	0.1 less than castings

°Applicable only when the specified magnesium range for castings is greater than 0.15%.

sic operations be applied to the same alloy, resulting in different characteristics, then additional digits are added to the designation.

4.1 Basic Temper Designations

F As Fabricated—Applies to the products of shaping processes in which no special control over thermal conditions or strain-hardening is employed. For wrought products, there are no mechanical property limits.

O Annealed (Wrought Products Only)—Applies to wrought products which are fully annealed to obtain the lowest strength condition.

H Strain Hardened (Wrought Products Only)—Applies to products which have their strength increased by strain-hardening, with or without supplementary thermal treatments to produce some reduction in strength. The H is always followed by two or more digits.

W Solution Heat-Treated—An unstable temper applicable only to alloys which spontaneously age at room temperature after solution heat-treatment. This designation is specific only when the period of natural aging is indicated; for example, W ½ h.

T Thermally Treated To Produce Stable Tempers Other Than **F, O,** or **H**—Applies to products which are thermally treated, with or without supplementary strain-hardening, to produce stable tempers. The T is always followed by one or more digits.

4.2 Subdivisions of Basic Tempers

4.2.1 Subdivisions of H Temper: Strain Hardened

4.2.1.1 The first digit following the H indicates the specific combination of basic operations, as follows:

H1 Strain Hardened Only—Applies to products which are strain hardened to obtain the desired strength without supplementary thermal treatment. The number following this designation indicates the degree of strain hardening.

H2 Strain Hardened and Partially Annealed—Applies to products which are strain hardened more than the desired final

Figure 5.3 *(Continued)*

amount and then reduced in strength to the desired level by partial annealing. For alloys that age soften at room temperature, the H2 tempers have the same minimum ultimate tensile strength as the corresponding H3 tempers. For other alloys, the H2 tempers have the same minimum ultimate tensile strength as the corresponding H1 tempers and slightly higher elongation. The number following this designation indicates the degree of strain hardening remaining after the product has been partially annealed.

H3 STRAIN HARDENED AND STABILIZED—Applies to products which are strain hardened and whose mechanical properties are stabilized by a low-temperature thermal treatment which results in slightly lowered tensile strength and improved ductility. This designation is applicable only to those alloys which, unless stabilized, gradually age soften at room temperature. The number following this designation indicates the degree of strain hardening before the stabilization treatment.

4.2.1.2 The digit following the designations H1, H2, and H3 indicates the degree of strain hardening. Numeral 8 has been assigned to indicate tempers having an ultimate tensile strength equivalent to that achieved by a cold reduction (temperature during reduction not to exceed 120°F (49°C) of approximately 75% following a full anneal. Tempers between 0 (annealed) and 8 are designated by numerals 1 through 7. Material having an ultimate tensile strength about midway between that of the 0 temper and that of the 8 temper is designated by the numeral 4; about midway between the 0 and 4 tempers by the numeral 2; and about midway between the 4 and 8 tempers by the numeral 6. Numeral 9 designates tempers whose minimum ultimate tensile strength exceeds that of the 8 temper by 2.0 ksi (14 MPa) or more. For two-digit H tempers whose second digit is odd, the standard limits for ultimate tensile strength are exactly midway between those of the adjacent two-digit H tempers whose second digits are even.

NOTE: For alloys which cannot be cold reduced, an amount sufficient to establish an ultimate tensile strength applicable to the 8 temper (75% cold reduction after full anneal), the 6 temper tensile strength may be established by a cold reduction of approximately 55% following a full anneal, or the 4 temper tensile strength may be established by a cold reduction of approximately 35% after a full anneal.

4.2.1.3 The third digit (Note 10), when used, indicates a variation of a two-digit temper. It is used when the degree of control of temper or the mechanical properties are different from, but close to, those for the two-digit H temper designation to which it is added, or when some other characteristic is significantly affected. (See Appendix for three-digit H tempers.)

NOTE: The minimum ultimate tensile strength of a three-digit H temper is at least as close to that of the corresponding two-digit H temper as it is to the adjacent two-digit H tempers.

4.2.2 SUBDIVISIONS OF T TEMPER: THERMALLY TREATED

4.2.2.1 Numerals 1 through 10 following the T indicate specific sequences of basic treatments, as follows (Note 5.8):

T1 COOLED FROM AN ELEVATED TEMPERATURE SHAPING PROCESS AND NATURALLY AGED TO A SUBSTANTIALLY STABLE CONDITION—Applies to products for which the rate of cooling from an elevated temperature shaping process, such as casting or ex-

Figure 5.3 *(Continued)*

trusion, is such that their strength is increased by room temperature aging.

T2 ANNEALED (CAST PRODUCTS ONLY)—Applies to cast products which are annealed to improve ductility and dimensional stability.

T3 SOLUTION HEAT TREATED AND THEN COLD WORKED—Applies to products which are cold worked to improve strength, or in which the effect of cold work in flattening or straightening is recognized in mechanical property limits.

T4 SOLUTION HEAT TREATED AND NATURALLY AGED TO A SUBSTANTIALLY STABLE CONDITION—Applies to products which are not cold worked after solution heat treatment, or in which the effect or cold work in flattening or straightening may not be recognized in mechanical property limits.

T5 COOLED FROM AN ELEVATED TEMPERATURE SHAPING PROCESS AND THEN ARTIFICIALLY AGED—Applies to products which are cooled from an elevated temperature shaping process, such as casting or extrusion, and then artificially aged to improve mechanical properties or dimensional stability or both.

T6 SOLUTION HEAT TREATED AND THEN ARTIFICIALLY AGED—Applies to products which are not cold worked after solution heat treatment, or in which the effect of cold work in flattening or straightening may not be recognized in mechanical property limits.

T7 SOLUTION HEAT TREATED AND THEN STABILIZED—Applies to products which are stabilized to carry them beyond the point of maximum strength to provide control of some special characteristics.

T8 SOLUTION HEAT TREATED, COLD WORKED, AND THEN ARTIFICIALLY AGED—Applies to products which are cold worked to improve strength, or in which the effect of cold work in flattening or straightening is recognized in mechanical property limits.

T9 SOLUTION HEAT TREATED, ARTIFICIALLY AGED, AND THEN COLD WORKED—Applies to products which are cold worked to improve strength.

T10 COOLED FROM AN ELEVATED TEMPERATURE SHAPING PROCESS, ARTIFICIALLY AGED, AND THEN COLD WORKED—Applies to products which are artificially aged after cooling from an elevated temperature shaping process, such as casting or extrusion, and then cold worked to improve strength further.

4.2.2.2 Additional digits (Note 5.9), the first of which shall not be zero, may be added to designations T1 through T10 to indicate a variation in treatment which significantly alters the characteristics of the product. (See Appendix for specific additional digits for T tempers.)

5. Notes

5.1 Producers of wrought aluminum and wrought aluminum alloys, and aluminum and aluminum alloy castings and foundry ingot, may register chemical composition limits and designations conforming to this standard with the Aluminum Association (AA) provided the aluminum or aluminum alloy is offered for sale, the complete chemical composition limits are registered, and the composition is significantly different from that of any aluminum or aluminum alloy for which a numerical designation already has been assigned. A numerical designation

Figure 5.3 *(Continued)*

assigned in conformance with this standard should be used only to indicate an aluminum or aluminum alloy having chemical composition limits identical to those registered with AA for that aluminum or aluminum alloy.

5.2 The aluminum content for unalloyed aluminum made by a refining process is the difference between 100.000% and the sum of all other metallic elements present in amounts of 0.0010% or more each, expressed to the third decimal; for unalloyed aluminum not made by a refining process, it is the difference between 100.00% and the sum of all other metallic elements present in amounts of 0.010% or more each, expressed to the second decimal.

5.3 A modification of the original alloy is limited to any one or a combination of the following:

(a) Change of not more than the following amounts in the arithmetic mean of the limits for an alloying element:

Arithmetic Mean of Limits for Alloying Elements in Original Alloy, %	Maximum Change, %
Up thru 1.0	0.15
Over 1.0 thru 2.0	0.20
Over 2.0 thru 3.0	0.25
Over 3.0 thru 4.0	0.30
Over 4.0 thru 5.0	0.35
Over 5.0 thru 6.0	0.40
Over 6.0	0.50

To determine compliance when limits are specified for a combination of two or more elements in one alloy composition, the mean of such a combination should be compared to the sum of the mean values of the same individual elements, or any combination thereof, in another alloy composition.

(b) Addition or deletion of not more than one alloying element with limits having an arithmetic mean of not more than 0.30%.

(c) Substitution of one alloying element for another element serving the same purpose.

(d) Change in limits for impurities.

(e) Change in limits for grain refining elements.

(f) Distinctive iron or silicon limits, or both, reflecting high purity base metal.

An alloy shall not be registered as a modification if it meets the requirements for a national variation.

5.4 A national variation has composition limits which are similar but not identical to those registered by another country, with differences such as:

(a) Differences in the arithmetic mean of limits for alloying elements not exceeding the following amounts:

Arithmetic Mean of Limits for Alloying Elements in Original Alloy or Modification, %	Maximum Difference, %
Up thru 1.0	0.15
Over 1.0 thru 2.0	0.20
Over 2.0 thru 3.0	0.25
Over 3.0 thru 4.0	0.30
Over 4.0 thru 5.0	0.35
Over 5.0 thru 6.0	0.40
Over 6.0	0.50

Figure 5.3 *(Continued)*

To determine compliance when limits are specified for a combination of two or more elements in one alloy composition, the mean of such a combination should be compared to the sum of the mean values of the same individual elements, or any combination thereof, in another alloy composition.

(b) Substitution of one alloying element for another element serving the same purpose.

(c) Different limits on impurities except for low iron. Low iron, reflecting high purity base metal, should be considered an alloy modification. See paragraph 5.3 (f).

(d) Different limits on grain refining elements.

(e) Inclusion of a minimum limit for iron or silicon, or both.

Wrought aluminum and wrought aluminum alloys meeting these requirements shall not be registered as a new alloy or alloy modification.

5.5 The serial letters are assigned internationally in alphabetical sequence starting with A but omitting I, O, and Q.

5.6 The serial letters are assigned in alphabetical sequence starting with A but omitting I, O, Q, and X, the X being reserved for experimental alloys.

5.7 Numerals 1 through 9 may be arbitrarily assigned as the third digit and registered with AA for an alloy and product to indicate a variation of a two-digit H temper provided the temper is used or is available for use by more than one user, mechanical property limits are registered, the characteristics of the temper are significantly different from those of all other tempers which have the same sequence of basic treatments and for which designations already have been assigned for the same alloy and product, and the following are also registered if characteristics other than mechanical properties are considered significant: (a) test methods and limits for the characteristics, or (b) the specific practices used to produce the temper. Zero has been assigned to indicate variations negotiated between the manufacturer and purchaser which are not used widely enough to justify registration.

5.8 A period of natural aging at room temperature may occur between or after the operations listed for tempers T3 through T10. Control of this period is exercised when it is metallurgically important.

5.9 Additional digits may be arbitrarily assigned and registered with AA for an alloy and product to indicate a variation of tempers T1 through T10 provided the temper is used or is available for use by more than one user; mechanical property limits are registered, the characteristics of the temper are significantly different from those of all other tempers which have the same sequence of basic treatments and for which designations already have been assigned for the same alloy and product, and the following are also registered if characteristics other than mechanical properties are considered significant: a. test methods and limits for the characteristics, or b. the specific practices used to provide the temper. Variations in treatment which do not alter the characteristics of the product are considered alternate treatments for which additional digits are not assigned.

APPENDIX

A1. Three-Digit H Tempers

A1.1 The following three-digit H temper designations have been assigned for wrought products in all alloys:

Figure 5.3 *(Continued)*

H111 Applies to products which are strain hardened less than the amount required for a controlled H11 temper.

H112 Applies to products which acquire some temper from shaping processes not having special control over the amount of strain hardening or thermal treatment, but for which there are mechanical property limits.

A1.2 The following three-digit H temper designations have been assigned for wrought products in alloys containing over a nominal 4% magnesium.

H311 Applies to products which are strain hardened less than the amount required for a controlled H31 temper.

H321 Applies to products which are strain hardened less than the amount required for a controlled H32 temper.

H323
H343 Applies to products which are specially fabricated to have acceptable resistance to stress corrosion cracking.

A1.3 The following three-digit H temper designations have been assigned for:

Patterned or Embossed Sheet	Fabricated from
H114	0 temper
H124, H224, H324	H11, H21, H31 temper, respectively
H134, H234, H334	H12, H22, H32 temper, respectively
H144, H244, H344	H13, H23, H33 temper, respectively
H154, H254, H354	H14, H24, H34 temper, respectively
H164, H264, H364	H15, H25, H35 temper, respectively
H174, H274, H374	H16, H26, H36 temper, respectively
H184, H284, H384	H17, H27, H37 temper, respectively
H194, H294, H394	H18, H28, H38 temper, respectively
H195, H295, H395	H19, H29, H39 temper, respectively

A2. Additional Digits for T Tempers

A2.1 The following specific additional digits have been assigned for stress-relieved tempers of wrought products:

T51 Stress Relieved by Stretching—Applies to the following products when stretched the indicated amounts after solution heat treatment or cooling from an elevated temperature shaping process.

Product	Stretch, Permanent Set, %
Plate	1.5-3
Rod, bar, shapes extruded tube	1-3
Drawn tube	0.5-3

Applies directly to plate and rolled or cold-finished rod and bar. These products receive no further straightening after stretching.

Applies to extruded rod, bar, shapes, and tube and to drawn tube when designated as follows:

T510 Products that receive no further straightening after stretching.

T511 Products that may receive minor straightening after stretching to comply with standard tolerances.

T52 Stress Relieved by Compressing—Applies to products which are stress relieved by compressing after solution heat treat-

Figure 5.3 (*Continued*)

ment, or cooling from an elevated temperature shaping process to produce a permanent set of 1-5%.

T54 STRESS RELIEVED BY COMBINED STRETCHING AND COMPRESSING—Applies to die forgings which are stress relieved by restriking cold in the finish die.

A2.2 The following temper designations have been assigned for wrought products heat treated from O or F temper to demonstrate response to heat-treatment.

T42 SOLUTION HEAT TREATED FROM THE O OR F TEMPER—To demonstrate response to heat treatment, and naturally aged to a substantially stable condition.

T62 SOLUTION HEAT TREATED FROM THE O OR F TEMPER—To demonstrate response to heat treatment, and artificially aged.

Temper designations T42 and T62 may also be applied to wrought products heat treated from any temper by the user when such heat treatment results in the mechanical properties applicable to these tempers.

Figure 5.3 *(Continued)*

One of the most important uses for copper is in the electric power distribution industries, where ETP no. 110 copper bus conductors are used to carry the electric power for all electrical applications. The power-distribution industries use such equipment as transformers, power stations, power-transmission lines, and electrical switch gear and control equipment. The electric motor industries are another large user of copper products.

Copper is one of the most important elements, with a specific gravity of 8.96 g/cm^3 and weight of 0.324 lb/in^3. It is the second-best conductor of electric current, exceeded only by silver. The copper metal is smelted from the oxide, sulfide, and carbonate compounds which are found in their natural states as cuprite, malachite, azurite, and bornite. The most important compounds are the oxides and the sulfates (blue vitriol), the latter being used for agricultural poisons and water purification.

Tables 5.58 through 5.63 list the chemical compositions, physical properties, and uses for the many alloys of copper. Tables 5.64 and 5.65 list the standard specifications for brass sheet, strip, plate, and rolled bar (ASTM B-36). Tables 5.66 and 5.67 list the standard specifications for phosphor bronze plate, sheet, strip, and rolled bar (ASTM B-103). Tables 5.68 and 5.69 list the standard specifications for phosphor bronze rod, bar, and shapes (ASTM B-139). Tables

(Text continued on page 276.)

TABLE 5.49 Chemical Composition Limits[a,b]

AA no.	UNC no.	Si	Fe	Cu	Mn	Mg	Cr	Zn		Ti	Other[c]		Aluminum[e]
											Each	Total[d]	min
1100	A91100	0.95	Si + Fe	0.05–0.20	0.05	—	—	0.10	—	—	0.05	0.15	99.0
2017	A92017	0.20–0.8	0.7	3.5–4.5	0.40–1.0	0.40–0.8	0.10	0.25	—	0.15	0.05	0.15	Remainder
2024	A92024	0.50	0.50	3.8–4.9	0.30–0.9	1.2–1.8	0.10	0.25	—	0.15	0.05	0.15	
2036	A92036	0.50	0.50	2.2–3.0	0.10–0.40	0.30–0.6	0.10	0.25	—	0.15	0.05	0.15	
2038	A92038	0.50–1.3	0.6	0.8–1.8	0.10–0.40	0.40–1.0	0.20	0.50	0.05V–0.05Ga	0.15	0.05	0.15	
2117	A92117	0.8	0.7	2.2–3.0	0.20	0.20–0.50	0.10	0.25	—	—	0.05	0.15	
3002	A93002	0.08	0.10	0.15	0.05–0.25	0.05–0.20	—	0.05	0.05V	0.03	0.03	0.10	
3003	A93003	0.6	0.7	0.05–0.20	1.0–1.5	—	—	0.10	—	—	0.05	0.15	
3004	A93004	0.30	0.7	0.25	1.0–1.5	0.8–1.3	—	0.25	—	—	0.05	0.15	
5005	A95005	0.30	0.7	0.20	0.20	0.50–1.1	0.10	0.25	—	—	0.05	0.15	
5052	A95052	0.25	0.40	0.10	0.10	2.2–2.8	0.15–0.35	0.10	—	—	0.05	0.15	
5083	A95083	0.40	0.40	0.10	0.40–1.0	4.0–4.9	0.05–0.25	0.25	—	0.15	0.05	0.15	
5086	A95086	0.40	0.50	0.10	0.20–0.7	3.5–4.5	0.05–0.25	0.25	—	0.15	0.05	0.15	
5182	A95182	0.20	0.35	0.15	0.20–0.50	4.0–5.0	0.10	0.25	—	0.10	0.05	0.15	
5252	A95252	0.08	0.10	0.10	0.10	2.2–2.8	—	0.05	0.05V	—	0.03	0.10	
5454	A95454	0.25	0.40	0.10	0.50–1.0	2.4–3.0	0.05–0.20	0.25	—	0.20	0.05	0.15	
5457	A95457	0.08	0.10	0.20	0.15–0.45	0.8–1.2	—	0.05	0.05V	—	0.03	0.10	
5657	A95657	0.08	0.10	0.10	0.03	0.6–1.0	—	0.05	0.05V–0.3Ga	—	0.02	0.05	
6009	A96009	0.6–1.0	0.50	0.15–0.6	0.20–0.8	0.40–0.8	0.10	0.25	—	0.10	0.05	0.15	
6010	A96010	0.8–1.2	0.50	0.15–0.6	0.20–0.8	0.6–1.0	0.10	0.25	—	0.10	0.05	0.15	
6053	A96053	[f]	0.35	0.10	—	1.1–1.4	0.15–0.35	0.10	—	—	0.05	0.15	
6061	A96061	0.40–0.8	0.7	0.15–0.40	0.15	0.8–1.2	0.04–0.35	0.25	—	0.15	0.05	0.15	
6063	A96063	0.20–0.6	0.35	0.10	0.10	0.45–0.9	0.10	0.10	—	0.10	0.05	0.15	
6111	A96111	0.7–1.1	0.40	0.50–0.9	0.15–0.45	0.50–1.0	0.10	0.15	—	0.10	0.05	0.15	
6463	A96463	0.20–0.6	015	0.20	0.05	0.45–0.9	—	0.05	—	—	0.05	0.15	
7021	A97021	0.25	0.40	0.25	0.10	1.2–1.8	0.05	5.0–6.0	0.08–0.18Zr	0.10	0.05	0.15	

7029	A97029	0.10	0.12	0.50–0.9	0.03	1.3–2.0	—	4.2–5.2	0.05V	0.05	0.03	0.10
7116	A97116	0.15	0.30	0.50–1.1	0.05	0.8–1.4	—	4.2–5.2	0.05V–0.03Ga	0.05	0.05	0.15
7129	A97129	0.15	0.30	0.50–0.9	0.10	1.3–2.0	0.10	4.2–5.2	0.05V–0.03Ga	0.05	0.05	0.15

[a] Composition in percent maximum unless shown as a range.

[b] For purposes of determining conformance to these limits, an observed value or a calculated value obtained from analysis is rounded off to the nearest unit in the last right-hand place of figures used in expressing the specified limit in accordance with the rounding-off method of ASTM E29.

[c] Analysis is required for elements other than aluminum for which specific limits are shown. Analysis for other elements is made when their presence is suspected to be, or in the course of routine analysis is indicated to be, in excess of the specified limits.

[d] Other elements total is the sum of those other metallic elements 0.010% or more, each expressed to the second decimal before determining the sum.

[e] The aluminum content for unalloyed aluminum not made by a refining process is the difference between 100.0% and the sum of all other metallic elements present in amounts of 0.010% or more each expressed to the second decimal before determining the sum.

[f] 45–65% of actual Mg.

SOURCE: Reprinted with permission, copyright 1992, Society of Automotive Engineers.

TABLE 5.50 Typical Heat Treatments for Aluminum Alloy Mill Products[a]

Alloy	Product	Solution heat treatment[b]		Precipitation heat treatment		
		Metal temperature[c] °C	Temper designation	Metal temperature[c] °C	Approx. time of temperature,[d] h	Temper designation
2036	Sheet	[e]	T4			
2038	Sheet	[e]	T4			
6009	Sheet	[e]	T4	200–210	1	T6[f]
6010	Sheet	[e]	T4	200–210	1	T6[f]
6061	Sheet	515–550	T4	155–165	18	T6
	Plate	515–550	T451	155–165	18	T651
	Extrusions, tube, rod, bar forgings	515–550[g]	T4	170–180	8	T6
6063	Extrusions, tube	[g]	T1	175–185[h]	3	T5
		515–525[g]	T4	170–180[i]	8	T6
6111	Sheet	[e]	T4	200–210	1	T6
6463	Extrusions	[g]	T1	175–185[h]	3	T5
		515–525[g]	T4	170–180[i]	8	T6
				[l]	[l]	T61
7021	Sheet	395–405[j]	W			
7029	Extrusions	480–520[k]	W	[m]	[m]	T5, T6
7116	Extrusions	425–540	W	[n]	[n]	T5
7129	Extrusions	480–520	S	[m]	[m]	T5, T6

[a] The times and temperatures shown are typical for various forms, sizes, and methods of manufacture and may not exactly describe the optimum treatment for a specific item.

[b] Material should be quenched in water or by high-velocity fans from the solution heat-treating temperature as rapidly as possible and with minimum delay after removal from the furnace. Unless otherwise indicated, when material is quenched by total immersion in water, the water should be at room

temperature and suitably cooled to remain below 35°C during the quench cycle. The use of high-velocity, high-volume jets of cold water is also effective for some material.

[c] The metal temperature should be attained as rapidly as possible. Where a temperature range exceeding 10°C is shown, a temperature range of 10° within the listed range should be selected and maintained during the time at temperature.

[d] The time at temperature will depend on the time required for load to reach temperature. The times shown are based on rapid heating with soaking time measured from the time the load reaches the 10°C range listed or selected.

[e] These alloys are supplied in the solution heat-treated condition. For optimum properties, subsequent reheat treatment is not recommended.

[f] Mechanical properties of material will meet tensile property limits of T6 temper as specified in Table 5.51.

[g] By suitable control of extrusion temperature, product may be quenched directly from extrusion press to provide specified properties for this temper. Some products may be adequately quenched in air blast at room temperature.

[h] An alternate treatment comprised of 1–2 h at 200–210°C may be used.

[i] An alternate treatment comprised of 6 h at 175–185°C may be used.

[j] Quenched at a minimum average cooling rate of 35°C/s as measured over the range 385–205°C.

[k] 10-min soak at temperature followed by cold water quench.

[l] A minimum of 8 h at room temperature followed by 2 h at 95–105°C plus 4 h at 155–165°C.

[m] 5 h at 95–105°C plus 5 h at 155–165°C.

[n] 5 h at 95–105°C plus 5 h at 160–170°C.

SOURCE: Reprinted with permission, copyright 1992, Society of Automotive Engineers.

TABLE 5.51 Typical Mechanical Properties and Comparative Characteristics

	Typical mechanical properties[a,c]									Comparative characteristics					
	Tension			Shear	Fatigue	Modulus	Resistance to corrosion					Weldability[q]		
	Strength		Elongation											
Alloy and temper[b]	Ultimate, MPa	Yield 0.2% offset, MPa	Percent in 50 mm (1.60 mm thick specimen)	Ultimate shearing strength, MPa	Endurance limit, MPa	Modulus[g] of elasticity, MPa × 10°	General[h]	Stress-corrosion cracking[i]	Toughness[n]	Workability (cold)[p]	Machinability[p]	Gas	Arc	Resistance spot and seam
1100-0	90	35	35	60	35[d]	69	A	A		A	E	A	A	B
2017-T4	425	275	20[k]	260	125[d]	75	D	C		C	B	N/A	N/A	N/A
2024-T4	470	325	20	285	140[d]	73	D	C		C	B	N/A	N/A	N/A
2036-T4	340	195	24	205	125[e]	71	C	A2[l]	A	B	C	—	B	B
2038-T4	325	170	25	205	125[e]	71	C	A2[l]		B	C	—	B	B
2117-T4	295	165	24[k]	195	95[d]	71	C	A		B	C	N/A	N/A	N/A
3002-0	95	40	33	70		69	A	A		A	E	A	A	B
3003-H14, H24	150	145	8	95	60[d]	69	A	A		B	D	A	A	A
3004-0	180	70	20	110	95[d]	69	A	A	B	A	D	B	A	B
-H32	215	170	10	115	105[d]	69	A	A		B	D	B	A	A
5005-0	125	40	25	75		69	A	A		A	E	A	A	B
5052-0	195	90	25	125	110[d]	70	A	A	A	A	D	A	A	B
-H32	230	195	12	140	115[d]	70	A	A		B	D	A	A	A
-H34	260	215	10	145	125[d]	70	A	A	B	B	C	A	A	A
5083-H321, H116	315	230	14[k]		160[d]	71	A	B		C	D	C	A	A
5086-H32	290	205	12			71	A	A		B	D	C	A	A
-H34	325	255	10		185[d]	71	A	B		B	C	C	A	A
-H112	270	130	14			71	A	A		A	D	C	A	B
5182-0	275	130	21	165	140[e]	71	A-B	A2[m]		A	D	C	A	B
-02	270	125	23			71	A-B	A2[m]		A	D	C	A	B
5252-H25	235	170	11	145		69	A	A		B	C	A	A	A
5454-0	250	115	22	160		70	A	A	A	A	D	C	A	B
-H32	275	205	10	165		70	A	A		B	D	C	A	A
-H34	305	240	10	180		70	A	A	B	B	C	C	A	A
5457-H25	180	160	12	110		69	A	A		A	E	A	A	B
5657-H25	160	140	12	95		69	A	A		B	D	A	A	A

6009-T4	220	125	25	150	115[e]	69	B	A2	A	A	C	A	A	A
6010-T4	290	165	24	195	125[e]	69	B	A2	A	B	C	A	A	A
6053-T61						69	A	A	—	—	C	N/A	N/A	N/A
6061-T4	240	145	22	165	95[d]	69	B	B	A	B	C	A	A	A
-T6, T651	310	275	12	205	95[d]	69	B	A	B	C	C	A	A	A
6063-T1	150	90	20	95	60[d]	69	A	A		B	D	A	A	A
-T5	185	145	12	115	70[d]	69	A	A		B	C	A	A	A
-T6	240	215	12	150	70[d]	69	A	A		C	C	A	A	A
6111-T1	290	160	26		69	69	B	A2	A	B	C	A	A	B
6463-T521	185	145	12			69	A	A		B	C	A	A	A
7021-T61	430	380	13		140[d]	71	B	A2[j]						
7029-T5, T6	430	380	15	270		70	B	A2[j]						
7116-T5	360	315	16				B	A1[j]		C				
7129-T6	430	380	15	270	145[f]	70	B	A2[j]						

[a] Typical properties are not guaranteed since in most cases they are averages for various sizes, product forms and methods of manufacture and may not be exactly representative of any particular product or size. These data are intended only as a basis for comparing alloys and tempers and should not be specified as engineering requirements or used for design purposes.

[b] Only the commonly used tempers are listed for the alloys shown. Other tempers of these alloys are available.

[c] The indicated typical mechanical properties for all except the O temper material are higher than the specified minimum properties. For O temper products, typical ultimate and yield values are slightly lower than specified (maximum) values.

[d] Based on 500,000,000 cycles of completely reversed stress using the RR Moore type of machine and specimen.

[e] Based on a single series of tests, 10,000,000 cycles sheet flexural specimens.

[f] Based on 50,000,000 cycles in a single series of tests using the RR Moore type of machine and specimen.

[g] Average of tension and compression modulii. Compression modulus is about 2% greater than tension modulus.

[h] General corrosion ratings are based on exposures to sodium chloride solution by intermittent spraying or immersion. Ratings A through D are relative ratings in decreasing order of merit. The ratings do not necessarily imply acceptable performance in the intended application.

[i] Stress-corrosion cracking ratings are based on *service experience* and on *laboratory tests* of specimens exposed to the 35% sodium chloride alternate immersion test for 2XXX, 6XXX, and copper containing 1XXX series alloys and total immersion in boiling in sodium chloride solution for 96 h for copper free 7XXX series alloys.

A No known instance of failure in service or in laboratory tests.

A2 Insufficient service experience; no known instance of failure in laboratory tests.

B No known instance of failure in service; limited failures in laboratory tests of short transverse specimens.

B2 Insufficient service experience; limited failures in laboratory service.

C Service failures with sustained tension stress acting in short transverse direction relative to grain structure; limited failures in laboratory tests of long transverse specimens.

D Limited service failures with sustained longitudinal or long transverse stress.

[j] Improved resistance to stress corrosion cracking can be realized by using controlled quenching and artificial aging practices in heat-treatable 7XXX aluminum alloys.

[k] Elongation in 50 mm apply for thicknesses up through 12.50 mm and in $5D$ ($5.65\sqrt{A}$) for thicknesses over 12.50 mm, where D and A are the diameter and cross-sectional area of the specimen. Values for elongations in $5D$ ($5.65\sqrt{A}$) are shown in brackets.

[l] This rating would be B2 for material exposed to elevated temperatures.

[m] This rating may be different for material held at elevated temperatures for long periods.

[n] Toughness ratings are based upon Kahn tear test of 1.60-mm-thick sheet specimens in both longitudinal and transverse directions. These data are based on a limited number of tests and should be used for general comparisons only.

Ratings: A over 175 000 N·m/m^2
B over 140 000 thru 175 000 N·m/m^2
C over 105 000 thru 140 000 N·m/m^2
D 0 through 105 000 N·m/m^2

[p] Ratings A through D for workability (cold) and A through E for machinability are relative ratings in decreasing order of merit.

[q] Ratings A through D for weldability are relative ratings as follows:

A Generally weldable by all commercial procedures and methods.

B Weldable with special techniques.

C Limited weldability due to crack sensitivity, loss in corrosion resistances, loss in mechanical properties.

D No commonly used welding methods have been developed.

N/A Rating not applicable for end use application requirements, that is, rivets.

SOURCE: Reprinted with permission, copyright 1992, Society of Automotive Engineers.

TABLE 5.52 Typical Physical Properties of SAE Casting Alloys

Alloy			Density		Approximate melting range[§]		Elec. cond.,	Therm. cond.	Coeff. of thermal expan., $\times 10^{-6}$			
UNS	ANSI	Temper	lb/in³	kg/m³	°F	°C	% IACS	W/(m · K)	68–212°F per °F	20–100°C per °C	68–572°F per °F	20–300°C per °C
A02010	201.0	T6	0.101	2800	995–1200	535–650	30	121	10.7	19.3	13.7	24.7
		T7	0.101	2800	995–1200	535–650	30	121	10.7	19.3	13.7	24.7
A02060	206.0	T4	0.101	2800	1010–1200	542–650	—	121	10.7	19.3	—	—
A02080	208.0	F	0.101	2800	970–1160	521–627	31	125	12.4	22.3	13.4	24.1
		T4	0.101	2800	970–1160	521–627	—	—	12.4	22.3	13.4	24.1
		T55	0.101	2800	970–1160	521–627	—	—	12.4	22.3	13.4	24.1
		T6	0.101	2800	970–1160	521–627	—	—	12.4	22.3	13.4	24.1
		T7	0.101	2800	970–1160	521–627	—	—	12.4	22.3	13.4	24.1
A02220	222.0	0	0.107	2960	965–1155	518–624	—	—	12.3	22.1	13.1	23.6
		T551	0.107	2960	965–1155	518–624	—	—	12.3	22.1	13.1	23.6
		T61	0.107	2960	965–1155	518–624	33	130	12.3	22.1	13.1	23.6
		T65	0.107	2960	965–1155	518–624	—	—	12.3	22.1	13.1	23.6
A02420	242.0	0	0.102	2820	990–1175	532–635	—	—	12.6	22.7	13.6	24.5
		T571*	0.102	2820	990–1175	532–635	34	134	12.6	22.7	13.6	24.5
		T61	0.102	2820	990–1175	532–635	—	—	12.6	22.7	13.6	24.5
		T77	0.102	2820	990–1175	532–635	38	151	12.6	22.7	13.6	24.5
A02950	295.0	T4	0.102	2820	970–1190	521–643	—	138	12.7	22.9	13.8	24.8
		T6	0.102	2820	970–1190	521–643	35	138	12.7	22.9	13.8	24.8
		T62	0.102	2820	970–1190	521–643	—	138	12.7	22.9	13.8	24.8
		T7	0.102	2820	970–1190	521–643	—	—	12.7	22.9	13.8	24.8
A02960	296.0	T4	0.101	2800	970–1170	521–632	—	130	12.2	22.0	13.3	23.9
		T6*	0.101	2800	970–1170	521–632	33	130	12.2	22.0	13.3	23.9
		T7	0.101	2800	970–1170	521–632	—	—	12.2	22.0	13.3	23.9
A03190	319.0	F	0.101	2800	960–1120	516–604	27	109	11.9	21.4	12.7	22.9
		T5	0.101	2800	960–1120	516–604	—	—	11.9	21.4	12.7	22.9
		T6	0.101	2800	960–1120	516–604	—	—	11.9	21.4	12.7	22.9

		T61	0.101	2800	960–1120	516–604	—	—	11.9	21.4	12.7	22.9
A23190	B319.0	T5	—	—	—	—	—	—	—	—	—	—
		T6	—	—	—	—	—	—	—	—	—	—
A03280	328.0	F	0.098	2720	1025–1105	552–596	30	121	11.9	21.4	12.9	23.2
		T6	0.098	2720	1025–1105	552–596	—	—	11.9	21.4	12.9	23.2
A03320	332.0	T5*	0.100	2770	970–1080	521–582	26	104	11.5	20.7	12.4	22.3
A03330	333.0	F*	0.100	2770	960–1085	516–585	26	104	11.4	20.5	12.4	22.3
		T5*	0.100	2770	960–1085	516–585	29	117	11.4	20.5	12.4	22.3
		T6*	0.100	2770	960–1085	516–585	29	117	11.4	20.5	12.4	22.3
		T7*	0.100	2770	960–1085	516–585	35	138	11.4	20.5	12.4	22.3
A03360	336.0	T551*	0.098	2720	1000–1050	538–566	29	117	11.0	19.8	12.0	21.6
		T65	0.098	2720	1000–1050	538–566	—	—	11.0	19.8	12.0	21.6
A03390	339.0	T551*	0.098	2720	—	—	—	117	—	—	—	—
A03540	354.0	T61	0.098	2720	1000–1105	538–596	32	125	11.6	20.9	12.7	22.9
A03550	355.0	T51	0.098	2720	1015–1150	546–621	43	167	12.4	22.3	13.7	24.7
		T6	0.098	2720	1015–1150	546–621	36	142	12.4	22.3	13.7	24.7
		T62*	0.098	2720	1015–1150	546–621	36	142	12.4	22.3	13.7	24.7
		T7	0.098	2720	1015–1150	546–621	42	163	12.4	22.3	13.7	24.7
		T71	0.098	2720	1015–1150	546–621	39	151	12.4	22.3	13.7	24.7
A33550	C355.0	T6	0.098	2720	1015–1150	546–621	36	142	12.4	22.3	13.7	24.7
		T61	0.098	2720	1015–1150	546–621	37	146	12.4	22.3	13.7	24.7
A03560	356.0	F	0.097	2685	1035–1135	557–613	—	—	11.9	21.4	12.9	23.2
		T51	0.097	2685	1035–1135	557–613	43	167	11.9	21.4	12.9	23.2
		T6	0.097	2685	1035–1135	557–613	39	151	11.9	21.4	12.9	23.2
		T7	0.097	2685	1035–1135	557–613	40	155	11.9	21.4	12.9	23.2
		T71	0.097	2685	1035–1135	557–613	—	—	11.9	21.4	12.9	23.2
A13560	A356.0	T6	0.097	2685	1035–1135	557–613	—	—	11.9	21.4	12.9	23.2
		T61	0.097	2685	1035–1135	557–613	39	151	11.9	21.4	12.9	23.2
		T7	0.097	2685	1035–1135	557–613	—	—	11.9	21.4	12.9	23.2
		T71	0.097	2685	1035–1135	557–613	—	—	11.9	21.4	12.9	23.2
A03570	357.0	T6	0.097	2685	1035–1135	557–613	39	151	11.9	21.4	12.9	23.2
A13570	A357.0	T61	0.097	2685	1035–1135	557–613	39	151	11.9	21.4	12.9	23.2
A03590	359.0	T61	0.097	2685	1045–1115	563–602	35	138	11.6	20.9	12.7	22.9
A03600	360.0	F	0.095	2630	1035–1105	557–596	—	—	12.2†	22.0†	—	—
A13600	A360.0	F	0.095	2630	1035–1105	557–596	29	113	12.2†	22.0†	—	—

TABLE 5.52 Typical Physical Properties of SAE Casting Alloys (*Continued*)

Alloy			Density		Approximate melting range§		Elec. cond.,	Therm. cond.	Coeff. of thermal expan., × 10^{-6}			
UNS	ANSI	Temper	lb/in³	kg/m³	°F	°C	% IACS	W/(m · K)	68–212°F per °F	20–100°C per °C	68–572°F per °F	20–300°C per °C
A03800	380.0	F	0.098	2720	1000–1100	538–593	23	96	12.1†	21.8†	—	—
A13830	A380.0	F	0.098	2720	1000–1100	538–593	—	100	—	—	—	—
A03830	383.0	F	0.098	2720	960–1080	516–582	23	96	11.7†	21.1†	—	—
A03840	384.0	F	0.098	2720	960–1080	516–582	23	96	11.7†	21.1†	—	—
A03900	390.0	F	—	—	—	—	—	—	—	—	—	—
A13900	A390.0	T5	0.099	2740	945–1200	507–649	25	134	10.0	18.0	—	—
		T6	0.099	2740	945–1200	507–649	—	—	10.0	18.0	—	—
		T7	0.099	2740	945–1200	507–649	—	—	10.0	18.0	—	—
A23900	B390.0	F	—	—	—	—	—	—	—	—	—	—
A04130	413.0	F	0.096	2660	1065–1080	574–582	—	—	11.9†	21.4†	—	—
A14130	A413.0	F	0.096	2660	1065–1080	574–582	31	121	11.9†	21.4†	—	—
A24430	B443.0	F	0.097	2685	1065–1170	574–632	37	146	12.3	22.1	13.4	24.1
A34430	C443.0	F	0.097	2685	1065–1170	574–632	37	142	12.9†	23.2†	—	—
A14440	A444.0	F	0.095	2635	1065–1145	574–618	41	159	12.1	21.8	13.2	23.8
A05140	514.0	F	0.096	2660	1085–1185	585–640	35	138	13.4	24.1	14.5	26.1
A05200	520.0	T4	0.093	2570	840–1120	449–604	21	88	13.7	24.7	14.8	26.6
A05350	535.0	F	0.095	2635	1020–1165	548–629	23	96	13.1	23.6	14.8	26.6
A07050	705.0	T5	0.100	2770	1105–1180	596–638	25	104	13.1	23.6	14.3	25.7
A07070	707.0	T5	0.100	2770	1085–1165	585–629	25	104	13.2	23.8	14.4	25.9
		T7	0.100	2770	1085–1165	585–629	—	—	13.2	23.8	14.4	25.9
A07100	710.0	T5	0.102	2820	1105–1195	596–646	35	138	13.4	24.1	14.6	26.3
A07120	712.0	T5	0.101	2800	1135–1200	613–649	35	138	13.7	24.7	14.8‡	26.6c
A07130	713.0	T5	0.102	2810	1100–1180	593–638	30	121	13.4‡	24.1‡	14.6‡	26.3c

* Chill cast samples; all other samples cast in green sand molds.
† For die cast alloys, data valid for temperature range of 68–392°F (20–200°C).
‡ Estimated value.
§ The approximate melting range data shown are a practical parameter of the alloy—not concise values. Normal and common composition and process variations can cause deviations from the values given.

SOURCE: Reprinted with permission, copyright 1992, Society of Automotive Engineers.

TABLE 5.53 Mechanical Property Limits of SAE Sand Casting Alloys*

Alloy			Min. tensile strength		Min. yield strength (0.2% offset)			
UNS	ANSI	Temper	ksi	MPa	ksi	MPa	Elongation % Min. in 4D	Brinell hardness[†] (500 kg)
A02010	201.0	T6	60.0	415	50.0	345	5.0	115–145
		T7	60.0	415	50.0	345	3.0	115–145
A02060	206.0	T4	40.0	275	24.0	165	8.0	—
A02080	208.0	F	19.0	130	12.0	85	1.5	40–70
		T55	21.0	145	—	—	—	—
A02220	222.0	0	23.0	160	—	—	—	—
		T61	30.0	205	—	—	—	100–130
A02420	242.0	0	23.0	160	—	—	—	—
		T571	29.0	200	—	—	—	—
		T61	32.0	220	20.0	140	—	90–120
		T77	24.0	165	13.0	90	1.0	—
A02950	295.0	T4	29.0	200	13.0	90	6.0	45–75
		T6	32.0	220	20.0	140	3.0	60–90
		T62	36.0	250	28.0	195	—	80–110
		T7	29.0	200	16.0	110	3.0	55–85
A03190	319.0	F	23.0	160	13.0	90	1.5	55–85
		T5	25.0	170	—	—	—	—
		T6	31.0	215	20.0	140	1.5	65–95
A23190	B319.0	T5	26.0[‡]	180[‡]	—	—	—	—
		T6	32.0[‡]	220[‡]	21.0[‡]	145[‡]	1.0[‡]	70–100[‡]
A03280	328.0	F	25.0	170	14.0	95	1.0	45–75
		T6	34.0	235	21.0	145	1.0	65–95

TABLE 5.53 Mechanical Property Limits of SAE Sand Casting Alloys* (*Continued*)

Alloy			Min. tensile strength		Min. yield strength (0.2% offset)			
UNS	ANSI	Temper	ksi	MPa	ksi	MPa	Elongation % Min. in 4D	Brinell hardness (500 kg)
A03550	355.0	T51	25.0	170	18.0	125	—	50–80
		T6	32.0	220	20.0	140	2.0	65–95
		T7	35.0	240	—	—	—	—
		T71	30.0	205	22.0	150	—	60–90
A33550	C355.0	T6	36.0	250	25.0	170	2.5	—
		T61	36.0[‡]	250[‡]	30.0[‡]	205[‡]	1.0[‡]	70–100[‡]
A03560	356.0	F	19.0	130	—	—	2.0	40–70
		T51	23.0	160	16.0	110	—	45–75
		T6	30.0	205	20.0	140	3.0	55–85
		T7	31.0	215	29.0	200	—	60–90
		T71	25.0	170	18.0	125	3.0	45–75
A13560	A356.0	T6	34.0	235	24.0	165	3.5	55–85
		T7	32.0[‡]	220[‡]	30.0[‡]	205[‡]	—	—
		T71	26.0[‡]	180[‡]	19.0[‡]	130[‡]	4.0[‡]	—
A03570	357.0	T6[§]	—	—	—	—	—	—
A13570	A357.0	T61[§]	—	—	—	—	—	—
A03590	359.0	T61[§]	—	—	—	—	—	—
A13900	A390.0	F	26.0[‡]	180[‡]	26.0[‡]	180[‡]	—	85–115[‡]
		T5	26.0[‡]	180[‡]	26.0[‡]	180[‡]	—	85–115[‡]
		T6	40.0[‡]	275[‡]	40.0[‡]	275[‡]	—	125–155[‡]
		T7	36.0[‡]	250[‡]	36.0[‡]	250[‡]	—	100–130[‡]
B24430	B443.0	F	17.0	115	6.0	40	3.0	25–55

A14440	A444.0	F	18.0‡	125‡	7.0‡	50‡	8.0‡	35–65‡
A05140	514.0	F	22.0	150	9.0	60	6.0	35–65
A05200	520.0	T4	42.0	290	22.0	150	12.0	60–90
A05350	535.0	F	35.0	240	18.0	125	9.0	60–90
A07050	705.0	T5	30.0	205	17.0	115	5.0	50–80
A07070	707.0	T5	33.0	230	22.0	150	2.0	60–90
		T7	37.0	255	30.0	205	1.0	65–95
A07100	710.0	T5	32.0	220	20.0	140	2.0	60–90
A07120	712.0	T5	34.0	235	25.0	170	4.0	60–90
A07130	713.0	T5	32.0	220	22.0	150	3.0	60–90

* Values represent properties obtained from 0.500 in diameter separately cast test bars as depicted in Fig. 8 of ASTM B 557, cast in green sand molds and tested in accordance with the procedures of ASTM B 557.

† Hardness values are given for information only; not required for acceptance.

‡ Preliminary value.

§ Mechanical properties for these alloys are dependent on casting process and heat treat procedures set for individual casting requirements. These alloys have generally been used in premium quality applications, and process techniques have not been standardized. Consult individual foundry for applicable property limits.

SOURCE: Reprinted with permission, copyright 1992, Society of Automotive Engineers.

TABLE 5.54 Typical Uses of SAE Aluminum Casting Alloys and Similar Specifications

Alloy designations			Type of casting*	Similar specifications			Typical uses and general data
UNS	ANSI	Former SAE		ASTM	Federal	AMS	
A02010	201.0	382	S	B26	—	—	Very high strength at room and elevated temperature; good impact strength and ductility; high cost premium casting alloy.
			PM	—	—	4229	
A02060	206.0	—	S	—	—	4237	High tensile and yield strength with moderate ductility; good fracture toughness in T4 temper, structural parts for automotive and aerospace applications.
			PM	—	—	—	
A02080	208.0	380	S	B26	QQ-A-601	—	Manifolds, valve bodies, and similar castings requiring pressure tightness.
			PM	B108	—	—	
A02220	222.0	34	S	B26	QQ-A-601	—	Primarily a piston alloy, but also used for aircooled cylinder heads and valve tappet guides.
			PM	B108	QQ-A-596	—	
A02420	242.0	39	S	B26	QQ-A-601	4222	Used primarily for aircooled cylinder heads, but also for pistons in high performance gasoline engines.
			PM	B108	QQ-A-596	—	
A02950	295.0	38	S	B26	QQ-A-601	4231	General structural castings requiring high strength and shock resistance.
A02960	296.0	—	PM	B108	QQ-A-596	4282	Modification of alloy 295.0 for use in permanent molds.
A03190	319.0	326	S	B26	QQ-A-601	—	General-purpose low-cost alloy; good foundry characteristics.
			PM	B108	QQ-A-596	—	
A23190	B319.0	329	S	—	—	—	General-purpose alloy similar to 319.0, but with lower ductility and improved machinability.
			PM	—	—	—	
A03280	328.0	327	S	B26	QQ-A-601	—	Similar to alloys 355.0 and 356.0, but lower ductility.
A03320	332.0	332	PM	B108	QQ-A-596	—	Primarily used for automotive and compressor pistons.

A03330	333.0	331	PM	B108	QQ-A-596	—	General-purpose low-cost permanent mold alloy used for engine parts, motor housings, flywheel housings, and regulator parts.
A03360	336.0	321	PM	B108	QQ-A-596	—	Piston alloy having low expansion.
A03390	339.0	334	PM	—	—	—	Piston alloy.
A03540	354.0	—	PM	B108	—	—	High-strength premium quality casting alloy.
				B686	—	—	
A03550	355.0	322	S	B26	QQ-A-601	4210	General use where high strength, medium ductility, and pressure tightness are required, such as pump bodies and liquid-cooled cylinder heads.
			PM	B108	QQ-A-596	4212	
				—	—	4214	
				—	—	4280	
				—	—	4281	
A33550	C355.0	335	S	B26	QQ-A-601	4215	Similar to alloy 355.0, but has greater ductility.
			PM	B108	QQ-A-596	—	
				B686	—	—	
A03560	356.0	323	S	B26	QQ-A-601	4217	For intricate castings requiring good strength and ductility.
			PM	B108	QQ-A-596	4284	
				—	—	4286	
A13560	A356.0	336	S	B26	QQ-A-601	4218	Similar to alloy 356.0, but has greater ductility.
			PM	B108	QQ-A-596	—	
				B686	—	—	
A03570	357.0	—	S	—	—	—	Similar to alloy A357.0, but has greater ductility.
			PM	B108	QQ-A-596	—	
A13570	A357.0	—	S	—	—	4219	High-strength structural alloy with good ductility.
			PM	B108	—	—	
				B686	—	—	
A03590	359.0	—	S	—	—	—	High-strength structural alloy with good ductility.
			PM	B108	—	—	
A03600	360.0	—	D	B85	—	—	Very good casting characteristics; good corrosion resistance; used in place of alloy 413 where higher mechanical properties are required.

TABLE 5.54 Typical Uses of SAE Aluminum Casting Alloys and Similar Specifications (*Continued*)

Alloy designations			Type of casting*	Similar specifications			Typical uses and general data
UNS	ANSI	Former SAE		ASTM	Federal	AMS	
A13600	A360.0	309	D	B85	QQ-A-591	4290	Excellent casting characteristics; suited for use in thin-walled or intricate castings produced in cold-chamber casting machine; high corrosion resistance; slightly higher mechanical properties than alloy 360.0.
A03800	380.0	308	D	B85	QQ-A-591	—	Similar to alloy A380.0, but suitable for use in either cold-chamber or gooseneck machines.
A13800	A380.0	306	D	B85	QQ-A-591	4291	Good casting characteristics and fair resistance to corrosion; not especially suited for thin sections; limited to cold-chamber machines.
A03830	383.0	383	D	B85	QQ-A-591	—	Similar to alloy 380.0, but with improved castability.
A03840	384.0	303	D	B85	QQ-A-591	—	General-purpose alloy with high fluidity; used for thin-walled castings or castings with large areas.
A03900	390.0	—	D	—	—	—	High wear resistance; used for cylinder blocks, transmission pump and air compressor housings, small engine crankcases, and air conditioner pistons.
A13900	A390.0	—	S PM	— —	— —	— —	Similar to 390.0, but formulated for sand and permanent mold casting.
A23900	B390.0	—	D	—	—	—	Similar to alloy 390.0.
A04130	413.0	—	D	B85	—	—	Good for large thin-wall die castings, difficult to machine and finish.
A14130	A413.0	305	D	B85	QQ-A-591	—	High corrosion resistance; excellent castability; used for complicated castings with thin sections, also difficult to machine and finish.
A24430	B443.0	35	S PM	B26 B108	QQ-A-601 QQ-A-596	— —	Used for intricate castings having thin sections; good corrosion resistance; fair strength and good ductility.

A34430	C443.0	304	D	B85	QQ-A-591	—	Good casting characteristics and resistance to corrosion.
A14440	A444.0	—	S	—	—	—	Good castability; excellent ductility for impact absorption; used for bridge railing posts and turbocharger compressor housings.
A05140	514.0	320	S	B26	QQ-A-601	—	Moderate strength; very high corrosion resistance.
A05200	520.0	324	S	B26	QQ-A-601	4240	High-strength structural alloy; requires special foundry and heat treat practice; susceptible to stress corrosion failure.
A05350	535.0	—	S	B26	QQ-A-601	—	Excellent shock and corrosion resistance, dimensional stability, and machinability; used in computer components, frame sections, optical equipment, and applications where stress rupture is a factor.
A07050	705.0	311	S	B26	QQ-A-601	—	High-strength general-purpose alloy; excellent machinability and dimensional stability; high corrosion resistance; can be anodized.
			PM	B108	QQ-A-596	—	
A07070	707.0	312	S	B26	QQ-A-601	—	Similar to alloy 705.0, but higher strength and lower ductility.
			PM	B108	QQ-A-596	—	
A07100	710.0	313	S	B26	QQ-A-601	—	High-strength general-purpose alloy similar to alloys 705.0 and 707.0; easily polished.
A07120	712.0	310	S	B26	QQ-A-601	—	General-purpose structural castings developing strengths equivalent to alloy 295.0 without requiring heat treatment, but casting characteristics slightly poorer than alloy 295.0.
A07130	713.0	315	S	B26	QQ-A-601	—	Similar to alloy 710.0.
			PM	B108	QQ-A-596	—	

* S—sand cast; PM—permanent mold; D—die cast.

SOURCE: Reprinted with permission, copyright 1992, Society of Automotive Engineers.

TABLE 5.55 SAE Aluminum Alloy Characteristics

Alloy designations			Foundry characteristics[a]						
				Pattern shrinkage allowance[b]					
UNS	ANSI	Former SAE	Type of casting	in/ft	%	Resistance to hot cracking[c]	Pressure tightness	Fluidity[d]	Solidification shrinkage tendency[e]
A02010	201.0	382	S	5/32	1.30	4	3	3	4
			PM	b	b	4	3	3	4
A02060	206.0	—	S	5/32	1.30	4	3	3	4
			PM	b	b	4	3	3	4
A02080	208.0	380	S	5/32	1.30	4	3	3	3
			PM	b	b	4	3	3	3
A02220	222.0	34	S	5/32	1.30	3	3	3	3
			PM	b	b	4	4	3	4
A02420	242.0	39	S	5/32	1.30	4	3	3	4
			PM	b	b	4	4	3	4
A02950	295.0	38	S	5/32	1.30	4	4	3	3
A02960	296.0	—	PM	b	b	4	3	3	3
A03190	319.0	326	S	5/32	1.30	2	2	2	2
			PM	b	b	2	2	2	3
A23190	B319.0	329	S	5/32	1.30	2	2	2	2
			PM	b	b	2	2	2	2
A03280	328.0	327	S	5/32	1.30	1	1	1	1
A03320	332.0	332	PM	b	b	1	2	1	2
A03330	333.0	331	PM	b	b	2	2	1	3
A03360	336.0	321	PM	b	b	1	2	1	3
A03390	339.0	334	PM	b	b	1	2	1	2
A03540	354.0	—	PM	b	b	2	1	1	3
A03550	355.0	322	S	5/32	1.30	1	1	1	1
			PM	b	b	1	1	2	2
A33550	C355.0	335	S	5/32	1.30	1	1	1	1
			PM	b	b	1	1	2	2
A03560	356.0	323	S	5/32	1.30	1	1	1	1
			PM	b	b	1	1	2	1

A13560	A356.0	336	S	5/32	1.30	1	1	1	1
			PM	b	b	1	1	2	1
A03570	357.0	—	S	5/32	1.30	1	1	1	1
			PM	b	b	1	1	2	1
A13570	A357.0	—	S	5/32	1.30	1	1	1	1
			PM	b	b	1	1	2	1
A03590	359.0	—	S	5/32	1.30	2	2	1	2
			PM	b	b	2	2	2	2
A03600	360.0	—	D	b	b	1	1	1	—
A13600	A360.0	309	D	b	b	1	1	1	—
A03800	380.0	308	D	b	b	1	1	1	—
A13800	A380.0	306	D	b	b	1	1	1	—
A03830	383.0	383	D	b	b	1	1	1	—
A03840	384.0	—	D	b	b	1	1	1	—
A03900	390.0	—	D	b	b	3	3	1	—
A13900	A390.0	—	S	5/32	1.30	3	3	1	3
			PM	b	b	3	3	1	3
A23900	B390.0	—	D	b	b	3	3	1	—
A04130	413.0	—	D	b	b	1	2	1	—
A14130	A413.0	305	D			1	2	1	—
A24430	B443.0	35	S	5/32	1.30	1	1	1	1
			PM	b	b	1	1	1	2
A34430	C443.0	304	D	b	b	2	3	3	—
A14440	A444.0	—	S	5/32	1.30	4	4	5	—
A05140	514.0	320	S	5/32	1.30	4	5	5	5
A05200	520.0	324	S	1/10	0.83	4	5	4	5
A05350	535.0	—	S	1/10	0.83	3	5	3	4
A07050	705.0	311	S	3/16	1.56	5	3	4	4
A07050	705.0	311	PM	b	b	5	4	4	5
A07070	707.0	312	S	3/16	1.56	5	3	4	4
			PM	b	b	5	4	4	5
A07100	710.0	313	S	3/16	1.56	5	3	4	4
A07120	712.0	310	S	3/16	1.56	5	3	4	4
A07130	713.0	315	S	3/16	1.56	5	3	4	4
			PM	b	b	5	4	4	5

TABLE 5.55 SAE Aluminum Alloy Characteristics (*Continued*)

Alloy		Other characteristics									
UNS	ANSI	Normally heat treated	Resistance to corrosion[f]	Machining[g]	Polishing[h]	Electro-plating[i]	Anodized appearance[j]	Chemical oxide coating[k] (protection)	Strength at elevated temperature[l]	Suitability for welding[m]	Suitability for brazing[n]
A02010	201.0	Yes	4	1	1	1	2	2	1	4	No
A02060	206.0	Yes	4	1	1	1	2	2	1	4	No
A02080	208.0	Yes	4	3	2	1	3	2	2	4	No
A02220	222.0	Yes	4	1	2	1	3	4	1	4	No
A02420	242.0	Yes	4	2	2	1	3	4	1	4	No
A02950	295.0	Yes	3	2	2	1	2	3	3	3	No
A02960	296.0	Yes	4	3	4	2	4	3	3	2	No
A03190	319.0	Yes	3	3	4	2	4	3	3	2	No
A23190	B319.0	Yes	3	3	4	2	4	3	3	2	No
A03280	328.0	Yes	3	4	5	2	4	2	2	2	No
A03320	332.0	Aged only	3	3	4	3	5	3	3	2	No
A03330	333.0	Yes	3	2	3	2	4	3	2	3	No
A03360	336.0	Yes	3	4	5	4	5	2	2	2	No
A03390	339.0	Aged only	3	3	4	3	5	3	3	2	No
A03540	354.0	Yes	3	4	4	2	4	3	2	3	No
A03550	355.0	Yes	3	3	3	1	4	2	2	2	No
A33550	C355.0	Yes	3	3	3	2	4	2	2	2	No
A03560	356.0	Yes	2	4	3	2	4	2	3	1	No
A13560	A356.0	Yes	2	3	3	1	4	2	3	1	No
A03570	357.0	Yes	2	3	3	1	4	2	3	1	No
A13570	A357.0	Yes	2	3	3	1	4	2	3	1	No
A03590	359.0	Yes	2	4	4	2	4	2	2	1	No
A03600	360.0	No	2	4	4	2	4	3	2	3	No
A13600	A360.0	No	3	3	3	1	4	3	2	3	No
A03800	380.0	No	4	3	3	1	4	5	2	4	No
A13800	A380.0	No	4	3	3	1	4	5	2	4	No
A03830	383.0	No	4	3	3	1	4	5	2	4	No
A03840	384.0	No	4	3	3	1	4	5	3	4	No

A03900	390.0	No	3	4	3	—	5	—	1	4	No
A13900	A390.0	Yes	3	4	3	—	5	—	1	4	No
A23900	B390.0	No	3	4	3	—	5	—	1	4	No
A04130	413.0	No	2	4	5	3	5	3	3	3	No
A14130	A413.0	No	3	4	5	3	5	3	3	3	No
A24430	B443.0	No	3	5	5	2	5	2	4	1	Ltd.
A34430	C443.0	No	2	5	5	2	4	3	5	1	No
A14440	A444.0	No	2	4	4	—	4	2	3	1	No
A05140	514.0	No	1	1	1	5	1	1	2	4	No
A05200	520.0	Yes	1	1	1	4	1	1	—[p]	5	No
A05350	535.0	Opt	1	1	1	—	1	1	3	4	No
A07050	705.0	Aged only	2	1	1	3	2	2	5	4	Yes
A07070	707.0	Yes	2	1	1	3	2	2	5	4	Yes
A07100	710.0	Aged only	2	1	1	2	2	3	5	4	Yes
A07120	712.0	Aged only	2	1	1	2	2	3	5	4	Yes
A07130	713.0	Aged only	2	1	1	2	2	3	5	4	Yes

NOTE: Type of casting: S—sand cast; PM—permanent mold; D—die cast.

[a] 1 indicates best of group; 5 indicates poorest of group.

[b] Not applicable to permanent mold and die castings. Allowances are for average sand castings. Shrinkage requirements will vary with intricacy of design and dimensions.

[c] Ability of alloy to withstand contraction stresses while cooling through hot-short or brittle temperature range.

[d] Ability of liquid alloy to flow readily in mold and fill thin sections.

[e] Decrease in volume accompanying freezing of alloy and measure of amount of compensating feed metal required in form of risers.

[f] Based on alloy resistance in 5% salt spray test (ASTM B117).

[g] Composite rating based on ease of cutting, chip characteristics, quality of finishing, and tool life. Ratings, in the case of heat treatable alloys, based on T6 temper. Other tempers, particularly the annealed temper, may have lower rating.

[h] Composite rating based on ease and speed of polishing and quality of finish provided by typical polishing procedure.

[i] Ability of casting to take and hold on electroplate applied by present standard methods.

[j] Rated on lightness of color, brightness, and uniformity of clear anodized coating applied in sulfuric acid electrolyte.

[k] Rated on combined resistance of coating and base alloy to corrosion.

[l] Rating based on tensile and yield strengths of temperature up to 500°F (260°C), after prolonged heating at testing temperatures.

[m] Based on ability of material to be fusion welded with filler rod of same alloy.

[n] Refers to suitability of alloy to withstand brazing temperatures without excessive distortion or melting.

[p] Not recommended for service at temperatures exceeding 200°F (93°C).

SOURCE: Reprinted with permission, copyright 1992, Society of Automotive Engineers.

TABLE 5.56 Mechanical Properties of Aluminum: Typical Properties

	Tension							
	Strength, psi		% Elong. in 2 in			Ultimate shear	Endurance	Mod. of
Alloy and temper	Ultimate	Yield	1/16 in (thick)	1/2 in (thick)	Brinell hardness[a]	strength, psi	limit, psi	elast., psi
EC-O	12,000	4,000	—	—	—	8,000	—	10.0×10^6
EC-H14	16,000	14,000	—	—	—	10,000	—	10.0×10^6
EC-H19	27,000	24,000	—		—	15,000	7,000	10.0×10^6
1060-O	10,000	4,000	43	—	19	7,000	3,000	10.0×10^6
1060-H14	14,000	13,000	12	—	26	9,000	5,000	10.0×10^6
1100-O	13,000	5,000	35	45	23	9,000	5,000	10.0×10^6
1100-H12	16,000	15,000	12	25	28	10,000	6,000	10.0×10^6
1100-H14	18,000	17,000	9	20	32	11,000	7,000	10.0×10^6
1100-H16	21,000	20,000	6	17	38	12,000	9,000	10.0×10^6
1100-H18	24,000	22,000	5	15	44	13,000	9,000	10.0×10^6
2011-T3[b]	55,000	43,000	—	15	95	32,000	18,000	10.2×10^6
2011-T8	59,000	45,000	—	12	100	35,000	18,000	10.2×10^6
2014-O	27,000	14,000	—	18	45	18,000	13,000	10.6×10^6
2014-T4, T451	62,000	42,000	—	20	105	38,000	20,000	10.6×10^6
2014-T6, T651[c]	70,000	60,000	—	13	135	42,000	18,000	10.6×10^6
2017-T4, T451	62,000	40,000	—	22	105	38,000	18,000	10.5×10^6
2024-O	27,000	11,000	20	22	47	18,000	13,000	10.6×10^6
2024-T3	70,000	50,000	18	—	120	41,000	20,000	10.6×10^6
2024-T4, T351[c]	68,000	47,000	20	19	120	41,000	20,000	10.6×10^6
2024-T36	72,000	57,000	13	—	130	42,000	18,000	10.6×10^6
2024-T81, T851	70,000	65,000	6	—	128	43,000	18,000	10.6×10^6
2024-O[d]	26,000	11,000	20	—	—	18,000	—	10.6×10^6
2024-T3[d,e]	65,000	45,000	18	—	—	40,000	—	10.6×10^6
2024-T4, T351[d,e]	64,000	42,000	19	—	—	40,000	—	10.6×10^6
2024-T36[d,e]	67,000	53,000	11	—	—	41,000	—	10.6×10^6
2024-T81, T851[d,e]	65,000	60,000	6	—	—	40,000	—	10.6×10^6
2024-T86[d,e]	70,000	66,000	6	—	—	42,000	—	10.6×10^6
2219-O[f]	25,000	11,000	18	—	—	—	—	10.6×10^6
2219-T31, T351[f]	52,000	36,000	17	—	—	—	—	10.6×10^6
2219-T81, T851	66,000	51,000	10	—	—	—	15,000	10.6×10^6
3003-O	16,000	6,000	30	40	28	11,000	7,000	10.0×10^6
3003-H12	19,000	18,000	10	20	35	12,000	8,000	10.0×10^6
3003-H14	22,000	21,000	8	16	40	14,000	9,000	10.0×10^6
3003-H16	26,000	25,000	5	14	47	15,000	10,000	10.0×10^6
3003-H18	29,000	27,000	4	10	55	16,000	10,000	10.0×10^6
3004-O	26,000	10,000	20	25	45	16,000	14,000	10.0×10^6
3004-H32	31,000	25,000	10	17	52	17,000	15,000	10.0×10^6
3004-H34	35,000	29,000	9	12	63	18,000	15,000	10.0×10^6
3004-H36	38,000	33,000	5	9	70	20,000	16,000	10.0×10^6
3004-H38	41,000	36,000	5	6	77	21,000	16,000	10.0×10^6
3004-O[d]	26,000	10,000	20	25	—	16,000	—	10.0×10^6
3004-H32[d]	31,000	25,000	10	17	—	17,000	—	10.0×10^6
3004-H34[d]	35,000	29,000	9	12	—	18,000	—	10.0×10^6
3004-H36[d]	38,000	33,000	5	9	—	20,000	—	10.0×10^6
3004-H38[d]	41,000	36,000	5	6	—	21,000	—	10.0×10^6

TABLE 5.56 Mechanical Properties of Aluminum: Typical Properties (*Continued*)

4032-T6	55,000	46,000	—	9	120	38,000	16,000	11.4×10^6
5005-O	18,000	6,000	25	—	28	11,000	—	10.0×10^6
5005-H14	23,000	22,000	6	—	—	19,000	—	10.0×10^6
5005-H32	20,000	17,000	11	—	36	14,000	—	10.0×10^6
5005-H34	23,000	20,000	8	—	41	14,000	—	10.0×10^6
5005-H36	26,000	24,000	6	—	46	15,000	—	10.0×10^6
5005-H38	29,000	27,000	5	—	51	16,000	—	10.0×10^6
5050-O	21,000	8,000	24	—	36	15,000	12,000	10.0×10^6
5050-H32	25,000	21,000	9	—	46	17,000	13,000	10.0×10^6
5050-H34	28,000	24,000	8	—	53	18,000	13,000	10.0×10^6
5050-H36	30,000	26,000	7	—	58	19,000	14,000	10.0×10^6
5050-H38	32,000	29,000	6	—	63	20,000	14,000	10.0×10^6
5052-O	28,000	13,000	25	30	47	18,000	16,000	10.2×10^6
5052-H32	33,000	28,000	12	18	60	20,000	17,000	10.2×10^6
5052-H34	38,000	31,000	10	14	68	21,000	18,000	10.2×10^6
5052-H36	40,000	35,000	8	10	73	23,000	19,000	10.2×10^6
5052-H38	42,000	37,000	7	8	77	24,000	20,000	10.2×10^6
5083-O	42,000	21,000	22	25	67	25,000	22,000	10.3×10^6
5083-H112	44,000	28,000	16	—	80	26,000	22,000	10.3×10^6
5083-H113	46,000	33,000	16	—	82	—	23,000	10.3×10^6
5083-H321	46,000	33,000	—	16	—	—	23,000	10.3×10^6
5083-H323	47,000	36,000	10	—	84	27,000	—	10.3×10^6
5086-O	38,000	17,000	22	30	60	23,000	21,000	10.3×10^6
5086-H32	42,000	30,000	12	16	72	25,000	22,000	10.3×10^6
5086-H34	47,000	37,000	10	14	82	27,000	23,000[h]	10.3×10^6
5086-H112	39,000	19,000	14	—	64	23,000	21,000[h]	10.3×10^6
5154-O	35,000	17,000	27	30	58	22,000	17,000	10.2×10^6
5154-H32	39,000	30,000	15	18	67	22,000	18,000	10.2×10^6
5154-H34	42,000	33,000	13	16	73	24,000	19,000	10.2×10^6
5154-H36	45,000	36,000	12	14	78	26,000	20,000	10.2×10^6
5154-H38	48,000	39,000	10	—	80	28,000	21,000	10.2×10^6
5154-H112	35,000	17,000	25	—	63	—	17,000	10.2×10^6
5454-O	36,000	17,000	22	25	62	23,000	—	10.2×10^6
5454-H32	40,000	30,000	10	18	73	24,000	—	10.2×10^6
5454-H34	44,000	35,000	10	16	81	26,000	—	10.2×10^6
5454-H112	36,000	18,000	18	—	62	23,000	—	10.2×10^6
5454-H311	38,000	26,000	14	—	70	23,000	—	10.2×10^6
5456-O	45,000	23,000	24	20	70	27,000	22,000	10.3×10^6
5456-H112	45,000	24,000	22	—	70	27,000	—	10.3×10^6
5456-H311	47,000	33,000	18	—	75	27,000	24,000	10.3×10^6
5456-H321	51,000	37,000	16	—	90	30,000	23,000	10.3×10^6
5456-H343	56,000	43,000	8	—	94	33,000	—	10.3×10^6
5457-O	19,000	7,000	22	—	32	12,000	—	10.0×10^6
5457-H32	22,000	19,000	9	—	40	14,000	—	10.0×10^6
5457-H34	25,000	22,000	8	—	45	15,000	—	10.0×10^6
5457-H36	28,000	26,000	7	—	51	17,000	—	10.0×10^6
5457-H38	30,000	27,000	6	—	55	18,000	—	10.0×10^6
6061-O	18,000	8,000	25	30	30	12,000	9,000	10.0×10^6
6061-T4, T451	35,000	21,000	22	25	65	24,000	14,000	10.0×10^6
6061-T6, T651	45,000	40,000	12	17	95	30,000	14,000	10.0×10^6

TABLE 5.56 Mechanical Properties of Aluminum: Typical Properties (*Continued*)

6061-O[d]	17,000	7,000	25	—	—	11,000	—	10.0×10^6
6061-T4, T451[d]	33,000	19,000	22	—	—	22,000	—	10.0×10^6
6061-T6, T651[d]	42,000	37,000	12	—	—	27,000	—	10.0×10^6
6063-O	13,000	7,000	—	—	25	10,000	8,000	10.0×10^6
6063-T4	25,000	13,000	22	—	—	16,000	—	10.0×10^6
6063-T5	27,000	21,000	12	22	60	17,000	10,000	10.0×10^6
6063-T6	35,000	31,000	12	18	73	22,000	10,000	10.0×10^6
6063-T832	42,000	39,000	12	—	95	27,000	—	10.0×10^6
6262-T9	58,000	55,000	—	10	120	35,000	13,000	10.0×10^6
7075-O	33,000	15,000	17	16	60	22,000	17,000	10.4×10^6
7075-T6, T651[g]	83,000	73,000	11	11	150	48,000	23,000	10.4×10^6
7075-O[d]	32,000	14,000	17	—	—	22,000	—	10.4×10^6
7075-T6, T651[d]	76,000	67,000	11	—	—	46,000	—	10.4×10^6
7079-T6, T651	78,000	68,000	—	14	145	45,000	23,000	10.4×10^6
7178-O	33,000	15,000	15	16	60	22,000	—	10.4×10^6
7178-T6, T651[c]	88,000	78,000	10	11	160	52,000	22,000	10.4×10^6

[a] 500-kg load; 10 mm ball.
[b] Sizes larger than 1½ in will have strengths slightly less than shown.
[c] Extruded shapes over ¾ in thick have strengths 15–20% higher than shown.
[d] These alloys are Alclad.
[e] Sheets thicker than 0.062 in will have strengths slightly higher than shown.
[f] Properties for sheets and plates only.
[g] Extruded products will have strengths approx. 10% higher.
[h] Applies to sheets and plates only.
SOURCE: Ryerson, Inc.

TABLE 5.57 Typical Characteristics and Applications of Wrought Aluminum

Alloy and temper	Resistance to corrosion		Workability (cold)[e]	Machinability[e]	Brazability[f]	Weldability[f]			Some applications of alloy
	General[a]	Stress-corrosion cracking[b]				Gas	Arc	Resistance spot and seam	
1060–0	A	A	A	E	A	A	A	B	
H12	A	A	A	E	A	A	A	A	Chemical equipment, railroad tank cars
H14	A	A	A	D	A	A	A	A	
H16	A	A	B	D	A	A	A	A	
H18	A	A	B	D	A	A	A	A	
1100–0	A	A	A	E	A	A	A	B	
H12	A	A	A	E	A	A	A	A	Sheet metal work, spun holloware, fin stock
H14	A	A	A	D	A	A	A	A	
H16	A	A	B	D	A	A	A	A	
H18	A	A	C	D	A	A	A	A	
1350–0	A	A	A	E	A	A	A	B	
H12, H111	A	A	A	E	A	A	A	A	
H14, H24	A	A	A	D	A	A	A	A	Electrical conductors
H16, H26	A	A	B	D	A	A	A	A	
H18	A	A	B	D	A	A	A	A	
2011–T3	D[c]	D	C	A	D	D	D	D	
T4, T451	D[c]	D	B	A	D	D	D	D	Screw-machine products
T8	D	B	D	A	D	D	D	D	
2014–0	—	—	—	D	D	D	D	B	
T3, T4, T451	D[c]	C	C	B	D	D	B	B	Truck frames, aircraft structures
T6, T651, T6510, T6511	D	C	D	B	D	D	B	B	
2017–T4, T451	D[c]	C	C	B	D	D	B	B	Screw-machine products, fittings

TABLE 5.57 Typical Characteristics and Applications of Wrought Aluminum (*Continued*)

Alloy and temper	Resistance to corrosion		Work-ability (cold)[e]	Machi-nability[e]	Brazability[f]	Weldability[f]			Some applications of alloy
	General[a]	Stress-corrosion cracking[b]				Gas	Arc	Resistance spot and seam	
2018–T61	—	—	—	B	—	—	—	—	Aircraft engine cylinders, heads, and pistons
2024–0	—	—	—	D	D	D	D	D	
T4, T3, T351, T3510, T3511	D[c]	C	C	B	D	C	B	B	
T361	D[c]	C	D	B	D	D	C	B	Truck wheels, screw-machine products, aircraft structures
T6	D	B	C	B	D	D	C	B	
T861, T81, T851, T8510 T8511	D	B	D	B	D	D	C	B	
T72	—	—	—	B	—	—	—	—	
2025–T6	D	C	—	B	D	D	B	B	Forgings, aircraft propellers
2117–T4	C	A	B	C	D	D	B	B	
2218–T61	D	C	—	—	—	—	—	C	Jet engine impellers and rings
T72	D	C	—	B	D	D	C	B	
2618–T61	D	C	—	B	D	D	C	B	Aircraft engines
3003–0	A	A	A	E	A	A	A	A	Cooking utensils, chemical equipment, pressure vessels, sheet metal work, builder's hardware, storage tanks
H12	A	A	A	E	A	A	A	A	
H14	A	A	B	D	A	A	A	A	
H16	A	A	C	D	A	A	A	A	
H18	A	A	C	D	A	A	A	A	
H25	A	A	B	D	A	A	A	A	

3004–0	A	A	A	D	B	B	A	B	Sheet metal work, storage tanks
H32	A	A	B	D	B	B	A	A	
H34	A	A	B	C	B	B	A	A	
H36	A	A	C	C	B	B	A	A	
H38	A	A	C	C	B	B	A	A	
3105–0	A	A	A	E	B	B	A	B	Residential siding, mobile homes, rain-carrying goods, sheet metal work
H12	A	A	B	E	B	B	A	A	
H14	A	A	B	D	B	B	A	A	
H16	A	A	C	D	B	B	A	A	
H18	A	A	C	D	B	B	A	A	
H25	A	A	B	D	B	B	A	A	
4032–T6	C	B	—	B	D	D	B	C	Pistons
5005–0	A	A	A	E	B	A	A	B	Appliances, utensils, architectural, electrical conductor
H12	A	A	A	E	B	A	A	A	
H14	A	A	B	D	B	A	A	A	
H16	A	A	C	D	B	A	A	A	
H18	A	A	C	D	B	A	A	A	
H32	A	A	A	E	B	A	A	A	
H34	A	A	B	D	B	A	A	A	
H36	A	A	C	D	B	A	A	A	
H38	A	A	C	D	B	A	A	A	
5050–0	A	A	A	E	B	A	A	B	Builder's hardware,refrigerator trim, coiled tubes
H32	A	A	A	D	B	A	A	A	
H34	A	A	B	D	B	A	A	A	
H36	A	A	C	C	B	A	A	A	
H38	A	A	C	C	B	A	A	A	
5052–0	A	A	A	D	C	A	A	B	Sheet metal work, hydraulic tube, appliances
H32	A	A	B	D	C	A	A	A	
H34	A	A	B	C	C	A	A	A	
H36	A	A	C	C	C	A	A	A	
H38	A	A	C	C	C	A	A	A	

TABLE 5.57 Typical Characteristics and Applications of Wrought Aluminum (*Continued*)

Alloy and temper	Resistance to corrosion: General[a]	Resistance to corrosion: Stress-corrosion cracking[b]	Workability (cold)[e]	Machinability[e]	Brazability[f]	Weldability[f]: Gas	Weldability[f]: Arc	Weldability[f]: Resistance spot and seam	Some applications of alloy
5056–0	A[d]	B[d]	A	D	D	C	A	B	Cable sheathing, rivets for magnesium, screen wire, zippers
H111	A[d]	B[d]	A	D	D	C	A	A	
H12, H32	A[d]	B[d]	B	D	D	C	A	A	
H14, H34	A[d]	B[d]	B	C	D	C	A	A	
H18, H38	A[d]	C[d]	C	C	D	C	A	A	
H192	B[d]	D[d]	D	B	D	C	A	A	
H392	B[d]	D[d]	D	B	D	C	A	A	
5083–0	A[d]	B[d]	B	D	D	C	A	B	Unfired, welded pressure vessels, marine, auto aircraft cryogenics, TV towers, drilling rigs, transportation equipment, missile components
H321	A[d]	B[d]	C	D	D	C	A	A	
H111	A[d]	B[d]	C	D	D	C	A	A	
5086–0	A[d]	A[d]	A	D	D	C	A	B	
H32, H116, H117	A[d]	A[d]	B	D	D	C	A	A	
H34	A[d]	B[d]	B	C	D	C	A	A	
H36	A[d]	B[d]	C	C	D	C	A	A	
H38	A[d]	B[d]	C	C	D	C	A	A	
H111	A[d]	A[d]	B	D	D	C	A	A	
5154–0	A[d]	A[d]	A	D	D	C	A	B	Welded structures, storage tanks, pressure vessels, saltwater service
H32	A[d]	A[d]	B	D	D	C	A	A	
H34	A[d]	A[d]	B	C	D	C	A	A	
H36	A[d]	A[d]	C	C	D	C	A	A	
H38	A[d]	A[d]	C	C	D	C	A	A	
5252–H24	A	A	B	D	C	A	A	A	Automotive and appliance trim
H25	A	A	B	C	C	A	A	A	
H28	A	A	C	C	C	A	A	A	

5454–0	A	A	A	D	D	C	A	B	Welded structures, pressure vessels, marine service
H32	A	A	B	D	D	C	A	A	
H34	A	A	B	C	D	C	A	A	
H111	A	A	B	D	D	C	A	A	
5456–0	A[d]	B[d]	B	D	D	C	A	B	High-strength welded structures, storage tanks, pressure vessels, marine applications
H111	A[d]	B[d]	C	D	D	C	A	A	
H321[g], H116	A[d]	B[d]	C	D	D	C	A	A	
5457–0	A	A	A	E	B	A	A	B	Anodized automotive and appliance trim
5657–H241	A	A	A	D	B	A	A	A	
H25	A	A	B	D	B	A	A	A	
H26	A	A	B	D	B	A	A	A	
H28	A	A	C	D	B	A	A	A	
6005–T5	B	A	C	C	A	A	A	A	Heavy-duty structures requiring good corrosion resistance—truck and marine, railroad cars, furniture, pipelines
6053–0	—	—	—	E	A	A	A	B	Wire and rod for rivets
T6, T61	A	A	—	C	A	A	A	A	
6061–0	B	A	A	D	A	A	A	B	Heavy-duty structures requiring good corrosion resistance—truck and marine, railroad cars, furniture, pipelines
T4, T451, T4510, T4511	B	B	B	C	A	A	A	A	
T6, T651, T652, T6510, T6511	B	A	C	C	A	A	A	A	
6063–T1	A	A	B	D	A	A	A	A	Pipe railing, furniture architectural extrusions
T4	A	A	B	D	A	A	A	A	
T5, T52	A	A	B	C	A	A	A	A	
T6	A	A	C	C	A	A	A	A	
T83, T831, T832	A	A	C	C	A	A	A	A	

TABLE 5.57 Typical Characteristics and Applications of Wrought Aluminum (*Continued*)

Alloy and temper	Resistance to corrosion		Work-ability (cold)[e]	Machi-nability[e]	Brazability[f]	Weldability[f]			Some applications of alloy
	General[a]	Stress-corrosion cracking[b]				Gas	Arc	Resistance spot and seam	
6151–T6, T652	—	—	—	—	—	—	—	—	Moderate strength intricate forgings for machine and automotive parts
6262–T6, T651, T6510, T6511	B	A	C	B	A	A	A	A	Screw-machine products
T9	B	A	D	B	A	A	A	A	
6463–T1	A	A	B	D	A	A	A	A	Extruded architectural and trim sections
T5	A	A	B	C	A	A	A	A	
T6	A	A	C	C	A	A	A	A	
7075–0	—	—	—	D	D	D	C	B	
T6, T651, T652, T6510, T6511	C[c]	C	D	B	D	D	C	B	Aircraft and other structures
T73, T7351	C	B	D	B	D	D	C	B	

[a] Ratings A through E are relative ratings in decreasing order of merit, based on exposures to sodium chloride solution by intermittent spraying or immersion. Alloys with A and B ratings can be used in industrial and seacoast atmospheres without protection. Alloys with C, D, and E ratings generally should be protected at least on faying surfaces.

[b] Stress-corrosion cracking ratings are based on service experience and on laboratory tests of specimens exposed to the 3.5% sodium chloride alternate immersion test.

A = No known instance of failure in service or in laboratory tests.
B = No known instance of failure in service; limited failures in laboratory tests of short transverse specimens.
C = Service failures with sustained tension stress acting in short transverse direction relative to grain structure; limited failures in laboratory tests of long transverse specimens.
D = Limited service failures with sustained longitudinal or long transverse stress.

[c] In relatively thick sections the rating would be E.

[d] This rating may be different for material held at elevated temperature for long periods.

[e] Ratings A through E for workability (cold) and A through E for machinability are relative ratings in decreasing order of merit.

[f] Ratings A through D for weldability and brazability are relative ratings defined as follows:

A = Generally weldable by all commercial procedures and methods.

B = Weldable with special techniques or for specific applications which justify preliminary trials or testing to develop welding procedure and weld performance.

C = Limited weldability because of crack sensitivity or loss in resistance to corrosion and mechanical properties.

D = No commonly used welding methods have been developed.

[g] Material in this temper is not recommended for, and should not be used in, applications requiring exposure to sea water.

SOURCE: Reprinted with permission, copyright 1992, Society of Automotive Engineers.

5.70 through 5.73 list the standard specifications for beryllium copper sheet, plate, strip, and rolled bar (ASTM B-194). Tables 5.74 through 5.76 list the ASTM standards for copper water tube.

ASTM-designated copper water tube must withstand an internal hydrostatic pressure sufficient to subject the tube to a fiber stress of 6000 psi, calculated from the following equation for thin-walled hollow cylinders under tension:

$$P = \frac{2\,St}{D - 0.8t}$$

where P = hydrostatic pressure, psi
t = tube wall thickness, in
D = outside diameter of the tube, in
S = allowable stress of the material, psi

Also, the tube must withstand an internal air pressure of 60 psig for 5 s without showing signs of leakage.

Table 5.77 presents the ASTM classification of coppers, and Table 5.78 lists the densities of copper alloys.

5.4 Magnesium Alloys

Magnesium and magnesium alloys have many applications where moderate strength and light weight are required. These alloys find many applications in military and commercial aircraft, as well as in rockets and missiles (aerospace vehicles).

Magnesium is the eighth most abundant element in the earth's crust. The metal is obtained by electrolysis of fused magnesium chloride derived from brines, wells, and seawater. Magnesium is a silvery white, light-weight metal which is also fairly tough. It is one-third lighter than aluminum. The metal tarnishes in air and easily burns when in the finely divided state with a dazzling white flame. The specific gravity of magnesium is 1.738 g/cm^3, and its density is 0.063 lb/in^3. Caution must be used when handling magnesium because of its flammability in air. Water should not be used to extinguish a magnesium fire.

Table 5.79 lists the specifications of wrought magnesium alloys. Table 5.80 lists the physical properties and characteristics of magnesium cast alloys. Tables 5.81 and 5.82 list the chemical and strength requirements of extruded magnesium bar, rod, and shapes (ASTM B-107).

5.5 Titanium Alloys

Titanium alloys have a high strength-to-weight ratio. They are used as armor plate in modern war planes and propeller shafts, rigging, and other parts of ships where high strength and resistance to salt water are required. Titanium metal is produced by reducing titanium tetrachloride with magnesium. Titanium is a lustrous, white metal with low density and good strength. The specific gravity of titanium is 4.54 g/cm^3, with a weight of 0.164 lb/in^3. The pure metal burns in air and is the only element that burns in nitrogen gas.

Titanium is used extensively in modern aircraft and aerospace vehicles, where a light-weight alloy with high strength finds many applications. Titanium is the ninth most abundant element in the earth's crust.

Table 5.83 lists the chemical requirements of titanium alloys (ASTM B-265). Table 5.84 lists the tensile and bend requirements of titanium alloys. These tables are for annealed titanium plate, sheet, and strip, which are classified as follows:

Grade 1 through grade 4: Unalloyed titanium

Grade 5: Titanium alloy (6% aluminum, 4% vanadium)

Grade 6: Titanium alloy (5% aluminum, 2.5% tin)

Grade 7: Unalloyed titanium plus palladium

Grade 9: Titanium alloy (3% aluminum, 2.5% vanadium)

Grade 11: Unalloyed titanium plus palladium

Grade 12: Titanium alloy (0.3% molybdenum, 0.8% nickel)

Table 5.85 lists the chemical and mechanical properties of wrought titanium alloys.

5.6 The Unified Numbering System (UNS) for Metals

The Unified Numbering System (UNS) provides a means of coordinating many nationally used numbering systems currently administered by societies, trade associations, and the producers of metals and alloys, thereby avoiding confusion caused by use of more than one identification number for the same material or by having the same number assigned to two or more entirely different materials.

Table 5.86 shows the primary series of numbers, and Table 5.87 lists the secondary division of some series of numbers. When you know the UNS number for a metal or alloy, you may use these tables to determine the prime material (metal) or classification of alloy represented by the UNS number.

5.7 Hardness Tests and Hardness Number Conversions

5.7.1 Brinell hardness numbers (HB)

The Brinell hardness system is one of the most widely used systems for indicating the hardness of metals and alloys. The Brinell hardness number of a material may be calculated from the following equation:

$$\mathrm{HB} = \frac{P}{\frac{\pi D}{2}\left(D - \sqrt{D^2 - d^2}\right)}$$

where HB = Brinell hardness number
P = load applied to the test ball, kg
D = diameter of ball, mm
d = measured diameter at the rim of the impression in the material, mm

The standard ball is 10 mm in diameter, and standard loads are 500, 1500, and 3000 kg. The test is not valid when the hardness of the test material is above the anticipated Brinell hardness number of 630.

5.7.2 Vickers hardness numbers (HV).

The Vickers hardness is determined by forcing a square-base diamond pyramid having an apex angle of 136° into the test specimen under a load ranging from 3 to 50 kg and then measuring the diagonals of the indentation created. The Vickers hardness is defined as the load per unit area of surface contact in kilograms per square millimeter and may be calculated from the average diagonal using the following equation:

$$\mathrm{HV} = \frac{2L \sin \frac{a}{2}}{d^2}$$

where HV = Vickers hardness number
d = length of average diagonal, mm
a = apex angle, 136°
L = load, kg

5.8 Tolerances (Size Variations) for Stock and Mill Sizes of Metals and Alloys (Plate, Sheet, Strip, Bar, Rounds, Hexagons, Tube, etc.)

5.8.1 Tolerances for carbon and alloy steel mill products

Tables 5.88 and 5.89 list thickness tolerances for hot-rolled carbon steel sheets. Tables 5.90 and 5.91 list thickness tolerances for cold-rolled carbon steel sheets. Table 5.92 lists thickness tolerances for galvanized carbon steel sheets. Table 5.93 lists thickness tolerances for hot-rolled carbon steel strip. Table 5.94 lists thickness tolerances for cold-rolled carbon steel strip. Table 5.95 lists tolerances for hot-wrought round, square, and round-cornered square bars of steel. Table 5.96 lists tolerances for hot-wrought hexagonal bars of steel. Table 5.97 lists tolerances for hot-wrought square- and round-edge flat bars of steel. Table 5.98 lists tolerances for cold-finished carbon steel bars, cold drawn or turned and polished (rounds, hexagons, squares, and flats). Table 5.99 lists size tolerances for cold-finished round bars, cold drawn, ground, and polished or turned, ground, and polished. Table 5.100 lists size tolerances for cold-finished alloy steel bars, cold drawn or turned and polished (rounds, squares, hexagons, or flats). Table 5.101 lists tolerances for tool steel bars. Table 5.102 lists tolerances for round carbon steel and alloy steel mechanical seamless tubing. Table 5.103 lists tolerances for round, drawn-over-mandrel carbon steel welded mechanical tubing.

5.8.2 Tolerances of stainless steel mill products

Table 5.104 lists tolerances for stainless steel sheets. Table 5.105 lists tolerances for stainless steel plates. Table 5.106 lists tolerances for stainless steel bars, hot-rolled rounds and squares. Table 5.107 lists tolerances for stainless steel hot-rolled hexagons and octagons. Table 5.108 lists tolerances for stainless steel hot-rolled flat bars. Table 5.109 lists tolerances for stainless steel centerless ground rounds and cold-drawn rounds. Table 5.110 lists tolerances for stainless steel cold-drawn squares, hexagons, and octagons.

Table 5.111 lists tolerances for stainless steel cold-drawn flats. Table 5.112 lists tolerances for stainless steel cold-drawn seamless mechanical tubing.

5.8.3 Tolerances of aluminum alloy mill products

Table 5.113 lists tolerances for aluminum alloy sheet and plate. Table 5.114 lists tolerances for aluminum alloy round wire and rods. Table 5.115 lists tolerances for aluminum alloy square, hexagon, and octagon wire and bars. Table 5.116 lists tolerances for aluminum alloy rectangular wire and bars. Table 5.117 lists tolerances for aluminum alloy screw-machine stock (round and hexagonal). Table 5.118 lists tolerances for aluminum alloy round drawn tubing (OD, ID, and wall thickness). Table 5.119 lists tolerances for aluminum alloy round extruded tubing (OD, ID, and wall thickness).

5.8.4 Tolerances of copper alloy mill products

Table 5.120 lists tolerances for copper mill products, cold-rolled (strip, sheet, bar, and plate). Table 5.121 lists tolerances for copper round rod, hexagonal and octagonal stock. Table 5.122 lists tolerances for copper round seamless tube (wall thickness).

5.9 Babbitt Metals for Bearings

Babbitt metal was formulated by Isaac Babbitt (1799–1862) and is a silver-colored, soft alloy of tin, copper, and antimony. (See Chap. 11, "Antifriction Bearings.")

5.10 Soldering Alloys

See Chap. 6, "Fastening and Joining Techniques."

5.11 Plastics (Thermoplastics and Thermoset Plastics)

Plastic materials are derived mainly from petroleum products. The types, trade names, and compositions of the various modern plastics form a long list, with more being developed as required to meet specific design and application needs in industry.

A *thermoplastic* is one in which the finished molded part may be remelted for remolding. A *thermoset* plastic is one in which the chemical reaction cannot be reversed, thus allowing the part to be cast only once. Thermoplastics are extruded, injection molded, and cast in dies. Thermoset plastics are usually compression molded. Some of the thermoplastics are also formulated for thermoset applications, such as the urethanes. Table 5.123 lists the common/trade names, suppliers, SAE symbols, and plastic "family" names for most plastics.

Common plastics and compositions. Listed here are some of the more prevalent plastics and compositions.

ABS (acrylonitrile-butadiene-styrene)
Acetal (Delrin, Celcon)
Acetate (cellulose)
Acrylic (Lucite, Plexiglas)
Benelex
Epoxy, epoxy glass
Diallyl phthalate, Melamine
Mylar (polyester film)
Nylon
Phenol formaldehyde
Phenolic laminates
Polycarbonate (Lexan)
Polyester glass
Polyethylene
Polypropylene
Polyimide
Polystyrene
Polysulfone
Polyurethane
Polyvinyl chloride (PVC)
Rtv (room-temperature vulcanizing) silicones
Styrofoam (polystyrene)
Teflon (PTFE, polytetrafluoroethylene)
Urea-formaldehyde

(Text continued on page 385.)

TABLE 5.58 General Information—Name, Nominal Composition, and Comparable Standards of Wrought Copper Alloys

Copper or copper alloy UNS no.*	Name[†]	Nominal composition percent by weight		SAE no.	ASTM standard no.[‡]	Former SAE no.
		Cu	Other			
C10200	Oxygen free copper (OF)	99.9	—	CA102	B75, B152, B280	—
C11000	Electrolytic tough pitch copper (ETP)	99.9	—	CA110	B3, B133, B152, B283	71, 83
C11100	Electrolytic tough pitch, anneal-resistant copper	99.9	(Trace elements)	CA111	—	71
C11300	Tough pitch copper with Ag (STP)	99.9	0.03 Ag	CA113	B152	71
C11400	Tough pitch copper with Ag (STP)	99.9	0.04 Ag	CA114	B152	71
C11500	Tough pitch copper with Ag (STP)	99.9	0.06 Ag	CA115	B152	—
C11600	Tough pitch copper with Ag (STP)	99.9	0.09 Ag	CA116	B152	71
C12000	Phosphorus-deoxidized copper (DLP)	99.9	0.0008 P	CA120	B68, B75, B152, B280	75
C12200	Phosphorus-deoxidized copper (DHP)	99.9	0.02 P	CA122	B68, B75, B152, B280	—
C14500	Phosphorus-deoxidized tellurium copper (DPTE)	99.5	0.5 Te, 0.008 P	CA145	B283, B301	—
C14700	Sulfur-bearing copper	99.7	0.3 S	CA147	B301	—
C15000	Zirconium copper	99.8	0.15 Zn	CA150	B301	—
C16200	Cadmium copper	99.0	1 Cd	CA162		—
C17000	Beryllium copper	98.0	1.7 Be	CA170	B194	—
C17200	Beryllium copper	98.0	1.9 Be	CA172	B194, B196	—
C17500	Beryllium copper	97.0	0.5 Be, 2.5 Co	CA175	B441, B534	—
C17600	Beryllium copper	97.0	0.4 Be, 1.5 Co, 1 Ag	CA176	B441	—

C18400	Chromium copper	99.0	0.8 Cr	CA184		—
C18700	Leaded copper	99.0	1 Pb	CA187	B301	—
C19200	High-copper alloy	99.0	1 Fe, 0.03 P	CA192	B111	—
C21000	Gilding, 95%	95.0	5 Zn	CA210	B36	—
C22000	Commercial bronze, 90%	90.0	10 Zn	CA220	B36, B135	—
C23000	Red brass, 85%	85.0	15 Zn	CA230	B36, B135	74D, 79A
C24000	Low brass, 80%	80.0	20 Zn	CA240	B36	79B
C26000	Cartridge brass, 70%	70.0	30 Zn	CA260	B36, B134 B135	70A, 74C, 80A
C26800	Yellow brass, 66%	66.0	34 Zn	CA268	B36	70C
C27000	Yellow brass, 65%	65.0	35 Zn	CA270	B134	80B
C33000	Low-leaded brass, (tube)	66.0	34 Zn, 0.5 Pb	CA330	B135	74B
C33100	Leaded brass	66.0	33 Zn, 1 Pb	CA331		
C34200	High-leaded brass	65.0	33 Zn, 2 Pb	CA342	B121	
C34500	Leaded brass	63.0	35 Zn, 2 Pb	CA345	B453	
C35000	Medium-leaded brass, 62%	63.0	36 Zn, 1 Pb	CA350	B121, B453	
C36000	Free-cutting brass	62.0	35 Zn, 3 Pb	CA360	B16	72
C37700	Forging brass	60.0	38 Zn, 2 Pb	CA377	B283	88
C46400	Naval brass, unhibited	60.0	39 Zn, 0.8 Sn	CA464	B21, B283	73
C46500	Naval brass, arsenical	60.0	40 Zn, 0.5 As	CA465		
C46600	Naval brass, antimonial	60.0	40 Zn, 0.5 Sb	CA466		
C46700	Naval brass, phosphorized	60.0	40 Zn, 0.5 P	CA467		
C51000	Phosphor bronze, 5% A	95.0	5 Sn, 0.2 P	CA510	B103, B139, B159	77A, 81
C51100	Phosphor bronze	96.0	4 Sn, 0.2 P	CA511	B103	
C52100	Phosphor bronze, 8% C	92.0	8 Sn, 0.2 P	CA521	B103	77C
C52400	Phosphor bronze, 10% D	90.0	10 Sn, 0.2 P	CA524	B103	
C54400	Phosphor bronze, B-2	88.0	4 Sn, 4 Zn, 4 Pb	CA544	B103, B139	—
C60800	Aluminum bronze	95.0	5 Al	CA608	B111	
C61400	Aluminum bronze, D	91.0	7 Al, 2 Fe	CA614	B150, B169	701D
C61800	Aluminum bronze	89.0	10 Al, 1 Fe	CA618		
C62300	Aluminum bronze	88.0	9 Al, 3 Fe	CA623	B150, B283	701B
C62400	Aluminum bronze	86.0	11 Al, 3 Fe	CA624		701B
C63000	Aluminum bronze	82.0	10 Al, 3 Fe, 5 Ni	CA630	B150, B283	701C
C64200	Aluminum silicon bronze	91.0	7 Al, 2 Si	CA642	B150, B283	

TABLE 5.58 General Information—Name, Nominal Composition, and Comparable Standards of Wrought Copper Alloys (*Continued*)

Copper or copper alloy UNS no.*	Name†	Nominal composition percent by weight		SAE no.	ASTM standard no.‡	Former SAE no.
		Cu	Other			
C65500	High silicon bronze, A	97.0	3 Si	CA655	B97, B98, B283	—
C67000	Manganese bronze, B	65.0	24 Zn, 4 Mn, 4 Al, 3 Fe	CA670	B138	—
C67300	Manganese bronze	60.0	34 Zn, 3 Mn, 2 Pb, 1 Si	CA673		—
C67400	Manganese bronze	58.0	37 Zn, 3 Mn, 1 Al, 1 Si	CA674		—
C67500	Manganese bronze, A	58.0	40 Zn, 0.3 Mn, 1 Fe, 1 Sn	CA675	B138	—
C70600	Copper nickel, 10%	90.0	10 Ni	CA706	B111, B171	—
C71000	Copper nickel, 20%	80.0	20 Ni	CA710	B111, B122	—
C71500	Copper nickel, 30%	70.0	30 Ni	CA715	B111, B122, B171	—
C75200	Nickel silver, 65–18	65.0	18 Ni, 17 Zn	CA752	B122, B151	—
C77000	Nickel silver, 55–18	55.0	18 Ni, 27 Zn	CA770	B122, B151	—

* Unified numbering system.

† Alloy names are shown for information only, and should not be used. Use the appropriate designation only. (Example: Copper Alloy UNS No. C21000 Copper Alloy.)

‡ ASTM standard numbers listed are only those forms or shapes covered in the specification for wrought copper or copper alloy.

SOURCE: Reprinted with permission, copyright 1992, Society of Automotive Engineers.

TABLE 5.59 Typical Physical Properties of Wrought Copper Alloys

Customary Units												
Copper or copper alloy	Melting point, °F			Coefficient of thermal expansion[b]							Modulus	
UNS no.	Liquidus	Solidus	Density[a]	68–212°F	68–392°F	68–572°F	Thermal conductivity[c]	Electrical resistivity[d]	Electrical conductivity[e]	Thermal capacity[f]	Elastic[g]	Rigid[h]
C10200	1981	—	.323	9.4	9.6	9.8	226	10.3	101	.092	17	6.4
C11000	1981	1949	.322	9.4	9.6	9.8	226	10.3	101	.092	17	6.4
C11100	1981	—	.322	9.4	9.6	9.8	224	10.3	101	.092	17	6.4
C11300	1981	—	.322	9.4	9.6	9.8	224	10.3	100	.092	17	6.4
C11400	1981	—	.322	9.4	9.6	9.8	224	10.4	100	.092	17	6.4
C11500	1981	—	.322	9.4	9.6	9.8	224	10.4	100	.092	17	6.4
C11600	1981	—	.322	9.4	9.6	9.8	224	10.4	99	.092	17	6.4
C12000	1981	—	.323	9.4	9.6	9.8	223	10.7	97	.092	17	6.4
C12200	1981	—	.323	9.4	9.5	9.8	196	12.2	85	.092	17	6.4
C14500	1960	1931[i]	.323	9.4	9.6	9.8	205	10.9	95	.092	17	6.4
C14700	1970	1953	.323	9.4	9.6	9.8	216	10.9	95	.092	17	6.4
C15000	1979	—	.323	9.4	9.6	9.8	212[k]	11.2[k]	93[k]	.092	17	6.4
C16200	1969	—	.321	9.4	9.6	9.8	208	11.9	87	.092	17	6.4
C17000	1800	1600	.298	9.3	9.4	9.9	—	47.2	22	—	19	7.3
C17200	1800	1600	.298	9.3	9.4	9.9	—	47.2	22	.100	19	7.3
C17500	1955	1885	.316	—	9.8	—	—	23.1	45	—	18	6.8
C17600	1930	1850	.316	—	9.8	—	—	19.0	50	—	18	6.8
C18400	1967	—	.321	9.4	9.6	9.8	187[k]	13.0[k]	80[k]	.092	19	7.2
C18700	1976	1947[j]	.323	9.4	9.6	9.8	218	10.6	98	.092	17	6.4
C19200	1983	—	.320	9.0	—	—	125	20.8	50	.092	17	6.4
C21000	1950	1920	.320	—	—	10.0	135	18.5	00	.090	17	6.4
C22000	1910	1870	.318	—	—	10.2	109	23.6	44	.090	17	6.4
C23000	1880	1810	.316	—	—	10.4	92	28.0	37	.090	17	6.4
C24000	1830	1770	.313	—	—	10.6	81	32.4	32	.090	16	6.0
C26000	1750	1680	.308	—	—	11.1	70	37.0	28	.090	16	6.0
C26800	1710	1660	.306	—	—	11.3	67	38.4	27	.090	15	5.6
C27000	1710	1660	.306	—	—	11.3	67	38.4	27	.090	15	5.6
C33000	1720	1660	.307	—	—	11.2	67	39.9	26	.090	15	5.6

TABLE 5.59 Typical Physical Properties of Wrought Copper Alloys (*Continued*)

Customary Units

Copper or copper alloy	Melting point, °F			Coefficient of thermal expansion[b]			Thermal	Electrical	Electrical	Thermal	Modulus	
UNS no.	Liquidus	Solidus	Density[a]	68–212°F	68–392°F	68–572°F	conductivity[c]	resistivity[d]	conductivity[e]	capacity[f]	Elastic[g]	Rigid[h]
C33100	1720	1660	.307	—	—	11.2	67	39.9	26	.090	15	5.6
C34200	1670	1630	.306	—	—	11.3	67	39.9	26	.090	15	5.6
C34500	1650	1625	.305	—	—	11.4	69	39.9	26	—	10	—
C35000	1650	1630	.305	—	—	11.4	67	39.9	26	.090	14	5.3
C36000	1650	1630	.307	—	—	11.4	67	39.9	26	.090	14	5.3
C37700	1640	1620	.305	—	—	11.5	69	38.4	27	.090	15	5.6
C46400	1650	1630	.304	—	—	11.8	67	39.9	26	.090	15	5.6
C46500	1650	1630	.304	—	—	11.8	67	39.9	26	.090	15	5.6
C46600	1650	1630	.304	—	—	11.8	67	39.9	26	.090	15	5.6
C46700	1650	1630	.304	—	—	11.8	67	39.9	26	.090	15	5.6
C51000	1920	1750	.320	—	—	9.9	40	69.1	15	.090	16	6.0
C51100	1945	1785	.320	—	—	9.9	48	52.0	20	.090	16	6.0
C52100	1880	1620	.318	—	—	10.1	36	79.8	13	.090	16	6.0
C52400	1830	1550	.317	—	—	10.2	29	94.3	11	.090	16	6.0
C54400	1830	1700	.321	—	—	9.6	50	54.6	19	.090	15	5.6
C60800	1945	1920	.295	—	—	10.0	46	60.0	17	.090	17.5	6.6
C61300	1915	1905	.285	—	—	9.0	39	74.1	14	.090	17	6.4
C61400	1915	1905	.285	—	—	9.0	39	74.1	14	.090	17	6.4
C61800	1910	1900	.274	—	—	9.0	37	79.8	13	—	17	—
C62300	1910	1890	.274	—	9.0	9.4	31	79.8	13	—	16	—
C62400	1910	1895	.274	—	9.0	9.2	34	79.8	13	—	16	—
C63000	1930	1890	.274	—	9.0	9.4	22	138.0	8	.090	17	6.4
C64200	1840	1800	.278	—	—	10.0	26	113.0	8	.090	16	6.0
C65500	1880	1780	.308	—	—	10.0	21	148.0	7	.090	15	5.6
C67000	1710	1665	.282	—	—	11.0	14	86.4	12	—	15	—
C67300	1620	1555	.299	—	—	11.0	—	86.4	12	—	15	—

C67400	1625	1550	.292	—	—	11.0	58	86.4	12	—	14	—
C67500	1630	1590	.302	—	—	11.8	61	43.2	24	.090	15	5.6
C70600	2100	2010	.323	—	—	9.5	26	115.0	9	.090	18	6.8
C71000	2192	2066	.323	—	—	9.1	21	160.0	6	.090	20	7.5
C71500	2260	2140	.323	—	—	9.0	17	225.0	5	.090	22	8.3
C75200	2030	1960	.316	—	—	9.0	19	173.0	6	.090	18	6.8
C77000	1930	—	.314	—	—	9.3	17	189.0	6	.090	18	6.8

[a] lb/in^3 at 68°F. See Table 2A for specific gravity (g/cm^3 at 20°C).
[b] Per °F at temperature range indicated (multiply factor given by 10^{-6}).
[c] Btu/ft^2/ft·h·°F at 68°F.
[d] (Annealed) ohms (circular mil/ft) at 68°F.
[e] (Annealed) percent IACS at 68°F (volume basis).
[f] (Specific heat) Btu/lb/°F at 68°F.
[g] (Tension) psi (multiply factor given by 10^6).
[h] Psi (multiply factor given by 10^6).
[i] Small amount of tellurium-rich constituent remains liquid down to 1575°F.
[j] Small amount of lead-rich constituent remains liquid down to 619°F.
[k] After precipitation-hardening heat treatment.
SOURCE: Reprinted with permission, copyright 1992, Society of Automotive Engineers.

TABLE 5.60 Fabrication Properties, Other Characteristics, and Typical Uses of Copper

Copper or copper alloy UNS no.	Approximate relative suitability for being worked*		Best temperature for hot working, °C	Approximate relative suitability* for being joined by						Resistance welding			Machinability‡	Type of chip†	Typical uses	Characteristics
	Cold	Hot		Soldering	Brazing	Oxyacetylene welding	Carbon arc welding	Gas-shielded arc welding	Coated-metal arc welding	Spot	Seam	Butt				
C10200	E	E	760–870	E	E	F	F	G	NR	NR	NR	G	20	L	Thermal and electrical conductors, electronic parts, glass-to-metal seals.	Oxygen-free 100% minimum electrical conductivity, excellent ductility, high purity, no out gassing. Not subject to hydrogen embrittlement. Designated for use where processing involves heating in a reducing atmosphere.
C11000	E	E	760–870	E	G	NR	F	F	NR	NR	NR	G	20	L	Electrical wiring and components, radiator fins, gaskets, washers, cold-heading wire, water deflectors, heat plugs, clock cases, plating anodes, screen wire.	Minimum electrical conductivity 100%, highest electrical conductivity of any metal except silver, has very high ductility. Will embrittle when heated to redness in a reducing atmosphere.
C11100	E	E	760–870	E	G	NR	F	F	NR	NR	NR	G	20	L	Radiator fins.	Has a softening temperature higher than the silver bearing coppers and electrolytic tough pitch copper.

C11300	E	E	760–780	E	G	NR	F	F	NR	NR	NR	G	20	L	Commutator bars, segments, collector rings and contacts, core and fin stock for radiators.	Minimum electrical conductivity 98%. Resistance to softening increased by presence of silver. Effect increases with increased silver added. Higher-silver-content copper used for continued exposure to somewhat higher temperature.
C11400	E	E	760–780	E	G	NR	F	F	NR	NR	NR	G	20	L		
C11500	E	E	760–870	E	G	NR	F	F	NR	NR	NR	G	20	L		
C11600	E	E	760–870	E	G	NR	F	F	NR	NR	NR	G	20	L		
C12000	E	E	760–870	E	E	G	G	E	NR	NR	NR	G	20	L	Electrical conductors, applications involving welding or brazing.	Regarded as an alternate to Copper UNS no. C10200. More resistant to embrittlement than Copper UNS no. C11000 high electrical conductivity.
C12200	E	E	760–870	E	E	G	G	E	NR	NR	NR	G	20	L	Tube, all types of hydraulic systems, fuel lines, vacuum lines, air conditioning, heat exchangers, anodes, air, gasoline, hydraulic, and oil lines, oil coolers, gauge lines.	Slightly improved mechanical properties. Electrical conductivity about 85%. Not subject to hydrogen embrittlement.
C14500	E	E	760–845	E	E	F	F	G	NR	NR	NR	G	80	S	Forgings and screw machine parts requiring high electrical and thermal conductivity, furnace brazing. Electrical connectors, motor and switch parts, soldering coppers, and welding torch tips.	Free-machining copper, combined with high electrical conductivity (90–96%).

TABLE 5.60 Fabrication Properties, Other Characteristics, and Typical Uses of Copper (*Continued*)

Copper or copper alloy UNS no.	Approximate relative suitability for being worked*		Best temperature for hot working, °C	Approximate relative suitability* for being joined by									Machinability‡	Type of chip†	Typical uses	Characteristics
										Resistance welding						
	Cold	Hot		Soldering	Brazing	Oxyacetylene welding	Carbon arc welding	Gas-shielded arc welding	Coated-metal arc welding	Spot	Seam	Butt				
C14700	E	E	760–870	E	E	NR	NR	NR	NR	NR	NR	G	80	S	Transformer and circuit-breaker terminals, studs, bolts, nuts, and current-carrying parts requiring fine machining.	Free-machining copper, combined with high electrical conductivity (90–96%).
C15000	E	E	760–870	E	G	F	F	F	NR	NR	NR	G	20	L	Resistance welding electrodes. Miscellaneous current-carrying components at elevated temperatures.	Precipitation hardened. Combined high strength and conductivity and resistance to softening at elevated temperatures.
C16200	E	G	760–870	E	E	F	F	G	NR	NR	NR	G	20	L	Electrical contacts and terminals, signal relays. Hard temper used for spring contact in small apparatus and resistance welding electrodes.	Moderate high strength and high electrical conductivity.
C17000	G	G	705–775	G	G	NR	F	G	NR	NR	NR	G	20	L	Leaf springs, electrical contacts, coil springs and bellows requiring severe forming distributor breaker arm, welding tips, and welding wheels.	Copper Alloy UNS nos. C17000, C17200, C17500, and C17600 can develop the highest mechanical properties by heat treatment. Complete range of properties.
C17200	G	G	705–775	G	G	NR	F	G	NR	NR	NR	G	20	L		
C17500	G	G	760–925	G	G	NR	F	G	NR	NR	NR	G	20	L		
C17600	G	G	760–925	G	G	NR	F	G	NR	NR	NR	G	20	L	Clips, welder tips, and wheels.	

C18400	E	E	900–925	G	G	NR	F	G	NR	NR	NR	G	20	L	Spot welding electrodes and wheels, flash welding dies, and commutator segments.	Precipitation hardened. Fairly high electrical conductivity. Resistance to softening at elevated temperatures.
C18700	G	NR	—	E	G	NR	NR	NR	NR	NR	NR	F	80	S	Screw machine parts requiring high electrical and thermal conductivity.	Free-machining copper, high electrical conductivity. Unsuited for hot working.
C19200	E	E	815–950	E	E	G		E	NR	NR	NR	G	20		Flexible hose, electrical terminals, fuse clips, gaskets, air-conditioning and heat-exchanger tubing.	Resistance to softening and also stress corrosion.
C21000	E	G	760–870	E	E	G	F	G	NR	NR	NR	G	20	L	Emblems, vitreous enamel base, ornamental trim, and jewelry.	Copper Alloy UNS nos. C21000, C22000, and C23000 are generally reddish in color, soft and malleable, higher annealing point than copper and slightly stronger and similar in corrosion resistance. Good for drawing and forming. Resistance to dezincification and season cracking is excellent.
C22000	E	G	760–870	E	E	G	F	G	NR	NR	NR	G	20	L	Emblems, vitreous enamel base, ornamental trim, jewelry, expansion plugs, valve parts, escutcheon fasteners, and spring clips.	
C23000	E	G	790–900	E	E	G	F	G	NR	F	NR	G	30	L	Radiator parts, heat-exchanger tubes, tube bends.	
C24000	E	F	815–900	E	E	G	F	G	NR	F	NR	G	30	L	Bellows and water temperature switch housing, flexible hose, pump lines.	Color is light golden, strength and ductility continue to increase.

TABLE 5.60 Fabrication Properties, Other Characteristics, and Typical Uses of Copper (*Continued*)

Copper or copper alloy UNS no.	Approximate relative suitability for being worked*		Best temperature for hot working, °C	Approximate relative suitability* for being joined by									Machinability‡	Type of chip†	Typical uses	Characteristics
	Cold	Hot		Soldering	Brazing	Oxyacetylene welding	Carbon arc welding	Gas-shielded arc welding	Coated-metal arc welding	Resistance welding: Spot	Resistance welding: Seam	Resistance welding: Butt				
C26000	E	F	730–845	E	E	G	F	F	NR	G	NR	G	30	L	Radiator tanks and lock-seam tubes, header plates, reflectors, lamp bases, terminals, ground straps, baffles, ammeter shells and speedometer counter-weights, washers, wheel covers, trim, carburetor parts.	Color is brass yellow. Greatest ductility of the copper-zinc series. Strength is higher than any of the preceding copper-zinc alloys.
C26800 C27000	E E	NR NR	— —	E E	E E	G G	F F	F F	NR NR	G G	NR NR	G G	30 30	L L	Radiator cores and tanks, lamp fixtures, socket shells, eyelets, fasteners and grommets, hinges, locks, pins, rivets, screws, and springs.	Strength increases and ductility decreases, but is still very good.
C33000	E	NR	—	E	G	F	F	F	NR	F	NR	F	60	M	Tube carburetor parts, oil cooler tube, radiator and ornamental work, pump and power cylinders and liners.	Provides some degree of machinability, together with moderate cold-working properties.
C33100	E	NR	—	E	G	NR	NR	NR	NR	NR	NR	F	70	M	Keys.	Intended for blanking, piercing, and machining.
C34200	E	NR	—	E	G	NR	NR	NR	NR	NR	NR	F	90	S	Clock plates and nuts, clock and watch backs, keys, gears, and wheels.	Provides increased machinability with moderate cold-working properties.

C34500	F	F	705–790	E	G	NR	NR	NR	NR	NR	NR	F	90	S	Screw-machine parts requiring roll threads, knurls, or staking operations.	Best combination of machinability and cold-working properties.
C35000	F	NR	—	E	G	NR	NR	NR	NR	NR	NR	F	70	M	Keys.	Intended for blanking, piercing, and machining.
C36000	NR	F	709–790	E	G	NR	NR	NR	NR	NR	NR	F	100	S	Automatic screw-machine parts and carburetor, magneto parts, radiator drums and other fittings, plugs, inserts, gears, pinions, locks.	The standard free-cutting brass and its machinability has become the standard by which other alloys are rated.
C37700	NR	E	650–815	E	G	NR	NR	NR	NR	NR	NR	F	80	S	Forgings and pressings of all kinds. Headings, air-conditioning tube fittings, convertible top hardware (latches, hinges, etc.), forged valve bodies.	Excellent hot-working properties and widely used as forging rod. At ordinary temperatures it is strong, hard, and free-cutting.
C46400	F	E	650–815	E	E	G	F	F	NR	G	F	G	30	L	Aircraft turnbuckle barrels and balls, cold headed parts, forgings, screw-machine parts, marine hardware, condenser plates, welding rod, nozzles, and fittings.	Excellent hot and fair cold-working properties of somewhat higher strength, good saltwater corrosion resistance.
C46500	F	E	650–815	E	E	G	F	F	NR	G	F	G	30	L		
C46600	F	E	650–815	E	E	G	F	F	NR	G	F	G	30	L		
C46700	F	E	650–815	E	E	G	F	F	NR	G	F	G	30	L		
C51000	E	NR	—	E	E	F	G	G	F	G	F	E	20	L	Springs, bearings, clips, contacts, switch parts, diaphragms, welding rod, thermostats, bellows, clutch disks, lock washers, fasteners.	C51000 and C52100 have a remarkable combination of strength, ductility and resilience, and fatigue resistance.
C51100	E	NR	—	E	E	F	G	G	F	G	F	E	20	L		
C52100	G	NR	—	E	E	F	G	G	F	G	F	E	20	L	Springs, clips, contacts, terminal wire and bushings, diaphragms, and bellows.	
C52400	G	NR	—	E	E	F	G	G	F	G	F	E	20	L		

TABLE 5.60 Fabrication Properties, Other Characteristics, and Typical Uses of Copper (*Continued*)

Copper or copper alloy UNS no.	Approximate relative suitability for being worked*		Best temperature for hot working, °C	Approximate relative suitability* for being joined by									Machinability‡	Type of chip†	Typical uses	Characteristics
	Cold	Hot		Soldering	Brazing	Oxyacetylene welding	Carbon arc welding	Gas-shielded arc welding	Coated-metal arc welding	Resistance welding: Spot	Resistance welding: Seam	Resistance welding: Butt				
C54400	G	NR	—	E	G	NR	NR	NR	NR	NR	NR	F	80	S	Bearings, bushings, gears, pinions, shafts, thrust washers, valve parts.	Free-cutting, good cold-working properties, also suitable for blanking, forming, and bending.
C60800	G	F	790–870	F	F	NR	—	G	G	G	G	G	20	—	Condenser, evaporator, and heat exchanger tubes, ferrules.	
C61300	G	G	785–925	F	F	NR	G	§	G	G	G	G	20	L	Gibs, wear strips, gears, bushings, nuts, bolts, and threaded members.	Good cold-working properties and corrosion resistance. High strength and ductility.
C61400	G	G	785–925	F	F	NR	G	§	G	G	G	G	20	L	Gibs, wear strips, gears, bushings, nuts, bolts, and threaded members.	Good cold-working properties and corrosion resistance. High strength and ductility.
C61800	F	G	760–885	F	G	NR	—	G	G	G	G	G	40	—	Bushings, bearings, corrosion applications, welding rod.	
C62300	F	G	730–815	F	F	NR	G	§	G	G	G	G	30	L	Valve guides, spark plug inserts, gears, valve seat inserts, oil plugs, and shifter forks.	Good hot-working properties; high strength retained well at elevated temperatures; acid and oxidation resistant.

C62400	NR	E	720–775	F	F	NR	G	§	G	G	G	G	30	L	Valve guides, spark plug inserts, gears, valve seat inserts, oil plugs, shifter forks, wear strips, ball bearings, and hydraulic valve components.	Excellent hot-working, poor cold-working properties; heat treated for high mechanical properties.
C63000	NR	G	705–760	F	F	NR	G	§	G	G	G	G	20	L	Retractable landing gear, propeller gears, large valve seat inserts, spacer bearings, high-pressure pump components.	Very high mechanical properties in the heat-treated condition; difficult to cold work; good hot-working properties, excellent corrosion resistance.
C64200	NR	E	705–760	F	F	NR	—	F	F	F	F	F	60	—	Valve stems, gears, bolts, nuts, valve bodies, and components.	Free machining, high strength, high corrosion resistance.
C65500	E	E	705–760	G	E	G	G	E	F	E	E	E	30	L	Hydraulic pressure lines, bolts, clamps, piston rings, rivets, and shafting.	Relatively high strength, marked ductility and capability for being both hot- and cold-worked and joined by all procedures. Excellent corrosion resistance.
C67000	NR	E	565–745	NR	F	NR	NR	§	G	G	F	G	30	S	Diesel injector nozzles; high pressure hydraulic applications, cams, pistons, and other components involving high mechanical loads and sliding contact.	High strength and good wear-resistant properties.
C67300	F	E	625–745	NR	G	NR	NR	NR	NR	NR	NR	F	70	S	Forged water pump impellers; gears, axial piston pump components, bushings, and bearings.	Hot-forgeable, free-cutting alloy having fairly high strength and good corrosion-resistant properties.

TABLE 5.60 Fabrication Properties, Other Characteristics, and Typical Uses of Copper (*Continued*)

Copper or copper alloy UNS no.	Approximate relative suitability for being worked*		Best temperature for hot working, °C	Approximate relative suitability* for being joined by						Resistance welding			Machinability‡	Type of chip†	Typical uses	Characteristics
	Cold	Hot		Soldering	Brazing	Oxyacetylene welding	Carbon arc welding	Gas-shielded arc welding	Coated-metal arc welding	Spot	Seam	Butt				
C67400	F	E	565–745	NR	F	NR	NR	§	G	G	F	G	30	L	Connecting rods, transmission synchronizing stop ring, door striker plates, shifter shoes, differential idler pins, forged water pump impellers, axial piston pump parts, bushings, and bearings.	Hot-forgeable, high-strength alloy with good wear-resistant properties and good corrosion resistance.
C67500	NR	E	625–790	E	E	G	F	F	NR	G	F	G	30	L	Clutch disks, pump rods, shafting, balls, valve stems, and bodies.	Strong, rigid, and abrasion resistant; adopted to hot forging and pressing, hot heading, and upsetting.
C70600	G	G	760–980	E	E	F	NR	E	G	G	G	E	20	L	Condenser and heat-exchanger tubes.	Used where requirements are severe. Strong, tough, and very resistant to general corrosion as well as stress-corrosion cracking; also serviceable at higher temperatures than copper and brasses. Well suited for condenser and heat exchanger tube.

C71000	G	G	760–980	E	E	G	NR	E	E	E	E	E	20	L	Condenser and heat-exchanger tubes, ferrules.	Copper Alloy UNS nos. C71000 and C71500 are used where requirements are severe. Strong, tough, and very resistant to general corrosion as well as stress-corrosion cracking; also serviceable at higher temperatures than copper and brasses. Well suited for condenser and heat-exchanger tube.
C71500	G	G	925–1035	E	E	G	NR	E	E	E	E	E	20	L	Automatic oil coolers, heat-exchanger tubes.	
C75200	E	NR	—	E	E	G	NR	F	NR	G	F	G	20	L	Rivets, screws, name plates, radio dials, etching stock, trim.	Copper Alloy UNS nos. C75200 and C77000 are manufactured in a wide range of nickel contents. Higher the nickel, the more silver white the alloy. 65% copper alloys have good cold-working properties and are used for cold drawing, spinning, forming, and stamping. The lower-copper-content alloys (55% Cu) are used for spring applications.
C77000	G	NR	—	E	E	G	NR	F	NR	G	F	G	30	L	Springs, resistance wire.	

* E = Excellent; G = Good; F = Fair; NR = Not recommended.

† S = Short; M = Medium; L = Long.

‡ Approximate relative machinability rating (free-cutting brass = 100).

§ Consumable electrode excellent. Tungsten are good, with ac preferred.

SOURCE: Reprinted with permission, copyright 1992, Society of Automotive Engineers.

TABLE 5.61 Chemical Composition of Cast Copper Alloys[a,p]

Copper alloy UNS no.[b]	Cu[c]	Sn	Pb	Zn[c]	Fe	Sb	Ni (incl. Co)	Mn	As	S	P	Al	Si
C83600	84.0–86.0[d]	4.0–6.0	4.0–6.0	4.0–6.0	0.30	0.25	1.0[d]	—	—	0.08	0.05[e]	0.005	0.005
C83800	82.0–83.8[d]	3.3–4.2	5.0–7.0	5.0–8.0	0.30	0.25	1.0[d]	—	—	0.08	0.03[e]	0.005	0.005
C85200	70.0–74.0	0.7–2.0	1.5–3.8	20.0–27.0	0.6	0.20	1.0	—	—	0.05	0.02	0.005	0.05
C85400	65.0–70.0	0.50–1.5	1.5–3.8	24.0–32.0	0.7	—	1.0	—	—	—	—	0.35	0.05
C85800	57.0 min[f]	1.5	1.5	31.0–34.0	0.50	0.05	0.50	0.25	0.05	0.05	0.01	0.50	0.25
C86200	60.0–66.0	0.20	0.20	22.0–28.0	2.0–4.0	—	1.0	2.5–5.0	—	—	—	3.0–4.9	—
C86300	60.0–66.0	0.20	0.20	22.0–28.0	2.0–4.0	—	1.0	2.5–5.0	—	—	—	5.0–7.5	—
C86500	55.0–60.0	1.0	0.40	36.0–42.0	0.40–2.0	—	1.0	0.10–1.5	—	—	—	0.50–1.5	—
C87200	89.0 min[f]	1.0	0.50	5.0	2.5	—	—	1.5	—	—	—	1.5	1.0–5.0
C87400	79.0 min[f]	—	1.0	12.0–16.0	—	—	—	—	—	—	—	0.8	2.5–4.0
C87500	79.0 min[f]	—	0.50	12.0–16.0	—	—	—	—	—	—	—	0.5	3.0–5.0
C87800[g]	80.0 min[h]	0.25	0.15	12.0–16.0	0.15	0.05	0.20	0.15	0.05	0.05	0.01	0.15	3.8–4.2
C87900	63.0 min[f]	0.25	0.25	30.0–60.0	0.40	0.05	0.50	0.15	0.05	0.05	0.01	0.15	0.8–1.2
C90300	86.0–89.0	7.5–9.0	0.30	3.0–5.0	0.20	0.20	1.0[d]	—	—	0.05	0.05[e]	0.005	0.005
C90500	86.0–89.0[d]	9.0–11.0	0.30	1.0–3.0	0.20	0.20	1.0[d]	—	—	0.05	0.05[e]	0.005	0.005
C90700	88.0–90.0[i]	10.0–12.0	0.50	0.50	0.15	0.20	0.50	—	—	0.05	0.30[e]	0.005	0.005
C92200	86.0–90.0[d]	5.5–6.5	1.0–2.0	3.0–5.0	0.25	0.25	1.0[d]	—	—	0.05	0.05[e]	0.005	0.005
C92300	85.0–89.0[d]	7.5–9.0	0.30–1.0	2.5–5.0	0.25	0.25	1.0[d]	—	—	0.05	0.05[e]	0.005	0.005
C92500	85.0–88.0	10.0–12.0	1.0–1.5	0.50	0.30	0.25	0.8–1.5	—	—	0.05	0.30[e]	0.005	0.005
C92700	86.0–89.0	9.0–11.0	1.0–2.5	0.7	0.20	0.25	1.0	—	—	0.05	0.25[e]	0.005	0.005
C92900	82.0–86.0[i]	9.0–11.0	2.0–3.2	0.25	0.20	0.25	2.8–4.0	—	—	0.05	0.50[e]	0.005	0.005
C93200	81.0–85.0[d]	6.3–7.5	6.0–8.0	2.0–4.0	0.20	0.35	1.0[d]	—	—	0.08	0.15[e]	0.005	0.005
C93500	83.0–86.0[d]	4.3–6.0	8.0–11.0	2.0	0.20	0.30	1.0[d]	—	—	0.08	0.05[e]	0.005	0.005
C93700	78.0–82.0[d]	9.0–11.0	8.0–11.0	0.8	0.15[j]	0.55	1.0[d]	—	—	0.08	0.15[e]	0.005	0.005
C93800	75.0–79.0[d]	6.3–7.5	13.0–16.0	0.8	0.15	0.8	1.0[d]	—	—	0.08	0.05[e]	0.005	0.005
C94300	68.5–73.5[d]	4.5–6.0	22.0–25.0	0.8	0.15	0.8	1.0[d]	—	—	0.08	0.05[e]	0.005	0.005

C94700	85.0–90.0	4.5–6.0	0.10[k]	1.0–2.5	0.25	0.15	4.5–6.0	0.20	—	0.05	0.05	0.005	0.005
C94800	84.0–89.0	4.5–6.0	0.30–1.0	1.0–2.5	0.25	0.15	4.5–6.0	0.20	—	0.05	0.05	0.005	0.005
C95200	86.0 min[i]	—	—	—	2.5–4.0	—	—	—	—	—	—	8.5–9.5	—
C95300	86.0 min[i]	—	—	—	0.8–1.5	—	—	—	—	—	—	9.0–11.0	—
C95400	83.0 min[f]	—	—	—	3.0–5.0	—	2.5	0.50	—	—	—	10.0–11.5	—
C95500	78.0 min[f]	—	—	—	3.0–5.0	—	3.0–5.0	3.5	—	—	—	10.0–11.5	—
C95800	79.0 min[f]	—	0.03	—	3.5–4.5[m]	—	4.0–5.0[m]	0.8–1.5	—	—	—	8.5–9.5	0.10
										Nb	C		
C96200	84.5–87.0	—	0.03	—	1.0–1.8	—	9.0–11.0	1.5	—	1.0	0.15	—	0.30

[a] These specification limits do not preclude the possible presence of other unnamed elements. However, analysis shall regularly be made only for the minor elements listed in the table plus all major elements except one. The major element which is not analyzed shall be determined by difference between the sum of those elements analyzed and 100%. By agreement between producer and consumer, analysis may be required and limits established for elements not specified.

[b] Unified Numbering System. For cross-reference to SAE, former SAE, ASTM, former ASTM, and former trade names, see SAE Information Report for Wrought and Cast Copper Alloys, SAE J461.

[c] In reporting chemical analyses by the use of instruments such as spectrograph, X-ray, and atomic absorption, copper may be indicated as "remainder." In reporting chemical analyses obtained by wet methods, zinc may be indicated as "remainder" on those alloys with over 2% zinc.

[d] In determining copper minimum, copper may be calculated at Cu + Ni.

[e] For continuous castings, phosphorus shall be 1.5% maximum.

[f] Total named elements shall be 99.5% minimum.

[g] Magnesium requirement is 0.01% maximum.

[h] Total named elements shall be 99.8% minimum.

[i] Cu + Sn + Pb + Ni + P shall be 99.5% minimum.

[j] The iron shall be 0.35% maximum when used for steel backed bearings.

[k] The mechanical properties of C94700 (heat treated) may not be attained if the lead content exceeds 0.01%.

[l] Total named elements shall be 99.0% minimum.

[m] Iron content shall not exceed nickel content.

[n] For welding grades, lead may not exceed 0.01%.

[p] Percent by mass (weight); maximum, unless shown as a range or minimum.

SOURCE: Reprinted with permission, copyright 1992, Society of Automotive Engineers.

TABLE 5.62 Mechanical Properties of Cast Copper Alloys

Copper alloy UNS no.*	SAE suffix[†,§]	ASTM standard no.	Casting method[‡,§] and condition	Tensile strength, min		Yield strength, min		Elongation, min, % in 50 mm (2 in)
				MPa	ksi	MPa	ksi	
						0.5% ext. under load		
C83600	A	B271, B584	Sand, centrifugal	205	30	95	14	20
C83600	B	B505	Continuous	250	36	130	19	15
C83600	C		Continuous	345	50	170	15	12
C83800	A	B271, B584	Sand, centrifugal	205	30	90	13	20
C83800	B	B505	Continuous	205	30	95	15	16
C85200		B271, B584	Sand, centrifugal	240	35	85	12	25
C85400		B271, B584	Sand, centrifugal	205	30	75	11	20
						0.2% Offset		
C85800		B176	Die[¶]	380	55	205	30	15
C86200		B271, B505, B584	Sand, centrifugal, cont.	620	90	310	45	18
C86300	A	B271, B584	Sand, centrifugal	760	110	415	60	12
C86300	B	B505	Continuous	760	110	425	62	14
C86500	A	B271, B584	Sand, centrifugal	450	65	170	25	20
C86500	B	B505	Continuous	485	70	170	25	25
						0.5% Ext. Under Load		
C87200		B271, B584	Sand, centrifugal	310	45	125	18	20
C87400		B271, B584	Sand, centrifugal	345	50	145	21	18
C87500		B271, B584	Sand, centrifugal	415	60	165	24	16
						0.2% Offset		
C87800		B176	Die[¶]	585	85	345	50	25
C87900		B176	Die[¶]	485	70	240	35	25

						0.5% Ext. Under Load		
C90300	A	B271, B584	Sand, centrifugal	275	40	125	18	20
C90300	B	B505	Continuous	305	44	150	22	18
C90500	A	B271, B584	Sand, centrifugal	275	40	125	18	20
C90500	B	B505	Continuous	305	44	170	25	10
C90700	A		Sand	240	35	125	18	10
C90700	B	B505	Continuous	275	40	170	25	10
C92200	A	B271, B584	Sand, centrifugal	235	34	110	16	24
C92200	B	B505	Continuous	260	38	130	19	18
C92300	A	B271, B584	Sand, centrifugal	250	36	110	16	18
C92300	B	B505	Continuous	275	40	130	19	16
C92500	A		Sand	240	35	125	18	10
C92500	B	B505	Continuous	275	40	165	24	10
C92700	A		Sand	240	35	125	18	10
C92700	B	B505	Continuous	260	38	140	20	8
C92900		B427, B505	Sand, continuous	310	45	170	25	8
C93200	A	B271, B584	Sand, centrifugal	205	30	95	14	15
C93200	B	B505	Continuous	240	35	140	20	10
C93500	A	B271, B584	Sand, centrifugal	195	28	85	12	15
C93500	B	B505	Continuous	205	30	110	16	12
C93700	A	B271, B584	Sand, centrifugal	205	30	85	12	15
C93700	B	B505	Continuous	240	35	140	20	6
C93700	C		Continuous	275	40	170	25	6
C93800	A	B271, B584	Sand, centrifugal	180	26	95	14	12
C93800	B	B505	Continuous	170	25	110	16	5
C94300	A	B271, B584	Sand, centrifugal	145	21	—	—	10
C94300	B	B505	Continuous	145	21	95	15	7
C94700	A	B505, B584	Sand, continuous	310	45	140	20	25
C94700	B	B505, B584	Sand, continuous (HT)	515	75	345	50	5
C94800		B505, B584	Sand, continuous	275	40	140	20	20

TABLE 5.62 Mechanical Properties of Cast Copper Alloys (*Continued*)

Copper alloy UNS no.*	SAE suffix[†,§]	ASTM standard no.	Casting method[‡,§] and condition	Tensile strength, min MPa	Tensile strength, min ksi	Yield strength, min 0.5% ext. under load MPa	Yield strength, min 0.5% ext. under load ksi	Elongation, min, % in 50 mm (2 in)
C95200	A	B148, B271	Sand, centrifugal	450	65	170	25	20
C95200	B	B505	Continuous	470	68	180	26	20
C95300	A	B148, B271	Sand, centrifugal	450	65	170	25	20
C95300	B	B505	Continuous	485	70	180	26	25
C95300	C	B148, B271, B505	Sand, centrifugal, cont. (HT)	550	80	275	40	12
C95400	A	B148, B271	Sand, centrifugal	515	75	205	30	12
C95400	B	B505	Continuous	585	85	220	32	12
C95400	C	B148, B271	Sand, centrifugal (HT)	620	90	310	45	6
C95400	D	B505	Continuous (HT)	655	95	310	45	10
C95500	A	B148, B271	Sand, centrifugal	620	90	275	40	6
C95500	B	B505	Continuous	655	95	290	42	10
C95500	C	B148, B271	Sand, centrifugal (HT)	760	110	415	60	5
C95500	D	B505	Continuous (HT)	760	110	425	62	8
C95800	A	B148, B271	Sand, centrifugal	585	85	240	35	15
C95800	B	B505	Continuous (3)	620	90	260	38	18
C96200		B369	Sand	310	45	170	25	20

* Unified Numbering System. For cross-reference to SAE, former SAE, former ASTM, and former trade names, see SAE Information Report for Wrought and Cast Copper Alloys, SAE J461.

† Suffix symbols may be specified to distinguish between two or more sets of mechanical properties, heat treatment, conditions, etc. as applicable.

‡ All alloys listed are in the "as cast" condition except those designated as heat treated (HT) and copper alloy UNS No. C95800 which is temper annealed.

§ Most commonly used method of casting is shown for each alloy. However, unless the purchaser specifies the method of casting or the mechanical properties by supplement to the UNS number, the supplier may use any method which will develop the properties indicated.

¶ Mechanical properties shown for die castings are typical, not minimum.

SOURCE: Reprinted with permission, copyright 1992, Society of Automotive Engineers.

TABLE 5.63 Typical Physical Properties of Cast Copper Alloys (Customary Units)

Copper alloy UNS no.	Melting point °F		Density lb/in^3	Specific gravity	Coefficient of thermal expansion 10^6 in/in/°F	Thermal conductivity % of Cu*	Electrical conductivity % IACS†	Modulus of elasticity 10^6 psi
	Liquidus	Solidus			(20–400°F)			
C83600	1840	1570	0.318	8.83	10.0	18	15	14
C83800	1840	1550	0.312	8.60	10.0	18	15	13
C85200	1725	1700	0.307	8.50	11.5	21	18	11
C85400	1725	1700	0.305	8.45	11.2	23	20	12
C85800	1650	1600	0.305	8.40	12.0	—	20	15
C86200	1725	1650	0.288	7.85	12.0	9	8	15
C86300	1690	1625	0.283	7.84	12.0	9	8	14
C86500	1620	1585	0.301	8.30	11.3	22	22	15
C87200	1780	1580	0.302	8.40	9.2	7	6	15
C87400	1680	1510	0.300	8.27	10.9	7	7	15
C87500	1680	1510	0.300	8.27	10.9	7	7	15
C87800	1680	1510	0.300	8.27	10.9	7	7	20
C87900	1700	1650	0.308	8.50	12.0	—	15	15
C90300	1830	1570	0.318	8.70	10.0	19	12	15
C90500	1830	1570	0.315	8.72	11.0	19	11	15
C90700	1830	1528	0.317	8.78	10.2	19	10	14
C92200	1810	1520	0.312	8.65	10.0	18	14	14
C92300	1830	1570	0.317	8.80	10.0	19	12	14
C92500	1830	1570	0.317	8.85	10.0	—	11	13
C92700	1800	1550	0.317	8.80	10.1	12	11	13

TABLE 5.63 Typical Physical Properties of Cast Copper Alloys (Customary Units) (*Continued*)

Copper alloy UNS no.	Melting point °F		Density lb/in^3	Specific gravity	Coefficient of thermal expansion 10^6 in/in/°F	Thermal conductivity % of Cu*	Electrical conductivity % IACS†	Modulus of elasticity 10^6 psi
	Liquidus	Solidus			(20–400°F)			
C92900	1880	1575	0.320	8.79	9.5	15	9	14
C93200	1800	1570	0.322	8.93	10.0	15	12	14
C93500	1830	1570	0.320	8.87	10.0	18	15	14.5
C93700	1705	1400	0.320	8.95	10.3	12	10	11
C93800	1730	1570	0.334	9.25	10.3	13	12	10
C94300	1750	1650	0.336	9.29	10.0	16	9	11
C94700	1880	1660	0.320	8.80	11.0	14	12	15
C94700 (HT)	1880	1660	0.320	8.80	11.0	15	15	15
C94800	1880	1660	0.320	8.80	11.0	10	12	15
C95200	1913	1907	0.276	7.64	9.0	13	11	15
C95300	1913	1904	0.272	7.53	9.0	16	15	16
C95300 (HT)	1913	1904	0.272	7.53	9.0	16	13	15
C95400	1900	1880	0.269	7.45	9.0	15	13	15.5
C95400 (HT)	1900	1880	0.269	7.45	9.2	15	12	16
C95500	1930	1900	0.272	7.53	9.0	11	8.5	16
C95500 (HT)	1930	1900	0.272	7.53	9.0	11	8	17
C95800	1940	1910	0.276	7.64	9.0	9	7	16.5
C96200	2100	2010	0.323	8.94	9.5	11	11	18

* Cu = 226 $Btu/ft^2/ft/h/°F$ at 68°F.

† International annealed copper standard.

SOURCE: Reprinted with permission, copyright 1992, Society of Automotive Engineers.

TABLE 5.64 Chemical Requirements

Copper alloy UNS	Copper, %	Lead, max, %	Iron, max, %	Zinc
C21000 (95 Cu, 5 Zn)	94.0 to 96.0	0.03	0.05	Remainder
C22000 (90 Cu, 10 Zn)	89.0 to 91.0	0.05	0.05	Remainder
C22600 (87.5 Cu, 12.5 Zn)	86.0 to 89.0	0.05	0.05	Remainder
C23000 (85 Cu, 15 Zn)	84.0 to 86.0	0.05	0.05	Remainder
C24000 (80 Cu, 20 Zn)	78.5 to 81.5	0.05	0.05	Remainder
C26000 (70 Cu, 30 Zn)	68.5 to 71.5	0.07	0.05	Remainder
C26800* (66 Cu, 34 Zn)	64.0 to 68.5	0.15	0.05	Remainder
C27200† (63 Cu, 37 Zn)	62.0 to 65.0	0.07	0.07	Remainder
C28000‡ (60 Cu, 40 Zn)	59.0 to 63.0	0.30	0.07	Remainder

* Material shall be free from beta constituent when examined at a magnification of 75 diameters.

† Small amounts of beta constituent, if present, may interfere in some instances with severe forming or drawing; therefore, suitability for forming or drawing should be established between manufacturer and purchaser.

‡ It is anticipated that this material will contain the beta constituent that may interfere with severe forming or drawing operations.

SOURCE: Reprinted with permission from the *Annual Book of ASTM Standards,* copyright 1992, American Society of Testing and Materials.

TABLE 5.65 Tensile Strength Requirements and Approximate Rockwell Hardness Values for Rolled Tempers

Rolled temper		Tensile strength, ksi*		Tensile strength, MPa†		Approximate Rockwell hardness‡							
						B scale				Superficial 30-T			
Temper designation						0.020 (0.508) to 0.036 in (0.914 mm) incl		Over 0.036 in (0.914 mm)		0.012 (0.305) to 0.028 in (0.711 mm) incl		Over 0.028 in (0.711 mm)	
Standard	Former	Min	Max	Min	Max	Min	Max	Min	Max	Min	Max	Min	Max
Copper Alloy UNS No. C21000													
M20	As hot rolled	32	42	220	290	—	—	—	—	—	—	—	—
H01	Quarter hard	37	47	255	325	20	48	24	52	34	51	37	54
H02	Half hard	42	52	290	355	40	56	44	60	46	57	48	59
H03	Three-quarter hard	46	56	315	385	50	61	53	64	52	60	54	62
H04	Hard	50	59	345	405	57	64	60	67	57	62	59	64
H06	Extra hard	56	64	385	440	64	70	66	72	62	66	63	67
H08	Spring	60	68	415	470	68	73	70	75	64	68	65	69
H10	Extra spring	61	69	420	475	69	74	71	76	65	69	66	70
Copper Alloy UNS No. C22000													
M20	As hot rolled	33	43	230	295	—	—	—	—	—	—	—	—
H01	Quarter hard	40	50	275	345	27	52	31	56	34	51	37	54
H02	Half hard	47	57	325	395	50	63	53	66	50	59	52	61
H03	Three-quarter hard	52	62	355	425	59	68	62	71	55	62	58	64
H04	Hard	57	66	395	455	65	72	68	75	60	65	62	67
H06	Extra hard	64	72	440	495	72	77	74	79	64	68	66	69
H08	Spring	69	77	475	530	76	79	78	81	67	69	68	70
H10	Extra spring	72	80	495	550	78	81	80	83	68	70	69	71
Copper Alloy UNS No. C22600													
H01	Quarter hard	42	52	290	355	29	58	29	58	39	58	39	58
H02	Half hard	48	58	330	400	52	68	52	68	54	64	54	64

H03	Three-quarter hard	53	63	365	435	61	73	61	73	59	68	59	68
H04	Hard	58	67	400	460	67	77	67	77	64	70	64	70
H06	Extra hard	65	73	450	505	74	81	74	81	68	73	68	73
H08	Spring	70	78	485	540	78	83	78	83	71	74	71	74
H10	Extra spring	74	82	510	565	81	86	81	86	73	76	73	76
Copper Alloy UNS No. C23000													
M20	As hot rolled	37	47	255	325	—	—	—	—	—	—	—	—
H01	Quarter hard	44	54	305	370	33	58	37	62	42	57	45	60
H02	Half hard	51	61	350	420	56	68	59	71	56	64	58	66
H03	Three-quarter hard	57	67	395	460	66	73	69	76	63	68	65	70
H04	Hard	63	72	435	495	72	78	74	80	67	71	68	72
H06	Extra hard	72	80	495	550	78	83	80	85	70	74	71	75
H08	Spring	78	86	540	595	82	85	84	87	74	76	75	77
H10	Extra spring	82	90	565	620	84	87	86	89	75	77	76	78
Copper Alloy UNS No. C24000													
M20	As hot rolled	41	51	285	350	—	—	—	—	—	—	—	—
H01	Quarter hard	48	58	330	400	38	61	42	65	42	57	45	60
H02	Half hard	55	65	380	450	59	70	62	73	56	64	58	66
H03	Three-quarter hard	61	71	420	490	69	76	72	79	63	68	65	70
H04	Hard	68	77	470	530	76	82	78	84	68	72	69	73
H06	Extra hard	78	87	540	600	83	87	85	89	72	75	73	76
H08	Spring	85	93	585	640	87	90	89	92	75	77	76	78
H10	Extra spring	89	97	615	670	88	91	90	93	76	78	77	79
Copper Alloy UNS No. C26000													
M20	As hot rolled	41	51	285	350	—	—	—	—	—	—	—	—
H01	Quarter hard	49	59	340	405	40	61	44	65	43	57	46	60
H02	Half hard	57	67	395	460	60	74	63	77	56	66	58	68
H03	Three-quarter hard	64	74	440	510	72	79	75	82	65	70	67	72
H04	Hard	71	81	490	560	79	84	81	86	70	73	71	74
H06	Extra hard	83	92	570	635	85	89	87	91	74	76	75	77
H08	Spring	91	100	625	690	89	92	90	93	76	78	76	78
H10	Extra spring	95	104	655	715	91	94	92	95	77	79	77	79

TABLE 5.65 Tensile Strength Requirements and Approximate Rockwell Hardness Values for Rolled Tempers (*Continued*)

Rolled temper		Tensile strength, ksi*		Tensile strength, MPa†		Approximate Rockwell hardness‡							
						B scale				Superficial 30-T			
Temper designation						0.020 (0.508) to 0.036 in (0.914 mm) incl		Over 0.036 in (0.914 mm)		0.012 (0.305) to 0.028 in (0.711 mm) incl		Over 0.028 in (0.711 mm)	
Standard	Former	Min	Max	Min	Max	Min	Max	Min	Max	Min	Max	Min	Max
Copper Alloy UNS No. C26800													
M20	As hot rolled	40	50	275	345	—	—	—	—	—	—	—	—
H01	Quarter hard	49	59	340	405	40	61	44	65	43	57	46	60
H02	Half hard	55	65	380	450	57	71	60	74	54	64	56	66
H03	Three-quarter hard	62	72	425	495	70	77	73	80	65	69	67	71
H04	Hard	68	78	470	540	76	82	78	84	68	72	69	73
H06	Extra hard	79	89	545	615	83	87	85	89	73	75	74	76
H08	Spring	86	95	595	655	87	90	89	92	75	77	76	78
H10	Extra spring	90	99	620	685	88	91	90	93	76	78	77	79
Copper Alloy UNS No. C27200													
M20	As hot rolled	41	51	285	350	—	—	—	—	—	—	—	—
H01	Quarter hard	49	59	340	405	40	61	44	65	43	57	46	60
H02	Half hard	56	66	385	455	57	74	60	76	54	67	56	68
H03	Three-quarter hard	63	73	435	505	71	78	74	81	64	70	66	71
H04	Hard	70	80	485	550	76	82	78	84	67	72	68	73
H06	Extra hard	81	91	560	625	82	87	85	89	71	75	72	76
Copper Alloy UNS No. C28000													
M20	As hot rolled	40	55	275	380	—	—	—	—	—	—	—	—
H01	Quarter hard	50	62	345	425	40	65	45	70	45	65	45	70
H02	Half hard	58	70	400	485	50	75	52	80	50	70	50	75

H03	Three-quarter hard	60	75	415	515	55	80	55	82	52	78	55	80
H04	Hard	70	85	485	585	60	85	60	87	55	80	55	82
H06	Extra hard	82	95	565	655	65	92	65	90	60	85	60	85

NOTE: Plate is generally available in only the as hot-rolled (M20) temper. Required properties for other tempers shall be agreed upon between the manufacturer and the purchaser at the time of placing the order.

* ksi = 1000 psi.

† MPa (megapascals).

‡ Rockwell hardness values apply as follows: the B scale values apply to metal 0.020 in (0.508 mm) and over in thickness, and the 30-T scale values apply to metal 0.012 in (0.305 mm) and over in thickness.

SOURCE: Reprinted with permission from the *Annual Book of ASTM Standards,* copyright 1992, American Society of Testing and Materials.

TABLE 5.66 Chemical Requirements

Element	Composition, %							
	Copper Alloy UNS No.							
	C51000	C51100	C51900	C52100	C52400	C53200*	C53400*	C54400*
Tin	4.2–5.8	3.5–4.9	5.0–7.0	7.0–9.0	9.0–11.0	4.0–5.5	3.5–5.8	3.5–4.5
Phosphorus	0.03–0.35	0.03–0.35	0.03–0.35	0.03–0.35	0.03–0.35	0.03–0.35	0.03–0.35	0.01–0.50
Iron, max	0.10	0.10	0.10	0.10	0.10	0.10	0.10	0.10
Lead	0.05 max	0.05 max	0.05 max	0.05 max	0.05 max	2.5–4.0	0.8–1.2	3.5–4.5
Zinc	0.30 max	0.30 max	0.30 max	0.20 max	0.20 max	0.20 max	0.30 max	1.5–4.5
Copper	Remainder	Remainder	Remainder	Remainder	Remainder	Remainder	Remainder	Remainder

* When specified for bearings, the phosphorus content shall be maintained from 0.01 to 0.15%.

SOURCE: Reprinted with permission from the *Annual Book of ASTM Standards,* copyright 1992, American Society of Testing and Materials.

TABLE 5.67 Tensile Strength Requirements and Approximate Rockwell Hardness Values

Temper designation[†]		Thickness, in (mm)	Tensile strength, ksi* (MPa)		Approximate Rockwell hardness	
Standard	Former		Min	Max	B scale	Superficial 30-T
		Copper Alloy UNS No. C51000				
M20	As hot rolled	Over 0.188 (4.775)	40 (275)	60 (415)	—	—
O60	Soft	Over 0.039 (0.991)	43 (295)	58 (400)	16–64	—
		Over 0.029 (0.737)			—	32–59
		Over 0.020 (0.508) to 0.039 (0.991) incl			12–60	—
		Over 0.010 (0.254) to 0.029 (0.737) incl			—	24–53
		0.003 (0.076) to 0.010 (0.254) incl				
H02	Half hard	Over 0.039 (0.991)	58 (400)	73 (505)	64–85	—
		Over 0.029 (0.737)			—	59–73
		Over 0.020 (0.508) to 0.039 (0.991) incl			60–82	—
		Over 0.010 (0.254) to 0.029 (0.737) incl			—	53–69
		0.003 (0.076) to 0.010 (0.254) incl				
H04	Hard	Over 0.039 (0.991)	76 (525)	91 (625)	86–93	—
		Over 0.029 (0.737)			—	73–78
		Over 0.020 (0.508) to 0.039 (0.991) incl			84–91	—
		Over 0.010 (0.254) to 0.029 (0.737) incl			—	71–75
		0.003 (0.076) to 0.010 (0.254) incl				
H06	Extra hard	Over 0.039 (0.991)	88 (605)	103 (710)	92–96	—
		Over 0.029 (0.737)			—	77–81
		Over 0.020 (0.508) to 0.039 (0.991) incl			89–95	—
		Over 0.010 (0.254) to 0.029 (0.737) incl			—	74–78
		0.003 (0.076) to 0.010 (0.254) incl				
H08	Spring	Over 0.039 (0.991)	95 (655)	110 (760)	94–98	—
		Over 0.029 (0.737)			—	79–82
		Over 0.020 (0.508) to 0.039 (0.991) incl			92–97	—

TABLE 5.67 Tensile Strength Requirements and Approximate Rockwell Hardness Values (*Continued*)

Temper designation[†]			Tensile strength, ksi* (MPa)		Approximate Rockwell hardness	
Standard	Former	Thickness, in (mm)	Min	Max	B scale	Superficial 30-T
		Copper Alloy UNS No. C51000 (*Continued*)				
		Over 0.010 (0.254) to 0.029 (0.737) incl			—	76–80
		0.003 (0.076) to 0.010 (0.254) incl				
H10	Extra spring	Over 0.039 (0.991)	100 (690)	114 (790)	95–99	—
		Over 0.029 (0.737)			—	80–83
		Over 0.020 (0.508) to 0.039 (0.991) incl			94–98	—
		Over 0.010 (0.254) to 0.029 (0.737) incl			—	77–81
		0.003 (0.076) to 0.010 (0.254) incl				
		Copper Alloy UNS Nos. C51100, C53200, C53400, and C54400				
M20	As hot rolled	Over 0.188 (4.775)	40 (275)	58 (415)	—	—
O60	Soft	Over 0.039 (0.991)	40 (275)	55 (380)	7–50	—
		Over 0.029 (0.737)			—	24–50
		Over 0.020 (0.508) to 0.039 (0.991) incl			0–45	—
		Over 0.010 (0.254) to 0.029 (0.737) incl			—	16–46
H02	Half hard	Over 0.039 (0.991)	55 (380)	70 (485)	60–81	—
		Over 0.029 (0.737)			—	57–73
		Over 0.020 (0.508) to 0.039 (0.991) incl			53–78	—
		Over 0.010 (0.254) to 0.029 (0.737) incl			—	52–71
H04	Hard	Over 0.039 (0.991)	72 (495)	87 (600)	82–90	—
		Over 0.029 (0.737)			—	71–77
		Over 0.020 (0.508) to 0.039 (0.991) incl			80–88	—
		Over 0.010 (0.254) to 0.029 (0.737) incl			—	69–75
H06	Extra hard	Over 0.039 (0.991)	84 (580)	99 (685)	88–94	—
		Over 0.029 (0.737)			—	75–80

		Over 0.020 (0.508) to 0.039 (0.991) incl			86–92	—
		Over 0.010 (0.254) to 0.029 (0.737) incl			—	73–78
H08	Spring	Over 0.039 (0.991)	91 (625)	105 (720)	90–96	—
		Over 0.029 (0.737)			—	77–81
		Over 0.020 (0.508) to 0.039 (0.991) incl			88–94	—
		Over 0.010 (0.254) to 0.029 (0.737) incl			—	75–79
H10	Extra spring	Over 0.039 (0.991)	96 (660)	109 (750)	92–97	—
		Over 0.029 (0.737)			—	78–82
		Over 0.020 (0.508) to 0.039 (0.991) incl			89–94	—
		Over 0.010 (0.254) to 0.029 (0.737) incl			—	76–80
		Copper Alloy UNS No. C51900				
O60	Soft	Over 0.039 (0.991)	48 (330)	63 (435)	22–66	—
		Over 0.029 (0.737)			—	35–64
		Over 0.020 (0.508) to 0.039 (0.991) incl			18–63	—
		Over 0.010 (0.254) to 0.029 (0.737) incl			—	25–57
H02	Half hard	Over 0.039 (0.991)	64 (440)	79 (545)	70–88	—
		Over 0.029 (0.737)			—	63–76
		Over 0.020 (0.508) to 0.039 (0.991) incl			65–85	—
		Over 0.010 (0.254) to 0.029 (0.737) incl			—	58–72
H04	Hard	Over 0.039 (0.991)	80 (550)	96 (660)	89–95	—
		Over 0.029 (0.737)			—	74–80
		Over 0.020 (0.508) to 0.039 (0.991) incl			86–93	—
		Over 0.010 (0.254) to 0.029 (0.737) incl			—	72–78
		Copper Alloy UNS No. C52100				
M20	As hot rolled	Over 0.188 (4.775)	50 (345)‡	78 (485)	—	—
O60	Soft	Over 0.039 (0.991)	53 (365)	67 (460)	29–70	—
		Over 0.029 (0.737)			—	38–68
		Over 0.020 (0.508) to 0.039 (0.991) incl			20–66	—
		Over 0.010 (0.254) to 0.029 (0.737) incl			—	27–62

TABLE 5.67 Tensile Strength Requirements and Approximate Rockwell Hardness Values (*Continued*)

Temper designation†			Tensile strength, ksi* (MPa)		Approximate Rockwell hardness	
Standard	Former	Thickness, in (mm)	Min	Max	B scale	Superficial 30-T
Copper Alloy UNS No. C52100 (*Continued*)						
H02	Half hard	Over 0.039 (0.991)	69 (475)	84 (580)	76–91	—
		Over 0.029 (0.737)			—	67–78
		Over 0.020 (0.508) to 0.039 (0.991) incl			69–88	—
		Over 0.010 (0.254) to 0.029 (0.737) incl			—	63–75
H04	Hard	Over 0.039 (0.991)	85 (585)	100 (690)	91–97	—
		Over 0.029 (0.737)			—	76–81
		Over 0.020 (0.508) to 0.039 (0.991) incl			89–95	—
		Over 0.010 (0.254) to 0.029 (0.737) incl			—	73–80
H06	Extra hard	Over 0.039 (0.991)	97 (670)	112 (770)	95–100	—
		Over 0.029 (0.737)			—	78–83
		Over 0.020 (0.508) to 0.039 (0.991) incl			93–98	—
		Over 0.010 (0.254) to 0.029 (0.737) incl			—	77–82
H08	Spring	Over 0.039 (0.991)	105 (720)	119 (820)	97–102	—
		Over 0.029 (0.737)			—	79–84
		Over 0.020 (0.508) to 0.039 (0.991) incl			95–100	—
		Over 0.010 (0.254) to 0.029 (0.737) incl			—	78–83
H10	Extra spring	Over 0.039 (0.991)	110 (760)	122 (830)	98–103	—
		Over 0.029 (0.737)			—	80–84
		Over 0.020 (0.508) to 0.039 (0.991) incl			96–101	—
		Over 0.010 (0.254) to 0.029 (0.737) incl			—	79–83
Copper Alloy UNS No. C52400						
M20	As hot rolled	Over 0.188 (4.775)	55 (380)	75 (515)	—	—
O60	Soft	Over 0.039 (0.991)	58 (400)	73 (505)	35–75	—

		Over 0.029 (0.737)			—	40–78
		Over 0.020 (0.508) to 0.039 (0.991) incl			25–71	—
		Over 0.010 (0.254) to 0.029 (0.737) incl			—	29–84
H02	Half hard	Over 0.039 (0.991)	76 (525)	91 (625)	78–95	—
		Over 0.029 (0.737)			—	67–80
		Over 0.020 (0.508) to 0.039 (0.991) incl			74–93	—
		Over 0.010 (0.254) to 0.029 (0.737) incl			—	63–77
H04	Hard	Over 0.039 (0.991)	94 (650)	109 (750)	94–101	—
		Over 0.029 (0.737)			—	78–82
		Over 0.020 (0.508) to 0.039 (0.991) incl			92–100	—
		Over 0.010 (0.254) to 0.029 (0.737) incl			—	75–81
H06	Extra hard	Over 0.039 (0.991)	107 (740)	122 (830)	98–103	—
		Over 0.029 (0.737)			—	80–84
		Over 0.020 (0.508) to 0.039 (0.991) incl			97–102	—
		Over 0.010 (0.254) to 0.029 (0.737) incl			—	79–83
H08	Spring	Over 0.039 (0.991)	115 (790)	129 (890)	99–104	—
		Over 0.029 (0.737)			—	81–85
		Over 0.020 (0.508) to 0.039 (0.991) incl			98–103	—
		Over 0.010 (0.254) to 0.029 (0.737) incl			—	80–84
H10	Extra spring	Over 0.039 (0.991)	120 (830)	133 (920)	100–105	—
		Over 0.029 (0.737)			—	82–86
		Over 0.020 (0.508) to 0.039 (0.991) incl			99–104	—
		Over 0.010 (0.254) to 0.029 (0.737) incl			—	81–85

NOTE: Plate is generally available in only the as hot-rolled (M20) temper. Required properties for other tempers shall be agreed upon between the manufacturer and the purchaser at the time of placing the order.

* ksi = 1000 psi.

† Standard designations defined in Practice B 601.

‡ Editorially corrected.

SOURCE: Reprinted with permission from the *Annual Book of ASTM Standards,* copyright 1992, American Society of Testing and Materials.

TABLE 5.68 Chemical Requirements

	Copper Alloy UNS No.				
Element, %	C51000*	C52100*	C52400*	C53400	C54400
Tin	4.2–5.8	7.0–9.0	9.0–11.0	3.5–5.8	3.5–4.5
Phosphorus	0.03–0.35	0.03–0.35	0.03–0.35	0.03–0.35	0.01–0.50
Iron, max*	0.10	0.10	0.10	0.10	0.10
Lead	0.05 max	0.05 max	0.05 max	0.8–1.2	3.5–4.5
Zinc	0.30 max	0.20 max	0.20 max	0.30 max	1.5–4.5
Copper	Remainder	Remainder	Remainder	Remainder	Remainder

* In the case of copper alloy UNS nos. C 51000, C 52100, and C 52400 rods 1.25 in and over in diameter, a maximum manganese content and maximum iron content of 1.2% may be permitted providing that the copper plus tin plus phosphorus plus iron plus manganese content is not less than 99.5%.

SOURCE: Reprinted with permission from the *Annual Book of ASTM Standards,* copyright 1992, American Society of Testing and Materials.

TABLE 5.69 Tensile Requirements for Rod and Bar

Temper designation		Diameter or distance between parallel surfaces, in	Tensile strength, ksi*		Elongation in 4 × diameter or thickness of specimen, min, %†
Standard	Former		min	max	
		Copper Alloy UNS No. C51000			
O60	Soft anneal	Rod: Round under ¼	40	58	—
H04	Hard	Rod: Round under ¼	80	128	—
		Round and hexagonal:			
		¼ to ½, incl	70	—	13
		over ½ to 1, incl	60	—	15
		over 1	55	—	18
		Bar: Square and rectangular:			
		¼ to ⅜, incl	60	—	10
		over ⅜	55	—	15
H08	Spring	Rod: Round:			
		0.026 to 1/16, incl	115	—	—
		over 1/16 to ⅛, incl	110	—	—
		over ⅛ to ¼, incl	105	—	3.5
		over ¼ to ⅜, incl	100	—	5.0
		over ⅜ to ½, incl	90	—	9.0
		Copper Alloy UNS No. C52100			
O60	Soft anneal	Rod: Round under ¼	53	68	—
H04	Hard	Rod: Round under ¼	105	150	—
		Round and hexagonal:			
		¼ to ½, incl	85	—	12
		over ½ to 1, incl	75	—	15
		over 1	60	—	20

TABLE 5.69 Tensile Requirements for Rod and Bar (*Continued*)

Temper designation		Diameter or distance between parallel surfaces, in	Tensile strength, ksi*		Elongation in 4 × diameter or thickness of specimen, min, %†
Standard	Former		min	max	
		Copper Alloy UNS No. C52100 (*Continued*)			
		Bar: Square and rectangular:			
		¼ to ⅜, incl	68	—	10
		over ⅜	60	—	15
		Copper Alloy UNS No. C52400			
O60	Soft anneal	Rod: Round under ¼	60	75	—
H04	Hard	Rod: Round under ¼	105	160	—
		Round and hexagonal:			
		¼ to ½, incl	95	—	10
		over ½ to 1, incl	85	—	12
		over 1	70	—	15
		Bar: Square and rectangular:			
		¼ to ⅜, incl	76	—	10
		over ⅜	70	—	15
		Copper Alloy UNS No. C 53400			
H04	Hard	Rod: Round and hexagonal:			
		1/16 to ¼, incl	65	—	8
		over ¼ to ½, incl	60	—	10
		over ½ to 1, incl	55	—	12
		over 1	50	—	15
		Bar: Square and rectangular:			
		¼ to ⅜, incl	55	—	10
		over ⅜	50	—	15

Copper Alloy UNS No. C 54400					
H04	Hard	Rod: Round and hexagonal:			
		1/16 to 1/4 incl	65	—	8
		over 1/4 to 1/2, incl	60	—	10
		over 1/2 to 1, incl	55	—	12
		over 1	50	—	15
		Bar: Square and rectangular:			
		1/4 to 3/8, incl	55	—	10
		over 3/8	50	—	15

* ksi = 1000 psi.

† In any case a minimum gauge length of 1 in shall be used.

SOURCE: Reprinted with permission from the *Annual Book of ASTM Standards,* copyright 1992, American Society of Testing and Materials.

TABLE 5.70 Chemical Requirements

Element	Composition, %	
	Copper Alloy UNS No. C17000	Copper Alloy UNS No. C17200
Beryllium	1.60–1.79	1.80–2.00
Additive elements:		
Nickel + cobalt, min	0.20	0.20
Nickel + cobalt + iron, max	0.6	0.6
Aluminum, max	0.20	0.20
Silicon, max	0.20	0.20
Copper	Remainder	Remainder

SOURCE: Reprinted with permission from the *Annual Book of ASTM Standards,* copyright 1992, American Society of Testing and Materials.

TABLE 5.71 Mechanical Property Requirements for Material in the Solution Heat-Treated or Solution Heat-Treated and Cold-Worked Condition

Temper designation[§]		Tensile strength, ksi* (MPa)	Elongation[†] in 2 in or 50 mm, min, %	Rockwell hardness[‡]		
Standard	Former			B scale	30T scale	15T scale
TB00	A	60–78 (410–540)	35	45–78	46–67	75–85
TD01	¼ H	75–88 (520–610)	10	68–90	62–75	83–89
TD02	½ H	85–100 (590–690)	5	88–96	74–79	88–91
TD04	H	100–120 (690–830)	2	96–102	79–83	91–94

* ksi = 1000 psi.

† Elongation requirement applies only to strip 0.004 in (0.102 mm) and thicker.

‡ The thickness of material that may be tested by use of the Rockwell hardness scales is as follows:

B scale	0.040 in (1.016 mm) and over
30T scale	0.020 to 0.040 in (0.508 to 1.016 mm), excl.
15T scale	0.015 to 0.020 in (0.381 to 0.508 mm), excl.

Hardness values shown apply only to direct determinations, not converted values.

§ Standard designations defined in Practice B 601.

SOURCE: Reprinted with permission from the *Annual Book of ASTM Standards,* copyright 1992, American Society of Testing and Materials.

TABLE 5.72 Mechanical Property Requirements after Precipitation Heat Treatment*

Temper designation		Tensile strength, ksi† (MPa)	Yield strength, ksi (MPa), min, 0.2% offset	Elongation in 2 in (50 mm), min, %‡	Rockwell hardness§, min		
Standard	Former				C scale	30N scale	15N scale
Copper Alloy UNS No. C17000							
TF00	AT	150–180¶ (1030–1240)	130 (890)	3	33	53	76.5
TH01	¼ HT	160–190¶ (1100–1310)	135 (930)	2.5	35	55	77
TH02	½ HT	170–200¶ (1170–1380)	145 (1000)	1	37	57	78.5
TH04	HT	180–210¶ (1240–1450)	155 (1070)	1	38	58	79.5
Copper Alloy UNS No. C17200							
TF00	AT	165–195¶ (1140–1340)	140 (960)	3	36	56	78
TH01	¼ HT	175–205¶ (1210–1410)	150 (1030)	2.5	36	56	79
TH02	½ HT	185–215¶ (1280–1480)	160 (1130)	1	38	58	79.5
TH04	HT	190–220¶ (1310–1520)	165 (1140)	1	38	58	80

* These values apply to mill products (Section 11). See 11.3 for exceptions in end products.

† ksi = 1000 psi.

‡ Applicable to material 0.004 in (0.102 mm) and thicker.

§ The thickness of material that may be tested by use of the Rockwell hardness scales is as follows:

C scale	0.040 in (1.016 mm) and over
30N scale	0.020 to 0.040 in (0.508 to 1.016 mm), excl.
15N scale	0.015 to 0.02 in (0.381 to 0.508 mm), excl.

Hardness values shown apply only to direct determinations, not converted values.

¶ The upper limits in the tensile strength column are for design guidance only.

SOURCE: Reprinted with permission from the *Annual Book of ASTM Standards,* copyright 1992, American Society of Testing and Materials.

TABLE 5.73 Mechanical Property Requirements—Mill-Hardened Condition*

Temper designation		Tensile strength, ksi[†] (MPa)	Yield strength, ksi (MPa), 0.2% offset	Elongation in 2 in (50 mm), min, %[‡]	Rockwell hardness,[§] min		
Standard	Former[†]				C scale	30N scale	15N scale
Copper Alloy UNS No. C17000							
TM00	AM	100–110[¶] (690–760)	70–95 (480–660)	18	18	37	67.5
TM01	¼ HM	110–120[¶] (760–830)	80–110 (550–760)	15	20	42	70
TM02	½ HM	120–135[¶] (830–930)	95–125 (660–860)	12	24	45	72
TM04	HM	135–150[¶] (930–1040)	110–135 (760–930)	9	28	48	75
TM05	SHM	150–160[¶] (1030–1100)	125–140 (860–970)	9	31	52	75.5
TM06	XHM	155–175[¶] (1070–1210)	135–165 (930–1140)	3	32	52	76
Copper Alloy UNS No. C17200							
TM00	AM	100–110[¶] (690–760)	70–95 (480–660)	16	R_B95	37	67.5
TM01	¼ HM	110–120[¶] (760–830)	80–110 (550–760)	15	20	42	70
TM02	½ HM	120–135[¶] (830–930)	95–125 (660–860)	12	23	44	72
TM04	HM	135–150[¶] (930–1030)	110–135 (760–930)	9	28	48	75

TABLE 5.73 Mechanical Property Requirements—Mill-Hardened Condition* (*Continued*)

Temper designation		Tensile strength, ksi† (MPa)	Yield strength, ksi (MPa), 0.2% offset	Elongation in 2 in (50 mm), min, %‡	Rockwell hardness,§ min		
Standard	Former†				C scale	30N scale	15N scale
Copper Alloy UNS No. C17200 (*Continued*)							
TM05	SHM	150–160¶ (1030–1100)	125–140 (860–970)	9	31	52	75.5
TM06	XHM	155–175¶ (1070–1210)	135–170 (930–1170)	4	32	52	76
TM08	XHMS	175–190¶ (1210–1310)	150–180 (1030–1240)	3	33	53	76.5

* These values apply to mill products (Section 11). See 11.3 for exceptions in end products.
† ksi = 1000 psi.
‡ Applicable to material 0.004 in (0.102 mm) and thicker.
§ The thickness of material that may be tested by use of the Rockwell hardness scales is as follows:

C scale	0.040 in (1.016 mm) and over
30N scale	0.020 to 0.040 in (0.508 to 1.016 mm), excl.
15N scale	0.015 to 0.020 in (0.381 to 0.508 mm), excl.

Hardness values shown apply only to direct determinations, not converted values.
¶ The upper limits in the tensile strength column are for design guidance only.
SOURCE: Reprinted with permission from the *Annual Book of ASTM Standards,* copyright 1992, American Society of Testing and Materials.

TABLE 5.74 Dimensions, Weights, and Tolerances in Diameter and Wall Thickness for Nominal or Standard Copper Water Tube Sizes (all tolerances are plus and minus except as otherwise indicated)

Nominal or standard size, in	Outside diameter, in	Average outside diameter tolerance,* in		Wall thickness and tolerances, in						Theoretical weight, lb/ft		
				Type K		Type L		Type M				
		Annealed	Drawn	Wall thickness	Tolerance†	Wall thickness	Tolerance†	Wall thickness	Tolerance†	Type K	Type L	Type M
¼	0.375	0.002	0.001	0.035	0.0035	0.030	0.003	‡	‡	0.145	0.126	‡
⅜	0.500	0.0025	0.001	0.049	0.005	0.035	0.004	0.025	0.002	0.269	0.198	0.145
½	0.625	0.0025	0.001	0.049	0.005	0.040	0.004	0.028	0.003	0.344	0.285	0.204
⅝	0.750	0.0025	0.001	0.049	0.005	0.042	0.004	‡	‡	0.418	0.362	‡
¾	0.875	0.003	0.001	0.065	0.006	0.045	0.004	0.032	0.003	0.641	0.455	0.328
1	1.125	0.0035	0.0015	0.065	0.006	0.050	0.005	0.035	0.004	0.839	0.655	0.465
1¼	1.375	0.004	0.0015	0.065	0.006	0.055	0.006	0.042	0.004	1.04	0.884	0.682
1½	1.625	0.0045	0.002	0.072	0.007	0.060	0.006	0.049	0.005	1.36	1.14	0.940
2	2.125	0.005	0.002	0.083	0.008	0.070	0.007	0.058	0.006	2.06	1.75	1.46
2½	2.625	0.005	0.002	0.095	0.010	0.080	0.008	0.065	0.006	2.93	2.48	2.03
3	3.125	0.005	0.002	0.109	0.011	0.090	0.009	0.072	0.007	4.00	3.33	2.68
3½	3.625	0.005	0.002	0.120	0.012	0.100	0.010	0.083	0.008	5.12	4.29	3.58
4	4.125	0.005	0.002	0.134	0.013	0.110	0.011	0.095	0.010	6.51	5.38	4.66
5	5.125	0.005	0.002	0.160	0.016	0.125	0.012	0.109	0.011	9.67	7.61	6.66
6	6.125	0.005	0.002	0.192	0.019	0.140	0.014	0.122	0.012	13.9	10.2	8.92
8	8.125	0.006	+0.002 −0.004	0.271	0.027	0.200	0.020	0.170	0.017	25.9	19.3	16.5
10	10.125	0.008	+0.002 −0.006	0.338	0.034	0.250	0.025	0.212	0.021	40.3	30.1	25.6
12	12.125	0.008	+0.002 −0.006	0.405	0.040	0.280	0.028	0.254	0.025	57.8	40.4	36.7

* The average outside diameter of a tube is the average of the maximum and minimum outside diameter, as determined at any one cross section of the tube.

† Maximum deviation at any one point.

‡ Indicates that the material is not generally available or that no tolerance has been established.

SOURCE: Reprinted with permission from the *Annual Book of ASTM Standards*, copyright 1992, American Society of Testing and Materials.

TABLE 5.75 Chemical Requirements

Copper UNS no.	Copper (incl silver), min %	Phosphorus, %
C10200	99.95	—
C10300	99.95*	0.001 to 0.005
C10800	99.95*	0.005 to 0.012
C12000	99.90	0.004 to 0.012
C12200	99.9	0.015 to 0.040

* Copper + silver + phosphorus.

SOURCE: Reprinted with permission from the *Annual Book of ASTM Standards,* copyright 1992, American Society of Testing and Materials.

TABLE 5.76 Mechanical Property Requirements

Temper designation			Rockwell hardness†		Tensile strength, min, ksi*	Average grain size, mm
Standard	Former	Form	Scale	Value		
O60	Annealed	Coils	F	50 max	30	0.040 min
O50	Annealed	Straight lengths	F	55 max	30	0.025 min
H	Drawn	Drawn	30 T	30 min	36	

* ksi = 1000 psi.

† Rockwell hardness tests shall be made on the inside surfaces of the tube. When suitable equipment is not available for determining the specified Rockwell hardness, other Rockwell scales and values may be specified subject to agreement between the purchaser and the supplier.

SOURCE: Reprinted with permission from the *Annual Book of ASTM Standards,* copyright 1992, American Society of Testing and Materials.

TABLE 5.77 Classification of Coppers

			Form in which copper is available[b]							
			From refiners				From fabricators			
Designations	Type of copper	UNS nos.[a]	Wire bars	Billets	Cakes	Ingots and ingot bars	Flat products	Pipe and tube	Rod and wire	Shapes
CATH	Electrolytic cathode		Cathodes only							
			Tough-Pitch Coppers							
ETP	Electrolytic tough pitch	C11000	x	x	x	x	x	x	x	x
RHC	Remelted, high-conductivity tough pitch	C11010	x	x	x	x	x	x	x	x
ETP	Electrolytic tough pitch (anneal resist)	C11100	x	x	x		x	x	x	x
CRTP	Chemically refined tough pitch	C11030	x	x	x	x	x	x	x	x
FRHC	Fire-refined, high-conductivity tough pitch	C11020	x	x	x	x	x	x	x	x
ETP[c]	Silver-bearing, tough pitch	C11300, C11400, C11500, C11600	x	x	x	x	x	x	x	x
FRTP	Fire-refined, tough pitch	C12500		x	x	x	x	x	x	x
FRSTP	Fire-refined tough pitch with silver	C12700, C12800, C12900, C1300		x	x	x	x			x
			Oxygen-Free Coppers (Without Use of Deoxidants)							
OFE	Oxygen-free, electronic	C10100	x	x	x		x	x	x	x
OF	Oxygen-free	C10200	x	x	x		x	x	x	x
OFS	Oxygen-free, silver-bearing	C10400, C10500, C10700	x	x	x		x	x	x	x
OFXLP	Oxygen-free, extra low phosphorus	C10300	x	x	x		x	x	x	x
OFLP	Oxygen-free, low phosphorus	C10800	x	x	x		x	x	x	x

TABLE 5.77 Classification of Coppers (*Continued*)

Designations	Type of copper	UNS nos.[a]	Form in which copper is available[b]							
			From refiners				From fabricators			
			Wire bars	Billets	Cakes	Ingots and ingot bars	Flat products	Pipe and tube	Rod and wire	Shapes
CATH	Electrolytic cathode		Cathodes only							
			Deoxidized Coppers							
DLP	Phosphorized, low-residual phosphorus	C12000	x	x		x	x	x	x	
DLPS[d]	Phosphorized, low-residual phosphorus silver-bearing	C12100	x	x		x	x	x	x	
DHP[e]	Phosphorized, high-residual phosphorus	C12200	x	x		x	x	x	x	
DHPS[d]	Phosphorized, high-residual phosphorus silver-bearing	C12300	x	x		x	x	x	x	
DPA	Phosphorized, arsenic-bearing	C14200	x			x	x			
DPTE[f]	Phosphorized, tellurium-bearing	C14500	x					x		
			Other Coppers							
	Sulfur-bearing	C14700	x					x		
	Zirconium-bearing	C15000	x	x		x		x		
PTE	Tellurium-bearing	C14500	x					x		

[a] The chemical compositions associated with these numbers are listed in the product specifications and in the Standard Designations for Copper and Copper Alloys.

[b] The x in the table indicates commercial availability.

[c] This includes types ETP, CRTP, and FRHC coppers to which silver has been added in amounts agreed upon.

[d] This includes oxygen-free copper to which phosphorus and silver have been added in amounts agreed upon.

[e] This includes oxygen-free copper to which phosphorus has been added.

[f] This includes oxygen-free tellurium-bearing copper to which phosphorus has been added in amounts agreed upon.

SOURCE: Reprinted with permission from the *Annual Book of ASTM Standards,* copyright 1992, American Society of Testing and Materials.

TABLE 5.78 Standard Densities

ASTM designation	Material	Copper or Copper Alloy UNS No.	Density, lb/in^3
B 36/B 336M	Copper-zinc alloy (brass)	C21000	0.320
		C22000	0.318
		C23000	0.316
		C24000	0.313
		C26000	0.308
		C26800	0.306
		C27200	0.305
B 96	Copper-silicon alloy	C65100	0.316
		C65500	0.308
		C65800	0.308
B 103	Copper-tin alloy (phosphor bronze)	C51000	0.320
		C51100	0.320
		C52100	0.318
		C52400	0.317
		C53200	0.323
		C53400	0.322
		C54400	0.320
B 121	Copper-zinc-lead alloy (leaded brass)	C33500	0.306
		C34000	0.306
		C34200	0.307
		C35000	0.305
		C35300	0.306
		C35340	0.306
		C35600	0.307
B 122	Copper-nickel-zinc alloy (nickel silver and copper-nickel alloy)	C70600	0.323
		C71000	0.323
		C71500	0.323
		C72200	0.323
		C72500	0.321
		C73500	0.319
		C74000	0.314
		C74500	0.313
		C75200	0.316
		C76200	0.310
		C77000	0.314
B 152	Copper UNS nos. C10100, C10200, C10300, C10400, C10500, C10700, C10800, C12000, C12200, C12300,	—	0.323
	C11000, C11300, C11400, C11600, C12500, C14200	—	0.322
B 169	Copper-aluminum alloy (aluminum bronze)	C60600	0.295
		C61000	0.281
		C61300	0.285
		C61400	0.285
B 194	Copper-beryllium alloy	C17000	0.297
		C17200	0.297
B 291	Copper-zinc-manganese alloy	C66700	0.308
B 422	Copper-nickel-silicon	C63800	0.299
		C64400	0.299
		C70250	0.318
		C72400	0.311
B 465	Copper-iron alloy	C19200	0.320
		C19400	0.322

TABLE 5.78 Standard Densities (*Continued*)

ASTM designation	Material	Copper or Copper alloy UNS no.	Density, lb/in^3
		C19500	0.322
		C19600	0.320
		C19700	0.319
B 534	Copper-cobalt-beryllium alloy	C17500	0.316
	Copper-nickel-beryllium alloy	C17510	0.317
B 591	Copper-zinc-tin alloys	C40500	0.319
		C40800	0.320
		C41100	0.318
		C41300	0.318
		C41500	0.318
		C42200	0.318
		C42500	0.316
		C43000	0.316
		C43400	0.316
B 592	Copper-zinc-aluminum-cobalt alloy	C68800	0.296
	Copper-aluminum-nickel alloy	C69000	0.296
B 740	Copper-nickel-tin alloys	C72700	0.321
		C72900	0.323
		C72650	0.320
B 16	Free-cutting brass	C36000	0.307
B 21	Naval brass	C46200	0.305
		C46400	0.304
		C48200	0.305
		C48500	0.305
B 98	Copper-silicon alloy	C65100	0.316
		C65500	0.308
		C65800	0.308
		C66100	0.308
B 124	Copper	C11000	0.323
	Copper tellurium	C14500	0.323
	Copper sulfur	C14700	0.323
	Forging brass	C37700	0.305
	Naval brass	C46400	0.304
	Medium-leaded naval brass	C48200	0.305
	Leaded naval brass	C48500	0.305
	Aluminum bronze	C61900	0.271
	Aluminum bronze, 9%	C62300	0.277
	Aluminum-nickel bronze	C63000	0.274
	Aluminum-silicon bronze	C64200	0.278
	Aluminum-silicon bronze, 6.7%	C64210	0.278
	High-silicon bronze (A)	C65500	0.308
	Manganese bronze (A)	C67500	0.302
	Nickel silver, 45-10	C77400	0.306
B 133	Copper		
	Deoxidized and oxygen-free	—	0.323
	Other classifications	—	0.321
B 138	Manganese bronze	C67000	0.286
		C67500	0.302
B 139	Phosphor bronze	C51000	0.320
		C52100	0.318

TABLE 5.78 Standard Densities (*Continued*)

ASTM designation	Material	Copper or Copper alloy UNS no.	Density, lb/in^3
		C52400	0.317
		C53400	0.322
		C54400	0.320
B 140	Leaded red brass	C31400	0.319
		C31600	0.320
		C32000	0.317
B 150	Aluminum bronze	C61300	0.285
	Aluminum bronze	C61400	0.285
	Aluminum bronze	C61900	0.270
	Aluminum bronze, 9%	C62300	0.276
	Aluminum bronze	C62400	0.269
	Aluminum-nickel bronze	C63000	0.274
	Aluminum-nickel bronze	C63200	0.276
	Aluminum-silicon bronze	C64200	0.278
	Aluminum-silicon bronze, 6.7%	C64210	0.278
B 151	Copper-nickel-zinc alloy (nickel silver) and copper-nickel alloy	C70600	0.323
		C71500	0.323
		C72000	0.323
		C74500	0.313
		C75200	0.317
		C75700	0.314
		C76400	0.315
		C77000	0.314
		C79200	0.314
		C79400	0.317
B 196	Copper-beryllium alloy	C17000	0.297
		C17200	0.297
		C17300	0.297
B 301	Free-cutting copper	C14500	0.323
		C14700	0.323
		C14710	0.323
		C14720	0.323
		C18700	0.323
B 371	Copper-zinc-silicon alloy	C69400	0.296
		C69700	0.300
B 411	Copper-nickel-silicon alloy	C64700	0.322
B 441	Copper-cobalt-beryllium	C17500	0.316
	Copper-nickel-beryllium	C17510	0.316
B 453	Copper-zinc-lead (leaded brass)	C33500	0.306
		C34000	0.306
		C34500	0.306
		C35000	0.305
		C35300	0.306
		C35600	0.307
B 455	Copper-zinc-lead (leaded brass)	C38000	0.305
		C38500	0.306

SOURCE: Reprinted with permission from the *Annual Book of ASTM Standards*, copyright 1992, American Society of Testing and Materials.

TABLE 5.79 Specifications of Magnesium Wrought Alloys

Alloy designation						
UNS	ASTM and SAE	Old SAE	Form	ASTM	AMS	Military or federal
M11311	AZ31B	510	Sheet and plate	B90	4375, 4376, 4377	QQ-M-44
			Bar, rod, shapes	B107	—	QQ-M-31
			Tube	B107	—	WW-T-825
			Forgings	B91	—	QQ-M-40
M11610	AZ61A	520	Bar, rod, shapes	B107	4350	QQ-M-31
			Tube	B107	4350	WW-T-825
			Wire (welding rod)	—	—	Mil-R-6944
			Forgings	B91	4358*	QQ-M-40
M11800	AZ80A	523	Bar, rod, shapes	B107	—	QQ-M-31
			Forgings	B91	4360*	QQ-M-40
M14141	LA141A		Sheet and plate	B90	—	—
M13310	HK31A	507	Sheet and plate	B90	4384, 4385	Mil-M-26075
M13210	HM21A		Sheet and plate	B90	4383, 4390	Mil-M-8917
			Forgings	—	4363	QQ-M-40
M13312	HM31A		Bar, rod, shapes	—	4388, 4389	Mil-M-8916
M15100	M1A	522	Bar, rod, shapes	B107	—	QQ-M-31
			Forgings	—	—	QQ-M-40
M16100	ZE10A	534	Sheet and plate	B90	—	Mil-M-46037
M16400	ZK40A		Bar, rod, shapes	B107	—	—
M16600	ZK60A	524	Bar, rod, shapes	B107	4352	QQ-M-31
			Tube	B107	4352	WW-T-825
			Forgings	B91	4362	QQ-M-40

* Noncurrent specifications.

SOURCE: Reprinted with permission from the *Annual Book of ASTM Standards*, copyright 1992, American Society of Testing and Materials.

TABLE 5.80 Physical Properties and Characteristics of Magnesium Sand-Casting Alloys

Alloy designation			Approximate melting range, °F (°C)				Foundry characteristics[c]					Other characteristics				
UNS	ASTM and SAE	Old SAE	Nonequilibrium solidus[a]	Solidus	Liquidus	Pattern shrinkage allowance, in/ft (mm/m)[b]	Pressure tightness	Fluidity[d]	Microporosity tendency[e]	Normally heat treated	Castability	Machining[f]	Electroplating[g]	Surface treatment[h]	Suitability to brazing[i]	Suitability to welding[j]
M10100[m]	AM100A	502	810 (432)	867 (464)	1100 (593)	5/32 (13.0)	2	1	2	Yes	2	1	2	2	No	1
M11630	AZ63A	50	685 (363)	850 (454)	1130 (610)	5/32 (13.0)	3	1	3	Yes	3	1	1	1	No	3
M11810[m]	AZ81A	505	790 (421)	882 (472)	1115 (602)	5/32 (13.0)	2	1	2	Yes	1	1	2	2	No	1
M11914[m]	AZ91C	504	785 (418)	875 (468)	1105 (596)	5/32 (13.0)	2	1	2	Yes	1	1	2	2	No	2
M11920[m]	AZ92A	500	770 (410)	830 (443)	1100 (593)	5/32 (13.0)	2	1	2	Yes	2	1	2	2	No	2
M12330[n]	EZ33A	506	— —	1010 (543)	1189 (643)	3/16 (15.5)	1	2	1	Yes	1	1	1	1	No	1
M13310[m]	HK31A	507	— —	1092 (589)	1204 (651)	7/32 (18.0)	1	2	1	Yes	1	1	1	1	—[k]	1
M13320[n]	HZ32A	—	— —	1026 (552)	1198 (648)	3/16 (15.5)	1	2	1	Yes	1	1	—[k]	2	—[k]	2
M18010[p]	K1A	—	— —	— —	1205 (652)	3/16 (15.5)	2	2	2	No	2	1	3	2	—[k]	1
M18210	QH21A	—	— —	1004 (539)	1184 (640)	3/16 (15.5)	2	2	2	Yes	1	1	2	1	No	—[k]
M18220[m]	QE22A	—	— —	1020 (549)	1190 (643)	5/32 (13.0)	2	2	2	Yes	1	1	2	1	—[k]	1
M16410[p]	ZE41A	—	— —	950 (510)	1184 (640)	3/16 (15.5)	—[k]	2	—[k]	Yes	1	1	1	1	No	2
M16630[p]	ZE63A	—	— —	510 (266)	950 (510)	3/16 (15.5)	1	2	1	Yes	1	1	—[k]	1	No	1
M16620	ZH62A	508	— —	— —	1169 (632)	5/32 (13.0)	2	2	2	Yes	2	1	1	1	No	—[k]
M16510	ZK51A	509	— —	1020 (549)	1185 (641)	5/32 (13.0)	3	2	3	Yes	3	1	2	2	No	3
M16610	ZK61A	513	— —	985 (529)	1175 (635)	5/32 (13.0)	3	2	3	Yes	3	1	2	1	No	3

[a] As measured on metal solidified under normal casting conditions.

[b] Allowance for average castings. Shrinkage requirements will vary with intricacy of design and dimensions. (1 in/ft × 8.333 = % shrinkage.)

[c] Rating of 1 indicates best of group; 3 indicates poorest of group.

[d] Ability of liquid alloy to flow readily in mold and fill thin sections.

[e] Based on radiographic evidence.

[f] Composite rating based on ease of cutting, chip characteristics, quality of finish, and tool life. Ratings, in the case of heat-treatable alloys, based on –T6 type temper. Other tempers, particularly the annealed temper, may have lower ratings.

[g] Ability of casting to take and hold an electroplate applied by present standard methods.

[h] Ability of castings to be cleaned in standard pickle solutions and to be conditioned for best paint adhesion.

[i] Refers to suitability of alloy to withstand brazing temperature without excessive distortion or melting.

[j] Based on ability of material to be fusion welded with filler rod of same alloy.

[k] Inexperience with these alloys under wide production conditions makes it undesirable to supply ratings at this time.

[m] Properties applicable for permanent mold and investment castings.

[n] Properties applicable for permanent mold castings also.

[p] Properties applicable for investment castings also.

SOURCE: Reprinted with permission from the *Annual Book of ASTM Standards,* copyright 1992, American Society of Testing and Materials.

TABLE 5.81 Chemical Requirements*

Alloy[†]		Composition, %										
UNS no.	ASTM no.	Magnesium	Aluminum	Manganese	Zinc	Zirconium, min	Silicon	Copper	Nickel	Iron	Calcium	Other impurities[‡]
M11311	AZ31B	Remainder	2.5–3.5	0.20–0.50	0.6–1.4	—	0.10	0.05	0.005	0.005	0.04	0.30
M11312	AZ31C	Remainder	2.4–3.6	0.15–0.35[§]	0.50–1.5	—	0.10	0.10	0.03	—	—	0.30
M11610	AC61A	Remainder	5.8–7.2	0.15–0.35	0.40–1.5	—	0.10	0.05	0.005	0.005	—	0.30
M11800	AZ80A	Remainder	7.8–9.2	0.12–0.35	0.20–0.8	—	0.10	0.05	0.005	0.005	—	0.30
M15100	M1A	Remainder	—	1.2–2.0	—	—	0.10	0.05	0.01	—	0.30	0.30
M16400	ZK40	Remainder	—	—	3.5–4.5	0.45	—	—	—	—	—	0.30
M16600	ZK60A	Remainder	—	—	4.8–6.2	0.45	—	—	—	—	—	0.30

NOTE: Analysis shall regularly be made only for the elements specifically mentioned in this table. If, however, the presence of other elements is suspected or indicated in the course of routine analysis to be in amounts greater than the specified limits, further analysis shall be made to determine that the total of these other elements is not in excess of the limits specified in the last column of the table. The following applies to all specified limits in this table: For purposes of acceptance and rejection, an observed value or a calculated value obtained from analysis should be rounded-off to the nearest unit in the last right-hand place of figures used in expressing the specified limit.

* Limits are in weight percent maximum unless shown as a range or otherwise stated.

[†] These alloy designations were established in accordance with Recommended Practice B 275.

[‡] Includes listed elements for which no specific limit is shown.

[§] Manganese minimum limit need not be met if iron is 0.005%, or less.

SOURCE: Reprinted with permission from the *Annual Book of ASTM Standards,* copyright 1992, American Society of Testing and Materials.

TABLE 5.82 Tensile Requirements

Alloy						Tensile strength, min		Yield strength (0.2% offset), min		Elongation in 2 in or 4 × dia. min, %
UNS no.	ASTM no.	Temper	Form	Specified diameter or thickness in[a,c]	Specified cross-sectional area, in^2 or OD of tube, in	ksi	(MPa)[d]	ksi	(MPa)[d]	
M11311	AZ31B	F	Bars, rods, shapes, and wire	0.249 and under	All	35.0	(241)	21.0	(145)	7
				0.250–1.499	All	35.0	(241)	22.0	(152)	7
				1.500–2.499	All	34.0	(234)	22.0	(152)	7
				2.500–4.999	All	32.0	(221)	20.0	(138)	7
			Hollow shapes	All	All	32.0	(221)	16.0	(110)	8
			Tubes	0.023–0.500	6.000 and under	32.0	(221)	16.0	(110)	8
				0.251–0.750		32.0	(221)	16.0	(110)	4
M11610	AZ61A	F	Bars, rods, shapes, and wire	0.249 and under	All	38.0	(262)	21.0	(145)	8
				0.250–2.499	All	39.0	(269)	24.0	(165)	9
				2.500–4.999	All	40.0	(276)	22.0	(152)	7
			Hollow shapes	All	All	36.0	(248)	16.0	(110)	7
			Tubes	0.028–0.750	6.000 and under	36.0	(248)	16.0	(110)	7
M11800	AZ80A	F	Bars, rods, shapes, and wire	0.249 and under	All	43.0	(296)	28.0	(193)	9
				0.250–1.499	All	43.0	(296)	28.0	(193)	8
				1.500–2.499	All	43.0	(296)	28.0	(193)	6
				2.500–4.999	All	42.0	(290)	27.0	(186)	4
M11800	AZ80A	T5	Bars, rods, shapes, and wire	0.249 and under	All	47.0	(324)	30.0	(207)	4
				0.250–2.499	All	48.0	(331)	33.0	(228)	4
				2.500–4.999	All	45.0	(310)	30.0	(207)	2

TABLE 5.82 Tensile Requirements (*Continued*)

Alloy						Tensile strength, min		Yield strength (0.2% offset), min		Elongation in 2 in or 4 × dia.
UNS no.	ASTM no.	Temper	Form	Specified diameter or thickness in[a,c]	Specified cross-sectional area, in^2 or OD of tube, in	ksi	(MPa)[c]	ksi	(MPa)[d]	min, %
M15100	M1A	F	Bars, rods, shapes, and wire	0.249 and under	All	30.0	(207)	[b]	—	2
				0.250–1.499	All	32.0	(221)	[b]	—	3
				1.500–2.499	All	32.0	(221)	[b]	—	2
				2.500–4.999	All	29.0	(200)	[b]	—	2
			Hollow shapes	All	All	28.0	(193)	[b]	—	2
			Tubes	0.028–0.750	6.000 and under	28.0	(193)	[b]	—	2
M16400	ZK40A	T5	Bars, rods, shapes, and wire	All	4.999 and under	40.0	(276)	37.0	(255)	4.0
			Hollow shapes	All	All	40.0	(276)	37.0	(255)	4.0
			Tubes	0.062–0.500	3.000 and under	40.0	(276)	36.0	(248)	4.0
M16600	ZK60A	F	Bars, rods, shapes, and wire	All	4.999 and under	43.0	(296)	31.0	(214)	5
					5.000–39.999	43.0	(296)	31.0	(214)	4
			Hollow shapes	All	All	40.0	(276)	28.0	(193)	5
			Tubes	0.028–0.750	3.000 and under	40.0	(276)	28.0	(193)	5
M16600	ZK60A	T5	Bars, rods, shapes, and wire	All	4.999 and under	45.0	(310)	36.0	(248)	4
			Hollow shapes	All	All	46.0	(317)	38.0	(262)	4
			Tubes	0.028–0.250	3.000 and under	46.0	(317)	38.0	(262)	4
				0.094–1.188	3.001–8.500	44.0	(303)	33.0	(228)	4

NOTE: For purposes of determining conformance with this specification, each value for tensile strength and yield strength shall be rounded to the nearest 100 psi and each value for elongation shall be rounded to the nearest 0.5%, both in accordance with the rounding method of Recommended Practice E 29.

[a] Intermediate dimensions shall be rounded off to the third decimal place in accordance with Recommended Practice E 29.

[b] Not required.

[c] Wall thickness of tubes.

[d] The values in megapascals are included for information only.

[e] Elongation of full-section and machined sheet-type specimens is measured in 2 in; of machined round specimens, in 4 × specimen dia.

[f] For material of such dimensions that a standard test specimen cannot be obtained, for wire less than 0.125 in diameter, or for material thinner than 0.062 in the test for elongation is not required.

SOURCE: Reprinted with permission from the *Annual Book of ASTM Standards,* copyright 1992, American Society of Testing and Materials.

TABLE 5.83 Chemical Requirements[a]

Element	Composition, %									
	Grade									
	1	2	3	4	5	6	7	9	11	12
Nitrogen, max	0.03	0.03	0.05	0.05	0.05	0.05	0.03	0.02	0.03	0.03
Carbon, max	0.10	0.10	0.10	0.10	0.10	0.10	0.10	0.10	0.10	0.08
Hydrogen,[b] max	0.015	0.015	0.015	0.015	0.015	0.020	0.015	0.015	0.015	0.015
Iron, max	0.20	0.30	0.30	0.50	0.40	0.50	0.30	0.25	0.20	0.30
Oxygen, max	0.18	0.25	0.35	0.40	0.20	0.20	0.25	0.15	0.18	0.25
Aluminum	—	—	—	—	5.5 to 6.75	4.0 to 6.0	—	2.5 to 3.5	—	—
Vanadium	—	—	—	—	3.5 to 4.5	—	—	2.0 to 3.0	—	—
Tin	—	—	—	—	—	2.0 to 3.0	—	—	—	—
Palladium	—	—	—	—	—	—	0.12 to 0.25	—	0.12 to 0.25	—
Molybdenum	—	—	—	—	—	—	—	—	—	0.2 to 0.4
Zirconium	—	—	—	—	—	—	—	—	—	—
Nickel	—	—	—	—	—	—	—	—	—	0.6 to 0.9
Residuals[c,d,e] (each), max	0.1	0.1	0.1	0.1	0.1	0.1	0.1	0.1	0.1	0.1
Residuals[c,d,e] (total), max	0.4	0.4	0.4	0.4	0.4	0.4	0.4	0.4	0.4	0.4
Titanium[f]	Remainder	Remainder	Remainder	Remainder	Remainder	Remainder	Remainder	Remainder	Remainder	Remainder

[a] Analysis shall be completed for all elements listed in this table for each grade. The analysis results for the elements not quantified in the table need not be reported unless the concentration level is greater than 0.1% each or 0.4% total.

[b] Lower hydrogen may be obtained by negotiation with the manufacturer.

[c] Need not be reported.

[d] A residual is an element present in a metal or an alloy in small quantities inherent to the manufacturing process but not added intentionally.

[e] The purchaser may, in the written purchase order, request analysis for specific residual elements not listed in this specification. The maximum allowable concentration for residual elements shall be 0.1% each and 0.4% maximum total.

[f] The percentage of titanium is determined by difference.

SOURCE: Reprinted with permission from the *Annual Book of ASTM Standards,* copyright 1992, American Society of Testing and Materials.

TABLE 5.84 Tensile and Bend Requirements

Grade	Tensile strength,* min		Yield strength,* 0.2% offset				Elongation in 2 in or 50 mm, min, %	Bend test†	
			min		max			Under 0.070 in (1.8 mm) in thickness	0.070 to 0.187 in (1.8 to 4.75 mm) in thickness
	ksi	MPa	ksi	MPa	ksi	MPa			
1	35	240	25	170	45	310	24	3*T*	4*T*
2	50	345	40	275	65	450	20	4*T*	5*T*
3	65	450	55	380	80	550	18	4*T*	5*T*
4	80	550	70	485	95	655	15	5*T*	6*T*
5	130	895	120	830	—	—	10‡,§	9*T*	10*T*
6	120	830	115	795	—	—	10‡	8*T*	9*T*
7	50	345	40	275	65	450	20	4*T*	5*T*
9	90	620	70	485	—	—	15¶	5*T*	6*T*
11	35	240	25	170	45	310	24	3*T*	4*T*
12	70	483	50	345	—	—	18	4*T*	5*T*

* Minimum and maximum limits apply to tests taken both longitudinal and transverse to the direction of rolling. Mechanical properties for conditions other than annealed or plate thickness over 1 in (25 mm) may be established by agreement between the manufacturer and the purchaser.

† *T* equals the thickness of the bend test specimen. Bend tests are not applicable to material over 0.187 in (4.75 mm) in thickness.

‡ For grades 5 and 6 the elongation on materials under 0.025 in (0.635 mm) in thickness may be obtained only by negotiation.

§ For grade 5, the elongation will be 8% minimum for thicknesses between 0.025 and 0.063 in.

¶ Elongation for continuous rolled and annealed (strip product from coil) for grade 9 shall be 12% minimum in the longitudinal direction and 8% minimum in the transverse direction.

SOURCE: Reprinted with permission from the *Annual Book of ASTM Standards,* copyright 1992, American Society of Testing and Materials.

TABLE 5.85 **Mechanical Properties of Wrought Titanium Alloys**

Nominal composition (%)	Condition	Room temperature: Tensile strength (ksi)	Room temperature: Yield strength (ksi)	Room temperature: Elongation (%)	Reduction in area (%)
Commercially Pure					
99.5 Ti	Annealed	48	35	30	55
99.2 Ti	Annealed	63	50	28	50
99.1 Ti	Annealed	75	65	25	45
99.0 Ti	Annealed	96	85	20	40
99.2 Ti[a]	Annealed	63	50	28	50
98.9[b]	Annealed	75	65	25	42
Alpha Alloys					
5 Al, 2.5 Sn	Annealed	125	117	16	40
5 Al, 2.5 Sn (low O_2)	Annealed	117	108	16	—
Near Alpha Alloys					
8 Al, 1 Mo, 1 V	Duplex annealed	145	138	15	28
11 Sn, 1 Mo, 2.25 Al, 5.0 Zr, 1 Mo, 0.2 Si	Duplex annealed	160	144	15	35
6 Al, 2 Sn, 4 Zr, 2 Mo	Duplex annealed	142	130	15	35
5 Al, 5 Sn, 2 Zr, 2 Mo, 0.25 Si	975°C (1785°F) (½ h), AC + 595°C (1100°F) (2 h), AC	152	140	13	—
6 Al, 2 Nb, 1 Ta, 1 Mo	As-rolled 2.5-cm (1-in) plate	124	110	13	34
6 Al, 2 Sn, 1.5 Zr, 1 Mo, 0.35 Bi, 0.1 Si	Beta forge + duplex anneal	147	137	11	—
Alpha-Beta Alloys					
8 Mn	Annealed	137	125	15	32
3 Al, 2.5 V	Annealed	100	85	20	—
6 Al, 4 V	Annealed	144	134	14	30
	Solution + age	170	160	10	25
6 Al, 4 V (low O_2)	Annealed	130	120	15	35
6 Al, 6 V, 2 Sn	Annealed	155	145	14	30
	Solution + age	185	170	10	20
7 Al, 4 Mo	Solution + age	160	150	16	22
6 Al, 2 Sn, 4 Zr, 6 Mo	Solution + age	184	170	10	23
6 Al, 2 Sn, 2 Zr, 2 Mo, 2 Cr, 0.25 Si	Solution + age	185	165	11	33
10 V, 2 Fe, 3 Al	Solution + age	185	174	10	19
Beta Alloys					
13 V, 11 Cr, 3 Al	Solution + age	177	170	8	—
	Solution + age	185	175	8	—
8 Mo, 8 V, 2 Fe, 3 Al	Solution + age	190	180	8	—
3 Al, 8 V, 6 Cr, 4 Mo, 4 Zr	Solution + age	210	200	7	—
	Annealed	128	121	15	—
11.5 Mo, 6 Zr, 4.5 Sn	Solution + age	201	191	11	—

[a] Also contains 0.2 Pd.
[b] Also contains 0.8 Ni and 0.3 Mo.
SOURCE: Titanium Metals Corp. of America and RMI Co.

TABLE 5.86 Primary Series of Numbers

	Nonferrous Metals and Alloys
A00001–A99999	Aluminum and aluminum alloys
C00001–C99999	Copper and copper alloys
E00001–E99999	Rare earth and rare earth-like metals and alloys (18 items; see Table 5.86)
L00001–L99999	Low-melting metals and alloys (15 items; see Table 5.86)
M00001–M99999	Miscellaneous nonferrous metals and alloys (12 items; see Table 5.86)
N00001–N99999	Nickel and nickel alloys
P00001–P99999	Precious metals and alloys (8 items; see Table 5.86)
R00001–R99999	Reactive and refractory metals and alloys (14 items; see Table 5.86)
Z00001–Z99999	Zinc and zinc alloys
	Ferrous Metals and Alloys
D00001–D99999	Specified mechanical properties steels
F00001–F99999	Cast irons and cast steels
G00001–G99999	AISI and SAE carbon and alloy steels
H00001–H99999	AISI H-steels
J00001–J99999	Cast steels (except tool steels)
K00001–K99999	Miscellaneous steels and ferrous alloys
S00001–S99999	Heat and corrosion resistant (stainless) steels
T00001–T99999	Tool steels
	Specialized Metals and Alloys
W00001–W99999	Welding filler metals, covered and tubular electrodes, classified by weld deposit composition (see Table 5.86)

SOURCE: Reprinted with permission from the *Annual Book of ASTM Standards,* copyright 1992, American Society of Testing and Materials.

TABLE 5.87 Secondary Division of Some Series of Numbers

E00001–E99999 Rare Earth and Rare Earth-Like Metals and Alloys	
E00000–E00999	Actinium
E01000–E20999	Cerium
E21000–E45999	Mixed rare earths*
E46000–E47999	Dysprosium
E48000–E49999	Erbium
E50000–E51999	Europium
E52000–E55999	Gadolinium
E56000–E57999	Nolmium
E58000–E67999	Lanthanum
E68000–E68999	Lutetium
E69000–E73999	Neodymium
E74000–E77999	Praseodymium
E78000–E78999	Promethium
E79000–E82999	Samarium
E83000–E84999	Scandium
E85000–E86999	Terbium
E87000–E87999	Thulium
E88000–E89999	Ytterbium
E90000–E99999	Yttrium
F00001–F9999 Cast Irons	
K00001–K99999 Miscellaneous Steels and Ferrous Alloys	
L00001–L99999 Low-Melting Metals and Alloys	
L00001–L00999	Bismuth
L01001–L01999	Cadmium
L02001–L02999	Cesium
L03001–L03999	Gallium
L04001–L04999	Indium
L05001–L05999	Lead
L06001–L06999	Lithium
L07001–L07999	Mercury
L08001–L08999	Potassium
L09001–L09999	Tubidium
L10001–L10999	Selenium
L11001–L11999	Sodium
L12001–L12999	Thallium
L13001–L13999	Tin
M00001–M99999 Miscellaneous Nonferrous Metals and Alloys	
M00001–M00999	Antimony
M01001–M01999	Arsenic
M02001–M02999	Barium
M03001–M03999	Calcium
M04001–M04999	Germanium
M05001–M05999	Plutonium
M06001–M06999	Strontium

M07001–M07999	Tellurium
M08001–M08999	Uranium
M10001–M19999	Magnesium
M20001–M29999	Manganese
M30001–M39999	Silicon
P00001–P99999 Precious Metals and Alloys	
P00001–P00999	Gold
P01001–P01999	Iridium
P02001–P02999	Osmium
P03001–P03999	Palladium
P04001–P04999	Platinum
P05001–P05999	Rhodium
P06001–P06999	Ruthenium
P07001–P07999	Silver
R00001–R99999 Reactive and Refractory Metals and Alloys	
R01001–R01999	Boron
R02001–R02999	Hafnium
R03001–R03999	Molybdenum
R04001–R04999	Niubium (columbium)
R05001–R05999	Tantalum
R06001–R06999	Thorium
R07001–R07999	Tungsten
R08001–R08999	Vanadium
R10001–R19999	Beryllium
R20001–R29999	Chromium
R30001–R39999	Cobalt
R40001–R49999	Rhenium
R50001–R59999	Titanium
R60001–R69999	Zirconium
W00001–W99999 Welding Filler Metals Classified by Weld Deposit Composition	
W00001–W09999	Carbon steel with no significant alloying elements
W10000–W19999	Manganese-molybdenum low-alloy steels
W20000–W29999	Nickel low-alloy steels
W30000–W39999	Austenitic stainless steels
W40000–W49999	Ferritic stainless steels
W50000–W59999	Chromium low-alloy steels
W60000–W69999	Copper-base alloys
W70000–W79999	Surfacing alloys
W80000–W89999	Nickel-base alloys
Z00001–Z99999 Zinc and Zinc Alloys	

* Alloys in which the rare earths are used in the ratio of their natural occurrence (that is, unseparated rare earths). In this mixture, cerium is the most abundant of the rare earth elements.

SOURCE: Reprinted with permission from the *Annual Book of ASTM Standards,* copyright 1992, American Society of Testing and Materials.

TABLE 5.88 Thickness Tolerances for Coils and Cut Lengths, Including Pickled Sheets

Specified width in inches	Specified thickness in inches					
	0.2299 to 0.1800	0.1799 to 0.0972	0.0971 to 0.0710	0.0709 to 0.0568	0.0567 to 0.0509	0.0508 to 0.0449
Over 12 to 20 incl.	0.007	0.007	0.006	0.006	0.005	0.005
Over 20 to 40 incl.	0.008	0.007	0.007	0.006	0.005	0.005
Over 40 to 48 incl.	0.009	0.008	0.007	0.006	0.006	0.005
Over 48 to 60 incl.	—	0.008	0.007	0.007	0.006	—
Over 60 to 72 incl.	—	0.008	0.008	0.007	0.007	—
Over 72		0.008	0.008			

NOTE: Thickness tolerances are over and under in inches.
SOURCE: Ryerson, Inc.

TABLE 5.89 Thickness Tolerances for Coils over 0.180 in Thick

Specified width in inches	Specified thickness in inches			
	0.5000 to 0.3751	0.3750 to 0.3125	0.3124 to 0.2300	0.2299 to 0.1800
Over 12 to 15 incl.	0.014	0.012	0.010	—
Over 15 to 20 incl.	0.015	0.014	0.011	—
Over 20 to 32 incl.	0.016	0.015	0.012	—
Over 32 to 40 incl.	0.017	0.016	0.013	—
Over 40 to 48 incl.	0.018	0.017	0.014	—
Over 48 to 60 incl.	0.019	0.019	0.015	0.011
Over 60 to 72 incl.	0.021	0.021	0.016	0.012

NOTE: Thickness tolerances are over and under in inches.
SOURCE: Ryerson, Inc.

TABLE 5.90 Thickness Tolerances for Coils and Cut Lengths—Over 12 in Wide

Specified width in inches	Specified thickness in inches					
	0.1419 to 0.0972	0.0971 to 0.0710	0.0709 to 0.0568	0.0567 to 0.0389	0.0388 to 0.0195	0.0194 to 0.0142
Over 12 to 15 incl.	0.005	0.005	0.005	0.004	0.003	0.002
Over 15 to 72 incl.	0.006	0.005	0.005	0.004	0.003	0.002
Over 72	0.007	0.006	0.005	0.004	0.003	—

NOTE: Thickness tolerances are over and under in inches.
SOURCE: Ryerson, Inc.

TABLE 5.91 Thickness Tolerances for Coils and Cut Lengths—2 to 12 in Wide

Specified width in inches	Specified thickness in inches			
	0.0821 to 0.0568	0.0567 to 0.0389	0.0388 to 0.0195	0.0194 to 0.0142
2 to 12 incl.	0.005	0.004	0.003	0.002

NOTE: Thickness tolerances are over and under in inches.
SOURCE: Ryerson, Inc.

TABLE 5.92 Thickness Tolerances for Coils and Cut Lengths

Specified widths in inches	Specified thickness in inches					
	0.1868 to 0.1009	0.1008 to 0.0748	0.0747 to 0.0606	0.0605 to 0.0426	0.0425 to 0.0232	0.0231 and thinner
To 32, incl.	0.008	0.007	0.006	0.005	0.004	0.003
Over 32 to 40	0.008	0.008	0.006	0.005	0.004	0.003
Over 40 to 60	0.009	0.008	0.006	0.005	0.004	0.003
Over 60 to 72	0.009	0.009	0.006	0.005	0.004	—

NOTE: Thickness tolerances are over or under in inches.

Thickness is measured at any point across the width not less than ⅜ in from a side edge. Regardless of whether total thickness tolerance is specified equally or unequally, over and under, the total tolerance should be equal to twice the tabular tolerances.

SOURCE: Ryerson, Inc.

TABLE 5.93 Thickness Tolerances for Coils and Cut Lengths

Specified width in inches	Specified thickness in inches						
	0.2299 to 0.2031	0.2030 to 0.1875	0.1874 to 0.1180	0.1179 to 0.0568	0.0567 to 0.0449	0.0448 to 0.0344	0.0343 to 0.0255
Up to 3½ incl.	—	0.006	0.005	0.004	0.003	0.003	0.003
Over 3½ to 6 incl.	—	0.006	0.005	0.005	0.003	0.003	—
Over 6 to 12 incl.	0.006	0.006	0.005	0.005	0.004	—	—

NOTE: Thickness tolerances are over and under in inches.

Thickness measurements are taken ⅜ in from edge of strip on 1 in or wider and at any place on the strip when narrower than 1 in. The given tolerances do not include crown.

SOURCE: Ryerson, Inc.

TABLE 5.94 Thickness Tolerances

Specified thickness in inches Under – To and incl.	Width in inches 1 to ½ excl.	Under 3 to 1 incl.	Under 3 to 6 incl.	Over 6 to 9 incl.	Over 9 to 12 incl.	Over 12 to 16 incl.	Over 16 to 20 incl.	Over 20 to 23$^{15}/_{16}$ incl.
0.250–0.200	0.003	0.004	0.0045	0.0045	0.005	0.0055	0.0055	0.0055
0.200–0.161	0.0025	0.0035	0.004	0.004	0.0045	0.0045	0.005	0.005
0.161–0.100	0.002	0.002	0.003	0.003	0.003	0.0035	0.0045	0.005
0.100–0.069	0.002	0.002	0.0025	0.003	0.003	0.0035	0.0035	0.0035
0.069–0.050	0.002	0.002	0.0025	0.0025	0.0025	0.003	0.003	0.003
0.050–0.040	0.002	0.002	0.0025	0.0025	0.0025	0.0025	0.0025	0.0025
0.040–0.035	0.002	0.002	0.002	0.002	0.002	0.002	0.002	0.002
0.035–0.032	0.0015	0.0015	0.002	0.002	0.002	0.002	0.002	0.002
0.032–0.029	0.0015	0.0015	0.0015	0.002	0.002	0.002	0.002	0.002
0.029–0.026	0.001	0.0015	0.0015	0.002	0.002	0.002	0.002	0.002
0.026–0.023	0.001	0.001	0.001	0.0015	0.0015	0.002	0.002	0.002
0.023–0.020	0.001	0.001	0.001	0.0015	0.0015	0.0015	0.0015	0.0015
0.020–0.017	0.00075	0.00075	0.00075	0.001	0.001	0.0015	0.0015	0.0015
0.017–0.015	0.00075	0.00075	0.00075	0.001	0.001	0.0015	0.0015	0.0015
0.015–0.013	0.00075	0.00075	0.00075	0.001	0.001	0.0015	0.0015	0.0015
0.013–0.012	0.00075	0.00075	0.00075	0.001	0.001	0.001	0.001	0.001
0.012–0.011	0.00075	0.00075	0.00075	0.001	0.001	0.001	0.001	0.001
0.011–0.009	0.00075	0.00075	0.00075	0.001	0.001	0.001	0.001	0.001
0.009–0.007	0.00075	0.00075	0.00075	—	—	—	—	—
0.007	0.00050	0.00050	0.00050	—	—	—	—	—

NOTE: Measure ⅜ in or more in from edge on 1 in or wider; and on narrower than 1 in at any place between the edges. Tolerances are plus or minus in inches.

SOURCE: Ryerson, Inc.

TABLE 5.95 Permissible Variations in Cross Section for Hot-Wrought Round, Square, and Round-Cornered Square Bars of Steel

Specified size, in	Permissible variation from specified size, in		Out-of-round or out-of-square, in*
	Over	Under	
To 5/16, incl	0.005	0.005	0.008
Over 5/16 to 7/16, incl	0.006	0.006	0.009
Over 7/16 to 5/8, incl	0.007	0.007	0.010
Over 5/8 to 7/8, incl	0.008	0.008	0.012
Over 7/8 to 1, incl	0.009	0.009	0.013
Over 1 to 1 1/8, incl	0.010	0.010	0.015
Over 1 1/8 to 1 1/4, incl	0.011	0.011	0.016
Over 1 1/4 to 1 3/8, incl	0.012	0.012	0.018
Over 1 3/8 to 1 1/2, incl	0.014	0.014	0.021
Over 1 1/2 to 2, incl	1/64	1/64	0.023
Over 2 to 2 1/2, incl	1/32	0	0.023
Over 2 1/2 to 3 1/2, incl	3/64	0	0.035
Over 3 1/2 to 4 1/2, incl	1/16	0	0.046
Over 4 1/2 to 5 1/2, incl	5/64	0	0.058
Over 5 1/2 to 6 1/2, incl	1/8	0	0.070
Over 6 1/2 to 8 1/4, incl	5/32	0	0.085
Over 8 1/4 to 9 1/2, incl	3/16	0	0.100
Over 9 1/2 to 10, incl	1/4	0	0.120

* Out-of-round is the difference between the maximum and minimum diameters of the bar, measured at the same cross section. Out-of-square is the difference in the two dimensions at the same cross section of a square bar between opposite faces.

SOURCE: Reprinted with permission from the *Annual Book of ASTM Standards,* copyright 1992, American Society of Testing and Materials.

TABLE 5.96 Permissible Variations in Cross Section for Hot-Wrought Hexagonal Bars of Steel

Specified sizes between opposite sides, in	Permissible variations from specified size, in		Out-of-hexagon (carbon steel and alloy steel) or out-of-octagon (alloy steel), in*
	Over	Under	
To 1/2, incl	0.007	0.007	0.011
Over 1/2 to 1, incl	0.010	0.010	0.015
Over 1 to 1 1/2, incl	0.021	0.013	0.025
Over 1 1/2 to 2, incl	1/32	1/64	1/32
Over 2 to 2 1/2, incl	3/64	1/64	3/64
Over 2 1/2 to 3 1/2, incl	1/16	1/64	1/16
Over 3 1/2 to 4 1/16, incl	5/64	1/64	5/64

* Out-of-hexagon or out-of-octagon is the greatest difference between any two dimensions at the same cross section between opposite faces.

SOURCE: Reprinted with permission from the *Annual Book of ASTM Standards,* copyright 1992, American Society of Testing and Materials.

TABLE 5.97 Permissible Variations in Thickness and Width for Hot-Wrought Square-Edge and Round-Edge Flat Bars[†]

Specified width, in	Permissible variations in thickness, for thickness given, over and under, in							Permissible variations in width, in	
	0.203 to 0.230, excl	0.230 to ¼, excl	¼ to ½, incl	Over ½ to 1, incl	Over 1 to 2, incl	Over 2 to 3, incl	Over 3	Over	Under
To 1, incl	0.007	0.007	0.008	0.010	—	—	—	1/64	1/64
Over 1 to 2, incl	0.007	0.007	0.012	0.015	1/32	—	—	1/32	1/32
Over 2 to 4, incl	0.008	0.008	0.015	0.020	1/32	3/64	3/64	1/16	1/32
Over 4 to 6, incl	0.009	0.009	0.015	0.020	1/32	3/64	3/64	3/32	1/16
Over 6 to 8, incl	*	0.015	0.016	0.025	1/32	3/64	1/16	⅛	3/32

* Flats over 6 to 8 in, incl, in width, are not available as hot-wrought steel bars in thickness under 0.230 in.

† When a square is held against a face and an edge of a square-edge flat bar, the edge shall not deviate by more than 3° or 5% of the thickness.

SOURCE: Reprinted with permission from the *Annual Book of ASTM Standards,* copyright 1992, American Society of Testing and Materials.

TABLE 5.98 Size Tolerances for Cold-Finished Carbon Steel Bars, Cold Drawn or Turned and Polished*

Size, in†	Maximum of carbon range 0.28% or less	Maximum of carbon range over 0.28% to 0.55%, incl	Maximum of carbon range to 0.55%, incl, stress relieved or annealed after cold finishing	Maximum of carbon range over 0.55% or all grades quenched and tempered or normalized and tempered before cold finishing
	All tolerances are in inches† and are minus			
	Rounds—Cold Drawn (to 4 in) or Turned and Polished			
To 1½, incl	0.002	0.003	0.004	0.005
Over 1½ to 2½, incl	0.003	0.004	0.005	0.006
Over 2½ to 4, incl	0.004	0.005	0.006	0.007
Over 4 to 6, incl	0.005	0.006	0.007	0.008
Over 6 to 8, incl	0.006	0.007	0.008	0.009
Over 8 to 9, incl	0.007	0.008	0.009	0.010
	Hexagons			
To ¾, incl	0.002	0.003	0.004	0.006
Over ¾ to 1½, incl	0.003	0.004	0.005	0.007
Over 1½ to 2½, incl	0.004	0.005	0.006	0.008
Over 2½ to 3⅛, incl	0.005	0.006	0.007	0.009
Over 3⅛ to 4, incl	0.005	0.006	—	—
	Squares‡			
To ¾, incl	0.002	0.004	0.005	0.007
Over ¾ to 1½, incl	0.003	0.005	0.006	0.008
Over 1½ to 2½, incl	0.004	0.006	0.007	0.009
Over 2½ to 4, incl	0.006	0.008	0.009	0.011
Over 4 to 5, incl	0.010	—	—	—
Over 5 to 6, incl	0.014	—	—	—
	Flats‡			
Width,† in				
To ¾, incl	0.003	0.004	0.006	0.008
Over ¾ to 1½, incl	0.004	0.005	0.008	0.010
Over 1½ to 3, incl	0.005	0.006	0.010	0.012
Over 3 to 4, incl	0.006	0.008	0.011	0.016
Over 4 to 6, incl	0.008	0.010	0.012	0.020
Over 6	0.013	0.015	—	—

* This table includes tolerances for bars that have been annealed, spheroidize annealed, normalized, normalized and tempered, or quenched and tempered before cold finishing. This table does not include tolerances for bars that are annealed, spheroidize annealed, normalized, normalized and tempered, or quenched and tempered after cold finishing; the producer should be consulted for tolerances for such bars.

† Width governs the tolerances for both width and thickness of flats. For example, when the maximum of carbon range is 0.28% or less, for a flat 2 in wide and 1 in thick, the width tolerance is 0.005 in and the thickness tolerance is the same, namely, 0.005 in.

‡ Tolerances may be ordered all plus, or distributed plus and minus with the sum equivalent to the tolerances listed.

SOURCE: Reprinted with permission from the *Annual Book of ASTM Standards,* copyright 1992, American Society of Testing and Materials.

TABLE 5.99 Size Tolerances for Cold-Finished Round Bars Cold Drawn, Ground, and Polished or Turned, Ground, and Polished

Size, in, cold drawn, ground, and polished	Turned, ground, and polished	Tolerances from specified size, minus only, in
To 1½, incl	To 1½, incl	0.001
Over 1½ to 2½, excl	Over 1½ to 2½, excl	0.0015
2½ to 3, incl	2½ to 3, incl	0.002
Over 3 to 4, incl	Over 3 to 4, incl	0.003
—	Over 4 to 6, incl	0.004*
—	Over 6	0.005*

* For nonresulfurized steels (steels specified to maximum sulphur limits under 0.08%) or for steels thermally treated, the tolerance is increased by 0.001 in.

SOURCE: Reprinted with permission from the *Annual Book of ASTM Standards,* copyright 1992, American Society of Testing and Materials.

TABLE 5.100 Size Tolerance for Cold-Finished Alloy Steel Bars, Cold Drawn or Turned and Polished

Size, in*	Maximum of carbon range 0.28% or less	Maximum of carbon range over 0.28% to 0.55%, incl	Maximum of carbon range to 0.55%, incl, stress relieved or annealed after cold finishing	Maximum of carbon range over 0.55% with or without stress relieving or annealing after cold finishing; also, all carbons, quenched and tempered (heat treated), or normalized and tempered, before cold finishing
	All tolerances are in inches and are minus			
	Rounds—Cold Drawn (to 4 in) or Turned and Polished			
To 1, incl, in coils	0.002	0.003	0.004	0.005
Cut lengths:				
To 1½, incl	0.003	0.004	0.005	0.006
Over 1½ to 2½, incl	0.004	0.005	0.006	0.007
Over 2½ to 4, incl	0.005	0.006	0.007	0.008
Over 4 to 6, incl	0.006	0.007	0.008	0.009
Over 6 to 8, incl	0.007	0.008	0.009	0.010
Over 8 to 9, incl	0.008	0.009	0.010	0.011
	Hexagons			
To ¾, incl	0.003	0.004	0.005	0.007
Over ¾ to 1½, incl	0.004	0.005	0.006	0.008
Over 1½ to 2½, incl	0.005	0.006	0.007	0.009
Over 2½ to 3⅛, incl	0.006	0.007	0.008	0.010
Over 3⅛ to 4, incl	0.006	—	—	—
	Squares			
To ¾, incl	0.003	0.005	0.006	0.008
Over ¾ to 1½, incl	0.004	0.006	0.007	0.009
Over 1½ to 2½, incl	0.005	0.007	0.008	0.010
Over 2½ to 4, incl	0.007	0.009	0.010	0.012
Over 4 to 5, incl	0.011	—	—	—
	Flats*			
To ¾, incl	0.004	0.005	0.007	0.009
Over ¾ to 1½, incl	0.005	0.006	0.009	0.011
Over 1½ to 3, incl	0.006	0.007	0.011	0.013
Over 3 to 4, incl	0.007	0.009	0.012	0.017
Over 4 to 6, incl	0.009	0.011	0.013	0.021
Over 6	0.014	—	—	—

* Width governs the tolerances for both width and thickness of flats. For example, when the maximum of carbon range is 0.28% or less, for a flat 2 in wide and 1 in thick, the width tolerance is 0.006 in and the thickness tolerance is the same, namely, 0.006 in.

SOURCE: Reprinted with permission from the *Annual Book of ASTM Standards,* copyright 1992, American Society of Testing and Materials.

TABLE 5.101 Tool Steel Bars: Size Tolerances

	Standard manufacturing tolerance, in, plus and minus	Precision tolerance, in, plus and minus
	Drill Rod Rounds	
0.500 to 1.500, incl.	0.001	0.0005
0.125 to 0.499, incl.	0.0005	0.00025
Up to 0.124, incl.	0.0003	0.0002
	Drill Rod Flats, Squares, Hexagons, Octagons	
1 to ¾ in incl.	Plus or minus 0.0015	—
Under ¾ to ¼ in	Plus or minus 0.001	—
Under ¼ in	Plus or minus 0.0005	—

SOURCE: Ryerson, Inc.

TABLE 5.102 Seamless Mechanical Tubing: Diameter and Wall-Thickness Tolerances—Cold Worked

Specified size of OD in inches	As drawn or finish annealed				Quenched and tempered		Wall thickness
	OD, in		ID, in		OD, in	ID, in	in %
	Over	Under	Over	Under	Over/under	Over/under	Over/under
3/16 to ½ excl[bc]	0.004	0.000	—	—	0.010	—	15
½ to 1½[abcd]	0.005	0.000	0.000	0.005	0.015	0.015	10
1½ to 3½[abcd]	0.010	0.000	0.000	0.010	0.030	0.030	10
3½ to 5½[ad]	0.015	0.000	0.005	0.015	0.045	0.045	10
5½ to 8 excl							
When wall less than 5% of OD[d]	0.030	0.030	0.035	0.035	—	—	10
When wall is from 5 to 7.5% of OD	0.020	0.020	0.025	0.025	—	—	10
When wall is over 7.5% of OD[a]	0.030	0.000	0.015	0.030	—	—	10
8 to 10¾ incl							
When wall less than 5% of OD[d]	0.045	0.045	0.050	0.050	—	—	10
When wall is from 5 to 7.5% of OD	0.035	0.035	0.040	0.040	—	—	10
When wall is over 7.5% of OD[a]	0.045	0.000	0.015	0.040	—	—	10
Over 10¾ to 12¾ incl							
When wall less than 5% of OD[d]	0.060	0.060	0.060	0.060	—	—	10
When wall is from 5 to 7.5% of OD	0.050	0.050	0.050	0.050	—	—	10
When wall is over 7.5% of OD[a]	0.045	0.045	0.045	0.045	—	—	10

[a] Many tubes with ID less than 50% of OD, or with wall thickness over 25% of OD, or weighing more than 90 lb/ft are difficult to draw over mandrel. Therefore, ID can vary over or under by an amount equal to 10% of wall and wall may vary 12½% over or under that specified.

[b] Footnote a doesn't apply for tubes less than ½ in (or less than ⅝ in when wall thickness is more than 20% of OD) that are not commonly drawn over mandrel. Therefore, the wall thickness can vary 15% over and under that specified and the ID is governed by the OD and wall thickness tolerances in table.

[c] For tubes less than ½ in (or less than ⅝ in when wall thickness is more than 20% of OD), which can be drawn over mandrel, the tolerances shown in the table apply, except that the wall thickness tolerances are 10% over and under the specified wall thickness.

[d] Tubing with wall thickness less than 3% of OD cannot be straightened properly without a certain amount of distortion. Consequently, an ovality tolerance of ½% over and under nominal OD applies in addition to the tolerances in above table.

SOURCE: Ryerson, Inc.

TABLE 5.103 Round, Drawn-over-Mandrel Carbon Steel Welded Mechanical Tubing

	Wall Thickness Tolerances									
	Outside diameter of tubing in inches									
	⅜ to ⅞		Over ⅞ to 1⅞		Over 1⅞ to 3¾		Over 3¾ to 5½		Over 5½ to 7¼	
Wall	Plus	Minus	Plus	Minus	Plus	Minus	Plus	Minus	Plus	Minus
22 (0.028)	0.002	0.002	0.002	0.002	0.002	0.002	—	—	—	—
20 (0.035)	0.002	0.002	0.002	0.002	0.002	0.002	—	—	—	—
18 (0.049)	0.002	0.003	0.002	0.003	0.002	0.003	—	—	—	—
16 (0.065)	0.002	0.002	0.002	0.003	0.002	0.003	0.004	0.004	—	—
14 (0.083)	0.002	0.002	0.002	0.003	0.003	0.003	0.004	0.005	—	—
13 (0.095)	0.002	0.002	0.002	0.003	0.003	0.003	0.004	0.005	0.004	0.005
12 (0.109)	0.002	0.003	0.002	0.004	0.003	0.003	0.005	0.005	0.005	0.005
11 (0.120)	0.003	0.003	0.002	0.004	0.003	0.003	0.005	0.005	0.005	0.005
10 (0.134)	—	—	0.002	0.004	0.003	0.003	0.005	0.005	0.005	0.005
9 (0.148)	—	—	0.002	0.004	0.003	0.003	0.005	0.005	0.005	0.005
8 (0.165)	—	—	0.003	0.004	0.003	0.004	0.005	0.006	0.005	0.006
7 (0.180)	—	—	0.004	0.004	0.003	0.005	0.006	0.006	0.006	0.006
6 (0.203)	—	—	0.004	0.005	0.004	0.005	0.006	0.007	0.006	0.007
5 (0.220)	—	—	—	—	0.004	0.006	0.007	0.007	0.007	0.007
4 (0.238)	—	—	—	—	0.005	0.006	0.007	0.007	0.007	0.007
3 (0.259)	—	—	—	—	0.005	0.006	0.007	0.007	0.007	0.007
2 (0.284)	—	—	—	—	0.005	0.006	0.007	0.007	0.007	0.007
1 (0.300)	—	—	—	—	0.006	0.006	0.008	0.008	0.008	0.008
0.320	—	—	—	—	0.007	0.007	0.008	0.008	0.008	0.008
0.344	—	—	—	—	0.008	0.008	0.009	0.009	0.009	0.009

OD and ID Tolerances				
OD size range in inches	OD inches*		ID inches*	
	Over	Under	Over	Under
Up to 0.499	0.004	0.000	—	—
0.500–1.699 incl.	0.005	0.000	0.000	0.005
1.700–2.099 incl.	0.006	0.000	0.000	0.006
2.100–2.499 incl.	0.007	0.000	0.000	0.007
2.500–2.899 incl.	0.008	0.000	0.000	0.008
2.900–3.299 incl.	0.009	0.000	0.000	0.009
3.300–3.699 incl.	0.010	0.000	0.000	0.010
3.700–4.099 incl.	0.011	0.000	0.000	0.011
4.100–4.499 incl.	0.012	0.000	0.000	0.012
4.500–4.899 incl.	0.013	0.000	0.000	0.013
4.900–5.299 incl.	0.014	0.000	0.000	0.014
5.300–5.549 incl.	0.015	0.000	0.000	0.015
5.550–5.999 incl.	0.010	0.010	0.010	0.010
6.000–6.499 incl.	0.013	0.013	0.013	0.013
6.500–6.999 incl.	0.015	0.015	0.015	0.015
7.000 and over	0.018	0.018	0.018	0.018

* When the wall thickness is less than 3% of the OD, an ovality tolerance of plus and minus ½% of the mean outside diameter is required. This tolerance is in addition to the OD and ID tolerances indicated above.

SOURCE: Ryerson, Inc.

TABLE 5.104 Stainless Steel Sheets: Standard Gauge Tolerances—All Finishes

Thickness in inches			Tolerance in inches (plus or minus)		
				Hand mill	
Under	Incl.	Gauge number	Continuous mill 48 in max. width	Over 48 to 60 in width incl.	Over 60 in width
0.1875 to 0.146		8 & 9	0.007	0.0105	0.014
0.146 to 0.131		10	0.006	0.009	0.012
0.131 to 0.115		11	0.005	0.0075	0.010
0.115 to 0.099		12	0.005	0.007	0.009
0.099 to 0.084		13	0.004	0.006	0.008
0.084 to 0.073		14	0.004	0.0055	0.007
0.073 to 0.059		15 & 16	0.003	0.0045	0.006
0.059 to 0.041		17 & 19	0.003	—	—
0.041 to 0.030		20 to 22	0.002	—	—
0.030 to 0.017		23 to 27	0.0015	—	—
0.017 to 0.008		28 to 34	0.0015	—	—
0.008 to 0.006		35 to 38	0.0015	—	—
0.006		39	0.001	—	—

SOURCE: Ryerson, Inc.

TABLE 5.105 Stainless Steel Plates: Thickness Tolerances

Thickness in inches	Thickness tolerance over variation* in inches			
	Widths to 84 in incl.	Widths over 84 to 120 in incl.	Widths over 120 to 144 in incl.	Widths over 144 in incl.
3/16 to 3/8 excl.	0.046	0.050	—	—
3/8 to 3/4 excl.	0.054	0.058	0.075	0.090
3/4 to 1 excl.	0.060	0.064	0.083	0.100
1 to 2 incl.	0.070	0.074	0.095	0.115
Over 2	OA	OA	OA	OA

* No plate shall vary more than 0.01 in under the thickness ordered. OA = On application. Spot grinding not to exceed 0.01 in under the specified thickness is permitted to remove surface imperfections.

SOURCE: Ryerson, Inc.

TABLE 5.106 Stainless Steel Bars: Hot-Rolled Rounds and Squares: Tolerances

Specified sizes, in	Variation from size, in		Out of round or square,* in
Over 5/16 to 7/16 incl.	+0.006	−0.006	0.009
Over 7/16 to 5/8 incl.	+0.007	−0.007	0.010
Over 5/8 to 7/8 incl.	+0.008	−0.008	0.012
Over 7/8 to 1 incl.	+0.009	−0.009	0.013
Over 1 to 1 1/8 incl.	+0.010	−0.010	0.015
Over 1 1/8 to 1 1/4 incl.	+0.011	−0.011	0.016
Over 1 1/4 to 1 3/8 incl.	+0.012	−0.012	0.018
Over 1 3/8 to 1 1/2 incl.	+0.014	−0.014	0.021
Over 1 1/2 to 2 incl.	+1/64	−1/64	0.023
Over 2 to 2 1/2 incl.	+1/32	−0	0.023
Over 2 1/2 to 3 1/2 incl.	+3/64	−0	0.035
Over 3 1/2 to 4 1/2 incl.	+1/16	−0	0.046
Over 4 1/2 to 5 1/2 incl.	+5/64	−0	0.058
Over 5 1/2 to 6 1/2 incl.	+1/8	−0	0.070
Over 6 1/2 to 8 incl.	+5/32	−0	0.085

* Out-of-round is the difference between the maximum and minimum diameters of the bar, measured at the same cross section. Out-of-square is the difference in the two dimensions at the same cross section of a square bar, each dimension being the distance between opposite faces.

SOURCE: Ryerson, Inc.

TABLE 5.107 Stainless Steel Hot-Rolled Hexagons and Octagons: Tolerances

Specified sizes measured between opposite sides, in	Variation from size, in		Maximum difference, three measurements for hexagons only, in
1/4 to 1/2 incl.	+0.007	−0.007	0.011
Over 1/2 to 1 incl.	+0.010	−0.010	0.015
Over 1 to 1 1/2 incl.	+0.021	−0.021	0.025
Over 1 1/2 to 2 incl.	+1/32	−1/32	1/32
Over 2 to 2 1/2 incl.	+3/64	−3/64	3/64
Over 2 1/2 to 3 1/2 incl.	+1/16	−1/16	1/16

SOURCE: Ryerson, Inc.

TABLE 5.108 Stainless Steel Hot-Rolled Flats: Tolerances

Specified widths, in	Variations from thickness for thickness given, in: ⅛ to ½, incl.	Over ½ to 1, incl.	Over 1 to 2, incl.	Variations from width, in: Over	Under
⅜ to 1 incl.	±0.008	±0.010	—	1/64	1/64
Over 1 to 2 incl.	±0.012	±0.015	±1/32	1/32	1/32
Over 2 to 4 incl.	±0.015	±0.020	±1/32	1/16	1/32
Over 4 to 6 incl.	±0.015	±0.020	±1/32	3/32	1/16
Over 6 to 8 incl.	±0.016	±0.025	±1/32	⅛	5/32
Over 8 to 10 incl.	±0.021	±0.031	±1/32	5/32	3/16

SOURCE: Ryerson, Inc.

TABLE 5.109 Stainless Steel Centerless Ground Rounds and Cold-Drawn Rounds: Tolerances

Sizes, in	Variation, in: Over	Under
3/32 to 5/16 excl.	0.001	0.001
5/16 to ½ excl.	0.0015	0.0015
½ to 1 excl.	0.002	0.002
1 to 1½ excl.	0.0025	0.0025
1½ to 4 incl.	0.003	0.003

SOURCE: Ryerson, Inc.

TABLE 5.110 Stainless Steel Cold-Drawn Squares, Hexagons, and Octagons: Tolerances

Specified size, in	Variations from size, in	
	Over	Under
3/32 to 5/16 excl.	0	0.002
5/16 to 1/2 excl.	0	0.003
1/2	0	0.004
Over 1/2 to 1 incl.	0	0.004
Over 1 to 2 incl.	0	0.006
Over 2 to 3 incl.	0	0.008
Over 3	0	0.010

SOURCE: Ryerson, Inc.

TABLE 5.111 Stainless Steel Cold-Drawn* Flats: Tolerances

Size width or thickness, in	Variations from width over or under, in		Variations from thickness over or under, in
	For thicknesses 1/4 and under	For thicknesses over 1/4	
Over 3/8 to 1 incl.	0.004	0.002	0.002
Over 1 to 2 incl.	0.006	0.003	0.003
Over 2 to 3 incl.	0.008	0.004	0.004
Over 3 to 4½ incl.	0.010	0.005	0.005

* When it is necessary to heat treat or heat treat and pickle after cold finishing, because of special hardness or mechanical property requirements, tolerances are double those shown in the table.

SOURCE: Ryerson, Inc.

TABLE 5.112 Cold-Drawn Annealed Seamless Mechanical Stainless Steel Tubing: Outside Diameter, Ovality, and Wall Thickness Variations

OD size, in	Variations from OD, in		Ovality, double OD tolerance when wall is:	Wall thickness, percent*,†	
	Over	Under		Over	Under
Under ½	0.005	0.005	Lighter than 0.015 in	15	15
½ to 1½ excl.	0.005	0.005	Lighter than 0.065 in	10	10
1½ to 3½ excl.	0.010	0.010	Lighter than 0.095 in	10	10
3½ to 5½ excl.	0.015	0.015	Lighter than 0.150 in	10	10
5½ to 8 excl.	0.030	0.030	Lighter than 0.240 in	10	10

* Tubes with wall thicknesses more than 25% of their outside diameter or with wall thicknesses greater than 1¼ in or weighing more than 90 lb/ft may vary in wall thickness plus and minus 12½%.

† For tubes with inside diameter less than ½ in (or less than ⅝ in when wall thickness is more than 20% of the outside diameter), which cannot be successfully drawn over a mandrel, the wall thickness may vary 15% over or under that specified and the inside diameter will be governed by the outside diameter and wall thickness variations.

SOURCE: Ryerson, Inc.

TABLE 5.113 Thickness Tolerances: Aluminum Alloy Sheet and Plate

	Width in inches						
Thickness in inches*	Up to 18	Over 18 to 36	Over 36 to 48	Over 48 to 54	Over 54 to 60	Over 60 to 66	Over 66 to 72
0.006–0.010	0.001	0.0015	0.0025	0.0025	—	—	—
0.011–0.017	0.0015	0.0015	0.0025	0.0035	—	—	—
0.018–0.028	0.0015	0.002	0.0025	0.0035	0.004	0.004	0.004
0.029–0.036	0.002	0.002	0.0025	0.004	0.005	0.005	0.005
0.037–0.045	0.002	0.0025	0.003	0.004	0.005	0.005	0.005
0.046–0.068	0.0025	0.003	0.004	0.005	0.006	0.006	0.006
0.069–0.076	0.003	0.003	0.004	0.005	0.006	0.006	0.006
0.077–0.096	0.0035	0.0035	0.004	0.005	0.006	0.006	0.006
0.097–0.108	0.004	0.004	0.005	0.005	0.007	0.007	0.007
0.109–0.125	0.0045	0.0045	0.005	0.005	0.007	0.007	0.007
0.126–0.140	0.0045	0.0045	0.005	0.005	0.007	0.010	0.012
0.141–0.172	0.006	0.006	0.008	0.008	0.009	0.012	0.014
0.173–0.203	0.007	0.007	0.010	0.010	0.011	0.014	0.016
0.204–0.249	0.009	0.009	0.011	0.011	0.013	0.016	0.018
0.250–0.320	0.013	0.013	0.013	0.013	0.015	0.018	0.020
0.321–0.438	0.019	0.019	0.019	0.019	0.020	0.020	0.023
0.439–0.625	0.025	0.025	0.025	0.025	0.025	0.025	0.025
0.626–0.875	0.030	0.030	0.030	0.030	0.030	0.030	0.030
0.876–1.125	0.035	0.035	0.035	0.035	0.035	0.035	0.035
1.126–1.375	0.040	0.040	0.040	0.040	0.040	0.040	0.040
1.376–1.625	0.045	0.045	0.045	0.045	0.045	0.045	0.045
1.626–1.875	0.052	0.052	0.052	0.052	0.052	0.052	0.052
1.876–2.250	0.060	0.060	0.060	0.060	0.060	0.060	0.060
2.251–2.750	0.075	0.075	0.075	0.075	0.075	0.075	0.075
2.751–3.000	0.090	0.090	0.090	0.090	0.090	0.090	0.090
3.001–4.000	0.110	0.110	0.110	0.110	0.110	0.110	0.110
4.001–5.000	0.125	0.125	0.125	0.125	0.125	0.125	0.125
5.001–6.000	0.135	0.135	0.135	0.135	0.135	0.135	0.135

	Width in inches							
Thickness in inches*	Over 72 to 78	Over 78 to 84	Over 84 to 90	Over 90 to 96	Over 96 to 132	Over 132 to 144	Over 144 to 156	Over 156 to 168
0.029–0.036	0.006	0.006	0.007	0.009	—	—	—	—
0.037–0.045	0.006	0.006	0.007	0.011	—	—	—	—
0.046–0.068	0.007	0.007	0.008	0.012	0.013	—	—	—
0.069–0.076	0.007	0.007	0.012	0.012	0.016	—	—	—
0.077–0.096	0.007	0.007	0.012	0.012	0.016	—	—	—
0.097–0.108	0.008	0.008	0.016	0.018	0.020	—	—	—
0.109–0.125	0.008	0.008	0.016	0.018	0.020			—
0.126–0.140	0.013	0.014	0.016	0.018	0.020	—	—	—
0.141–0.172	0.015	0.016	0.017	0.019	0.023	—	—	—
0.173–0.203	0.017	0.017	0.017	0.022	0.026	—	—	—
0.204–0.249	0.018	0.018	0.018	0.024	0.028	—	—	—
0.250–0.320	0.020	0.020	0.020	0.025	0.030	0.035	0.042	0.053
0.321–0.438	0.023	0.025	0.025	0.026	0.033	0.038	0.045	0.057
0.439–0.625	0.030	0.030	0.030	0.035	0.035	0.043	0.049	0.067

TABLE 5.113 Thickness Tolerances: Aluminum Alloy Sheet and Plate (*Continued*)

	Width in inches (*Continued*)							
Thickness in inches*	Over 72 to 78	Over 78 to 84	Over 84 to 90	Over 90 to 96	Over 96 to 132	Over 132 to 144	Over 144 to 156	Over 156 to 168
0.626–0.875	0.037	0.037	0.037	0.045	0.045	0.054	0.059	0.077
0.876–1.125	0.045	0.045	0.045	0.055	0.055	0.065	0.070	0.088
1.126–1.375	0.052	0.052	0.052	0.065	0.065	0.075	0.080	0.098
1.376–1.625	0.060	0.060	0.060	0.075	0.075	0.085	0.090	0.108
1.626–1.875	0.070	0.070	0.070	0.088	0.088	—	—	—
1.876–2.250	0.080	0.080	0.080	0.100	0.100	—	—	—
2.251–2.750	0.100	0.100	0.100	0.125	0.125	—	—	—
2.751–3.000	0.120	0.120	0.120	0.150	0.150	—	—	—
3.001–4.000	0.140	0.140	0.140	0.160	0.160	—	—	—
4.001–5.000	0.150	0.150	0.150	0.160	—	—	—	—
5.001–6.000	0.160	0.160	0.160	0.170	—	—	—	—

* Sheets have a thickness less than 0.250 in, plates 0.250 in and larger.

NOTE: All tolerances are plus and minus. When a dimension tolerance is specified other than as an equal bilateral tolerance, the value of the standard tolerance is that which would apply to the mean of the maximum and minimum dimensions permissible under the tolerance. Standard tolerances conform to or are within those specified in "Recommended Standards for Wrought Aluminum Mill Products," as issued by The Aluminum Association.

SOURCE: Ryerson, Inc.

TABLE 5.114 Diameter Tolerances: Aluminum Alloy Round Wire and Rods

	Allowable deviation from specified diameter, in			
			Rolled rod*	
Specified diameter in inches	Drawn wire*	Cold-finished rod*	Plus	Minus
Up to 0.035	0.0005	—	—	—
0.036–0.064	0.001	—	—	—
0.065–0.374	0.0015	—	—	—
0.375–0.500	—	0.0015	—	—
0.501–1.000	—	0.002	—	—
1.001–1.500	—	0.0025	—	—
1.501–2.000	—	0.004	0.006	0.006
2.001–3.000	—	0.006	0.008	0.008
3.001–3.499	—	0.008	0.012	0.012
3.500–5.000	—	0.012	0.031	0.016
5.001–8.000	—	—	0.062	0.031

* Tolerances are plus and minus.

SOURCE: Ryerson, Inc.

TABLE 5.115 Distance Across Flats Tolerances: Aluminum Alloy Square, Hexagonal, and Octagonal Wire and Bars

Specified distance across flats in inches	Allowable deviation from specified distance across flats, in		
	Drawn wire*	Cold-finished bar*	Rolled bar*
Up to 0.035	0.001	—	—
0.036–0.064	0.0015	—	—
0.065–0.374	0.002	—	—
0.375–0.500	—	0.002	—
0.501–1.000	—	0.0025	—
1.001–1.500	—	0.003	—
1.501–2.000	—	0.005	0.016
2.001–3.000	—	0.008	0.020
3.001–4.000	—	—	0.020

* All tolerances are plus or minus.
SOURCE: Ryerson, Inc.

TABLE 5.116 Thickness and Width Tolerances: Aluminum Alloy Rectangular Wire and Bars

Specified thickness and width in inches	Allowable deviation from specified thickness and width, in			
	Drawn wire and cold-finished bar*		Rolled bar*	
	Thickness	Width	Thickness	Width
Up to 0.035	0.001	—	—	—
0.036–0.064	0.0015	—	—	—
0.065–0.500	0.002	0.002	0.006	—
0.501–0.750	0.0025	0.0025	0.008	0.016
0.751–1.000	0.0025	0.0025	0.012	0.016
1.001–1.500	0.003	0.003	0.016	0.016
1.501–2.000	0.005	0.005	0.016	0.031
2.001–3.000	0.008	0.008	0.020	0.031
3.001–4.000	—	0.010	—	—
4.001–6.000	—	—	—	0.047
6.001–10.000	—	—	—	0.062

NOTE: Standard tolerances conform to, or are within those specified in "Recommended Standards for Wrought Aluminum Mill Products," as issued by The Aluminum Association.
* All tolerances are plus or minus.
SOURCE: Ryerson, Inc.

TABLE 5.117 Diameter Tolerances and Distance Across Flats Tolerances: Aluminum Alloy Round and Hexagonal Screw-Machine Stock

Round stock		Hexagonal stock	
Specified diameter in inches	Allowable deviation from specified diameter, in	Specified distance across flats in inches	Allowable deviation from specified distance across flats, in
0.125–0.500	0.0015	0.125–0.500	0.002
0.501–1.000	0.002	0.501–1.000	0.0025
1.001–1.500	0.0025	1.001–1.500	0.003
1.501–2.000	0.004	1.501–2.000	0.005
2.001–2.500	0.006	2.001–3.000	0.008
2.501–3.000	0.008		
3.001–3.375	0.012		

NOTE: All tolerances are plus or minus. Standard tolerances conform to those specified in "Recommended Standards for Wrought Aluminum Products," as issued by The Aluminum Association.

SOURCE: Ryerson, Inc.

TABLE 5.118 Aluminum Alloy Round Drawn Tubing: Tolerances
(a) Diameter Tolerances

Specified OD or ID, in	Allowable deviation of mean diameter from specified diameter (size), in	Allowable deviation of diameter at any point from specified diameter (ovalness), in*	
		Not heat treated†	Heat treated†
Under 0.501	0.003	0.003	0.006
0.501–1.000	0.004	0.004	0.008
1.001–2.000	0.005	0.005	0.010
2.001–3.000	0.006	0.006	0.012
3.001–5.000	0.008	0.008	0.016
5.001–6.000	0.010	0.010	0.020
6.001–8.000	0.015	0.015	0.030
8.001–10.000	0.020	0.020	0.040
10.001–12.000	0.025	0.025	0.050

(b) Wall Thickness Tolerances

Specified wall thickness, in	Allowable deviation of mean wall thickness from specified wall thickness, in	Allowable deviation of wall thickness at any point from specified wall thickness (eccentricity)	
		Not heat treated‡	Heat treated
0.010–0.035	0.002	0.002	Plus or minus 10% of specified wall thickness min. ±0.003
0.036–0.049	0.003	0.003	
0.050–0.083	0.004	0.004	
0.084–0.120	0.005	0.006	
0.121–0.203	0.006	0.008	
0.204–0.300	0.008	0.012	
0.301–0.375	0.015	0.020	
0.376–0.500	0.020	0.030	

* Not applicable to annealed (–0 temper) tubing, coiled tubing, or tubing having a wall thickness less than 0.020 in or 2½% of the OD—or equivalent round diameter (dia. of a circle having a circumference equal to the perimeter of a tube).

† For the –T8 tempers of 6063 alloy, the tolerances for non-heat-treated apply.

‡ For coiled tubing, use tolerances in heat treated column.

NOTE: All tolerances are plus or minus. Standard tolerances conform to, or are within those specified in "Recommended Standards for Wrought Aluminum Mill Products," as issued by The Aluminum Association. When outside diameter, inside diameter, and wall thickness are all specified, standard tolerances are applicable to any two of these dimensions, but not to all three. When a dimension tolerance is specified other than as an equal bilateral tolerance, the value of the standard tolerance is that which would apply to the mean of the maximum and minimum dimensions permissible under the tolerance. Mean diameter is the average of two diameter measurements taken at right angles to each other at any point along the length. Mean wall thickness is the average of two measurements taken opposite each other. When dimensions specified are outside and inside, rather than wall thickness, the allowable deviation at any point (eccentricity) is plus or minus 10% of the mean wall thickness, but not less than ±0.003 in.

SOURCE: Ryerson, Inc.

TABLE 5.119 Aluminum Alloy Round Extruded Tubing: Tolerances
(a) Diameter Tolerances

Specified OD or ID, in	Allowable deviation of mean diameter from specified diameter (size), in	Allowable deviation of diameter at any point from specified diameter (ovalness), in
0.500–0.999	0.010	0.020
1.000–1.999	0.012	0.025
2.000–3.999	0.015	0.030
4.000–5.999	0.025	0.050
6.000–7.999	0.035	0.075
8.000–9.999	0.045	0.100
10.000–11.999	0.055	0.125
12.000–13.999	0.065	0.150
14.000–15.999	0.075	0.175
16.000–17.999	0.085	0.200

(b) Wall Thickness Tolerances

	Allowable deviation of mean wall thickness from specified wall thickness in inches				Allowable deviation of wall thickness at any point from mean wall thickness (eccentricity)
	Outside diameter in inches				
Specified wall thickness, in	Under 1.250	1.250–2.999	3.000–4.999	5.000 and over	
Under 0.047	0.006	—	—	—	Plus or minus 10% of mean wall thickness max. ±0.060 min. ±0.010
0.047–0.061	0.007	0.008	0.008	0.010	
0.062–0.077	0.008	0.008	0.009	0.012	
0.078–0.124	0.009	0.009	0.010	0.015	
0.125–0.249	0.009	0.009	0.013	0.020	
0.250–0.374	0.011	0.011	0.016	0.025	
0.375–0.499	—	0.015	0.021	0.035	
0.500–0.749	—	0.020	0.028	0.045	
0.750–0.999	—	—	0.035	0.055	
1.000–1.499	—	—	0.045	0.065	
1.500–2.000	—	—	—	0.075	
2.001–2.499	—	—	—	0.085	±0.120
2.500–2.999	—	—	—	0.095	
3.000–3.499	—	—	—	0.105	
3.500–4.000	—	—	—	0.115	

NOTE: All tolerances are plus or minus. Tolerances are applicable to the average shape; wider tolerances may be required for some shapes and closer tolerances may be possible for others. When outside diameter, inside diameter, and wall thickness (or their equivalent dimensions in other-than-round tube) are all specified, standard tolerances are applicable to any two of these dimensions, but not to all three. When a dimension tolerance is specified other than as an equal bilateral tolerance, the value of the standard tolerance is that which would apply to the mean of the maximum and minimum dimensions permissible under the tolerance. Mean diameter is the average of two diameter measurements taken at right angles to each other at any point along the length. Not applicable in the annealed (–0) temper or if wall thickness is less than 2½ percent of the outside diameter or equivalent round diameter. The equivalent round diameter is the diameter of a circle having a circumference equal to the perimeter of the tube. The mean wall thickness of round tube is the average of two measurements taken opposite each other. The mean wall thickness of other-than-round tube is the average of two measurements taken opposite each other at approximate center line of tube and perpendicular to the longitudinal axis of the cross section. When dimensions specified are outside and inside, rather than wall thickness itself, allowable deviation of any point (eccentricity) applies to mean wall thickness. Standard tolerances conform to or are within those specified in "Recommended Standards for Wrought Aluminum Mill Products," as issued by The Aluminum Association.

SOURCE: Ryerson, Inc.

TABLE 5.120 Copper Mill Products: Thickness Tolerances (in inches)

Thickness, in	Width, in							
	Up to 8 incl.	Over 8 to 12 incl.	Over 12 to 14 incl.	Over 14 to 20 incl.	Over 20 to 28 incl.	Over 28 to 36 incl.	Over 36 to 48 incl.	Over 48 to 60 incl.
Nonrefractory Alloys								
	Strip				*Sheet*			
Up to 0.004 incl.	0.0003	0.0006	0.0006	—	—	—	—	—
Over 0.004 to 0.006 incl.	0.0004	0.0008	0.0008	0.0013	—	—	—	—
Over 0.006 to 0.009 incl.	0.0006	0.0010	0.0010	0.0015	—	—	—	—
Over 0.009 to 0.013 incl.	0.0008	0.0013	0.0013	0.0018	0.0025	0.003	0.0035	0.004
Over 0.013 to 0.017 incl.	0.0010	0.0015	0.0015	0.002	0.0025	0.003	0.0035	0.0045
Over 0.017 to 0.021 incl.	0.0013	0.0018	0.0018	0.002	0.003	0.0035	0.004	0.005
Over 0.021 to 0.026 incl.	0.0015	0.002	0.002	0.0025	0.003	0.0035	0.004	0.005
Over 0.026 to 0.037 incl.	0.002	0.002	0.002	0.0025	0.0035	0.004	0.005	0.006
Over 0.037 to 0.050 incl.	0.002	0.0025	0.0025	0.003	0.004	0.005	0.006	0.007
Over 0.050 to 0.073 incl.	0.0025	0.003	0.003	0.0035	0.005	0.006	0.007	0.008
Over 0.073 to 0.130 incl.	0.003	0.0035	0.0035	0.004	0.006	0.007	0.008	0.010
Over 0.130 to 0.188 incl.	0.0035	0.004	0.004	0.0045	0.007	0.008	0.010	0.012
	Bar		*Plate*					
Over 0.188 to 0.205 incl.	0.0035	0.004	0.004	0.0045	0.007	0.008	0.010	0.012
Over 0.205 to 0.300 incl.	0.004	0.0045	0.0045	0.005	0.009	0.010	0.012	0.014
Over 0.300 to 0.500 incl.	0.0045	0.005	0.005	0.006	0.012	0.013	0.015	0.018
Over 0.500 to 0.750 incl.	0.0055	0.007	0.007	0.009	0.015	0.017	0.019	0.023
Over 0.750 to 1.00 incl.	0.007	0.009	0.009	0.011	0.018	0.021	0.024	0.029
Over 1.00 to 1.50 incl.	0.022	0.022	0.022	0.022	0.022	0.025	0.029	0.036
Over 1.50 to 2.00 incl.	0.026	0.026	0.026	0.026	0.026	0.030	0.036	0.044

Refractory Alloys								
	Strip				*Sheet*			
Up to 0.004 incl.	0.0004	0.0008	0.0008	—	—	—	—	—
Over 0.004 to 0.006 incl.	0.0006	0.0010	0.0010	0.0015	—	—	—	—
Over 0.006 to 0.009 incl.	0.0008	0.0013	0.0013	0.002	—	—	—	—
Over 0.009 to 0.013 incl.	0.0010	0.0015	0.0015	0.0025	—	—	—	—
Over 0.013 to 0.017 incl.	0.0013	0.002	0.002	0.0025	—	—	—	—
Over 0.017 to 0.021 incl.	0.0015	0.0025	0.0025	0.003	—	—	—	—
Over 0.021 to 0.026 incl.	0.002	0.0025	0.0025	0.003	0.004	0.005	0.006	0.007
Over 0.026 to 0.037 incl.	0.0025	0.003	0.003	0.0035	0.005	0.006	0.007	0.008
Over 0.037 to 0.050 incl.	0.003	0.0035	0.0035	0.004	0.006	0.007	0.008	0.010
Over 0.050 to 0.073 incl.	0.0035	0.004	0.004	0.0045	0.007	0.008	0.010	0.012
Over 0.073 to 0.130 incl.	0.004	0.0045	0.0045	0.005	0.008	0.010	0.012	0.014
Over 0.130 to 0.188 incl.	0.0045	0.005	0.005	0.006	0.010	0.012	0.014	0.016
	Bar		*Plate*					
Over 0.188 to 0.205 incl.	0.0045	0.005	0.005	0.006	0.010	0.012	0.014	0.016
Over 0.205 to 0.300 incl.	0.005	0.006	0.006	0.007	0.012	0.014	0.016	0.018
Over 0.300 to 0.500 incl.	0.006	0.007	0.007	0.008	0.015	0.017	0.019	0.023
Over 0.500 to 0.750 incl.	0.008	0.010	0.010	0.012	0.019	0.021	0.024	0.029
Over 0.750 to 1.00 incl.	0.010	0.012	0.012	0.015	0.023	0.026	0.030	0.037
Over 1.00 to 1.50 incl.	0.028	0.028	0.028	0.028	0.028	0.032	0.037	0.045
Over 1.50 to 2.00 incl.	0.033	0.033	0.033	0.033	0.033	0.038	0.045	0.055

SOURCE: Vincent, Inc.

TABLE 5.121 Copper Round Rod, Hexagonal and Octagonal Stock: Tolerances

Diameter or distance between parallel surfaces, in	Nonrefractory alloys		Refractory alloys	
	Round	Hexagonal, octagonal	Round	Hexagonal, octagonal
Up to 0.150 incl.	0.0013	0.0025	0.002	—
Over 0.150 to 0.500 incl.	0.0015	0.003	0.002	0.004
Over 0.500 to 1.00 incl.	0.002	0.004	0.003	0.005
Over 1.00 to 2.00 incl.	0.0025	0.005	0.004	0.006
Over 2.00	0.15%*	0.30%*	0.20%*	0.40%*

* Expressed to the nearest 0.001 in.

SOURCE: Vincent, Inc.

TABLE 5.122 Copper Round Seamless Tube: Wall-Thickness Tolerances

Wall thickness, in	Outside diameter, in						
	1/32 to 1/8 incl.	Over 1/8 to 5/8 incl.	Over 5/8 to 1 incl.	Over 1 to 2 incl.	Over 2 to 4 incl.	Over 4 to 7 incl.	Over 7 to 10 incl.
Nonrefractory Alloys							
Up to 0.018	0.002	0.001	0.0015	0.002	—	—	—
Incl. 0.018 to 0.025	0.003	0.002	0.002	0.0025	—	—	—
Incl. 0.025 to 0.035	0.003	0.0025	0.0025	0.003	0.004	—	—
Incl. 0.035 to 0.058	0.003	0.003	0.0035	0.0035	0.005	0.007	—
Incl. 0.058 to 0.083	—	0.0035	0.004	0.004	0.006	0.008	0.010
Incl. 0.083 to 0.120	—	0.004	0.005	0.005	0.007	0.009	0.011
Incl. 0.120 to 0.165	—	0.005	0.006	0.006	0.008	0.010	0.012
Incl. 0.165 to 0.220	—	0.007	0.0075	0.008	0.010	0.012	0.014
Incl. 0.220 to 0.284	—	—	0.009	0.010	0.012	0.014	0.016
Incl. 0.284 to 0.380	—	—	0.011	0.012	0.014	0.016	0.018
Incl. 0.380 and over	—	—	—	5%*	5%*	6%*	6%*
Refractory Alloys							
Up to 0.018	0.0025	0.0015	0.002	0.0025	—	—	—
Incl. 0.018 to 0.025	0.004	0.0025	0.0025	0.003	—	—	—
Incl. 0.025 to 0.035	0.004	0.003	0.003	0.004	0.005	—	—
Incl. 0.035 to 0.058	0.004	0.004	0.0045	0.0045	0.0065	0.009	—
Incl. 0.058 to 0.083	—	0.0045	0.005	0.005	0.0075	0.010	0.013
Incl. 0.083 to 0.120	—	0.005	0.0065	0.0065	0.009	0.011	0.014
Incl. 0.120 to 0.165	—	0.007	0.007	0.0075	0.010	0.013	0.015
Incl. 0.165 to 0.220	—	—	0.009	0.010	0.013	0.015	0.018
Incl. 0.220 to 0.284	—	—	0.012	0.013	0.015	0.018	0.020
Incl. 0.284 to 0.380	—	—	—	0.015	0.018	0.020	0.023
Incl. 0.380 and over	—	—	—	6%*	6%*	8%*	8%*

* Expressed to the nearest 0.001 in.
SOURCE: Vincent, Inc.

TABLE 5.123 Common Plastics

Common/trade name	Supplier	SAE symbol	Plastic "family" name
ABS	Generic Name	ABS	Acrylonitrile/butadiene/styrene
Absafil	Wilson Fiberfil International	ABS	Acrylonitrile/butadiene/styrene
Acetal	Generic Name	POM	Polyoxymethylene: polyformaldehyde
Aclar	Ausimont	PCTFE	Polychlorotrifluoroethylene
Acrylic	Generic Name	PMMA	Poly (methyl methacrylate)
Acrylite	Cyro Industries	PMMA	Poly (methyl methacrylate)—"acrylic"
Adiprane	Uniroyal Inc.	PUR	Polyurethane, thermoset (unsaturated)
Alathon	E.I. Dupont de Nemours & Co.	PE	Polyethylene
Alton	International Polymers	PPS + PTFE	Polyphenylene sulfide + polytetrafluoroethylene
Ampol	American Polymers Inc.	CA	Cellulose acetate
Andrez	Unknown	SB	Styrene-butadiene
Apex	Teknor Apex Co.	PVC	Poly (vinyl chloride)
Araldrite	Ciba-Geigy Corp.	EP	Epoxide: epoxy
Aramid	Generic Name	PARA	Polyarylamid (polyaramide)
Ardel	Union Carbide Corp.	PAT	Polyester, thermoplastic—"polyarylate"
Arloy	Arco Chemical Co.	PC + SMA	Polycarbonate + styrene maleic anhydride
Arylon	E.I. Dupont de Nemours & Co.	PAT	Polyester, thermoplastic—"polyarylate"
Astrel	Amoco Chemicals Corp.	PASU	Polyarylsulfone
Azdel	Azdel Inc.	PP	Polypropylene
Bakelite	Union Carbide Corp.	PF	Phenol-formaldehyde
Bayblend	Mobay Chemical Corp.	ABS + PC	Acrylonitrile/butadiene/styrene + polycarbonate
Bayflex	Mobay Chemical Corp.	PUR	Polyurethane, thermoset
Bayflex	Mobay Chemical Corp.	TPU	Thermoplastic elastomer
Bexloy C	E.I. Dupont de Nemours & Co.	PA+	Polyamide (amorphous) blend
Bexloy K & J	E.I. Dupont de Nemours & Co.	PBT + PET	Polybutylene terephthalate + polyethylene terephthalate

BMC	Generic Name	UP	Polyester, thermoset (unsaturated)
Butvar	Monsanto Co.	PVB	Poly (vinyl butyral)
Cadon	Monsanto Co.	ABS	Acrylonitrile/butadiene/styrene
Cadon	Monsanto Co.	ABS + SMA	Acrylonitrile/butadiene/styrene + styrene maleic anhydride
Cadon	Monsanto Co.	SMA	Styrene maleic anhydride
Calibre	Dow Chemical Co.	PC	Polycarbonate
Capron	Allied Engineered Plastics	PA	Polyamide—"nylon"
Castethane	Dow Chemical Co.	PUR	Polyurethane, thermoset
Celanese	Celanese Engineering Resins	PA	Polyamide—"nylon"
Celanese N	Celanese Engineering Resins	PA + RUBBER	Polyamide + rubber
Celanex	Celanese Engineering Resins	PBT	Polyester, thermoplastic—"polybutylyne terephthalate"
Celanex	Celanese Engineering Resins	PBT + PET	Polybuthylene terephthalate + polyethylene terephthalate
Celanex	Celanese Engineering Resins	PBT + RUBBER	Polybutylene terephthalate + rubber
Celcon	Celanese Engineering Resins	POM	Polyoxymethylene: polyformaldehyde—"acetal"
Celcon C	Celanese Engineering Resins	POM + RUBBER	Polyoxymethylene + rubber
Cellidor	Bayer AG	CA	Cellulose acetate
Cellidor	Bayer AG	CAP	Cellulose acetate propionate
Cellidor	Bayer AG	CP	Cellulose propionate
Centrex	Monsanto Co.	ASA	Acrylonitrile/styrene/acrylate
Corvel	Polymer Corp.	EP	Epoxide
Cyanaprene	American Cyanamid Co.	PUR	Polyurethane, thermoset (unsaturated)
Cycolac	Borg-Warner Chemicals Inc.	ABS	Acrylonitrile/butadiene/styrene
Cycoloy	Borg-Warner Chemicals Inc.	ABS + TPU	Acrylonitrile/butadiene/styrene + thermoplastic polyurethane
Cycoloy EHA	Borg-Warner Chemicals Inc.	ABS + PC	Acrylonitrile/butadiene/styrene + polycarbonate
Cycovin K	Borg-Warner Chemicals Inc.	ABS – PVC	Acrylonitrile/butadiene/styrene + polyvinyl chloride
Cymel	American Cyanamid Co.	MF	Melamine-formaldehyde
Cytor	Unknown	TPU	Polyurethane, thermoplastic
Daplen	Chemie Linz AG	PP	Polypropylene
Dapon	Chemie Linz AG	DAP	Poly (diallyl phthalate)

TABLE 5.123 Common Plastics (*Continued*)

Common/trade name	Supplier	SAE symbol	Plastic "family" name
Delrin	E.I. Dupont de Nemours & Co.	POM	Polyoxymethylene: polyformaldehyde—"acetal"
Delrin AF	E.I. Dupont de Nemours & Co.	POM + PTFE	Polyoxymethylene + polytetra-fluoroethylene
Delrin ST	E.I. Dupont de Nemours & Co.	POM + RUBBER	Polyoxymethylene + rubber
Delrin T	E.I. Dupont de Nemours & Co.	POM + RUBBER	Polyoxymethylene + rubber
Derakane	Dow Chemical Co.	UP	Polyester, thermoset (unsaturated)
Desmopan	Bayer AG	PUR	Polyurethane, thermoset (unsaturated)
Diakon	ICI Hyde Group	PMMA	Poly (methyl methacrylate)—"acrylic"
Diaron	Reichold Chemicals Inc.	MF	Melamine-formaldehyde
DKE + 450	Sumitoma Corp. of America	PVC + PMMA	Polyvinyl chloride = polymethyl methacrylate
Duraflex	Shell Chemical Co.	PB	Polybutene-1
Durathon	Bayer AG	PS	Polystyrene
Durel	Celanese Engineering Resins	PAT	Polyester, thermoplastic—"polyarylate"
Durethan	Bayer AG	PA	Polyamide—"nylon"
Durez	Occidental Chemical Corp.	DAP	Poly (diallyl phthalate)
Durez	Occidental Chemical Corp.	PF	Phenol-formaldehyde
Durilite	Unknown	EC	Ethyl cellulose
Dylan	Arco Chemical Co.	PE	Polyethylene
Dylark	Arco Chemical Co.	SMA	Styrene/maleic anhydride
Dylark	Arco Chemical Co.	SMA + PS	Styrene/maleic anhydride + high impact polystyrene
Dylen	Arco Chemical Co.	PS	Polystyrene
Dynyl	Phone Poulenc Inc.	PEBA	Thermoplastic polyester—"polyether block amide"
Econol	Sohio Chemical Co.	PAT	Polyester, thermoplastic—"polyarylate"
Elkcel	Carborundum Co.	POB	Poly-*p*-oxybenzoate
Elemid	Borg-Warner Chemicals Inc.	ABS + PA	Acrylonitrile/butadiene/styrene + polyamide
Elexar	Shell Chemical Co.	SB	Styrene-butadiene

Elexar	Shell Chemical Co.	TES	Thermoplastic elastomer—"styrene block copolymer"
Elvax	E.I. Dupont de Nemours & Co.	EVAC	Ethylene/vinyl acetate
Envex	Rogers Corp.	PI	Polyamide
Epon	Shell Chemical Co.	EP	Epoxide: epoxy
Epotuf	Reichold Chemicals Inc.	EP	Epoxide: epoxy
Escorene	Exxon Chemical Americas	PE	Polyethylene
Escorene	Exxon Chemical Americas	PP	Polypropylene
Estamid (ester)	Dow Chemical Co.	PEBA	Polyester, thermoplastic—"polyether block amide"
Estane	B.G. Goodrich Chemical Group	ABS + TPU	Acrylonitrile/butadiene/styrene + thermoplastic polyurethane
Estane	B.G. Goodrich Chemical Group	TPU	Thermoplastic elastomer—"polyurethane"
Ethocel	Dow Chemical Co.	CA	Cellulose acetate
Ethocel	Dow Chemical Co.	CAB	Cellulose acetate butyrate
Ethocel	Dow Chemical Co.	CAP	Cellulose acetate propionate
Ethocel	Dow Chemical Co.	CP	Cellulose propionate
Ethocel	Dow Chemical Co.	EC	Ethyl cellulose
Evanol	Unknown	PVAL	Poly (vinyl alcohol)
Ferroflex	Ferro Corp.	TPO	Thermoplastic elastomer—"polyolefinic"
Fluon	ICI Americas Inc.	PTFE	Polytetrafluoroethylene
Fluorocomp	LNP Corp./ICI Americas	FEP	Perfluoro (ethylene/propylene)
Formion	A. Schulman Inc.	EMA	Ethylene methacrylate acid
Formvar	Monsanto Co.	PVFM	Poly (vinyl formal)
Forsacryl	Unknown	SAN	Styrene-acrylonitrile
Fortiflex	Soltex Polymer Corp.	PE	Polyethylene
Fortron	Celanese Engineering Resins	PPS	Poly (phenylene sulfide)
Geloy 1200	General Electric Co.	ASA + PVC	Acrylonitrile/styrene/acrylate + polyvinyl chloride
Geloy 1320	General Electric Co.	ASA + PMMA	Acrylonitrile/styrene/acrylate + polymethyl methacrylate
Gelva	Monsanto Co.	PVAC	Poly (vinyl acetate)
Gelvatol	Monsanto Co.	PVAL	Poly (vinyl alcohol)
Gemax	General Electric Co.	PBT + PPE	Polybutylene terephthalate + polyphenylene ether

TABLE 5.123 Common Plastics (*Continued*)

Common/trade name	Supplier	SAE symbol	Plastic "family" name
Gemon	General Electric Co.	PI	Polyimide
Geon	B.G. Goodrich Chemical Group	PVC	Poly (vinyl chloride)
Geon	B.G. Goodrich Chemical Group	VCVDC	Vinyl chloride/vinylidene chloride
Gracon	W.R. Grace Co.	PVC	Poly (vinyl chloride)
Grilon	Emser Industries Inc.	PA + RUBBER	Polyamide + rubber
Halon	Allied Engineered Plastics	PCTFE	Polychlorotrifluoroethylene
Halon	Allied Engineered Plastics	PTFE	Polytetrafluoroethylene
Hi-Fax	Himont U.S.A. Inc.	PE	Polyethylene
Hostadur	American Hoechst Corp.	PET	Polyester, thermoplastic—"polyethylene terephthalate"
Hostaflon	American Hoechst Corp.	PTFE	Polytetrafluoroethylene
Hostaform	American Hoechst Corp.	POM	Polyoxymethylene: polyformaldehyde—"acetal"
Hostalen	American Hoechst Corp.	PE	Polyethylene
Hostalen	American Hoechst Corp.	PEOX	Poly (ethylene oxide)
Hostalen	American Hoechst Corp.	PP	Polypropylene
Hostalite Z	American Hoechst Corp.	PVC + CPE	Polyvinyl chloride + chlorinated polyethylene
Hycar	B.G. Goodrich Chemical Group	PVC + NBR	Polyvinyl chloride + nitrile butadiene rubber
Hytrel	E.I. Dupont de Nemours & Co.	TEEE	Thermoplastic elastomer—"ether ester block copolymer"
Impet	Celanese Engineering Resins	PET	Polyester thermoplastic—"poly (ethylene terephthalate)"
Ionomer	Generic name	EMA	Ethylene/methacrylic acid
Isomin	Unknown	MF	Melamine-formaldehyde
Isoplast	Dow Chemical Co.	RTPU	Thermoplastic elastomer—"rigid polyurethane"
Kadel	Amoco Chemicals Corp.	PEEK	Polyether-etherketone
Kamax	Rohm & Haas Co.	PI	Polyamide
Kel-F	3M Company	PCTFE	Polychlorotrifluoroethylene
Kinel	Rhone Poulenc Inc.	PI	Polyamide

Kralastic FVM	Uniroyal Inc.	ABS + PVC	Acrylonitrile/butadiene/styrene + polyvinyl chloride
Kraton	Shell Chemical Co.	TES	Thermoplastic elastomer—"styrene block copolymer"
Kydex	Rohm & Haas Co.	PVC + PMMA	Polyvinyl chloride + polymethyl methacrylate
Kynar	Pennwalt Corp.	PVDF	Poly (vinylidene fluoride)
K-Resins	Phillips Chemical Co.	SB	Styrene-butadiene
Lexan	General Electric Co.	PC	Polycarbonate plastics
Lexan	General Electric Co.	PC + PE	Polycarbonate + polyethylene
Lomod	General Electric Co.	TEEE	Thermoplastic elastomer—"ether ester block copolymer"
Lupolen	BASF Wyandotte Corp.	PE	Polyethylene
Luran	BASF Wyandotte Corp.	ASA	Acrylonitrile/styrene/acrylate
Luran	BASF Wyandotte Corp.	SAN	Styrene/acrylonitrile
Lustran	Monsanto Co.	ABS	Acrylonitrile/butadiene/styrene
Lustran	Monsanto Co.	ABS + PVC	Acrylonitrile/butadiene/styrene + polyvinyl chloride
Lustran	Monsanto Co.	SAN	Styrene/acrylonitrile
Lustrex	Polysar Inc.	PS	Polystyrene
Luvican	BASF Wyandotte Corp.	PVK	Polyvinylcarbazole
Macroblend	Mobay Chemical Corp.	PC + PBT	Polycarbonate + polybutylene terephthalate
Macroblend	Mobay Chemical Corp.	PC + PET	Polycarbonate + polyethylene terephthalate
Macrolon	Mobay Chemical Corp.	PC	Polycarbonate plastics
Marlex	Phillips Chemical Co.	PE	Polyethylene
Marlex	Phillips Chemical Co.	PP	Polypropylene
Melmac	Phillips Chemical Co.	MF	Melamine-formaldehyde
Merlon	Mobay Chemical Corp.	PC	Polycarbonate plastics
Merlon T	Mobay Chemical Corp.	PC + PE	Polycarbonate + polyethylene
Microthane	Unknown	EVAC	Ethylene/vinyl acetate
Mindel	Union Carbide Corp.	PARA	Polyarylamid (polyaramide)
Mindel	Union Carbide Corp.	PPSU	Poly (phenylene sulfone)
Mindel A	Union Carbide Corp.	ABS – PPSU	Acrylonitrile/butadiene/styrene + polyphenylene sulfone
Mindel B	Union Carbide Corp.	PET + PPSU	Polyethylene terephthalate + polyphenylene sulfone

TABLE 5.123 Common Plastics (*Continued*)

Common/trade name	Supplier	SAE symbol	Plastic "family" name
Moplen	Himont-Italia	PP	Polypropylene
N5	Thermofil Inc.	PA + SAN	Polyamide + styrene/acrylonitrile
Nitrocellulose	Generic name	CN	Cellulose nitrate
None	—	AB	Acrylonitrile/butadiene
None	—	ABA	Acrylonitrile/butadiene/acrylate
None	—	AMMA	Acrylonitrile/methyl methacrylate
None	—	CF	Cresol formaldehyde
None	—	CMC	Carboxymethyl cellulose
None	—	CPVC	Chlorinated poly (vinyl chloride)
None	—	CS	Casein
None	—	EEA	Ethylene/ethyl acrylate
None	—	ETFE	Ethylene/tetrafluoroethylene
None	—	FF	Fluran formaldehyde
None	—	PA + EMA	Polyamide + ethylene methacrylic acid (ionomer)
None	—	PAE	Polyarylether
None	—	PB	Polybutene-1
None	—	PFF	Phenol furfurol
None	—	PPOX	Poly (propylene oxide)
None	—	PVCA	Poly (vinyl chloride acetate)
None	—	PVP	Polyvinylpyrrolidone
None	—	SI	Silicone
None	—	SMS	Styrene/A-methylstyrene
None	—	VCE	Vinyl chloride/ethylene
None	—	VCEMA	Vinyl chloride/ethylene/methyl acrylate
None	—	VCMA	Vinyl chloride/methyl acrylate

Noryl	General Electric Co.	PPE	Polyphenylene ether plastics
Noryl	General Electric Co.	PPE + PS	Polyphenylene ether + high impact polystyrene
Noryl GTX	General Electric Co.	PA +PPE	Polyamide + polyphenylene ether
Novodur	Mobay Chemical Corp.	ABS	Acrylonitrile/butadiene/styrene
Novolen	BASF Wyandotte Corp.	PP	Polypropylene
Nycoa 1900	Nylon Corp. of America	PA + EMA	Polyamide + ethylene methacrylic acid—“ionomer”
Nydur BC	Unknown	PA + RUBBER	Polyamide + rubber
Nydur KL	Unknown	PA + RUBBER	Polyamide + rubber
Nylon	Generic name	PA	Polyamide—“nylon”
Oleflo	Avisun	PP	Polypropylene
Oppanol B	BASF Wyandotte Corp.	PIB	Polyisobutylene
Oroglas	Rohm & Haas Co.	PMMA	Poly (methyl methacrylate)—“acrylic”
Orthane	Eagle Picher Plastics Div.	TPU	Polyurethane, thermoplastic
Ozo	Unknown	PVC + NBR	Polyvinyl chloride + nitrile butadiene rubber
Paracril	Uniroyal Inc.	PVC + NBR	Polyvinyl chloride + nitrile butadiene rubber
Paxon	Allied Engineered Plastics	PE	Polyethylene
Pebax	Atochem U.S.A. Inc.	PEBA	Polyester, thermoplastic—“polyether block amide”
Pellethane	Dow Chemical Co.	ABS + TPU	Acrylonitrile/butadiene/styrene + thermoplastic polyurethane
Pellethane	Dow Chemical Co.	TPU	Thermoplastic elastomer—“polyurethane”
Penton	Hercules Inc.	CPE	Chlorinated polyethylene
Petlon	Mobay Chemical Corp.	PBT	Polyester, thermoplastic—“polybutylene terephthalate”
Petlon	Mobay Chemical Corp.	PET	Polyester, thermoplastic—“polyethylene terephthalate”
Petra	Allied Engineered Plastics	PBT	Polyester, thermoplastic—“polybuthylene terephthalate”
Petra	Allied Engineered Plastics	PET	Polyester, thermoplastic—“polyethylene terephathalate”
Phenolic	Generic name	PF	Phenol-formaldehyde
Piso	Celanese Engineering Resins	PISU	Polymidesulfone
Plaskon	Plaskon Electronic Mtls. Inc.	UF	Urea-formaldehyde
Plenco	Plastics Engineering Co.	PF	Phenol-formaldehyde
Plexiglas	Rohm & Haas Co.	PMMA	Poly (methyl methacrylate)—“acrylic”

TABLE 5.123 Common Plastics (*Continued*)

Common/trade name	Supplier	SAE symbol	Plastic "family" name
Pliolite	Goodyear Tire & Rubber Co.	SB	Styrene-butadiene
Pliovic	Goodyear Tire & Rubber Co.	PVC	Poly (vinyl chloride)
Pocan	Bayer AG/Mobay	PBT + RUBBER	"Polybutylene terephthalate" + rubber
Pocan B	Bayer AG/Mobay	PBT	Polyester, thermoplastic—"polybutylene terephthalate"
Polycomp	LNP Corp./ICI Americas	PPS + PTFE	Polyphenylene sulfide + fluoroethylene
Polyfort	A. Schulman Inc.	PE	Polyethylene
Polyfort	A. Schulman Inc.	PP	Polypropylene
Polypur	A. Schulman Inc.	TPU	Thermoplastic elastomer—"polyurethane"
Polystyrol	BASF Wyandotte Corp.	PS	Polystyrene
Polystyrol	BASF Wyandotte Corp.	SB	Styrene/butadiene
Polystyrol SB	BASF Wyandotte Corp.	PS	Polystyrene, high impact
Polytrope	A. Schulman Inc.	TPO	Thermoplastic elastomer—"polyolefinic"
Polyvin	A. Schulman Inc.	PVC	Poly (vinyl chloride)
Poly-Dap	DAP	DAP	Poly (diallyl phthalate)
Premi-Glas	Premix Inc.	UP	Polyester, unsaturated thermoset
Prevex	Borg-Warner Chemicals Inc.	PPE	Polyphenylene ether plastics
Prevex	Borg-Warner Chemicals Inc.	PPE + PS	Polyphenylene ether + high impact polystyrene
Profax	Himont U.S.A. Inc.	PP	Polypropylene
Proloy	Borg-Warner Chemicals Inc.	ABS + PC	Acrylonitrile/butadiene/styrene + polycarbonate
Pyralin	E.I. Dupont de Nemours & Co.	PI	Polyimide
Radel	Union Carbide Corp.	PPSU	Polyphenylene sulfone
Renflex	Research Polymers Inc.	TPO	Thermoplastic elastomer—"polyolefinic"
Rilsan	Atochem U.S.A. Inc.	PA	Polyamide—"nylon"
Riteflex BP	Celanese Engineering Resins	TEEE	Thermoplastic elastomer—"ether ester block copolymer"
Ropet	Rohm & Haas Co.	PET + PMMA	Polyethylene terephthalate + polymethyl methacrylate

Rovel	Dow Chemical Co.	AES	Acrylonitrile/ethylene/styrene
Rynite	E.I. Dupont de Nemours & Co.	PBT	Polyester, thermoplastic—“polybutylene terephthalate”
Rynite	E.I. Dupont de Nemours & Co.	PET	Polyester, thermoplastic—“polybutylene terephthalate”
Rynite SST	E.I. Dupont de Nemours & Co.	PET + RUBBER	Polyethylene terephthalate + rubber
Ryton	Phillips Chemical Co.	PPS	Poly (phenylene sulfide)
Santoprene	Monsanto Co.	TPO	Thermoplastic elastomer—“polyolefinic”
Saran	Dow Chemical Co.	PVDC	Poly (vinylidene chloride)
Selar	E.I. Dupont de Nemours & Co.	PA + PE	Polyamide + polyethylene
Selectron	PPG Industries Inc.	UP	Polyester unsaturated thermoset
Skanopal	Penstorp Inc.	UF	Urea-formaldehyde
Skybond	Monsanto Co.	PI	Polyimide
SMC	Generic name	UP	Polyester, thermoset (unsaturated)
Solair	Soltex Polymer Corp.	PE	Polyethylene
Spectrim	Dow Chemical Co.	PUR	Polyurethane, thermoset
Styrolux	Westlake Plastics Co.	SB	Styrene-butadiene
Styron	Dow Chemical Co.	PS	Polystyrene
Surlyn	E.I. Dupont de Nemours & Co.	EMA	Ethylene/methacrylic acid—“ionomer”
Tedlar	E.I. Dupont de Nemours & Co.	PVF	Poly (vinyl fluoride)
Teflon	E.I. Dupont de Nemours & Co.	FEP	Perfluoro (ethylene/propylene)
Teflon	E.I. Dupont de Nemours & Co.	PTFE	Polytetrafluoroethylene
Teflonz	E.I. Dupont de Nemours & Co.	FEP	Tetrafluoroethylene/hexafluoro propylene
Teflonz	E.I. Dupont de Nemours & Co.	FEP	Tetrafluoroethylene/hexafluoro propylene
Telcar	Teknor Apex Co.	TPO	Thermoplastic elastomer—“polyolefinic”
Tenite	Eastman Chemical Products Inc.	CA	Cellulose acetate
Tenite	Eastman Chemical Products Inc.	CAB	Cellulose acetate butyrate
Tenite	Eastman Chemical Products Inc.	CAP	Cellulose acetate propionate
Tenite	Eastman Chemical Products Inc.	CP	Cellulose propionate
Tenite	Eastman Chemical Products Inc.	PP	Polypropylene
Terblend SKR	BASF Wyandotte Corp.	ASA + PC	Acrylonitrile/styrene/acrylate + polycarbonate

TABLE 5.123 Common Plastics (*Continued*)

Common/trade name	Supplier	SAE symbol	Plastic "family" name
Terlukan	Bayer AG	ABS	Acrylonitrile/butadiene/styrene
Tetran	Pennwalt Corp.	PTFE	Polytetrafluoroethylene
Texin	Mobay Chemical Corp.	PC + TPU	Polycarbonate + thermoplastic polyurethane
Texin	Mobay Chemical Corp.	TPU	Polyurethane, thermoplastic
Thermo	Unknown	CPE	Chlorinated polyethylene
Thermocomp AL	LNP Corp./ICI Americas	AS + PTFE	Acrylonitrile/butadiene/styrene + polytetra fluoroethylene
Thermocomp KL	LNP Corp./ICI Americas	POM + PTFE	Polyoxymethylene + polytetra fluoroethylene
Torlon	Amoco Chemicals Corp.	PAI	Polyamide-imide
TPE	Generic name	—	Thermoplastic elastomer
TPX	Mitsui & Co.	PMP	Poly (4-methylpentene-1)
Triax 1000	Monsanto Co.	ABS + PA	Acrylonitrile/butadiene/styrene + polyamide
Trosiplast	Kay-Fries Inc.	PVC	Poly (vinyl chloride)
Tuf-Flex	American Hoechst Corp.	PS	Polystyrene, high impact
Tyril	Dow Chemical Co.	SAN	Styrene/acrylonitrile
Tyrin	Dow Chemical Co.	CPE	Chlorinated polyethylene
Udel	Union Carbide Corp.	PPSU	Poly (phenylene sulfone)
Ultadur	BASF Wyandotte Corp.	PET	Poly (ethylene terephthalate)
Ultaform	BASF Wyandotte Corp.	POM	Polyoxymethylene: polyformaldehyde—"acetal"
Ultamid KR	BASF Wyandotte Corp.	PA + RUBBER	Polyamide + rubber
Ultem	General Electric Co.	PEI	Polyetherimide
Ultradur	BASF Wyandotte Corp.	PBT	Polyester, thermoplastic—"polybutylene terephthalate"
Ultradur KR	BASF Wyandotte Corp.	PBT + RUBBER	Polybutylene terephthalate + rubber
Ultramid	BASF Wyandotte Corp.	PA	Polyamide—"nylon"

Ultrason	BASF Wyandotte Corp.	PESU	Polyether sulfone
Ultrason	BASF Wyandotte Corp.	PPSU	Poly (phenylene sulfone)
Ultrex	Spiratex Co.	PE	Polyethylene
Unichem	Colorite Plastics Co.	PVC	Poly (vinyl chloride)
Uyex	Eastman Chemical Products Inc.	CAB	Cellulose acetate butyrate
Valox	General Electric Co.	PBT	Polyester, thermoplastic—"polybutylene terephthalate"
Valox	General Electric Co.	PBT + PET	Polybutylene terephthalate + "polyethylene terephthalate"
Valox	General Electric Co.	PBT + RUBBER	Polybutylene terephthalate + rubber
Valox	General Electric Co.	PC + PBT	Polycarbonate + polybutylene terephthalate
Valox	General Electric Co.	PC + PET	Polycarbonate + terephthalate
Valox	General Electric Co.	PET	Polyester, thermoplastic—"polyethylene terephthalate"
Vandor PB	Celanese Engineering Resins	PBT + RUBBER	Polybutylene terephthalate + rubber
Vectra	Celanese Engineering Resins	ARP	Polyester, thermoplastic—"liquid crystal polymer"
Vedril	Vedril Spa (Spanish)	PMMA	Poly (methyl methacrylate)—"acrylic"
Vespel	E.I. Dupont de Nemours & Co.	PARA	Polyarylamid (polyaramide)—"aramid"
Vespel	E.I. Dupont de Nemours & Co.	PI	Polyimide
Vibrin-Mat	U.S. Rubber Co.	UP	Polyester, thermoset (unsaturated)
Victrex	ICI Americas Inc.	PESU	Polyethersulfone
Victrex Peek	ICI Americas Inc.	PEEK	Polyetherketone
Victrex Pek	ICI Americas Inc.	PEK	Polyetherketone
Vinoflex	BASF Wyandotte Corp.	PVC	Poly (vinyl chloride)
Vinylite	Canadian Resins & Chemical Ltd	PVAC	Poly (vinyl acetate)
Vinylite	Canadian Resins & Chemical Ltd	PVB	Poly (vinyl butyral)
Vinylite	Canadian Resins & Chemical Ltd	PVC	Poly (vinyl chloride)
Vinylite	Canadian Resins & Chemical Ltd	VCVAC	Vinyl chloride/vinyl acetate
Vistaflex	Esso Chemicals (Europe)	TPO	Thermoplastic elastomer—"polyolefinic"

TABLE 5.123 Common Plastics (*Continued*)

Common/trade name	Supplier	SAE symbol	Plastic "family" name
Vydyne	Monsanto Co.	PA	Polyamide "nylon"
Vynite	Allied Engineered Plastics	PVC + NBR	Polyvinyl chloride + nitrile butadiene rubber
Vythene	Alpha Chemicals & Plastics CRP	PVC + PU	Polyvinyl chloride + polyurethane
Wellamid	Wellman Inc.	PA	Polyamide—"nylon"
Wellite	Wellman Inc.	PBT	Polyester, thermoplastic—"polybutylene terephthalate"
Wellpet	Wellman Inc.	PET	Polyester, thermoplastic—"polyethylene terephthalate"
Xenoy	General Electric Co.	PC + PBT	Polycarbonate + polybutylene terephthalate
XMC	Generic name	UP	Polyester, thermoset (unsaturated)—50% glass
Xydar	Dartco	ARP	Polyester, thermoplastic—"liquid crystal polymer"
Zytel	E.I. Dupont de Nemours & Co.	PA	Polyamide—"nylon"
Zytel ST	E.I. Dupont de Nemours & Co.	PA + RUBBER	Polyamide + rubber

SOURCE: Reprinted with permission, copyright 1992, Society of Automotive Engineers.

Common plastics and typical uses

Acetal (Delrin, Celcon) *Properties:* High modulus of elasticity, low coefficient of friction, excellent abrasion and impact resistance, low moisture absorption, excellent machinability, ablative. *Typical uses:* Bearings, gears, antifriction parts, electrical components, washers, seals, insulators, cams.

Acetate (Cellulose) *Properties:* Odorless, tasteless, nontoxic, grease resistant, high impact strength. *Typical uses:* Badges, blister packaging, displays, optical covers, book covers.

Acrylic (Plexiglas, Lucite) *Properties:* Unusual optical clarity, high tensile strength, weatherability, good electrical properties, ablative. *Typical uses:* Displays, signs, models, lenses, electrical and electronic parts.

Benelex (Laminate) *Properties:* High compressive strength, machinable, resists corrosion (alkalis or acids), good electrical insulation, high flexural, shear, and tensile strength. *Typical uses:* Work surfaces, electrical panels and switch gear, bus braces (low voltage only), neutron shielding.

Diallyl phthalate, Melamine *Properties:* High strength, chemical resistant, low water absorption, medium-high temperature use. *Typical uses:* Terminal blocks and strips, dishware, automotive applications, aerospace applications.

Epoxy glass *Properties:* High strength, high-temperature applications, flame retardant, low coefficient of thermal expansion, low water absorption. *Typical uses:* High-quality printed-circuit boards, microwave stripline applications, VHF and UHF applications, electrical insulation, services in temperature range –400 to 500°F.

Mylar (polyester film, polyethylene terephthalate) *Properties:* High dielectric strength, chemical resistance, high mechanical strength, moisture resistant, temperature range –70° to 105°C, does not embrittle with age. *Typical uses:* Electrical and industrial applications, graphic arts applications.

Nylon *Properties:* Wear resistant, low friction, high tensile strength, excellent impact resistance, high fatigue resistance, easy machining, corrosion resistant, lightweight. *Typical uses:* Bearings, bushings, valve seats, washers, seals, cams, gears, guides, wheels, insulators, wear parts.

Phenol formaldehyde (Bakelite) *Properties:* Wear resistant, rigid, moldable to precise dimensions, strong, excellent electrical properties, economical, will not support combustion. *Typical uses:* Electrical and electronic parts, handles, housings, insulator parts, mechanism parts, parts that are to resist temperatures to 250°C.

Phenolic laminates *Properties:* Immune to common solvents, lightweight, strong, easily machined. *Typical uses:* Bearings, machined parts, insulation, gears, cams, sleeves, electrical and electronic parts.

Polycarbonate (Lexan) *Properties:* Virtually unbreakable, weather resistant, optically clear, lightweight, self-extinguishing, thermoformable, machinable, solvent cementable. *Typical uses:* High voltage insulation, impact resistant injection moldings, glazing, bulletproof, glazing, plumbing fittings. The strongest thermoplastic.

Polyester glass *Properties:* Extremely tough, high dielectric strength, heat resistant, low water absorption, antitracking electrically, self-extinguishing, machinable. *Typical uses:* Insulators and bus braces, switch phase barriers, general electrical insulation, mechanical insulated push rods for switches and breakers, contact blocks, terminal blocks.

Polyethylene *Properties:* Transparent in thin sheets, water resistant. *Typical uses:* Bags for food storage, vapor barriers in construction, trays, rollers, gaskets, seals, radiation shielding.

Polypropylene *Properties:* Good tensile strength, low water absorption, excellent chemical resistance, stress-crack resistant, electrical properties. *Typical uses:* Tanks, ducts, exhaust systems, gaskets, laboratory and hospital ware, wire coating, sporting goods.

Polystyrene *Properties:* Outstanding electrical properties, excellent machinability, ease of fabrication, excellent chemical resistance, oil resistant, clarity, rigidity, hardness, dimensional stability. *Typical uses:* Lighting panels, tote boxes, electronic components, door panels (refrigerators), drip pans, displays, furniture components.

Polysulfone *Properties:* Tough, rigid, high-strength, high-temperature thermoplastic, temperature range −150° to +300°F, excellent electrical characteristics, good chemical resistance, low creep and cold-flow properties, capable of being repeatedly autoclaved. *Typical uses:* Food-processing and medical industries, electrical and electronics, appliance, automotive, aircraft, and aerospace uses.

Polyurethane *Properties:* Elastomeric to rock-hard forms available, high physical characteristics, toughness, durability, broad hardness range, withstands severe use, abrasion resistant, weather resistant, radiation resistant, temperature range –80° to 250°F, resistant to common solvents, available also in foam types. *Typical uses:* Replaces a host of materials that are not performing well; extremely broad range of usage; replaces rubber parts, plastic parts, and some metallic parts.

Polyvinyl chloride (PVC) *Properties:* Corrosion resistant, formable, lightweight, excellent electrical properties, impact resistant, low water absorption, cementable, machinable, weldable. *Typical uses:* Machined parts, nuts, bolts, PVC pipe and fittings, valves, strainers.

RTV silicone rubber *Properties:* Resistant to temperature extremes (–75° to 400°F), excellent electrical characteristics, weather resistant, good chemical resistance, FDA, USDA, and UL approved. *Typical uses:* General-purpose high-quality sealant, gasket cement, food contact surfaces, electrical insulation, bonding agent, glass-tank construction, and countless other applications.

Styrofoam *Properties:* Low water absorption, floats, thermal insulator, extremely lightweight. *Typical uses:* Insulation board for homes and buildings, cups, containers, thermos containers, shock absorbing packaging, plates (food), flotation logs.

Teflon (PTFE) *Properties:* Unexcelled chemical resistance, cryogenic service, electrical insulation, very low friction, high dielectric strength, very low dissipation factor, very high resistivity, machinability. *Typical uses:* Valve components, gaskets (with caution, due to cold flow), pump parts, seal rings, insulators (electrical), terminals, bearings, rollers, bushings, electrical tapes, plumbing tapes, machined parts, bondable with special etchant preparations.

Urea-formaldehyde *Properties:* Hard, strong, molds accurately, low water absorption, excellent electrical properties, ablative, economical, will not support combustion. *Typical uses:* Electrical and electronic parts, insulators, small parts, housings.

5.11.1 General mechanical properties of plastics

Tablc 5.124 shows the mechanical strength "ranges" of the common plastics. The figures in the table reflect both "filled" and "unfilled" types. The fillers are commonly fiberglass, carbon fibers, mica, etc.

5.12 Elastomers (Rubber and Synthetics)

Table 5.125 lists the properties of elastomers.

5.13 Insulating Materials

Table 5.126 lists the properties of insulating materials.

5.14 Properties of Materials: General and Specific

Table 5.127 lists the properties of various metals and alloys. Table 5.128 lists the properties of other metals and alloys. Table 5.129 lists the coefficients of linear expansion for common materials. Table 5.130 lists the properties of common woods. Table 5.131 lists the chemical symbols for metals. Table 5.132 lists the standard pipe dimensions.

5.15 Material Specification Sheets and Analysis Reports

Figures 5.4 through 5.9 present sample material specification sheets from material manufacturers, a material analysis sheet, and a material conformation test report from a materials testing laboratory. All manufacturers of plastic materials provide the material specification sheets when so requested. Material analysis sheets are likewise supplied by metal providers, forges, and foundrys when so requested. The material test report is generated by one of the various materials test laboratories nationwide, but it must be purchased by the company requesting the analysis.

Due to the large amount of imported materials, many of which do not meet the requirements of the SAE, ASTM, AISI, ASM, and ANSI, material confirmation by way of laboratory analysis is becoming a common practice. This is becoming such a necessity because many of the imported materials and hardware are failing in service.

For example, one company that had a cracking problem due to welding a pin that was specified as type 304 austenitic stainless steel decided to have the material analyzed at a materials testing laboratory. The results of the test were astounding. The material was found by analysis to conform to *no* known type of American stainless steel standard, let alone type 304. The material was unidentifiable as a standard grade of stainless steel and also had a sulfur content that was 10 times higher than that allowed for type 304 stainless. This is the reason the pin cracked when it was welded.

Materials that do not conform to the American standards, as specified on the engineering drawings, pose a serious safety problem for manufacturers of industrial and consumer products and their users. When in doubt about a material's performance, have the material analyzed at a testing laboratory. The material supplier is responsible for the specifications of the material which it sells. If you order a type 304L stainless steel per SAE or ASTM specifications, the material *must* conform to these specifications, both chemically and mechanically.

Counterfeit hardware such as bolts and nuts and counterfeit materials, both metals and plastics, are a common problem in industry today. The U.S. Congress is in the process of passing laws to protect the unwary users and manufacturers against these practices. Large companies with materials testing facilities usually have no problem with this phenomenon. Small and medium-sized companies without materials testing facilities should be aware of these problems and take steps to prevent them from occurring.

TABLE 5.124 Mechanical Properties of Plastics

Plastic	Tensile strength, lb/in²	Compressive strength, lb/in²	Flexural yield, lb/in²
ABS	3000 / 9000	6000 / 22,000	5000 / 28,000
Acetal	6000 / 12,000	10,000 / 19,000	12,000 / 29,000
Acetate (cellulose)	4400 / 8000	—	5000 / 11,000
Epoxy glass	9000 / 21,000	24,000 / 41,000	9000 / 61,000
Epoxy resin	3000 / 14,000	14,000 / 26,000	13,000 / 22,000
Nylon	7000 / 26,000	12,000 / 30,000	6000 / 42,000
Phenolic resins	4000 / 10,000	10,000 / 35,000	4000 / 18,000
Polycarbonate	7000 / 26,000	8000 / 22,000	13,000 / 33,000
Polyester glass	3000 / 52,000	11,000 / 52,000	5000 / 82,000
Polyethylene	500 / 5600	1500 / 5600	1500 / 7200
Polypropylene	2700 / 15,000	3600 / 8200	4000 / 12,000
Polystyrene	1500 / 22,000	3000 / 23,000	2500 / 27,000
Polysulfone	10,000 / 12,000	13,000 / 15,000	14,000 / 16,000
Polyurethane	4000 / 12,000	19,000 / 21,000	700 / 20,000
Polyvinyl chloride (PVC)	5000 / 8000	7000 / 14,000	9000 / 17,000
Rigid Teflon (TFE)	4000 / 7000	4500 / 7500	7000 / 10,000

TABLE 5.125 Elastomer Properties

Base	Weight, lb/in^3	Tensile strength, lb/in^2	Percent elongation in 2 in	Durometer	Temperature range, °F
Acrylic	0.039 0.041	1900 2100	400 500	40 90	−40 +350
Butyl	0.032 0.034	2400 2600	450 550	30 100	−65 +250
Fluorocarbon	0.045 0.075	2400 2600	250 350	60 95	−40 +500
Natural rubber	0.032 0.034	3400 3600	550 650	30 100	−65 +212
Synthetic rubber	0.032 0.034	3400 3600	550 650	40 80	−65 +212
Neoprene	0.043 0.045	2900 3100	550 650	40 100	−65 +212
Nitrile	0.035 0.037	2900 3100	550 650	20 90	−65 +300
Silicone	0.035 0.037	1400 1600	650 750	20 90	−120 +600
Urethane	0.038 0.040	4400 4600	600 700	50 100	−65 +212

TABLE 5.126 Properties of Insulating Materials

Material	Specific gravity	Thermal resistivity, W•cm²/cm•°C	Dielectric constant	Electrical resistivity, Ω•cm
Air	0.00129	4,000	1	—
Asbestos paper	2.0–2.8	400	—	1.6×10^{11}
Asphalt	1.1–1.5	140	2.7	6×10^{14}
Bakelite resin	1.25	300–600	4.5–7.5	2×10^{16}
Buna S (RH-RW)	0.94	520	2.9	10^{15}
Butyl	0.91	520	2.4	10^{17}
Concrete	1.8–2.5	50–100	—	—
Cork	0.22–0.26	1800	—	—
Enamel (wire)	—	—	5	10^{14}
Glass (common)	2.4–2.8	90–100	5.5–9.1	9×10^{13}
Mica	2.9–3.2	280	5.7	10^{15}
Neoprene	1.5–1.24	520	9	10^{11}
Paper (dry)	0.7–1.15	800	1.7–2.6	5×10^{4}
Paper (in cable)	—	700	3.4–3.5	5×10^{4}
Paraffin	0.89	385–400	2.1	10^{16}
Porcelain (wet process)	2.3–2.5	100	4.4	3×10^{14}
PVC	1.2–1.7	600	6.5–12	5×10^{12}
Polyethylene	0.92	300–400	2.25	10^{16}

TABLE 5.126 Properties of Insulating Materials (*Continued*)

Silicone rubber	$\frac{1.4}{2.1}$	$\frac{350}{450}$	$\frac{3.2}{3.5}$	10^{14}
Teflon (TFE)	$\frac{2.1}{2.3}$	400	2	10^{16}
Varnished cloth	1.25	$\frac{600}{900}$	5	3×10^{14}
Water	1.00	170	80	—
Wood (maple)	$\frac{0.62}{0.75}$	550	4.4	3×10^{10}

TABLE 5.127 Properties of Various Metals and Alloys

Material	Relative resistivity* at 20°C	Density g/cm^3	Thermal conductivity at 20°C W/cm•°C	Thermal expansion × 10^{-6}/°C, in	Melting, °C
Aluminum	1.54	2.70	2.22	23.6	660
Beryllium	2.3	1.85	1.46	11.6	1277
Bismuth	67.0	9.80	0.084	13.3	271
Brass, yellow	3.7	8.47	1.17	20.3	930
Cadmium	4.3	8.65	0.92	29.8	321
Carbon, graphite	790	2.25	0.24	0.6–4.3	Sublimes
Chromium	7.4	7.19	0.67	6.2	1875
Cobalt	3.6	8.85	0.69	13.8	1495
Columbium (see Niobium)					
Constantan	29.0	8.9	0.21	14.9	1290
Copper, hard drawn	1.03	8.94	3.91	16.8	1083
Gallium	4.7	5.91	0.29	18.0	30
Germanium	2.7×10^6	5.33	0.59	5.75	937
Gold	1.36	19.32	2.96	14.2	1063
Inconel, 17–16–8	56.9	8.51	0.15	11.5	1425
Indium	4.9	7.31	0.24	33.0	156
Invar, 64–36	46.0	8.00	0.11	0–2	1425
Iron	5.6	7.87	0.75	11.8	1536
Lead	12.0	11.34	0.35	29.3	327
Magnesium	2.58	1.74	1.53	27.1	650
Mercury	55.6	13.55	0.082	—	–38.9
Molybdenum	3.3	10.22	1.42	4.9	2610
Monel, 67–30	27.9	8.84	0.26	14.0	1325
Nichrome, 80–20	62.5	8.4	0.134	13.0	1400
Nickel	5.5	8.89	0.61	13.3	1440
Niobium	7.2	8.57	0.52	7.31	2468
Palladium	6.3	12.02	0.70	11.8	1552
Phosphor bronze 95–5	6.4	8.86	0.71	17.8	1000
Platinum, 99.9%	6.16	21.45	0.69	8.9	1769
Silicon	10^{11}	2.33	1.25	2.5	1420
Silver	0.922	10.49	4.18	19.7	961
Steel, 0.4–0.5 C	7–12	7.8	0.5	11.0	1480
Steel, stainless 304	42	7.9	0.16	17.0	1430
Steel, stainless 410	33	7.7	0.24	11	1500
Tantalum	7.4	16.6	0.54	6.6	3000
Thorium	8.1	11.6	0.37	12.5	1750
Tin	7.0	7.30	0.63	23	232
Titanium	24.2	4.51	0.41	8.4	1670
Tungsten	3.2	19.3	1.67	4.6	3410
Uranium	17.5	18.7	0.3	6.8–14.1	1132
Zinc	3.5	7.14	1.10	27	420
Zirconium	23	6.5	0.21	5.8	1852

* Standard resistivity of 100% IACS copper at 20°C = 1.7241×10^{-6} Ω·cm.

TABLE 5.128 Other Common Metals and Alloys

Metal	Density g/cm^3	Weight, lb/in^3	Young's modulus (E), tension, lb/in^2	Torsional modulus (G), lb/in^2	Poisson's ratio	Electrical resistivity, Ω•cm
Aluminum (pure)	2.70	0.098	9×10^6	—	0.33	2.6×10^{-6}
Aluminum alloy (high strength)	2.78	0.101	$10–11 \times 10^6$	—	0.33	2.8×10^{-6}
Antimony	6.69	0.242	11.3×10^6	2.9×10^6	—	3.1×10^{-6}
Beryllium copper (C170) alloy	8.4	0.303	19×10^6	—	0.29	3.1×10^{-6}
Bismuth	9.75	0.352	—	—	—	119×10^{-6}
Brass (80Cu/20Zn)	8.6	0.311	16×10^6	6×10^6	0.34	7×10^{-6}
Cadmium	8.65	0.312	10.1×10^6	3.5×10^6	—	7.5×-6
Cast iron (gray)	7.2	0.260	14×10^6	5.6×10^6	0.21	—
Chromium	7.19	0.260	—	—	—	2.6×10^{-6}
Copper	8.96	0.324	17×10^6	6.4×10^6	0.34	1.72×10^{-6}
Gold	19.32	0.698	11.4×10^6	—	—	2.44×10^{-6}
Iron	7.87	0.284	28×10^6	11.2×10^6	0.30	10×10^{-6}
Iron (malleable)	7.85	0.284	25×10^6	11.5×10^6	0.17	—
Lead	11.35	0.410	2.4×10^6	—	0.43	22×10^{-6}
Lithium	0.53	0.019	—	—	—	9×10^{-6}
Magnesium (cast)	1.74	0.063	6.5×10^6	2.4×10^6	0.35	44×10^{-6}
Mercury	13.55	0.490	—	—	—	96×10^{-6}
Molybdenum	10.22	0.369	—	—	—	5.7×10^{-6}
Nickel	8.90	0.322	30×10^6	10.6×10^6	0.32	7.8×10^{-6}
Palladium	12.02	0.434	—	—	—	11×10^{-6}
Phosphor bronze	8.90	0.322	16×10^6	6×10^6	0.35	10×10^{-6}
Platinum	21.45	0.775	24.2×10^6	9.3×10^6	—	10×10^{-6}
Silver	10.50	0.379	11.2×10^6	3.8×10^6	—	1.6×10^{-6}
Steel (medium carbon)	7.80	0.282	30×10^6	11.4×10^6	0.30	15×10^{-6}
Steel (stainless 300 type)	8.03	0.290	28×10^6	11.4×10^6	0.28	30×10^{-6}
Steel (stainless 400 type)	7.75	0.280	29×10^6	12.6×10^6	0.28	30×10^{-6}
Tin	7.31	0.264	7×10^6	2.4×10^6	—	11.5×10^{-6}
Titanium	4.54	0.164	16×10^6	—	—	—
Tungsten	19.30	0.697	51.5×10^6	21.5×10^6	—	5.51×10^{-6}
Zinc	7.13	0.258	14.5×10^6	5×10^6	0.11	6×10^{-6}

TABLE 5.129 Coefficients of Linear Expansion for Common Materials

Metal, alloy, or other material	Linear expansion	
	in per 1°F	in per 1°C
Aluminum, wrought	0.0000128	0.0000231
Brass	0.0000104	0.0000188
Bronze	0.0000101	0.0000181
Copper	0.0000093	0.0000168
Cast iron, gray	0.0000059	0.0000106
Wrought iron	0.0000067	0.0000120
Lead	0.0000159	0.0000286
Magnesium alloy	0.0000160	0.0000290
Nickel	0.0000070	0.0000126
Cast steel	0.0000061	0.0000110
Hard steel	0.0000073	0.0000132
Medium steel	0.0000067	0.0000120
Soft steel	0.0000061	0.0000110
Stainless steel	0.0000099	0.0000178
Zinc, rolled	0.0000173	0.0000263
Concrete	0.0000079	0.0000143
Granite	0.0000047	0.0000084
Marble	0.0000056	0.0000100
Plaster	0.0000092	0.0000166
Slate	0.0000058	0.0000104
Fir	0.0000021	0.0000037
Maple	0.0000036	0.0000064
Oak	0.0000027	0.0000049
Pine	0.0000030	0.0000054
Plate glass	0.0000050	0.0000089
Hard rubber	0.0000044	0.0000080
Porcelain	0.0000009	0.0000016
Silver	0.0000104	0.0000188
Tin	0.0000148	0.0000269
Tungsten	0.0000024	0.0000043

TABLE 5.130 Properties of Common Woods

Name	Density, g/cm³	Density, lb/ft³	Modulus of elasticity, lb/in² × 10⁶
Ash, white	0.64	39.8	1.77
Birch, paper	0.60	37.5	1.59
Cedar, eastern	0.49	30.7	0.87
Cherry, black	0.53	33.3	1.49
Cyprus	0.48	30.1	1.44
Ebony, African	0.77	48.0	1.43
Eucalyptus, Australian	0.83	51.8	2.64
Fir, Douglas	0.51	32.0	1.93
Gum, black	0.55	34.5	1.19
Hemlock, eastern	0.43	27.0	1.20
Hickory, shagbark	0.84	52.2	2.17
Ironwood, black	1.01	67.3	2.99
Locust, black	0.71	44.2	2.06
Mahogany, African	0.67	41.7	1.53
Maple, sugar	0.68	42.2	1.83
Oak, black	0.67	41.8	1.64
Oak, red	0.66	41.1	1.81
Oak, white	0.71	44.3	1.78
Pine, longleaf	0.64	39.8	2.06
Poplar, yellow	0.43	26.7	1.50
Redwood	0.44	27.2	1.36
Spruce, white	0.43	27.0	1.42
Teak, Indian	0.58	36.3	1.70
Walnut, black	0.56	35.1	1.69

TABLE 5.131 Chemical Symbols for Metals

Metal	Symbol	Metal	Symbol
Aluminum	Al	Manganese	Mn
Antimony	Sb	Mercury	Hg
Beryllium	Be	Molybdenum	Mo
Bismuth	Bi	Nickel	Ni
Boron	B	Platinum	Pt
Cadmium	Cd	Selenium	Se
Carbon	C	Silicon	Si
Chromium	Cr	Silver	Ag
Cobalt	Co	Tellurium	Te
Copper	Cu	Tin	Sn
Gold	Au	Titanium	Ti
Iridium	Ir	Tungsten	W
Iron	Fe	Vanadium	V
Lead	Pb	Zinc	Zn
Lithium	Li	Zirconium	Zr
Magnesium	Mg		

TABLE 5.132 Standard Pipe Sizes

To determine the weight per linear foot of a pipe, use the relationship

$$W = \pi\left(\frac{OD}{2}\right)^2 - \pi\left(\frac{ID}{2}\right)^2 \times 12 \times \text{density}$$

Nominal pipe size	OD, in	ASA pipe schedules (wall thickness, in)					
		40	60	80	100	120	160
⅛	0.405	0.068		0.095			
¼	0.540	0.088		0.119			
⅜	0.675	0.091		0.126			
½	0.840	0.109		0.147			
¾	1.050	0.113		0.154			
1	1.315	0.133		0.179			
1¼	1.660	0.140		0.191			
1½	1.900	0.145		0.200			
2	2.375	0.154		0.218			
2½	2.875	0.203		0.276			
3	3.500	0.216		0.300			
3½	4.000	0.226		0.318			
4	4.500	0.237		0.337		0.438	0.531
5	5.563	0.258		0.375		0.500	0.625
6	6.625	0.280		0.432		0.562	0.719
8	8.625	0.322	0.406	0.500	0.594	0.719	0.906
10	10.750	0.365	0.500	0.594	0.719	0.844	1.125
12	12.750	0.406	0.562	0.688	0.844	1.000	1.312

LEXAN® High Modulus 500 Grade

resin

LEXAN 500 resin is a member of the LEXAN family of polycarbonate resins particularly suited to applications requiring high rigidity combined with toughness and impact strength.

LEXAN 500 resin has the highest combination of rigidity and impact strength available in any thermoplastic, plus excellent dimensional stability, low mold shrinkage, and colorability.

LEXAN 500 resin also has these additional advantages:

Mechanical:
- Flexural modulus increased nearly 50% over standard LEXAN resins

Flammability:
- Listed 94 V-0* at 1/16" (1.6 mm) per UL Std. 94
- Listed 94 5V* at 1/8" (3.2 mm) per UL Std. 94

Molding:
- Reduced mold shrinkage allows for the production of more precise parts.

Typical Property Values

English Units (SI Units)

PROPERTY	ASTM TEST METHOD	LEXAN 500 resins**
PHYSICAL		
Specific Gravity	D792	1.25
Specific Volume, in³/lb(cm³/g)	—	22.2(0.80)
Weight/volume, lbs/in³(g/cm³)	—	0.045(1.25)
Water Absorption, %	D570	
24 hrs @ 73°F(23°C)		0.12
Equilibrium, 73°F(23°C)		0.31
Mold Shrinkage, in/in(mm/mm)	D955	0.002-0.004**
Transmittance, %	D1003	Not applicable
Haze, %	D1003	Not applicable
Refractive Index	—	Not applicable
THERMAL		
Deflection Temperature, °F(°C)	D648	
@ 66 psi(0.46 MPa)		295(146)
@ 264 psi(1.84 MPa)		288(142)
Specific Heat, btu/lb/°F(kj/kgK)	—	0.29(1.20)
Thermal Conductivity, Btu-in/h-ft²-°F (W/km)	—	1.41(0.20)
Coefficient of Thermal Expansion in/in/°F(m/m/°C)	D696	1.79×10^{-5}(3.22×10^{-5})
Vicat Softening Temperature, °F(°C)	D1525	310(154)
Flammability Ratings		
ASTM D635*	D635	AEB <0.5"
UL Standard 94* 1/16"(1.6 mm)	UL 94	94 V-0
UL Standard 94* 1/8"(3.2 mm)	UL 94	94 V-0/94 5V
Oxygen Index	D2863	32.5
ELECTRICAL		
Dielectric Strength, volts/mi.(kV/mm)	D149	
Short time, 125 mils(3.2 mm)		450(17.7)
Dielectric Constant	D150	
60H		3.10
10⁶H		3.05
Power Factor	D150	
60H		0.0008
10⁶H		0.0075
Volume Resistivity, ohm-cm	D257	
@ 73°F, dry(23°C)		$>10^{16}$
Arc Resistance, sec	D495	
Stainless Steel Electrodes		5-10
Tungsten Electrodes		120
MECHANICAL		
Tensile Strength, psi(MPa)	D638	
Yield		9,600(66)
Ultimate		8,000(55)
Elongation, %	D638	
Yield		8-9
Rupture		10-20
Tensile Modulus, 10⁵ psi(MPa)	D638	4.50(3,100)
Flexural Strength, psi(MPa)	D790	15,000(100)
Flexural Modulus, 10⁵ psi(MPa)	D790	5.0(3,400)
Compressive Strength, psi(MPa)	D695	14,000(96)
Compressive Modulus, 10⁵ psi(MPa)	D695	5.20(3,600)
Shear Strength, psi(MPa)	D732	
Yield		8,500(58)
Shear Modulus, 10⁵ psi(MPa)	—	1.47(1,000)
Izod Impact Strength, ft-lbs/in(J/m)	D256	
Notched, ⅛" thick(3.2 mm)		2(100)
Unnotched, ⅛" thick(3.2 mm)		40(2,000)
Tensile Impact Strength, ft-lbs/in²(kJ/m²)	D1822	
S-type		75(158)
Falling Dart Impact Strength, ft-lbs, (J), ⅛" thick(3.2 mm)		75(102)
Fatigue Strength, psi @ 2.5mm cycles(MPa)	D671	2,000(14.0)
Rockwell Hardness	D785	
M		85
R		124
Deformation Under Load, %	D621	
4000 psi, @ 73°F(27 MPa @ 23°C)		0.2
4000 psi, @ 158°F(27 MPa @ 70°C)		0.4
Taber Abrasion Resistance, mg weight loss/1000 cycles	D1044	11

* This rating is not intended to reflect hazards of this or any other material under actual fire conditions.

** .002-.004 in/in for parts up to 8" in length.
.0025-.0045 in/in for parts 8"-16" in length.
.0035-.0055 in/in for parts over 16" in length.
Property values may vary slightly for some colors.

Figure 5.4 Material specification sheet—plastic.

500 Family Engineering Thermoplastics VALOX® resin

500 Family. A 30% glass reinforced thermoplastic polyester alloy offering:

Property Advantages
- Improved flatness • Appearance • Minimum sink marks
- Low coefficient of thermal expansion • UL 94 V-0 capabilities

Processing Advantage
- Good flow

Typical Property Values — English Units (SI Units)

PROPERTY	UNITS	ASTM TEST METHOD	VALOX 508 VCT resin 30% Glass Reinforced PBT Alloy	VALOX 553 VCT resin 30% Glass Reinforced PBT Alloy UL 94 V-0 Recognized
PHYSICAL				
Specific Gravity		D792	1.50	1.58
Specific Volume	in³/lb(cm³/kg)	D892	18.5(668)	17.6(635)
Water Absorption 24 hours	%	D570	.06	.07
Mold Shrinkage	in/in x 10^{-3}			
Flow Direction	(mm/mm x 10^{-3})			
30-90 mil(0.76-2.3 mm)			3-5	3-5
90-180 mil(2.3-4.6 mm)			5-6	5-6
Cross Flow Direction				
30-90 mil(0.76-2.3 mm)			4-7	4-7
90-180 mil(2.3-4.6 mm)			7-10	7-10
MECHANICAL				
Tensile Strength	psi(MPa)	D638	16,000(110)	18,000(124)
Elongation at Break	%	D638#	—	5
Flexural Strength	psi(MPa)	D790	24,500(170)	28,000(190)
Flexural Modulus	psi(MPa)	D790	1,000,000(6,900)	1,000,000(6,900)
Compressive Strength	psi(MPa)	D695	16,700(115)	19,550(135)
Shear Strength	psi(MPa)	D732	8,260(57)	8,940(61)
Izod Impact Strength		D256		
Notched, ⅛" thick(3.2 mm)	ft lb/in(J/m)		2.0(107)	1.4(75)
Unnotched, ⅛" thick(3.2 mm)	ft lb/in(J/m)		12(640)	12(640)
Rockwell Hardness R-scale		D785	119	118
THERMAL				
Heat Deflection Temp.		D648		
@ 66 psi(0.46 MPa)	°F(°C)		420(215)	400(204)
@ 264 psi(1.82 MPa)	°F(°C)		350(176)	320(160)
Coeff. of Thermal Expansion				
Mold Direction x 10^{-5}	in/in°F(m/m/°C)			
Range: -40 → 100F(-40 → 40°C)			1.3(2.3)	1.2(2.2)
Range: 140 → 280°F(60 → 140°C)			0.9(1.6)	1.2(2.2)
ELECTRICAL				
Dielectric Strength 1/16"(1.6 mm)	V/mil(kV/mm)	D149	740(29)	650(26)
1/8"(3.2 mm)	V/mil(kV/mm)		600(24)	480(19)
Dielectric Constant 100 Hz		D150	3.6	3.8
10^6 Hz			3.6	3.7
Dissipation Factor 100 Hz		D150	.0014	.002
10^6 Hz			.02	.02
Volume Resistivity	ohm-cm x 10^{16} (ohm-m x 10^{14})	D257	5.9	4.3
UL				
Flammability†		UL 94	HB/.058"	V-0/.033"
Arc Resistance	sec	D495	62/.124"	94/.058"
High Voltage Arc Tracking Rate	in/min	UL 746A	1.8/.124"	7.8/.124"
High Ampere Arc Ignition	arcs	UL 746A	15/.124"	15/.124"
Hot Wire Ignition	sec	UL 746A	66/.124"	70/.124"
Comparative Track Index (CTI)	volts	UL 746A	145/.124"	145/.124"
UL Temp. Index		UL 746B		
Elec. Properties	°C		125/.058"	125/.058"
Mech. Properties with impact	°C		110/.058"	110/.058"
Mech. Properties without impact	°C		125/.058"	125/.058"

† This rating is not intended to reflect hazards presented by this or any other material under actual fire conditions
# ASTM D638 type V @ 0.5"/min.

Figure 5.5 Material specification sheet—plastic.

CODE COMPLIANCE

ANSI Z 26.1-1966—
Safety Code for Safety Glazing Materials for Glazing Motor Vehicles Operating on Land Highways; Items 4 and 5, rigid plastics, ≥0.125" thickness; Items 6 and 7, flexible plastics, 0.060 inch to 0.187 inch thickness.

ANSI Z 97.1-1966/72—
Performance Specifications and Methods of Test for Safety Glazing Material Used in Buildings; ≥0.099 inch thickness.

Because of variations in local building codes, it is difficult to generalize on compliance of LUCITE cast acrylic sheet for all applications. However, specific building code information will be supplied on request.

TYPICAL PHYSICAL PROPERTIES OF LUCITE® CAST ACRYLIC SHEET

PROPERTY		ASTM	"LUCITE" CAST ACRYLIC SHEET
	Specific Gravity	D792	1.19
OPTICAL	Refractive Index	D542	1.49
	Light Transmittance	D1003	
	☐ Parallel		91%
	☐ Total		92%
	☐ Haze		1%
	Spectral Transmission	Beckman	
	☐ 290 to 330 nm, 0.250" sheet, max. percent	DU-792	5%
MECHANICAL	Tensile Strength	D638	
	☐ Rupture		10.8M psi (760 kg/cm²)
	☐ Modulus of Elasticity		427M psi (3 x 10⁴ kg/cm²)
	☐ Elongation at Rupture		4.5%
	Flexural Strength	D790	
	☐ Rupture		14.9M psi (1,050 kg/cm²)
	☐ Modulus of Elasticity		427M psi (3 x 10⁴ kg/cm²)
	Compressive Strength	D695	
	☐ Yield		17.9M psi (1,260 kg/cm²)
	☐ Modulus of Elasticity		427M psi (3 x 10⁴ kg/cm²)
	Shear Strength	D732	8.9M psi (630 kg/cm²)
	Impact Strength	D256	
	☐ Charpy Unnotched		7.0 ft. lb./in.² (0.48 kg/cm²)
	Rockwell Hardness	D785	M-100
THERMAL	Hot Forming Temperature		275-350°F (135-175°C)
	Heat Distortion Temperature 3.6°F (2°C)/Min-264 psi	D648	203°F (95°C)
	Coefficient of Thermal Expansion (ave. value)	D696	3.9 x 10⁻⁵ in./in./°F (7 x 10⁻⁵ cm/cm/°C)
	Maximum Recommended Continuous Service Temperature		180°F (82°C)
	Coefficient of Thermal Conductivity		1.45 Btu in./ft.² hr. °F (5 x 10⁻⁴ Cal/sec. cm² °C/cm)
	Shrinkage, max. percent		2.5%
	Specific Heat		0.35 Btu/lb. °F (0.35 Cal/gr °C)
ELECTRICAL	Surface Resistivity, 82°F (28°C), 75% RH	D257	>10¹⁴ ohm
	Volume Resistivity	D257	4 x 10¹¹ ohm/mil (10¹⁵ ohm/cm)
	Dielectric Strength, Short Time Test	D149	0.42 kv/mil (20 kv/mm)
	Dielectric Constant	D150	
	☐ 60 cycles		4
	☐ 10³ cycles		3
	☐ 10⁶ cycles		3
	Power Factor	D150	
	☐ 60 cycles		0.06
	☐ 10³ cycles		0.04
	☐ 10⁶ cycles		0.02
	Arc Resistance	D495	No Tracking
MISCELLANEOUS	Water Absorption (Wt. Gain on Immersion for 24 hrs.)	D570	0.3%
	Soluble Matter Lost after Immersion	D570	0.0%
	Odor		None
	Taste		None
COMBUSTIBILITY*	Smoke Density Rating	D2843	13.5%
	Factor	E84	
	0.118"		385
	0.236"		530
	Fuel Contribution Factor		11,300 Btu/lb. (6,265 cal/g)
	Auto Ignition Temperature	D1929	750°F
	Rate of Flame Spread	E84	
	0.118"		140
	0.236"		110
		E162	
	0.118"		219
	0.236"		249
		D635	
	0.118"		1.18 in./min.
	0.236"		0.71 in./min.

*"Lucite" cast acrylic sheet is combustible like many other synthetic and natural building materials. Small scale tests are not intended to reflect hazards under actual fire conditions

The Du Pont Company assumes no obligation or liability for any advice furnished or for any results obtained with respect to this information. All such advice is given and accepted at the buyer's risk. The disclosure of information herein is not a license to operate under, or a recommendation to infringe, any patent of Du Pont or others. Du Pont warrants that the use or sale of any material which is described herein and is offered for sale by Du Pont does not infringe any patent covering the material itself, but does not warrant against infringement by reason of the use thereof in combination with other materials or in the operation of any process.

Figure 5.6 Material specification sheet—plastic.

HAYSITE DIVISION
SYNTHANE-TAYLOR CORPORATION
P. O. BOX 6180
5599 NEW PERRY HIGHWAY
ERIE, PA U.S.A. 16512
TELEPHONE (814) 868-3691
An Alco Standard Corporate Partner

BULLETIN 143
9-75

GRADE ETR-FR-C

GPO-3

FIBERGLASS REINFORCED POLYESTER SHEETS, MOLDED PARTS AND COMPOUNDS

DESCRIPTION

A track-resistant, flame retardant random glass fibre mat reinforced polyester laminate. Physical and electrical properties exceed NEMA GPO-2 requirements, ASTM specification D1532-67T for polyester glass-mat laminates, and meet NEMA GPO-3 requirements. This grade is recognized by Underwriters' Laboratories as acceptable for sole support of current-carrying parts. (File E27875)

ETR-FR-C is U.L. rated 94V-0 & 180 seconds arc resistance.

PROPERTIES

Specific Gravity	1.82
Barcol Hardness	59
Compressive Strength, Flatwise, PSI	34,952
Tensile Strength, PSI	10,300
Flexural Strength, PSI	20,400
Impact Strength, IZOD, Ft. Lb./In. Notch	
Edgewise	8.0
Flatwise	15.0
Water Absorption, Percent	0.37
Bonding Strength, PSI	1,300
Shear Strength, PSI	14,200
Modulus of Elasticity in Flexure, x 10^6, PSI	1.59
Thermal Conductivity	
CAL/SEC/CM²/CM/°C	1.31×10^{-3}
BTU/HR/FT²/IN/°F	3.79

Arc Resistance, Seconds	180
Dielectric Strength, Perpendicular to Laminations	
Short Time, VPM, in oil	400
Dielectric Strength, Parallel to Laminations,	
Step by Step, KV	59.1
D24/23, KV	38.0
Dielectric Constant, Condition A	
@ 60 cycles	4.73
@ 1 KC	4.69
Dissipation Factor, Condition A	
@ 60 cycles	.0160
@ 1 KC	.0107
Flame Retardance	
*Sec. Ign./Sec. Burn	120/35
**Sec. Ign./Sec. Burn	30/1
***Track Resistance, Min.	400
Flammability, U.L. Subject 94	94V-0

*NEMA Standard Publication 240-1961, LPI-7.07A (Thickness 1/2" to 2" Incl.)
**ASTM D635-56T, NEMA LPI-7.07 (Thickness 1/16" to less than 1/2")
***NEMA Inclined Plane Method, similar to ASTM D-2303-64T

GENERAL INFORMATION

Color: Red

Thickness: 1/32" thru 2"

Standard Sheet Size: 3' x 6'; (4' x 8' some thicknesses)
(4' x 5' or special size panels can be run upon request. Contact HAYSITE for exact pricing.)

Approximate weight per square foot,
1/8" thickness – 1.2 lbs.

Unless otherwise indicated, all properties published in our data bulletins are based on tests performed on standard ASTM test samples and according to standard ASTM test methods. Values shown are for test samples made from production materials and they are believed to be conservative. NO WARRANTY IS TO BE CONSTRUED, HOWEVER. Parts may vary considerably from this standard test data. Where specific or unusual applications arise, tests should be made on actual parts.

Sample of plastics specification sheet.

Figure 5.7 Material specification sheet—plastic.

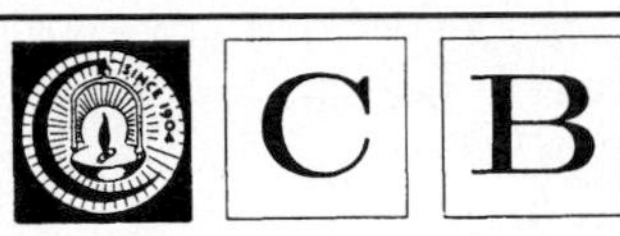

CRESCENT BRASS MFG. CORP.

Seventh, Spruce and Bingaman Streets, Reading, Pa. 19602
P.O. Box 1218, Reading, Pa. 19603

PA: Area Code 215/372-7834
Out of State: 800/523-8171

CERTIFICATE OF ANALYSIS

CUSTOMER: ____________

PURCHASE ORDER: SW1-139

MATERIAL: 131

DATE: March 6, 1981

INVOICE: 40114

PART NO: C-7130 & C-7131

We certify that the above castings are produced from material of the following chemical composition:

COPPER	92.21
TIN	1.28
LEAD	1.76
ZINC	Balance
IRON	.05
ANTIMONY	.01
NICKEL	.13
SILICON	
ALUMINUM	
MANGANESE	
PHOSPHORUS	.001
SULPHUR	.001

Ivan L. Jeffery

All contracts made contingent upon strikes, fires, accidents or causes beyond our control. Quotations are for immediate acceptance and subject to change without notice. All contracts and quotations made by agents are subject to approval of this company. We will not be responsible for loss or damage to customers' patterns, while in our possession or in transit, caused by fire, theft or by any other causes

Figure 5.8 Certificate of analysis—metal alloy.

DR. WM. B. D. PENNIMAN
1866-1938
DR. ARTHUR LEE BROWNE
1867-1933

EXECUTIVE STAFF

PHILIP M. AIDI
ALLEN W. THOMPSON
DANTE G. BERETTA
J. ADRIAN BUTT
DONALD W. SMITH

PENNIMAN & BROWNE, INC.
CHEMISTS-ENGINEERS-INSPECTORS
6252 FALLS ROAD
BALTIMORE. MARYLAND 21209

ESTABLISHED
1896

CABLE ADDRESS
"BALTEST"

TELEPHONE
825-4131
AREA CODE 301

ENGINEERING DIVISION

REPORT OF TEST

Attn: Mr. R.A. Walsh, R & D

July 25, 1979

No. 791553

Sample of Aluminum Castings

Client Powercon Corp.

Marks or Other Data Physical & Chemical Analysis - two castings to verify Alloy 356 T 6 Condition.

Tensile Test

Sample No.	1	2
Tensile Strength, psi.	33,755	34,735
Yield Strength, psi.	21,960	24,025
Elongation % in 1"	7.5	7.5

Chemical Analysis

Sample	1	2
Silicon	6.55	6.68
Iron	0.098	0.10
Copper	0.15	0.17
Manganese	0.024	0.023
Magnesium	0.23	0.25
Zinc	0.047	0.066
Titanium	0.085	0.080

Both samples meet chemical & physical requirements for Aluminum Alloy 356 in the T6 Condition.

PENNIMAN & BROWNE, INC.

spl

J.A. Butt

FORM 30 L/B

Figure 5.9 Materials laboratory test report—metal alloy.

Chapter 6

Fastening and Joining Techniques and Hardware

6.1 Bolts, Screws, Nuts, and Washers

Bolts and screws are the most commonly used types of fastening devices. The thread on a bolt or screw may be compared to an inclined plane wrapped around a cylinder, thus assuming the form of one of the basic machines. Many different thread form standards are used throughout the world, but this chapter addresses only the forms in common use, such as the 60° V thread form for the U.S. Customary (inch) system and the metric (ISO) standard. The other basic thread forms and their geometry are shown in Chap. 7, "Machining, Machine Tools, and Practices."

Threaded fasteners have countless applications in industry, and in many cases, their performance is critical. Failure of a threaded fastener such as a heavily loaded bolt or bolts can cause severe injury, property damage, and death in critical applications. It is for these reasons that standards of performance have been devised and specified in the various American standards, such as those of the American National Standards Institute (ANSI), the American Society of Testing and Materials (ASTM), the Society of Automotive Engineers (SAE), the Industrial Fasteners Institute (IFI), the American Iron and Steel Institute (AISI), and others. In recent years, it has been discovered that "counterfeit" bolts are being imported on a large scale into the United States. False head markings and inferior steels have been found, and these have contributed to a number of failures in critical applications. Figure 6.1 shows a typical counterfeit bolt which failed during its installation process. This is a direct indication of improperly processed or poor-quality material. In other cases cited, failure was through the threaded section of such bolts or the result of cracking due to improper heat treatment combined with faulty material. I have personally witnessed at least three imported-bolt failures under normal operation within a time span of only 1 year.

Not only are the counterfeit fasteners causing problems, but improper materials specifications also have been noted. Recently, I had a sample of stainless steel that had cracked during the welding process analyzed. The material was specified as type AISI 304 stainless steel, but when analyzed at a materials testing laboratory, the specimen did not conform to *any* known American stainless steel series and also contained 10 times the minimum amount of sulfur allowed for type 304 stainless steel.

As a precautionary procedure, hardware and materials which are used in critical applications should be certified and, if necessary, analyzed to ensure its conformity to SAE, AISI, ASTM, or other applicable American standards. This will help prevent the problems associated with fastener and materials failures and protect American manufacturers against the possibility of lawsuits.

Government legislation is in progress to control and hopefully eliminate these problems.

6.1.1 Dimensions of bolts, screws, nuts, and washers

Basic dimensions for the most commonly used American standard bolts are shown in Fig. 6.2. Basic dimensions for the most commonly used American standard machine screws are shown in Fig. 6.3. Basic dimensions for American standard miniature screws are shown in Fig. 6.4.

The dimensions shown in these figures are the most important ones needed for machining clearances and tool/design engineering purposes. The complete dimensional specifications and applicable tolerances for all standard hardware or fasteners should be obtained from the fastener handbooks distributed by the Industrial Fasteners Institute (IFI) (see Sec. 23.1).

The design specifications for strength of all types of threaded fasteners are shown in a subsection to follow. In addition, the normal tightening torques required for bolts and screws will be shown in another subsection to follow. Calculation procedures for bolts and screws will likewise be presented in a later subsection.

Figure 6.5 shows the basic dimensions for metric hex cap screws. Figure 6.6 shows samples of miniature metric screws with a machinist's scale for size comparisons. Figure 6.7 shows the dimensions of American standard hex nuts and jamb nuts. Figure 6.8 shows the dimensions of metric standard nuts, type 1. Figure 6.9 shows the dimensions of American standard flat washers. Figure 6.10 shows dimensions of metric standard flat washers.

Figure 6.11 shows dimensions of American standard shoulder bolts and socket head cap screws, which are widely used in tooling applications as well as in other mechanical design applications.

Standard shoulder screw mechanical data

Thread class	UNC-3A (ANSI/ASME B1.3) (No plating allowance is provided.)
Material	Alloys of chrome, nickel, molybdenum, or vanadium
Hardness	32 to 43 Rockwell C at the surface
Ultimate tensile strength	140,000 lb/in^2 based on minimum thread neck area
Shear strength	84,000 lb/in^2 in thread neck and shoulder areas

Figure 6.12 shows the head marking standard for SAE-graded bolts together with the tensile strength requirements and proof load ratings. Figure 6.13 shows the head marking standard for ASTM-graded bolts together with the tensile strength requirements and proof load ratings.

6.1.2 Grade classification and strength of standard bolts, screws, and nuts

Table 6.1 shows the mechanical requirements and SAE identification markings for the different strength grades of bolts, screws, studs, sems, and U bolts. Table 6.2 shows the proof loads and tensile strength requirements for the different grades of threaded bolts and screws. Table 6.3 shows the strength requirements (allowable tensile loads) for machine screws only. Table 6.4 shows the proof loads and hardness requirements for the different grades of standard hex nuts.

(Text continued on page 426.)

Figure 6.1 Failure of the head of a suspected counterfeit bolt.

	Hex Bolts				Hex Cap Screw (Finished Hex Bolts)				Round Head Square Neck Bolts				Countersunk Bolts			
Nominal size	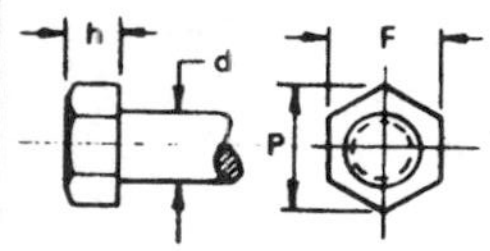				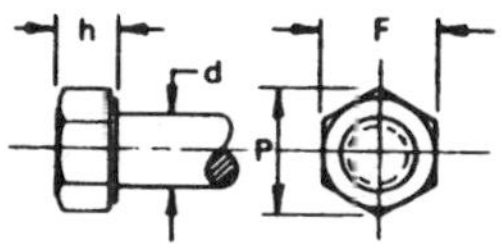				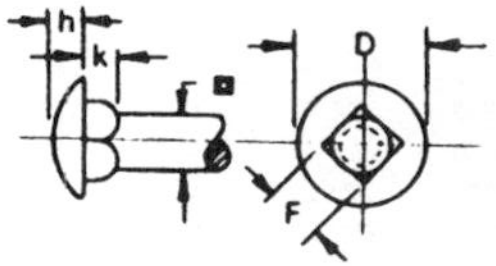				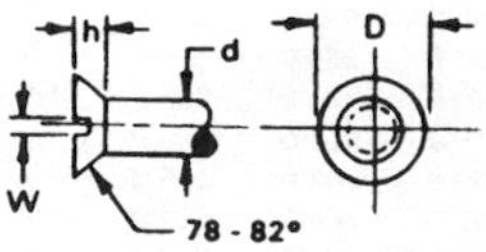			
Basic Dia.	d	F	P	h	d	F	P	h	D	F	h	k	d	D	h	W ♦
0.2500 - 1/4	0.260	0.438	0.505	0.188	0.2500	0.438	0.505	0.163	0.594	0.260	0.145	0.156	0.260	0.493	0.150	0.064
0.3125 - 5/16	0.324	0.500	0.577	0.235	0.3125	0.500	0.577	0.211	0.719	0.324	0.176	0.187	0.324	0.618	0.189	0.072
0.3750 - 3/8	0.388	0.562	0.650	0.268	0.3750	0.562	0.650	0.243	0.844	0.388	0.208	0.219	0.388	0.740	0.225	0.081
0.4375 - 7/16	0.452	0.625	0.722	0.316	0.4375	0.625	0.722	0.291	0.969	0.452	0.239	0.250	0.452	0.803	0.226	0.081
0.5000 - 1/2	0.515	0.750	0.866	0.364	0.5000	0.750	0.866	0.323	1.094	0.515	0.270	0.281	0.515	0.935	0.269	0.091
0.5625 - 9/16	—	—	—	—	0.5625	0.812	0.938	0.371	—	—	—	—	—	—	—	----
0.6250 - 5/8	0.642	0.938	1.083	0.444	0.6250	0.938	1.083	0.403	1.344	0.642	0.344	0.344	0.642	1.169	0.336	0.116
0.7500 - 3/4	0.768	1.125	1.299	0.524	0.7500	1.125	1.299	0.483	1.594	0.768	0.406	0.406	0.768	1.402	0.403	0.131
0.8750 - 7/8	0.895	1.312	1.516	0.604	0.8750	1.312	1.516	0.563	1.844	0.895	0.469	0.469	0.895	1.637	0.470	0.147
1.0000 - 1	1.022	1.500	1.732	0.700	1.0000	1.500	1.732	0.627	2.094	1.022	0.531	0.531	1.022	1.869	0.537	0.166
1.1250 - 1-1/8	1.149	1.688	1.949	0.780	1.1250	1.688	1.949	0.718	—	—	—	—	1.149	2.104	0.604	0.178
1.2500 - 1-1/4	1.277	1.875	2.165	0.876	1.2500	1.875	2.165	0.813	—	—	—	—	1.277	2.337	0.671	0.193
1.3750 - 1-3/8	1.404	2.062	2.382	0.940	1.3750	2.062	2.382	0.878	—	—	—	—	1.404	2.571	0.738	0.208
1.5000 - 1-1/2	1.531	2.250	2.598	1.036	1.5000	2.250	2.598	0.974	—	—	—	—	1.531	2.804	0.805	0.240
1.7500 - 1-3/4	1.785	2.625	3.031	1.196	1.7500	2.625	3.031	1.134	—	—	—	—	—	—	—	—
2.0000 - 2	2.039	3.000	3.464	1.388	2.0000	3.000	3.464	1.263	—	—	—	—	—	—	—	—

Note: ♦ **Minimum dimensions of slot widths. All other tabulated values are maximum dimensions.** ■ **diameters same as hex bolts (d) of same basic size.**

Figure 6.2 Dimensions for American standard bolts.

Nominal Size		Fillister Head			Binding Head			Pan Head			Countersunk			Undercut C'sunk		
		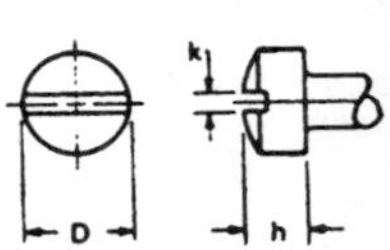			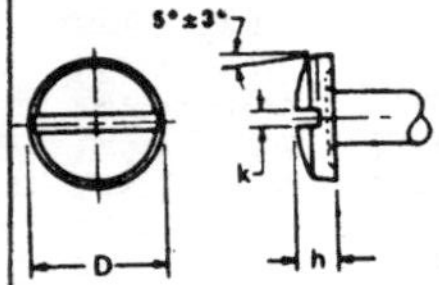			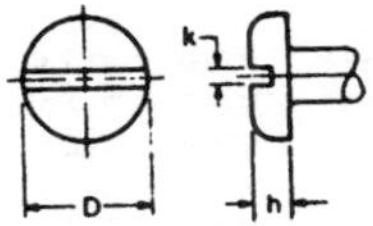			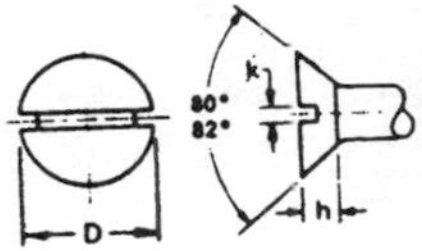			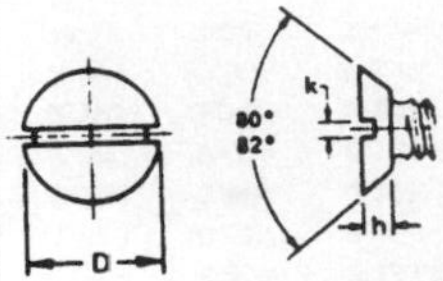		
	Basic Dia.	D	h	k♦	D	h	k♦	D	h	k♦	D	h	k♦	D	h	k♦
0 -	0.0600	0.096	0.055	0.016	0.126	0.032	0.016	0.116	0.039	0.016	0.119	0.035	0.016	0.119	0.025	0.016
1 -	0.0730	0.118	0.066	0.019	0.153	0.041	0.019	0.142	0.046	0.019	0.146	0.043	0.019	0.146	0.031	0.019
2 -	0.0860	0.140	0.083	0.023	0.181	0.050	0.023	0.167	0.053	0.023	0.172	0.051	0.023	0.172	0.036	0.023
3 -	0.0990	0.161	0.095	0.027	0.208	0.059	0.027	0.193	0.060	0.027	0.199	0.059	0.027	0.199	0.042	0.027
4 -	0.1120	0.183	0.107	0.031	0.235	0.068	0.031	0.219	0.068	0.031	0.225	0.067	0.031	0.225	0.047	0.031
5 -	0.1250	0.205	0.120	0.035	0.263	0.078	0.035	0.245	0.075	0.035	0.252	0.075	0.035	0.252	0.053	0.035
6 -	0.1380	0.226	0.132	0.039	0.290	0.087	0.039	0.270	0.082	0.039	0.279	0.083	0.039	0.279	0.059	0.039
8 -	0.1640	0.270	0.156	0.045	0.344	0.105	0.045	0.322	0.096	0.045	0.332	0.100	0.045	0.332	0.070	0.045
10 -	0.1900	0.313	0.180	0.050	0.399	0.123	0.050	0.373	0.110	0.050	0.385	0.116	0.050	0.385	0.081	0.050
12 -	0.2160	0.357	0.205	0.056	0.454	0.141	0.056	0.425	0.125	0.056	0.438	0.132	0.056	0.438	0.092	0.056
1/4-	0.2500	0.414	0.237	0.064	0.525	0.165	0.064	0.492	0.144	0.064	0.507	0.153	0.064	0.507	0.107	0.064
5/16-	0.3125	0.518	0.295	0.072	0.656	0.209	0.072	0.615	0.178	0.072	0.635	0.191	0.072	0.635	0.134	0.072
3/8-	0.3750	0.622	0.335	0.081	0.788	0.253	0.081	0.740	0.212	0.081	0.762	0.230	0.081	0.762	0.161	0.081
7/16-	0.4375	0.625	0.368	0.081	—	—	—	0.863	0.247	0.081	0.812	0.223	0.081	0.812	0.156	0.081
1/2-	0.5000	0.750	0.412	0.091	—	—	—	0.987	0.281	0.091	0.875	0.223	0.091	0.875	0.156	0.091

Note: ♦ Minimum dimensions of slot widths. All other tabulated values are maximum dimensions.

Figure 6.3 Dimensions for standard machine screws.

Size	Thds/in	Basic dia.	Fillister			Binding			Pan			100° Flat Head		
			D	h	k♦	D	h	k♦	D	h	k♦	D	h	k♦
30 UNM	318	0.0118	0.021	0.012	0.003	—	—	—	0.025	0.010	0.003	0.023	0.007	0.003
40 UNM	254	0.0157	0.025	0.016	0.003	0.041	0.010	0.004	0.033	0.012	0.004	0.029	0.008	0.003
50 UNM	203	0.0197	0.033	0.020	0.004	0.051	0.012	0.005	0.041	0.016	0.005	0.037	0.011	0.004
60 UNM	169	0.0236	0.041	0.025	0.005	0.062	0.016	0.007	0.051	0.020	0.007	0.045	0.013	0.005
80 UNM	127	0.0315	0.051	0.032	0.007	0.082	0.020	0.008	0.062	0.025	0.008	0.056	0.016	0.007
100 UNM	102	0.0394	0.062	0.040	0.008	0.103	0.025	0.012	0.082	0.032	0.012	0.072	0.019	0.008
120 UNM	102	0.0472	0.082	0.050	0.012	0.124	0.032	0.015	0.103	0.040	0.015	0.092	0.025	0.012

Note: ♦ Minimum dimensions of slot widths. All other tabulated values are maximum dimensions.

Figure 6.4 Dimensions for standard miniature screws.

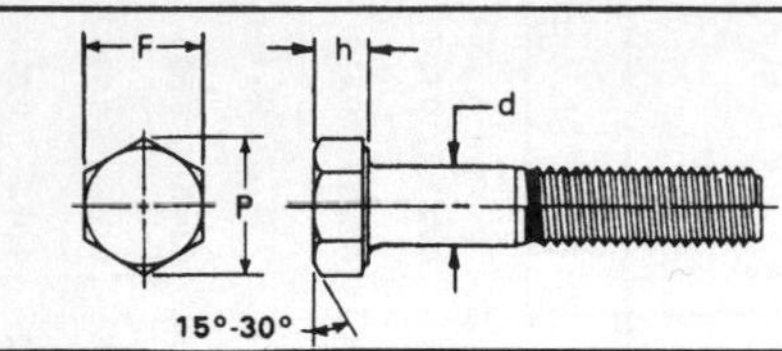

Diameter & thread pitch	d	F	P	h
M5 - 0.8	5.00	8.00	9.24	3.65
M6 - 1	6.00	10.00	11.55	4.15
M8 - 1.25	8.00	13.00	15.01	5.50
M10 - 1.50	10.00	16.00	18.48	6.63
M12 - 1.75	12.00	18.00	20.78	7.76
M14 - 2	14.00	21.00	24.25	9.09
M16 - 2	16.00	24.00	27.71	10.32
M20 - 2.5	20.00	30.00	34.64	12.88
M24 - 3	24.00	36.00	41.57	15.44
M30 - 3.5	30.00	46.00	53.12	19.48
M36 - 4	36.00	55.00	63.51	23.38

Note: Tabulated dimensions are in millimeters and are maximum values.

Figure 6.5 Dimensions for metric hex-cap screws.

Figure 6.6 Miniature metric screws.

Size	Flats	Points	Thickness
#0	5/32	0.180	0.050
#1	5/32	0.180	0.050
#2	3/16	0.217	0.066
#3	3/16	0.217	0.066
#4	1/4	0.289	0.098
#5	5/16	0.361	0.114
#6	5/16	0.361	0.114
#8	11/32	0.397	0.130
#10	3/8	0.433	0.130
1/4	7/16	0.505	0.226 0.163-jamb nut
5/16	1/2	0.577	0.273 0.195-jamb nut
3/8	9/16	0.650	0.337 0.227-jamb nut
7/16	11/16	0.794	0.385 0.260-jamb nut
1/2	3/4	0.866	0.448 0.323-jamb nut
5/8	15/16	1.083	0.559 0.387-jamb nut
3/4	1 1/8	1.299	0.665 0.446-jamb nut
7/8	1 5/16	1.516	0.776 0.510-jamb nut
1	1 1/2	1.732	0.887 0.575-jamb nut

Figure 6.7 Dimensions for American standard hex and jamb nuts.

Size	Flats	Points	Thickness
M1.6x0.35	3.20	3.70	1.30
M2x0.4	4.00	4.62	1.60
M2.5x0.45	5.00	5.77	2.00
M3x0.5	5.50	6.35	2.40
M3.5x0.6	6.00	6.93	2.80
M4x0.7	7.00	8.08	3.20
M5x0.8	8.00	9.24	4.70
M6x1	10.00	11.55	5.20
M8x1.25	13.00	15.01	6.80
M10x1.5	16.00	18.48	8.40
M12x1.75	18.00	20.78	10.80
M14x2	21.00	24.25	12.80
M16x2	24.00	27.71	14.80
M20x2.5	30.00	34.64	18.00
M24x3	36.00	41.57	21.50
M30x3.5	46.00	53.12	25.60
M36x4	55.00	63.51	31.00

Note: Tabulated dimensions are in millimeters. 1 mm = 0.03937"

Figure 6.8 Dimensions for metric standard nuts, hexagonal.

Size	Outside Diameter	Thickness
#0	3/16	0.028
#1	7/32	0.028
#2	1/4	0.036
#3	5/16	0.036
#4	3/8	0.045
#5	13/32	0.045
#6	7/16	0.045
#8	1/2	0.045
#10	9/16	0.045
1/4	47/64	0.071
5/16	7/8	0.071
3/8	1	0.071
7/16	1 1/8	0.071
1/2	1 1/4	0.112
5/8	1 3/4	0.112
3/4	2	0.112
7/8	2 1/4	0.174
1	2 1/2	0.174

Figure 6.9 Dimensions for American standard flat washers.

Size	Series	Outside Diameter	Thickness
1.6	Narrow	4.00	0.70
	Regular	5.00	0.70
	Wide	6.00	0.90
2	Narrow	5.00	0.90
	Regular	6.00	0.90
	Wide	8.00	0.90
2.5	Narrow	6.00	0.90
	Regular	8.00	0.90
	Wide	10.00	1.20
3	Narrow	7.00	0.90
	Regular	10.00	1.20
	Wide	12.00	1.40
3.5	Narrow	9.00	1.20
	Regular	10.00	1.40
	Wide	15.00	1.75
4	Narrow	10.00	1.20
	Regular	12.00	1.40
	Wide	16.00	2.30
5	Narrow	11.00	1.40
	Regular	15.00	1.75
	Wide	20.00	2.30
6	Narrow	13.00	1.75
	Regular	18.80	1.75
	Wide	25.40	2.30
8	Narrow	18.80	2.30
	Regular	25.40	2.30
	Wide	32.00	2.80
10	Narrow	20.00	2.30
	Regular	28.00	2.80
	Wide	39.00	3.50
12	Narrow	25.40	2.80
	Regular	34.00	3.50
	Wide	44.00	3.50
14	Narrow	28.00	2.80
	Regular	39.00	3.50
	Wide	50.00	4.00
16	Narrow	32.00	3.50
	Regular	44.00	4.00
	Wide	56.00	4.60
20	Narrow	39.00	4.00
	Regular	50.00	4.60
	Wide	66.00	5.10
24	Narrow	44.00	4.60
	Regular	56.00	5.10
	Wide	72.00	5.60
30	Narrow	56.00	5.10
	Regular	72.00	5.60
	Wide	90.00	6.40
36	Narrow	66.00	5.60
	Regular	90.00	6.40
	Wide	110.00	8.50

Figure 6.10 Dimensions for metric standard flat washers.

Nominal size		Shoulder screws d	D	h	s	T	L	Cap screws d	D	h	s
4	0.1120	—	—	—	—	—	—	0.1120	0.183	0.112	0.094
5	0.1250	—	—	—	—	—	—	0.1250	0.205	0.125	0.094
6	0.1380	—	—	—	—	—	—	0.1380	0.226	0.138	0.109
8	0.1640	—	—	—	—	—	—	0.1640	0.270	0.164	0.141
10	0.1900	—	—	—	—	—	—	0.1900	0.312	0.190	0.156
1/4	0.2500	0.2480	0.375	0.188	0.125	0.190-24	0.375	0.2500	0.375	0.250	0.188
5/16	0.3125	0.3105	0.438	0.219	0.156	0.250-20	0.438	0.3125	0.469	0.312	0.250
3/8	0.3750	0.3730	0.562	0.250	0.188	0.312-18	0.500	0.3750	0.562	0.375	0.312
7/16	0.4375	—	—	—	—	—	—	0.4375	0.656	0.438	0.375
1/2	0.5000	0.4980	0.750	0.312	0.250	0.375-16	0.625	0.5000	0.750	0.500	0.375
5/8	0.6250	0.6230	0.875	0.375	0.312	0.500-13	0.750	0.6250	0.938	0.625	0.500
3/4	0.7500	0.7480	1.000	0.500	0.375	0.625-11	0.875	0.7500	1.125	0.750	0.625
7/8	0.8750	—	—	—	—	—	—	0.8750	1.312	0.875	0.750
1	1.0000	0.9980	1.312	0.625	0.500	0.750-10	1.000	1.0000	1.500	1.000	0.750
1-1/8	1.1250	—	—	—	—	—	—	1.1250	1.688	1.125	0.875
1-1/4	1.2500	1.2480	1.750	0.750	0.625	0.875-9	1.125	1.2500	1.875	1.250	0.875
1-3/8	1.3750	—	—	—	—	—	—	1.3750	2.062	1.375	1.000
1-1/2	1.5000	1.4980	2.125	1.000	0.875	1.125-7	1.500	1.5000	2.250	1.500	1.000
1-3/4	1.7500	1.7480	2.375	1.125	1.000	1.250-7	1.750	1.7500	2.625	1.750	1.250
2	2.0000	1.9980	2.750	1.250	1.250	1.500-6	2.000	2.0000	3.000	2.000	1.500

Note: All tabulated dimensions are maximum values. See text for materials, hardness, etc.

Figure 6.11 American standard socket-head shoulder screws and socket-head cap screws.

SAE bolt head markings

SAE bolt head markings	Diameter, in.	Tensile strength, psi	Proof load, psi	
	1/4 - 3/4 7/8 - 1 1/2	74,000 psi 60,000	55,000 psi 33,000	Grade 2, *low or medium-carbon steel
	1/4 - 1 1 1/8 - 1 1/2	120,000 105,000	85,000 74,000	Grade 5, *medium carbon steel (Q/T)†
	-	120,000	85,000	Grade 5.1, screws
	1/4 - 1	120,000	85,000	Grade 5.2, low-carbon martensitic steel (Q/T)
	1/4 - 1 1/2	150,000	120,000	Grade 8, medium-carbon alloy steel (Q/T)
	1/4 - 1	150,000	120,000	Grade 8.2, low-carbon martensitic steel (Q/T)

*Highest usage grades †(Q/T) designates quenched and tempered

Figure 6.12 SAE bolt-head grade markings.

ASTM bolt head markings	Diameter, in.	Tensile strength, psi	Proof load, psi	
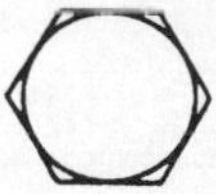	1/4 - 4	A & B-60,000 min. B-100,000 max.		A307 carbon steel
	1/4 - 1 1 1/8 - 1 1/2 1 3/4 - 3	120,000 105,000 90,000	85,000 74,000 55,000	A449 medium-carbon steel (Q/T)
 A325	1/2 - 1 1 1/8 - 1 1/2	120,000 105,000	85,000 74,000	A325 Type 1 medium carbon steel (Q/T)
 A325	1/2 - 1 1 1/8 - 1 1/2	120,000 105,000	85,000 74,000	A325 Type 2 low carbon martensitic steel (Q/T)
 A325	1/2 - 1 1 1/8 - 1 1/2	120,000 105,000	85,000 74,000	A325 Type 3 weathering steel (Q/T)
 A490	1/2 - 1 1/2	150,000	120,000	A490 alloy steel (Q/T)
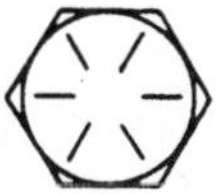	1/4 - 4	150,000	120,000	A354 grade BD alloy steel (Q/T)

(Q/T) designates quenched and tempered

Figure 6.13 ASTM bolt-head grade markings.

TABLE 6.1 Mechanical Requirements and Identification Marking for Bolts, Screws, Studs, Sems, and U Bolts[j]

Grade designation	Products	Nominal size dia, in	Full-size bolts, screws, studs, sems: Proof load (stress), lb/in²	Full-size bolts, screws, studs, sems: Tensile strength (stress) min, lb/in²	Machine test specimens of bolts, screws, and studs: Yield[a] strength (stress) min, lb/in²	Machine test specimens of bolts, screws, and studs: Tensile strength (stress) min, lb/in²	Machine test specimens of bolts, screws, and studs: Elongation[f] min, %	Machine test specimens of bolts, screws, and studs: Reduction of area min, %	Surface hardness: Rockwell 30N max	Core hardness: Rockwell Min	Core hardness: Rockwell Max	Grade identification marking[i]
1	Bolts, screws, studs	¼ to 1½	33,000[k]	60,000	36,000[b]	60,000	18	35	—	B70	B100	None
2	Bolts, screws, studs	¼ to ¾[c]	55,000[k]	74,000	57,000	74,000	18	35	—	B80	B100	
		Over ¾ to 1½	33,000	60,000	36,000[b]	60,000	18	35	—	B70	B100	None
4	Studs	¼ to 1½	65,000	115,000	100,000	115,000	10	35	—	C22	C32	None
5	Bolts, screws, studs	¼ to 1	85,000	120,000	92,000	120,000	14	35	54	C25	C34	
		Over 1 to 1½	74,000	105,000	81,000	105,000	14	35	50	C19	C30	
5.1[d]	Sems,[h] bolts, screws	No. 6 to ⅝	85,000	120,000	—	—	—	—	59.5[g]	C25	C40[g]	
		No. 6 to ½										
5.2	Bolts, screws	¼ to 1	85,000	120,000	92,000	120,000	14	35	56	C26	C36	

TABLE 6.1 Mechanical Requirements and Identification Marking for Bolts, Screws, Studs, Sems, and U Bolts[j] (*Continued*)

Grade designation	Products	Nominal size dia, in	Full-size bolts, screws, studs, sems		Machine test specimens of bolts, screws, and studs				Surface hardness	Core hardness		Grade identification marking[i]
			Proof load (stress), lb/in²	Tensile strength (stress) min, lb/in²	Yield[a] strength (stress) min, lb/in²	Tensile strength (stress) min, lb/in²	Elongation[f] min, %	Reduction of area min, %	Rockwell 30N max	Rockwell Min	Rockwell Max	
7[e]	Bolts, screws	¼ to 1½	105,000	133,000	115,000	133,000	12	35	54	C28	C34	
8	Bolts, screws, studs	¼ to 1½	120,000	150,000	130,000	150,000	12	35	58.6	C33	C39	
8.1	Studs	¼ to 1½	120,000	150,000	130,000	150,000	10	35	—	C32	C38	None
8.2	Bolts, screws	¼ to 1	120,000	150,000	130,000	150,000	10	35	58.6	C33	C39	

[a] Yield strength is stress at which a permanent set of 0.2% of gauge length occurs.
[b] Yield point shall apply instead of yield strength at 0.2% offset.
[c] Grade 2 requirements for sizes ¼ through ¾ in apply only to bolts and screws 6 in and shorter in length and to studs of all lengths. For bolts and screws longer than 6 in, grade 1 requirements shall apply.
[d] Grade 5 material heat treated before assembly with a hardened washer is an acceptable substitute.
[e] Grade 7 bolts and screws are roll threaded after heat treatment.
[f] Hex washer head and hex flange products without assembled washers shall have a core hardness not exceeding Rockwell C38 and a surface hardness not exceeding Rockwell 30N 57.5.
[g] Sems and similar products without washers.
[h] Not applicable to studs or slotted and cross-recess head products.
[i] Proof load test: Requirements in these grades only apply to stress relieved products.
SOURCE: Reprinted with permission, copyright 1992, Society of Automotive Engineers.

TABLE 6.2 Proof Load and Tensile Strength Requirements*

Nominal dia of product and threads per in	Stress area, in²	Grade 1		Grade 2		Grade 4		Grades 5 and 5.2†		Grade 5.1		Grade 7		Grades 8, 8.1, and 8.2†	
		Proof load, lb	Tensile strength min, lb	Proof load, lb	Tensile strength min, lb	Proof load, lb	Tensile strength min, lb	Proof load, lb	Tensile strength min, lb	Proof load, lb	Tensile strength min, lb	Proof load, lb	Tensile strength min, lb	Proof load, lb	Tensile strength min, lb
Coarse-Thread Series—UNC															
No. 6–32	0.00909	—	—	—	—	—	—	—	—	750	1,100	—	—	—	—
8–32	0.0140	—	—	—	—	—	—	—	—	1,200	1,700	—	—	—	—
10–24	0.0175	—	—	—	—	—	—	—	—	1,500	2,100	—	—	—	—
12–24	0.0242	—	—	—	—	—	—	—	—	2,050	2,900	—	—	—	—
¼–20	0.0318	1,050	1,900	1,750	2,350	2,050	3,650	2,700	3,800	2,700	3,800	3,350	4,250	3,800	4,750
5⁄16–18	0.0524	1,750	3,150	2,900	3,900	3,400	6,000	4,450	6,300	4,450	6,300	5,500	6,950	6,300	7,850
⅜–16	0.0775	2,550	4,650	4,250	5,750	5,050	8,400	6,600	9,300	6,600	9,300	8,150	10,300	9,300	11,600
7⁄16–14	0.1063	3,500	6,400	5,850	7,850	6,900	12,200	9,050	12,800	9,050	12,800	11,200	14,100	12,800	15,900
½–13	0.1419	4,700	8,500	7,800	10,500	9,200	16,300	12,100	17,000	12,100	17,000	14,900	18,900	17,000	21,300
9⁄16–12	0.182	6,000	10,900	10,000	13,500	11,800	20,900	15,500	21,800	15,500	21,800	19,100	24,200	21,800	27,300
⅝–11	0.226	7,450	13,600	12,400	16,700	14,700	25,400	19,200	27,100	19,200	27,100	23,700	30,100	27,100	33,900
¾–10	0.334	11,000	20,000	18,400	24,700	21,700	38,400	28,400	40,100	—	—	35,100	44,400	40,100	50,100
⅞–9	0.462	15,200	27,700	15,200	27,700	30,000	53,100	39,300	55,400	—	—	48,500	61,400	55,400	69,300
1–8	0.606	20,000	36,400	20,000	36,400	39,400	69,700	51,500	72,700	—	—	63,600	80,600	72,700	90,900
1⅛–7	0.763	25,200	45,800	25,200	45,800	49,600	87,700	56,500	80,100	—	—	80,100	101,500	91,600	114,400
1¼–7	0.969	32,000	58,100	32,000	58,100	63,000	111,400	71,700	101,700	—	—	101,700	127,700	116,300	145,400
1⅜–6	1.155	38,100	69,300	38,100	69,300	75,100	132,800	85,500	121,300	—	—	121,300	153,600	138,600	173,200
1½–6	1.405	46,400	84,300	46,400	84,300	91,300	161,600	104,000	147,500	—	—	147,500	186,900	168,600	210,800

TABLE 6.2 Proof Load and Tensile Strength Requirements* (*Continued*)

Nominal dia of product and threads per in	Stress area, in²	Grade 1		Grade 2		Grade 4		Grades 5 and 5.2†		Grade 5.1		Grade 7		Grades 8, 8.1, and 8.2†	
		Proof load, lb	Tensile strength min, lb	Proof load, lb	Tensile strength min, lb	Proof load, lb	Tensile strength min, lb	Proof load, lb	Tensile strength min, lb	Proof load, lb	Tensile strength min, lb	Proof load, lb	Tensile strength min, lb	Proof load, lb	Tensile strength min, lb
Fine-Thread Series—UNF															
No. 6–40	0.01015	—	—	—	—	—	—	—	—	850	1,200	—	—	—	—
8–36	0.01474	—	—	—	—	—	—	—	—	1,250	1,750	—	—	—	—
10–32	0.0200	—	—	—	—	—	—	—	—	1,700	2,400	—	—	—	—
12–28	0.0258	—	—	—	—	—	—	—	—	2,200	3,100	—	—	—	—
¼–28	0.0364	1,200	2,200	2,000	2,700	2,350	4,200	3,100	4,350	3,100	4,350	3,800	4,850	4,350	5,450
5/16–24	0.0580	1,900	3,500	3,200	4,300	3,750	6,700	4,900	6,950	4,900	6,950	6,100	7,700	6,950	8,700
⅜–24	0.0878	2,900	5,250	4,800	6,500	5,700	10,100	7,450	10,500	7,450	10,500	9,200	11,700	10,500	13,200
7/16–20	0.1187	3,900	7,100	6,550	8,800	7,700	13,650	10,100	14,200	10,100	14,200	12,500	15,800	14,200	17,800
½–20	0.1599	5,300	9,600	8,800	11,800	10,400	18,400	13,600	19,200	13,600	19,200	16,800	21,300	19,200	24,000
9/16–18	0.203	6,700	12,200	11,200	15,000	13,200	23,300	17,300	24,400	17,300	24,400	21,300	27,000	24,400	30,400
⅝–18	0.256	8,450	15,400	14,100	18,900	16,600	29,400	21,800	30,700	21,800	30,700	26,900	34,000	30,700	38,400
¾–16	0.373	12,300	22,400	20,500	27,600	24,200	42,900	31,700	44,800	—	—	39,200	49,500	44,800	56,000
⅞–14	0.509	16,800	30,500	16,800	30,500	33,100	58,500	43,300	61,100	—	—	53,400	67,700	61,100	76,400
1–12	0.663	21,900	39,800	21,900	39,800	43,100	76,200	56,400	79,600	—	—	69,600	88,200	79,600	99,400
1–14 uns	0.679	22,400	40,700	22,400	40,700	44,100	78,100	57,700	81,500	—	—	71,300	90,300	81,500	101,900
1⅛–12	0.856	28,200	51,400	28,200	51,400	55,600	98,400	63,300	89,900	—	—	89,900	113,800	102,700	128,400
1¼–12	1.073	35,400	64,400	35,400	64,400	69,700	123,400	79,400	112,700	—	—	112,700	142,700	128,800	161,000
1⅜–12	1.315	43,400	78,900	43,400	78,900	85,500	151,200	97,300	138,100	—	—	138,100	174,900	157,800	197,200
1½–12	1.581	52,200	94,900	52,200	94,900	102,800	181,800	117,000	166,000	—	—	166,000	210,300	189,700	237,200

* Proof loads and tensile strengths are computed by multiplying the proof load stresses and tensile strength stresses by the stress area of the thread.

The stress area of sizes and thread series may be computed from the formula: $A_6 = 0.7854\left[D - \frac{0.9743}{n}\right]^2$, where D equals nominal diameter in inches and n equals threads per inch.

† Grades 5.2 and 8.2 applicable to sizes ¼ through 1 in.

SOURCE: Reprinted with permission, copyright 1992, Society of Automotive Engineers.

TABLE 6.3 Tensile Load Requirements for Machine Screws

Nominal size or basic major dia of thread and threads per in		Stress area, in^2	Tensile strength,* lb, min	
			Grade 60M	Grade 120M
No. 4–40	0.112	0.00604	360	720
4–48	0.112	0.00661	390	780
5–40	0.125	0.00796	470	940
5–44	0.125	0.00830	490	980
6–32	0.138	0.00909	550	1100
6–40	0.138	0.01015	600	1200
8–32	0.164	0.0140	850	1700
8–36	0.164	0.01474	880	1750
10–24	0.190	0.0175	1050	2100
10–32	0.190	0.0200	1200	2400
12–24	0.216	0.0242	1450	2900
12–28	0.216	0.0258	1550	3100
¼–20	0.250	0.0318	1900	3800
¼–28	0.250	0.0364	2200	4350
5/16–18	0.312	0.0524	3,150	6,300
5/16–24	0.312	0.0580	3,500	6,950
⅜–16	0.375	0.0775	4,650	9,300
⅜–24	0.375	0.0878	5,250	10,500
7/16–14	0.438	0.1063	6,400	12,800
7/16–20	0.438	0.1187	7,100	14,200
½–13	0.500	0.1419	8,500	17,000
½–20	0.500	0.1599	9,600	19,200
9/16–12	0.562	0.182	10,900	21,800
9/16–18	0.562	0.203	12,200	24,400
⅝–11	0.625	0.226	13,600	27,100
⅝–18	0.625	0.256	15,400	30,700
¾–10	0.750	0.334	20,100	40,100
¾–16	0.750	0.373	22,400	44,800

* Tensile strength values for grade 60M and grade 120M are based on 60,000 and 120,000 lb/in^2, respectively.

SOURCE: Reprinted with permission, copyright 1992, Society of Automotive Engineers.

TABLE 6.4 Proof Load and Hardness Requirements for Nuts*

Nut grade	Nut size dia, in	Proof load stress, lb/in²† — Thread series: UNC 8 UN	UNF, 12 UN and finer	Rockwell hardness
2‡	¼ to 1½	90,000	90,000	C32 max
5	¼ to 1	120,000	109,000	C32 max
	Over 1 to 1½	105,000	94,000	C32 max
8	¼ to ⅝	150,000	150,000	C24–C32
	Over ⅝ to 1			C26–C34
	Over 1 to 1½			C26–C36

* Values listed are not normally applicable to jam, slotted, castle, heavy, or thick nuts.

† The proof load in pounds for a nut is computed by multiplying the proof load stress for the nut grade, size, and thread series, and the stress area for the applicable size and thread.

‡ Normally applicable to square nuts only. Also, square nuts normally available in Grade 2 only.

SOURCE: Reprinted with permission, copyright 1992, Society of Automotive Engineers.

6.1.3 Tightening torques and clamp loads of the different grades and sizes of machine bolts

Table 6.5 shows the tightening torques and clamp loads produced for class 2, 5, and 8 steel bolts. These three classes of bolts are used most commonly in industry. Class 2 bolts are for noncritical general commercial applications, class 5 bolts are used extensively where more tightening loads are required than allowable with class 2 bolts, and class 8 bolts are used where critical highly loaded bolt connections are required. Note that American standard hex nuts are produced in classes 2, 5, and 8 according to Table 6.4, which shows the proof load stress ratings for all three classes. A nut should be of the same or higher strength class as the bolt used for each particular application.

Calculating tightening torque values and clamp loads for standard bolts. The clamp load ranges shown in Table 6.5 are for applications developing 100 and 75 percent of the minimum yield strength for each respective bolt series. Torque values listed in this table are given in pounds-feet (lb·ft). In Table 6.5, the maximum clamp load was determined using the minimum yield strength (lb/in²) allowable for each bolt or screw grade (see Figs. 6.12 to 6.16). The minimum

TABLE 6.5 Tightening Torque Ranges for American Standard Steel Bolts (Hardware, Dry, Nonlubricated, and Zinc Plated)

	SAE grade 2		SAE grade 5		SAE grade 8	
Bolt size	Tightening torque range, lb·ft	Clamp load range, lb	Tightening torque range, lb·ft	Clamp load range, lb	Tightening torque range, lb·ft	Clamp load range, lb
¼–20	5.7–4.3	1,813–1,360	9.1–6.9	2,926–2,195	12.9–9.7	4,134–3,101
¼–28	6.5–4.9	2,075–1,556	10.5–7.9	3,349–2,512	14.8–11.1	4,732–3,549
5/16–18	11.7–8.8	2,987–2,240	18.8–14.1	4,821–3,616	26.2–20.0	6,812–5,109
5/16–24	12.9–9.7	3,306–2,480	20.8–15.6	5,336–4,002	29.5–22.1	7,540–5,655
⅜–16	20.7–15.5	4,418–3,314	33.4–25.1	7,130–5,348	47.2–35.4	10,075–7,556
⅜–24	23.5–17.6	5,005–3,754	37.9–28.4	8,078–6,059	53.5–40.1	11,414–8,561
7/16–14	33.1–24.9	6,059–4,544	53.5–40.1	9,780–7,335	75.6–56.7	13,819–10,364
7/16–20	37.0–27.8	6,766–5,075	59.7–44.8	10,920–8,190	84.4–63.3	15,431–11,573
½–13	50.6–37.9	8,088–6,066	81.6–61.2	13,055–9,791	1115.3–86.5	18,447–13,835
½–20	57.0–42.7	9,114–5,835	91.9–69.0	14,711–11,033	130.0–97.4	20,787–15,590
9/16–12	73.0–54.7	10,374–7,780	117.7–88.1	16,744–12,558	166.4–124.8	23,660–17,745
9/16–18	81.4–61.0	11,571–8,678	131.3–98.1	18,676–14,007	185.6–139.2	26,390–19,793
⅝–11	100.6–75.5	12,882–9,662	162.4–121.8	20.792–15,594	229.5–172.1	29,380–22,035
⅝–18	114–85.5	14,592–10,944	184–138	23,552–17,664	260.0–195.0	33,280–24,960
¾–10	178.5–133.9	19,038–14,279	288–216	30,728–23,046	407.1–305.3	43,420–35,368
¾–16	199–149.5	21,261–15,946	321.7–241.3	34,316–25,737	454.6–341.0	48,490–45,045
⅞–9	288–216	26,334–19,751	464.9–348.7	42,504–31,878	656.9–492.7	60,060–45,045
⅞–14	317–238	29,013–19,751	512.2–384.1	46,828–35,121	723.7–542.8	66,170–49,628
1–8	432–324	34,542–25,907	696.9–522.7	55,752–41,814	984.8–738.6	78,780–59,085
1–12	472–354	37,791–28,343	761.1–571.8	60,996–45,747	1077–808	86,190–64,643

clamp load shown in Table 6.5 was determined by reducing the maximum clamp load by 25 percent.

Example For a grade 5 bolt of ½ to 13 size, the minimum yield strength is 92,000 lb/in² according to Table 6.1. Stress area of a ½ to 13 bolt is 0.1419 in² (see figures in the following thread section). Then, the clamp load L is

$$\begin{aligned} L &= \text{minimum yield strength} \times \text{stress area of bolt} \\ &= 92{,}000 \times 0.1419 \\ &= 13{,}055 \text{ lb} \end{aligned}$$

The tightening torque is calculated from

$$T = KLD$$

where T = tightening torque, lb·in
K = dynamic coefficient of friction, min = 0.15 (dry and zinc plated)
L = clamp load, lb
D = nominal bolt diameter, in

Then,

$$\begin{aligned} T &= 0.15 \times 13{,}055 \times 0.50 \\ &= 979 \text{ lb·in, or } 81.6 \text{ lb·ft} \end{aligned}$$

which agrees with the maximum torque value shown in Table 6.5 for this particular bolt (½ to 13, grade 5).

Note: Do not specify torque loads as foot pounds (ft·lb) or inch pounds (in·lb) because these are measures of energy or work, not torque. Also, do not specify torque loads as pounds per foot (lb/ft) because this is a force measurement per linear distance and not a torque load. The metric equivalent of U.S. Customary torque loads given in pounds-feet (lb·ft) is newton-meters (N·m).

The tightening torques and clamp loads for any machine bolt or screw may be effectively calculated using this procedure. To find the minimum yield strength of the material from which the bolt or screw is made, see Chap. 5, "Materials and Their Uses." Tightening torques and clamp loads for bolts or screws made from stainless steels or nonferrous alloys may thus be calculated. Because of the general nature of the torque equation and unknown coefficients of dynamic friction for various material combinations, it is advisable to reduce the minimum yield strength of each material by 25 to 30 percent prior to making the torque calculation from the calculated clamp load. Thus, if the minimum yield strength of the material from which the bolt is made is 45,000 lb/in^2, reduce this value by 25 to 30 percent, calculate the allowable clamp load, and then calculate the torque required to produce this clamp load.

Controlling preload on a threaded fastener

Turn of nut or head method. The bolt or screw is first torqued to 60 to 80 percent of its minimum yield strength (see preceding calculation method). Then the nut or the head of the bolt (when a nut is not used, as in a tapped hole) is tightened an additional half turn (180°). This amount of additional turn usually puts the bolt or screw into or beyond its yield strength point.

This method takes into account the recommendations of some authorities that the bolt should be tightened to its yield strength and is a reliable way to control preload on a threaded fastener. Structural steel joints have been preloaded as described by the construction and structures industries for more than 50 years. This method is quick and economical for the majority of applications found throughout industry. In a critical application, an accurate torque wrench should be used.

6.1.4 Set, self-tapping, thread-forming, and wood screws

Figures 6.14 and 6.15 show the American standard socket set screws with dimensions and applications data. The size of the hex wrench required for each set-screw size is also shown. Figure 6.16 shows a chart of the standard self-tapping and thread-forming screws. Types AB, A, B, BF, and C are thread-forming, while types D, F, G, T, BF, and BT are thread-cutting or self-tapping. Type U is a spiral screw type that is driven or press-fit into the appropriate-sized hole. All thread forms shown are 60° V thread.

Holes for self-tapping and thread-forming screws. Extensive tables of recommended hole sizes for self-tapping and thread-forming screws are available from screw manufacturers. Because of the great variety of materials and thickness ranges possible for applying these types of screws, no tables are given here. In actual practice, you may measure the outside diameter of the screw thread and the root diameter and then take the mean difference to find an approximate hole diameter for the particular screw and material combination. A few trial combinations will give you the exact drill size to use for your application.

Figure 6.17 shows American standard wood screws and their dimensions. Wood screws are used by pattern makers and in wooden form blocks for vacuum-forming equipment applications (vacuum-forming plastics). Head styles of the various machine screws are shown in Fig. 6.18.

6.1.5 Wrench clearances for design applications

An important point that is sometimes forgotten in basic mechanical design work is wrench clearances. Figures 6.19 and 6.20 show an extensive listing of required clearances for open-end, box, and socket wrenches. Allowances should be made in initial design work to allow for more clearance than shown in the figures when possible. Tabulated dimensions shown in the figures are minimum allowables. No allowances have been made for torquing devices, since these are extensive and variable according to manufacturer. Figure 6.21 shows the dimensions and mechanical properties of hex keys (Allen wrenches).

Figure 6.22 shows the wrench openings for American standard nuts. Figure 6.23 is a photograph of a sample of hardware components showing some of the screws, bolts, nuts, washers, pins, and special fasteners that are used throughout industry. The numbers and styles of standard hardware components are enormous, and new components are being developed constantly. Hardware manufacturers produce catalogs that show the dimensions and mechanical properties of their particular fasteners or hardware components. The fastener handbooks available from the Industrial Fasteners Institute (IFI) are among the most complete and technically correct for both the inch series and metric components (see Chap. 23).

6.2 Thread Systems: American Standard and Metric (60° V)

The international standard screw threads consist of the unified inch series and the metric series. The metric series is standardized into the M and MJ profiles. The unified series is designated as UN (unified national). Another unified profile is designated as UNR, which has a rounded root on the external thread. The metric profile MJ also has a rounded root on the external thread and a larger minor diameter of both the internal and external threads. Both the UNR and MJ profiles are used for applications requiring high fatigue strength; they are also employed in aerospace applications.

A constant-pitch unified series is also standardized and consists of 4, 6, 8, 12, 16, 20, 28, and 32 threads per inch. These are used for sizes over 1 in diameter, and the 8UN, 12UN, and 16UN are the *preferred* pitches. Figure 6.24 shows that both the unified and metric M series use the same profile geometry. The other common screw thread systems are shown in Chap. 7 of this *Handbook* and include the Acme, stub Acme, Whitworth, buttress, and others.

The unified threads are further classified as UN A for external threads and UN B for internal threads. The UN series contains three fit classes, 1A, 2A, and 3A for external threads and 1B, 2B, and 3B for internal threads. A typical engineering drawing call-out for a coarse external class 2 thread in ¼ to 20 size would be

0.250–20UNC–2A

A ¼ to 20 size class 2 tapped hole would be shown as

0.250–20UNC–2B

Thread fit classes. Unified thread series and interference-fit threads.

Unified thread series

1A	External, loose fit for easy assembly and noncritical uses
2A	External, general applications where plating may be applied
3A	External, tight fit used for great accuracy; no plating allowance provided
1B	Internal, loose fit for easy assembly and noncritical uses
2B	Internal, general applications where plating may be applied
3B	Internal, tight fit used for great accuracy; no plating allowance provided

Class 5 interference-fit threads

Class 5 external

NC5 HF	For driving in hard ferrous materials over 160 BHN
NC5 CSF	For driving in copper alloys and soft ferrous materials under 160 BHN
NC5 ONF	For other nonferrous materials, any hardness

Class 5 internal

NC5 IF	Entire ferrous material range
NC5 INF	Entire nonferrous material range

(Text continued on page 442.)

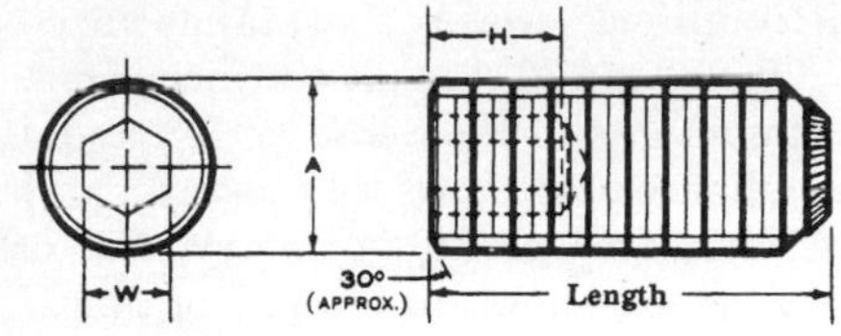

size	threads per inch		A			C		D		F		H	W
	UNC	UNF	max.	min. UNC	min. UNF	max.	min.	max.	min.	max.	min.	min.	nom.
#0	....	80	.0600	....	.0568	.033	.027	.040	.037	.017	.013	.022	.028
#1	64	72	.0730	.0692	.0695	.040	.033	.049	.045	.021	.017	.028	.035
#2	56	64	.0860	.0819	.0822	.047	.039	.057	.053	.024	.020	.028	.035
#3	48	56	.0990	.0945	.0949	.054	.045	.066	.062	.027	.023	.040	.050
#4	40	48	.1120	.1069	.1075	.061	.051	.075	.070	.030	.026	.040	.050
#5	40	44	.1250	.1199	.1202	.067	.057	.083	.078	.033	.027	.050	.0625
#6	32	40	.1380	.1320	.1329	.074	.064	.092	.087	.038	.032	.050	.0625
#8	32	36	.1640	.1580	.1585	.087	.076	.109	.103	.043	.037	.062	.0781
#10	24	32	.1900	.1828	.1840	.102	.088	.127	.120	.049	.041	.075	.0937
¼	20	28	.2500	.2419	.2435	.132	.118	.156	.149	.0565	.0585	.100	.125
5/16	18	24	.3125	.3038	.3053	.172	.156	.203	.195	.082	.074	.125	.1562
3/8	16	24	.3750	.3656	.3678	.212	.194	.250	.241	.0987	.0887	.150	.1875
7/16	14	20	.4375	.4272	.4294	.252	.232	.296	.287	.114	.104	.175	.2187
½	13	20	.5000	.4891	.4919	.291	.270	.343	.334	.130	.120	.200	.250
9/16	12	18	.5625	.5511	.5538	.332	.309	.390	.379	.1456	.1356	.200	.250
5/8	11	18	.6250	.6129	.6163	.371	.347	.468	.456	.164	.148	.250	.3125
¾	10	16	.7500	.7371	.7406	.450	.425	.562	.549	.1955	.1795	.300	.375
7/8	9	14	.8750	.8611	.8647	.530	.502	.656	.642	.2267	.2107	.400	.500
1	8	12	1.0000	.9850	.9886	.609	.579	.750	.734	.260	.240	.450	.5625
1⅛	7	12	1.1250	1.1086	1.1136	.689	.655	.843	.826	.291	.271	.450	.5625
1¼	7	12	1.2500	1.2336	1.2386	.767	.733	.937	.920	.3225	.3025	.500	.625
1⅜	6	12	1.3750	1.3568	1.3636	.848	.808	1.031	1.011	.3537	.3337	.500	.625
1½	6	12	1.5000	1.4818	1.4886	.926	.886	1.125	1.105	.385	.365	.600	.750

Figure 6.14 Socket set-screw dimensions.

Point Types

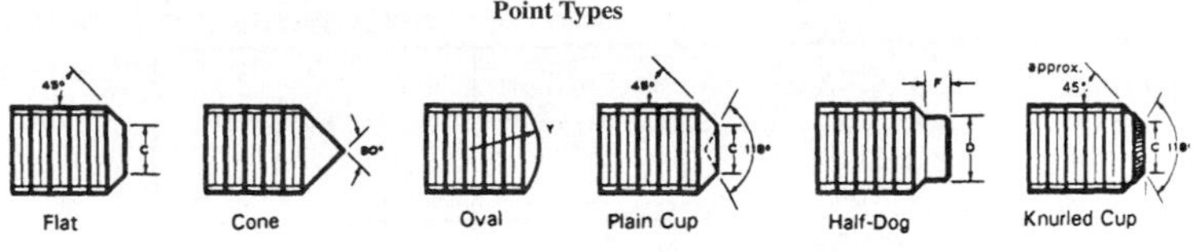

Application Data

Y	tap drill size			recommended seating torques – Pound-inches								
				regular and LOC-WEL screws			self-locking with NYLOK					
rad.	size	UNC	UNF	min. screw length	alloy steel	stain-less	min. screw length	alloy steel	stain-less	min. screw length	alloy steel	stain-less
.047	#0	....	1.25mm	3/32	.5	.4	3/32	.4	.3	1/8	.5	.4
.055	#1	1.5mm	1.5mm	3/32	1.5	1.2	1/8	1.2	1.0	5/32	1.5	1.2
.062	#2	#50	1.85mm	3/32	1.5	1.2	1/8	1.2	1.0	5/32	1.5	1.2
.078	#3	#46	2.1mm	3/32	5	4	5/32-3/16	4	3	7/32	5	4
.084	#4	2.3mm	#42	3/32	5	4	5/32-3/16	4	3	7/32	5	4
.093	#5	#37	#37	5/32	9	7	3/16	7	6	1/4	9	7
.109	#6	#33	#32	1/8	9	7	3/16	7	6	1/4	9	7
.125	#8	#29	3.5mm	1/8	20	16	1/4	16	13	5/16	20	16
.141	#10	#24	#20	5/32	33	26	1/4-5/16	28	22	3/8	33	26
.188	1/4	#6	5.5mm	3/16	87	70	1/4-7/16	52	42	1/2	87	70
.234	5/16	G	I	1/4	165	130	5/16-7/16	90	72	5/8	165	130
.281	3/8	O	8.6mm	5/16	290	230	3/8-1/2	200	160	3/4	290	230
.328	7/16	9.4mm	25/64	3/8	430	340	7/16-3/4	300	240	7/8	430	340
.375	1/2	27/64	11.5mm	1/2	620	500	1/2-3/4	500	400	7/8	620	500
.422	9/16	31/64	1/2	1/2	620	500	1/2-3/4	500	400	7/8	620	500
.468	5/8	17/32	14.5mm	9/16	1,225	980	5/8-7/8	980	780	1	1,225	980
.562	3/4	21/32	17.5mm	5/8	2,125	1,700	3/4-1 1/8	1,700	1,360	1 1/4	2,125	1,700
.656	7/8	49/64	20.5mm	3/4	5,000	4,000	3/4-1 1/4	3,650	2,920	1 5/16	5,000	4,000
.750	1	7/8	23.5	7/8	7,000	5,600	7/8-1 5/16	5,200	4,160	1 1/2	7,000	5,600
.044	1 1/8	25mm	1 3/64	1	7,000	5,600	....	....	....	....	....	....
.938	1 1/4	1 7/64	1 11/64	1 1/8	9,600	7,700	....	....	....	....	....	....
1.032	1 3/8	1 7/32	1 19/64	1 1/4	9,600	7,700	....	....	....	....	....	....
1.125	1 1/2	34mm	36mm	1 1/4	11,320	9,100	....	....	....	....	....	....

Figure 6.15 Set-screw point types.

Type	ANSI Standard
	AB
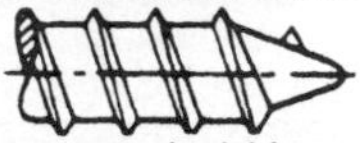 Not Recommended-Use type AB	A
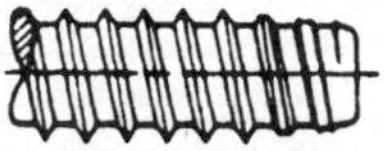	B
	BP
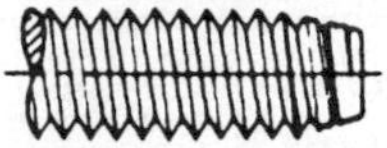	C
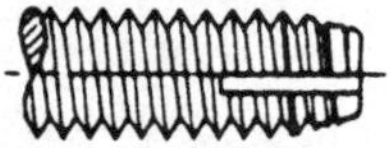	D
	F
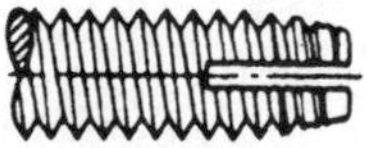	G
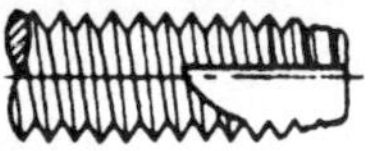	T
	BF
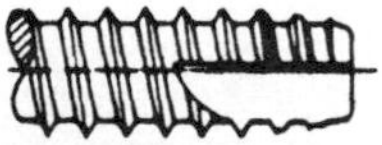	BT
	U

Figure 6.16 Self-tapping and thread-forming screw types.

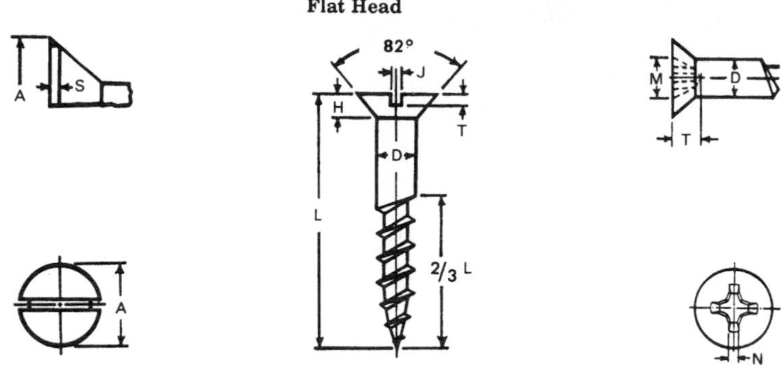

SLOTTED | **PHILLIPS**

	D	A			S	H		J		T			D	M		T	N	
Nominal Size	Basic Diameter of Screw	Head Diameter			Flat on Min Screw	Height of Head		Width of Slot		Depth of Slot		Number Threads per Inch	Basic Diameter of Screw	Diameter of Recess		Depth of Recess	Width of Recess	Driver Size
		Max Sharp	Min Sharp	Absolute Min with Max S		Max	Min	Max	Min	Max	Min			Max	Min	Max	Min	
0	0.060	0.119	0.105	0.099	0.002	0.035	0.026	0.023	0.016	0.015	0.010	32	0.060	0.069	0.056	0.043	0.014	0
1	0.073	0.146	0.130	0.123	0.003	0.043	0.033	0.026	0.019	0.019	0.012	28	0.073	0.077	0.064	0.051	0.015	0
2	0.086	0.172	0.156	0.147	0.003	0.051	0.040	0.031	0.023	0.023	0.015	26	0.086	0.102	0.089	0.063	0.017	1
3	0.099	0.199	0.181	0.171	0.004	0.059	0.048	0.035	0.027	0.027	0.017	24	0.099	0.107	0.094	0.068	0.018	1
4	0.112	0.225	0.207	0.195	0.004	0.067	0.055	0.039	0.031	0.030	0.020	22	0.112	0.128	0.115	0.089	0.018	1
5	0.125	0.252	0.232	0.220	0.005	0.075	0.062	0.043	0.035	0.034	0.022	20	0.125	0.154	0.141	0.086	0.027	2
6	0.138	0.279	0.257	0.244	0.005	0.083	0.069	0.048	0.039	0.038	0.024	18	0.138	0.174	0.161	0.106	0.029	3
7	0.151	0.305	0.283	0.268	0.005	0.091	0.076	0.048	0.039	0.041	0.027	16	0.151	0.189	0.176	0.121	0.031	2
8	0.164	0.332	0.308	0.292	0.006	0.100	0.084	0.054	0.045	0.045	0.029	15	0.164	0.204	0.191	0.136	0.032	2
9	0.177	0.358	0.334	0.316	0.006	0.108	0.091	0.054	0.045	0.049	0.032	14	0.177	0.214	0.201	0.146	0.033	2
10	0.190	0.385	0.359	0.340	0.007	0.116	0.098	0.060	0.050	0.053	0.034	13	0.190	0.258	0.245	0.146	0.034	3
12	0.216	0.438	0.410	0.389	0.008	0.132	0.112	0.067	0.056	0.060	0.039	11	0.216	0.283	0.270	0.171	0.036	3
14	0.242	0.491	0.461	0.437	0.009	0.148	0.127	0.075	0.064	0.068	0.044	10	0.242	0.303	0.290	0.191	0.039	3
16	0.268	0.544	0.512	0.485	0.010	0.164	0.141	0.075	0.064	0.075	0.049	9	0.268	0.327	0.314	0.216	0.045	3
18	0.294	0.597	0.563	0.534	0.011	0.180	0.155	0.084	0.072	0.083	0.054	8	0.294	0.378	0.365	0.230	0.062	4
20	0.320	0.650	0.614	0.582	0.012	0.196	0.170	0.084	0.072	0.090	0.059	8	0.320	0.393	0.380	0.245	0.065	4
24	0.372	0.756	0.716	0.679	0.013	0.228	0.198	0.094	0.081	0.105	0.069	7	0.372	0.424	0.411	0.276	0.069	4

Figure 6.17 American standard wood screw dimensions.

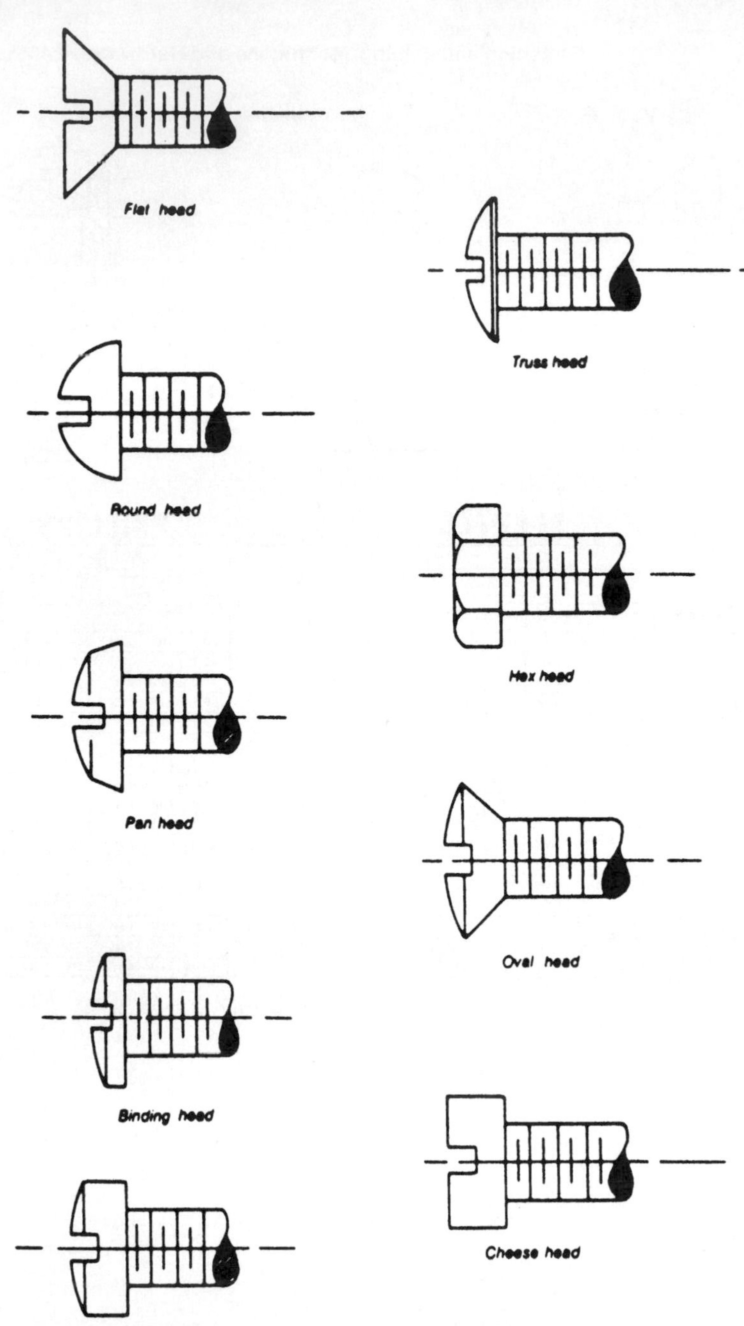

Figure 6.18 Head styles of standard machine screws.

Clearances for Open-End Wrench 15° and Socket Wrench (Standard Length)

(Derived from SAE Aeronautical Standard)

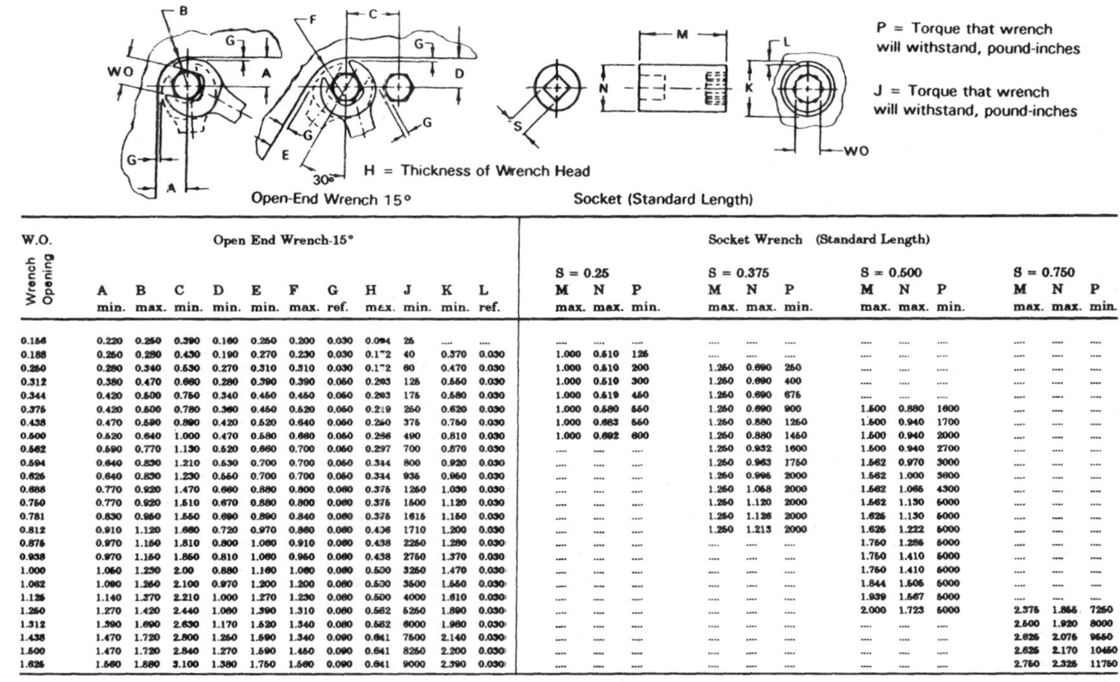

W.O.	Open End Wrench-15°											Socket Wrench (Standard Length)											
												S = 0.25			S = 0.375			S = 0.500			S = 0.750		
Wrench Opening	A	B	C	D	E	F	G	H	J	K	L	M	N	P	M	N	P	M	N	P	M	N	P
	min.	max.	min.	min.	min.	max.	ref.	max.	min.	min.	ref.	max.	max.	min.	max.	max.	min.	max.	max.	min.	max.	max.	min.
0.156	0.220	0.250	0.390	0.160	0.250	0.200	0.030	0.094	25	....	....	....	....	....	....	....	....	....	....	....	....	....	....
0.188	0.250	0.280	0.430	0.190	0.270	0.230	0.030	0.172	40	0.370	0.030	1.000	0.510	125	....	....	....	....	....	....	....	....	....
0.250	0.280	0.340	0.530	0.270	0.310	0.310	0.030	0.172	60	0.470	0.030	1.000	0.510	200	1.250	0.690	250	....	....	....	....	....	....
0.312	0.380	0.470	0.660	0.280	0.390	0.390	0.050	0.203	125	0.550	0.030	1.000	0.510	300	1.250	0.690	400	....	....	....	....	....	....
0.344	0.420	0.500	0.750	0.340	0.450	0.450	0.050	0.203	175	0.580	0.030	1.000	0.519	450	1.250	0.690	675	....	....	....	....	....	....
0.375	0.420	0.500	0.780	0.360	0.450	0.520	0.050	0.219	250	0.620	0.030	1.000	0.580	550	1.250	0.690	900	1.500	0.880	1600	....	....	....
0.438	0.470	0.590	0.890	0.420	0.520	0.640	0.050	0.250	375	0.750	0.030	1.000	0.683	550	1.250	0.880	1250	1.500	0.940	1700	....	....	....
0.500	0.520	0.640	1.000	0.470	0.580	0.660	0.050	0.266	490	0.810	0.030	1.000	0.692	600	1.250	0.880	1450	1.500	0.940	2000	....	....	....
0.562	0.590	0.770	1.130	0.520	0.660	0.700	0.050	0.297	700	0.870	0.030	....	....	....	1.250	0.932	1600	1.500	0.940	2700	....	....	....
0.594	0.640	0.830	1.210	0.530	0.700	0.700	0.050	0.344	800	0.920	0.030	....	....	....	1.250	0.963	1750	1.562	0.970	3000	....	....	....
0.625	0.640	0.830	1.230	0.550	0.700	0.700	0.050	0.344	936	0.950	0.030	....	....	....	1.250	0.995	2000	1.562	1.000	3600	....	....	....
0.688	0.770	0.920	1.470	0.660	0.880	0.800	0.060	0.375	1250	1.030	0.030	....	....	....	1.250	1.058	2000	1.562	1.065	4300	....	....	....
0.750	0.770	0.920	1.510	0.670	0.880	0.800	0.060	0.375	1500	1.120	0.030	....	....	....	1.250	1.120	2000	1.562	1.130	5000	....	....	....
0.781	0.830	0.950	1.550	0.690	0.890	0.840	0.060	0.375	1615	1.150	0.030	....	....	....	1.250	1.128	2000	1.625	1.130	5000	....	....	....
0.812	0.910	1.120	1.660	0.720	0.970	0.860	0.060	0.436	1710	1.200	0.030	....	....	....	1.250	1.213	2000	1.625	1.222	5000	....	....	....
0.875	0.970	1.150	1.810	0.800	1.060	0.910	0.060	0.438	2250	1.280	0.030	....	....	....	....	....	....	1.750	1.285	5000	....	....	....
0.938	0.970	1.150	1.850	0.810	1.060	0.950	0.060	0.438	2750	1.370	0.030	....	....	....	....	....	....	1.750	1.410	5000	....	....	....
1.000	1.060	1.230	2.00	0.880	1.160	1.060	0.060	0.500	3250	1.470	0.030	....	....	....	....	....	....	1.750	1.410	5000	....	....	....
1.062	1.090	1.250	2.100	0.970	1.200	1.200	0.060	0.500	3500	1.550	0.030	....	....	....	....	....	....	1.844	1.505	5000	....	....	....
1.125	1.140	1.370	2.210	1.000	1.270	1.230	0.060	0.500	4000	1.610	0.030	....	....	....	....	....	....	1.939	1.567	5000	....	....	....
1.250	1.270	1.420	2.440	1.060	1.390	1.310	0.080	0.562	5250	1.890	0.030	....	....	....	....	....	....	2.000	1.723	5000	2.375	1.865	7250
1.312	1.390	1.690	2.630	1.170	1.520	1.340	0.080	0.562	6000	1.980	0.030	....	....	....	....	....	....	....	....	....	2.500	1.920	8000
1.438	1.470	1.720	2.800	1.250	1.590	1.340	0.090	0.641	7500	2.140	0.030	....	....	....	....	....	....	....	....	....	2.625	2.075	9550
1.500	1.470	1.720	2.840	1.270	1.590	1.450	0.090	0.641	8250	2.200	0.030	....	....	....	....	....	....	....	....	....	2.625	2.170	10450
1.625	1.560	1.880	3.100	1.380	1.750	1.560	0.090	0.641	9000	2.390	0.030	....	....	....	....	....	....	....	....	....	2.750	2.325	11750

Note: P = Torque that wrench will withstand, pound-inches. No allowances have been made for torque devices. H = wrench head thickness. J = Torque that wrench will withstand, pound-inches. Tabulated dimensions are in inches.

Figure 6.19 Wrench clearance chart.

Wrench Clearances for Standard Box Wrenches - 12 Point Type
(Derived from SAE Aeronautical Standard)

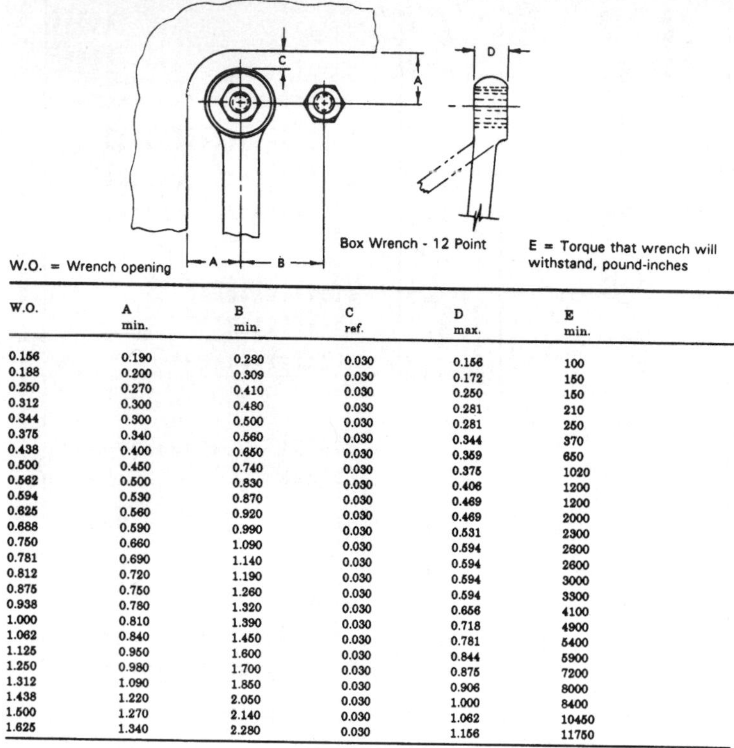

W.O.	A min.	B min.	C ref.	D max.	E min.
0.156	0.190	0.280	0.030	0.156	100
0.188	0.200	0.309	0.030	0.172	150
0.250	0.270	0.410	0.030	0.250	150
0.312	0.300	0.480	0.030	0.281	210
0.344	0.300	0.500	0.030	0.281	250
0.375	0.340	0.560	0.030	0.344	370
0.438	0.400	0.650	0.030	0.359	650
0.500	0.450	0.740	0.030	0.375	1020
0.562	0.500	0.830	0.030	0.406	1200
0.594	0.530	0.870	0.030	0.469	1200
0.625	0.560	0.920	0.030	0.469	2000
0.688	0.590	0.990	0.030	0.531	2300
0.750	0.660	1.090	0.030	0.594	2600
0.781	0.690	1.140	0.030	0.594	2600
0.812	0.720	1.190	0.030	0.594	3000
0.875	0.750	1.260	0.030	0.594	3300
0.938	0.780	1.320	0.030	0.656	4100
1.000	0.810	1.390	0.030	0.718	4900
1.062	0.840	1.450	0.030	0.781	5400
1.125	0.950	1.600	0.030	0.844	5900
1.250	0.980	1.700	0.030	0.875	7200
1.312	1.090	1.850	0.030	0.906	8000
1.438	1.220	2.050	0.030	1.000	8400
1.500	1.270	2.140	0.030	1.062	10450
1.625	1.340	2.280	0.030	1.156	11750

Figure 6.20 Box wrench clearance chart.

Dimensions and Properties of Hex Keys - (Allen Wrenches - inches)

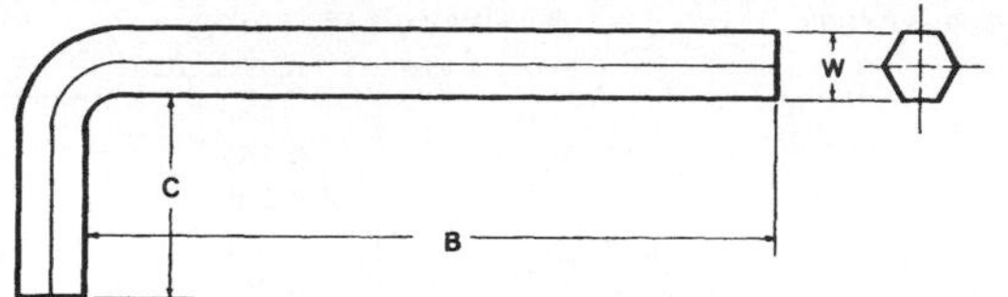

	DIMENSIONS					MECHANICAL PROPERTIES	
	key size W		B nom.		C nom.	torsional shear strength Lb-ins min.	torsional yield Lb-ins min.
dash no.	max.	min.	short arm	long arm			
1	.028	.0275	1.219	2.594	.219	1.2	1.1
2	.035	.0345	1.219	2.672	.344	2.4	2.1
3	.050	.049	1.656	2.844	.531	7	6.0
4	1/16	.0615	1.750	3.000	.562	12	11
5	5/64	.0771	1.875	3.188	.609	26	23
6	3/32	.0927	2.000	3.375	.656	46	40
7	7/64	.1077	2.125	3.562	.703	73	63
8	1/8	.1235	2.250	3.750	.750	108	94
9	9/64	.1391	2.375	3.960	.796	154	134
10	5/32	.1547	2.500	4.125	.844	210	183
11	3/16	.1860	2.750	4.500	.938	364	317
12	7/32	.2172	3.000	4.875	1.031	580	502
13	1/4	.2480	3.250	5.250	1.125	860	750
14	5/16	.3110	3.750	6.000	1.250	1,685	1,465
15	3/8	.3730	4.250	6.750	1.375	2,900	2,520
16	7/16	.4355	4.750	7.500	1.500	4,400	3,860
17	1/2	.4975	5.250	8.250	1.625	6,600	5,750
18	9/16	.5600	5.750	9.000	1.750	9,200	8,000
19	5/8	.6225	6.250	9.750	1.875	12,650	11,000
20	3/4	.7470	7.250	11.250	2.125	20,800	18,100
21	7/8	.8720	8.250	12.750	2.375	29,200	25,400
22	1	.9970	9.250	14.250	2.625	43,700	38,000
23	1 1/4	1.243	11.250	....	3.000	71,900	62,500
24	1 1/2	1.493	13.250	....	3.500	124,000	108,000
25	1 3/4	1.743	15.250	....	4.000	198,000	172,000
26	2	1.993	17.250	....	4.500	276,000	240,000

Figure 6.21 Hex-key table, Allen wrenches.

Maximum Width Across Flats of Nut	Wrench Opening	
	Minimum	Maximum
5/32	0.158	0.163
3/16	0.190	0.195
7/32	0.220	0.225
1/4	0.252	0.257
9/32	0.283	0.288
5/16	0.316	0.322
11/32	0.347	0.353
3/8	0.378	0.384
7/16	0.440	0.446
1/2	0.504	0.510
9/16	0.566	0.573
5/8	0.629	0.636
11/16	0.692	0.699
3/4	0.755	0.763
13/16	0.818	0.826
7/8	0.880	0.888
15/16	0.944	0.953
1	1.006	1.015
1-1/16	1.068	1.077
1-1/8	1.132	1.142
1-1/4	1.257	1.267
1-5/16	1.320	1.331
1-3/8	1.383	1.394
1-7/16	1.446	1.457
1-1/2	1.508	1.520
1-5/8	1.634	1.646
1-11/16	1.696	1.708
1-13/16	1.822	1.835
1-7/8	1.885	1.898
2	2.011	2.025
2-1/16	2.074	2.088
2-3/16	2.200	2.215
2-1/4	2.262	2.277
2-3/8	2.388	2.404
2-7/16	2.450	2.466
2-9/16	2.576	2.593
2-5/8	2.639	2.656
2-3/4	2.766	2.783
2-13/16	2.827	2.845
2-15/16	2.954	2.973
3	3.016	3.035

Note: Wrenches are marked with the "Nominal size of wrench", which is equal to the basic or maximum width across the flats of the corresponding nut.

Figure 6.22 Wrench openings for American standard nuts.

Figure 6.23 Samples of various hardware items.

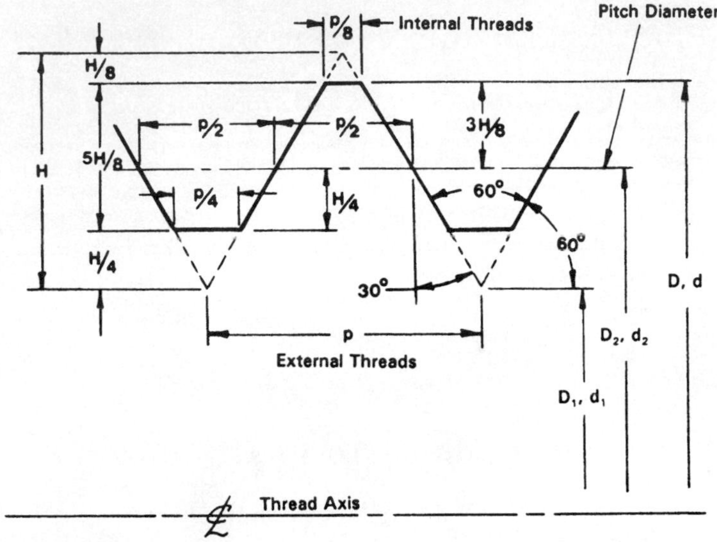

Basic Thread Profile for Unified (UN) and Metric (M) Threads (ISO 68)

$D,(d)$ = basic major diameter of internal (external) thread
$D_1,(d_1)$ = basic minor diameter of internal (external) thread
$D_2,(d_2)$ = basic pitch diameter of internal (external) thread
p = pitch
$H = 0.5\sqrt{3}\,p$

Figure 6.24 Basic thread profiles (unified and metric).

Interference-fit threads are commonly used on threaded studs to ensure a tight, vibration-resistant fit. The internal thread of a class 5 interference-fit application should be lubricated for best results when torquing the stud or externally threaded part into the class 5 fit tapped hole.

6.2.1 Unified and metric thread data

Unified national tap drill sizes. You may calculate the tap drill diameter for 75 and 100 percent thread for the unified and metric M profile series using the following equations. For unified national threads,

$$D_{\mathrm{td}} = D_{\mathrm{m}} - \frac{0.947}{n} \qquad \text{(Tap drill diameter for 75 percent thread)}$$

$$D_{\text{td}} = D_{\text{m}} - \frac{1.299}{n} \qquad \text{(Tap drill diameter for 100 percent thread)}$$

For metric threads, M profile,

$$D_{\text{d}} = D_{\text{M}} - \frac{(\%T)(p)}{76.98}$$

$$\%T = \frac{76.98}{p}(D_{\text{M}} - D_{\text{d}})$$

In the preceding equations, symbolism is as follows. For unified threads,

D_{td} = diameter of tap drill, in

D_{m} = major diameter of external thread or tap diameter, in

n = number of threads per inch

For metric threads,

D_{d} = drilled hole diameter, mm

D_{M} = basic major diameter, mm

$\%T$ = percent of thread (i.e., 70 percent = 0.70, etc)

p = pitch of thread, mm

Note: Recommended percent of thread is usually taken as 70 to 75 percent for a general class 2 type fit, which allows for electroplatings such as zinc, cadmium, chrome, nickel, etc.

Unified national coarse (UNC) screw thread data are presented in Fig. 6.25. Unified national fine (UNF) screw thread data are presented in Fig. 6.26. Metric M profile thread data are presented in Fig. 6.27. American national drill sizes are shown in Fig. 6.28. Both number and letter size drills are indicated with their decimal equivalents.

The standard limits of size for both American and unified national series screw threads are fully covered in Table 6.6. The four sections of the table are extracted from National Bureau of Standards Handbook H-28 and are in general agreement with current ANSI standards. The table covers or includes sizes 0–80 through 3–16UN.

Other screw thread systems are shown with their basic geometries and dimensions in Fig. 7.56.

Engagement of threads. The length of engagement of a stud end or bolt end E can be stated in terms of the major diameter D of the thread. In general,

- For a steel stud in cast iron or steel, $E = 1.50D$.
- For a steel stud in hardened steel or high-strength bronze, $E = D$.
- For a steel stud in aluminum or magnesium alloys subjected to shock loads, $E = 2.00D + 0.062$.
- For a steel stud as above, subjected to normal loads, $E = 1.50D + 0.062$.

Load to break a threaded section. For screws or bolts,

$$P_b = SA_{ts}$$

where P_b = load to break the screw or bolt, pounds-force (lbf)
S = ultimate tensile strength of screw or bolt material, lb/in^2
A_{ts} = tensile stress area of screw or bolt thread, in^2

Tensile stress area calculation. The tensile stress area A_{ts} of screws and bolts is derived from

$$A_{ts} = \frac{\pi}{4}\left(D - \frac{0.9743}{n}\right) \qquad \text{(For inch-series threads)}$$

where A_{ts} = tensile stress area, in^2
D = basic major diameter of thread, in
n = number of threads per inch

Note: You may select the stress areas for unified bolts or screws by using Figs. 6.25 and 6.26, while the metric stress areas may be derived by converting millimeters to inches for each metric fastener and using the preceding equation.

6.3 Rivets

Rivets form a large class of fastening devices and are manufactured in many types and varieties and various materials. Rivets are made from carbon steels, aluminum alloys, brass, copper, bronze, and other materials agreed on by the manufacturer and purchaser.

Head forms for standard rivets include button, truss, brazier, coopers, oval, and flush. Flush-head rivets are provided in the following countersunk head angles: 60°, 78°, 90°, 100°, 120°, 144°, and 150°. The most common countersunk forms are the 90° and 100° types. To employ these types of rivets, a countersinking tool is used to cut the recess for the flush head. When the material is thin, a process known as *dimpling* and *double-dimpling* is employed.

Figure 6.29 shows the dimpling methods, in which a dimpling tool is used to produce the countersunk recess for the rivet. This method is used on aerospace vehicles to attach the "skins," or outer metal layers, on the craft. Modern methods of adhesive bonding are being used extensively in conjunction with spot welding to manufacture large sections of aerospace vehicles in lieu of riveting. But riveting is still used for many fastening applications throughout industry and the construction trades.

Rivets are made for blind-hole applications in the form of pull-stem pop rivets, drive-stem rivets, and explosive rivets. Other forms include solid-stem, tubular, and semitubular rivets.

Rivet edge distance. The position or location of rivets from the edge of a part is normally $2d$, where d is the rivet shank diameter, with an absolute minimum of $1.5d$. The lateral spacing between rivets is known as *pitch* and is determined by the load requirements of the riveted joint. See Fig. 6.30 for an illustration of edge distance.

Rivet symbols on engineering drawings take the forms shown in Fig. 6.31 (rivet symbols). These symbols are encountered frequently on aerospace vehicle assembly drawings.

6.3.1 Basic stresses in riveted joints

Calculate the three loads that bear on rivets and riveted joints as follows:

1. Single-shear tensile load F_s (see Fig. 6.32) is

$$F_s = nAS_s$$

where n = number of rivets
A = cross-sectional area of one rivet, in^2
S_s = allowable shearing stress of the rivet, lb/in^2

2. Bearing-stress tensile load F_b (see Fig. 6.33) is

$$F_b = nA_1S_b$$

where n = number of rivets
A_1 = projected bearing area (diameter of rivet $\times\, t$)
S_b = allowable bearing stress of the material, lb/in^2

3. Safe load F_t based on tensile stress (see Fig. 6.34) is

$$F_t = nA_2S_t$$

where n = number of rivets
A_2 = area of plate between rivets, in^2
S_t = allowable tensile strength of the material, lb/in^2

The *least* of the three calculated loads will be the safe tensile load for the riveted joint.

In machine design, allowable design stresses for structural-steel and plain-steel rivets used for riveted joints generally are

- 11,000 lb/in^2, tensile
- 8800 lb/in^2, shear
- 19,000 lb/in^2, compressive or bearing

These values are well below the ultimate allowable stresses listed in the ASME Boiler Code and are therefore conservative.

Rivet placement, pitch, and sizing requirements on complex, heavily loaded, dynamic structures are usually determined by the structural designer in collaboration with stress analysts and dynamics engineers.

Other manufacturing techniques such as welding, spot welding, and structural adhesive bonding have replaced riveting in many applications. Nevertheless, riveting is still employed in a great number of industrial applications. The types and varieties of rivets are numerous, and a complete description and dimensional data, as well as materials specifications, are contained in the Industrial Fasteners Institute handbooks on fasteners in both the U.S. Customary and metric units.

6.3.2 General sizing of rivets

For rivet sizing (general, noncritical applications), the following approximations may be used:

$$d = 1.25\sqrt{t} \quad \text{to} \quad 1.45\sqrt{t}$$

where d is the diameter of rivet shank in inches or millimeters (use next larger size) and t is the material thickness in inches.

(Text continued on page 465.)

Screw thread data, Unified National Coarse (UNC)

Thread	Tap Drill	Decimal in	Stress Area in^2	Basic Pitch Diameter, in
#1–64	#53	0.0595	0.0026	0.0629
#2–56	#50	0.0700	0.0037	0.0744
#3–48	#47	0.0785	0.0048	0.0855
#4–40	#43	0.0890	0.0060	0.0958
#5–40	#38	0.1015	0.0080	0.1088
#6–32	#36	0.1065	0.0090	0.1177
#8–32	#29	0.1360	0.0140	0.1437
#10–24	#25	0.1495	0.0175	0.1629
1/4–20	#7	0.2010	0.0318	0.2175
5/16–18	F	0.2570	0.0524	0.2764
3/8–16	5/16	0.3125	0.0775	0.3344
7/16–14	T	0.3580	0.1063	0.3911
1/2–13	27/64	0.4219	0.1419	0.4500
9/16–12	31/64	0.4844	0.1820	0.5084
5/8–11	17/32	0.5312	0.2260	0.5660
3/4–10	41/64	0.6406	0.3340	0.6850
7/8–9	49/64	0.7656	0.4620	0.8028
1–8	7/8	0.8750	0.6060	0.9188

Figure 6.25 Screw thread data (UNC).

Thread	Tap drill	Decimal in	Stress Area in^2	Basic Pitch Diameter, in
#0–80	3/64	0.0469	0.0018	0.0519
#1–72	#53	0.0595	0.0027	0.0640
#2–64	#50	0.0700	0.0039	0.0759
#3–56	#45	0.0820	0.0052	0.0874
#4–48	#42	0.0935	0.0066	0.0985
#5–44	#37	0.1040	0.0083	0.1102
#6–40	#33	0.1130	0.0102	0.1218
#8–36	#29	0.1360	0.0147	0.1460
#10–32	#21	0.1590	0.0200	0.1697
1/4–28	#3	0.2130	0.0364	0.2268
5/16–24	I	0.2720	0.0580	0.2854
3/8–24	Q	0.3320	0.0878	0.3479
7/16–20	25/64	0.3906	0.1187	0.4050
1/2–20	29/64	0.4531	0.1599	0.4675
9/16–18	33/64	0.5156	0.2030	0.5264
5/8–18	9/16	0.5625	0.2560	0.5889
3/4–16	11/16	0.6875	0.3730	0.7094
7/8–14	13/16	0.8125	0.5090	0.8286
1–12	29/32	0.9063	0.6630	0.9459

Figure 6.26 Screw thread data (UNF).

Metric thread data, M profile, internal and external

Thread Designation Dia. × Pitch, mm	Tap Drill, mm	Pitch Dia. 6H, Internal, mm	Pitch Dia. 6g, External, mm
M1.6 × 0.35	1.25	1.373	1.291
M2 × 0.4	1.60	1.740	1.654
M2.5 × 0.45	2.05	2.208	2.117
M3 × 0.5	2.50	2.675	2.580
M3.5 × 0.6	2.90	3.110	3.004
M4 × 0.7	3.30	3.545	3.433
M5 × 0.8	4.20	4.480	4.361
M6 × 1	5.00	5.350	5.212
M8 × 1.25	6.70	7.188	7.042
M8 × 1	7.00	7.350	7.212
M10 × 1.5	8.50	9.026	8.862
M10 × 1.25	8.70	9.188	9.042
M10 × 0.75	—	9.513	9.391
M12 × 1.75	10.20	10.863	10.679
M12 × 1.5	—	11.026	10.854
M12 × 1.25	10.80	11.188	11.028
M12 × 1	—	11.350	11.206
M14 × 2	12.00	12.701	12.503
M14 × 1.5	12.50	13.026	12.854
M15 × 1	—	14.350	14.206
M16 × 2	14.00	14.701	14.503
M16 × 1.5	14.50	15.026	14.854
M17 × 1	—	16.350	16.206
M18 × 1.5	16.50	17.026	16.854
M20 × 2.5	17.50	18.376	18.164
M20 × 1.5	18.50	19.026	18.854
M20 × 1	—	19.350	19.206
M22 × 2.5	19.50	20.376	20.164
M22 × 1.5	20.50	21.026	20.854
M24 × 3	21.00	22.051	21.803
M24 × 2	22.00	22.701	22.493
M25 × 1.5	—	24.026	23.854

Figure 6.27 Metric thread data.

Drill No.	Decimal	Drill No.	Decimal	Drill No.	Decimal
97	0.0059	56	0.0465	15	0.180
96	0.0063	55	0.052	14	0.182
95	0.0067	54	0.055	13	0.185
94	0.0071	53	0.0595	12	0.189
93	0.0075	52	0.0635	11	0.191
92	0.0079	51	0.067	10	0.1935
91	0.0083	50	0.070	9	0.196
90	0.0087	49	0.073	8	0.199
89	0.0091	48	0.076	7	0.201
88	0.0095	47	0.0785	6	0.204
87	0.010	46	0.076	5	0.2055
86	0.0105	45	0.082	4	0.209
85	0.011	44	0.086	3	0.213
84	0.0115	43	0.089	2	0.221
83	0.012	42	0.0935	1	0.228
82	0.0125	41	0.096	A	0.234
81	0.013	40	0.098	B	0.238
80	0.0135	39	0.0995	C	0.242
79	0.0145	38	0.1015	D	0.246
78	0.016	37	0.104	E	0.250
77	0.018	36	0.1065	F	0.257
76	0.020	35	0.110	G	0.261
75	0.021	34	0.111	H	0.266
74	0.0225	33	0.113	I	0.272
73	0.024	32	0.116	J	0.277
72	0.025	31	0.120	K	0.281
71	0.026	30	0.1285	L	0.290
70	0.028	29	0.136	M	0.295
69	0.0292	28	0.1405	N	0.302
68	0.033	27	0.144	O	0.316
67	0.032	26	0.147	P	0.323
66	0.035	25	0.1495	Q	0.332
65	0.035	24	0.152	R	0.339
64	0.035	23	0.154	S	0.348
63	0.037	22	0.157	T	0.358
62	0.038	21	0.159	U	0.368
61	0.039	20	0.161	V	0.377
60	0.040	19	0.166	W	0.386
59	0.041	18	0.1695	X	0.397
58	0.042	17	0.173	Y	0.404
57	0.043	16	0.177	Z	0.413

Figure 6.28 Drill sizes (American national standard).

TABLE 6.6 Standard Limits of Size: Unified and American Screw Threads

Nominal size and threads per inch	Series designation	External									Internal						
		Class	Allowance, in	Major diameter limits, in			Pitch diameter limits, in			Minor diameter, in	Class	Minor diameter limits, in		Pitch diameter limits, in			Major diameter, in
				Max*	Min	Min†	Max*	Min	Tolerance			Min	Max	Min	Max	Tolerance	Min
No. 0–80 to ½–13																	
0–80	NF	2A	0.0005	0.0595	0.0563		0.0514	0.0496	0.0018	0.0442	2B	0.0465	0.0514	0.0519	0.0542	0.0023	0.0600
		3A	0.0000	0.0600	0.0568		0.0519	0.0506	0.0013	0.0447	3B	0.0465	0.0514	0.0519	0.0536	0.0017	0.0600
1–64	NC	2A	0.0006	0.0724	0.0686		0.0623	0.0603	0.0020	0.0532	2B	0.0561	0.0623	0.0629	0.0655	0.0026	0.0730
		3A	0.0000	0.0730	0.0692		0.0629	0.0614	0.0015	0.0538	3B	0.0561	0.0623	0.0629	0.0648	0.0019	0.0730
1–72	NF	2A	0.0006	0.0724	0.0689		0.0634	0.0615	0.0019	0.0554	2B	0.0580	0.0635	0.0640	0.0665	0.0025	0.0730
		3A	0.0000	0.0730	0.0695		0.0640	0.0626	0.0014	0.0560	3B	0.0580	0.0635	0.0640	0.0659	0.0019	0.0730
2–56	NC	2A	0.0006	0.0854	0.0813		0.0738	0.0717	0.0021	0.0635	2B	0.0667	0.0737	0.0744	0.0772	0.0028	0.0860
		3A	0.0000	0.0860	0.0819		0.0744	0.0728	0.0016	0.0641	3B	0.0667	0.0737	0.0744	0.0765	0.0021	0.0860
2–64	NF	2A	0.0006	0.0854	0.0816		0.0753	0.0733	0.0020	0.0662	2B	0.0691	0.0753	0.0759	0.0786	0.0027	0.0860
		3A	0.0000	0.0860	0.0822		0.0759	0.0744	0.0015	0.0668	3B	0.0691	0.0753	0.0759	0.0779	0.0020	0.0860
3–48	NC	2A	0.0007	0.0983	0.0938		0.0848	0.0825	0.0023	0.0727	2B	0.0764	0.0845	0.0855	0.0885	0.0030	0.0990
		3A	0.0000	0.0990	0.0945		0.0855	0.0838	0.0017	0.0734	3B	0.0764	0.0845	0.0855	0.0877	0.0022	0.0990
3–56	NF	2A	0.0007	0.0983	0.0942		0.0867	0.0845	0.0022	0.0764	2B	0.0797	0.0865	0.0874	0.0902	0.0028	0.0990
		3A	0.0000	0.0990	0.0949		0.0874	0.0858	0.0016	0.0771	3B	0.0797	0.0865	0.0874	0.0895	0.0021	0.0990
4–40	NC	2A	0.0008	0.1112	0.1061		0.0950	0.0925	0.0025	0.0805	2B	0.0849	0.0939	0.0958	0.0991	0.0033	0.1120
		3A	0.0000	0.1120	0.1069		0.0958	0.0939	0.0019	0.0813	3B	0.0849	0.0939	0.0958	0.0982	0.0024	0.1120
4–48	NF	2A	0.0007	0.1113	0.1068		0.0978	0.0954	0.0024	0.0857	2B	0.0894	0.0968	0.0985	0.1016	0.0031	0.1120
		3A	0.0000	0.1120	0.1075		0.0985	0.0967	0.0018	0.0864	3B	0.0894	0.0968	0.0985	0.1008	0.0023	0.1120
5–40	NC	2A	0.0008	0.1242	0.1191		0.1080	0.1054	0.0026	0.0935	2B	0.0979	0.1062	0.1088	0.1121	0.0033	0.1250
		3A	0.0000	0.1250	0.1199		0.1088	0.1069	0.0019	0.0943	3B	0.0979	0.1062	0.1088	0.1113	0.0025	0.1250
5–44	NF	2A	0.0007	0.1243	0.1195		0.1095	0.1070	0.0025	0.0964	2B	0.1004	0.1079	0.1102	0.1134	0.0032	0.1250
		3A	0.0000	0.1250	0.1202		0.1102	0.1083	0.0019	0.0971	3B	0.1004	0.1079	0.1102	0.1126	0.0024	0.1250
6–32	NC	2A	0.0008	0.1372	0.1312		0.1169	0.1141	0.0028	0.0989	2B	0.104	0.114	0.1177	0.1214	0.0037	0.1380
		3A	0.0000	0.1380	0.1320		0.1177	0.1156	0.0021	0.0997	3B	0.1040	0.1140	0.1177	0.1204	0.0027	0.1380
6–40	NF	2A	0.0008	0.1372	0.1321		0.1210	0.1184	0.0026	0.1065	2B	0.111	0.119	0.1218	0.1252	0.0034	0.1380
		3A	0.0000	0.1380	0.1329		0.1218	0.1198	0.0020	0.1073	3B	0.1110	0.1186	0.1218	0.1243	0.0025	0.1380

8–32	NC	2A	0.0009	0.1631	0.1571		0.1428	0.1399	0.0029	0.1248	2B	0.130	0.139	0.1437	0.1475	0.0038	0.1640
		3A	0.0000	0.1640	0.1580		0.1437	0.1415	0.0022	0.1257	3B	0.1300	0.1389	0.1437	0.1465	0.0028	0.1640
8–36	NF	2A	0.0008	0.1632	0.1577		0.1452	0.1424	0.0028	0.1291	2B	0.134	0.142	0.1460	0.1496	0.0036	0.1640
		3A	0.0000	0.1640	0.1585		0.1460	0.1439	0.0021	0.1299	3B	0.1340	0.1416	0.1460	0.1487	0.0027	0.1640
10–24	NC	2A	0.0010	0.1890	0.1818		0.1619	0.1586	0.0033	0.1379	2B	0.145	0.156	0.1629	0.1672	0.0043	0.1900
		3A	0.0000	0.1900	0.1828		0.1629	0.1604	0.0025	0.1389	3B	0.1450	0.1555	0.1629	0.1661	0.0032	0.1900
10–32	NF	2A	0.0009	0.1891	0.1831		0.1688	0.1658	0.0030	0.1508	2B	0.156	0.164	0.1697	0.1736	0.0039	0.1900
		3A	0.0000	0.1900	0.1840		0.1697	0.1674	0.0023	0.1517	3B	0.1560	0.1641	0.1697	0.1726	0.0029	0.1900
12–24	NC	2A	0.0010	0.2150	0.2078		0.1879	0.1845	0.0034	0.1639	2B	0.171	0.181	0.1889	0.1933	0.0044	0.2160
		3A	0.0000	0.2160	0.2088		0.1889	0.1863	0.0026	0.1649	3B	0.1710	0.1807	0.1889	0.1922	0.0033	0.2160
12–28	NF	2A	0.0010	0.2150	0.2085		0.1918	0.1886	0.0032	0.1712	2B	0.177	0.186	0.1928	0.1970	0.0042	0.2160
		3A	0.0000	0.2160	0.2095		0.1928	0.1904	0.0024	0.1722	3B	0.1770	0.1857	0.1928	0.1959	0.0031	0.2160
12–32	NEF	2A	0.0009	0.2151	0.2091		0.1948	0.1917	0.0031	0.1768	2B	0.182	0.190	0.1957	0.1998	0.0041	0.2160
		3A	0.0000	0.2160	0.2100		0.1957	0.1933	0.0024	0.1777	3B	0.1820	0.1895	0.1957	0.1988	0.0031	0.2160
¼–20	UNC	1A	0.0011	0.2489	0.2367		0.2164	0.2108	0.0056	0.1876	1B	0.196	0.207	0.2175	0.2248	0.0073	0.2500
		2A	0.0011	0.2489	0.2408	0.2367	0.2164	0.2127	0.0037	0.1876	2B	0.196	0.207	0.2175	0.2223	0.0048	0.2500
		3A	0.0000	0.2500	0.2419		0.2175	0.2147	0.0028	0.1887	3B	0.1960	0.2067	0.2175	0.2211	0.0036	0.2500
¼–28	UNF	1A	0.0010	0.2490	0.2392		0.2258	0.2208	0.0050	0.2052	1B	0.211	0.220	0.2268	0.2333	0.0065	0.2500
		2A	0.0010	0.2490	0.2425		0.2258	0.2225	0.0033	0.2052	2B	0.211	0.220	0.2268	0.2311	0.0043	0.2500
		3A	0.0000	0.2500	0.2435		0.2268	0.2243	0.0025	0.2062	3B	0.2110	0.2190	0.2268	0.2300	0.0032	0.2500
¼–32	NEF	2A	0.0010	0.2490	0.2430		0.2287	0.2255	0.0032	0.2107	2B	0.216	0.224	0.2297	0.2339	0.0042	0.2500
		3A	0.0000	0.2500	0.2440		0.2297	0.2273	0.0024	0.2117	3B	0.2160	0.2229	0.2297	0.2328	0.0031	0.2500
5/16–18	UNC	1A	0.0012	0.3113	0.2982		0.2752	0.2691	0.0061	0.2431	1B	0.252	0.265	0.2764	0.2843	0.0079	0.3125
		2A	0.0012	0.3113	0.3026	0.2982	0.2752	0.2712	0.0040	0.2431	2B	0.252	0.265	0.2764	0.2817	0.0053	0.3125
		3A	0.0000	0.3125	0.3038		0.2764	0.2734	0.0030	0.2443	3B	0.2520	0.2630	0.2764	0.2803	0.0039	0.3125
5/16–24	UNF	1A	0.0011	0.3114	0.3006		0.2843	0.2788	0.0055	0.2603	1B	0.267	0.277	0.2854	0.2925	0.0071	0.3125
		2A	0.0011	0.3114	0.3042		0.2843	0.2806	0.0037	0.2603	2B	0.267	0.277	0.2854	0.2902	0.0048	0.3125
		3A	0.0000	0.3125	0.3053		0.2854	0.2827	0.0027	0.2614	3B	0.2670	0.2754	0.2854	0.2890	0.0036	0.3125

TABLE 6.6 Standard Limits of Size: Unified and American Screw Threads (*Continued*)

Nominal size and threads per inch	Series designation	External									Internal						
				Major diameter limits, in			Pitch diameter limits, in					Minor diameter limits, in		Pitch diameter limits, in			Major diameter, in
		Class	Allowance, in	Max*	Min	Min†	Max*	Min	Tolerance	Minor diameter, in	Class	Min	Max	Min	Max	Tolerance	Min
No. 0–80 to ½–13																	
5/16–32	NEF	2A	0.0010	0.3115	0.3055		0.2912	0.2880	0.0032	0.2732	2B	0.279	0.286	0.2922	0.2964	0.0042	0.3125
		3A	0.0000	0.3125	0.3065		0.2922	0.2898	0.0024	0.2742	3B	0.2790	0.2847	0.2922	0.2953	0.0031	0.3125
3/8–16	UNC	1A	0.0013	0.3737	0.3595		0.3331	0.3266	0.0065	0.2970	1B	0.307	0.321	0.3344	0.3429	0.0085	0.3750
		2A	0.0013	0.3737	0.3643	0.3595	0.3331	0.3287	0.0044	0.2970	2B	0.307	0.321	0.3344	0.3401	0.0057	0.3750
		3A	0.0000	0.3750	0.3656		0.3344	0.3311	0.0033	0.2983	3B	0.3070	0.3182	0.3344	0.3387	0.0043	0.3750
3/8–24	UNF	1A	0.0011	0.3739	0.3631		0.3468	0.3411	0.0057	0.3228	1B	0.330	0.340	0.3479	0.2553	0.0074	0.3750
		2A	0.0011	0.3739	0.3667		0.3468	0.3430	0.0038	0.3228	2B	0.330	0.340	0.3479	0.3528	0.0049	0.3750
		3A	0.0000	0.3750	0.3678		0.3479	0.3450	0.0029	0.3239	3B	0.3300	0.3372	0.3479	0.3516	0.0037	0.3750
3/8–32	NEF	2A	0.0010	0.3740	0.3680		0.3537	0.3503	0.0034	0.3357	2B	0.341	0.349	0.3547	0.3591	0.0044	0.3750
		3A	0.0000	0.3750	0.3690		0.3547	0.3522	0.0025	0.3367	3B	0.3410	0.3469	0.3547	0.3580	0.0033	0.3750
7/16–14	UNC	1A	0.0014	0.4361	0.4206		0.3897	0.3826	0.0071	0.3485	1B	0.360	0.376	0.3911	0.4003	0.0092	0.4375
		2A	0.0014	0.4361	0.4258	0.4206	0.3897	0.3850	0.0047	0.3485	2B	0.360	0.376	0.3911	0.3972	0.0061	0.4375
		3A	0.0000	0.4375	0.4272		0.3911	0.3876	0.0035	0.3499	3B	0.3600	0.3717	0.3911	0.3957	0.0046	0.4375
7/16–20	UNF	1A	0.0013	0.4362	0.4240		0.4037	0.3975	0.0062	0.3749	1B	0.383	0.395	0.4050	0.4131	0.0081	0.4375
		2A	0.0013	0.4362	0.4281		0.4037	0.3995	0.0042	0.3749	2B	0.383	0.395	0.4050	0.4104	0.0054	0.4375
		3A	0.0000	0.4375	0.4294		0.4050	0.4019	0.0031	0.3762	3B	0.3830	0.3916	0.4050	0.4091	0.0041	0.4375
7/16–28	UNEF	2A	0.0011	0.4364	0.4299		0.4132	0.4096	0.0036	0.3926	2B	0.399	0.407	0.4143	0.4189	0.0046	0.4375
		3A	0.0000	0.4375	0.4310		0.4143	0.4116	0.0027	0.3937	3B	0.3990	0.4051	0.4143	0.4178	0.0035	0.4375
1/2–12	N	2A	0.0016	0.4984	0.4870		0.4443	0.4389	0.0054	0.3962	2B	0.410	0.428	0.4459	0.4529	0.0070	0.5000
		3A	0.0000	0.5000	0.4886		0.4439	0.4419	0.0040	0.3978	3B	0.4100	0.4223	0.4459	0.4511	0.0052	0.5000
1/2–13	UNC	1A	0.0015	0.4985	0.4822		0.4485	0.4411	0.0074	0.4041	1B	0.417	0.434	0.4500	0.4597	0.0097	0.5000
		2A	0.0015	0.4985	0.4876	0.4822	0.4485	0.4435	0.0050	0.4041	2B	0.417	0.434	0.4500	0.4565	0.0065	0.5000
		3A	0.0000	0.5000	0.4891		0.4500	0.4463	0.0037	0.4056	3B	0.4170	0.4284	0.4500	0.4548	0.0048	0.5000

½–20 to 1⅛–12

½–20	UNF	1A	0.0013	0.4987	0.4865		0.4662	0.4598	0.0064	0.4374	1B	0.446	0.457	0.4675	0.4759	0.0084	0.5000
		2A	0.0013	0.4987	0.4906		0.4662	0.4619	0.0043	0.4374	2B	0.446	0.457	0.4675	0.4731	0.0056	0.5000
		3A	0.0000	0.5000	0.4919		0.4675	0.4643	0.0032	0.4387	3B	0.4460	0.4537	0.4675	0.4717	0.0042	0.5000
½–28	UNEF	2A	0.0011	0.4989	0.4924		0.4757	0.4720	0.0037	0.4551	2B	0.461	0.470	0.4768	0.4816	0.0048	0.5000
		3A	0.0000	0.5000	0.4935		0.4768	0.4740	0.0028	0.4562	3B	0.4610	0.4676	0.4768	0.4804	0.0036	0.5000
⁹⁄₁₆–12	UNC	1A	0.0016	0.5609	0.5437		0.5068	0.4990	0.0078	0.4587	1B	0.472	0.490	0.5084	0.5186	0.0102	0.5625
		2A	0.0016	0.5609	0.5495	0.5437	0.5068	0.5016	0.0052	0.4587	2B	0.472	0.490	0.5084	0.5152	0.0068	0.5625
		3A	0.0000	0.5625	0.5511		0.5084	0.5045	0.0039	0.4603	3B	0.4720	0.4843	0.5084	0.5135	0.0051	0.5625
⁹⁄₁₆–18	UNF	1A	0.0014	0.5611	0.5480		0.5250	0.5182	0.0068	0.4929	1B	0.502	0.515	0.5264	0.5353	0.0089	0.5625
		2A	0.0014	0.5611	0.5524		0.5250	0.5205	0.0045	0.4929	2B	0.502	0.515	0.5264	0.5323	0.0059	0.5625
		3A	0.0000	0.5625	0.5538		0.5264	0.5230	0.0034	0.4943	3B	0.5020	0.5106	0.5264	0.5308	0.0044	0.5625
⁹⁄₁₆–24	NEF	2A	0.0012	0.5613	0.5541		0.5342	0.5303	0.0039	0.5102	2B	0.517	0.527	0.5354	0.5405	0.0051	0.5625
		3A	0.0000	0.5625	0.5553		0.5354	0.5325	0.0029	0.5114	3B	0.5170	0.5244	0.5354	0.5392	0.0038	0.5625
⅝–11	UNC	1A	0.0016	0.6234	0.6052		0.5644	0.5561	0.0083	0.5119	1B	0.527	0.546	0.5660	0.5767	0.0107	0.6250
		2A	0.0016	0.6234	0.6113	0.6052	0.5644	0.5589	0.0055	0.5119	2B	0.527	0.546	0.5660	0.5732	0.0072	0.6250
		3A	0.0000	0.6250	0.6129		0.5660	0.5619	0.0041	0.5135	3B	0.5270	0.5391	0.5660	0.5714	0.0054	0.6250
⅝–12	N	2A	0.0016	0.6234	0.6120		0.5693	0.5639	0.0054	0.5212	2B	0.535	0.553	0.5709	0.5780	0.0071	0.6250
		3A	0.0000	0.6250	0.6136		0.5709	0.5668	0.0041	0.5228	3B	0.5350	0.5463	0.5709	0.5762	0.0053	0.6250
⅝–18	UNF	1A	0.0014	0.6236	0.6105		0.5875	0.5805	0.0070	0.5554	1B	0.565	0.578	0.5889	0.5980	0.0091	0.6250
		2A	0.0014	0.6236	0.6149		0.5875	0.5828	0.0047	0.5554	2B	0.565	0.578	0.5889	0.5949	0.0060	0.6250
		3A	0.0000	0.6250	0.6163		0.5889	0.5854	0.0035	0.5568	3B	0.5650	0.5730	0.5889	0.5934	0.0045	0.6250
⅝–24	NEF	2A	0.0012	0.6238	0.6166		0.5967	0.5927	0.0040	0.5727	2B	0.580	0.590	0.5979	0.6031	0.0052	0.6250
		3A	0.0000	0.6250	0.6178		0.5979	0.5949	0.0030	0.5739	3B	0.5800	0.5809	0.5979	0.6018	0.0039	0.6250
¹¹⁄₁₆–12	N	2A	0.0016	0.6859	0.6745		0.6318	0.6264	0.0054	0.5837	2B	0.597	0.615	0.6334	0.6405	0.0071	0.6875
		3A	0.0000	0.6875	0.6761		0.6334	0.6293	0.0041	0.5853	3B	0.5970	0.6085	0.6334	0.6387	0.0053	0.6875
¹¹⁄₁₆–24	NEF	2A	0.0012	0.6863	0.6791		0.6592	0.6552	0.0040	0.6352	2B	0.642	0.652	0.6604	0.6656	0.0052	0.6875
		3A	0.0000	0.6875	0.6803		0.6604	0.6574	0.0030	0.6364	3B	0.6420	0.6494	0.6604	0.6643	0.0039	0.6875
¾–10	UNC	1A	0.0018	0.7482	0.7288		0.6832	0.6744	0.0088	0.6255	1B	0.642	0.663	0.6850	0.6965	0.0115	0.7500
		2A	0.0018	0.7482	0.7353	0.7288	0.6832	0.6773	0.0059	0.6255	2B	0.642	0.663	0.6850	0.6927	0.0077	0.7500
		3A	0.0000	0.7500	0.7371		0.6850	0.6806	0.0044	0.6273	3B	0.6420	0.6545	0.6850	0.6907	0.0057	0.7500
¾–12	N	2A	0.0017	0.7483	0.7369		0.6942	0.6887	0.0055	0.6461	2B	0.660	0.678	0.6959	0.7031	0.0072	0.7500
		3A	0.0000	0.7500	0.7386		0.6959	0.6918	0.0041	0.6478	3B	0.6600	0.6707	0.6959	0.7013	0.0054	0.7500

TABLE 6.6 Standard Limits of Size: Unified and American Screw Threads (*Continued*)

Nominal size and threads per inch	Series designation	External									Internal						
				Major diameter limits, in			Pitch diameter limits, in					Minor diameter limits, in		Pitch diameter limits, in			Major diameter, in
		Class	Allowance, in	Max*	Min	Min†	Max*	Min	Tolerance	Minor diameter, in	Class	Min	Max	Min	Max	Tolerance	Min
½–20 to 1⅛–12																	
¾–16	UNF	1A	0.0015	0.7485	0.7343		0.7079	0.7004	0.0075	0.6718	1B	0.682	0.696	0.7094	0.7192	0.0098	0.7500
		2A	0.0015	0.7485	0.7391		0.7079	0.7029	0.0050	0.6718	2B	0.682	0.696	0.7094	0.7159	0.0065	0.7500
		3A	0.0000	0.7500	0.7406		0.7094	0.7056	0.0038	0.6733	3B	0.6820	0.6908	0.7094	0.7143	0.0049	0.7500
¾–20	UNEF	2A	0.0013	0.7487	0.7406		0.7162	0.7118	0.0044	0.6874	2B	0.696	0.707	0.7175	0.7232	0.0057	0.7500
		3A	0.0000	0.7500	0.7419		0.7175	0.7142	0.0033	0.6887	3B	0.6960	0.7037	0.7175	0.7218	0.0043	0.7500
13/16–12	N	2A	0.0017	0.8108	0.7994		0.7567	0.7512	0.0055	0.7086	2B	0.722	0.740	0.7584	0.7656	0.0072	0.8125
		3A	0.0000	0.8125	0.8011		0.7584	0.7543	0.0041	0.7103	3B	0.7220	0.7329	0.7584	0.7638	0.0054	0.8125
13/16–16	UN	2A	0.0015	0.8110	0.8016		0.7704	0.7655	0.0049	0.7343	2B	0.745	0.759	0.7719	0.7782	0.0063	0.8125
		3A	0.0000	0.8125	0.8031		0.7719	0.7683	0.0036	0.7358	3B	0.7450	0.7533	0.7719	0.7766	0.0047	0.8125
13/16–20	UNEF	2A	0.0013	0.8112	0.8031		0.7787	0.7743	0.0044	0.7498	2B	0.758	0.770	0.7800	0.7857	0.0057	0.8125
		3A	0.0000	0.8125	0.8044		0.7800	0.7767	0.0033	0.7512	3B	0.7580	0.7662	0.7800	0.7843	0.0043	0.8125
⅞–9	UNC	1A	0.0019	0.8731	0.8523		0.8009	0.7914	0.0095	0.7368	1B	0.755	0.778	0.8028	0.8151	0.0123	0.8750
		2A	0.0019	0.8731	0.8592	0.8523	0.8009	0.7946	0.0063	0.7368	2B	0.755	0.778	0.8028	0.8110	0.0082	0.8750
		3A	0.0000	0.8750	0.8611		0.8028	0.7981	0.0047	0.7387	3B	0.7550	0.7681	0.8028	0.8089	0.0061	0.8750
⅞–12	N	2A	0.0017	0.8733	0.8619		0.8192	0.8137	0.0055	0.7711	2B	0.785	0.803	0.8209	0.8281	0.0072	0.8750
		3A	0.0000	0.8750	0.8636		0.8209	0.8168	0.0041	0.7728	3B	0.7850	0.7952	0.8209	0.8263	0.0054	0.8750
⅞–14	UNF	1A	0.0016	0.8734	0.8579		0.8270	0.8189	0.0081	0.7858	1B	0.798	0.814	0.8286	0.8392	0.0106	0.8750
		2A	0.0016	0.8734	0.8631		0.8270	0.8216	0.0054	0.7858	2B	0.798	0.814	0.8286	0.8356	0.0070	0.8750
		3A	0.0000	0.8750	0.8647		0.8286	0.8245	0.0041	0.7874	3B	0.7980	0.8068	0.8286	0.8339	0.0053	0.8750
⅞–16	UN	2A	0.0015	0.8735	0.8641		0.8329	0.8280	0.0049	0.7968	2B	0.807	0.821	0.8344	0.8407	0.0063	0.8750
		3A	0.0000	0.8750	0.8656		0.8344	0.8308	0.0036	0.7983	3B	0.8070	0.8158	0.8344	0.8391	0.0047	0.8750
⅞–20	UNEF	2A	0.0013	0.8737	0.8656		0.8412	0.8368	0.0044	0.8124	2B	0.821	0.832	0.8425	0.8482	0.0057	0.8750
		3A	0.0000	0.8750	0.8669		0.8425	0.8392	0.0033	0.8137	3B	0.8210	0.8287	0.8425	0.8468	0.0043	0.8750
15/16–12	UN	2A	0.0017	0.9358	0.9244		0.8817	0.8760	0.0057	0.8336	2B	0.847	0.865	0.8834	0.8908	0.0074	0.9375
		3A	0.0000	0.9375	0.9261		0.8834	0.8793	0.0011	0.8353	3B	0.8470	0.8575	0.8834	0.8889	0.0055	0.9375
5/16–16	UN	2A	0.0015	0.9360	0.9266		0.8954	0.8904	0.0050	0.8593	2B	0.870	0.884	0.8969	0.9034	0.0065	0.9375
		3A	0.0000	0.9375	0.9281		0.8969	0.8932	0.0037	0.8608	3B	0.8700	0.8783	0.8969	0.9013	0.0049	0.9375

$^{15}/_{16}$–20	UNEF	2A	0.0014	0.9361	0.9280		0.9036	0.8991	0.0045	0.8748	2B	0.883	0.895	0.9050	0.9109	0.0059	0.9375
		3A	0.0000	0.9375	0.9294		0.9050	0.9016	0.0034	0.8762	3B	0.8830	0.8912	0.9050	0.9094	0.0044	0.9375
1–8	UNC	1A	0.0020	0.9980	0.9755		0.9168	0.9067	0.0101	0.8446	1B	0.865	0.890	0.9188	0.9320	0.0132	1.0000
		2A	0.0020	0.9980	0.9830	0.9755	0.9168	0.9100	0.0068	0.8446	2B	0.865	0.890	0.9188	0.9276	0.0088	1.0000
		3A	0.0000	1.0000	0.9850		0.9188	0.9137	0.0051	0.8466	3B	0.8650	0.8797	0.9188	0.9254	0.0066	1.0000
1–12	UNF	1A	0.0018	0.9982	0.9810		0.9441	0.9353	0.0088	0.8960	1B	0.910	0.928	0.9459	0.9573	0.0114	1.0000
		2A	0.0018	0.9982	0.9868		0.9441	0.9382	0.0059	0.8960	2B	0.910	0.928	0.9459	0.9535	0.0076	1.0000
		3A	0.0000	1.0000	0.9886		0.9459	0.9415	0.0044	0.8978	3B	0.9100	0.9198	0.9459	0.9516	0.0057	1.0000
1–16	UN	2A	0.0015	0.9985	0.9891		0.9579	0.9529	0.0050	0.9218	2B	0.932	0.946	0.9594	0.9659	0.0065	1.0000
		3A	0.0000	1.0000	0.9906		0.9594	0.9557	0.0037	0.9233	3B	0.9320	0.9408	0.9594	0.9643	0.0049	1.0000
1–20	UNEF	2A	0.0014	0.9986	0.9905		0.9661	0.9616	0.0045	0.9373	2B	0.946	0.957	0.9675	0.9734	0.0059	1.0000
		3A	0.0000	1.0000	0.9919		0.9675	0.9641	0.0034	0.9387	3B	0.9460	0.9537	0.9675	0.9719	0.0044	1.0000
1$^{1}/_{16}$–12	UN	2A	0.0017	1.0608	1.0494		1.0067	1.0010	0.0057	0.9586	2B	0.972	0.990	1.0084	1.0158	0.0074	1.0625
		3A	0.0000	1.0625	1.0511		1.0084	1.0042	0.0042	0.9603	3B	0.9720	0.9823	1.0084	1.0139	0.0055	1.0625
1$^{1}/_{16}$–16	UN	2A	0.0015	1.0610	1.0516		1.0204	1.0154	0.0050	0.9843	2B	0.995	1.009	1.0219	1.0284	0.0065	1.0625
		3A	0.0000	1.0625	1.0531		1.0219	1.0182	0.0037	0.9853	3B	0.9950	1.0033	1.0219	1.0268	0.0049	1.0625
1$^{1}/_{16}$–18	NEF	2A	0.0014	1.0611	1.0524		1.0250	1.0203	0.0047	0.9929	2B	1.002	1.015	1.0264	1.0326	0.0062	1.0625
		3A	0.0000	1.0625	1.0538		1.0264	1.0228	0.0036	0.9943	3B	1.0020	1.0105	1.0264	1.0310	0.0046	1.0625
1⅛–7	UNC	1A	0.0022	1.1228	1.0982		1.0300	1.0191	0.0109	0.9475	1B	0.970	0.998	1.0322	1.0463	0.0141	1.1250
		2A	0.0022	1.1228	1.1064	1.0982	1.0300	1.0228	0.0072	0.9475	2B	0.970	0.998	1.0322	1.0416	0.0094	1.1250
		3A	0.0000	1.1250	1.1086		1.0322	1.0268	0.0054	0.9497	3B	0.9700	0.9875	1.0322	1.0393	0.0071	1.1250
1⅛–8	N	2A	0.0021	1.1229	1.1079	1.1004	1.0417	1.0348	0.0069	0.9695	2B	0.900	1.015	1.0438	1.0528	0.0090	1.1250
		3A	0.0000	1.1250	1.1100		1.0438	1.0386	0.0052	0.9716	3B	0.9900	1.0047	1.0438	1.0505	0.0067	1.1250
1⅛–12	UNF	1A	0.0018	1.1232	1.1060		1.0691	1.0601	0.0090	1.0210	1B	1.035	1.053	1.0709	1.0826	0.0117	1.1250
		2A	0.0018	1.1232	1.1118		1.0691	1.0631	0.0060	1.0210	2B	1.035	1.053	1.0709	1.0787	0.0078	1.1250
		3A	0.0000	1.1250	1.1136		1.0709	1.0664	0.0045	1.0228	3B	1.0350	1.0448	1.0709	1.0768	0.0059	1.1250
1⅛–16 to 1¾–12																	
1⅛–16	UN	2A	0.0015	1.1235	1.1141		1.0829	1.0779	0.0050	1.0468	2B	1.057	1.071	1.0844	1.0909	0.0065	1.1250
		3A	0.0000	1.1250	1.1156		1.0844	1.0807	0.0037	1.0483	3B	1.0570	1.0658	1.0844	1.0893	0.0049	1.1250
1⅛–18	NEF	2A	0.0014	1.1236	1.1149		1.0875	1.0828	0.0047	1.0554	2B	1.065	1.078	1.0889	1.0951	0.0062	1.1250
		3A	0.0000	1.1250	1.1163		1.0889	1.0853	0.0036	1.0568	3B	1.0650	1.0730	1.0889	1.0935	0.0046	1.1250
1$^{3}/_{16}$–12	UN	2A	0.0017	1.1858	1.1744		1.1317	1.1259	0.0058	1.0836	2B	1.097	1.115	1.1334	1.1409	0.0075	1.1875
		3A	0.0000	1.1875	1.1761		1.1334	1.1291	0.0043	1.0853	3B	1.0970	1.1073	1.1334	1.1390	0.0056	1.1875
1$^{3}/_{16}$	UN	2A	0.0015	1.1860	1.1766		1.1454	1.1403	0.0051	1.1093	2B	1.120	1.134	1.1469	1.1535	0.0066	1.1875
		3A	0.0000	1.1875	1.1781		1.1469	1.1431	0.0038	1.1108	3B	1.1200	1.1283	1.1469	1.1519	0.0050	1.1875
1$^{3}/_{16}$–18	NEF	2A	0.0015	1.1860	1.1773		1.1499	1.1450	0.0049	1.1178	2B	1.127	1.140	1.1514	1.1577	0.0063	1.1875
		3A	0.0000	1.1875	1.1788		1.1514	1.1478	0.0036	1.1193	3B	1.1270	1.1355	1.1514	1.1561	0.0047	1.1875

TABLE 6.6 Standard Limits of Size: Unified and American Screw Threads (*Continued*)

Nominal size and threads per inch	Series designation	External									Internal						
				Major diameter limits, in			Pitch diameter limits, in					Minor diameter limits, in		Pitch diameter limits, in			Major diameter, in
		Class	Allowance, in	Max*	Min	Min†	Max*	Min	Tolerance	Minor diameter, in	Class	Min	Max	Min	Max	Tolerance	Min
1⅛–16 to 1¾–12																	
1¼–7	UNC	1A	0.0022	1.2478	1.2232		1.1550	1.1439	0.0111	1.0725	1B	1.095	1.123	1.1572	1.1716	0.0144	1.2500
		2A	0.0022	1.2478	1.2314	1.2232	1.1550	1.1476	0.0074	1.0725	2B	1.095	1.123	1.1572	1.1668	0.0096	1.2500
		3A	0.0000	1.2500	1.2336		1.1572	1.1517	0.0055	1.0747	3B	1.0950	1.1125	1.1572	1.1644	0.0072	1.2500
1¼–8	N	2A	0.0021	1.2479	1.2329	1.2254	1.1667	1.597	0.0070	1.0945	2B	1.115	1.140	1.1688	1.1780	0.0092	1.2500
		3A	0.0000	1.2500	1.2350		1.1688	1.1635	0.0053	1.0966	3B	1.1150	1.1297	1.1688	1.1757	0.0069	1.2500
1¼–12	UNF	1A	0.0018	1.2482	1.2310		1.1941	1.1849	0.0092	1.1460	1B	1.160	1.178	1.1959	1.2079	0.0120	1.2500
		2A	0.0018	1.2482	1.2368		1.1941	1.1879	0.0062	1.1460	2B	1.160	1.178	1.1959	1.2039	0.0080	1.2500
		3A	0.0000	1.2500	1.2386		1.1959	1.1913	0.0046	1.1478	3B	1.1600	1.1698	1.1959	1.2019	0.0060	1.2500
1¼–16	UN	2A	0.0015	1.2485	1.2391		1.2079	1.2028	0.0051	1.1718	2B	1.182	1.196	1.2094	1.2160	0.0066	1.2500
		3A	0.0000	1.2500	1.2406		1.2094	1.2056	0.0038	1.1733	3B	1.1820	1.1908	1.2094	1.2144	0.0050	1.2500
1¼–18	NEF	2A	0.0015	1.2485	1.2398		1.2124	1.2075	0.0049	1.1803	2B	1.190	1.203	1.2139	1.2202	0.0063	1.2500
		3A	0.0000	1.2500	1.2413		1.2139	1.2103	0.0036	1.1818	3B	1.1900	1.1980	1.2139	1.2186	0.0047	1.2500
1⁵⁄₁₆–12	UN	2A	0.0017	1.3108	1.2994		1.2567	1.2509	0.0058	1.2086	2B	1.222	1.240	1.2584	1.2659	0.0075	1.3125
		3A	0.0000	1.3125	1.3011		1.2584	1.2541	0.0043	1.2103	3B	1.2220	1.2323	1.2584	1.2640	0.0056	1.3125
1⁵⁄₁₆–16	UN	2A	0.0015	1.3110	1.3016		1.2704	1.2653	0.0051	1.2343	2B	1.245	1.259	1.2719	1.2785	0.0066	1.3125
		5A	0.0000	1.3125	1.3031		1.2719	1.2681	0.0038	1.2358	3B	1.2450	1.2533	1.2719	1.2769	0.0050	1.3125
1⁵⁄₁₆–18	NEF	2A	0.0015	1.3110	1.3023		1.2749	1.2700	0.0049	1.2428	2B	1.252	1.265	1.2764	1.2827	0.0063	1.3125
		3A	0.0000	1.3125	1.3038		1.2764	1.2728	0.0036	1.2443	3B	1.2520	1.2605	1.2764	1.2811	0.0047	1.3125
1⅜–6	UNC	1A	0.0024	1.3726	1.3453		1.2643	1.2523	0.0120	1.1681	1B	1.195	1.225	1.2667	‡1.2822	‡0.0155	1.3750
		2A	0.0024	1.3726	1.3544	1.3453	1.2643	1.2563	0.0080	1.1681	2B	1.195	1.225	1.2667	1.2771	0.0104	1.3750
		3A	0.0900	1.3750	1.3568		1.2667	1.2607	0.0060	1.1705	3B	1.1950	1.2146	1.2667	1.2745	0.0078	1.3750
1⅜–8	N	2A	0.0022	1.3728	1.3578	1.3503	1.2916	1.2844	0.0072	1.2194	2B	1.240	1.265	1.2938	1.3031	0.0093	1.3750
		3A	0.0000	1.3750	1.3600		1.2938	1.2884	0.0054	1.2216	3B	1.2400	1.2547	1.2938	1.3008	0.0070	1.3750
1⅜–12	UNF	1A	0.0019	1.3731	1.3559		1.3190	1.3096	0.0094	1.2709	1B	1.285	1.303	1.3209	1.3332	0.0123	1.3750
		2A	0.0019	1.3731	1.3617		1.3190	1.3127	0.0063	1.2709	2B	1.285	1.303	1.3209	1.3291	0.0082	1.3750
		3A	0.0000	1.3750	1.3636		1.3209	1.3162	0.0047	1.2728	3B	1.2850	1.2948	1.3209	1.3270	0.0061	1.3750

$1\frac{3}{8}$–16	UN	2A	0.0015	1.3735	1.3641		1.3329	1.3278	0.0051	1.2968	2B	1.307	1.321	1.3344	1.3410	0.0066	1.3750
		3A	0.0000	1.3750	1.3656		1.3344	1.3306	0.0038	1.2983	3B	1.3070	1.3158	1.3344	1.3394	0.0050	1.3750
$1\frac{3}{8}$–18	NEF	2A	0.0015	1.3735	1.3648		1.3374	1.3325	0.0049	1.3053	2B	1.315	1.328	1.3389	1.3452	0.0063	1.3750
		3A	0.0000	1.3750	1.3663		1.3389	1.3353	0.0036	1.3068	3B	1.3150	1.3230	1.3389	1.3436	0.0047	1.3750
$1\frac{7}{16}$–12	UN	2A	0.0018	1.4357	1.4243		1.3816	1.3757	0.0059	1.3335	2B	1.347	1.365	1.3834	1.3910	0.0076	1.4375
		3A	0.0000	1.4375	1.4261		1.3834	1.3790	0.0044	1.3353	3B	1.3470	1.3573	1.3834	1.3891	.0057	1.4375
$1\frac{7}{16}$–16	UN	2A	0.0016	1.4359	1.4265		1.3953	1.3901	0.0052	1.3592	2B	1.370	1.384	1.3969	1.4037	0.0068	1.4375
		3A	0.0000	1.4375	1.4281		1.3969	1.3930	0.0039	1.3608	3B	1.3700	1.3783	1.3969	1.4020	0.0051	1.4375
$1\frac{7}{16}$–18	NEF	2A	0.0015	1.4360	1.4273		1.3999	1.3949	0.0050	1.3678	2B	1.377	1.390	1.4014	1.4079	0.0065	1.4375
		3A	0.0000	1.4375	1.4288		1.4014	1.3977	0.0037	1.3693	3B	1.3770	1.3855	1.4014	1.4062	0.0048	1.4375
$1\frac{1}{2}$–6	UNC	1A	0.0024	1.4976	1.4703		1.3893	1.3772	0.0121	1.2931	1B	1.320	1.350	1.3917	1.4075	0.0158	1.5000
		2A	0.0024	1.4976	1.4794	1.4703	1.3893	1.3812	0.0081	1.2931	2B	1.320	1.350	1.3917	1.4022	0.0105	1.5000
		3A	0.0000	1.5000	1.4818		1.3917	1.3856	0.0061	1.2955	3B	1.3200	1.3396	1.3917	1.3996	0.0079	1.5000
$1\frac{1}{2}$–8	N	2A	0.0022	1.4978	1.4828	1.4753	1.4166	1.4093	0.0073	1.3444	2B	1.365	1.390	1.4188	1.4283	0.0095	1.5000
		3A	0.0000	1.5000	1.4850		1.4188	1.4133	0.0055	1.3466	3B	1.3650	1.3797	1.4188	1.4259	0.0071	1.5000
$1\frac{1}{2}$–12	UNF	1A	0.0019	1.4981	1.4809		1.4440	1.4344	0.0096	1.3959	1B	1.410	1.428	1.4459	1.4584	0.0125	1.5000
		2A	0.0019	1.4981	1.4867		1.4440	1.4376	0.0064	1.3959	2B	1.410	1.428	1.4459	1.4542	0.0083	1.5000
		3A	0.0000	1.5000	1.4886		1.4459	1.4411	0.0048	1.3978	3B	1.4100	1.4198	1.4459	1.4522	0.0063	1.5000
$1\frac{1}{2}$–16	UN	2A	0.0016	1.4984	1.4890		1.4578	1.4526	0.0052	1.4217	2B	1.432	1.446	1.4594	1.4662	0.0068	1.5000
		3A	0.0000	1.5000	1.4906		1.4594	1.4555	0.0039	1.4233	3B	1.4320	1.4408	1.4594	1.4645	0.0051	1.5000
$1\frac{1}{2}$–18	NEF	2A	0.0015	1.4985	1.4898		1.4624	1.4574	0.0050	1.4303	2B	1.440	1.452	1.4639	1.4704	0.0065	1.5000
		3A	0.0000	1.5000	1.4913		1.4639	1.4602	0.0037	1.4318	3B	1.4400	1.4480	1.4639	1.4687	0.0048	1.5000
$1\frac{9}{16}$–16	N	2A	0.0016	1.5609	1.5515		1.5203	1.5151	0.0052	1.4842	2B	1.495	1.509	1.5219	1.5287	0.0068	1.5625
		3A	0.0000	1.5625	1.5531		1.5219	1.5180	0.0039	1.4858	3B	1.4950	1.5033	1.5219	1.5270	0.0051	1.5625
$1\frac{9}{16}$–18	NEF	2A	0.0015	1.5610	1.5523		1.5249	1.5199	0.0050	1.4928	2B	1.502	1.515	1.5264	1.5329	0.0065	1.5625
		3A	0.0000	1.5625	1.5538		1.5264	1.5227	0.0037	1.4943	3B	1.5020	1.5105	1.5264	1.5312	0.0048	1.5625
$1\frac{5}{8}$–8	N	2A	0.0022	1.6228	1.6078	1.6003	1.5416	1.5342	0.0074	1.4694	2B	1.490	1.515	1.5438	1.5535	0.0097	1.6250
		3A	0.0000	1.6250	1.6100		1.5438	1.5382	0.0056	1.4716	3B	1.4900	1.5047	1.5438	1.5510	0.0072	1.6250
$1\frac{5}{8}$–12	UN	2A	0.0018	1.6232	1.6118		1.5691	1.5632	0.0059	1.5210	2B	1.535	1.553	1.5709	1.5785	0.0076	1.6250
		3A	0.0000	1.6250	1.6136		1.5709	1.5665	0.0044	1.5228	3B	1.5350	1.5448	1.5709	1.5766	0.0057	1.6250

TABLE 6.6 Standard Limits of Size: Unified and American Screw Threads (*Continued*)

Nominal size and threads per inch	Series designation	External									Internal						
				Major diameter limits, in			Pitch diameter limits, in					Minor diameter limits, in		Pitch diameter limits, in			Major diameter, in
		Class	Allowance, in	Max*	Min	Min†	Max*	Min	Tolerance	Minor diameter, in	Class	Min	Max	Min	Max	Tolerance	Min
1⅝–16 to 1¾–12																	
1⅝–16	UN	2A	0.0016	1.6234	1.6140		1.5828	1.5776	0.0052	1.5467	2B	1.557	1.571	1.5844	1.5912	0.0068	1.6250
		3A	0.0000	1.6250	1.6156		1.5814	1.5805	0.0039	1.5483	3B	1.5570	1.5658	1.5844	1.5895	0.0051	1.6250
1⅝–18	NEF	2A	0.0015	1.6235	1.6148		1.5874	1.5824	0.0050	1.5553	2B	1.565	1.578	1.5889	1.5954	0.0065	1.6250
		3A	0.0000	1.6250	1.6163		1.5889	1.5852	0.0037	1.5568	3B	1.5650	1.5730	1.5889	1.5937	0.0048	1.6250
1 11/16–16	N	2A	0.0016	1.6859	1.6765		1.6453	1.6400	0.0053	1.6092	2B	1.620	1.634	1.6469	1.6538	0.0069	1.6875
		3A	0.0000	1.6875	1.6781		1.6469	1.6429	0.0040	1.6108	3B	1.6200	1.6283	1.6469	1.6521	0.0052	1.6875
1 11/16–18	NEF	2A	0.0015	1.6860	1.6773		1.6499	1.6448	0.0051	1.6178	2B	1.627	1.640	1.6514	1.6580	0.0066	1.6875
		3A	0.0000	1.6875	1.6788		1.6514	1.6476	0.0038	1.6193	3B	1.6270	1.6355	1.6514	1.6563	0.0049	1.6875
1¾–5	UNC	1A	0.0027	1.7473	1.7165		1.6174	1.6040	0.0134	1.5019	1B	1.534	1.568	1.6201	1.6375	0.0174	1.7500
		2A	0.0027	1.7473	1.7268	1.7165	1.6174	1.6085	0.0089	1.5019	2B	1.534	1.568	1.6201	1.6317	0.0116	1.7500
		3A	0.0000	1.7500	1.7295		1.6201	1.6134	0.0067	1.5046	3B	1.5340	1.5575	1.6201	1.6288	0.0087	1.7500
1¾–8	N	2A	0.0023	1.7477	1.7327	1.7252	1.6665	1.6590	0.0075	1.5943	2B	1.615	1.640	1.6688	1.6786	0.0098	1.7500
		3A	0.0000	1.7300	1.7350		1.6688	1.6632	0.0056	1.5966	3B	1.6150	1.6297	1.6688	1.6762	0.0074	1.7500
1¾–12	UN	2A	0.0018	1.7482	1.7368		1.6941	1.6881	0.0060	1.6460	2B	1.660	1.678	1.6959	1.7037	0.0073	1.7500
		3A	0.0000	1.7500	1.7386		1.6959	1.6914	0.0045	1.6478	3B	1.6600	1.6698	1.6959	1.7017	0.0053	1.7500
1¾–16 to 3–16																	
1¾–16	UNEF	2A	0.0016	1.7484	1.7390		1.7078	1.7025	0.0053	1.6717	2B	1.682	1.696	1.7094	1.7163	0.0069	1.7500
		3A	0.0000	1.7500	1.7406		1.7094	1.7054	0.0040	1.6733	3B	1.6820	1.6906	1.7094	1.7146	0.0052	1.7500
1 13/16–16	N	2A	0.0016	1.8109	1.8015		1.7703	1.7650	0.0053	1.7342	2B	1.745	1.759	1.7719	1.7788	0.0069	1.8125
		3A	0.0000	1.8125	1.8031		1.7719	1.7679	0.0040	1.7358	3B	1.7450	1.7533	1.7719	1.7771	0.0052	1.8125
1⅞–8	N	2A	0.0023	1.8727	1.8577	1.8502	1.7915	1.7838	0.0077	1.7193	2B	1.740	1.765	1.7938	1.8038	0.0100	1.8750
		3A	0.0000	1.8750	1.8600		1.7938	1.7881	0.0057	1.7216	3B	1.7400	1.7547	1.7938	1.8013	0.0075	1.8750
1⅞–12	UN	2A	0.0018	1.8732	1.8618		1.8191	1.8131	0.0060	1.7710	2B	1.785	1.803	1.8209	1.8287	0.0078	1.8750
		3A	0.0000	1.8750	1.8636		1.8209	1.8164	0.0045	1.7728	3B	1.7850	1.7948	1.8209	1.8267	0.0058	1.8750
1⅞–16	UN	2A	0.0016	1.8734	1.8640		1.8328	1.8275	0.0053	1.7967	2B	1.807	1.821	1.8344	1.8413	0.0069	1.8750
		3A	0.0000	1.8750	1.8656		1.8344	1.8304	0.0040	1.7983	3B	1.8070	1.8158	1.8344	1.8396	0.0052	1.8750

1 15/16–16	N	2A	0.0016	1.9359	1.9265		1.8953	1.8899	0.0054	1.8592	2B	1.870	1.884	1.8969	1.9039	0.0070	1.9375
		3A	0.0000	1.9375	1.9281		1.8969	1.8929	0.0040	1.8608	3B	1.8700	1.8783	1.8969	1.9021	.0052	1.9375
2–4½	UNC	1A	0.0029	1.9971	1.9641		1.8528	1.8385	0.0143	1.7245	1B	1.759	1.795	1.8557	1.8743	0.0186	2.0000
		2A	0.0029	1.9971	1.9751	1.9641	1.8528	1.8433	0.0095	1.7245	2B	1.759	1.795	1.8557	1.8681	0.0124	2.0000
		3A	0.0000	2.0000	1.9780		1.8557	1.8486	0.0071	1.7274	3B	1.7590	1.7861	1.8557	1.8650	0.0093	2.0000
2–8	N	2A	0.0023	1.9977	1.9827	1.9752	1.9165	1.9087	0.0078	1.8443	2B	1.865	1.890	1.9188	1.9289	0.0101	2.0000
		3A	0.0000	2.0000	1.9850		1.9188	1.9130	0.0058	1.8466	3B	1.8650	1.8797	1.9188	1.9264	0.0076	2.0000
2–12	UN	2A	0.0018	1.9982	1.9868		1.9441	1.9380	0.0061	1.8960	2B	1.910	1.928	1.9459	1.9538	0.0079	2.0000
		3A	0.0000	2.0000	1.9886		1.9459	1.9414	0.0045	1.8978	3B	1.9100	1.9198	1.9459	1.9518	0.0059	2.0000
2–16	UNEF	2A	0.0016	1.9984	1.9890		1.9578	1.9524	0.0054	1.9217	2B	1.932	1.946	1.9594	1.0664	0.0070	2.0000
		3A	0.0000	2.0000	1.9906		1.9594	1.9554	0.0040	1.9233	3B	1.9320	1.9408	1.9594	1.9646	0.0052	2.0000
2 1/16–16	N	2A	0.0016	2.0609	2.0515		2.0203	2.0149	0.0054	1.9842	2B	1.995	2.009	2.0219	2.0289	0.0070	2.0625
		3A	0.0000	2.0625	2.0531		2.0219	2.0179	0.0040	1.9858	3B	1.9950	2.0033	2.0219	2.0271	0.0052	2.0625
2 1/8–8	N	2A	0.0024	2.1226	2.1076	2.1001	2.0414	2.0335	0.0079	1.9692	2B	1.990	2.015	2.0438	2.0540	0.0102	2.1250
		3A	0.0000	2.1250	2.1100		2.0438	2.0379	0.0059	1.9716	3B	1.9900	2.0047	2.0438	2.0515	0.0077	2.1250
2 1/8–12	UN	2A	0.0018	2.1232	2.1118		2.0691	2.0630	0.0061	2.0210	2B	2.035	2.053	2.0709	2.0788	0.0079	2.1250
		3A	0.0000	2.1250	2.1136		2.0709	2.0664	0.0045	2.0228	3B	2.0350	2.0448	2.0709	2.0768	0.0059	2.1250
2 1/8–16	UN	2A	0.0016	2.1234	2.1140		2.0828	2.0774	0.0054	2.0467	2B	2.057	2.071	2.0844	2.0914	0.0070	2.1250
		3A	0.0000	2.1250	2.1156		2.0844	2.0803	0.0041	2.0483	3B	2.0570	2.0658	2.0844	2.0896	0.0052	2.1250
2 3/16–16	N	2A	0.0016	2.1859	2.1765		2.1453	2.1399	0.0054	2.1092	2B	2.120	2.134	2.1469	2.1539	0.0070	2.1875
		3A	0.0000	2.1875	2.1781		2.1469	2.1428	0.0041	2.1108	3B	2.1200	2.1283	2.1469	2.1521	0.0052	2.1875
2 1/4–4½	UNC	1A	0.0029	2.2471	2.2141		2.1028	2.0882	0.0146	1.9745	1B	2.009	2.045	2.1057	2.1247	0.0190	2.2500
		2A	0.0029	2.2471	2.2251	2.2141	2.1028	2.0931	0.0097	1.9745	2B	2.009	2.045	2.1057	2.1183	0.0126	2.2500
		3A	0.0000	2.2500	2.2280		2.1057	2.0984	0.0073	1.9774	3B	2.0090	2.0361	2.1057	2.1152	0.0095	2.2500
2 1/4–8	N	2A	0.0024	2.2476	2.2326	2.2251	2.1664	2.1584	0.0080	2.0942	2B	2.115	2.140	2.1688	2.1792	0.0104	2.2500
		3A	0.0000	2.2500	2.2350		2.1688	2.1628	0.0060	2.0966	3B	2.1150	2.1297	2.1688	2.1766	0.0078	2.2500
2 1/4–12	UN	2A	0.0018	2.2482	2.2368		2.1941	2.1880	0.0061	2.1460	2B	2.160	2.178	2.1959	2.2038	0.0079	2.2500
		3A	0.0000	2.2500	2.2386		2.1959	2.1914	0.0045	2.1478	3B	2.1600	2.1698	2.1959	2.2018	0.0059	2.2500
2 1/4–16	UN	2A	0.0016	2.2484	2.2390		2.2078	2.2024	0.0054	2.1717	2B	2.182	2.196	2.2094	2.2164	0.0070	2.2500
		3A	0.0000	2.2500	2.2406		2.2094	2.2053	0.0041	2.1733	3B	2.1820	2.1908	2.2094	2.2146	0.0052	2.2500
2 5/16–16	N	2A	0.0017	2.3108	2.3014		2.2702	2.2647	0.0055	2.2341	2B	2.245	2.259	2.2719	2.2791	0.0072	2.3125
		3A	0.0000	2.3125	2.3031		2.2719	2.2678	0.0041	2.2358	3B	2.2450	2.2533	2.2719	2.2773	0.0054	2.3125

TABLE 6.6 Standard Limits of Size: Unified and American Screw Threads (*Continued*)

Nominal size and threads per inch	Series designation	External									Internal						
		Class	Allowance, in	Major diameter limits, in			Pitch diameter limits, in			Minor diameter, in	Class	Minor diameter limits, in		Pitch diameter limits, in			Major diameter, in
				Max*	Min	Min†	Max*	Min	Tolerance			Min	Max	Min	Max	Tolerance	Min
1¾–16 to 3–16																	
2⅜–12	UN	2A	0.0019	2.3731	2.3617		2.3190	2.3128	0.0062	2.2709	2B	2.285	2.303	2.3209	2.3290	0.0081	2.3750
		3A	0.0000	2.3750	2.3636		2.3209	2.3163	0.0046	2.2728	3B	2.2850	2.2948	2.3209	2.3269	0.0060	2.3750
2⅜–16	UN	2A	0.0017	2.3733	2.3639		2.3327	2.3272	0.0055	2.2966	2B	2.307	2.321	2.3344	2.3416	0.0072	2.3750
		3A	0.0000	2.3750	2.3656		2.3344	2.3303	0.0041	2.2983	3B	2.3070	2.3158	2.3344	2.3398	0.0054	2.3750
2 7/16–16	N	2A	0.0017	2.4358	2.4264		2.3953	2.3897	0.0055	2.3591	2B	2.370	2.384	2.3969	2.4041	0.0072	2.4375
		3A	0.0000	2.4375	2.4281		2.3969	2.3928	0.0041	2.3608	3B	2.3700	2.3783	2.3969	2.4023	0.0054	2.4375
2½–4	UNC	1A	0.0031	2.4969	2.4612		2.3345	2.3190	0.0155	2.1902	1B	2.229	2.267	2.3376	2.3578	0.0202	2.5000
		2A	0.0031	2.4969	2.4731	2.4612	2.3345	2.3241	0.0104	2.1902	2B	2.229	2.267	2.3376	2.3511	0.0135	2.5000
		3A	0.0000	2.5000	2.4762		2.3376	2.3298	0.0078	2.1933	3B	2.2290	2.2594	2.3376	2.3477	0.0101	2.5000
2½–8	N	2A	0.0024	2.4976	2.4826	2.4751	2.4164	2.4082	0.0082	2.3442	2B	2.365	2.390	2.4188	2.4294	0.0106	2.5000
		3A	0.0000	2.5000	2.4850		2.4188	2.4127	0.0061	2.3466	3B	2.3650	2.3797	2.4188	2.4268	0.0080	2.5000
2½–12	UN	2A	0.0019	2.4981	2.4867		2.4440	2.4378	0.0062	2.3959	2B	2.410	2.428	2.4459	2.4540	0.0081	2.5000
		3A	0.0000	2.5000	2.4886		2.4459	2.4413	0.0046	2.3978	3B	2.4100	2.4198	2.4459	2.4519	0.0060	2.5000
2½–16	UN	2A	0.0017	2.4983	2.4889		2.4577	2.4522	0.0055	2.4216	2B	2.432	2.446	2.4594	2.4666	0.0072	2.5000
		3A	0.0000	2.5000	2.4906		2.4594	2.4553	0.0041	2.4233	3B	2.4320	2.4408	2.4594	2.4648	0.0054	2.5000
2⅝–12	UN	2A	0.0019	2.6231	2.6117		2.5690	2.5628	0.0062	2.5209	2B	2.535	2.553	2.5709	2.5790	0.0081	2.6250
		3A	0.0000	2.6250	2.6136		2.5709	2.5663	0.0046	2.5228	3B	2.5350	2.5448	2.5709	2.5769	0.0060	2.6250
2⅝–16	UN	2A	0.0017	2.6233	2.6139		2.5827	2.5772	0.0055	2.5466	2B	2.557	2.571	2.5844	2.5916	0.0072	2.6250
		3A	0.0000	2.6250	2.6156		2.5844	2.5803	0.0041	2.5483	3B	2.5570	2.5658	2.5844	2.5898	0.0054	2.6250
2⅜–4	UNC	1A	0.0032	2.7468	2.7111		2.5844	2.5686	0.0158	2.4401	1B	2.479	2.517	2.5876	2.6082	0.0206	2.7500
		2A	0.0032	2.7468	2.7230	2.7111	2.5844	2.5739	0.0105	2.4401	2B	2.479	2.517	2.5876	2.6013	0.0137	2.7500
		3A	0.0000	2.7500	2.7262		2.5876	2.5797	0.0079	2.4433	3B	2.4790	2.5094	2.5876	2.5979	0.0103	2.7500
2¾–8	N	2A	0.0025	2.7475	2.7325	2.7250	2.6663	2.0580	0.0083	2.5941	2B	2.615	2.640	2.6688	2.6796	0.0108	2.7500
		3A	0.0000	2.7500	2.7350		2.6688	‡2.6625	‡0.0063	2.5966	3B	2.6150	2.6297	2.6688	2.6769	0.0081	2.7500
2¾–12	UN	2A	0.0019	2.7481	2.7367		2.6940	2.6878	0.0062	2.6459	2B	2.660	2.678	2.6959	2.7040	0.0081	2.7500
		3A	0.0000	2.7500	2.7386		2.6959	2.6913	0.0046	2.6478	3B	2.6600	2.6698	2.6959	2.7019	0.0060	2.7500

2¾–16	UN	2A	0.0017	2.7483	2.7389		2.7077	2.7022	0.0055	2.6716	2B	2.682	2.696	2.7094	2.7166	0.0072	2.7500
		3A	0.0000	2.7500	2.7406		2.7094	2.7053	0.0041	2.6733	3B	2.6820	2.6908	2.7094	2.7148	0.0054	2.7500
2⅞–12	UN	2A	0.0019	2.8731	2.8617		2.8190	2.8127	0.0063	2.7709	2B	2.785	2.803	2.8209	2.8291	0.0082	2.8750
		3A	0.0000	2.8750	2.8636		2.8209	2.8162	0.0047	2.7728	3B	2.7850	2.7948	2.8209	2.8271	0.0062	2.8750
2⅞–16	UN	2A	0.0017	2.8733	2.8639		2.8327	2.8271	0.0056	2.7966	2B	2.807	2.821	2.8344	2.8417	0.0073	2.8750
		3A	0.0000	2.8750	2.8656		2.8344	2.8302	0.0042	2.7983	3B	2.8070	2.8158	2.8344	2.8399	0.0055	2.8750
3–4	UNC	1A	0.0032	2.9968	2.9611		2.8344	2.8183	0.0161	2.6901	1B	2.729	2.767	2.8376	2.8585	0.0209	3.0000
		2A	0.0032	2.9968	2.9730	2.9611	2.8344	2.8237	0.0107	2.6901	2B	2.729	2.767	2.8376	2.8515	0.0139	3.0000
		3A	0.0000	3.0000	2.9762		2.8376	2.8296	0.0080	2.6933	3B	2.7290	2.7594	2.8376	2.8480	0.0104	3.0000
3–8	N	2A	0.0026	2.9974	2.9824	2.9749	2.9162	2.9077	0.0085	2.8440	2B	2.865	2.890	2.9188	2.9299	0.0111	3.0000
		3A	0.0000	3.0000	2.9850		2.9188	2.9124	0.0064	2.8466	3B	2.8650	2.8797	2.9188	2.9271	0.0083	3.0000
3–12	UN	2A	0.0019	2.9981	2.9867		2.9440	2.9377	0.0063	2.8959	2B	2.910	2.928	2.9459	2.9541	0.0082	3.0000
		3A	0.0000	3.0000	2.9886		2.9459	2.9412	0.0047	2.5978	3B	2.9100	2.9198	2.9459	2.9521	0.0062	3.0000
3–16	UN	2A	0.0017	2.9983	2.9889		2.9577	2.9521	0.0056	2.9216	2B	2.932	2.946	2.9594	2.9667	0.0073	3.0000
		3A	0.0000	3.0000	2.9906		2.9594	2.9552	0.0042	2.9233	3B	2.9320	2.9408	2.9594	2.9649	0.0055	3.0000

* For class 2A threads having an additive finish, the maximum is increased to the basic size, the value being the same as for class 3A shown in this column.

† For unfinished hot-rolled material.

SOURCE: Extracted from National Bureau of Standards Handbook H28 (1967), Part I (Screw-Thread Standards for Federal Services), which is in general agreement with *American Standard Unified Screw Threads* (ASA B1.1-1960).

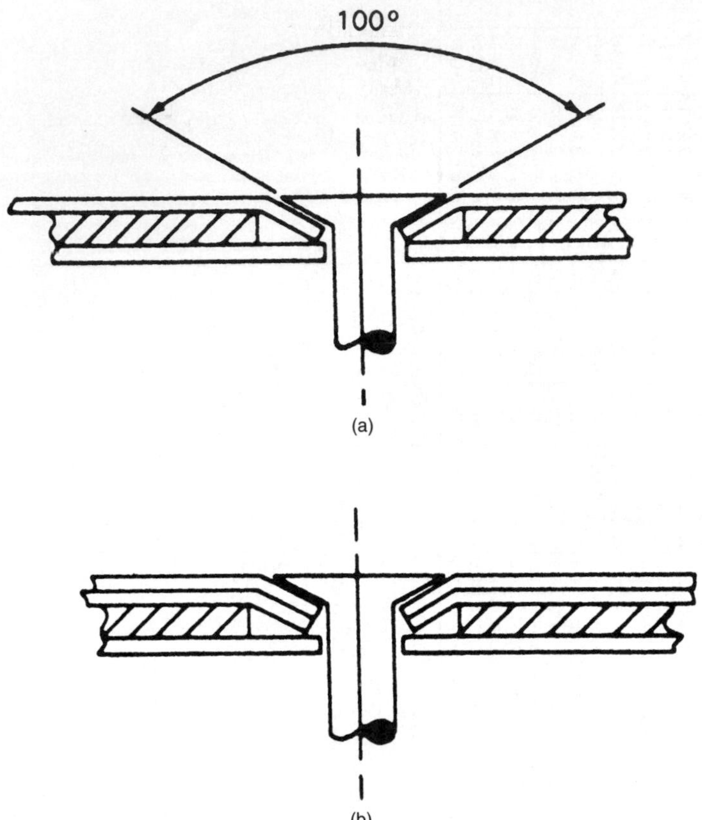

Figure 6.29 (*a*) Dimpling. (*b*) Double dimpling.

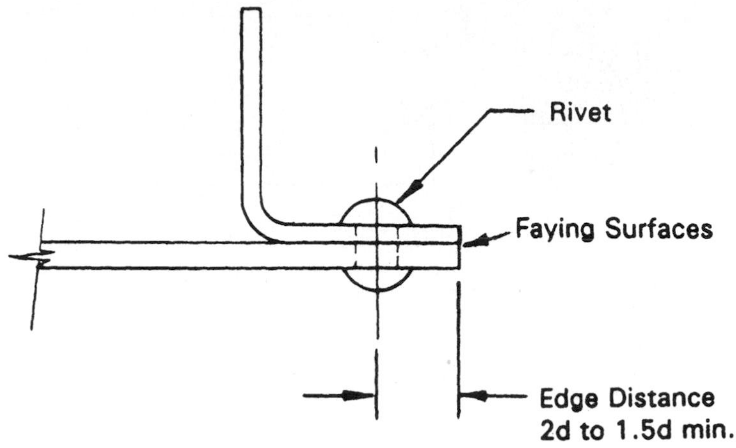

Figure 6.30 Rivet edge distance.

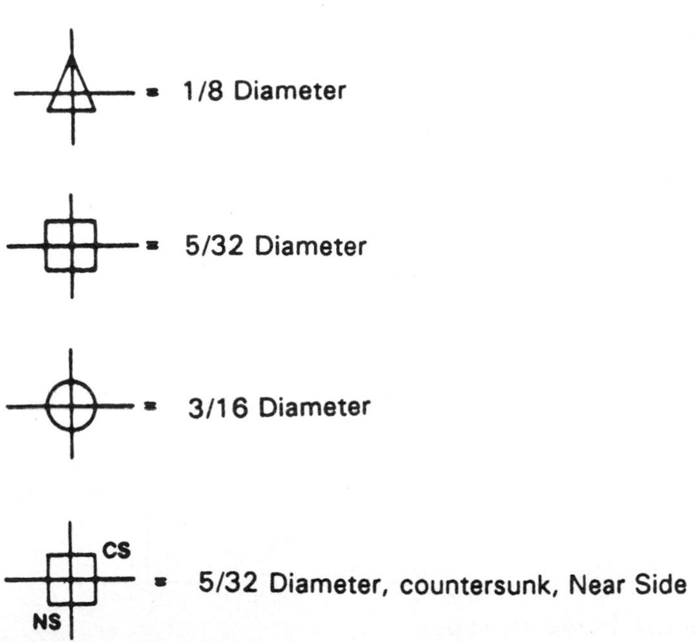

Figure 6.31 Standard rivet symbols.

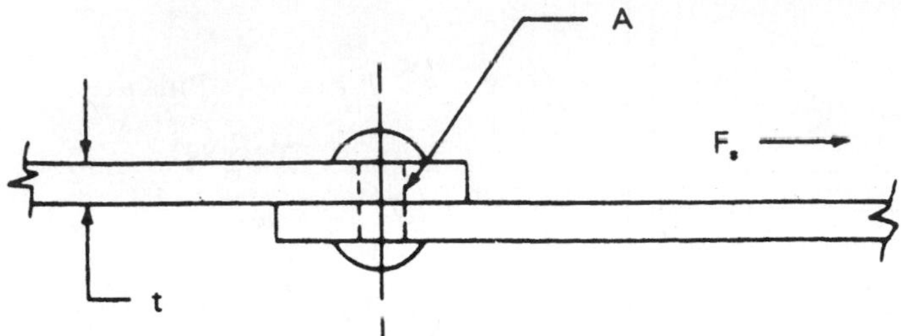

Figure 6.32 Single-shear area.

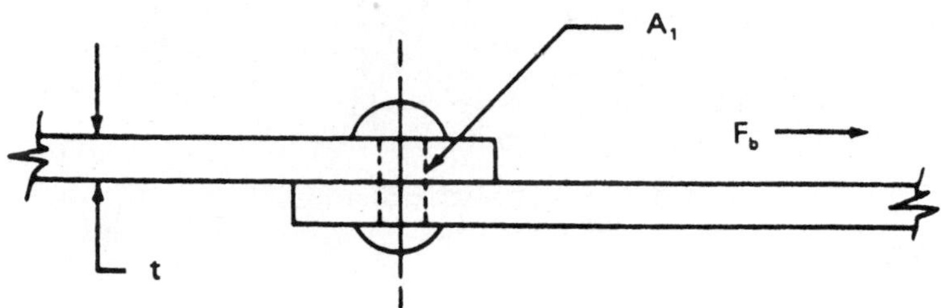

Figure 6.33 Pitch and bearing-stress area.

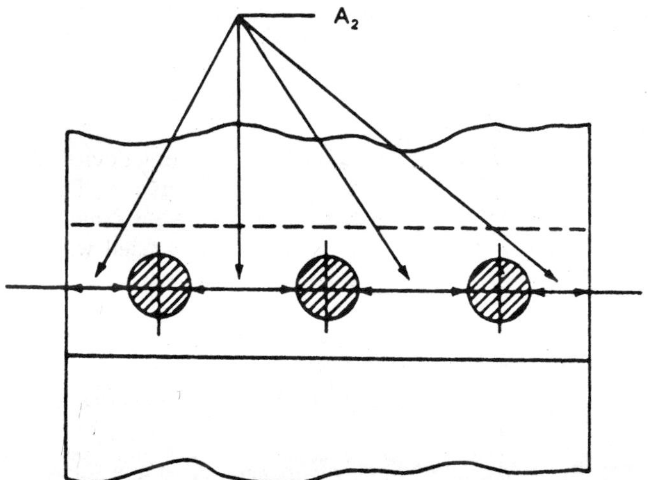

Figure 6.34 Pitch and bend areas.

6.4 Pins

Pins of various types are used throughout industry. Pins are available in different sizes, styles, and materials. This section details the most popular pins used in all types of design and assembly applications. The common-usage pins include

- Clevis pins
- Cotter pins
- Spring pins (roll pins)
- Spiral spring pins
- Taper pins
- Dowel pins
- Grooved pins
- Quick-release pins

6.4.1 Clevis pins

Clevis pins are used where a quickly detachable pin is of benefit from a design and manufacturing standpoint. Figure 6.35 shows the sizes and dimensions of standard clevis pins. The clevis pin may be made of various materials such as carbon steel, stainless steel, aluminum alloy, and other materials.

6.4.2 Cotter pins

Cotter pins are very common and economical fastening devices that see countless uses and applications throughout industry. The two most common types of cotter pins and their sizes and dimensions are shown in Fig. 6.36. The cotter pin is normally used with the standard clevis pin.

6.4.3 Spring pins (roll pins)

The slotted type of spring pin (sometimes called a *roll pin*) is used in applications where economy is important. This type of pin has been used to replace the tapered pin, dowel pin, and grooved pin in many applications because of its low cost and ease of preparation and assembly into holes with loose tolerances. Spring-temper carbon steel is usually used for these pins, but they are also available in other materials. Figure 6.37 shows the sizes, dimensions, and recommended hole diameters for spring-pin applications, along with the double-shear values for design reference. Placement of the slot in relation to shock loads for this type of pin can affect its performance and shock-absorbing qualities.

6.4.4 Spiral spring pins (coiled spring pins)

The spiral spring pin was developed after the standard slotted spring pin in order to provide more shock resistance and a tighter fit in drilled holes. These pins are made for standard, light-duty, and heavy-duty applications and are produced in various materials to suit the application. I have conducted studies of slotted spring pins and spiral spring pins and have found that the heavy-duty slotted spring pin will withstand more shock-loading cycles than the standard spiral spring pin. Figure 6.38 shows the sizes, dimensions, recommended hole sizes, and double-shear values for these pins.

6.4.5 Taper pins

The standard taper pin was widely used before the advent of the spring pins and grooved pins. This pin type is still used in some industrial applications. Figure 6.39 shows the standard sizes and dimensions of taper pins.

6.4.6 Dowel pins (hardened and ground machine type)

The hardened and ground dowel pin is used widely in tooling applications and a wide range of indexing applications where great accuracy is required. Figure 6.40 shows the available standard sizes and dimensions of this important class of pin.

6.4.7 Grooved pins

The solid groove pin is one of the most popular fastening devices in use today. Its applications are limitless, and its use is economical, practical, and easy to implement. The hole diameter required for its application is not as critical as that for other solid pins. Seven standard styles or types are recognized as American national standards. Figure 6.41 shows the different types, sizes, and dimensions. Figure 6.42 shows the standard lengths. Figure 6.43 shows the recommended hole sizes. And Fig. 6.44 gives the standard minimum double-shear loads for these pins.

6.4.8 Quick-release pins

The quick-release pin is available in many types and finds use in design applications where a quick release action of a fastened joint or part is required. Most of these types of pins contain a push-button release action that allows the pin to be removed by a straight pulling action after the release button is pressed. The quick-release pin series is available in carbon steel, alloy steels, and stainless steels. Applications include tool engineering, aerospace vehicles, and many other applications where a strong, quick-release fastener is required. The quick-release pin is normally used for shear-loading applications only.

6.5 Retaining Rings

Retaining rings have many uses in the design and maintenance of modern equipment, including

- Shaft retention
- Bearing retention
- Retention of parts on shafts
- Spring retention
- Vertical and horizontal shaft support

The standard retaining ring is normally made of spring steel, although other materials such as beryllium-copper alloys and stainless steels are sometimes used. Figure 6.45 shows some of the main retaining types.

The allowable thrust loads for each type of retaining ring must be obtained from the retaining ring manufacturers' handbooks. The calculation procedures for various applications are also shown in these handbooks. There are at least 25 to 30 different types of retaining rings. The critical dimensions for machining the grooves that hold the retaining ring in place are also obtained from the manufacturers' handbooks. Figure 6.46 shows a typical page from the Waldes retaining ring handbook. This sample page is for the 5100 external type ring, and the typical machining dimensions for the retaining groove may be seen under "Groove Dimensions" in the table. Dimensions and application data are also shown.

Note that electroplating thickness can interfere with the proper functioning of the ring in the groove. Overplating can cause the ring to come out of the retaining groove during operation of the mechanism on which the ring is used. Therefore, specify a maximum plating thickness of 0.0002 in (0.2 mil) or allow additional clearance for the ring in the groove when the part is to be electroplated.

Figure 6.47 shows a retaining ring interchangeability chart for various manufacturers and also lists the appropriate military standard numbers.

6.5.1 X-washers (split washers)

An X-washer is a unique type of retaining ring. It is used in applications similar to those for the standard spring retaining ring except that it may be installed with a pair of common pliers, as shown in Fig. 6.48. The dimensions and sizes of the presently available X-washer series are also shown in Fig. 6.48. The X-washer is sometimes called a *split washer* and may be listed as such in fastener catalogs, although that is an incorrect name.

An X-washer is normally used for a one-time-only application. Once the washer is installed on a shaft and removed with pliers, it should not be reused. Although applicable only for one-time installations, these devices are suitable and economical for many applications in product design and manufacturing. The fact that these washers may be installed and removed with common pliers, and not special tools, is an asset in their application.

6.6 Set-Collars, Clamp-Collars, and Split-Collars

These devices have many uses in product design and manufacturing. They are used to retain shafts, to withstand high-thrust loads, and to space parts, and they are often welded to plate cams, plate sprockets, and indexing plates to form a hub by which the part is retained on a shaft. The standard set-collar is simply a machined ring with set screws that hold the ring on a shaft or cylindrical end of a part. Figure 6.49 shows the standard set-collar sizes and dimensions. These collars are normally made from low-carbon steel with zinc plating as a finish.

(Text continued on page 483.)

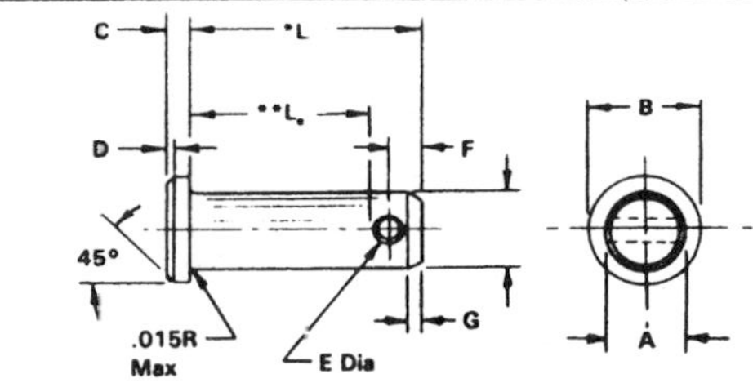

	A		B	C	D	E				
Basic Pin Diameter	Shank Diameter Max	Min	Head Diameter Max	Head Height Max	Head Chamfer ± 0.01	Hole Diameter Max	Min	F	G	Cotter Pin Size
0.188	0.186	0.181	0.32	0.07	0.02	0.088	0.073	0.09	0.055	1/16
0.250	0.248	0.243	0.38	0.10	0.03	0.088	0.073	0.09	0.055	1/16
0.312	0.311	0.306	0.44	0.10	0.03	0.119	0.104	0.12	0.071	3/32
0.375	0.373	0.368	0.51	0.13	0.03	0.119	0.104	0.12	0.071	3/32
0.438	0.436	0.431	0.57	0.16	0.04	0.119	0.104	0.12	0.071	3/32
0.500	0.496	0.491	0.63	0.16	0.04	0.151	0.136	0.15	0.089	1/8
0.625	0.621	0.616	0.82	0.21	0.06	0.151	0.136	0.15	0.089	1/8
0.750	0.746	0.741	0.94	0.26	0.07	0.182	0.167	0.18	0.110	5/32
0.875	0.871	0.866	1.04	0.32	0.09	0.182	0.167	0.18	0.110	5/32
1.000	0.996	0.991	1.19	0.35	0.10	0.182	0.167	0.18	0.110	5/32

*L = Total length under head
**L_e = Length of effective grip
Effective grip lengths must be selected from manufacturer's catalogs.

Figure 6.35 Standard clevis-pin dimensions.

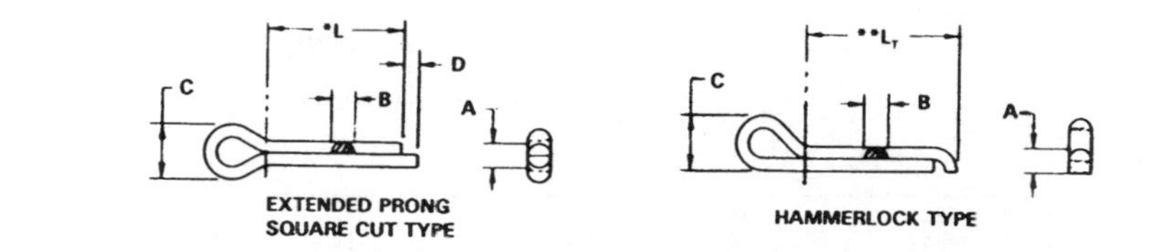

Basic Pin Diameter	Total Shank Diameter A	Wire Width Maximum B	Head Diameter Minimum C	Extended Prong Length, Minimum D	Recommended Hole Size
0.031	0.032	0.032	0.06	0.01	0.047
0.047	0.048	0.048	0.09	0.02	0.062
0.062	0.060	0.060	0.12	0.03	0.078
0.078	0.076	0.076	0.16	0.04	0.094
0.094	0.090	0.090	0.19	0.04	0.109
0.109	0.104	0.104	0.22	0.05	0.125
0.125	0.120	0.120	0.25	0.06	0.141
0.141	0.134	0.134	0.28	0.06	0.156
0.156	0.150	0.150	0.31	0.07	0.172
0.188	0.176	0.176	0.38	0.09	0.203
0.219	0.207	0.207	0.44	0.10	0.234
0.250	0.225	0.225	0.50	0.11	0.266
0.312	0.280	0.280	0.62	0.14	0.312
0.375	0.335	0.335	0.75	0.16	0.375
0.438	0.406	0.406	0.88	0.20	0.438
0.500	0.473	0.473	1.00	0.23	0.500
0.625	0.598	0.598	1.25	0.30	0.625
0.750	0.723	0.723	1.50	0.36	0.750

* L = Length
** L_T = Total length
Allow extra length for spreading and securing
Available lengths to be selected from manufacturer's catalogs.

Figure 6.36 Cotter-pin dimensions.

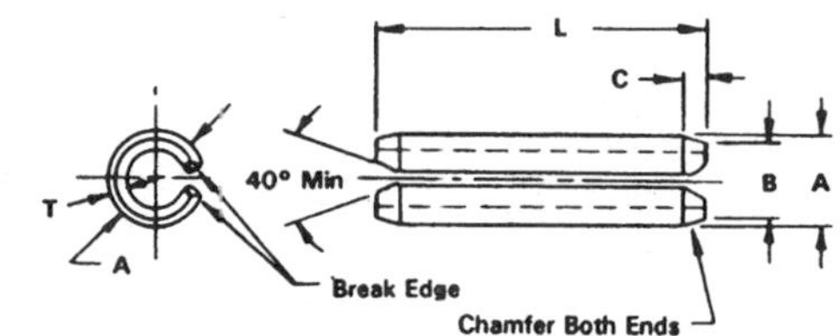

	A		B	C	T					
Basic Pin Diameter	Pin Diameter Max	Pin Diameter Min	Chamfer Dia.	Chamfer Lth.	Stock Thickness	Hole Diameter Recommended Max	Hole Diameter Recommended Min	Double Shear Load, Lb. ♦ AISI 1070 1095 & 420	Double Shear Load, Lb. ♦ AISI 302	Double Shear Load, Lb. ♦ Beryllium Copper
0.062	0.069	0.066	0.059	0.028	0.012	0.065	0.062	425	350	270
0.078	0.086	0.083	0.075	0.032	0.018	0.081	0.078	650	550	400
0.094	0.103	0.099	0.091	0.038	0.022	0.097	0.094	1,000	800	660
0.125	0.135	0.131	0.122	0.044	0.028	0.129	0.125	2,100	1,500	1,200
0.141	0.149	0.145	0.137	0.044	0.028	0.144	0.140	2,200	1,600	1,400
1.156	0.167	0.162	0.151	0.048	0.032	0.160	0.156	3,000	2,000	1,800
0.188	0.199	0.194	0.182	0.055	0.040	0.192	0.187	4,400	2,800	2,600
0.219	0.232	0.226	0.214	0.065	0.048	0.224	0.219	5,700	3,550	3,700
0.250	0.264	0.258	0.245	0.065	0.048	0.256	0.250	7,700	4,600	4,500
0.312	0.328	0.321	0.306	0.080	0.062	0.318	0.312	11,500	7,100	6,800
0.375	0.392	0.385	0.368	0.095	0.077	0.382	0.375	17,600	10,000	10,100
0.438	0.456	0.448	0.430	0.095	0.077	0.445	0.437	20,000	12,000	12,200
0.500	0.521	0.513	0.485	0.110	0.094	0.510	0.500	25,800	15,500	16,800
0.625	0.650	0.640	0.608	0.125	0.125	0.636	0.625	46,000	18,800	.....
0.750	0.780	0.769	0.730	0.150	0.150	0.764	0.750	66,000	23,200	.....

Length L, is selected from manufacturer's catalogs. ♦ Other materials may be available.

Figure 6.37 Spring-pin dimensions.

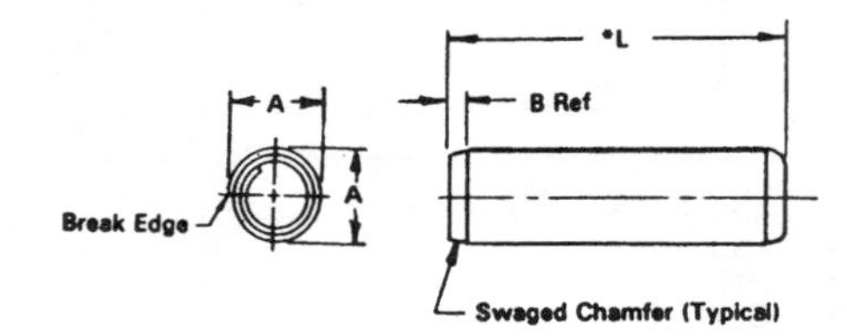

	A			B								
Basic Pin Diameter	Pin Diameter Std Duty Max	Pin Diameter Heavy Duty Max	Pin Diameter Light Duty Max	Chamfer Length Ref.	Hole Size Max	Hole Size Min	Double Shear Load, Min., Lb ♦ Std Duty 1070, 1095 and 420	Std Duty 302	Heavy Duty 1070, 1095 and 420	Heavy Duty 302	Light Duty 1070, 1095 and 420	Light Duty 302
0.031	0.035	.....	.....	0.024	0.032	0.031	75	60	.....	.....	.....	.....
0.047	0.052	.....	.....	0.024	0.048	0.046	170	140	.....	.....	.....	.....
0.062	0.072	0.070	0.073	0.028	0.065	0.061	300	250	450	350	.....	135
0.078	0.088	0.086	0.089	0.032	0.081	0.077	475	400	700	550	.....	225
0.094	0.105	0.103	0.106	0.038	0.097	0.093	700	550	1,000	800	375	300
0.109	0.120	0.118	0.121	0.038	0.112	0.108	950	750	1,400	1,125	525	425
0.125	0.138	0.136	0.139	0.044	0.129	0.124	1,250	1,000	2,100	1,700	675	550
0.156	0.171	0.168	0.172	0.048	0.160	0.155	1,925	1,550	3,000	2,400	1,100	875
0.188	0.205	0.202	0.207	0.055	0.192	0.185	2,800	2,250	4,400	3,500	1,500	1,200
0.219	0.238	0.235	0.240	0.065	0.224	0.217	3,800	3,000	5,700	4,600	2,100	1,700
0.250	0.271	0.268	0.273	0.065	0.256	0.247	5,000	4,000	7,700	6,200	2,700	2,200
0.312	0.337	0.334	0.339	0.080	0.319	0.308	7,700	6,200	11,500	9,200	4,440	3,500
0.375	0.403	0.400	0.405	0.095	0.383	0.370	11,200	9,000	17,600	14,000	6,000	5,000
0.438	0.469	0.466	0.471	0.095	0.446	0.431	15,200	13,000	22,500	18,000	8,400	6,700
0.500	0.535	0.532	0.537	0.110	0.510	0.493	20,000	16,000	30,000	24,000	11,000	8,800
0.625	0.661	0.658	.....	0.125	0.635	0.618	31,000	25,000	46,000	37,000	.....	.....
0.750	0.787	0.784	.....	0.150	0.760	0.743	45,000	36,000	66,000	53,000	.....	.....

* Length L is selected from manufacturer's catalogs. ♦ Other materials may be available.

Figure 6.38 Spiral-spring-pin dimensions.

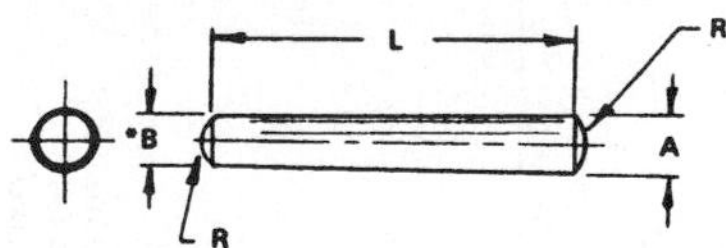

Pin Size Number and Basic Pin Dia		A Major Diameter (Large end)				R End Crown Radius Maximum
		Commercial Class		Precision Class		
		Max	Min	Max	Min	
7/0	0.0625	0.0638	0.0618	0.0635	0.0625	0.072
6/0	0.0780	0.0793	0.0773	0.0790	0.0780	0.088
5/0	0.0940	0.0953	0.0933	0.0950	0.0940	0.104
4/0	0.1090	0.1103	0.1083	0.1100	0.1090	0.119
3/0	0.1250	0.1263	0.1243	0.1260	0.1250	0.135
2/0	0.1410	0.1423	0.1403	0.1420	0.1410	0.151
0	0.1560	0.1573	0.1553	0.1570	0.1560	0.166
1	0.1720	0.1733	0.1713	0.1730	0.1720	0.182
2	0.1930	0.1943	0.1923	0.1940	0.1930	0.203
3	0.2190	0.2203	0.2183	0.2200	0.2190	0.229
4	0.2500	0.2513	0.2493	0.2510	0.2500	0.260
5	0.2890	0.2903	0.2883	0.2900	0.2890	0.299
6	0.3410	0.3423	0.3403	0.3420	0.3410	0.351
7	0.4090	0.4103	0.4083	0.4100	0.4090	0.419
8	0.4920	0.4933	0.4913	0.4930	0.4920	0.502
9	0.5910	0.5923	0.5903	0.5920	0.5910	0.601
10	0.7060	0.7073	0.7053	0.7070	0.7060	0.716
11	0.8600	0.8613	0.8593	.....	.....	0.870
12	1.0320	1.0333	1.0313	.....	.....	1.042
13	1.2410	1.2423	1.2403	.....	.....	1.251
14	1.5210	1.5223	1.5203	.....	.....	1.531

* B dimension varies per length. Length L to be selected from manufacturer's catalogs.

Figure 6.39 Taper-pin dimensions.

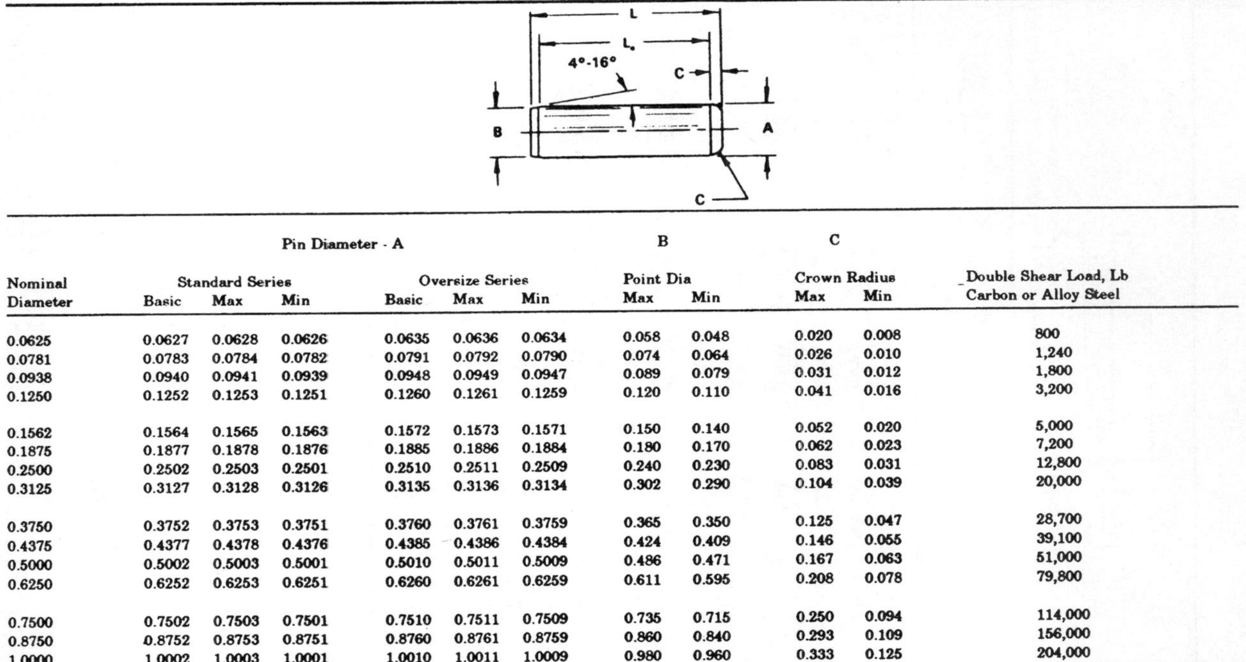

Nominal Diameter	Pin Diameter - A: Standard Series Basic	Standard Series Max	Standard Series Min	Oversize Series Basic	Oversize Series Max	Oversize Series Min	B: Point Dia Max	Point Dia Min	C: Crown Radius Max	Crown Radius Min	Double Shear Load, Lb Carbon or Alloy Steel
0.0625	0.0627	0.0628	0.0626	0.0635	0.0636	0.0634	0.058	0.048	0.020	0.008	800
0.0781	0.0783	0.0784	0.0782	0.0791	0.0792	0.0790	0.074	0.064	0.026	0.010	1,240
0.0938	0.0940	0.0941	0.0939	0.0948	0.0949	0.0947	0.089	0.079	0.031	0.012	1,800
0.1250	0.1252	0.1253	0.1251	0.1260	0.1261	0.1259	0.120	0.110	0.041	0.016	3,200
0.1562	0.1564	0.1565	0.1563	0.1572	0.1573	0.1571	0.150	0.140	0.052	0.020	5,000
0.1875	0.1877	0.1878	0.1876	0.1885	0.1886	0.1884	0.180	0.170	0.062	0.023	7,200
0.2500	0.2502	0.2503	0.2501	0.2510	0.2511	0.2509	0.240	0.230	0.083	0.031	12,800
0.3125	0.3127	0.3128	0.3126	0.3135	0.3136	0.3134	0.302	0.290	0.104	0.039	20,000
0.3750	0.3752	0.3753	0.3751	0.3760	0.3761	0.3759	0.365	0.350	0.125	0.047	28,700
0.4375	0.4377	0.4378	0.4376	0.4385	0.4386	0.4384	0.424	0.409	0.146	0.055	39,100
0.5000	0.5002	0.5003	0.5001	0.5010	0.5011	0.5009	0.486	0.471	0.167	0.063	51,000
0.6250	0.6252	0.6253	0.6251	0.6260	0.6261	0.6259	0.611	0.595	0.208	0.078	79,800
0.7500	0.7502	0.7503	0.7501	0.7510	0.7511	0.7509	0.735	0.715	0.250	0.094	114,000
0.8750	0.8752	0.8753	0.8751	0.8760	0.8761	0.8759	0.860	0.840	0.293	0.109	156,000
1.0000	1.0002	1.0003	1.0001	1.0010	1.0011	1.0009	0.980	0.960	0.333	0.125	204,000

Note: Sizes 0.0781 and 0.1562 diameter not recommended for new design.
L = Total pin length; L_e = Length of engagement.
Dowel pins listed are available in nominal lengths from 0.1875 to 6.000 inches.
Consult the manufacturer's catalogs for available lengths.

Figure 6.40 Dowel-pin dimensions.

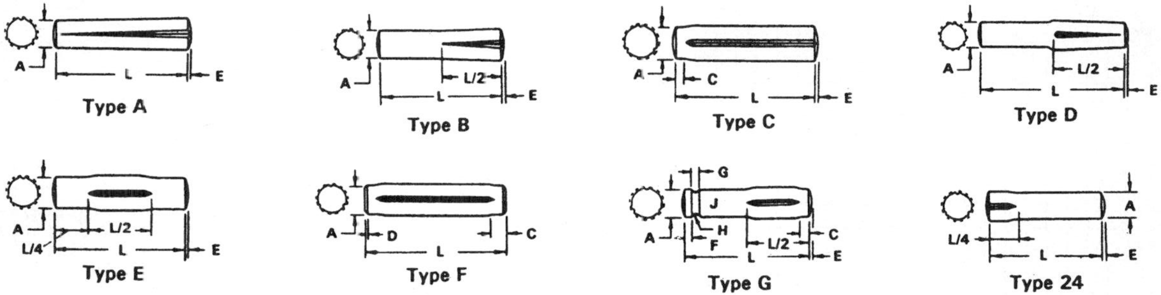

Basic Pin Diameter	A Max	C Ref.	D Min.	E Max	F Min.	G Max.	H Ref.	J Max
0.0312	0.0312	0.015	.....	.....	.....	.....	.....	.....
0.0469	0.0469	0.031	.....	.....	.....	.....	.....	.....
0.0625	0.0625	0.031	0.016	0.0115	.....	.....	.....	.....
0.0781	0.0781	0.031	0.016	0.0137	.....	.....	.....	.....
0.0938	0.0938	0.031	0.016	0.0141	0.028	0.041	0.016	0.067
0.1094	0.1094	0.031	0.016	0.0160	0.028	0.041	0.016	0.082
0.1250	0.1250	0.031	0.016	0.0180	0.059	0.041	0.031	0.088
0.1563	0.1563	0.062	0.031	0.0220	0.059	0.057	0.031	0.109
0.1875	0.1875	0.062	0.031	0.0230	0.059	0.057	0.031	0.130
0.2188	0.2188	0.062	0.031	0.0270	0.091	0.072	0.047	0.151
0.2500	0.2500	0.062	0.031	0.0310	0.091	0.072	0.047	0.172
0.3125	0.3125	0.094	0.047	0.0390	0.122	0.104	0.062	0.214
0.3750	0.3750	0.094	0.047	0.0440	0.122	0.135	0.062	0.255
0.4375	0.4375	0.094	0.047	0.0520	0.185	0.135	0.094	0.298
0.5000	0.5000	0.094	0.047	0.0570	0.185	0.135	0.094	0.317

Figure 6.41 Grooved-pin dimensions.

Nominal Length	Nominal Size														
	1/32	3/64	1/16	5/64	3/32	7/64	1/8	5/32	3/16	7/32	1/4	5/16	3/8	7/16	1/2
1/8	Y	Y	Y												
1/4	Y	Y	Y	Y	Y	Y	Y								
3/8	Y	Y	Y	Y	X	X	X	X	X						
1/2	Y	Y	Y	Y	X	X	X	X	X	X	X				
5/8		Y	Y	Y	X	X	X	X	X	X	X	X			
3/4			Y	Y	X	X	X	X	X	X	X	X	X		
7/8			Y	Y	X	X	X	X	X	X	X	X	X	X	
1			Y	Y	X	X	X	X	X	X	X	X	X	X	X
1-1/4					X	X	X	X	X	X	X	X	X	X	X
1-1/2							X	X	X	X	X	X	X	X	X
1-3/4								X	X	X	X	X	X	X	X
2								X	X	X	X	X	X	X	X
2-1/4									X	X	X	X	X	X	X
2-1/2										X	X	X	X	X	X
2-3/4										X	X	X	X	X	X
3										X	X	X	X	X	X
3-1/4											X	X	X	X	X
3-1/2												X	X	X	X
3-3/4													X	X	X
4													X	X	X
4-1/4													X	X	X
4-1/2														X	X

Note: Carbon steel pins are normally available in the marked sizes by X and Y. X designates all types of pins; Y designates all types except type G. Other lengths may be available from different manufacturers.

Figure 6.42 Sizes and lengths of standard grooved pins.

Recommended Hole Sizes For Grooved Pins			
Nominal Pin Size	Drill Size	Hole Diameter	
		Max	Min
1/32	1/32	0.0324	0.0312
3/64	3/64	0.0482	0.0469
1/16	1/16	0.0640	0.0625
5/64	5/64	0.0798	0.0781
3/32	3/32	0.0956	0.0938
7/64	7/64	0.1113	0.1094
1/8	1/8	0.1271	0.1250
5/32	5/32	0.1587	0.1563
3/16	3/16	0.1903	0.1875
7/32	7/32	0.2219	0.2188
1/4	1/4	0.2534	0.2500
5/16	5/16	0.3166	0.3125
3/8	3/8	0.3797	0.3750
7/16	7/16	0.4428	0.4375
1/2	1/2	0.5060	0.5000

Figure 6.43 Hole sizes for grooved pins.

Nominal Pin Size	Double Shear Load, Min, lb			
	Material			
	Low Carbon Steel	Alloy Steel (Rockwell C45 to 50)	Corrosion Resistant Steel	Brass
1/32	104	202	143	64
3/64	220	430	300	136
1/16	402	785	540	250
5/64	624	1,215	860	386
3/32	896	1,750	1,240	555
7/64	1,222	2,380	1,685	757
1/8	1,600	3,115	2,200	990
5/32	2,494	4,860	3,440	1,540
3/16	3,588	6,990	4,960	2,220
7/32	4,884	9,520	6,760	3,020
1/4	6,380	12,430	8,840	3,950
5/16	9,970	19,420	13,750	6,170
3/8	11,620	27,950	19,800	9,050
7/16	15,820	38,060	27,000	12,100
1/2	20,600	49,700	35,200	15,800

Figure 6.44 Shear loads for grooved pins.

Retaining Ring Types

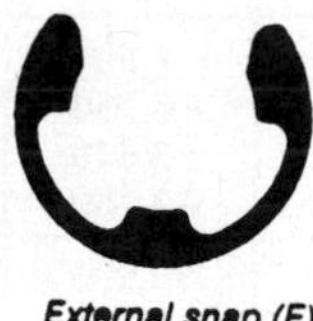

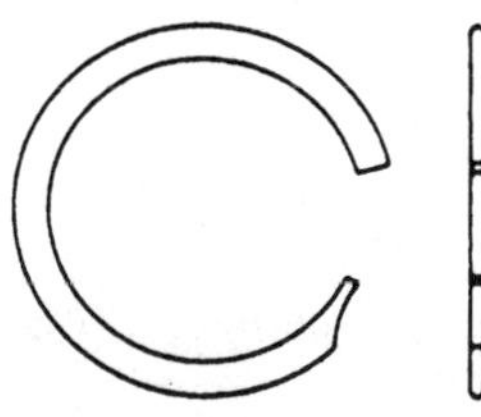

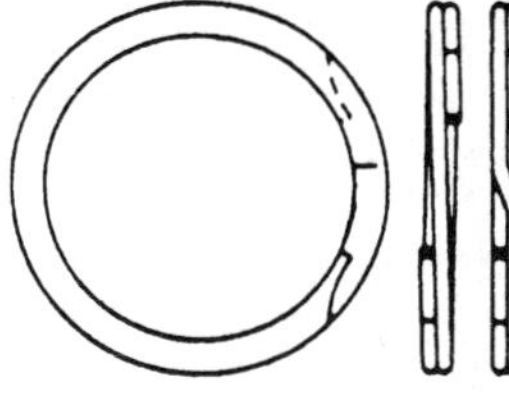

Figure 6.45 Retaining-ring styles.

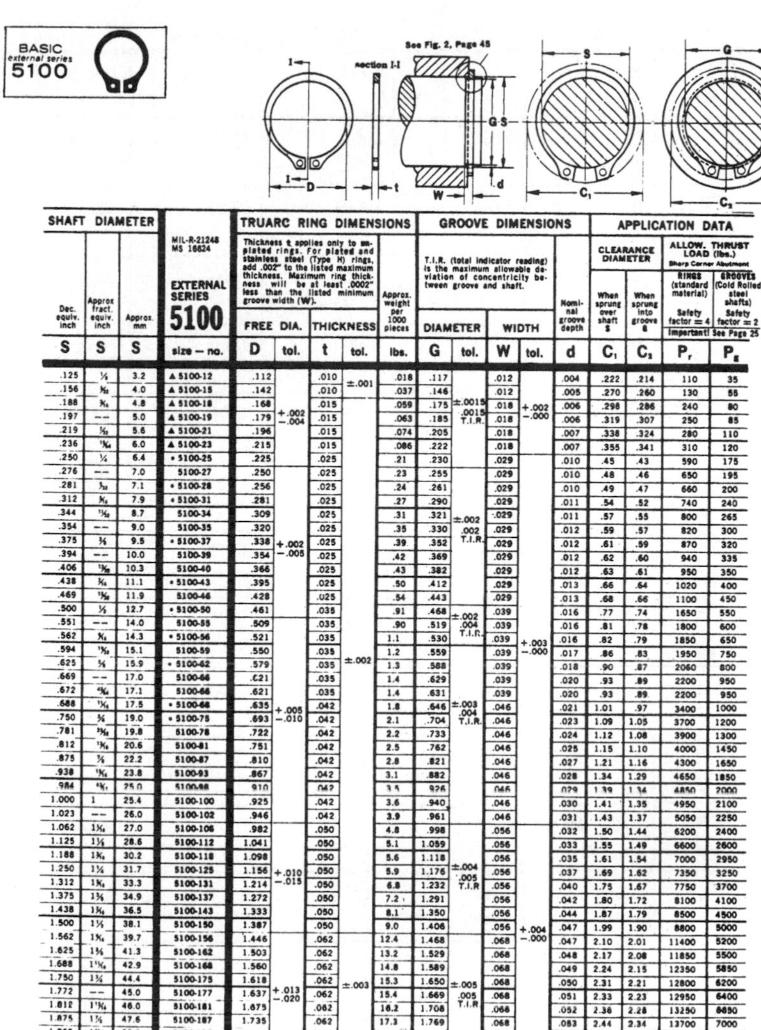

SHAFT DIAMETER | MIL-R-21248 MS 16824 EXTERNAL SERIES 5100 | TRUARC RING DIMENSIONS | GROOVE DIMENSIONS | APPLICATION DATA

Thickness t applies only to unplated rings. For plated and stainless steel (Type H) rings, add .002" to the listed maximum thickness. Maximum ring thickness will be at least .0002" less than the listed minimum groove width (W).

T.I.R. (total indicator reading) is the maximum allowable deviation of concentricity between groove and shaft.

ALLOW. THRUST LOAD (lbs.) Sharp Corner Abutment. Important! See Page 25

Dec. equiv. inch S	Approx fract. equiv. inch S	Approx. mm S	size — no.	FREE DIA. D	tol.	THICKNESS t	tol.	Approx. weight per 1000 pieces lbs.	DIAMETER G	tol.	WIDTH W	tol.	Nominal groove depth d	CLEARANCE DIAMETER When sprung over shaft C_1	CLEARANCE DIAMETER When sprung into groove C_2	RINGS (standard material) Safety factor = 4 P_r	GROOVES (Cold Rolled steel shafts) Safety factor = 2 P_g
.125	1/8	3.2	▲ 5100-12	.112		.010	±.001	.018	.117		.012		.004	.222	.214	110	35
.156	5/32	4.0	▲ 5100-15	.142		.010		.037	.146		.012		.005	.270	.260	130	55
.188	3/16	4.8	▲ 5100-18	.168		.015		.059	.175	±.0015 .0015 T.I.R.	.018	+.002 −.000	.006	.298	.286	240	80
.197	--	5.0	▲ 5100-19	.179	+.002 −.004	.015		.063	.185		.018		.006	.319	.307	250	85
.219	7/32	5.6	▲ 5100-21	.196		.015		.074	.205		.018		.007	.338	.324	280	110
.236	15/64	6.0	▲ 5100-23	.215		.015		.086	.222		.018		.007	.355	.341	310	120
.250	1/4	6.4	• 5100-25	.225		.025		.21	.230		.029		.010	.45	.43	590	175
.276	--	7.0	5100-27	.250		.025		.23	.255		.029		.010	.48	.46	650	195
.281	9/32	7.1	• 5100-28	.256		.025		.24	.261		.029		.010	.49	.47	660	200
.312	5/16	7.9	• 5100-31	.281		.025		.27	.290		.029		.011	.54	.52	740	240
.344	11/32	8.7	5100-34	.309		.025		.31	.321		.029		.011	.57	.55	800	265
.354	--	9.0	5100-35	.320		.025		.35	.330	±.002 .002 T.I.R.	.029		.012	.59	.57	820	300
.375	3/8	9.5	• 5100-37	.338	+.002 −.005	.025		.39	.352		.029		.012	.61	.59	870	320
.394	--	10.0	5100-39	.354		.025		.42	.369		.029		.012	.62	.60	940	335
.406	13/32	10.3	5100-40	.366		.025		.43	.382		.029		.012	.63	.61	950	350
.438	7/16	11.1	• 5100-43	.395		.025		.50	.412		.029		.013	.66	.64	1020	400
.469	15/32	11.9	5100-46	.428		.025		.54	.443		.029		.013	.68	.66	1100	450
.500	1/2	12.7	• 5100-50	.461		.035		.91	.468		.039		.016	.77	.74	1650	550
.551	--	14.0	5100-55	.509		.035		.90	.519	±.002 .004 T.I.R.	.039		.016	.81	.78	1800	600
.562	9/16	14.3	• 5100-56	.521		.035		1.1	.530		.039	+.003 −.000	.016	.82	.79	1850	650
.594	19/32	15.1	5100-59	.550		.035		1.2	.559		.039		.017	.86	.83	1950	750
.625	5/8	15.9	• 5100-62	.579		.035	±.002	1.3	.588		.039		.018	.90	.87	2060	800
.669	--	17.0	5100-66	.621		.035		1.4	.629		.039		.020	.93	.89	2200	950
.672	43/64	17.1	5100-66	.621		.035		1.4	.631		.039		.020	.93	.89	2200	950
.688	11/16	17.5	• 5100-68	.635	+.005 −.010	.042		1.8	.646	±.003 .004 T.I.R.	.046		.021	1.01	.97	3400	1000
.750	3/4	19.0	• 5100-75	.693		.042		2.1	.704		.046		.023	1.09	1.05	3700	1200
.781	25/32	19.8	5100-78	.722		.042		2.2	.733		.046		.024	1.12	1.08	3900	1300
.812	13/16	20.6	5100-81	.751		.042		2.5	.762		.046		.025	1.15	1.10	4000	1450
.875	7/8	22.2	5100-87	.810		.042		2.8	.821		.046		.027	1.21	1.16	4300	1650
.938	15/16	23.8	5100-93	.867		.042		3.1	.882		.046		.028	1.34	1.29	4650	1850
.984	63/64	25.0	5100-98	.910		.042		3.5	.926		.046		.029	1.39	1.34	4850	2000
1.000	1	25.4	5100-100	.925		.042		3.6	.940		.046		.030	1.41	1.35	4950	2100
1.023	--	26.0	5100-102	.946		.042		3.9	.961		.046		.031	1.43	1.37	5050	2250
1.062	1 1/16	27.0	5100-106	.982		.050		4.8	.998		.056		.032	1.50	1.44	6200	2400
1.125	1 1/8	28.6	5100-112	1.041		.050		5.1	1.059		.056		.033	1.55	1.49	6600	2600
1.188	1 3/16	30.2	5100-118	1.098		.050		5.6	1.118		.056		.035	1.61	1.54	7000	2950
1.250	1 1/4	31.7	5100-125	1.156	+.010 −.015	.050		5.9	1.176	±.004 .005 T.I.R	.056		.037	1.69	1.62	7350	3250
1.312	1 5/16	33.3	5100-131	1.214		.050		6.8	1.232		.056		.040	1.75	1.67	7750	3700
1.375	1 3/8	34.9	5100-137	1.272		.050		7.2	1.291		.056		.042	1.80	1.72	8100	4100
1.438	1 7/16	36.5	5100-143	1.333		.050		8.1	1.350		.056		.044	1.87	1.79	8500	4500
1.500	1 1/2	38.1	5100-150	1.387		.050		9.0	1.406		.056	+.004 −.000	.047	1.99	1.90	8800	5000
1.562	1 9/16	39.7	5100-156	1.446		.062		12.4	1.468		.068		.047	2.10	2.01	11400	5200
1.625	1 5/8	41.3	5100-162	1.503		.062		13.2	1.529		.068		.048	2.17	2.08	11850	5500
1.688	1 11/16	42.9	5100-168	1.560		.062		14.8	1.589		.068		.049	2.24	2.15	12350	5850
1.750	1 3/4	44.4	5100-175	1.618		.062	±.003	15.3	1.650		.068		.050	2.31	2.21	12800	6200
1.772	--	45.0	5100-177	1.637	+.013 −.020	.062		15.4	1.669	±.005 .005 T.I.R	.068		.051	2.33	2.23	12950	6400
1.812	1 13/16	46.0	5100-181	1.675		.062		16.2	1.708		.068		.052	2.38	2.28	13250	6650
1.875	1 7/8	47.6	5100-187	1.735		.062		17.3	1.769		.068		.083	2.44	2.34	13700	7000
1.969	1 31/32	50.0	5100-196	1.819		.062		18.0	1.857		.068		.056	2.54	2.43	14350	7800
2.000	2	50.8	5100-200	1.850		.062		19.0	1.886		.068		.057	2.55	2.44	14600	8050

Figure 6.46 Sample "Truarc" ring data sheet.

	Roto Clip	Waldes	I.R.R.	Anderton	Mil Standard
	E	5133	1000	1500	16633
	BE	5131	1001	1501	16634
	RE	5144	1200	1540	3215
	C	5103	2000	1800	16632
	HO	5000	3000	1300	16625
	BHO	5001	3001	1301	16629
	VHO	5002	—	1302	16631
	SH	5100	3100	1400	16624
	BSH	5101	3101	1401	16628
	VSH	5102	—	1402	16630
	HOI	5008	4000	1308	16627
	SHI	5108	4100	1408	16626
	SHF	5555	7100	1440	90707
	SHR	5160	—	1460	3217
	SHM	5560	—	—	—

Figure 6.47 Retaining-ring interchangeability table.

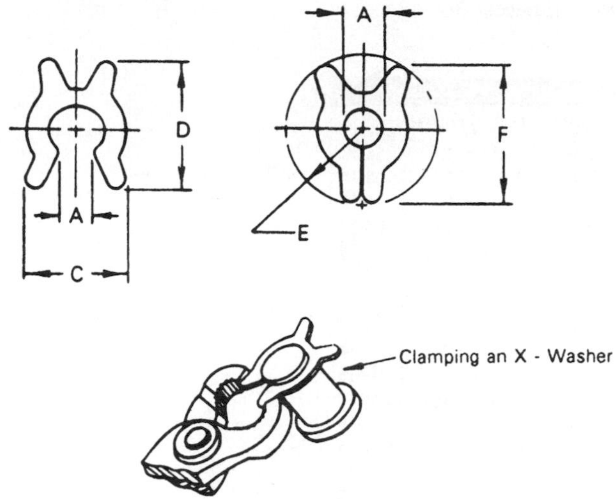

X - Washer Dimensions

A	B*	C	D	E	F
.086	.025	.320	.406	.210	.406
.098	.055	.364	.490	.297	.475
.130	.055	.430	.575	.359	.556
.164	.065	.523	.687	.422	.665
.190	.065	.593	.745	.437	.730
.222	.075	.622	.776	.469	.775
.256	.075	.698	.905	.500	.890
.285	.075	.822	.986	.563	.984
.317	.089	.872	1.100	.609	1.078
.347	.089	.948	1.190	.688	1.188
.381	.089	1.060	1.297	.797	1.281

Note: B* = thickness (inches)

Figure 6.48 X-washer dimensional sizes.

DIMENSIONS			
BORE	O. D.	WIDTH	SET SCREW
3/16	7/16	1/4	8-32
1/4	1/2	9/32	10-32
5/16	5/8	11/32	10-32
3/8	3/4	3/8	1/4-20
7/16	7/8	7/16	1/4-20
1/2	1"	7/16	1/4-20
9/16	1"	7/16	1/4-20
5/8	1-1/8	1/2	5/16-18
11/16	1-1/4	9/16	5/16-18
3/4	1-1/4	9/16	5/16-18
13/16	1-5/16	9/16	5/16-18
7/8	1-1/2	9/16	5/16-18
15/16	1-5/8	9/16	5/16-18
1"	1-5/8	5/8	5/16-18
1-1/16	1-3/4	5/8	5/16-18
1-1/8	1-3/4	5/8	5/16-18
1-3/16	2"	11/16	3/8-16
1-1/4	2"	11/16	3/8-16
1-5/16	2-1/8	11/16	3/8-16
1-3/8	2-1/8	3/4	3/8-16
1-7/16	2-1/4	3/4	3/8-16
1-1/2	2-1/4	3/4	3/8-16
1-9/16	2-1/2	13/16	3/8-16
1-5/8	2-1/2	13/16	3/8-16
1-11/16	2-1/2	13/16	3/8-16
1-3/4	2-3/4	7/8	1/2-13
1-13/16	2-3/4	7/8	1/2-13
1-7/8	2-3/4	7/8	1/2-13
1-15/16	3"	7/8	1/2-13
2"	3"	7/8	1/2-13
2-1/16	3"	7/8	1/2-13
2-1/8	3"	7/8	1/2-13
2-3/16	3-1/4	15/16	1/2-13
2-1/4	3-1/4	15/16	1/2-13
2-5/16	3-1/4	15/16	1/2-13
2-3/8	3-1/4	15/16	1/2-13
2-7/16	3-1/2	1"	1/2-13
2-1/2	3-1/2	1"	1/2-13
2-9/16	3-3/4	1-1/8	1/2-13
2-5/8	3-3/4	1-1/8	1/2-13
2-11/16	4"	1-1/8	1/2-13
2-3/4	4"	1-1/8	1/2-13
2-13/16	4-1/4	1-1/8	1/2-13
2-7/8	4-1/4	1-1/8	1/2-13
2-15/16	4-1/4	1-1/8	1/2-13
3"	4-1/4	1-1/8	1/2-13

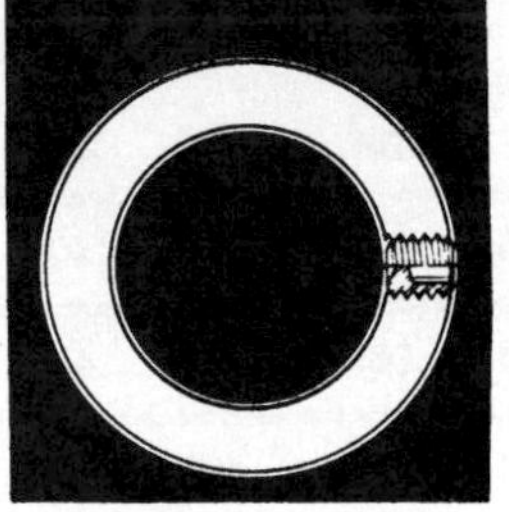

Figure 6.49 Set-collars (*Ruland, Inc.*).

Clamp-collars are similar to set-collars, except that they have a slit through one wall and are clamped on a shaft by tightening the clamp screw provided on the collar. These types of collars are also made with internal threads for adjustment and a more positive clamping force. Clamp-collars are normally made of carbon steels, aluminum alloys, and stainless steels. Figure 6.50 shows the sizes and dimensions of standard clamp-collars, and Fig. 6.51 shows the data for the internally threaded clamp-collar series.

Split-collars and threaded split-collars are also available and widely used in machine design. The data for these types of clamping collars are shown in Figs. 6.52 and 6.53.

Note: Figures 6.49 through 6.53 were extracted from the Ruland catalog of collars and couplings (Ruland Manufacturing Company, Inc., Watertown, MA 02172).

6.7 Machinery Bushings, Shims, and Arbor Spacers

6.7.1 Machinery bushings

Machinery bushings are a special form of flat washer commonly made of low-carbon mild steel. They are used as spacers between gears, pulleys, and sprockets and as filler spacers for parts mounted on shafts. These bushings are manufactured in the following gauges and diameters:

- 18 gauge, 0.048 in
- 14 gauge, 0.075 in
- 10 gauge, 0.134 in
- 3⁄16 in, 0.1875 in

Inside diameters range from 0.500 through 3.00 in.

6.7.2 Steel shims

Steel shims are thin steel rings with a plain center hole that are used for building up gears and bearings and to provide proper clearance between mating parts. Figure 6.54 lists the sizes and thicknesses normally available for steel shims.

6.7.3 Steel arbor spacers

Steel arbor spacers are thin steel rings with a keyway center hole that are used for accurately spacing milling cutters, slitter knives, and gang saws on keyway arbors. Steel shims and steel arbor spacers are made of AISI 1010, fully hardened, cold-rolled low-carbon steel. Figure 6.54 also lists the sizes and thicknesses of steel arbor spacers.

6.8 Specialty Fasteners

The specialty fastener component lines available today are great in numbers and types. This section will detail only those specialty fasteners which have become common and which are used widely in new product design and manufacturing.

Figure 6.23 shows a variety of standard and specialty fasteners. At the bottom center of Fig. 6.23 is an eye bolt, and immediately above this is a penta-head bolt and its socket wrench. This five-sided-head bolt is used to make equipment tamperproof, since any standard wrench will not grip the head for removal. The lower right of Fig. 6.23 shows a variety of swage nuts. The lower left shows a slotted spring washer, which is used to maintain pressure on joints that have a central pivot point. Almost half the fasteners in Fig. 6.23 can be considered specialty fasteners. A partial listing of some of the common specialty fasteners would include

- Acorn nuts
- Floating nuts
- Plastic bolts
- Split lock nuts
- SEMS
- Weld nuts
- Various plastic washers
- Sealing washers
- T-slot nuts and bolts
- Push nuts (Pal nuts)
- Various types of weld studs
- Sheet metal nuts
- Nylok bolts

6.8.1 Specialty fasteners in common use

Figure 6.55 shows the different types of SEMS (screw and captive washer assemblies) available today. Note that on the SEM, the screw is either thread-forming or thread-tapping. This makes this class of fastener useful and economical in rapid-assembly applications such as automotive equipment manufacturing. SEMS are specified in American National Standards Institute. Standard ANSI/ASME B18.13.

Figure 6.56 shows some of the widely used Tinnerman types of speed-nuts, which are made of high-carbon, spring-tempered steel. These types of speed-nuts are produced in sizes from 6–32 through 5⁄16–18 or larger in special cases. The Tinnerman type U and J nuts are used widely to fasten sheet metal screw covers onto sheet metal enclosures. The flat and round types are used on through-bolt sheet metal applications, such as automotive equipment and electronic chassis work. These are economical, efficient fasteners whose applications are limitless.

Another specialty type of fastener that is used widely is the swage nut. The swage nut is produced in several different styles, one of which is shown in Fig. 6.57*a*. The swage nut is extremely useful in applications where the thread cannot be produced efficiently or effectively in a parent metal that must be fastened to another part. Swage nuts are used in switch-gear equipment where copper bus bars are fastened together and it is not practical to tap the soft copper bars for bolting. These nuts are also used on thin sheet metal parts where a strong joint is required and not enough material thickness is available for tapping the sheet metal. The swage nut is normally made from carbon steel with zinc or cadmium plating, stainless steels, and aluminum alloys. Figure 6.57*a* shows a typical PEM-type nut.

The Rivnut and Plusnut, which are produced by B.F. Goodrich Company are shown in Fig. 6.57*b* and *c*. These types of "blind" fasteners have countless applications in industry and are also produced with sealed ends for liquid-proofing applications. The Rivnut is widely used in the aerospace industry.

6.8.2 Electroplating fasteners

High-quality fasteners such as the Unbrako series of socket-head cap screws and shoulder bolts, which use the UNR thread profile, may be precision plated according to Table 6.7. Other types of fasteners also may use the plating specifications shown in Table 6.7. For more complete information on electroplating, see Chap. 19, "Plating Practices and Finishes."

(Text continued on page 497.)

DIMENSIONS			
BORE	O.D.	WIDTH	CLAMP SCREW
1/8	1/2	.235	4-40
3/16	9/16	.235	4-40
1/4	5/8	.281	4-40
5/16	11/16	.281	4-40
3/8	7/8	.343	6-32
7/16	15/16	.343	6-32
1/2	1-1/8	.406	8-32
9/16	1-1/4	.437	10-32
5/8	1-5/16	.437	10-32
11/16	1-3/8	.437	10-32
3/4	1-1/2	1/2	1/4-28
13/16	1-5/8	1/2	1/4-28
7/8	1-5/8	1/2	1/4-28
15/16	1-3/4	1/2	1/4-28
1	1-3/4	1/2	1/4-28
1-1/16	1-7/8	1/2	1/4-28
1-1/8	1-7/8	1/2	1/4-28
1-3/16	2-1/16	1/2	1/4-28
1-1/4	2-1/16	1/2	1/4-28
1-5/16	2-1/8	9/16	1/4-28
1-3/8	2-1/4	9/16	1/4-28
1-7/16	2-1/4	9/16	1/4-28
1-1/2	2-3/8	9/16	1/4-28
1-9/16	2-3/8	9/16	1/4-28
1-5/8	2-5/8	11/16	5/16-24
1-11/16	2-3/4	11/16	5/16-24
1-3/4	2-3/4	11/16	5/16-24
1-13/16	2-7/8	11/16	5/16-24
1-7/8	2-7/8	11/16	5/16-24
1-15/16	3	11/16	5/16-24
2	3	11/16	5/16-24
2-1/16	3-1/8	3/4	5/16-24
2-1/8	3-1/4	3/4	5/16-24
2-3/16	3-1/4	3/4	5/16-24
2-1/4	3-1/4	3/4	5/16-24
2-5/16	3-3/8	3/4	5/16-24
2-3/8	3-1/2	3/4	5/16-24
2-7/16	3-1/2	3/4	5/16-24
2-1/2	3-3/4	7/8	3/8-24
2-9/16	3-7/8	7/8	3/8-24
2-5/8	3-7/8	7/8	3/8-24
2-11/16	4	7/8	3/8-24
2-3/4	4	7/8	3/8-24
2-13/16	4-1/4	7/8	3/8-24
2-7/8	4-1/4	7/8	3/8-24
2-15/16	4-1/4	7/8	3/8-24
3	4-1/4	7/8	3/8-24

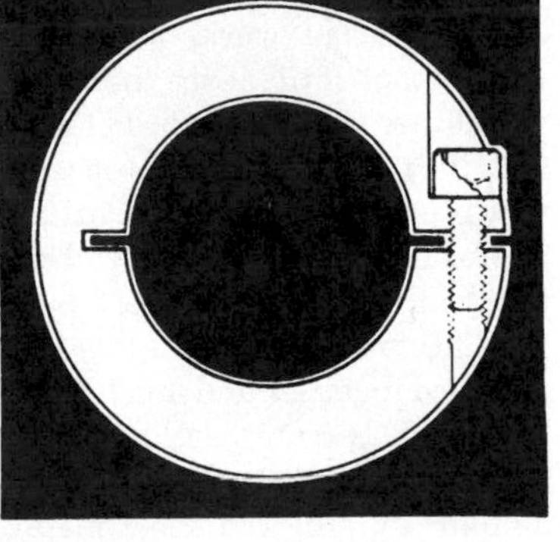

Figure 6.50 Clamp-collars (*Ruland, Inc.*).

DIMENSIONS			
THREADED BORE	O.D.	WIDTH	CLAMP SCREW
8-32	1/2	.235	4-40
10-24	9/16	.235	4-40
10-32	9/16	.235	4-40
1/4-20	5/8	.281	4-40
1/4-28	5/8	.281	4-40
5/16-18	11/16	.281	4-40
5/16-24	11/16	.281	4-40
3/8-16	7/8	.343	6-32
3/8-24	7/8	.343	6-32
7/16-14	15/16	.343	6-32
7/16-20	15/16	.343	6-32
1/2-13	1-1/8	.406	8-32
1/2-20	1-1/8	.406	8-32
5/8-11	1-5/16	.437	10-32
5/8-18	1-5/16	.437	10-32
3/4-10	1-1/2	1/2	1/4-28
3/4-16	1-1/2	1/2	1/4-28
7/8-9	1-5/8	1/2	1/4-28
7/8-14	1-5/8	1/2	1/4-28
1-8	1-3/4	1/2	1/4-28
1-12	1-3/4	1/2	1/4-28
1-14	1-3/4	1/2	1/4-28
1-1/8-7	1-7/8	1/2	1/4-28
1-1/8-12	1-7/8	1/2	1/4-28
1-1/4-7	2-1/16	1/2	1/4-28
1-1/4-12	2-1/16	1/2	1/4-28
1-3/8-6	2-1/4	9/16	1/4-28
1-3/8-12	2-1/4	9/16	1/4-28
1-1/2-6	2-3/8	9/16	1/4-28
1-1/2-12	2-3/8	9/16	1/4-28
1-3/4-16	2-3/4	11/16	5/16-24
2"-12	3	11/16	5/16-24

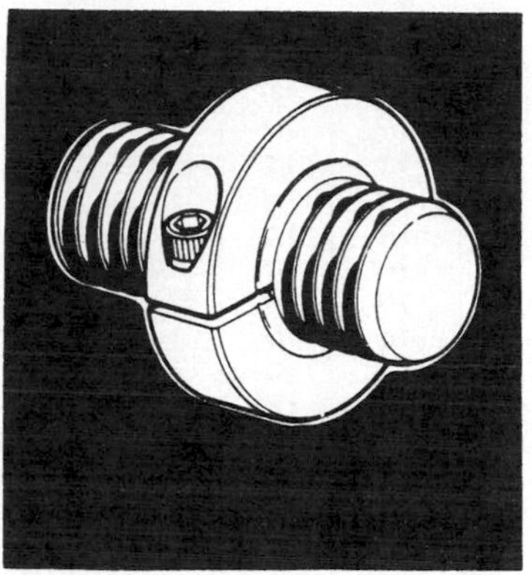

Figure 6.51 Threaded clamp-collars (*Ruland, Inc.*).

DIMENSIONS			
BORE	O.D.	WIDTH	CLAMP SCREW
1/8	1/2	.235	4-40
3/16	8/16	.235	4-40
1/4	5/8	.281	4-40
5/16	11/16	.281	4-40
3/8	7/8	.343	6-32
7/16	15/16	.343	6-32
1/2	1-1/8	.406	8-32
9/16	1-1/4	.437	10-32
5/8	1-5/16	.437	10-32
11/16	1-3/8	.437	10-32
3/4	1-1/2	1/2	1/4-28
13/16	1-5/8	1/2	1/4-28
7/8	1-5/8	1/2	1/4-28
15/16	1-3/4	1/2	1/4-28
1	1-3/4	1/2	1/4-28
1-1/16	1-7/8	1/2	1/4-28
1-1/8	1-7/8	1/2	1/4-28
1-3/16	2-1/16	1/2	1/4-28
1-1/4	2-1/16	1/2	1/4-28
1-5/16	2-1/8	9/16	1/4-28
1-3/8	2-1/4	9/16	1/4-28
1-7/16	2-1/4	9/16	1/4-28
1-1/2	2-3/8	9/16	1/4-28
1-9/16	2-3/8	9/16	1/4-28
1-5/8	2-5/8	11/16	5/16-24
1-11/16	2-3/4	11/16	5/16-24
1-3/4	2-3/4	11/16	5/16-24
1-13/16	2-7/8	11/16	5/16-24
1-7/8	2-7/8	11/16	5/16-24
1-15/16	3	11/16	5/16-24
2	3	11/16	5/16-24
2-1/16	3-1/8	3/4	5/16-24
2-1/8	3-1/4	3/4	5/16-24
2-3/16	3-1/4	3/4	5/16-24
2-1/4	3-1/4	3/4	5/16-24
2-5/16	3-3/8	3/4	5/16-24
2-3/8	3-1/2	3/4	5/16-24
2-7/16	3-1/2	3/4	5/16-24
2-1/2	3-3/4	7/8	3/8-24
2-9/16	3-7/8	7/8	3/8-24
2-5/8	3-7/8	7/8	3/8-24
2-11/16	4	7/8	3/8-24
2-3/4	4	7/8	3/8-24
2-13/16	4-1/4	7/8	3/8-24
2-7/8	4-1/4	7/8	3/8-24
2-15/16	4-1/4	7/8	3/8-24
3	4-1/4	7/8	3/8-24

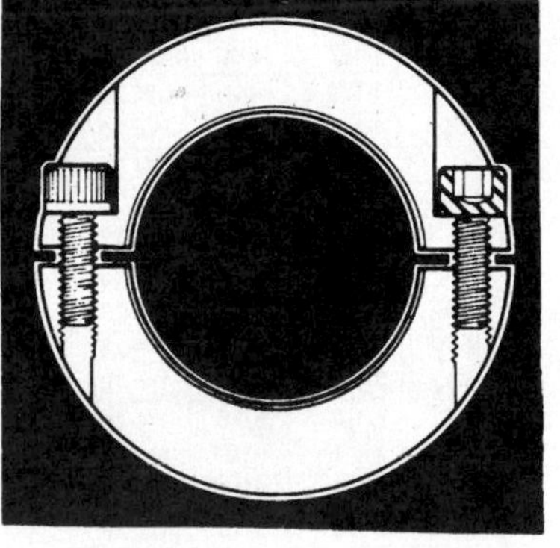

Figure 6.52 Split-collars (*Ruland, Inc.*).

DIMENSIONS			
BORE	O.D.	WIDTH	CLAMP SCREW
8-32	1/2	.235	4-40
10-24	9/16	.235	4-40
10-32	9/16	.235	4-40
1/4-20	5/8	.281	4-40
1/4-28	5/8	.281	4-40
5/16-18	11/16	.281	4-40
5/16-24	11/16	.281	4-40
3/8-16	7/8	.343	6-32
3/8-24	7/8	.343	6-32
7/16-14	15/16	.343	6-32
7/16-20	15/16	.343	6-32
1/2-13	1-1/8	.406	8-32
1/2-20	1-1/8	.406	8-32
5/8-11	1-5/16	.437	10-32
5/8-18	1-5/16	.437	10-32
3/4-10	1-1/2	1/2	1/4-28
3/4-16	1-1/2	1/2	1/4-28
7/8-9	1-5/8	1/2	1/4-28
7/8-14	1-5/8	1/2	1/4-28
1-8	1-3/4	1/2	1/4-28
1-12	1-3/4	1/2	1/4-28
1-14	1-3/4	1/2	1/4-28
1-1/8-7	1-7/8	1/2	1/4-28
1-1/8-12	1-7/8	1/2	1/4-28
1-1/4-7	2-1/16	1/2	1/4-28
1-1/4-12	2-1/16	1/2	1/4-28
1-3/8-6	2-1/4	9/16	1/4-28
1-3/8-12	2-1/4	9/16	1/4-28
1-1/2-6	2-3/8	9/16	1/4-28
1-1/2-12	2-3/8	9/16	1/4-28
1-3/4-16	2-3/4	11/16	5/16-24
2"-12	3	11/16	5/16-24

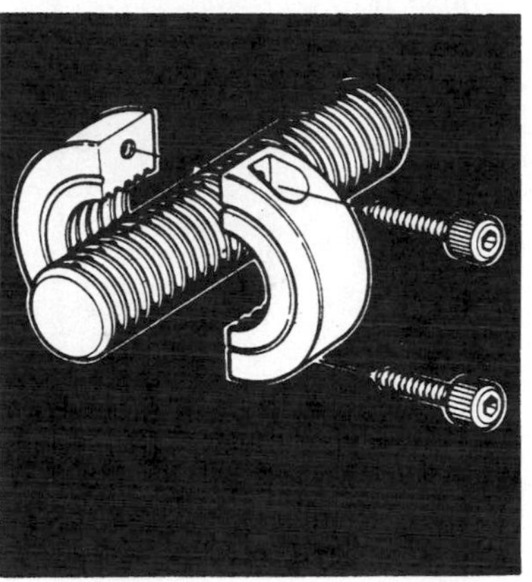

Figure 6.53 Split threaded clamp-collars (*Ruland, Inc.*).

Sizes and Thicknesses of Steel Shims - (Inches)

ID	OD	Thickness Ranges
0.375	0.625	0.001 0.002 0.003 0.004 0.005 0.006 0.007 0.008 0.010 0.012 0.015 0.020 0.025 0.031 0.047
0.500	0.750	0.0062 0.093 0.125 (These thicknesses available in all ID and OD sizes)
0.625	1.000	
0.750	1.125	
0.875	1.375	
1.000	1.500	
1.125	1.625	
1.250	1.750	
1.375	1.875	
1.500	2.125	
1.750	2.750	
2.000	2.750	

Sizes and Thicknesses of Steel Arbor Spacers - (Inches)

ID	OD	Thickness Ranges
0.500	0.750	0.001 0.002 0.003 0.004 0.005 0.006 (These thicknesses available for diameters listed)
0.625	1.000	
0.750	1.125	
0.875	1.375	
1.000	1.500	
1.250	1.750	
1.500	2.125	
2.000	2.250	
0.750	1.125	0.007 0.008 0.010 0.012 0.015 0.020 (These thicknesses available for diameters listed)
0.875	1.375	
1.000	1.500	
1.250	1.750	
1.500	2.125	
2.000	2.750	
1.000	1.500	0.025 0.031 0.047 0.062 0.093 0.125 (These thicknesses available for diameters listed)
1.250	1.750	
1.500	2.125	
2.000	2.750	

Figure 6.54 Steel shims and arbor spacers.

SEMS - by SHAKEPROOF
(Pre-assembled lock washer and screw units)

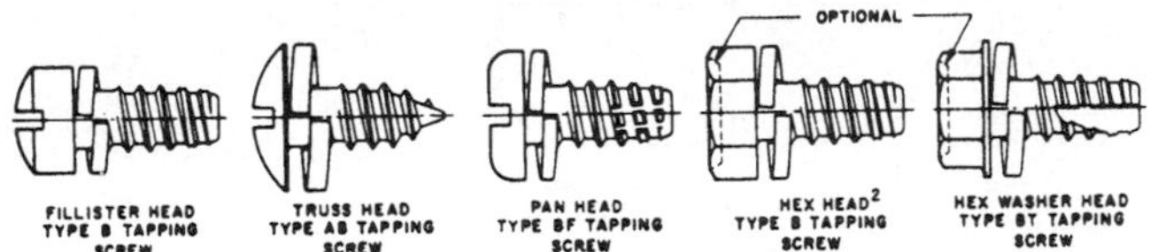

REPRESENTATIVE EXAMPLES OF HELICAL SPRING LOCK WASHER SEMS

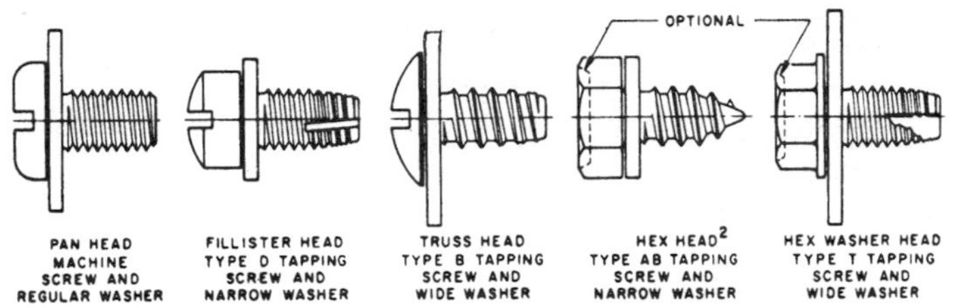

REPRESENTATIVE EXAMPLES OF PLAIN WASHER SEMS

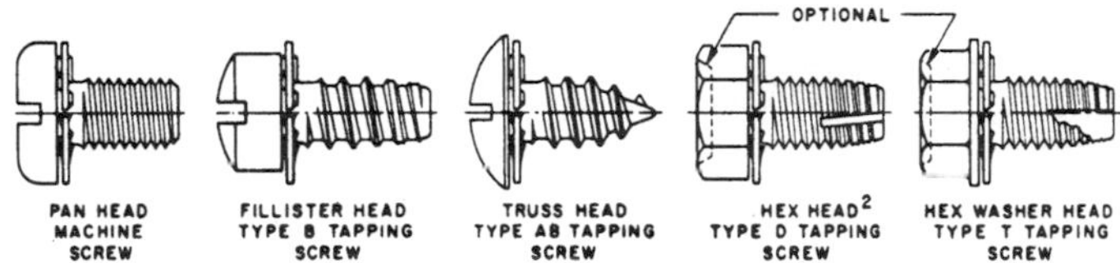

REPRESENTATIVE EXAMPLES OF INTERNAL TOOTH LOCK WASHER SEMS

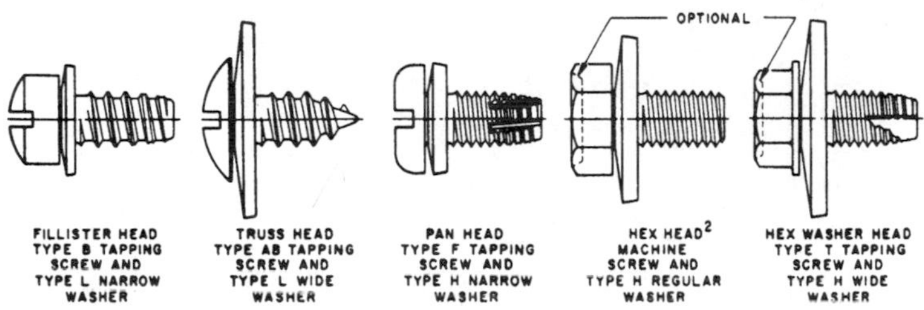

REPRESENTATIVE EXAMPLES OF CONICAL SPRING WASHER SEMS

Figure 6.55 Types of SEMS.

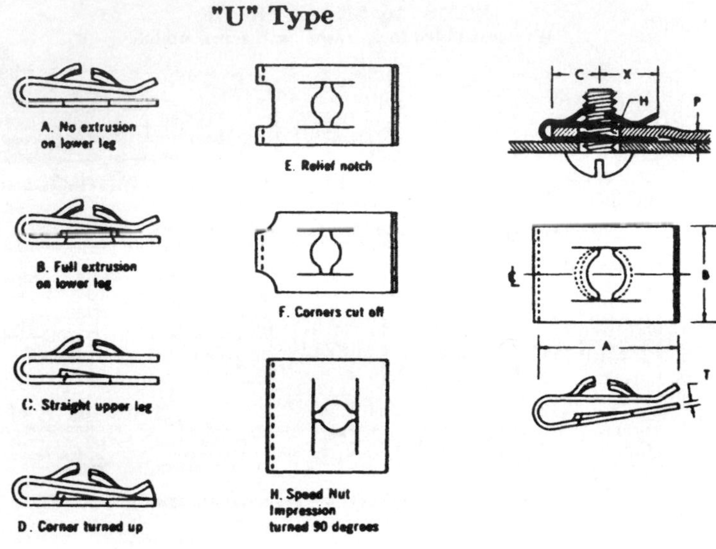

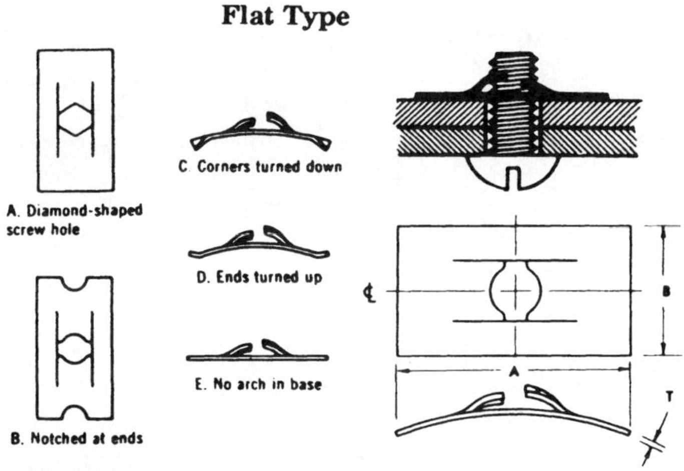

Figure 6.56 Tinnerman speed-nuts.

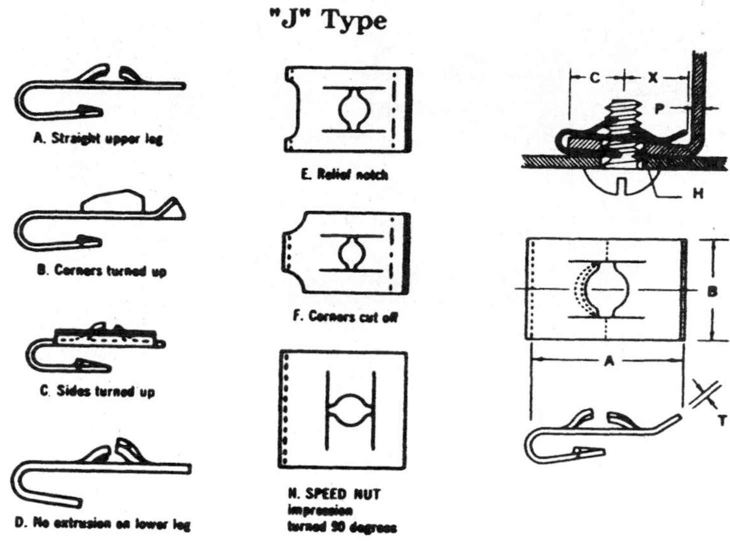
"J" Type
A. Straight upper leg
B. Corners turned up
C. Sides turned up
D. No extrusion on lower leg
E. Relief notch
F. Corners cut off
H. SPEED NUT impression turned 90 degrees
C
X
P
H
B
A
T

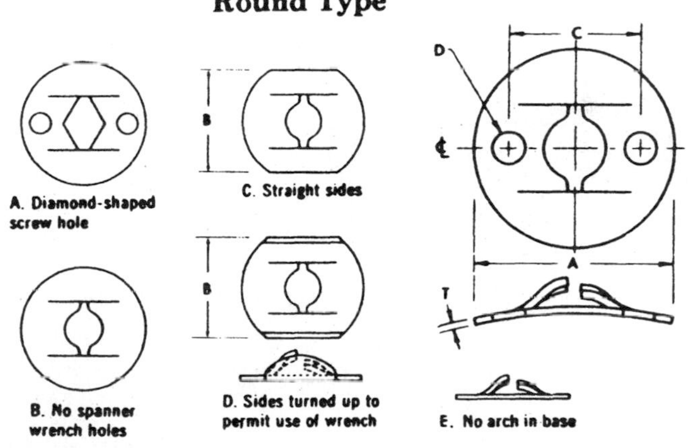
Round Type
A. Diamond-shaped screw hole
B. No spanner wrench holes
C. Straight sides
D. Sides turned up to permit use of wrench
E. No arch in base
B
B
C
D
A
T

Figure 6.56 *(Continued)*

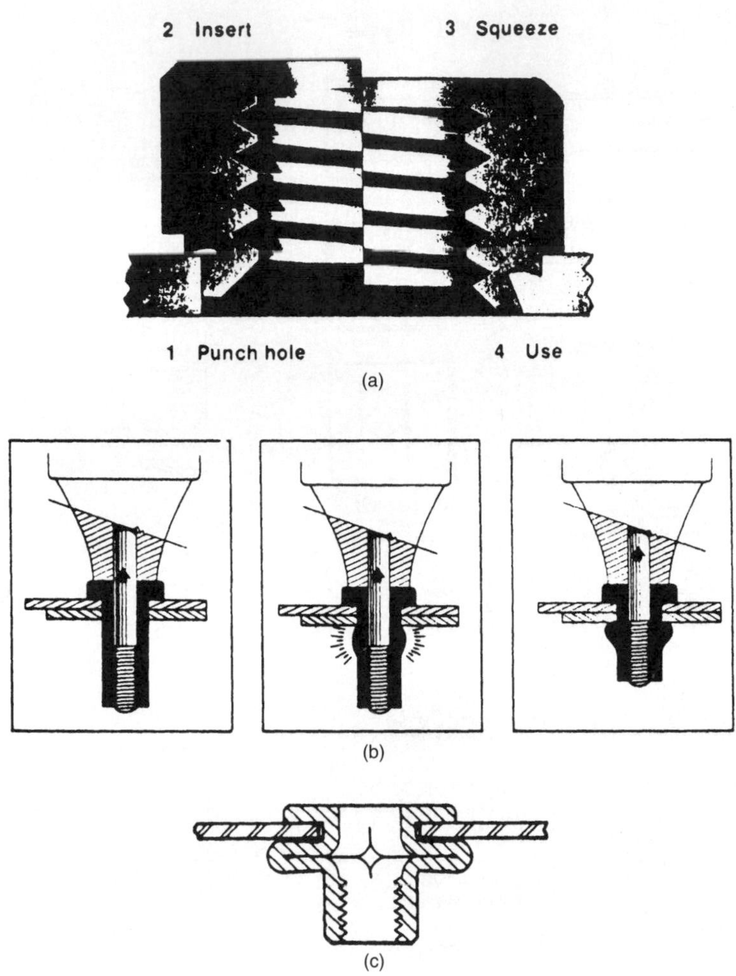

Figure 6.57 (*a*) Clinch or swage nut. (*b*) Rivnut installation. (*c*) Installed Plusnut.

TABLE 6.7 Precision Plating Specifications for Fasteners

Type	Thickness (minimum), in			Pre- or postplate treatments or instructions	Typical specifications
	A	B	C		
Cadmium	0.0002	0.0003	0.0005	Clear postplate dip	AMS 2400 and QQ-P-416, type I
Cadmium	0.0002	0.0003	0.0005	Olive drab chromate	QQ-P-416, type II
Cadmium	0.0002	0.0003	0.0005	Iridescent dichromate	QQ-P-416, type II
Zinc	0.0002	0.0003	0.0005	Clear bright	ASTM B633, type III
Zinc	0.0002	0.0003	0.0005	Olive drab chromate	ASTM B633, type II
Zinc	0.0002	0.0003	0.0005	Iridescent dichromate	ASTM B633, type II
Zinc	0.0002	0.0003	0.0005	Supplementary phosphate	ASTM B633, type IV
Silver	0.0002	0.0003	0.0005	Nickel strike	AMS 2410, AMS 2411
Black oxide	Alloy or carbon steel	18-8 stainless			AMS 2485, Mil-C-13924
Dull nickel	0.0002	0.0003	0.0005		AMS 2403
Copper	0.0002	0.0003	0.0005		AMS 2418
Tin	0.0002	0.0003	0.0005		AMS 2408, Mil-T-10727, type I
Phosphate (class A) (Parker-Lubrite)	Dry	Nondrying oil		Manganese phosphate	AMS 2481, DOD-P-16232
Phosphate (class B) (Parkerizing)	Dry	Drying oil		Zinc phosphate	AMS 2480, DOD-P-16232
Cadmium	0.0002	0.0003	0.0005	Black dye over olive drab chromate	QQ-P-416 type II except color
Cadmium	0.0002	0.0003	0.0005	Fluoborate bath, bake at 375° for 23 h, iridescent dichromate	NAS 672

TABLE 6.7 Precision Plating Specifications for Fasteners (*Continued*)

Type	Thickness (minimum), in			Pre- or postplate treatments or instructions	Typical specifications
	A	B	C		
Silver	0.0002	0.0003	0.0005	Copper strike	AMS 2412
Nickel	0.0002 NI			Thermal treat 630°	AMS 2416
Cadmium	0.0001 CD				
Vacuum cadmium	0.0002	0.0003	0.0005		Mil-C-8837, type I
Cadmium	0.0002	0.0003	0.0005	Supplementary phosphate	QQ-P-416, type III
Vacuum cadmium	0.0002	0.0003	0.0005	Iridescent dichromate “Cronak” or equivalent	Mil-C-8837, type II
Molydisulfide coating				Available with a variety of carriers, concentrations, and treatments to customer requirements	
Passivation				For austenitic series stainless steel	QQ-P-35
Passivation				For 400 series stainless steel	
Cadmium	0.0002	0.0003	0.0005	Clear postplate dip	AMS 2401
Sermetel					AMS 2506
“Metric” blue dye					
IVD aluminum	0.0010	0.0005	0.0003	Supplementary chromate	Mil-C-83488, type II

6.9 Welding, Brazing, and Soldering

Welding, brazing, and soldering are all important methods of joining and fastening metals and alloys. This section will detail the various methods or processes and materials used in these three types of joining techniques.

6.9.1 Welding

Welding is a fusion process for joining metals. The heat of application causes mixing of the joint metals or of the filler metal and the joint metal. The resulting joint is as strong as the parent metal, provided the weld is made correctly.

Numerous welding methods or techniques are in common use for a vast array of applications. Modern welding methods or techniques are catagorized in Fig. 6.58, which shows the process and the American Welding Society (AWS) designation. Both welding and cutting processes for metals are shown in Fig. 6.58.

Although the list of processes shown in Fig. 6.58 is extensive, the majority of welding is done by the following methods:

- Stick welding (fluxed rod)—SMAW
- MIG (metal inert gas) welding—GMAW
- TIG (tungsten inert gas) welding—GTAW
- Stud arc welding—SW

Whether the welding process is gas or arc, the welder may proceed to do the weld in the *forward* or *backward* direction, as shown in Fig. 6.59. The direction of welding is left to the judgment of the welder based on the configuration of object being welded. When the welder is looking down at the welded joint, this is normally called *in-position welding*. When the welder is looking up at the joint, this is called *out-of-position welding*. Any orientation not looking down at the weld can be considered as out-of-position welding.

Each of the various welding processes produces physical characteristics that allow the process to be identified by direct eye inspection. Figure 6.60 shows an assembly welded using the MIG process (GMAW). Here the weld is rather rough looking and was difficult to clean mechanically. The welding heat setting and the diameter of the weld wire play important roles in producing a neat, clean weld that is also mechanically sound. Figure 6.61 shows the same type of joint (using the same parts) that has been welded using the TIG process (GTAW). It is immediately apparent that the TIG process is more advantageous in this application, from the point of view of both strength and cosmetic appearance. This joint is comprised of parts manufactured from AISI 304 type stainless steel. Figure 6.61 shows the welded assembly "sand-blasted" after welding. The TIG weld in this application was made efficiently and correctly by a skilled welder. Welding is an art as well as a science, and a good welder needs a great deal of practice and experience.

In a welded assembly of numerous parts, the welder's skill and experience play an important role in producing an acceptable final weld assembly. Many welded assemblies require additional machining after the welding process because of the strains produced when the welded joints cool to room temperature. Allowance must be made in the design of such an assembly to accommodate these welding distortions, which are sometimes unavoidable.

Welding procedures and electrode sizes. The correct electrode size is one that, when used with the proper amperage and travel speed, produces a weld of the required size in the least amount of time. The electrode diameter selected for use depends largely on the thickness of the material to be welded, the position in which welding is to be performed, and the type of joint to be welded. In general, larger electrodes will be selected for applications involving thicker materials and for welding in the flat position in order to take advantage of their higher deposition rates.

For welding in the horizontal, vertical, and overhead positions, the molten weld metal tends to flow out of the joint due to gravity. This can be controlled by using small electrodes to reduce the weld pool size. Electrode manipulation and increased travel speed along the weld joint also aid in controlling the weld pool size.

Weld groove design also must be considered when electrode size is selected. The experience of the welder often has a bearing on the size of the electrode. This is particularly true for out-of-position welding, since the welder's skill determines the size of the molten pool that the welder can control.

Welds that are larger than necessary are more costly and, in certain instances, are actually harmful to the joint. Any sudden change in section size or in the contour of a weld, such as that caused by overwelding, creates stress concentrations. An improperly welded assembly of parts will distort upon cooling, and an experienced welder can prevent this to a certain degree by applying the welds at the correct points and in the correct sequences. Tooling fixtures and weld jigs play an important role in controlling the distortion of welded assemblies when they are designed and applied properly.

Shielded-metal arc welding can be accomplished with either alternating current (ac) or direct current (dc) when the appropriate electrode is used. The melting rate of any given electrode is directly related to the electrical energy supplied to the arc via the welding controller apparatus.

Direct current (dc) always supplies a steadier arc and smoother metal transfer than alternating current (ac). Most covered electrodes operate better on reverse polarity (electrode positive), although some are suitable for and are even designed for straight-polarity welding (electrode negative). Reverse polarity produces deeper weld penetration, while straight polarity produces a higher electrode melting rate. Direct current is particularly suitable for thin-section welding and is preferred for vertical and overhead welding (out-of-position welding). If *arc blow* is a problem when welding with dc, change the current to ac.

For SMAW, ac offers advantages over dc; one is the absence of arc blow, and the other is the cost of the power source for producing the weld (the welding machine or apparatus). Without arc blow, larger electrodes and higher welding currents can be used.

Welding technique. In SMAW welding, you first select the proper equipment, materials, and tools for the job. The type of welding current and its polarity must then be selected, and the power source set accordingly. The power source must be set to give the proper voltampere (VA) characteristic for the size and type of electrode being used.

Strike the arc, for the weld to begin, by tapping the end of the electrode near the beginning of the weld joint; then quickly move it to produce an arc of proper length at the beginning of the weld joint. Then move the electrode uniformly along the joint, keeping a constant arc length, as the electrode melts to produce the welded joint. A good deal of practice is required, especially in out-of-position type weld joints. To break the welding arc, when the weld joint is completed, stop the forward motion of the electrode and abruptly withdraw the electrode away from the joint or move the electrode into the weld pool quickly to kill the arc and abruptly remove it, thus breaking the arc.

Note: Complete welding procedures and data for all welding processes are prepared by the American Welding Society (AWS) and are available in handbook form in their *Welding Handbook*, eighth edition, in three volumes.

Weld strength: Related equations and tables. Here we will present the equations for determining the approximate strengths of welded joints. Any equation involving a process with many variables, such as welding, can only be an approximation. With this in mind, therefore, one should allow a factor of safety when designing and calculating the strengths of welded joints.

Fillet welds. Refer to Fig. 6.62*a*. The basic welding equations for the fillet weld are as follows

$$h = 0.707l$$

$$hL = \frac{P}{S_i}$$

$$A = \frac{P}{S_i}$$

$$L = \frac{P}{S_i h}$$

where l = leg dimension of fillet weld, in
L = length of fillet weld, in
h = weld throat height, in
P = load, lb
S_i = induced stress, lb/in^2
A = throat area, in^2

Butt welds (primary). Refer to Fig. 6.62*b*. The tensile stress in a butt weld induced by a tensile load P is

$$S_t = \frac{P}{td}$$

where S_t = tensile stress, lb/in^2
P = tensile load, lb
t = material thickness, in
d = width of butt welded joint, in

For minimum leg sizes for fillet welds, see Fig. 6.63*b*. For allowable design strengths and shear forces for fillet welds and partial-penetration groove welds, see Fig. 6.63*a*.

Example The allowable unit force for a fillet weld with a 0.25-in leg, using 80,000-lb/in^2 weld rod or wire, is $16,500 \times 0.25 = 4125$ lb/in. Thus, if the weld joint is 3-in long, the force allowable is $4125 \times 3 = 12,375$ lb.

Plug welds. Plug welds (Fig. 6.64) are useful in sheet metal and structural design applications. Plug welds are used primarily for shear loads, although they are not limited to this type of load. A plug weld may be subjected to a combination of shear and tensile loads. The typical sizes of plugs welds are shown in Fig. 6.63*c* for various applications or combinations of material thicknesses. Figure 6.64 illustrates a typical plug weld.

Note: It should be noted that the preceding weld-strength figures and tables, allowables, and examples are for *static* loads only. When the welded members are dynamically or cyclically loaded, a factor of safety should be applied. A safety factor of 3 should be applied for general dynamic conditions. In other words, if the weld joint was calculated to withstand a load of 3000 pounds force, for dynamic conditions this load should be reduced to a 1000 pounds force maximum. (Divide the calculated load by 3 to arrive at the allowable load with the factor of safety applied.)

Specifying welds. The type of welding, weld-rod strength and type, fillet or bead size, location, and length of welds all must be specified on the welding drawings of a part or assembly. Standard weld symbols recognized by the American Welding Society (AWS) should be used on the engineering drawings (see "standard weld symbols," below).

Thin-section parts or any part or assembly that may pose a weld-distortion problem should be reviewed in coordination with the welding department or welder prior to final design or beginning the work. Experienced welders usually know or can determine welding sequences to prevent distortion or keep it to a minimum. Welding-sequence instructions may be required on the welding drawing.

Secondary machining operations are usually performed on a welded part or assembly after the welding operation to correct unavoidable distortion or dimensional changes that take place during welding. To reduce cost and save welding time, the amount of welding on a part or assembly should be kept to a minimum, in accordance with the strength requirements of the design or sealing requirements.

(Text continued on page 507.)

Process	Designation
Arc welding (AW)	
Atomic-hydrogen welding	AHW
Bare-metal arc welding	BMAW
Carbon arc welding	CAW
-gas	CAW-G
-shielded	CAW-S
-twin	CAW-T
Flux-cored arc welding	FCAW
-electrogas	FCAW-EG
Gas-metal arc welding	GMAW
-electrogas	GMAW-EG
-pulsed arc	GMAW-P
-short circuiting arc	GMAW-S
Gas-tungsten arc welding	GTAW
-pulsed arc	GTAW-P
Plasma arc welding	PAW
Plasma gas-metal arc welding	PAW-GMAW
Shielded-metal arc welding	SMAW
Stud arc welding	SW
Submerged arc welding	SAW
-series	SAW-S
Solid-State Welding (SSW)	
Cold welding	CW
Diffusion welding	DFW
Explosive welding	EXW
Forge welding	FOW
Friction welding	FRW
Hot press welding	HPW
Roll welding	ROW
Ultrasonic welding	USW
Other Welding	
Electron-beam welding	EBW
Electroslag welding	ESW
Flow welding	FLOW
Induction welding	IW
Laser beam welding	LBW
Thermite welding	TW
Oxyfuel Gas Welding (OFW)	
Air acetylene welding	AAW
Oxyacetylene welding	OAW
Oxyhydrogen welding	OHW
Pressure gas welding	PGW
Resistance Welding (RW)	
Flash welding	FW
High frequency resistance welding	HFRW
Percussion welding	PEW
Projection welding	RPW
Resistance seam welding	RSEW
Resistance spot welding	RSW
Upset welding	UW

Metal Cutting Processes and Designations

Process	Designation
Thermal Oxygen Cutting (OC)	
Chemical flux cutting	FOC
Metal powder cutting	POC
Oxyfuel gas cutting	OFC
-oxyacetylene	OFC-A
-oxyhydrogen	OFC-H
-oxynatural gas	OFC-N
-oxypropane	OFC-P
Oxygen arc cutting	AOC
Oxygen lance cutting	LOC
Arc cutting (AC)	
Air-carbon arc cutting	AAC
Carbon arc cutting	CAC
Gas-metal arc cutting	GMAC
Gas-tungsten arc cutting	GTAC
Metal arc cutting	MAC
Plasma arc cutting	PAC
Shielded-metal arc cutting	SMAC
Other cutting	
Electron-beam cutting	EBC
Laser beam cutting	LBC

Recognized by The American Welding Society (AWS)

Figure 6.58 Welding processes and designations.

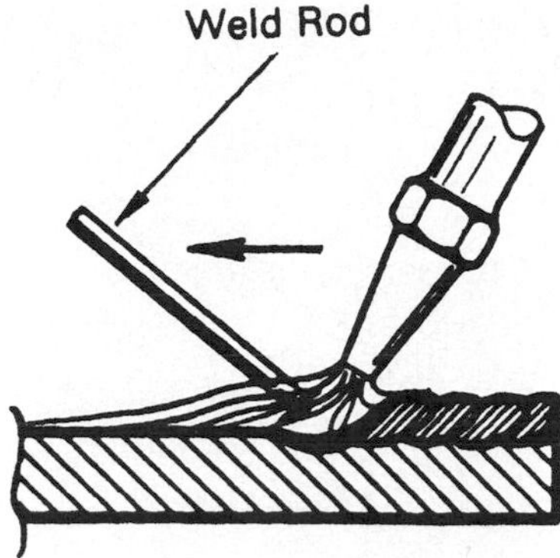

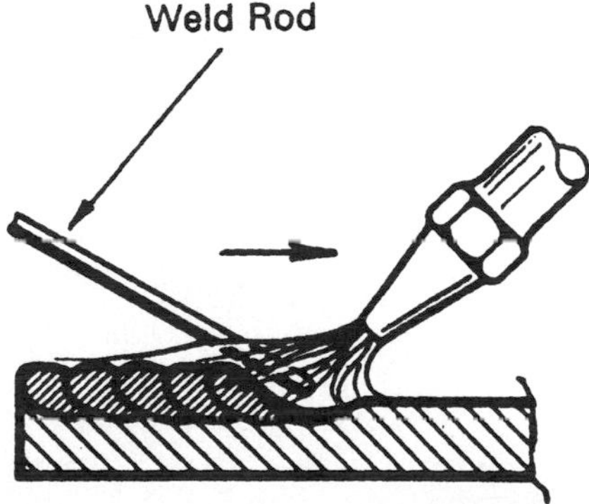

Figure 6.59 (*a*) Forward. (*b*) Backward.

Figure 6.60 MIG-welded assembly.

Figure 6.61 TIG-welded assembly.

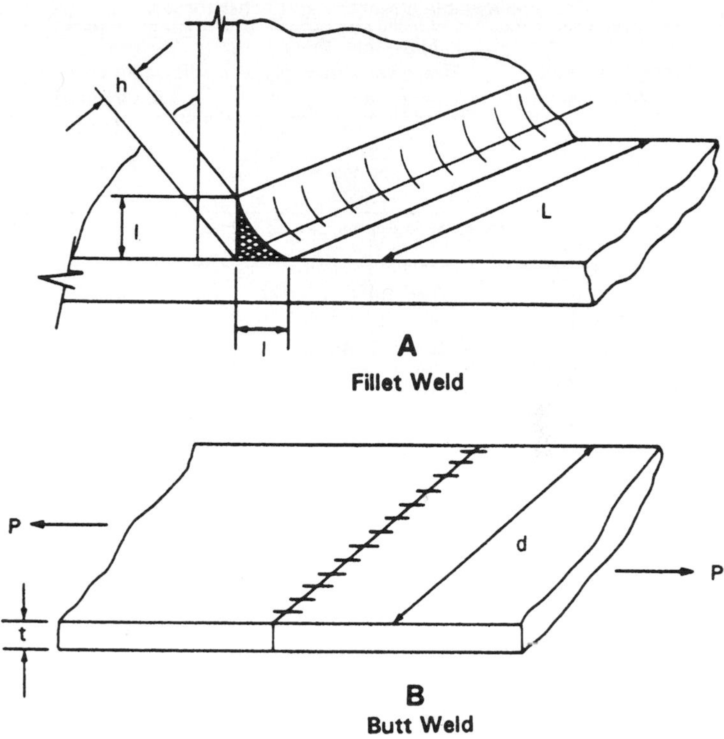

Figure 6.62 (*a*) Fillet. (*b*) Butt.

Design-allowable strengths and shear forces.

Strength of Weld* Rod or Wire Metal, psi	Allowable Shear Stress on Throat (h), psi	Allowable Unit Force, lb/Linear in.
60,000	17,000	12,500 × l
80,000	23,000	16,500 × l
100,000	29,000	21,000 × l
120,000	35,000	25,000 × l

*For intermediate weld-rod strengths, interpolation may be used. In the above table h = weld throat, l = length of leg of the fillet

(a)

Minimum leg size (fillet weld).

Thickness of Thicker Plate (t), in	Minimum* Leg Size (l), in
Up to 1/4	1/8
> 1/4 to 1/2	3/16
> 1/2 to 3/4	1/4
> 3/4 to 1 1/2	5/16
> 1 1/2 to 2 1/2	3/8

*Also minimum throat (h) of partial penetration groove weld. Leg of weld (l) should not exceed thickness of thinner plate.

(b)

Plug weld sizes (diameters).

Gauge or Thickness of Thinner Member, in	Plug-weld Hole Diameter, in
1/16 or #16 gauge	1/4 to 3/8
3/32 or #13 gauge	1/2
1/8 or #11 gauge	5/8
3/16 or #7 gauge	5/8
1/4	3/4
3/8	1
1/2	1 1/4

(c)

Figure 6.63 (*a*) Allowable shear. (*b*) Leg sizes. (*c*) Plug sizes.

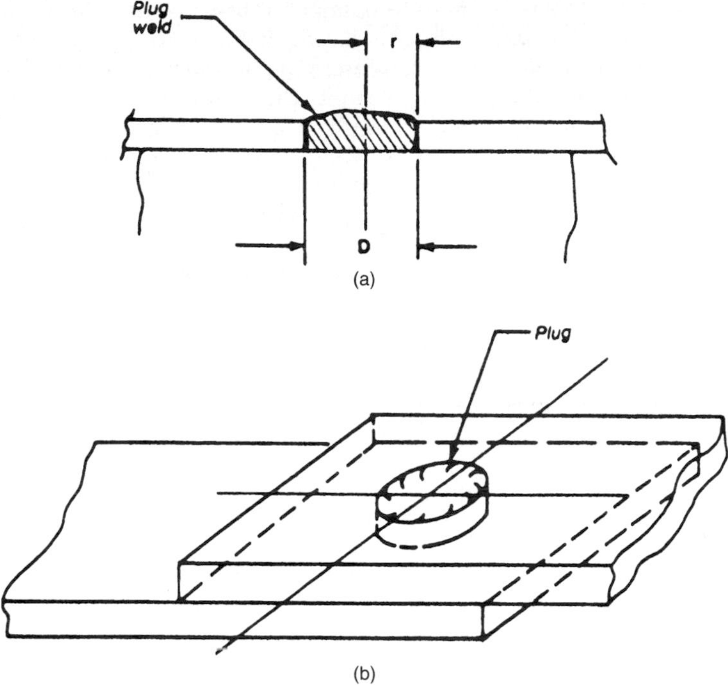

Figure 6.64 (*a*) Section of plug. (*b*) Plug-welded plates.

Standard weld symbols. The basic weld symbols shown in Fig. 6.65 should be used on all welding drawings, especially if the welded part is sent to an outside vendor or subcontractor. If in-house symbols are used, these should be noted on the welding drawings so that outside vendors or subcontractors know their exact meaning. The symbols shown in Fig. 6.65 are those recognized by the American Welding Society (AWS), the American Iron and Steel Institute (AISI), ASME, SAE, and other authorities and specification agencies.

Elements of the welding symbol. When a weld is specified on an American standard engineering drawing, it should conform to certain characteristics, which are shown in Fig. 6.66. In this way, uniformity and complete understanding are maintained between the welder and the design engineer. Typical welding drawing call-outs or symbols are shown in Fig. 6.67 with an explanation of their meaning.

Types of weld joints. There are many types of weld joints or designs, and the basic ones are shown in Fig. 6.68. The various joints have been designed for different applications and strengths. Other characteristics are designed into the weld joint, such as minimal out-gassing, dynamic strength, deep penetration, pressure-vessel applications, and others. Weld joints that require special preparation, such as machining, filing, or grinding, are more expensive to produce and are thus used for special applications. The majority of industrial welding consists of the simple fillet- and butt-welded joints, followed by the single V and double V joints.

Welding applications data. Welding is one of the most common and important means of fastening. Its applications are limitless, and the technology is constantly changing. Given here is a listing of various welding process applications that are helpful in design as well as welding work.

Thin-gauge metal welding. Small welding flames or small arcs are required for welding thin-gauge metals. The TIG process is especially useful for producing small, accurate welds on thin materials, under 11 gauge (0.1196 in). To prevent buckling of large-area, thin materials, *heat sinks* are useful. Heat sinks may take the form of wet burlap bags or large blocks of metal clamped to the welded parts or sections. Applying *tack welds* in a specified sequence also may help to prevent buckling of large, thin sections prior to beginning the final seams.

Preheating. Large sections or masses of metal usually require a preheat stage, where the parts are heated a few hundred degrees Fahrenheit prior to beginning the welding process. This prevents thermal shock and minimizes distortion and possible cracking of the welds.

Air cooling. Welded parts or assemblies are normally allowed to cool to ambient temperature after the welding process is completed. Do not water quench welded parts immediately after welding. Because of the high temperatures generated in the welding process, cracking or distortion may occur. Changes in the grain structure of the metal may occur if the hot, welded part is suddenly cooled by water quenching.

Welding bases or platforms. A flat, level area is required for welding large assemblies. This is usually provided by structural beams embedded in the weld shop floor. The beams must be straight and leveled with a transit or leveling instrument. For smaller welded parts and assemblies, the standard welding table is used. Figure 6.69 shows a typical steel-grid welding table, which is used in many welding departments. This type of table is level and has square openings where different types of clamping and squaring tools may be attached to hold the welded assembly prior to the welding operation.

Notice the screening and plastic shielding located around the welding table area. This shielding prevents the intense ultraviolet radiation generated by the welding arc from reaching the eyes of other personnel. The intensity of the welding arc radiation is high enough to damage the membrane covering the human cornea and eyeball. It is not necessary to look directly at the welding arc for damage to occur to the eye. The arc rays can penetrate the side of the eye indirectly and cause damage. The usual effect of looking at a welding arc is the feeling that sand has entered the eye. This usually begins to show some hours after exposure to the arc, either directly or indirectly, and is the result of scar-tissue formation in the damaged eye tissues.

Welding stainless steels. The electrode used to weld stainless steels also should be stainless steel, matching the application. Types AISI 300 through 303 should not be welded, since these are machining grades. Type AISI 304 is a preferred stainless steel for welding applications, with AISI type 304L a special low-carbon grade for critical applications such as those used on aerospace vehicles. Too much carbon or sulfur in a stainless steel produces cracking during the welding process. AISI types 308, 309S, 310S, 316, and 316L are also suitable for welding applications, because they are low in carbon content. AISI types 316 and 316L stainless steels are used widely in highly corrosive environments such as chemical and food-processing applications. The 300 series stainless steels are austenitic (nonmagnetic) and cannot be hardened by heat-treatment procedures. See Chap. 5 for more information on stainless steels.

Welding carbon and alloy steels. The low-carbon grades from AISI 1010 through 1020 are readily weldable because they are low in carbon content. Some of the medium-carbon grades are weldable with caution, while the high-carbon grades are not recommended for welding (AISI 1045–1095). The higher carbon content in the steel causes cracking during the welding process. Low-alloy- and alloy-grade steels are weldable according to type and welding process employed. See Chap. 5 for more data on the low-alloy and alloy steels, including tool steels.

Cutting metals. Oxyacetylene cutting (OFC-A) is the most common welding process for cutting ferrous metals. Most ferrous metals cut cleanly using this method, except the stainless steels, high-manganese steels, and special alloy steels. To cut these difficult materials, special techniques are required wherein the molten metal can be blown away from the flame or arc during the cutting process. Laser beam cutting (LBC) is a modern method of cutting difficult materials and extremely thin materials. Figure 6.70 shows a small part made of carbon steel which was cut using the laser beam method. This part is approximately 2 in long and 0.25 in thick. The quantity required did not justify building a stamping die for this part, and milling the part from stock was expensive; therefore, laser beam cutting was selected for the method of manufacture.

Many branches of industry rely on the welding processes for producing their equipment and machinery economically. Figure 6.71 shows a typical electrical power-distribution industry lineup of switch gear which relies heavily on the welding processes to fasten and join the many sheet metal parts and structures required.

6.9.2 Brazing

Brazing employs a nonferrous filler metal, usually in wire or paste form, to join metal parts at a temperature above approximately 800°F but below the melting point of the base metals being joined. Various fluxes are used in the brazing process to remove oxides on the base-metal parts so that the filler metal can adhere to them strongly. Sal ammoniac is a good general-purpose flux for brazing copper, phosphor-bronze, and stainless steels.

The brazing of tungsten alloys to various base metals is accomplished by pretinning the brazing surfaces of the tungsten-alloy part in a nitrogen-atmosphere furnace before joining the tungsten-alloy part with the base-metal part. This is done because it is extremely difficult to remove oxide layers that form on the tungsten part unless it is pretinned and protected from the atmosphere. Many of the various designs of electrical contact points are brazed to their base-metal mountings, although riveting is sometimes employed.

Brazing heat. Heat for brazing parts may be supplied by the following methods:

- Torch brazing
- Furnace brazing
- Resistance brazing
- Dip brazing
- Vacuum-furnace brazing
- Induction brazing

When there is an unusual condition in the brazing method or process, a brazing specialist should be consulted. So many brazing materials and fluxes are available that only an expert in the field may be able to solve your particular brazing problem.

In the normal brazing process, a suitable brazing wire or paste is selected, and the parts to be brazed are set up or clamped into position (brazing fixtures are sometimes employed) after the joint has been fluxed with the proper flux for the application. Heat is applied to the parts to be joined, and when they are hot enough, the filler wire is fed into the brazed joint, where a wetting action takes place, and the joint is filled with the melted brazing filler. The joint is then allowed to air cool to room temperature. The method of fluxing and applying the filler metal is critical for a well-brazed joint. It requires considerable skill and practice to braze a difficult joint or complicated setup. Excess brazing filler should not be used on any brazed joint because it wastes material and produces an inefficient joint.

Brazing pastes and alloys. Brazing and soldering alloys are available as wire, strip, preformed shapes, and pastes. Brazing pastes are applied to the joint prior to heating and are therefore applicable for manual as well as automated processing. Flux is also compounded in some of the brazing pastes, making their use easily applicable to production operations.

Lucas-Milhaupt (Handy and Harman Company) produces an extensive array of pastes for soldering and brazing in their Handy-Flo series 110, 120, 210, 310, 320, and 330, which are listed in Fig. 6.72. Other standard Handy and Harman brazing materials are outlined in Fig. 6.73. With some of the new brazing products, it is now possible to join ceramics, diamonds, and other difficult to wet materials.

6.9.3 Soldering

The use of lead or tin base alloys having melting points below 800°F for joining metal parts is known as *soft soldering*. Such joints usually do not have great mechanical strength, although they may be required to carry electric currents.

The three basic standard soldering alloys are

- 60 percent tin, 40 percent lead—melting point 375°F
- 50 percent tin, 50 percent lead—melting point 420°F
- 40 percent tin, 60 percent lead—melting point 460°F

A number of other alloys are available, and these will be shown in later figures. The standard 60-40 solder is useful for most electrical/electronic soldering, and a small amount of antimony may be added for improving quality and strength. The electronic wire solders are usually made with a rosin flux core. The flux is noncorrosive and nonconducting and may be removed after the soldering operation with naphtha, Varsol, or enamel paint thinners. Rosin-cored solders can be stored for extensive periods without degradation of the rosin flux core.

Preforms are also produced in soldering alloys. A *preform* is a stamped shape, made of solder alloy, that will fit a particular device or application. Some of the delicate soldering operations would be difficult or impossible without preforms.

Figure 6.74 shows a typical printed circuit board which had been automatically soldered in a "wave" soldering operation. This board was taken from a piece of automotive equipment that failed in service. All the copper foil lines on the printed circuit board are covered with solder, with the termination points neatly made.

Solder compositions which are recognized by the American Society for Testing and Materials (ASTM) are shown in Table 6.8. These alloys run from low-lead to high-tin content and are designed for various applications. The melting temperatures are also given in the table.

Soldering aluminum. Aluminum soldering employs a soldering alloy of 60 to 75 percent tin, the remainder being zinc. Special aluminum fluxes are available, and the process is carried out at a temperature of 550 to 775°F.

Commercial and high-purity aluminums are easiest to solder, with wrought alloys that contain no more than 1 percent magne-

(Text continued on page 523.)

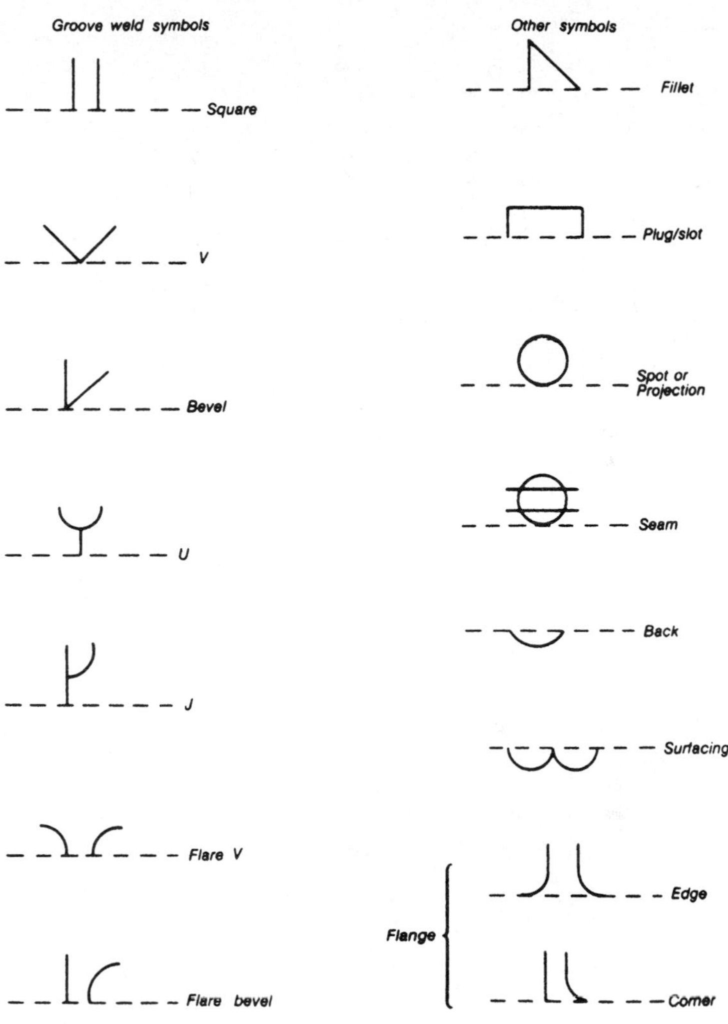

Figure 6.65 Weld symbols.

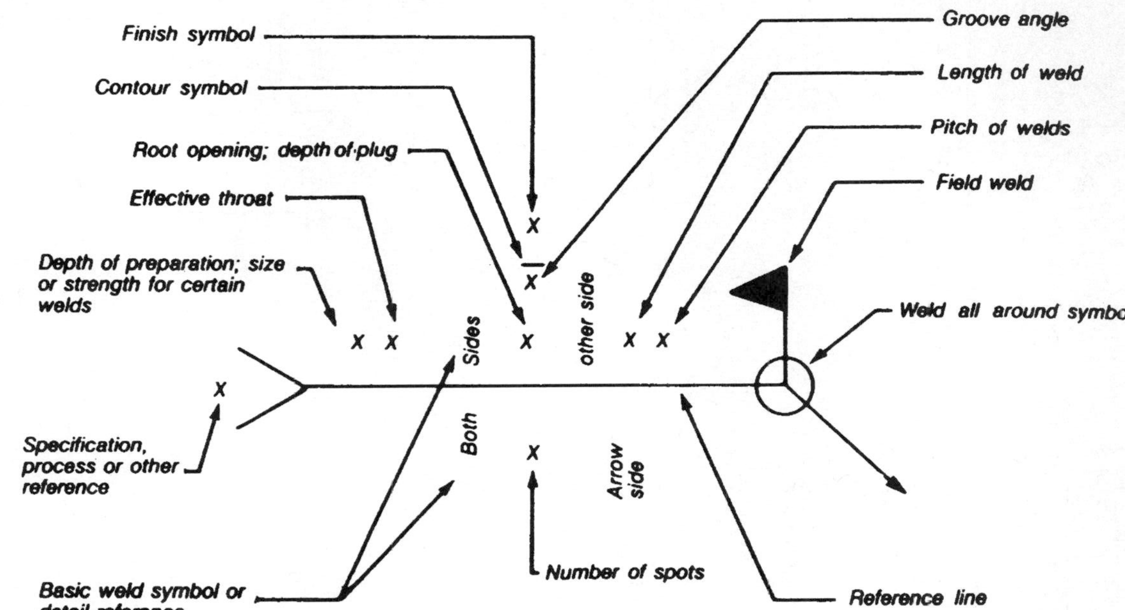
Standard locations of elements of a welding symbol
Finish symbol
Contour symbol
Root opening; depth of plug
Effective throat
Depth of preparation; size or strength for certain welds
Specification, process or other reference
Basic weld symbol or detail reference
Groove angle
Length of weld
Pitch of welds
Field weld
Weld all around symbol
Reference line
Number of spots
Sides
Both
other side
Arrow side
X

Figure 6.66 Elements of the welding symbol.

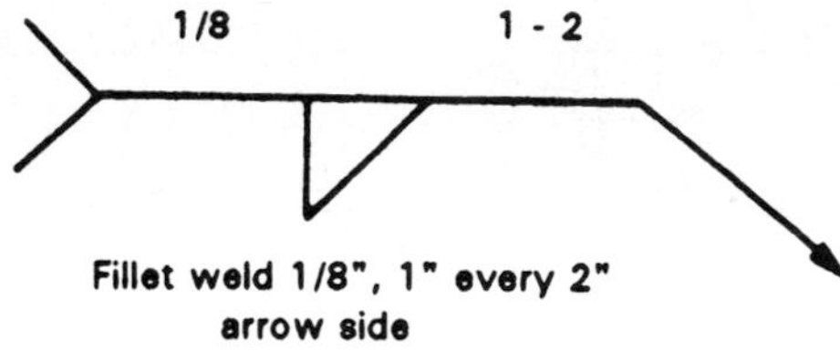

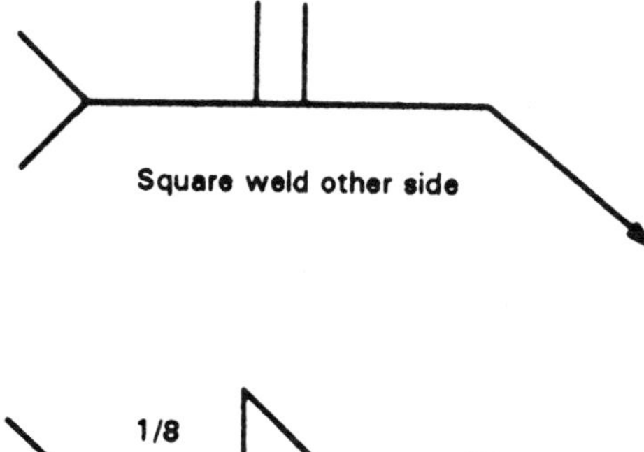

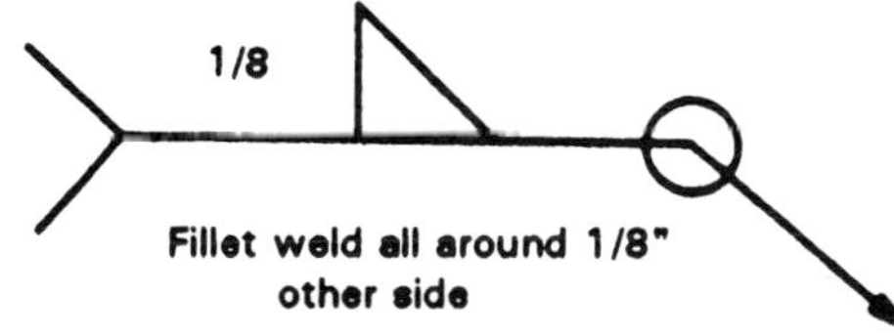

Figure 6.67 Typical weld call-outs (welding drawings).

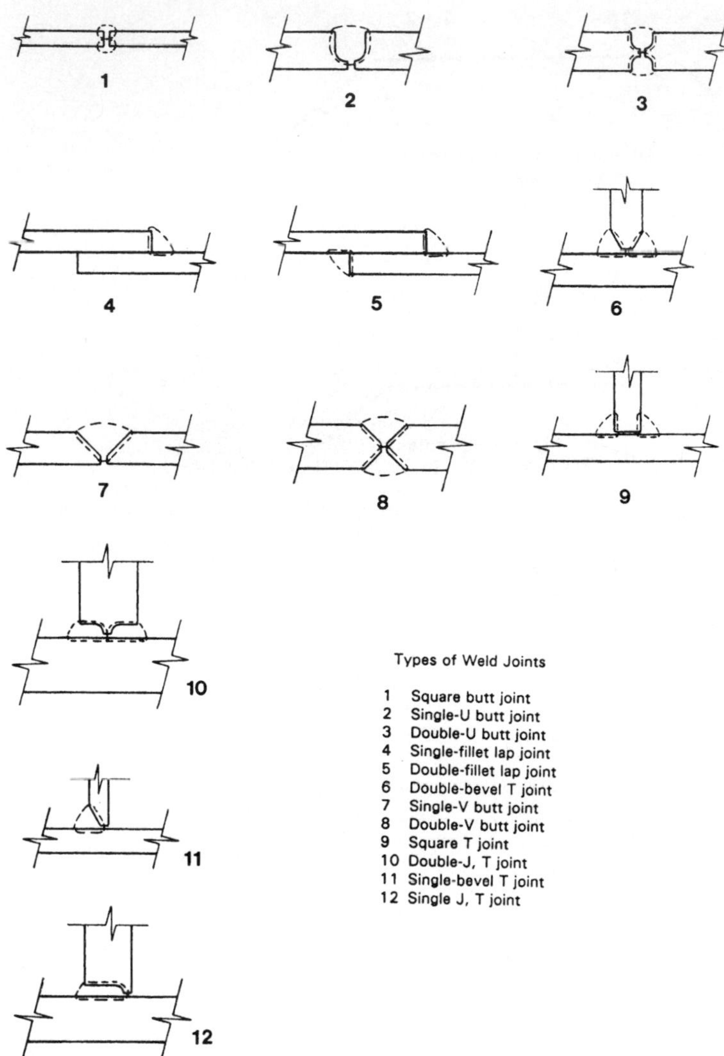

Figure 6.68 Basic weld-joint geometry.

Figure 6.69 A cast iron grid welding table.

Figure 6.70 A laser-cut steel part.

Figure 6.71 Switch gear equipment fabricated from sheet steel (*Powercon Corporation, Severn, Maryland*).

HEATING METHODS	110	120	210	310	320	330
Torch	•	•	•			
Induction	•	•	•			
Resistance	•	•	•			
Vacuum Brazing				•	•	•
Atmospheric Furnace	•	•	•	•	•	•
Infrared, Hot plate						
Oven						
TEMPERATURE RANGE						
300 - 500° F 149-260° C						
500 - 1000° F 260-524° C						•
1000 - 1500° F 524-815° C	•	•		•	•	•
1500 - 2000° F 815-1093° C			•	•	•	•
Includes Flux	•	•	•			
Can Be Boron Modified	•	•	•			
MATERIALS JOINED						
Copper	•	•	•	•	•	•
Brass	•	•		•	•	
Cold rolled steels	•	•	•	•	•	•
Stainless Steel	•	•	•	•	•	•
Non-ferrous alloys	•	•	•	•	•	•
Tungsten Carbide	•	•	•			

Figure 6.72 Brazing paste properties.

H & H Alloy Designations	AWS A 5.8	AMS Spec.	Federal Spec. QQ-B-654A	Solidus °F	Solidus °C	Liquidus °F	Liquidus °C	Nominal Compositions % Ag	Cu	Zn	Others	Comments
Easy-Flo 45	BAg-1	4769B	VII	1125	605	1145	620	45	15	16	24Cd	Versatile alloy; for Fe&Ni base alloys
Easy-Flo	BAg-1a	4770F	IV	1160	625	1175	635	50	15.5	16.5	18Cd	For ferrous, non-ferrous, dissimilar metals.
Easy-Flo 35	BAg-2	4768D	VIII	1125	605	1295	700	35	26	21	18Cd	Gen. purpose for larger gaps.
Easy-Flo 30	BAg-2a			1125	605	1310	710	30	27	23	20Cd	For ferrous, non-ferrous, dissimilar metals.
Easy-Flo 3	BAg-3	4771D	V	1170	630	1270	690	50	15.5	15.5	16Cd/3Ni	For tungsten carbide brazing. Al-Bronze to steel. Stainless Steels.
Sil-Fos 5	BCuP-3			1190	643	1495	812	5	89		6P	Same as Sil-Fos.
Sil-Fos	BCuP-5		BCuP-5	1190	643	1475	801	15	80		5P	For Cu or Cu alloys — Not for Fe Alloys.
Sil-Fos 6	BCuP-4			1190	643	1325	718	6.0	86.5		7.5P	
Sil-Fos 18				1191	643	1191	643	17.75	75		7.25P	
69-014				1215	657	1270	687		86.7		6.3P/7Sn	
70-873				1245	674	1285	696		87.3		7.1P/5.6Sn	
Fos-Flo 7	BCuP-2			1310	709	1460	793		92.75		7.25P	Low cost alloy for copper & copper alloys.
Fos-Flo 8				1350	732	1350	732		91.5		8.5P	
Braze 300	BAg-20		BAg-20	1250	675	1410	765	30	38	32		For steel & non-ferrous alloys melting above 1450°F; Ni-Ag knife handle
Braze 380	BAg-34			1200	650	1330	720	38	32	28	2 Sn	Cd free. For small gaps, Fe, Cu alloys.
Braze 403	BAg-4		BAg-4	1220	660	1435	780	40	30	28	2Ni	For tungsten carbides — stainless food handling equip. (no Cd).
Braze 404				1220	660	1580	860	40	30	25	5Ni	Brazing carbides & stainless steels.
Braze 450	BAg-5		BAg-5	1225	665	1370	745	45	30	25		For band instruments (Cu alloys), brass lamps.
Braze 495	BAg-22			1260	680	1290	700	49	16	23	7.5Mn/4.5Ni	For brazing of carbides and stainless steel.
Braze 505	BAg-24			1220	660	1305	705	50	20	28	2Ni	For Ni & Fe base alloys — retards interface corrosion (no Cd).
Braze 541	BAg-13	4772E		1340	725	1575	855	54	40	5	1Ni	For stainless steels used at elevated temps.
Braze 559	BAg-13a	4765A	BAg-13a	1420	770	1640	895	56	42		2Ni	Atmosphere brazing for high temp (NoZn).
Braze 560	BAg-7		BAg-7	1145	620	1205	650	56	22	17	5Sn	Food handling equipment (Cd free).
Braze 600				1245	675	1325	720	60	25	15		For Monel & other nickel alloys.
Braze 603	BAg-18	4773B	BAg-18	1115	600	1325	720	60	30		10Sn	Low temp. seals on vacuum parts.
Braze 630	BAg-21	4774B		1275	690	1475	800	63	28.5		6Sn/2.5Ni	Stainless steel food equip./400 stainless.
Braze 650	BAg-9		BAg-9	1240	670	1325	720	65	20	15		For silverware, Fe and Ni alloys.
Braze 720	BAg-8			1435	780	1435	780	72	28			Electronics where Cd & Zn not tolerated.
Hi-Temp 095	4764B			1615	880	1770	925		52.5		38Mn, 9.5Ni	High strength for carbides, steels.
Hi-Temp 870				1760	960	1885	1030		87		10Mn, 3 Co	High temperature strength for carbides, tool steel, stainless and nickel alloys.
Premabraze 616	BVAg-29			1155	625	1305	705	61.5	24		14.5 In	For ferrous, non-ferrous in vacuum.
Premabraze 130	BAu4	4787B		1742	950	1742	950				82 Au, 18 Ni	Oxidation resistant to 1500°F, service.

Figure 6.73 Standard brazing materials.

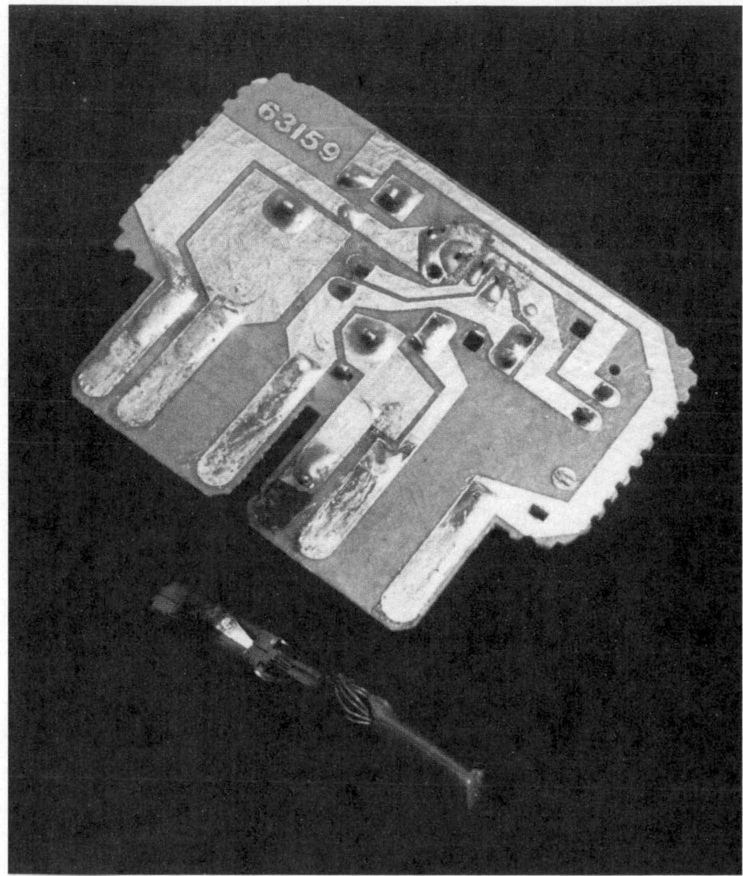

Figure 6.74 An electrically damaged PC board with solder-coated foil.

TABLE 6.8 ASTM Standard Solder Compositions

	Composition, %*,†												Melting Range‡			
													Solidus		Liquidus	
Alloy grade	Sn 1	Pb 2	Sb 3	Ag 4	Cu 5	Cd 6	Al 7	Bi 8	As 9	Fe 10	Zn 11	Ni 12	°F	°C	°F	°C
Section 1: Solder Alloys Containing Less than 0.2% Lead																
Sn96	Rem	0.10	0.12 max	3.4–3.8	0.08	0.005	0.005	0.15	0.01 max	0.02	0.005	—	430	221	430	221
Sn95	Rem	0.10	0.12	4.4–4.8	0.08	0.005	0.005	0.15	0.01	0.02	0.005	—	430	221	473	245
Sn94	Rem	0.10	0.12	5.4–5.8	0.08	0.005	0.005	0.15	0.01	0.02	0.005	—	430	221	536	280
Sb5	94.0 min	0.20	4.5–5.5	0.015	0.08	0.03	0.005	0.15	0.05	0.04	0.005	—	450	233	464	240
E	Rem	0.10	0.05	0.25–0.75	3.0–5.0	0.005	0.005	0.02	0.05	0.02	0.005	—	440	225	660	349
HA	Rem	0.10	0.5–4.0	0.1–3.0	0.1–2.0	0.005	0.005	0.15	0.05	0.02	0.5–4.0	—	420	216	440	227
HB	Rem	0.10	4.0–6.0	0.05–0.5	2.0–5.0	0.005	0.005	0.15	0.05	0.02	0.01	0.05–2.0	460	238	660	349
Section 2: Solder Alloys Containing Lead																
Sn70	69.5–71.5	Rem	0.50	0.015	0.08	0.001	0.005	0.25	0.03	0.02	0.005	—	361	183	377	193
Sn63	62.5–63.5	Rem	0.50	0.015	0.08	0.001	0.005	0.25	0.03	0.02	0.005	—	361	183	361	183
Sn62	61.5–62.5	Rem	0.50	1.75–2.25	0.08	0.001	0.005	0.25	0.03	0.02	0.005	—	354	179	372	189
Sn60	59.5–61.5	Rem	0.50	0.015	0.08	0.001	0.005	0.25	0.03	0.02	0.005	—	361	183	374	190
Sn50	49.5–51.5	Rem	0.50	0.015	0.08	0.001	0.005	0.25	0.025	0.02	0.005	—	361	183	421	216
Sn45	44.5–46.5	Rem	0.50	0.015	0.08	0.001	0.005	0.25	0.025	0.02	0.005	—	361	183	441	227
Sn40A	39.5–41.5	Rem	0.50	0.015	0.08	0.001	0.005	0.25	0.02	0.02	0.005	—	361	183	460	238
Sn40B	39.5–41.5	Rem	1.8–2.4	0.015	0.08	0.001	0.005	0.25	0.02	0.02	0.005	—	365	185	448	231
Sn35A	34.5–36.5	Rem	0.50	0.015	0.08	0.001	0.005	0.25	0.02	0.02	0.005	—	361	183	447	247
Sn35B	34.5–36.5	Rem	1.6–2.0	0.015	0.08	0.001	0.005	0.25	0.02	0.02	0.005	—	365	185	470	243

TABLE 6.8 ASTM Standard Solder Compositions (*Continued*)

	Composition, %*,†												Melting Range‡			
													Solidus		Liquidus	
Alloy grade	Sn 1	Pb 2	Sb 3	Ag 4	Cu 5	Cd 6	Al 7	Bi 8	As 9	Fe 10	Zn 11	Ni 12	°F	°C	°F	°C
Section 2: Solder Alloys Containing Lead																
Sn30A	29.5–31.5	Rem	0.50	0.015	0.08	0.001	0.005	0.25	0.02	0.02	0.005	—	361	183	491	255
Sn30B	29.5–31.5	Rem	1.4–1.8	0.015	0.08	0.001	0.005	0.25	0.02	0.02	0.005	—	365	185	482	250
Sn25A	24.5–26.5	Rem	0.50	0.015	0.08	0.001	0.005	0.25	0.02	0.02	0.005	—	361	183	511	266
Sn25B	24.5–26.5	Rem	1.1–1.5	0.015	0.08	0.001	0.005	0.25	0.02	0.02	0.005	—	365	185	504	263
Sn20A	19.5–21.5	Rem	0.50	0.015	0.08	0.001	0.005	0.25	0.02	0.02	0.005	—	361	183	531	277
Sn20B	19.5–21.5	Rem	0.8–1.2	0.015	0.08	0.001	0.005	0.25	0.02	0.02	0.005	—	363	184	517	270
Sn15	14.5–16.5	Rem	0.50	0.015	0.08	0.001	0.005	0.25	0.02	0.02	0.005	—	437	225	554	290
Sn10A	9.0–11.0	Rem	0.50	0.015	0.08	0.001	0.005	0.25	0.02	0.02	0.005	—	514	268	576	302
Sn10B	9.0–11.0	Rem	0.20	1.7–2.4	0.08	0.001	0.005	0.03	0.02	0.02	0.005	—	514	268	570	299
Sn5	4.5–5.5	Rem	0.50	0.015	0.08	0.001	0.005	0.25	0.02	0.02	0.005	—	586	308	594	312
Sn2	1.5–2.5	Rem	0.50	0.015	0.08	0.001	0.005	0.25	0.02	0.02	0.005	—	601	316	611	322
Ag1.5	0.75–1.25	Rem	0.40	1.3–1.7	0.30	0.001	0.005	0.25	0.02	0.02	0.005	—	588	309	588	309
Ag2.5	0.25	Rem	0.40	2.3–2.7	0.30	0.001	0.005	0.25	0.02	0.02	0.005	—	580	304	580	304
Ag5.5	0.25	Rem	0.40	5.0–6.0	0.30	0.001	0.005	0.25	0.02	0.02	0.005	—	580	304	716	380

* Limits are % max unless shown as a range or stated otherwise.

† For purposes of determining conformance to these limits, an observed value or calculated value obtained from analysis shall be rounded to the nearest unit in the last right-hand place of figures used in expressing the specified limit, in accordance with the rounding method of Practice E 29.

‡ Temperatures given are approximations and for information only.

SOURCE: Reprinted with permission, from the *Annual Book of ASTM Standards,* copyright 1992, American Society of Testing and Materials.

sium or manganese the next easiest. The heat-treatable alloys are more difficult. Forged and cast aluminum alloys are not recommended for soldering, although it may be possible to a limited extent. The low-temperature brazing alloys may do the job more efficiently, with a higher-strength joint possible.

Ultrasonic soldering. The following metals and alloys may be soldered ultrasonically: aluminum, brass, copper, germanium, magnesium, silicon, and silver.

6.10 Adhesive Bonding

Adhesive bonding is used very frequently in modern manufacturing operations. The methods are generally fast, strong, and economical when used in the proper manner on appropriate articles. Entire fuselage sections are bonded or cemented on modern aircraft to replace riveting. The method not only affords lighter weight but also is stronger and requires no maintenance. The bonding strength of cyanoacrylate adhesives is on the order of thousands of pounds of tension for 1 in^2 of bonded surface area.

Structural adhesives. Following is a list of the various types of adhesives used in industrial applications:

- Hot-melt adhesives, thermoplastic resins—100 percent solids
- Dispersion or solution adhesives, thermoplastic resins—20 to 50 percent solids
- Silicone adhesives, thermoset—100 percent solids (rubber-like with high impact and peel strengths)
- Anaerobic adhesives, thermoset—100 percent solids, liquid (thread-locking uses such as Loctite series adhesives)
- Phenolic or urea adhesives, thermoset resins—100 percent solids or solution
- Epoxy adhesives, thermoset—100 percent solids, liquid
- Polyurethane adhesives, thermoset—100 percent solids, liquid
- Cyanoacrylate adhesives, thermoset—100 percent solids, liquid (hazard of bonding skin on contact; almost instant set; 30 s to 5 min cure; high strength)

- Modified acrylic adhesives, thermoset—100 percent solids, liquid or paste (fast cure, 3 to 60 s)

Weldbonding. A combination of spot welding and adhesive bonding, this process is used on aerospace assemblies to cut costs, reduce weight, and increase strength. The method affords lighter weight than riveting, is stronger, yields air- and fuel-tight joints, and produces a smooth exterior surface that reduces wind resistance. The structural adhesives are applied prior to the spot-welding operation; then the bonded and welded assembly is oven cured at an elevated temperature for a predetermined time interval.

Chapter

7

Machining, Machine Tools, and Practices

Machine tools and cutting tools have advanced in great strides in the past 40 years. What at one time was a difficult operation on a machine tool such as a lathe or milling machine has become commonplace and greatly simplified with the advent of microprocessor controls, advanced positioning and control techniques, and modern cutting-tool materials. Chapter 1 described some of the modern equipment that is standard in many companies throughout the nation and the world. This chapter discusses other types of equipment, controls, and cutting tools together with their applications to machining and metalworking practices.

Over the past 40 years, we have progressed in our cutting tools from high-carbon steel, high-speed steel, cobalt matrix, and solid carbides to cemented or sintered carbides, ceramics, silicon nitride, cubic boron nitride, and special cutting tool coatings such as titanium nitride, titanium carbide, aluminum oxide, and others. The advantages of these new technologies in cutting tools have been increased production rates coupled with cost savings. Cutting tool technology is changing constantly, with new types of cutters, mills, drills, reamers, etc. being introduced to the market at a steady pace.

This chapter will show the latest types of cutting tools together with the important speeds and feeds recommended for them. Also shown are the typical speeds and feeds for the popular and widely used high-speed steel (HSS) and cobalt-matrix tools. The speeds and feeds tables for the various materials and machining methods are provided by the manufacturers who produce the cutting tools. Their research and development efforts, coupled with their experience and expertise, will be appreciated by those who use these tables.

A typical machined detail part is shown in Fig. 7.1. Producing this part required stock cutoff, drilling, turning, boring, counterboring, broaching, facing, end milling, deburring, and finally, zinc plating. A typical part such as that shown in Fig. 7.1 can now be produced more rapidly than was possible in the past and at relatively less cost due to the advances in cutting and machine tool technologies.

7.1 Turning and Boring

Turning is the machining process used to generate external, cylindrical forms by removing material, usually with a single-point cutting tool. *Boring* is essentially internal turning to generate internal shapes. The common turning machines include engine lathes, single-spindle automatic lathes, horizontal turret lathes, automatic screw machines, Swiss-type automatic screw machines, multiple-spindle automatic bar and chucking machines, and computer-controlled automatic turning centers. The single-point tool is moved parallel to the machine spindle for straight or contour turning of the outside diameter and turning or boring of an internal surface. Form tools, both flat and circular, were at one time fed into the workpiece to produce the desired contour on the part. Knurling produces a controlled rough surface pattern on the periphery of the part, either diamond shaped or straight, in coarse, medium, or fine texture.

7.1.1 Turning and boring tool materials.

High-speed steel (HSS), cast nonferrous alloys (Stellite and Tantung), and cemented carbides (sintered carbides) are among the most widely used turning, milling, and boring tool bit materials. The more advanced materials used for turning, boring, and milling operations include the following families:

- Tungsten carbides, coated (aluminum oxide and titanium nitride) and uncoated
- Cermets (*cer*amics with *met*allic binders)—titanium carbide and titanium nitride with a metallic binder

- Ceramics—alumina base (aluminum oxide) and silicon nitride base ceramics
- Polycrystallines—polycrystalline diamond and cubic boron nitride

Popular grades of HSS and Tantung (cast-alloy) tool bits

HSS and cobalt ground tool bits

M-2 HSS: General-purpose tool bit material. Works extremely well on mild steel, alloys, and tool steels and is an excellent finishing tool. Hardness: Rockwell C63 to C65.

5% cobalt: For heavy cuts on castings and forgings. A T-4 type of tungsten high-speed steel which withstands higher heat than M-2 types. Hardness: Rockwell C64 to C66.

10% cobalt: A superior type of high-speed steel used for heavy cuts in hard materials. Hardness: Rockwell C64.5 to C67.5.

Cobalt M-34: For heavy cuts on castings and forgings. A T-4 type of tungsten HSS which withstands higher heat than M-2 types.

Cobalt M-43: A superior type of HSS which is excellent for high-heat applications and for heavy cuts in hard materials.

Tantung tool bits. *Tantung G:* A cast-alloy cutting tool material composed of chromium, tungsten, columbium, and carbon in a cobalt matrix. These materials have the ability to retain cutting hardness at temperatures up to 1500°F. As a cutting tool, Tantung G is excellent for all turning, boring, facing, milling, and cutoff applications on most metal and nonmetallic materials. Performs best at cutting speeds of 100 to 250 surface feet per minute (sfpm). Hardness: Rockwell C60 to C63 and transverse rupture strength of 300,000 psi, minimum.

Note: Typical modern high-speed turning and boring tool materials and insert forms are shown following the speeds and feeds tables in this section.

7.1.2 Turning tool types, terms and definitions, and grinding

Single-point tools. A typical set of turning tools of HSS is shown in Fig. 7.2, together with a straight-shank lathe toolholder. The unground and ground tool bits are shown under the toolholder, followed by the different configurations of basic cutting bits. The cutting bit types are as follows:

- A Left-hand turning tool
- B Round-nose turning tool
- C Right-hand turning tool
- D Left-hand facing tool
- E Threading tool
- F Right-hand facing tool
- G Cutoff tool

Applications for the cutting tools are shown in Fig. 7.3 and include turning, facing, threading, cutoff, boring, and inside threading. The important geometric form angles relating to single-point cutting tools which are ground from HSS and cast-alloy bit-stock materials (Tantung, Tantung G, Stellite, etc.) are shown in Fig. 7.4.

7.1.3 Tool nomenclature

A single-point tool contains several geometric elements which are classified and defined by the American National Standards Institute (ANSI) B94.50-1975 (R1986), *Single-Point Cutting Tools, Basic Nomenclature and Definitions for.* The basic definitions may be summarized as follows:

The *size* of a tool of square or rectangular section is expressed by giving, in the order named, the width of the shank w, the height of shank h, and the total tool length l in inches, such as $0.75 \times 1.50 \times 8$ in.

The *shank* is that part of the tool on one end of which the point is formed or the tip or bit is supported. It is supported on the tool post of the machine.

The *base* is that surface of the shank which bears against the support and takes the tangential pressure of the cut.

The *heel* consists of the areas adjacent to the intersection of the base and flank.

The *face* is the surface on which the chip apparently impinges as it is separated from the workpiece. It may be provided with a narrow land ground along the cutting edge to support the built-up edge. This land is usually of less rake than that of the balance of the face. The face rake is then often greater than normal. For sintered-carbide tools, the land may be ground to a negative rake.

The *tool point* is all that part of the tool which is shaped to produce the cutting edges and face.

The *cutting edge* is the portion of the face edge along which the chip is separated from the workpiece. It consists usually of the side-cutting edge, the nose, and the end-cutting edge.

The *nose* is the corner, arc, or chamfer joining the side-cutting and the end-cutting edges.

The *flank* of the tool is the surface or surfaces below and adjacent to the cutting edge.

The *neck* is an extension of the shank of reduced cross-sectional area. A small point, as required in boring operations, is sometimes attached to the shank by a neck.

The *flat* or *drag* is the straight portion of the end-cutting edge at 0° intended to eliminate feed marks and produce a smooth machined surface.

A typical single-point carbide-tipped turning tool is shown in Fig. 7.4, and the angles shown are *normal,* that is, taken with reference to the cutting edges, since these are the ones specified in grinding a single-point tool. If a land is used, the rake of the land is given, followed by the rake of the face, such as –3 (12). This indicates a land rake of 3° negative with a positive side rake of 12°.

7.1.4 Tool angles (see Fig. 7.5)

The tool angles shown in Fig. 7.5 are defined as follows:

Back-rake angle: The angle between the face of the tool and the base of the shank or holder. This is usually measured in a plane through the side-cutting edge and at right angles to the base. It is positive if the face slopes downward from the point toward the shank, tending to reduce the included angle of the tool point. It is negative if the face slopes upward toward the shank.

Side-rake angle: The angle between the face of the tool and the base of the shank or holder. It is usually measured in a plane perpendicular to the base and to the side-cutting edge and hence is *normal side rake.*

Side-relief angle: The angle between the portion of the side flank immediately below the side-cutting edge and a line drawn through this cutting edge perpendicular to the base. It is usually measured in a plane at right angles to the side flank and hence is *normal side relief.*

End-relief angle: The angle between the portion of the end flank immediately below the end-cutting edge and a line drawn through that cutting edge perpendicular to the base. It is usually measured in a plane at right angles to the end flank and hence is *normal end relief.*

Clearance angle: The angle between a plane perpendicular to the base of the tool or holder and that portion of the flank immediately below the relieved flank. Side-clearance angle is measured in the plane of the back-rake angle. The clearance angle is greater than its corresponding relief angle, except when only one plane exists on the flank, in which case the clearance and relief angles coincide.

Side-cutting-edge angle: The angle between the straight side-cutting edge and the side of the tool shank or holder.

End-cutting-edge angle: The angle between the cutting edge on the end of the tool and a line at right angles to the side of the tool shank.

Note: As the setting of the tool or holder is changed in relation to the workpiece, the *effective working angles* will no longer agree with the tool angles.

Tool character. An abbreviated, convenient designation system for specifying the angles of single-point cutting tools is shown in Fig. 7.6. These angles are considered *normal* as used in most tool specifications and in grinding operations.

Working angles. Working angles are the angles between the tool and the workpiece. These angles depend on the shape of the tool as well as on its position relative to the workpiece. These angles are defined as follows:

Setting angle: The angle made by the straight portion of the shank of a tool or holder with the machined portion of the workpiece, commonly 90°.

Entering angle: The angle that the side-cutting edge of a tool makes with the machined surface of the workpiece, which is 90° in the case of a tool with 0° side-cutting-edge angle effective.

True rake angle: The slope of the tool face toward the tool base, from the active cutting edge in the direction of chip flow.

Cutting angle: The angle between the face of the tool and a tangent to the machined surface at the point of action. This angle is equal to 90° minus the true rake angle.

Lip angle: The included angle of the tool material between the face and the relieved flank. According to the direction of measurement, it may represent the *end lip angle, side lip angle,* or *true lip angle.*

Working relief angle: The angle between the relieved ground flank of the tool and a line tangent to the machined surface passing through the active cutting edge.

Working end-cutting-edge angle: The angle between the end-cutting edge and a plane tangent to the machined surface at the point of cutting.

7.1.5 Selection of tool geometry

Rake angles. The rake-angle combination varies greatly according to tool material, workpiece material, and cost. Thermally efficient cutting is improved with positive rake angles or at least positive rake angles with respect to chip flow or true rake. It should be understood that a high positive rake results in a more fragile cutting edge and must often be compromised for tool durability. As cutting speeds increase, the rake angle has less effect on tool pressures. Therefore, in using tool materials which can be operated at higher cutting speeds, it becomes possible to use less positive rake angles or even negative rakes to increase tool strength and economize on tool maintenance. Prismatic-insert and throwaway-insert tools are greatly simplified in use and maintenance by using negative rake angles, although more cutting power and increased cutting forces are required.

Combining negative back rake with positive side rake allows safer cutting through slots or keyways, thus placing the initial impact loads on a portion of the cutting edge removed from the nose of the tool bit.

Relief angles. Side and end relief angles vary between 5 and 15° for cutting metals and may run higher for some of the nonmetallic materials. Increased relief angles reduce cutting forces and result in a cleaner cut on low-tensile-strength materials. Reduced relief angles give more support to the cutting edge of the tool and are indicated for cutting high-strength metals. A wear land of excessive width may be the result of too small a relief angle, and tool breakage downward from the cutting edge may result from too large a relief angle.

Cutting-edge angles. The shape of the workpiece often determines the side-cutting-edge angle. Side-cutting-edge angles of approximately 15° will reduce the cutting power requirement, increase tool life, and aid in controlling the chip. A greater angle increases the chip thickness or makes an increase in feed possible. A decreased side-cutting-edge angle reduces the force at right angles to the workpiece and is required on thin-wall or long, slender workpieces.

End-cutting-edge angles of 6 to 15° are common. An angle of less than 6° may cause excessive forces normal to the work surface and lead to rapid dulling of the cutting tool. Angles greater than 15° may weaken the tool point but are used for tracing tools that must "in-feed" while operating. In all cases, the end-cutting-edge angle should be a minimum of 4° in relation to the surface of the workpiece.

A modification of the end-cutting-edge angle to 0° for a distance a little greater than the feed will produce a *drag,* or flattening, effect on the tool feed mark. If this modification is used, it must have a relief angle under it.

Nose radius. A small nose radius reduces cutting forces and is indicated on long, slender parts or thin-walled sections. Large nose radii make the tool stronger and are indicated for roughing operations. Large radii are also generally used for machining cast iron and similar materials which produce a crumbling chip.

Chipbreaker. A *chipbreaker* is a small step or groove in the face of a tool or a separate piece attached to the tool or toolholder that causes the chip to break into small sections or curl. The three common types of chipbreakers are those which are ground into the tool point, those which are attached to the tool point, and those which are preformed into an insert. Figure 7.7 shows a typical removable insert toolholder and support for an engine lathe. The removable cutting insert shown mounted on the end of the toolholder has a chipbreaker groove formed into its perimeter.

Figure 7.8 shows a typical modern engine lathe with its ACU-RITE III digital read-out panel at the upper left. Sensors on the lathe send digital electronic signals to the read-out panel so that the operator can set all the controls and movements to a precision of ±0.0005 in without reading the vernier dials on the machine. This allows higher productivity, with less chance of machine operator errors due to incorrect reading of the mechanical verniers on the machine's controls. The toolholder clamp knob for clamping the toolholder shown in Figure 7.7 can be seen directly to the right of the three-jaw chuck. Figure 1.3 provides a detail view of this lathe's gear control panel.

Figure 7.9 shows a typical engine lathe operational setup to machine a large aluminum alloy part. Notice the short broken chips produced by the chipbreaker on the cutting tool.

Cutting angles for single-point cutting tools (HSS, cast alloy, and carbide)

Cutting angles for high-speed-steel cutting tools. Figure 7.10 shows the recommended cutting angles for high-speed-steel (HSS) lathe tool bits. Figure 7.11 shows the recommended cutting angles for cast-alloy (Stellite, Tantung/Tantung G, etc) lathe tool bits. Figure 7.12 shows the recommended cutting angles for carbide lathe bit tools.

7.1.6 Grinding/sharpening of HSS, cast-alloy, and carbide tool bits

Proper grinding and sharpening of standard tool-bit materials should produce a surface condition that promotes a substantial increase in the number of workpieces produced per grind. First, grind the tool bit to the proper angles using an aluminum oxide wheel of 40 to 60 grit, followed by a 320-grit aluminum oxide wheel. The second step should only remove a minimal amount of material, on the order of 0.0005 to 0.001 in. If hand honing of the tool is attempted, a hard Arkansas or medium India stone should be used. An experienced operator is required for hand honing tool bits.

(*Text continued on page 542.*)

Figure 7.1 Machined steel part, zinc plated.

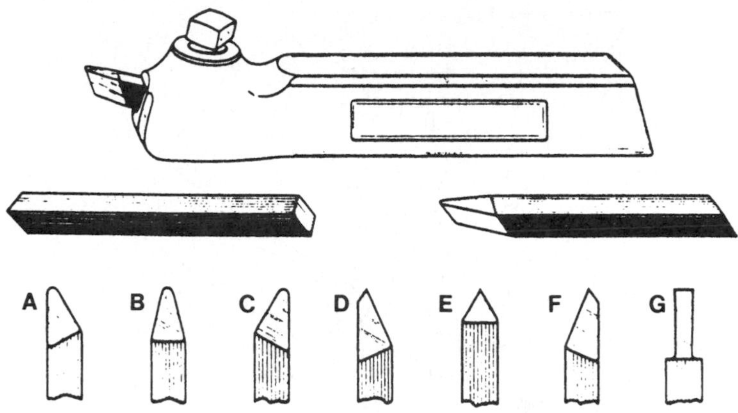

Figure 7.2 Standard lathe cutting tools.

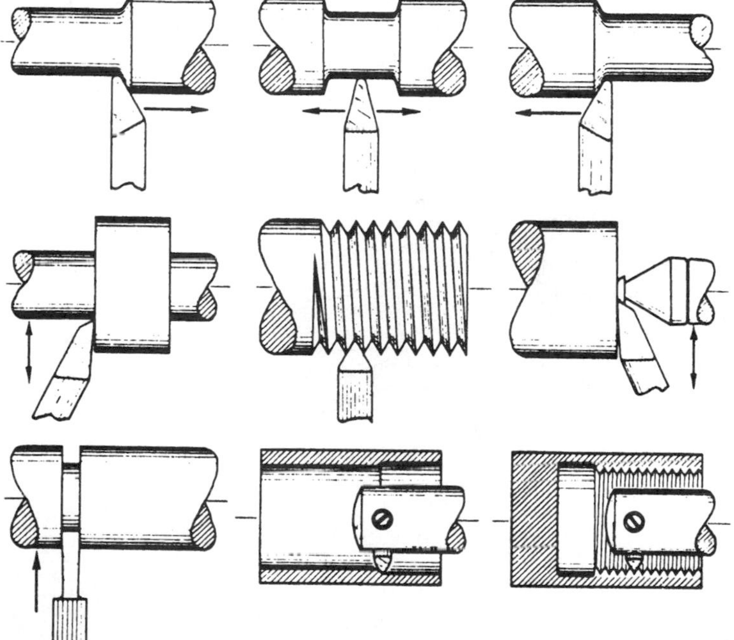

Figure 7.3 Turning operations.

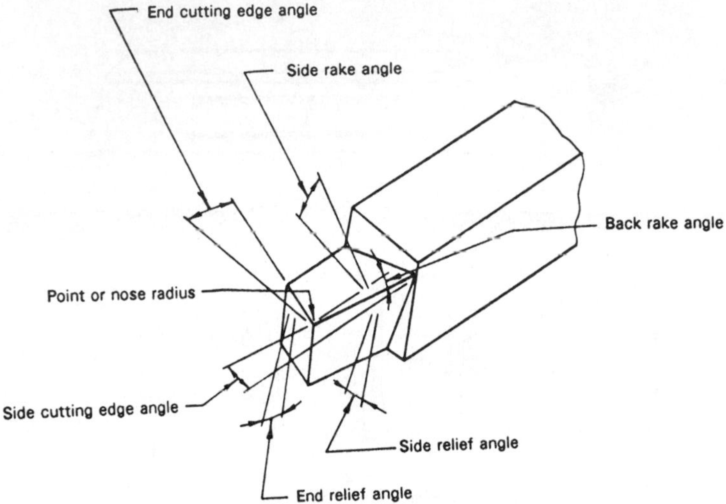

Figure 7.4 Form angles of single-point cutting tool.

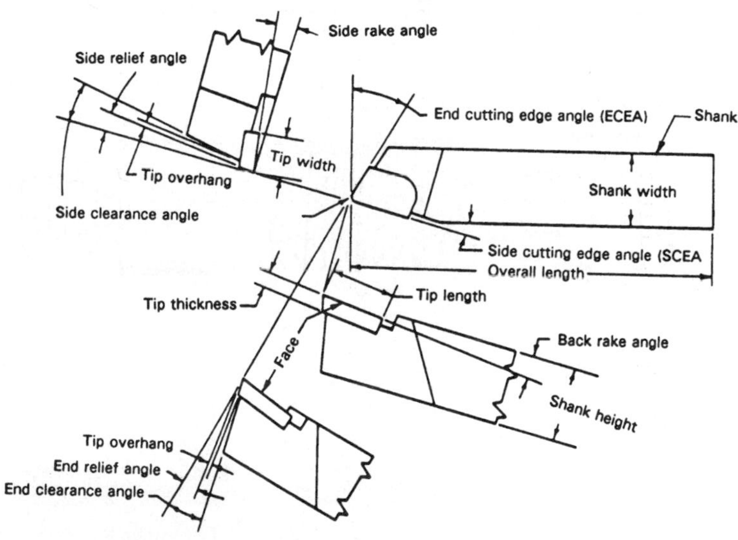

Figure 7.5 Tool angles and definitions.

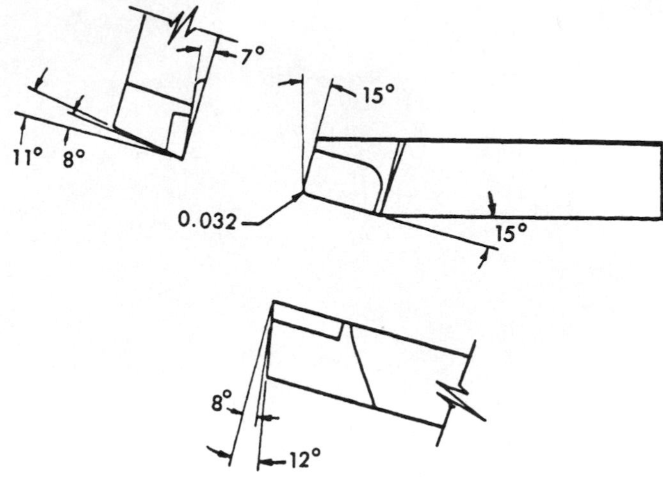

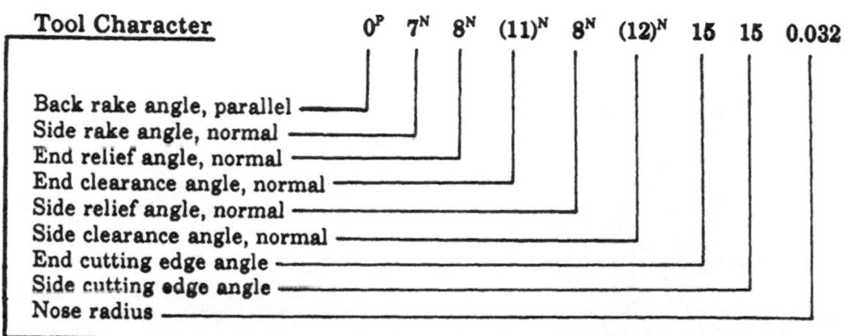

Figure 7.6 Tool character system.

Figure 7.7 Close-up view of turning insert and toolholder.

Figure 7.8 Typical engine lathe with digital control panel.

Figure 7.9 Ongoing turning operation.

Recommended Angles for HSS (High-speed-steel) Single-point Tools - (Tabular data in degrees)

Material	Side-relief angle	Front-relief angle	Back-rake angle	Side-rake angle
High-speed, alloy and high-carbon tool steels and stainless steels	7 - 9 (8)	6 - 8 (8)	0 - 7 (0)	8 - 10 (8)
SAE steels:				
1020, 1035, 1040	8 - 10 (8)	8 - 10 (8)	0 - 12 (0)	8 - 12 (8)
1045, 1095	7 - 9 (8)	8 - 10 (8)	0 - 12 (0)	8 - 12 (8)
1112, 1120	7 - 9 (8)	7 - 9 (8)	0 - 14 (0)	10 - 14 (10)
1314, 1315	7 - 9 (8)	7 - 9 (8)	0 - 14 (0)	10 - 16 (10)
1335	7 - 9 (8)	7 - 9 (8)	0 - 14 (0)	10 - 16 (10)
3115, 3120, 3130	7 - 9 (8)	7 - 9 (8)	0 - 10 (0)	8 - 12 (8)
3135, 3140	7 - 9 (8)	7 - 9 (8)	0 - 10 (0)	8 - 10 (8)
3250, 4140, 4340	7 - 9 (8)	7 - 9 (8)	0 - 8 (0)	8 - 10 (8)
6140, 6145	7 - 9 (8)	7 - 9 (8)	0 - 8 (0)	8 - 10 (8)
Aluminum & alloys	12 - 14 (14)	(14)	(0)	(15)
Phenol formaldahyde (Bakelite)	(14)	(14)	(0)	(10)
Brass, free-cutting	10 - 12 (10)	8 - 10 (10)	(0)	1 - 8 (8)
Bronzes-cast, red, yellow	8 - 10 (10)	8 - 10 (10)	(0)	-4 to +6 (+6)
Bronze, free-cutting	8 - 10 (10)	8 - 10 (10)	(0)	2 - 6 (6)
Phosphor-bronze, hard	8 - 10 (10)	6 - 10 (10)	(0)	0 - 6 (6)
Cast iron, gray	8 - 10 (8)	6 - 8 (8)	0 - 5 (0)	8 - 12 (8)
Copper	12 - 14 (12)	12 - 14 (12)	0 - 16 (0)	12 - 20 (12)
Copper alloys:				
Hard	8 - 10 (10)	6 - 10 (10)	(0)	0 - 8 (8)
Soft	10 - 12 (12)	8 - 12 (12)	0 - 2 (0)	0 - 10 (10)
Fiber	14 - 16 (14)	12 - 14 (14)	0 - 2 (0)	0 - 10 (10)
Formica	14 - 16 (14)	10 - 14 (14)	0 - 16 (0)	10 - 12 (12)
Nickel iron	14 - 16 (14)	10 - 14 (14)	0 - 8 (0)	12 - 15 (15)
Micarta	14 - 16 (14)	10 - 14 (14)	0 - 16 (0)	10 - 15 (15)
Monel and nickel	14 - 16 (14)	12 - 14 (14)	0 - 10 (0)	12 - 15 (15)
Nickel silvers	10 - 14 (14)	10 - 14 (14)	0 - 10 (0)	0 - 10 (10)
Rubber, hard and plastics	18 - 20 (20)	14 - 20 (20)	(0)	0 - 20 (20)

NOTE: Angles in parentheses are recommended as a starting point.

Figure 7.10 Angles for HSS single-point tools.

Recommended Cutting Angles for Cast-Alloy Tools * - (Tabular data in degrees)

Material	Back-rake angle	Side-rake angle	Side-relief angle	Front-relief angle	Side-cutting-edge angle	End-cutting-edge angle
Steel	8 - 20 **	8 - 20 **	6	6	10	15
Cast steel	8	8	6	6	10	15
Cast iron	0	4	6	6	10	15
Bronze	4	4	6	6	10	10
Stainless steel	8 - 20 **	8 - 20 **	6	6	10	15

* Stellite 98M-2 turning tools & Tantung/Tantung "G"
** Angles depend on grade and type of steel. Soft materials require more positive rake than hard materials.
Boring tools use the same rake but greater relief to clear the workpiece.

Figure 7.11 Angles for cast-alloy tools.

Recommended Angles for Carbide Single-point Tools - (Tabular data in degrees)

Material	Normal end relief	Normal side relief	Normal back rake	Normal side rake
Aluminum & magnesium alloys	6 - 10 (10)	6 - 10 (10)	0 to 10 (10)	10 to 20 (15)
Copper	6 - 8 (8)	6 - 8 (8)	0 to 4 (0)	15 to 20 (15)
Brass and bronze	6 - 8 (8)	6 - 8 (8)	0 to -5 (0)	+8 to -5 (+8)
Cast iron	5 - 8 (6)	5 - 8 (6)	0 to -7 (0)	+6 to -7 (-6)
Low carbon steels to SAE 1020	5 - 10 (6)	5 - 10 (6)	0 to -7 (0)	+6 to -7 (+6)
Carbon steels, SAE 1025 and above	5 - 8 (6)	5 - 8 (6)	0 to -7 (0)	+6 to -7 (+6)
Alloy steels	5 - 8 (6)	5 - 8 (6)	0 to -7 (0)	+6 to -7 (+6)
Free machining steels SAE 1100 and 1300	5 - 10 (6)	5 - 10 (6)	0 to -7 (0)	+6 to -7 (+6)
Stainless steels, austenitic	5 - 10 (6)	5 - 10 (6)	0 to -7 (0)	+6 to -7 (+6)
Stainless steels, hardenable grades	5 - 8 (6)	5 - 8 (6)	0 to -7 (0)	+6 to -7 (+6)
High nickel alloys (Monel, Inconel, etc.)	5 - 10 (8)	5 - 10 (8)	0 to -3 (0)	+6 to +10 (+10)
Titanium alloys	5 - 8 (6)	5 - 8 (6)	0 to -5 (0)	+6 to -5 (+6)

NOTE: Angles in parantheses are recommended as a starting point.

Figure 7.12 Angles for carbide tools.

7.1.7 Turning operation calculations

Cutting speed. Cutting speed is given in surface feet per minute (sfpm) and is the speed of the workpiece in relation to the stationary tool bit at the cutting point surface. The cutting speed is given by the simple relation

$$S = \frac{\pi d_f \,(\text{rpm})}{12} \qquad \text{for inch units}$$

and

$$S = \frac{\pi d_f \,(\text{rpm})}{1000} \qquad \text{for metric units}$$

where S = cutting speed, sfpm or m/min
d_f = diameter of work, in or mm
rpm = revolutions per minute of the workpiece

When the cutting speed (sfpm) is given for the material, the revolutions per minute (rpm) of the workpiece or lathe spindle can be found from

$$\text{rpm} = \frac{12S}{\pi d_f} \qquad \text{for inch units}$$

and

$$\text{rpm} = \frac{1000S}{\pi d_f} \qquad \text{for metric units}$$

Example A 2-in-diameter metal rod has an allowable cutting speed of 300 sfpm for a given depth of cut and feed. At what revolutions per minute (rpm) should the machine be set to rotate the work?

$$\text{rpm} = \frac{12S}{\pi d_f} = \frac{12(300)}{3.14 \times 2} = \frac{3600}{6.283} = 573 \text{ rpm}$$

Set the machine speed to the next lowest even speed that the machine is capable of attaining.

Lathe cutting time. The time required to make any particular cut on a lathe may be found using two methods. When the cutting speed is given, the following simple relation may be used:

$$T = \frac{\pi d_f L}{12FS} \qquad \text{for inch units}$$

and $$\mathrm{T} = \frac{\pi d_f L}{1000FS} \qquad \text{for metric units}$$

where T = time for the cut, min
d_f = diameter of work, in or mm
L = length of cut, in or mm
F = feed, ipr (inches per revolution) or mmpr (millimeters per revolution)
S = cutting speed, sfpm (surface feet per minute) or m/min

Example What is the cutting time in minutes for one pass over a 10″ length of 2.25-in-diameter rod when the cutting speed allowable is 250 sfpm with a feed of 0.03 ipr?

$$T = \frac{\pi d_f L}{12FS} = \frac{3.1416(2.25)10}{12(0.03)250} = \frac{70.686}{90} = 0.785 \text{ min, or } 47 \text{ s}$$

When the revolutions per minute of the machine is known, the cutting time may be found from

$$T = \frac{L}{F(\text{rpm})}$$

where L = length of work, in
T = cutting time, min
F = feed, ipr (inches per revolution)
rpm = spindle speed or workpiece speed, rpm

Volume of metal removed. The volume of metal removed during a lathe cutting operation can be calculated as follows:

$$V_r = 12C_d FS \qquad \text{for inch units}$$

and $$V_r = C_d FS \qquad \text{for metric units}$$

where V_r = volume of metal removed, in^3 or cm^3
C_d = depth of cut, in or mm
F = feed, ipr or mmpr
S = cutting speed, sfpm or m/min

Note: $1 \text{ in}^3 = 16.387 \text{ cm}^3$

Example With a depth of cut of 0.25 in and a feed of 0.125 in, what volume of material is removed in 1 min when the cutting speed is 120 sfpm?

$$V_r = 12C_dFS = 12 \times 0.25 \times 0.125 \times 120 = 45 \text{ in}^3$$

For convenience, the chart shown in Fig. 7.13 may be used for quick calculations of volume of material removed for various depths of cut, feeds, and speeds.

Machine power requirements (horsepower or kilowatts). It is often necessary to know the machine power requirements for an anticipated feed, speed, and depth of cut for a particular material or class of materials to see if the machine is capable of sustaining the desired production rate. The following simple formulas for calculating required horsepower are approximate only because of the complex nature and many variables involved in cutting any material.

The following formula is for approximating machine power requirements for making a particular cut:

$$\text{hp} = dfSC$$

where hp = required machine horsepower
d = depth of cut, in
f = feed, ipr
S = cutting speed, sfpm
C = power constant for the particular material (see Fig. 7.16)

Example With a depth of cut of 0.06 in and a feed of 0.025 in, what is the power requirement for turning aluminum-alloy bar stock at a speed of 350 sfpm?

$$\text{hp} = dfSC = 0.06 \times 0.025 \times 350 \times 4 \qquad \text{(see Fig. 7.16)}$$

$$= 2.1$$

For the metric system, the kilowatt requirement is $2.1 \times 0.746 = 1.76$ kW.

Note: 0.746 kW = 1 hp or 746 W = 1 hp.

The national manufacturers of cutting tools provide the users of their materials with various devices for quickly approximating the various machining calculations shown in the preceding formulas. Samples of some of the devices available for these calculations are shown in Figs. 7.14 and 7.15.

Although formulas and calculators are available for doing the various machining calculations, it is to be cautioned that these calculations are approximations and that the following factors must be taken into consideration when metals and other materials are cut at high powers and speeds using modern cutting tools.

1. Available machine power
2. Condition of the machine
3. Size, strength, and rigidity of the workpiece
4. Size, strength, and rigidity of the cutting tool

Prior to beginning a large production run of turned parts, sample pieces are run in order to determine the exact feeds and speeds required for a particular material and cutting tool combination.

Power constants. Figure 7.16 shows a table of constants for various materials which may be used when calculating the approximate power requirements of the cutting machines.

7.1.8 Speeds, cuts, and feeds

HSS, cast-alloy, and carbide tools (see Fig. 7.17). The surface speed (sfpm), depth of cut (in), and feed (ipr) for various materials using HSS, cast-alloy, and carbide cutting tools are shown in Fig. 7.17. In all cases, especially where combinations of values are selected that have not been used previously on a given machine, the selected values should have their required horsepower or kilowatts calculated. Use the approximate calculations shown previously, or use one of the machining calculators available from the cutting tool manufacturers. The method indicated earlier for calculating the required horsepower gives a conservative value that is higher than the actual power required. In any event, on a manually controlled machine, the machinist or machine operator will know if the selected speed, depth of cut, and feed are more than the given machine can tolerate and can make corrections accordingly. On CNC/DNC-controlled automatic turning centers and other automatic machines, the cutting parameters must be selected carefully, with the machine operator carefully watching the first trial program run so that he or she may intervene if problems of overloading or tool damage occur.

Modern high-speed insert-type cutting tools. Figures 7.18 to 7.48 show the recommended speeds, depths of cut, and feeds for modern types of insert cutting tools which are widely used throughout industry today. These new cutting tools allow higher cutting speeds and greater productivity than previously possible. Also included at the beginning of each speed and feed table are the types and designations for the materials and their important cutting characteristics together with tool-application considerations.

Tables of speeds and feeds for turning and boring inserts

Low-carbon and free-machining steels. 1100 series, 1008, 1010, 1018, and 1200 series, leaded steels, and steels with free-machining additives (see Fig. 7.18).

Material characteristics. Low-carbon, soft and gummy; difficult chip control; torn finish is common; high-speed capability. Free-machining, easy to machine; high-speed capability; high depths of cut achievable; easy chip control.

Tool-application considerations

Condition: Torn finish (built-up edge)

Remedy: Increase speed; use cermets; use PVD-coated grade with sharp edge; use positive-rake inserts; increase coolant concentration.

Condition: Difficult chip control

Remedy: Increase speed; change lead angle to redirect chip away from workpiece.

Condition: Burrs and sharp edges

Remedy: Change cutting path; use PVD-coated grade with sharp edge; use positive-rake or high-positive-rake inserts.

Medium/high-carbon steels and alloy steels. 1045, 1085, 1541, 1561, 1572, and 4000 series, 4300 series, 5100 series, 8600 series, 52100, and 300M (see Figs. 7.19 through 7.23).

Material characteristics. Higher chrome, nickel, and molybdenum content, work hardening. Higher carbon content, abrasive but achieves surface finish easier. Higher nickel content, more carbon and alloy, more difficult to machine.

(*Text continued on page 556.*)

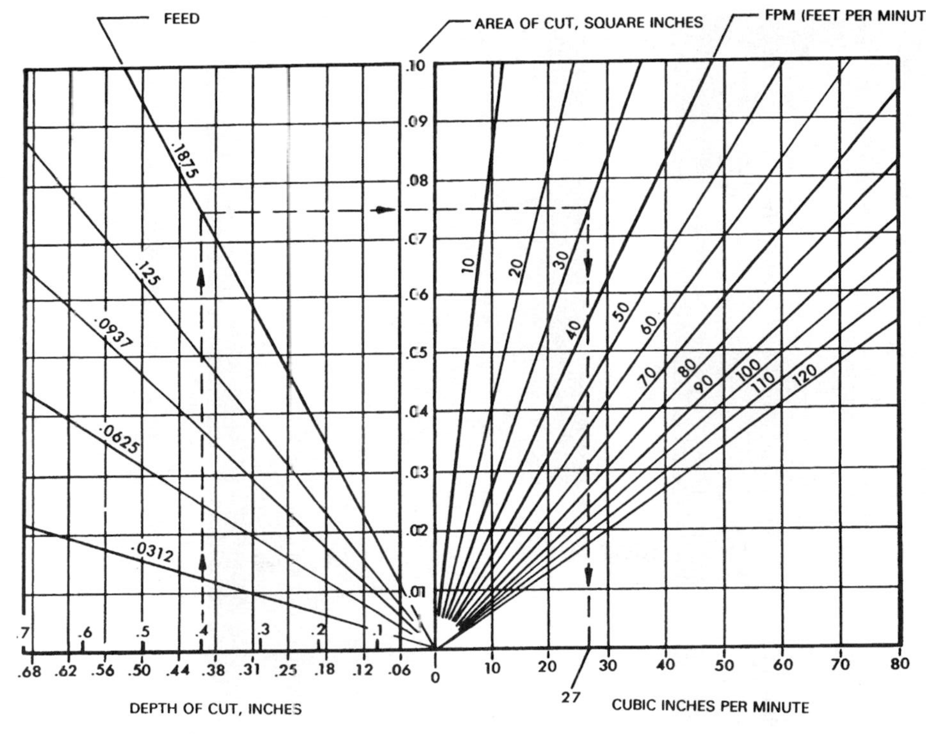

Figure 7.13 Metal-removal rate (mrr) chart.

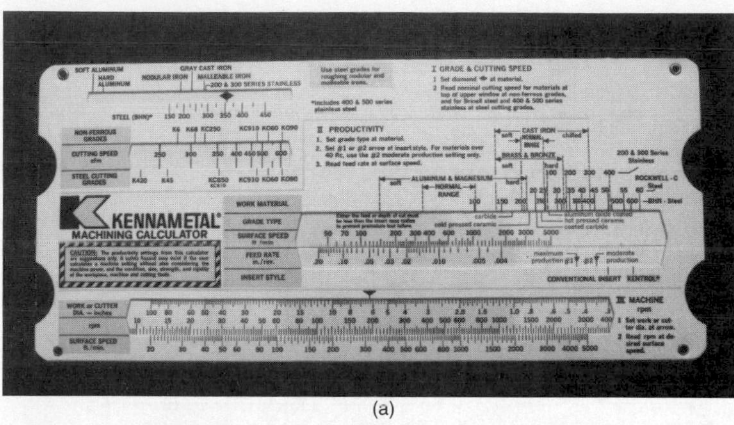

(a)

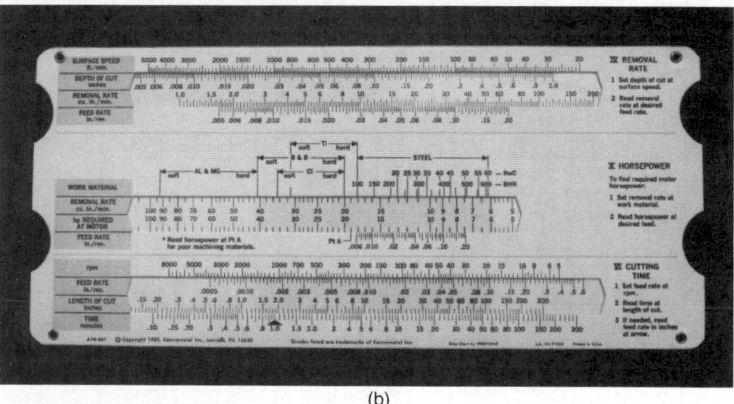

(b)

Figure 7.14 (*a*) Typical machining calculator (front side). (*b*) Typical machining calculator (rear side).

Figure 7.15 Machining calculator.

Power Constants for Various Metals and Alloys

Material	Constant
SAE Steels:	
1005 - 1029	6
1030 - 1050	7
1053 - 1095	8
1211 - 1215	6
1314 - 1345	6
1330 - 1350	9
1524 - 1552	9
4130 - 4820	9
5120 - 52100	10
Cast steels	9
SAE Stainless steels:	
30303, 51403, 51410, 51416 51431, 51430F, 51440F	10
30302, 30304, 30309,30316 30321, 51431, 51501	11
51420, 51420F, 51440A, B, C	12
Cast irons:	
Hard	4
Medium	3
Soft	3
Semi-steel	3
Malleable irons:	
Hard	5
Medium	4
Soft	3

Material	Constant
Titanium & alloys:	
Pure	4
Alpha alloys	7
Beta alloys	8
Copper	4
Zinc alloys	3
Monel	12
Brass & bronze:	
Hard	10
Soft	4
Aluminum alloys:	
Cast	3
Bar stock	4
Magnesium alloys	3

Figure 7.16 Power constant table.

Recommended Cuts, Feeds and Speeds for Metals and Nonmetallic Turning - (For HSS, Cast-Alloys and Carbide Tools)

Class	Material or SAE No.	Cutting Tool Material	Depth of Cut: 0.005-0.015 Feed: 0.002-0.005	Depth of Cut: 0.015-0.094 Feed: 0.005-0.015	Depth of Cut: 0.094-0.187 Feed: 0.015-0.030	Depth of Cut: 0.187-0.375 Feed: 0.030-0.050	Depth of Cut: 0.375-0.750 Feed: 0.050-0.090
Free-cutting steels	1112, 11L17	HSS	....	250 - 350	175 - 250	80 - 150	55 - 75
	1120	Cast-alloys	....	425 - 550	315 - 400	215 - 300	100 -210
	1315, etc.	Sintered carbides	750 - 1,500	600 - 750	450 - 600	350 - 450	175 - 350
Carbon & low-alloy steels	1010, 1020	HSS	....	225 - 300	150 - 200	75 - 125	45 - 65
	1025, etc.	Cast-alloys	....	375 - 500	275 - 350	180 - 250	100 - 175
		Sintered carbides	700 - 1,200	550 - 700	400 - 550	300 - 400	150 - 300
Medium alloy steels	1030	HSS	....	200 - 275	125 - 175	70 - 120	40 - 60
	1050	Cast-alloys	....	325 - 400	230 - 300	160 - 225	80 - 150
		Sintered cvarbides	600 - 1,000	450 - 600	350 - 450	250 - 350	125 - 250
High-alloy steels	1060	HSS	....	175 - 250	125 - 175	65 - 100	35 - 55
	1095	Cast-alloys	....	250 - 350	200 - 250	150 - 200	65 - 150
	1350	Sintered carbides	500 - 750	400 - 500	300 - 400	200 - 300	100 -200
Chromium-nickel steels	3120, 3450	HSS	....	150 - 200	100 - 125	50 - 75	30 - 50
	5140, 52100	Cast-alloy	....	230 - 315	165 - 225	110 - 160	55 - 110
		Sintered carbides	425 - 550	325 - 425	250 - 325	175 - 250	75 - 175
Molybdenum steels	4130	HSS	....	160 - 210	110 - 140	60 - 80	35 - 55
	4615	Cast-alloys	....	250 - 325	160 - 225	120 - 150	65 - 100
		Sintered carbides	475 - 650	350 - 475	275 - 350	200 - 275	100 - 200
Chrome, vanadium and stainless steels	6120	HSS	....	100 - 150	80 - 100	50 - 75	30 - 50
	6150, 18Cr-5Ni	Cast-alloys	....	210 - 250	170 - 200	110 - 165	55 - 100
	6195	Sintered carbides	375 - 500	300 - 375	250 - 300	175 - 250	75 - 175
Tungsten steels	7260	HSS	....	120 - 150	75 - 120	40 - 75	25 - 40
	18-4-1 annealed	Cast-alloys	....	130 - 175	110 - 130	80 - 100	35 - 80
		Sintered carbides	325 - 400	250 - 325	200 - 250	150 - 200	50 - 150
Special steels	12-14% Mn.	HSS	....	....	....	....	....
		Cast-alloys	....	....	....	....	....
		Sintered carbides	200 - 250	125 - 200	75 - 125	50 - 75	....

Figure 7.17 Cuts, feeds, and speeds table.

Special steels	Si. elect., sheet ingot iron, etc.	HSS	400 - 500	300 - 400	200 - 300	150 - 200	....
		Cast-alloys	....	500 - 600	350 - 450	250 - 300	....
		Sintered carbide	1,000 - 1,200	800 - 1,000	600 - 800	500 - 600	....
Cast iron	Soft gray	HSS	....	120 - 150	90 - 120	75 - 90	35 - 75
		Cast-alloys	....	225 - 300	160 - 220	125 - 160	70 - 125
		Sintered carbides	450 - 600	350 - 450	250 - 350	200 - 250	100 - 200
	Medium and malleable	HSS	....	120 - 150	90 - 120	60 - 90	30 - 60
		Cast-alloys	....	100 - 225	150 - 190	120 - 150	60 - 120
		Sintered carbides	350 - 450	250 - 350	200 - 250	150 - 200	75 - 150
	Hard alloys	HSS	....	90 - 125	60 - 90	40 - 60	20 - 40
		Cast-alloys	....	120 - 170	80 - 120	55 - 80	35 - 55
		Sintered carbides	250 - 300	150 - 250	100 - 150	75 - 100	50 - 75
	Chilled	HSS	10 - 15	....	....	....	....
		Cast-alloys	....	....	....	....	....
		Sintered carbides	30 - 50	10 - 30	....	....	....
Copper base alloys	Leaded, free - cutting, soft brass and bronze	HSS	....	300 - 400	225 - 300	150 - 255	100 - 150
		Cast-alloys	....	500 - 600	400 - 500	325 - 400	200 - 325
		Sintered carbides	1,000 - 1,250	800 - 1,000	650 - 800	500 - 650	300 - 500
	Normal brass, bronze low alloy	HSS	....	275 - 350	225 - 275	150 - 225	100 - 150
		Cast-alloys	....	375 - 425	325 - 375	250 - 325	175 - 250
		Sintered carbides	700 - 800	600 - 700	500 - 600	400 - 500	200 - 400
	Tough copper, high tin & alum. bronzes, gilding.	HSS	....	100 - 150	75 - 100	50 - 75	35 - 50
		Cast-alloys	....	225 - 300	180 - 225	125 - 180	75 - 125
		Sintered carbides	500 - 600	400 - 500	300 - 400	200 - 300	100 - 200
Light alloys	Magnesium	HSS	500 - 750	350 - 500	275 - 350	200 - 275	125 - 200
		Cast-alloys	700 - 1,000	500 - 700	400 - 500	300 - 400	200 - 300
		Sintered carbides	1,250 - 2,000	800 - 1,250	600 - 800	500 - 600	300 - 500
	Aluminum	HSS	350 - 500	225 - 350	150 - 225	100 - 150	50 - 100
		Cast-alloys	450 - 650	300 - 450	225 - 300	150 - 225	75 - 150
		Sintered carbides	700 - 1,000	450 - 700	300 - 450	200 - 300	100 - 200
Titanium	Pure & low alloys	HSS	....	100 - 160	70 - 110	50 - 75	....
		Cast-alloys	....	165 - 375	110 - 250	75 - 165	....
		Sintered carbides	550 - 900	375 - 600	250 - 400	165 - 265	....

	Alpha alloys	HSS	....	30 - 75	20 - 50	....	....
		Cast-alloys	....	75 - 110	50 - 75	....	....
		Sintered carbides	165 - 450	110 - 300	75 - 200	50 - 135	....
	Beta alloys	HSS	....	30 - 40	20 - 25	....	....
		Cast-alloys	....	40 - 90	25 - 60	....	....
		Sintered carbides	125 - 225	90 - 150	60 - 100	40 - 70	....
Plastics	Thermoplastic, thermosetting	HSS	....	....	....	....	....
		Cast-alloys	....	....	....	....	....
		Sintered carbides	650 - 1,000	400 - 650	250 - 400	150 - 250	....
Abrasives	Glass, hard rubber, green ceramics, marble.	HSS	....	....	....	....	....
		Cast-alloys	....	....	....	....	....
		Sintered carbides	150 - 250	75 - 150	....	....	....

NOTE: It is possible that a combination of speeds, feeds and cuts may be so selected for a given application, that a higher horsepower may be required than is available at the lathe spindle. In all cases, especially where combinations of values are selected that have not been used previously on a given machine, the selected values should have their required horsepower calculated. See the subsection (Horsepower requirements) for calculating required horsepower when speed, feed and cut are given.
Values of depth of cut are in inches; feeds are given in ipr (inches per revolution) and speed is given in sfpm (surface feet per minute).

Figure 7.17 (*Continued*)

suggested grades and machining conditions for free-machining and low carbon steels

free-machining and low carbon steels	machining conditions	finishing	roughing	general purpose starting conditions
free-machining and low carbon steels: AISI: 1008, 1010, 1018, 1020, 1026, 1108, 1117, 1141, 1151, 10L18, 10L45, 10L50, 11L44, 12L14 and Ledloy steel based on a machinability index range of 80-100 and a hardness of 100-200 BHN	**depth of cut inches (mm)**	.020-.100 (0,5-2,5)	.100-.300 (2,5-7,6)	.060-.250 (1,5-6,3)
	feed rate ipr (mm/rev.)	.006-.011 (0,15-0,28)	.010-.045 (0,25-1,1)	carbides .014 (0,35) cermets .012 (0,3) ceramics .010 (0,25)
	grades	**surface speed—sfm (m/min.)**		
	KC910	600-1500 (185-455)	500-1400 (150-425)	900 (275)
	KC950	500-1300 (150-395)	400-1200 (120-365)	850 (260)
	KC990	500-1200 (150-365)	450-1200 (135-365)	800 (245)
	KC810	400-800 (120-245)		650 (200)
	KC850		300-800 (90-245)	600 (185)
	KT125	450-1500 (135-455)		950 (290)
	KT150	400-1000 (120-305)		800 (245)
	KT175		350-950 (105-290)	700 (215)
	KC730	300-750 (90-230)	250-650 (75-200)	500 (150)
	KC720	250-600 (75-185)	200-550 (60-170)	350 (105)
	K060	1200-1500 (365-455)		1300 (395)
	K090	1200-1800 (365-550)		1450 (440)
	KY4000	800-3000 (245-915)	700-2500 (215-760)	1500 (455)
	supplemental uncoated carbide grade			
	K420	250-450 (75-135)	200-350 (60-105)	300 (90)

Figure 7.18 (Reproduced with permission of Kennametal Inc.)

suggested grades and machining conditions for medium and high carbon steels

medium and high carbon steels	machining conditions	finishing	roughing	general purpose starting conditions
medium and high carbon steels: AISI: 1045, 1525, 1085, 1541, 1090, 1561, 1055, 1080, 1095, 1572 based on a machinability index range of 55-70 and a hardness of 150-325 BHN	**depth of cut inches (mm)**	.010-.100 (0,25-2,5)	.100-.300 (2,5-7,6)	.050-.200 (1,2-4,0)
	feed rate ipr (mm/rev.)	.006-.012 (0,15-0,3)	.008-.030 (0,2-0,75)	carbides .012 (0,30) cermets .010 (0,25) ceramics .010 (0,25)
	grades	**surface speed—sfm (m/min.)**		
	KC910	500-1350 (150-410)		750 (230)
	KC990	650-1000 (200-305)	550-900 (170-275)	750 (230)
	KC950	400-800 (120-245)	400-700 (120-215)	600 (185)
	KC810	300-700 (90-215)		500 (150)
	KC850	250-700 (75-215)	250-600 (75-185)	400 (120)
	KT125	550-1000 (170-305)		800 (245)
	KT150	450-850 (135-260)		600 (185)
	KT175	400-800 (120-245)	350-700 (105-215)	550 (170)
	KC740	250-700 (75-215)		650 (200)
	KC710	250-600 (75-185)	200-500 (60-150)	350 (105)
	KC720	200-500 (60-150)	150-450 (45-135)	300 (90)
	K090	800-1500 (245-455)		1100 (335)
	supplemental uncoated carbide grade			
	K420	200-400 (60-120)	150-300 (45-90)	250 (75)

Figure 7.19 (Reproduced with permission of Kennametal Inc.)

suggested grades and machining conditions for *alloy* steels (medium carbon)

	machining conditions	finishing	roughing	general purpose starting conditions
medium carbon *alloy* steel: AISI: 1345, 4140, 4150, 4340, 52100, M-50, 8640, and Rycut 40, Cr-Mo alloy and Super-Kut steels based on a machinability index range of 50-70 and a hardness of 200-325 BHN	**depth of cut inches (mm)**	.015-.100 (0,4-2,5)	.100-.300 (2,5-7,6)	.06-.200 (1,5-5,0)
	feed rate ipr (mm/rev.)	.003-.008 (0,08-0,2)	.008-.020 (0,2-0,5)	carbides .012 (0,3) cermets .010 (0,25) ceramics .010 (0,25)
	grades	**surface speed—sfm (m/min.)**		
	KC910	500-900 (150-275)		700 (215)
	KC990	400-800 (120-245)	300-700 (90-215)	600 (185)
	KC950	450-750 (135-230)	325-700 (100-215)	600 (185)
	KC810	200-400 (60-120)	150-350 (45-105)	300 (90)
	KC850	275-550 (85-170)	175-500 (55-150)	450 (135)
	KT125	325-750 (100-230)		550 (170)
	KT150	300-700 (90-215)		500 (150)
	KT175	200-600 (60-185)	200-500 (60-150)	400 (120)
	KC740	175-450 (55-135)		300 (90)
	KC710	175-400 (55-120)	125-350 (40-105)	300 (90)
	KC720		80-250 (25-75)	175 (55)
	K090	750-1350 (230-410)		1000 (305)
	supplemental uncoated carbide grade			
	K420	150-300 (45-90)	150-300 (45-90)	200 (60)

Figure 7.20 (Reproduced with permission of Kennametal Inc.)

suggested grades and machining conditions for *alloy* steels (low carbon)

	machining conditions	finishing	roughing	general purpose starting conditions
low carbon *alloy* steel: AISI: 4012, 4023, 4320, 8620, E-9310, 94B15, 4422, 5120, 8622, 8822 based on a machinability index range of 45-70 and a hardness of 160-325 BHN	**depth of cut inches (mm)**	.010-.100 (0,25-2,5)	.100-.500 (2,5-12,7)	.150 (3,8)
	feed rate ipr (mm/rev.)	.004-.010 (0,1-0,25)	.010-.030 (0,25-0,75)	carbides .015 (0,38) cermets .012 (0,3) ceramics .010 (0,25)
	grades	**surface speed—sfm (m/min.)**		
	KC910	450-1100 (135-335)		750 (230)
	KC990	400-1000 (120-305)	500-950 (150-290)	650 (200)
	KC950	500-800 (150-245)	400-700 (120-215)	600 (185)
	KC810	300-750 (90-230)	250-600 (75-185)	400 (120)
	KC850	250-750 (75-230)	200-600 (60-185)	400 (120)
	KT125	450-1000 (135-305)		800 (245)
	KT150	400-900 (120-275)		700 (215)
	KT175	350-850 (105-260)		600 (185)
	KC740	250-600 (75-185)		400 (120)
	KC710	250-700 (75-215)	200-500 (60-150)	325 (100)
	KC720		100-300 (30-90)	200 (60)
	K090	750-1400 (230-425)		900 (275)
	Kyon 4000	800-3000 (245-915)	700-2500 (215-760)	1500 (455)
	supplemental uncoated carbide grade			
	K420	200-400 (60-120)	150-350 (45-105)	250 (75)

Figure 7.21 (Reproduced with permission of Kennametal Inc.)

suggested grades and machining conditions for preheat-treated *alloy* steels

preheat-treated *alloy* steels and bearing steels: AISI: 4330, 4140, 4150, 8640, 4340, and stress-proof steel; based on a machinability index range of 40-55 and a hardness of 35-50 Rc (325-480 BHN)	machining conditions	finishing	roughing	general purpose starting conditions
	depth of cut inches (mm)	.003-.060 (0,08-1,5)	.060-.250 (1,5-6,3)	.010-.080 (0,4-2,0)
	feed rate ipr (mm/rev.)	.003-.014 (0,08-0,35)	.006-.024 (0,15-0,6)	.010 (0,25)
	grades	surface speed—sfm (m/min.)		
	KC950	175-500 (55-150)	125-400 (40-120)	250 (75)
	KC850		100-275 (30-85)	175 (55)
	KT125	200-600 (60-185)		350 (105)
	KC730	75-225 (25-70)		150 (45)
	K090	600-1100 (185-335)		850 (260)
	KD120	550-800 (170-245)		600 (185)
	KD200	700-1000 (215-305)	600-850 (185-260)	750 (230)

Figure 7.22 (Reproduced with permission of Kennametal Inc.)

suggested grades and machining conditions for heat-treated steels

heat-treated steels and bearing steels: AISI: 4330, 300-M, ETD-180, 52100, 17-4 PH, and Hy Tuff steel; based on a machinability index range of 10-40 and a hardness of 50-65 Rc (480-750 BHN)	machining conditions	finishing	roughing	general purpose starting conditions
	depth of cut inches (mm)	.003-.060 (0,08-1,5)	.060-.250 (1,5-6,3)	.015-.080 (0,4-2,0)
	feed rate ipr (mm/rev.)	.003-.014 (0,08-0,35)	.006-.024 (0,15-0,6)	solid CBN's .015 (0,38) tipped CBN's .009 (0,23) ceramics .006 (0,15)
	grades	surface speed—sfm (m/min.)		
	KC730	50-150 (15-45)		70 (20)
	K090	250-750 (75-230)		350 (105)
	KD050	290-675 (90-205)		500 (150)
	KD120	225-575 (70-175)		400 (120)
	KD200	275-600 (85-185)	175-400 (50-120)	400 (120)
	supplemental uncoated carbide grade			
	K68	40-125 (12-40)		60 (18)

Figure 7.23 (Reproduced with permission of Kennametal Inc.)

Tool-application considerations

Condition: Crater wear

Remedy: Use aluminum oxide–coated grade; reduce speed; use more free-cutting chip control; use cermets; increase coolant pressure; reduce feed.

Condition: Flank wear

Remedy: Use TiC/alumina ceramics; use aluminum oxide–coated grade; increase feed; increase coolant concentration; increase depth of cut.

Condition: Thermal deformation

Remedy: Use more wear-resistant grade; reduce speed; reduce feed.

Tool steels (see Figs. 7.24 through 7.27)
Material characteristics. Abrasive, work hardening, and tough, hard-to-break chips.

Tool-application considerations

Condition: Flank wear

Remedy: Use aluminum oxide–coated grade; reduce speed; increase feed.

Condition: Crater wear

Remedy: Use aluminum oxide–coated grade; use cermets; reduce speed; reduce feed.

Condition: Dull surface finish

Remedy: Increase speed; use positive-rake inserts (PVD-coated); use cermets; increase coolant concentration.

Gray cast iron. Gray, classes 20, 25, 30, 45, and 60, high tensile (see Fig. 7.28).
Material characteristics. Abrasive, potential scale and inclusions, tendency to break out during exit from cut, potential for chatter on thin-wall sections.

Tool-application considerations

Condition: Excessive edge wear

Remedy: Use harder grade or aluminum oxide–coated grades; use ceramics; increase feed to reduce in-cut time.

Condition: Chipping

Remedy: Increase lead angle; use stronger grade; use prehoned inserts or inserts with edge preparation.

Condition: Workpiece break-out

Remedy: Use sharp inserts or PVD-coated grades; use lower feed rate during exit; increase speed; increase lead angle; use positive geometries for finish cuts.

Condition: Workpiece chatter

Remedy: Use sharp inserts or PVD-coated grades; use positive-rake inserts; increase lead angle; increase feed to stabilize workpiece.

Ductile cast iron. Nodular/ductile, malleable (see Figs. 7.29 and 7.30). *Material characteristics.* Abrasive, difficult to machine, good surface finishes difficult to achieve.

Tool-application considerations

Condition: Edge wear

Remedy: Use harder grades; apply aluminum oxide–coated grades; consider ceramics and cermets for finishing; increase feed to reduce in-cut time.

Condition: Crater wear

Remedy: Apply aluminum oxide–coated grades; apply geometries that are free-cutting; lower speed (sfpm).

Condition: Torn or dull surface finish

Remedy: Apply ceramics, cermets, or PVDs at higher speeds and lower feeds; increase lead angle; increase coolant concentration.

Hardened irons (see Fig. 7.31)
Material characteristics. Highly abrasive, high cutting forces.

Tool-application considerations

Condition: Excessive edge wear

Remedy: Apply alumina-based ceramics or cubic boron nitride (CBN) grades; feed above 0.004 ipr; increase lead angles or use round inserts; check coolant application.

Condition: Catastrophic breakage

Remedy: Increase lead angles or use round inserts; use large nose radii; repair toolholder; reduce feeds.

Austenitic stainless steels. 200 and 300 series (see Fig. 7.32). *Material characteristics.* Work hardens rapidly; small depths of cut are difficult; usually abrasive rather than hard; tough and stringy chips.

Tool-application considerations

Condition: Depth-of-cut notch

Remedy: Increase lead angle; use tougher grade; feed over 0.005 ipr.

Condition: Built-up edge

Remedy: Increase speed; use cermets; use positive-rake inserts (PVD-coated).

Condition: Workpiece glazing

Remedy: Increase depth of cut; reduce nose radius; use sharp PVD-coated grades.

Condition: Dull surface finish

Remedy: Increase speed; reduce feed; increase positive rake.

Ferritic/martensitic stainless steels. 400 series and precipitation-hardening PH grades (see Fig. 7.33).

Material characteristics. Brittle, stringy chips; high cutting forces; high work hardening (especially PH stainless grades).

Tool-application considerations

Condition: Built-up edge

Remedy: Increase speed; use cermets; use positive-rake inserts (PVD-coated); increase coolant concentration.

Condition: Workpiece glazing

Remedy: Increase depth of cut; reduce nose radius; use positive-rake inserts (PVD-coated); increase coolant concentration.

Condition: Depth-of-cut notch

Remedy: Increase lead angle; use tougher grade; feed over 0.005 ipr.

Condition: Torn or dull surface finish

Remedy: Increase speed; reduce feed; use positive-rake inserts (PVD-coated); increase coolant concentration.

High-temperature alloys. Iron, nickel, and cobalt base (see Figs. 7.34 through 7.36).

suggested grades and machining conditions for tool steels

tool steels: *hot-worked* AISI: H10, H11, H21, H13, H24 *cold-worked* S5, O1, D2, A2, A10 based on a machinability index range of 40-60 and a hardness of 150-250 BHN	machining conditions	finishing	roughing	general purpose starting conditions
	depth of cut inches (mm)	.015-.100 (0,40-2,5)	.100-.300 (2,5-7,6)	.050-.200 (1,25-5,0)
	feed rate ipr (mm/rev.)	.003-.006 (0,08-0,15)	.005-.018 (0,12-0,45)	carbides .010 (0,25) cermets .008 (0,2) ceramics .008 (0,2)
	grades	surface speed—sfm (m/min.)		
	KC910	500-950 (150-290)		725 (220)
	KC990	425-850 (130-260)	400-600 (120-185)	600 (185)
	KC950	450-725 (135-220)	400-550 (120-170)	500 (150)
	KC850		275-500 (85-150)	400 (120)
	KT125	600-950 (185-290)		750 (230)
	KT150	500-800 (150-245)		600 (185)
	KT175	300-700 (90-215)	250-600 (75-185)	400 (120)
	KC740	275-575 (85-175)		400 (120)
	KC720		150-300 (45-90)	225 (70)
	KC710	190-400 (60-120)	150-300 (45-90)	250 (75)
	K090	600-1200 (185-365)		1050 (320)

Figure 7.24 (Reproduced with permission of Kennametal Inc.)

suggested grades and machining conditions for tool steels

tool steels: *high speed* T1, M2, T5, M30, M10, M4, T2 based on a machinability index range of 35-60 and a hardness of 150-225 BHN	machining conditions	finishing	roughing	general purpose starting conditions
	depth of cut inches (mm)	.015-.100 (0,4-2,5)	.100-.300 (2,5-7,6)	.060-.200 (1,5-5,0)
	feed rate pr (mm/rev.)	.003-.010 (0,08-0,25)	.008-.030 (0,2-0,75)	.012 (0,3)
	grades	surface speed—sfm (m/min.)		
	KC910	500-900 (150-275)		625 (190)
	KC990	400-800 (120-245)	400-550 (120-170)	550 (170)
	KC950	400-700 (120-215)	300-550 (90-170)	450 (135)
	KC850		250-450 (75-135)	350 (105)
	KT125	500-850 (150-260)		625 (190)
	KT150	450-750 (135-230)		425 (130)
	KT175	200-600 (60-185)		325 (100)
	KC740	275-550 (85-170)		375 (115)
	KC710	175-350 (55-105)	140-280 (45-85)	225 (70)
	KC720		140-275 (45-85)	200 (60)
	K090	550-1000 (170-305)		900 (275)
M3, M4, M7, M15, M41, M46, M48, T15 with a hardness of 225-400 BHN	KC910	200-475 (60-145)		350 (105)
	KC990	175-425 (55-130)	150-375 (45-115)	325 (100)
	KC950	170-400 (50-120)	140-350 (45-105)	300 (90)
	KC850	125-300 (40-90)	100-275 (30-85)	225 (70)
	KT125	250-500 (75-150)		400 (120)
	KC720	40-175 (12-55)		100 (30)
	K090	400-850 (120-260)		700 (215)

Figure 7.25 (Reproduced with permission of Kennametal Inc.)

tool steels:	machining conditions	finishing	roughing	general purpose starting conditions
tool steels: heat-treated based on a machinability index range of 5-40 and a hardness of 55-68 Rc (570-780 BHN)	**depth of cut inches (mm)**	.003-.060 (0,08-1,5)	.060-.250 (1,5-6,3)	.015-.080 (0,4-2,0)
	feed rate ipr (mm/rev.)	.003-.014 (0,08-0,35)	.006-.024 (0,15-0,6)	solid CBN's .012 (0,3) tipped CBN's .008 (0,2) ceramics .005 (0,13)
	grades	**surface speed—sfm (m/min.)**		
	K090	220-475 (65-145)		300 (90)
	KD050	220-560 (65-170)		350 (105)
	KD120	200-400 (60-120)		300 (90)
	KD200	175-400 (55-120)	150-350 (45-105)	250 (75)
	supplemental uncoated carbide grade			
	K68	20-90 (6-25)		50 (15)

Figure 7.26 (Reproduced with permission of Kennametal Inc.)

suggested grades and machining conditions for tool steels

tool steels:	machining conditions	finishing	roughing	general purpose starting conditions
tool steels: wrought high carbon/low alloy W1, W2, L2, P20, P6 based on a machinability index range of 45-65 and a hardness of 190-230 BHN	**depth of cut inches (mm)**	.015-.100 (0,4-2,5)	.100-.300 (0,25-7,6)	.060-.200 (1,5-5,0)
	feed rate ipr (mm/rev.)	.003-.010 (0,08-0,3)	.005-.018 (0,12-0,45)	carbides .010 (0,25) cermets .008 (0,2) ceramics .008 (0,2)
	grades	**surface speed—sfm (m/min.)**		
	KC910	550-950 (170-290)		750 (230)
	KC990	500-875 (150-265)	450-625 (135-190)	600 (185)
	KC950	475-775 (145-235)	425-600 (130-185)	550 (170)
	KC850		300-550 (90-170)	425 (130)
	KT125	650-1000 (200-305)		775 (235)
	KT150	525-825 (160-250)		625 (190)
	KT175	325-725 (100-220)		450 (135)
	KC740	300-600 (90-185)		425 (130)
	KC710	225-475 (70-145)	200-425 (60-130)	300 (90)
	K090	700-1300 (215-395)		1100 (335)

Figure 7.27 (Reproduced with permission of Kennametal Inc.)

suggested grades and machining conditions for gray cast iron

gray cast iron:	machining conditions	finishing	roughing	general purpose starting conditions
gray cast iron: high tensile—class 20, 30, 35, 45, 55 and 60 based on a machinability index range of 68-78 and a hardness of 175-320 BHN	**depth of cut inches (mm)**	.015-.100 (0,4-2,5)	.100-.500 (2,5-12,7)	.050-.250 (1,25-6,3)
	feed rate ipr (mm/rev.)	.004-.015 (0,1-0,4)	.008-.030 (0,2-0,75)	carbides .015 (0,32) Kyon 3000 .015 (0,32) K060/K090 .010 (0,25)
	grades	**surface speed—sfm (m/min.)**		
	KC910	475-1200 (145-365)		650 (200)
	KC990	400-1000 (120-305)	400-1000 (120-305)	650 (200)
	KC250		200-500 (60-150)	350 (105)
	KC730	400-700 (120-215)	300-500 (90-150)	450 (135)
	KC720		200-500 (60-150)	300 (90)
	K313/K68	300-600 (90-185)	250-450 (75-135)	300 (90)
	K060	1200-2400 (365-730)		1500 (455)
	K090	1200-2800 (365-855)		1600 (490)
	Kyon 3000	650-4000 (200-1220)	700-3250 (215-990)	2400 (730)

Figure 7.28 (Reproduced with permission of Kennametal Inc.)

suggested grades and machining conditions for ductile cast iron

ductile cast iron: nodular/ductile, ferritic/pearlitic, pearlitic/martensitic based on a machinability index range of 40-50 and a hardness of 140-260 BHN	**machining conditions**	**finishing**	**roughing**	**general purpose starting conditions**
	depth of cut inches (mm)	.015-.100 (0,4-2,5)	.100-.500 (2,5-12,7)	.050-.175 (1,25-4,4)
	feed rate ipr (mm/rev.)	.003-.020 (0,08-0,5)	.008-.030 (0,2-0,75)	carbides .012 (0,3) cermets .010 (0,25) Kyon 4000 .012 (0,3) K060/K090 .010 (0,25)
	grades	**surface speed—sfm (m/min.)**		
	KC910	450-1000 (135-305)	400-850 (120-260)	750 (230)
	KC990	400-800 (120-245)	400-800 (120-245)	645 (195)
	KC950		375-750 (115-230)	600 (185)
	KC850		200-550 (60-170)	400 (120)
	KC810	225-600 (70-185)	225-600 (70-185)	500 (150)
	KC250		135-300 (40-90)	175 (55)
	KT125	800-1200 (245-365)		850 (260)
	KT150	700-1000 (215-305)		750 (230)
	KT175	550-800 (170-245)	550-800 (170-245)	600 (185)
	KC730	350-600 (105-185)		400 (120)
	KC720		300-500 (90-150)	400 (120)
	Kyon 4000	1000-3500 (305-1065)	900-3000 (275-915)	2000 (610)
	K090	850-1500 (260-455)		1100 (335)
	K060	850-1500 (260-455)		1000 (305)

Figure 7.29 (Reproduced with permission of Kennametal Inc.)

ductile cast iron: nodular/ductile, ferritic/pearlitic, pearlitic/martensitic based on a machinability index range of 40-50 and a hardness of 270-400 BHN	**machining conditions**	**finishing**	**roughing**	**general purpose starting conditions**
	depth of cut inches (mm)	.010-.100 (0,25-2,5)	.100-.500 (2,5-12,7)	.050-.175 (1,25-4,4)
	feed rate ipr (mm/rev.)	.003-.020 (0,08-0,5)	.008-.030 (0,2-0,75)	carbides .010 (0,25) Kyon 4000 .010 (0,25) K060/K090.008 (0,2)
	grades	**surface speed—sfm (m/min.)**		
	KC910	350-650 (105-200)	325-550 (100-170)	450 (135)
	KC990	300-600 (90-185)	250-500 (75-150)	400 (120)
	KC950	250-450 (75-135)	250-450 (75-135)	350 (105)
	KC850	180-400 (55-120)	180-300 (55-90)	250 (75)
	KC730	175-350 (55-105)		250 (75)
	Kyon 4000	800-2500 (245-760)	800-2000 (245-610)	1600 (490)
	K090	650-1200 (200-365)		900 (275)

Figure 7.30 (Reproduced with permission of Kennametal Inc.)

suggested grades and machining conditions for hardened cast irons

	machining conditions	finishing	roughing	general purpose starting conditions
hardened irons: based on a machinability index range of 40-60 and a hardness of 400-525 BHN	**depth of cut inches (mm)**	.003-.060 (0,08-1,5)	.060-.250 (1,5-6,3)	.030-.125 (0,75-3,2)
	feed rate ipr (mm/rev.)	.003-.012 (0,08-0,3)	.008-.014 (0,2-0,35)	solid CBN's .010 (0,25) tipped CBN's .007 (0,18) ceramics .005 (0,13)
	grades	**surface speed—sfm (m/min.)**		
	K090	200-600 (60-185)	180-550 (55-170)	250 (75)
	KD120	275-900 (85-275)		400 (120)
	KD200	250-750 (75-230)	225-700 (70-125)	300 (90)
	K313		55-85 (15-25)	65 (20)
525-700 BHN	K090	75-300 (25-90)		125 (40)
	KD120	100-450 (30-135)		300 (90)
	KD220	75-375 (25-115)		225 (70)
	KD200	80-400 (25-120)	180-350 (55-105)	250 (75)

Figure 7.31 (Reproduced with permission of Kennametal Inc.)

suggested grades and machining conditions for austenitic stainless steel

	machining conditions	finishing	roughing	general purpose starting conditions
austenitic stainless steel: 300 series AISI: 303, 201, 316L, 302, 321, 347, 384	**depth of cut inches (mm)**	.020-.100 (0,5-2,5)	.100-.500 (2,5-12,7)	.060-.175 (1,5-4,4)
based on a machinability index range of 35-55 and a hardness of 135-275 BHN	**feed rate ipr (mm/rev.)**	.003-.015 (0,08-0,4)	.006-.030 (0,15-0,75)	carbides .014 (0,35) cermets .012 (0,3)
	grades	**surface speed—sfm (m/min.)**		
	KC850	375-750 (115-230)	250-500 (75-150)	500 (150)
	KT125	500-950 (150-290)		700 (215)
	KT150	400-850 (120-260)		650 (200)
	KT175	375-850 (115-260)	350-800 (105-245)	600 (185)
	KC730	300-650 (90-200)	250-575 (75-175)	525 (160)
	KC720	200-400 (60-120)	175-325 (55-100)	275 (85)

Figure 7.32 (Reproduced with permission of Kennametal Inc.)

suggested grades and machining conditions for ferritic/martensitic stainless steel

	machining conditions	finishing	roughing	general purpose starting conditions
ferritic/martensitic stainless steel: wrought 400 series and PH stainless	**depth of cut inches (mm)**	.015-.100 (0,4-2,5)	.100-.500 (2,5-12,7)	.060-.175 (1,5-4,4)
AISI: 410, 416, 416F, 420, 430, 440, 440C	**feed rate ipr (mm/rev.)**	.003-.015 (0,08-0,4)	.006-.017 (0,15-0,42)	carbides .015 (0,38) cermets .012 (0,3)
based on a machinability index range of 40-55 and a hardness of 135-300 BHN	**grades**	**surface speed—sfm (m/min.)**		
	KC950	450-650 (135-200)	450-550 (135-170)	500 (150)
	KC850		250-450 (70-135)	325 (100)
	KC250		200-400 (60-120)	300 (90)
	KT125	600-900 (185-275)		750 (230)
	KT150	550-800 (170-245)		675 (205)
	KC730	250-500 (75-150)	240-400 (75-120)	350 (105)
	KC720	150-350 (45-105)	125-300 (40-90)	200 (60)
300-450 BHN	KC950	400-550 (120-170)	400-500 (120-150)	450 (135)
	KC850		180-350 (55-105)	280 (80)
	KC250		150-300 (45-90)	225 (70)
	KT125	500-800 (150-245)		675 (205)
	KT150	500-700 (150-215)		600 (185)
	KC730	250-450 (75-135)	250-350 (75-105)	300 (90)
	KC720	120-275 (35-85)	100-250 (30-75)	175 (55)

Figure 7.33 (Reproduced with permission of Kennametal Inc.)

Material characteristics. Relatively poor tool life; small depths of cut are difficult; work hardens rapidly; usually abrasive rather than hard; tough and stringy chips.

Tool-application considerations

Condition: Depth-of-cut notch

Remedy: Increase lead angle; use tougher grade; use 0.015-in or greater depth of cut; feed over 0.005 ipr; increase coolant concentration.

Condition: Built-up edge

Remedy: Increase speed; change cutting tool material; use positive-rake inserts (PVD-coated); do not overrun cutting edge; increase coolant concentration.

Condition: Workpiece glazing

Remedy: Increase depth of cut; increase feed rate; reduce nose radius; use positive-rake inserts (PVD-coated).

Condition: Torn or dull surface finish

Remedy: Increase speed; reduce feed; use positive-rake inserts (PVD-coated); increase coolant concentration.

Titanium alloys. Pure, alpha, alpha-beta, and beta alloys (see Fig. 7.37).

Material characteristics. Relatively poor tool life; chips tend to gall and weld to cutting edge; requires lower cutting speeds than steels of equal hardness; usually abrasive; tough and stringy; low thermal conductivity.

Tool-application considerations

Condition: Depth-of-cut notch

Remedy: Increase lead angle; use 0.015-in or greater depth of cut; remove embrittled surface from mill stock; feed over 0.005 ipr; increase coolant concentration.

Condition: Built-up edge

Remedy: Keep a sharp edge; use positive-rake inserts (PVD-coated); increase coolant concentration.

Condition: Workpiece glazing

Remedy: Increase depth of cut; reduce nose radius; use positive-rake inserts (PVD-coated); index cutting edge.

Condition: Torn or dull surface finish

Remedy: Index cutting edge; reduce feed; use positive-rake inserts (PVD-coated); increase speed; increase coolant concentration.

High-silicon and free-machining aluminum (see Fig. 7.38)

Free-machining aluminum. 1000, 1100, 1200, and 1300 series; 2011 through 2024 series; 3000 series. 1050 to 1350: Almost pure. 2011 to 2024: 2024 is popular (screw-machine products, aircraft parts); contains copper, manganese, and magnesium.

Material characteristics. Soft and gummy.

Tool-application considerations

Condition: Built-up edge

Remedy: Increase speed; use positive-rake inserts (PVD-coated); use coolants designed for machining aluminum; J polish top of insert.

Condition: Torn or dull surface finish

Remedy: Increase speed; reduce feed; use positive-rake inserts (PVD-coated); use coolant designed for aluminum; use polycrystalline diamond tools; J polish top of insert.

High-silicon aluminum. 4000, 5000, 6000, and 7000 series (7000 series uses zinc, zirconium, and titanium as alloying additives). 4000 series: Contains silicon for heat resistance and wear. 5000 series: Contains chromium. 6000 series: 6061 typical, contains silicon, copper, magnesium, and chromium. 7000 series: Contains copper, magnesium, chromium, and zinc (aircraft parts).

Material characteristics. Abrasive and tough.

Tool-application considerations

Condition: Edge wear

Remedy: Use coated grade; use polycrystalline diamond tools; increase coolant concentration.

Condition: Built-up edge/surface finish

Remedy: Increase speed; increase coolant concentration.

Nonferrous alloys and nonmetallics (see Figs. 7.39 and 7.40)

Nonferrous metals. Free-machining and high-strength copper alloys, brass, zinc, and magnesium.

Material characteristics. Easily machined; high machining speeds; positive chip control with magnesium to reduce fire hazards.

Caution: Fire hazard is present when machining magnesium at high speeds.

Nonmetallics. Nylons, acrylics, phenolics, and resin materials.

Material characteristics. Easily machined; high machining speeds; machine with polycrystalline diamonds whenever possible; center height of cutting is important.

Tool-application considerations

Condition: Built-up edge

Remedy: Increase speed; use positive-rake inserts; J polish top of inserts.

Condition: Poor surface finish

Remedy: Increase speed; use polycrystalline diamond inserts; use positive-rake inserts; J polish top of inserts; use positive chip control.

Miscellaneous work materials. Suggested grades and machining conditions for these materials are given in Figs. 7.41 through 7.48.

7.1.9 Grades of cutting inserts (for use with Figs. 7.18 through 7.48)

Charts 7.1 through 7.4 give the composition and application descriptions of the cutting inserts shown in Figs. 7.18 through 7.48. The insert grades described in the charts are those of Kennametal, Inc., with the charts also listing the ANSI and ISO equivalents as reference.

Selection of speed, feed, and depth of cut: Procedures. Use the preceding speed, feed, and depth of cut figures as a basis for these choices. Useful tool life is influenced most by cutting speed. The feed rate is the next most influential factor in tool life, followed by the depth of cut (doc).

(Text continued on page 575.)

suggested grades and machining conditions for high-temperature alloys (nickel base)

high-temperature alloys (nickel base)	machining conditions	finishing	roughing	general purpose starting conditions
nickel 200, Monel, R405, Monel K500, Inconel 600, Inconel 625/901/X750/718, Waspalloy	depth of cut inches (mm)	.010-.060 (0,25-1,5)	.060-.250 (1,5-6,3)	.100 (2,5)
based on a machinability index range of 10-35 and a hardness of 125-250 BHN	feed rate ipr (mm/rev.)	.004-.012 (0,1-0,3)	.004-.010 (0,1-0,25)	(all grades) .006 (0,15)
	grades	surface speed—sfm (m/min.)		
	KC950	250-350 (75-105)		300 (90)
	KC250		50-200 (15-60)	150 (45)
	KT150	100-500 (30-150)		350 (105)
	KC730	90-300 (25-90)		175 (55)
	KC720		60-200 (20-60)	150 (45)
	K313/K68	75-250 (25-75)		150 (45)
	K090	600-1000 (185-305)		850 (260)
	Kyon 2100	500-1200 (150-365)		800 (245)
	Kyon 2000		400-750 (120-230)	700 (215)
200-450 BHN	KC950	100-200 (30-60)	65-150 (20-45)	150 (45)
Inconel 718, Hastelloy C, Rene 95, Waspalloy	KC730	90-275 (25-85)		175 (55)
	KC720		60-140 (20-45)	95 (30)
	K313/K68	75-225 (25-70)		150 (45)
	K090	600-1300 (185-395)		850 (260)
	Kyon 2100	500-950 (150-290)		800 (245)
	Kyon 2000		300-700 (90-215)	700 (215)
	KD120	400-600 (120-185)		500 (150)
	supplemental uncoated carbide grade			
	K1		50-100 (15-30)	75 (25)

Figure 7.34 (Reproduced with permission of Kennametal Inc.)

suggested grades and machining conditions for high-temperature alloys (iron base)

high-temperature alloys (iron base)	machining conditions	finishing	roughing	general purpose starting conditions
Waspalloy A286, 19-9 DL, Discaloy, 16-25-6, Incoloy 800	depth of cut inches (mm)	.010-.100 (0,25-2,5)	.100-.250 (2,5-6,3)	.060-.200 (1,5-5,0)
based on a machinability index range of 15-30 and a hardness of 180-250 BHN	feed rate ipr (mm/rev.)	.003-.012 (0,08-0,3)	.006-.020 (0,15-0,5)	(all grades) .008 (0,2)
	grades	surface speed—sfm (m/min.)		
	KC950	225-450 (70-135)	180-375 (55-115)	300 (90)
	KC250		150-250 (45-75)	175 (55)
	KC730	150-350 (45-105)	40-300 (12-90)	250 (75)
	K313/K68	100-300 (30-90)	40-250 (12-75)	200 (60)
	Kyon 2100	350-750 (105-230)		550 (170)
	Kyon 2000		225-600 (70-185)	500 (150)
250-350 BHN	KC950	175-425 (55-130)	150-350 (45-105)	300 (90)
	KC250		100-200 (30-60)	175 (55)
	KC730	100-300 (30-90)	90-225 (30-70)	200 (60)
	K313/K68	100-250 (30-75)	90-200 (30-60)	150 (45)
	K090	325-750 (100-230)		600 (185)
	Kyon 2100	300-700 (90-215)		550 (170)
	Kyon 2000		175-550 (55-170)	450 (135)
	supplemental uncoated carbide grade			
	K1		50-105 (15-30)	75 (25)

Figure 7.35 (Reproduced with permission of Kennametal Inc.)

suggested grades and machining conditions for high-temperature alloys (cobalt base)

high-temperature alloys (cobalt base) Haynes 188, Stellite F, 5816, Haynes 25 (L605), J1650	**machining conditions**	**finishing**	**roughing**	**general purpose starting conditions**
	depth of cut inches (mm)	.010-.060 (0,25-1,5)	.060-.250 (1,5-6,3)	.100 (2,5)
based on a machinability index range of 6-15 and a hardness of 150-250 BHN	**feed rate ipr (mm/rev.)**	.002-.008 (0,05-0,2)	.005-.010 (0,12-0,25)	(all grades) .005 (0,12)
	grades	**surface speed—sfm (m/min.)**		
	KC730	50-125 (15-40)	30-110 (10-35)	90 (30)
	KC720		25-90 (8-25)	60 (20)
	K313/K68	40-100 (12-30)	30-100 (10-30)	75 (25)
250-450 BHN	KC730	40-120 (12-35)	25-100 (8-30)	80 (25)
	KC720		20-80 (6-25)	50 (15)
	K313/K68	35-100 (10-30)	25-80 (8-25)	65 (20)
	K090	250-800 (75-245)		500 (150)
	KD120	300-800 (90-245)		500 (150)
	KD200	275-725 (85-220)		500 (150)
450-750 BHN	KC730	30-90 (10-30)	20-75 (6-25)	60 (20)
	K090	200-650 (60-200)	190-550 (60-170)	300 (90)
	KD120	200-700 (60-215)		450 (135)
	KD200	180-625 (55-190)	175-500 (55-150)	400 (120)
	supplemental uncoated carbide grade			
	K1		20-50 (6-15)	30 (10)

Figure 7.36 (Reproduced with permission of Kennametal Inc.)

suggested grades and machining conditions for titanium alloys

titanium unalloyed (98.9-99.5% pure)	**machining conditions**	**finishing**	**roughing**	**general purpose starting conditions**
based on a machinability index range of 20-40 and a hardness of 100-200 BHN	**depth of cut inches (mm)**	.010-.060 (0,25-1,5)	.060-.250 (1,5-6,3)	.040-.150 (1,0-3,8)
	feed rate ipr (mm/rev.)	.004-.010 (0,1-0,25)	.008-.015 (0,2-0,4)	(all grades) .006 (0,15)
	grades	**surface speed—sfm (m/min.)**		
	KC730	325-500 (100-150)	275-450 (80-140)	400 (120)
	KC720	225-375 (70-110)	180-300 (60-90)	300 (90)
	K313	275-400 (80-125)	230-350 (70-110)	350 (110)
titanium—alloyed Ti-6Al-4V Ti-5Al-2.5Sn 250-350 BHN	KC730	170-300 (50-90)	140-275 (40-80)	200 (60)
	KC720	120-325 (40-100)	90-200 (25-60)	150 (40)
	K313	140-250 (40-75)	120-225 (40-70)	200 (60)
350-450 BHN	KC730	50-200 (15-60)	40-150 (10-50)	140 (40)
	KC720	40-175 (10-55)	30-150 (10-45)	100 (30)
	K313	50-175 (10-50)	35-130 (10-40)	120 (35)

Figure 7.37 (Reproduced with permission of Kennametal Inc.)

suggested grades and machining conditions for free-machining and high-silicon aluminum

	machining conditions	finishing	roughing	general purpose starting conditions
non-ferrous, free-machining aluminum alloys: AA: 2024-T4, 2014-T6, 6061-T6, 2011-T3, 3003-H18, and A2, Alcan, Alcoa 510, and Duralumin aluminums based on a machinability index range of 70-100 and a hardness of 50-150 BHN	**depth of cut inches (mm)**	.010-.150 (0,25-3,8)	.150-.350 (3,8-8,8)	.060-.200 (1,5-5,0)
	feed rate ipr (mm/rev.)	.003-.016 (0,08-0,4)	.008-.025 (0,2-0,62)	(all grades) .018 (0,45)
	grades	**surface speed—sfm (m/min.)**		
	KD100	1000-10,000 (305-3050)		2500 (760)
	KC730	200-3000 (60-915)	700-2600 (215-795)	1800 (550)
	KT125	900-2600 (275-795)	700-2300 (215-700)	1600 (490)
	K313	650-2200 (200-670)	650-2000 (200-610)	1600 (490)
high-silicon aluminum (hypereutectic): A380, A390, A380-1, A390-1, A380-2. 50-150 BHN	KD100	2000-3000 (610-915)	1200-2500 (365-760)	1700 (520)

Figure 7.38 (Reproduced with permission of Kennametal Inc.)

suggested grades and machining conditions for non-ferrous, free-machining alloys

	machining conditions	finishing	roughing	general purpose starting conditions
non-ferrous machining alloys: copper, brass, zinc based on a machinability index range of 70-100 and a hardness of 50-150 BHN	**depth of cut inches (mm)**	.015-.100 (0,4-2,5)	.100-.300 (2,5-7,5)	.060-.200 (1,5-5,0)
	feed rate ipr (mm/rev.)	.006-.014 (0,15-0,35)	.008-.030 (0,2-0,75)	(all grades) .010 (0,25)
	grades	**surface speed—sfm (m/min.)**		
	KC990		700-2200 (215-670)	1200 (365)
	KC850		300-1000 (90-305)	700 (215)
	KT125	1000-2000 (305-610)		1400 (425)
	KC730	450-1500 (135-455)	375-1300 (115-395)	900 (275)
	KT150		800-1400 (245-425)	1000 (305)
	KT175		650-1200 (200-365)	800 (245)
	KC720		150-550 (45-170)	300 (90)
	KD100	1000-3000 (305-915)	900-2600 (275-795)	1700 (520)
	K313	375-1750 (115-535)	350-1450 (105-440)	850 (260)
magnesium 60-90 BHN ***NOTE: Fire hazard present when machining magnesium at high speeds.***	KD100	1000-3500 (305-1065)		2000 (610)
	KC730	600-3000 (185-915)		1650 (505)
	K313	550-2600 (170-795)		1450 (440)

Figure 7.39 (Reproduced with permission of Kennametal Inc.)

suggested grades and machining conditions for non-metallic materials

	machining conditions	finishing	roughing	general purpose starting conditions
carbon and graphite composites: brush alloys, Kevlar, graphite 270-400 BHN	**depth of cut inches (mm)**	.005-.030 (0,12-0,75)	.030-.250 (0,75-6,3)	.075 (1,9)
	feed rate ipr (mm/rev.)	.005-.014 (0,12-0,35)	.010-.060 (0,25-1,5)	.008 (0,2)
	grades	**surface speed—sfm (m/min.)**		
	KD100	1800-4300 (550-1310)		2500 (760)
	KC730	425-950 (130-290)	350-850 (105-260)	650 (200)
glass and ceramics: macor, mica 200-250 BHN	**depth of cut inches (mm)**	.005-.050 (0,12-1,2)		.050 (1,2)
	feed rate ipr (mm/rev.)	.005-.010 (0,12-0,25)		.008 (0,2)
	grades	**surface speed—sfm (m/min.)**		
	KD100	750-3300 (230-1005)		1650 (505)
nylon, plastics, rubbers, phenolics and resins 0-200 BHN	**depth of cut inches (mm)**	.005-.020 (0,12-0,5)	.020-.200 (0,5-5,0)	.050 (1,2)
	feed rate ipr (mm/rev.)	.003-.012 (0,08-0,3)	.006-.015 (0,15-0,35)	.005 (0,12)
	grades	**surface speed—sfm (m/min.)**		
	KD100	500-2400 (150-730)		1300 (395)
	KC730	325-750 (100-230)	300-700 (90-215)	550 (170)

Figure 7.40 (Reproduced with permission of Kennametal Inc.)

suggested grades and machining conditions

	machining conditions	finishing	roughing	general purpose starting conditions
zirconium: 150-300 BHN, Zr-2% HS (grade 11), Zircaloy 2	**depth of cut inches (mm)**	.010-.050 (0,25-1,2)	.050-.250 (1,2-6,3)	.050-.100 (1,2-2,5)
	feed rate ipr (mm/rev.)	.005-.010 (0,12-0,25)	.010-.020 (0,25-0,5)	.008 (0,2)
	grades	**surface speed—sfm (m/min.)**		
	KC730	180-320 (55-100)	160-300 (50-90)	225 (70)
	KC710	140-240 (45-75)	125-225 (40-70)	175 (55)

Figure 7.41 (Reproduced with permission of Kennametal Inc.)

	machining conditions	finishing	roughing	general purpose starting conditions
manganese: wrought 140-220 BHN	**depth of cut inches (mm)**	.010-.050 (0,25-1,2)	.050-.200 (1,2-5,0)	.100 (2,5)
	feed rate ipr (mm/rev.)	.005-.010 (0,12-0,25)	.006-.018 (0,15-0,45)	.008 (0,2)
	grades	**surface speed—sfm (m/min.)**		
	KC730	150-325 (45-100)	125-300 (40-90)	200 (60)
	KC720	100-200 (30-60)	90-175 (25-55)	125 (40)
	K313	125-250 (40-75)	90-200 (30-60)	150 (45)

Figure 7.42 (Reproduced with permission of Kennametal Inc.)

	machining conditions	finishing	roughing	general purpose starting conditions
depleted uranium: wrought 150-180 BHN	**depth of cut inches (mm)**	.010-.040 (0,25-1,0)	.040-.20 (1,0-5,0)	.080 (2,0)
	feed rate ipr (mm/rev.)	.005-.013 (0,12-0,3)	.005-.015 (0,12-0,4)	.006 (0,15)
	grades	**surface speed—sfm (m/min.)**		
	KC730	135-300 (40-90)	110-250 (35-75)	175 (55)
	K313	125-225 (40-70)	75-150 (25-45)	110 (35)

Figure 7.43 (Reproduced with permission of Kennametal Inc.)

tin alloys as cast: 15-30 (500 Kg) ASTM 823, alloys 1,2,3,11	machining conditions	finishing	roughing	general purpose starting conditions
	depth of cut inches (mm)	.010-.050 (0,25-1,2)	.050-.300 (1,2-7,6)	.100 (2,5)
	feed rate ipr (mm/rev.)	.006-.012 (0,15-0,3)	.008-.015 (0,2-0,4)	.008 (0,2)
	grades	surface speed—sfm (m/min.)		
	KC730	750-900 (230-275)	625-775 (190-235)	700 (215)
	K313	500-750 (150-230)	400-625 (120-190)	600 (185)

Figure 7.44 (Reproduced with permission of Kennametal Inc.)

suggested grades and machining conditions

lead alloys, cast: ASTM B23, alloys 7, 8, 13, 15	machining conditions	finishing	roughing	general purpose starting conditions
	depth of cut inches (mm)	.025-.100 (0,62-2,5)	.100-.300 (2,5-7,6)	.100 (2,5)
	feed rate ipr (mm/rev.)	.005-.010 (0,12-0,25)	.005-.012 (0,12-0,3)	.008 (0,2)
	grades	surface speed—sfm (m/min.)		
	KC730	850-1250 (260-380)	750-900 (230-275)	850 (260)
	K313	750-1000 (230-305)	700-900 (215-275)	800 (245)

Figure 7.45 (Reproduced with permission of Kennametal Inc.)

zinc alloys cast: 80-100 BHN, AMS 4803 140-220 BHN ILZRO 12	machining conditions	finishing	roughing	general purpose starting conditions
	depth of cut inches (mm)	.020-.150 (0,5-3,8)	.150-.200 (3,8-5,0)	.080 (2,0)
	feed rate ipr (mm/rev.)	.006-.012 (0,15-0,3)	.008-.018 (0,2-0,45)	.008 (0,2)
	grades	surface speed—sfm (m/min.)		
	KC730	750-1250 (230-380)	650-1050 (200-320)	800 (245)
	K313	725-1200 (220-365)	625-1000 (190-305)	750 (230)

Figure 7.46 (Reproduced with permission of Kennametal Inc.)

compacted graphite iron: 175-250 BHN	machining conditions	finishing	roughing	general purpose starting conditions
	depth of cut inches (mm)	.004-.014 (0,3-0,35)	.008-.024 (0,2-0,6)	.060 (1,5)
	feed rate ipr (mm/rev.)	.004-.014 (0,1-0,35)	.008-.024 (0,2-0,6)	.008 (0,2)
	grades	surface speed—sfm (m/min.)		
	K090	1000-1500 (305-455)		1100 (335)
	KC910	400-750 (120-230)	350-675 (105-205)	500 (150)
	KC990	325-650 (100-200)	280-625 (85-190)	450 (135)
	KC730	150-300 (45-90)		225 (70)
	KC850		180-375 (55-115)	250 (75)

Figure 7.47 (Reproduced with permission of Kennametal Inc.)

tungsten alloys	machining conditions	finishing	roughing	general purpose starting conditions
	depth of cut inches (mm)	.010-.050 (0,25-1,2)	.050-.200 (1,2-5,0)	.100 (2,5)
	feed rate ipr (mm/rev.)	.005-.010 (0,12-0,25)	.006-.018 (0,15-0,45)	.008 (0,2)
	grades	surface speed—sfm (m/min.)		
	KC730	300-500 (90-150)	200-400 (60-120)	275 (85)
	K313	225-400 (70-120)	175-375 (55-115)	250 (75)

Figure 7.48 (Reproduced with permission of Kennametal Inc.)

tungsten carbide grades

CVD ceramic (Al_2O_3) coated carbide grades			
grades	**composition and application**	**ANSI**	**ISO**
KC990	**composition:** A multi-layer ceramic coated grade with high-strength substrate, CVD coated with TiC/N and alternating layers of Al_2O_3 and TiN. **application:** Engineered for heavy roughing to finishing of steels, stainless steels and irons at ceramic coated speeds. Coating carbide inserts with multiple layers of ceramic and TiN offers greater productivity, versatility and reliability.	C2-C4 C6-C8	K05-K25 M10-M25 P05-P25
KC950	**composition:** A multi-layered ceramic coated carbide grade with a tough cobalt enriched substrate, CVD coated with TiC/Al_2O_3/TiN. **application:** Used for high-speed roughing and finishing of steels, ferritic and martensitic stainless steels and irons. Cobalt enriched substrate offers high strength at the cutting edge while maintaining high resistance to crater wear and abrasive wear.	C2-C3 C6-C7	K10-K20 M10-M25 P05-P25
KC910	**composition:** A ceramic coated carbide grade having a very thermal-deformation-resistant substrate. **application:** The TiC/Al_2O_3 CVD coating is engineered to have excellent abrasion resistance and resistance to edge buildup for long tool life in high-speed finishing and light-roughing operations of carbon steels, alloy steels, tool steels, ferritic and martensitic stainless steels, and all cast irons.	C3-C4 C7-C8	K01-K15 M05-M20 P01-P20
CVD tri-phase coated carbide grades			
KC850	**composition:** A TiC/TiC-N/TiN coating on an extra-strong cobalt enriched substrate. **application:** For your toughest jobs on a wide variety of materials. Used for interrupted cuts and heavy to moderate roughing of carbon and alloy steels, tool steels, stainless steels, alloy cast irons and ductile irons. Excellent thermal and mechanical shock resistance makes KC850 ideally suited for applications requiring maximum edge strength.	C5-C7	M25-M45 P25-P45
KC250	**composition:** A TiC/TiC-N/TiN coated grade on a substrate which has excellent toughness. **application:** For operations of low to moderate speeds and light to heavy roughing of stainless steels, high-temperature alloys and cast irons.	C1-C2	K25-K35 M30-M45
KC810	**composition:** A TiC/TiC-N/TiN coating on a thermal-deformation-resistant substrate. **application:** This is a good grade for finishing to moderate roughing at moderate speeds. It displays a good balance of wear resistance and strength for general purpose machining of carbon steels, alloy steels and tool steels.	C6-C7	M15-M35 P10-P30

Chart 7.1 (Reproduced with permission of Kennametal Inc.)

PVD TIN (titanium nitride) coated carbide grades			
grades	**composition and application**	**ANSI**	**ISO**
KC710	**composition:** A PVD coated grade that has good toughness and thermal shock resistance with good crater wear resistance and resistance to buildup on the cutting edge. **application:** Greatly improved productivity and higher speed capability in comparison with uncoated carbide when turning, boring and milling most steels.	C5-C6	M15-M25 P15-P25
KC720	**composition:** A tough, durable PVD coated carbide grade. **application:** Developed for cutting high-temperature alloys, stainless steels and low-carbon steels at low to moderate speeds. Its unique mechanical and thermal shock resistant properties and resistance to edge buildup enable KC720 to deliver superior performance and reliability on difficult operations like cutoff operations, and milling high-temperature alloys with coolant.	C1-C2 C5	K25-K35 M30-M40 P25-P45
KC730	**composition:** A PVD coated carbide grade. **application:** For machining high-temperature alloys, aerospace materials, refractory metals and 200 and 300 series stainless steels. The substrate offers superior thermal deformation resistance, depth of cut notch resistance and edge strength. The uniformly dense PVD coating increases wear resistance, reduces problems with edge buildup and provides an unusually good combination of properties for machining difficult-to-machine materials and aluminum.	C2-C4	K05-K15 M05-M15
KC740	**composition:** A hard, crater resistant PVD coated carbide grade. **application:** For precision machining of carbon and alloy steels at medium to high speeds. Excellent resistance to buildup on the cutting edge.	C7-C8	P05-P15
uncoated carbide grades			
K1	**composition:** A very tough WC/Co unalloyed grade. **application:** For roughing through heavy interruptions when turning or milling stainless steels, cast irons and cast steels, rough cast nonferrous alloys and most high-temperature alloys including titanium.	C1	K20-K30
K68	**composition:** A tough WC/Co unalloyed grade. **application:** K68 has excellent edge wear resistance for machining stainless steels, cast irons, nonferrous metals, nonmetals and most high-temperature alloys.	C2-C3	K05-K15 M10-M20
K313	**composition:** An unalloyed WC/Co fine-grained grade. **application:** Exceptional edge wear resistance combined with very high strength for machining nonmetals, nonferrous metals including aluminum, stainless steels, cast irons and most high-temperature alloys including titanium.	C2-C4	K05-K15 M10-M20
K420	**composition:** A tough WC/TaC/TiC/Co alloyed steel cutting grade. **application:** K420 has superior edge strength and thermal shock resistance for milling or turning through severe interruptions at high chip loads; also used for heavy roughing and semi-finishing of all soft to moderately hard steels.	C5-C6	M25-M40 P30-P40

Chart 7.2 (Reproduced with permission of Kennametal Inc.)

cermet (CERamics with METallic binders) grades

grades	composition and application	ANSI	ISO
KT125	**composition:** A wear-resistant TiC/TiN-base grade. **application:** Used for high-speed, precision turning and boring of carbon steels, alloy steels, stainless steels and malleable (ductile) cast irons.	C4 C7-C8	M01-M10 P01-P05
KT150	**composition:** A general purpose TiC/TiN-base grade. **application:** Used for semi-finish turning, boring and milling of malleable (ductile) cast irons, stainless steels, carbon steels and alloy steels.	C3-C4 C7-C8	M05-M15 P01-P10
KT175	**composition:** A tough TiC/TiN-base grade. **application:** Used for milling, rough turning and boring of carbon steels, alloy steels, stainless steels and malleable (ductile) cast irons.	C2-C4 C6-C8	M10-M20 P10-P20

ceramic grades

alumina-base ceramics			
grades	**composition and application**	**ANSI**	**ISO**
Kyon 2100	composition: A cold pressed sialon material. application: Exhibits reliable performance during high speed machining of high temperature super alloys, including tough applications where scale or interrupted cuts occur.	C3-C4	K01-K10
Kyon 4000	**composition:** Aluminum Oxide (Al_2O_3) reinforced with silicon-carbide whiskers and zirconium oxide. **application:** Excellent chemical wear resistance and toughness. For high-speed roughing and finishing of ductile cast iron and low carbon steels.	C1-C3 C5-C7	P05-P20 M05-M20
K090	**composition:** A grade (black) composed of alumina and 30% TiC. **application:** High toughness and thermal shock resistance for machining carbon steels, alloy steels, tool steels and stainless steels to 60 Rc (653 BHN).	C3-C4 C7-C8	K01-K10 M10 P01-P20
K060	**composition:** A pure alumina-based ceramic grade (white). **application:** Excellent abrasion resistance for machining soft cast irons and steels to 35 Rc (330 BHN).	C3-C4 C7-C8	K01-K05 P01-P05
silicon nitride-base ceramics			
Kyon 3000	**composition:** An advanced silicon nitride (sialon) grade. **application:** Having excellent abrasion resistance combined with good toughness and thermal shock resistance. It is used for high productivity milling and turning of gray cast irons at high speeds (800-4000 sfm).	C1-C3	K05-K20
Kyon 2000	**composition:** An advanced silicon nitride (sialon) grade. **application:** Excellent thermal shock resistance combined with fracture toughness for high-speed roughing of nickel-base alloys where scale and/or interruptions are present.	C1-C3	K05-K20

Chart 7.3 (Reproduced with permission of Kennametal Inc.)

polycrystalline grades

polycrystalline diamond (PCD)			
grades	**composition and application**	**ANSI**	**ISO**
KD100	**composition:** This material is a polycrystalline diamond (PCD) tip brazed on a standard carbide insert. **application:** It is ultra hard and has excellent wear resistance for improved size control (workpiece tolerance) and surface finish. It is unsurpassed for tool life on highly abrasive nonmetals and nonferrous metals.	C3-C4	K01-K10 M10
polycrystalline cubic boron nitride (CBN)			
KD200	**composition:** A solid CBN structure having multiple cutting edges. **application:** It has excellent wear, high thermal and mechanical shock resistance. It is recommended for high-speed rough machining on hardened ferrous materials 50-65 Rc (480-740 BHN)	C1-C2 C6-C7	K05-K20 M10-M15 P05-P20
KD120	**composition:** A CBN tip brazed on a standard carbide insert. **application:** It has excellent wear resistance and can be used to semi-finish and finish machine hardened ferrous materials 50-65 Rc (480-740 BHN). This can be held in standard toolholders.	C3-C4 C7-C8	K01-K05 M01-M05 P01-P05
KD220	**composition:** Another CBN tip on a standard insert for maximum application flexibility whose toughness approaches KD200. **application:** It is well suited for light roughing of ni-hards, hi-chrome irons, chilled cast irons, hard facing alloys and hardened tool steels 50-65 Rc (480-740 BHN).	C7	K01-K05 M01-M05 P01-P05
KD050	**composition:** The most wear resistant CBN tip on a standard carbide insert. **application:** Designed for precision finishing of hardened tool steels 50-65 Rc (480-740 BHN) where the maximum depth of cut is .060.	C8	P01

Chart 7.4 (Reproduced with permission of Kennametal Inc.)

When the depth of cut exceeds approximately 10 times the feed rate, a further increase in depth of cut has little effect on tool life. In selecting the cutting conditions for a turning or boring operation, the first step is to select the depth of cut, followed by selection of the feed rate and then the cutting speed. Use the preceding horsepower/kilowatt equations to determine the approximate power requirements for a particular depth of cut, feed rate, and cutting speed to see if the machine can handle the power required. You also may use one of the cutting tool manufacturers' machining calculators, samples of which are shown in Figs. 7.14 and 7.15. Many production and tooling engineers prefer to use the calculators provided by the manufacturer who supplies their cutting tools, together with production trial runs on any particular part, in determining the final machining parameters.

Select the heaviest depth of cut and feed rate that the machine can sustain, considering its horsepower or kilowatt rating, in conjunction with the required surface finish desired on the workpiece.

Relation of speed to feed. The following general rules apply to most turning and boring operations:

- If the tool shows a built-up edge, increase feed or increase speed.
- If the tool shows excessive cratering, reduce feed or reduce speed.
- If the tool shows excessive edge wear, increase feed or reduce speed.

Caution: The productivity settings from the machining calculators and any handbook speed and feed tables are suggestions and guides only. *A safety hazard may exist* if the user calculates or uses a table-selected machine setting *without also considering* the machine power and the condition, size, strength, and rigidity of the workpiece, machine, and cutting tools.

Turning, boring, and threading inserts. Figure 7.49 shows a sample of some of the typical cutting inserts available today. The versatile 80° diamond inserts are shown in the center area of the figure (two inserts) to the left and right of the lower center triangle. Various types and styles of toolholders for the inserts are produced by the insert manufacturers to hold the disposable inserts rigidly in position during the cutting operation. Figure 7.50 shows samples of typical turning and boring toolholders, and Fig. 7.51 shows a modern toolholder with a multipurpose, double-ended cutting insert. With the one insert, finishing, facing, and cutoff operations may be performed according to the orientation angle of the toolholder in relation to the workpiece.

7.1.10 ANSI and ISO identification systems for turning, boring, and milling inserts

Removable turning, boring, and milling inserts are identified and specified according to the American National Standards Institute (ANSI) and the International Standards Organization (ISO) systems shown in Figs. 7.52 and 7.53, respectively. Sample drawings of various types of inserts are shown in Fig. 7.54. The identification code is listed at the top right of each insert and may be referenced back to the ANSI identification system (Fig. 7.52).

7.1.11 Thread turning

Thread-turning inserts are available in different styles or types for turning external and internal thread systems such as UN series, 60° metric, Whitworth (BSW), Acme, ISO, American buttress, etc. Figure 7.55 shows some of the typical thread-cutting inserts.

The defining dimensions and forms for various thread systems are shown in Fig. 7.56 with indications of their normal industrial uses. The dimensions in the figure are in U.S. Customary and metric systems as indicated. In all parts of the figure, P = pitch, reciprocal of threads-per-inch (for U.S. Customary) or millimeters (for metric).

Figure 7.56*a* defines the ISO thread system: M (metric) and UN (unified national). *Typical uses:* All branches of the mechanical industries. Figure 7.56*b* defines the UNJ thread system (controlled-root radii). *Typical uses:* Aerospace industries. Figure 7.56*c* defines the Whitworth system (BSW). *Typical uses:* Fittings and pipe couplings for water, sewer, and gas lines. Presently replaced by ISO system. Figure 7.56*d* defines the American buttress system, 7° face. *Typical uses:* Machine design. Figure 7.56*e* defines the NPT (American national pipe thread) system. *Typical uses:* Pipe threads, fittings, and couplings. Figure 7.56*f* defines the BSPT (British standard pipe thread) system. *Typical uses:* Pipe thread for water, gas, and steam lines. Figure 7.56*g* defines the Acme thread system, 29°. *Typical uses:* Mechanical industries for motion-transmission screws. Figure 7.56*h* defines the stub Acme thread system, 29°. *Typical uses:* Same as Acme, but used where normal Acme thread is too deep. Figure 7.56*i* defines the API 1:6 tapered-thread system. *Typical uses:* Petroleum industries. Figure 7.56*j* defines the TR DIN 103 thread system. *Typical uses:* Mechanical industries for motion-transmission screws. Figure 7.56*k* defines the RD DIN 405 (round) thread system. *Typical uses:* Pipe couplings and fittings in the fire-protection and food industries.

Threading operations. Prior to cutting (turning) any particular thread, the following should be determined:

- Machining toward the spindle (standard helix)
- Machining away from the spindle (reverse helix)
- Helix angle (see following equation)
- Insert and toolholder
- Insert grade
- Speed (sfpm)
- Number of thread passes
- Method of in-feed

Calculating the thread helix angle. To calculate the helix angle of a given thread system, use the following simple equation (see Fig. 7.57):

$$\tan \alpha = \frac{p}{\pi D_e}$$

where $\tan \alpha$ = natural tangent of the helix angle, degrees
D_e = effective diameter of thread, in or mm
$\pi = 3.1416$
p = pitch of thread, in or mm

Example Find the helix angle of a unified national coarse 0.375-16 thread.

$$p = 1/16 = 0.0625$$

(The pitch is the reciprocal of the number of threads per inch in the U.S. Customary system.)

$$D_e = 0.375 \text{ in}$$

Therefore,

$$\tan \alpha = \frac{0.0625}{3.1416 \times 0.375} = \frac{0.0625}{1.1781} = 0.05305$$

$$\arctan 0.05305 = 3.037° \quad \text{or} \quad 3°2.22'$$

The helix angle of any helical thread system can be found by using the preceding procedure.

Cutting procedures for external and internal threads: Machine setups. Figure 7.58 illustrates the methods for turning the external thread systems (standard and reverse helix). Figure 7.59 illustrates the methods for turning the internal thread systems (standard and reverse helix).

Problems in thread cutting

Problem	Possible remedy
Burr on crest of thread	1. Increase surface feet per minute (rpm). 2. Use positive rake. 3. Use full-profile insert (NTC type).
Poor tool life	1. Increase surface feet per minute (rpm). 2. Increase chip load. 3. Use more wear-resistant tool.

Built-up edge	1. Increase surface feet per minute (rpm). 2. Increase chip load. 3. Use positive rake, sharp tool. 4. Use coolant or increase concentration.
Torn threads on workpiece	1. Use neutral rake. 2. Alter infeed angle. 3. Decrease chip load. 4. Increase coolant concentration. 5. Increase surface feet per minute (rpm).

In-feed methods for thread cutting

0° in-feed angle. When the in-feed angle is 0°, cutting occurs on both sides of the thread form, which places all the cutting edge in the cut and helps protect the edge from chipping. *Disadvantages:* May produce difficult-to-handle chip; the tip of the tool may chip when cutting high-tensile-strength materials; burring is increased; and chatter problems may develop.

Large in-feed angle (15 to 30°). Cutting with the leading edge of the tool produces an easy-to-handle chip, and reduced burr problems occur on the trailing edge of the tool. *Disadvantages:* Trailing edge of tool may drag and tend to chip; torn or poor surface occurs when cutting soft, gummy materials such as low-carbon steels (1020, etc.) and low-alloy aluminums or pure aluminum.

Small in-feed angle (5 to 10°). Tool cuts from both sides and is protected from chipping; chip is easy to handle. *Disadvantages:* Similar to 0° in-feed, but less in magnitude because cutting forces are equalized and chip is easy to control.

Standard thread systems and standard hardware (American National Standards Institute, ANSI). See Chap. 8, "ANSI Standards Applicable to Machining and Metalworking Practices." Also see Chap 6, "Fastening and Joining Techniques and Hardware."

7.1.12 Modern turning centers and standard lathe machine tools

The modern DNC (direct numerical control) turning center has replaced many types of older machine tools such as the automatic screw machines, small turret lathes, and profiling equipment. Figures 7.60 and 7.61 show typical automatic CNC turning centers.

A sample of typical parts produced on this type of machine tool is shown in Fig. 7.62. The controllers of these machines can be seen in the photographs. The spindle and coolant line can be seen near the center of the machine shown in Fig. 7.60. The bar-stock material is fed through the spindle and clamped in position for cutting by a collet-type mechanism at the spindle.

Figure 7.63 shows a typical small turret lathe used to produce small parts when the production rates do not warrant the use of a DNC turning center. Figure 7.64 shows a typical geared-head engine lathe equipped with digital read-out panel used for setting the controls and movements of the machine. The digital read-out panel is shown in the upper left of the photograph and reads to four decimal places (±0.0005 in). Engine lathes of this type have been the major basic machines used in the metalworking industries for many years, together with the standard milling machines. It has often been said that the engine lathe can produce almost any type of detail part requiring machining when equipped with the proper accessories and auxiliary devices.

7.2 Milling

Milling is a machining process for generating machined surfaces by removing a predetermined amount of material progressively

Figure 7.49 A variety of cutting insert types.

(*Text continued on page 596.*)

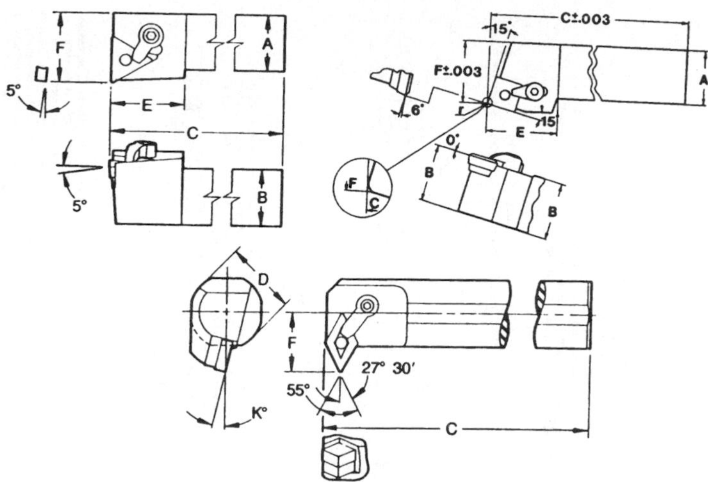

Figure 7.50 Typical insert toolholders.

Figure 7.51 A convertible insert and toolholder.

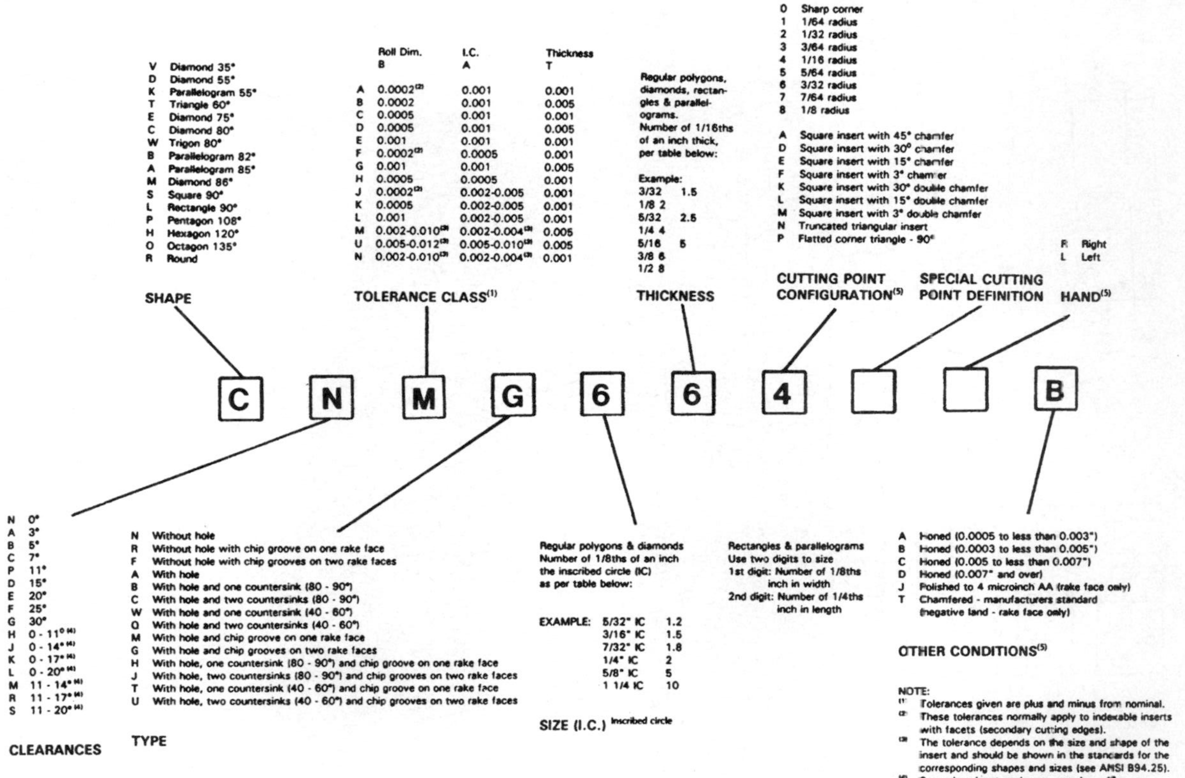

Figure 7.52 ANSI cutting insert identification system.

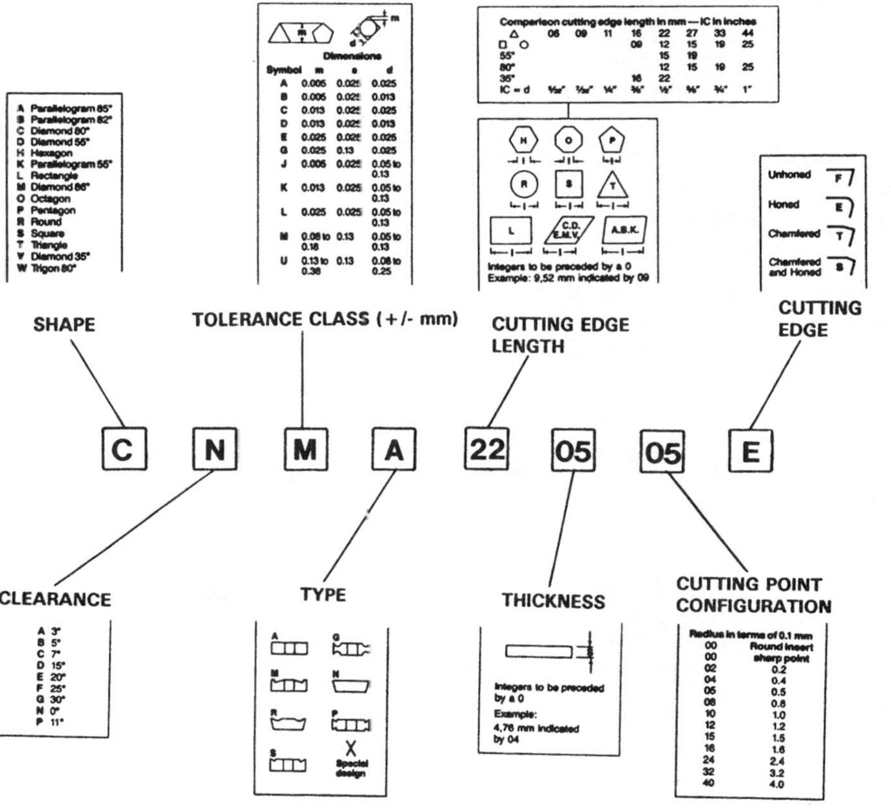

Figure 7.53 ISO cutting insert identification system.

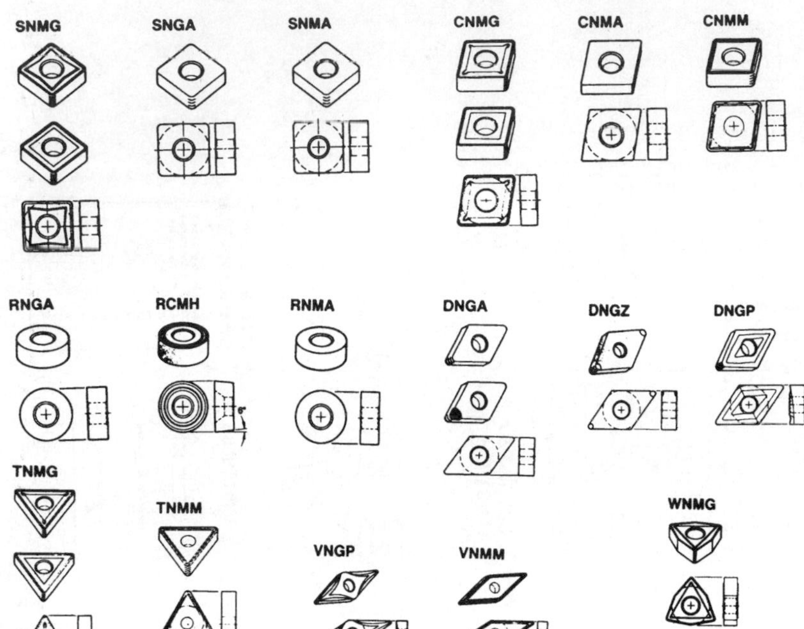

Figure 7.54 Sample inserts with identification codes.

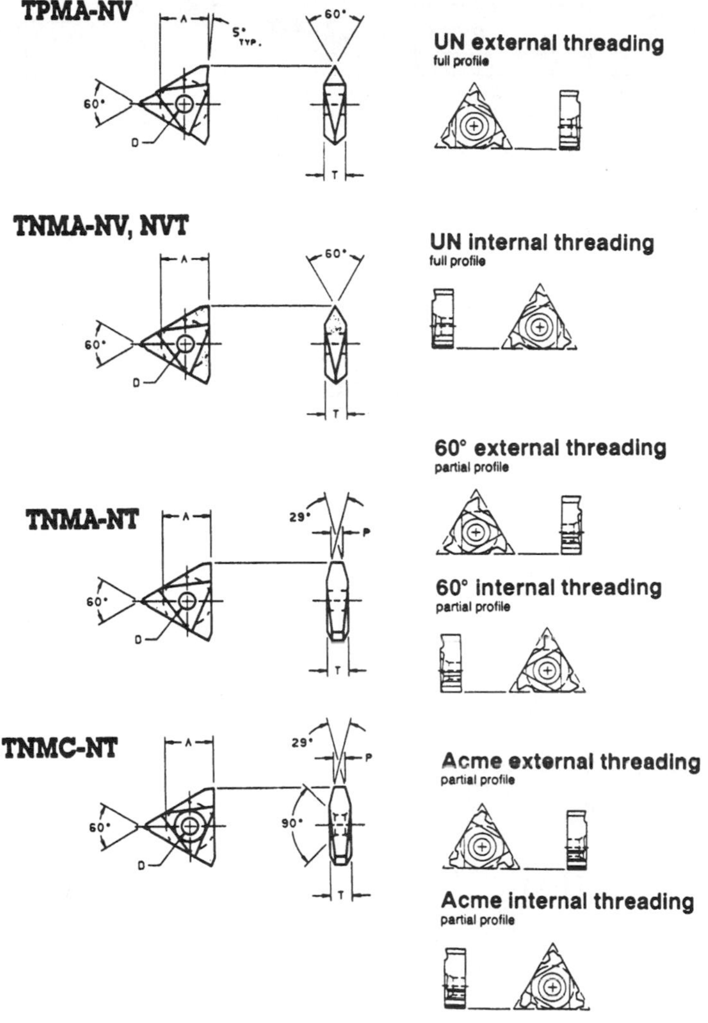

Figure 7.55 Sample inserts and thread-cutting inserts.

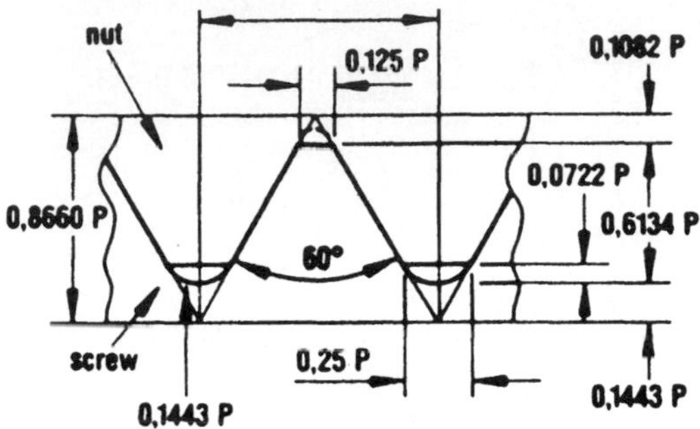

(A) ISO - M (Metric)
UN (Unified National)

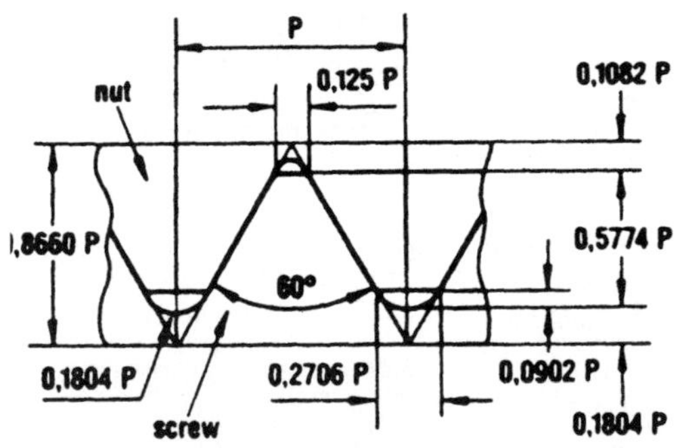

(B) UNJ
(Controlled root radii)

Figure 7.56 Thread systems and dimensional geometry.

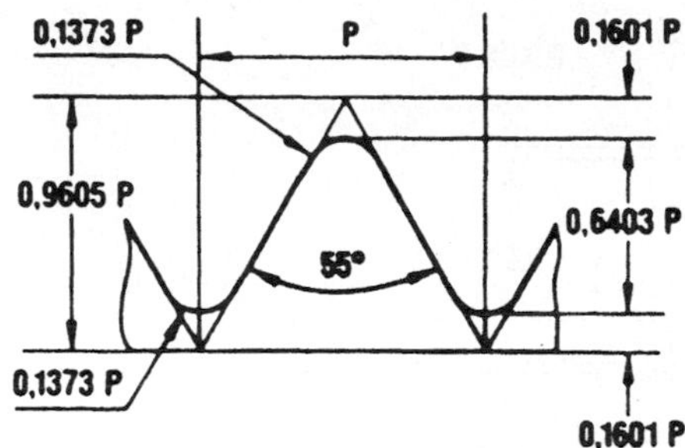

(C) Whitworth (BSW)

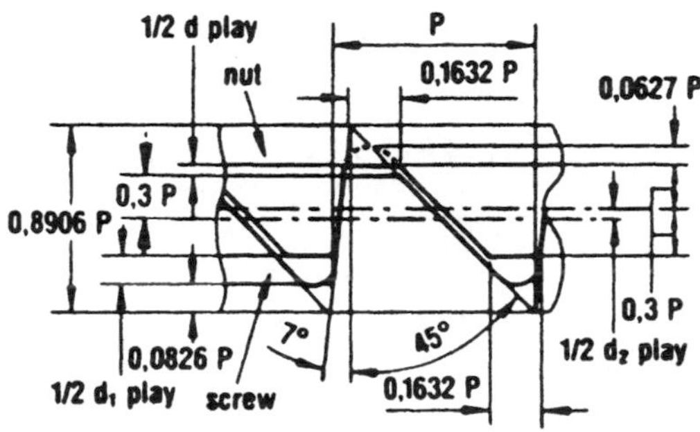

(D) American Buttress (7° face)

Figure 7.56 *(Continued)*

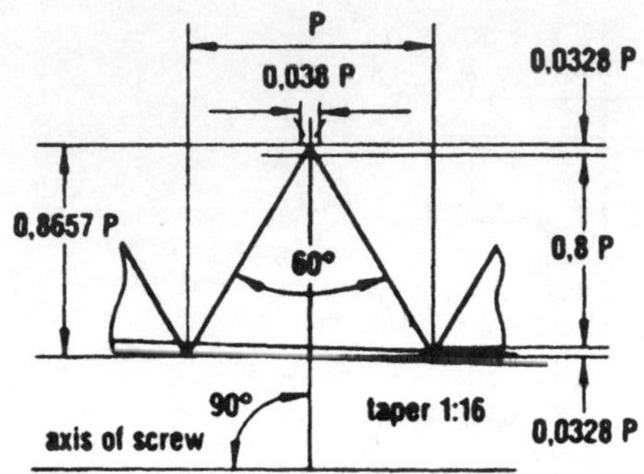

(E) NPT
(American National Pipe Thread)

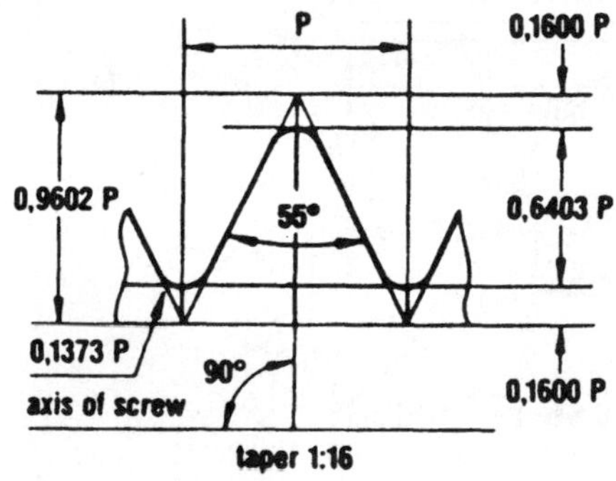

(F) BSPT
(British Standard Pipe Thread)

Figure 7.56 *(Continued)*

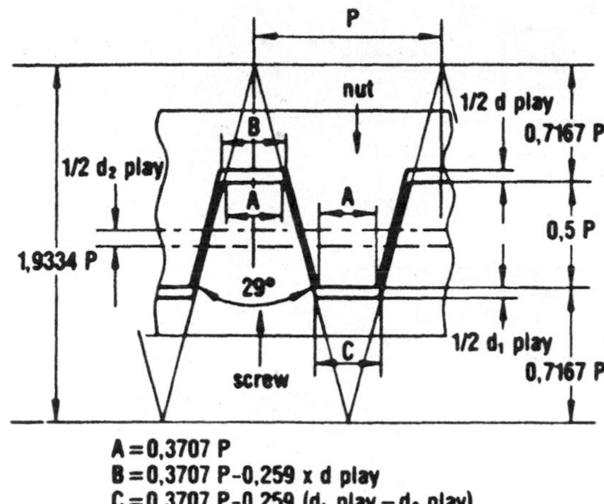

(G) Acme (29°)

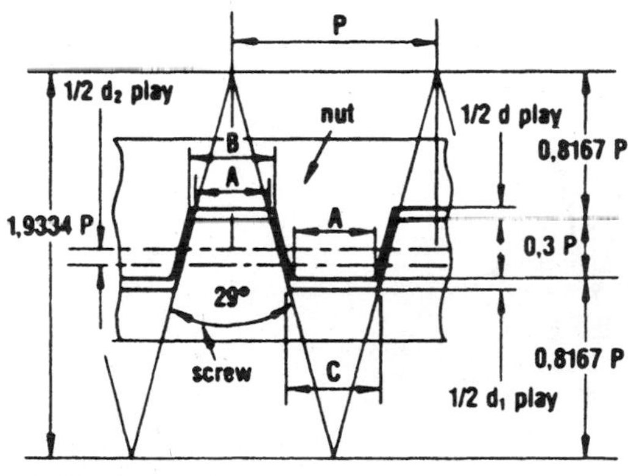

(H) Acme (Stub - 29°)

Figure 7.56 *(Continued)*

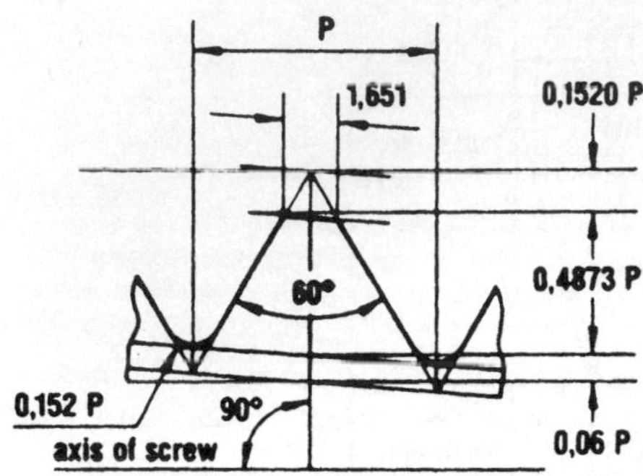

(I) API
Taper: 1:6 (V-0.38" R)

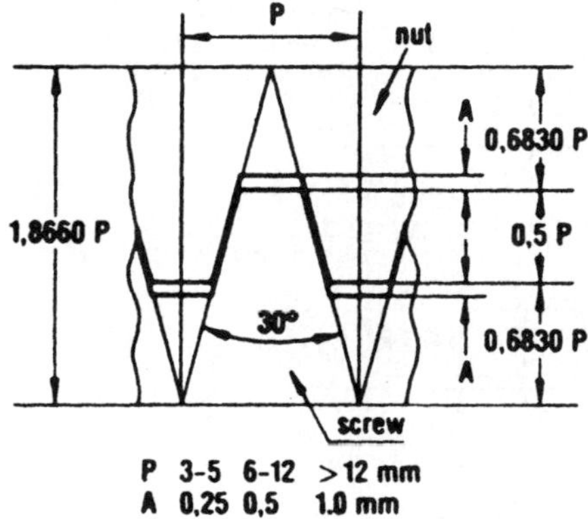

(J) TR DIN 103

Figure 7.56 *(Continued)*

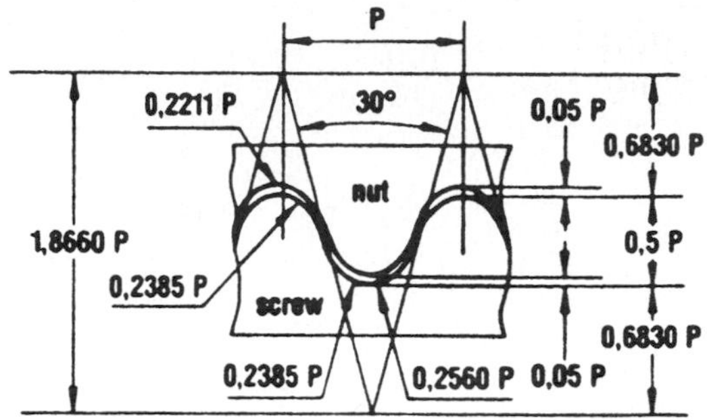

(K) RD DIN 405 (Round)

Figure 7.56 *(Continued)*

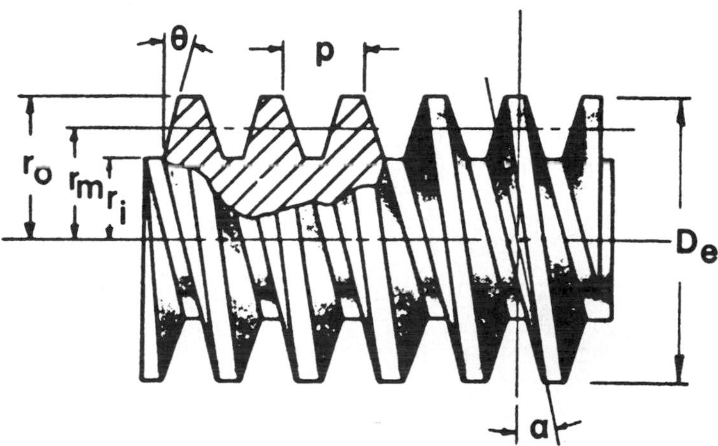

Figure 7.57 Calculating the helix angle.

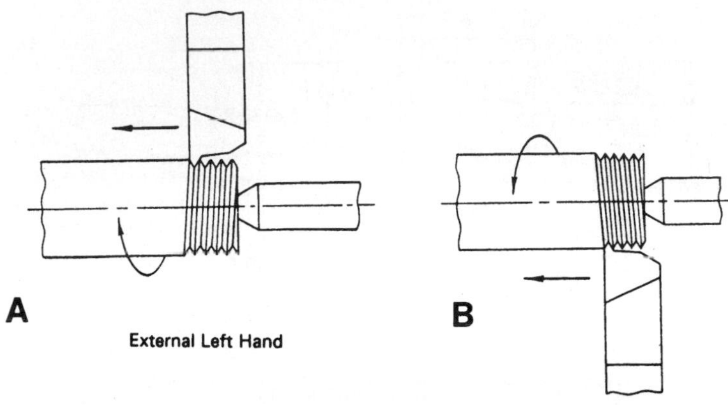

Feed Direction Towards Spindle (Standard Helix)

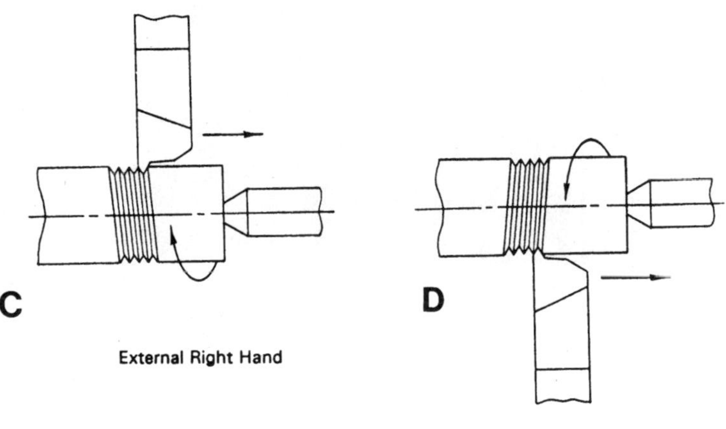

Feed Direction Away from Spindle (Reverse Helix)

Figure 7.58 Thread-cutting procedures, external.

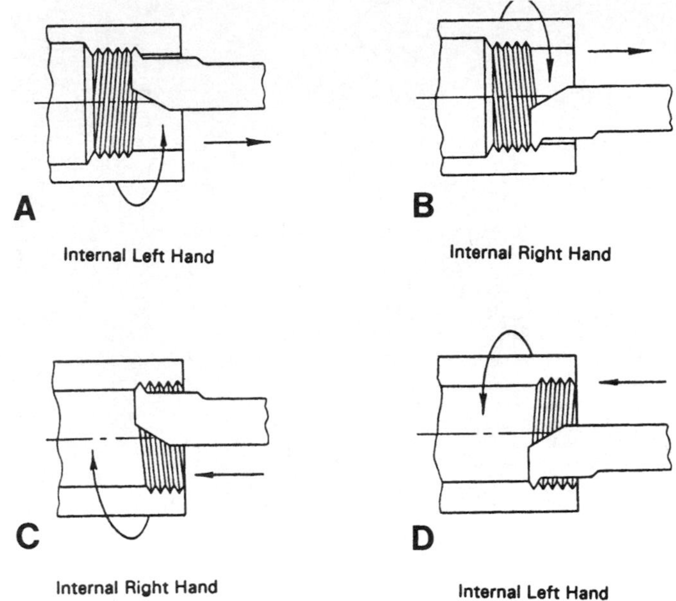

Figure 7.59 Thread-cutting procedures, internal.

Figure 7.60 Modern CNC turning center.

Figure 7.61 Modern CNC turning center.

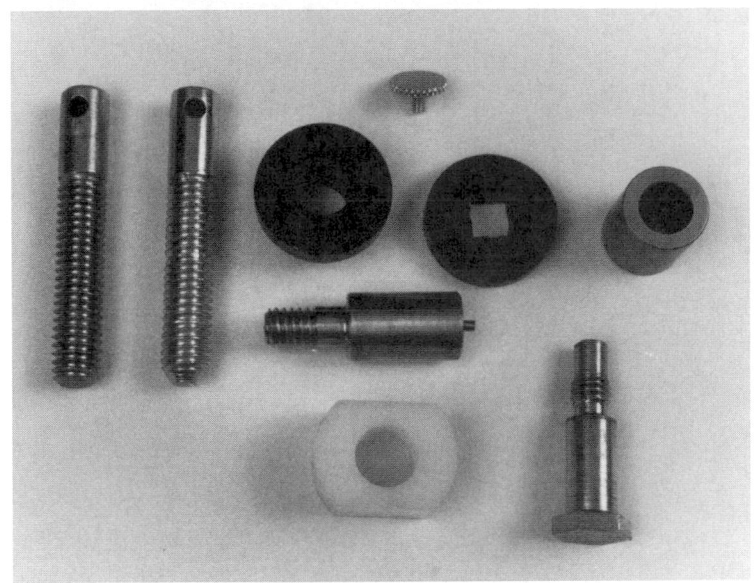
Figure 7.62 Typical CNC machined parts (turned, milled, etc.).

Figure 7.63 A small production manual turret lathe.

Figure 7.64 Large geared-head engine lathe with digital panel.

from the workpiece. The milling process employs relative motion between the workpiece and the rotating cutting tool to generate the required surfaces. In some applications the workpiece is stationary and the cutting tool moves, while in others the cutting tool and the workpiece are moved in relation to each other and to the machine. A characteristic feature of the milling process is that each tooth of the cutting tool takes a portion of the stock in the form of small, individual chips.

Typical cutting tool types for milling-machine operations are shown in Figs. 7.65 and 7.66.

Milling methods

- Peripheral milling (slab milling)
- Face milling and straddle milling
- End milling
- Single-piece milling

- String or “gang” milling
- Slot milling
- Profile milling
- Thread milling
- Worm milling
- Gear milling

Modern milling machines have many forms, but the most common types are shown in Fig. 7.67. The well-known and highly popular Bridgeport-type milling machine is shown in Fig. 7.68. The Bridgeport machine is often used in tool and die making operations and in model shops, where prototype work is done. The great stability and accuracy of the Bridgeport makes this machine popular with many experienced machinists and die makers. The Bridgeport shown in Fig. 7.68*a* is equipped with digital sensing controls and read-out panel, reading to ±0.0005 in. An ongoing Bridgeport milling operation is shown in Fig. 7.68*b*, and the digital read-out panel can be seen at the upper right side of the machine.

A ball-end milling operation is shown in Fig. 7.69, where an aluminum alloy part is being cut on a Bridgeport-type machine. This aluminum part is being manufactured without the use of a cutting solution or coolant. Many of the better grades of aluminum alloys, such as 2024, 6061, and 7075, can be considered free-machining and are often cut without coolants and at high surface speeds (see speeds and feeds section). When cutting solutions and coolants are used for turning or milling aluminum alloys, special formulations are available and may be used (see coolants and cutting solutions section).

A large vertical milling machine is shown in Fig. 7.70. This machine is set up to straddle-mill copper-alloy castings using face mills in a parallel, stacked array in order to make two cuts on two surfaces with one pass of the part through the cutters. In this application, the cast copper parts are positioned in pneumatic clamps in a “gang” or string arrangement. Many parts are thus cut in a single traverse of the horizontal table. Mass-production techniques such as these allow parts to be manufactured more quickly and at less cost. The milling cutters on this machine are of the face-mill removable-carbide insert type, the inserts being made of tungsten carbide with a titanium nitride or titanium carbide coating.

The modern machining center is being used to replace the conventional milling machine in many industrial applications. Figure 7.71 shows a machining center, with its control panel at the right side of the machine. Machines such as these generally cost $250,000 or more depending on the accessories and auxiliary equipment obtained with the machine. These machines are the modern "workhorses" of industry and cannot remain idle for long periods owing to their cost. As described in Chap. 1, these machines are computer-controlled and make their own tool changes automatically during ongoing machining operations. Figure 7.72 shows a typical "gang-milling" operation of aluminum cast parts which are finish bored, drilled, and then tapped while being held in a pneumatically actuated clamping fixture. The pneumatic line can be seen coming into the fixture at the lower right side of the photograph. Four coolant lines are shown directed at the machine spindle in the cutting tool location. These coolant lines move with the tool and spindle during the cutting operation. One needs to see these machines in actual operation to appreciate the great speed and accuracy with which they perform their programmed (CNC) machining functions.

The modern machining center may be equipped for three-, four-, or five-axis operation. The normal or common operations usually call for three-axis machining, while more involved machining procedures require four- or even five-axis operation. Three-axis operation consists of x and y table movements and z-axis vertical spindle movements. The four-axis operation includes the addition of spindle rotation with three-axis operation. Five-axis operation includes a horizontal fixture for rotating the workpiece on a horizontal axis at a predetermined speed (rpms), together with the functions of the four-axis machine. This allows all types of screw threads to be machined on the part and other operations such as producing a worm for worm-gear applications, segment cuts, arcs, etc. Very complex parts may be mass produced economically on a three-, four-, or five-axis machining center, all automatically, using CNC (computer numerical control).

The control panels on these machining centers contain a microprocessor that is, in turn, controlled by a host computer, generally located in the tool or manufacturing engineering office; the host computer controls one or more machines with direct numerical control (DNC) or distributed numerical control. Various machining programs are available for writing the operational instructions sent to the controller on the machining center. Figure 7.73 shows a detailed view of a typical microprocessor (CNC) control panel used on a machining center. This particular control panel is from an Enshu 550-V machining center, a photograph of which appears in Fig. 1.2.

7.2.1 Milling Calculations

The following calculation methods and procedures for milling operations are intended to be guidelines and not *absolute* because of the many variables encountered in actual practice.

Metal-removal rates. The *metal-removal rate R* (sometimes *mrr*) for all types of milling is equal to the volume of metal removed by the cutting process in a given time, usually expressed as cubic inches per minute (in^3/min). Thus,

$$R = WHf$$

where R = metal-removal rate, in^3/min.
W = width of cut, in
H = depth of cut, in
f = feed rate, ipm (in/min)

In peripheral or slab milling, W is measured parallel to the cutter axis and H perpendicular to the axis. In face milling, W is measured perpendicular to the axis and H parallel to the axis.

Feed rate. The speed or rate at which the workpiece moves past the cutter is the *feed rate f,* which is measured in inches per minute (ipm). Thus,

$$f = F_t N C_{rpm}$$

Where f = feed rate, ipm
F_t = feed per tooth (chip thickness), in (also called cpt)
N = number of cutter teeth
C_{rpm} = rotation of the cutter, rpms

Feed per tooth. Production rates of milled parts are directly related to the feed rate that can be used. The feed rate should be as high as possible, considering machine rigidity and power available at the cutter. To prevent overloading the machine drive motor, the *feed per tooth allowable* F_t may be calculated from

$$F_t = \frac{K\text{hp}_c}{NC_{\text{rpm}}WH}$$

where hp_c = horsepower available at the cutter (80 to 90 percent of motor rating), i.e., if motor nameplate states 15 hp, then hp available at the cutter is 0.8 to 0.9 × 15 (80 to 90 percent represents motor efficiency)
K = machinability factor (see Fig. 7.74)

Other symbols are as in preceding equation.

Figure 7.75 gives the suggested feed per tooth for milling using high-speed-steel (HSS) cutters for the various cutter types. For carbide, cermets, and ceramic tools, see the figures in the feeds and speeds section.

Cutting speed. The *cutting speed* of a milling cutter is the peripheral linear speed resulting from the rotation of the cutter. The cutting speed is expressed in feet per minute (fpm, or ft/min) or surface feet per minute (sfpm or sfm) and is determined from

$$S = \frac{\pi D(\text{rpm})}{12}$$

where S = cutting speed, fpm or sfpm (sfpm is also termed spm)
D = outside diameter of the cutter, in
rpm = rotational speed of cutter, rpms

The required rotational speed of the cutter may be found from the following simple equation:

$$\text{rpm} = \frac{S}{(D/12)\pi} \qquad \text{or} \qquad \frac{S}{0.26D}$$

When it is necessary to increase the production rate, it is better to change the cutter material rather than to increase the cutting speed. Increasing the cutting speed alone may shorten the life of the cutter, since the cutter is usually being operated at its maximum speed for optimal productivity.

General rules for selection of the cutting speed

- Use lower cutting speeds for longer tool life.
- Take into account the Brinell hardness of the material.
- Use the lower range of recommended cutting speeds when starting a job.
- For a fine finish, use a lower feed rate in preference to a higher cutting speed.

Number of teeth: Cutter. The number of cutter teeth N required for a particular application may be found from the simple expression (not applicable to carbide or other high-speed cutters)

$$N = \frac{f}{F_t C_{rpm}}$$

where f = feed rate, ipm
F_t = feed per tooth (chip thickness), in
C_{rpm} = rotational speed of cutter, rpms
N = number of cutter teeth

An industry-recommended equation for calculating the number of cutter teeth required for a particular operation is

$$N = 19.5\sqrt{R} - 5.8$$

where N = number of cutter teeth
R = radius of cutter, in

This simple equation is suitable for HSS cutters only and is not valid for carbide, cobalt cast alloy, or other high-speed cutting tool materials.

Figure 7.76 gives recommended cutting speed ranges (sfpm) for HSS cutters. See the figures in feeds and speeds section for carbide, cermet, ceramic, and other high-speed advanced cutting materials.

Milling horsepower. Ratios for metal removal per horsepower (cubic inches per minute per horsepower at the milling cutter) have been given for various materials (see Fig. 7.74). The general equation is

$$K = \frac{\text{in}^3/\text{min}}{\text{hp}_c} = \frac{WHf}{\text{hp}_c}$$

where K = metal removal factor, $\text{in}^3/\text{min}/\text{hp}_c$ (see Fig. 7.74)
hp_c = horsepower at the cutter
W = width of cut, in
H = depth of cut, in
f = feed rate, ipm

The total horsepower required at the cutter may then be expressed as

$$\text{hp}_c = \frac{\text{in}^3/\text{min}}{K} \qquad \text{or} \qquad \frac{WHf}{K}$$

The K factor varies with type and hardness of material, and for the same material varies with the feed per tooth, increasing as the chip thickness increases. The K factor represents a particular rate of metal removal and not a general or average rate. For a quick approximation of total power requirements at the machine motor, see Fig. 7.77, which gives the maximum metal-removal rates for different horsepower-rated milling machines cutting different materials.

7.2.2 Feeds and speeds for milling with advanced cutting tool materials

This section presents the feeds and speeds with which materials may be milled using the carbide, cermet, ceramic, and advanced cutting tool materials such as cubic boron nitride (CBN) that are widely used in industry today. Cutting tool technology has advanced rapidly, and new tools and materials are being made available at a rapid pace. Nevertheless, the data presented here are the latest available at the date of publication of this *Handbook*.

Modern theory of milling. The key characteristics of the milling process are

- Simultaneous motion of cutter rotation and feed movement of the workpiece

- Interrupted cut
- Production of tapered chips

It was common practice for many years in the industry to mill *against* the direction of feed. This was due to the type of tool materials then available (HSS) and the absence of antibacklash devices on the machines. This method became known as *conventional* or *up milling* and is illustrated in Fig. 7.78*b*. *Climb milling* or *down milling* is now the preferred method of milling with advanced cutting tool materials such as carbides, cermets, CBN, etc. Climb milling is illustrated in Fig. 7.78*a*. Here, the insert enters the cut with some chip load and proceeds to produce a chip that thins as it progresses toward the end of the cut. This allows the heat generated in the cutting process to dissipate into the chip. Climb-milling forces push the workpiece toward the clamping fixture, in the direction of the feed. Conventional-milling (up-milling) forces are against the direction of feed and produce a lifting force on the workpiece and clamping fixture.

The angle of entry is determined by the position of the cutter centerline in relation to the edge of the workpiece. A negative angle of entry β is preferred and is illustrated in Fig. 7.79*b*, where the centerline of the cutter is below the edge of the workpiece. A negative angle is preferred because it ensures contact with the workpiece at the strongest point of the insert cutter. A positive angle of entry will increase insert chipping. If a positive angle of entry must be employed, use an insert with a honed or negative land.

Figure 7.80 shows an eight-tooth cutter climb-milling a workpiece using a negative angle of entry, and the feed, or advance, per revolution is 0.048 in with a chip load per tooth of 0.006 in. The following milling formulas will allow you to calculate the various milling parameters.

In the following formulas,

$$nt = \text{number of teeth or inserts in the cutter}$$

$$\text{cpt} = \text{chip load per tooth or insert, in}$$

$$\text{ipm} = \text{feed, inches per minute}$$

$$\text{fpr} = \text{feed (advance) per revolution, in}$$

$$D = \text{cutter effective cutting diameter, in}$$

rpm = revolutions per minute

sfpm = surface feet per minute (also termed sfm)

$$\text{sfpm} = \frac{\pi D(\text{rpm})}{12} \qquad \text{rpm} = \frac{12(\text{sfpm})}{\pi D} \qquad \text{fpr} = \frac{\text{ipm}}{\text{rpm}}$$

$$\text{ipm} = \text{cpt} \times \text{nt} \times \text{rpm} \qquad \text{cpt} = \frac{\text{ipm}}{nt(\text{rpm})} \quad \text{or} \quad \frac{\text{fpr}}{nt}$$

Example Given a cutter of 5 in diameter, eight teeth, 500 sfpm, and 0.007 cpt,

$$\text{rpm} = \frac{12 \times 500}{3.1415 \times 5} = 382$$

$$\text{ipm} = 0.007 \times 8 \times 382 = 21.4 \text{ in}$$

$$\text{fpr} = \frac{21.4}{382} = 0.056 \text{ in}$$

Slotting. Special consideration is given for slot milling, and the following equations may be used effectively to calculate chip load per tooth (cpt) and inches per minute (ipm):

$$\text{cpt} = \frac{\left(\dfrac{\sqrt{(D-x)x}}{r}\right)\left(\dfrac{\text{ipm}}{\text{rpm}}\right)}{\text{number of effective teeth}}$$

$$\text{ipm} = \text{rpm} \times \text{number of effective teeth} \left(\frac{\text{cpt}}{\dfrac{\sqrt{(D-x)x}}{r}}\right)$$

where D = diameter of slot cutter, in
r = radius of cutter, in
x = depth of slot, in
cpt = chip load per tooth, in
ipm = feed, inches per minute
rpm = rotational speed of cutter, rpms

Milling horsepower for advanced cutting tool materials

Horsepower consumption. It is advantageous to calculate the milling operational horsepower requirements before starting a job. Lower-

(Text continued on page 617.)

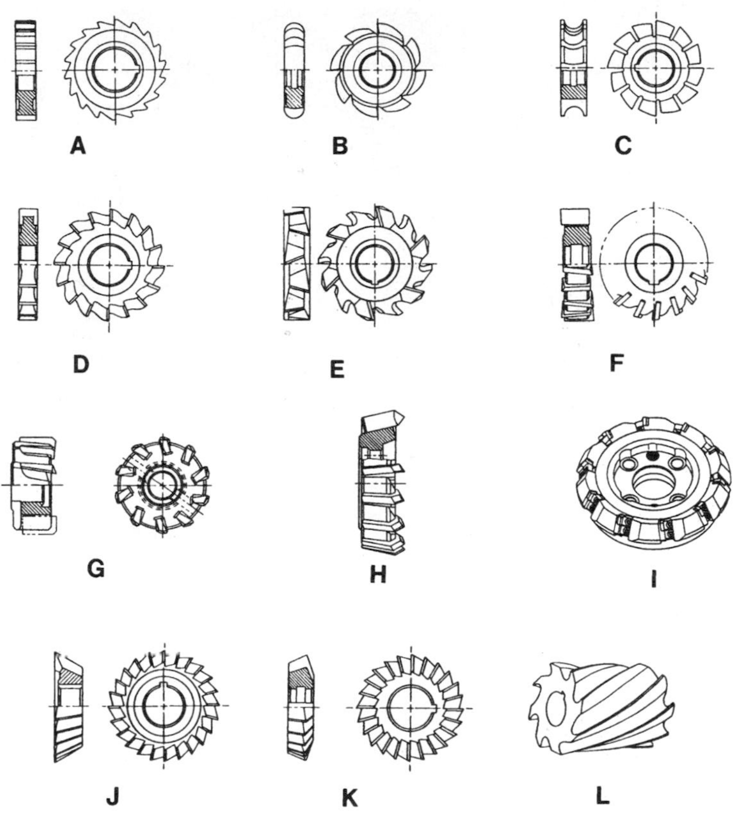

Milling Cutter Styles - High-Speed Steel and Carbide Insert

A Disk type milling cutter
B Convex half-round milling cutter
C Concave half-round milling cutter
D Three-side milling cutter
E Staggered-tooth milling cutter
F Inserted blade milling cutter
G Face milling cutter
H Face milling head
I Double-angle carbide insert milling cutter
J Single-angle milling cutter
K Double-angle milling cutter
L Left hand slab milling cutter

Figure 7.65 Typical milling cutters.

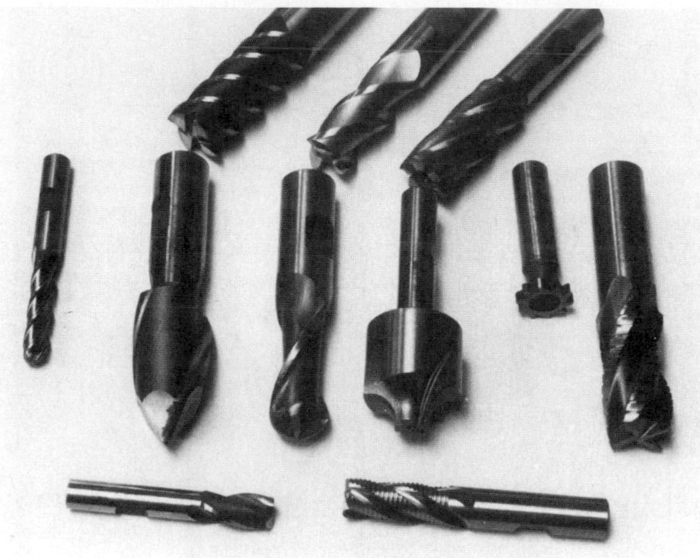

Figure 7.66 Samples of end-milling cutters.

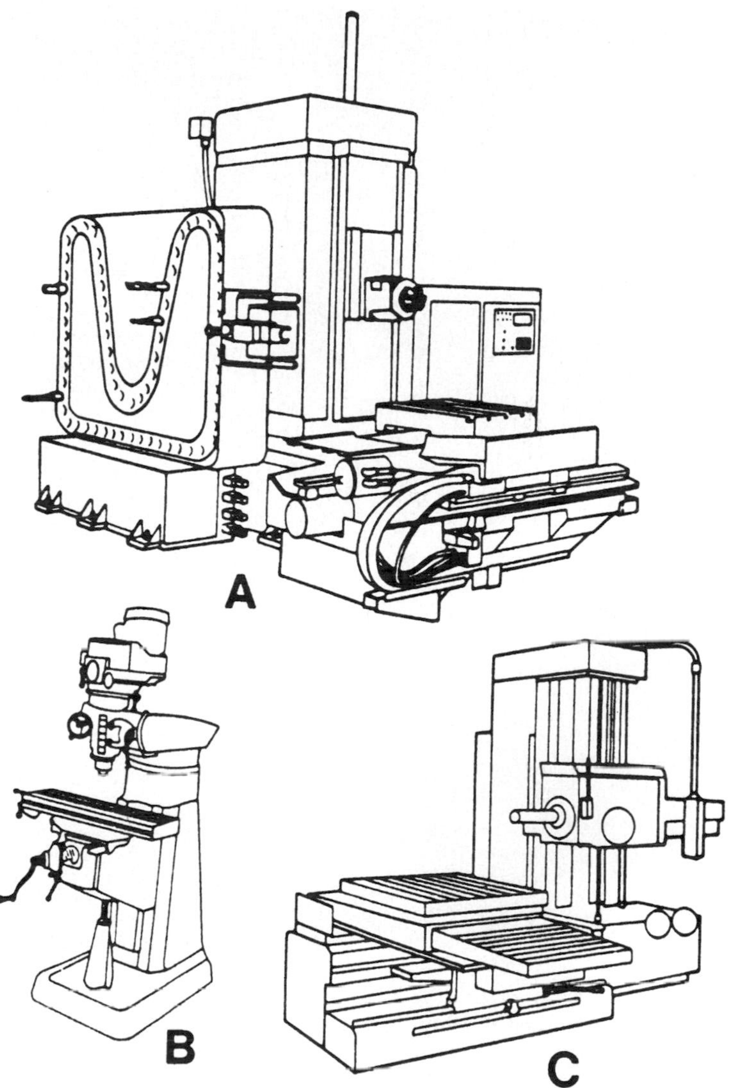

Figure 7.67 Types of milling machines.

(a)

Figure 7.68 (*a*) The popular Bridgeport universal milling machine. (*b*) Close-up of milling operation showing digital panel.

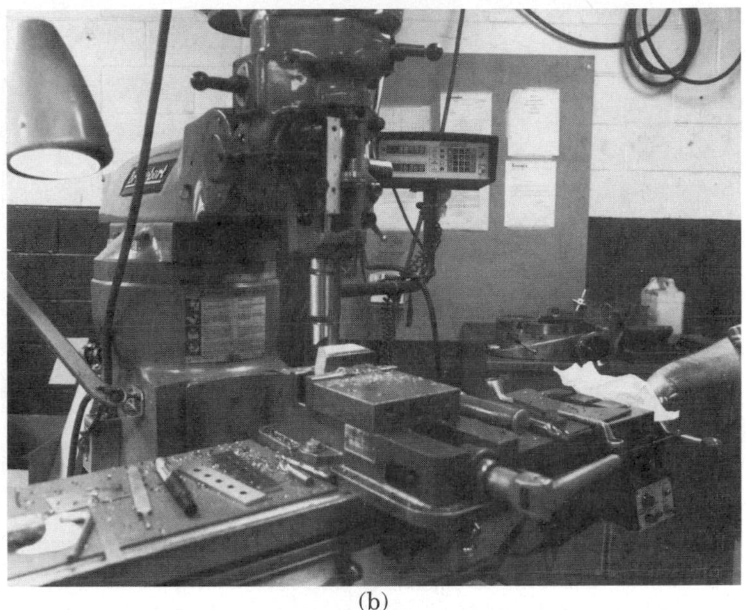

(b)

Figure 7.68 (*Continued*)

Figure 7.69 Close-up of ball-milling operation on an aluminum-alloy part.

Figure 7.70 Large milling machine, shown straddle-milling production parts.

Figure 7.71 Vertical machining center in operation.

Figure 7.72 Close-up of production milling, pallet-mounted parts.

Figure 7.73 The CNC control panel of a vertical machining center.

(K) Factor for Various Materials

Material	K(in³/min/(hp$_c$))
Cold drawn steel, SAE 1112, 1120, 1315	1.0
Forged and alloy steel, SAE 3120, 1020, 2320, 2345, 150-300 BHN	0.63 - 0.87
Alloy steel, 300 - 400 BHN	0.5
Malleable iron and cold drawn steel, SAE 6140	0.9
Cast irons:	
Soft	1.5
Medium	0.8 - 1.0
Hard	0.6 - 0.8
Stainless steel, AISI 416, free-machining	1.1
Stainless steel, austenitic, AISI 303, free-machining	0.83
Stainless steel, austenitic, AISI 304	0.72
Tool steel	0.51
Bronze and brass:	
Soft	1.7- 2.5
Medium	1.0 - 1.4
Hard	0.6 - 1.0
Aluminum and magnesium	2.5 - 4.0
Monel metal	0.55
Copper, annealed	0.84
Nickel	0.53
Titanium & alloys	0.75 - 1.1

NOTE: "K" values are in cubic inches per minute per cutter horsepower (in³/min/hp$_c$)

Figure 7.74 *K* factor table.

Suggested Feed per Tooth for Milling - High-Speed Steel Cutters (Tabulated Data in Inches)

Material	Face mills	Helical mills	Slot/side mills	End mills	Form-relieved cutters
Magnesium & alloys	0.022	0.018	0.013	0.011	0.007
Aluminum & Alloys	0.022	0.018	0.013	0.011	0.007
Free-cutting brasses & bronzes	0.022	0.018	0.013	0.011	0.007
Medium brasses & bronzes	0.014	0.011	0.008	0.007	0.004
Hard brasses & bronzes	0.009	0.007	0.006	0.005	0.003
Copper	0.012	0.010	0.007	0.006	0.004
Cast iron, soft (150-180 Bhn)	0.016	0.013	0.009	0.008	0.005
Cast iron, medium (180-220 Bhn)	0.013	0.010	0.007	0.007	0.004
Cast iron, hard (220-300 Bhn)	0.011	0.008	0.006	0.006	0.003
Malleable iron	0.012	0.010	0.007	0.006	0.004
Cast steel	0.012	0.010	0.007	0.006	0.004
Low-carbon steel, free-machining	0.012	0.010	0.007	0.006	0.004
Low-carbon steels	0.010	0.008	0.006	0.005	0.003
Medium-carbon steels	0.010	0.008	0.006	0.005	0.003
Alloy steel, ann'ld (180-220 Bhn)	0.008	0.007	0.005	0.004	0.003
Alloy steel, tough (220-300 Bhn)	0.006	0.005	0.004	0.003	0.002
Alloy steel, hard (300-400 Bhn)	0.004	0.003	0.003	0.002	0.002
Stainless steels, free-machining	0.010	0.008	0.006	0.005	0.003
Stainless steels	0.006	0.005	0.004	0.003	0.002
Monel metal	0.008	0.007	0.005	0.004	0.003
Titanium & alloys	0.008	0.007	0.005	0.004	0.003
Machinable plastics	0.013	0.010	0.008	0.007	0.004

NOTE: Tabular data in inches. For feed per tooth in millimeters, multiply tabular data by 25.4. For carbon-steel cutters, multiply tabular data by 0.50 or divide by 2. Source: Cincinnati Milicron, Inc.

Figure 7.75 Milling feed table, HSS.

Milling Cutting Speeds for Various Materials (sfpm) Surface feet per minute (High-speed steel tools only)

Material	High-speed steel tools Rough	Finish
Cast iron	50 - 60	80 - 110
Semisteel	40 - 50	65 - 90
Malleable iron	80 - 100	110 - 130
Cast steel	45 - 60	70 - 90
Copper	100 - 150	150 - 200
Brass	200 - 300	200 - 300
Bronze	100 - 150	150 - 180
Aluminum	400 - 450	700 - 750
* Magnesium	600 - 800	1,000 - 1,500
SAE steels:		
1020 (coarse feed), low-carbon	60 - 80	60 - 80
1020 (fine feed), low-carbon	100 - 120	100 - 120
1035, medium-carbon	75 - 90	90 - 120
1330, alloy steel	90 - 110	90 - 110
1050, Med-high-carbon	60 - 80	100 - 125
2315, nickel steel	90 - 110	90 - 110
3150, nickel-chromium	50 - 60	70 - 90
4150, chrome-molybdenum	40 - 50	70 - 90
4340, nickel-chrome-molybdenum	40 - 50	60 - 70
Stainless steel	60 - 80	100 - 120
Titanium, hard alloy	80 - 100	110 - 130

NOTE: Tabular data ranges are in sfpm (surface feet per minute for HSS cutters only).
* A fire hazard is present when machining magnesium at high-speeds.

Figure 7.76 Milling cutting speeds, HSS.

Milling-Machine Horsepower Ratings - for maximum metal removal rates (in³/min) for HSS (high-speed steel cutters)

Workpiece Material	Rated hp of Machine: 3	5	7.5	10	15	20	25	30	40	50
	Max. Metal Removal (in³/min)									
Aluminum	2.7	5.5	8.7	12	18	27	37	48	69	91
Brass, soft	2.4	4.7	7.5	10	16	24	32	41	60	79
Bronze, hard	1.7	3.3	5.3	7.3	11	17	23	30	43	56
Bronze, very hard	0.78	1.6	2.5	3.4	5.3	7.8	11	15	20	26
Cast iron, soft	1.6	3.2	5.2	7.1	11	16	22	28	41	54
Cast iron, hard	1	2	3.3	4.6	7	10	14	18	26	35
Cast iron, chilled	0.78	1.6	2.5	3.4	5.3	7.8	10	13	19	26
Malleable iron	1	2.1	3.4	4.7	7.3	11	14	18	26	36
Steel, soft	1	2	3.3	4.6	7	10	14	18	26	35
Steel, medium	0.78	1.6	2.5	3.4	5.3	7.8	10	13	19	26
Steel, hard	0.56	1.1	1.8	2.5	3.9	5.7	7.7	10	14	19

NOTE: Data source - Kearney & Trecker Corp.

Figure 7.77 Milling machine horsepower ratings.

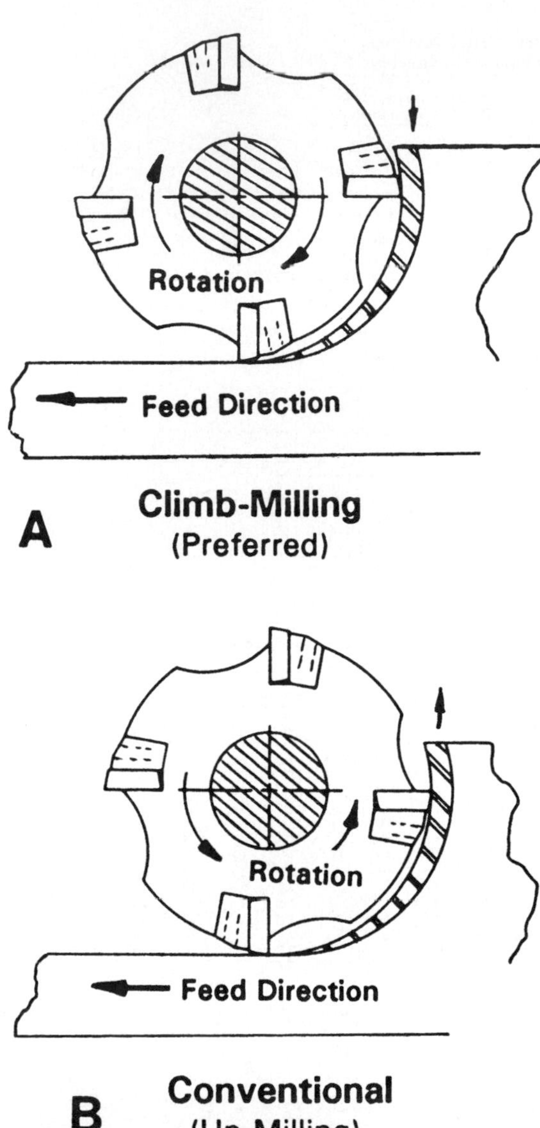

Figure 7.78 Climb- and up-milling.

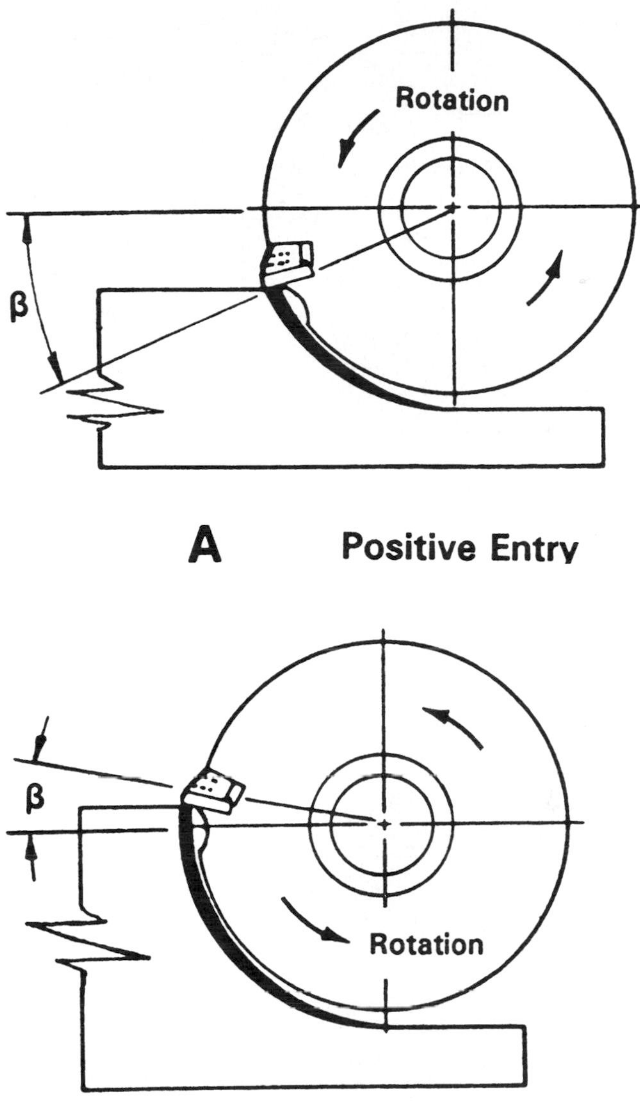

Figure 7.79 Milling entry angles.

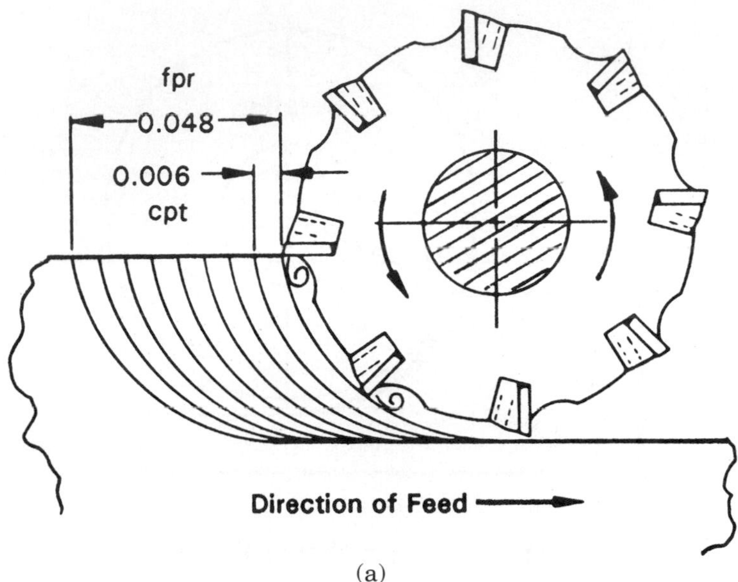

(a)

Power Constant Factor (P_f) for Milling Various Materials

P_f = cubic inches of metal removal per single horsepower

Material	P_f Factor
Free-machining aluminum alloys	0.20
Gray cast irons	0.25
Non-ferrous free-machining alloys	0.45
Alloy cast irons and ductile irons	0.50
Martensitic stainless steels	0.81
Titanium	0.87
Free-machining carbon steel	0.89
Standard carbon steel	0.92
Alloy steels	0.95
Austenitic stainless steel	0.96
High-temperature alloys	1.00
Tool steels	1.05
Cobalt based alloys	1.20

Note: The P_f factors will vary per feed rate (ipm) and Brinell hardness (Bhn).
The P_f factors in the table are for normal feed rates and material hardness ranges to 285 Bhn.
A 15 hp spindle-rated mill should be able to machine 15 x 0.92 = 13.8 cubic inches of standard plain carbon steel per minute.

(b)

Figure 7.80 (*a*) Milling principle. (*b*) Power constants for milling.

horsepower machining centers take advantage of the ability of the modern cutting tools to cut at extremenly high surface speeds (sfpm). Knowing your machine's speed and feed limits could be critical to your obtaining the desired productivity goals. The condition of your milling machine is also critical to obtaining these productivity goals. Older machines with low-spindle-speed capability should use the uncoated grades of carbide cutters and inserts.

Horsepower calculation. A popular equation used in industry for calculating horsepower at the spindle is

$$\text{hp} = \frac{M_{rr} P_f}{E_s}$$

where M_{rr} = metal removal rate, in^3/min
P_f = power constant factor (see Fig. 7.80*a*)
E_s = spindle efficiency, 0.80 to 0.90 (80 to 90 percent)

Note: The spindle efficiency is a reflection of losses from the machine's motor to actual power delivered at the cutter and must be taken into account, as the equation shows.

A table of P_f factors is shown in Fig. 7.80*a* and represents the number of cubic inches of material that may be removed per each (1) horsepower input at the spindle or cutter for different types of materials.

Note: The metal removal rate (M_{rr}) = depth of cut × width of cut × ipm = in^3/min.

Axial cutting forces at various lead angles. Axial cutting forces vary as you change the lead angle of the cutting insert. The 0° lead angle produces the minimum axial force into the part. This is advantageous for weak fixtures and thin web sections. The 45° lead angle loads the spindle with the maximum axial force, which is advantageous when using the older machines.

Tangential cutting forces. The use of a tangential force equation is appropriate for finding the approximate forces that fixtures, part walls or webs, and the spindle bearings are subjected to during the milling operation. The tangential force is easily calculated when you have determined the horsepower being used at the spindle or cutter. It is important to remember that the tangential forces decrease as the spindle speed (rpms) increases, i.e., at higher surface feet per minute. The ability of the newer advanced cutting tools to operate at higher speeds thus produces fewer fixture and web-deflecting forces with a decrease in horsepower requirements for any particular machine. Some of the new high-speed cutter inserts can operate efficiently at speeds of 10,000 sfpm or higher when machining such materials as free-machining aluminum and magnesium alloys.

The tangential force developed during the milling operations may be calculated from

$$t_f = \frac{126{,}000\text{hp}}{D(\text{rpm})}$$

where t_f = tangential force, pounds force
hp = horsepower at the spindle or cutter
D = effective diameter of cutter, in
rpm = rotational speed in revolutions per minute

The preceding calculation procedure for finding the tangential forces developed on the workpiece being cut may be used in conjunction with the clamping fixture types and clamping calculations shown in Chap. 9, "Tooling Practices."

7.2.3 Feeds and speeds tables: Advanced cutting tools and inserts

The following speeds and feeds tables are for use with the advanced cutting tool materials and inserts. These tables are reproduced with the permission of Kennametal, Inc.

Note: Figure 7.95 shows how to apply the range of conditions given in the feeds and speeds tables.

Free-machining carbon steels: See Fig. 7.81.

Plain carbon steels: See Fig. 7.82.

Tool steels: See Fig. 7.83.

Alloy steels: See Fig. 7.84

Cast irons (gray, nodular, and malleable): See Fig. 7.85.

Alloy cast irons and ductile irons: See Fig. 7.86.

Austenitic stainless steels: See Fig. 7.87.

Martensitic and ferritic stainless steels: See Fig. 7.88

Cobalt-base alloys: See Fig. 7.89.

High-temperature alloys: See Fig. 7.90.

Titanium: See Fig. 7.91.

Free-machining aluminum alloys: See Fig. 7.92.

Nonferrous free-machining alloys: See Fig. 7.93.

Nonmetallics: See Fig. 7.94.

How to apply the range of conditions for the preceding feeds and speeds tables is shown in Fig. 7.95. Figure 7.95*a* describes the characteristics of the Kennametal insert grades shown in the speeds and feeds tables. A chart of carbide-insert grade comparisons for different manufacturers is shown in Fig. 7.95*b*. Insert-grade comparisons may be made using this chart, although the chart is a guide *only* and indicates those grades having similar properties under most conditions. It is not intended to imply that all cross-referenced grades are exact duplicates in physical and metallurgical characteristics or that they perform equally in the same applications.

Cutter speed (rpm) from surface speed (sfpm). A time saving table of surface speed versus cutter speed is shown in Fig. 7.96 for cutter diameters from 0.25 through 5 in. For cutter speed (rpm) values when the surface speed is greater than 200 sfpm, use the simple equation

$$\text{rpm} = \frac{12(\text{sfpm})}{\pi D}$$

where D is the effective diameter of cutter in inches.

7.2.4 Milling accessories

Many types of accessories are available for various milling capabilities, and a few basic ones are shown here. Figure 7.97 shows the widely used horizontal dividing and angle-setting tool. With this accessory, you may divide the circle into an equal number of divisions or set any horizontal angle from a particular baseline or starting point. The vernier on this device will set an angle within ±15 minutes of arc. The clamping table or surface of this device can be rotated a full 360°.

(*Text continued on page 627.*)

work material	grade	starting conditions for general purpose milling		range of conditions	
		speed (sfm)	feed (cpt)	speed (sfm)	feed (cpt)
free-machining carbon steels: AISI 1100 and 1200 series steels suggested machining conditions based on a machinability index range of 80-100 and a hardness range of 140-190 BHN	K420	400	.008	300-600	.005-.012
	K2884	450	.006	300-700	.004-.010
	KC950	600	.007	450-1500	.004-.010
	KC850	500	.008	450-1200	.004-.015
	KC710	500	.006	350-1200	.004-.010
	KT150	400	.005	350-1400	.003-.008

Figure 7.81 (Reproduced with permission of Kennametal Inc.)

work material	grade	starting conditions for general purpose milling		range of conditions	
		speed (sfm)	feed (cpt)	speed (sfm)	feed (cpt)
plain carbon steels: AISI 1000 series steels suggested machining conditions based on a machinability index range of 80-100 and a hardness range of 185-240 BHN	K420	400	.007	300-600	.005-.012
	K2884	450	.005	300-700	.004-.010
	KC950	600	.006	450-1500	.004-.010
	KC850	500	.007	450-1200	.004-.015
	KC710	500	.005	350-1200	.004-.010
	KT150	400	.004	350-1400	.003-.008

Figure 7.82 (Reproduced with permission of Kennametal Inc.)

work material	grade	starting conditions for general purpose milling		range of conditions	
		speed (sfm)	feed (cpt)	speed (sfm)	feed (cpt)
tool steels: wrought high speed, shock-resistant hot and cold worked material suggested machining conditions based on a machinability index range of 40-60 and a hardness range of 200-330 BHN	K420	350	.006	300-500	.005-.010
	K2884	400	.005	300-500	.004-.008
	KC950	500	.006	400-1000	.004-.008
	KC850	400	.007	400-800	.004-.010
	KC710	400	.005	300-800	.004-.008
	KT150	350	.004	250-800	.003-.006
330-450 BHN	KT150	300	.003	200-600	.003-.006
	K090	900	.004	700-1500	.003-.006
450-700 BHN	K090	500	.004	400-700	.003-.006
	KD120	600	.004	400-800	.003-.008
	KD200	600	.006	250-800	.003-.010

Figure 7.83 (Reproduced with permission of Kennametal Inc.)

work material	grade	starting conditions for general purpose milling		range of conditions	
		speed (sfm)	feed (cpt)	speed (sfm)	feed (cpt)
alloy steels: AISI 1300, 4000, 5000, 6000, 8000 and 9000 series steels. suggested machining conditions based on a machinability index range of 80-100 and a hardness range of 190-330 BHN	K1	300	.005	200-400	.004-.010
	K420	400	.006	300-600	.005-.012
	K2884	400	.005	300-600	.004-.010
	KC950	550	.006	400-1200	.004-.010
	KC850	450	.007	400-1000	.004-.012
	KC710	400	.005	350-900	.004-.009
	KT150	400	.004	300-1000	.003-.006
330-450 BHN	KT150	400	.003	200-600	.003-.006
	K090	900	.004	700-1800	.003-.006
450-700 BHN	K090	700	.004	450-1500	.003-.006
	KD120	600	.004	350-800	.003-.008
	KD200	600	.006	250-900	.003-.010

Figure 7.84 (Reproduced with permission of Kennametal Inc.)

work material	grade	starting conditions for general purpose milling		range of conditions	
		speed (sfm)	feed (cpt)	speed (sfm)	feed (cpt)
cast irons: gray, nodular, malleable. suggested machining conditions based upon a machinability index range of 68-78 and a hardness range of 190-330 BHN	K8735	400	.005	300-500	.003-.012
	KC950	800	.008	700-1800	.004-.015
	KC910	700	.006	700-1800	.003-.012
	KT150	1500	.005	300-2500	.003-.010
	K090	2500	.004	1500-4500	.003-.008
	Kyon 3000	2500	.006	1500-4500	.004-.012
330-450 BHN	K090	1200	.004	1000-3000	.003-.008
	Kyon 3000	1200	.006	1000-3000	.004-.012
450-700 BHN	K090	700	.004	500-1500	.003-.008
	Kyon 3000	700	.006	500-1500	.004-.012
	KD120	400	.005	300-600	.004-.010
	KD200	500	.008	300-900	.004-.015

Figure 7.85 (Reproduced with permission of Kennametal Inc.)

work material	grade	starting conditions for general purpose milling		range of conditions	
		speed (sfm)	feed (cpt)	speed (sfm)	feed (cpt)
alloy cast irons and ductile irons: that produce a curled chip; suggested machining conditions based on a hardness range of 140-260 BHN	K45 K420 K2884	475	.005	300-600	.004-.012
	KC060	700	.006	600-1000	.004-.012
	KC910	700	.005	600-1300	.004-.010
	KC850	550	.008	400-1000	.005-.015
	KC250	475	.008	400-700	.005-.015
	KT150	1000	.005	300-1800	.003-.010
	K090	1500	.004	1200-3000	.003-.008

Figure 7.86 (Reproduced with permission of Kennametal Inc.)

work material	grade	starting conditions for general purpose milling		range of conditions	
		speed (sfm)	feed (cpt)	speed (sfm)	feed (cpt)
austenitic stainless steels: wrought 200 and 300 series stainless steels; suggested machining conditions based upon a machinability index range of 35-50 and a hardness range of 140-190 BHN	K1 K68 K8735 K313	400	.005	300-650	.004-.010
	KC850	600	.007	300-1000	.005-.015
	KC250	500	.007	300-700	.005-.015
	KT150	700	.005	400-1200	.003-.010
	K090	1200	.005	900-1800	.003-.008

Figure 7.87 (Reproduced with permission of Kennametal Inc.)

work material	grade	starting conditions for general purpose milling		range of conditions	
		speed (sfm)	feed (cpt)	speed (sfm)	feed (cpt)
martensitic and ferritic stainless steels: wrought 400 and 500 series and PH stainless steels; suggested machining conditions based upon a machinability index range of 45-55 and a hardness range of 175-210 BHN	K45 K420 K2884	400	.005	225-600	.004-.010
	KC950	650	.006	450-900	.004-.010
	KC850	600	.008	400-800	.005-.012
	KC250	450	.008	300-700	.005-.015
	KT150	700	.005	500-1000	.003-.010
	K090	1200	.005	900-2000	.003-.008

Figure 7.88 (Reproduced with permission of Kennametal Inc.)

work material	grade	starting conditions for general purpose milling		range of conditions	
		speed (sfm)	feed (cpt)	speed (sfm)	feed (cpt)
cobalt based: (example) Haynes alloy 25 Stellite	K1 K68 K8735 K313	80	.005	60-150	.003-.008
	K090	1000	.005	800-1500	.003-.008
	KD200	850	.007	400-1200	.005-.010

Figure 7.89 (Reproduced with permission of Kennametal Inc.)

work material	grade	starting conditions for general purpose milling		range of conditions	
		speed (sfm)	feed (cpt)	speed (sfm)	feed (cpt)
high-temperature alloys: iron and nickel base; suggested machining conditions based on a machinability index range of 15-30 and a hardness range of 200-260 BHN (example) Inconel 718, Incoloy 901, Waspaloy A286	K1 K68 K8735 K313	100	.007	90-300	.003-.015
	KC250	200	.007	150-270	.005-.015
	KT150	600	.005	450-1200	.003-.010
	K090	1000	.005	900-1800	.003-.008
	Kyon 2000	1200	.006	700-1600	.004-.012
260-450 BHN	K1 K68 K8735 K313	100	.005	90-225	.003-.010
	KC250	110	.005	90-150	.003-.012
	KT150	400	.005	300-900	.003-.010
	K090	900	.004	700-1500	.003-.008
	Kyon 2000	800	.005	700-1200	.004-.012
	KD120	700	.004	600-900	.004-.010

Figure 7.90 (Reproduced with permission of Kennametal Inc.)

work material	grade	starting conditions for general purpose milling		range of conditions	
		speed (sfm)	feed (cpt)	speed (sfm)	feed (cpt)
titanium: Ti_6Al_4V	K68	200	.005	150-450	.003-.010
	K1 K313	175	.006	125-400	.004-.015

Figure 7.91 (Reproduced with permission of Kennametal Inc.)

work material	grade	starting conditions for general purpose milling		range of conditions	
		speed (sfm)	feed (cpt)	speed (sfm)	feed (cpt)
free-machining aluminum alloys: suggested machining conditions based upon a machinability index range of 70-100 and a hardness range of 80-120 BHN	K68	2000	.007	1000-10000	.005-.015
	K8735	2000	.009	1000-10000	.004-.018
	KT150	2000	.005	1000-10000	.003-.012
	KD100	3000	.005	1000-10000	.003-.010
high silicon aluminum (hypereutectic)	KD100	2000	.005	1200-3000	.003-.015

Figure 7.92 (Reproduced with permission of Kennametal Inc.)

work material	grade	starting conditions for general purpose milling		range of conditions	
		speed (sfm)	feed (cpt)	speed (sfm)	feed (cpt)
non-ferrous free machining alloys: copper, zinc, and brass alloys suggested machining conditions based upon a machinability index range of 70-100 and a hardness range of 80-120 BHN	K68	1000	.007	300-2000	.005-.015
	K8735	1000	.009	300-2000	.004-.018
	KT150	1000	.005	300-2000	.003-.012
	KD100	2500	.005	1800-3500	.003-.010

Figure 7.93 (Reproduced with permission of Kennametal Inc.)

work material	grade	starting conditions for general purpose milling		range of conditions	
		speed (sfm)	feed (cpt)	speed (sfm)	feed (cpt)
non-ferrous free machining alloys: copper, zinc, and brass alloys suggested machining conditions based upon a machinability index range of 70-100 and a hardness range of 80-120 BHN	K68	1000	.007	300-2000	.005-.015
	K8735	1000	.009	300-2000	.004-.018
	KT150	1000	.005	300-2000	.003-.012
	KD100	2500	.005	1800-3500	.003-.010

Figure 7.94 (Reproduced with permission of Kennametal Inc.)

how to apply range of conditions		
condition	**speed**	**feed**
roughing	↓	↑
finishing	↑	↓
end milling	↑	↓
slotting	↑	↓
hard material	↓	→
soft material	↑	↑
scale	↓	↑
tool life	↓	→
heavy d.o.c.	↓	↓

lower = ↓
higher = ↑
same = →

(a)

Figure 7.95 (*a*) Applying range of conditions, milling tables. (Reproduced with permission of Kennametal Inc.) (*b*) Insert designations, characteristics, and applications. (*c*) Carbide insert grade comparison.

grade	composition and characteristics	milling application
K1	Best mechanical strength and shock resistance.	Excellent general purpose grade at lower surface speeds. Highly recommended for end milling and for machining titanium.
K68	More wear and abrasion resistant than K8735.	Moderate feed and speed milling of cast iron, high-temperature alloys, 300 series stainless steels, plastics, and aluminum.
K420	Tougher than K2884 . . . excellent thermal shock resistance.	Moderate feed and speed milling of all steels.
K2884	Primary uncoated steel milling grade . . . more wear and abrasion resistant than K420.	Moderate feed and speed milling of steels, alloy steels, and 400 and 500 series stainless steels.
K8735	Primary uncoated cast iron milling grade . . . slightly tougher than K68 . . . superior resistance to built-up edge.	Moderate feed and speed milling of cast, ductile, and malleable iron, 300 series stainless steel, plastic, and aluminum.
K313	New Fine Grain Grade—more wear resistant than K68 yet tougher.	Mills nickel and cobalt-based alloys, titanium, cast iron, and 300 series stainless steels with excellent tool life.
KC210	TiC/TiC-N/TiN coatings . . . higher speed, more wear resistant than KC250.	Moderate speed finish milling of 300 series stainless steels; and cast, ductile, and malleable iron. Good for wiper inserts.
KC250	TiC/TiC-N/TiN coatings . . . much tougher than KC210, higher speed than K1.	Low speed, rough milling of irons, steels, and stainless steels. Good for roughing through scale.
KC710	New PVD coated grade—PVD (physical vapor deposition), TiN coating . . . good edge wear resistance with strong substrate.	Low to moderate feeds at a broad range of speeds. Excellent on steel, alloy steels, stainless steels, and ductile and nodular irons.
KC810	TiC/TiC-N/TiN coatings . . . edge wear resistance and speed comparable to KC850 but not as tough as KC850.	Good wear resistance and strength for moderate milling of all steels.
KC850	TiC/TiC-N/TiN coatings on a cobalt enriched substrate . . . toughest coated grade . . . higher speed than KC250.	Moderate to high feeds. Excellent on all steels, all stainless steels, and alloyed cast irons.
KC950	TiC/Al_2O_3/TiN coatings on a tough, cobalt enriched, heat resistant carbide substrate.	Moderate to high speed milling of steels and cast irons. Especially good in crankshaft milling.
KT150	TiC/TiN cermet composition . . . resistant to wear and built-up edge.	Semi-finishing to finishing conditions. Good on aluminum, steels, and stainless steels.
Kyon 2000	Sialon (silicon nitride) . . . excellent edge wear resistance, depth of cut notch resistance, and shock resistance.	Moderate feed and high speed milling of nickel-base alloys.
Kyon 3000	Sialon . . . excellent edge wear, shock, and abrasion resistance.	Moderate to very high feeds and speeds when milling gray cast iron.
K090	Composite ceramic . . . aluminum oxide and titanium carbide . . . high edge wear resistance.	High speed finishing at two to three times the speed of carbides on hard cast irons, alloy steels, and nickel-base alloys.
KD100	Polycrystalline diamond tipped . . . superior edge wear resistance and resistance to built-up edge.	High speed milling of abrasive, non-ferrous materials such as high silicon aluminum and non-metallics.
KD200	Solid CBN (cubic boron nitride).	For close tolerance milling of hardened ferrous materials.

(b)

Figure 7.95 *(Continued)*

Carbide Grade Comparison

KENNA-METAL	IMCO	ADAMAS	CARB-OLOY	CARMET	NEW-COMBER	SANDVIC	SECO	FIRTH STERLING	TRW	VAL-ENITE	VR/WESSON	WALMET
UNCOATED GRADES												
K1	IC-10	B	44A	CA-3	N-10	—	—	H-6	CQ-12	VC-1	VR-54	WA-1
K68	MG-10	PWX	820	CA-310	—	H10	G-27	H-17	CQ-22	VC-27	RAM-1	WA-110
K68	IC-20	A	883	CA-4	N-22	H20	H-13	H-21	CQ-2	VC-2	2A5	WA-2
K313	IC-40	AAA	999	CA-8	N-40	H05	—	HF	CQ-4	VC-4	—	WA-4
K420	IC-50	434	390	CA-740	N-50	—	S6	T-04	CY-12	—	2A7	WA-54
K420	IC-55	499	370	CA-720	N-55	S6	S6	T-12	CY-16	VC-5	VR-75	WA-5
K2884	IC-67	548	—	CA-717	N-60	SIP	S2	T-25	CY-14	VC-6	VR-73	WA-47
K313	IC-70	490	350	—	N-70	SIP	SIG	T-25	CY-31	VC-8	—	WA-73
COATED GRADES												
KC730	IC-202	ACT-2	523	CA9443	NT-2	GC315	TP-15	TC	027	VN2	630	P2
KC810	IC-552	ACT-5	550	CA9720	NT-5	GC1025	TP-35	HN	715	VN5	660	P5
KC850	IC-672	ACT-7	518	—	NT-6	—	TP-25	TC1	714	—	670	P47
KC910	IC-554	ROXIDE	570	—	NAO2	GC015	—	CC46	918	V01	—	A60
KC950	IC-674	—	545	—	—	GC415	—	CC44	—	V05	680	A62

This grade selection chart is intended to be used as a guide to grade selection of various manufacturers.
It indicates those grades having similar characteristics under most general conditions. It is not intended to imply that all comparable grades are exact duplicates in physical and metallurgical properties, or that they perform exactly the same on all applications.

(c)

Figure 7.95 *(Continued)*

CUTTER SPEEDS IN REVOLUTIONS PER MINUTE

	Surface speed (ft. per min.)															
Diameter of cutter (in.)	25	30	35	40	50	55	60	70	75	80	90	100	120	140	160	180	200
	Cutter revolutions per minute																
1/4	382	458	535	611	764	851	917	1,070	1,147	1,222	1,376	1,528	1,834	2,139	2,445	2,750	3,056
5/16	306	367	428	489	611	672	733	856	917	978	1,100	1,222	1,466	1,711	1,955	2,200	2,444
3/8	255	306	357	408	509	560	611	713	764	815	916	1,018	1,222	1,425	1,629	1,832	2,036
7/16	218	262	306	349	437	481	524	611	656	699	786	874	1,049	1,224	1,398	1,573	1,748
1/2	191	229	268	306	382	420	459	535	573	611	688	764	917	1,070	1,222	1,375	1,528
5/8	153	184	214	245	306	337	367	428	459	489	552	612	736	857	979	1,102	1,224
3/4	127	153	178	203	254	279	306	357	381	408	458	508	610	711	813	914	1,016
7/8	109	131	153	175	219	241	262	306	329	349	392	438	526	613	701	788	876
1	95.5	115	134	153	191	210	229	267	287	306	344	382	458	535	611	688	764
1-1/4	76.3	91.8	107	123	153	168	183	214	230	245	274	306	367	428	490	551	612
1-1/2	63.7	76.3	89.2	102	127	140	153	178	191	204	230	254	305	356	406	457	508
1-3/4	54.5	65.5	76.4	87.3	109	120	131	153	164	175	196	218	262	305	349	392	436
2	47.8	57.3	66.9	76.4	95.5	105	115	134	143	153	172	191	229	267	306	344	382
2-1/2	38.2	45.8	53.5	61.2	76.3	84.2	91.7	107	114	122	138	153	184	213	245	275	306
3	31.8	38.2	44.6	51	63.7	69.9	76.4	89.1	95.3	102	114	127	152	178	208	228	254
3-1/2	27.3	32.7	38.2	44.6	54.5	60	65.5	76.4	81.8	87.4	98.1	109	131	153	174	196	218
4	23.9	28.7	33.4	38.2	47.8	52.6	57.3	66.9	71.7	76.4	86	95.6	115	134	153	172	191
5	19.1	22.9	26.7	30.6	38.2	42	45.9	53.5	57.3	61.1	68.8	76.4	91.7	107	122	138	153

Figure 7.96 Cutter revolutions per minute from surface speed.

Figure 7.97 Horizontal dividing and angle-setting head.

The device shown in Fig. 7.98 will allow the setting of a compound angle because the clamping table on this device can be rotated both horizontally and vertically and both directions are controlled by a vernier setting. This device is similar to a compound sine plate but is perhaps more convenient and easier to use, although the compound sine plate is more accurate owing to the fact that it is set using Jo-blocks. Previous chapters of this *Handbook* explain the use and setting practices of compound sine plates and simple sine plates.

Quick answers to milling calculations can be obtained by using the various cutting tool manufacturers calculators, a sample of which is shown in Fig. 7.99. With these devices, all the basic milling calculations can be done, including the required horsepower needed for a particular milling operation. When a device such as this is not available to the tool or manufacturing engineer or machinist, the calculations may be performed by using the equations and charts presented in this section. This device is similar to the turning and boring calculator shown in the turning and boring section (Sec. 7.1), except that it has been designed for use in milling operations.

Standard dividing and indexing head procedures are shown in Sec. 7.12.8

Machining calculations. Although the modern machining centers can set angles and compound angles through the programmed controller on these machines, the basic accessories are nonetheless important when used on manually set machines, such as those used for small production runs and in prototype and model shops. Many of the machining procedures and calculations would indeed be complex without the use of the modern machining center equipped for four- or five-axis operations.

It should be apparent that the basic milling machine and machining center also can be used for drilling and jig-boring operations, although on a limited scale in relation to the available horsepower and physical size of the machine. Figure 7.100 illustrates some of the basic cutting tools used on mills and machining centers. In the figure, parts *a, b,* and *c* are drill bits which have been coated with titanium nitride, part *d* is a typical ball-end mill, part *e* is a high-speed close-spiral tap, while parts *f, g,* and *h* are a newer type end mill design used for roughing operations at high speed, where large volumes of material are removed very rapidly. In parts *f, g,* and *h,* notice the threadlike grooves in the spiral flutes, which allow a rapid roughing operation to be performed. A close examination of the photograph will reveal the line on the tools which shows where the titanium nitride coating ends. The titanium nitride coating imparts a gold-colored finish on these cutting tools which is not apparent in the black and white photograph.

7.3 Drills and Drilling

Drilling is a machining operation for producing round holes in metallic and nonmetallic materials. A *drill* is a rotary-end cutting tool with one or more cutting edges or lips and one or more straight or helical grooves or flutes for the passage of chips and cutting fluids and coolants. When the depth of the drilled hole reaches three or four times the drill diameter, a reduction must be made in the drilling feed and speed. A coolant-hole drill can produce drilled depths to eight or more times the diameter of the drill. The gundrill can produce an accurate hole to depths of more than 100 times the diameter of the drill with great precision.

Enlarging a drilled hole for a portion of its depth is called *countersinking,* while a counterbore for cleaning the surface a small amount around the hole is called *spotfacing.* Cutting an angular bevel at the perimeter of a drilled hole is also termed *countersinking.* Countersinking tools are available to produce 82°, 90°, and 100° countersinks and other special angles.

Drills are classified by material, length, shape, number, and type of helix or flute, shank, point characteristics, and size series. Most drills are made for right-hand rotation. Right-hand drills, as viewed from their point, with the shank facing away from your view, are rotated in a counterclockwise direction in order to cut. Left-hand drills cut when rotated clockwise in a similar manner.

7.3.1 Drill terminology

Figure 7.100*a* to *c* shows common twist drills made of high-speed steel and coated with titanium nitride. The line just above the flutes shows the limit of the titanium nitride coating. Figure 7.101 shows the standard twist drill form with the appropriate terminology describing its characteristic features.

Drill types or styles

- HSS jobber drills
- Solid-carbide jobber drills
- Carbide-tipped screw-machine drills
- HSS screw-machine drills
- Carbide-tipped glass drills
- HSS extralong straight-shank drills (24 in)
- Taper-shank drills (0 through number 7 ANSI taper)
- Core drills
- Coolant-hole drills
- HSS taper-shank extralong drills (24 in)
- Aircraft extension drills (6 and 12 in)
- Gun drills

- HSS half-round jobber drills
- Spotting and centering drills
- Parabolic drills
- S-point drills
- Square solid-carbide die drills
- Spade drills
- Miniature drills
- Microdrills and microtools

American national standard tapers. Figure 7.102 shows the American national standard taper geometry and dimensions for ANSI tapers 1 through 7. Taper nunber 0 is not listed in the national standards. Table 7.1 accompanies Fig. 7.102 and lists the detail dimensions.

7.3.2 Drill point styles and angles

Over a period of many years, the metalworking industry has developed many different drill point styles for a wide variety of applications from drilling soft plastics to drilling the hardest types of metal alloys. All the standard point styles and special points are shown in Fig. 7.103, including the important point angles which differentiate these different points. New drill styles are being introduced periodically, but the styles shown in Fig. 7.103 include some of the newer types as well as the commonly used older configurations.

The old practice of grinding drill points by hand and eye is, at the least, ineffective with today's modern drills and materials. For a drill to perform accurately and efficiently, modern drill-grinding machines such as the models produced by the Darex Corporation are required. Models are also produced which are also capable of sharpening taps, reamers, end mills, and countersinks. Metal-cutting tool sharpening and grinding practices are not detailed in this *Handbook.* The tool suppliers and tool sharpening vendors are equipped to sharpen all the cutting tools they distribute in a more accurate and efficient manner than can be done by hand in modern machine shops. High-speed-steel and cobalt-based turning bits are an exception to this modern grinding and sharpening practice, in that the machinist or machine operator occasionally dresses or hones such a cutting tool.

Recommended general uses for drill point angles shown in Fig. 7.103 are shown below. Figure 7.103*k* illustrates web thinning of a standard twist drill.

Typical uses

A	Copper and medium to soft copper alloys
B	Molded plastics, Bakelite, etc.
C	Brasses and soft bronzes
D	Alternate for G, cast irons, die castings, and aluminum
E	Crankshafts and deep holes
F	Manganese steel and hard alloys (point angle 125 to 135°)
G	Wood, fiber, hard rubber, and aluminum
H	Heat-treated steels and drop forgings
I	Split point, 118° or 135° point, self-centering (CNC applications)
J	Parabolic flute for accurate, deep holes and rapid cutting
K	Web thinning (thin the web as the drill wears from resharpening; this restores the chisel point to its proper length)

Other drill styles which are used today include the helical or S-point, which is self-centering and permits higher feed rates, and the chamfered point, which is effective in reducing burr generation in many materials.

Drills are produced from high-speed steel (HSS), solid carbide, or with carbide brazed inserts. Drill systems are made by many of the leading tool manufacturers which allow the use of removable inserts of carbide, cermet, ceramics, and cubic boron nitride (CBN). Many of the HSS twist drills used today have coatings such as titanium nitride, titanium carbide, aluminum oxide, and other tremendously hard and wear-resistant coatings. These coatings can increase drill life by as much as three to five times over premium HHS and plain-carbide drills.

7.3.3 Classification of high-speed steels

Figure 7.104 shows the chemical composition and characteristics of the M and T series of high-speed steels. The classification shown applies to drills, turning tools, mills, and other tools made of high-speed steels and is of great value in selecting the proper type of HSS tool for the intended application in machining.

7.3.4 Conversion of surface speed to revolutions per minute for drills

Fractional drill sizes. Figure 7.105 shows the standard fractional drill sizes and the revolutions per minute of each fractional drill size for various surface speeds. The drilling speed tables that follow give the allowable drilling speed (sfpm) of the various materials. From these values, the correct rpm setting for drilling can be ascertained using the speed/rpm tables given here.

Wire drill sizes (1 through 80). See Fig. 7.106.

Letter drill sizes. See Fig. 7.107.

7.3.5 Tap drill sizes for producing unified inch screw threads, metric and pipe threads

Tap drills for unified inch screw threads. See Fig. 7.108.

Tap-drill sizes for producing metric screw threads. See Fig. 7.109.

Tap-drill sizes for pipe threads (taper and straight pipe). See Fig. 7.110.

Equation for obtaining tap-drill sizes for cutting taps

$$D_h = D_{bm} - 0.0130\left(\frac{\%\text{ of full thread desired}}{n_i}\right)$$ for unified inch-size threads

$$D_{h1} = D_{bm1} - \left(\frac{\%\text{ of full thread desired}}{76.98}\right)$$ for metric series threads

where D_h = drilled hole size, in
D_{h1} = drilled hole size, mm
D_{bm} = basic major diameter of thread, in
D_{bm1} = basic major diameter of thread, mm
n_i = number of threads per inch

Note: In the preceding equations, use the percentage whole number; i.e., for 84 percent, use 84.

Example What is the drilled hole size in inches for a ⅜-16 tapped thread with 84 percent of full thread?

$$D_h = 0.375 - 0.0130 \times \frac{84}{16} = 0.375 - 0.06825 = 0.30675 \text{ in}$$

0.30675 in is then the decimal equivalent of the required tap drill for 84 percent of full thread. Use the next closest drill size, which would be letter size N (0.302 in). The diameters of the American standard wire and letter-size drills are shown in Fig. 7.111. For metric tapped holes, use the recommended metric drill size in the tables or the closest American standard drill size.

When producing the tapped hole, be sure that the correct class of fit is satisfied, i.e., class 2B, 3B, interference fit, etc. The different classes of fits for the thread systems are shown in the section of standards of the American National Standards Institute (ANSI) and the American Society of Mechanical Engineers (ASME); see Chap. 8, "ANSI Standards Applicable to Machining and Metalworking Practices." Certain fit classes allow for electroplating and other characteristics which are determined by the design engineer, who selects the class of fit for a particular application.

7.3.6 Speeds and feeds, drill geometry, and cutting recommendations for drills

The composite drilling table shown in Fig. 7.112 has been derived from data originated by the Society of Manufacturing Engineers (SME) and various major drill manufacturers. Figure 7.113 illustrates the standard drill point and split point together with the chisel edge angle range in common use.

7.3.7 Spade drills

Spade drills are used to produce holes ranging from 1 in to over 6 in in diameter. Very deep holes can be produced with spade drills, including core drilling, counterboring, and bottoming to a flat or other shape. The spade drill consists of the spade drill bit and holder. The holder may contain coolant holes through which coolant can be delivered to the cutting edges, under pressure, which cools the spade and flushes the chips from the drilled hole. Typical spade drills, holders, and terminology and spade geometry are shown in Fig. 7.114.

(Text continued on page 658.)

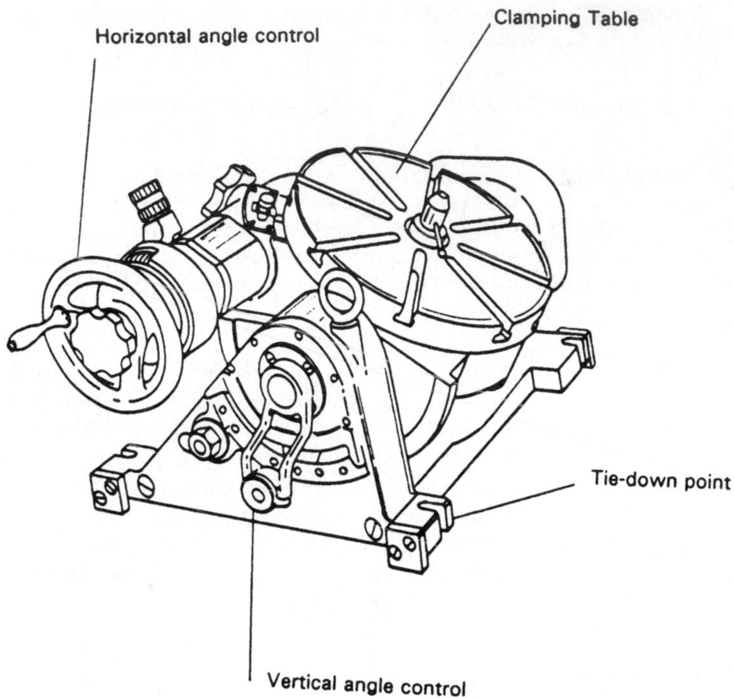

Figure 7.98 Vertical and horizontal angle-setting device.

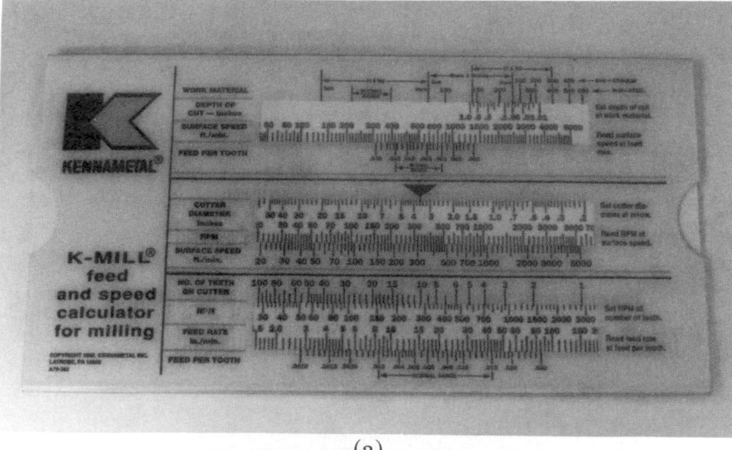

(a)

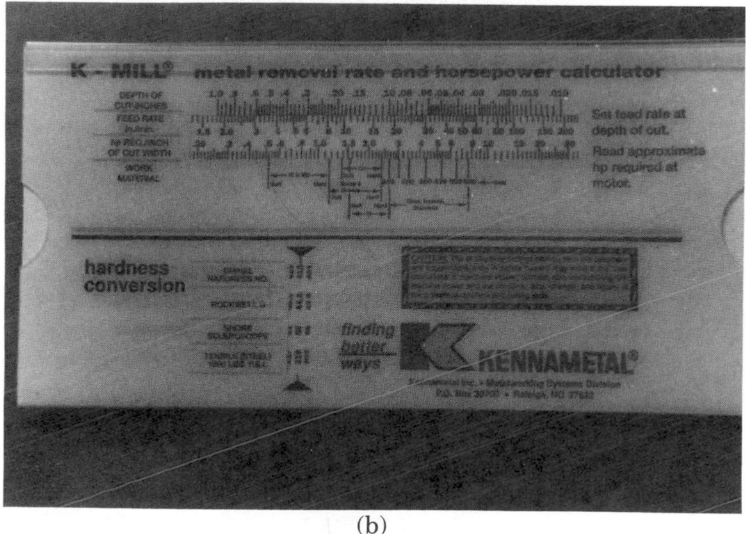

(b)

Figure 7.99 (*a*) Milling feed and speed calculator (front side). (*b*) Milling feed and speed calculator (rear side).

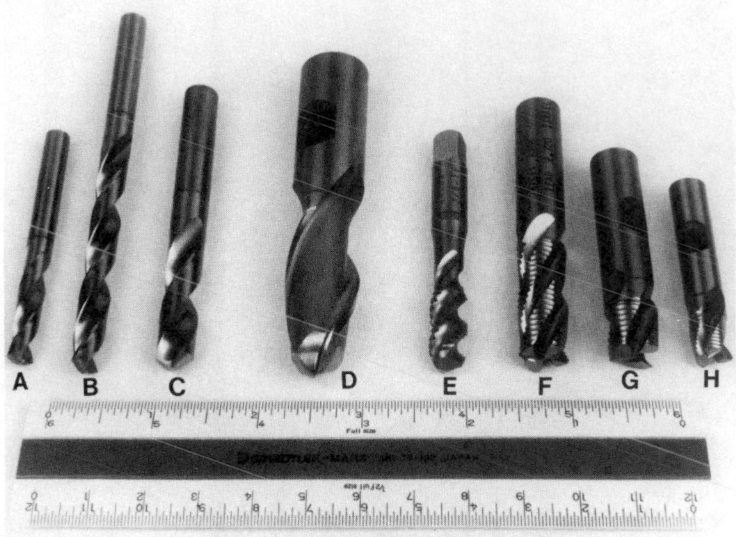

Figure 7.100 Titanium nitride–coated drills and end mills.

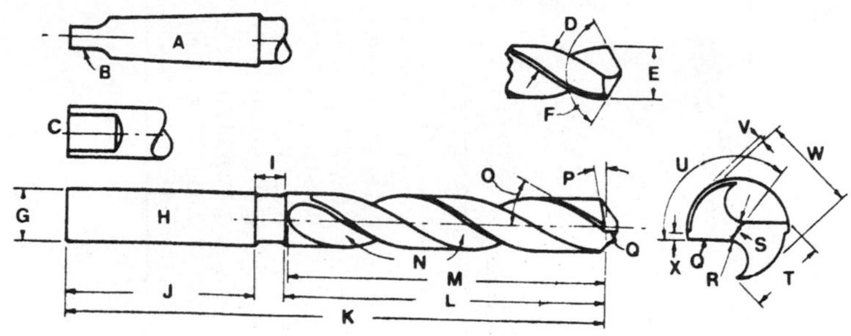

Twist Drill Features

A Taper shank
B Tang
C Tang drive
D Land width
E Drill diameter
F Point angle
G Shank diameter
H Straight shank
I Neck
J Shank length
K Overall length
L Body
M Flute length
N Flutes
O Helix angle
P Lip relief angle
Q Lip
R Web
S Chisel edge
T Land
U Chisel edge angle
V Body diameter clearance
W Clearance diameter
X Margin

Figure 7.101 Twist-drill features.

TABLE 7.1 Detail Dimensions* for American National Standard Tapers

	Shank							Tang			Tang Slot					
American national standard taper number	Diam. of plug at small end	Diam. at end of socket	Whole length	Depth	Depth of drilled hole	Depth of reamed hole	Standard plug depth	Thickness	Length	Radius	Radius	Width	Length	End of socket to tang slot	Taper per inch	Taper per foot	American national standard taper number
	D	*A*	*B*	*S*	*G*	*H*	*P*	*t*	*T*	*R*	*a*	*W*	*L*	*K*			
0†	0.25200	0.35610	2 11/32	2 7/32	2 1/16	2 1/32	2	5/32	1/4	5/32	3/64	11/64	9/16	1 15/16	0.052050	0.62460	0‡
1	0.36900	0.47500	2 9/16	2 7/16	2 3/16	2 5/32	2 1/8	13/64	3/8	3/16	3/64	7/32	3/4	2 1/16	0.049882	0.59858	1
2	0.57200	0.70000	3 1/8	2 15/16	2 21/32	2 39/64	2 9/16	1/4	7/16	1/4	1/16	17/64	7/8	2 1/2	0.049951	0.59941	2
3	0.77800	0.93800	3 7/8	3 11/16	3 5/16	3 1/4	3 3/16	5/16	9/16	9/32	5/64	21/64	1 3/16	3 1/16	0.050196	0.60235	3
4	1.02000	1.23100	4 7/8	4 5/8	4 3/16	4 1/8	4 1/16	15/32	5/8	5/16	3/32	31/64	1 1/4	3 7/8	0.051938	0.62326	4
4 1/2	1.26600	1.50000	5 3/8	5 1/8	4 5/8	4 9/16	4 1/2	9/16	11/16	3/8	1/8	37/64	1 3/8	4 5/16	0.052000	0.62400	4 1/2
5	1.47500	1.74800	6 1/8	5 7/8	5 5/16	5 1/4	5 3/16	5/8	3/4	3/8	1/8	21/32	1 1/2	4 15/16	0.052626	0.63151	5
6	2.11600	2.49400	8 9/16	8 1/4	7 13/32	7 21/64	7 1/4	3/4	1 1/8	1/2	5/32	25/32	1 3/4	7	0.052138	0.62565	6
7	2.75000	3.27000	11 5/8	11 1/4	10 5/32	10 5/64	10	1 1/8	1 3/8	3/4	3/16	1 5/32	2 5/8	9 1/2	0.052000	0.62400	7

* Table agrees with American nuclear standards for taper shanks except for angle and undercut of tang.

† Size 0 taper shank not listed in American national standards.

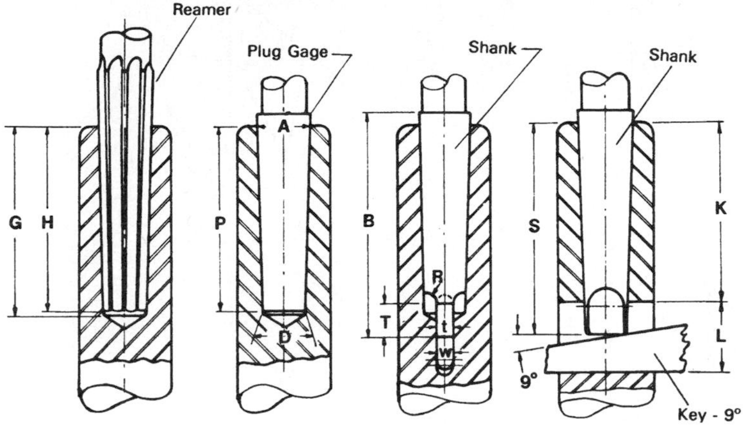

Figure 7.102 American national standard tapers.

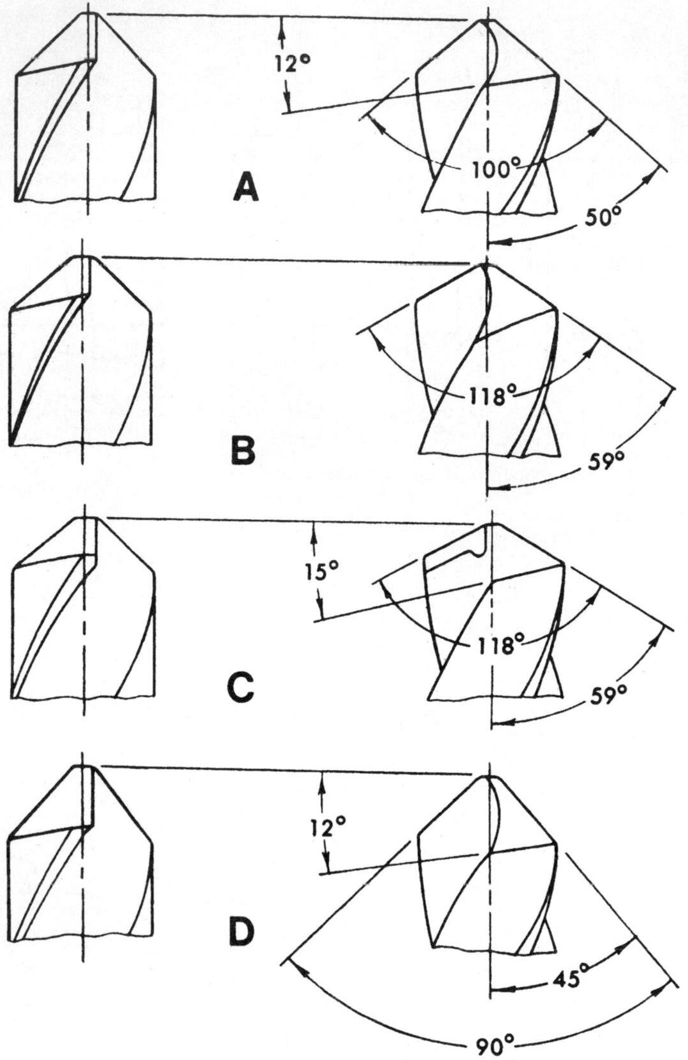

Figure 7.103 Drill-point styles and angles.

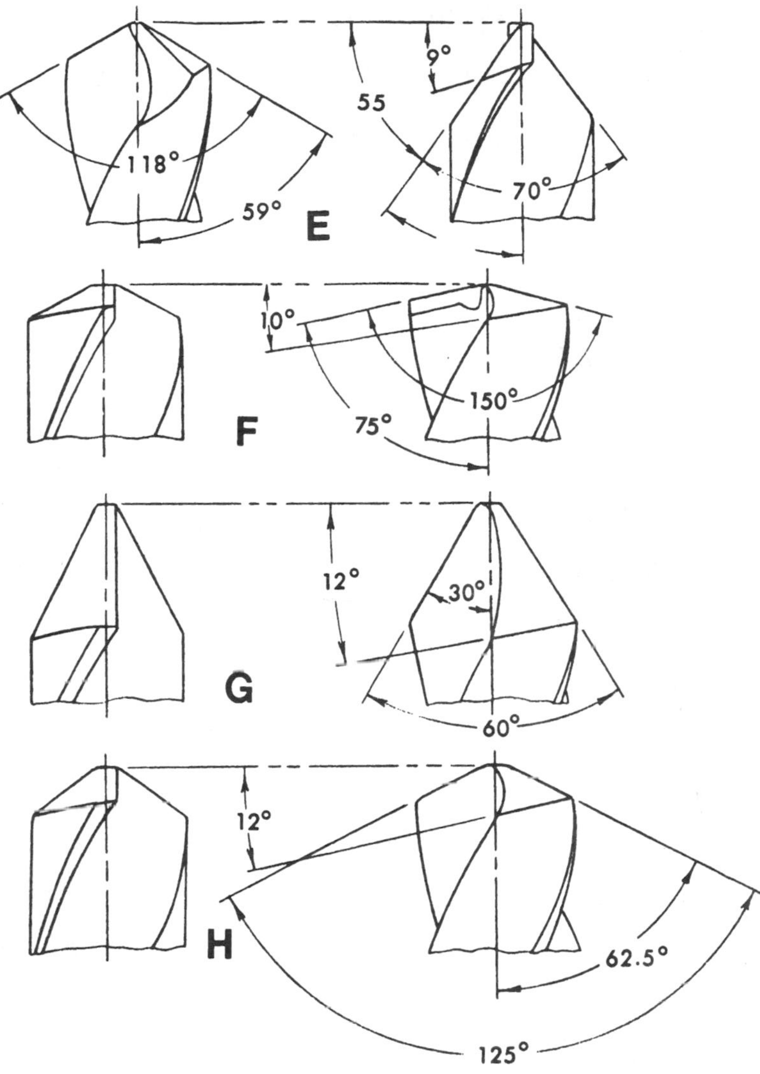

Figure 7.103 *(Continued)*

Chemical Composition						Comparative Physical Properties *			
AISI - SAE Grade	Tungsten	Chromium	Vanadium	Molybdenum	Cobalt	Red Hardness	Abrasion Resistance	Edge Strength	Grinding Ability
M - 1	1.5	4.0	1.0	8.5	-	10	10	18	18
M - 2	6.0	4.0	2.0	5.0	-	10	11	17	17
M - 3-1	6.0	4.0	2.4	6.0	-	10	14	12	8
M - 3-2	6.0	4.0	3.0	6.0	-	10	17	11	6
M - 4	5.5	4.5	4.0	4.5	-	10	18	8	5
M - 7	1.7	4.0	2.0	8.75	-	10	12	17	14
M - 10	-	4.0	2.0	8.0	-	10	10	17	17
M - 15	6.5	4.5	5.0	3.0	5.0	13	19	9	2
M - 30	2.0	4.0	1.0	8.0	5.0	13	10	14	14
M - 34	2.0	4.0	2.0	8.5	8.0	15	11	14	14
M - 36	6.0	4.0	2.0	6.0	9.0	16	11	14	14
M - 42	1.5	3.75	1.15	9.5	8.0	17	19	15	14
T - 1	18.0	4.0	1.0	-	-	10	10	16	18
T - 2	18.0	4.0	2.0	-	-	10	11	15	17
T - 3	18.0	4.0	3.0	-	-	10	14	8	7
T - 4	18.0	4.0	1.0	-	5.0	13	10	11	14
T - 5	18.0	4.0	2.0	-	8.0	15	11	11	14
T - 6	22.0	4.5	1.5	-	12.0	20	10	11	14
T - 15	13.0	4.5	5.0	-	5.0	17	20	9	2

* Comparative Range of Physical Properties:
0 - 4 = Poor; 5 - 8 = Fair; 9 - 12 = Good; 13 - 16 = Very Good; 17 - 20 = Excellent

Figure 7.104 Classification of high-speed steels (HSS).

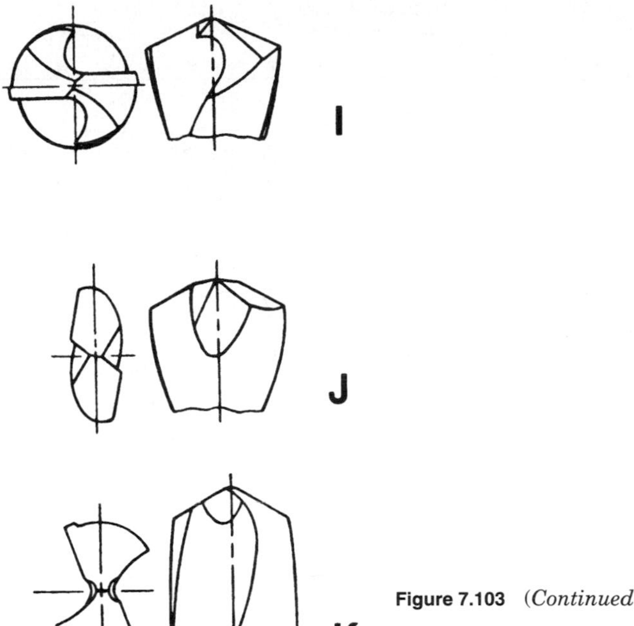

Figure 7.103 *(Continued)*

FRACTIONAL SIZE DRILLS

Surface Feet per Minute

Diam. Inches	10'	12'	15'	20'	25'	30'	35'	40'	45'	50'	60'	70'	80'	90'	100'
	Revolutions per Minute														
1/64	2445	2934	3667	4889	6112	7334	8556	9778	11001	12223	14668	17112	19557	22001	24446
1/32	1222	1467	1833	2445	3056	3667	4278	4889	5500	6112	7334	8556	9778	11001	12223
3/64	815	978	1222	1630	2037	2445	2852	3259	3667	4074	4889	5704	6519	7334	8149
1/16	611	733	917	1222	1528	1833	2139	2445	2750	3056	3667	4278	4889	5500	6112
5/64	489	587	733	978	1222	1467	1711	1956	2200	2445	2934	3422	3911	4400	4889
3/32	407	489	611	815	1019	1222	1426	1630	1833	2037	2445	2852	3259	3667	4074
7/64	349	419	524	698	873	1048	1222	1397	1572	1746	2095	2445	2794	3143	3492
1/8	306	367	458	611	764	917	1070	1222	1375	1528	1833	2139	2445	2750	3056
9/64	272	326	407	543	679	815	951	1086	1222	1358	1630	1901	2173	2445	2716
5/32	244	293	367	489	611	733	856	978	1100	1222	1467	1711	1956	2200	2445
11/64	222	267	333	444	556	667	778	889	1000	1111	1333	1556	1778	2000	2222
3/16	204	244	306	407	509	611	713	815	917	1019	1222	1426	1630	1833	2037
13/64	188	226	282	376	470	564	658	752	846	940	1128	1316	1504	1692	1880
7/32	175	210	262	349	437	524	611	698	786	873	1048	1222	1397	1572	1746
15/64	163	196	244	326	407	489	570	652	733	815	978	1141	1304	1467	1630
1/4	153	183	229	306	382	458	535	611	688	764	917	1070	1222	1375	1528
9/32	136	163	204	272	340	407	475	543	611	679	815	951	1086	1222	1358
5/16	122	147	183	244	306	367	428	489	550	611	733	856	978	1100	1222
11/32	111	133	167	222	278	333	389	444	500	556	667	778	889	1000	1111
3/8	102	122	153	204	255	306	357	407	458	509	611	713	815	917	1019
13/32	94	113	141	188	235	282	329	376	423	470	564	658	752	846	940
7/16	87	105	131	175	218	262	306	349	393	437	524	611	698	786	873
15/32	81	98	122	163	204	244	285	326	367	407	489	570	652	733	815
1/2	76	92	115	153	191	229	267	306	344	382	458	535	611	688	764
9/16	68	81	102	136	170	204	238	272	306	340	407	475	543	611	679
5/8	61	73	92	122	153	183	214	244	275	306	367	428	489	550	611
11/16	56	67	83	111	139	167	194	222	250	278	333	389	444	500	556
3/4	51	61	76	102	127	153	178	204	229	255	306	357	407	458	509
13/16	47	56	71	94	118	141	165	188	212	235	282	329	376	423	470
7/8	44	52	65	87	109	131	153	175	196	218	262	306	349	393	437
15/16	41	49	61	81	102	122	143	163	183	204	244	285	326	367	407
1	38	46	57	76	95	115	134	153	172	191	229	267	306	344	382
1-1/8	34	41	51	68	85	102	119	136	153	170	204	238	272	306	340
1-1/4	31	37	46	61	76	92	107	122	138	153	183	214	244	275	306
1-3/8	28	33	42	56	69	83	97	111	125	139	167	194	222	250	278
1-1/2	25	31	38	51	64	76	89	102	115	127	153	178	204	229	255
1-5/8	24	28	35	47	59	71	82	94	106	118	141	165	188	212	235
1-3/4	22	26	33	44	55	65	76	87	98	109	131	153	175	196	218
1-7/8	20	24	31	41	51	61	71	81	92	102	122	143	163	183	204
2	19	23	29	38	48	57	67	76	86	95	115	134	153	172	191
2-1/4	17	20	25	34	42	51	59	68	76	85	102	119	136	153	170
2-1/2	15	18	23	31	38	46	53	61	69	76	92	107	122	138	153
2-3/4	14	17	21	28	35	42	49	56	63	69	83	97	111	125	139
3	13	15	19	25	32	38	45	51	57	64	76	89	102	115	127
3-1/2	11	13	16	22	27	33	38	44	49	55	65	76	87	98	109

For speeds higher than tabulated, multiply all values by 10 or 100. For speeds lower than tabulated, divide all values by 10

Figure 7.105 Drill rpm/surface speed, fractional drills.

WIRE SIZE DRILLS

Surface Feet per Minute

Diam. No.	10'	12'	15'	20'	25'	30'	35'	40'	45'	50'	60'	70'	80'	90'	100'
	Revolutions per Minute														
41	398	477	597	796	995	1194	1393	1592	1790	1990	2387	2785	3183	3581	3979
42	409	490	613	817	1021	1226	1430	1634	1838	2043	2451	2860	3268	3677	4085
43	429	515	644	858	1073	1288	1502	1717	1931	2146	2575	3004	3434	3863	4292
44	444	533	666	888	1110	1332	1555	1777	1999	2221	2665	3109	3554	3999	4442
45	466	559	699	932	1165	1397	1630	1863	2096	2329	2795	3261	3726	4192	4658
46	472	566	707	943	1179	1415	1650	1886	2122	2358	2830	3301	3773	4244	4716
47	487	584	730	973	1216	1460	1703	1946	2190	2433	2920	3406	3893	4379	4866
48	503	603	754	1005	1256	1508	1759	2010	2262	2513	3016	3518	4021	4523	5026
49	523	628	785	1046	1308	1570	1831	2093	2355	2617	3140	3663	4186	4710	5233
50	546	655	819	1091	1364	1637	1910	2183	2456	2729	3274	3820	4366	4911	5457
51	570	684	855	1140	1425	1710	1995	2280	2565	2851	3421	3991	4561	5131	5701
52	602	722	902	1203	1504	1805	2105	2406	2707	3008	3609	4211	4812	5414	6015
53	642	770	963	1284	1605	1926	2247	2568	2889	3207	3848	4490	5131	5773	6414
54	694	833	1042	1389	1736	2083	2431	2778	3125	3473	4167	4862	5556	6251	6945
55	735	881	1102	1469	1836	2204	2571	2938	3306	3673	4408	5142	5877	6611	7346
56	821	986	1232	1643	2054	2464	2875	3286	3696	4108	4929	5751	6572	7394	8215
57	888	1066	1332	1777	2221	2665	3109	3553	3997	4452	5342	6232	7122	8013	8903
58	909	1091	1364	1819	2274	2728	3183	3638	4093	4547	5456	6367	7275	8186	9095
59	932	1118	1397	1863	2329	2795	3261	3726	4192	4658	5590	6521	7453	8388	9316
60	955	1146	1432	1910	2387	2865	3342	3820	4297	4775	5729	6684	7639	8594	9549
61	979	1175	1469	1959	2449	2938	3428	3918	4407	4897	5876	6856	7835	8815	9794
62	1005	1206	1508	2010	2513	3016	3518	4021	4523	5025	6030	7035	8040	9045	10050
63	1032	1239	1549	2065	2581	3097	3613	4129	4646	5160	6192	7224	8256	9288	10320
64	1061	1273	1592	2122	2653	3183	3714	4244	4775	5305	6366	7427	8488	9549	10610
65	1091	1310	1637	2183	2728	3274	3820	4365	4911	5455	6546	7637	8728	9819	10910
66	1157	1389	1736	2315	2894	3472	4051	4630	5207	5790	6948	8106	9264	10422	11580
67	1194	1432	1790	2387	2984	3581	4178	4775	5371	5970	7164	8358	9552	10746	11940
68	1232	1479	1848	2464	3080	3696	4313	4929	5545	6160	7392	8624	9856	11088	12320
69	1308	1570	1962	2616	3270	3924	4578	5232	5887	6530	7836	9142	10488	11754	13060
70	1364	1637	2046	2728	3410	4093	4775	5457	6139	6820	8184	9548	10912	12276	13640
71	1469	1763	2204	2938	3673	4407	5142	5070	0011	7305	8838	10311	11784	13257	14730
72	1528	1833	2272	3056	3820	4584	5348	6112	6875	7640	9168	10696	12224	13752	15280
73	1592	1910	2387	3183	3979	4775	5570	6366	7162	7960	9552	11144	12736	14328	15920
74	1698	2037	2546	3395	4244	5093	5942	6791	7639	8510	10212	11914	13616	15318	17020
75	1819	2183	2728	3638	4547	5457	6366	7276	8185	9095	10914	12733	14552	16371	18190
76	1910	2292	2865	3820	4775	5730	6684	7639	8594	9550	11460	13370	15280	17190	19100
77	2122	2546	3183	4244	5305	6366	7427	8488	9549	10610	12732	14854	16976	19098	21220
78	2387	2865	3581	4775	5968	7162	8356	9549	10743	11935	14322	16709	19096	21483	23870
79	2634	3161	3951	5269	6586	7903	9220	10537	11854	13170	15804	18438	21072	23706	26340
80	2829	3395	4244	5659	7074	8488	9903	11318	12732	14150	16980	19810	22640	25470	28300

For speeds higher than tabulated, multiply all values by 10 or 100. For speeds lower than tabulated, divide all values by 10.

Figure 7.106 Drill rpm/surface speed, wire-size drills.

LETTER SIZE DRILLS

	Surface Feet per Minute														
	10'	12'	15'	20'	25'	30'	35'	40'	45'	50'	60'	70'	80'	90'	100'
Letter Size	Revolutions per Minute														
A	163	196	245	326	408	490	571	653	735	818	982	1145	1309	1472	1636
B	160	193	241	321	401	481	562	642	722	803	963	1124	1284	1445	1605
C	158	189	237	316	395	473	552	631	710	789	947	1105	1262	1420	1578
D	155	186	233	311	388	466	543	621	699	778	934	1089	1245	1400	1556
E	153	183	229	306	382	458	535	611	687	764	917	1070	1222	1375	1528
F	149	178	223	297	372	446	520	595	669	743	892	1040	1189	1337	1486
G	146	176	220	293	366	439	512	585	659	732	878	1024	1170	1317	1463
H	144	172	215	287	359	431	503	574	646	718	862	1005	1149	1294	1436
I	140	169	211	281	351	421	492	562	632	702	842	983	1123	1264	1404
J	138	165	207	276	345	414	483	552	621	690	827	965	1103	1241	1379
K	136	163	204	272	340	408	476	544	612	680	815	951	1087	1223	1359
L	132	158	198	263	329	395	461	527	593	659	790	922	1054	1185	1317
M	129	155	194	259	324	388	453	518	583	648	777	907	1036	1166	1295
N	126	152	190	253	316	379	442	506	569	633	759	886	1012	1139	1265
O	121	145	181	242	302	363	423	484	544	605	725	846	967	1088	1209
P	118	142	177	237	296	355	414	473	532	592	710	828	946	1065	1183
Q	115	138	173	230	288	345	403	460	518	575	690	805	920	1035	1150
R	113	135	169	225	282	338	394	451	507	564	676	789	902	1014	1127
S	110	132	165	220	274	329	384	439	494	549	659	769	878	988	1098
T	107	128	160	213	267	320	373	427	480	533	640	746	853	959	1066
U	104	125	156	208	259	311	363	415	467	519	623	727	830	934	1038
V	101	122	152	203	253	304	355	405	456	507	608	709	810	912	1013
W	99	119	148	198	247	297	346	496	445	495	594	693	792	891	989
X	96	115	144	192	240	289	337	385	433	481	576	672	769	865	962
Y	95	113	142	189	236	284	331	378	425	473	567	662	756	851	945
Z	92	111	139	185	231	277	324	370	416	462	555	647	740	832	925

For speeds higher than tabulated, multiply all values by 10 or 100. For speeds lower than tabulated, divide all values by 10.

Figure 7.107 Drill rpm/surface speed, letter-size drills.

Tap size	Tap drill size	Decimal equiv. of tap drill, in	Theoretical percent of thread, %	Probable mean over-size, in	Probable hole size, in	Probable percent of thread,* %
0–80	56	0.0465	83	0.0015	0.0480	74
	3/64	0.0469	81	0.0015	0.0484	71
	1.20 mm	0.0472	79	0.0015	0.0487	69
	1.25 mm	0.0492	67	0.0015	0.0507	57
1–64	54	0.0550	89	0.0015	0.0565	81
	1.45 mm	0.0571	78	0.0015	0.0586	71
	53	0.0595	67	0.0015	0.0610	59
1–72	1.5 mm	0.0591	77	0.0015	0.0606	68
	53	0.0595	75	0.0015	0.0610	67
	1.55 mm	0610	67	0.0015	0.0606	68
2–56	51	0.0670	82	0.0017	0.0687	74
	1.75 mm	0.0689	73	0.0017	0.0706	66
	50	0.0700	69	0.0017	0.0717	62
	1.80 mm	0.0709	65	0.0017	0.0726	58
2–64	50	0.0700	79	0.0017	0.0717	70
	1.80 mm	0.0709	74	0.0017	0.0726	66
	49	0.0730	64	0.0017	0.0747	56
3–48	48	0.0760	85	0.0019	0.0779	78
	5/64	0.0781	77	0.0019	0.0800	70
	47	0.0785	76	0.0019	0.0804	69
	2.00 mm	0.0787	75	0.0019	0.0806	68
	46	0.0810	67	0.0019	0.0829	60
	45	0.0820	63	0.0019	0.0839	56
3–56	46	0.0810	78	0.0019	0.0829	69
	45	0.0820	73	0.0019	0.0839	65
	2.10 mm	0.0827	70	0.0019	0.0846	62
	2.15 mm	0.0846	62	0.0019	0.0865	54
4–40	44	0.0860	80	0.0020	0.0880	74
	2.20 mm	0.0866	78	0.0020	0.0886	72
	43	0.0890	71	0.0020	0.0910	65
	2.30 mm	0.0906	66	0.0020	0.0926	60
4–48	2.35 mm	0.0925	72	0.0020	0.0926	72
	42	0.0935	68	0.0020	0.0955	61
	3/32	0.0938	68	0.0020	0.0958	60
	2.40 mm	0.0945	65	0.0020	0.0965	57
5–40	40	0.0980	83	0.0023	0.1003	76
	39	0.0995	79	0.0023	0.1018	71
	38	0.1015	72	0.0023	0.1038	65
	2.60 mm	0.1024	70	0.0023	0.1047	63

Figure 7.108 Tap-drill sizes, unified inch screw threads.

Tap size	Tap drill size	Decimal equiv. of tap drill, in	Theoretical percent of thread, %	Probable mean over-size, in	Probable hole size, in	Probable percent of thread,* %
5–44	38	0.1015	79	0.0023	0.1038	72
	2.60 mm	0.1024	77	0.0023	0.1047	69
	37	0.1040	71	0.0023	0.1063	63
6–32	37	0.1040	84	0.0023	0.1063	78
	36	0.1065	78	0.0023	0.1088	72
	7⁄64	0.1095	70	0.0026	0.1120	64
	35	0.1100	69	0.0026	0.1126	63
	34	0.1100	67	0.0026	0.1136	60
6–40	34	0.1110	83	0.0026	0.1136	75
	33	0.1130	77	0.0026	0.1156	69
	2.90 mm	0.1142	73	0.0026	0.1168	65
	32	0.1160	68	0.0026	0.1186	60
8–32	3.40 mm	0.1339	74	0.0029	0.1368	67
	29	0.1360	69	0.0029	0.1389	62
8–36	29	0.1360	78	0.0029	0.1389	70
	3.5 mm	0.1378	72	0.0029	0.1407	65
10–24	27	0.1440	85	0.0032	0.1472	79
	3.70 mm	0.1457	82	0.0032	0.1489	76
	26	0.1470	79	0.0032	0.1502	74
	25	0.1495	75	0.0032	0.1527	69
	24	0.1520	70	0.0032	0.1552	64
10–32	5⁄32	0.1563	83	0.0032	0.1595	75
	22	0.1570	81	0.0032	0.1602	73
	21	0.1590	76	0.0032	0.1622	68
12–24	11⁄64	0.1719	82	0.0035	0.1754	75
	17	0.1730	79	0.0035	0.1765	73
	16	0.1770	72	0.0035	0.1805	66
12–28	16	0.1770	84	0.0035	0.1805	77
	15	0.1800	78	0.0035	0.1835	70
	4.60 mm	0.1811	75	0.0035	0.1846	67
	14	0.1820	73	0.0035	0.1855	66
1⁄4–20	9	0.1960	83	0.0038	0.1998	77
	8	0.1990	79	0.0038	0.2028	73
	7	0.2010	75	0.0038	0.2048	70
	13⁄64	0.2031	72	0.0038	0.2069	66
1⁄4–28	5.40 mm	0.2126	81	0.0038	0.2164	72
	3	0.2130	80	0.0038	0.2168	72
5⁄16–18	F	0.2570	77	0.0038	0.2608	72
	6.60 mm	0.2598	73	0.0038	0.2636	68
	G	0.2610	71	0.0041	0.2651	66
5⁄16–24	H	0.2660	86	0.0041	0.2701	78
	6.80 mm	0.2677	83	0.0041	0.2718	75

Figure 7.108 *(Continued)*

Tap size	Tap drill size	Decimal equiv. of tap drill, in	Theoretical percent of thread, %	Probable mean over-size, in	Probable hole size, in	Probable percent of thread,* %
	I	0.2720	75	0.0041	0.2761	67
⅜–16	7.80 mm	0.3071	84	0.0044	0.3115	78
	7.90 mm	0.3110	79	0.0044	0.3154	73
	5/16	0.3125	77	0.0044	0.3169	72
	O	0.3160	73	0.0044	0.3204	68
8–24	21/64	0.3281	87	0.0044	0.3325	79
	8.40 mm	0.3307	82	0.0044	0.3351	74
	Q	0.3320	79	0.0044	0.3364	71
	8.50 mm	0.3346	75	0.0044	0.3390	67
7/16–14	T	0.3580	86	0.0046	0.3626	81
	23/64	0.3594	84	0.0046	0.3640	79
	9.20 mm	0.3622	81	0.0046	0.3668	76
	9.30 mm	0.3661	77	0.0046	0.3707	72
	U	0.3680	75	0.0046	0.3726	70
	9.40 mm	0.3701	73	0.0046	0.3747	68
7/16–20	W	0.3860	79	0.0046	0.3906	72
	25/64	0.3906	72	0.0046	0.3952	65
½–13	10.50 mm	0.4134	87	0.0047	0.4181	82
	27/64	0.4219	78	0.0047	0.4266	73
½–20	29/64	0.4531	72	0.0047	0.4578	65
9/16–12	15/32	0.4688	87	0.0048	0.4736	82
	31/64	0.4844	72	0.0048	0.4892	68
9/16–18	½	0.5000	87	0.0048	0.5048	80
⅝–11	17/32	0.5313	79	0.0049	0.5362	75
⅝–18	9/16	0.5625	87	0.0049	0.5674	80
¾–10	41/64	0.6406	84	0.0050	0.6456	80
	21/32	0.6563	72	0.0050	0.6613	68
¾–16	11/16	0.6875	77	0.0050	0.6925	71
	17.50 mm	0.6890	75	0.0050	0.6940	69
⅞–9	49/64	0.7656	76	0.0052	0.7708	72
⅞–14	51/64	0.7969	84	0.0052	0.8021	79
1–8	55/64	0.8594	87	0.0059	0.8653	83
	⅞	0.8750	77	0.0059	0.8809	73
1–12	29/32	0.9063	87	0.0059	0.9122	81
	59/64	0.9219	72	0.0060	0.9279	67
1–14	59/64	0.9219	84	0.0060	0.9279	78
1⅛–7	31/32	0.9688	84	0.0062	0.9750	81
	63/64	0.9844	76	0.0067	0.9911	72
1⅛–12	1 1/32	1.0313	87	0.0071	1.0384	80

Figure 7.108 *(Continued)*

Metric Tap size	Tap drill size	Decimal equiv. of tap drill, in	Theoretical percent of thread, %	Probable mean over-size, in	Probable hole size, in	Probable percent of thread,* %
M1.6 × 0.35	1.20 mm	0.0472	88	0.0014	0.0486	80
	1.25 mm	0.0492	77	0.0014	0.0506	69
M2 × 0.4	1/16	0.0625	79	0.0015	0.0640	72
	1.60 mm	0.0630	77	0.0017	0.0647	69
	52	0.0635	74	0.0017	0.0652	66
M2.5 × 0.45	2.05 mm	0.0807	77	0.0019	0.0826	69
	46	0.0810	76	0.0019	0.0829	67
	45	0.0820	71	0.0019	0.0839	63
M3 × 0.5	40	0.0980	79	0.0023	0.1003	70
	2.5 mm	0.0984	77	0.0023	0.1007	68
	39	0.0995	73	0.0023	0.1018	64
M3.5 × 0.6	33	0.1130	81	0.0026	0.1156	72
	2.9 mm	0.1142	77	0.0026	0.1163	68
	32	0.1160	71	0.0026	0.1186	63
M4 × 0.7	3.2 mm	0.1260	88	0.0029	0.1289	80
	30	0.1285	81	0.0029	0.1314	73
	3.3 mm	0.1299	77	0.0029	0.1328	69
M4.5 × 0.75	3.7 mm	0.1457	82	0.0032	0.1489	74
	26	0.1470	79	0.0032	0.1502	70
	25	0.1495	72	0.0032	0.1527	64
M5 × 0.8	4.2 mm	0.1654	77	0.0032	0.1686	69
	19	0.1660	75	0.0032	0.1692	68
M6 × 1	10	0.1935	84	0.0038	0.1973	76
	9	0.1960	79	0.0038	0.1998	71
	5 mm	0.1968	77	0.0038	0.2006	70
	8	0.1990	73	0.0038	0.2028	65
M7 × 1	A	0.2340	81	0.0038	0.2378	74
	6 mm	0.2362	77	0.0038	0.2400	70
	B	0.2380	74	0.0038	0.2418	66
M8 × 1.25	6.7 mm	0.2638	80	0.0041	0.2679	74
	17/64	0.2656	77	0.0041	0.2697	71
	H	0.2660	77	0.0041	0.2701	70
	6.8 mm	0.2677	74	0.0041	0.2718	68
M10 × 1.5	8.4 mm	0.3307	82	0.0044	0.3351	76
	Q	0.3320	80	0.0044	0.3364	75
	8.5 mm	0.3346	77	0.0044	0.3390	71
M12 × 1.75	10.25 mm	0.4035	77	0.0047	0.4082	72
	Y	0.4040	76	0.0047	0.4087	71
	13/32	0.4062	74	0.0047	0.4109	69
M14 × 2	15/32	0.4688	81	0.0048	0.4736	76
	12 mm	0.4724	77	0.0048	0.4772	72

Figure 7.109 Tap-drill sizes, metric screw threads.

Metric Tap size	Tap drill size	Decimal equiv. of tap drill, in	Theoretical percent of thread, %	Probable mean over-size, in	Probable hole size, in	Probable percent of thread,* %
M16 × 2	35/64	0.5469	81	0.0049	0.5518	76
	14 mm	0.5512	77	0.0049	0.5561	72
M20 × 2.5	11/16	0.6875	78	0.0050	0.6925	74
	17.5 mm	0.6890	77	0.0052	0.6942	73
M24 × 3	13/16	0.8125	86	0.0052	0.8177	82
	21 mm	0.8268	76	0.0054	0.8322	73
	53/64	0.8281	76	0.0054	0.8335	73
M30 × 3.5	1 1/32	1.0312	83	0.0071	1.0383	80
	25.1 mm	1.0394	79	0.0071	1.0465	75
	1 3/64	1.0469	75	0.0072	1.0541	70
M36 × 4	1 17/64	1.2656	74	Reaming recommended		

Figure 7.109 (*Continued*)

Taper pipe		Straight pipe	
Thread	Drill	Thread	Drill
1/8–27	R	1/8–27	S
1/4–18	7/16	1/4–18	29/64
3/8–18	37/64	3/8–18	19/32
1/2–14	23/32	1/2–14	47/64
3/4–14	59/64	3/4–14	15/16
1–11 1/2	1 5/32	1–11 1/2	1 3/16
1 1/4–11 1/2	1 1/2	1 1/4–11 1/2	1 33/64
1 1/2–1 1/2	1 47/64	1 1/2–11 1/2	1 3/4
2–11 1/2	2 7/32	2–11 1/2	2 7/32
2 1/2–8	2 5/8	2 1/2–8	2 21/32
3–8	3 1/4	3–8	3 9/32
3 1/2–8	3 3/4	3 1/2–8	3 25/32
4–8	4 1/4	4–8	4 9/32

Figure 7.110 Pipe taps.

Drill No.	Decimal	Drill No.	Decimal	Drill No.	Decimal
97	0.0059	56	0.0465	15	0.180
96	0.0063	55	0.052	14	0.182
95	0.0067	54	0.055	13	0.185
94	0.0071	53	0.0595	12	0.189
93	0.0075	52	0.0635	11	0.191
92	0.0079	51	0.067	10	0.1935
91	0.0083	50	0.070	9	0.196
90	0.0087	49	0.073	8	0.199
89	0.0091	48	0.076	7	0.201
88	0.0095	47	0.0785	6	0.204
87	0.010	46	0.076	5	0.2055
86	0.0105	45	0.082	4	0.209
85	0.011	44	0.086	3	0.213
84	0.0115	43	0.089	2	0.221
83	0.012	42	0.0935	1	0.228
82	0.0125	41	0.096	A	0.234
81	0.013	40	0.098	B	0.238
80	0.0135	39	0.0995	C	0.242
79	0.0145	38	0.1015	D	0.246
78	0.016	37	0.104	E	0.250
77	0.018	36	0.1065	F	0.257
76	0.020	35	0.110	G	0.261
75	0.021	34	0.111	H	0.266
74	0.0225	33	0.113	I	0.272
73	0.024	32	0.116	J	0.277
72	0.025	31	0.120	K	0.281
71	0.026	30	0.1285	L	0.290
70	0.028	29	0.136	M	0.295
69	0.0292	28	0.1405	N	0.302
68	0.033	27	0.144	O	0.316
67	0.032	26	0.147	P	0.323
66	0.035	25	0.1495	Q	0.332
65	0.035	24	0.152	R	0.339
64	0.035	23	0.154	S	0.348
63	0.037	22	0.157	T	0.358
62	0.038	21	0.159	U	0.368
61	0.039	20	0.161	V	0.377
60	0.040	19	0.166	W	0.386
59	0.041	18	0.1695	X	0.397
58	0.042	17	0.173	Y	0.404
57	0.043	16	0.177	Z	0.413

Figure 7.111 Drill sizes (American national standard).

Speeds, Feeds, Drill Geometry and Cutting Recommendations for Standard Drill Types *

Material Type	Hardness Bhn	Tool Grade	Drill Type	PA-deg.	LRf deg.	HA-deg.	Point Type	sfpm Speed	ipr Feed x 10^{-3}
Low-alloy steels	to 300	M-1, M-2	A	118-135	7-10	25-30	Split	50-60	3-7
4130, 4340, ,4140	300-400	M-1, M-2	A	118-135	7-10	25-30	split	40-50	2-6
	400-500	Cobalt	B	118-135	7-10	25-30	split	25-40	1-4
	over 500	C-2	C	118	7-10	0	notched	75-100	0.5-2
Die steels	to 300	M-1, M-2	A	118-135	7-10	25-30	split	45-55	3-7
Hot-work	300-400	M-1, M-2	A	118-135	7-10	25-30	split	35-50	2-6
	400-500	Cobalt	B	118-135	7-10	25-30	split	25-35	1-4
	over 500	C-2	C	118	7-10	0	Notched	70-90	0.5-2
Stainless steels (Austenitic) 300	135-185	M-1, M-2	A	118-135	7-10	25-30	split	70-90	2-6
Stainless steels	150-250	M-1, M-2	A	118-135	7-10	25-30	split	50-70	3-7
(Martensitic) 400	250-450	M-1, M-2	A	118-135	7-10	25-30	split	30-40	2-6
	over 450	Cobalt	B	118-135	7-10	25-30	split	20-30	1-4
Stainless steels	to 200	M-1, M-2	A	118-135	7-10	25-30	split	50-60	3-7
Precipitation	200-350	M-1, M-2	A	118-135	7-10	25-30	split	35-45	2-6
hardening 17-7PH, etc.	over 350	Cobalt	B	118-135	7-10	25-30	split	20-30	1-4
Nickel-cobalt steels	to 400	M-1, M-2	A	118-135	7-10	25-30	split	55-65	2-6
High-strength	400-500	Cobalt	B	118-135	7-10	25-30	split	30-40	1-4
	over 500	C-2	C	118	7-10	0	notched	70-90	0.5-2
High-temperature Cobalt-base alloys	to 300	Cobalt	B	118-135	7-10	25-30	split	15-25	1-4
High-temperature	to 250	Cobalt	B	118-135	7-10	25-30	split	20-30	2-6
Iron-base alloys	over 250	Cobalt	B	118-135	7-10	25-30	split	15-25	2-6
High-temperature	to 265	Cobalt	B	118-135	7-10	25-30	split	20-30	2-6
Nickel-base alloys	265-330	Cobalt	B	118-135	7-10	25-30	split	20-25	2-5
	over 330	Cobalt	B	118-135	7-10	25-30	split	15-20	1-4

Figure 7.112 Drilling recommendation table.

Magnesium & alloys	All	M-1, M-2	A	118-135	7-10	25-30	split	150-350	2-7
Aluminum & alloys 2024, 6061, 7075, etc.	All	M-1, M-2	A	118-135	7-10	25-30	split	175-400	2-7
Titanium	to 250	M-34, M-42	B	135	7-12	30-38	split	25-30	5-7
Titanium Alpha alloys	250-300	M-34, M-42	B	135	7-12	30-38	split	20-25	5-7
Titanium Alpha-Beta alloys	to 350 over 350	M-34, M-42 M-34, M-42	B B	135 135	7-12 7-12	30-38 30-38	split split	20-25 15-25	5-7 5-7
Titanium Beta alloys	to 350 over 350	M-34, M-42 M-34, M-42	B B	135 135	7-12 7-12	30-38 30-38	split split	15-20 15-17	1-4 0.5-2
Beryllium copper	250	C-2	D	90-118	10-15	25-30	split	30-45	2-8
Tungsten & alloys	to 350	C-2, C-3	D	90-118	7-10	25-30	notched	200-250	1-4
Brass, free-machining	All	M-1, M-2	A	118	7-10	25-30	standard	100-250	4-10
Bronzes, common	All	M-1, M-2	A	118	7-10	25-30	standard	200-250	3-15
Bronze, phosphur	Hard	M-1, M-2	A	118	7-10	25-30	notched	75-150	2-6
Copper	All	M-1, M-2	A	90-118	7-10	25-30	standard	100-250	1-5
Cast iron Soft to medium	soft-med.	M-1, M-2	A	118	7-10	25-30	std or split	75-150	2-8
Cast iron Hard	Hard	C-2	D	118	7-10	25-30	std or split	40-75	1-5
Zinc	All	M-1, M-2	A	118	7-10	25-30	standard	200-250	3-10
Low-carbon steels	to 300	M-1, M-2	A	118	7-10	25-30	standard	80-100	3-10
Thermoplastics	Medium	M-1, M-2	E	60-90	12-16	17	standard	100-150	2-15

Thermosetting plastics	Soft	M-1, M-2	E	60-90	12-16	17	standard	150	3-8
	Hard	M-1, M-2	E	60-90	12-16	17	standard	100	2-6

NOTE:
Drill Types: A = AIAA type B or C; B = Heavy duty cobalt; C = Carbide tipped; D = Solid carbide; E = Standard with wide, polished flutes.

Coolants and cutting fluids are recommended in the Coolant & Cutting Fluid Section of the handbook.

* Tabular data in the table is for drills of 0.125 through 0.500" diameter and hole depths of 1 to 3 drill diameters.
Adjustments must be made for other conditions, by interpolation or trial drilling. (Smaller drills have a lower ipr feed rate; larger drills have a higher ipr feed rate).

Drill geometry: PA = Point angle, degrees; LRf = Lip relief angle, degrees; HA = helix angle, degrees

Tabular data for ipr - Feed is given in powers of ten notation, i.e. 2 = .002"; 6 = .006"; 0.5 = 0.0005", etc.

Figure 7.112 *(Continued)*

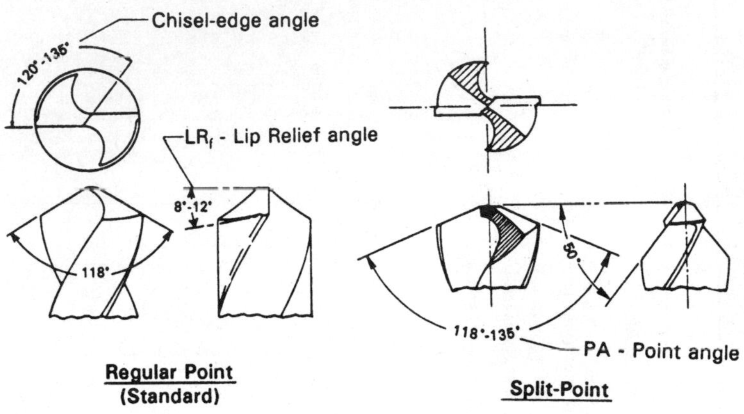

Figure 7.113 Standard and split points.

Spade Drill Terminology & Features

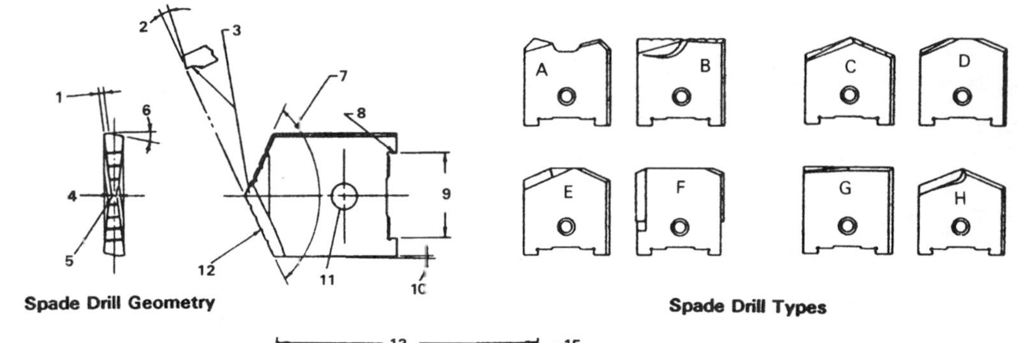
1
2
3
4
5
6
7
8
9
10
11
12
Spade Drill Geometry
1- Circular OD land, radial land or margin
2- Front clearance/lip relief
3- Chip curler/gullet
4- Web
5- Chisel edge
6- OD clearance/radial relief
7- Point angle
8- Locating ears
9- Locating slot
10- Back taper
11- Screw hole
12- Chipbreaker grooves
13- Flute length
14-Locating flats
15- Coolant inlet (pipe thread)
16- Coolant holes
17- Shank
18- Coolant inductor
19- Blade screw
20- Body diameter
13
14
15
16
17
18
19
20
Spade Drill Holder

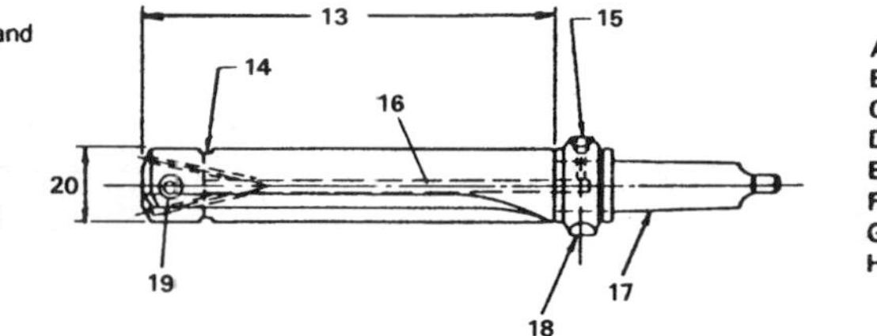
A
B
C
D
E
F
G
H
Spade Drill Types
A- Spur-core blade
B- Facing blade (flat bottom)
C- Regular blade
D- Standard core blade
E- Standard carbide core blade
F- Core blade with carbide edges
G- Counterbore
H- Regular carbide blade

Figure 7.114 Spade drills.

The standard point angle on a spade drill is 130°. The rake angle ranges from 10 to 12° for average-hardness materials. The rake angle should be 5 to 7° for hard steels and 15 to 20° for soft, ductile materials. The back-taper angle should be 0.001 to 0.002 in per inch of blade depth. The outside diameter clearance angle is generally between 7 to 10°.

The cutting speeds for spade drills are normally 10 to 15 percent lower than those for standard twist drills. See the tables of drill speeds and feeds in the preceding section for approximate starting speeds. Heavy feed rates should be used with spade drilling. The table shown in Fig. 7.115 gives recommended feed rates for spade drilling various materials.

Horsepower and thrust forces for spade drilling. The following simplified equations will allow you to calculate the approximate horsepower requirements and thrust needed to spade drill various materials with different diameter spade drills. In order to do this, you must find the feed rate for your particular spade drill diameter, as shown in Fig. 7.115, and then select the P factor for your material, as tabulated in Fig. 7.116.

The following equations may then be used to estimate the required horsepower at the machine's motor and the thrust required in pounds force for the drilling process.

$$C_{hp} = P\left(\frac{\pi D^2}{4}\right)FN$$

$$T_p = 148{,}500PFD$$

$$M_{hp} = \frac{C_{hp}}{e}$$

$$F = \frac{f_m}{N} \qquad \text{and} \qquad f_m = FN$$

where C_{hp} = horsepower at the cutter
M_{hp} = required motor horsepower
T_p = Thrust for spade drilling, pounds force
D = drill diameter, in
F = feed, ipr (see Fig. 7.115 for ipr/diameter/material)
P = power factor constant (see Fig. 7.116)
f_m = feed, ipm
N = spindle speed, rpm

e = drive motor efficiency factor (0.90 for direct belt drive to the spindle; 0.80 for geared head drive to the spindle)

Note: The P factors must be increased by 40 to 50 percent for dull tools, although dull cutters should not be utilized if productivity is to remain high.

7.3.8 Microdrills

Drills below 0.020 in in diameter are considered to be *microdrills.* Microdrills as small as 0.0016 in in diameter are available as stock items from the drill supply vendors. Microdrills are manufactured from high-speed steel, cobalt-base carbides, and solid-tungsten carbides, and a limited selection is available in diamond and CBN surfaces. Some of the standard commercially available microdrill sizes are listed in Fig. 7.117.

In order to use microdrills, special machines have been developed for controlling these extremely small and fragile tools. Holes of great precision may be made in many materials using the appropriate machine tools and microdrills designed for microdrilling. Needless to say, a microdrilling operation is conducted under a high-magnification viewing device, with the hand motions of the operator greatly reduced in magnitude by linkage translators on the microdrilling machine.

Specialty flat-style microdrill geometry and terminology are shown in Fig. 7.118, together with the various types of microdrilling tools. The microdrilled hole usually requires additional operations such as countersinking, reaming, counterboring, etc. Figure 7.119 gives the preferred dimensions for the special flat-type microdrills that are usually custom made for various applications. Materials for these special microdrills may be of HSS, cobalt-base carbides, or tungsten carbides.

Solid-carbide square die drills. For cold drilling extremely accurate holes in hard steels from Rockwell R_c40 to R_c70, the carbide square die drill is standardized in sizes from 0.09375 through 0.5000 in diameter. These are available from national drill distributors and are ideally suited for mold and die repair and maintenance.

7.3.9 Drilling problems and solutions

Problem	Causes	Remedy
Outer corners breakdown	Revolutions per minute too high Poor lip relief	Reduce feed and speed Check lip relief
Cutting lips chip	Feed too high High lip relief	Reduce feed Check lip relief
Cracks in cutting lips	Running too hot	Repoint drill Check feed and speed
Drill breaks	Improper point Flutes clogging	Use proper point Check feed
Drill splits up center	Feed too high Lip relief wrong	Reduce feed Correct relief
Drill will not penetrate	Reverse chisel	Check chisel angle
Rough hole	Dull point No lubricant	Repoint drill Use lubricant
Oversize hole	Unequal length on cutting lips	Repoint drill
Loose spindle	Inspect spindle	
Chips change form while drilling	Improper point	Repoint drill
Margins chip	Oversize bushing	Change bushing

7.4 Reaming

A *reamer* is a rotary cutting tool, either cyclindrical or conical in shape, used for enlarging drilled holes to accurate dimensions, normally on the order of ±0.0001 in and closer. Reamers usually have two or more flutes which may be straight or spiral in either left-hand or right hand spiral. Reamers are made for manual or machine operation. Figure 7.120 shows reamer geometry and terminology.

Reamers are made in various forms, including

- Hand reamers
- Machine reamers
- Left-hand flute

- Right-hand flute
- Expansion reamers
- Chucking reamers
- Stub screw-machine reamers
- End-cutting reamers
- Jobbers reamers
- Shell reamers
- Combined drill and reamer

Most reamers are produced from premium-grade HSS. Reamers are also produced in cobalt alloys, and these may be run at speeds 25 percent faster than HSS reamers. Reamer feeds depend on the type of reamer, the material and amount to be removed, and the final finish required. Material-removal rates depend on the size of the reamer and material, but general figures may be used on a trial basis and are summarized below:

Hole diameter	Material to be removed
Up to 0.500 in diameter	0.005 in for finishing
More than 0.500 in diameter	0.015 in for finishing
Up to 0.500 in diameter	0.015 in for semifinished holes
More than 0.500 in diameter	0.030 in for semifinished holes

This is an important consideration when using the expansion reamer owing to the maximum amount of expansion allowed by the adjustment on the expansion reamer.

7.4.1 Machine speeds and feeds for HSS reamers (see Fig. 7.121)

Note: Cobalt-alloy and carbide reamers may be run at speeds 25 percent faster than those shown in Fig. 7.121.

Carbide-tipped and solid-carbide chucking reamers are also available and afford greater effective life than HHS and cobalt reamers without losing their nominal size dimensions. Speeds and feeds for carbide reamers are generally similar to those for the cobalt-alloy types.

7.4.2 Sharpening reamers

It would be difficult, if not impossible, to hand sharpen any type of reamer. Reamer sharpening machines are produced by various manufacturers (Darex), and sharpening facilities are available nationwide for this purpose.

Standard reamer sizes are produced and may be purchased separately or in sets for various applications. Some of the more common types of reamers are shown in Fig. 7.121*a*.

7.4.3 Forms of reamers

Other forms of reamers include the following:

Morse taper reamers. These reamers are used to produce and maintain holes for American standard Morse taper shanks. They usually come in a set of two, one for roughing and the other for finishing the tapered hole.

Taper-pin reamers. Taper-pin reamers are produced in HSS with straight, spiral, and helical flutes. They range in size from pin size 7/0 through 14 and include 21 different sizes to accommodate all standard taper pins.

Dowel-pin reamers. Dowel-pin reamers are produced in HSS for standard length and jobbers' lengths in 14 different sizes from 0.125 through 0.500 in. The nominal reamer size is slightly smaller than the pin diameter to afford a force fit.

Helical-flute die-makers' reamers. These reamers are used as milling cutters to join closely drilled holes. They are produced from HSS and are available in 16 sizes ranging from size AAA through O.

Reamer blanks. Reamer blanks are available for use as gages, guide pins, or punches. They are made of HSS in jobbers' lengths from 0.015 through 0.500 in diameters. Fractional sizes through 1.00 in diameter and wire-gage sizes are also available.

Shell reamers (see Fig. 7.121*a*). These reamers are designed for mounting on arbors and are best suited for sizing and finishing operations. Most shell reamers are produced from HSS. The inside hole in the shell reamer is tapered ⅛ in per foot and fits the taper on the reamer arbor.

Expansion reamers (see Fig. 7.121*a*). The hand expansion reamer has an adjusting screw at the cutting end which allows the reamer flutes to expand within certain limits. The recommended expansion limits are listed below for sizes through 1.00 in diameter:

Reamer size: 0.25 to 0.625 in diameter Expansion limit = 0.010 in

Reamer size: 0.75 to 1.000 in diameter Expansion limit = 0.013 in

Note: Expansion reamer stock sizes up to 3.00 in diameter are available.

7.5 Broaching

Broaching is a precision machining operation wherein a broach tool is either pulled or pushed through a hole in a workpiece or over the surface of a workpiece to produce a very accurate shape such as round, square, hexagonal, spline, keyway, and so on. Keyways in gear and sprocket hubs are broached to an exact dimension so that the key will fit with very little clearance between the hub of the gear or sprocket and the shaft. The cutting teeth on broaches are increased in size along the axis of the broach so that as the broach is pushed or pulled through the workpiece, a progressive series of cuts is made to the finished size in a single pass.

Broaches are driven or pulled by manual arbor presses and horizontal or vertical broaching machines. A single stroke of the broaching tool completes the machining operation. Broaches are commonly made from premium-quality HSS and are supplied either in single tools or as sets in graduated sizes and different shapes. Figure 7.122 shows a number of different types of broaches such as keyway, square, and hexagonal.

Broaches may be used to cut internal or external shapes on workpieces. Blind holes also can be broached with specially designed broaching tools. The broaching tool teeth along the length of the broach are normally divided into three separate sections. The teeth of a broach include roughing teeth, semifinishing teeth, and finishing teeth. All finishing teeth of a broach are the same size, while the semifinishing and roughing teeth are progressive in size up to the finishing teeth.

Figure 7.123 shows the terminology and geometry of broaching teeth. A broaching tool must have sufficient strength and stock-removal and chip-carrying capacity for its intended operation. An interval-pull broach must have sufficient tensile strength to withstand the maximum pulling forces that occur during the pulling operation. An internal-push broach must have sufficient compressive strength as well as the ability to withstand buckling or breaking under the pushing forces that occur during the pushing operation.

Broaches are produced in sizes ranging from 0.050 to as large as 20 in or more. The term *button broach* was used for broaching tools which produced the spiral lands that form the "rifling" in gun barrels from small to large caliber. Broaches may be rotated to produce a predetermined spiral angle during the pull or push operations.

7.5.1 Calculation of pull forces during broaching

The allowable pulling force P is determined by first calculating the cross-sectional area at the minimum root of the broach. The allowable pull in pounds force is determined from

$$P = \frac{A_r F_y}{f_s}$$

where A_r = minimum tool cross section, in^2
F_y = tensile yield strength or yield point of tool steel, psi
f_s = factor of safety (generally 3 for pull broaching)

The minimum root cross section for a round broach is

$$A_r = \frac{\pi D_r^2}{4} \quad \text{or} \quad 0.7854 D_r^2$$

where D_r = minimum root diameter, in

The minimum pull-end cross section A_p is

$$A_p = \frac{\pi}{4} D_p^2 - W D_p \quad \text{or} \quad 0.7854 D_p^2 - W D_p$$

where D_p = pull-end diameter, in
W = pull-slot width, in

7.5.2 Calculation of push forces during broaching

Knowing the length L and the compressive yield point of the tool steel used in the broach, the following relations may be used in designing or determining the maximum push forces allowed in push broaching.

If the length of the broach is L and the minimum tool diameter is D_r, the ratio L/D_r should be less than 25 so that the tool will not bend under maximum load. Most push broaches are short enough that the maximum compressive strength of the broach material will allow much greater forces than the forces applied during the broaching operation.

If the L/D_r ratio is greater than 25, compressive broaching forces may bend or break the broach tool if they exceed the maximum allowable force for the tool. The maximum allowable compressive force (pounds force) for a long push broach is determined from the following equation:

$$P = \frac{5.6 \times 10^7 D_r^4}{(f_s)L^2}$$

where L is measured from the push end to the first tooth in inches.

7.5.3 Minimum forces required for broaching different materials

For flat surface broaches,

$$F = WnR\psi$$

For round-hole internal broaches,

$$F = \frac{\pi DnR}{2}\psi$$

For spline-hole broaches,

$$F = \frac{nSWR}{2}\psi$$

where F = minimum pulling or pushing force required, lbf (pounds force)

W = width of cut per tooth or spline, in

D = hole diameter before broaching, in
R = rise per tooth, in
n = maximum number of broach teeth engaged in the workpiece
S = number of splines (for splined holes only)
ψ = broaching constant (see Fig. 7.124 for values)

Referring to Fig. 7.123, typical rake and relief angles are specified in Fig. 7.125.

7.6 Vertical Boring and Jig Boring

The increased demand for accuracy in producing large parts initiated the refined development of modern vertical and jig boring machines. Although the modern CNC machining centers can handle small to medium-sized jig boring operations, very large and heavy work of high precision is done on modern CNC jig boring machines or vertical boring machines. Also, any size work which requires extreme accuracy is usually jig bored. The modern jig boring machines are equipped with high-precision spindles and *x/y* coordinate table movements of high precision and may be CNC controlled with digital read-out panels. For a modern jig boring operation that is CNC/DNC controlled, the circle diameter and number of equally spaced holes or other geometric pattern is entered into the DNC program and the computer calculates all the coordinates and orientation of the holes from a reference point. This information is either sent to the CNC jig boring machine's controller or the machine operator can load this information into the controller, which controls the machine movements to complete the machining operation. A typical jig-boring machine is illustrated in Fig. 7.126.

Extensive tables of jig boring coordinates are not necessary with the modern CNC jig boring or vertical boring machines. Figures 7.127 and 7.128 are for manually controlled machines, where the machine operator makes the movements and coordinate settings manually.

Vertical boring machines with tables up to 192 in in diameter are produced for machining very large and heavy workpieces.

For manually controlled machines with vernier or digital readouts, a table of jig boring dimensional coordinates is shown in Fig. 7.127 for dividing a 1-in circle into a number of equal divisions. Since the dimensions or coordinates given in the table are for *xy* table movements, the machine operator may use these directly to make the appropriate machine settings after converting the coordinates for the required circle diameter to be divided.

Figure 7.128 is a coordinate diagram of a jig bore layout for 11 equally spaced holes on a 1-in-diameter circle. The coordinates are taken from the table in Fig. 7.127. If a different-diameter circle is to be divided, simply multiply the coordinate values in the table by the diameter of the required circle; i.e., for an 11-hole circle of 5-in diameter, multiply the coordinates for the 11-hole circle by 5. Thus the first hole x dimension would be $5 \times 0.50000 = 2.50000$ in, and so on.

7.7 Grinding, Lapping, Honing, and Superfinishing (Surface Finishes)

7.7.1 Grinding

The *grinding* process is an abrasive machining operation where material is removed from a workpiece in small chips or particles by the mechanical action of abrasive particles of irregular shape, size, and hardness. Grinding can be a rough or a precision operation for producing smooth surfaces, either flat, cylindrical, or irregularly shaped. The medium of the grinding operation is the grinding wheel, which is used for both external and internal grinding procedures. Grinding wheel shapes and other specifications are defined by the following ANSI standards:

ANSI B74.2-1982, *Shapes and sizes of grinding wheels*

ANSI B74.3-1986, *Shapes and sizes of diamond and cubic boron nitride abrasive products*

ANSI B74.13-1990, *Markings for identifying grinding wheels and other bonded abrasives*

Other ANSI standards define chemical analysis, bulk density, size of abrasive grains, and other specifications for grinding products and testing procedures.

An ideal grinding abrasive has the ability to fracture before serious dulling occurs and offers maximum resistance to point wear. Each abrasive has a special crystal structure and fracture characteristics, making it suitable for grinding operations on specific materials.

(*Text continued on page 682.*)

Recommended Feed Rates for Spade Drilling- (ipr, inches per revolution)

Material	Hardness Bhn	Feed - ipr Spade Drill Diameter, inches					
		1-1.25	1.25-2	2-3	3-4	4-5	5-8
Plain carbon steels	100-225	.012	.015	.018	.022	.025	.030
	225-275	.010	.013	.015	.018	.020	.025
	275-325	.008	.010	.013	.015	.018	.020
Free-machining steels	100-240	.014	.016	.018	.022	.025	.030
	240-325	.010	.014	.016	.020	.022	.025
Free-machining alloy steels	150-250	.014	.016	.018	.022	.025	.030
	250-325	.012	.014	.016	.018	.020	.025
	325-375	.010	.012	.014	.016	.018	.020
Alloy steels	125-180	.012	.015	.018	.022	.025	.030
	180-225	.010	.012	.016	.018	.022	.025
	225-325	.009	.010	.013	.015	.018	.020
	325-400	.006	.006	.010	.012	.014	.016
Grey cast iron	110-160	.020	.022	.026	.028	.030	.034
	160-240	.012	.014	.016	.018	.020	.022
	240-325	.010	.012	.016	.018	.018	.018
Ductile & nodular iron	140-190	.014	.016	.018	.020	.022	.024
	190-250	.012	.014	.016	.018	.018	.020
	250-325	.010	.012	.016	.018	.018	.018
Malleable iron- ferritic	110-160	.014	.016	.018	.020	.022	.024
Malleable iron- pearlitic	160-280	.011	.013	.015	.018	.018	.018
Stainless steels- free-machining							
Ferritic & austenitic (screw stock)	-------	.016	.018	.020	.022	.024	.026
Martensitic (440F, etc.)	-------	.012	.014	.016	.016	.018	.020

Stainless steels							
Ferritic & austenitic (200 & 300 series)	-------	.012	.014	.016	.018	.020	.020
Martensitic (400 series)	-------	.010	.012	.012	.014	.016	.018
Copper alloys							
Soft (ETP-110, etc)	-------	.016	.018	.020	.026	.028	.030
Hard (bronzes)	-------	.010	.012	.014	.016	.018	.018
Aluminum alloys (free-machining)	-------	.020	.022	.024	.028	.030	.040
Magnesium alloys (general) **	-------	.024	.026	.030	.034	.040	.050
High-temperature alloys (general)	-------	.008	.010	.012	.012	.014	.014
Titanium alloys (general)	-------	.008	.010	.012	.014	.014	.016
Tool steels							
Water-hardening & shock resisting	150-250	.012	.-14	.016	.018	.020	.022
Cold work	200-250	.007	.008	.009	.010	.011	.012
Hot work	150-250	.012	.013	.015	.016	.018	.020
High-speed steels	200-250	.010	.012	.013	.015	.017	.018

NOTE: Hardness ranges are Brinell hardness numbers. Tabular data is in inches of feed per revolution, ipr.
** A fire hazard exists when machining or drilling magnesium & alloys.

Figure 7.115 Feed rates for spade drills.

"P" Factors for Spade Drilling Various Materials

Material	Hardness Bhn	"P" Factor
Plain carbon & alloy steels	90-200	0.75
	200-275	0.92
	300-375	1.02
	375-450	1.18
	45-52R_C	1.45
Gray cast irons	-------	0.25
Alloy cast irons & ductile irons	-------	0.50
Stainless steel (austenitic)	-------	0.96
Stainless steels (martensitic)	-------	0.81
Titanium alloys	-------	0.87
Aluminum alloys	-------	0.20
Magnesium alloys	-------	0.15
Copper alloys	Soft - R_B 20-80	0.42
	Hard - R_B 80-100	0.75
Tool steels	-------	1.10
Cobalt based alloys	-------	1.25
High-temperature alloys	-------	1.45
Non-ferrous free-machining alloys	-------	0.45

Note: Where no hardness range is given, the maximum hardness is 300 Bhn. For harder materials, use a higher "P" factor.

Figure 7.116 *P* factor table.

Standard Size Microdrills - High-Speed Steel and Cobalt

High-Speed Steel Microdrills

Diameter inches	mm	Flute lth.
0.0059	0.15	0.0469
0.0063	0.16	0.0469
0.0067	0.17	0.0625
0.0071	0.18	0.0625
0.0075	0.19	0.0625
0.0079	0.20	0.0625
0.0083	0.21	0.0625
0.0087	0.22	0.0625
0.0091	0.23	0.0625
0.0094	0.24	0.0781
0.0098	0.25	0.0781
0.0102	0.26	0.0781
0.0106	0.27	0.0781
0.0110	0.28	0.0938
0.0114	0.29	0.0938
0.0118	0.30	0.0938
0.0126	0.32	0.0938
0.0134	0.34	0.0938
0.0142	0.36	0.1875
0.0150	0.38	0.1875
0.0157	0.40	0.1875
0.0165	0.42	0.1875
0.0173	0.44	0.1875
0.0181	0.46	0.1875
0.0189	0.48	0.1875
0.0197	0.50	0.1875

Note: Drill points are 118°. Shank size is same as drill diameter. Drills 0.38mm and less are 0.75" long, all others 0.875".

Cobalt Microdrills

Diameter inches	mm	Flute lth.
0.0019	0.05	0.0158
0.0024	0.06	0.0158
0.0028	0.07	0.0158
0.0032	0.08	0.0197
0.0035	0.09	0.0197
0.0039	0.10	0.0276
0.0043	0.11	0.0276
0.0047	0.12	0.0276
0.0051	0.13	0.0394
0.0055	0.14	0.0394
0.0059	0.15	0.0394
0.0063	0.16	0.0552
0.0067	0.17	0.0552
0.0071	0.18	0.0552
0.0075	0.19	0.0552
0.0079	0.20	0.0709
0.0083	0.21	0.0709
0.0087	0.22	0.0709
0.0091	0.23	0.0709
0.0094	0.24	0.0709
0.0098	0.25	0.0867
0.0102	0.26	0.0867
0.0106	0.27	0.0867
0.0110	0.28	0.0867
0.0114	0.29	0.0867
0.0118	0.30	0.0867
0.0122	0.31	0.1103
0.0126	0.32	0.1103
0.0130	0.33	0.1103
0.0134	0.34	0.1103
0.0138	0.35	0.1103

Diameter inches	mm	Flute lth.
0.0142	0.36	0.1103
0.0146	0.37	0.1103
0.0150	0.38	0.1103
0.0154	0.39	0.1142
0.0157	0.40	0.1142
0.0161	0.41	0.1142
0.0165	0.42	0.1142
0.0169	0.43	0.1142
0.0173	0.44	0.1142
0.0177	0.45	0.1142
0.0181	0.46	0.1142
0.0185	0.47	0.1142
0.0189	0.48	0.1142
0.0193	0.49	0.1576
0.0197	0.50	0.1576

Note: Cobalt drills are for extremely accurate drilling jobs. Right hand spiral, 118° points and 25° helix angle. All shank diameters are 1mm and total length 25mm.

Figure 7.117 Microdrills.

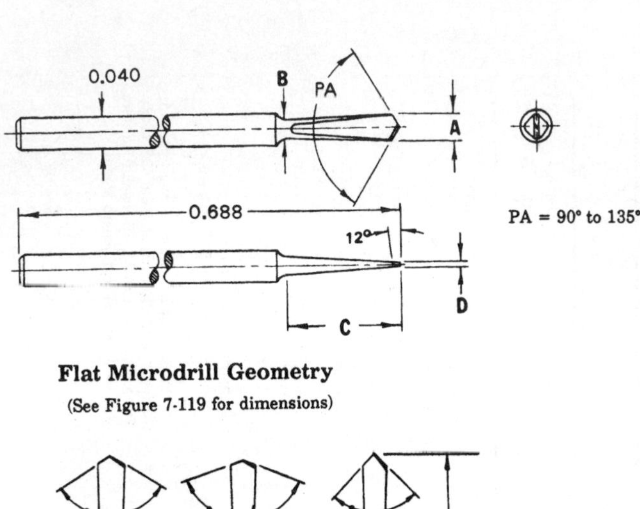

Flat Microdrill Geometry

(See Figure 7-119 for dimensions)

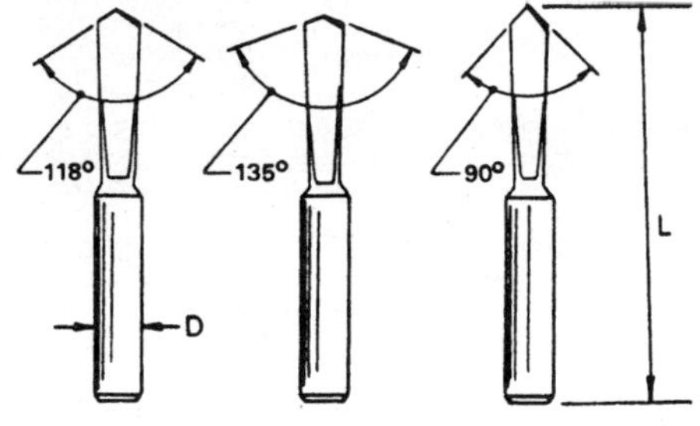

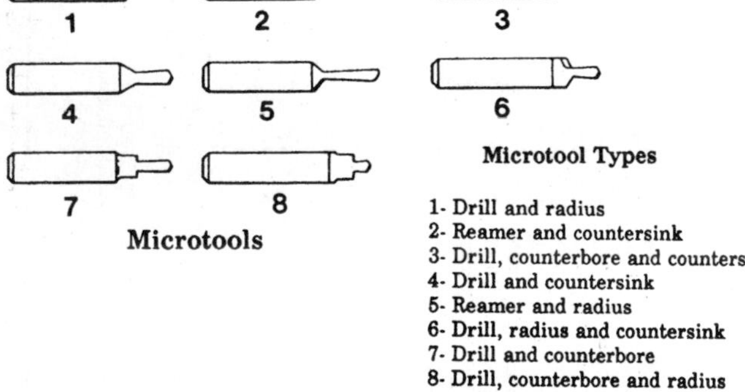

Microtools

Microtool Types

1- Drill and radius
2- Reamer and countersink
3- Drill, counterbore and countersink
4- Drill and countersink
5- Reamer and radius
6- Drill, radius and countersink
7- Drill and counterbore
8- Drill, counterbore and radius

Microdrills and Microtools

Figure 7.118 Geometry of microdrills and microtools.

Flat Microdrill Dimensions - Refer to Figure 7-118 for drill geometry.

Diameter A	Back Taper B	Length C	Web Thickness D
0.0010	0.0001	0.0070	0.0005-0.00075
0.0020	0.0001	0.0140	0.0011-0.0015
0.0030	0.0002	0.0210	0.0016-0.0020
0.0040	0.0002	0.0280	0.0018-0.0022
0.0050	0.0003	0.0350	0.0020-0.0024
0.0060	0.0003	0.0420	0.0022-0.0026
0.0070	0.0004	0.0490	0.0024-0.0028
0.0080	0.0004	0.0560	0.0026-0.0030
0.0090	0.0005	0.0630	0.0028-0.0032
0.0100	0.0005	0.0700	0.0030-0.0034
0.0110	0.0006	0.0770	0.0032-0.0036
0.0120	0.0006	0.0840	0.0038-0.0042
0.0130	0.0007	0.0910	0.0042-0.0046
0.0140	0.0007	0.0980	0.0044-0.0048
0.0150	0.0008	0.1050	0.0046-0.0050
0.0160	0.0008	0.1120	0.0048-0.0052
0.0170	0.0009	0.1190	0.0050-0.0054
0.0180	0.0009	0.1260	0.0053-0.0058
0.0190	0.0010	0.1330	0.0056-0.0060
0.0200	0.0010	0.1400	0.0060-0.0064

Note: These microdrill sizes and dimensions are for custom made flat microdrills. See Figure 7-117 for modern standard size microdrills of HSS and cobalt alloy.

Figure 7.119 Flat microdrill dimensions.

Reamer Features

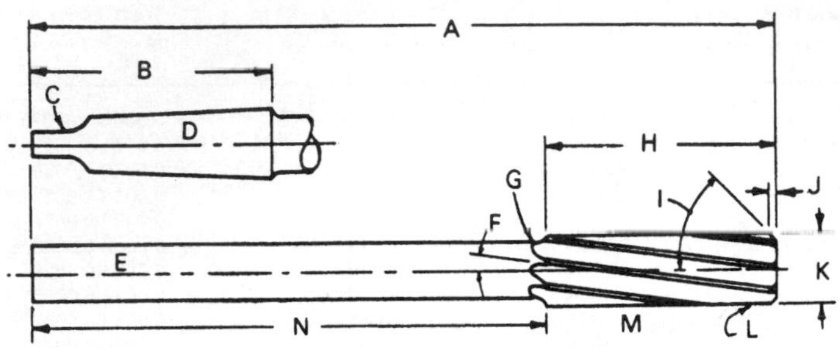

Chucking Reamer - Straight & Taper Shank

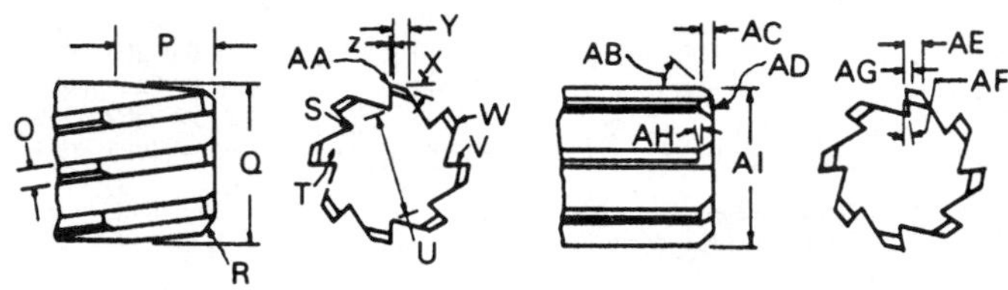

Hand Reamer **Machine Reamer**

A Overall length
B Shank length
C Tang
D Taper shank
E Straight shank
F Helix angle
G Cutter sweep
H Flute length
I Chamfer angle
J Chamfer length
K Actual size
L Body
M Helix flutes, Right hand shown
N Shank length
O Land width
P Starting taper
Q Actual size diameter
R Bevel
S Flute
T Land
U Core diameter
V Cutting face
W Heel
X Relief angle
Y Relieved land
Z Margin
AA Cutting edge
AB Chamfer angle
AC Chamfer length
AD Chamfer relief
AE Land width
AF Radial rake angle
AG Margin
AH Chamfer relief angle
AI Actual size diameter

Figure 7.120 Reamer features.

Machine Speeds and Feeds for HSS Reamers- (sfpm and ipr)

Material	Speed (sfpm)	Feed Code (ipr)
Steel - 150 Bhn	80	1
Steel - 200 Bhn	55	2
Steel - 250 Bhn	35	3
Steel - 300 Bhn	30	3
Steel - 350 Bhn	17	4
Steel - 400 Bhn	10	4
Steel, cast	25	3
Steel, forged alloys	30	3
Steel, low carbon	75	2
Steel, high carbon	45	4
Steel, stainless	15	3
Steel, tool	35	4
Titanium	40	1
Zinc alloy	150	1
Aluminum & alloys	150	1
Brass, leaded	175	1
Brass, red & yellow	150	1
Bronzes	160	1
Copper	45	3
Cast iron, chilled	10	4
Cast iron, hard	50	3
Cast iron, pearlitic	60	1
Cast iron, soft	95	1
Malleable iron	65	2
Monels	30	3
Nickels	40	3
Plastic, hard	50	1
Plastic, soft	65	3

Feed Code, ipr (inches per revolution)

Reamer Diameter	Code 1	Code 2	Code 3	Code 4
0.125"	0.006	0.005	0.004	0.003
0.500"	0.012	0.010	0.007	0.005
1.00"	0.020	0.015	0.012	0.008
2.00"	0.032	0.025	0.020	0.012
2.25 - 2.50"	0.043	0.035	0.028	0.018
2.75 - 3.00"	0.055	0.045	0.035	0.024

Note: Reamer feeds may be interpolated for intermediate sizes than those shown in the table. Cobalt reamers may be run at speeds 25% faster than those shown in the table for HSS.

(a)

Figure 7.121 (*a*) Speeds and feeds, HSS reamers. (*b*) Typical reamer types.

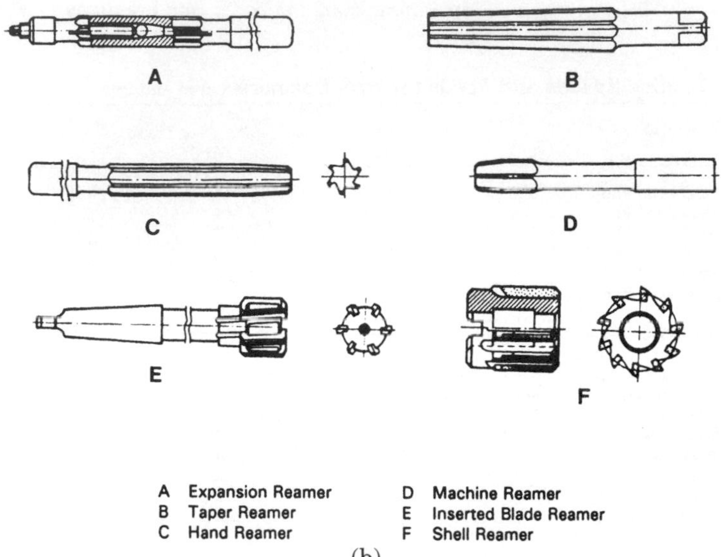

(b)

Figure 7.121 (*Continued*)

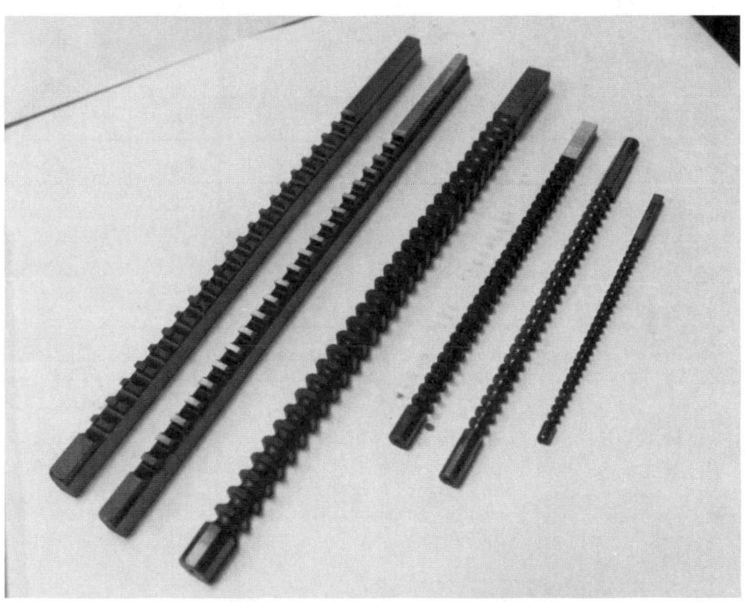

Figure 7.122 Keyway, square, and hexagonal broaches.

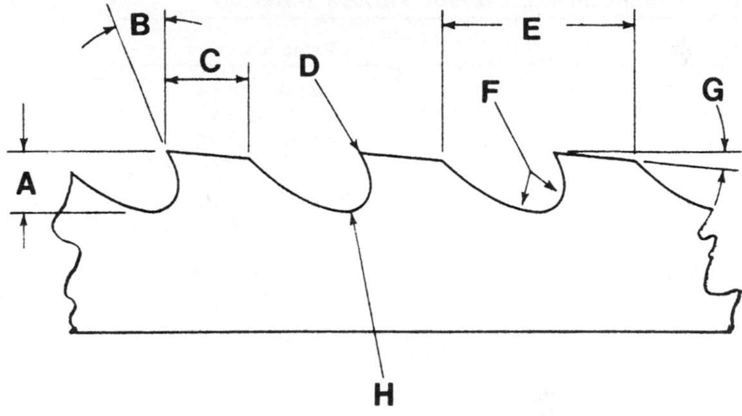

Broach Terminology and Geometry

A Gullet Depth
B Face Angle
C Land
D Cutting Edge
E Pitch
F Tooth Gullet
G Rake Angle
H Root Radius

Figure 7.123 Broach terminology.

Broaching Constants (ψ) for Various Materials

Material	Value of ψ
Aluminum	200,000 - 300,000
Babbitt	25,000 - 35,000
Brass	200,000 - 300,000
Bronze	300,000 - 350,000
Cast irons	200,000 - 350,000
High-temperature alloys	350,000 - 600,000
Mild steels	350,000 - 450,000
Steel castings	350,000 - 400,000
Titanium	325,000 - 375,000
Zinc alloys	200,000 - 250,000

Note: The tabular values given in the table have a limited value due to the many variables involved in broaching, such as chipbreakers, lubricating and cutting fluid effects and other factors which tend to increase or reduce the required cutting force as calculated using the preceding equations.

Figure 7.124 Broaching constants.

Typical HSS Broach Rake angles and Relief Angles - Degrees)

Material	Rake Angle (Degrees)	Relief Angle (Degrees)
Aluminum	6 - 10	------
Babbitt	8 - 10	------
Brass	-5 to 5	2 - 3
Bronze	0	1 - 2
Cast iron	6 - 10	2 - 5
Copper	12 - 15	2 - 3
Aluminum bronze	12 - 15	2 - 3
Steels: SAE		
1035	15	1 - 2
1112	15	2 - 3
4140	8 - 15	1 - 3
5140	18 - 20 (finishing)	1 - 2
Stainless steels: AISI		
303	15	0.5 - 2
304, 304L	15	0.5 - 2
316	12 - 15	0.5 - 2
410	12 - 15	0.5 - 2
430	15 - 20	0.5 - 2
440	12- 15	0.5 - 2
Titanium:		
Soft	5 - 15	2 - 4
Hard	12 - 15	2.5 - 3
Zinc	6	------

Figure 7.125 Rake angles, broaches.

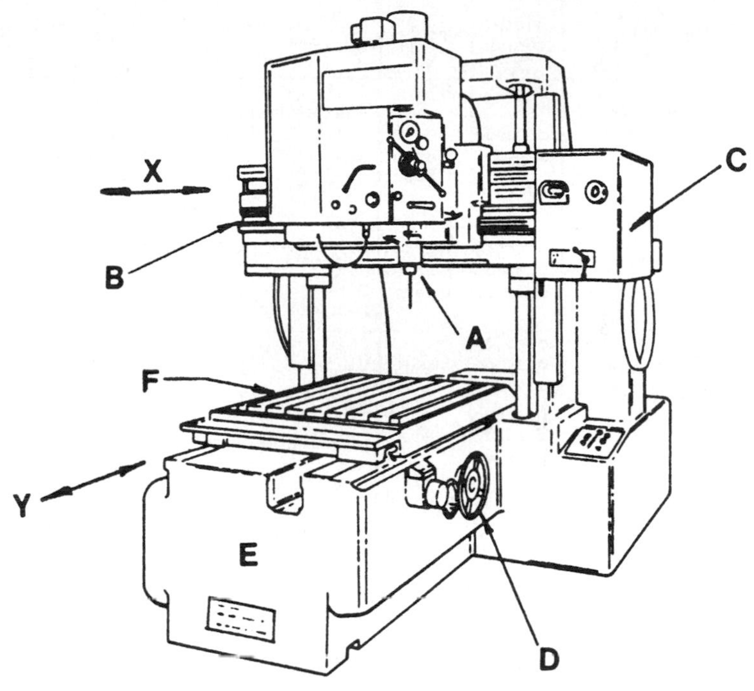

Typical Jig Boring Machine- NC or CNC

A High precision spindle
B X axis ways
C Controller
D Manual table positioning control
E Front
F Horizontal clamping table
X X axis movement
Y Y axis movement

Figure 7.126 Jig-boring machine.

Jig Boring Coordinates for Dividing the Circle

Hole No.	Horizontal X	Vertical Y
Three holes:		
1	0.50000	
2	0.75000	0.43301
3	....	0.86602
Five holes:		
1	0.50000	
2	0.34549	0.47553
3, 5	0.55902	0.18164
4	....	0.58778
Six holes:		
1, 3, 6	0.50000	
2, 4, 5	0.25000	0.43301
Seven holes:		
1	0.50000	
2	0.18826	0.39091
3, 7	0.42300	0.09655
4, 6	0.33923	0.27052
5	....	0.43388
Eight holes:		
1	0.50000	
2, 5, 6	0.14645	0.35355
3, 4, 7, 8	0.35355	0.14645
Nine holes:		
1	0.50000	
2	0.11698	0.32139
3, 9	0.29620	0.17101
4, 8	0.33682	0.05939
5, 7	0.21984	0.26200
6	....	0.34202
Ten holes:		
1	0.50000	
2, 6, 7	0.09549	0.29389
3, 5, 8, 10	0.25000	0.18164
4, 9	0.30902	
Eleven holes:		
1	0.50000	
2	0.07937	0.27032
3, 11	0.21292	0.18450
4, 10	0.27887	0.04009
5, 9	0.25626	0.11704
6, 8	0.15233	0.23701
7	....	0.28172
Twelve holes:		
1	0.50000	
2, 7, 8	0.06699	0.25000
3, 6, 9, 12	0.18301	0.18301
4, 5, 10, 11	0.25000	0.06699
Thirteen holes:		
1	0.50000	
2	0.05727	0.23236
3, 13	0.15870	0.17913
4, 12	0.22376	0.08486
5, 11	0.23757	0.02885
6, 10	0.19695	0.13594
7, 9	0.11121	0.21190
8	....	0.23932
Fourteen holes:		
1	0.50000	
2, 8, 9	0.04951	0.21694
3, 7, 10, 14	0.13875	0.17397
4, 6, 11, 13	0.20048	0.09655
5, 12	0.22252	
Fifteen holes:		
1	0.50000	
2	0.04323	0.20337
3, 15	0.12221	0.16820
4, 14	0.18005	0.10396
5, 13	0.20677	0.02173
6, 12	0.19774	0.06425
7, 11	0.15451	0.13912
8, 10	0.08456	0.18994
9	....	0.20790
Sixteen holes:		
1	0.50000	
2, 9, 10	0.03806	0.19134
3, 8, 11, 16	0.10839	0.16221
4, 7, 12, 15	0.16221	0.10839
5, 6, 13, 14	0.19134	0.03806
Seventeen holes:		
1	0.50000	
2	0.03377	0.18062
3, 17	0.09672	0.15623
4, 16	0.14664	0.11073
5, 15	0.17674	0.05028
6, 14	0.18296	0.01695
7, 13	0.16449	0.08190
8, 12	0.12379	0.13580
9, 11	0.06637	0.17134
10	....	0.18374
Eighteen holes:		
1	0.50000	
2, 10, 11	0.03016	0.17101
3, 9, 12, 18	0.08682	0.15038
4, 8, 13, 17	0.13302	0.11162
5, 7, 14, 16	0.16318	0.05939
6, 15	0.17364	

Figure 7.127 Jig-boring coordinates.

Hole No.	Horizontal X	Vertical Y	Hole No.	Horizontal X	Vertical Y
Nineteen holes:			11, 15	0.07076	0.11634
1	0.50000		12, 14	0.03673	0.13112
2	0.02709	0.16235	13	....	0.13616
3, 19	0.07834	0.14475	Twenty-four holes:		
4, 18	0.12110	0.11148	1	0.50000	
5, 17	0.15073	0.06612	2, 13, 14	0.01704	0.12941
6, 16	0.16403	0.01358	3, 12, 15, 24	0.04995	0.12059
7, 15	0.15956	0.04039	4, 11, 16, 23	0.07946	0.10355
8, 14	0.13779	0.09003	5, 10, 17, 22	0.10355	0.07946
9, 13	0.10110	0.12989	6, 9, 18, 21	0.12059	0.04995
10, 12	0.05344	0.15567	7, 8, 19, 20	0.12941	0.01704
11	....	0.16460	Twenty-five holes:		
Twenty holes:			1	0.50000	
1	0.50000		2	0.01508	0.12434
2, 11, 12	0.02447	0.15451	3, 25	0.04677	0.11653
3, 10, 13, 20	0.07102	0.13938	4, 24	0.07367	0.10140
4, 9, 14, 19	0.11062	0.11062	5, 23	0.09657	0.07989
5, 8, 15, 18	0.13938	0.07102	6, 22	0.11340	0.05337
6, 7, 16, 17	0.15451	0.02447	7, 21	0.12312	0.02348
Twenty-one holes:			8, 20	0.12508	0.00787
1	0.50000		9, 19	0.11920	0.03873
2	0.02221	0.14738	10, 15	0.10582	0.06716
3, 21	0.06467	0.13428	11, 17	0.08580	0.09136
4, 20	0.10138	0.10925	12, 16	0.06038	0.10983
5, 19	0.12908	0.07452	13, 15	0.03116	0.12140
6, 18	0.14530	0.03317	14	....	0.12532
7, 17	0.14862	0.01114	Twenty-six holes:		
8, 16	0.13874	0.05445	1	0.50000	
9, 15	0.11652	0.09293	2, 14, 15	0.01454	0.11966
10, 14	0.08397	0.12314	3, 13, 16, 26	0.04273	0.11270
11, 13	0.04393	0.14242	4, 12, 17, 25	0.06848	0.09920
12	....	0.14904	5, 11, 18, 24	0.09022	0.07993
Twenty-two holes:			6, 10, 19, 23	0.10673	0.05601
1	0.50000		7, 9, 20, 22	0.11703	0.02885
2, 12, 13	0.02025	0.14086	8, 21	0.12054	
3, 11, 14, 22	0.05912	0.12946	Twenty-seven holes:		
4, 10, 15, 21	0.09321	0.10755	1	0.50000	
5, 9, 16, 20	0.11971	0.07695	2	0.01348	0.11530
6, 8, 17, 19	0.13655	0.04009	3, 27	0.03971	0.10910
7, 18	0.14232		4, 26	0.06379	0.09699
Twenty-three holes:			5, 25	0.08444	0.07967
1	0.50000		6, 24	0.10054	0.05805
2	0.01854	0.13490	7, 23	0.11121	0.03329
3, 23	0.05425	0.12489	8, 22	0.11589	0.00675
4, 22	0.08593	0.10562	9, 21	0.11433	0.02016
5, 21	0.11125	0.07853	10, 20	0.10660	0.04598
6, 20	0.12830	0.04560	11, 19	0.09312	0.06933
7, 19	0.13585	0.00930	12, 18	0.07462	0.08893
8, 18	0.13331	0.02771	13, 17	0.05210	0.10374
9, 17	0.12091	0.06264	14, 16	0.02678	0.11297
10, 16	0.09951	0.09295	15	....	0.11608

Figure 7.127 (*Continued*)

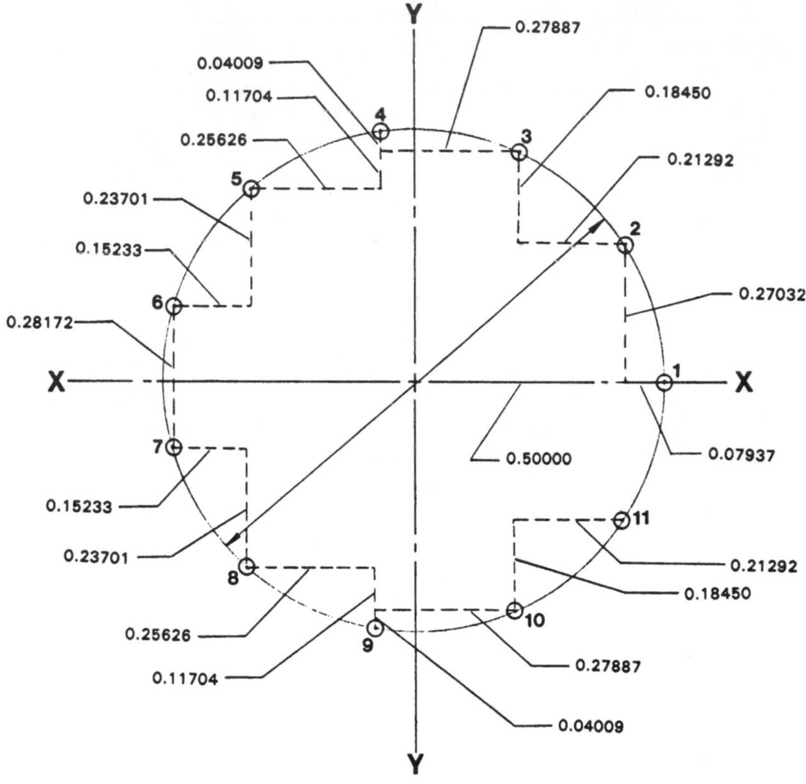

Figure 7.128 Coordinate diagram.

Grinding wheels are composed of abrasive grains of preselected size bonded together with different bonding media. Five important considerations must be given to the selection of a grinding wheel to suit a particular application:

1. Abrasive type
2. Grain size
3. Bonding media
4. Grade or hardness of the wheel
5. Structure

Wheel abrasives

Natural abrasives: Corundum, emery, and diamond (corundum is natural aluminum oxide containing varying amounts of impurities).

Manufactured abrasives: Synthesized diamond, silicon carbide, aluminum oxide, and cubic boron nitride (CBN). These abrasives all have well-defined physical and chemical characteristics.

Grain size: Abrasive grains vary from 6 to 8 coarse grit to 1000 to 2000 grit for polishing and lapping.

Designation of grinding wheels. A standard marking system defined by ANSI 74.13-1990 for the identification of grinding wheels (excluding diamond and cubic boron nitride) is shown in Fig. 7.129. From this marking system, you may determine the characteristics of the grinding wheel from its markings, as defined by Fig. 7.129.

A standard marking system defined by ANSI B74.3-1986 for the identification of diamond and CBN is shown in Fig. 7.130. From this marking system, you may determine the characteristics of diamond and CBN grinding wheels.

Grinding wheel speeds. The most efficient operating speeds in surface feet per minute (sfpm) for general use are summarized in Fig. 7.131. The manufacturer of your particular wheel may recommend a different surface speed based on its experience with its product. Too low a speed will result in wasted abrasive and lower efficiency, and too high a speed may result in too hard grinding action and breakage of the grinding wheel. Do not exceed the maximum speed in revolutions per minute that is marked on each wheel. Severe injury can result from the flying fragments of a broken grinding wheel.

Some of the standard shapes of grinding wheels are shown in Fig. 7.132. ANSI B74.2-1982 defines shapes and sizes, although different forms and shapes may be produced by some wheel manufacturers. Standard types and shapes of diamond or CBN grinding wheels are shown in Fig. 7.133. As can be seen from Figs. 7.132 and 7.133, many shapes and sizes are available for a multitude of grinding operations, from roughing to tool and die finishes.

It is difficult in a modern machining and metalworking handbook to give the exact type or number of grinding wheel to use for any specific application because of the many variables that arise in actual production situations. The data given in this section are for reference and approximate applicational uses. The manufacturer of the grinding wheels and abrasives employed should be contacted for precise applications on any grinding operation.

Modern machine grinding equipment has been developed to a high degree over the past 40 years. Figure 7.134 shows a modern surface grinder used in tool and die making and other precision applications. In this machine, the grinding wheel is stationary, and the table traverses from left to right and reverses itself in a continuous travel until the final finish is produced on the workpiece. The grinding wheel moves vertically in exact increments to produce the required cut and surface finish. This type of machine is used for flat-surface grinding only.

Figure 7.135 shows a Brown and Sharpe cylindrical grinding machine in which the workpiece is rotated at the same time the grinding wheel is making the required surface finish on the cylindrical part.

The final quality or surface texture of machined and ground parts is usually given on the engineering drawing in root mean square (RMS) numbers. An illustration of the finish texture according to the RMS system is shown in Fig. 7.136. These finishes range from 500 to 2 RMS, with the numbers representing microinches (μin) average. 500 RMS would represent a roughing operation on a milling machine or shaper to a superfinishing operation of 2 μm, average or RMS (root mean square). Finishes finer than 2 RMS can be made using polishing compounds such as cerium oxide or rouge. Cerium oxide and rouge are used extensively in the optical industries for polishing lenses and reflecting mirrors. For finishes of higher RMS values (ranging from 5 to 3 μin), compounds such as aluminum oxide powder may be used.

A convenient table of surface feet per minute converted to revolutions per minute of the grinding wheel is shown in Fig. 7.137. The figures in the table may be calculated using the following equation for converting surface feet per minute (sfpm) to revolutions per minute (rpm):

$$\text{sfpm} = \frac{\pi D(\text{rpm})}{12} \qquad \text{and} \qquad \text{rpm} = \frac{12(\text{sfpm})}{\pi D}$$

Characteristics of grinding

Wheel speed: As wheel speed is increased, less work is required of each individual abrasive grain, and this promotes slower wheel wear.

Work speed: This is the speed at which the workpiece traverses the wheel or rotates about a center.

In-feed rates: The rate at which the wheel enters the workpiece during the grinding action. High in-feed rates increase wheel wear and produce a rougher finish than low in-feed rates.

Traverse or cross-feed: This is the rate at which the workpiece is moved across the face of the wheel. It is not the same as work speed.

Material to be ground. Materials to be ground are either metallic or nonmetallic, and the metallics are divided into low- or high-tensile types. Aluminum oxide wheels are generally used for grinding metallic materials, while diamond and CBN are used to grind the extremely hard metallics as well as ceramics and other hard nonmetallics. Silicon carbide wheels are generally used to grind the softer-grade nonmetallics. Specific and specialized grinding applications should be referred to the grinding wheel manufacturer. Arbitrarily selecting a grinding wheel or relying on handbook listings of specific grinding wheels for exact operations may not be the best solution to your grinding requirements, especially as far as productivity and wheel wear are concerned.

Grinding wheel dressing. There are various forms of grinding wheel dressing tools available. Some of the many types of grinding wheel dressers include

- Helical hooded dressers
- Abrasive wheel dressers
- Single-stone diamond dressers
- Multiple-point diamond dressers
- T-type diamond hand dressers
- Diamond stick dressers (silicon carbide)
- Dressing sticks for diamond and CBN grinding wheels
- Ball bearing dressers (for extremely accurate dressing)
- Diamond surface grinder wheel dressers (diamond nib)

7.7.2 Lapping

Lapping is a final finishing operation which results in four major improvements to a workpiece:

1. Extreme accuracy of dimension
2. Correction of minor imperfections
3. Better surface finish
4. Close fit between mating or faying surfaces.

In normal lapping operations, less heat is generated than in most other finishing operations. In manual and semiautomatic machine lapping, the end results depend on the following major factors:

- Type of lap material
- Type of lapping medium or compound
- Speed of the lapping motion
- The material to be lapped

Lap materials. Cast iron is the most efficient machine lapping material. Other materials used for hand lapping include soft steel, bronze, brass, lead, leather, and various cloths. Leather and cloth are used for polishing. The material of the lap should be softer than the material that is being lapped.

Lapping media

- Silicon carbide—for rapid stock removal
- Fused aluminum oxide—for soft steel and nonferrous alloys
- Unfused aluminum oxide—for excellent polishing action
- Diamond—for precious stones and tungsten carbides

The manufacturers who produce the lapping media also provide the proper mixtures and viscosities of the lapping solutions.

Lapping speeds. Efficient lapping speeds range from 300 to 8000 sfpm. Higher speeds will improve the surface finish. Lapping pressures range between 1 and 3 psi for soft materials to 10 psi for hard materials. In manual lapping, the final surface finish depends on the skill of the operator and the lapping media. New materials which can be used for lapping include cerium oxide and microfine aluminum oxides of optical grade. There are no known materials other than optical rouge and cerium oxide for producing ultrafine finishes on glass and metallic materials.

7.7.3 Honing

Honing is a low-speed abrading process using bonded abrasive sticks for removing stock from metallic and nonmetallic materials. Honing corrects surface errors produced by other machining or grinding operations. Honing has its most important function in the final finishing of internal cylindrical surfaces.

Honing speeds. Figure 7.138 gives the approximate honing speeds for cast irons and steels, which are the most commonly honed materials. The combined rotation and reciprocation of a hone produces a cross-hatched surface finish on an internal cylindrical part.

Honing abrasives. Honing sticks are produced with the following abrasives: silicon carbide, aluminum oxide, CBN, and diamond. Silicon carbide is used to hone cast irons and nonferrous materials, aluminum oxide is used to hone steels, and diamond and CBN are used on surfaces that have been chromium plated and other extremely hard materials.

Surfaces as fine as 3 to 4 μin are obtainable using 500 grit silicon carbide on steel parts. Grain sizes for manual and power stroke honing range from 150 to 1200 grit, according to the honing media and the application.

7.7.4 Superfinishing

Utilizing a bonded stick for cylindrical parts or a cup wheel for flat and spherical workpieces with an abrasive action, superfinishing may be performed. *Superfinishing* produces a highly wear-resistant finish on parts that are applicable for the superfinishing process. The objective in superfinishing is the removal of fragmentation or smear metal irregularities to restore surface geometry and the surface of the workpiece by eliminating surface stresses and burns. Stock removal may range from 0.0002 to 0.001 in. Scratch patterns of 30 μin RMS or more to a mirror finish may be produced.

General-purpose and high-production superfinishing machines are available to produce a superfinish on almost any symmetrical type of workpiece. The superfinishing stone is ground to the contour of the part to be superfinished, such as a cylindrical outside surface.

Superfinishing is possible on the hardest of steels and other metallic alloys. Very fine mesh aluminum oxide is employed for many superfinishing applications.

Superfinishing speeds. The recommended speed for most superfinishing operations is from 50 to 60 sfpm at a pressure on the stone contact area of 10 to 35 psi. Superfinishing times are suprisingly fast, with steel of hardness R_c35 being finished from 20 to 1 μin in approximately 2 min under average pressure and with 500 mesh aluminum oxide as the abrasive media. The use of optical-grade cerium oxide also may improve the finish after the aluminum oxide operation is completed.

7.8 Files and Sharpening Stones

7.8.1 Files

Common hand files are generally divided into three catagories:

- American-pattern machinists' files
- Swiss-pattern files
- Special-purpose files

The correct selection and proper use of hand files require extensive experience to produce first-class results. The cutting efficiency of hand files is a function of tooth design, construction, material, and pattern of the teeth. Most files are made of high-carbon steel, heat treated to extreme hardness.

The standard files are either single-cut or double-cut, with some patterns being wavy or curved. Among the many types and designs of hand files, a new class of files has been introduced within recent years. These include the sintered-diamond Swiss-pattern files which contain diamond crystals on their surfaces of varying grades of fineness. These relatively new files will cut any material efficiently and are excellent for tool and die hand-working procedures on extremely hard steels.

Figure 7.139 shows the American-pattern standard machinists' files and their common uses and characteristics. Figure 7.140 shows the standard Swiss-pattern files with their characteristics and uses.

Files are characterized by coarseness grade and type of cut.

Coarseness grades

- Bastard cut—for heavy material removal with coarse finish
- Second cut—for light removal with fair finish
- Smooth cut—for fine finishing work

Cut types

- Single cut—used with light pressure for smooth finishes or to sharpen cutting surfaces
- Double cut—for use with heavier pressure to produce a rougher finish

Die sinkers' files. These specialized files are used for dressing and finishing dies and are supplied in cut 0 and cut 2 with the same general types as Swiss-pattern files.

Die sinkers' rifler files. These specialized files are used in die and mold work, instrument work, and other fine filing jobs. Figure 7.141 shows die sinkers' rifler files with their associated trade number designations. These files are available in cut numbers 0, 2, and 4. Most Swiss-pattern and die sinkers' files are available in various coarseness grades ranging from number 00 through 6. Number 00 is the coarsest and number 6 is the finest grade. Presently, these specialized files are produced with sintered-diamond and CBN surfaces for working the hardest steel dies and molds.

Figure 7.142 shows an assortment of Swiss-pattern files in 4-in length. The file at the top of Fig. 7.142 is a sintered-diamond equaling needle file. The diamond needle files come in the following shapes:

- Equaling, flat
- Half-round
- Three-square
- Round
- Knife

The diamond needle files have the following grades of coarseness:

- Fine—200/300 grit
- Medium—140/170 grit
- Coarse—100/120 grit

Rotary files and burrs. Rotary files and burrs are made from high-grade carbon steel as well as solid carbide. They are available in various shank diameters, including 3⁄32, 1⁄8, and 1⁄4 in. Rotary files and burrs are made in the following shapes: ball, cone, 60° cone, 90° cone, inverted cone, cylindrical flat end, cylindrical radius end, flame, oval, 14° taper radius end, tree-shape pointed end, and tree-shape radius end. Both rotary files and burrs are made in single-cut and double-cut forms, with various degrees of coarseness.

7.8.2 Sharpening stones

Sharpening stones are made from the following abrasive types:

India stone—Aluminum oxide; used where close tolerances and smooth cutting edges are required

Silicon carbide—Fastest cutting sharpening stone used where speed is essential and moderate tolerances are permitted

Arkansas—A natural stone recommended for final finishing that produces the highest precision edge possible

Boron carbide—Next to diamond in hardness and will cut any material except diamond; used to dress carbide cutting tools

Sharpening stones are made in file form also, with many different shapes available, such as those shown for the Swiss-pattern files in Fig. 7.140.

7.9 Knurling

Knurls are usually hob-cut to obtain sharp, perfectly formed teeth. Most knurls, either diamond or straight, are made from quality HSS (type M-4) or cobalt alloy (M-48). The knurls fit either revolving or stationary head knurling tools for use on lathe machines. The knurling tools are made in different sizes for use on lathes with swings of 7 through 36 in.

Standard face diamond knurls are available in sizes ranging from 12, 16, 20, 24, 25, 30, 40, 50, to 80 teeth per inch. Standard straight knurls are available in sizes ranging from 12, 16, 20, 24, 25, 30, 40, 50, to 80 teeth per inch.

Straight knurling is a form of serrating. Both diamond and straight knurls are machined into a part either for gripping purposes, ornamental purposes, or both. Straight or diamond knurls are a necessity for parts such as thumb screws and the like, where the knurl provides a firm gripping surface. Knurl patterns are available in the following forms:

- Straight
- 30° diagonal right-hand and left-hand (in sets to produce a diamond pattern)
- 30° diamond male
- 30° diamond female (indented knurl)
- Diametral pitch knurls

The knurl is machined into the part on the lathe as either a narrow band, where the knurling tool is in-fed into the workpiece, or as a continuous knurl, using the lathe carriage to automatically traverse the workpiece as in turning a screw thread.

7.10 JIC and ISO Carbide Codes

The Joint Industrial Council (JIC) carbide classification code system is shown in Fig. 7.143. Since this system evolved around the early cemented and sintered carbide grades, no provision was made for the newer, more advanced cutting tool materials. Also, the wide variety of cemented carbide compositions prevented the universal acceptance of a single classification system. Nevertheless, two grade-classification systems are presently accepted: the JIC system and the International Standards Organization (ISO) system. The ISO carbide grade-classification system is shown in Fig. 7.144.

Reference may be made to all the modern advanced cutting tool materials in subsections 7.1, "Turning and Boring," and 7.2, "Milling." The Kennametal material tables also reference the JIC and ISO classifications for the cutting grades shown in the tables.

(Text continued on page 706.)

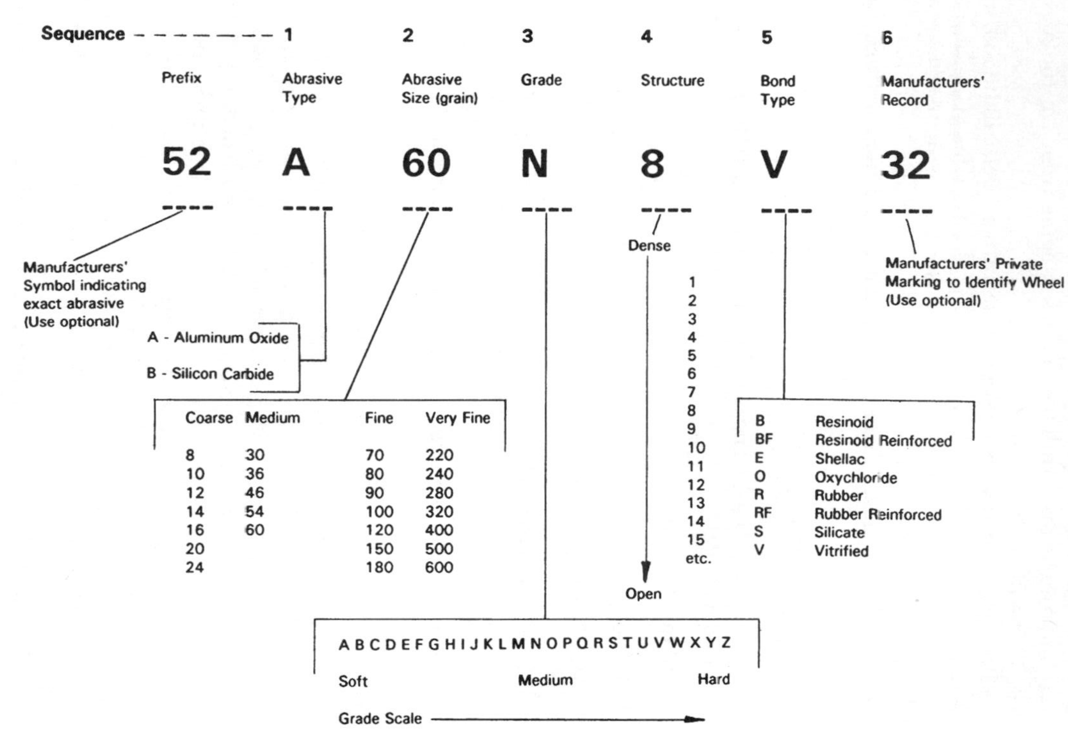

Figure 7.129 Grinding wheel marking system.

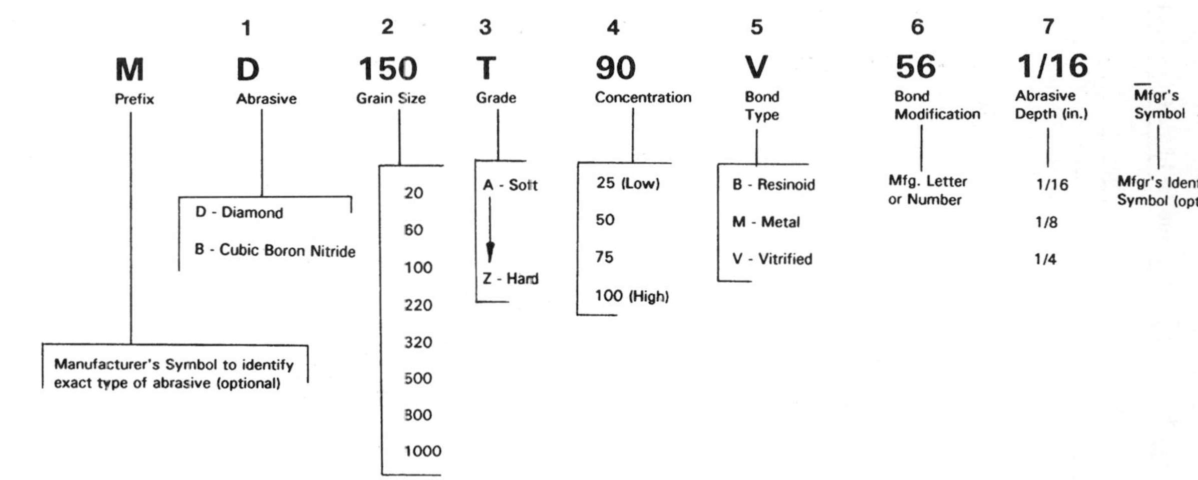

Figure 7.130 Marking system for diamond and CBN.

Efficient Grinding Wheel Operating Speeds in Surface Feet Per Minute (sfpm)	
Type of Operation	**sfpm**
Cutlery (large-offhand)	4,000-5,000
Cut-off (Rubber, shellac, resinoid)	9,000-16,000
Cylinders (Including hemming)	2,500-5,000
Cylindrical grinding	5,000-12,000
Disc grinding	4,000-5,500
Internal grinding	4,000-12,000
Knife grinding (machine knives)	3,500-4,500
Portable grinding	6,500 12,500
Snagging (vitrified small hole)	5,000-6,000
Snagging (resinoid and rubber)	7,000-9,500 - 12,500
Surface grinding	4,000-6,500
Tool grinding	5,000-6,000
Weld grinding	9,500-14,200

Note: The higher speeds are permitted only where bearings, protection devices and machine rigidity are adequate for the intended operation.
To convert sfpm to rpm use the following equation: rpm = (12 x sfpm)/(π x D)
Where: sfpm = surface feet per minute; π = 3.1416 and D = wheel diameter, inches.
CAUTION: Do not operate the grinding wheel above its marked maximum rpm limit.

Figure 7.131 Grinding wheel speeds.

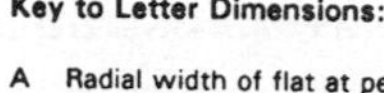

Key to Letter Dimensions:

A Radial width of flat at periphery
B Depth of blind hole bushing
D Diameter - overall
E Thickness of hole
F Depth of recess, one side
G Depth of recess, other side
H Hole diameter
J Diameter of outside flat
K Diameter of inside flat

N Depth of relief one side
O Depth of relief other side
P Diameter of recess
R Radius
S Length of cylindrical section
T Thickness, overall
U Width of edge
V Face angle
W Wall thickness at grinding face

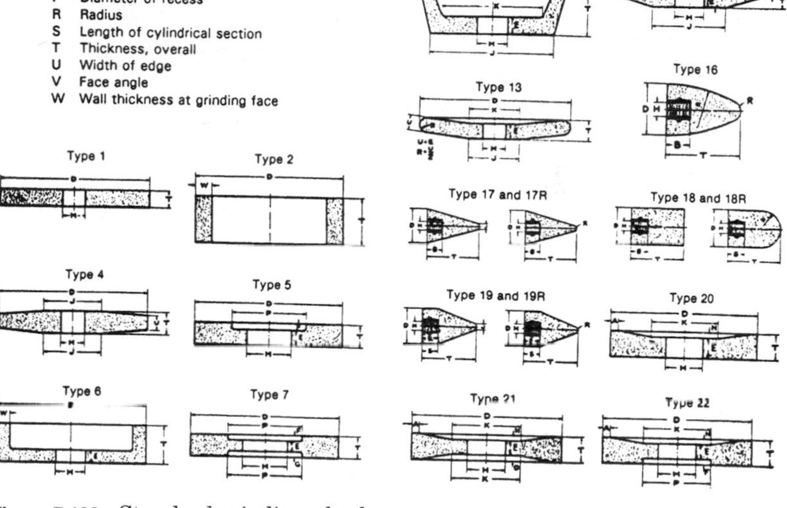

Figure 7.132 Standard grinding wheels.

Standard Types of Diamond or CBN Wheels - Norton Company (Abrasives Marketing Group) Worcester, Massachusetts

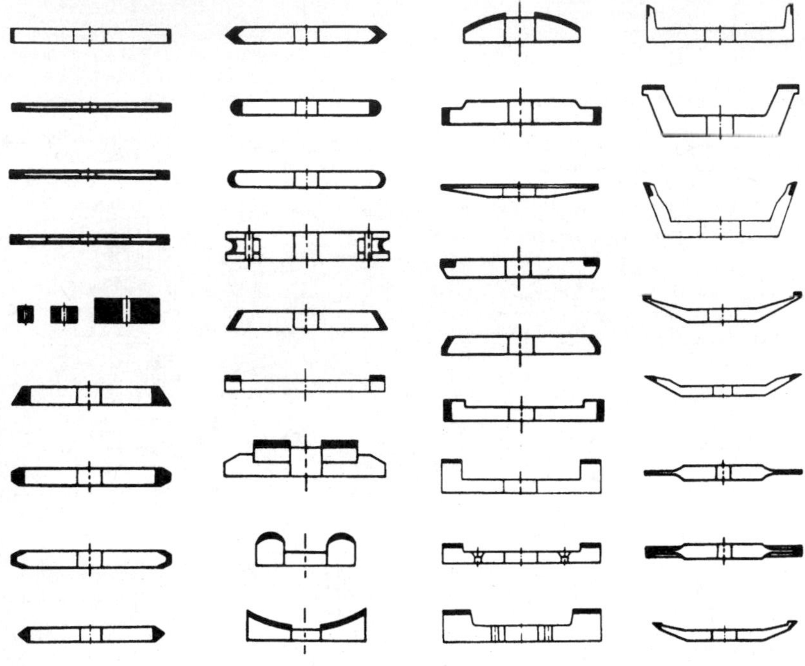

Figure 7.133 Diamond and CBN wheels.

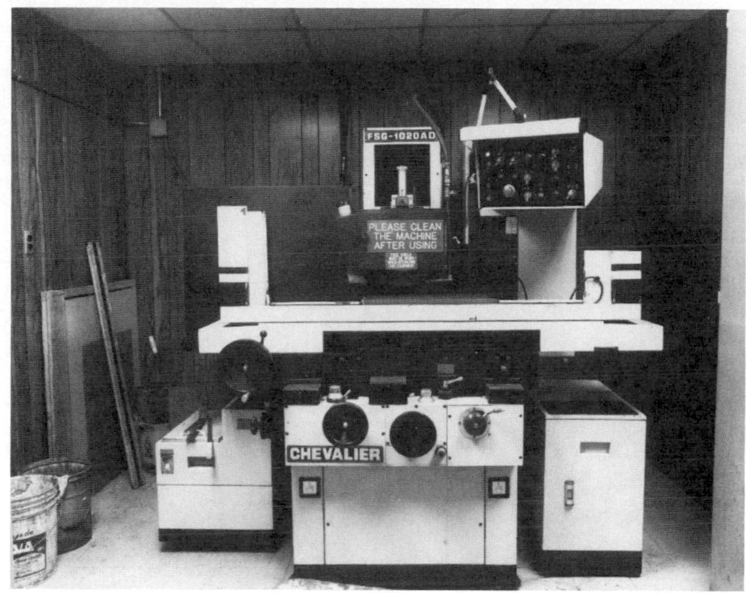

Figure 7.134 Modern automatic surface grinder.

Figure 7.135 Cylindrical grinding machine.

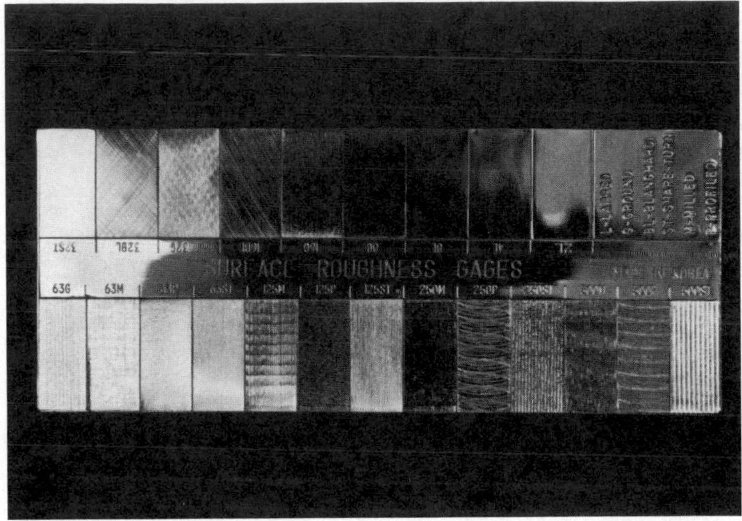

Figure 7.136 Surface roughness gages.

Revolutions per Minute for Various Grinding Speeds in sfpm - Surface feet per minute
(Wheel diameters from 1" to 72" diameter)

Wheel Diameter, Inch	Peripheral (Surface) Speed, Feet per Minute																Wheel Diameter, Inch
	4,000	4,500	5,000	5,500	6,000	6,500	7,000	7,500	8,000	8,500	9,000	9,500	10,000	12,000	14,000	16,000	
	Revolutions per Minute																
1	15,279	17,189	19,099	21,008	22,918	24,828	26,738	28,648	30,558	32,468	34,377	36,287	38,197	45,837	53,476	61,115	1
2	7,639	8,594	9,549	10,504	11,459	12,414	13,369	14,324	15,279	16,234	17,189	18,144	19,099	22,918	26,738	30,558	2
3	5,093	5,730	6,366	7,003	7,639	8,276	8,913	9,549	10,186	10,823	11,459	12,096	12,732	15,279	17,825	20,372	3
4	3,820	4,297	4,775	5,252	5,730	6,207	6,685	7,162	7,639	8,117	8,594	9,072	9,549	11,459	13,369	15,279	4
5	3,056	3,438	3,820	4,202	4,584	4,966	5,348	5,730	6,112	6,494	6,875	7,257	7,639	9,167	10,695	12,223	5
6	2,546	2,865	3,183	3,501	3,820	4,138	4,456	4,775	5,093	5,411	5,730	6,048	6,366	7,639	8,913	10,186	6
7	2,183	2,456	2,728	3,001	3,274	3,547	3,820	4,093	4,365	4,638	4,911	5,184	5,457	6,548	7,639	8,731	7
8	1,910	2,149	2,387	2,626	2,865	3,104	3,342	3,581	3,820	4,058	4,297	4,536	4,775	5,730	6,685	7,639	8
9	1,698	1,910	2,122	2,334	2,546	2,759	2,971	3,183	3,395	3,608	3,820	4,032	4,244	5,093	5,942	6,791	9
10	1,528	1,719	1,910	2,101	2,292	2,483	2,674	2,865	3,056	3,247	3,438	3,629	3,820	4,584	5,348	6,112	10
12	1,273	1,432	1,592	1,751	1,910	2,069	2,228	2,387	2,546	2,706	2,865	3,024	3,183	3,820	4,456	5,093	12
14	1,091	1,228	1,364	1,501	1,637	1,773	1,910	2,046	2,183	2,319	2,456	2,592	2,728	3,274	3,820	4,365	14
16	955	1,074	1,194	1,313	1,432	1,552	1,671	1,790	1,910	2,029	2,149	2,268	2,387	2,865	3,342	3,820	16
18	849	955	1,061	1,167	1,273	1,379	1,485	1,592	1,698	1,804	1,910	2,016	2,122	2,546	2,971	3,395	18
20	764	859	955	1,050	1,146	1,241	1,337	1,432	1,528	1,623	1,719	1,814	1,910	2,292	2,674	3,056	20
22	694	781	868	955	1,042	1,129	1,215	1,302	1,389	1,476	1,563	1,649	1,736	2,083	2,431	2,778	22
24	637	716	796	875	955	1,035	1,114	1,194	1,273	1,353	1,432	1,512	1,592	1,910	2,228	2,546	24
26	588	661	735	808	881	955	1,028	1,102	1,175	1,249	1,322	1,396	1,469	1,763	2,057	2,351	26
28	546	614	682	750	819	887	955	1,023	1,091	1,160	1,228	1,296	1,364	1,637	1,910	2,183	28
30	509	573	637	700	764	828	891	955	1,019	1,082	1,146	1,210	1,273	1,528	1,783	2,037	30
32	477	537	597	657	716	776	836	895	955	1,015	1,074	1,134	1,194	1,432	1,671	1,910	32
34	449	506	562	618	674	730	786	843	899	955	1,011	1,067	1,123	1,348	1,573	1,798	34
36	424	477	531	584	637	690	743	796	849	902	955	1,008	1,061	1,273	1,485	1,698	36
38	402	452	503	553	603	653	704	754	804	854	905	955	1,005	1,206	1,407	1,608	38
40	382	430	477	525	573	621	668	716	764	812	859	907	955	1,146	1,337	1,528	40
42	364	409	455	500	546	591	637	682	728	773	819	864	909	1,091	1,273	1,455	42
44	347	391	434	477	521	564	608	651	694	738	781	825	868	1,042	1,215	1,389	44
46	332	374	415	457	498	540	584	623	664	706	747	789	830	996	1,163	1,329	46
48	318	358	398	438	477	517	557	597	637	676	716	756	796	955	1,114	1,273	48
53	288	324	360	396	432	468	504	541	577	613	649	685	721	865	1,009	1,153	53
60	255	286	318	350	382	414	446	477	509	541	573	605	637	764	891	1,019	60
72	212	239	265	292	318	345	371	398	424	451	477	504	531	637	743	849	72

Figure 7.137 Rpm/surface speed table.

Honing Speeds - sfpm (surface feet per minute)

Material	Hardness R_C	Bore Character	sfpm
Steel	15-35	Interrupted	150
	15-35	Plain	80
	35-50	Interrupted	80
	35-50	Plain	60
	50-65	Interrupted	80
	50-65	Plain	50
Cast Irons	15-50	Interrupted	200
	15-50	Plain	110
	50-65	Interrupted	110
	50-65	Plain	60

Note: Tabular values are approximate and should be used as a guide.
Observe the honing action and take appropriate steps to refine the operation.

Figure 7.138 Honing speeds.

American Pattern Machinists' Files - Description and Uses

File Cross-Section	Name	Tooth Characteristic	General Uses
	Flat	Usually bastard cut. Also second- cut and smooth.	General purpose and lathe filing
	Hand	One edge smooth. Bastard, second-cut and smooth.	Finishing flat surfaces
	Pillar	One edge smooth. Bastard, second-cut and smooth	Keyways, slots and narrow work
	Warding	Usually bastard. also second-cut and smooth	Filing ward notches in keys and narrow work.
	Square	Bastard, second-cut and smooth.	Enlarging holes or recesses, mortises, keyways and splines.
	Three-Square	Sharp edges. Bastard, second-cut and smooth.	Filing acute angles, corners, grooves and notches.
	Round	Usually bastard. Also second-cut and smooth	Enlarging holes and shaping curved surfaces.
	Half-Round	Usually bastard. Also second-cut and smooth	Concave corners, crevices and round holes.
	Knife	Usually bastard. Also second-cut and smooth	Cleaning out acute angles, corners and slots.

Note: Many variations are available including, Long angle lathe files, aluminum flat files, aluminum half-round files, regular taper saw files, chain saw files and cantsaw files.

Figure 7.139 Machinists' files.

Swiss Pattern Files - Description and Uses

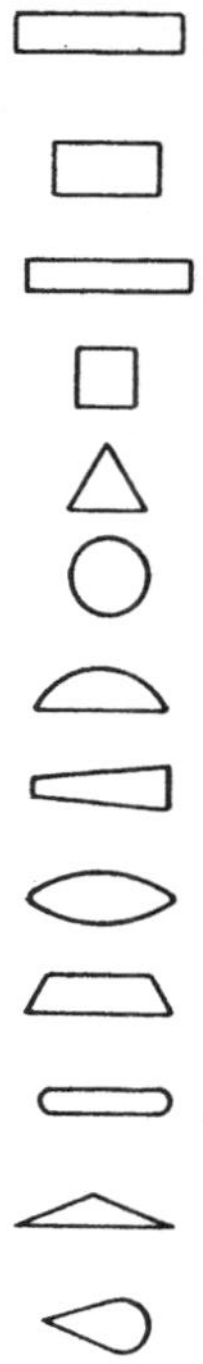

File Cross-Section	Name	Tooth Characteristic	General Uses
	Hand	Double-cut on two flat faces and one edge. Other edge smooth.	Flat surfaces
	Pillar	Double-cut on two flat faces. Both edges smooth.	Flat surfaces and slots
	Warding	Double-cut on two flat faces. Single-cut on two edges.	Slots
	Square	Double-cut	Corners and holes.
	Three-Square	Double-cut three faces. Single-cut on edges	Corners and holes
	Round	Double-cut	Corners and holes
	Half-Round	Double-cut	Corners and holes
	Knife	Double-cut on flat faces. Single-cut on edges	Slots
	Crossing	Double-cut	Corners and holes
	Barrette	Cut on wide flat face. Other	Corners, flat surfaces, burring gear teeth.
	Crochet	Double-cut	Slots, flat surfaces and rounded corners.
	Cant	Double-cut three faces. Single cut on two sharp edges	Corners
	Pippin	Double-cut	Rounded corners and holes.

Figure 7.140 Swiss-pattern files.

Die Sinkers' Rifler Files - Shape and Trade Number are Shown at Each File

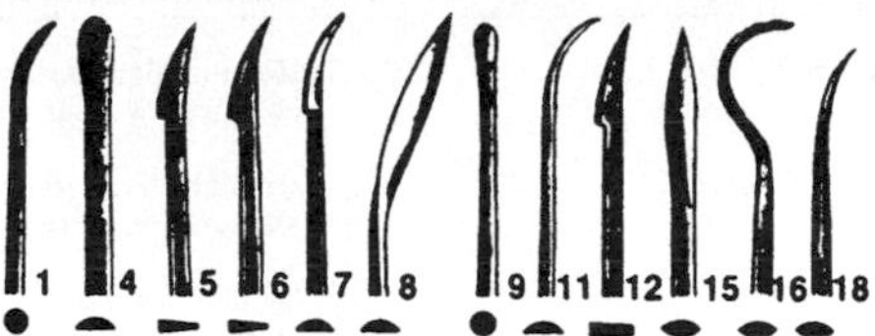

Note: Files are double-ended and approximately 6.5 inches length
Available in Cut Numbers 0, 2 or 4.

Figure 7.141 Die sinkers' rifler files.

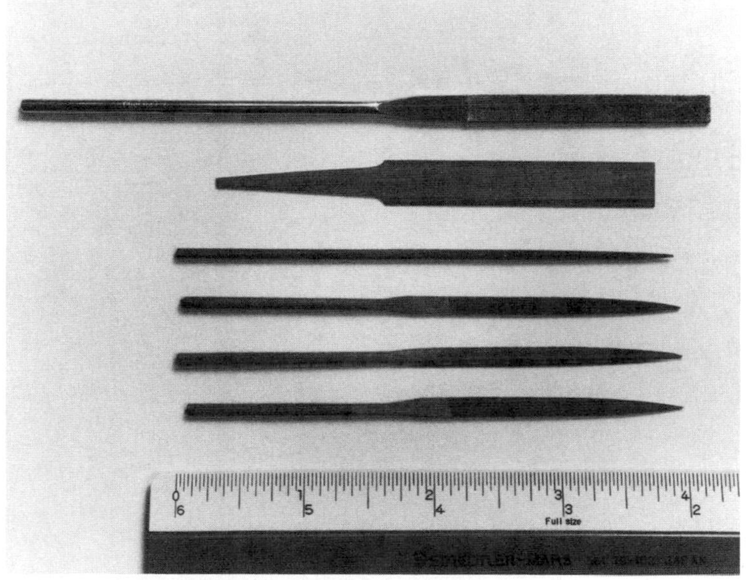

Figure 7.142 Swiss-pattern file samples, 4-in size (top is a diamond-grit file).

JIC Carbide-Classification Code

Code	Application	Carbide Characteristics
C-1	Roughing	Medium-high shock resistance Medium-low wear resistance
C-2	General purpose	Medium shock resistance Medium wear resistance
C-3	Finishing	Medium-low shock resistance Medium-high wear resistance
C-4	Precision finishing	Low shock resistance High wear resistance
C-5	Roughing	High resistance to cutting temperatures Shock and cutting load Medium wear resistance
C-6	General purpose	Medium-high shock resistance Medium wear resistance Medium shock resistance
C-7	Finishing	Medium shock resistance Medium wear resistance
C-8	Precision finishing	Very high wear resistance Low shock resistance

Note: Hardness increases from top to bottom; toughness increases from bottom to top

Figure 7.143 JIC carbide code.

ISO Carbide Classification System - International Standards Organization

Main Machining Group	Color Marking	Application Group	Operations and Working conditions
P Group: steel cast steel, long chip malleables	Blue	P01	High precision turning and boring. High cutting speeds. Good surface finish and vibration-free machining
		P10	Turning, thread cutting and milling. High cutting speeds. Small/medium chip cross-section
		P20	Turning, milling, medium cutting speeds and medium chip cross-section. Planing - small chip.
		P30	Turning, milling, planing. Medium to low cutting speeds. Medium/large chip cross-section. Unfavorable conditions
		P40	Planing, turning, milling, shaping. Low cutting speeds. Large chip cross-section. High rake angles. Unfavorable conditions
		P50	Where highest demands are made on carbide toughness. Turning, planing and shaping. Low cutting speeds. Large chips and high rakes. Unfavorable conditions.
M Group: steel, cast steel austenitic manganese steels, cast iron alloys, austenitic steels, malleable cast iron, free-cutting steels.	Yellow	M10	Turning. Medium-high cutting speeds. Small to medium chip cross-section.
		M20	Turning, milling. Medium cutting speeds and medium chip cross-section.
		M30	Turning, milling, planing. Medium cutting speeds. Medium/large chip cross-section.
		M40	Turning, form turning, parting off and recessing - for automatics.
K Group: cast iron, chilled cast irons, short chip malleables hardened steels, nonferrous metals and nonmetallic materials.	Red	K01	Turning, precision turning/boring. Finish milling and scraping.
		K10	Turning, milling, boring, countersinking. reaming, scraping and broaching.
		K20	Turning, milling, planing, countersinking. scraping, reaming and broaching under tougher conditions than K10.
		K30	Turning, milling, planing, shaping under unfavorable conditions. High rakes.
		K40	Turning, milling, planing, shaping under unfavorable conditions. High rakes.

Note: Cutting speed and wear resistance increase from bottom to top; feed and carbide toughness increase from top to bottom.

Figure 7.144 ISO carbide classification system.

7.11 Cutting Fluids and Coolants for Machining Operations

Cutting fluids and machining coolants have been developed over the past 15 to 20 years which are very different than those used previously in industry. Many of the modern cutting fluids and coolants are designed and formulated to be environmentally safe and biodegradable. Some cutting fluids have been developed for use on specific types of materials, while others are suitable for a very wide range of different materials and cutting conditions. Some of the modern cutting fluids are supplied in aerosol cans and are sprayed on the workpiece while the machining operation is being performed. These spray-application fluids adhere strongly to the workpiece and allow easier machinability while preventing corrosion on the workpiece, such as rusting on ferrous materials.

Combination cutting fluids and coolants are being produced which may be used for most of the high-speed machining operations afforded by the advanced cutting tool materials. With the advent of universal-type cutting/coolant combination fluids, the inventory of cutting fluids and coolants can be kept to a minimum within a manufacturing facility or machine shop.

The older types of coolants and cutting fluids are not ineffective, but they are outdated performance-wise, and some are environmentally unsafe for disposal into any sewage system. Lard oils, kerosene, and other older cutting oils are difficult to degrade chemically in the sewage-treatment plants.

A list of typical cutting fluids and coolants used many years ago with various materials in industrial machining applications follows:

Cast iron	Usually worked dry
Mild steel	Oil or soapy water
Hard steels	Mineral lard oil
Monel metal	Dry or mineral lard oil
Bronze	Dry or mineral lard oil
Brass	Dry (kerosene or turpentine was used on the harder compositions)
Copper	Dry or mixture of lard oil and turpentine
Babbitt	Dry or mixture of lard oil and kerosene
Aluminum	Dry or mixture of lard oil and kerosene or plain kerosene
Threading	Mineral lard oil

Coolants

- Lard oil—One of the oldest and best lubricants/coolants
- Mineral lard oil mixtures—More fluid and cheaper than lard oils
- Soluble oils—Specially prepared mineral oils mixed with water
- Soda water mixtures—Made by mixing 1 lb sodium carbonate, 1 qt lard oil, 1 qt soft soap, and 8 to 10 gal water; boil the mixture for 30 min and allow to cool before using.

Many of these outdated cutting fluids and coolants accounted for the smoke that was produced during the cutting operations. Bear in mind that during the period that these fluids were used, the only cutting tool materials were heat-treated high-carbon and alloy steels and early variations of HSS.

Modern coolants/cutting fluids. Cutting oils are divided into three basic types: petroleum oils, fixed (animal or vegetable) oils, and synthetic oils. Chemical additives give oils additional or enhanced properties such as resistance to oxidation and foaming and the ability to perform under extreme pressures and temperatures.

Some of the modern coolants/cutting fluids and compounds include

Nonhazardous cutting compounds—Biodegradable, contain no 1,1,1-trichloroethane

Plumbers' lard oil—Used for mixing with mineral oils

Wax cut cutting oil—Chlorinated waxes suspended in clear oil

Medium-duty soluble oil—Used where tool life and surface finish are critical

Thred Kut—Heavy-duty brown sulfochlorinated cutting oil, antiweld, antiwear solution.

Sulfur-base cutting oils—Used for all metals and high-alloy steels

Kleen Kut soluble oil—Water-soluble emulsion, economical; mixed with water at 5% to 10% concentration

Thred Kut 99—A dark, heavy sulfochlorinated fatty oil for machining and grinding soft, tough, and stringy metals such as stainless steels, low-carbon steels, jet-engine alloys, and monel metals

Trampol-X cutting fluid—Economical, water-soluble, and efficient cutting fluid/coolant for all types of machining operations; designed to withstand recycling in central coolant systems

Synthetic coolant—Heavy-duty synthetic cutting and grinding concentrate for machining ferrous alloys, aluminum, and brasses

Blasocut—A high-efficiency cutting/coolant fluid for all types of machining operations; used in central coolant systems and fed at high pressures into the tool and workpiece cutting area; water-soluble; made in Switzerland; frequently used on turning center and machining center CNC machines.

7.12 Calculations for Common Machining Problems

7.12.1 Drill-point advance

When drilling a hole, it is often useful to know the distance from the cylindrical end of the drilled hole to the point of the drill for any angle point and any diameter drill. Refer to Fig. 7.145, where the advance t is calculated from

$$\tan\left(\frac{180-\alpha}{2}\right) = \frac{t}{D/2}$$

then

$$t = \frac{D}{2}\tan\left(\frac{180-\alpha}{2}\right)$$

where D = diameter of drill, in
α = drill-point angle

Example What is the advance t for a 0.785-in-diameter drill with a 118° point angle?

$$t = \frac{0.875}{2}\tan\left(\frac{180-118}{2}\right) \qquad \textbf{Note}: \frac{180-\alpha}{2} = \measuredangle\theta \text{ (reference)}$$

$$= 0.4375 \tan 31^\circ$$

$$= 0.4375 \times 0.60086 = 0.2629 \text{ in}$$

7.12.2 Tapers

Finding taper angles under a variety of given conditions is an essential part of machining mathematics. Following are a variety of taper problems with their associated equations and solutions.

For taper in inches per foot, see Fig. 7.146*a*. If the taper in inches per foot is denoted by *T*, then

$$T = \frac{12(D_1 - D_2)}{L}$$

where D_1 = diameter of larger end, in
D_2 = diameter of smaller end, in
L = length of tapered part along axis, in
T = taper, in/ft

Also, to find the angle θ, use the relationship

$$\tan\theta = \frac{12(D_1 - D_2)}{L}$$

then find arctan θ for angle θ.

Example $D_1 = 1.255$ in, $D_2 = 0.875$ in, and $L = 3.5$ in. Find angle θ.

$$\tan\theta = \frac{1.255 - 0.875}{3.5} = \frac{0.380}{0.875} = 0.43429$$

$$= 0.43429$$

And arctan 0.43429 = 23.475° or 23°28.5′.

Figure 7.146*b* shows a taper angle of 27.5° in 1 in, and the taper per inch is therefore 0.4894. This is found simply by solving the triangle formed by the axis line, which is 1 in long, and half the taper angle, which is 13.75°. Solve one of the right-angled triangles formed by the tangent function:

$$\tan 13.75° = x/1$$

$$\text{and} \qquad x = \tan 13.75° = 0.2447$$

$$\text{and} \qquad 2 \times 0.2447 = 0.4894$$

as shown in Fig. 7-146*b*.

The taper in inches per foot is equal to 12 times the taper in inches per inch. Thus, in Fig. 7.146*b*, the taper per foot is 12 × 0.4894 = 5.8728 in.

7.12.3 Typical taper problems

1. Set two disks of known diameter and a required taper angle at the correct center distance L (see Fig. 7.147).

Given: Two disks of known diameter d and D and the required angle θ. Solve for L.

$$L = \frac{D - d}{2\left(\sin \frac{\theta}{2}\right)}$$

2. Find the angle of the taper when given the taper per foot (see Fig. 7.148).

Given: Taper per foot T. Solve for angle θ.

$$\theta = 2\left(\arctan \frac{T}{24}\right)$$

3. Find the taper per foot when the diameters of the disks and the length between them are known (see Fig. 7.149).

Given: d, D, and L. Solve for T.

$$T = \tan\left(\arcsin \frac{D - d}{L}\right) \times 24$$

4. Find the angle of the taper when the disk dimensions and their center distance is known (see Fig. 7.150).

Given: d, D, and L. Solve for angle θ.

$$\theta = 2\left(\arcsin \frac{D - d}{2L}\right)$$

5. Find the taper in inches per foot measured at right angles to one side when the disk diameters and their center distance are known (see Fig. 7.151).

Given: d, D, and L. Solve for T, in inches per foot.

$$T = \tan\left[2\left(\arcsin \frac{D - d}{2L}\right)\right] \times 12$$

6. Set a given angle with two disks in contact when the diameter of the smaller disk is known (see Fig. 7.152).

Given: d and θ. Solve for D, diameter of the larger disk.

$$D = \left(\frac{2d \sin \frac{\theta}{2}}{1 - \sin \frac{\theta}{2}} \right) + d$$

Figure 7.153 shows an angle-setting template which may be easily constructed in any machine shop. Angles of extreme precision are possible to set using this type of tool. The diameters of the disks may be machined precisely, and the center distances between the disks may be set with a gage or Jo-blocks. Also, any angle may be repeated when a record is kept of the disk diameters and the precise center distance. The angle θ, taper per inch, or taper per foot may be calculated using some of the preceding equations.

7.12.4 Checking angles and notches with plugs

A machined plug may be used to check the correct width of an angular opening or machined notch or to check templates or parts which have corners cut off or in which the body is notched with a right angle. This is done using the following techniques and simple equations.

In Figs. 7.154, 7.155, and 7.156, $D = a + b - c$ (right-angle notches). To check the width of a notched opening, see Fig. 7.157 and the following equation:

$$D = W \tan \left(45^\circ - \frac{\theta}{2} \right)$$

When the correct size plug is inserted into the notch, it should be tangent to the opening indicated by the dashed line.

Also, the equation for finding the correct plug diameter that will contact all sides of an oblique or non-right-angle triangular notch is as follows (see Fig. 7.158):

$$D = \frac{2W}{\left(\cot \frac{A}{2} + \right) + \left(\cot \frac{C}{2} \right)}$$

where W = width of notch, in
A = angle A
B = angle B

7.12.5 Finding diameters

When the diameter of a part is too large to measure accurately with a micrometer or vernier caliper, you may use a 90° or any convenient included angle on the tool (which determines angle A) and measure the height H as shown in Fig. 7.159. The simple equation for calculating the diameter D for any angle A is as follows:

$$D = H \frac{2}{\csc A - 1} \qquad (\textbf{Note}:\ \text{Cosecant } 45° = 1.4142)$$

Thus the equation for measuring the diameter D with a 90° square reduces to

$$D = 4.828H$$

Then, if the height H measured was 2.655 in, the diameter of the part would be

$$D = 4.828 \times 2.655 = 12.818 \text{ in}$$

When measuring large gears, a more convenient angle for the measuring tool would be 60°, as shown in Fig. 7.160. In this case, the calculation becomes simple. When the measuring angle of the tool is 60° (angle A = 30°), the diameter D of the part is $2H$.

For measuring either inside or outside radii on any type of part such as a casting or a broken segment of a wheel, the calculation for the radius of the part is as follows (see Figs. 7.161 and 7.162):

$$r = \frac{4b^2 + c^2}{8b}$$

where r = radius of part, in
b = chordal height, in
c = chord length, in

The chord should be made from a precisely measured piece of tool steel flat, and the chordal height b may be measured with an inside telescoping gage or micrometer.

(Text continued on page 721.)

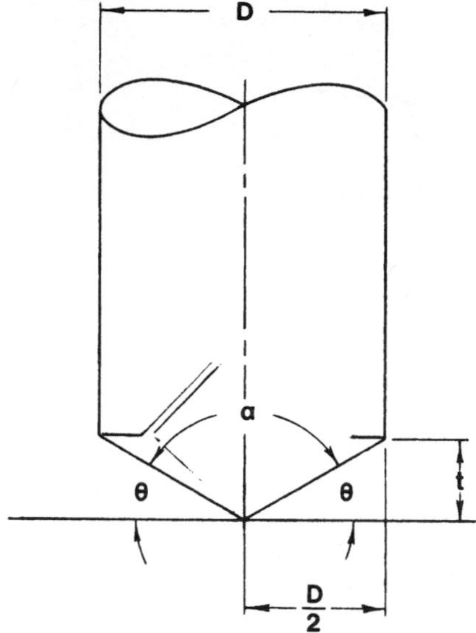

Figure 7.145 Drill advance.

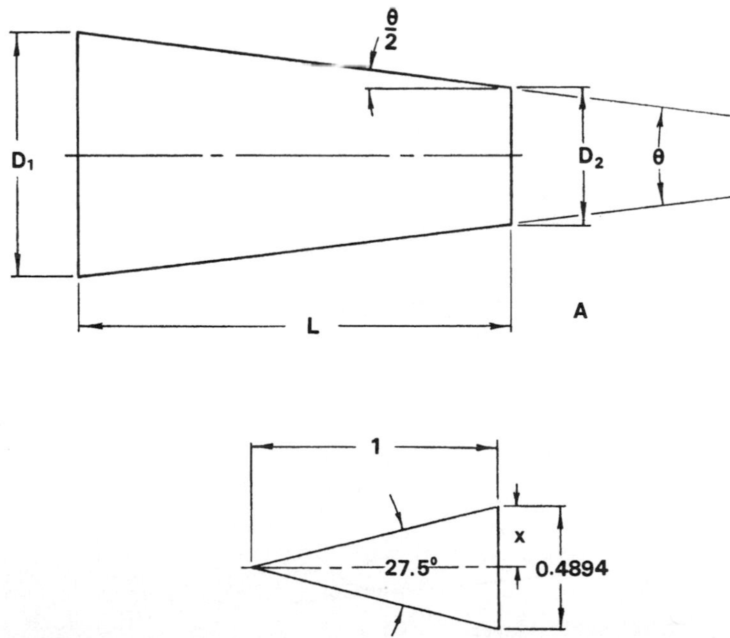

Figure 7.146 Taper angles.

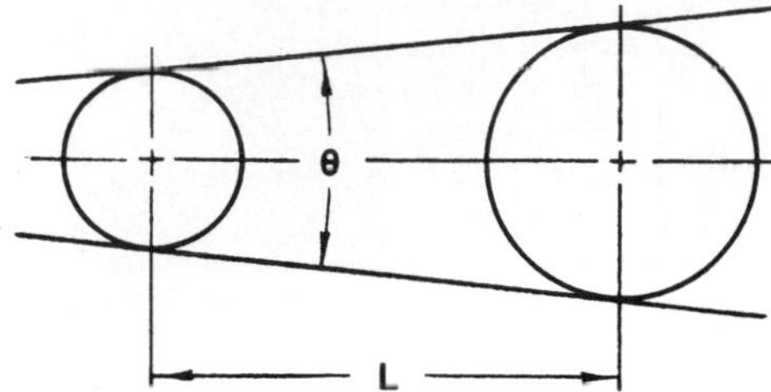

Figure 7.147 Taper.

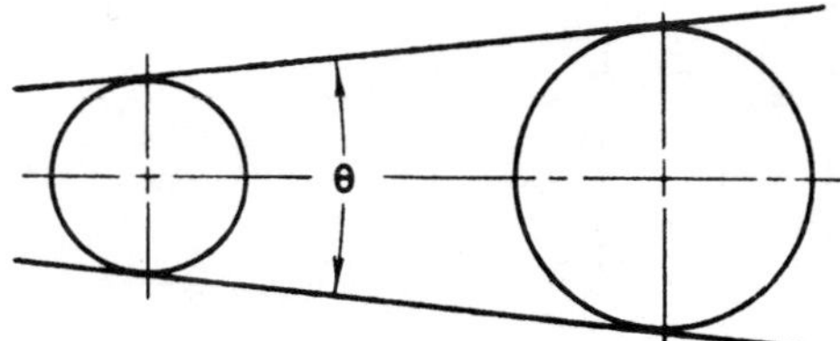

Figure 7.148 Angle of taper.

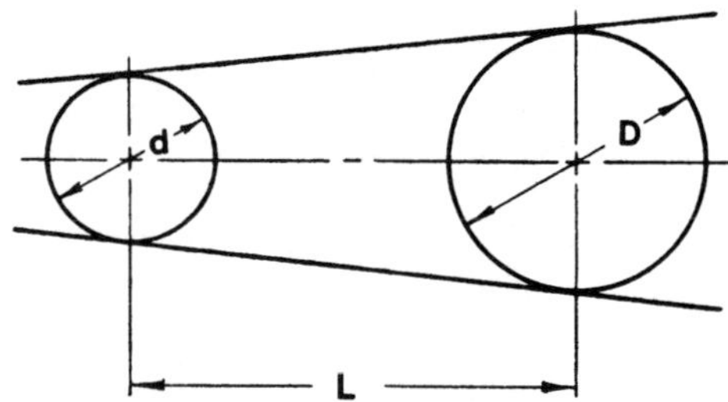

Figure 7.149 Taper per foot.

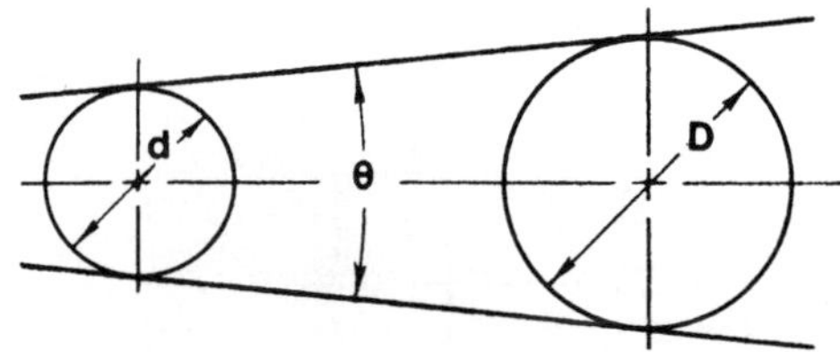

Figure 7.150 Angle of taper.

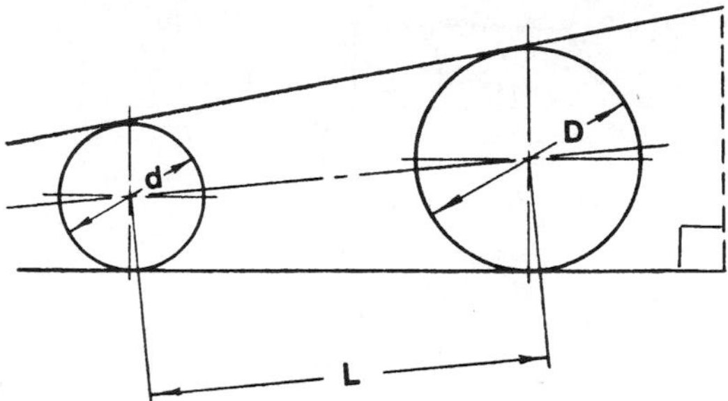

Figure 7.151 Taper in inches per foot.

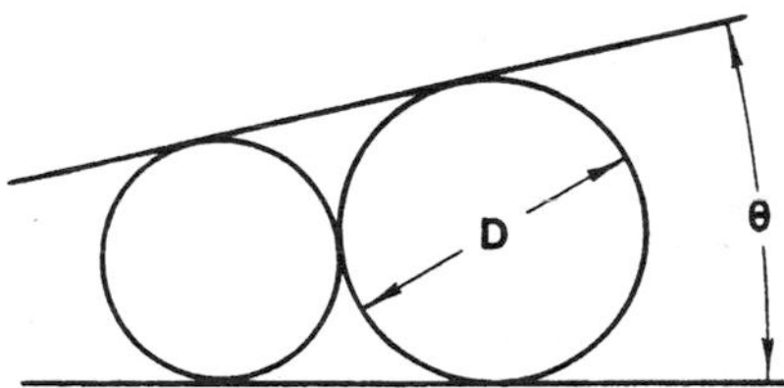

Figure 7.152 Setting a given angle.

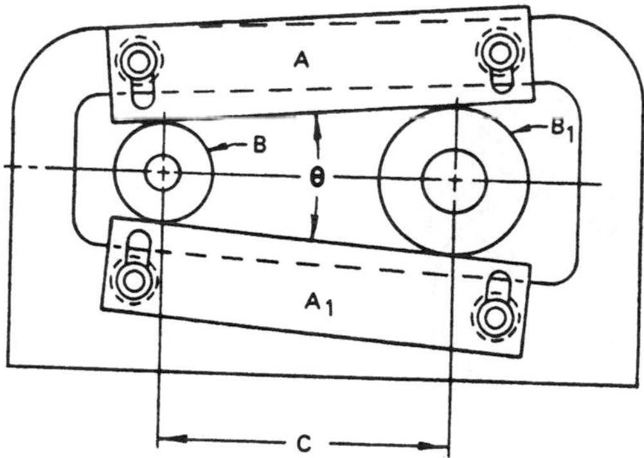

Figure 7.153 Angle-setting template.

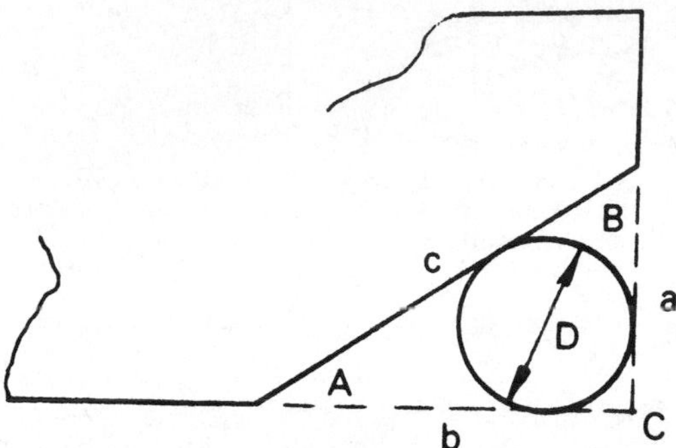

Figure 7.154 Right-angle notch.

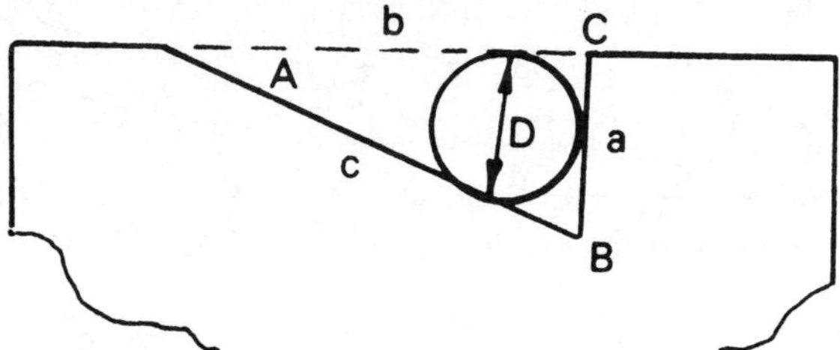

Figure 7.155 Right-angle notch.

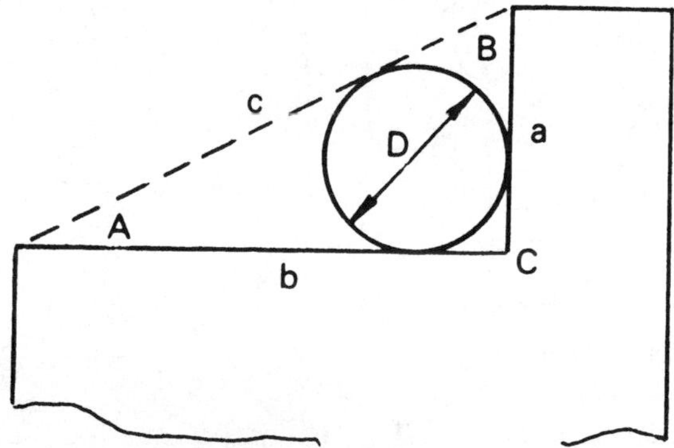

Figure 7.156 Right-angle notch.

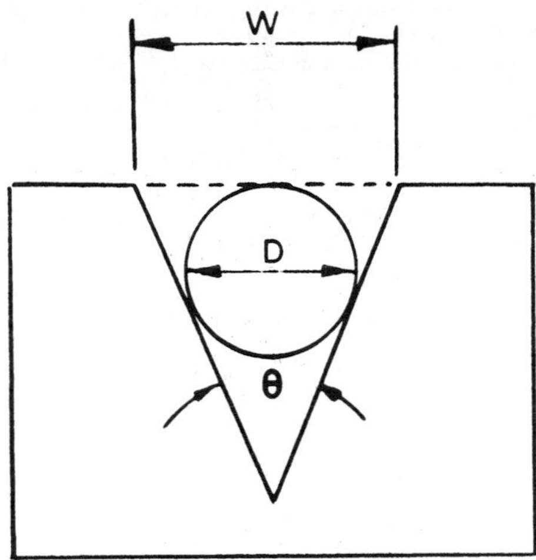

Figure 7.157 Width of notched opening.

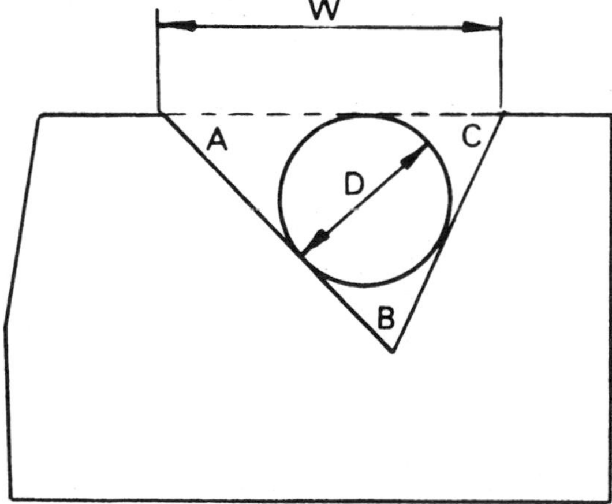

Figure 7.158 Finding plug diameter.

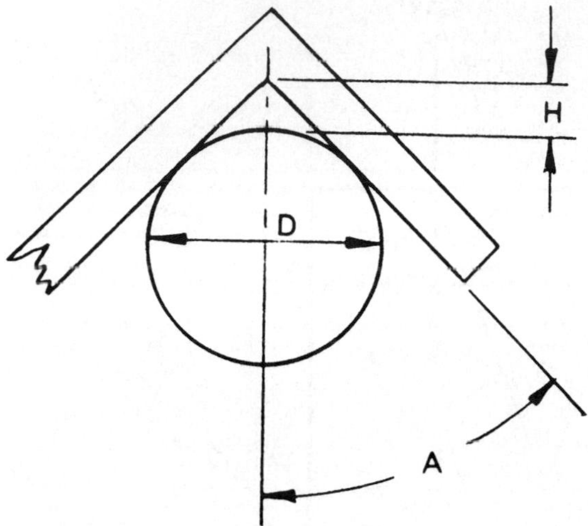

Figure 7.159 Finding the diameter.

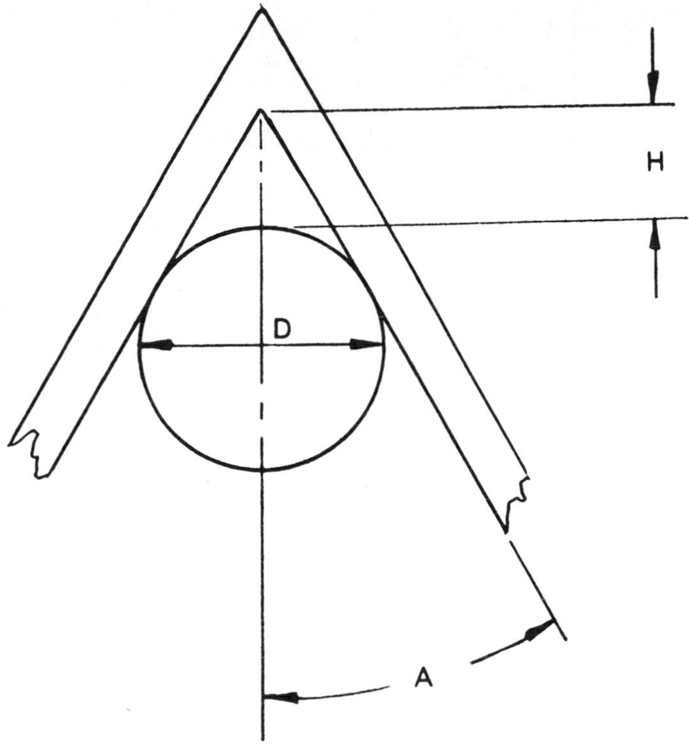

Figure 7.160 Finding the diameter.

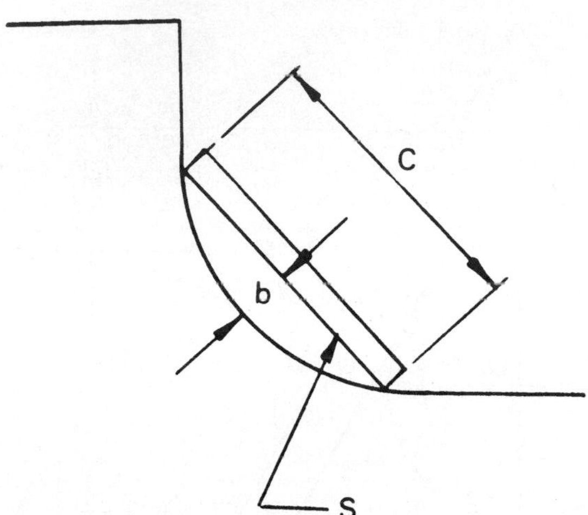

Figure 7.161 Finding the radius.

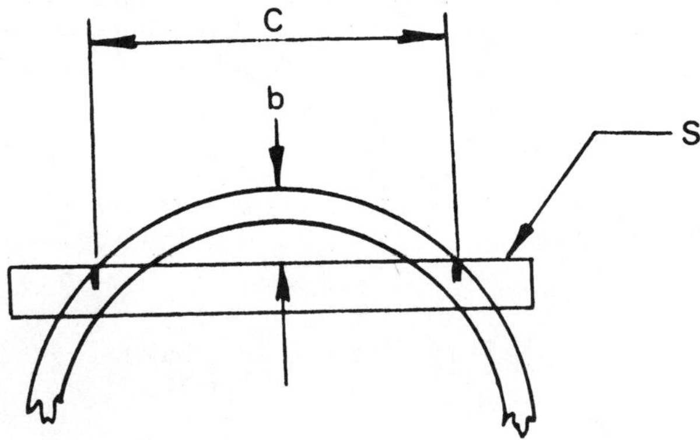

Figure 7.162 Finding the radius.

7.12.6 Measuring radius of arc by measuring over rolls or plugs

Another accurate method of finding or checking the radius on a part is illustrated in Figs. 7.163 and 7.164. In this method, we may calculate either an inside or an outside radius by the following equations:

$$r = \frac{(L + D)^2}{8D} \qquad \text{(for convex radii, Fig. 7.163)}$$

$$r = \frac{(L + D)^2}{8(h - D)} + \frac{h}{2} \qquad \text{(for concave radii, Fig. 7.164)}$$

where L = length over rolls or plugs, in
D = diameter of rolls or plugs, in
h = height of concave high point above the rolls or plugs, in

For accuracy, the rolls or plugs must be placed on a tool plate or plane table and the distance L across the rolls measured accurately. The diameter D of the rolls or plugs also must be measured precisely and the height h measured with a telescoping gage or inside micrometers.

7.12.7 Measuring dovetail slides

The accuracy of machining of dovetail slides and their given widths may be checked using cylindrical rolls (such as a drill rod) or wires and the following equations (see Fig. 7.165):

$$x = D\left(\cot \frac{\theta}{2}\right) + a \qquad \text{(For male dovetails, Fig. 7.165}a\text{)}$$

$$y = b - D\left(1 + \cot \frac{\theta}{2}\right) \qquad \text{(For female dovetails, Fig. 7.165}b\text{)}$$

Note: $c = h \cot \theta$. Also, the diameter of the rolls or wire should be sized so that the point of contact e is below the corner or edge of the dovetail.

7.12.8 Universal dividing heads

The precision universal dividing head is a precision milling attachment used to divide the circumference of circular work and to equally space the divisions. This milling tool may be used for milling spur gear teeth (using the appropriate cutter), pinion gears, splines, and spacing holes on a given circle. Other types of milled parts which may be produced using the universal dividing head include hexagonal nuts, octagons, pentagons, and other polygon shapes.

Refer to Fig. 7.166, in which *A* denotes the dividing head, *B* the indexing plates, and *C* the tail stock center. Work may be mounted between the head and tail stock centers or held in a chuck or collet, either of which is placed on the head spindle. Rotating the head crank causes the head stock spindle to rotate at a ratio of 40:1. This ratio and an index plate with a series of equally spaced holes (to measure and stop the crank rotation) make it possible to divide the circumference of the workpiece into the required number of equal divisions or sections.

The index plates (*C*) have different hole series, such as 15, 16, 17, 18, 19, 20, 21, 23, 27, 29, 31, 33, 37, 39, 41, 43, 47, and 49. An index chart of all possible divisions is supplied with the universal dividing head. These dividing heads are usually supplied in either left-hand or right-hand models, according to your particular setup and requirements. The precision dividing head usually can hold the angular divisions to within 10 seconds of arc.

Some dividing-head models are equipped with index plates and a series of change gears to alter the ratio of divisions. Instructions for the use of each particular dividing head must be obtained from the manufacturer. A precision dividing head is a necessary machine tool accessory in any model shop, machine shop, or tool and die operation which requires precise division of a circle.

7.13 Taps and Dies for Threading Operations

The tapping of threaded holes and the die cutting of external threads with the use of taps and dies are performed most efficiently and economically when the correct type of tap or die is used. The number of flutes on the tap and the style of flutes are important in the efficient removal of material that is cut in the tapping process. Four flute taps dispose of the cut material in shallow or large-diameter holes or when the material breaks into small chips but are not efficient in cutting stringy materials for deep or small-diameter holes.

Taps are available in spiral-point form, which allows the tap to push the cut material ahead of the tap on through holes. Spiral-flute and high-spiral-flute designs are made to pull the cut material up and out of the tapped hole during the tapping procedure. Thread-forming taps are also available which do not produce chips, since the forming of the thread is a metal deforming or displacement process.

Some of the typical standard types of taps and dies are shown in Fig. 7.167. To produce a full thread to the bottom of a drilled hole, a standard set of taps is used, which includes the taper tap, plug tap, and bottoming tap used in the order listed to produce a fully threaded blind hole.

7.13.1 Available types of taps and dies

Taps

- Two-flute taps
- Three-flute taps
- Four-flute taps
- Cut-thread taps
- Ground taps
- 30° spiral-flute taps
- 52° spiral-flute taps
- Spiral-point taps
- Straight and tapered pipe taps
- Interrupted-thread taps
- Pulley taps
- Nut taps
- Combined tap and drill

Dies

- Round adjustable dies
- Thread-cone dies (acorn type)
- Hexagon rethreading dies (standard thread and pipe thread)
- Square bolt dies
- Square pipe dies
- Locknut-thread round adjustable dies

Taps and dies are made from carbon-steel, HSS, and solid carbide (plain or titanium nitride coated). Taps and dies are made for American standard unified threads, ISO metric threads, Acme threads, BA (British Association) threads, and other special thread forms used in industry. Most taps and dies are available in either right-hand or left-hand thread.

Although taps are produced in both cut-thread and ground-thread forms, the ground-thread tap is preferred for the following reasons:

1. The ground-thread tap will produce more than five times the number of holes than will the cut tap.
2. Although the ground-thread tap is more costly, it is more economical due to its long wear ability.
3. A ground tap will produce a more accurate tapped hole.
4. It requires less machine power to use the ground tap on a size-to-size basis.
5. The cut-thread tap is usually not suitable for producing class 3B tapped holes.

The application of the proper cutting fluid is critical to economical and successful tapping operations. Various modern types of cutting fluids are produced for tapping and die-cutting threads on different materials. It is essential to use the proper type of cutting fluid for each specific type of tapping and die-cutting operation. The proper cutting fluids and cutting fluid direction and pressure are important on high-speed tapping operations as performed on the CNC turning centers and machining centers.

7.13.2 Speeds for tapping

The normal tapping speed for any particular material, when using a HSS ground-thread or carbide tap, should be the same as the drilling speed for the equivalent drill diameter. See Subsection 7.3 for the cutting speeds and revolutions per minute required for different materials and drill diameters to arrive at the required tapping speed or revolutions per minute.

7.13.3 Thread lead tolerances

Ground-thread taps should always be used when a threaded assembly must carry a heavy load. The thread lead tolerance on cut-thread taps is much broader than the close-tolerance thread lead produced by the ground-thread tap and will cause the threads to not maintain a full thread-bearing condition, which is detrimental to the strength of the tapped and threaded assembly. In other words, if the thread leads of the male thread do not coincide closely with the thread leads of the nut or tapped hole, a weak threaded assembly results or may not assemble easily.

The thread lead tolerances of cut-thread and ground-thread taps is as follows:

- Cut-thread tap lead tolerance = ±0.0030 in/in.
- Ground-thread tap lead tolerance = ±0.0005 in/in.

Pitch-diameter tolerance ranges of cut-thread and ground-thread taps are as follows (actual tolerance depends on the thread size):

- Cut-thread pitch-diameter tolerance range = 0.001 to 0.0055 in/in.
- Ground-thread pitch-diameter tolerance range = 0.0005 to 0.0025 in/in.

7.13.4 Limit numbers for ground-thread taps (American UN thread system, ANSI)

All American standard listed ground-thread taps are marked with the capital letter G to designate ground thread. The letter G is followed by either the letter H or the letter L. The letter H designates *above* the basic pitch-diameter limits, and the letter L designates *below* the basic pitch-diameter limits. The number following the letter H or L designates the pitch-diameter limits. The number is a code number that references the actual dimensional limits of the basic pitch diameter. Figure 7.168 shows the H or L code number with the associated pitch-diameter limit dimensions.

Example A tap marked GH2 indicates a ground-thread tap with pitch-diameter limits of 0.0005 to 0.0010 in *over* the basic pitch diameter on sizes 1 in and under.

Note: Do not confuse these limit codes with the class of fit for a particular thread size. These tap-limit numbers are not related to the class of fit.

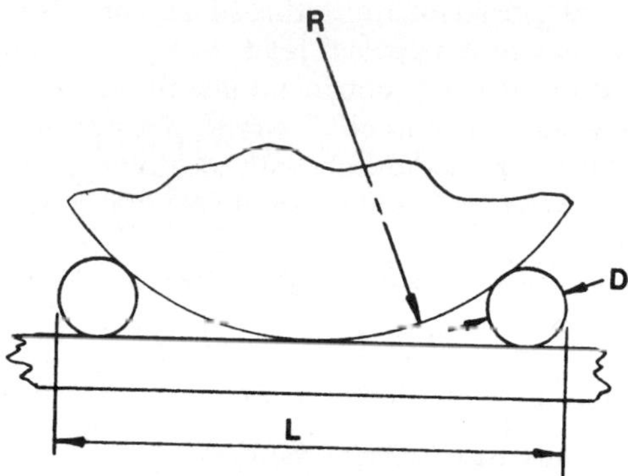

Figure 7.163 Finding the radius.

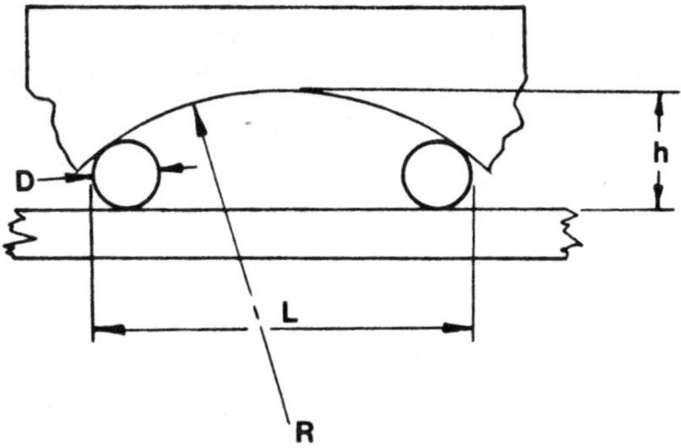

Figure 7.164 Finding the radius.

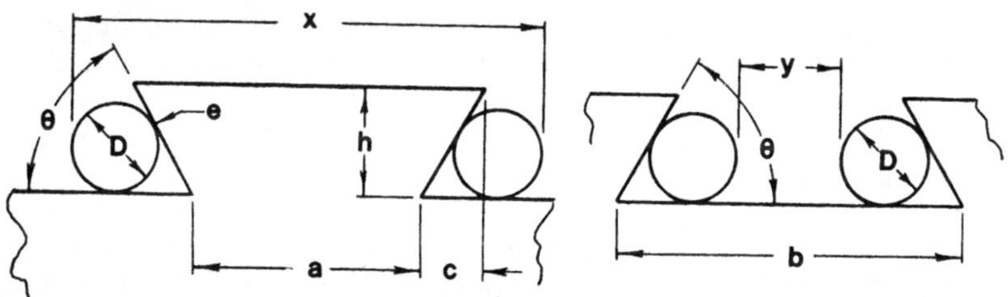

Figure 7.165 Measuring dovetail slides.

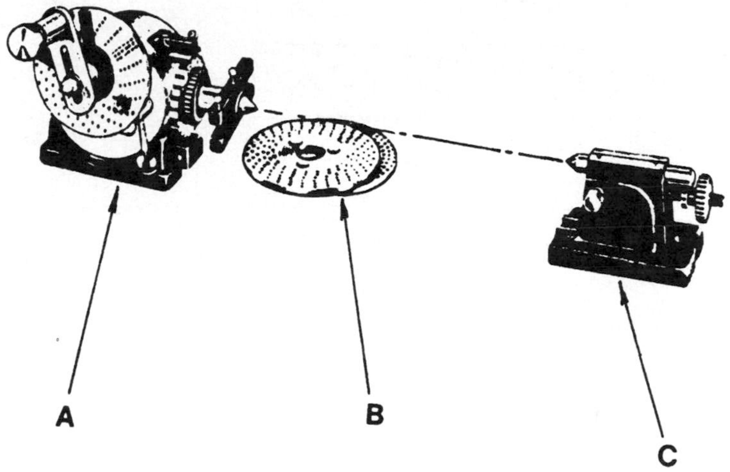

Figure 7.166 Universal dividing head.

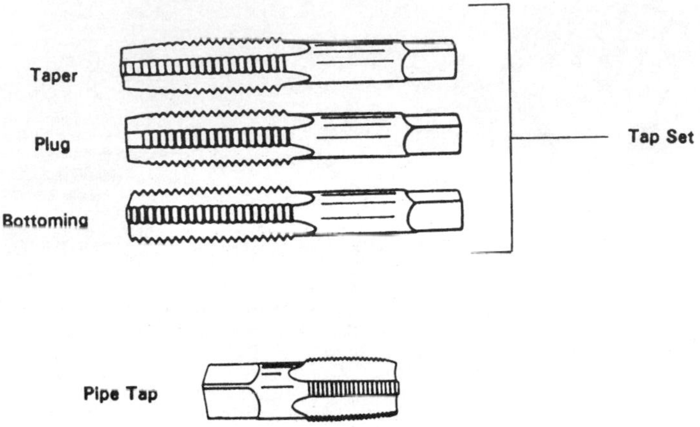

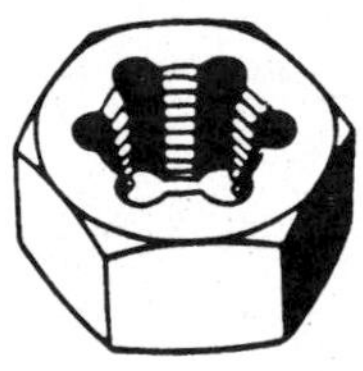

Hexagon Rethreading Die

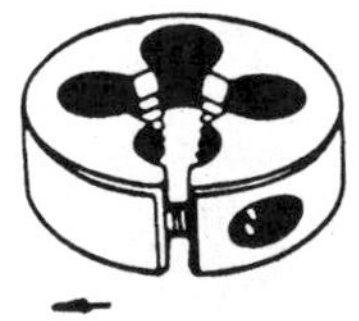

Round Adjustable Die

Solid Square Bolt Die

Cone or Acorn Die

Figure 7.167 Typical standard taps and dies.

Limit Number Codes for Ground-Thread Taps - Pitch Diameter Limits

Limit Number Code	Pitch Diameter Limits	Tap Size
L1	Basic to basic minus 0.0005"	All to 1" diameter
H1	Basic to basic plus 0.0005"	"
H2	Basic plus 0.0005" to 0.001"	"
H3	Basic plus 0.001" to 0.0015"	"
H4	Basic plus 0.0015" to 0.002"	"
H5	Basic plus 0.002" to 0.0025"	"
H6	Basic plus 0.0025" to 0.003"	"
H7	Basic plus 0.003" to 0.0035"	"
H4	Basic plus 0.001" to 0.002"	Over 1" to 1.500" diameter

Note: The limit code number divided by 2 equals in thousandths of an inch, the amount that the maximum tap pitch diameter is above basic in the H series and the amount that the minimum tap pitch diameter is under basic in the L series.

Figure 7.168 Limit number codes for ground-thread taps.

7.13.5 Limit numbers for ground-thread ISO metric taps

When the tap basic pitch diameter is over the basic thread pitch diameter by even multiples of 0.0005 in, the tap will be marked with the letter D. When the tap basic pitch diameter is under the basic thread pitch diameter by even multiples of 0.0005 in, the tap will be marked with the letters DU. The letters D and DU are followed by the limit number, which is determined as follows:

The D limit number: Amount the tap pitch diameter high limit is over basic pitch diameter, divided by 0.0005 in.

The DU limit number: Amount the tap pitch diameter low limit is under basic pitch diameter, divided by 0.0005 in.

Examples M12 × 1.75, marked D6 limit: The maximum tap pitch diameter equals basic pitch diameter plus 0.0030 in (6 × 0.0005 = 0.0030 in). Tap pitch diameter tolerance is minus 0.0012 in.

M6 × 1, marked DU4 limit: The minimum tap pitch diameter equals basic pitch diameter minus 0.0020 in (4 × 0.0005 = 0.0020 in). Tap pitch diameter tolerance is plus 0.0010 in.

Note: See ANSI/ASME Standard B94.9-1987, *Taps, cut and ground threads.*

Tap markings. All taps are marked with the nominal thread size, number of threads per inch, and the symbol to identify the thread form. On multiple thread lead taps, the lead is marked in fractions and type of lead, such as double, triple, etc. Also, the hand of the thread is marked on the tap, i.e., LH for left hand and RH for right hand.

Example A ¼–20 unified national coarse double-lead left-hand tap would be marked

¼–20UNC Double LH ⅒ in lead

See Chap. 6, "Fastening and Joining Techniques and Hardware."

7.13.6 Thread gauges (external and internal)

As shown in the preceding section on taps and dies, taps are made with ground thread forms which have pitch-diameter limits. Note also that the round adjustable dies for cutting external threads may be set with their set screw to cut the thread larger by a few thousandths of an inch. With these capabilities on the taps and dies, any particular class of fit for a particular thread size and pitch may be produced (i.e., 1, 2, 3, 1A, 2A, 3A, 1B, 2B, and 3B). Classes 1, 1A, and 1B are loose-tolerance threads; 2, 2A, and 2B are moderate or common tolerance; and 3, 3A, and 3B are close-tolerance thread fits.

In all production applications of thread cutting such as tapped holes, threaded rods, or hardware such as bolts, screws, and nuts, a method for controlling the class of fit must be employed. To accomplish this, inspection procedures using thread gages are employed.

Some of the gauges used for the quality-control inspection of threaded parts include

- Work-plug gages—Thread-setting plugs [American (inch) and metric]
- Thread-ring gages [American (inch) and metric]
- Working thread-plug gages [American (inch) and metric]

Note: Thread-setting plugs are used to check the ring gages for wear.

Chapter

8

American National Standards Applicable to Machinery, Machining, and Metalworking Practices

The American National Standards Institute (ANSI) issues standards in the form of published pamphlets which define the geometry, dimensions, inspection limits, test procedures and other control data, and specifications important to the design and manufacture of thousands of items. Components, materials, and specifications such as screw-thread systems, bolts, screws, washers, nuts, splines, pins, cutting tools, mechanical devices, various equipment and machinery, and a host of other items of importance to the machining, metalworking, and mechanical industries are all defined and specified in the various American national standards.

The purpose of these standards is to define the various physical, chemical, electrical, and mechanical characteristics of materials, components, systems, assemblies of equipment, and inspection and testing procedures. The American national standards provide a means for obtaining order and conformity among American manufactured products.

On August 24, 1969, the American Standards Association (ASA) was restructured as the United States of America Standards Institute, and standards that were approved as American standards were designated as USA standards. On October 6, 1969, the name was then changed to American National Standards Institute (ANSI). The present standards designation is ANSI instead of ASA or USAS.

The American National Standards Institute (ANSI) works in collaboration with other national organizations such as the American Society of Testing and Materials (ASTM), the Society of Automotive Engineers (SAE), the American Welding Society (AWS), the American Society of Mechanical Engineers (ASME), the American Gear Manufacturers Association (AGMA), the American Iron and Steel Institute (AISI), the Institute of Electrical and Electronics Engineers (IEEE), and others in an effort to consolidate the American standards data and publications generated by these other national organizations. The metalworking industries and other industries nationwide depend on the combined national standards of all the various American societies, institutes, and associations in order to have guidelines, specifications, and design and test procedures for manufacturing their products.

Many products and materials are required by purchasing specifications to conform to the various American standards and will not be accepted by a purchaser unless they do conform to the specified standards. For example, when a design engineer specifies a material on his or her design drawing of a spring, the material as listed on the drawing may be

0.156-in-diameter music wire per ASTM-A228

When the material is delivered to the spring manufacturer, it should conform to the specifications of this standard designation (ASTM-A228), both physically and chemically. If this specified material were to be tested and analyzed at a materials test laboratory, it would be required to conform to the ASTM-A228 specification. Failure of the material to conform to the specification could result in part failure in service. In American industry today, this problem of failure to conform to American standard specifications is becoming more prevalent and is evident in the hardware failures found in counterfeit bolts, screws, and nuts and in the materials failures found in nonconforming ferrous and nonferrous alloys being imported into the United States in ever-increasing quantities. A photograph of a counterfeit bolt which broke during installation can be seen in Fig. 6.1. The failure of imported and sometimes domestically produced parts and hardware that contain various types of screw threads that are not made to the ANSI standards also causes problems for product manufacturers in the form of excessively loose or binding fits. Imported roller chain also has been cited as not conforming to ANSI standard specifications, with breakages noted well below the standard tensile strength allowables.

The designations of the various ANSI standards which are of prime importance to the machining, metalworking, and mechanical industries are listed in this chapter by subject catagory. It was the author's and publisher's decision to not include extracts of the various ANSI standards in this *Handbook* for the following reasons:

- The basic standards applicable to the machining, metalworking, and mechanical industries are too extensive to republish.
- The standards are being revised constantly to keep pace with changing technologies.
- Whenever a standard is revised, in effect, the handbook containing these standards would be out of date and contain obsolete data.

Companies that rely on the data contained in the national standards published by ANSI and the other standards organizations should keep copies of the standards that apply to their work in the standards or engineering departments of their organizations. The ANSI standards listed in this chapter are considered by the author to be the main, basic standards required for the machining and metalworking industries. Standards from the ASTM and SAE for materials are extracted in Chap. 5, "Materials and Their Uses."

Most of the national associations, societies, and institutes that generate American standards applicable to the metalworking and electromechanical industries are listed in Chap. 23 of this *Handbook,* together with their current addresses. Standards may be purchased directly from these organizations, and most of the listed organizations have catalogs available which specify the various technical publications they produce.

8.1 Listing of ANSI Standards by Category

1. Thread systems
2. Fastening and joining devices
3. Machining practices
4. Tools and tooling

5. Mechanical components
6. Welding
7. Heat treatment
8. Tolerances and fits
9. Drawing symbols and formats
10. Gaging and inspection

Category 1: Thread systems

ANSI B1.9-1973, Buttress inch screw threads

ANSI B1.10-1958 (R1988), Unified miniature screw threads

ANSI B1.11-1958 (R1989), Microscope objective thread

ANSI B1.18M-1982 (R1987), Metric screw threads for commercial mechanical fasteners—Boundary profile defined

ANSI B1.20.3-1976 (R1982), Dryseal pipe threads (inch)

ANSI B1.20.4-1976 (R1982), Dryseal pipe threads (metric translation of B1.20.3-1976)

ANSI/ASME B1.1-1989, Unified inch screw threads (UN and UNR thread form)

ANSI/ASME B1.5-1988, Acme screw threads

ANSI/ASME B1.7M-1984, Screw threads, definitions and letter symbols for

ANSI/ASME B1.8-1988, Stub Acme screw threads

ANSI/ASME B1.12-1987, Screw threads—Class 5 interference fit thread

ANSI/ASME B1.13M-1983 (R1989), Metric screw threads—M profile

ANSI/ASME B1.20.1-1983, Pipe threads (general purpose), inch

ANSI/ASME B1.20.7-1966 (R1983), Hose coupling screw threads

Category 2: Fastening and joining devices

ANSI B18.1.1-1972 (R1989), Small solid rivets (0.4375 in diameter and under)

ANSI B18.1.2-1972 (R1989), Large rivets (0.500 in diameter and over)

ANSI B18.2.1-1981, Square and hex bolts and screws, inch series

ANSI B18.2.3.1M-1979 (R1989), Screws, metric hex cap

ANSI B18.2.3.2M-1979 (R1989), Screws, metric formed hex

ANSI B18.2.3.3M-1979 (R1989), Screws, metric heavy hex

ANSI B18.2.3.5M-1979 (R1989), Bolts, metric hex

ANSI B18.2.3.6M-1979 (R1989), Bolts, metric heavy hex

ANSI B18.2.3.7M-1979 (R1989), Bolts, metric heavy hex structural

ANSI B18.2.3.8M-1981, Screws, metric hex lag

ANSI B18.2.4.1M-1979 (R1989), Hex nuts, style 1, metric

ANSI B18.2.4.2M-1979 (R1989), Hex nuts, style 2, metric

ANSI B18.2.4.3M-1979 (R1989), Hex nuts, slotted, metric

ANSI B18.2.4.4M-1982, Nuts, metric hex flange

ANSI B18.2.4.5M-1979 (R1990), Hex jam nuts, metric

ANSI B18.2.4.6M-1979 (R1990), Hex nuts, heavy, metric

ANSI B18.5.2.1M-1981, Bolts, metric round head, short square neck

ANSI B18.6.1-1981, Wood screws, inch series

ANSI B18.6.2-1972 (R1983), Slotted head cap screws, square head set screws, and slotted headless set screws

ANSI B18.6.3-1972 (R1983), Slotted and recessed head machine screws and machine screw nuts

ANSI B18.6.4-1981, Screws, tapping and metallic drive, inch series, thread forming and cutting

ANSI B18.7-1972 (R1980), Semitubular rivets, full tubular rivets, split rivets, and rivet caps, general purpose

ANSI B18.8.1-1972 (R1983), Clevis pins and cotter pins

ANSI B18.8.2-1978 (R1989), Pins—Taper pins, dowel pins, straight pins, grooved pins, and spring pins, inch series

ANSI B18.9-1958 (R1989), Plow bolts

ANSI B18.11-1961 (R1983), Miniature screws

ANSI B18.17-1968 (R1983), Wing nuts, thumb screws, and wing screws

ANSI B18.22M-1981, Washers, metric plain

ANSI B18.22.1-1965 (R1981), Plain washers

ANSI/ASME B18.1.3M-1983 (R1989), Metric small solid rivets

ANSI/ASME B18.2.2-1987, Square and hex nuts, inch series

ANSI/ASME B18.2.3.4M-1984, Screws, metric hex flange

ANSI/ASME B18.2.3.9M-1984, Metric heavy hex flange screws

ANSI/ASME B18.3-1986, Socket cap, shoulder and set screws, inch series

ANSI/ASME B18.3.1M-1986, Screws, socket head cap, metric series

ANSI/ASME B18.3.3M-1986, Hexagon socket head shoulder screws, metric series

ANSI/ASME B18.3.4M-1986, Screws, hexagon socket button head cap, metric

ANSI/ASME B18.3.5M-1986, Hexagon socket flat countersunk head cap screws, metric series

ANSI/ASME B18.3.6M-1986, Screws, hexagon socket set, metric series

ANSI/ASME B18.5.2.2M-1982, Bolts, metric round head square neck

ANSI/ASME B18.6.5M-1986, Metric thread forming and thread cutting tapping screws

ANSI/ASME B18.6.7M-1985, Metric machine screws

ANSI/ASME B18.13-1987, Screw and washer assemblies—SEMS, inch series

ANSI/ASME B18.15-1985, Forged eyebolts

ANSI/ASME B18.21.1-1990, Lock washers

ANSI/ASME B18.21.2M-1990, Lock washers, metric series

Category 3: Machining

ANSI B5.8-1972 (R1988), Chucks and chuck jaws

ANSI B5.10-1981 (R1987), Machine tapers

ANSI B5.16-1952 (R1986), Accuracy of engine and tool room lathes

ANSI B17.1-1967 (R1989), Keys and keyseats

ANSI B17.2-1967 (R1978), Woodruff keys and keyseats

ANSI B74.2-1982, Shapes and sizes of grinding wheels and shapes, sizes, and identification of mounted wheels, specifications for

ANSI B74.13-1990, Markings for identifying grinding wheels and other bonded abrasives

ANSI B94.2-1983 (R1988), Reamers

ANSI B94.3-1965 (R1984), Straight cutoff blades for lathes and screw machines

ANSI B94.7-1980 (R1987), Hobs

ANSI B94.8-1967 (R1987), Inserted blade milling cutter bodies

ANSI B94.11M-1979 (R1987), Twist drills, straight shank and taper shank combined drills and countersinks

ANSI B94.21-1986 (R1987), Gear shaper cutters

ANSI B94.49-1975 (R1986), Spade drill blades and spade drill holders

ANSI/ASME B5.1M-1985, T-slots—Their bolts, nuts, and tongues

ANSI/ASME B94.6-1984, Knurling

ANSI/ASME B94.9-1987, Taps, cut and ground threads

ANSI/ASME B94.19-1985, Milling cutters and end mills

Category 4: Tools and tooling accessories

ANSI B5.25-1978 (R1986), Punch and die sets, inch

ANSI B5.25M-1980 (R1986), Punch and die sets, metric

ANSI B94.14-1968 (R1987), Punches—Basic head type

ANSI B94.14.1-1977 (R1984), Punches—Basic head type, metric

ANSI B94.33-1974 (R1986), Jig bushings

ANSI B107.6-1978 (R1987), Box, open end, combination and flare nut wrenches, inch series

ANSI B107.9-1978 (R1987), Box, open end, combination and flare nut wrenches, metric series

ANSI B107.10M-1982 (R1988), Socket wrenches, handles and attachments for hand, inch and metric series

ANSI/ASME B107.5M-1987, Socket wrenches, hand, metric

ANSI/ASME B107.8M-1984, Adjustable wrenches

ANSI/ASME B107.19-1987, Pliers, retaining ring

Category 5: Mechanical components

ANSI B29.2M-1982 (R1987), Inverted tooth (silent) chains and sprockets

ANSI B29.6M-1983 (R1988), Steel detachable link chains and sprockets

ANSI B29.10M-1981 (R1987), Heavy duty offset sidebar transmission roller chains and sprocket teeth

ANSI B29.15-1973 (R1987), Heavy duty roller type conveyor chains and sprocket teeth

ANSI B29.19-1976 (R1987), A and CA550 and 620 roller chains, attachments and sprockets

ANSI B92.1-1970 (R1982), Involute splines and inspection, inch version

ANSI B92.2M-1981 (R1989), Involute splines, metric module

ANSI/ASME B29.1M-1986, Precision power transmission roller chains, attachments and sprockets

Category 6: Welding

ANSI/AWS D9.1-90, Sheet metal welding code

ANSI/AWS D10.12-89, Recommended practices and procedures for welding low-carbon steels

ANSI/AWS D11.2-89, Guide for welding iron castings

ANSI/AWS D14.2-86, Machine tool weldments, specification for metal cutting

Category 7: Heat treatment

ANSI/SAE AMS 2728, Heat treatment of wrought copper beryllium alloy parts

ANSI/SAE AMS 2756, Gas nitriding of steel parts

ANSI/SAE AMS 2757, Gaseous nitrocarburizing

ANSI/SAE AMS 2759, Heat treatment of steel parts, general requirements

ANSI/SAE AMS 2759/3, Heat treatment of precipitation corrosion resisting and maraging steel parts

ANSI/SAE AMS 2759/4, Heat treatment of austenitic corrosion resistant steel parts

ANSI/SAE AMS 2759/5, Heat treatment of martensitic corrosion resistant steel parts

ANSI/SAE AMS 2759/6, Heat treatment and gas nitriding of low-alloy steel parts

ANSI/SAE AMS 2760A, Heat treatment—Carbon, low-alloy, and specialty steels

ANSI/SAE AMS 2770D, Heat treatment of aluminum alloy parts

ANSI/SAE AMS 2775A, Case hardening of titanium and titanium alloys

Category 8: Tolerances and fits

ANSI B4.1-1967 (R1987), Preferred limits and fits for cylindrical parts

ANSI B4.2-1978 (R1984), Preferred metric limits and fits

ANSI B4.3-1978 (R1984), General tolerances for metric dimensioned products

ANSI B89.3.1-1972 (R1988), Out-of-roundness, measurement of

ANSI B89.6.2-1973 (R1988), Temperature and humidity environment for dimensional measurement

ANSI Y14.5M-1982 (R1988), Dimensioning and tolerancing

ANSI/ASME B1.22M-1985, Gages and gaging practice for MJ series metric screw threads

ANSI/ASME B107.17M-1985, Gages, wrench openings, reference

Category 9: Drawing symbols and formats

ANSI Y10.20-1975 (R1988), Mathematic signs and symbols for use in physical sciences and technology

ANSI Y14.1-1980 (R1987), Drawing sheet size and format

ANSI Y14.7.1-1971 (R1988), Gear drawing standards—Part 1, For spur, helical, double helical, and rack

ANSI Y14.7.2-1978 (R1989), Gear and spline drawing standards—Part 2, Bevel and hypoid gears

ANSI Y14.17-1966 (R1987), Fluid power diagrams

ANSI Y14.36-1978 (R1987), Surface texture symbols

ANSI Y32.10-1967 (R1987), Graphic symbols for fluid power diagrams

Category 10: Gaging and inspection

ANSI B4.4M-1981 (R1987), Inspection of workpieces

ANSI B89.3.1-1972 (R1988), Out-of-roundness, measurement of

ANSI/ASME B1.2-1983, Gages and gaging for unified screw threads

ANSI/ASME B1.3M-1986, Gaging systems for dimensional acceptability, inch and metric screw threads (UN, UNR, UNJ, M, and MJ)

ANSI/ASME B1.16M-1984, Gages and gaging for metric M screw threads

ANSI/ASME B1.19M-1984, Gages for metric screw threads for commercial mechanical fasteners—Boundary profile defined

ANSI/ASME B107.17M-1985, Gages, wrench openings, reference

8.2 Standards and Approval Agencies and Acronyms

AGA	American Gas Association
AGMA	American Gear Manufacturers Association
AHAM	Association of Home Appliance Manufacturers
AMCA	Air Movement and Control Association
ANSI	American National Standards Institute
ARA	American Refrigeration Association
ARL	Applied Research Laboratories
ASHRAE	American Society of Heating, Refrigeration, and Air-Conditioning Engineers
ASME	American Society of Mechanical Engineers
ASSE	American Society of Sanitary Engineering
CEC	California Energy Commission
CGA	Canadian Gas Association
CSA	Canadian Standards Association
DIN	Deutschland Ingineering Normalization (German Engineering/Industrial Standard)
DOT	Department of Transportation
ETL	ETL Testing Laboratories
FSEC	Florida Solar Energy Center
FM	Factory Mutual
GAMA	Gas Appliance Manufacturers Association
HVI	Home Ventilating Institute
IAPMO	International Association of Plumbing and Mechanical Officials
NEC	National Electrical Code
NEMA	National Electrical Manufacturers Association
NFPA	National Fire Protection Association
NSF	National Sanitation Foundation
OPEI	Outdoor Power Equipment Institute
OSHA	Occupational Safety and Health Administration
SRCC	Solar Rating and Certification Corporation

UL	Underwriters' Laboratories
USDA	United States Department of Agriculture
AEC	Atomic Energy Commission
AN	Army-Navy Standard
ASA	American Standards Association (Now ANSI)
IEC	International Electrotechnical Commission
ISO	International Standards Organization
JAN	Joint Army-Navy Standard
MS	Military Standard
NASA	National Aeronautics and Space Administration
USAS	USA Standard (Now ANSI)

8.3 Approval Associations and Their Trademarks

See Fig. 8.1.

UL Listed

Products or systems are evaluated by Underwriters Laboratories with respect to hazards to life and property. Listing signifies that production samples of the product have been found to comply with the established requirements.

UL Recognized

An evaluation by Underwriters Laboratories of component parts which will be used later in a complete product or system. These would be factory-installed components in UL listed equipment.

CSA Certified

Product or system has been evaluated by Canadian Standards Association through examination, testing, and inspection, and complies with applicable standards of safety and/or performance.

Static Control

This refers to products and materials that discourage the formation of static electricity or are designed to drain static charges to the ground.

OSHA

The product is designed to meet the requirements of the Occupational Safety and Health Administration, which sets standards necessary or appropriate to provide safe or healthful employment and places of employment.

FM

Factory Mutual System is a group of mutual insurance companies that provides insurance from fire, explosion, accidents and other hazards. Services include fire prevention, inspection, research and consultation.

ANSI

Product meets the requirements of the American National Standards Institute, an organization which coordinates safety, engineering, and industrial standards.

OSHA/ANSI

Product meets requirements of Occupational Safety and Health Administration and American National Standards Institute.

Explosionproof

Product may be used in at least one of the hazardous locations defined by the National Electrical Code. These are classified according to the nature of the hazard.

Federal Specification

These specifications describe essential and technical requirements for items, materials, or services bought by the U S Government.

Military Specification

These specifications describe requirements for products bought by the U S armed forces.

Figure 8.1 Trademarks of approval associations.

Chapter

9

Tooling, Die Making, Molds, Jigs, and Fixtures

9.1 Definitions

Tooling. *Tooling* is a general term used to encompass many different processes involving the design and manufacture of special tools, dies, molds, jigs, and fixtures. The most common type of tooling consists of dies that are used to stamp or blank sheet metal parts for mass production. The use of a stamping or blanking die makes it possible to produce thousands of parts with consistent dimensional accuracy at a rapid pace. This ensures that the die-produced parts will fit correctly into their next assembly stage, such as in a complex mechanical device or mechanism, and have interchangeability.

The production of detail parts from a tooling device such as a stamping die reduces the overall cost of producing industrial and consumer products in relation to the cost of the die versus the number of parts to be made on the die. Complex tooling devices are relatively expensive to produce and usually must be justified by the number of parts they produce during a set time interval. As a general rule, thousands of parts should be produced yearly to justify tooling costs and maintenance of the tools.

Die making. One of the most common tooling procedures is the design and production of dies, i.e., *die making*. Industry uses a great variety of dies, including

- Stamping, blanking, and punching dies
- Bending and forming dies
- Combination or progressive dies
- Forging dies
- Dies for die casting metals and metal alloys
- Beading dies (a form of bending die)
- Extrusion dies
- Drawing dies (for wire, rod, and bar)
- Wire-form dies

Molds. There are many different types of molds that fall under the general definition of tooling. *Molds* are used to produce metal and metal-alloy parts and various types of plastic parts. In die casting, the mold is referred to as a *die*. The various types of molds made from metals, usually tool steels, include

- Die-casting molds
- Chill-casting molds
- Permanent casting molds
- Slush-casting molds
- Thermoplastic injection molds
- Thermoset plastic compression molds

Molds are also made from special tooling epoxies (see Sec. 9.6.4).

Jigs. *Jigs* are defined as tooling devices used as patterns (templates) for producing parts, match plates for drilling holes, and other devices used to guide or control a machining process. The process of *pin routing* uses a template or jig to guide the action of the high-speed routing cutter while it is cutting a stack of thin-gage sheet metal parts. A drilling or reaming jig may be designed to clamp previously die-stamped parts which are to receive a secondary machining operation such as reaming or additional drilling.

Specially hardened drill bushings are incorporated as part of the drill jig to guide the drill accurately as the part is jig drilled. Jigs allow parts to be produced with dimensional accuracy and consistency. Clamping and clamping devices are an important part of the jigging process. A subsection detailing clamping devices and clamping calculations will be presented in a later part of this chapter (see Sec. 9.8).

Fixtures. One of the most important aspects of tooling is the design and application of fixtures. A tooling *fixture* may be defined as a manufacturing aid or assembly device that is necessary in the production of mass-produced parts and assemblies. Various common types of fixtures are used in industrial applications, including

- Subassembly fixtures
- Assembly fixtures
- Welding fixtures
- Machining fixtures
- Wiring fixtures (for wire harnesses)

The design of tooling fixtures is limited only by the imagination and ingenuity of the tool designer. Fixtures for subassembly of small parts may weigh only a few ounces, while the assembly fixtures used to produce large aircraft and aerospace vehicles may weigh more than 100 tons. Tooling fixtures are an absolute necessity for the interchangeability of complex mass-produced products. Vast sums of money are spent each year by the automotive industry alone to produce the tooling fixtures required to assemble automotive equipment. The application of clamps and holding devices on tooling fixtures is an important part of tool design. The clamps and holding devices may be mechanical, electromechanical, pneumatic, or hydraulic and must be an integral part of the complete fixture. Safety and versatility must be kept in mind when designing the clamping and holding devices used on tooling fixtures.

9.2 Tool-Steel Characteristics, Heat Treatment, and Selection

To ensure that the proper tool steel is selected for each different type of tooling device and that its capabilities are developed to full potential, the producers of the various tool steels are prepared to advise tool designers or engineers on the mechanical properties and conditions of service under which the finished tools operate best. The word *tool* throughout this chapter denotes any of the tooling devices previously described.

The majority of tool-steel applications may be categorized under a small number of groups or types of operations: cutting, shearing, forming, drawing, bending, extruding, rolling, and ramming or battering. For each of these groups, certain metallurgic characteristics are of utmost importance. Cutting tools must possess high hardness and extreme strength, high resistance to the effects of elevated temperatures, and high wear resistance. Shearing tools require high wear resistance combined with toughness, and these characteristics must be balanced properly, depending on the tool design, thickness of the stock being sheared, and temperature of the shearing operation. Forming tools must possess high toughness and high strength, and many require high resistance to the softening effect of elevated temperatures. In battering or raming tools, high toughness is the most important characteristic.

Heat treatment plays an important role in attaining these desired characteristics. It should be kept in mind that tools are actually being processed, not steels. To ensure that proper heat-treatment procedures are employed, this section will present tables that list guidelines for forging, annealing, hardening, tempering, and normalizing the commonly used tool steels to which AISI designations have been assigned. These guidelines, which include temperature ranges, heating rates, cooling rates, and time at temperature, should be adapted to fit the specific application.

9.2.1 Identification and classification of tool steels

Table 9.1 shows the identification and type classification of tool steels. Figure 9.1 provides a list of the main tool-steel groups.

9.2.2 Heat treatment of tool steels

Tables 9.2 and 9.3 list the typical heat treatment of tool steels along with supplement notes and explanations (also see Sec. 5.1.1, "Tool Steels").

Tool steels are either carbon or alloy steels, which are capable of being hardened and tempered, and they are usually melted in electric furnaces and produced under tool-steel practices to meet their

Type of Tool-Steel	Designation
High-speed tool steels	M - molybdenum types T - tungsten types
Hot-work tool-steels	H H1 to H19 - chromium types H20 to H39 - tungsten types H40 to H59 - molybdenum types
Cold-work tool-steels	D - high-carbon high-chromium types A - medium-alloy air-hardening types O - oil-hardening types
Shock-resisting tool-steels	S
Mold tool-steels	P
Special-purpose tool-steels	L - low-alloy types F - carbon-tungsten types
Water-hardening tool-steels	W

Figure 9.1 Main tool-steel groups.

special requirements. Special care should be taken when using the heat-treatment data shown in Tables 9.2 and 9.3, and this is outlined as follows.

Forging. The information shown in the tables is for those occasions when a consumer is unable to purchase the desired size and must forge from a larger size. The temperature at which to start forging is given as a range, the higher side of which should be used for larger sections and heavy or rapid reductions and the lower side for smaller sections and lighter reductions. As the alloy content of the steel increases, the time of soaking at forging temperatures increases proportionately. Likewise, as the alloy content increases, it becomes more necessary to cool slowly from the forging temperature. With very high alloy steels, such as high-speed steels and air-hardening steels, this slow cooling is imperative in order to prevent cracking. Either furnace cooling or burying in an insulating material, such as lime, mica, or silocel, is satisfactory.

Annealing. The information shown in the tables on annealing is intended for those instances where a finished tool must be softened

(*Text continued on page 758.*)

TABLE 9.1 Identification and Type Classification of Tool Steels

Type	Identifying elements, % C	W	Mo	Cr	V	Co
	High Speed: Tungsten Types (1)					
T1	0.75 (2)	18.00	—	4.00	1.00	—
T2	0.80	18.00	—	4.00	2.00	—
T4	0.75	18.00	—	4.00	1.00	5.00
T5	0.80	18.00	—	4.00	2.00	8.00
T6	0.80	20.00	—	4.50	1.50	12.00
T8	0.75	14.00	—	4.00	2.00	5.00
T15	1.50	12.00	—	4.00	5.00	5.00
	High Speed: Molybdenum Types (1)					
M1	0.85 (2)	1.50	8.50	4.00	1.00	—
M2	0.85: 1.00 (2)	6.00	5.00	4.00	2.00	—
M3 class 1	1.05	6.00	5.00	4.00	2.40	—
M3 class 2	1.20	6.00	5.00	4.00	3.00	—
M4	1.30	5.50	4.50	4.00	4.00	—
M6	.80	4.00	5.00	4.00	1.50	12.00
M7	1.00	1.75	8.75	4.00	2.00	—
M10	0.85: 1.00 (2)	—	8.00	4.00	2.00	—
M30	0.80	2.00	8.00	4.00	1.25	5.00
M33	0.90	1.50	9.50	4.00	1.15	8.00
M34	0.90	2.00	8.00	4.00	2.00	8.00
M36	0.80	6.00	5.00	4.00	2.00	8.00
M41	1.10	6.75	3.75	4.25	2.00	5.00
M42	1.10	1.50	9.50	3.75	1.15	8.00
M43	1.20	2.75	8.00	3.75	1.60	8.25
M44	1.15	5.25	6.25	4.25	2.00	12.00
M46	1.25	2.00	8.25	4.00	3.20	8.25
M47	1.10	1.50	9.50	3.75	1.25	5.00

Type	Identifying elements, % C	Mn or Si	W	Mo	Cr	V	Co	Other
	Cold Work: Medium-Alloy Air-Hardening Types (1)							
A2	1.00	—	—	1.00	5.00	—	—	—
A3	1.25	—	—	1.00	5.00	1.00	—	—
A4	1.00	2.00 Mn	—	1.00	1.00	—	—	—
A6	0.70	2.00 Mn	—	1.25	1.00	—	—	—
A7	2.25	—	1.00 (3)	1.00	5.25	4.75	—	—
A8	0.55	—	1.25	1.25	5.00	—	—	—
A9	0.50	—	—	1.40	5.00	1.00	—	1.50 Ni
A10 (4)	1.35	1.80 Mn: 1.25 Si	—	1.50 —	—	—	—	1.80 Ni
	Cold Work: Oil-Hardening Types							
01	0.90	1.00	.50	—	.50	—	—	—
02	0.90	1.60	—	—	—	—	—	—
06 (4)	1.45	0.80 Mn: 1.00 Si	 —	25	—	—	—	—
07	1.20	—	1.75	—	.75	—	—	—
—	—							
W5	1.10	—	—	—	0.50	—	—	—
	Shock-Resisting Types							
S1	0.50	—	2.50	—	1.50	—	—	—
S2	0.50	1.00 Si	—	0.50	—	—	—	—
S5	0.55	0.80 Mn: 2.00 Si	—	0.40	—	—	—	—
S6	0.45	1.40 Mn: 2.25 Si	—	0.40	1.50	—	—	—
S7	0.50	—	—	1.40	3.25	—	—	—

Hot Work: Chromium Types (1)						
H10	0.40	—	2.50	3.25	0.40	—
H11	0.35	—	1.50	5.00	0.40	—
H12	0.35	1.50	1.50	5.00	0.40	—
H13	0.35	—	1.50	5.00	1.00	—
H14	0.40	5.00	—	5.00	—	—
H19	0.40	4.25	—	4.25	2.00	4.25
Hot Work: Tungsten Types						
H21	0.35	9.00	—	3.50	—	—
H22	0.35	11.00	—	2.00	—	—
H23	0.30	12.00	—	12.00	—	—
H24	0.45	15.00	—	3.00	—	—
H25	0.25	15.00	—	4.00	—	—
H26	0.50	18.00	—	4.00	1.00	—
Hot Work: Molybdenum Types						
H42	0.60	6.00	5.00	4.00	2.00	—
Cold Work: High-Carbon High-Chromium Types (1)						
D2	1.50	—	1.00	12.00	1.00	—
D3	2.25	—	—	12.00	—	—
D4	2.25	—	1.00	12.00	—	—
D5	1.50	—	1.00	12.00	—	3.00
D7	2.35	—	1.00	12.00	4.00	—

Special-Purpose Low-Alloy Types								
L2	0.50/1.10 (5)	—	—	—	1.00	0.20	—	—
L6	0.70	—	—	0.25 (3)	0.75	—	—	1.50 Ni
Water-Hardening Types								
W1	0.60/1.40 (5)	—	—	—	—	—	—	—
W2	0.60/1.40 (5)	—	—	—	—	0.25	—	—
W5	1.10	—	—	—	0.50	—	—	—
Mold Types								
P2	0.07	—	—	0.20	2.00	—	—	0.50 Ni
P3	0.10	—	—	—	0.60	—	—	1.25 Ni
P4	0.07	—	—	0.75	5.00	—	—	—
P5	0.10	—	—	—	2.25	—	—	—
P6	0.10	—	—	—	1.50	—	—	3.50 Ni
P20	0.35	—	—	0.40	1.70	—	—	—
P21	0.20	—	—	—	—	—	—	4.00 Ni: 1.20 A1

(1) Some of the types can be produced with a sulfur addition to improve machinability.
(2) Other carbon contents may be available.
(3) Optional.
(4) Contains free graphite in the microstructure to improve machinability.
(5) Various carbon contents are available.

TABLE 9.2 Typical Heat Treatments for Tool Steels

Tool steel type	Forging		Annealing			Hardening		
	Start, °F	Do not forge below °F	Temp., °F	Cooling rate, °F Max/h	Brinell hardness	Heating rate	Preheat temp., °F	Hardening temp., °F
High Speed: Tungsten Types								
T1	1950–2150	1750	1600–1650	40	217–255	Rapid from preheat	1500–1600	2300–2375(a)
T2	1950–2150	1750	1600–1650	40	223–255	Rapid from preheat	1500–1600	2300–2375(a)
T4	1950–2150	1750	1600–1650	40	229–269	Rapid from preheat	1500–1600	2300–2375(a)
T5	1950–2150	1800	1600–1650	40	235–285	Rapid from preheat	1500–1600	2325–2375(a)
T6	1950–2150	1800	1600–1650	40	248–302	Rapid from preheat	1500–1600	2325–2375(a)
T8	1950–2150	1800	1600–1650	40	229–255	Rapid from preheat	1500–1600	2300–2375(a)
T15	1950–2150	1800	1600–1650	40	241–277	Rapid from preheat	1500–1600	2200–2300(a)
High Speed: Molybdenum Types								
M1	1900–2100	1700	1500–1600	40	207–235	Rapid from preheat	1350–1550	2150–2225(a)
M2	1900–2100	1700	1600–1650	40	212–241	Rapid from preheat	1350–1550	2175–2250(a)
M3 (1; 2)	1900–2100	1700	1600–1650	40	223–255	Rapid from preheat	1350–1550	2200–2250(a)
M4	1900–2100	1700	1600–1650	40	223–255	Rapid from preheat	1350–1550	2200–2250(a)
M6	1900–2100	1700	1600	40	248–277	Rapid from preheat	1450	2150–2200(a)
M7	1900–2100	1700	1500–1600	40	217–255	Rapid from preheat	1350–1550	2150–2225(a)
M10	1900–2100	1700	1500–1600	40	207–255	Rapid from preheat	1350–1550	2150–2225(a)
M30	1900–2100	1700	1600–1650	40	235–269	Rapid from preheat	1350–1550	2200–2250(a)
M33	1900–2100	1700	1600–1650	40	235–269	Rapid from preheat	1350–1550	2200–2250(a)
M34	1900–2100	1700	1600–1650	40	235–269	Rapid from preheat	1350–1500	2200–2250(a)
M36	1900–2100	1700	1600–1650	40	235–269	Rapid from preheat	1350–1550	2225–2275(a)
M41	1900–2100	1700	1600–1650	40	235–269	Rapid from preheat	1350–1550	2175–2220(a)
M42	1900–2100	1700	1600–1650	40	235–269	Rapid from preheat	1350–1550	2125–2175(a)
M43	1900–2100	1700	1600–1650	40	248–269	Rapid from preheat	1350–1550	2100–2150(a)
M44	1900–2100	1700	1600–1650	40	248–285	Rapid from preheat	1350–1550	2190–2240(a)
M46	1900–2100	1700	1600–1650	40	235–269	Rapid from preheat	1350–1550	2175–2225(a)
M47	1900–2100	1700	1600–1650	40	235–269	Rapid from preheat	1350–1550	2150–2200(a)
Hot Work: Chromium Types								
H10	1950–2100	1650	1550–1650	40	192–229	Moderate from preheat	1500	1850–1900
H11	1950–2100	1650	1550–1650	40	192–235	Moderate from preheat	1500	1825–1875

TABLE 9.2 Typical Heat Treatments for Tool Steels (*Continued*)

Hardening		Tempering					
Minutes at temp.	Quench medium (b)	Temp., °F	Tempered Rc hardness	Depth of hardening	Heat-treat distortion	Hardening safety	Resist. to decarb.
High Speed: Tungsten Types							
2–5	O, A, or S	1000–1100(c)	65–60	Deep	A or S = low; O = medium	High	High
2–5	O, A, or S	1000–1100(c)	66–61	Deep	A or S = low; O = medium	High	High
2–5	O, A, or S	1000–1100(c)	66–62	Deep	A or S = low; O = medium	Medium	Medium to high
2–5	O, A, or S	1000–1100(c)	65–60	Deep	A or S = low; O = medium	Medium	Low
2–5	O, A, or S	1000–1100(c)	65–60	Deep	A or S = low; O = medium	Medium	Low
2–5	O, A, or S	1000–1100 (c)	65–60	Deep	A or S = low; O = medium	Medium	Medium
2–5	O, A, or S	1000–1200(c)	68–63	Deep	A or S = low; O = medium	Medium	Medium
High Speed: Molybdenum Types							
2–5	O, A, or S	1000–1100(c)	65–60	Deep	A or S = low; O = medium	Medium	Low
2–5	O, A, or S	1000–1100(c)	65–60	Deep	A or S = low; O = medium	Medium	Medium
2–5	O, A, or S	1000–1100(c)	66–61	Deep	A or S = low; O = medium	Medium	Medium
2–5	O, A, or S	1000–1100(c)	66–61	Deep	A or S = low; O = medium	Medium	Medium
2–5	O, A, or S	1000–1100(c)	66–61	Deep	A or S = low; O = medium	Medium	Low
2–5	O, A, or S	1000–1100(c)	66–61	Deep	A or S = low; O = medium	Medium	Low
2–5	O, A, or S	1000–1100(c)	65–60	Deep	A or S = low; O = medium	Medium	Low
2–5	O, A, or S	1000–1100(c)	65–60	Deep	A or S = low; O = medium	Medium	Low
2–5	O, A, or S	1000–1100(c)	65–60	Deep	A or S = low; O = medium	Medium	Low
2–5	O, A, or S	1000–1100(c)	65–60	Deep	A or S = low; O = medium	Medium	Low
2–5	O, A, or S	1000–1100(c)	65–60	Deep	A or S = low; O = medium	Medium	Low
2–5	O, A, or S	1000–1100(d)	70–65	Deep	A or S = low; O = medium	Medium	Low
2–5	O, A, or S	950–1100(d)	70–65	Deep	A or S = low; O = medium	Medium	Low
2–5	O, A, or S	950–1100(d)	70–65	Deep	A or S = low; O = medium	Medium	Low
2–5	O, A, or S	1000–1160(d)	70–62	Deep	A or S = low; O = medium	Medium	Low
2–5	O, A, or S	975–1050(d)	69–67	Deep	A or S = low; O = medium	Medium	Low
2–5	O, A, or S	975–1100(d)	70–65	Deep	A or S = low; O = medium	Medium	Low
Hot Work: Chromium Types							
15–40(e)	A	1000–1200(c)	56–39	Deep	Very low	Highest	Medium
15–40(e)	A	1000–1200(c)	54–38	Deep	Very low	Highest	Medium

TABLE 9.2 Typical Heat Treatments for Tool Steels (*Continued*)

Tool steel type	Forging: Start, °F	Forging: Do not forge below °F	Annealing: Temp., °F	Annealing: Cooling rate, °F Max/h	Annealing: Brinell hardness	Hardening: Heating rate	Hardening: Preheat temp., °F	Hardening: Hardening temp., °F
H12	1950–2100	1650	1550–1650	40	192–235	Moderate from preheat	1500	1825–1875
H13	1950–2100	1650	1550–1650	40	192–229	Moderate from preheat	1500	1825–1900
H14	1950–2150	1700	1600–1650	40	207–235	Moderate from preheat	1500	1850–1950
H19	1900–2100	1650	1600–1650	40	207–241	Rapid from preheat	1500	2000–2200(a)
Hot Work: Tungsten Types								
H21	1950–2150	1650	1600–1650	40	207–235	Rapid from preheat	1500	2000–2200(a)
H22	1950–2150	1650	1600–1650	40	207–235	Rapid from preheat	1500	2000–2200(a)
H23	1950–2150	1800	1600–1650	40	212–255	Rapid from preheat	1550	2200–2300(a)
H24	1950–2150	1750	1600–1650	40	217–241	Rapid from preheat	1500	2000–2250(a)
H25	1950–2150	1700	1600–1650	40	207–235	Rapid from preheat	1500	2100–2300(a)
H26	1950–2150	1750	1600–1650	40	217–241	Rapid from preheat	1600	2150–2300(a)
Hot Work: Molybdenum Type								
H42	1900–2050	1700	1550–1650	40	207–235	Rapid from preheat	1350–1550	2050–2225(a)
Cold Work: High-Carbon High-Chromium Types								
D2	1850–2000	1700	1600–1650	40	217–255	Very slowly	1500	1800–1875
D3	1850–2000	1700	1600–1650	40	217–255	Very slowly	1500	1700–1800
D4	1850–2000	1700	1600–1650	40	217–255	Very slowly	1500	1775–1850
D5	1850–2000	1700	1600–1650	40	223–255	Very slowly	1500	1800–1875
D7	2050–2125	1800	1600–1650	40	235–262	Very slowly	1500	1850–1950
Cold Work: Medium-Alloy Air-Hardening Types								
A2	1850–2000	1650	1550–1600	40	201–235	Slowly	1450	1700–1800
A3	1850–1950	1650	1550–1600	40	207–229	Slowly	1450	1750–1850
A4	1850–2000	1650	1360–1400	25	200–241	Slowly	1250	1500–1600
A6	1900–2050	1600	1350–1375	25	217–248	Slowly	1200	1525–1600
A7	1925–2100	1800	1600–1650	25	235–269	Very slowly	1500	1750–1800
A8	1950–2100	1700	1550–1600	40	192–241	Slowly	1450	1800–1850
A9	1950–2100	1700	1550–1600	25	212–248	Slowly	1450	1800–1875
A10	1800–1925	1600	1410–1460	15	235–269	Slowly	1200	1450–1500
Cold Work: Oil-Hardening Types								
O1	1800–1950	1550	1400–1450	40	183–212	Slowly	1200	1450–1500
O2	1800–1925	1550	1375–1425	40	183–217	Slowly	1200	1400–1475
O6	1800–1950	1500	1410–1450	20	183–217	Slowly	—	1450–1500
O7	1800–2000	1600	1450–1500	40	192–217	Slowly	1200	W=1450–1525(b) O=1500–1625(b)
Shock-Resisting Types								
S1	1850–2050	1600	1450–1500	40	183–229	Slowly	1200	1650–1750
S2	1850–2050	1600	1400–1450	40	192–217	Slowly	1200	1550–1650
S5	1850–2050	1600	1425–1475	25	192–229	Slowly	1400	1600–1700
S6	1850–2050	1600	1475–1525	25	192–229	Slowly	1400	1650–1750
S7	1950–2050	1700	1500–1550	25	187–223	Slowly	1200–1300	1700–1750

TABLE 9.2 Typical Heat Treatments for Tool Steels (*Continued*)

Hardening		Tempering					
Minutes at temp.	Quench medium (b)	Temp., °F	Tempered Rc hardness	Depth of hardening	Heat-treat distortion	Hardening safety	Resist. to decarb.
15–40(e)	A	1000–1200(c)	55–38	Deep	Very low	Highest	Medium
15–40(e)	A	1000–1200(c)	53–38	Deep	Very low	Highest	Medium
15–40(e)	A	1100–1200(c)	47–40	Deep	Low	Highest	Medium
2–5	A or O	1000–1300(c)	57–40	Deep	A = low; O = medium	High	Medium
Hot Work: Tungsten Types							
2–5	A or O	1100–1250	54–36	Deep	A = low O = medium	High	Medium
2–5	A or O	1100–1250	52–39	Deep	A = low; O = medium	High	Medium
2–5	O	1200–1350(c)	47–34	Deep	Medium	High	Medium
2–5	O	1050–1200(c)	55–45	Deep	A = low; O = medium	High	Medium
2–5	A or O	1050–1250(c)	44–35	Deep	A = low; O = medium	High	Medium
2–5	O, A, or S	1050–1250(c)	58–43	Deep	S, A = low; O = medium	High	Medium
Hot Work: Molybdenum Type							
15–45(e)	O, A, or S	1050–1200(c)	60–50	Deep	S, A = low; O = medium	Medium	Medium
Cold Work: High-Carbon High-Chromium Types							
15–45(e)	A	400–1000	61–54	Deep	Lowest	Highest	Medium
15–45(e)	O	400–1000	61–54	Deep	Very low	High	Medium
15–45(e)	A	400–1000	61–54	Deep	Lowest	Highest	Medium
15–45(e)	A	400–1000	61–54	Deep	Lowest	Highest	Medium
30–60(e)	A	300–1000	65–58	Deep	Lowest	Highest	Medium
Cold Work: Medium-Alloy Air-Hardening Types							
20–45(e)	A	350–1000	62–57	Deep	Lowest	Highest	Medium
25–60(e)	A	350–1000	65–57	Deep	Lowest	Highest	Medium
15–90(e)	A	350–800	62–54	Deep	Lowest	Highest	Medium to high
20–45(e)	A	300–800	60–54	Deep	Lowest	Highest	Medium to high
30–60(e)	A	300–1000	67–57	Deep	Lowest	Highest	Medium
20–45(e)	A	350–1100	60–50	Deep	Lowest	Highest	Medium
20–45(e)	A	950–1150	56–35	Deep	Lowest	Highest	Medium
30–60(e)	A	350–80	62–55	Deep	Lowest	Highest	Medium to high
Cold Work: Oil-Hardening Types							
10–30	O	350–500	62–57	Medium	Very low	Very high	High
5–20	O	350–500	62–57	Medium	Very low	Very high	High
10–30	O	350–600	63–58	Medium	Very low	Very high	High
10–30	O or W	350–550	64–58	Medium	W = high O = very low	W = low O = very high	High
Shock-Resisting Types							
15–45	O	400–1200	58–40	Medium	Medium	High	Medium
5–20	B or W	350–800	60–50	Medium	High	Low	Low
5–20	O	350–800	60–50	Medium	Medium	High	Low
10–30	O	400–600	56–54	Medium	Medium	High	Low
15–45(e)	A or O	400–1150	57–45	Deep	A = lowest; O = low	A = highest; O = high	Medium

TABLE 9.2 Typical Heat Treatments for Tool Steels (*Continued*)

	Forging		Annealing			Hardening		
Tool steel type	Start, °F	Do not forge below °F	Temp., °F	Cooling rate, °F Max/h	Brinell hardness	Heating rate	Preheat temp., °F	Hardening temp., °F
				Special Purpose: Low-Alloy Types				
L2	1800–2000	1550	1400–1450	40	163–197	Slowly	—	W=1450–1550 O=1550–1700
L6	1800–2000	1550	1400–1450	40	183–255	Slowly	—	1450–1550
				Water-Hardening Types				
W1	1800–1950(f)	1500	1360–1450(f)	40	156–201	Slowly	(g)	1400–1550(h)
W2	1800–1950(f)	1500	1360–1450(f)	40	156–201	Slowly	(g)	1400–1550(h)
W5	1800–1950(f)	1500	1360–1450(f)	40	163–201	Slowly	(g)	1400–1525(h)
						Hardening		
						Carburizing temp., °F		Hardening temp., °F
				Mold Types				
P2	1850–2050	1550	1350–1500	40	103–123	1650–1700		1525–1550(i)
P3	1850–2050		1350–1500	40	109–137	1650–1700		1475–1525(i)
P4	1850–2050	1600	1600–1650	25	116–128	1775–1825		1775–1825(i)
P5	1850–2050	1550	1550–1600	40	105–131	1650–1700		1550–1600(i)
P6	1950–2150	1700	1550	15	183–217	1650–1700		1450–1500(i)
P20	1850–2050	1600	1400–1450	40	149–212	1600–1650		1500–1600
						Solution Treating		
						Heating rate	Preheat temp.	Solution temp., °F
P21	2000–2100	1750		Do not anneal		Slowly	Do not preheat	1300–1350

TABLE 9.2 Typical Heat Treatments for Tool Steels (*Continued*)

Hardening		Tempering					
Minutes at temp.	Quench medium (b)	Temp., °F	Tempered Rc hardness	Depth of hardening	Heat-treat distortion	Hardening safety	Resist. to decarb.
Special Purpose: Low-Alloy Types							
10–30	O or W	350–1000	63–45	O = medium	O = medium W = high	O = medium W = low	High
10–30	O	350–1000	62–45	Medium	Low	High	High
Water-Hardening Types							
10–30	B or W	350–650	64–50	Shallow	High	Low	Highest
10–30	B or W	350–650	64–50	Shallow	High	Low	Highest
10–30	B or W	350–650	64–50	Shallow	High	Low	Highest
Mold Types							
15	O	350–500	64–58(k)	Medium	Low	High	High
15	O	350–500	64–58(k)	Medium	Low	High	High
15	A	350–900	64–58(k)	Medium	Very low	High	High
15	O or W	350–500	64–58(k)		W = high O = low	High	High
15	A or O	350–450	61–58(k)		A = very low, O = low	High	High
15	O	900–1100	37–28	Medium	Low	High	High
		Aging					
		Temp., °F	Hardness Rc				
60–180	A or O	950–1025	40–30	Deep	Lowest	Highest	High

TABLE 9.3 Notes and Explanations for Table 9.2

(a) When the high temperature heating is carried out in a salt bath, the range of temperatures should be about 25°F lower than that shown.

(b) A = air quench
B = brine quench
O = oil quench
S = salt bath quench
W = water quench

(c) Double tempering recommended for not less than 1 h at temperature each temper.

(d) Triple tempering recommended for not less than 1 h at temperature each temper.

(e) Times shown apply to open furnace heat treatment. For pack hardening, a common rule is to heat for ½ h per inch of cross section of the pack.

(f) Forging, normalizing, and annealing temperatures of carbon tool steels are given as ranges because they vary with carbon content. The following temperatures are recommended:

Forging
0.50 to 1.25% C: the range shown
1.25 to 1.40% C: low side of range

Normalizing
0.60 to 0.75% C: 1500°F
0.75 to 0.90% C: 1450°F
0.90 to 1.10% C: 1600°F
1.10 to 1.40% C: 1600 to 1700°F

Annealing
0.60 to 0.90% C: 1360 to 1400°F
0.90 to 1.40% C: 1400 to 1450°F

(g) For large tools and tools having intricate sections, preheating at 1050–1200°F is recommended.

(h) Varies with carbon content as follows:
0.60–0.80% C: 1450–1550°F
0.85–1.05% C: 1425–1550°F
1.10–1.40% C: 1400–1525°F

(i) After carburizing

(k) Carburized case hardness

SOURCE: "AISI Steel Products Manual—Tool Steels," April 1976.

for additional machining or where the user has performed a forging operation. The annealing temperature is given as a range, the upper limit of which should be used for large sections and the lower limit for smaller sections. The length of time the steel is held, after being uniformly heated through at the annealing temperature, varies from about 1 h for light sections and small furnace charges of carbon or low-alloy tool steel to about 4 h for heavy sections and large furnace charges of high-alloy steel.

Normalizing. The purpose of *normalizing* after forging is to refine the grain structure and to produce a uniform structure throughout the forging. Normalizing should not be confused with low-temperature (about 1200°F) annealing, which is used for relief of residual stresses resulting from heavy machining, bending, and forming.

Steels that can be normalized are O1 (1600°F), O2 (1550°F), O6 (1600°F), and O7 (1650°F); L2 (1600–1650°F) and L6 (1600°F); W1, W2, and W5 (1450–1700°F); and P20 and P21 (1650°F).

The length of time the steel is held after being uniformly heated through at the normalizing temperature varies from about 15 min for a small section to about 1 h for large sizes. Cooling from the normalizing temperature is done in still air.

Other factors of concern to heat treaters. Other properties of the tool steels which are of concern to the heat treater are depth of hardening, distortion in heat treating, safety in hardening, and resistance to decarburization. A qualitative evaluation of these properties is also presented in Tables 9.2 and 9.3, comparing all the tool steels relative to one another rather than within any particular class. The following general observations may be helpful.

Depth of hardening. This relates to the depth of hardness penetration of the individual tool steels. The hardenability ratings are based on the use of the particular quenching medium recommended. Carbon tool steels in group W are very shallow hardening steels and are generally quenched in water. The hardenability increases in tool steels as the alloy content increases (except for cobalt and tungsten). The hardenability increases with carbon content until excess carbide appears, and then it begins to decrease with further increases in carbon. For large tool or die sections, it is imperative that a high-alloy steel be selected if high strength is to be developed throughout the section in the finished part. For the P steels which are used in the carburized and hardened condition, the core hardenability is rated as low, medium, or high.

Distortion in heat treating. This rates the tool steels on the basis of the distortion normally obtained in hardening the respective grades from the normally recommended hardening temperatures. Distortion in heat treating is important in intricately designed tools that must maintain their shape after hardening. The steels rated lowest or very low usually can be machined very close to finish size prior to heat treatment so that little grinding will be required after the hardening operation.

In general, water-hardening steels exhibit the most distortion, while air-hardening steels exhibit the least. It is important to note, however, that carbon tool steels and other shallow-hardening types may distort very little in heat treatment when the hardened case is small in comparison with the unhardened core for any particular tool or die design.

Safety in hardening. This deals with the overall freedom from heat-treating difficulties which may be experienced in handling the tool-steel grades in question. The ratings apply particularly to freedom from cracking when complicated or intricate sections are being hardened. The air- and oil-hardening steels prove superior to the water-hardening steels in this respect.

When designing machine parts and tools which require heat treatment, the design engineer should allow generous filleting at changes in section and eliminate the use of sharp angles as far as possible. The greater the symmetry of design, the less hazardous is the heat treatment.

Resistance to carburization. This influences the type of heat-treating equipment selected, as well as the amount of material that should be removed from the surface after hardening. Both these factors concern the economics of tool-steel use. The ratings are intended to apply at the hardening temperature normally recommended. Those steels which are rated low must be protected in some way from decarburization during the heating cycle.

Additional heat-treatment data. See Sec. 5.1.1.

9.2.3 Selection of tool steels

The tool steels listed in the preceding tables are generally available. The relative availability within a group, however, will vary depending on whether the steel is designed for specific applications or finds use in general applications. Experience indicates that in the majority of cases the choice is not limited to a single type of tool steel or even to a particular family of tool steels for a workable solution to an individual tooling problem. It is desirable to select a tool steel that will give the most economical overall performance when weighed against expected productivity, ease of fabrication, and cost.

The majority of tool-steel applications can be divided into a small number of groups or types of operations, such as cutting, shearing, forming, drawing, extruding, rolling, and battering. The following characteristic descriptions of the tool steels are intended as a guide, and it must be understood that the proper selection of a tool steel for a specific application cannot always be made with 100 percent assurance. Because of this, consultation with the steel producer is recommended. The following list describes the characteristics of the major tool-steel types.

A. Cold-work tool steels (medium alloy, air hardening). These steels show a minimum of distortion during heat treatment and have greater safety in hardening than the oil-hardening grades. Dies which could crack during heat treatment when made from oil-hardening grades generally can be handled safely when made from the air-hardening group. The low-carbon types A8 and A9 offer greater shock resistance than the other steels in this group but are lower in wear resistance. Type A7 exhibits maximum abrasion resistance but should be restricted to lower-toughness applications.

D. Cold-work tool steels (high carbon, high chromium). These steels are more wear resistant than the medium-alloy air-hardening steels used where long-run dies are required. Of the group, D1, D2, and D5 have the greater toughness but the least abrasion resistance. These steels, being very wear-resistant, are difficult to machine and grind, and a minimum of stock should be allowed for grinding after hardening. These grades are all air-hardening and show little distortion or movement during heat treatment. Wear resistance increases as the carbon and vanadium contents increase.

E. Special-purpose tool steels (carbon-tungsten types). These are often called *finishing steels* and provide relatively high wear resistance in water-hardening steels. These steels are typically used for wire, bar, or tube cold-drawing dies, finishing tools, and fine-cutting-edge tools such as broaches, taps, and reamers. F2 is recommended where high wear resistance and sharp cutting edge capability are required. These steels are somewhat difficult to grind after hardening because of their wear and abrasion resistance.

H. Hot-work tool steels. These steels are chromium-, tungsten-, and molybdenum-based. The chromium-based types are air-hardening, showing very little distortion during heat treatment. The tungsten- and molybdenum-based steels are either air- or oil-hardening and show more distortion during oil quenching. These are high-heat-resisting steels with moderate wear resistance. The tungsten types (H20 to H39) are for those hot-work applications where resistance to the softening effect of elevated temperature is of greatest importance and a lesser degree of toughness is allowed. The molybdenum types (H40 to H59) offer excellent high-heat resistance but should be restricted to those applications where less ductility is acceptable. A wide range of hot-work tools are made from these steels for die-casting dies, extrusion-press parts, forging dies, hot punches, and shears.

L. Special-purpose tool steels (low alloy). These steels have deeper hardening characteristics than the W group and have similar properties to O1 and O2 as general-purpose tool steels but exhibit a greater tendency to distort during heat treatment. Of the group, L6 has greater toughness, at the sacrifice of wear resistance. High-carbon type L3 may be used for short-run and special-purpose tools and dies.

M. High-speed tool steels (molybdenum base). These steels are commonly used for high-speed cutting-tool applications. They decarburize better than the tungsten type and are somewhat more critical in their heat treatment. Vanadium and cobalt are added, as is the case with the tungsten types, with corresponding advantages and disadvantages. The M2 type is considered the molybdenum counterpart of T1 as a general-purpose cutting-tool material. The series beginning with M41 has the characteristic of exceptionally high hardness in heat treatment. These steels are also used for cold-header die inserts, punches, and thread-rolling and blanking dies. The steels in this group are *underhardened* for these applications in order to increase toughness.

O. Cold-work tool steels (oil hardening). All these steels listed under the symbol O are low-alloy types that must be oil quenched in heat treatment. Types O1 and O2 are widely used tool steels for many types of die applications, having greater hardenability and generally less distortion during heat treatment than the water-hardening steels. These steels will harden throughout in sections up to 2.50 in thick with relative freedom from distortion and cracking during heat treatment. Type O7 attains the greatest wear or abrasion resistance but is usually used in special applications.

P. Special-purpose tool steels (mold steels). These steels are generally considered as plastic-mold steels but have found other applications outside the mold-making field. These steels are usually supplied at very low hardness to facilitate machining and other processing prior to carburizing to develop the required surface properties for injection and compression molds for plastics. Types P20 and P21 are usually supplied in the hardened condition so that they may be machined and put into immediate service. These types are suitable for plastic molds, zinc die-casting dies, and holder blocks.

S. Shock-resisting tool steels. These steels contain less carbon but higher alloy content and are therefore tougher than water-hardening grades. They have less wear resistance than the water-hardening steels but are used where punching, shearing, or trimming is being performed. Type S1 has the greatest wear resistance in the group and may be carburized for even greater hardness and wear resistance, but with a loss in toughness. Because of the moderately high hardening temperatures and rapid quenching required, these steels are subject to distortion during heat treatment.

T. High-speed tool steels (tungsten base). These steels are generally used for metal-cutting tools, although type T1 is sometimes used as a die material because of its high strength and wear resistance. Type T1 has been an established general-purpose high-speed steel (HSS) for many years. See Sec. 7.3.3, "Classification of High-Speed Steels," for compositions of both the T and M types of HSS and characteristics.

W. Water-hardening tool steels. Being low in alloy content, these steels are shallow-hardening, developing a tough case with a hard core. They are quenched in water or brine, are subject to distortion, and do not retain their properties above 350°F. Water-hardening tool steels are used for short production runs in all types of tools and dies. Their shallow hardenability adapts them well for cold-heading dies. Although used for many applications, they are limited in their properties and capabilities.

9.3 Dies, Molds, and Die-Making Procedures

The stamping, punching, or blanking die is the most common type of tooling employed by industry. These types of dies consist of a male punch and a female die block. The material to be punched, stamped, or blanked is placed between the die sections, and a force is applied to the punch or male portion of the die set. As the material is being punched, compressive and tensile stresses are developed within the stock material until a cutting and then shearing

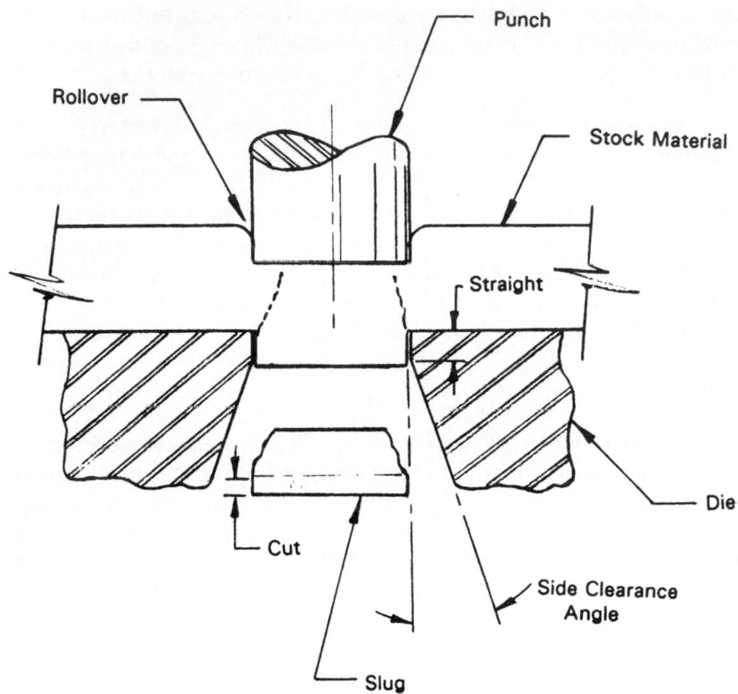

Figure 9.2 Punch action.

action takes place, forcing the punched portion of the material out of the female die block. Figure 9.2 illustrates a typical punching operation.

A portion of the stock is cut cleanly, while the remainder is broken by the shear forces developed within the material. Figure 9.3 shows a typical punched edge with the cut and sheared sections clearly defined. The shiny section is the cut portion, while the remainder is shear fractured. The proportion of the cleanly cut section in relation to the irregular shear-fractured section is a function of the material hardness and the die clearance. Soft materials will have approximately 30 percent or more of the stock cut and the remainder shear fractured, while hard materials will have only 10 to 20 percent of the stock thickness cleanly cut and the remainder shear fractured.

Figure 9.3 Punched edge.

The female die block must have an angular side clearance below the die cutting *straight* in order for the punched part to fall out or clear the female die after the punching operation is completed. Figure 9.4 shows a typical blanking die set, separated to show the parts. In the figure, the parts of the die set are labled and defined as follows:

A	Male portion of die
B	Top plate of the die set
C	Guidepost bushing
D	Bottom plate of the die set
E	Gate (for stock material)
F	Stripper or shoulder bolt
G	Opening in stripper plate
H	Guidepost
I	Die spring
J	Female die
K	Stripper plate

The die set shown in Fig. 9.4 was designed and built for blanking polycarbonate (Lexan) plastic material, 0.05 in thick. The plastic stock was cut in uniform strips to fit the die gate so that it could be fed progressively into the die during each blanking operation with the production of a minimum amount of scrap.

Figure 9.4 Blanking die, separated.

9.3.1 Manual die making (blanking dies)

Prior to the modern EDM methods of punching and blanking, the die maker used the manual method, which consisted of the following process steps:

1. The male portion or punch section of the die was machined to the proper shape and dimensions from the selected tool steel.
2. The finished male portion or punch was then heat treated to the required hardness and temper.
3. The heat-treated male portion was then set against the face or surface of the soft or annealed female die block and a high pressure applied. This step produced a sharp outline of the male portion into the surface of the female die block.
4. The die maker then machined the female die block close to the outline impression made by step 3 (to within a few thousandths of an inch).

Note: The male portion and female die block were drilled and pinned (mounted) into the die set prior to step 3.

5. With the male and female portions aligned and set, pressure was applied to the die set, forcing the male portion into the female die block a small distance. This procedure shaved the close-machined edges of the female die block and rolled the die material inward.
6. The female portion was then carefully hand filed to remove the rolled and shaved burrs produced by step 5.
7. Step 6 was repeated until the male portion had progressed into the female die block approximately two times the thickness of the stock material to be stamped.
8. The correct side clearance angle was then filed in the female die block, below the cutting straight. Angular side clearances range between 0.5 and 2.0° per side, according to stock thickness. The height of the cutting straight is 0.125 in for all stock 0.125 in thick and less and usually equal to the stock thickness for all stock above 0.125 in.
9. The proper die clearance was then applied to the male punch or female die block by hand filing the appropriate die member.

Note: As a general rule in die stamping or punching,

- For punching holes in parts, the punch (male) is made to the exact size of the punched hole or area, and the correct die clearance is filed or cut in the female die block (Fig. 9.5*a*).
- For stamping or blanking a part outline, the female die block is made to the exact part size, and the punch (male) is filed smaller according to the required die clearance (Fig. 9.5*b*).

9.3.2 EDM (electric discharge machining) die-making procedures

Electric-discharge machining (EDM) has replaced much of the work of the die maker in many companies where EDM machines are employed. In the EDM process, which includes both *wire* and *ram* methods, an electrically charged electrode (wire or solid form) does the actual cutting of the metal (usually tool steel). A typical EDM machine is shown in Fig. 1.4. The hand production of dies is still practiced where the cost of the EDM machine cannot be justified on a production basis.

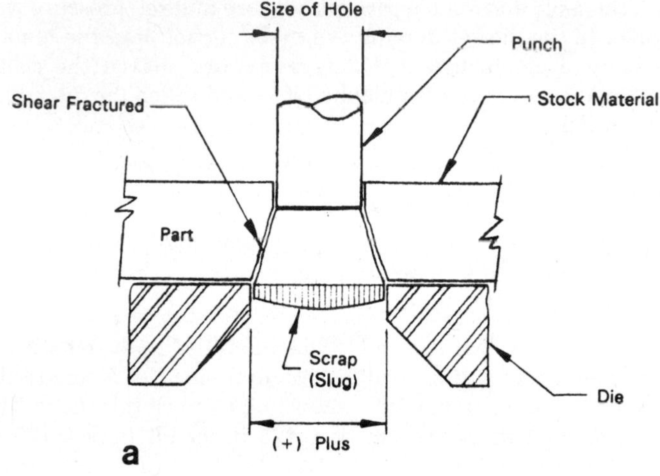

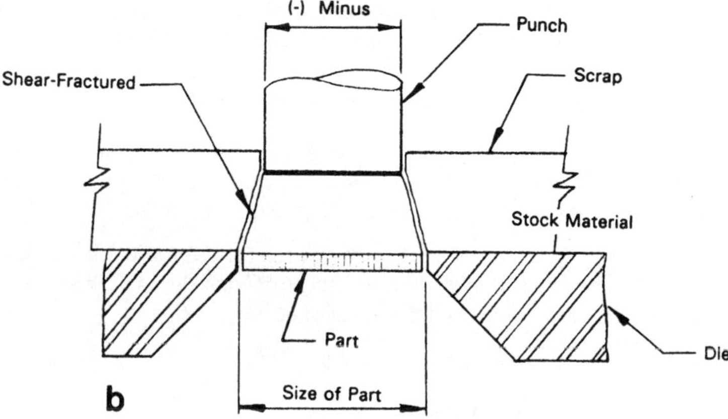

Figure 9.5 (*a*) Punching holes. (*b*) Punching a part.

The wire EDM machine is usually employed when making punching and blanking dies with complex outlines, where extreme accuracy is required. As an example of the accuracy of the EDM wire process, see Fig. 9.6. The die set in the figure was manufactured (wire EDM cut) of prehardened tool steel and was produced in less than 8 h. The hand production of a small die set with a complex shape such as that shown in the figure would have taken an expert die maker as long as 5 to 8 days of tedious work. This small sample die set was cut with a total die clearance of 0.0005 in and is capable of punching a thin sheet of paper. The only additional work required after wire EDM cutting of the male and female portions was to surface grind the two die parts. The two portions of the die are separated and shown with a thin piece of paper, which was cut using hand pressure. A die set such as this would be difficult to produce by manual methods of die making owing to its small size and intricate pattern.

Another example of EDM machining is given in Fig. 9.7, which shows the teeth of a ratchet which was wire cut from 0.188-in-thick cold-rolled steel sheet stock. The sharp edges of the ratchet teeth are typical of an EDM-cut material. The movements of the EDM machine are determined by a CNC controller on the machine which has been programmed by the tool engineering department. The program to cut this ratchet was loaded into the EDM machine's controller memory and the program run to produce the part to

Figure 9.6 A sample die set, wire EDM cut from hardened tool steel.

Figure 9.7 A ratchet plate, CNC, EDM wire cut from mild steel. Note the sharp, accurate cut edges.

great accuracy. The holes shown in the ratchet were die punched after the teeth were EDM cut.

The wire EDM machines produced in the 1980s have been improved to the point where the cutting speeds have increased two to four times their original rates. The cutting section of a typical wire EDM machine is shown in Fig. 9.8. The wire can be seen running vertically between the wire guides and feed mechanism. During the cutting operation, cutting/cooling fluid is allowed to flow over the part, in the vicinity of the wire, where it contacts the material being cut. When tool steels are being cut on the wire EDM, they may be cut in the annealed condition and later heat treated or they may be cut in the fully hardened condition to prevent the distortion that may occur during heat treatment. This characteristic of wire EDM cutting allows the tool engineer to use grades or types of tool steels for die making which would otherwise distort in heat treatment by cutting the dies in the fully hardened condition.

The newer types of wire EDM machines are designed so that the wire guides are controlled independently and are able to move so that tapered sides may be cut into the die. Thus a conical slug or other taper-sided outline can be cut from a die block.

EDM die-making procedures are similar to the manual method of making dies, except the tool-steel die members (punch and die

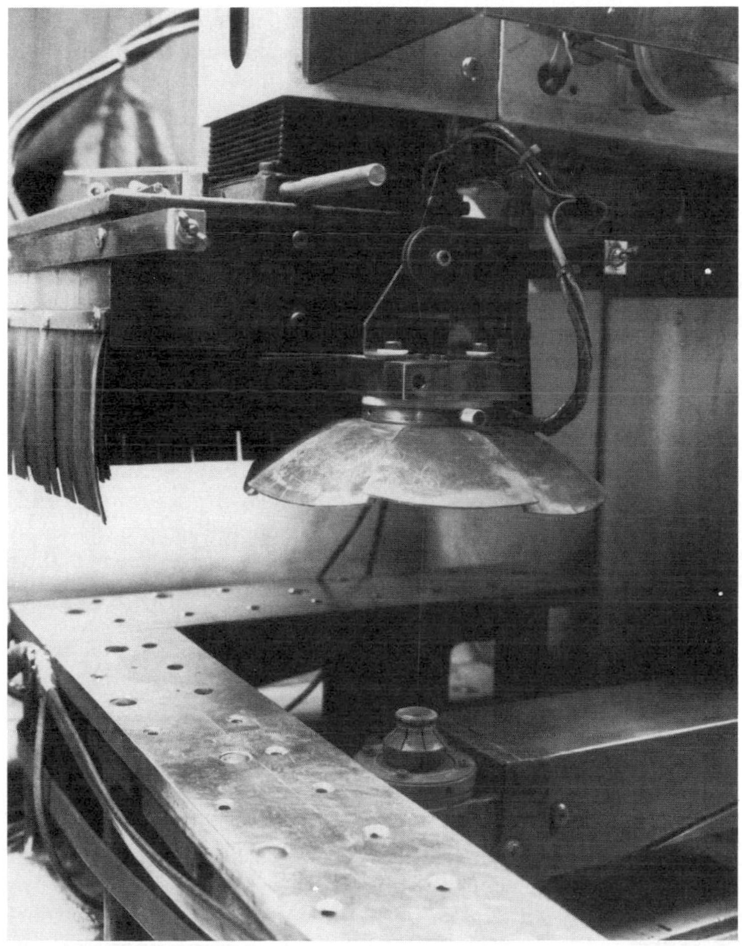

Figure 9.8 Close-up of wire EDM. Note the wire guides.

block) are produced on the wire EDM machine, with the tool steel either being heat treated or in the soft condition. It is usually found that the wire EDM will cut the tool-steel die members cleaner when they are in the fully heat-treated condition.

After the die members have been cut with the proper die clearance, the die parts are mounted in the die set with shims placed around the mated male and female die members to ensure that the die clearance is the same all around. The dies are then drilled and pinned, with additional shoulder bolts or socket-head cap screws employed in addition to the alignment pins to hold all the members securely in alignment. The basic die set consisting of top and bottom plates (die shoe), guideposts, and guide bushings plus an optional top shank may be ordered in many different styles and sizes from suppliers such as Danly or Dieco and others. Photographs and illustrations of typical standard and special die sets are shown in other subsections.

9.3.3 EDM mold making (ram EDM)

Molds that are machined from tool steels are presently being made using ram EDM machines. In this process, the cavity of the mold is produced in a positive shape from a carbon-type material. This form, or positive, is then used in the ram EDM process to machine the cavity of the mold by the electric-discharge process. The ram, or electrode (positive form), is placed under a cutting/cooling fluid with the tool-steel mold block and is moved downward into the tool-steel block as the electric-discharge cutting operation progresses. A hollow or cavity with the exact shape of the ram or electrode is thus produced to great accuracy and a fine surface finish in the tool steel mold block.

Molds or dies are produced with this method for manufacturing plastic parts (injection or compression molding process) as well as for die casting and powder-metal processing. Large amounts of material are machined accurately at a relatively rapid rate in the newer ram EDM process. When the mold cavities have been cut, the die or mold maker must polish the mold and add gates, ejectors, and other requirements to complete the final mold assembly. The P type special-purpose tool steels are usually selected for production of molds for plastic parts, while other types of tool steels are selected for die-casting dies, permanent steel molds, and powder-metal dies.

9.3.4 Samples of dies, drawings, and stamped or blanked parts

A typical high-quality die set is shown in Fig. 9.9. This is a heavy-duty, long-production-run type of stamping die for producing heavy-gage cold-rolled steel parts. The male and female die element tool-steel materials were selected and heat treated with great care and assembled accurately by the die maker. The tool-steel die elements were cut on the wire EDM machine using a sophisticated CNC program designed by the tool engineering department. The CNC program was then loaded into the EDM machine's controller and the dies accurately cut with the tool-steel die elements having been heat treated previously.

Figure 9.10 shows another finished die set with its required protective shield surrounding the die. Industry regulations call for protective shields on dies where an operator may accidentally come into hand contact with the moving parts of the die during the blanking, punching, forming, or drawing operations. The design

Figure 9.9 A typical high-quality blanking die set.

Figure 9.10 Finished die set with required hand protection shield (clear Lexan plastic).

and addition of the protective die shields are an important part of die design today and are necessary for worker safety.

Figure 9.11 shows two typical blanked parts. The upper part in the figure is made of a low-strength aluminum alloy (3003-H14), and the 50 percent cut or burnished section can be seen over the shear-fractured section. The part below is made of C-1018 cold-rolled steel, and a double cut or burnish is evident. The double cut alternating between the shear-fractured areas is characteristic of a close die clearance per side of 1 to 2 percent of the total stock thickness. This type of blanked edge may not be suitable for certain types of applications, and a secondary operation such as *shaving* may be required to finish the part edges.

In Sec. 9.5.1 figures will be presented for calculating the tonnage required on the press for stamping parts. To calculate the tonnage requirements, we must know the perimeter of the part in linear inches or millimeters. Figure 9.12 shows a measuring tool used to determine the perimeter of irregularly shaped parts. This tool is

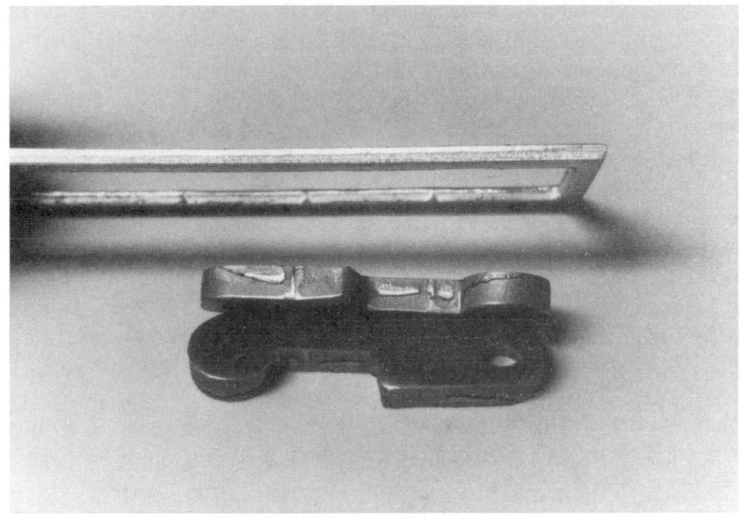

Figure 9.11 Typical blanked parts, edge characteristics.

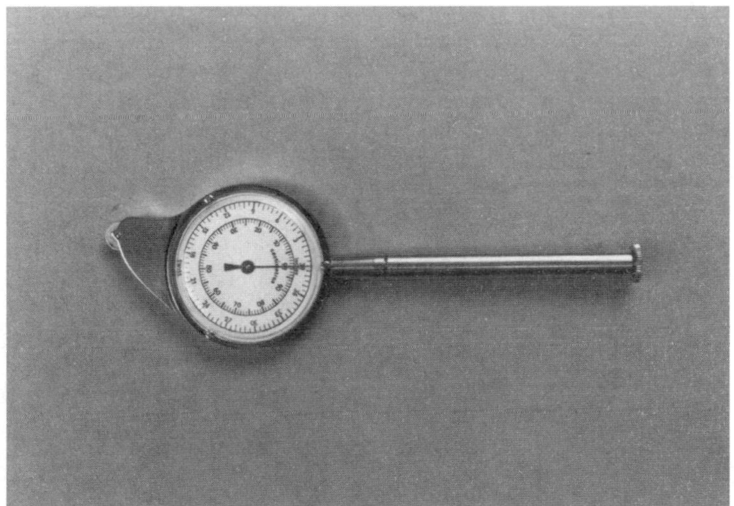

Figure 9.12 Linear measuring device.

sometimes called a *map measuring tool.* To use the tool, the scale is zeroed, and the small wheel at the end of the tool is placed at a starting point on the perimeter of the part to be measured. Tracing the tool around the perimeter of the part by rolling the wheel on the part outline will give a direct scale measurement in inches or millimeters on the dial of the tool. From this measurement, the tonnage requirements may be calculated using procedures shown in a later section.

The modern die-making and design processes utilize CNC and computer programs not only to control the EDM machines but also to produce the die drawings. A computer-generated drawing is possible using the various computer-aided design (CAD) systems available today. The computer CAD program sends the output information for the drawing to a plotter or laser printer, where a clean, neat drawing is produced. Figure 9.13 presents an example of a CAD drawing produced by a modern tool and die design and engineering department.

9.3.5 Steel-rule dies

Steel-rule dies make use of low-cost materials and are employed in many industrial applications. These are single-element tools that consist of a steel-rule cutting section only. Printers rule or similar steel strip is employed and bent to the shape of the part to be punched or cut. The sharp edges of the steel-rule members are operated against a flat metal platen or a hard wood or plastic block and produce the blanked part by a cutting or cleaving action.

Steel-rule dies are used to blank paper, cardboard, fiber, rubber, felt, leather, and similar materials (gaskets are a good example). Figure 9.14 shows an exploded view of steel-rule die construction. The steel rules that do the actual cutting should be hardened to Rockwell C52 to C55, although this high a hardness may not be required for some materials. The stripper portion of the die is usually 0.312 to 0.375 in thick, extending slightly above the height of the steel-rule cutters, and is made of neoprene, cork sheet, or rubber.

9.4 Die Clearances and Stamping Data

Figure 9.15 shows the different types of edges produced on punched and blanked parts with different die clearances. This figure is typical of the low-carbon steels, which are frequently used for many types of die stamped, pierced, or blanked parts.

Figure 9.16 shows samples of typical slugs produced in the piercing or punching of hard copper (ETP 110, hard drawn). The figure clearly shows the effect of die clearance and the characteristic edges produced by the cutting (burnishing) and shear-fracture

SECTION - A-A

POS	QTY	PART NAME	MATERIAL	DIMENSIONS	HARDNESS
.					
.17	1	PIVOT	CRS	.938x1.25x4.0	
.16	5	STRIPPER BOLT	9-0814-56	1/2⌀x1.75	DANLY
.					
.14	2	LOCATOR	02 STEEL	.380⌀x1	
.13	8	DOWEL PIN	.375x2 1/4	.375⌀x2.5	DANLY
.12	22	SHCS	3/8-16x2	3/8-16x2	DANLY
.11	12	SPRING	9-2008-26	1 1/4⌀x1 1/2	DANLY
.10	8	STRIPPER BOLT	9-0816-56	1/2⌀x2	DANLY
.9	1	DIE SET	1410-2F-1	#1410-2F-1	DANLY
.					
.7	1	SPACER	CRS	1/2x6.312x9.497	
.6	1	DIE	A2-484	1.5x5.281x0.9	60...62
.5	1	PRESSURE PAD	CRS	3/4x6 5/16x10.475	
.4	1	STRIPPER	A2-484	3/4x7 5/16x9.187	
.3	1	PUNCH	A2-484	1.5x6.375x9.497	58...60
.2	1	DIE	A2-484	1.5x3.29x9.187	60...62
.1	4	KEY	CRS	1x1x8	

Figure 9.13 Typical CAD drawing of a die set.

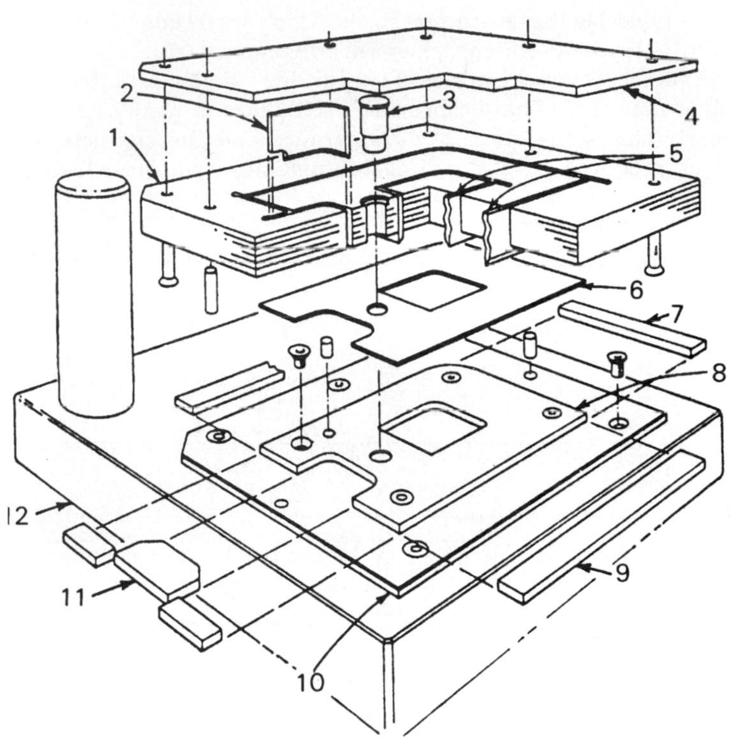

1	Plywood	7	Neoprene
2	Steel rule	8	Die plate
3	Punch	9	Neoprene
4	Steel subplate	10	Steel subplate
5	Steel rule	11	Neoprene
6	Blank	12	Die shoe

Note: Neoprene inserts are cut and glued in those areas where stripping action is required.

Figure 9.14 Typical steel-rule die.

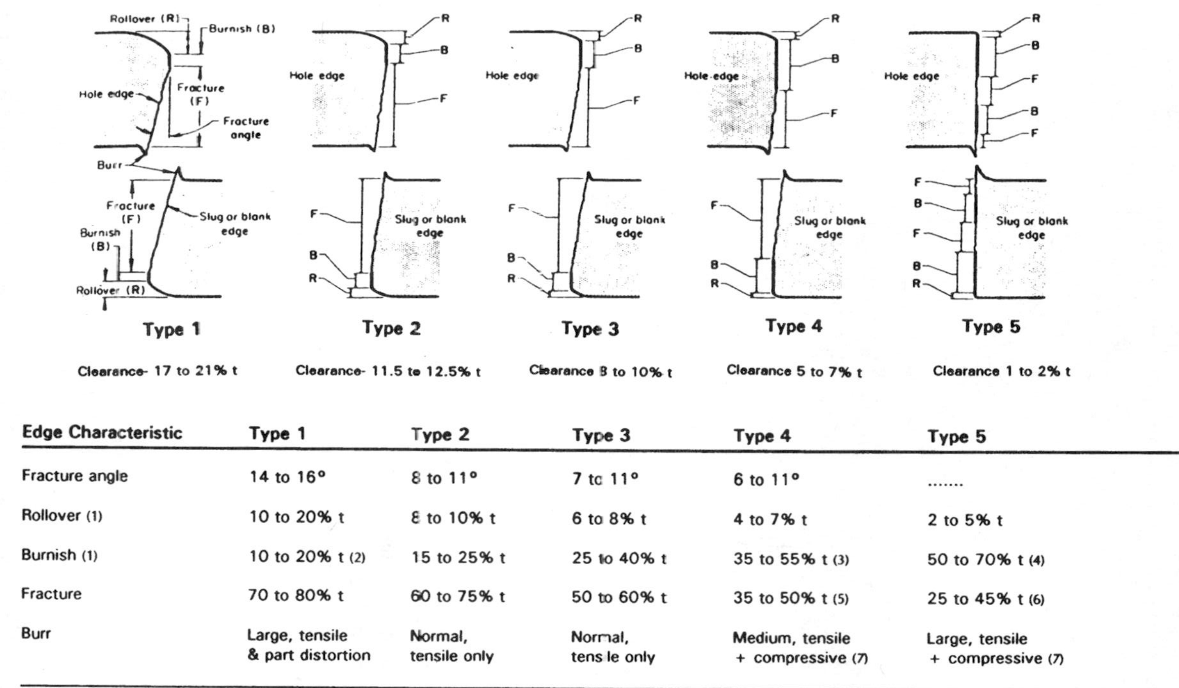

Edge Characteristic	Type 1	Type 2	Type 3	Type 4	Type 5
Fracture angle	14 to 16°	8 to 11°	7 to 11°	6 to 11°	....
Rollover (1)	10 to 20% t	8 to 10% t	6 to 8% t	4 to 7% t	2 to 5% t
Burnish (1)	10 to 20% t (2)	15 to 25% t	25 to 40% t	35 to 55% t (3)	50 to 70% t (4)
Fracture	70 to 80% t	60 to 75% t	50 to 60% t	35 to 50% t (5)	25 to 45% t (6)
Burr	Large, tensile & part distortion	Normal, tensile only	Normal, tensile only	Medium, tensile + compressive (7)	Large, tensile + compressive (7)

Note: (1) Rollover plus burnish approx. equals punch penetration before fracture, (2) Burnish on edge of slug or blank may be small and irregular or absent, (3) With spotty secondary shear, (4) In two separate portions, alternating with fracture, (5) With rough surface, (6) In two separate portions, alternating with burnish, (7) Amount of compressive burr depends on die sharpness.

Figure 9.15 Edge characteristics.

Figure 9.16 Typical die-punched slugs.

actions. (The cut or burnished section is indicated by *a* and the shear-fracture section by *b* in the figure.) These slugs are typical of type 1 and type 2 edges, as shown in Fig. 9.15.

Figure 9.17 gives punch-to-die clearances for piercing or blanking various metals and alloys to produce the five types of edge characteristics shown in Fig. 9.15. Clearances shown in Fig. 9.17 are based on data published on piercing by Danly Machine Corporation and on blanking by the American Society of Tool and Manufacturing Engineers (ASTME).

The tabular die-clearance data shown in Fig. 9.17 is given per side as a percentage of the stock thickness. For example, if we were punching stainless steel whose stock thickness was 0.050 in and we desired a type 3 edge, the total die clearance would be $0.05 \times (0.09$ to $0.11) \times 2 = 0.009$ to 0.011 in total die clearance, or 0.0045 to 0.0055 in clearance per side.

Another method that has been used for many years in industry for die clearances is outlined below.

Work Piece Material	Clearance per side, % of stock thickness *				
	Edge Type 1	Edge Type 2	Edge Type 3	Edge Type 4	Edge Type 5
Low-carbon steel	21 max	11.5-12.5	8-10	5-7	1-2
High-carbon steel	25 max	17-19	14-16	11-13	2.5-5
Stainless steel	23 max	12.5-13.5	9-11	3-5	1-2
Aluminum alloys: Up to 33,000 psi TS	17 max	8-10	6-8	2-4	0.5-1
Over 33,000 psi TS	20 max	12.5-14	9-10	5-6	0.5-1
Brass, annealed	21 max	8-10	6-8	2-3	0.5-1
Brass, half-hard	24 max	9-11	6-8	3-5	0.5-1.5
Phosphor bronze	25 max	12.5-13.5	10-12	3.5-5	1.5-2.5
Copper, annealed	25 max	8-9	5-7	2-4	0.5-1
Copper, half-hard	25 max	9-11	6-8	3-5	1-2
Lead	22 max	8-10	6.5-7.5	4-6	1.5-2.5
Magnesium alloys	16 max	5-7	3.5-4.5	1.5-2.5	0.5-1

NOTE: * Tabular data is clearance per side as % of stock thickness. Also, for clearances that produce edges of types 1, 2 and 3, it is usually necessary to use ejector punches or other devices to prevent the slug or blanked part from adhering to the punch.

Figure 9.17 Die clearances for piercing or various metals and alloys (for five types of edge characteristics as shown in Fig. 9.15).

Die Clearances per Side as a Percentage of Stock Thickness (Group Method)

Material group	Clearance per side, percent of stock thickness t
Group 1: 1100 and 5052 aluminum alloys (all tempers); 3003-0; etc.	4.5% t
Group 2: 2024 and 6061 aluminum alloys (all tempers); brass (all tempers); cold-rolled steel, soft; stainless steel, soft; copper, soft; BeCu, soft	6.0% t
Group 3: Cold-rolled steel, half hard; stainless steel, half hard and full hard; copper, hard	7.5% t
Group 4: Nonmetallic materials (general)	1.25% t

Note: Angular side clearance (one side) = 0.5 to 2 percent. Angular side clearance is cut below the die straight (see previous data for die-straight heights or thicknesses).

9.4.1 Calculation of punch dimensions

Punch dimensions may be estimated from the following: When the diameter of a pierced round hole is equal to the stock thickness, the unit compressive stress on the punch is four times the unit shear stress on the cut area of the stock from the equation

$$1 = \frac{4S_s t}{S_c d}$$

where S_c = unit compressive stress on the punch, psi
S_s = unit shear stress on the stock, psi
t = stock thickness, in
d = diameter of punched hole, in

The diameters of most punched holes are greater than stock thickness, and a value for the ratio d/t of 1.1 is recommended. The maximum allowable length of a punch can be calculated from the following equation:

$$L = \frac{\pi d}{8} \sqrt{\frac{Ed}{S_s t}}$$

where d/t = 1.1 or higher
E = modulus of elasticity of the punch material, psi

Other terms were previously defined.

The punching of holes with diameters less than stock thickness is generally achieved by using high-compressive-strength tool steels, guided punches, greater than average die clearances, shear added to the punch or dies, and prevention of stock slippage or movement during punching.

9.4.2 Standard die sets

Die sets are available from the major die supply manufacturers such as Danly and Dieco. Figures 9.18 and 9.19 show some of the most commonly used die sets that are available as stock items. In Fig. 9.18, the die-sets are identified as follows:

a Round series, back-post AS-31

b Round series, center-post AS-32

c Four-post series AS-37

d Diagonal-post AS-AS-35

e Long, narrow series, two-post AS-41 and three-post AS-42

In Fig. 9.19, the die sets are identified as follows:

a Four-post series AS-67

b Two-post AS-63

c Demountable two-post AS-39 or four-post AS-40

The top and bottom plates of a die set are called the *top shoe* and *bottom shoe,* respectively.

If a special size or configuration for a die set is not available commercially, the die set may be custom-made by the die maker. In this case, the material and size of the top and bottom shoes and the optional *shank* are determined by the tool engineer. To complete the basic die set, guideposts and guide bushings must be selected. The guide bushings are available in plain or ball-bearing types.

9.4.3 Guide pins and guide bushings for die sets

When a die maker is building a custom die set, the guide pins and guide bushings are selected from commercially available types, which may be either plain or ball-bearing types. Guide pins and guide bushings are produced in various diameters and lengths, which must be determined by the design of the die set and the press used for the die operation.

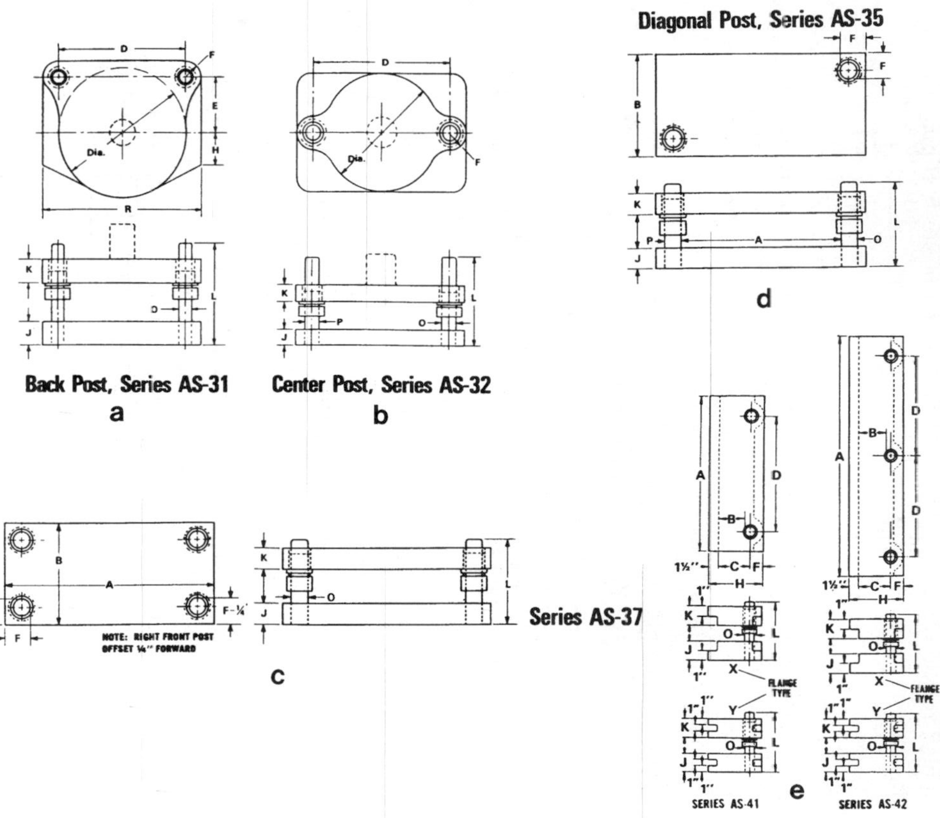

Figure 9.18 Danly die sets, types.

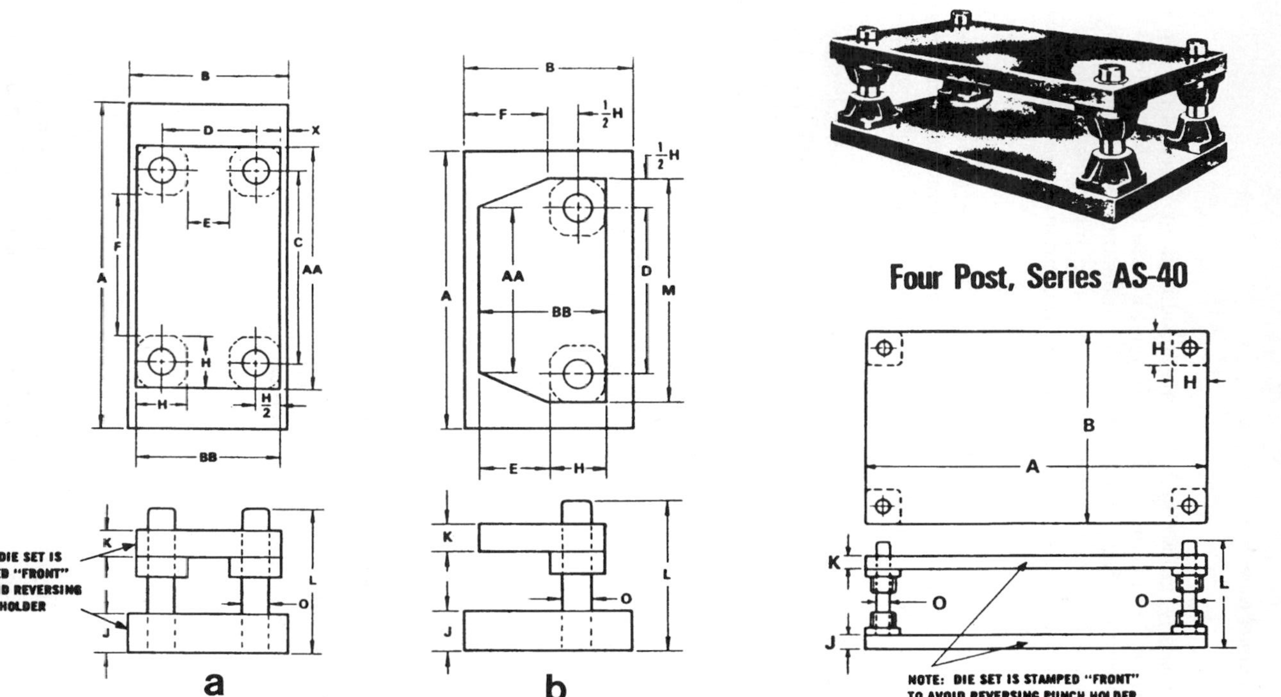
NOTE: DIE SET IS STAMPED "FRONT" TO AVOID REVERSING PUNCH HOLDER
a
b
Four Post, Series AS-40
NOTE: DIE SET IS STAMPED "FRONT" TO AVOID REVERSING PUNCH HOLDER
c

Figure 9.19 Danly die sets, types.

Ball-bearing guide bushings are produced in three different types for different operating conditions. Figure 9.20 shows three types of ball-bearing guide bushings (*b*) and samples of typical die sets (*a*) which may use either plain or ball-bearing guide bushings. Selection of the correct type of ball-bearing guide bushing may be determined from the following descriptions:

Type I: Preloaded type. Recommended for use with high-production, long-life dies. All the balls remain in contact with the post and bushing in preloaded conditions throughout the press stroke.

Type II: Relieving type. Recommended when it is desirable that the ball cage does not leave the bushing at any time. Provides for safe operation and prevents foreign objects from falling into the bushing.

Type III: Disengaging type. Used where the ball cage can be permitted to leave the bushing with each stroke. This is the most economical type because of the short length, and it is used for general applications which require long press strokes.

These types of bushings should be ordered as complete sets (guidepost, ball cage, and bushing) to ensure proper fit of the components.

Important factors in designing and building any die set are

- Available stroke of the press
- Open height of the die set
- Minimum shut height (at depleted punch and die life)
- Maximum shut height (new punch and die sections)
- Dimension of the punch holder
- Dimension of the die holder
- Guidepost length
- Bushing length

Figure 9.21 shows the relations of these factors. The tool design engineer and die maker must determine the dimensions of all the factors listed and shown in Fig. 9.21 to produce the die correctly.

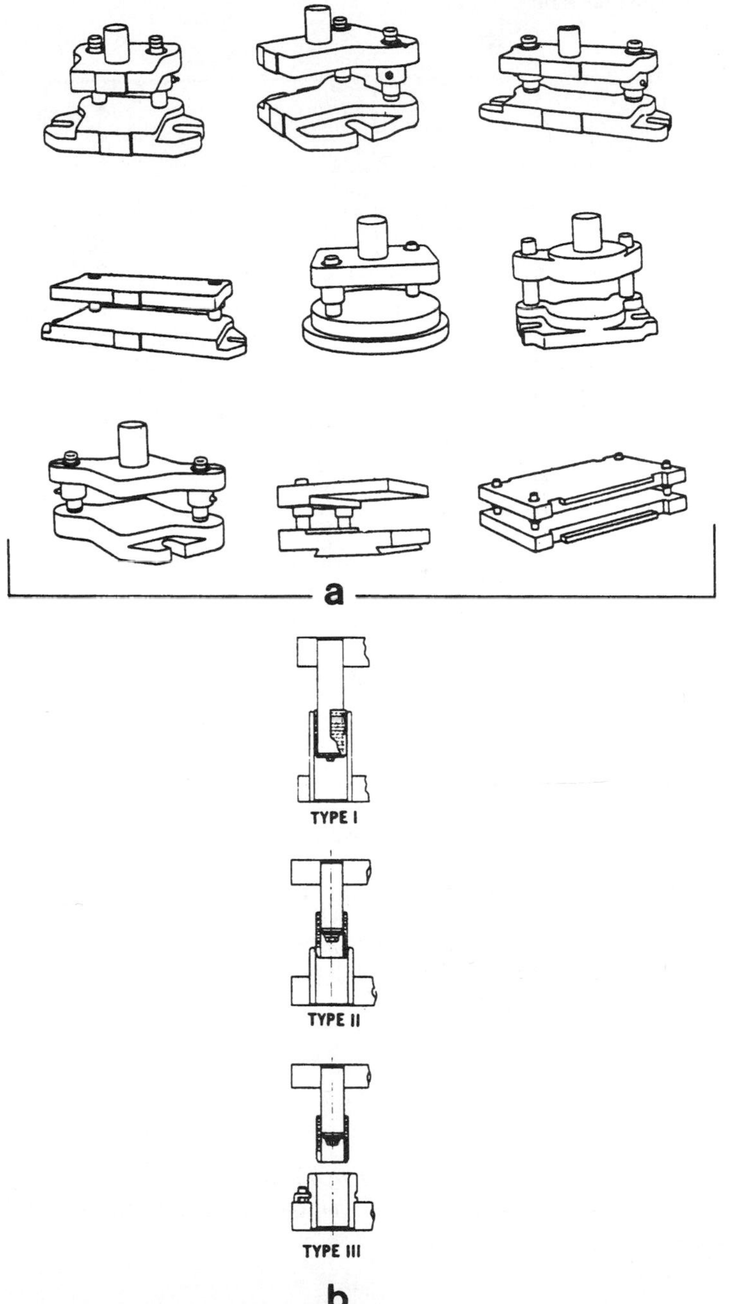

Figure 9.20 (*a*) Die sets. (*b*) Ball-bearing guide bushings.

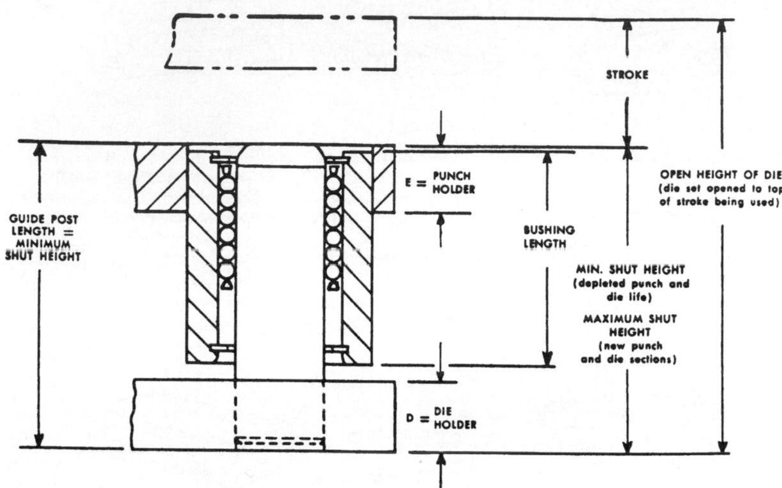

Figure 9.21 Die set variable characteristics.

9.5 Punching and Blanking Forces

9.5.1 Force required for punching or blanking

The simple equation for calculating the punching or blanking force P in pounds for a given material and thickness is given as

$$P = SLt \qquad \text{For any shape or aperture}$$

$$P = S\pi Dt \qquad \text{For round holes}$$

where P = force required to punch or blank, pounds-force (lbf)
S = shear strength of material, psi (see Fig. 9.22)
L = sheared length, in
D = diameter of hole, in
t = thickness of material, in

9.5.2 Stripping forces

Stripping forces vary from 2.5 to 20 percent of the punching or blanking forces. A frequently used equation for determining the stripping forces is

$$F_s = 3500Lt$$

where F_s = stripping force, lbf
L = perimeter of cut (sheared length), in
t = thickness of material, in

Note: This equation is approximate and may not be suitable for all conditions of punching and blanking due to the many variables encountered in this type of metalworking.

9.5.3 Shear strengths of various materials

The shear strength (in pounds per square inch) of the material to be punched or blanked is required in order to calculate the force required to punch or blank any particular part. Figure 9.22 lists the average shear strengths of various materials, both metallic and nonmetallic. If you require the shear strength of a material that is not listed in Fig. 9.22 or in Chap. 5, "Materials and Their Uses," an approximation of the shear strength may be made as follows (for relatively ductile materials only): Go to Chap. 5, "Materials and Their Uses," and find the *ultimate tensile strength* of the given material. Take 45 to 55 percent of this value as the approximate shear strength. For example, if the ultimate tensile strength of the given material is 75,000 psi,

$$\text{Shear strength} = 0.45 \times 75{,}000 = 30{,}750 \text{ psi approximately (low value)}$$

$$= 0.55 \times 75{,}000 = 41{,}250 \text{ psi approximately (high value)}$$

Manufacturers' standard gages for steel sheets. The decimal equivalents of the American standard manufacturers' gages for steel sheets is shown in Fig. 9.23. Sheet steels in the United States are purchased to these gage equivalents, and tools and dies are designed for this standard gaging system.

9.6 Bending, Forming, and Progressive Die Operations and Data

Bending and forming dies are used to shape sheet metal parts by the action of bending or drawing the metal. Of concern to the die designer are allowable inside bend radii for various materials and gages and permissible limits in the drawing or progressive forming of shapes with regular or irregular cross sections.

Material	Shear Strength, psi
Carbon Steels:	
SAE 1010 HR	21,500
SAE 1020 HR	32,000
SAE 1045 QT	55,000
SAE 1045 A	44,000
SAE 1095 QT	90,000
SAE 1095 A	63,000
SAE 1117 HR	32,000
Alloy Steels:	
SAE 4130 N	43,500
SAE 4130 T (150,000)	90,000
SAE 4140 N	66,500
SAE 3120 HT-D (800°F)	95,000
SAE 3140 HT-D (800°F)	130,000
SAE 3250 HT-D (800°F)	165,000
Stainless Steels:	
AISI 201	52,000
AISI 301	50,000
AISI 302	41,000
AISI 304	38,500
AISI 310	42,750
AISI 316	38,250
AISI 321	38,250
Cold rolled S/S strip (full hard)	
AISI 300 Series	112,000
Stainless Steels: Annealed	
AISI 410	33,750
AISI 416	33,750
AISI 440C	49,500
AISI 430	33,750
Monel Metal:	
70,000 UTS	42,900
110,000 UTS	65,500
K Monel:	
155,500 UTS	98,500
Nickel:	
68,000 UTS	52,300
121,000 UTS	75,300
Inconel Alloys:	
80,000 UTS	59,000
100,000 UTS	66,000
150,000 UTS	80,000
175,000 UTS	87,000

Figure 9.22 Shear strengths of metallic and nonmetallic materials, psi.

Copper and Alloys:	
CA 110 (ETP 110)	22,000-28,000
CA 210 (Guilding)	26,000-37,000
CA 220 (Bronze)	28,000-38,000
CA 230 (Red brass)	31,000-42,000
CA 260 (Cartridge brass)	33,000-44,000
CA 268 (Yellow brass)	33,000-43,000
Beryllium copper: Strip & sheet	
C 17200 (25)	34,200-54,000
C 17000 (165)	34,200-94,500
C 17510 (3)	24,750-67,500
C 17500 (10)	24,750-67,500
C 17410 (174) HT	58,500
Beryllium Nickel:	
UNS-N033 HT	123,750
Aluminum and Alloys:	
1100-O	9,000
1100-H18	13,000
2014-O	18,000
2014-T4, T451	38,000
2014-T6, T651	42,000
2024-O	18,000
2024-T3, T4, T351	41,000
3003-O	11,000
3003-H14	14,000
3003-H18	16,000
5052-O	18,000
5052-H32, H38	60,000-77,000
6061-O	12,000
6061-T4, T451	24,000
6061-T6, T651	30,000
7075-O	22,000
7075-T6, T651	48,000
7178-O	23,000
7178-T6, T651	53,300
Magnesium Alloys:	
Soft (annealed)	19,000
Hardened	28,500 max.
Titanium & Alloys:	
Pure	27,000-49,500
Typical alloys	45,000-77,000
Nonmetallics:	
Polyester-glass (GPO-1, 2 & 3)	12,000-17,000
Polycarbonate (Lexan)	6,000-10,000
Cycolac	4,400-7,400
ABS (Acrylonitrile Butadene Styrene)	1,500-4,000
Acetal (Delrin)	3,000-6,000
Acetate (Cellulose)	2,000-4,000
Epoxy-glass	4,000-10,000
Nylon	3,000-12,000

Figure 9.22 *(Continued)*

Phenolic resins (cloth)	26,000 (Hot-blanked)
Paper	3,500-6,400
Mica	10,000
Teflon, rigid (TFE)	1,500-3,000
Hard rubber	20,000
Polystyrene	10,000 max.
Asbestos board	5,000

Notes: For metallic materials- when the tabulated shear values are given in ranges, the shear values run from the an soft condition to the hardest condition. Interpolate intermediate values between ranges. For nonmetallic materials- t value ranges are given from soft to hard grades or glass-filled grades.

A = annealed; HR = hot-rolled; N = normalized; T = tempered; HT-D = heat treated and drawn (tempered); QT = quen tempered; UTS = ultimate tensile strength; HT = heat-treated.

Figure 9.22 *(Continued)*

The die cavities used for forming metals may be ram EDM cut, as explained in an earlier section, or they may be cut using the CNC machining centers in profiling operations. The male portion of the die may be machined by various methods such as turning and milling on the modern CNC turning and machining centers or on engine lathes and manually controlled milling machines such as the Bridgeport machine.

Progressive forming, bending, and blanking die design and die making are complex arts as well as technologies that require considerable skill, knowledge, and practical experience. This section will present some of the basic information and data important to die design and die making.

9.6.1 Typical forming and progressive dies and parts

Forming and bending dies may be made for very simple operations or for complex, multistaged operations used to blank, form, or bend complex sheet metal parts. Figure 9.24 shows a very simple forming die used to produce a raised indent on an electrical contact finger made of beryllium-copper alloy. In the figure, the small forming die is shown at the left, with samples of two finger contacts. Part usage per year did not justify the cost of producing a complex blanking and bending progressive die to produce these parts. Production of the parts shown required the following sequence of operations:

- Beryllium-copper strip was purchased in correct slit widths (soft condition).
- The two holes were strippit punched from the correct cut length of the part.

Standard Gage Number	Ounces/Ft^2	Lb/Ft^2	Thickness (Inches)
3	160	10.0000	0.2391
4	150	9.3750	0.2242
5	140	8.7500	0.2092
6	130	8.1250	0.1943
7	120	7.5000	0.1793
8	110	6.8750	0.1644
9	100	6.2500	0.1495
10	90	5.6250	0.1345
11	80	5.0000	0.1196
12	70	4.3750	0.1046
13	60	3.7500	0.0897
14	50	3.1250	0.0747
15	45	2.8125	0.0673
16	40	2.5000	0.0598
17	36	2.2500	0.0538
18	32	2.0000	0.0478
19	28	1.7500	0.0418
20	24	1.5000	0.0359
21	22	1.3750	0.0329
22	20	1.2500	0.0299
23	18	1.1250	0.0269
24	16	1.0000	0.0239
25	14	0.87500	0.0209
26	12	0.75000	0.0179
27	11	0.68750	0.0164
28	10	0.62500	0.0149
29	9	0.56250	0.0135
30	8	0.50000	0.0120
31	7	0.43750	0.0105
32	6.5	0.40625	0.0097
33	6	0.37500	0.0090
34	5.5	0.34375	0.0082
35	5	0.31250	0.0075
36	4.5	0.28125	0.0067
37	4.25	0.26562	0.0064
38	4	0.25000	0.0060

Note: Thickness equivalents are based on 0.0014945 in. per ounce per sq. ft.; 0.023912 in. per pound per sq. ft. (Reciprocal of 41.820 lb. per sq. ft. per inch thick); 3.443329 in. per lb. per sq. in.

Figure 9.23 Manufacturers' standard gages for steel sheets.

- The raised indent was then formed on the end of the part using the small forming die shown in the figure.
- The punched and indented part was then bent to shape on a small press brake.

Figure 9.24 A small forming die and parts.

- The part was then heat treated to correct hardness (for spring action).
- The part was deburred by tumbling.
- Silver plating was then applied to the finished part.

Typical examples of punched, blanked, and formed sheet metal parts are shown in Figs. 9.25 and 9.26. Figure 9.25 shows a stainless steel sheet metal part that required spring action. The material selected for this application was AISI 301 spring-temper stainless steel. This part was preslit to proper width, shear cut to length, punched, beaded for stiffness, and finally bent on the press brake. Figure 9.26 shows a part made from no. 11 gage low-carbon steel in a multistaged progressive die. This part required punching, blanking, bossing, and bending operations. The progressive die used for this type of part is complex and costly. The shear and forming marks are clearly evident on the surfaces of the part.

A simple progressive punching and blanking die is shown in Fig. 9.27. The part strip and piece part are shown at the bottom of the figure; the dimensions are in millimeters. The punching, blanking, and part dropoff slot are shown in section *A-A,* progressing from right to left. A heavy-duty die set with an upper shank was used to make the die set shown in the figure.

Figure 9.25 Die-punched stainless steel part.

Figure 9.26 Die-punched mild-carbon-steel part.

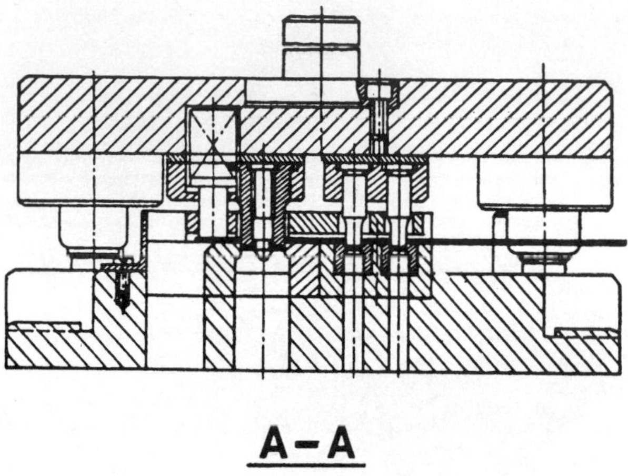

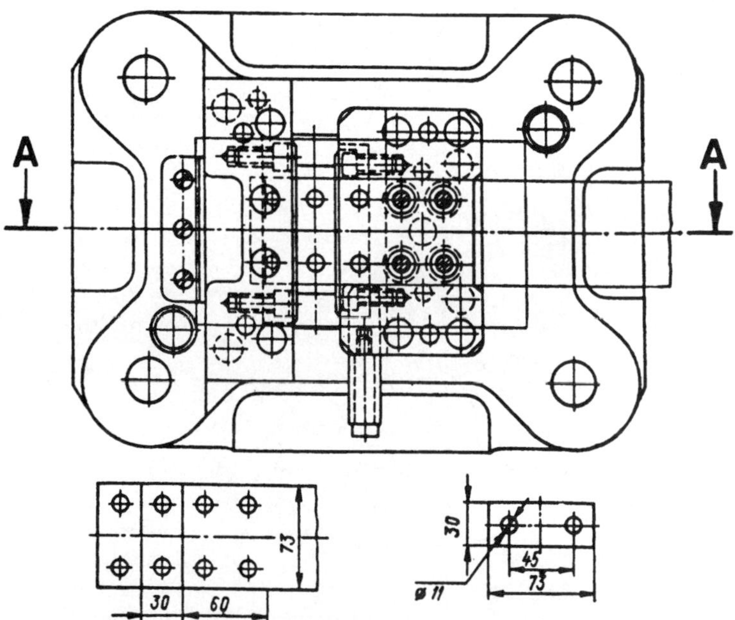

Figure 9.27 Progressive die with part samples.

A drawing die is shown in Fig. 9.28*a*, with the parts identified as follows:

1. Drawing punch

2. Drawing die block

3. Clamp ring (or holder)

A compound die for piercing and drawing is shown in Fig. 9.28*b*, with the parts identified as follows:

1. Shear punch and drawing die block

2. Piercing die

3. Shearing die block

4. Clamping ring

5. Draw punch

6. Dimensioned finished part (millimeters)

See Sec. 9.6.5 for drawing and forming shapes and appropriate equations for drawing and forming calculations.

Methods for applying springs to die sets are shown in Fig. 9.29. Here, the springs are shown with methods of applying preload, with adjustment. Parts *c* and *e* of the figure illustrate the use of Belleville disk springs in place of the standard helical die springs. Helical die springs may be made with either round or rectangular spring wire, although the rectangular wire types are usually employed in American die-making practice because of their higher power-to-weight ratios. The application of Belleville disk springs and helical springs may be further studied by referring to Chap. 13, "Springs."

9.6.2 Bend radii for various metals and alloys

The minimum bend radii allowed for forming metals and alloys are important factors in die design and die making. A bend radius that is too small for a particular metal and gage may cause cracking or rupture of the part being formed. A radius that is too large may not meet the requirements of the part design. This is especially true when a hole is close to the edge or flange of a part and would interfere with the inside bend radius by running past the tangent point

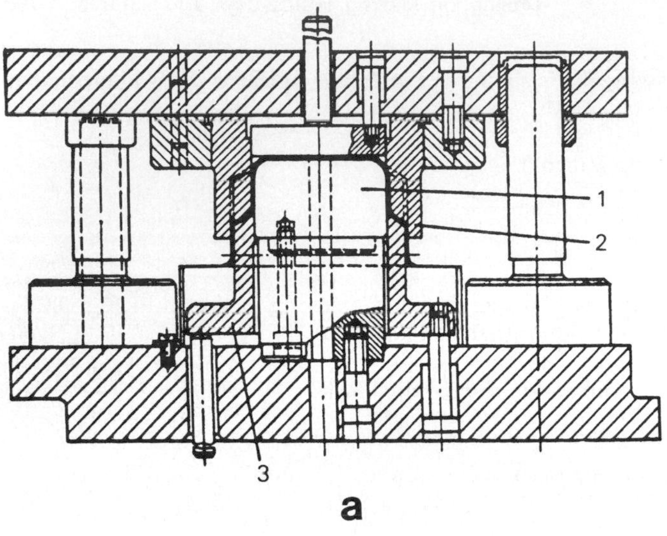

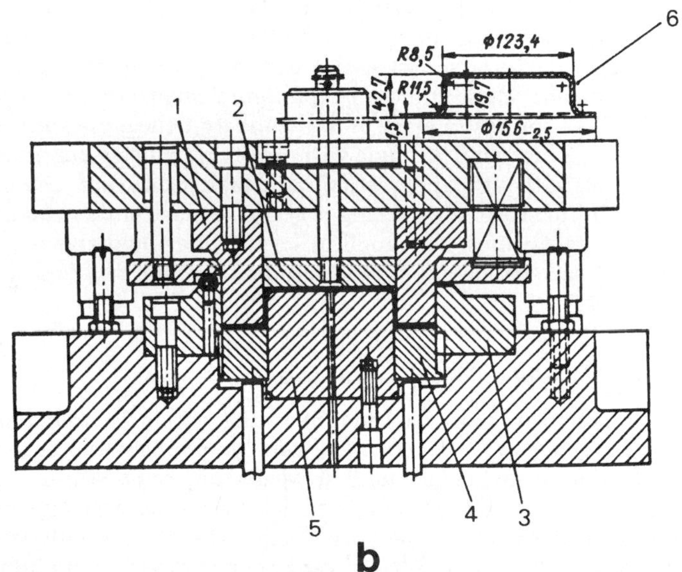

Figure 9.28 A complex drawing die.

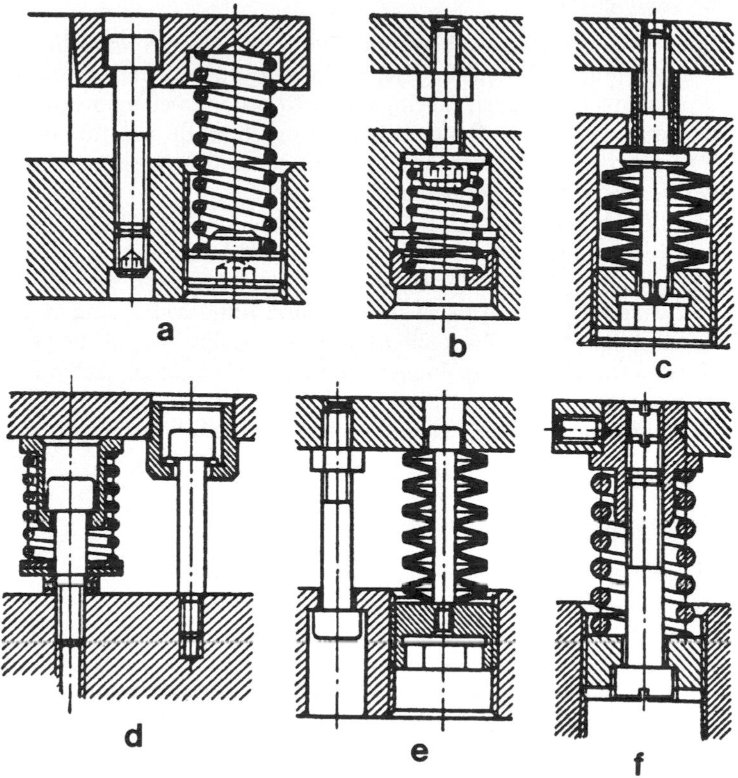

Figure 9.29 Die spring applications.

of the radius. This would cause "pulling" of the hole when the part is bent, with subsequent hole deformation.

Minimum bend radii for various metals and alloys are shown in Fig. 9.30. These bend radii are for cold bending the metals at room temperature (70°F), and at a 90° angle. These minimum bend radii are for an axis of the bend that is at 90° to the direction of rolling of the metal (commonly called *grain direction*). Larger bend radii are required when the bend axis is at 45° or parallel to the direction of rolling of the metal. The tables in Fig. 9.30 list the minimum bend radii as a multiple of the metal thickness. Thus a tabulated bend radius of 3.5 for 0.063-in-thick material indicates that the bend radius is actually equal to $3.5 \times 0.063 = 0.22$ in. In other words, we are multiplying the tabulated values times the material thickness to arrive at the minimum bend radius in inches.

9.6.3 Springback

When a sheet of metal is bent, either in a die or on a press brake, the bent flange will tend to open to a larger angle when the bending pressure is removed (springback). In order to compensate for this characteristic, the flange is usually overbent by a certain number of degrees so that the metal will assume the correct angle of bend when the bending pressure is removed.

The harder the material, the greater is the amount of springback on the workpiece. Quarter-hard cold-rolled steel will exhibit approximately 1 to 2° of springback; half-hard has approximately 3 to 4°; hard steels have more than 5°; and annealed spring steels may have as much as 15 to 20° of springback. The size of the bend radius on the part also influences the amount of springback on all materials.

The amount of springback will depend on the following factors:

- Type of material
- Hardness of material and temper
- Radius of bend
- Gage of material

For practical die-making procedures, which must make allowances for springback of bent materials, trial pieces of material are usually bent to the desired radius in a press brake at 90° and the actual springback is measured with a protractor. The 90° bend angle will open to a larger angle when the bending pressure is removed from the part.

Springback is not a problem when bending sheet metal parts or bar stock on a press brake because the brake operator can adjust the stroke of the press brake to form the correct angle. Once the stroke of the brake is determined and set, all parts made of the same material will bend to the correct angle, providing the gage or hardness of the material does not change during the operation.

To eliminate springback in forming-die designs, the punch or die may be shaped and angled to provide overbend of the part, thus eliminating springback.

9.6.4 Nonmetallic dies and materials

Plastic materials are used for some die and mold applications. Their use is not recommended unless the specifications for the

Minimum Bend Radii for Metals and Alloys- Given in Multiples of Material Thickness (inches)

Material		Thickness, inches						
		0.015	0.031	0.063	0.093	0.125	0.188	0.250
Carbon steels:								
SAE 1010		S	S	S	S	S	0.5	0.5
SAE 1020-1025		0.5	0.5	1.0	1.0	1.0	1.1	1.25
SAE 1070 & 1095		3.75	3.0	2.6	2.7	2.5	2.7	2.8
Alloy steels:								
SAE 4130 & 8630		0.5	2.0	1.5	1.7	1.5	1.7	1.9
Stainless steels:								
AISI 301, 302, 304 (A)		0.5					0.5	0.75
AISI 316 (A)		0.5					0.5	0.75
AISI 410, 430 (A)		1.0					1.0	1.25
AISI 301, 302, 304 (CR) ¼ H		0.5		0.5	1.0		1.0	1.25
AISI 316 ¼ H		1.0					1.0	1.25
AISI 301, 302, 304 ½ H		1.0					1.0	1.25
AISI 316 ½ H		2.0	2.0	3.0	2.0	2.0	2.0	2.5
AISI 301, 302, 304 H		2.0	2.0	1.5	1.5	1.5	1.5	1.5
Aluminum alloys:								
1100	O	0	0	0	0	0	0	0
	H12	0	0	0	0	0	3.0	6.0
	H14	0	0	0	0	0	3.0	6.0
	H1	0	0	2.0	3.0	4.0	8.0	16.0
	H18	1.0	2.0	4.0	6.0	8.0	16.0	24.0
2014 & Alclad	O	0	0	0	0	0	3.0	6.0
	T6	2.0	4.0	8.0	15.0	20.0	36.0	64.0
2024 & Alclad	O	0	0	0	0	0	3.0	6.0
	T3	2.0	4.0	8.0	15.0	20.0	30.0	48.0
3003, 5005,	O	0	0	0	0	0	0	0
5357, 5457	H12/H32	0	0	0	0	0	3.0	6.0
	H14/H34	0	0	0	1.0	2.0	4.0	8.0

Figure 9.30 Table of minimum bend radii.

	H16/H36	0	1.0	3.0	5.0	6.0	12.0	24.0
	H18/H38	1.0	2.0	5.0	9.0	12.0	24.0	40.0
5050, 5052,	O	0	0	0	0	2.0	3.0	4.0
5652	H32	0	0	2.0	3.0	4.0	6.0	12.0
	H34	0	0	2.0	4.0	5.0	9.0	16.0
	H36	1.0	1.0	4.0	5.0	8.0	18.0	24.0
	H38	1.0	2.0	6.0	9.0	12.0	24.0	40.0
6061	O	0	0	0	0	2.0	3.0	4.0
	T6	1.0	2.0	4.0	6.0	9.0	18.0	28.0
7075 & Alclad	O	0	0	2.0	3.0	5.0	9.0	18.0
	T6	2.0	4.0	12.0	18.0	24.0	36.0	64.0
7178	O	0	0	2.0	3.0	5.0	9.0	18.0
	T6	2.0	4.0	12.0	21.0	28.0	42.0	80.0
Copper & alloys:								
ETP #110	soft	S	S	S	S	0.5	0.5	1.0
	hard	S	1.0	1.5	2.0	2.0	2.0	2.0
Alloy 210	¼ H	S	S	S	S	S	0.5	1.0
	½ H	S	S	S	S	S	1.0	1.5
	H	S	S	S	S	S	....	....
	EH	S	0.5	0.5	0.5	0.5	....	....
Alloy 260	¼ H	S	s	S	S	S	0.5	1.0
	½ H	S	S	S	0.3	0.3	....	....
	H	S	0.5	0.5	0.5	1.0	....	....
	EH	2.0	2.0	1.5	2.0	2.0	....	....
Alloy 353	¼ H	S	S	S	S	S	0.5	1.0
	½ H	S	0.5	0.5	0.7	0.3	....	....
	H	2.0	2.0	1.5	2.0	2.0	....	....
	EH	6.0	6.0	4.0	4.0	4.0	....	....
Magnesium sheet @ 70°F:								
	AZ31B-O (S.B.)	3.0	—	—	—	—	—	3.0
	AZ31B-O	5.5	—	—	—	—	—	5.5

AZ31B-H24	8.0	—	—	—	—	—	8.0
HK31A-O	6.0	—	—	—	—	—	6.0
HK31A-H24	13.0	—	—	—	—	—	13.0
HM21A-T8	9.0	—	—	—	—	—	9.0
HM21A-T81	10.0	—	—	—	—	—	10.0
LA141A-O	3.0	—	—	—	—	—	3.0
ZE10A-O	5.5	—	—	—	—	—	5.5
ZE10A-H24	8.0	—	—	—	—	—	8.0
Titanium & alloys @ 70°F:							
Pure (A)	3.0	3.0	3.0	3.5	3.5	3.5	3.5
Ti-8Mn (A)	4.0	4.0	4.0	4.0	5.0	5.0	5.0
Ti-5Al-2.5Sn (A)	5.5	5.5	5.5	5.5	6.0	6.0	6.0
Ti-6Al-4V (A)	4.5	4.5	4.5	5.0	5.0	5.0	5.0
Ti-6Al-4V (ST)	7.0						7.0
Ti-6Al-6V-2Sn (A)	4.0						4.0
Ti-13V-11Cr-3Al (A)	3.0	3.0	3.0	3.5	3.5	3.5	3.5
Ti-4Al-3Mo-1V (A)	3.5	3.5	3.5	4.0	4.0	4.0	4.0
Ti-4Al-3Mo-1V (ST)	5.5	5.5	5.5	6.0	6.0	6.0	6.0

Note: S = sharp bend; 0 = sharp bend; S.B. = special bending quality; A = annealed; ST = solution treated; H = hard; EH = extra hard; Magnesium sheet may be bent at temperatures to 800°F; titanium may be bent at temperatures to 1,000°F; on copper and alloys, direction of bending is at 90° to direction of rolling (bend radii must be increased 10-20% @ 45° and 25-35% parallel to direction of rolling). The tabulated values of the minimum bend radii are given in multiples of the material thickness. The values of the bend radii should be tested on a test specimen prior to die-design or production bending finished parts.

Figure 9.30 *(Continued)*

plastic materials are within the physical limits of the application requirements. Figure 9.31 shows the range of properties available in cast unfilled plastics that may be used for tooling. Shrinkage during hardening, weathering, permanence, and dimensional stability must be considered when using plastic materials for tooling applications.

Phenolics are used for die models, stretch-form dies, duplicate masters, and semipermanent molds. The phenolics are limited to the casting applications and are brittle and react with various other materials.

Epoxies are used for capped forming tools, metal-bonding tools, vacuum-forming tools, molding dies, and all plastic impact tools. Drawing dies having a metallic core and capped with a working face of epoxy are used in the appliance, automotive, and aerospace industries. Epoxy molding dies are being made to mold cycloaliphatic resins, which are two-part epoxy systems. Cycloaliphatic resins (an epoxy) are now used widely for electrical insulators and support details and structures for live current–carrying parts in medium- and high-voltage applications in the switchgear industry. In effect, epoxy materials are molded in specially formulated epoxy molds. Special *release agents* are required to separate the cast epoxy part from the mold cavity. For long production runs, metal molds are made from tool steels. The plastic molding processes are discussed in Chap. 18, "Castings, Moldings, Extrusions, and Powder-Metal Technology."

Ethyl-cellulose compounds, which are thermoplastic materials, have been used for drop-hammer dies and other applications.

Properties of Major Tooling Plastics ♦

Property	Phenolic	Epoxy	Ethyl-cellulose
Specific gravity	1.30-1.32	1.11-1.23	1.09-1.17
Tensile strength, 10^3 psi	6-9	9-12	2-8
Modulus of elasticity, 10^5 psi	4.5	4.5	1.0-3.0
Compressive strength, 10^3 psi	12-15	15-18	10-35
Flexural strength, 10^3 psi	11-17	14-19	4-12
Impact (Izod) ft-lbs/in notch	0.25-0.40	0.45-1.7	2.0-8.0
Hardness, Rockwell	M93-120	M80-100	R50-115
Dimensional stability	Fair	Excellent	Good
Machinability	Excellent	Good	Good
Acid resistance	Good	Good	Poor
Alkali resistance	Poor	Excellent	Excellent
Solvent resistance	Fair	Excellent	Poor

Note: ♦ Per ASTM test methods.

Figure 9.31 Tooling plastics.

9.6.5 Drawing and forming shapes and equations

The diameter of the circular blank for producing simple drawn cylindrical parts may be approximated from

$$D = 1.13\sqrt{F} = 1.13\sqrt{\Sigma f}$$

where D = diameter of blank, in or mm
F = Total area of part to be drawn, in^2 or mm^2
Σf = sum of the individual areas of the drawn part, in^2 or mm^2

Equations for determining the blank diameters for many different drawn-part configurations are compiled in Fig. 9.32. These configurations are intended for material thickness and blank diameter ranges determined by the ratio $S/D \times 100 = 0.06$ to 2.0 using ductile metals or alloys in the soft or annealed condition (where S = material thickness, in or mm, and D = blank diameter, in or mm). The ratio of material thickness and blank diameter times 100 must fall within the range of 0.06 to 2.0 in order for the blank diameter D equations shown in Fig. 9.32 to be valid.

Example: A blank that is 5.00 in in diameter and 0.125 in thick would fall within the range of $0.125/5.00 \times 100 = 2.5$, which is *outside* the range of 0.06 to 2.0, as explained previously. A blank that is 4.00 in in diameter and 0.062 in thick would fall within the range of $0.062/4.00 \times 100 = 1.55$, which is *inside* the range of 0.06 to 2.0, making the equations valid for this combination of material thickness and blank diameter.

Figure 9.33 shows the step equations used to determine the drawn height at each step in the drawing process when we know the blank diameter, the drawing coefficients ($m_1, \ldots, m_n$), the workpiece diameter ($d_1, \ldots, d_n$), and the other variables indicated in the equations. Figures 9.34 through 9.39 give the drawing coefficients when we know the $S/D \times 100$ range, as well as approximations for the first drawing step height (h_1). The designations for the symbols shown in the equations in Fig. 9.33 are as follows:

D = diameter of the blank, in or mm
$d_1, d_2, \ldots, d_n$ = workpiece diameter for each operation, in or mm, proceeding from larger to smaller diameter as drawing steps increase
$a_1, a_2, \ldots, a_n$ = bevel dimensions for each operation (profile 3 only)

(*Text continued on page 812.*)

Figure	Drawn Profile	Diameter of Blank, D
1	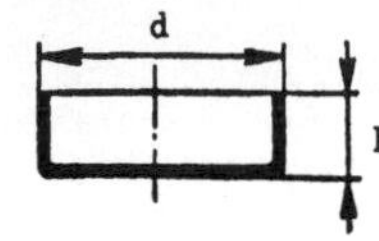 d, h	$\sqrt{d^2 + 4dh}$
2	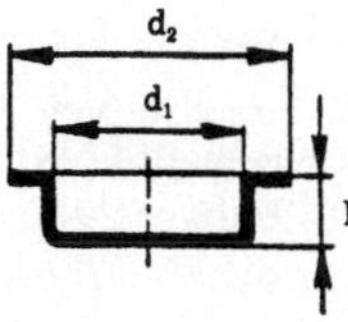 d_2, d_1, h	$\sqrt{d_2^2 + 4d_1h}$
3	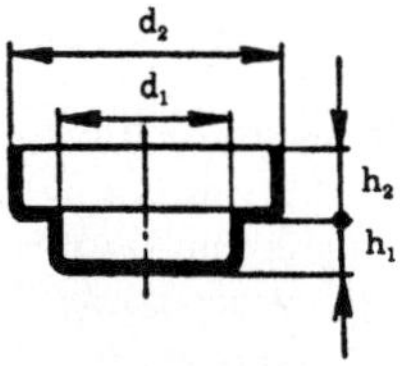 d_2, d_1, h_2, h_1	$\sqrt{d_2^2 + 4(d_1h_1 + d_2h_2)}$
4	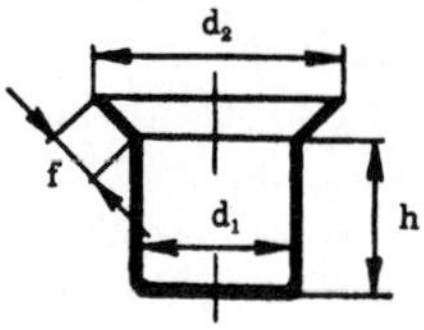 d_2, f, d_1, h	$\sqrt{d_1^2 + 4d_1h + 2f(d_1 + d_2)}$

Figure 9.32 Equations for determining blank diameters, drawing operations.

Figure	Drawn Profile	Diameter of Blank, D
5	d2, r, d1	$\sqrt{d_1^2 + 2\pi r d_1 + 8r^2}$
6	d3, d2, r, d1	$\sqrt{d_1^2 + 2\pi r d_1 + 8r^2 + d_3^2 - d_2^2}$
7	d3, d2, h, r, d1	$\sqrt{d_1^2 + 2\pi r d_1 + 8r^2 + 4d_2 h + d_3^2 - d_2^2}$
8	d3, f, d2, h, r, d1	$\sqrt{d_1^2 + 2\pi r d_1 + 8r^2 + 4d_2 h + 2f\left(d_2 + d_3\right)}$

Figure 9.32 *(Continued)*

Figure	Drawn Profile	Diameter of Blank, D
9		$\sqrt{d_1^2 + 2\pi r d_1 + 8r^2 + 4d_2 h}$ or $\sqrt{d_2^2 + 4d_2 H - 1.72rd_2 - 0.56r^2}$ *
10		$\sqrt{d_1^2 + 2\pi r\left(d_1 + d_2\right) + 4\pi r^2}$
11		$\sqrt{d_1^2 + 2\pi r\left(d_1 + d_2\right) + 4d_2 h + 4\pi r^2}$
12		$\sqrt{d_1^2 + 4d_2 h + 2\pi r\left(d_1 + d_2\right) + 4\pi r^2 + d_1^2 - d_3^2}$ or $\sqrt{d_4^2 + 4d_2 H - 3.44rd_2}$ *

Figure 9.32 *(Continued)*

Figure	Drawn Profile	Diameter of Blank, D
13	d_2, f, d_1	$\sqrt{d_1^2 + 2f(d_1 + d_2)}$
14	d_3, d_2, f, d_1	$\sqrt{d_1^2 + 2f(d_1 + d_2) + d_3^2 - d_2^2}$
15	d_2, h, f, d_1	$\sqrt{d_1^2 + 2f(d_1 + d_2) + 4d_2 h}$
16	d, f	$\sqrt{2df}$

Figure 9.32 *(Continued)*

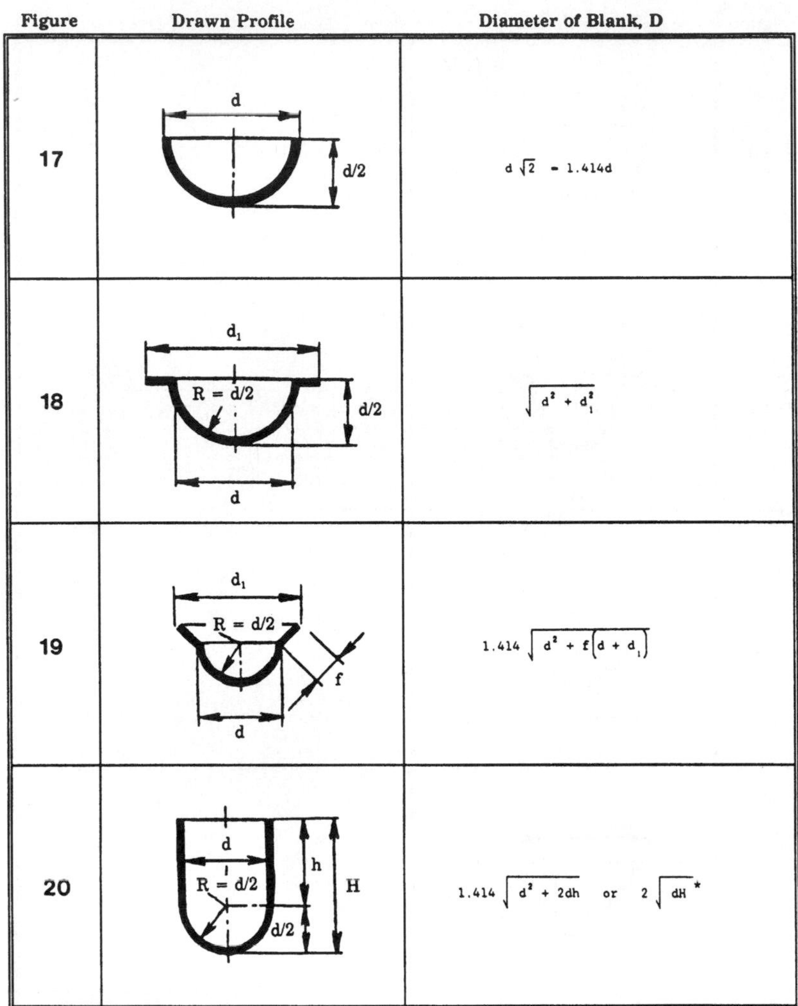

Figure	Drawn Profile	Diameter of Blank, D
17		$d\sqrt{2} = 1.414d$
18		$\sqrt{d^2 + d_1^2}$
19		$1.414\sqrt{d^2 + f(d + d_1)}$
20		$1.414\sqrt{d^2 + 2dh}$ or $2\sqrt{dH}$ *

Figure 9.32 *(Continued)*

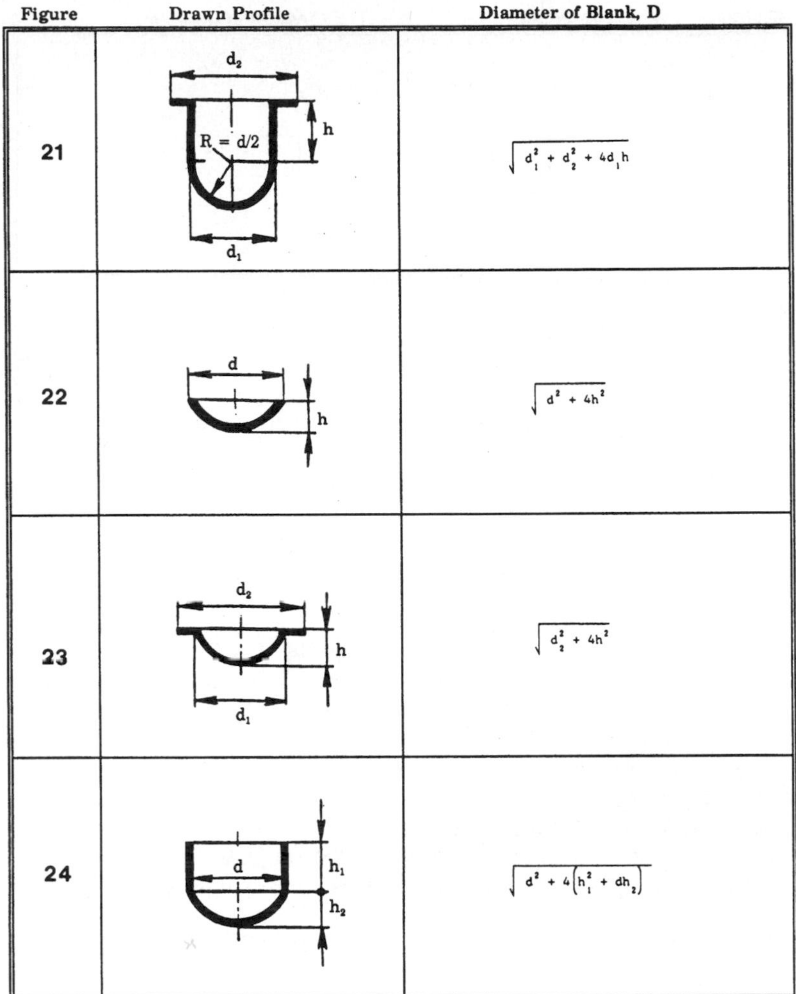

Figure	Drawn Profile	Diameter of Blank, D
21		$\sqrt{d_1^2 + d_2^2 + 4d_1h}$
22		$\sqrt{d^2 + 4h^2}$
23		$\sqrt{d_2^2 + 4h^2}$
24		$\sqrt{d^2 + 4\left(h_1^2 + dh_2\right)}$

Figure 9.32 *(Continued)*

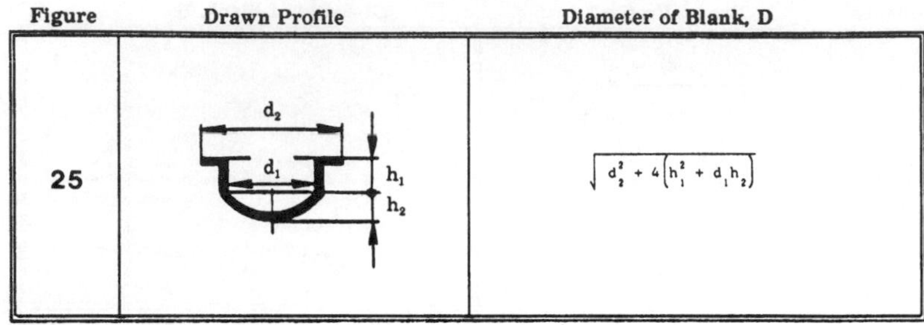

Figure	Drawn Profile	Diameter of Blank, D
25		$\sqrt{d_2^2 + 4\left(h_1^2 + d_1 h_2\right)}$

Figure 9.32 *(Continued)*

$m_1, m_2, \ldots, m_n$ = drawing coefficients for each operation (see Figs. 9.34 to 9.39)

$S, S_1, \ldots, S_n$ = blank thickness and wall thickness for each operation, in or mm

$d\phi$ = flange diameter, in or mm (for profile 6 only)

$r_1, r_2, \ldots, r_n$ = inside radius or corner radius for each operation, in or mm

The equations shown in Fig. 9.33 allow the tool designer to calculate the dimensions for the dies required in each step of the drawing operation. Some profile heights will require only one or two steps, while others will require more than two successive drawing steps. The most critical variables used in the drawing operations are the drawing coefficients ($m_1, m_2, \ldots, m_n$) and the first-step relative value of h/d for flanged parts. These values must be determined accurately using the tables in Figs. 9.34 through 9.39.

The drawing-process calculations for cylindrical parts consist of

1. Determination of the deformation limit (coefficients $m_1, m_2, \ldots, m_n$).
2. Determination of the required number of steps.
3. Calculation of the drawn part dimensions for every step.

The deformation limits are determined by practical drawing coefficients m that were derived from experiments and proved by actual practice. The drawing coefficient for the first step is

$$m_1 = d_1/D$$

(Text continued on page 818.)

Figure	Workpiece Profile	Operation	Equation for Profile Height
1		**Step 1**	$h_1 = 0.25\left(\frac{D}{m_1} - d_1\right)$
		Step 2	$h_2 = 0.25\left(\frac{D}{m_1 m_2} - d_2\right)$
		Step n	$h_n = 0.25\left(\frac{D}{m_1 m_2 \ldots m_n} - d_n\right)$
2		**Step 1**	$h_1 = 0.25\left(\frac{D}{m_1} - d_1\right) + 0.43\frac{r_1}{d_1}\left(d_1 + 0.32\, r_1\right)$
		Step 2	$h_2 = 0.25\left(\frac{D}{m_1 m_2} - d_2\right) + 0.43\frac{r_2}{d_2}\left(d_2 + 0.32\, r_2\right)$
		Step n	$h_n = 0.25\left(\frac{D}{m_1 m_2 \ldots m_n} - d_n\right) + 0.43\frac{r_n}{d_n}\left(d_n + 0.32\, r_n\right)$

Figure 9.33 Equations for calculating the profile height h at each drawing step.

Figure	Workpiece Profile	Operation	Equation for Profile Height
3	45°, a, h, d	Step 1	$h_1 = 0.25\left(\frac{D}{m_1} - d_1\right) + 0.57\frac{a_1}{d_1}\left(d_1 + 0.86\,a_1\right)$
		Step 2	$h_2 = 0.25\left(\frac{D}{m_1 m_2} - d_2\right) + 0.57\frac{a_2}{d_2}\left(d_2 + 0.86\,a_2\right)$
		Step n	$h_n = 0.25\left(\frac{D}{m_1 m_2 \ldots m_n} - d_n\right) + 0.57\frac{a_n}{d_n}\left(d_n + 0.86\,a_n\right)$
4	0.5d, h, d	Step 1	$h_1 = 0.25\frac{D}{m_1}$
		Step 2	$h_2 = 0.25\frac{D}{m_1 m_2}$
		Step n	$h_n = 0.25\frac{D}{m_1 m_2 \ldots m_n}$

Figure 9.33 *(Continued)*

Figure	Workpiece Profile	Operation	Equation for Profile Height
5	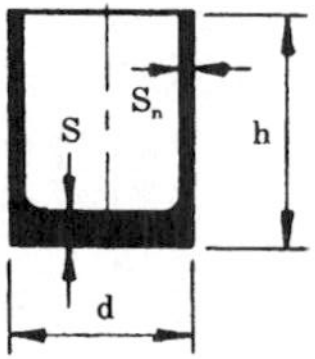 S, S_n, h, d	Step 1	$h_1 = 0.25\left(\frac{D}{m_1} - d_1\right)\frac{S}{S_1} + S$
		Step 2	$h_2 = 0.25\left(\frac{D}{m_1 m_2} - d_2\right)\frac{S}{S_2} + S$
		Step n	$h_n = 0.25\left(\frac{D}{m_1 m_2 \ldots m_n} - d_n\right)\frac{S}{S_n} + S$
6	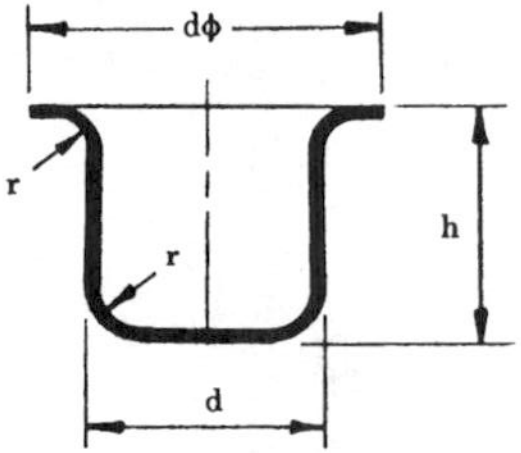 dϕ, r, r, h, d	Step 1	$h_1 = 0.25\left(\frac{D}{m_1} - \frac{d\phi^2}{d_1} + 3.44\, r_1\right)$
		Step 2	$h_2 = 0.25\left(\frac{D}{m_1 m_2} - \frac{d\phi^2}{d_2} + 3.44\, r_2\right)$
		Step n	$h_n = 0.25\left(\frac{D}{m_1 m_2 \ldots m_n} - \frac{d\phi^2}{d_n} + 3.44\, r_n\right)$

Figure 9.33 *(Continued)*

Coefficient Step	Coefficient Values for Relative Blank Thickness S/D x 100				
	2.0 - 1.5	1.5 - 1.0	1.0 - 0.5	0.5 - 0.2	0.2 - 0.06
m_1	0.46-0.50	0.50-0.53	0.53-0.56	0.56-0.58	0.58-0.60
m_2	0.70-0.72	0.72 0.74	0.74-0.76	0.76-0.78	0.78-0.80
m_3	0.72-0.74	0.74-0.76	0.76-0.78	0.78-0.80	0.80-0.82
m_4	0.74-0.76	0.76-0.78	0.78-0.80	0.80-0.82	0.82-0.84

Note: Tabulated values are the drawing coefficients. S = material thickness and D = blank diameter.

Figure 9.34 Drawing coefficients for cylindrical parts without flanges (profiles 1–5 of Fig. 9.33).

Relative Dia. of Flange, dϕ/d	Coefficient Values for Relative Blank Thickness S/D x 100				
	2.0 - 1.5	1.5 - 1.0	1.0 - 0.5	0.5 - 0.2	0.2 - 0.06
1.1	0.50	0.53	0.55	0.57	0.59
1.3	0.49	0.51	0.53	0.54	0.55
1.5	0.47	0.49	0.50	0.51	0.52
1.8	0.45	0.46	0.47	0.48	0.48
2.0	0.42	0.43	0.44	0.45	0.45
2.2	0.40	0.41	0.42	0.42	0.42
2.5	0.37	0.38	0.38	0.38	0.38
2.8	0.33	0.34	0.34	0.35	0.35

Note: Tabulated values are the drawing coefficients. S = material thickness and D = blank diameter.

Figure 9.35 Drawing coefficients for cylindrical part with flanges (profile 6 of Fig. 9.33).

Relative Dia. of Flange dϕ/d	Value of (h/d) for Relative Blank Thickness S/D x 100				
	2.0 - 1.5	1.5 - 1.0	1.0 - 0.5	0.5 - 0.2	0.2 - 0.06
1.1	0.90-0.75	0.82-0.60	0.70-0.57	0.62-0.50	0.52-0.45
1.3	0.80-0.65	0.72-0.56	0.60-0.50	0.53-0.45	0.47-0.40
1.5	0.70-0.58	0.63-0.50	0.53-0.45	0.48-0.40	0.42-0.35
1.8	0.58-0.48	0.53-0.42	0.44-0.37	0.39-0.34	0.35-0.29
2.0	0.51-0.42	0.46-0.36	0.38-0.32	0.34-0.29	0.30-0.25
2.2	0.45-0.35	0.40-0.31	0.38-0.27	0.29-0.25	0.26-0.22
2.5	0.35-0.28	0.32-0.25	0.27-0.22	0.23-0.20	0.21-0.17
2.8	0.27-0.22	0.24-0.19	0.21-0.17	0.18-0.15	0.16-0.13

Note: Tabulated values are the values of h/d. (see profile 6 of Figure 9-29).
The larger tabulated values correspond to the larger radii r = (10-12)S for S/D x 100 = 2.0-1.5; r = (20-25)S for S/D x 100 = 0.2-0.06. The smaller tabulated values correspond to the smaller radii for bottom and flange where r = approx. (4-8)S. S is the material thickness and D is the blank diameter.

Figure 9.36 Approximate value of the first step relative depth (h/d) for cylindrical parts with flange (profile 6 of Fig. 9.33).

Blank Diameter (millimeters)	Height of Part (h_1) in 1st Step using Coefficients m_1 0.45	0.48	0.50	0.53	0.55	0.58	0.60 - (coefficients)
30	13	12	11	10	9.5	9	....
40	18	16	15	14	13	12	....
50	22	20	19	17	16	15	....
60	26	24	22	20	19	18	....
70	31	28	26	24	22	20	19
80	35	32	30	27	26	23	22
90	40	36	34	30	29	26	24
100	44	40	37	34	32	29	27
120	....	48	45	40	38	35	32
150	....	60	55	50	48	44	40
180	....	72	67	60	58	52	50
200	....	80	75	68	64	58	55

Note: Tabulated values are the height of the part in 1st drawing step, millimeters. (for profile 1, Fig.9-29)

Figure 9.37 Height of cylindrical part (h_1) for the listed drawing coefficients (profile 1 of Fig. 9.33).

Blank Diameter (millimeters)	Height of Part (h_1) in 1st Step using Cocfficients m_1 0.45	0.48	0.50	0.53	0.55	0.59	0.60 - (coefficients)
30	14	13	13	11	10	10	....
40	19	17	16	15	14	13	....
50	23	21	20	17	16	15	....
60	28	26	24	22	21	20	....
70	33	30	28	26	24	22	21
80	37	34	32	29	28	25	24
90	42	38	36	32	32	29	27
100	47	43	40	37	35	32	30
120	....	52	49	44	42	39	36
150	....	65	60	55	53	49	45
180	....	77	72	65	63	57	55
200	....	88	81	74	70	64	61

Note:Tabulated values are the height of the part in 1st drawing step, millimeters. (for profile 2, Fig. 9-29)

Figure 9.38 Height of cylindrical part (h_1) for the listed drawing coefficients (profile 2 of Fig. 9.33).

Blank Diameter (millimeters)	Height of Part (h_1) in 1st Step using Coefficients m_1						
	0.48	0.50	0.53	0.55	0.58	0.60	0.62 - (coefficients)
120	53	50	45	43	40	37	....
150	66	61	56	52	50	46	....
180	79	74	67	65	59	57	....
200	88	83	76	72	66	63	58
250	110	103	95	90	83	78	73
300	132	122	114	108	98	92	86
350	154	144	134	126	116	108	102
400	176	166	152	144	132	123	115
450	198	184	172	162	148	140	130
500	220	205	190	180	165	155	145
550	242	226	210	198	182	172	160
600	264	244	228	216	200	185	173

Note: Tabulated values are the height of the part in 1st drawing step, millimeters. (for profile 3, Fig. 9-29)

Figure 9.39 Height of cylindrical part (h_1) for the listed drawing coefficients (profile 3 of Fig. 9.33).

For the second step,

$$m_2 = d_2/d_1$$

Dimensions for the first step are

$$d_1 = m_1 D$$

For the second step,

$$D_2 = m_2 d_2$$

where D = blank diameter, in or mm
d = part diameter, in or mm
m = drawing coefficient

In this way, knowing the coefficient m, we can determine the dimensions and number of steps.

Note: The dimensions used in Figs. 9.34 through 9.39 are given in millimeters. The drawing coefficients are dimensionless values (multipliers).

9.6.6 General rules for die stamping and forming operations

Some of the *basic* rules and dimensions for stamping and forming operations are shown in Figs. 9.40 through 9.44. The edge-distance recommendations shown in Fig. 9.40 for die-stamping metals are easy to apply during punching or stamping operations, but these distances (*A* and *B*) are often reduced when the gage of the metal is below 0.020 in.

Figure 9.41 shows the common methods of relieving the bending stresses on intermediately flanged parts and parts with angle-notched ends. Figure 9.42 shows methods for minimum flanges and stiffening ribs on the heel of die-formed parts. Light-gage sheet metal parts can be made quite strong with the addition of heel-applied stiffening webs. The load-carrying ability of thin-gage sheet metal parts such as angles is greatly increased with the addition of these die-formed stiffening webs.

Figure 9.43 shows a 90° formed *bead,* which is common in thin sheet metal parts for obtaining stiffness without adding another member to the part. Automotive and aerospace sheet metal parts frequently contain stiffening beads and "lightening holes." See Chap. 16, "Sheet Metal Practices and Layout," for additional information on sheet metal bending and forming.

Figure 9.44 shows a 60° flat-bottomed bead. Such beads are normally larger than the 90° types shown in Fig. 9.43 and are used on large sheet metal parts.

Forces required for die bending. The force for die forming a flange (edge bending) may be calculated from

$$P = \frac{lt^2}{2W}(S_t) \qquad \text{(See Fig. 9.42)}$$

The force required for V bending with a centrally located load may be calculated from

$$P = \frac{lt^2}{W}(S_t)$$

The force for bending channel and U bends may be calculated from

$$P = \frac{2lt^2}{W}(S_t)$$

where P = bending force, lbf
l = length of bend, in
t = material thickness, in
W = width of unsupported material, in
S_t = ultimate tensile strength of the material, psi (see Chap. 5)

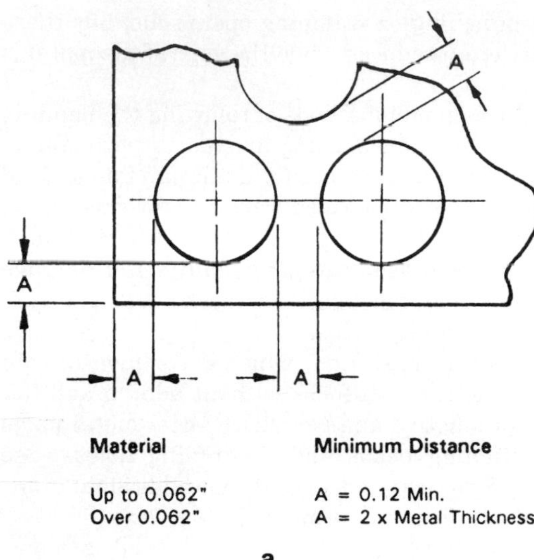

Material	Minimum Distance
Up to 0.062"	A = 0.12 Min.
Over 0.062"	A = 2 x Metal Thickness

a

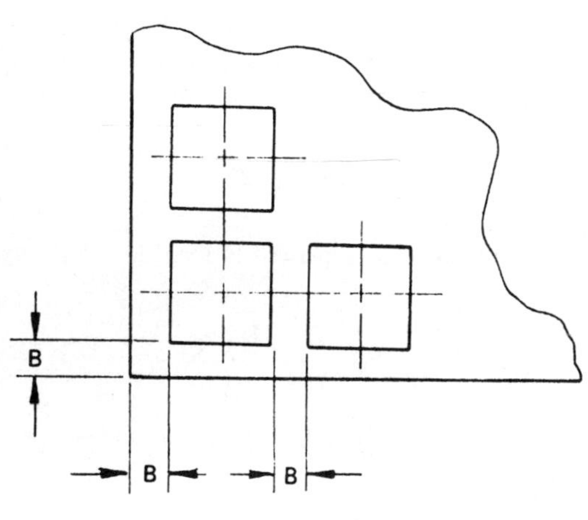

Material	Minimum Distance
Up to 0.090"	B = 0.18"
Over 0.090"	B = 2 x Metal Thickness

b

Figure 9.40 (*a*) Minimum edge. (*b*) Minimum edge.

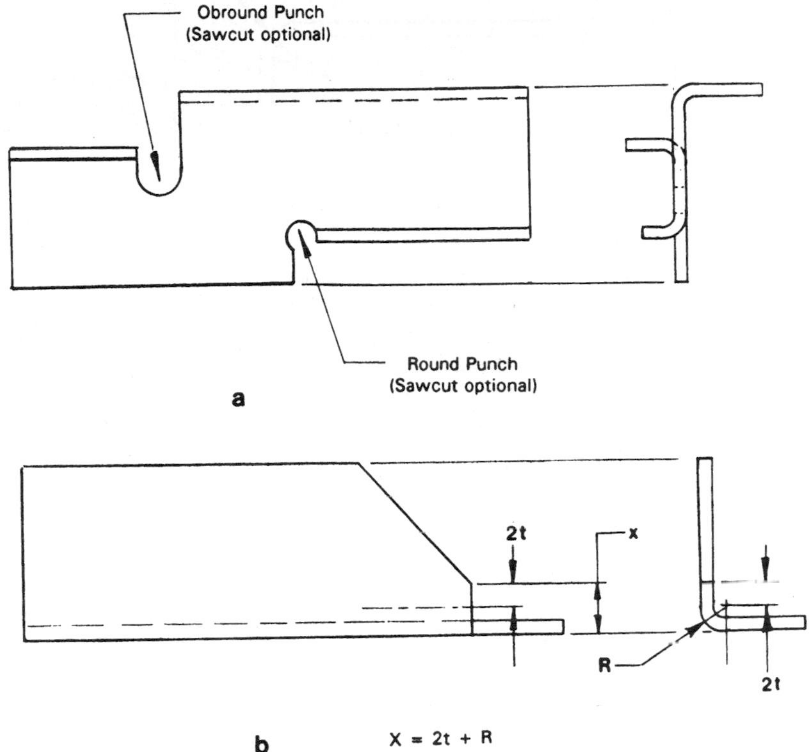

Figure 9.41 (*a*) Bend relief notches. (*b*) Notch limits.

9.7 Jigs and Fixtures

A *jig* is a tool that may be used as a guide to form (cut, grind, or file) the outline of a part. Jigs are also used with drill bushings to accurately drill and/or ream holes in a part. The jig is positioned accurately on the part to be drilled prior to drilling the holes. Stamped parts may thus be mass produced with additional drilled or reamed holes, making the parts accurate and interchangeable at the next-assembly stage of manufacture. A drilling-guide tool is sometimes called a *drill fixture*. Either term, *jig* or *fixture,* is sometimes used interchangeably in industry when used for a drilling or reaming operation.

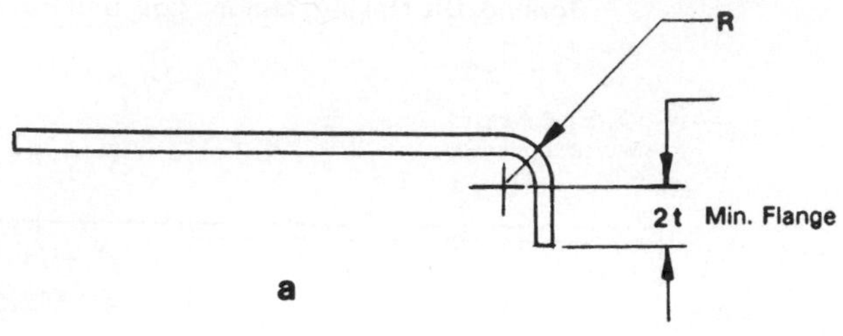

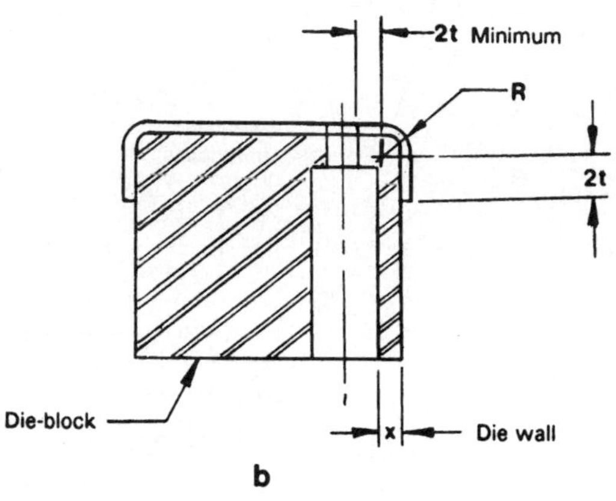

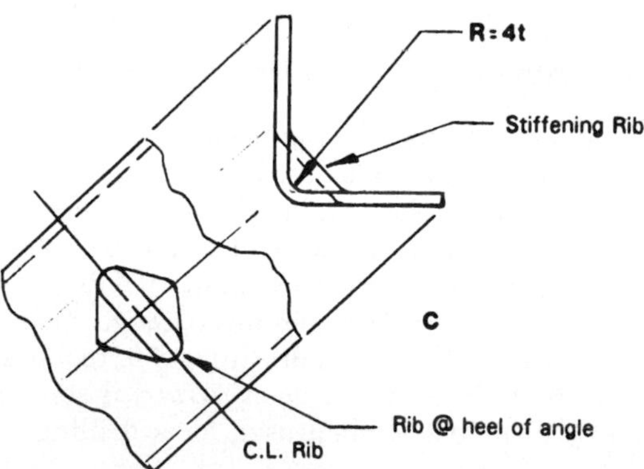

Figure 9.42 (*a*) Minimum flange. (*b*) Edge distance. (*c*) Rib.

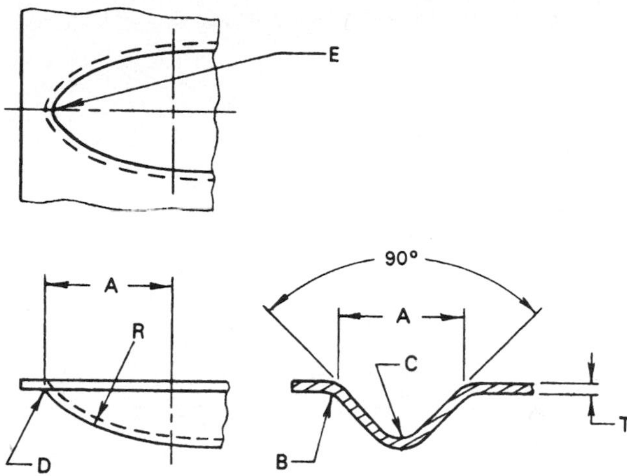

A	B (Radius)	C (Radius)	D (Radius)	E (Radius)
0.25	2T	2T	4T	T
0.38	2T	2T	4T	T
0.50	2T	2T	4T	2T
0.62	4T	4T	4T	2T
0.75	5T	5T	4T	3T
1.00	5T	5T	4T	3T

Figure 9.43 Stiffening beads.

Different size drill bushings used in jigs and fixtures are shown in Fig. 9.45. The drill bushing is one of the most common parts used in tooling work. The drill bushing is available in different types and sizes to accommodate the different size drills and reamers. The bushing type may be plain cylindrical, flanged, press fit, or lock-in, according to the intended application. The correct definitions of drill bushing types are as follows:

- Headless press fit, type P
- Standard head, type H
- Slip/fixed, type SF

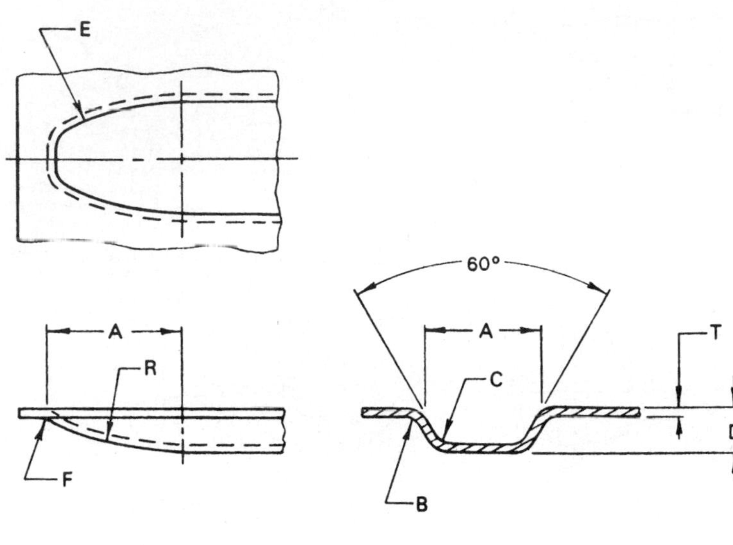

A	B (Radius)	C (Radius)	D	E (Radius)	F (Radius)
1.00	3T	2T	0.25	4T	4T
1.50	3T	2T	0.31	4T	4T

Figure 9.44 Stiffening beads.

Figure 9.45 shows the plain bushing (P), flanged bushing (H), and lock-in bushing (SF). The lock-in or slip/fixed type of drill bushing is used when the production rates are high so that the bushing may be replaced easily as it wears during operation. Drill bushings are made of quality-grade tool steels with hardness ranges of Rockwell C50 to C60.

9.7.1 Tooling fixtures

A *tooling fixture* is a device used to accurately and efficiently aid the manufacturing processes. Fixtures are made in countless varieties and designs, including those for

- Assembly and subassembly
- Welding

Figure 9.45 Drill bushings.

- Machining
- Machining pallets (quick-interchangeable fixtures)
- Heat treating
- Plating
- Wiring and cable harnesses

Tooling fixtures may weigh less than 1 oz or more than 100 tons. Large assembly fixtures, such as those used in the final assembly of aerospace vehicles or construction machinery, require the use of transits, optical/laser levels, and theodolites in order to position the critical parts accurately during construction of the fixture.

The properly designed tooling fixture has many requirements, such as

- Dimensional stability
- Dimensional accuracy

- Ease of manufacture
- Efficiency in use
- Practicality
- Cost-effectiveness
- Safety in operation

A typical small assembly fixture is shown in Fig. 9.46. The pneumatically actuated clamps used on this fixture are evident in the photograph. Holding clamps are important elements in the design of many fixtures. Section 9.8 will be useful to the tooling fixture designer and shows various clamp designs and calculation techniques for their application. Safety to manufacturing personnel is of prime importance when clamping devices are used on any tooling fixture, especially those clamping devices which are pneumatically or hydraulically actuated.

Figure 9.47 shows a large assembly fixture which is used to assemble electromechanical devices that must be totally inter-

Figure 9.46 Pneumatic assembly fixture.

Figure 9.47 Large assembly fixture.

changeable. This fixture weighs more than half a ton and has leveling ball jacks anchored into a concrete floor.

Figure 7.72 shows a typical pneumatically actuated machining fixture in use on a CNC-controlled vertical machining center. Figure 9.48 shows a drawing of a typical machining fixture that is actuated by a manual screw mechanism. The fixture drawing was generated by a CAD system and drawn on an automatic ink-pen plotter.

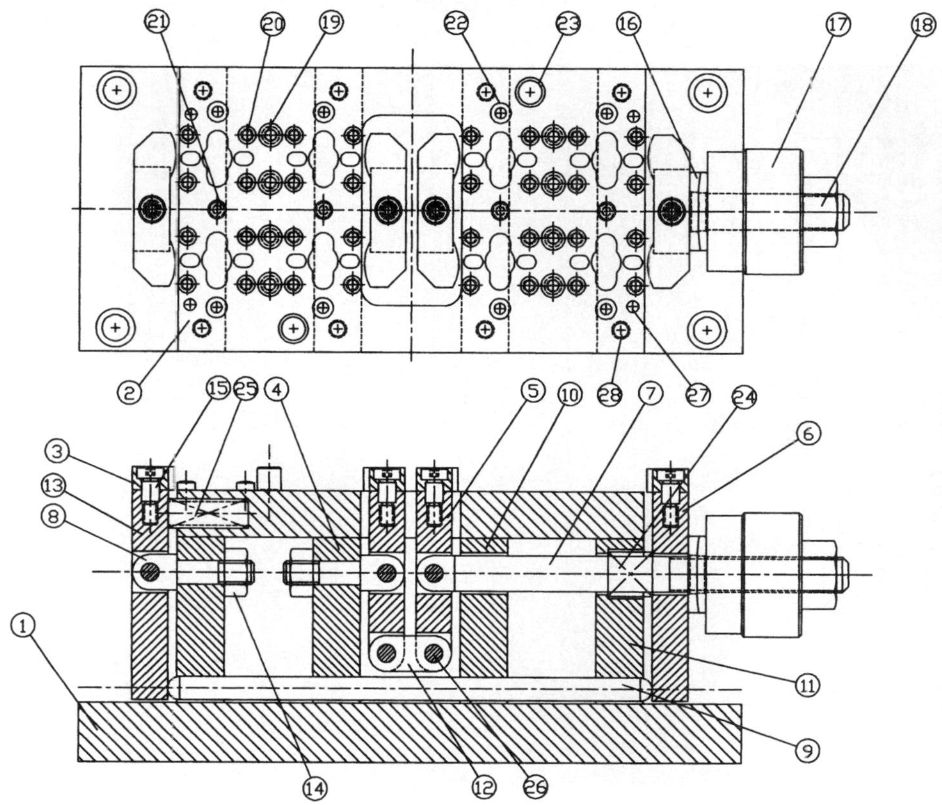

Figure 9.48 CAD drawing of a typical machining fixture.

POS	QTY	PART NAME	MATERIAL	DIMENSIONS	HARDNESS
28	8	SHCS	9-1236-41	3/8x4 1/2	DANLY
27	2	DOWEL PIN	7-0832-1	ø1/4x2	DANLY
26	5	DOWEL PIN	7-1228-1	ø3/8x1 3/4	DANLY
25	1	SPRING	LC-072H-6		LEE
24	1	SPRING	LC-082M-3		LEE
23	2	BUSHING	10063	.5x.625	STEVENS
22	8	LOCATING PIN	CL-7A-SLP-3		CARR LANE
21	4	REST BUTTON	CL-14-RB	3/8x1/2	CARR LANE
20	32	LOCATOR BUTTON	CL-2-SLB	3/8x3/16	CARR LANE
19	8	REST BUTTON	CL-1-RB	1/2x1/2	CARR LANE
18	1	LOCK NUT	LN-750	3/4-10	VLIER
17	1	HOLLOW CYLINDER	CY2129-25	7415 LB	VLIER
16	1	SPHERICAL WASHER	CL-5-SW	3/4 DIA	CARR LANE
15	4	SHOULDER SCREW	CL-14-SS	1/2x.375	CARR LANE
14	2	NUT		3/8-13	
13	1	CLAMP LEVER	1018 STEEL	.75x1.75x4 7/16	
12	1	LINK	1045 STEEL	.75x.75x1.75	RC 38-40
11	1	SUPPORT BAR	1018 STEEL	1x3.5x6	
10	1	SUPPORT BAR	1018 STEEL	1x3.5x6	
9	1	PUSH ROD	O1 STEEL	ø1/2x10.25	RC 38-40
8	2	SWING BOLT	O1 STEEL	ø3/4x2.625	
7	1	PULL ROD	O1 STEEL	ø3/4x9 1/4	
6	1	CLAMP LEVER	1018 STEEL	.75x1.75x4 7/16	
5	2	CLAMP LEVER	1018 STEEL	.75x1.75x3 13/16	
4	2	SUPPORT BAR	1018 STEEL	1x3.5x6	
3	4	ADJUSTIBLE CLAMP	1045 STEEL	.5x.875x3.218	RC 40-45
2	1	TOP PLATE	1018 STEEL	1x6x9.875	
1	1	BASE PLATE	1018 STEEL	1 1/4x6x14	

Figure 9.48 *(Continued)*

The design and application of tooling fixtures are as important to manufacturing processes as the design of the product that requires these fixtures for production, and in most cases, the fixtures are more difficult to design and have closer tolerances than the product itself.

9.7.2 Pallets

A *pallet* is a quickly removable indexed machining fixture that is used when maximum productivity of machined parts is required. In order for a palletizing system to be cost-effective, the cost of multiple pallets is weighed against the number of machined parts required for any particular job or production run.

The use of multiple pallets reduces machine "down time" drastically and makes the machined parts cost-effective when quantities are large enough to warrant a palletizing system.

In a palletized system, the machine operator loads multiple parts into different pallets while the machine tool is machining parts on a previously loaded pallet. All the pallets are pin indexed to fit the bed of the machine tool at a precise location relative to the zero position of the cutting tool or spindle centerline. In effect, the machine operator is using the normal idle time (while the CNC machine tool is operating) to load pallets (machining fixtures that hold multiple parts and which are quick changing).

A palletizing system is usually expensive to implement but is totally justified if it produces parts which are cost-effective, when the cost to produce the parts meets or exceeds expected price goals and specifications.

9.8 Clamping Mechanisms and Calculation Procedures

Clamping mechanisms are an integral part of nearly all tooling fixtures. Countless numbers of clamping designs may be used by the tooling fixture designer and tool maker, but only the basic types are described in this section. With these basic clamp types, it is possible to design a vast number of different tools. Both manual and pneumatic/hydraulic clamping mechanisms are shown, together with the equations used to calculate each basic type. The forces generated by the pneumatic and hydraulic mechanisms may be calculated initially by using the equations shown in Chap. 20.

The basic clamping mechanisms used by many tooling fixture designers are outlined in Fig. 9.49, types 1 through 12. These basic clamping mechanisms also may be used for other mechanical design applications.

Eccentric clamp, round (Fig. 9.49, type 12). The eccentric clamp, such as that shown in Fig. 9.49, type 12, is a fast-action clamp compared with threaded clamps, but threaded clamps have higher clamping

(*Text continued on page 837.*)

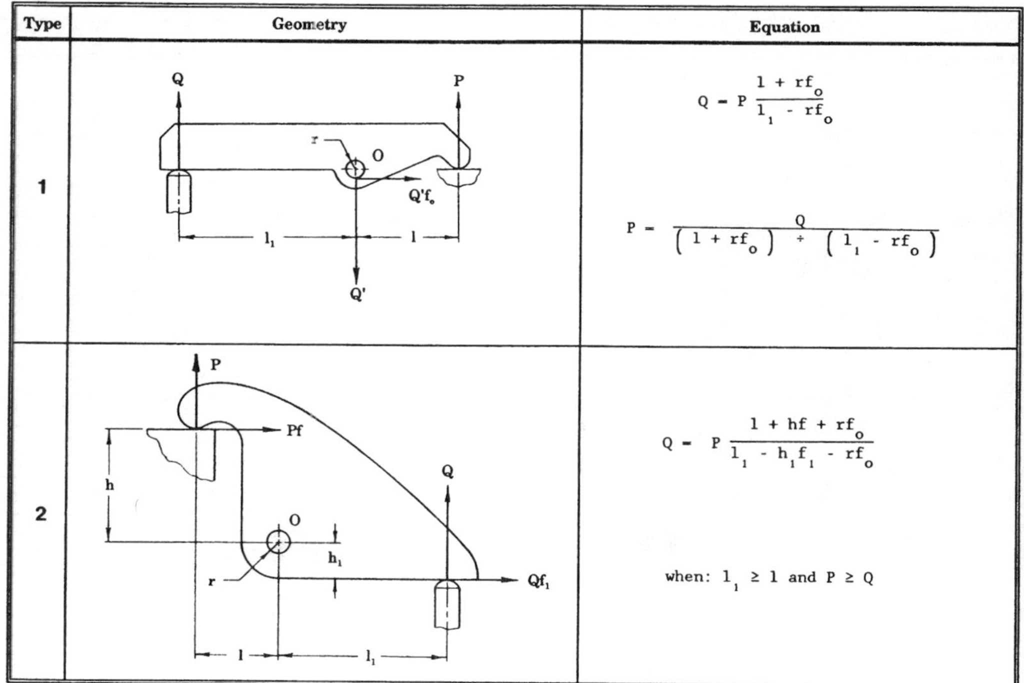

Type	Geometry	Equation
1		$Q = P \frac{l + rf_o}{l_1 - rf_o}$ $P = \frac{Q}{\left(l + rf_o\right) \div \left(l_1 - rf_o\right)}$
2		$Q = P \frac{l + hf + rf_o}{l_1 - h_1 f_1 - rf_o}$ when: $l_1 \geq l$ and $P \geq Q$

Figure 9.49 Basic clamping mechanisms (lever, cam, screw, pneumatic, and hydraulic).

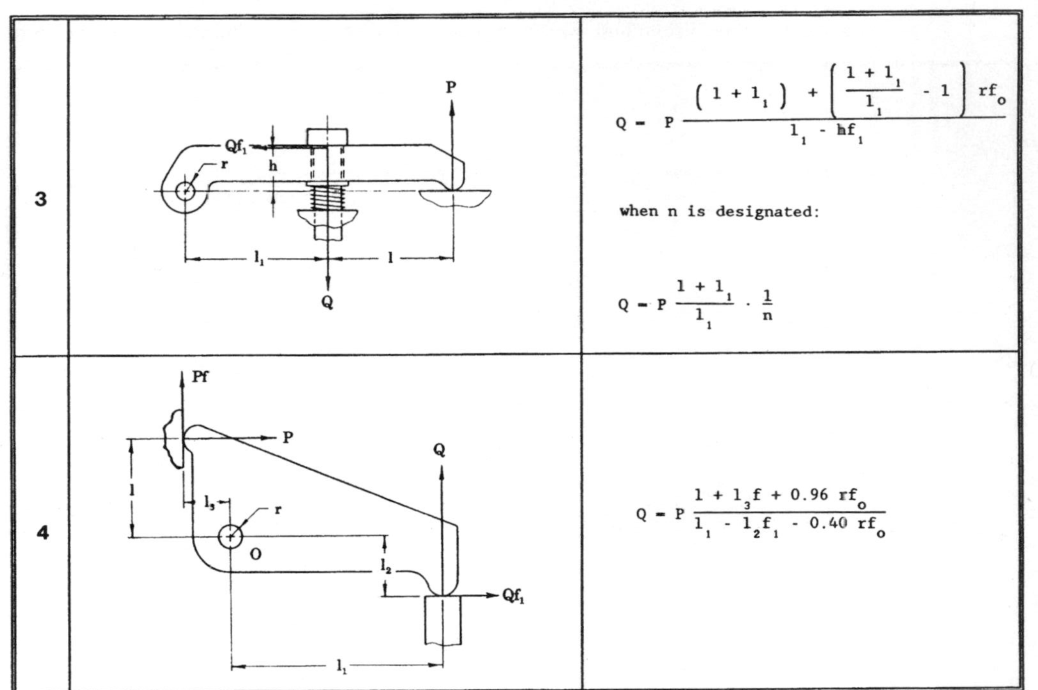

$$Q = P\,\frac{(l + l_1) + \left(\frac{l + l_1}{l_1} - 1\right) rf_o}{l_1 - hf_1}$$

when n is designated:

$$Q = P\,\frac{l + l_1}{l_1} \cdot \frac{1}{n}$$

$$Q = P\,\frac{l + l_3 f + 0.96\ rf_o}{l_1 - l_2 f_1 - 0.40\ rf_o}$$

Figure 9.49 *(Continued)*

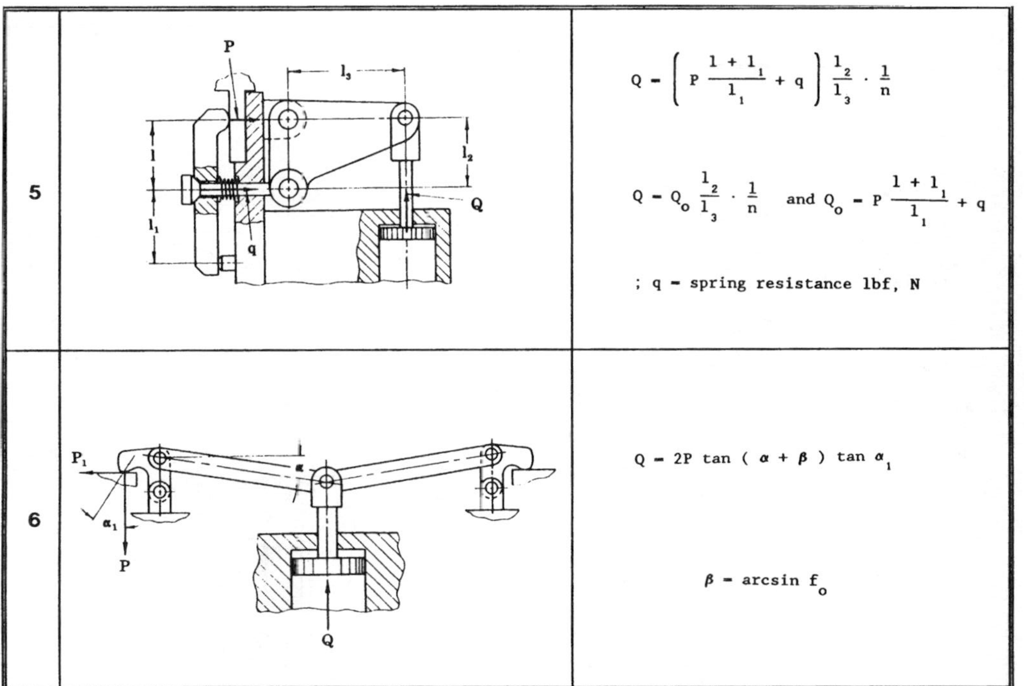

5		$Q = \left(P \frac{l + l_1}{l_1} + q \right) \frac{l_2}{l_3} \cdot \frac{1}{n}$ $Q = Q_o \frac{l_2}{l_3} \cdot \frac{1}{n}$ and $Q_o = P \frac{l + l_1}{l_1} + q$; q = spring resistance lbf, N
6		$Q = 2P \tan(\alpha + \beta) \tan \alpha_1$ $\beta = \arcsin f_o$

Figure 9.49 *(Continued)*

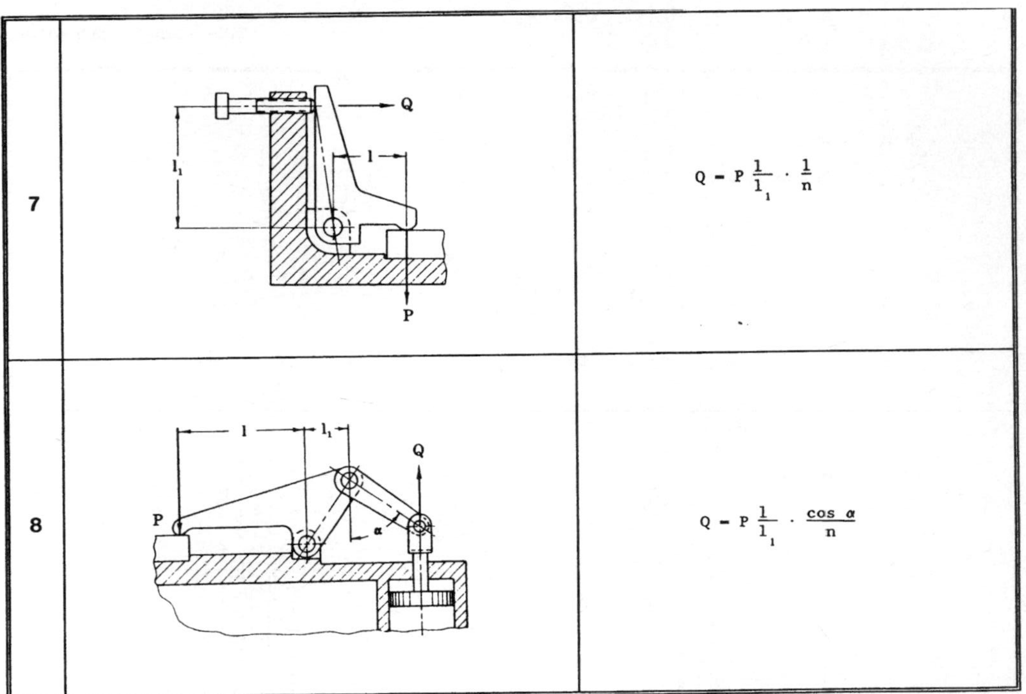

Figure 9.49 *(Continued)*

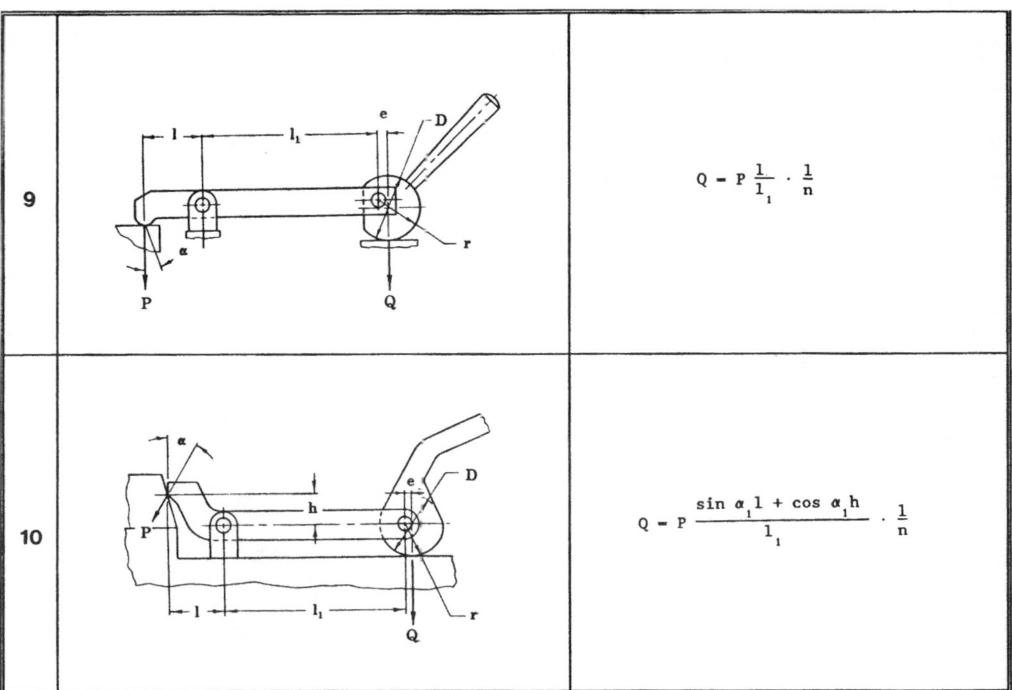

9	$Q = P \frac{l}{l_1} \cdot \frac{1}{n}$
10	$Q = P \frac{\sin \alpha_1 l + \cos \alpha_1 h}{l_1} \cdot \frac{1}{n}$

Figure 9.49 *(Continued)*

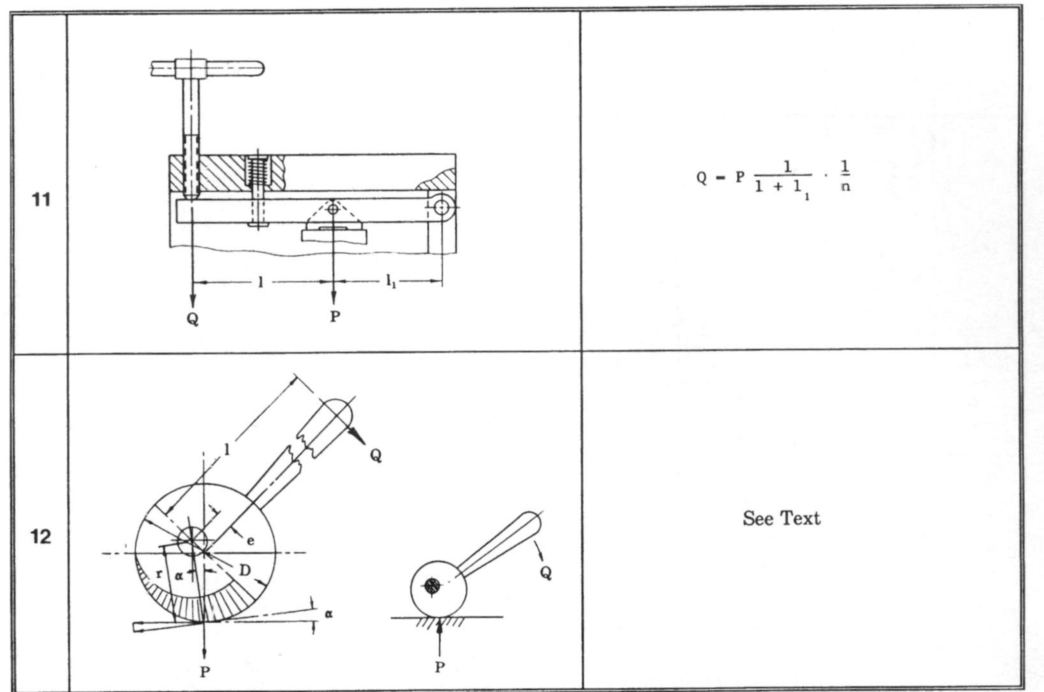

NOTE: f_o = coefficient of friction (axels and pivot pins) = 0.1 to 0.15 ; f = coefficient of friction of clamped surface = tan ϕ ; ϕ_1 = arctan f ; n = efficiency coefficient, 0.98 to 0.84, (determined by frictional losses in pivots and bearings, 0.98 for the best bearings through 0.84 for no bearings, (in order to avoid the use of complex, lengthy equations, the value of "n" can be taken as a mean between the limits shown) ; q = spring resistance or force, pounds or Newtons, (lbf or N).

Figure 9.49 *(Continued)*

forces. The eccentric clamp usually develops clamping forces that are 10 to 15 times higher than the force applied to the handle.

The ratio of the handle length to the eccentric radius normally does not exceed 5 to 6, while for a swinging clamp or strap clamp (threaded clamps), the ratio of the handle length to the thread pitch diameter is 12 to 15. The round eccentrics are relatively cheap and have a wide range of applications in tooling.

The angle α in Fig. 9.49, type 12, is the rising angle of the round eccentric clamp. Because this angle changes with rotation of the eccentric, the clamping force is not proportional at all handle rotation angles. The clamping stroke of the round eccentric at 90° of its handle rotation equals the roller eccentricity *e*. The machining allowance for the clamped part or blank x must be less than the eccentricity *e*. To provide secure clamping, eccentricity $e \geq$ x to 1.5x is suggested.

The round eccentric clamp is supposed to have a self-holding characteristic to prevent loosening in operation. This property is gained by choosing the correct ratio of the roller diameter *D* to the eccentricity *e*. The holding ability depends on the coefficient of static friction. In design practice, the coefficient of friction *f* would normally be 0.1 to 0.15, and the self-holding quality is maintained when *f* exceeds tan α.

The equation for determining the clamping force P is

$$P = Ql \frac{l}{[\tan(\alpha + \phi_1) + \tan\phi_2]r}$$

Then the necessary handle torque ($M = Pl$) is

$$M = P[\tan(\alpha + \phi_1) + \tan\phi_2]r$$

where r = distance from pivot point to contact point of the eccentric and the machined part surface, in or mm

α = rotation angle of the eccentric at clamping (reference only)

$\tan\phi_1$ = friction coefficient at the clamping point

$\tan\phi_2$ = friction coefficient in the pivot axle

l = handle length, in or mm

Q = force applied to handle, lbf or Newtons

D = diameter of eccentric blank or disc, in or mm

P = clamping force, lbf or Newtons

Note: $\tan(\alpha + \phi_1) \approx 0.2$ and $\tan\phi_2 \approx 0.05$ in actual practice.

See Fig. 9.50 for listed clamping forces for the eccentric clamp shown in Fig. 9.49, type 12.

The cam lock. Another clamping device that may be used instead of the eccentric clamp is the standard cam lock. In this type of clamping device, the clamping action is more uniform than in the round eccentric, although it is more difficult to manufacture. A true camming action is produced with this type of clamping device. The method for producing the cam geometry is shown in Fig. 9.51. The layout shown is for a cam surface generated in 90° of rotation of the device, which is the general application. Note that the cam angle should not exceed 9° in order for the clamp to function properly and be self-holding. The cam wear surface should be hardened to approximately Rockwell C30 to C50, or according to the application and the hardness of the materials which are being clamped. The cam geometry may be developed using CAD, and the program for machining the cam lock may be loaded into the CNC of a wire EDM machine.

9.9 Molds

Tooling practice also includes the design and manufacture of various types of molds. Molds are made for casting metals and alloys and for injection and compression molding plastics. Injection molding is used for thermoplastics, while compression molding is used for the thermoset plastics. See Chap. 5, "Materials and Their Uses," and Chap. 18, "Castings, Moldings, Extrusions, and Powder-Metal Technology," for more information on the various casting alloys and plastics used in molding processes.

Figure 9.52 shows a typical machined form used to make the tooling epoxy mold to mold other types of epoxy plastics. Forms or master patterns such as that shown in Fig. 9.52 are normally made of 2024 or 7075 aluminum alloys, although other materials may be used. The high-quality aluminum alloys were used on this master pattern owing to their excellent strength and easy machinability. This particular master pattern was machined on a CNC machining center and assembled by a master die maker.

Figure 9.53 shows another master pattern used for making tooling epoxy molds. In this example, the pattern was produced on a CNC-controlled turning center using a program written by the tool engineering department. It should be noted that no additional fin-

D mm (inches)	Clamping Force, P (Newtons)						
	490	**735**	**980**	**1225**	**1470**	**1715**	**1960**
40 (1.58")	2.65	3.97	5.40	6.67	8.00	9.37	10.64
50 (1.98")	3.34	5.00	6.67	8.39	10.01	11.77	13.68
60 (2.36")	4.02	6.03	8.00	10.01	11.97	14.03	16.48
70 (2.76")	4.71	7.06	9.42	11.77	14.08	16.48	18.79

NOTE: Tabulated values are torques (Newton-meters).
To convert clamping forces in Newtons to pounds-force, multiply table values by 0.2248, (i.e. 1960 N = 1960 x 0.2248 = 441 lbf).
To convert tabulated torques in Newton-meters to pounds-feet, multiply values by 0.7376, (i.e. 18.79 N-m = 18.79 x 0.7376 = 13.9 lbs-ft).

Figure 9.50 Torque values for listed clamping forces—eccentric clamps (type 12, Fig. 9.49).

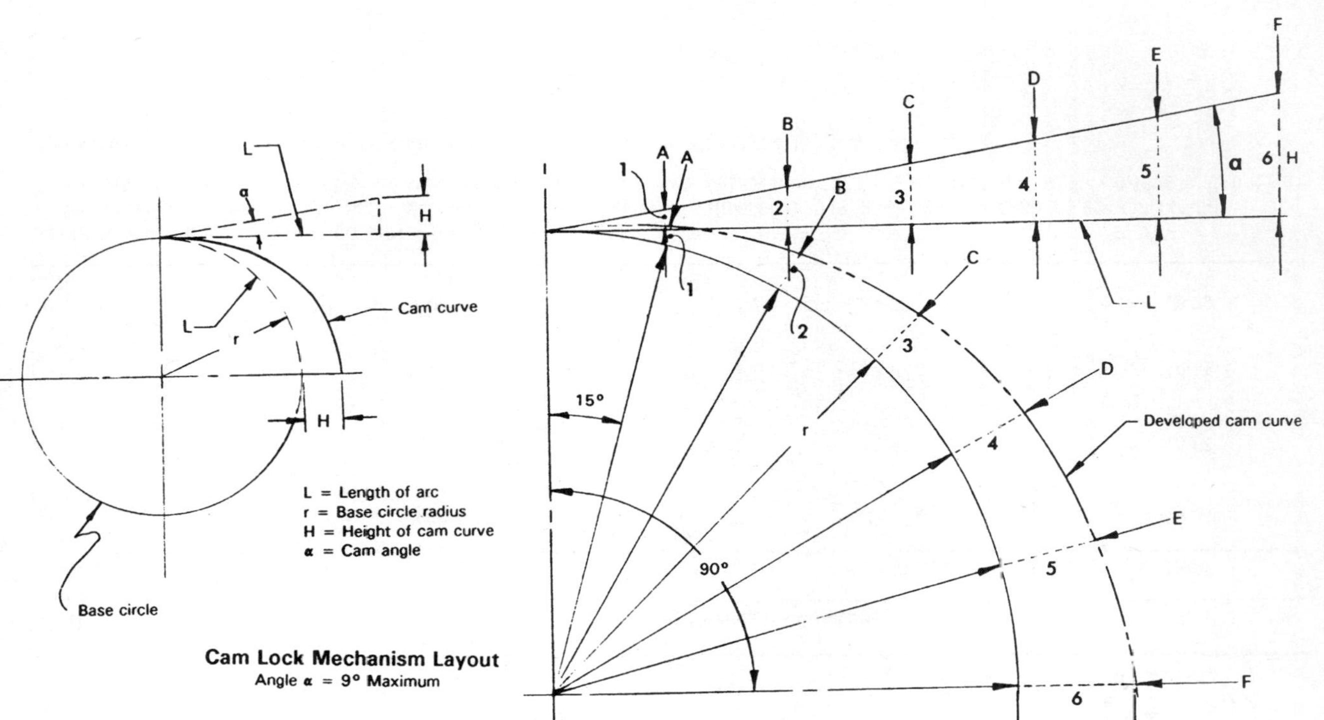

Figure 9.51 Determining cam geometry.

Figure 9.52 A mold form.

ishing was required on this master pattern. The extremely smooth and polished surfaces were produced with carbide cutting tools in a multiple-pass operation.

9.10 Force Gage for Tooling Applications

It is often necessary to know the pressures or forces actually required to operate specific types of tooling devices. This information is of benefit to the tool design engineer and master die maker. Strain gages and "load cells" are normally required to determine accurately the forces applied to various components in operation. A simple, inexpensive type of hydraulic force gage may be constructed by the die maker for this application. Figure 9.54 shows two hydraulic force gages with different ranges, as indicated on the dials of the gages.

To construct this type of force gage, the end of the piston must be exactly 1 in^2 in area. The detail parts for manufacturing such a gage are shown in Fig. 9.55. The force range of such a gage is

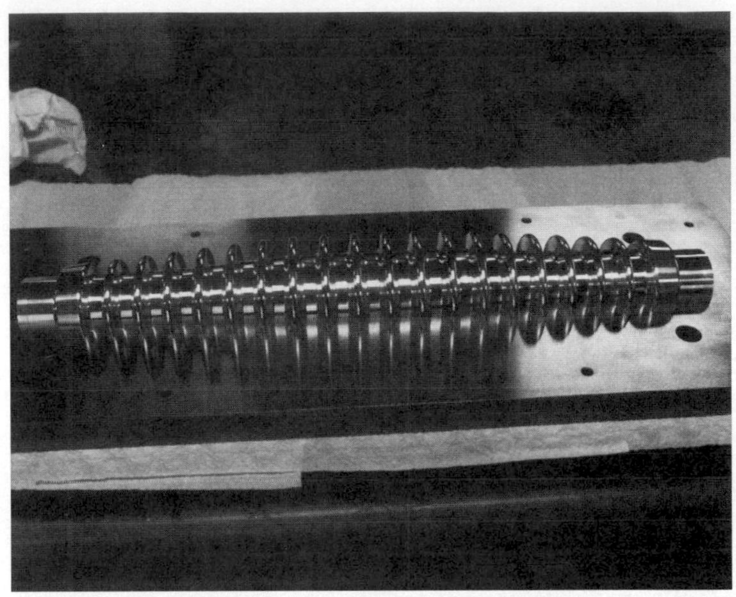

Figure 9.53 Master metal pattern for producing plastic molds.

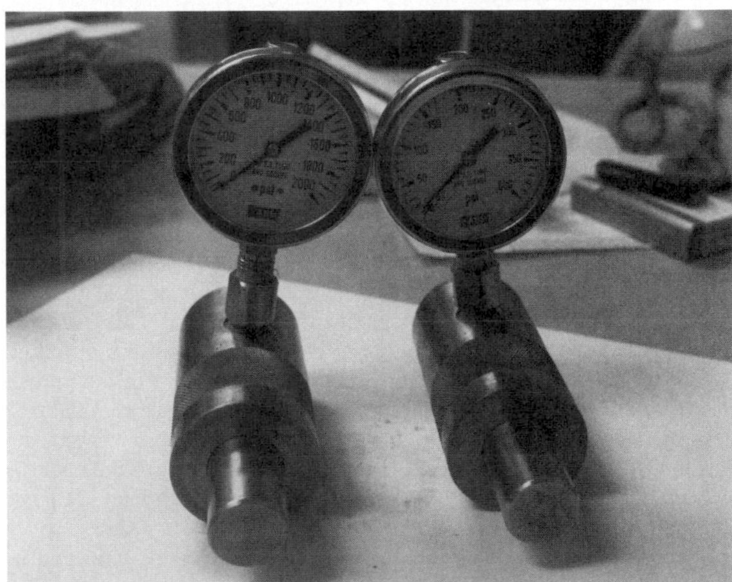

Figure 9.54 Two hydraulic force gages.

changed merely by changing the hydraulic gage, and the accuracy of this gage is limited by the accuracy of the hydraulic gage itself (normally ±3 to 5 percent). This simple gage has many applications in mechanical design, tool engineering, and die making.

9.11 The Five Major Rules of Die Making

Tooling practices and die making are exacting arts and sciences. The tool design engineer and tool and die maker require great skill, knowledge, and experience. Several designs may be possible for any particular tooling and die-making problem, but there is usu-

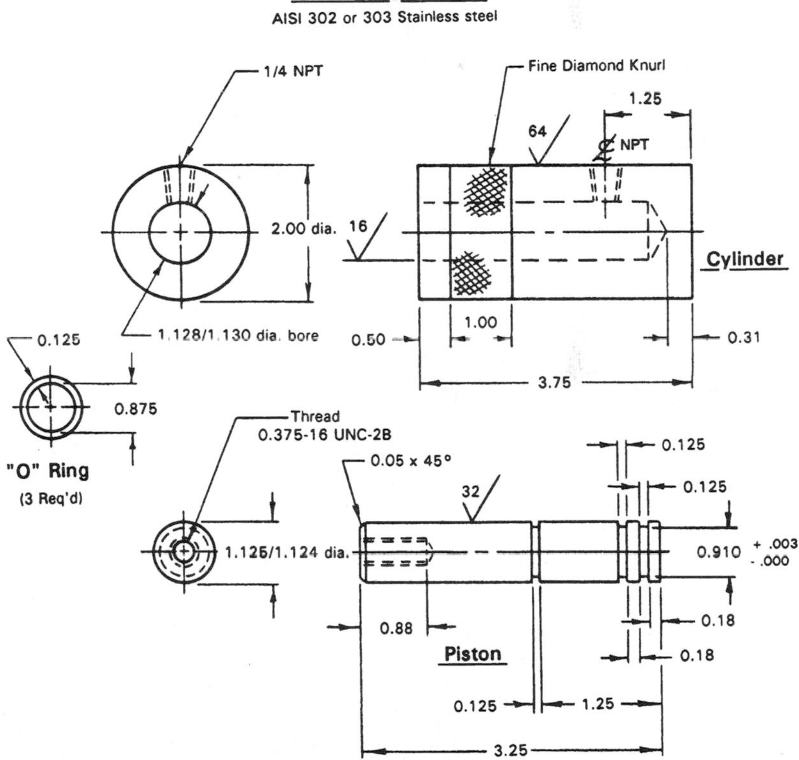

Figure 9.55 Detail of the gages shown in Fig. 9.54.

ally only one solution that is best for the given conditions and tooling objectives. With this in mind, the following five major tooling and die-making rules will help the new tool designer and die maker to achieve his or her goals:

1. Define the stamping or die-making problem correctly.
2. Select the design that is best for all conditions.
3. Permit the fabrication of the die parts without difficulty.
4. The finished parts of the die must be assembled easily by the die maker.
5. The tool or die must function well and solve the stamping, tool, or die problem exactly as intended.

Clean and precise working drawings of the die and all its parts must be produced by the tool engineering department, and the die maker must transform these drawings into an accurate, working die using the information provided by the tooling engineer and the die maker's own experience and skill.

The production of functional and accurate parts, through tooling, is the *beginning* of, and the most important part of, a sometimes long and complex process that determines the success of the finished product.

Chapter

10

Gears

Gears are used in most types of machinery and countless mechanisms throughout industry, including the automotive, scientific, and aerospace industries. Gears are a basic machine element and one of the basic simple machines, such as the lever, wheel and axle, inclined plane or wedge, and a few others. Gears have been in use by human beings for over 3000 years in one form or another. Figure 10.1*a* is a common spur gear section with the terminology of the various features listed. More detailed illustrations, equations, and explanations of the different gear types will be given in the following subsections.

The method used to manufacture a gear depends on machinery available, design specifications or requirements, cost of production, and type of material from which the gear is to be made. Some of the methods used for producing different types of gears are as follows:

- Low-load, low-speed gears—die stamping
- Small, low-cost gears—die casting of zinc, aluminum, or brass
- Small, low-load, precision gears—molded plastics such as acetal (Delrin), nylon (Zytel), and polycarbonate (Lexan)
- Medium to small, moderate-load, quiet-operation gears—phenolic fiber materials, machined
- Small, accurate metallic gears—extruded metal shapes that are cut off to size

- Small to medium, moderate- to high-load gears—powder-metal technology for producing iron or mild steel and stainless steel gears which are self-lubricating due to the porous nature of sintered powder-metal components, wherein the lubricant is infused into the gear material
- Accurate and high-load gears—for machine-tool uses, shaving and grinding of the gear teeth
- Control gears—usually made from medium-alloy, medium-carbon steels using shaving and/or grinding methods
- Automotive gears—usually cut from low-alloy steel forgings by hobbing, shaping, shaving, or grinding
- Aerospace power gears—usually made of high-alloy steel and fully hardened by case carburizing or nitriding
- General industrial gears—fully hardened steel or alloy-steel gears made by hobbing, shaving, planing, milling, or grinding, according to the application

Gear manufacturing methods. There are many methods for manufacturing gears, including hobbing, shaping, grinding, shaving, lapping, honing, broaching, die casting, cold forming, EDM cutting, laser cutting, powder metallurgy, molding, die stamping, water-jet cutting, milling, forging, rolling, fly cutting, and extruding.

10.1 Gears in Common Use and Manufacturing Methods

The types of gears in common use are shown in Fig. 10.1*b*. The method of manufacturing gears varies according to many parameters, including size of the gear, material, heat treatment, quantity to be produced, accuracy, tooth surface texture or finish, sound-producing characteristics, load-carrying capacity, speed of operation, and configuration. These parameters must be considered in selecting the most economical method or methods consistent with the desired end results. Some of the methods used to manufacture gears are illustrated in Fig. 10.2. A detailed description of each of the major gear production methods is given below.

Hobbing. Hobbing is the generation of a toothed gear by advancing a rack-profiled tool in relation to the rotation of the gear blank. The curve of the gear-tooth profile is developed by successive advancing positions of the rack teeth of the hobbing tool. The material of the gear is removed by a series of progressive rack-shaped cutting faces that are positioned around the tool as elements of a cylinder. The rack sections around the tool advance in a helical path so that the rotation of the tool about its axis provides the linear motion of the rack section with respect to the gear being cut (see Fig. 10.2*d*). The generation of the face width of the gear is accomplished by continuous rotation of the tool while it is advanced across the face of the gear. Hobbing can be used as either a roughing or finishing operation and is suited for the manufacture of large segments of the different types of gears produced such as spur, helical, and worm gears.

Shaping. Shaping of gear teeth is accomplished by using a circular form cutter with properly relieved teeth. The cutter rotates in timed relationship with the workpiece, while each stroke of the cutter produces a small portion of the tooth form or profile. Shaping can be used to produce many different types of gears, including internal and external gears of either the spur or helical types, racks, noncircular face gears, double helicals, and gear teeth that end close to a shoulder. Shaping can be used as a roughing or finishing operation (see Fig. 10.2*c* for the shaving motions).

Grinding. There are three different methods of grinding gears. In the first method, a continuously formed grinding wheel resembling a large-diameter worm is fed into the workpiece similar to the hobbing method. As the wheel is fed into the workpiece, it generates both sides of the tooth profile or form (see Fig. 10.2*g*). The second method uses a grinding wheel with the proper tooth-space form dressed on its perimeter. A gear tooth space is formed by the action of the grinding wheel turning on its own axis while traversing along the face of the gear in a reciprocating motion. The grinding wheel is fed progressively into the workpiece until full depth is obtained. In this process, the gear is indexed one tooth at a time (see Fig. 10.2*f*). In the third process, two disk-type grinding wheels are positioned so that their axes are perpendicular to the profiles of a rack tooth, and the working faces of the grinding wheels serve as the rack profiles. Involute tooth profiles are generated by three simultaneous motions of the grinding wheels.

Shaving. Shaving is a free-cutting machining process performed on a machine specially designed for this purpose. The shaving cutter is usually in the form of a precision quality gear with several grooves or slots from tip to root in the normal plane of the teeth. Each tooth of the cutter thus has multiple cutting edges. The helix angle of the cutter teeth is usually different from the helix angle of the workpiece (gear blank). During the shaving process, the workpiece and cutter are rotated in tight mesh, the cutter being the driving member. Variations of this basic process are used by various gear-shaving machines. Shaving is used most commonly for finishing external spur and helical gears, but it can be used for internal gears when the configuration and size allow for proper shaving cutter design. Gears to be finished by shaving may be produced by any of the usual gear-cutting processes (see Fig. 10.2*h*).

Milling. Milling of gears is accomplished by a form of milling cutter with a profile that matches that of a single space on the gear to be cut. The cutter travels axially across the gear blank, thus form cutting the adjacent tooth flanks or sides. The gear blank is indexed one tooth at a time with a device such as a universal dividing head until all teeth in the gear have been cut. External spur, helical, and bevel gears may be produced using this method (see Fig. 10.2*b*). Gear teeth also may be formed by special end mills with the proper profile, as shown in Fig. 10.2*a*.

Bevel gears also may be produced by the action shown in Fig. 10.2*e*, where a bevel gear is being cut by the action of reciprocating cutting tools.

10.2 Gear Action and Definitions

As an example, take two spur gears as a set, with a ratio of 4 to 3 (4:3). This means that the gear to pinion tooth ratio is 4 to 3. The smaller gear is called the *pinion*, and the larger is called the *gear*. The distance between the gear centerlines or shafts is called the *center distance*.

For the two spur gears to mesh properly, they must have the same tooth spacing. The *tooth spacing* is measured along the *pitch circle*, and the tooth spacing term *circular pitch* is defined as the circumference of the pitch circle divided by the number of teeth in the pinion or gear. The pitch circles of two meshed gears must be *tangent* (touching at one common point called the *pitch point*). The two-gear set will have the same circular pitch only if the ratio of the pitch-circle radii is the same as the tooth ratio. As such,

$$\frac{\text{Radius of gear pitch circle}}{\text{Radius of pinion pitch circle}} = \frac{\text{number of teeth in gear}}{\text{number of teeth in pinion}}$$

Dividing the pitch-circle circumference of a gear by the number of teeth in the gear determines the circular pitch.

To keep the angular velocity of the driven gear to the angular velocity of the driving gear constant, a tooth-form curve called the *involute* is normally used in gearing practice. The involute curve is well suited for designing and manufacturing gears because of the relative ease of generating and producing this curve on many machine tools using the methods outlined in the preceding section. Other tooth-form curves also will produce uniform angular velocity between meshed gears, but the involute-curve system is in common use for the reasons given above. When the gear tooth profiles are correct to produce uniform velocity between the driver and driven gears, the tooth profiles are said to be *conjugate.* See Secs. 2.1.4, "The Involute Function," 2.3, "Geometric Construction, and 3.5, "Involute Function Calculations."

Any line perpendicular to the involute tooth profile is called a *line of pressure* because it is in the direction of the force when the mating drive gear tooth is in contact at that point. All the lines of pressure for each involute gear tooth are *tangent* to the base circle. When the involute gear and pinion rotate together in proper mesh, their two lines of pressure through the point of contact always lie along the same line. This line is called the *line of action,* is tangent to both base circles, and contains the pitch point.

The *pressure angle* is defined as the angle at a pitch point between a line perpendicular to the involute tooth surface and a line tangent to the pitch circle. The pressure angle of an involute gear tooth is determined by the size ratio between the base circle and the pitch circle (see Fig. 10.3). Two common pressure angles used by the gear industry are 14.5 and 20°. The pressure angle is equal to the profile angle between the tangent to the involute profile and the radial line through the pitch point. The cosine of the pressure angle is equal to the ratio of the base-circle radius to the pitch-circle radius. When the base circle is chosen to be approximately 94 percent of the size of the pitch circle, the pressure angle becomes approximately 20° ($\cos 20° = 0.9397$). Many modern gears use a 20° pressure angle.

Dynamic loads imposed on gear teeth in actual operation must be accounted for in gear design procedures. Usually, an allowance is made for the effective dynamic load and then close controls are specified on gear tooth accuracy. Innacurate and poorly finished teeth and backlash account for peak dynamic loads on gear teeth during operation. Also, the gears should be operated above or below the resonance point, especially in spur gear systems. See Chap. 14,

"Power Transmission Systems and Components" (14.3, "Shafts"), for calculating the critical speeds of various shafts.

10.3 Pressure Angles and the Diametral Pitch System

Pressure angles. The two most common pressure angles used by many gear manufacturers are the 14.5 and 20°. The 20° pressure-angle gears are generally recognized as having a higher load-carrying capacity, but the 14.5° pressure-angle gears are less sensitive to backlash owing to center distance variations and are smoother and quieter in operation, provided that the teeth are not undercut.

Diametral pitch system. The *diametral pitch* of a gear is the number of teeth in the gear for each inch of pitch diameter. Therefore, the diametral pitch determines the size of the gear teeth on each particular gear. Figure 10.4 shows the various tooth dimensions for different diametral pitches of spur gears. Figure 10.5 is a full-scale representation of the various involute teeth of the 14.5 and 20° diametral pitch systems. This figure may be used to check the diametral pitch of a gear you wish to compare or measure.

Note: Spur and helical gears are normally made with involute teeth, and they are normally interchangeable, size for size. Involute profile gears are generally interchangeable, while noninvolute gears are not.

10.4 Ratios for the Various Gear Systems or Arrangements

The ratios that are possible using the various gear systems or forms are shown in Fig. 10.6, but the power-transmitting capacity of different gear arrangements is variable to a marked extent. It is difficult to determine the upper power limit of gear systems because of such variables as type of material, form of gear, size of equipment available to produce the proposed gear, life requirements, lubrication limits, etc.

10.5 Module Gear System (Metric Standard)

Because the metric (SI) system is used throughout the world, American gear manufacturers have been cutting metric gears using the

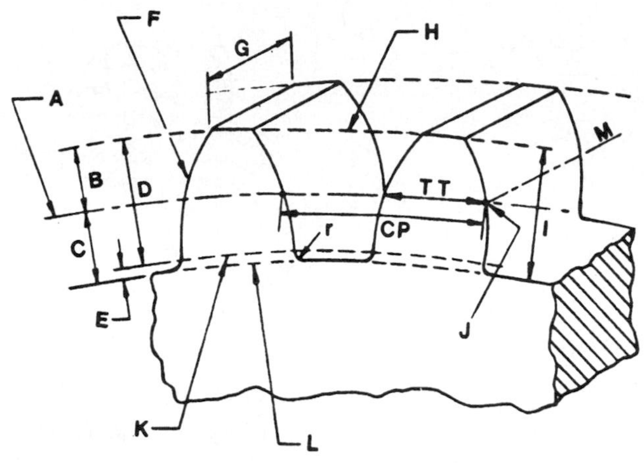

Spur Gear Terminology

A Pitch Circle
B Addendum
C Dedendum
D Working Depth
E Clearance
F Toothe Profile (involute)
G Face Width
H Addendum Circle (O.D. gear)
I Whole Depth
J Pitch Point
K Working Depth Circle
L Root or Dedendum Circle
CP Circular Pitch
M Line of Contact
TT Tooth Thickness

(a)

Parallel Axes	Intersecting Axes	Nonintersecting Nonparallel Axes
Spur, external	Straight bevel	Crossed-helical
Spur, internal	Zerol bevel	Single-enveloping worm
Helical, external	Spiral bevel	Double-enveloping worm
Helical, internal	Face gear	Hypoid
		Spiroid

(b)

Figure 10.1 (*a*) Spur gear terminology. (*b*) Common gear types.

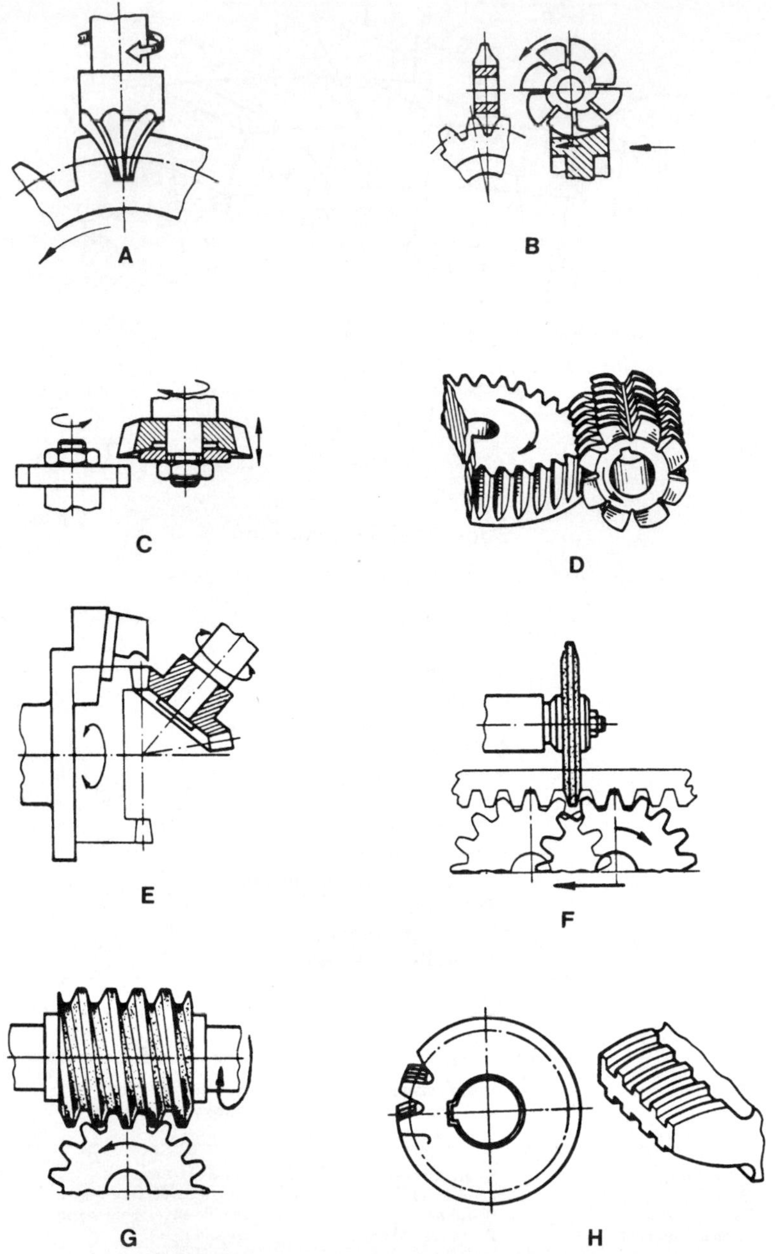

Figure 10.2 Methods of gear manufacture: (*a*) end milling, (*b*) side milling, (*c*) shaper cutting, (*d*) hobbing, (*e*) reciprocating cutting, (*f*) profile grinding, (*g*) helically profiled grinding, (*h*) shaving.

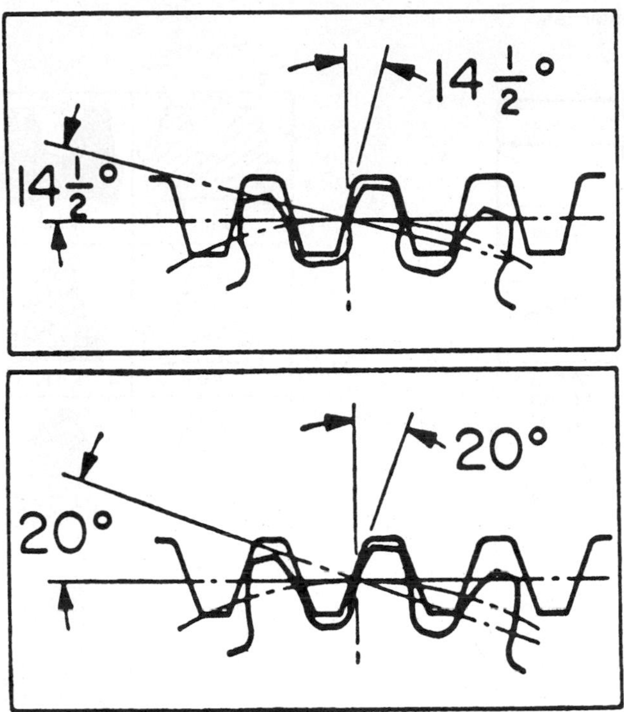

Figure 10.3 Two common pressure angles.

Diametral Pitch	Circular Pitch (Inches)	Thickness of Tooth on Pitch Line (Inches)	Depth to be Cut in Gear (Inches) (Hobbed Gears)	Addendum (Inches)
3	1.0472	.5236	.7190	.3333
4	.7854	.3927	.5393	.2500
5	.6283	.3142	.4314	.2000
6	.5236	.2618	.3565	.1667
8	.3927	.1963	.2696	.1250
10	.3142	.1571	.2157	.1000
12	.2618	.1309	.1798	.0833
16	.1963	.0982	.1348	.0625
20	.1571	.0785	.1120	.0500
24	.1309	.0654	.0937	.0417
32	.0982	.0491	.0708	.0312
48	.0654	.0327	.0478	.0208
64	.0491	.0245	.0364	.0156

Figure 10.4 Gear cutting table.

20°P.A.	14½°P.A.
64 D.P.	
48 D.P.	48 D.P.
32 D.P.	32 D.P.
24 D.P.	24 D.P.
20 D.P.	20 D.P.
16 D.P.	16 D.P.
12 D.P.	12 D.P.
10 D.P.	10 D.P.

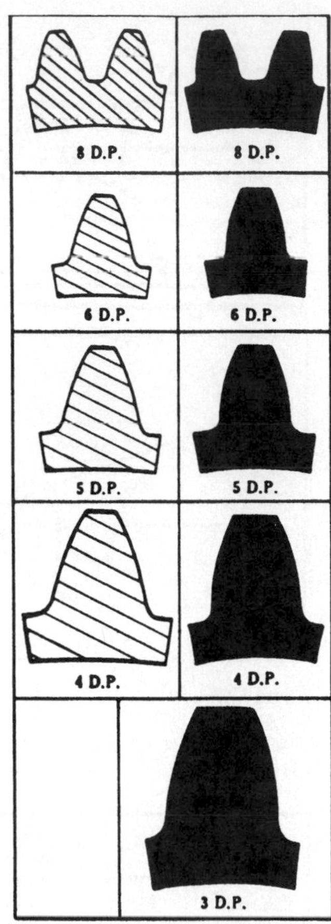

Figure 10.5 Full-scale gear teeth, comparison gage.

Arrangement Type	Min. No. of Toothed Parts	Ratio Range		
		5:1	50:1	100:1
Single Reduction:				
Spur	2	Yes	No	No
Helical	2	Yes	No	No
Bevel	2	Yes	No	No
Hypoid	2	Yes	Yes	Yes
Face	2	Yes	No	No
Worm	2	Yes	Yes	Yes
Spiroid	2	No	Yes	Yes
Planoid	2	Yes	No	No
Simple Planetary	3	Yes	No	No
Fixed Differential	5	No	Yes	Yes

Figure 10.6 Gear-ratio chart.

module system of measuring and producing gears for some years. *Module* is defined as the pitch diameter, in millimeters, divided by the number of teeth in the gear. The module is equal to the circular pitch in inches converted to millimeters times 0.3183. To find the outside diameter of a metric gear, add 2 to the number of teeth and multiply the sum by the module number (the diameter will be given in millimeters). Figure 10.7 shows the equivalents of diametral pitch, circular pitch, and module. Both the *diametral pitch* and the *module* are actually tooth-size dimensions that cannot be measured directly on a gear. Diametral pitch and module are reference values used to calculate other dimensions on a gear, the values of which can be measured with measuring tools and instruments.

The following relationships are true for all spur gears:

- Circular pitch = $\pi \times$ module (metric)
- Circular pitch = π/diametral pitch (U.S. Customary)
- Pitch diameter = number of teeth $\times$ module (metric)
- Pitch diameter = number of teeth/diametral pitch (U.S. Customary)

Equivalent DP, CP, and module.

Diametral pitch	Circular pitch	Module
¾	4.1888	33.8661
0.7854	4	32.3397
0.8467	3.7106	30
1	3.1415	25.3995
1.0160	3.0922	25
1.0472	3	24.2548
1¼	2.5133	20.3196
1.2700	2.4737	20
1.4111	2.2264	18
1½	2.0944	16.9330
1.5708	2	16.1698
1.5875	1.9790	16
1.6933	1.8553	15
1¾	1.7952	14.5140
1.8143	1.7316	14
1.9538	1.6079	13
2	1.5708	12.6998
2.0944	1½	12.1274
2.1166	1.4842	12
2¼	1.3963	11.2887
2.3090	1.3606	11
2½	1.2560	10.1598
2.5400	1.2369	10
2.8222	1.1132	9
3	1.0472	8.4665
3.1416	1	8.0849
3.1749	0.9895	8
3½	0.8976	7.2570
3.6285	0.8658	7
4	0.7854	6.3499
4.1888	¾	6.0637
4.2333	0.7421	6
5	0.6283	5.0799
5.0799	0.6184	5
6	0.5236	4.2333
6.2832	½	4.0425
6.3499	0.4947	4
8	0.3927	3.1749
8.4665	0.3711	3
10	0.3142	2.5400

Figure 10.7 Gear measurement systems.

Mathematically,

$$\text{Module} = \frac{25.400}{\text{diametral pitch}}$$

$$\text{Diametral pitch} = \frac{25.400}{\text{module}}$$

Gear types, geometries, measurements, and calculations. The following sections will detail all the commonly used gear forms or types with their individual geometries, measurements, and basic calculations which may be used to select the gear type and system required for your particular application. These sections on the various types of gears are intended for use by designers and machine shop personnel or machinists who wish to know the basic facts about the different gear types or systems. These sections are not intended for use in the production or manufacture of all the different types of gears owing to the many types of specialized machinery, complex procedures, and tooling required in the production of complex gears and gear systems.

The design and production of accurate and complex gears constitute a complex science as well as an art. Each different gear manufacturer uses different machinery, tooling, and specialized procedures to produce their gears.

We will therefore present only those aspects of gear design, processing, and calculations which are of interest and general need to the designer, machinist, and other personnel within the metalworking industries who are not gear design engineers and specialists in gearing systems. Gear design engineering texts are listed in the Bibliography for reference.

10.6 Spur Gears

Spur gears are the most common gears found in industry. They are manufactured in both external and internal forms, the external form being the most widely used. Simple and complex forms of planetary (epicyclic) gearing use the internal and external forms of the spur gear in different combinations. Helical gears are also used in epicyclic gear systems.

Refer to Fig. 10.8 for the complete terminology for external spur gears. The pitch diameter for the tooth-cutting operation on a spur

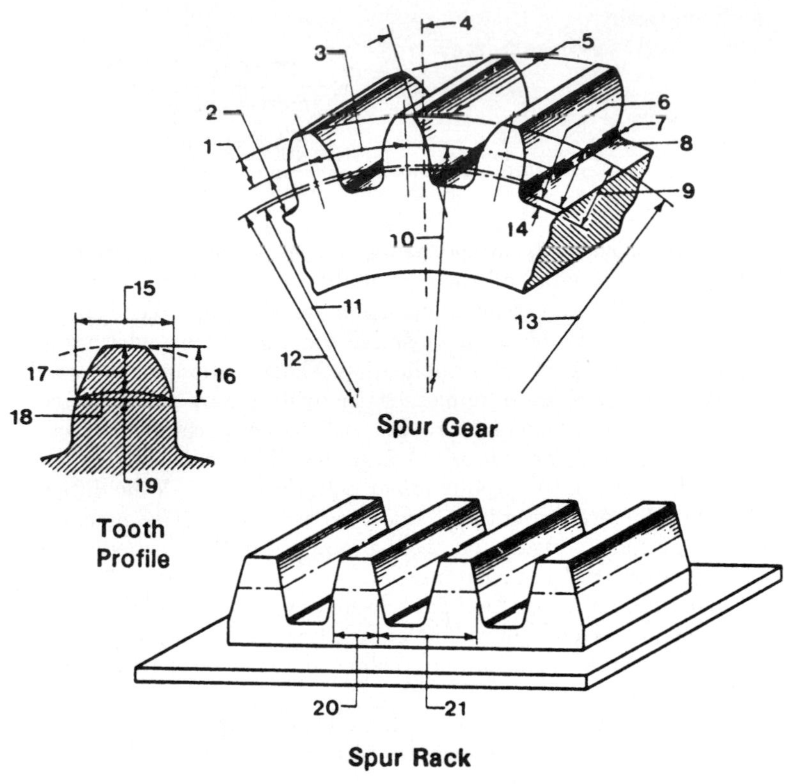

Spur Gear Terminology

1 Addendum
2 Dedendum
3 Circular pitch
4 Pressure angle (PA)
5 Face width
6 Addendum of mating gear
7 Tooth fillet
8 Working depth
9 Whole depth
10 Pitch diameter
11 Base circle diameter
12 Form diameter
13 Outside diameter
14 Clearance
15 Chordal thickness
16 Chordal addendum
17 Addendum
18 Arc thickness
19 Rise of arc
20 Tooth thickness
21 Circular pitch

Figure 10.8 Spur gear, external.

gear is given in the preceding section. In a spur gear system, the operating pitch diameter is

$$\text{Pitch diameter (operating) of pinion} = \frac{2 \times \text{operating center distance}}{\text{ratio} + 1}$$

$$\text{Pitch diameter of gear} = \text{ratio} \times \text{pitch diameter (operating) of pinion}$$

The ratio is

$$\text{Ratio} = \frac{\text{number of teeth in gear}}{\text{number of teeth in pinion}}$$

Spur gear formulas for full-depth involute teeth (see Fig. 10.9). All the basic dimensions for standard spur gears may be calculated and then specified by using the equations shown in Fig. 10.9. Of interest to the designer who specifies the gear dimensions are the basic equations used to determine the tooth loads on the gears, both static and dynamic. Gear failure can occur as a result of tooth breakage or surface failure in operation. An important equation for calculating the tooth loads on spur gears is the Barth revision of the Lewis equation, which considers beam strength but not wear. The minimum load for wear on gear teeth is shown in a later subsection, where the K factor for determining the limiting load may be calculated when the physical properties of the gear material are accurately known.

Lewis equation (Barth revision). For metallic spur gears, the modified Lewis equation is

$$W = \frac{SFY}{P}\left(\frac{600}{600 + V}\right)$$

where W = tooth load, lb (along the pitch line)
S = safe material stress allowable (static), psi (see Fig. 10.10)
F = face width, in
Y = tooth-form factor (see Fig. 10.11)
P = diametral pitch (dimensionless quantity)
D = pitch diameter, in
V = pitch-line velocity, ft/min = $0.262 \times PD \times$ rpm (the equation for W is valid for pitch-line velocities to 1500 ft/min)

SPUR GEAR FORMULAS

FOR FULL DEPTH INVOLUTE TEETH

To Obtain	Having	Formula
Diametral Pitch (P)	Circular Pitch (p)	$P = \frac{3.1416}{p}$
	Number of Teeth (N) & Pitch Diameter (D)	$P = \frac{N}{D}$
	Number of Teeth (N) & Outside Diameter (D_o)	$P = \frac{N + 2}{D_o}$ (Approximate)
Circular Pitch (p)	Diametral Pitch (P)	$p = \frac{3.1416}{P}$
Pitch Diameter (D)	Number of Teeth (N) & Diametral Pitch (P)	$D = \frac{N}{P}$
	Outside Diameter (D) & Diametral Pitch (P)	$D = D_o - \frac{2}{P}$
Base Diameter (D_b)	Pitch Diameter And Pressure Angle	$D_b = D\cos\phi$
Number of Teeth (N)	Diametral Pitch (P) & Pitch Diameter (D)	$N = P \times D$
Tooth Thickness (t) @Pitch Diameter (D)	Diametral Pitch (P)	$t = \frac{1.5708}{P}$
Addendum (a)	Diametral Pitch (P)	$a = \frac{1}{P}$
Outside Diameter (D_o)	Pitch Diameter (D) & Addendum (a)	$D_o = D + 2a$
Whole Depth (h_t) (20P & Finer)	Diametral Pitch (P)	$h_t = \frac{2.2}{P} + .002$
Whole Depth (h_t) (Coarser than 20P)	Diametral Pitch (P)	$h_t = \frac{2.157}{P}$
Working Depth (h_K)	Addendum	$h_K = 2(a)$
Clearance (c)	Whole Depth (h_t) Addendum (a)	$c = h_t - 2a$
Dedendum (b)	Whole Depth (h_t) & Addendum (a)	$b = h_t - a$
Contact Ratio (M_c)	Outside Radii, Base Radii, Center Distance and Pressure Angle	$M_c = \frac{\sqrt{R_o^2 - R_b^2} + \sqrt{r_o^2 - r_b^2} - C\sin\phi}{P\cos\phi}$ *
Root Diameter (D_r)	Pitch Diameter and Dedendum	$D_r = D - 2b$
Center Distance (C)	Pitch Diameter or No. of Teeth and Pitch	$C = \frac{D_1 + D_2}{2}$ or $\frac{N_1 + N_2}{2P}$

* R_O = Outside Radius, Gear
r_O = Outside Radius, Pinion
R_b = Base Circle Radius, Gear
r_b = Base Circle Radius, Pinion

Figure 10.9 Spur gear equations.

Values of Safe Static Stress (S), psi

Material		(s) Lb. per Sq. In.
Plastic		5000
Bronze		10000
Cast Iron		12000
Steel	.20 Carbon (Untreated)	20000
	.20 Carbon (Case-hardened)	25000
	.40 Carbon (Untreated)	25000
	.40 Carbon (Heat-treated)	30000
	.40 C. Alloy (Heat-treated)	40000

Figure 10.10 Safe static stress.

Number of Teeth	14½° Full Depth Involute	20° Full Depth Involute
10	0.176	0.201
11	0.192	0.226
12	0.210	0.245
13	0.223	0.264
14	0.236	0.276
15	0.245	0.289
16	0.255	0.295
17	0.264	0.302
18	0.270	0.308
19	0.277	0.314
20	0.283	0.320
22	0.292	0.330
24	0.302	0.337
26	0.308	0.344
28	0.314	0.352
30	0.318	0.358
32	0.322	0.364
34	0.325	0.370
36	0.329	0.377
38	0.332	0.383
40	0.336	0.389
45	0.340	0.399
50	0.346	0.408
55	0.352	0.415
60	0.355	0.421
65	0.358	0.425
70	0.360	0.429
75	0.361	0.433
80	0.363	0.436
90	0.366	0.442
100	0.368	0.446
150	0.375	0.458
200	0.378	0.463
300	0.382	0.471
Rack	0.390	0.484

Figure 10.11 *Y* factors, spur gears.

For nonmetallic spur gears,

$$W = \frac{SFY}{P}\left(\frac{150}{200 + V} + 0.25\right)$$

Note: S values of 6000 psi and above may be used for phenolic gears, and 5000 psi may be used for some of the thermoset types of plastics commonly used for molding gears. S is the safe static stress allowable, the values of which have a safety factor incorporated (see Fig. 10.10). Also see Sec. 10.14, "Gear Materials and Hardness Ranges."

Most stock spur gears are cut to operate at a standard center distance, which was defined previously. Figure 10.12*a* lists the average *backlash* when the spur gears are mounted at the calculated center distance. Alterations in the calculated center distance will occur during manufacturing processes, and these, in turn, alter the backlash. The approximate relationship between center distance and backlash change for 14.5 and 20° pressure-angle gears can be calculated as follows:

- For 14.5°, change in center distance = 1.933 × change in backlash, i.e., change in backlash = change in center distance/1.933.
- For 20°, change in center distance = 1.374 × change in backlash, i.e., change in backlash = change in center distance/1.374.

Thus it is apparent that 14.5° PA (pressure-angle) gears will have a smaller change in backlash than 20° PA gears for a given change in the center distance.

Spur gear milling cutters. Spur gears may be cut on a milling machine or a CNC machining center using the appropriate milling cutter, which has an involute profile. These cutters are available in 14.5° and 20° pressure angles and come in different diametral pitch sizes and a cutter series (from 1 to 8) for the number of teeth required in the particular gear. Diametral pitch sizes are available from 1 through 48, with 8 cutters available in each diametral pitch for cutting spur gears with different numbers of teeth. Therefore, more than 400 cutters are available to cover all standard sizes of spur gears from the largest to the smallest. The machine tool catalogs list the cutters with their diametral pitches and series number so that you may select the proper cutter for your application. Figure 10.12*b* shows a typical spur gear milling cutter.

The individual cutters for each diametral pitch have the following teeth-cutting ranges:

Cutter 1: 135 teeth to a rack

Cutter 2: 55 teeth to 134 teeth

Cutter 3: 35 teeth to 54 teeth

Cutter 4: 26 teeth to 34 teeth

Cutter 5: 21 teeth to 25 teeth

Cutter 6: 17 teeth to 20 teeth

Cutter 7: 14 teeth to 16 teeth

Cutter 8: 12 teeth to 13 teeth

Figure 10.2*b* shows a spur gear milling cutter in operation, where the cutter axis is at right angles to the axis of the spur gear being cut.

Undercut. When the number of teeth in a gear is small, the tip of the mating gear tooth may interfere with the lower portion of the tooth profile. To prevent this, the generating process removes material at this point. This results in loss of a portion of the involute adjacent to the tooth base, reducing tooth contact and tooth strength.

Undercutting occurs during tooth generation on 14.5° PA gears when the number of teeth is less than 32 and on 20° PA gears when the number of teeth is less than 18. This condition becomes worse as the number of teeth decreases, so it is recommended that the minimum number of teeth be 16 for 14.5° PA and 13 for 20° PA spur gears. See Fig. 10.13 for a typical spur rack or gear and Fig. 10.8 for spur gear terminology.

In a similar manner, *internal* spur gear teeth may interfere when the pinion gear is too near the size of the mating internal gear. Therefore, for 14.5° PA gears, the difference in teeth number between the gear and pinion should not be less than 15. For 20° PA, the difference in teeth number should not be less than 12. See Fig. 10.15 for internal spur gear terminology.

Stem pinions. When a spur stem pinion is required to have a small number of teeth (5 to 10), undercutting of the teeth is minimized by using special enlarged pitch diameters. A spur stem pinion with a small number of teeth allows high ratios to be obtained, which are not normally available in standard spur gear sets. These special spur stem pinions are not intended for operation with internal spur gears or 11-tooth pinions, but they will operate satisfactorily with all other standard spur gears of the same pressure angle. See Fig. 10.14 for a typical spur stem pinion with special enlarged pitch diameter.

10.7 Internal Gears

An external spur or helical gear may be meshed with an internal spur or helical gear, respectively. The external gear must not be larger than 66 to 67 percent of the pitch diameter of the internal gear. If the internal gear is to have 88 teeth, the external gear should have $0.66 \times 88 = 58$ teeth maximum (see the preceding subsection on "Undercut"). This generalization is not valid on epicyclic gear systems (planetary gears).

An internal gear is necessary for epicyclic gear systems, and the short center distances afforded are beneficial to compact gear systems where space is limited (see Sec. 10.17, "Epicyclic Gears"). Internal gears cannot be hobbed normally, but they can be shaped, milled, cast, or broached (size permitting). Figure 10.15 shows the basic terminology used for internal spur gears.

All the simple equations used for external spur gears apply to internal spur gears, except those which apply to center distance. The equations for internal spur gear center distance are

$$\text{Center distance} = \frac{\text{pitch diameter of gear} - \text{pitch diameter of pinion}}{2}$$

$$\text{Pitch diameter (operating) of pinion} = \frac{2 \times \text{operating center distance}}{\text{ratio} - 1}$$

$$\text{Pitch diameter (operating) of gear} = \frac{2 \times \text{operating center distance} \times \text{ratio}}{\text{ratio} - 1}$$

10.8 Helical Gears

Helical gears are used to transmit power or motion and force between shafts that are parallel. When helical gears are used in the parallel-shaft arrangement, they must be opposite hand one from each other; that is, if a left-hand pinion is used, a right-hand gear must be selected, and if a right-hand pinion is used, a left-hand gear must be selected.

Single helical gear sets impose both thrust and radial loads on their support bearings. Helical gear teeth are normally made with an involute profile in the *transverse* plane (the transverse plane is a cross-sectional plane that is perpendicular to the gear axis). Small changes in center distance do not affect the action of helical gear sets. Helical gears may be made by hobbing, milling, shaping, or casting, with powder-metal technology occasionally applied successfully. Finishing is accomplished by grinding, shaving, lapping, rolling, or burnishing.

The size of helical gear teeth may be specified by module for the metric system or by diametral pitch (DP) for the U.S. Customary system. Helical gears can be hobbed with standard spur gear hobs. Helical gears are mainly produced with a 20° pressure angle, although pressure angles of 22.5 and 25° are also used for higher load-transmitting capabilities.

Figure 10.16 shows the terminology of a helical gear and rack. In the transverse plane, the elements of a helical gear are the same as those of a spur gear. The equations for helical gear calculations are shown in Fig. 10.17. Additional helical gear relational equations are

Normal circular pitch = circular pitch × cosine helix angle

Normal module = transverse module × cosine helix angle

Normal diametral pitch = transverse diametral pitch/cosine helix angle

Axial pitch = circular pitch/tangent helix angle

Axial pitch = normal circular pitch/sine helix angle

Figure 10.18 shows the relationship between transverse diametral pitch and normal diametral pitch for 45° helix angle helical gears. Figure 10.19 illustrates the helix angle, normal and axial planes, and axial circular pitch p and normal circular pitch p_n.

An important equation for calculating the tooth loads on helical gears operating on parallel shafts is the Lewis equation modified to compensate for the difference between spur and helical gears with modified tooth-form factors Y, as shown in Fig. 10.20.

(*Text continued on page 873.*)

Diametral Pitch	Backlash (Inches)	Diametral Pitch	Backlash (Inches)
3	.013	8-9	.005
4	.010	10-13	.004
5	.008	14-32	.003
6	.007	33-64	.0025
7	.006		

(a)

(b)

Figure 10.12 (*a*) Spur gear backlash. (*b*) Spur gear milling cutter.

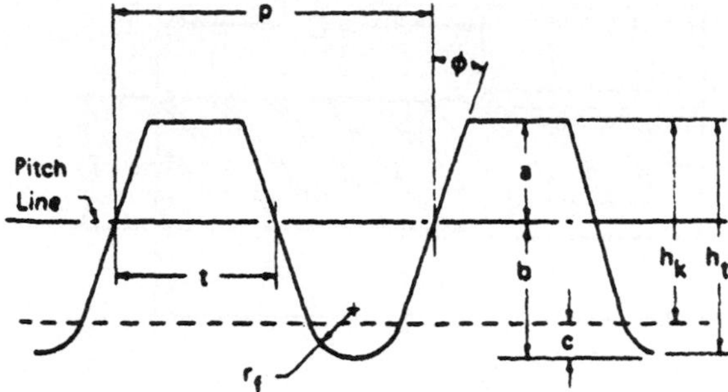

a Addendum
b Dedendum
c Clearance
h_k Working Depth
h_t Whole Depth
p Circular Pitch
r_f Fillet Radius
t Circular Tooth Thickness
ϕ Pressure Angle

Figure 10.13 Spur rack or gear teeth.

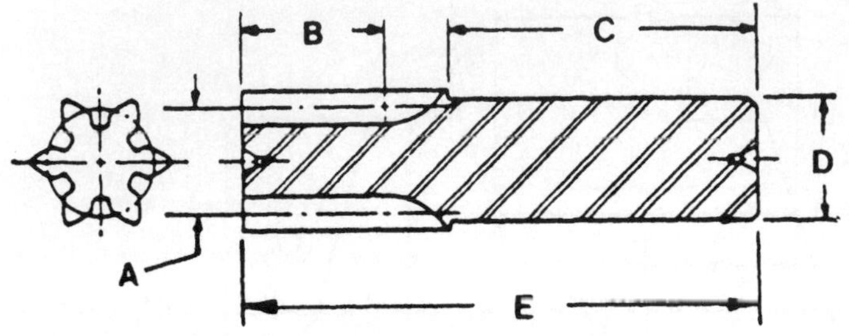

A Pitch Diameter (special)
B Face
C Stem Length
D Stem Diameter
E Overall Length

Figure 10.14 Spur stem pinion.

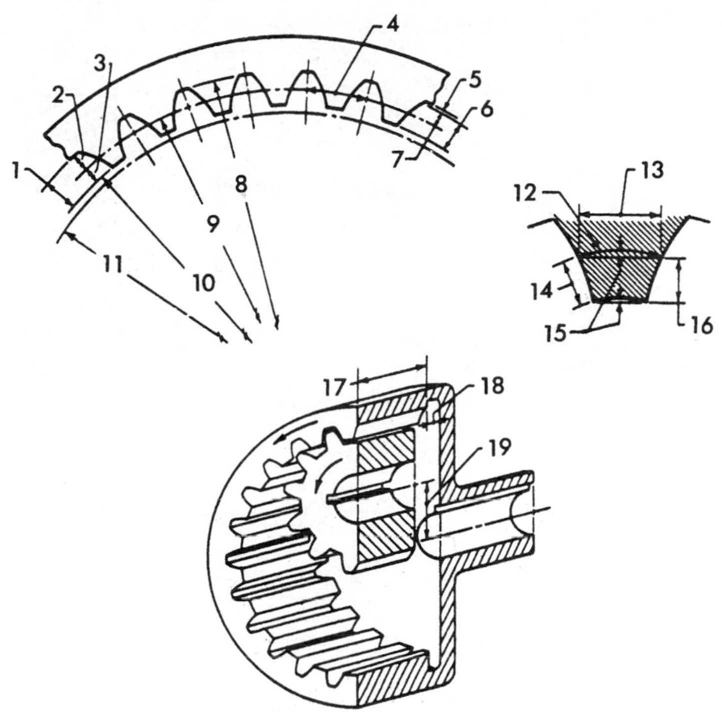

1	Whole depth	11	Base circle diameter
2	Dedendum	12	Arc thickness
3	Addendum	13	Chordal thickness
4	Circular pitch	14	Addendum
5	Clearance	15	Rise of arc
6	Working depth	16	Chordal addendum
7	Addendum of mating gear	17	Width of face
8	Root diameter	18	Cutter clearance
9	Pitch diameter	19	Center distance
10	Inside diameter		

Figure 10.15 Internal gear and pinion terminology.

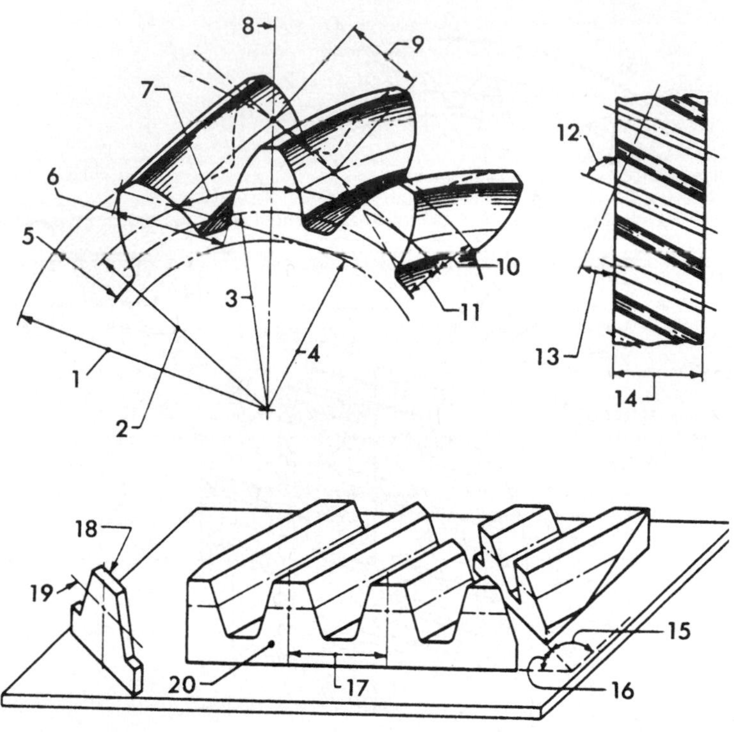

1 Outside diameter
2 Pitch diameter
3 Form diameter
4 Base circle diameter
5 Whole depth
6 Base pitch or normal pitch
7 Transverse circular pitch
8 Axis of gear
9 Normal circular pitch
10 Addendum
11 Dedendum
12 Lead angle
13 Helix angle
14 Face width
15 Lead angle
16 Helix angle
17 Circular pitch
18 Normal plane
19 Normal pitch line
20 Front plane

Figure 10.16 Helical gear and rack terminology.

To Obtain	Having	Formula
Transverse Diametral Pitch (P)	Number of Teeth (N) & Pitch Diameter (D)	$P = \frac{N}{D}$
	Normal Diametral Pitch (P_n) Helix Angle (ψ)	$P = P_N \text{Cos}\psi$
Pitch Diameter (D)	Number of Teeth (N) & Transverse Diametral Pitch (p)	$D = \frac{N}{P}$
Normal Diametral Pitch (P_N)	Transverse Diametral Pitch (P) & Helix Angle (ψ)	$P_N = \frac{P}{\text{Cos}\psi}$
Normal Circular Tooth Thickness (τ)	Normal Diametral Pitch (P_N)	$\tau = \frac{1.5708}{P_N}$
Transverse Circular Pitch (p_t)	Diametral Pitch (P) (Transverse)	$p_t = \frac{\pi}{P}$
Normal Circular Pitch (p_n)	Transverse Circular Pitch (p)	$p_n = p_t \text{Cos}\psi$
Lead (L)	Pitch Diameter and Pitch Helix Angle	$L = \frac{\pi D}{\text{Tan}\psi}$

Figure 10.17 Helical gear equations.

P Transverse Diametral Pitch	P_N Normal Diametral Pitch
24	33.94
20	28.28
16	22.63
12	16.97
10	14.14
8	11.31
6	8.48

Relationship of Pitches for 45° Helix Angle

Example:

Normal P_N = P/cos 45°

= 24/0.707

= 33.94

Figure 10.18 Transverse and normal diametral pitch relations.

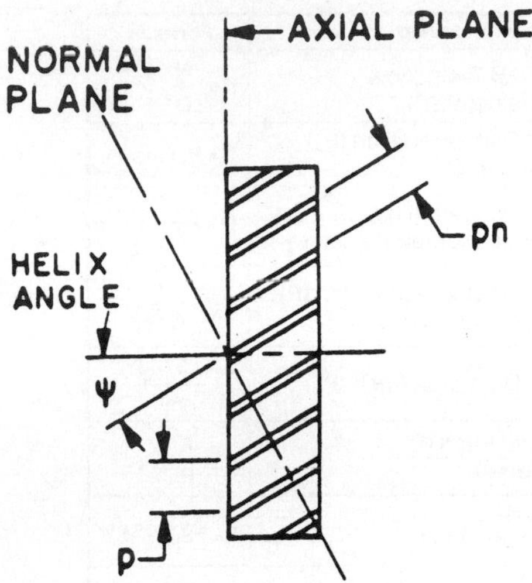

Figure 10.19 Axial and normal circular pitch.

VALUES OF TOOTH FORM FACTOR (Y)

FOR 14½° P.A. – 45° HELIX ANGLE GEAR			
No. of Teeth	Factor Y	No. of Teeth	Factor Y
8	.295	25	.361
9	.305	30	.364
10	.314	32	.365
12	.327	36	.367
15	.339	40	.370
16	.342	48	.372
18	.345	50	.373
20	.352	60	.374
24	.358	72	.377

Figure 10.20 Tooth-form factors for helical gears.

Lewis equation for helical gears (modified)

$$W = \frac{SFY}{P_N}\left(\frac{600}{600 + V}\right)$$

where W = tooth load, lb (along pitch line)
S = safe material stress (static), psi (see Fig. 10.21)
F = face width, in
Y = tooth-form factor (see Fig. 10.20)
P_N = normal diametral pitch (see Fig. 10.18)
D = pitch diameter, in
V = Pitch-line velocity, ft/min = $0.262 \times D \times$ rpm

The data contained in Sec. 10.6, "Spur Gears," also pertain to helical gears which are cut to the diametral pitch system. The helix angle ψ is the angle between any helix and an element of its cylinder. In helical gears, it is at the pitch diameter unless otherwise specified. The helical tooth form is normally involute in the plane of rotation and can be developed in a manner similar to that of the spur gear. The lead L is the axial advance of a helix for one complete turn of 360°. The normal diametral pitch P_N is the diametral pitch as calculated in the normal plane.

Note: Helical gears of the same hand operate with their axes at right angles, while helical gears of opposite hand operate with their axes parallel.

When helical gears are operated with their axes at right angles, the tooth load is concentrated at a point, with the result that small loads produce very high pressures. The tooth load that may be applied to these types of drives is limited to a large degree.

As a result of the design of the helical gear tooth, an axial or thrust load is developed which must be absorbed by the use of proper bearings at the appropriate ends of the gears (see Fig. 10.22 for location of thrust bearings for the various helical gear arrangements). The magnitude of the thrust load is based on the horsepower to be transmitted and may be calculated from

$$\text{Axial thrust load (lb)} = \frac{126{,}050 \times \text{hp}}{\text{rpm} \times \text{pitch diameter}}$$

Helical gears with a helix angle of 45°, which is common, produce a tangential force equal in magnitude to the axial thrust load. A separating force is also developed in the gear set which is also based on the calculated horsepower as follows:

$$\text{Separating force (lb)} = \text{axial thrust load (lb)} \times 0.26$$

Note: The preceding equations are based on a helix angle of 45° and a normal pressure angle of 14.5° (common in most helical gears).

Helical gear systems have advantages over or offer the following benefits relative to spur gear systems:

- Improved tooth strength
- Increased contact ratio due to axial tooth overlap
- Greater load-carrying capacity, size for size
- Smoother and quieter operating characteristics

A typical helical gear set is shown in Fig. 10.22*b*.

10.9 Straight Miter and Bevel Gears

Bevel gear teeth are tapered in both tooth thickness and tooth height. At one end the tooth is large, while at the other end it is small. The actual tooth dimension is usually specified for the large end of the tooth, which is at the far end of the gear-set intersection, away from the pitch apex (see Fig. 10.23*a*). Most straight-tooth bevel and miter gears are cut with a generated tooth form having a localized lengthwise tooth bearing known as the *coniflex* tooth form. The localization of tooth contact permits minor adjustment of the gears at assembly and allows for some displacement due to deflection under operating loads without concentration of the load at the end of the tooth. The coniflex system results in an increase in gear life and quieter operation.

Most miter and bevel gears are mounted with their shaft axes at 90°, although other angles of intersection are used occasionally. Figure 10.23*a* shows the terminology of the miter and bevel gear set. A typical straight bevel gear set is shown in Fig. 10.23*b*.

Straight miter and bevel gear formulas (see Fig. 10.24). The tooth-load equations for straight miter and bevel gears are as follows:

Lewis equation (modified). For miter and bevel gears,

$$W = \frac{SFY}{P}\left(\frac{600}{600 + V}\right)0.75$$

where W = tooth load, lb (along the pitch line)
S = safe material stress (static), psi (see Fig. 10.25)
F = face width, in
Y = tooth-form factor (see Fig. 10.26)
P = diametral pitch (dimensionless quantity)
D = pitch diameter, in
V = pitch-line velocity, ft/min = $0.26 \times D \times$ rpm

The average backlash is given in Fig. 10.27 when the miter or bevel gear set is mounted at the exact mounting distance.

Thrust loads. The axial thrust loads developed by straight-tooth miter and bevel gears always tend to separate the gears according to the following equations:

$$\text{Gear thrust (lbf)} = \frac{126{,}050 \times \text{hp}}{\text{rpm} \times \text{pitch diameter}} \times \tan\alpha \cos\beta$$

$$\text{Pinion thrust (lbf)} = \frac{126{,}050 \times \text{hp}}{\text{rpm} \times \text{pitch diameter}} \times \tan\alpha \sin\beta$$

where α = tooth-pressure angle
β = ½ pitch angle (see Fig. 10.23)

Also, pitch angle is determined from

$$\text{Pitch angle (pinion)} = \arctan \frac{N_P}{N_G}$$

$$\text{Pitch angle (gear)} = 90° - \text{pitch angle of pinion}$$

The 20° pressure-angle straight miter and bevel gear is the most common and popular gear in present use. The correctly rated thrust bearings must be selected from the calculated loads using the preceding equations for thrust loads.

The circular pitch and the pitch diameters of miter and bevel gears are calculated in the same way as those for spur gears. The pitch-cone angles may be calculated using one of the following equations:

$$\tan \text{pitch angle (pinion)} = \frac{\text{number of teeth in pinion}}{\text{number of teeth in gear}}$$

$$\tan \text{pitch angle (gear)} = \frac{\text{number of teeth in gear}}{\text{number of teeth in pinion}}$$

When the shaft angle is less than 90°,

$$\text{tan pitch angle (pinion)} = \frac{\text{sin shaft angle}}{\text{ratio} + \text{cos shaft angle}}$$

$$\text{tan pitch angle (gear)} = \frac{\text{sin shaft angle}}{1/\text{ratio} + \text{cos shaft angle}}$$

When the shaft angle is more than 90°,

$$\text{tan pitch angle (pinion)} = \frac{\sin(180° - \text{shaft angle})}{\text{ratio} - \cos(180° - \text{shaft angle})}$$

$$\text{tan pitch angle (gear)} = \frac{\sin(180° - \text{shaft angle})}{1/\text{ratio} - \cos(180° - \text{shaft angle})}$$

In all cases,

$$\text{Pitch angle (pinion)} + \text{pitch angle (gear)} = \text{shaft angle}$$

10.10 Spiral Miter and Bevel Gears

Spiral miter and bevel gears have a lengthwise curvature similar to Zerol gears. The difference is that spiral bevel gears have an appreciable angle with the axis of the gear. Spiral bevel gear teeth do not have a true helical spiral, and they look like helical bevel gears. Spiral bevel gears are generated by the same machines that cut Zerol gears, except that the cutting tool is set at an angle to the axis of the spiral bevel gear. Spiral bevel gears are made to 16, 17.5, 20, and 22.5° pressure angles, but the 20° pressure is considered as an industry standard.

VALUES OF SAFE STATIC STRESS (s)

Material		(s) Lb. per Sq. In.
Bronze		10000
Cast Iron		12000
Steel	.20 Carbon (Untreated)	20000
	.20 Carbon (Case-hardened)	25000
	.40 Carbon (Untreated)	25000
	.40 Carbon (Heat-treated)	30000
	.40 C. Alloy (Heat-treated)	40000

Figure 10.21 Values of safe static stress.

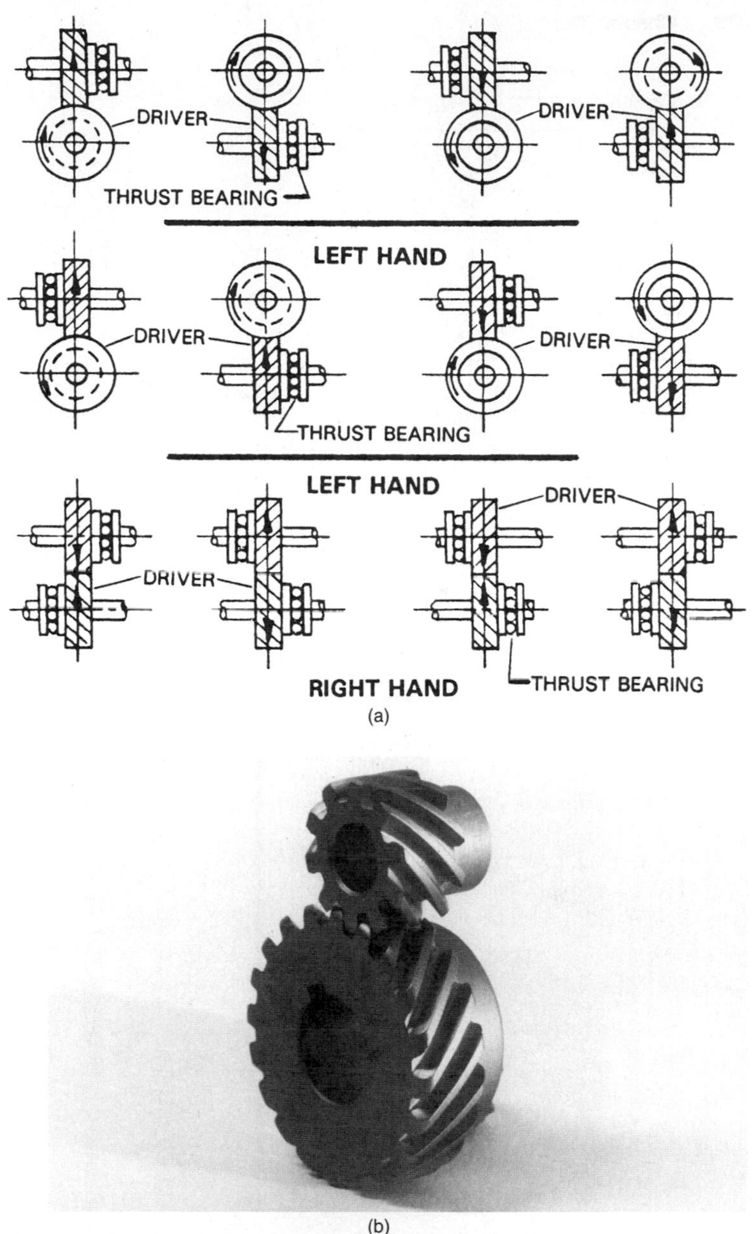

Figure 10.22 (*a*) Location of thrust bearings for helical gear sets. (*b*) Typical helical gear set.

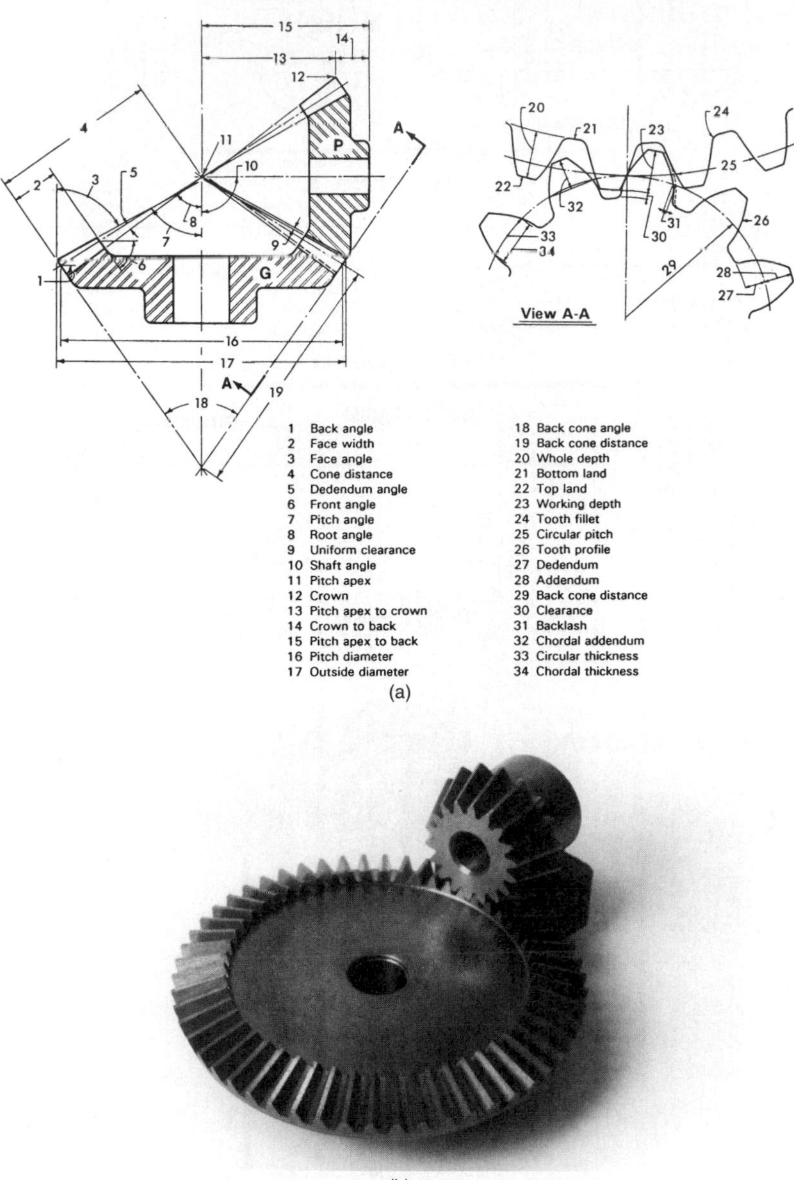

Figure 10.23 (*a*) Bevel gear terminology. (*b*) A typical straight bevel gear set.

STRAIGHT TOOTH MITER AND BEVEL GEAR FORMULAS

TO OBTAIN	HAVING	FORMULA	
		Pinion	Gear
Pitch Diameter (D.d)	No. of Teeth and Diametral Pitch (P)	$d = \frac{n}{P}$	$D = \frac{n}{P}$
Whole Depth (h_t)	Diametral Pitch (P)	$h_t = \frac{2.188}{P} = .002$	$h_t = \frac{2.188}{P} = .002$
Addendum (a)	Diametral Pitch (P)	$a = \frac{1}{P}$	$a = \frac{1}{P}$
Dendendum (b)	Whole Depth (h_t) & Addendum (a)	$b = h_t - a$	$b = h_t - a$
Clearance	Whole Depth (n_t) & Addendum (a)	$c = h_t - 2a$	$c = h_t - 2a$
Circular Tooth Thickness (τ)	Diametral Pitch (P)	$\tau = \frac{1.5708}{P}$	$\tau = \frac{1.5708}{P}$
Pitch Angle	Number of Teeth In Pinion (N_P) and Gear (N_G)	$L_P = \tan^{-1}\left(\frac{N_P}{N_G}\right)$	$L_G = 90 - L_P$
Outside Diameter (D_O, d_O)	Pinion & Gear Pitch Diameter ($D_P + D_G$) Addendum (a) & Pitch Angle ($L_P + L_G$)	$d_o = D_P + 2a(\cos L_P)$	$D_o = D_G + 2a(\cos L_G)$

Figure 10.24 Miter and bevel gear equations.

Material		(s) Lb. per Sq. In.
Cast Iron		10000
Steel	.20 Carbon (Untreated)	12000
	.20 Carbon (Case-hardened)	25000
	.40 Carbon (Untreated)	25000
	.40 Carbon (Heat-treated)	30000
	.40 C. Alloy (Heat-treated)	40000

Figure 10.25 Values of safe static stress.

TOOTH FORM FACTOR (Y)

20°P.A.—Long Addendum Pinions
Short Addendum Gears

No. Teeth Pinion	RATIO 1		1.5		2		3		4		6	
	Pin.	Gear	Pin.	Gear	Pin.	Gear	Pin.	Gear	Pin.	Gear	Pin.	Gear
12	–		–	–	.345	.283	.355	.302	.358	.305	.361	.324
14	–		.349	.292	.367	.301	.377	.317	.380	.323	.405	.352
16	.333		.367	.311	.386	.320	.396	.333	.402	.339	.443	.377
18	.342		.383	.328	.402	.336	.415	.346	.427	.364	.474	.399
20	.352		.402	.339	.418	.349	.427	.355	.456	.386	.500	.421
24	.371		.424	.364	.443	.368	.471	.377	.506	.405	–	–
28	.386		.446	.383	.462	.386	.509	.396	.543	.421	–	–
32	.399		.462	.396	.487	.402	.540	.412	–	–	–	–
36	.408		.477	.408	.518	.415	.569	.424	–	–	–	–
40	.418		–	–	.543	.424	.594	.434	–	–	–	–

Figure 10.26 *Y* factors, bevel gears.

Diametral Pitch	Backlash (Inches)
4	.008
5	.007
6	.006
8	.005
10	.004
12-20	.003
24-48	.002

Figure 10.27 Backlash in bevel gears.

For spiral miter and bevel gears, the direction of axial thrust loads developed in operation is determined by the hand and the direction of rotation. Figure 10.28 shows the arrangements possible for spiral miter and bevel gears and the appropriate locations for the thrust bearings. The thrust bearings must be rated to withstand the imposed loads in operation (see Chap. 11, "Antifriction Bearings").

Thrust loads for spiral miter and bevel gear sets are calculated using the equations shown in Fig. 10.29 (see also Fig. 10.23*a*). The spiral angle γ for spiral miter and bevel gears is normally 35°, as produced by many gear manufacturers.

10.11 Worm Gears

Worms and worm gears are used to transmit power or motion between nonintersecting shafts at right angles (90°) to each other. Worm gear drives are the smoothest and quietest form of gearing when properly applied and maintained. Worm gear drives should be considered for the following requirements:

- High-ratio speed reduction
- Limited space
- Right-angle, nonintersecting shafts
- Good resistance to backdriving
- Transmission of high torques

The terminology of standard worm gearing is illustrated in Fig. 10.30. A typical worm gear set is shown in Fig. 10.31. The formulas for worm gearing are shown in Fig. 10.32.

When operating, worm gears produce thrust loadings. Figure 10.33 indicates the direction of thrust of worms and worm gears when they are rotated. To absorb the thrust loads, thrust bearings should be located as indicated in the figure.

Efficiency of worm gearing. A commonly used efficiency equation for worm gears is

$$\text{Efficiency } E = \frac{\tan\gamma\,(1 - f\tan\gamma)}{f + \tan\gamma}$$

where γ = worm-lead angle, degrees
f = coefficient of sliding or dynamic friction

Note: For a bronze worm gear and hardened-steel worm, $f = 0.03$ to 0.05 for initial estimates.

Another commonly used efficiency equation for worm gearing is

$$\text{Efficiency } E = \frac{1 - f\tan\gamma}{1 + \dfrac{f}{\tan\gamma}}$$

where γ = lead angle, degrees
f = coefficient of dynamic friction

Note: $\tan \gamma = \text{lead}/(\pi D_w)$, where lead is the number of threads in worm times circular pitch and D_w is the pitch diameter of worm in inches. The number of leads in a worm is normally 1 to 4 and determines the gear ratio of the worm gear set as follows:

$$R = \frac{N_g}{L}$$

where N_g = number of teeth in the worm wheel
L = number of leads on the worm, usually 1 to 4

Therefore, if a worm has 2 leads and the worm wheel has 40 teeth, the ratio is 40/2 = 20, and the ratio is 20:1.

The output torque of the worm gear shaft will be

$$\text{Output torque} = E \text{ (efficiency)} \times \text{worm torque} \times \text{ratio } (R)$$

Example If 100 pound-inches of torque is applied to the worm shaft and the efficiency is 85 percent, the output torque of the worm wheel shaft will be

$$T_o \text{ (output torque)} = 0.85 \times 100 \times 20 = 1700 \text{ pound-inches or } 142 \text{ pounds-feet}$$

The output revolutions per minute (rpm_o) are then

$$\text{rpm}_o = \text{worm rpm/ratio}$$

If the worm were rotating at 600 rpm, the worm wheel rpm (rpm_o) would be

$$\text{rpm}_o = 600/20 = 30 \text{ rpm}$$

The torques (forces) and speeds can be altered at the input or output, but there is no gain of power or energy (work), only a loss that is determined by the efficiency of the worm gear drive. Efficiencies are calculated using one or the other of the preceding efficiency equations.

Strength of worm gears. The Lewis equation for the strength of worm gears is

$$F = sbyP_c = \frac{sby\pi}{P_d}$$

where F = permissible tangential load, lbf (see the equations for gear loads on bearings in Sec. 10.15)
P_c = normal circular pitch
P_d = normal diametral pitch
b = face width of gear, in
y = tooth-form factor (see Fig. 10.34)
s = allowable bending stress, psi, which is calculated from

$$s = s_1\left(\frac{1200}{1200 + V_g}\right)$$

where s_1 = 0.30 × ultimate strength of worm gear material, psi
V_g = pitch-line velocity of the gear, ft/min

AGMA horsepower rating. Permissible horsepower inputs which produce normal wear rates in worm gear units are given by

$$\text{hp} = \frac{n}{R} KJV_f$$

where hp = horsepower of input
n = worm speed, rpm
R = transmission ratio = rpm worm/rpm gear
K = pressure constant (see Fig. 10.35)
$J = R/(R + 2.5)$
V_f = velocity factor, which may be determined from

$$V_f = \frac{450}{450 + V_p + \dfrac{3V_p}{R}}$$

In the velocity factor relationship, V_p = pitch line velocity of worm (ft/min).

The AGMA recommendation for input horsepower limit of plain worm gear units, for worm gear speeds of 2000 rpm, is given by

$$\text{hp} = \frac{9.5C^{1.7}}{R + 5}$$

where hp = permissible input power
C = center distance, in
R = transmission ratio = rpm worm/rpm gear

Dynamic load F_d. This may be approximated from the equation

$$F_d = \left(\frac{1200 + V_g}{1200}\right)F$$

where F = actual tangential load, lbf (see equations for forces in gear systems, Sec. 10.15.1)
V_g = pitch-line velocity of the gear, ft/min

Note: The dynamic load should not exceed the endurance load F_1, as set out in the following Lewis equation:

$$F_1 = \frac{s_1 b y \pi}{P_d}$$

where P_d = diametral pitch
s_1 = 0.33 times ultimate strength of worm gear material, psi

See previous matter for other symbols.

Note: Quality worm gear systems for power transmission should have ground and polished steel worms and tough phosphor-bronze worm gears. The less efficient, more economical worm gear set consists of a steel worm and cast iron worm gear.

10.12 Other Gear Systems

The preceding data and information were for the gear systems used most commonly today. Other gear systems are used in industry, although not as frequently as the previously detailed systems. Among the other systems of gearing in use are the following:

- Zerol bevel gears
- Hypoid gears
- Face gears
- Crossed-helical gears
- Double-enveloping worm gears
- Spiroid gears

The following subsections provide descriptions of these gear systems.

(Text continued on page 892.)

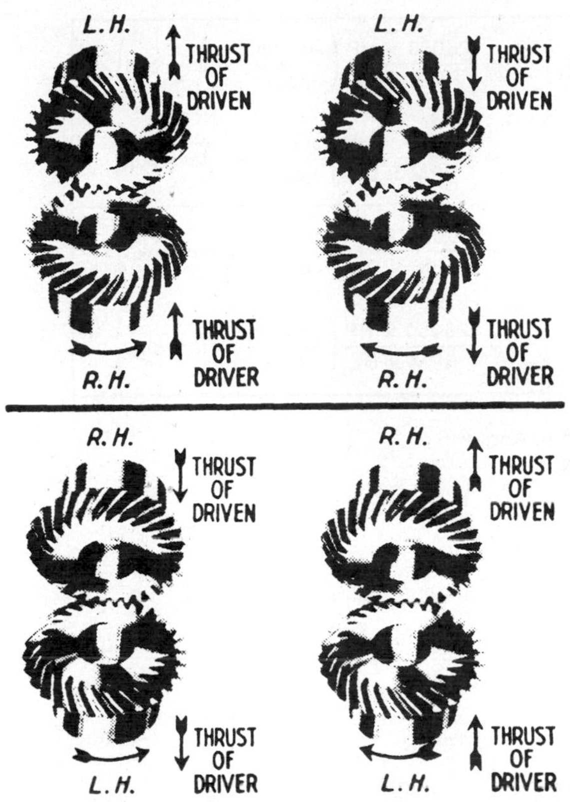

Figure 10.28 Direction of thrust on spiral bevel gear sets.

R.H. SPIRAL 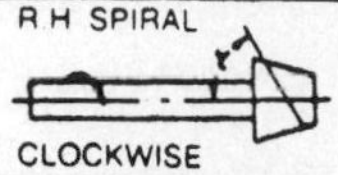 CLOCKWISE	$T_p = \dfrac{126{,}050 \times HP}{RPM \times D}\left(\dfrac{\tan\alpha \sin\beta}{\cos\gamma} - \tan\gamma \cos\beta\right)$
L.H. SPIRAL 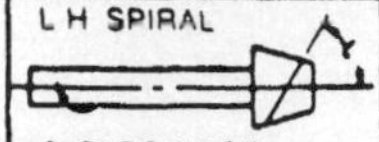 C. CLOCKWISE	$T_G = \dfrac{126{,}050 \times HP}{RPM \times D}\left(\dfrac{\tan\alpha \cos\beta}{\cos\gamma} + \tan\gamma \sin\beta\right)$
L.H. SPIRAL 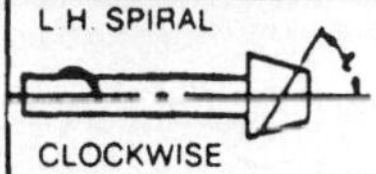 CLOCKWISE	$T_p = \dfrac{126{,}050 \times HP}{RPM \times D}\left(\dfrac{\tan\alpha \sin\beta}{\cos\gamma} + \tan\gamma \cos\beta\right)$
R.H. SPIRAL  C. CLOCKWISE	$T_G = \dfrac{126{,}050 \times HP}{RPM \times D}\left(\dfrac{\tan\alpha \cos\beta}{\cos\gamma} + \tan\gamma \sin\beta\right)$

α = Tooth Pressure Angle

β = 1/2 Pitch Angle

$$\text{Pitch Angle} = \tan^{-1}\left(\frac{N_p}{N_G}\right)$$

γ = Spiral Angle = 35°

Figure 10.29 Thrust load equations, spiral bevel gears.

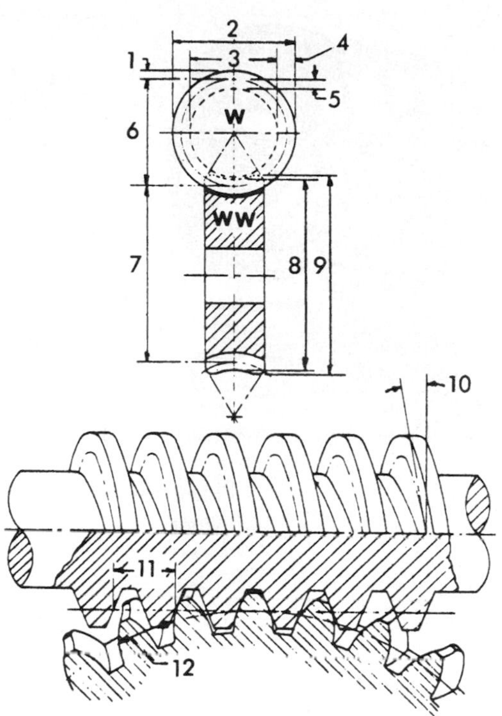

1 Addendum
2 Outside diameter
3 Root diameter
4 Whole depth
5 Dedendum
6 Pitch diameter (worm)
W Worm
7 Pitch diameter (worm wheel)
8 Throat diameter
9 Maximum diameter
10 Lead angle of worm
11 Linear pitch
12 Circular pitch
WW Worm wheel

Figure 10.30 Worm gear terminology.

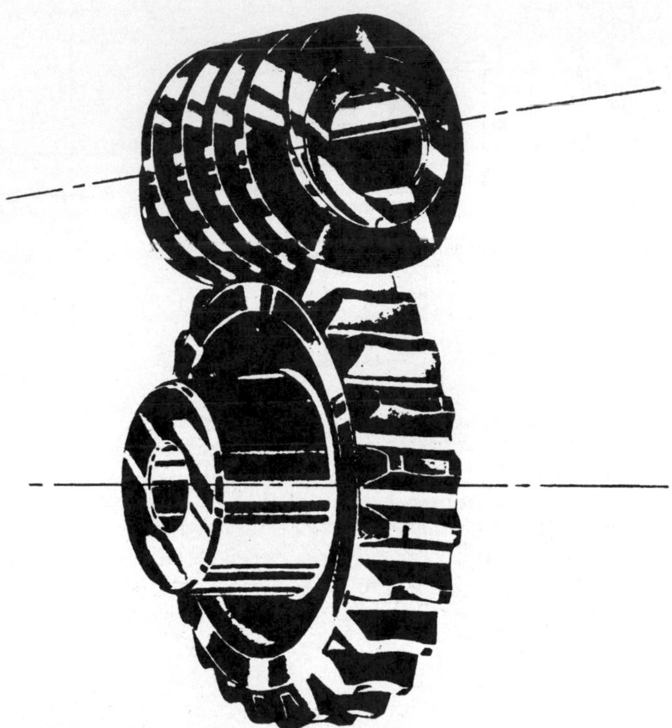

Figure 10.31 Typical worm gear set.

TO OBTAIN	HAVING	FORMULA
Circular Pitch (p)	Diametral Pitch (P)	$P = \frac{3.1416}{P}$
Diametral Pitch (P)	Circular Pitch (p)	$P = \frac{3.1416}{P}$
Lead (of Worm)	Number of Threads in Worm & Circular Pitch (p)	$L = P$ (Number of Threads)
Addendum (a)	Diametral Pitch (P)	$a = \frac{1}{P}$
Pitch Diameter of Worm (D_W)	Outside Diameter (d_o) & Addendum (a)	$D_W = d_o - 2a$
Pitch Diameter of Worm Gear (D_G)	Circular Pitch (p) & Number of Teeth (N)	$D_G = \frac{N_P}{3.1416}$
Center Distance Between Worm and Worm Gear (CD)	Pitch Diameter of Worm (D_W) & Worm Gear (D_G)	$CD = \frac{P_W + D_G}{2}$
Whole Depth of Teeth (h_T)	Circular Pitch (p)	$h_T = .6866\,p$
	Diametral Pitch (P)	$h_T = \frac{2.157}{P}$
Bottom Diameter of Worm (d_r)	Whole Depth (hT) & Outside Diameter (d_w)	$d_r = d_o - 2\,h_T$
Throat Diameter of Worm Gear (D_T)	Pitch Diameter of Worm Gear (D) & Addendum (a)	$D_T = D + 2a$
Lead Angle of Worm (γ)	Pitch Diameter of Worm (D) & The Lead (L)	$\gamma = \tan^{-1}\left(\frac{L}{3.1416d}\right)$
Ratio	No. of Teeth on Gear (N_G) and Number of Threads on Worm	$\text{Ratio} = \frac{N_G}{\text{No. of Threads}}$

Figure 10.32 Worm and worm gear equations.

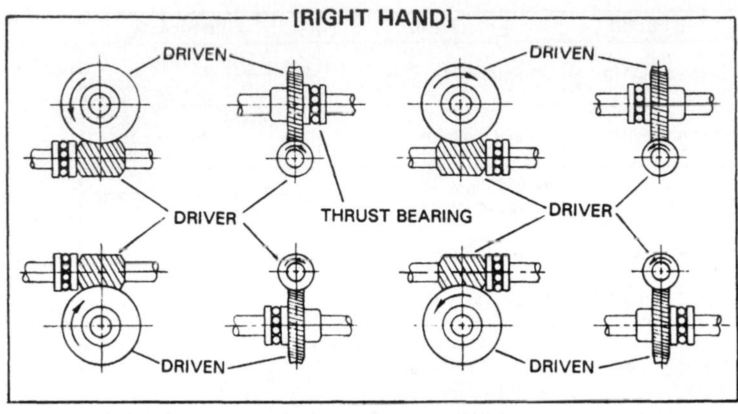

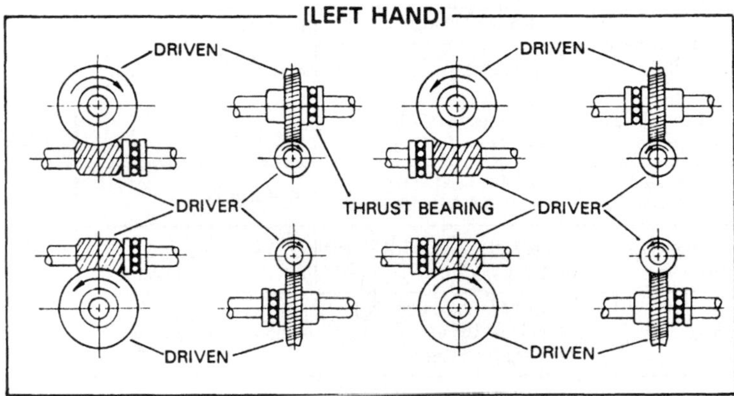

Figure 10.33 Location of thrust bearings on worm gear sets.

Form Factors y – for use in Lewis strength equation

Number of Teeth	$14\frac{1}{2}°$ Full-Depth Involute or Composite	20° Full-Depth Involute	20° Stub Involute
12	0.067	0.078	0.099
13	0.071	0.083	0.103
14	0.075	0.088	0.108
15	0.078	0.092	0.111
16	0.081	0.094	0.115
17	0.084	0.096	0.117
18	0.086	0.098	0.120
19	0.088	0.100	0.123
20	0.090	0.102	0.125
21	0.092	0.104	0.127
23	0.094	0.106	0.130
25	0.097	0.108	0.133
27	0.099	0.111	0.136
30	0.101	0.114	0.139
34	0.104	0.118	0.142
38	0.106	0.122	0.145
43	0.108	0.126	0.147
50	0.110	0.130	0.151
60	0.113	0.134	0.154
75	0.115	0.138	0.158
100	0.117	0.142	0.161
150	0.119	0.146	0.165
300	0.122	0.150	0.170
Rack	0.124	0.154	0.175

Figure 10.34 Form factors for worm gears.

Pressure constants, K.

Center distance, C, in	Constant, K
1	0.0125
2	0.025
3	0.04
4	0.09
5	0.17
6	0.29
7	0.45
8	0.66
9	0.99
10	1.20
15	4.0
20	8.0

Interpolate for intermediate values.

Figure 10.35 Pressure constants, worm gears.

10.12.1 Zerol bevel gears

Zerol bevel gears are similar to straight bevel gears except that they have a curved tooth. Zerol bevel gears have 0° spiral angle. The machinery used to make Zerol gears is different from that used to make straight bevel gears. Zerol gear teeth may be finished by grinding or lapping and are favored over straight bevel gears where high accuracy and full hardness are important. These gears are preferred in high-speed applications.

Zerol gears are usually made with a 20° pressure angle; 22.5 and 25° pressure angles are used when the numbers of teeth are small. The calculations for pitch diameter and pitch-cone angle are the same as those for straight bevel gears.

10.12.2 Hypoid gears

Hypoid gears resemble bevel gears and spiral bevel gears and are used on crossed-axis shafts. The distance between a hypoid pinion axis and the axis of a hypoid gear is called the *offset*. Hypoid pinions may have as few as five teeth in a high-ratio set. Ratios can be obtained with hypoid gears that are not available with bevel gears. High ratios are easy to obtain with the hypoid gear system.

Hypoid gears are matched to run together, just as Zerol or spiral bevel gear sets are matched. The geometry of hypoid teeth is defined by the various dimensions used to set up the machines to cut the teeth.

10.12.3 Face gears

Face gears have teeth cut on the face end of a gear. They are not normally thought of as bevel gears, but functionally, they are related most closely to bevel gears.

A spur pinion and a face gear are mounted with intersecting shafts, usually at 90°. The pinion bearings carry radial loads, while the face-gear bearings have both radial and thrust loads.

The formulas for determining the dimensions of a pinion to run with a face gear are the same as those of a pinion running with a mating gear on parallel axes. The pressure angles and pitches used are similar to spur gear or helical gear practices.

10.12.4 Crossed-helical gears

Crossed-helical gears are essentially nonenveloping worm gears. Both gears are cylindrical in shape. Crossed-helical gears are mounted on axes that do not intersect and are usually at 90°. The bearings for crossed-helical gears have both radial and thrust loads (see Fig. 10.22).

A point contact is made between two spiral gears at 90° to each other. As the gears revolve, this point travels across the tooth in a sloping line. After the gears have "worn in" for a period of time, the original point contact spreads to a line contact along the length of the gear faces. This increases their load-carrying capacity considerably. When the crossed-helical gear set is new, the load-carrying capacity is very limited, until this wear-in process has taken effect.

Some of the basic formulas for crossed-helical gears are

$$\text{Shaft angle} = \text{helix angle of driver} \pm \text{helix angle of driven}$$

$$\text{Normal module} = \text{normal circular pitch}/\pi$$

$$\text{Normal diametral pitch} = \frac{\pi}{\text{normal circular pitch}}$$

$$\text{Pitch diameter} = \frac{\text{number of teeth} \times \text{normal module}}{\cos \text{helix angle}}$$

$$\text{Center distance} = \frac{\text{pitch diameter, driver} + \text{pitch diameter, driven}}{2}$$

$$\text{Cosine of helix angle} = \frac{\text{number of teeth} \times \text{normal circular pitch}}{\pi \times \text{pitch diameter}}$$

10.12.5 Double-enveloping worm gears

The double-enveloping worm gear is like the single-enveloping worm gear (see Sec. 10.11), except that the worm envelops the worm gear. This worm gear system has more tooth surface in contact (area contact), and this allows it to carry higher loads than single-enveloping worm gears. The only double-enveloping worm gear drive system in current use is the cone-drive design (Ex-Cell-O Corp.).

In both single- and double-enveloping worm gears, it is generally recommended that the worm or pinion diameter be made a function of the center distance. Therefore,

$$\text{Pitch diameter of worm} = \frac{(\text{center distance})^{0.875}}{2.2}$$

This equation merely recommends a good proportion of worm-to-gear diameter to obtain the best power capacity. Instrument gear designers often use different proportions, according to their intended application.

The helix angle of a single- or double-enveloping worm gear may be obtained from the following general formula:

$$\text{tan center helix angle of gear} = \frac{\text{pitch diameter of gear}}{\text{pitch diameter of worm} \times \text{ratio}}$$

10.12.6 Spiroid gears

The spiroid gear systems operate on nonintersecting, nonparallel shafts or axes. The spiroid pinion is tapered and resembles a worm, while the gear member is a face gear with teeth curved in a lengthwise direction; the inclination to the tooth is similar to a helix angle but is not a true helical spiral. Figure 10.36*a* illustrates a spiroid gear set and its terminology.

The spiroid gear family has helicon, planoid, and spiroid gears. The helicon is a spiroid with no taper in the pinion. The planoid is used for lower ratios than the spiroid, and its offset is less. The spiroid pinion may be made by hobbing, milling, rolling, or thread chasing. The spiroid gear is usually made by hobbing, using specially adapted machines and hobbing tools.

Spiroid gears are used in a wide variety of applications from aerospace actuators to automotive systems and appliances. High ratio in compact arrangements, low cost when mass produced, and good load-carrying characteristics make the hypoid gear system attractive in many applications. The fact that this type of gearing system can be made with lower-cost machine tools and manufacturing processes is an important design and manufacturing consideration.

10.13 Gear Teeth Gages

When a replacement gear is required for a machine or mechanism, you must determine the diametral pitch or relative size of the tooth and its pressure angle. The 14.5 and 20° pressure-angle involute tooth form will be found in common use throughout industry. If you do not know the manufacturer or the cross-reference to the catalog number usually found on the gear hub, you may use a gear tooth gage to find the diametral pitch and pressure angle. A typical gear tooth gage is shown in Fig. 10.36*b* for both 14.5 and 20° pressure-angle involute teeth. When measuring a bevel or miter gear, the gage must be used at the large end of the tooth on the perimeter of the gear, as shown in Fig. 10.37. When measuring a helical gear, the gear tooth gage must be held perpendicular to the gear axis or shaft, as shown in Fig. 10.38. When the gage can be rolled along the perimeter of the gear being measured without a mismatch, you have found the correct diametral pitch or relative tooth size. Counting the number of teeth in the gear or pinion and measuring the approximate pitch diameter will allow you to find a matching gear to replace the one in question or the entire set.

Figure 10.39 shows some of the common gear types found in wide use for a variety of applications. The following gear types are represented:

A	Miter gear, 45°
B	Pinion of a straight bevel gear set
C	Typical spur gear
D	Spur stem pinion, eight teeth—12-DP special modified involute tooth
E	Helical pinion, left-hand 45° helix angle
F	Worm from a worm gear set, right hand

10.14 Gear Materials and Hardness Ranges

10.14.1 Plastic gears and materials

Plastic gears find widespread use in many applications where low loads and speeds are specified. The thermoplastics such as polycarbonates, polyamides, and acetals are popular for low-strength applications where lubrication may be minimal or where the gears come into contact with the ambient surroundings such as in food or drug-handling machinery. Thermoset plastics such as the laminated phenolic fabric materials may be used in relatively high-strength applications such as automotive timing gears, air compressors, household appliances, bottling machinery, and calculating machinery. Bakelite, another thermoset plastic, is also used to compression mold gears for low-strength, high-volume applications. The thermoplastics are usually injection molded, while the thermoset plastics are usually compression molded. Thermoplastics may be remelted for remolding, while thermoset plastics have a one-way chemistry that does not allow their remelting for remolding. In general, thermoset plastics are harder than thermosetting plastics and usually more rigid and heat resistant. Figure 10.40 lists the physical properties of some of the commonly used thermoplastic and thermoset plastic materials for gearing applications.

10.14.2 Ferrous and nonferrous gear materials and characteristics/processes

Table 10.1 lists the typical gear materials: wrought steel. Commonly used quenchants for ferrous gear materials are listed in Table 10.2. Table 10.3 lists typical Brinell hardness ranges and strengths for annealed, normalized, and tempered steel gearing. Table 10.4 lists typical Brinell hardness ranges and strengths for quenched and tempered alloy-steel gearing. Table 10.5 lists typical effective case depth specifications for carburized gearing. Table 10.6 lists minimum hardness and tensile strength requirements for gray cast iron gearing. Table 10.7 lists the mechanical properties of ductile iron gearing. Table 10.8 describes the machinability of common gear materials. Table 10.9 describes the mechanical properties of cast bronze alloys for gearing. Refer to Chap. 5, "Materials and Their Uses," for data relative to heat treatment of steels and alloy steels.

10.14.3 Gear quality numbers (AGMA)

The AGMA gear quality number refers to the accuracy and tolerances that are permissible in manufacturing each particular gear in terms of its specialized use. The AGMA quality numbers for racks and gears are shown in Table 10.10 for each particular application. The permissible tolerances for the different quality numbers may be obtained from the AGMA standards, which show the type of gear and the permissible tolerances and inspection dimensions.

10.14.4 AGMA gear specification sample sheet

For indicating the basic gear data and manufacturing and inspection data when specifying a particular gear, the gear drawing should contain this specification data in a form similar to that shown in Table 10.11.

(Text continued on page 922.)

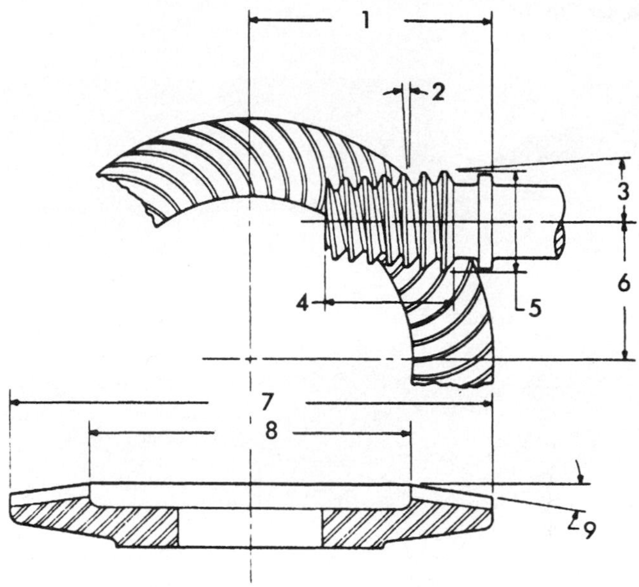

1	Pinion mounting distance	6	Center distance
2	Thread angle	7	Gear O.D.
3	Pinion taper angle	8	Gear I.D.
4	Pinion length	9	Gear taper angle
5	Pinion O.D.		

(a)

(b)

Figure 10.36 (*a*) Spiroid gear terminology. (*b*) Typical gear tooth gage.

Figure 10.37 Use of the gear tooth gage, bevel gears.

Figure 10.38 Use of the gear tooth gage, helical gears.

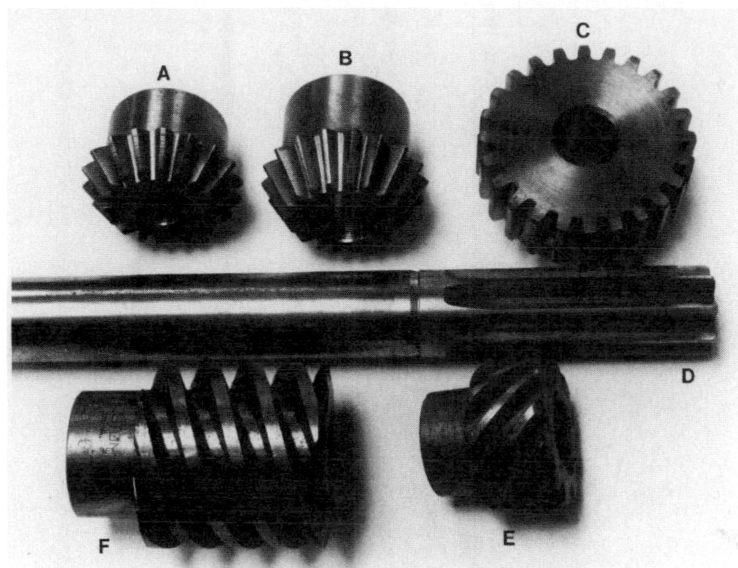

Figure 10.39 Typical common gears.

Properties	Polycarbonate	Polyamide	Acetal	Phenolic Fabric - LE	
				Crosswise	Lengthwise
Tensile strength, psi x 10^3	9 - 11	8.5 - 11	10	9.5	13.5
Flex. strength, psi x 10^3	11 - 13	14.5	13.5	15	
Elongation %	60 - 100	60 - 300	15 - 75	-	-
Impact strength, ft-lbs/in	12 - 16	0.9 - 2	1.4 - 2.3	1	1.25
Water absorbtion %/24 Hrs	0.3	1.5	0.4	See note 2	
Heat resistance °F (continuous)	250 - 275	250	175	250	
Trade names	Lexan	Nylon, Zytel	Delrin	Phenolite, Ryertex, Textolite	

NOTES: 1 Tabulated data are average values (see material specification sheet for exact data)
2 0.125", 1.3%; 0.25", 0.95%; 0.50", 0.70%; 1" and over, 0.55%
3 Source: General Electric Company, Plastics Division.

Figure 10.40 Physical properties of plastics used for gears.

TABLE 10.1 Typical Gear Materials—Wrought Steel

Common alloy-steel grades	Common heat-treatment practice*	General remarks/application
1045	T-H, I-H, F-H	Low hardenability
4130	T-H	Marginal hardenability
4140	T-H, T-H&N, I-H, F-H	Fair hardenability
4145	T-H, T-H&N, I-H, F-H	Medium hardenability
8640	T-H, T-H&N, I-H, F-H	Medium hardenability
4340	T-H, T-H&N, I-H, F-H	Good hardenability in heavy sections
Nitralloy 135 Mod.	T-H&N	Special heat treatment
Nitralloy G	T-H&N	Special heat treatment
4150	I-H, F-H, T-H, TH&N	Quench crack sensitive Good hardenability
4142	I-H, F-H, T-H&N	Used when 4140 exhibits marginal hardenability
4350†	T-H, I-H, F-H	Quench crack sensitive, excellent hardenability in heavy sections
1020	C-H	Very low hardenability
4118	C-H	Fair core hardenability
4620	C-H	Good case hardenability
8620	C-H	Fair core hardenability
4320	C-H	Good core hardenability
8822	C-H	Good core hardenability in heavy sections
3310†	C-H	Excellent hardenability
4820	C-H	(in heavy sections)
9310	C-H	for all three grades

* C-H = carburize harden; F-H = flame harden; I-H = induction harden; T-H = through harden; T-H&N = through harden then nitride

† Recognized, but not current standard grade.

SOURCE: Extracted from AGMA standard: ANSI/AGMA 2004-B89 (revision of AGMA 240.01) with the permission of the publisher, American Gear Manufacturers Association, 1500 King Street, Suite 201, Alexandria, Virginia 22314.

TABLE 10.2 Commonly Used Quenchants for Ferrous Gear Materials

Material grade	Quenchant	Remarks
1020	Water or brine	Carburized and quenched with good quench agitation.
4118 4620 8620 8822 4320	Oil	Carburized and quenched in well-agitated conventional oil at 80–160°F (27–71°C) is normally required. For finer pitched gearing, hot oil at 275–375°F (135–190°C) may be used to minimize distortion. Some loss in core hardness will also result from hot oil quench.
3310 9310	Oil	Carburized and quenched in hot oil at 275–375°F (135–190°C). This is the preferred quench. In larger sections, conventional oil can be used.
1045 4130 8630	Water, oil, or polymer	Type of quenchant depends on chemistry and section size. Large sections normally require water or low-concentration polymer. Smaller sections can be processed in well-agitated oil.
1141 1541	Oil or polymer	Good response in well-agitated conventional oil or polymer. Induction- or flame-hardened parts normally quenched in polymer.
4140 4142 4145	Oil or polymer	Same as above; however, thin sections or sharp corners can represent a crack hazard. Hot oil should be considered in these cases. With proper equipment, air quench can be used for flame-hardened parts.
		These are high-hardenability steels which can be crack sensitive in moderate to thin sections. Hot oil is often used. High-concentration polymer should be used with caution.

4150 4340 4345 4350	Oil or polymer	If conventional oil is used, parts are often removed warm and tempered promptly after quench. Crack sensitivity applies also to flame- or induction-hardened parts, with high-concentration polymer being the usual quenchant. Oil is sometimes used, and air quench can be applied for flame hardening with proper equipment.
Gray or ductile iron	Oil, polymer, or air	Quench medium depends on alloy content. High-alloy irons can be air quenched to moderate hardness levels. Unalloyed or low-alloy irons require oil or polymer. In this section parts and flame- or induction-hardened surfaces can be crack sensitive.

SOURCE: Extracted from AGMA standard: ANSI/AGMA 2004-B89 (revision of AGMA 240.01) with the permission of the publisher, American Gear Manufacturers Association, 1500 King Street, Suite 201, Alexandria, Virginia 22314.

TABLE 10.3 Typical Brinell Hardness Ranges and Strengths for Annealed, Normalized, and Tempered Steel Gearing

	Annealed heat treatment[†]			Normalized and tempered[‡]		
Typical alloy steels specified*	Brinell hardness range, HB	Tensile strength minimum, ksi (MPa)	Yield strength minimum, ksi (MPa)	Brinell hardness range, HB	Tensile strength minimum, ksi (MPa)	Yield strength minimum, ksi (MPa)
1045	159–201	80 (550)	50 (345)	159–201	80 (550)	50 (345)
4130 8630	156–197	80 (550)	50 (345)	167–212	90 (620)	60 (415)
4140 4142 8640	187–229	95 (655)	60 (415)	262–302	130 (895)	85 (585)
4145 4150	197–241	100 (690)	60 (415)	285–331	140 (965)	90 (620)
4340 4350 type	212–255	110 (760)	65 (450)	302–341	150 (1035)	95 (655)

* Steels shown in order of increased hardenability.

[†] Hardening by quench and tempering results in a combination of properties generally superior to that achieved by anneal or normalize and temper, i.e., impact, ductility, etc.

[‡] Hardness and strengths able to be obtained by normalizing and tempering are also a function of controlling section size and tempering temperature considerations.

SOURCE: Extracted from AGMA standard: ANSI/AGMA 2004-B89 (revision of AGMA 240.01) with the permission of the publisher, American Gear Manufacturers Association, 1500 King Street, Suite 201, Alexandria, Virginia 22314.

TABLE 10.4 Typical Brinell Hardness Ranges and Strengths for Quenched and Tempered Alloy Steel Gearing

Alloy steel grade*	Heat treatment	Hardness range, HB†	Tensile strength minimum, ksi (MPa)	Yield strength minimum, ksi (MPa)
4130	Water	212–248	100 (690)	75 (515)
	quench and	up to		
8630	temper	302–341	145 (1000)	125 (860)
4140	Oil	241–285‡	120 (830)	95 (655)
8640	quench and	up to		
	temper	341–388		
4142				
4145		341–388	170 (1170)	150 (1035)
4150				
4340	Oil	277–321	135 (930)	110 (760)
	quench and	up to		
4350	temper	363–415§	180 (1240)	145 (1000)

* Steels shown in order of increased hardenability, 4350 being the highest. These steels can be ordered to H band hardenability ranges.

† Hardness range is dependent on controlling section size and quench severity.

‡ It is difficult to cut teeth in 4100 series steels above 341 HB and 4300 series steels above 375 HB. (4340 and 4350 provide advantage due to higher tempering temperatures and microstructure considerations)

§ High specified hardness is used for special gearing, but costs should be evaluated due to reduced machinability.

SOURCE: Extracted from AGMA standard: ANSI/AGMA 2004-B89 (revision of AGMA 240.01) with the permission of the publisher, American Gear Manufacturers Association, 1500 King Street, Suite 201, Alexandria, Virginia 22314.

TABLE 10.5 Typical Effective Case Depth Specifications for Carburized Gearing

Normal diametral pitch*	Normal tooth thickness†	Range of normal diametral pitch	Range of normal circular pitch	Effective case depth (inches) to RC 50‡	
				Spur, helical bevel, and miter§	Worms with ground threads¶
16	0.098	17.5–13.7	0.180–0.230	0.010–0.020	0.020–0.030
14	0.112	17.5–13.7	0.180–2.300	0.010–0.020	0.020–0.030
12	0.131	13.7–10.5	0.230–0.300	0.015–0.025	0.025–0.040
10	0.157	10.5–8.5	0.300–0.370	0.020–0.030	0.035–0.050
8	0.198	8.5–7.5	0.370–0.480	0.025–0.040	0.040–0.055
7	0.224	7.5–6.5	0.370–0.480	0.025–0.040	0.040–0.055
6	0.251	6.5–5.2	0.480–0.600	0.030–0.050	0.045–0.060
5	0.314	5.2–4.3	0.600–0.728	0.040–0.060	0.045–0.060
4	0.393	4.3–3.7	0.728–0.860	0.050–0.070	0.045–0.060
3.5	0.449	3.7–3.1	0.860–1.028	0.060–0.080	0.060–0.075
3.0	0.523	3.1–2.8	1.026–1.200	0.070–0.090	0.075–0.090
2.75	0.571	2.8–2.6	1.026–1.200	0.070–0.090	0.075–0.090
2.5	0.628	2.6–2.3	1.200–1.400	0.080–0.105	0.075–0.090
2.25	0.698	2.3–2.2	1.200–1.400	0.080–0.105	0.075–0.090
2.0	0.785	2.2–1.9	1.428–1.676	0.090–0.125	0.075–0.090

1.75	0.897	1.9–1.6	1.676–1.976	0.105–0.140	0.075–0.090
1.5	1.047	1.6–1.3	1.976–2.400	0.120–0.155	0.075–0.090
1.25	1.256	1.3–1.1	2.400–2.828	0.145–0.180	0.075–0.090
1.0	1.570	1.1 & less	2.828 & more	0.170–0.205	0.075–0.090
0.75	2.094	1.1 & less	2.325 & more	0.170–0.205	0.075–0.090

* All case depths are based on normal diametral pitch. All other pitch measurements should be converted before specifying a case depth.

† Gears with thin top lands may be subject to excessive case depth at the tips. Land width should be calculated before a case is specified.

‡ Case at root is typically 50–70 percent of case at midtooth. The case depth for bevel and miter gears is calculated from the thickness of the tooth's small end. For gearing requiring maximum performance, detailed studies must be made of the application, loading, and manufacturing procedures to determine the required effective case depth. For further details, refer to AGMA 2001-B88.

§ To convert above data to metric, multiply values given by 25.4 to determine mm equivalent.

¶ Worm and ground-thread case depths allow for grinding. Unground worm gear cases may be decreased accordingly. For very heavily loaded coarse pitch ground thread worms, heavier case depth than shown in table may be required.

SOURCE: Extracted from AGMA standard: ANSI/AGMA 2004-B89 (revision of AGMA 240.01) with the permission of the publisher, American Gear Manufacturers Association, 1500 King Street, Suite 201, Alexandria, Virginia 22314.

TABLE 10.6 Minimum Hardness and Tensile Strength Requirements for Gray Cast Iron

ASTM class number*	Brinell hardness	Tensile strength, ksi (MPa)
20	155	20 (140)
30	180	30 (205)
35	205	35 (240)
40	220	40 (275)
50	250	50 (345)
60	285	60 (415)

* See ASTM A48 for additional information.

SOURCE: Extracted from AGMA standard: ANSI/AGMA 2004-B89 (revision of AGMA 240.01) with the permission of the publisher, American Gear Manufacturers Association, 1500 King Street, Suite 201, Alexandria, Virginia 22314.

TABLE 10.7 Mechanical Properties of Ductile Iron

ASTM grade designation*	Former AGMA class	Recommended heat treatment	Brinell hardness range	Min. tensile strength, ksi (MPa)	Min. yield strength, ksi (MPa)	Elongation in 2 in (50 mm), percent min
60-40-18	A-7-a	Annealed ferritic	170 max.	60 (415)	40 (275)	18.0
65-45-12	A-7-b	As-cast or annealed ferritic-pearlitic	156–217	65 (450)	45 (310)	12.0
80-55-06	A-7-c	Normalized ferritic-pearlitic	187–255	80 (550)	55 (380)	6.0
100-70-03	A-7-d	Quench and tempered pearlitic	241–302	100 (690)	70 (485)	3.0
120-90-02	A-7-e	Quench and tempered martensitic	Range specified	120 (830)	90 (620)	2.0

* See ASTM A536 or SAE J434 for further information.

NOTE: Other tensile properties and hardnesses should be used only by agreement between gear manufacturer and casting producer.

SOURCE: Extracted from AGMA standard: ANSI/AGMA 2004-B89 (revision of AGMA 240.01) with the permission of the publisher, American Gear Manufacturers Association, 1500 King Street, Suite 201, Alexandria, Virginia 22314.

TABLE 10.8 Machinability of Common Gear Materials

Material grades	Low-carbon carburizing steel grades, remarks
1020	Good machinability, as rolled, as forged, or normalized.
4118 4620 8620 8822	Good machinability, as rolled or as forged. However, normalized is preferred. Inadequate cooling during normalizing can result in gummy material, reduced tool life, and poor surface finish. Quench and temper as a prior treatment can aid machinability. The economics of the pretreatments must be considered.
3310 4320 4820 9310	Fair to good machinability if normalized and tempered, annealed or quenched and tempered. Normalizing without tempering results in reduced machinability.
Material grades	**Medium-carbon through hardened steel grades, remarks**
1045 1141 1541	Good machinability if normalized.
4130 4140 4142	Good machinability if annealed, or normalized and tempered to approximately 255 HB or quenched and tempered to approximately 321 HB. Over 321 HB, machinability is fair. Above 363 HB,machinability is poor. Inadequate (slack) quench with subsequent low tempering temperature may produce a part which meets the specified hardness but produces a mixed microstructure which results in poor machinability.
4145 4150 4340 4345 4350	Remarks for medium-carbon alloy steel (above) apply. However, the higher carbon results in lower machinability. Sulfur additions aid the machinability of these grades. 4340 machinability is good up to 363 HB. The higher carbon level in 4145, 4150, 4345, and 4350 makes them more difficult to machine and should be specified only for heavy sections. Inadequate (slack) quench can seriously affect machinability in these steels.
Material grades	**Other gear material, remarks**
Gray irons	Gray cast irons have good machinability. Higher-strength gray cast irons [above 50 ksi (345 MPa) tensile strength] have reduced machinability.
Ductile irons	Annealed or normalized ductile cast iron has good machinability. The “as cast” (not heat treated) ductile iron has fair machinability. Quenched and tempered ductile iron has good machinability up to 285 HB and fair machinability up to 352 HB. Above 352 HB, machinability is poor.

TABLE 10.8 Machinability of Common Gear Materials (*Continued*)

Material grades	Other gear material, remarks
Gear bronzes and brasses	All gear bronzes and brass have good machinability. The very high strength heat-treated bronzes [above 110 ksi (760 MPa) tensile strength] have fair machinability.
Austenitic stainless steel	All austenitic stainless steel grades only have fair machinability. Because of work-hardening tendencies, feeds and speeds must be selected to minimize work hardening.

NOTE: Coarse-grain steels are more machinable than fine grain. However, gear steels are generally used in the fine-grain condition since mechanical properties are improved and distortion during heat treatment is reduced. Increasingly cleaner steels are now also being specified for gearing. However, if sulfur content is low, less than 0.015%, machinability may decrease appreciably.

SOURCE: Extracted from AGMA standard: ANSI/AGMA 2004-B89 (revision of AGMA 240.01) with the permission of the publisher, American Gear Manufacturers Association, 1500 King Street, Suite 201, Alexandria, Virginia 22314.

TABLE 10.9 Mechanical Properties of Cast Bronze Alloys*

Copper alloy UNS no.[†]	Former AGMA type	Casting method and condition[‡]	Minimum tensile strength,[§] ksi (MPa)	Minimum yield strength,[§] ksi (MPa)	Minimum percent elongation in 2 in (50 mm)	Typical hardness[¶] HB 500 kgf	HB 3000 kgf
C86200	MNBR 3	Sand, centrifugal, continuous	90 (620)	45 (310)	18	—	180
C86300	MNBR 4	Sand, centrifugal,	110 (760)	60 (415)	12	—	225
		continuous	110 (760)	62 (425)	14	—	225
C86500	MNBR 2	Sand, centrifugal	65 (450)	25 (170)	20	112	—
C86500	MNBR 2	Continuous	70 (485)	25 (170)	25	112	—
C90700	BRONZE 2	Sand	35 (240)	18 (125)	10	70	—
C90700	BRONZE 2	Continuous	40 (275)	25 (170)	10	80	—
C90700	BRONZE 2	Centrifugal	50 (345)	28 (195)	12	100	—
C92500	BRONZE 5	Sand	35 (240)	18 (125)	10	70	—
C92500	BRONZE 5	Continuous	40 (275)	24 (165)	10	80	—
C92700	BRONZE 3	Sand	35 (240)	18 (125)	10	70	—
C92700	BRONZE 3	Continuous	38 (260)	20 (140)	8	80	—
C92900	—	Sand, continuous	45 (310)	25 (170)	8	90	—
C95200	ALBR 1	Sand, centrifugal	65 (450)	25 (170)	20	—	125
C95200	ALBR 1	Continuous	68 (470)	26 (180)	20	—	125
C95300	ALBR 2	Sand, centrifugal	65 (450)	25 (170)	20	—	140
C95300	ALBR 2	Continuous	70 (485)	26 (180)	25	—	140

C95300	ALBR 2	Sand, centrifugal	80 (550)	40 (275)	12	—	160
C95300	ALBR 2	Continuous (HT)	80 (550)	40 (275)	12	—	160
C95400	ALBR 3	Sand, centrifugal (HT)	75 (515)	30 (205)	12	—	160
C95400	ALBR 3	Continuous	85 (585)	32 (220)	12	—	160
C95400	ALBR 3	Sand, centrifugal (HT)	90 (620)	45 (310)	6	—	190
C95400	ALBR 3	Continuous (HT)	95 (655)	45 (310)	10	—	190
C95500	ALBR 4	Sand, centrifugal	90 (620)	40 (275)	6	—	190
C95500	ALBR 4	Continuous	95 (655)	45 (290)	10	—	190
C95500	ALBR 4	Sand, centrifugal (HT)	110 (760)	60 (415)	5	—	200
C95500	ALBR 4	Continuous (HT)	110 (760)	62 (425)	8	—	200

* For rating of worm gears in accordance with AGMA 6034-A87, the materials factor k_s will depend on the particular casting method employed.

† Unified numbering system. For cross-reference to SAE, former SAE & ASTM, see SAE Information Report SAE J461. For added copper alloy information, also see SAE J462.

‡ Refer to ASTM B427 for sand and centrifugal cast C90700 alloy and sand cast C92900.

§ Minimum tensile strength and yield strength shall be reduced 10% for continuous cast bars having a cross section of 4 in (102 mm) or more (see ASTM B505, Table 3 footnote).

¶ BHN at other load levels (1000 or 1500 kgf) may be used if approved by purchaser.

SOURCE: Extracted from AGMA standard: ANSI/AGMA 2004-B89 (revision of AGMA 240.01) with the permission of the publisher, American Gear Manufacturers Association, 1500 King Street, Suite 201, Alexandria, Virginia 22314.

TABLE 10.10 AGMA Applications and Quality Numbers for Racks and Gears

Gearing application	Quality no.*	Gearing application	Quality no.*
Aerospace		Cement industry	
Actuators	7–11	(continued)	
Control gearing	7–11	Electric dragline	
Engine accessories	10–13	Cast gear	3
Engine power	10–13	Cut gear	6–8
Engine starting	10–13	Electric locomotive	6–8
Loading hoist	7–11	Electric shovel	
Propeller feathering	10–13	Cast gear	3
Small engines	12–13	Cut gear	6–8
Agriculture		Elevator	5–6
Baler	3–7	Locomotive crane	
Beet harvester	5–7	Cast gear	3
Combine	5–7	Cut gear	5–6
Corn picker	5–7	(Plant operation)	
Cotton picker	5–7	Air separator	5–6
Farm elevator	3–7	Ball mill	5–7
Field harvester	5–7	Compeb mill	5–6
Peanut harvester	3–7	Conveyor	5–6
Potato digger	5–7	Cooler	5–6
Air compressor	10–11	Elevator	5–6
Automotive industry	10–11	Feeder	5–6
Baling machine	5–7	Filter	5–6
Bottling industry		Kiln	5–6
Capping	6–7	Kiln slurry agitator	5–6
Filling	6–7	Overhead crane	5–6
Labeling	6–7	Pug, rod, and tube mills	5–6
Washer, sterilizer	6–7	Pulverizer	5–6
Brewing industry		Raw and finish mill	5–6
Agitator	6–8	Rotary dryer	5–6
Barrel washer	6–8	Slurry agitator	5–6
Cookers	6–8	Chewing gum industry	
Filling machine	6–8	Chicle grinder	6–8
Mash tubs	6–8	Coater	6–8
Pasteurizer	6–8	Mixer-kneader	6–8
Racking machine	6–8	Molder-roller	6–8
Brick-making machinery	5–7	Wrapper	6–8
Bridge machinery	5–7	Chocolate industry	
Briquette machines	5–7	Glazer, finisher	6–8
Cement industry		Mixer, mill	6–8
Quarry operation		Molder	6–8
Conveyor	5–6	Presser, refiner	6–8
Crusher	5–6	Tampering	6–8
Diesel electric		Wrapper	6–8
locomotive	8–9	Clay-working machinery	5–7

TABLE 10.10 AGMA Applications and Quality Numbers for Racks and Gears (*Continued*)

Gearing application	Quality no.*	Gearing application	Quality no.*
Construction equipment		Computing and accounting machines (continued)	
Backhoe	6–8	Typewriter	8
Cranes		Cranes	
Open gearing	3–6	Boom hoist	5–6
Enclosed gearing	6–8	Gantry	5–6
Ditch digger	3–8	Load hoist	5–7
Transmission	6–8	Overhead	5–6
Drag line	5–8	Ship	5–7
Dumpster	6–8	Crushers	
Paver loader	3	Ice, feed	6–8
Transmission	8	Portable and stationary	6–8
Mixer	3–5	Rock, ore, coal	6–8
Swing gear	3–5	Dairy industry	
Mixing bucket	3	Bottle washer	6–7
Shaker	8	Homogenizer	7–9
Shovels		Separator	7–9
Open gearing	3–6	Dish washer	
Enclosed gearing	6–8	Commercial	5–7
Stationary mixer		Distillery industry	
Transmission	8	Agitator	5–7
Drum gears	3–5	Bottle filler	5–7
Stone crusher		Conveyor, elevator	6–7
Transmission	8	Grain pulverizer	6–8
Conveyor	6	Mash tub	5–7
Truck mixer		Mixer	5–7
Transfer case	9	Yeast tub	5–7
Drum gears	3–5	Electric furnace	
Commercial meters		Tilting gears	5–7
Gas	7–9	Electronic instrument control and guidance systems	
Liquid, water, milk	7–9	Accelerometer	10–12
Parking	7–9	Airborne temperature recorder	12–14
Computing and accounting machines		Aircraft instrument	12
Accounting-billing	9–10	Altimeter-stabilizer	9–11
Adding machine-calculator	7–9	Analog computer	10–12
Addressograph	7	Antenna assembly	7–9
Bookkeeping	9–10	Antiaircraft detector	12
Cash register	7	Automatic pilot	9–11
Comptometer	6–8	Digital computer	10–12
Computing	10–11	Gun data computer	12–14
Data processing	7–9		
Dictating machine	9		

TABLE 10.10 AGMA Applications and Quality Numbers for Racks and Gears (*Continued*)

Gearing application	Quality no.*	Gearing application	Quality no.*
Electronic instrument control and guidance systems (continued)		Machine-tool industry	
Gyro caging mechanism	10–12	Hand motion (but not indexing and positioning)	6–9
Gyroscope-computer	12–14	Power drives	
Pressure transducer	12–14	0–800 fpm	6–8
Radar, sonar, tuner	10–12	800–2000 fpm	8–10
Recorder, telemeter	10–12	2000–4000 fpm	10–12
Servo system component	9–11	Over 4000 fpm	12 & Up
Sound detector	9	Indexing and positioning	
Transmitter, receiver	10–12	Approximate positioning	6–10
Engines		Accurate indexing and positioning	12 & Up
Combustion			
Engine accessories	10–12	Marine industry	
Supercharger	10–12	Anchor hoist	6–8
Timing gearings	10–12	Cargo hoist	7–8
Transmission	8–10	Conveyor	5–7
Farm equipment		Davit gearing	5–7
Milking machine	6–8	Elevator	6–7
Separator	8–10	Small propulsion	10–12
Sweeper	4–6	Steering gear	8
Flour mill industry		Winch	5–8
Bleacher	7–8	Metalworking	
Grain cleaner	7–8	Bending roll	5–7
Grinder	7–8	Draw bench	6–8
Hulling	7–8	Forge press	5–7
Milling, scouring	7–8	Punch press	5–7
Polisher	7–8	Roll lathe	5–7
Separator	7–8	Mining and preparation	
Foundry industry		Breaker	5–6
Conveyor	5–6	Car dump	5–6
Elevator	5–6	Concentrator	5–6
Ladle	5–6	Continuous miner	6–7
Molding machine	5–6	Conveyor	5–7
Overhead cranes	5–6	Cutting machine	6–10
Sand mixer	5–6	Drag line	
Sand slinger	5–6	Open gearing	3–6
Tumbling mill	5–6	Enclosed gearing	6–8
Home appliances		Drills	5–6
Blender	6–8	Drier	5–6
Mixer	7–9	Electric locomotive	6–8
Timer	8–10	Elevator	5–6
Washing machine	8–10	Feeder	6–8

TABLE 10.10 AGMA Applications and Quality Numbers for Racks and Gears (*Continued*)

Gearing application	Quality no.*
Mining and preparation (continued)	
Flotation	5–6
Grizzly	5–7
Hoists, skips	7–8
Loader (underground)	5–8
Rock drill	5–6
Rotary car dump	6–8
Screen (rotary)	7–8
Screen (shaking)	7–8
Separator	5–6
Sedimentation	5–6
Shaker	6–8
Shovel	3–8
Tipple gearing	5–7
Washer	6–8
Paper and pulp	
Bag machines	6–8
Box machines	6–8
Building paper	6–8
Calendar	6–8
Chipper	6–8
Coating	6–8
Envelope machines	6–8
Food container	6–8
Glazing	6–8
Log conveyor-elevator	5–7
Mixer, agitator	6–8
Paper machine	
Auxiliary	8–9
Main drive	10–12
Press, couch, drier rolls	6–8
Slitting	10–12
Steam drum	6–8
Varnishing	6–8
Wall paper machines	6–8
Paving industry	
Aggregate drier	5–7
Aggregate spreader	5–7
Asphalt mixer	5–7
Asphalt spreader	5–7
Concrete batch mixer	5–7
Photographic equipment	
Aerial	10–12
Commercial	8–10
Printing industry	
Press	
Book	9–11
Flat	9–11
Magazine	9–11
Newspaper	9–11
Roll reels	6–7
Rotary	9–11
Pump industry	
Liquid	10–12
Rotary	6–8
Slush-duplex-triplex	6–8
Vacuum	6–8
Quarry industry	
Conveyor-elevator	6–7
Crusher	5–7
Rotary screen	7–8
Radar and missile	
Antenna elevating	8–10
Data gear	10–12
Launch pad azimuth	8
Ring gear	9–12
Rotating drive	10–12
Railroads	
Construction hoist	5–7
Wrecking crane	6–8
Rubber and plastics	
Boot and shoe machines	6–8
Drier, press	6–8
Extruder, strainer	6–8
Mixer, tuber	6–8
Refiner, calender	5–7
Rubber mill, scrap cutter	5–7
Tire building	6–8
Tire chopper	5–7
Washer, banbury mixer	5–7
Small power tools	
Bench grinder	6–8
Drills-saws	7–9

TABLE 10.10 AGMA Applications and Quality Numbers for Racks and Gears (*Continued*)

Gearing application	Quality no.*	Gearing application	Quality no.*
Small power tools (continued)		Steel industry (continued)	
Hair clipper	7–9	Blooming mill rack and pinion	5–6
Hedge clipper	7–9	Blooming mill side guard	5–6
Sander, polisher	8–10	Car haul	5–6
Sprayer	6–8	Coil conveyor	5–6
Space navigation		Coil dump	5–6
Sextant and star tracker	14 & Up	Crop conveyor	5–6
Steel industry		Edger drives	5–6
Miscellaneous drives		Electrolytic line	6–7
Bessemer tilt-car dump	5–6	Flange machine ingot buggy	5–6
Coke pusher, distributor	5–6	Leveler	6–7
Conveyor, door lift	5–6	Magazine pusher	6–7
Electric furnace tilt	5–6	Mill shear drives	6–7
Hot metal car tilt	5–6	Mill table drives (under 800 ft/min)	5–6
Hot metal charger	5–6	Mill table drives (over 800–1800 ft/min)	6–7
Jib hoist, dolomite machine	5–6	Mill table drives (over 1800 ft/min)	8
Larry car, mud gun	5–6	Nail and spike machine	5–6
Mixing bin, mixer tilt	5–6	Piler	5–6
Ore crusher, pig machine	5–6	Plate mill rack and pinion	5–6
Pulverizer, quench car	5–6	Plate mill side guards	5–6
Shaker, sinter conveyor	5–6	Plate turnover	5–6
Sinter machine skip hoist	5–6	Preheat furnace pusher	5–6
Slag crusher, slag shovel	5–6	Processor	6–7
Primary and secondary rolling mill drives		Pusher rack and pinion	5–6
Blooming and plate mill	5–6	Rotary furnace	5–6
Heavy-duty hot mill drives	5–6	Shear depress table	5–6
Slabbing and strip mill	5–6	Slab squeezer	5–6
Hot mill drives		Slab squeezer rack and pinion	5–6
Sendzimer-stekel	7–8	Slitter, side trimmer	6–7
Tandem-temper-skin	6–7	Tension reel	6–7
Cold mill drives		Tilt table, upcoiler	5–6
Bar, merchant, rail, rod	5–6	Transfer car	5–6
Structural, tube	5–6	Wire drawing machine	6–7
Auxiliary and miscellaneous drives		Precision gear drives	
Annealing furnace car	5–6		
Bending roll	5–6		
Blooming mill manipulator	5–6		

TABLE 10.10 AGMA Applications and Quality Numbers for Racks and Gears (*Continued*)

Gearing application	Quality no.*	Gearing application	Quality no.*
Steel industry (continued)		Steel industry (continued)	
Diesel electric gearing	8–9	Overhead hoist	5–6
Flying shear	9–10	Pickler building	5–6
Shear timing gears	9–10	Pig machine, sand house	5–6
High speed reels	8–9	Portable hoist	5–6
Locomotive timing		Scale pit, shipping	5–6
gears	9–10	Scrap balers and shears	5–6
Pump gears	8–9	Scrap preparation	5–6
Tube reduction gearing	8–9	Service shops	5–6
Turbine	9–10	Skull cracker	5–6
Overhead cranes		Slab handling	5–6
Billet charger, cold mill	5–6	Miscellaneous	
Bucket handling	5–6	Clocks	6
Car repair shop	5–6	Counters	7–9
Cast house, coil storage	5–6	Fishing reel	6
Charging machine	5–6	Gauges	8–10
Cinder yard, hot top	5–6	IBM card puncher, sorter	8
Coal and ore bridges	5–6	Metering pumps	7–8
Electric furnace charger	5–6	Motion-picture equipment	8
Hot metal, ladle	5–6	Popcorn machine, comm.	6–7
Hot mill, ladle house	5–6	Pumps	5–7
Jib crane, motor room	5–6	Sewing machine	8
Mold yard, rod mill	5–6	Slicer	7–8
Ore unloader, stripper	5–6	Vending machines	6–7

* Quality numbers are inclusive from the highest to the lowest number shown.

SOURCE: Extracted from AGMA standard 390.03 with the permission of the publisher, American Gear Manufacturers Association, 1500 King Street, Suite 201, Alexandria, Virginia 22314.

TABLE 10.11 AGMA Design Manual for Fine-Pitch Gearing: Recommended Minimum Fine-Pitch Spur and Helical Gear Specifications for General Applications (See Note 1)

Arranged for printing on a standard form drawing or for application to drawing by rubber stamp; for proper use of capital or lowercase lettering, see Note 2.

	Spur Gear Data			
Basic Specification Data	Number of teeth	(*N*)		
	Diametral pitch	(*P*)		
	Pressure angle	(ϕ)		
	Standard pitch diameter	(*N*/*P*)	(Ref.)	
	Tooth form (per AGMA 207.05)			
	Max. calc. cir. thickness on std. pitch circle			
Mfg. and Inspection Data	Gear testing radius			
	AGMA quality number			
	Total composite tolerance			
	Tooth-to-tooth composite tolerance			
	Outside diameter			
	Master gear basic cir. tooth thickness at std. pitch circle		(Ref.)	
	Master gear number of teeth		(Ref.)	

	Helical Gear Data*			
BASIC SPECIFICATION DATA	NUMBER OF TEETH	(N)		
	NORMAL DIAMETRAL PITCH	(P_n)		
	NORMAL PRESSURE ANGLE	(ϕ_n)		
	HELIX ANGLE—HAND	ψ		
	STANDARD PITCH DIAMETER	$(N/P_n \cos \psi)$	(Ref.)	
	TOOTH FORM (PER AGMA 207.05)			
	MAX. CALC. NORMAL CIR. THICKNESS ON STD. PITCH CIRCLE			
MFG. AND INSPECTION DATA	GEAR TESTING RADIUS			
	AGMA QUALITY NUMBER			
	TOTAL COMPOSITE TOLERANCE			
	TOOTH-TO-TOOTH COMPOSITE TOLERANCE			
	LEAD			
	OUTSIDE DIAMETER			
	MASTER GEAR BASIC NORMAL CIR. TOOTH THICKNESS AT STD. PITCH CIRCLE		(Ref.)	
	MASTER GEAR NUMBER OF TEETH		(Ref.)	

* If desired, a combination format covering both spur and helical gears can be used by specifying the helix angle equal to zero degrees. This permits standardization on the helical drawing format for both spur and helical gears.

NOTE 1: For data on the determination of spur and helical tooth proportions, see Section 4 or Standard AGMA 207.05. For data on inspection, see Section 10. For data on quality number, see Section 6 or AGMA 390.03.

NOTE 2: The use of all uppercase letters or both uppercase and lowercase letters is optional. The spur gear format illustrates the proper use of both uppercase and lowercase letters. The helical format illustrates the use of all upper case (capital) letters.

SOURCE: Extracted from AGMA standard 370.01 (R-1978) with the permission of the publisher, American Gear Manufacturers Association, 1500 King Street, Suite 201, Alexandria, Virginia 22314.

10.15 Forces and Wear Loads in Gearing Systems

When gears are in operation, different types of mechanical loads are produced by the different types of gears. Loads encountered in the various gear systems include radial loads, axial loads (tangential), and thrust loads. Heavy wearing loads on the tooth surfaces are also produced. The wearing loads and calculation procedures for them are shown in the next section. All the basic types of gear loads will be presented in the next section, which will allow designers to calculate the forces produced on the gear system shaft support bearings in order to be able to select the properly rated bearings. Calculation procedures in the following section will allow for the proper selection of gear material and hardness, which will satisfy the maximum wear loads permissible for the various gear systems and materials.

10.15.1 Forces in gear systems (bearing loads)

Determination of forces in bearing systems. In determining the forces developed by machine elements commonly encountered in bearing applications, the following equations are used.

Spur gearing (see Fig. 10.41). Tangential force is

$$F_{3g}\text{, newtons} = \frac{(1.91 \times 10^7)P}{P_{dg}\ \text{rpm}_g}$$

$$F_{3g}\text{, pounds-force} = \frac{(1.26 \times 10^5)P}{P_{dg}\ \text{rpm}_g}$$

Separating force is

$$F_{2g} = F_{3g} \tan \phi_p \cos\gamma_f$$

Single-helical gearing (see Fig. 10.42). Tangential force is

$$F_{3g}\text{, newtons} = \frac{(1.91 \times 10^7)P}{P_{dg}\ \text{rpm}_g}$$

$$F_{3g}\text{, pounds-force} = \frac{(1.26 \times 10^5)P}{P_{dg}\ \text{rpm}_g}$$

Separating force is

$$F_{2g} = \frac{F_{3g} \tan \phi_g}{\cos \psi_g}$$

Thrust force is

$$F_{1g} = F_{3g} \tan \psi_g$$

Note that for double-helical (herringbone) gearing, $F_{1g} = 0$.

Straight bevel and zerol gearing (0° spiral). In straight bevel and zerol gearing, the gear forces tend to push the pinion and gear out of mesh so that the direction of the thrust and separating forces is always the same regardless of the direction of rotation.

In calculating the tangential force F_{3p} or F_{3g} for bevel gearing, use the pinion or gear *mean* diameter M_{dp} or M_{dg} instead of the pitch diameter P_{dp} or P_{dg}. The mean diameter is calculated from

$$M_{dg} = P_{dg} - b \sin \gamma_g$$

$$M_{dp} = P_{dp} - b \sin \gamma_p$$

In straight bevel and zerol gearing, $F_{3p} = F_{3g}$ (see Fig. 10.43).

At the *pinion,* tangential force is

$$F_{3p}, \text{ newtons} = \frac{(1.91 \times 10^7)P}{M_{dp} \text{ rpm}_p}$$

$$F_{3p}, \text{ pounds-force} = \frac{(1.26 \times 10^5)P}{M_{dp} \text{ rpm}_p}$$

Thrust force is

$$F_{1p} = F_{3p} \tan \phi_p \cos \gamma_p$$

Separating force is

$$F_{2p} = F_{3p} \tan \phi_p \cos \gamma_p$$

At the *gear,* tangential force is

$$F_{3g}, \text{ newtons} = \frac{(1.91 \times 10^7)P}{M_{dg} \text{ rpm}_g}$$

$$F_{3g}, \text{ pounds-force} = \frac{(1.26 \times 10^5)P}{M_{dg} \text{ rpm}_g}$$

Thrust force is

$$F_{1g} = F_{3g} \tan \phi_g \sin \gamma_g$$

Separating force is

$$F_{2g} = F_{3g} \tan \phi_g \cos \gamma_g$$

Spiral bevel and hypoid gearing. In spiral bevel and hypoid gearing, the direction of the thrust and separating forces depends on spiral angle, hand of spiral, direction of rotation, and whether the gear is *driving* or *driven.*

The hand of the spiral is determined by noting whether the tooth curvature on the near face of the gear (Fig. 10.44) inclines to the left or right from the shaft axis. Direction of rotation is determined by viewing toward the gear or pinion apex.

In spiral bevel gearing (Fig. 10.45),

$$F_{3p} = F_{3g}$$

In hypoid gearing,

$$F_{3p} = \frac{F_{3g} \cos \psi_p}{\cos \psi_g}$$

The hypoid-pinion effective working diameter is

$$M_{dp} = M_{dg}\left(\frac{n_p}{n_g}\right)\left(\frac{\cos \psi_g}{\cos \psi_p}\right)$$

The hypoid-gear effective working diameter is

$$M_{dg} = P_{dg} - b \sin \psi_g$$

Thrust and separating-force equations are summarized in Fig. 10.46. The cases listed include driving member rotating either clockwise or counterclockwise.

Straight worm gearing (see Fig. 10.47). For the worm, tangential force is

$$F_{3w}\text{, newtons} = \frac{(1.91 \times 10^7)P}{P_{dw}\ \text{rpm}_w}$$

$$F_{3w}\text{, pounds-force} = \frac{(1.26 \times 10^5)P}{P_{dw}\ \text{rpm}_w}$$

Thrust force is

$$F_{1w}\text{, newtons} = \frac{(1.91 \times 10^7)P\eta}{P_{dg}\ \text{rpm}_g}$$

$$F_{1w}\text{, pounds-force} = \frac{(1.26 \times 10^5)P\eta}{P_{dg}\ \text{rpm}_g}$$

or

$$F_{1w} = \frac{F_{3w}\eta}{\tan \lambda}$$

Separating force is

$$F_{2w} = \frac{F_{3w} \sin \phi}{\cos \phi \sin \lambda + \mu \cos \lambda}$$

For the worm gear, tangential force is

$$F_{3g}\text{, newtons} = \frac{(1.91 \times 10^7)P\eta}{P_{dg}\ \text{rpm}_g}$$

$$F_{3g}\text{, pounds-force} = \frac{(1.26 \times 10^5)P\eta}{P_{dg}\ \text{rpm}_g}$$

or

$$F_{3g} = \frac{F_{3w}\eta}{\tan \lambda}$$

Thrust force is

$$F_{1g}\text{, newtons} = \frac{(1.91 \times 10^7)P}{P_{dw}\ \text{rpm}_w}$$

$$F_{1g}\text{, pounds-force} = \frac{(1.26 \times 10^5)P}{P_{dw}\ \text{rpm}_w}$$

Separating force is

$$F_{2g} = \frac{F_{3w} \sin \phi}{\cos \phi \sin \lambda + \mu \cos \lambda}$$

where $\lambda = \tan^{-1}\left(\dfrac{P_{dg}}{g_r P_{dw}}\right)$ or $\lambda = \tan^{-1}\left(\dfrac{L}{\pi P_{dw}}\right)$

and

$$\eta = \frac{\cos \phi - \mu \tan \lambda}{\cos \phi + \mu \cot \lambda}$$

In the metric system, the coefficient of friction μ is approximately

$$\mu = (5.34 \times 10^{-7})V_s^3 + \frac{0.146}{V_s^{0.09}} - 0.103$$

and $$V_s\text{, meters/second} = \frac{P_{du}\text{rpm}_w}{(1.91 \times 10^4)\cos\lambda}$$

In the U.S. customary (inch) system,

$$\mu = (7 \times 10^{-14})V_s^3 + \frac{0.235}{V_s^{0.09}} - 0.103$$

and $$V_s\text{, feet/minute} = \frac{P_{dw}\text{rpm}_w}{3.82\cos\lambda}$$

The approximations are for the coefficient of friction as given in AGMA standard 440.04, October 1971, Table 4, for the rubbing-velocity range 0.015 to 15 m/s (3 to 3000 ft/min).

Nomenclature (bearing forces)

C = center distance of gears, in or mm
F_b = belt or chain pull, lbf or N
F_1 = thrust force, lbf or N
F_{1g}, F_{1p}, F_{1w} = thrust force on gear, pinion, or worm, lbf or N
F_2 = separating force, lbf or N
F_{2g}, F_{2p}, F_{2w} = separating force on gear, pinion, or worm, lbf or N
F_3 = tangential force, lbf or N
F_{3g}, F_{3p}, F_{3w} = tangential force on gear, pinion, or worm, lbf or N
L = lead or axial advance of a helix for one complete revolution, in or mm
M_d = mean diameter or effective working diameter, of sprocket, pulley, or sheave, in or mm
M_{dg}, M_{dp}, M_{dw} = mean diameter or effective working diameter of gear, pinion, or worm, respectively, in or mm
P = power, hp or kW
P_{dg}, P_{dp}, P_{dw} = pitch diameter of gear, pinion, or worm, in or mm
V_s = surface or rubbing velocity, ft/min or m/s
b = tooth length, in or mm
f_{cb} = belt or chain pull factor
g_r = gearing ratio
n_g, n_p, n_s = number of teeth in gear, pinion, or sprocket
p' = pitch or distance between equally spaced tooth surfaces along the pitch line, in or mm
γ = for bevel gearing—pitch angle of gear, degrees; for

hypoid gearing—face angle of pinion and root angle of gear, degrees

η = efficiency
λ = worm gearing lead angle, degrees
μ = coefficient of dynamic friction
ϕ = normal tooth-pressure angle for gear or pinion, degrees
ψ = for helical gearing—helix angle for gear or pinion, degrees; spiral angle for gear or pinion, degrees
rpm = rotation, revolutions per minute

Vertical, horizontal, radial reactions—Shaft on two supports. The following equations will be useful for determining the resultant reactions at the bearing points in gear, V-belt, or chain/sprocket systems. The bearings may be selected using values obtained from these equations.

Referring to Fig. 10.48, the vertical-reaction component force at bearing B is

$$R_{LBv} = \frac{1}{x}\left[\begin{matrix} x_1\,(F_{2g}\cos\theta_1 + F_{3g}\sin\theta_1) + \tfrac{1}{2}\,(P_{dg} - b\sin\gamma_g)\,F_{1g}\cos\theta_1 \\ + x_2 F\cos\theta_2 + M\cos\theta_3 \end{matrix}\right]$$

Horizontal-reaction component force at bearing B is

$$R_{LBh} = \frac{1}{x}\left[\begin{matrix} x_1\,(F_{2g}\sin\theta_1 + F_{3g}\cos\theta_1) + \tfrac{1}{2}\,(P_{dg} - b\sin\gamma_g)\,F_{1g}\sin\theta_1 \\ + x_2\,F\sin\theta_2 + M\sin\theta_3 \end{matrix}\right]$$

Vertical-reaction component force at bearing A is

$$R_{LAv} = F_{2g}\cos\theta_1 + F_{3g}\sin\theta_1 + F\cos\theta_2 - R_{LBv}$$

Horizontal-reaction component force at bearing A is

$$R_{LAh} = F_{2g}\sin\theta_1 - F_{3g}\cos\theta_1 + F\sin\theta_2 - R_{LBh}$$

The resultant radial reactions are

$$TR_{LA} = \sqrt{(R_{LAv})^2 + (R_{LAh})^2}$$

and

$$TR_{LB} = \sqrt{(R_{LBv})^2 + (R_{LBh})^2}$$

Nomenclature for preceding reaction equations is as follows:

x = bearing spread, in or mm
A, B = bearing-position subscripts
x_1, x_2 = linear distance (positive or negative), in or mm
F_{1g}, F_{2g}, F_{3g} = thrust, separating and tangential forces on the gear, sheave, or sprocket; i.e., F_1 = thrust, F_2 = separating force, and F_3 = tangential force and g denotes gear, sheave, or sprocket, lbf or N
R_L = reaction-component of force, lbf or N
TR_L = resultant radial reaction, lbf or N
M = moment, N·mm or lbf·in
γ = bevel-gearing pitch angle of gear or pinion
$\theta_1, \theta_2, \theta_3$ = gear mesh-angle relative to the plane of reference as shown in Fig. 10.48

10.16 Gear Loads and Design Procedures

The following subsections will aid the designer in selecting the correct gear sizes and gear materials for most general applications. The design procedures consist of a series of equations which are used to size the gears and then check the dynamic and wear loads to make certain that these loads are within the allowable stress limits for each particular design and material. The gear systems

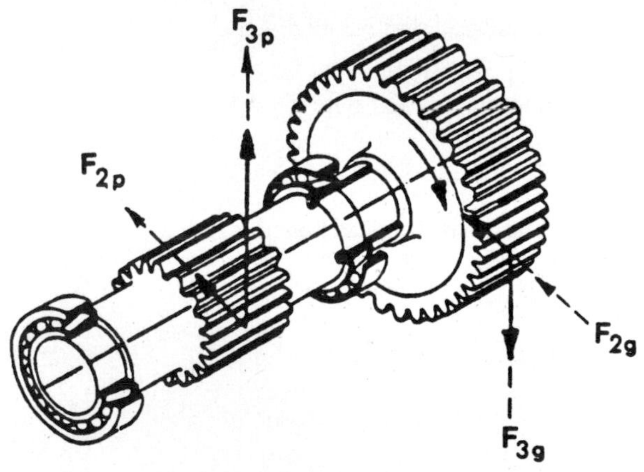

Figure 10.41 Forces in spur gears.

(*Text continued on page 935.*)

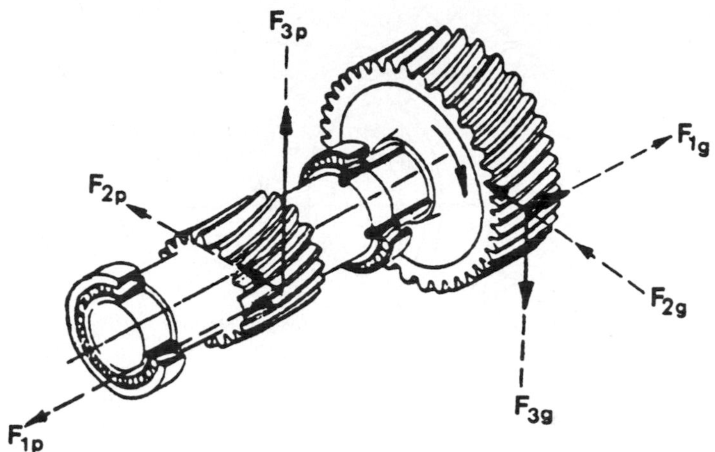

Figure 10.42 Forces in helical gears.

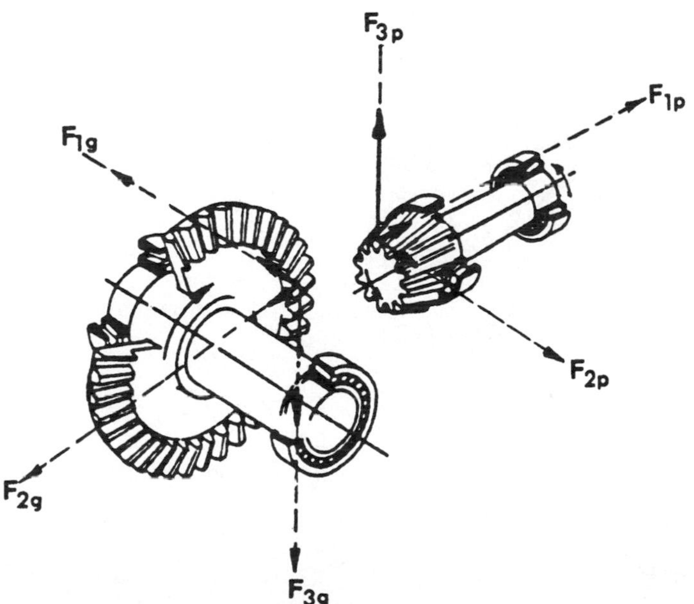

Figure 10.43 Forces in straight bevel and zerol gears.

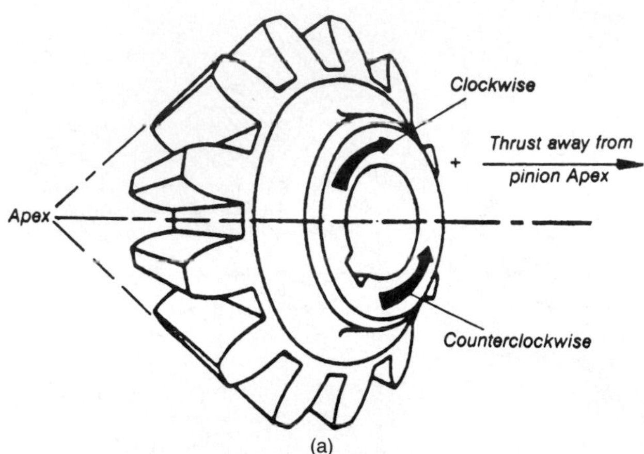

(a)

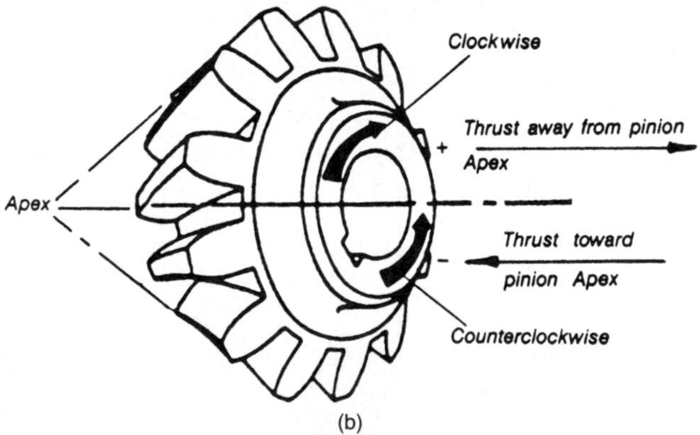

(b)

Figure 10.44 (*a*) Direction of thrust, straight bevel gears. (*b*) Direction of thrust, spiral bevel gears.

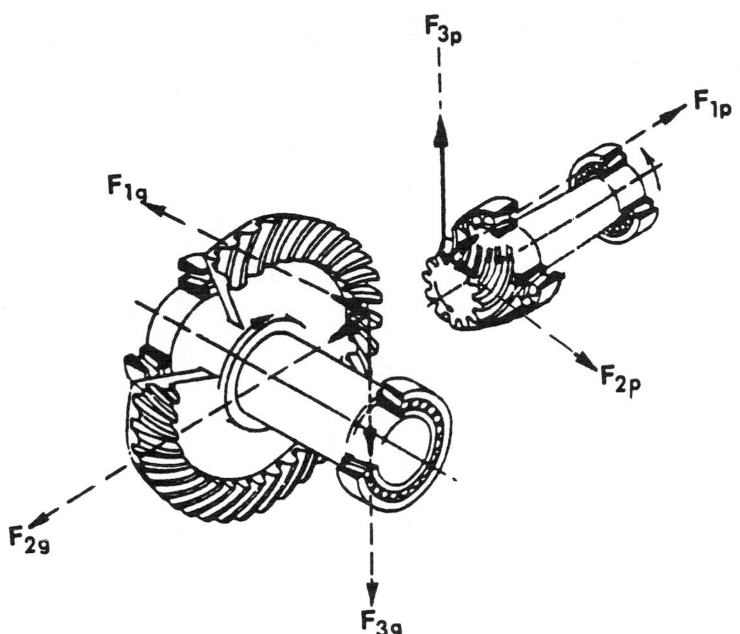

Figure 10.45 Forces in spiral bevel gears.

Driving-member rotation	Thrust force	Separating force
Right-hand spiral—clockwise	$F_{1p} = \frac{F_{3p}}{\cos \psi_p}(\tan \phi_p \sin \gamma_p - \sin \psi_p \cos \gamma_p)$, driving gear	$F_{2p} = \frac{F_{3p}}{\cos \psi_p}(\tan \phi_p \cos \gamma_p + \sin \psi_p \sin \gamma_p)$, driving gear
Left-hand spiral—counterclockwise	$F_{1g} = \frac{F_{3g}}{\cos \psi_g}(\tan \phi_g \sin \gamma_g + \sin \psi_g \cos \gamma_g)$, driven gear	$F_{2g} = \frac{F_{3g}}{\cos \psi_g}(\tan \phi_g \cos \gamma_g - \sin \psi_g \sin \gamma_g)$, driven gear
Right-hand spiral—counterclockwise	$F_{1p} = \frac{F_{3p}}{\cos \psi_p}(\tan \phi_p \sin \gamma_p + \sin \psi_p \cos \gamma_p)$, driving gear	$F_{2p} = \frac{F_{3p}}{\cos \psi_p}(\tan \phi_p \cos \gamma_p - \sin \psi_p \sin \gamma_p)$, driving gear
Left-hand spiral—clockwise	$F_{1g} = \frac{F_{3g}}{\cos \psi_g}(\tan \phi_g \sin \gamma_g - \sin \psi_g \cos \gamma_g)$, driven gear	$F_{2g} = \frac{F_{3g}}{\cos \psi_g}(\tan \phi_g \cos \gamma_g + \sin \psi_g \sin \gamma_g)$, driven gear

Figure 10.46 Thrust and separating force equations, spiral bevel and hypoid gearing.

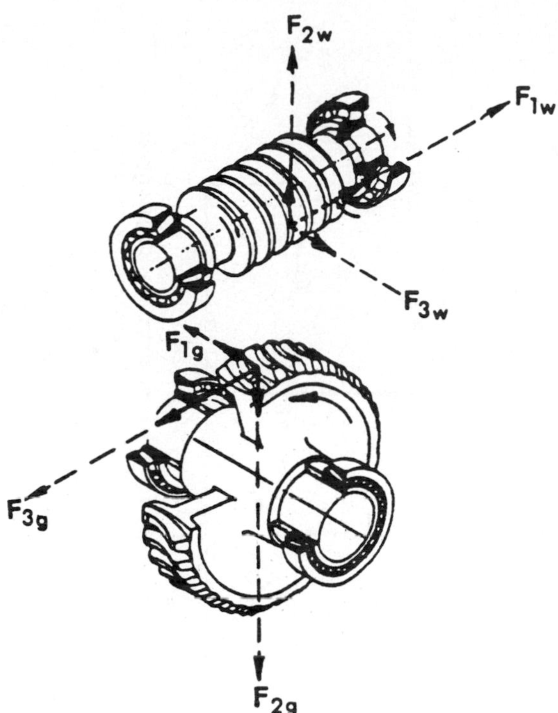

Figure 10.47 Forces in worm gears.

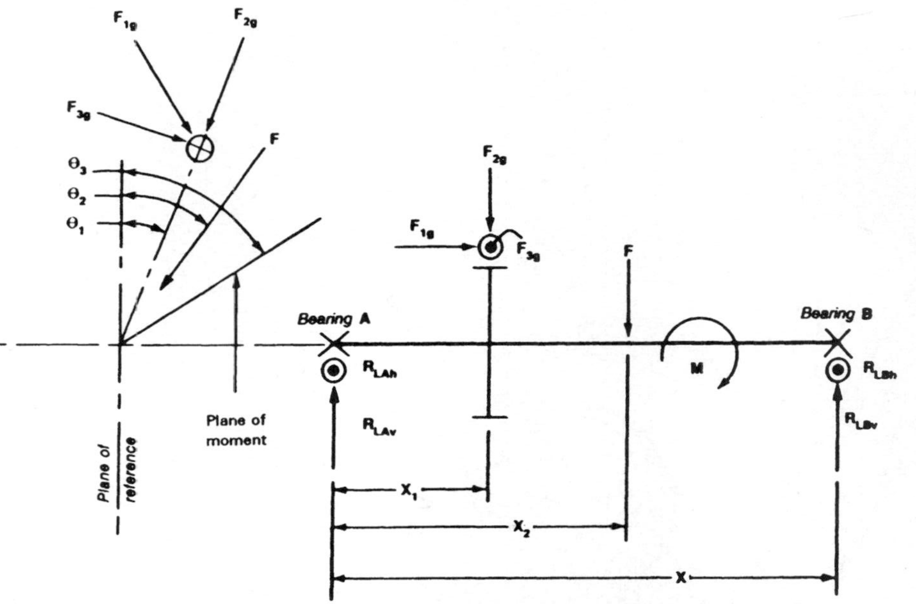

Note: Shown in this section are equations for the case of a shaft on two supports with gear forces F_1 (tangential), F_2 (separating) and F_3 (thrust), an external radial load F and an external moment M. The loads are applied at arbitrary angles (θ_1, θ_2, and θ_3) relative to the reference plane indicated in the above figure. Using the principles of superposition, the equations for radial and horizontal reactions (R_{LA} and R_{LB}) can be expanded to include any number of gears, external forces, or moments. Use signs as determined from the gear force equations.

Figure 10.48 Application of load diagram, gearing systems.

for which the equations have been developed include spur gears, helical gears, bevel gears, spiral bevel gears, and worm gears.

10.16.1 Spur gear loads and design procedures

A typical set of spur gears is shown in Fig. 10.49, from which the gear terminology and geometric features can be seen. The proportions for standard gear teeth are shown in Fig. 10.50.

Note: $P_c = \pi D/N \qquad P_d = N/D \qquad \text{and} \qquad P_c \times P_d = \pi$

where P_c = circular pitch, in
P_d = diametral pitch (dimensionless quantity)
N = number of teeth
D = pitch diameter, in

Interference of spur gear teeth. To avoid involute profile *overlap* of teeth in spur gears, the maximum addendum radius for each gear must be equal to or less than

$$\sqrt{(\text{radius of base circle})^2 + (\text{center distance})^2 (\sin \phi)^2}$$

where ϕ = pressure angle, degrees

Allowable tooth stresses. The allowable tooth stress s_a depends on the gear material and the pitch-line velocity as follows:

$$s_a = s_o\left(\frac{600}{600 + V}\right) \qquad \text{for } V \text{ less than 2000 ft/min}$$

$$s_a = s_o\left(\frac{1200}{1200 + V}\right) \qquad \text{for } V \text{ from 2000 to 4000 ft/min}$$

$$s_a = s_o\left(\frac{78}{78\sqrt{V}}\right) \qquad \text{for } V \text{ greater than 4000 ft/min}$$

where s_a = allowable stress, psi
s_o = 0.33 × ultimate strength of material
V = pitch-line velocity, ft/min

Precise s_o values may be obtained from the materials tables shown in Tables 10.3, 10.7, and 10.9, as well as from Chap. 5. s_o is the endurance strength of the material.

Note: s_o values are approximate for the following materials:

Cast iron = 8000 psi

Bronze = 12,000 psi

Steels = 10,000 to 50,000 psi

Actual operating tooth stress. If the diametral pitch is known,

$$\frac{P_d^2}{y} = \frac{sk\pi^2}{F} \qquad \text{and} \qquad s = \frac{F(P_d)^2}{yk\pi^2}$$

where s = actual stress (must be $\leqq s_a$), psi (see equation above)
k = 4 (as an upper limit)
F = transmitted force, lbf
= $2M_t/D$, where M_t = torque of weaker gear, lb·in, and
D = pitch diameter, in
P_d = diametral pitch
y = tooth-form factor (see Fig. 10.51)

If the pitch diameter is unknown,

$$s = \frac{2M_t P_d^3}{k\pi^2 yN}$$

where s = actual stress, psi (must be $\leqq s_a$)
M_t = torque of weaker gear, lb·in
k = 4 (as an upper limit)
N = number of teeth on the weaker gear (~15 minimum)
P_d = diametral pitch
y = tooth-form factor (see Fig. 10.51)

Note: The largest possible P_d will provide the most economical design. In general, when diameters are known, design for the largest number of teeth possible; when diameters are unknown, design for the smallest pitch diameters possible.

Dynamic tooth loads (Buckingham equation). The dynamic load F_d equation approximating a detailed dynamic analysis is given as

$$F_d = \frac{0.05V(bC + F)}{0.05V + \sqrt{bC + F}} + F$$

where F_d = dynamic load, lbf
V = pitch-line velocity, ft/min
F = transmitted force, lbf = $2M_t/D$; also = gear torque/pitch radius of gear
b = face width of gear, in
C = constant (deformation factor); see Fig. 10.52

Wear tooth loads. To ensure durability in a gear *pair,* the profiles of the teeth must not have excessive contact stress as determined by the wear load F_w:

$$F_w = D_p b K_1 Q$$

where D_p = pitch diameter of smaller gear (pinion), in
b = face width of gear, in
K_1 = stress factor for fatigue (see Fig. 10.53 and next equation)
$Q = 2N_g/(N_p + N_g)$
N_g = number of teeth on gear
N_p = number of teeth on pinion

$$K_1 = \frac{s_{es}^2 \sin \phi}{1.4}\left(\frac{1}{E_p} + \frac{1}{E_g}\right)$$

where s_{es} = surface endurance limit of a gear pair, psi (see Fig. 10.53)
E_p = modulus of elesticity of pinion material, psi (see Chap. 5)
E_g = modulus of elasticity of gear material, psi (see Chap. 5)
ϕ = pressure angle, degrees

Note: s_{es} may be estimated from

$$s_{es} = 400 \times (\text{BHN}) - 10{,}000$$

where BHN is the average Brinell hardness number of the pinion and gear for values up to 350 BHN. Then, the wear load F_w must be equal to or greater than the dynamic load F_d. Also, K_1 factors for various materials and tooth forms are shown in Fig. 10.53, as recommended by Buckingham.

The preceding calculation procedures will establish the tentative or preliminary gear design. Final design decisions should be deter-

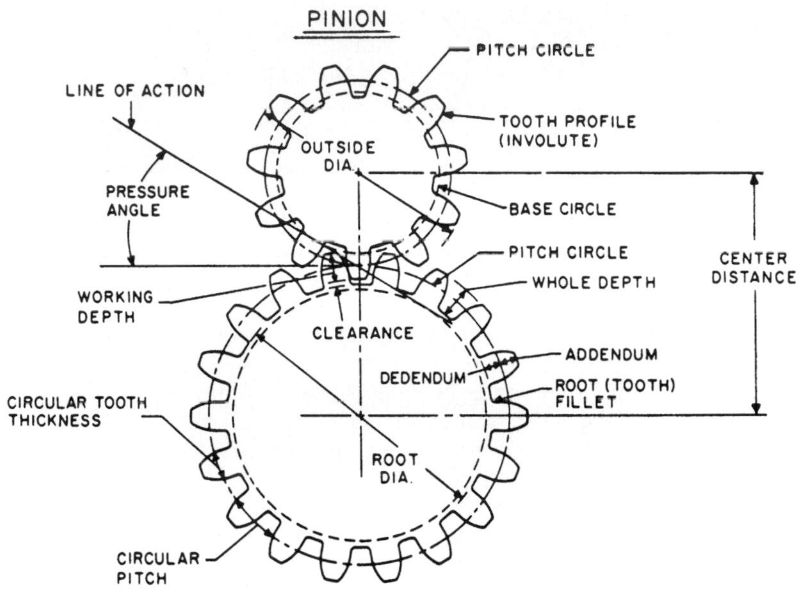

Figure 10.49 Typical set of spur gears and terminology.

Tooth Type	14.5° Composite	14.5° Full Depth Involute	20° Full Depth Involute	20° Stub Involute
Addendum	$1/P_d$	$1/P_d$	$1/P_d$	$0.8/P_d$
Minimum dedendum	$1.157/P_d$	$1.157/P_d$	$1.157/P_d$	$1/P_d$
Whole depth	$2.157/P_d$	$2.157/P_d$	$2.157/P_d$	$1.8/P_d$
Clearance	$0.157/P_d$	$0.157/P_d$	$0.157/P_d$	$0.2/P_d$

Note: In the composite tooth form, the middle third of the tooth profile has an involute shape, while the remainder is cycloidal.

Figure 10.50 Proportions of standard gear teeth.

Gear Tooth Form Factor (y) - for use in Lewis strength equations

Number of Teeth	14.5° Full-Depth Involute or Composite	20° Full-Depth Involute	20° Stub Involute
12	0.067	0.078	0.099
13	0.071	0.083	0.103
14	0.075	0.088	0.108
15	0.078	0.092	0.111
16	0.081	0.094	0.115
17	0.084	0.096	0.117
18	0.086	0.098	0.120
19	0.088	0.100	0.123
20	0.090	0.102	0.125
21	0.092	0.104	0.127
23	0.094	0.106	0.130
25	0.097	0.108	0.133
27	0.099	0.111	0.136
30	0.101	0.114	0.139
34	0.104	0.118	0.142
38	0.106	0.122	0.145
43	0.108	0.126	0.147
50	0.110	0.130	0.151
60	0.113	0.134	0.154
75	0.115	0.138	0.158
100	0.117	0.142	0.161
150	0.119	0.146	0.165
300	0.122	0.150	0.170
Rack	0.124	0.154	0.175

Figure 10.51 Gear tooth-form factor.

Values of the Deformation Factor C - for dynamic load calculations

Materials		Involute	Tooth Error - inches			
Pinion	Gear	tooth form	0.0005	0.001	0.002	0.003
Cast iron	Cast iron	14.5°	400	800	1600	2400
Steel	Cast iron	14.5°	550	1100	2200	3300
Steel	Steel	14.5°	800	1600	3200	4800
Cast iron	Cast iron	20° Full Depth	415	830	1660	2490
Steel	Cast iron	20° Full Depth	570	1140	2280	3420
Steel	Steel	20° Full Depth	830	1660	3320	4980
Cast iron	Cast iron	20° Stub	430	860	1720	2580
Steel	Cast iron	20° Stub	590	1180	2360	3540
Steel	Steel	20° Stub	860	1720	3440	5160

Figure 10.52 Values of the deformation factor.

Values for (s_{es}) and (K_1) for Various Materials - for use in wear load equations

Average Brinell Hardness Number of Steel Pinion and Steel Gear		Surface Endurance Limit (s_{es})	Stress Fatigue Factor K_1 14.5°	20°
150		50,000	30	41
200		70,000	58	79
250		90,000	96	131
300		110,000	144	196
350		130,000	206	281
400		150,000	268	366
Brinell Hardness Number (BHN)				
Steel Pinion	**Gear**			
150	Cast Iron	50,000	44	60
200	Cast Iron	70,000	87	119
250	Cast Iron	90,000	144	196
150	Phos. Bronze	50,000	46	62
200	Phos. Bronze	65,000	73	100
Cast Iron Pinion	Cast Iron Gear	80,000	152	208
Cast Iron Pinion	Cast Iron Gear	90,000	193	284

Figure 10.53 Constants for various gear materials.

mined by appropriate tests on the gear system in actual operation as weighed against the tentative design and expected or specified performance criteria.

10.16.2 Helical gear loads and design procedures

The following procedures are for helical gears operating on parallel shafts only, which is the normal function for helical gears. Remember that helical gears operating on parallel shafts must be of opposite hand to each other, i.e., LH pinion with a RH gear and RH pinion with a LH gear.

Virtual number of teeth. The *virtual* number of teeth N_f on a helical gear is the number of teeth that *could* be generated on the ellipse formed by taking a cross section through the gear in the *normal* plane (see Figs. 10.16 and 10.19). Therefore,

$$N_f = \frac{N}{\cos^3 \psi}$$

where N = actual number of teeth
ψ = helix angle, degrees (see Figs. 10.16 and 10.19)

Strength design. These procedures are similar to those for spur gears (Sec. 10.16.1). Analyzing the tooth normal to the helix, the normal load F_n using the Lewis equation is

$$F_n = s\left(\frac{b}{\cos \psi}\right) \frac{\pi y}{(P_d/\cos \psi)}$$

Then the tangential forces F on the teeth are

$$F = \frac{sby\pi}{(P_d/\cos \psi)} = \frac{sk\pi^2 y}{(P_d/\cos \psi)^2 \cos \psi} \qquad \text{(when standard pitch is in the normal plane)}$$

$$\text{or } F = \frac{sby\pi \cos \psi}{P_d} = \frac{sk\pi^2 y \cos \psi}{P_d^2} \qquad \text{(when standard pitch is in the diametral plane)}$$

where F = tangential force, lbf
$K = b/P_c$ (limited to a maximum of ~6)

P_d = diametral pitch in plane of rotation (dimensionless rotation)
y = tooth-form factor, based on the virtual number of teeth N_f above
s = allowable stress, psi

When the pressure angle ϕ is standard in the normal plane, the y factors from Fig. 10.51 for spur gears may be used. When the pressure angle ϕ is standard in the diametral plane, the y factors of Fig. 10.51 are considered approximate. A more accurate value of y is not usually necessary when using these procedures, since corrections can be made as you proceed through the calculations.

Allowable stress is given by

$$s = s_o\left(\frac{78}{78 + \sqrt{V}}\right)$$

where s_o = 0.33 × ultimate strength of material, psi
V = pitch-line velocity, ft/min

In checking the gear design strength, the pitch diameter is either known or unknown. If the pitch diameter P_d is known,

$$\frac{P_d^2}{y} = \frac{s_o k \pi^2 \cos\psi}{F}\left(\frac{78}{78 + \sqrt{V}}\right)$$

where $k = b/P_c$
F = tangential force = torque/pitch radius, lbf
V = pitch-line velocity, ft/min
s_o = see following equation

$$s_o = \frac{s}{\left(\frac{78}{78 + \sqrt{V}}\right)}$$

where s = allowable stress, psi (see equation above)

If the pitch diameter P_d is unknown,

$$s_1 = \frac{2TP_d^3}{ky\pi^2 N \cos\psi}$$

where s_1 = actual induced stress, psi
T = resisting torque of weaker gear, lb·in
N = actual number of teeth on the weaker gear

The preceding helical gear equations are a first approximation for determining possible pitch P_d and face width b, which are then checked for dynamic and wear loads using the following equations.

Limiting endurance beam strength. The beam strength F_o is derived from the Lewis equation, with no velocity factor, and is

$$F_o = \frac{s_o b y \pi \cos \psi}{P_d} \qquad \text{an allowed value}$$

Then the limiting endurance strength F_o must be equal to or greater than the dynamic load F_d, which is

$$F_d = F + \frac{0.05V\,(Cb\cos^2\psi + F)\cos\psi}{0.05V + \sqrt{Cb\cos^2\psi + F}} \qquad \text{(use preceding symbols)}$$

and values of C may be obtained from the spur gear section (Fig. 10.52)

Limiting wear load. The wear load F_w for helical gears is calculated from the Buckingham equation:

$$F_w = \frac{D_p b Q K_1}{\cos^2\psi} \qquad \text{(an allowed value)}$$

Where D_p = pitch diameter of the pinion, in
Q = see following equation
K_1 = see following equation

$$Q = \frac{2D_g}{D_p + D_g} = \frac{2N_g}{N_p + N_g} \qquad (N_p \text{ and } N_g \text{ are actual number of teeth})$$

$$K_1 = \frac{s_{es}^2 \sin\phi_n}{1.4}\left(\frac{1}{E_p} + \frac{1}{E_g}\right)$$

where s_{es} = surface endurance limit (see Sec. 10.15.1)

Then the limiting wear load F_w must be equal to or greater than the dynamic load F_d, and the endurance load F_o must be equal to or greater than the dynamic load F_d.

Note: F_o and F_w are allowable values that cannot be exceeded.

10.16.3 Bevel gear loads and design procedures

Strength design of straight-tooth bevel gears may be based on a modified Lewis equation which takes into account the tapered teeth of the bevel gear. The permissible force F that may be transmitted is then given as

$$F = \frac{sby\pi}{P_d}\left(\frac{L - b}{L}\right)$$

where F = force transmitted, lbf
s = allowable bending stress, psi
y = tooth-form factor for bevel gears (use 75 percent of the values shown for spur gears in Fig. 10.51 as an approximation)
L = cone distance, in (see Fig. 10.23 and following equation)
b = face width of gear, in
P_d = diametral pitch based on the largest part of the tooth cross section (at the perimeter of the bevel gear). This is the point where a gear tooth gauge is used to measure the diametral pitch of a straight-tooth bevel gear (see Fig. 10.37).

$$L = \sqrt{R_p^2 + R_g^2} \qquad \text{inches (shaft angle} = 90°)$$

where R_p = pitch radius of pinion, in
R_g = pitch radius of gear, in

For improved producibility and operation of straight-tooth bevel gears, the face width b should generally not be greater than $L/3$, where L is the cone distance.

When designing for strength, the diameter of the gear may be either known or unknown. When the diameter is known, use the modified Lewis equation:

$$\frac{P_d}{y} = \frac{sb\pi}{F}\left(\frac{L - b}{L}\right) \qquad \text{(an allowed value)}$$

where F = transmitted force (lbf) = torque of weaker gear/weaker gear pitch radius. The terms on the right side of this equation can be determined after the gear material has been specified.

The allowable stress s is calculated as explained in the following equations, while the preceding equation yields an allowable value for P_d/y, which must be satisfied (must equal the right side of equation numerically) by selecting an appropriate value for P_d.

When the diameter is unknown, use the following form of the Lewis equation for calculating the actual stress s:

$$s = \frac{2P_d^2T}{\pi byN}\left(\frac{L}{L-b}\right)$$ actual stress, psi (must be less than allowable stress)

In the preceding equation, you may substitute values for b and $L/(L - b)$ as follows: Let

$$b = \frac{N_p}{6P_d}\sqrt{1+R^2} \qquad \text{and} \qquad \frac{L}{L-b} = \frac{3}{2}$$

where N = actual number of teeth in weaker gear
N_p = number of teeth on the pinion
R = ratio of the angular velocity A_{vp} of the pinion to the angular velocity A_{vg} of the gear, i.e., $R = A_{vp}/A_{vg}$

The design procedures shown for strength are a first approximation which must be checked for wear loads and dynamic loads as shown in the equations that follow.

The allowable stress s for average conditions may be calculated as follows:

$$s = s_o\left(\frac{1200}{1200+V}\right)$$ psi (for cut-teeth gears)

or $$s = s_o\left(\frac{78}{78+\sqrt{V}}\right)$$ psi (for generated teeth)

where $s_o = 0.33 \times$ ultimate strength of material, psi
V = pitch-line velocity, ft/min ($0.262 \times$ pitch diameter $\times$ rpm)

The virtual number of teeth N_f in a straight-tooth bevel gear is

$$N_f = \frac{N}{\cos \alpha}$$

where N = actual number of teeth
α = pitch angle or half-cone angle, degrees

Limiting wear load. The limiting wear load F_w may be approximated from

$$F_w = \frac{0.75 D_p b K_1 Q}{\cos\alpha} \qquad \text{(an allowed value)}$$

where D_p, b, K_1, and Q are the same as for spur gears, except that Q is based on the virtual number of teeth N_f and α is the pitch angle of the pinion in degrees.

Limiting endurance load. The limiting endurance load F_o may be calculated from

$$F_o = \frac{s_o b y \pi}{P_d}\left(\frac{L-b}{L}\right) \qquad \text{(an allowed value)}$$

Dynamic load. The dynamic load F_d may be approximated from

$$F_d = \frac{0.05V(bC+F)}{0.05V+\sqrt{bC+F}}$$

Symbols are the same as those for spur gears, and y is taken as 75 percent of the values shown in Fig. 10.51.

Finally, F_d must be equal to or less than F_w and be equal to or less than F_o.

Note: F_w and F_o are allowed values which must not be exceeded by the dynamic load F_d.

AGMA standard recommended horsepower rating and wear equations for bevel gears are as follows: For peak load,

$$\text{hp} = \frac{snD_p b y \pi(L-0.5b)}{126{,}000\, P_d L}\left(\frac{78}{78+\sqrt{V}}\right)$$

where s = 250 times BHN of weaker gear (for gears hardened and also not hardened after cutting)
s = 300 times BHN of weaker gear if it is case hardened
n = speed of the pinion, rpm

Other symbols were defined in the preceding sections.

For wear (durability),

$$\text{hp} = 0.8C_mC_Bb \qquad \text{(for straight bevel gears)}$$

$$\text{hp} = C_mC_Bb \qquad \text{(for spiral bevel gears)}$$

where C_m = material factor from Fig. 10.54
C_B = see following equation
b = face width of gear, in

$$C_B = \frac{D_p^{1.5}n}{233}\left(\frac{78}{78+\sqrt{V}}\right) \qquad \text{and} \qquad n = \text{rpm of pinion}$$

10.16.4 Worm gear loads and design procedures

The worm drive consists of a threaded worm in mesh with a gear called the *worm wheel.* The worm normally may have from one to four leads or threads. The axial pitch P_a of the worm is equal to the circular pitch P_c of the gear or worm wheel. The lead is the axial distance a point on the worm helix advances per revolution.

The following relationships exist in worm gearing:

$$\tan\alpha = \frac{\text{lead}}{\pi D_w} = \frac{P_cN_w}{\pi D_w} \qquad \text{and} \qquad \frac{\text{rpm}_w}{\text{rpm}_g} = \frac{N_g}{N_w} = \frac{D_g}{D_w\tan\alpha}$$

where α = lead angle of worm, degrees
D_w = worm pitch diameter, in
D_g = gear pitch diameter, in
N_w = number of threads on the worm
N_g = number of teeth in the gear (worm wheel)

Worm gear strength design. The following strength equation is based on the Lewis equation:

$$F = sbyP_{nc} = \frac{sby\pi}{P_{nd}}$$

where P_{nc} = normal circular pitch, in
P_{nd} = normal diametral pitch in plane normal to tooth
F = permissible tangential load, lbf
s = allowable stress, psi

$$s = s_o\left(\frac{1200}{1200+V_g}\right)$$

where $s_o = 0.33 \times$ ultimate strength of material, psi
V_g = pitch line velocity of the gear, ft/min

Dynamic load. The dynamic load F_d for the worm gear is estimated from

$$F_d = \left(\frac{1200 + V_g}{1200}\right)F$$

where F = actual transmitted tangential load, lbf

Endurance load. The endurance load F_o for the worm gear is

$$F_o = \frac{s_o b y \pi}{P_{nd}}$$

Wear load. The wear load F_w for the worm gear is

$$F_w = D_g b B$$

where D_g = pitch diameter of gear, in
b = gear face width, in
B = constant from Fig. 10.55

The values of constant B listed in Fig. 10.55 are for worm lead angles up to 10°. For lead angles between 10 and 25°, increase B by 25 percent (multiply the given values by 1.25). For lead angles over 25°, increase B by 50 percent (multiply given values by 1.50).

Note: F_o and F_w are allowable values which must not be exceeded by the dynamic load F_d.

AGMA horsepower rating equations for worm gears are as follows: From a wear standpoint,

$$\text{hp} = \frac{n}{R} KQm \qquad \text{(wear check)}$$

where hp = input horsepower
n = rpm of worm
R = transmission ratio = rpm worm/rpm gear
K = pressure constant per center distance (see Fig. 10.56)
$Q = R/(R + 2.5)$

m = velocity factor, estimated from

$$m = \frac{450}{450 + V_w + 3V_w/R}$$

where V_w = pitch line velocity of the worm, ft/min

AGMA design equations

$$D_w \approx \frac{C}{2.2} \approx 3P_c$$

$$b \approx 0.73D_w$$

$$L \approx P_c\left(4.5 + \frac{N_g}{50}\right)$$

where D_w = pitch diameter of worm, in
C = center distance between worm and gear, in
b = face width of gear, in
P_c = circular pitch of gear, in
L = axial length of worm, in

The preceding equations are for approximating the preliminary proportions of the worm gear unit.

AGMA recommendations for the limiting horsepower rating of plain worm gear units from the standpoint of heat dissipation are as follows: For worm gear speeds to 2000 rpm,

$$\text{hp} \approx \frac{9.5C^{1.5}}{R + 5} \qquad \text{(heat check)}$$

where hp = permissible input horsepower
C = center distance, in
R = transmission ratio (see previous symbols)

Note: For efficiency equations of worm gear sets, see Sec. 10.11.

10.17 Epicyclic Gearing

Epicyclic gearing, also called *planetary gearing,* is found in many variations and arrangements to meet a broad range of speed-ratio requirements. Some of the most often used epicyclic systems are

Gear		Pinion		
Material	Brinell (BHN)	Material	Brinell (BHN)	C_m
Annealed Steel	160-200	Heat-Treated Steel	210-245	0.30
Heat-Treated Steel	245-280	Heat-Treated Steel	285-325	0.40
Heat-Treated Steel	285-325	Heat-Treated Steel	335-360	0.50
Heat-Treated Steel	210-245	Oil or Surface Hdn'd St'l	500	0.40
Heat-Treated Steel	285-325	Case-Hardened Steel	550	0.60
Oil or Surface Hdn'd St'l	500	Case-Hardened Steel	550	0.90
Case-Hardened Steel	550	Case-Hardened Steel	550	1.00

Note: If cast iron teeth are strong enough, they will nct fail by wear. If steel teeth satisfy the wear requirements, they will have enough strength.

Figure 10.54 Material factors (C_m) for various gear material combinations.

Material Combination Constants (B) for Worm Gear Pairs

Worm	Gear	B
Hardened Steel	Cast Iron	50
Steel, 250 BHN	Phosphor Bronze	60
Hardened Steel	Phosphor Bronze	80
Hardened Steel	Chilled Phos. Bronze	120
Hardened Steel	Antimony Bronze	120
Cast Iron	Phosphor Bronze	150

Note: The tabulated values for (B) are for lead angles up to 10°.
For lead angles between 10° and 25°, multiply (B) value by 1.25.
For lead angles greater than 25°, multiply (B) values by 1.50.

Figure 10.55 Material combination constants, worm gears.

Pressure Constant (K) Dependent on Center Distance

Center Distance C, (inches)	K
1	0.0125
2	0.025
3	0.04
4	0.09
5	0.17
6	0.29
7	0.45
8	0.66
9	0.99
10	1.20
15	4.0
20	8.0
30	29.0
40	66.0
50	120.0

Note: To find values of (K) for intermediate values of center distance (C), use interpolation.

Figure 10.56 Pressure constants.

described in this section, together with the basic calculations used to specify the gears employed in these systems.

In general, the epicyclic gear train consists of a central "sun" gear, several "planets" meshing with and spaced uniformly around the sun gear, and an "annulus" or ring gear meshing with the planet gears. The sun and planet gears are externally toothed, while the ring gear is internally toothed. The name *epicyclic* is derived from the fact that points on the planet gears describe epicycloidal curves in space during rotation.

Epicyclic gear systems consist of either external/internal spur gears or external/internal helical gears. When helical gears are used in epicyclic systems, the hand of the internal teeth is the same as that of the external teeth; internal left-hand gears mesh with external left-hand gears and internal right-hand gears mesh with external right-hand gears.

A simple epicyclic gear system is shown in Fig. 10.57, together with the six arrangements possible for this system. The figure lists the six variations, with their corresponding speed-ratio equations. The diagram to the right in the figure is called the *gear train schematic diagram* and is the simplified system used to describe the action of the gear system and to show its parts with the gear numbers used in the ratio equations. N_1 represents gear number 1, and the number of teeth in the gear is substituted in the ratio equation. You may select the ratio first and then the number of teeth in the first gear to solve for the number of teeth in the second gear. Or you may select the number of teeth in both gears, N_1 and N_2, and solve for the ratio.

Epicyclic gear systems will not assemble unless the number of teeth in each gear is selected properly. If the planet gears are equally spaced around the sun gear, the following equations must be satisfied for assembly to be possible:

$$N_R = N_S + 2N_P$$

$$\frac{N_R + N_S}{\text{Number of planets}} = \text{an integer}$$

where N_R = number of ring or annulus teeth
N_S = number of sun gear teeth
N_P = number of planet gear teeth

The sum of the ring gear and sun gear teeth must be equally divisible by the number of planet gears in the system or the gears will not assemble. The tooth load at each planet gear is balanced between the sun-planet mesh and the planet-ring mesh. This tangential driving load is calculated from

$$F_t = \frac{126{,}050P_h}{n_s d_s(\text{no. of planets})}$$

where F_t = tangential driving force, lbf
n_s = rpm of the sun gear
d_s = pitch diameter of the sun gear, in
P_h = horsepower transmitted

The preceding equation shows the theoretical value of the tangential force, but in actual practice, this load may increase greatly due to dimensional tooth errors. With modern machinery, cutting-tool materials, and CNC controls, this may be less of a problem than in the past.

Figure 10.58 shows the three most common forms of epicyclic gearing. In the figure, illustration *A* shows the *planetary* system, *B* shows the *star* system, and *C* shows the *solar* system. In these figures, numeral 1 indicates the ring gear, numeral 2 the planet gear, numeral 3 the sun gear, and the letter *C* indicates the carrier of the planet gears. If you refer back to Fig. 10.57, it can be seen that by fixing or holding a specified gear motionless, the system will react or perform according to the table and the speed-ratio equations.

Another type of epicyclic gearing system is shown in Fig. 10.59. In this system, gears 2 and 4 are joined on a common shaft with the carrier *C,* with gears 1 and 3 being the input or output. The carrier is also an output in two of the configurations shown in the table, where the speed ratios of the different configurations of this system of gearing are shown.

The derivations of the speed ratios of the different types of epicyclic gear systems are rather complicated and will not be explained in this section. Rather, samples of different types of epicyclic systems are shown together with their speed-ratio equations for your applications or reference. Some of the texts listed in the Bibliography cover epicyclic gear systems in greater detail.

An interesting epicyclic system is known as *Humpage's bevel gears* and is illustrated in Fig. 10.60 together with the speed-ratio equation for this system. In the figure, the input is at gear 1 and the output is at gear 4, whose shaft passes through a hole in gear 5 (which is fixed). Gears 2 and 3 are the planets, and only one set is shown, although the system must have at least two or three sets for dynamic balance if the system is for high-speed use.

Speed-ratio definition and number of teeth in epicyclic systems. The speed ratios, by convention, are usually taken as greater than unity. If we refer back to Fig. 10.57, in the first row the input member is gear number 1, the fixed member is the carrier, the output is gear number 2, and there are three planet gears. If the ring gear has 48 teeth and the sun gear has 15 teeth, this will satisfy the previous equation stating that in a simple epicyclic system the sum of the teeth in the ring and sun gears must be equally divisible by the number of planet gears. This tells us if the system can be assembled properly, i.e.,

$$\frac{\text{Number of teeth in ring gear} + \text{number of teeth in sun gear}}{\text{3 sun gears}} = 21 \text{ (an integer)}$$

For a better example of ratios and numbers of teeth in epicyclic systems, refer to Fig. 10.61. This figure represents an actual production sample of an epicyclic system used in a portable electric screwdriver. This system is the same as that shown in Fig. 10.57, line 3, where the sun gear is the input, the ring gear is fixed (integral with the housing), and the carrier C is the output. The sun gear in this system has 6 teeth and the internal ring gear has 42 teeth, which satisfies the previous equation. The speed ratio of this system is given from Fig. 10.57 as

$$\begin{aligned} R &= 1 + \frac{N_2}{N_1} \\ &= 1 + \frac{42}{6} \\ &= 1 + 7 = 8 \end{aligned}$$

The speed-ratio is therefore 8 to 1, and the configuration of the system tells us that for each 8 revolutions of the sun gear (the input), the carrier (output) will rotate 1 revolution. This system is thus a speed-reduction type. The equation also tells us that the output will rotate in the same direction as the input (since its sign is positive). Figure 10.61 shows only one stage of the entire system. If you look at Fig. 10.62, you will see the first stage, which consists of three planet gears attached to the carrier plate. The six-tooth sun gear, which is the input for the second stage, is attached at the center of the carrier plate of the first stage and can just be seen in Fig. 10.62. Figure 10.63 is a cross section through the housing of this two-stage epicyclic system showing the ring gear (integral to the housing), the carrier plates with planets attached, and the sun gears. Since this is a two-stage system, the total speed ratio is $8 \times 8 = 64$ to 1. The total speed ratio of a multistage system is equal to the product of the ratios of the stages. If this were a three-stage system, the final ratio would be $8 \times 8 \times 8 = 512$ to 1. It can then be realized that the epicyclic gear systems or trains offer large speed ratios in limited spaces (either speed-increasing or speed-reduction, including changes in rotational direction from input to output).

Following is a selection of epicyclic gear systems with different configurations and speed ratios. Figures 10.64 and 10.65 are examples of *coupled planetary drives.* Figures 10.66 and 10.67 are examples of *fixed-differential drives.* The gear train schematic diagram and speed-ratio equation are shown in each of the figures, together with a typical cross section taken through the epicyclic-drive housing.

Epicyclic drive train calculations (simple planetary systems). Figure 10.68 is a representation of the epicyclic system shown in Fig. 10.57, line 3, where the sun gear is the input, the ring gear is held stationary, and the output is taken from the rotating carrier. This is also shown in Fig. 10.63 (one stage of the system) and in Figs. 10.61 and 10.62. The ratio equation was given as $R = 1 + (N_2/N_1)$. We will substitute the symbols of the ratio equation as follows:

$$N_1 = A \qquad N_2 = C$$

where A = size of driver (sun), pitch diameter (in), or number of teeth
C = size of fixed ring gear, pitch diameter (in), or number of teeth
R = rotation of driver (sun gear) for each revolution of the carrier (output)

(*Text continued on page 967.*)

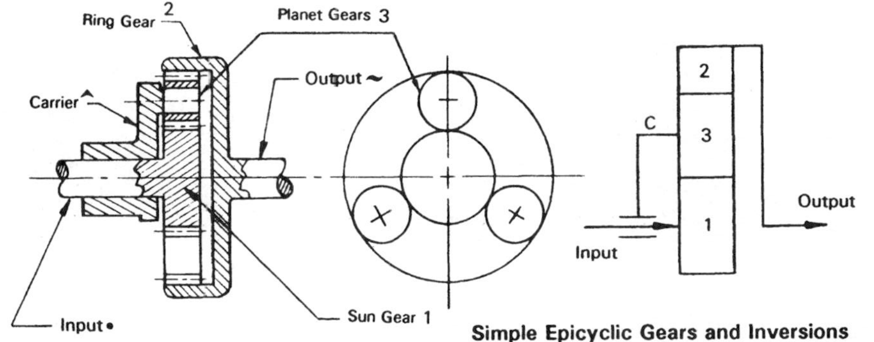

Simple Epicyclic Gears and Inversions

Input Member	Fixed Member	Output Member	Speed-ratio Equation
•1	C ^	2 ~	$R = -N_2/N_1$
2	C	1	$R = -N_1/N_2$
1	2	C	$R = 1 + (N_2/N_1)$
2	1	C	$R = 1 + (N_1/N_2)$
C	2	1	$R = 1/(1 + (N_2/N_1))$
C	1	2	$R = 1/(1 + (N_1/N_2))$

Note: The minus sign indicates opposite rotation from input.

Figure 10.57 Planetary (epicyclic) gear systems.

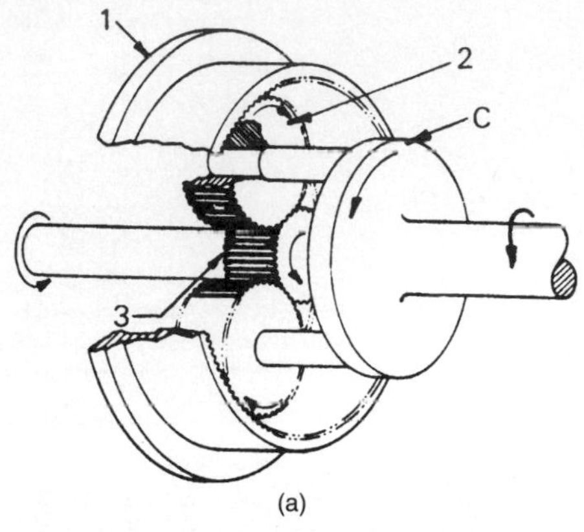

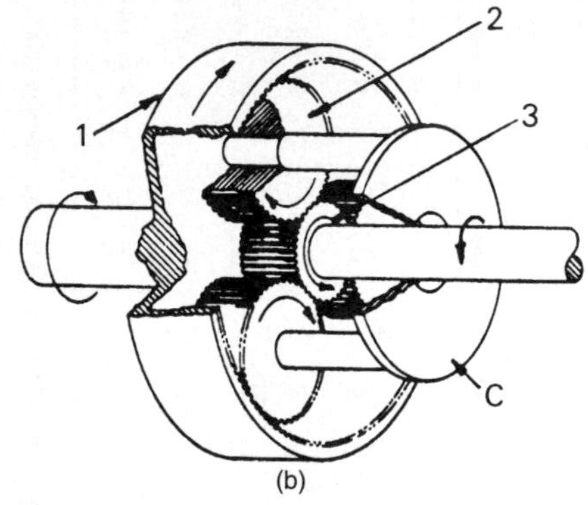

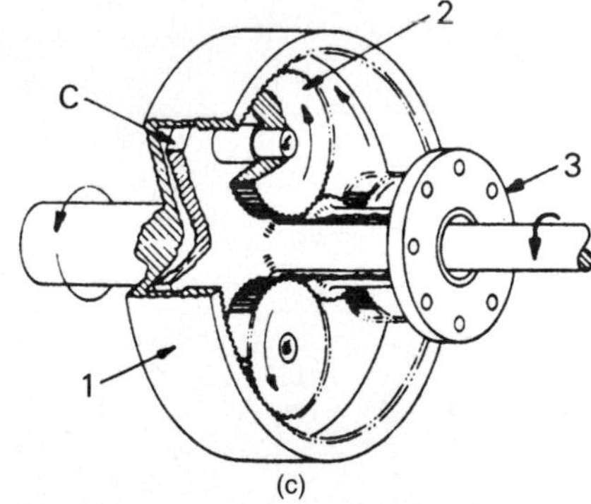

Figure 10.58 Three common epicyclic gear systems.

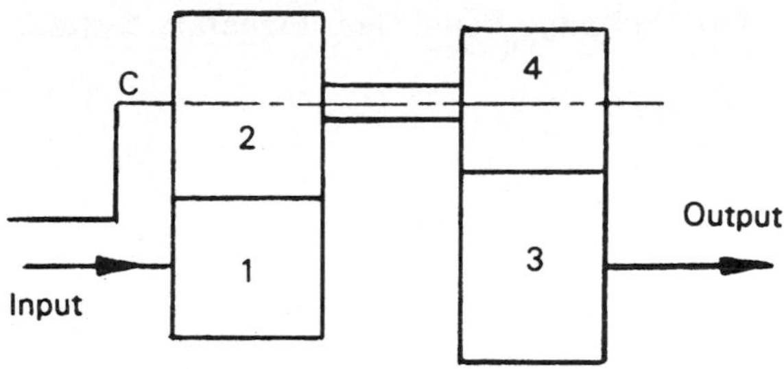

Input Member	Fixed Member	Output Member	Speed-ratio Equation
1	C	3	$R = N_2N_3/N_1N_4$
1	3	C	$R = 1 - [(N_2N_3)/(N_1N_4)]$
3	1	C	$R = 1 - [(N_1N_4)/(N_2N_3)]$
3	C	1	$R = N_4N_1/N_3N_2$
C	1	3	$R = 1/\{1 - [(N_1N_4)/(N_2N_3)]\}$
C	3	1	$R = 1/\{1 - [(N_2N_3)/(N_1N_4)]\}$

Figure 10.59 Commonly used epicyclic gear system.

The Humpage Bevel Gear Planetary System

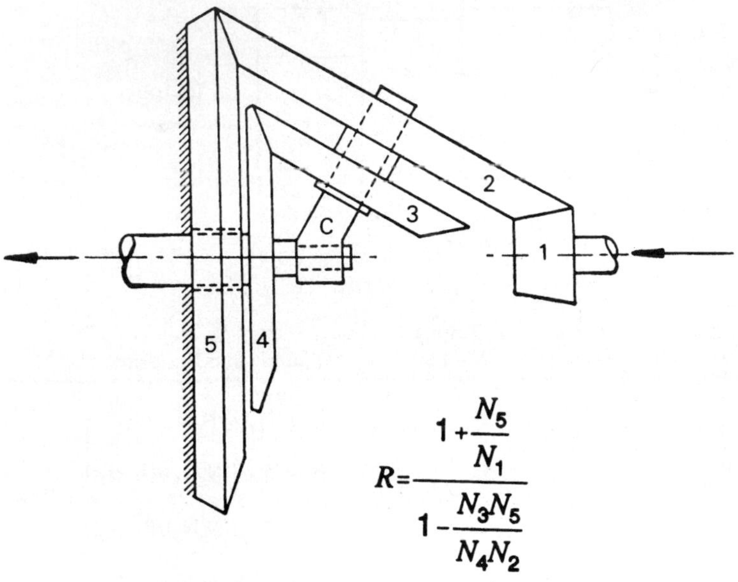

$$R = \frac{1 + \dfrac{N_5}{N_1}}{1 - \dfrac{N_3 N_5}{N_4 N_2}}$$

Figure 10.60 Humpage's epicyclic gear system.

Figure 10.61 View of an actual epicyclic gear system.

Figure 10.62 Epicyclic system, showing stages.

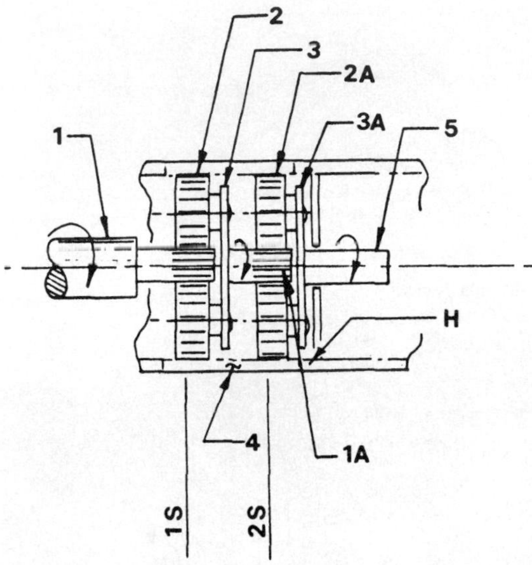

1 Input and sun gear
1A 2nd stage sun gear
2 1st stage planet gears
2A 2nd stage planet gears
3 1st stage carrier plate
3A 2nd stage carrier plate
4 Internal ring gear
5 Output
H Housing
1S 1st stage
2S 2nd stage

Figure 10.63 Cross section through a two-stage epicyclic system.

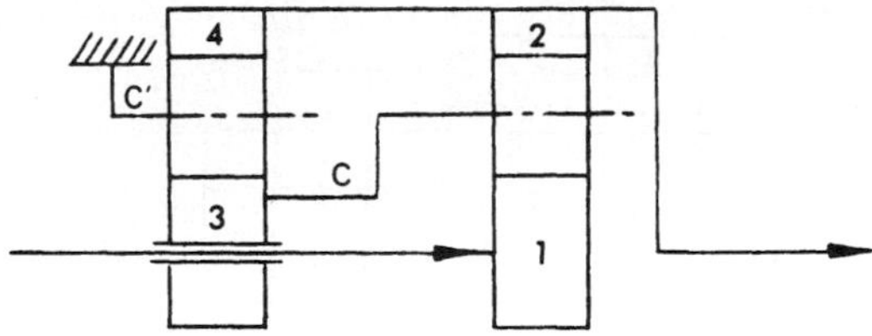

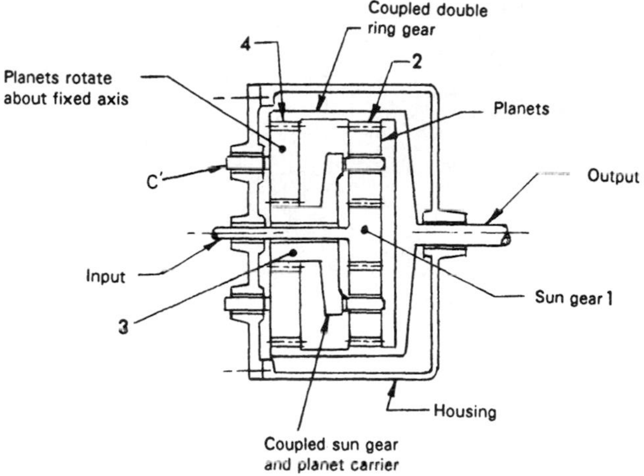

$$R = \left(1 + \frac{N_2}{N_1}\right)\left(-\frac{N_4}{N_3}\right) - \frac{N_2}{N_1}$$

Figure 10.64 Epicyclic system, coupled planetary drive.

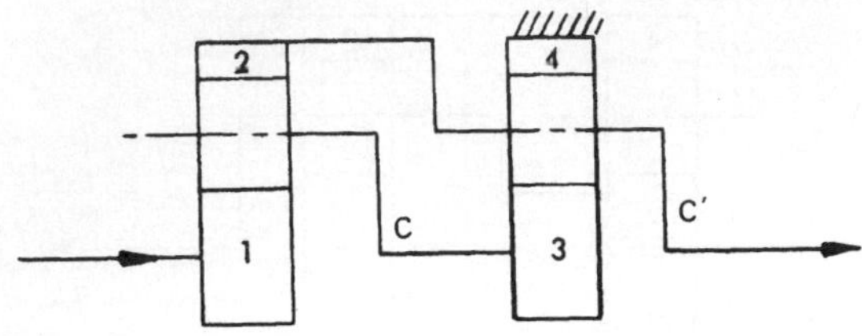

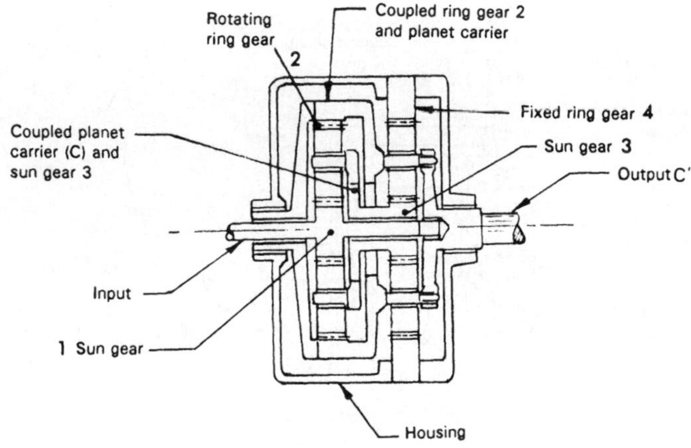

$$R = 1 + \frac{N_4}{N_3}\left(1 + \frac{N_2}{N_1}\right)$$

Figure 10.65 Epicyclic system, coupled planetary drive.

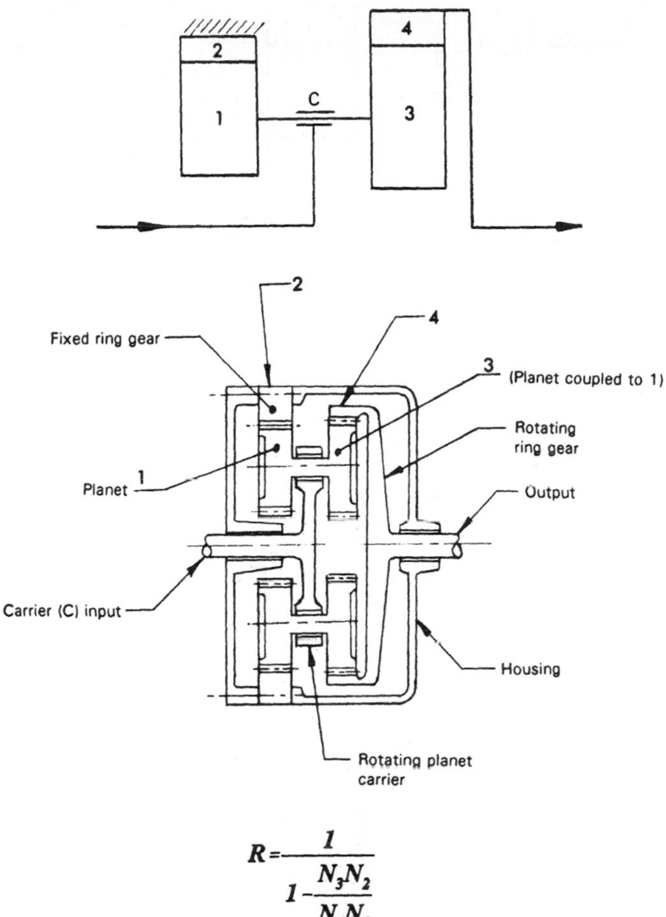

$$R = \frac{1}{1 - \dfrac{N_3 N_2}{N_4 N_1}}$$

Figure 10.66 Epicyclic system, fixed-differential drive.

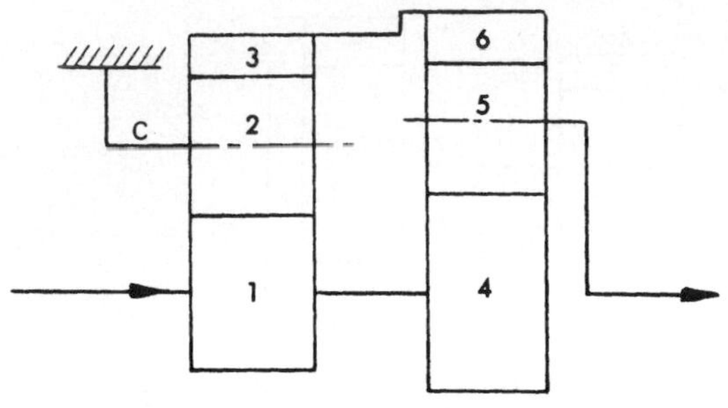

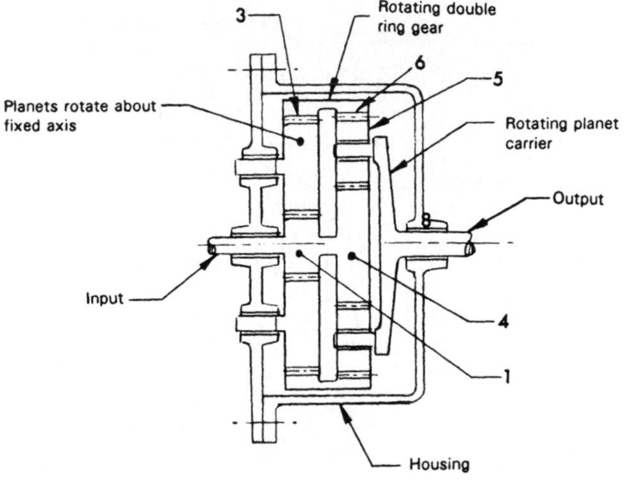

$$R = \frac{1 + \frac{N_4}{N_6}}{\frac{N_4}{N_6} - \frac{N_1}{N_3}}$$

Figure 10.67 Epicyclic system, fixed-differential drive.

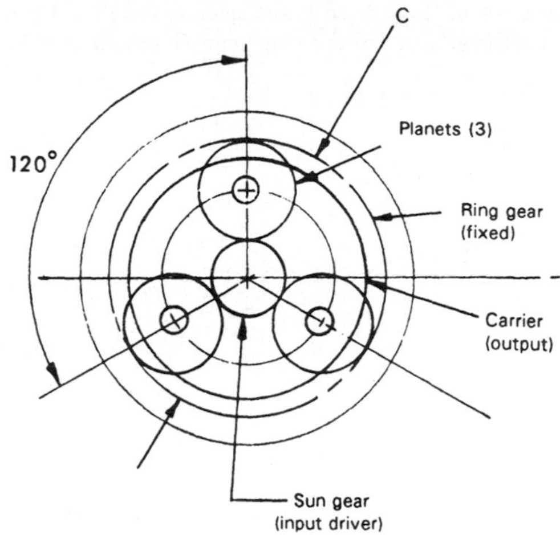

Figure 10.68 Epicyclic gear system.

Example We require a planetary spur gear drive with a 6:1 ratio and teeth of 20 diametral pitch. We would like to limit the number of teeth in the driver (sun gear) to 12. The ratio of 6 to 1 means that the driver or sun gear must make six revolutions for each revolution of the output (carrier).

Solution We are given

Ratio = 6:1

Diametral pitch required = 20

Desired number of teeth in the driver (sun gear) = 12

The pitch diameter of the driver is then (use spur gear relations)

$$D_p = \frac{N}{P_d}$$

$$= \frac{12}{20} = 0.60 \text{ in}$$

where N = number of teeth in sun gear
D_p = pitch diameter, in
P_d = diametral pitch (dimensionless ratio)

Therefore, the pitch diameter of the 12-tooth sun gear is 0.60 in. Then calculate the number of teeth required in the ring gear (fixed) for the 6:1 ratio from

$$R = 1 + \frac{C}{A}$$

$$6 = 1 + \frac{C}{12}$$

$$\frac{C}{12} = 5$$

$$C = 12 \times 5$$

$C = 60$ teeth required in the ring gear

The pitch diameter of the ring gear with 60 teeth and 20 diametral pitch is

$$D_p = \frac{N}{P_d}$$

$$= \frac{60}{20} = 3.00 \text{ in pitch diameter of ring gear}$$

The pitch diameter of the planet gears must now be found from (see Fig. 10.69)

$$\frac{3.00 - 0.6}{2} = D_p$$

$$\frac{2.4}{2} = d$$

$D_p = 1.2$ in pitch diameter of planet gears

The number of teeth in the planet gears may now be found from

$$D_p = \frac{N}{P_d}$$

$$1.2 = \frac{N}{20}$$

$N = 24$ teeth

As a check, refer to Fig. 10.70 and the following:

$$R = 1 + \frac{C}{A}$$

$$= 1 + \frac{60}{12}$$

$$= 1 + 5 = 6 \quad \text{(so the ratio is 6 to 1, as was required)}$$

As a check for assembly of this system, the number of teeth in ring gear plus the number of teeth in sun gear divided by the number of planets must be equal to an integer. Thus

$$\frac{60 + 12}{3} = 24 \text{ (so the system will assemble)}$$

Another example of the epicyclic system calculation procedure occurs when we wish to design a system for a limited-space application. Knowing the maximum desired pitch diameter of the ring gear and the required ratio, we may proceed as follows.

Example We wish to employ an epicyclic system as depicted in Fig. 10.57, line 3, and Figs. 10.61 and 10.62. The reduction or ratio is to be 20 to 1, driver to follower. The maximum pitch diameter of the ring gear (fixed) is not to exceed 2.00 in because of space limitations and a low power-handling ability. The recommended minimum number of teeth in the driver (sun gear) is to be 13.

Solution First, with a 20 to 1 ratio and a minimum number of sun gear teeth of 13, we proceed to find the number of teeth required in the fixed gear from

$$R = 1 + \frac{C}{A} \qquad \text{(see preceding symbols)}$$

$$20 = 1 + \frac{C}{13}$$

$$19 = \frac{C}{13}$$

$$C = 247 \text{ teeth}$$

If we allow this number of teeth in the fixed gear whose pitch diameter is not to exceed 2.00 in, then the diametral pitch of the teeth must be

$$D_p = \frac{N}{P_d}$$

$$2.00 = \frac{247}{P_d}$$

$$P_d = \frac{247}{2.00} = 123.5 \qquad \text{(which is too small)}$$

Next, we will try a two-stage reduction. If the two-stage final reduction is 20 to 1, then each stage must have a reduction of

$$\sqrt{20} = 4.47 \quad \text{(for two stages)} \qquad \text{and} \qquad \sqrt[3]{20} = 2.71 \quad \text{(for three stages)}$$

Then,

$$R = 1 + \frac{C}{A} \qquad \text{(for two-stage reduction)}$$

$$4.47 = \frac{C}{13}$$

$$C = 45.11 \qquad \text{(round off to 45 teeth)}$$

Now, the diametral pitch with 45 teeth on a 2.00-in pitch diameter is

$$D_p = \frac{N}{P_d}$$

$$2.00 = \frac{45}{P_d}$$

$$P_d = 22.5 \qquad \text{(use 24 as a diametral pitch)}$$

Then the actual pitch diameter of the ring gear (fixed) will be

$$D_p = \frac{N}{P_d}$$

$$= \frac{45}{24} = 1.875 \text{ in} \qquad \text{(the actual pitch diameter of our fixed ring gear)}$$

Now we know the number of teeth in the sun gear (driver) and the ring gear, the pitch diameter of the ring gear, and the number of stages we need. Next, we proceed to find the pitch diameter D_p of the sun gear (driver), the pitch diameter of the planet gears, and the number of teeth in the planet gears (all gears have a diametral pitch of 24). The pitch diameter of the sun gear is

$$D_p = \frac{N}{P_d}$$

$$= \frac{13}{24} = 0.542 \text{ in pitch diameter}$$

Then, we find the pitch diameter of the planet gears from

$$D_p = \frac{1.875 - 0.542}{2} = 0.667 \text{ in} \qquad \text{(see Fig. 10.71)}$$

The number of teeth in each planet gear is therefore

$$D_p = \frac{N}{P_d}$$

$$0.667 = \frac{N}{24}$$

$$N = 0.667 \times 24 = 16.008 \qquad \text{(call this 16 teeth; see Fig. 10.72)}$$

Check the ratio equation against the number of teeth in the sun gear (driver) and the ring gear (fixed) from

$$R = 1 + \frac{C}{A}$$

$$= 1 + \frac{45}{13}$$

$$= 1 + 3.462$$

$$= 4.462 \text{ ratio of each stage}$$

The actual final ratio will then be

$$R \times R = \text{final reduction}$$

$$4.462 \times 4.462 = 19.91$$

The actual fit of the pitch diameters is then (see Fig. 10.73)

$$0.667 + 0.667 + 0.542 = 1.876 \qquad \text{(1.875 was calculated)}$$

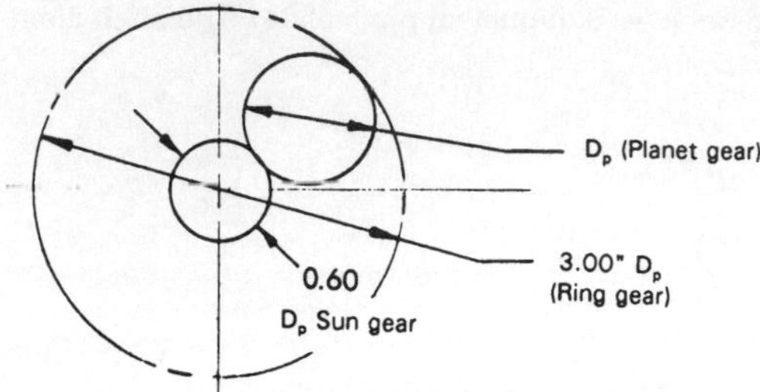

Figure 10.69 Finding pitch diameters.

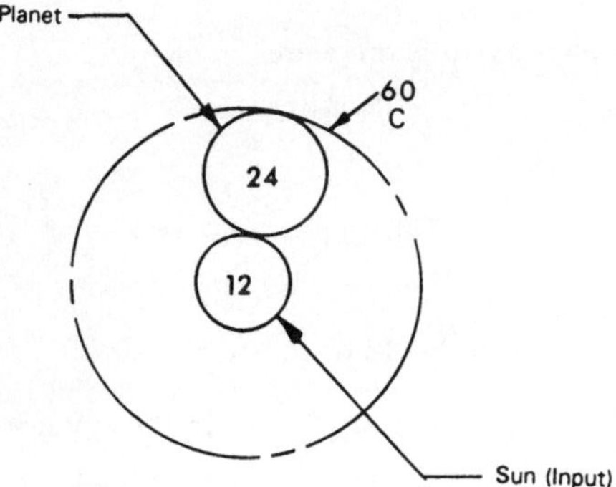

Figure 10.70 Checking pitch diameters.

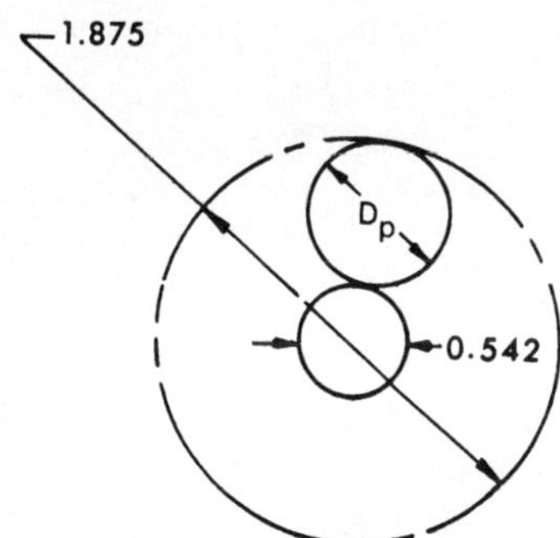

Figure 10.71 Finding pitch diameter of planets.

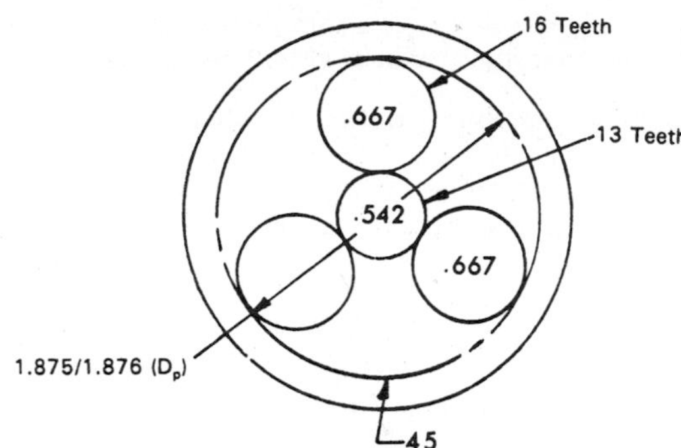

Figure 10.72 Finding the number of teeth in gears.

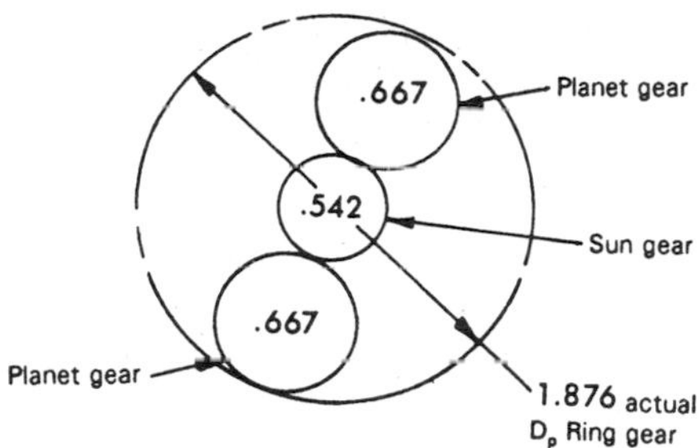

Figure 10.73 Fit of the pitch diameters.

Therefore, the fit of the pitch diameters is very close to the theoretical value.

As a last check, we will see if the epicyclic system can be assembled. The assembly check was given previously as the number of teeth in the ring gear plus the number of teeth in the sun gear divided by the number of planets must equal an integer. Therefore,

$$\frac{45 + 13}{3} = \frac{58}{3} = 19.333$$

Thus, we cannot use three planet gears in this system. We may use two planet gears only because $(45 + 13)/2 = 29$ (an integer). To make this system work with three planet gears, the number of teeth in the ring and sun gears, and possibly the ratio, must be adjusted and the system reevaluated to keep the pitch diameter of the ring gear at a maximum of

2.00 in and at the same time maintain a standard diametral pitch such that the gears may be cut using standard hobs or milling cutters.

To keep a standard diametral pitch and maintain the other requirements of this system, helical gears may be used. Since the helical gears' transverse diametral pitch is a function of the cosine of the helix angle, altering the helix angle directly affects the pitch diameter. See Fig. 10.17 helical gear equations.

Conclusion. Because of the double-stage reduction in the preceding epicyclic system, the actual load on the teeth of the stage 1 planet gears may be low enough to use a material such as acetal (Delrin), nylon (Zytel), or polycarbonate (Lexan) for the planet gears. In the case of the electric screwdriver epicyclic system shown in Figs. 10.61 and 10.62, plastic planet gears were used. Note that the forces on the teeth are higher in the second-stage gears, which are thus made of metal, as is the entire internal tooth ring gear, which is part of the gear system housing. As the reduction stages progress away from the input sun gear, the forces on the gear teeth of the succeeding stages become higher.

10.18 Gear Train Calculations

Speed ratios of gear trains. The speed ratios of gears are inversely proportional to their pitch diameters (see Fig. 10.74):

$$\text{Speed ratio} = \frac{\text{product of driven}}{\text{product of drivers}} = \frac{D_1 \times D_2 \times D_3}{d_1 \times d_2 \times d_3}$$

The speed ratio of a gear train also can be found if the number of teeth in each gear is known (see Fig. 10.75):

$$\frac{n_4}{n_1} = \frac{N_1}{N_2}\frac{N_3}{N_4}$$

where

n_1 = speed of gear 1, rpm

n_4 = speed of gear 4, rpm

N_1, N_2, N_3, and N_4 = number of teeth in gears 1 through 4

Additional ratios can be inserted into the tooth-ratio side of the equation for longer gear trains comprising more gears.

The reverse problem of finding the number of teeth each gear must have if the *ratio* of the gear train is to equal an arbitrarily chosen value is more difficult. All given ratios cannot be produced exactly by a gear train because the individual gears must contain an integral number of teeth. We can approximate the desired ratio with a degree of accuracy that is suitable for almost all applications. The method used to accomplish this was shown by M. F. Spots (Spots, 1953) and is shown in detail by the following.

The given arbitrary ratio between the first and last shaft is represented by G. Let u/w be a common fraction whose value is close to G. Then the ratio G may be exactly represented by

$$G = \frac{uh - j}{wh}$$

where j is an integer and h has the value obtained by solving the equation

$$h = \frac{j}{u - wG}$$

In the equation for G, the numerator and denominator must be integers that may be factored into terms suitable as the numbers of teeth in the gears of the train. Note, however, that the equation for h does not generally yield an integer. The numerator and denominator in the equation for G also will not be integers generally However, if an integer h' whose value is close to h is used, an approximate value G' of the ratio is obtained that may be very close to the exact value. Then,

$$G' = \frac{uh' - j}{wh'}$$

An example showing the use of the preceding three equations follows.

Example If the shaft on the left in Fig. 10.75 is to revolve 3.62 revolutions for each revolution of the output shaft on the right, find the proper number of teeth for each gear in the train N_1, N_2, N_3, and N_4.

$$G = \frac{1}{3.62} = 0.2762431$$

Suitable values for u/w can be found on a calculator by placing the given value for G on the display and multiplying successive integers by G until the product is very close to an integer. Thus,

$$wG \approx u$$

For example, $40 \times G$ is close to 11, so a suitable fraction u/w is $^{11}/_{40}$. Let $j = 1$. Then,

$$h = \frac{1}{11 - 40\,(0.2762431)} = -20.111$$

Now, if we suppose that $h' = -20$, then

$$G' = \frac{uh' - j}{wh'}$$

$$= \frac{(11)(-20) - 1}{40\,(-20)} = \frac{-220 - 1}{-800} = \frac{221}{800} = \frac{(13 \times 17)}{(20 \times 40)} = 0.27265$$

(See Sec. 2.8 tables for factors and primes.)

In the preceding equation for G, the numbers 221 and 800 are to be factored as shown: (13×17) and (20×40). Use the factors and primes tables to find the factors of the numerator and denominator. In the preceding equation for G which was solved and factored as 13×17 and 20×40, this then represents the number of teeth in the four gears in the train shown in Fig. 10.75:

Gears:

13 teeth
17 teeth (N_1 and N_3)
20 teeth
40 teeth (N_2 and N_4)

The preceding method for finding the number of teeth required in a preselected ratio gear train has many practical uses when working with gear systems.

We will now substitute the calculated values for the number of teeth into the basic ratio equation to see what the actual ratio is as compared with what we originally desired (we wanted a ratio of 3.62, input to output):

$$\frac{n_4}{n_1} = \frac{N_1}{N_2}\frac{N_3}{N_4}$$

$$\frac{1}{3.62} = \frac{13 \times 17}{20 \times 40}$$

$$0.2762 = 0.2762$$

As you can see, the solution for the preselected ratio of 1/3.62 is satisfied.

Note: More accuracy could be obtained by using a more appropriate value of $u/w = 11/40$, if one exists, or by going to a six-gear system and finding three factors in the numerator and denominator of G'.

Force ratios for gear trains. Refer to Fig. 10.76, which is a gear train with a weight suspended from one end and an applied force at the other end (which is required to balance the weight load). Here, *A, B, C,* and *D* are the pitch circles of the gears in the train. Then,

$$F = \frac{W \times r \times r_1 \times r_2}{R \times r_1 \times R_2} \qquad \text{and} \qquad W = \frac{F \times R \times R_1 \times R_2}{r \times r_1 \times r_2}$$

where F = force, lbf or N
W = weight, lb or (kg·g)N
r, r_1, r_2 = pitch radius, in or mm
R, R_1, R_2 = pitch radius, in or mm

Note: If the weight at W is 50 kg, the SI force is $50 \times 9.81 = 490.5$ N, which is equivalent to a weight of 50 kg suspended at point W; i.e., the weight of a mass of W kg is equal to a force of Wg N, where $g = 9.81$ m/s^2 (the acceleration of gravity).

Differential gears. Differential gear systems are in a general sense an arrangement where the normal ratio of the unit can be changed by driving into the unit with a second drive. There may be two inputs and one output or one input and two outputs. One of the most common uses of the differential gear drive is in the rear-end drives of automobiles. When an automobile goes around a corner, one wheel must make more turns than the other (the wheel on the outside of the curve makes more revolutions than the inside wheel). Fixed differential drives were shown in a previous section (see Figs. 10.66 and 10.67).

The typical automotive differential is shown in Figs. 10.77 and 10.78. In Fig. 10.78, the gears in the differential are of the spiral bevel type, which allows a higher load capability over conventional straight bevel gears and quieter operation

10.19 Sprockets (Geometry and Dimensioning)

Figure 10.79 shows the geometry of ANSI standard roller chain sprockets and the derivation of the dimensions for design engi-

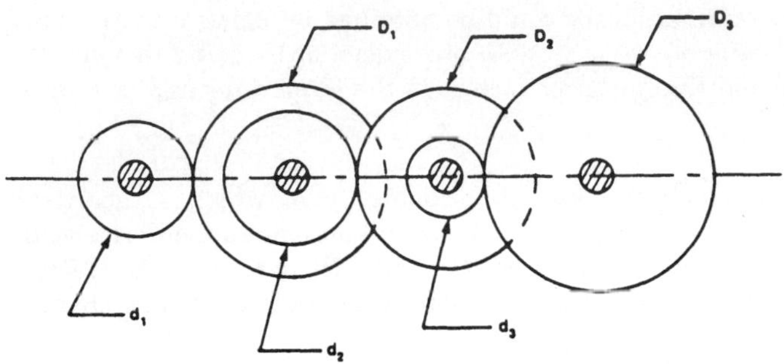

Figure 10.74 Gear train speed ratio.

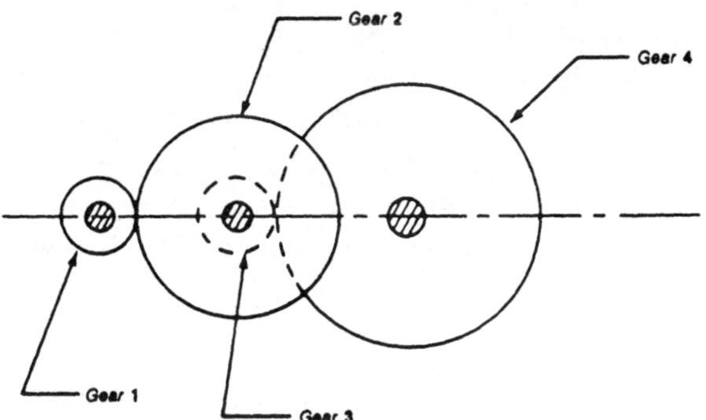

Figure 10.75 Gear train speed ratio.

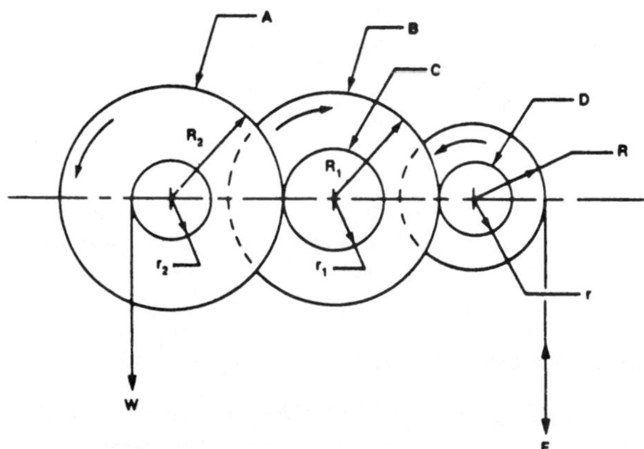

Figure 10.76 Gear train force ratio.

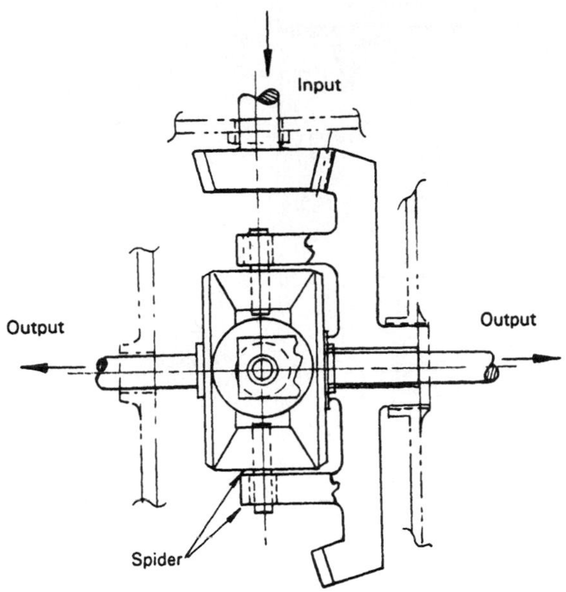

Figure 10.77 Typical differential gear system.

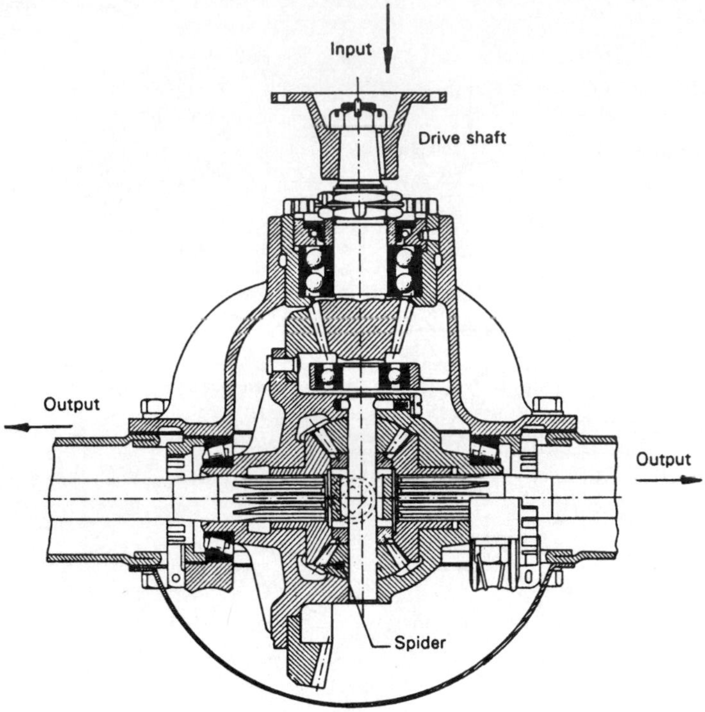

Input
Drive shaft
Output
Output
Spider

Figure 10.78 Common automotive differential gear train.

S
M
c
B
90°
90°
F
z
E
A
T
V
a
J
H
e
b
y
R
e
180°
N
x
W
180°
N
360°
N

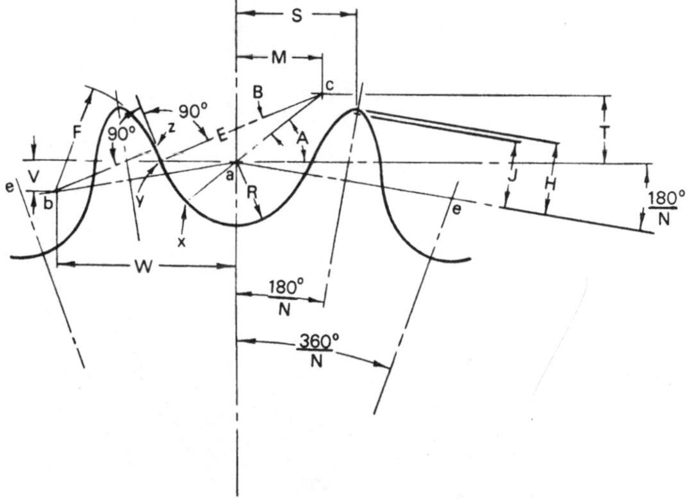

Figure 10.79 Geometry of ANSI roller-chain sprockets.

neering or tool engineering use. With the following relational data and equations, dimensions may be derived for input to CNC machining centers or EDM machines for either manufacturing the different-sized sprockets or producing the dies to stamp and shave the sprockets.

The equations for calculating sprockets are as follows:

P = pitch (ae) N = number of teeth D_r = nominal roller diameter

$$D_s = \text{seating curve diameter} = 1.005D_r + 0.003 \text{ (in)} \qquad R = \frac{1}{2D_s}$$

$$A = 35° + \left(\frac{60°}{N}\right) \qquad B = 18° - \left(\frac{56°}{N}\right) \qquad ac = 0.8D_r$$

$$M = 0.8D_r \cos\left[35° + \left(\frac{60°}{N}\right)\right]$$

$$T = 0.8D_r \sin\left[35° + \left(\frac{60°}{N}\right)\right] \qquad E = 1.3025D_r + 0.0015 \text{ (in)}$$

$$\text{Chord } xy = (2.605D_r + 0.003) \sin\left[9° - \left(\frac{28°}{N}\right)\right] \text{ (in)}$$

$$yz = D_r\left\{1.4 \sin\left[17° - \left(\frac{64°}{N}\right)\right] - 0.8 \sin\left[18° - \left(\frac{56°}{N}\right)\right]\right\}$$

Length of line between a and b = $1.4D_r$

$$W = 1.4D_r \cos\left(\frac{180°}{N}\right) \qquad V = 1.4D_r \sin\left(\frac{180°}{N}\right)$$

$$F = D_r\left\{0.8 \cos\left[18° - \left(\frac{56°}{N}\right)\right] + 1.4 \cos\left[17° - \left(\frac{64°}{N}\right)\right] - 1.3025\right\} - 0.0015 \text{ in}$$

$$H = \sqrt{F^2 - (1.4D_r - 0.5P)^2}$$

$$S = 0.5P \cos\left(\frac{180°}{N}\right) + H \sin\left(\frac{180°}{N}\right)$$

Approximate outside diameter of sprocket when J is $0.3P$

$$= P\left[0.6 + \cot\left(\frac{180°}{N}\right)\right]$$

Outside diameter of sprocket with tooth pointed

$$= p\ \cot\left(\frac{180°}{N}\right) + \cos\,(180°N)(D_s - D_r) + 2H$$

$$\text{Pressure angle for new chain} = xab = 35° - \left(\frac{120°}{N}\right)$$

$$\text{Minimum pressure angle} = xab - B = 17° - \left(\frac{64°}{N}\right)$$

$$\text{Average pressure angle} = 26° - \left(\frac{92°}{N}\right)$$

The seating-curve data for the preceding equations is shown in Fig. 10.80.

10.20 Ratchets

See Sec. 14.7.

10.21 Gear Design Programs for PCs and CAD Stations

The Gleason Machine Division offers a service for gear system calculations when you require a computer analysis of the gear tooth design. Also available from the Gleason Machine Division are computer programs that will assist you with a gear tooth design analysis:

- Dimension sheet: Calculation of the basic tooth geometry, contact ratios, stress analysis and data, bearing thrust loads, etc.
- Summary: Calculation of cutting and grinding machine setup data to produce the selected tooth geometry
- Tooth contact analysis: A special analysis program that determines the tooth contact pattern and transmission motion errors based on specified cutting tools and gear tooth geometry

- Undercut check program
- Loaded-tooth contact analysis
- FEA (finite element analysis)

Programs are also available from various sources for use on personal computers (PCs) to perform various gear design functions and to solve various other gear problems.

10.22 Keyways and Set Screws for Gear Shafts

Standard keyways and set screws for various shaft diameters are shown in Fig. 10.81. For more design data on shafts and shafting, see Sec. 14.3.

10.23 Calculations for Power, Torque, Force, and Revolutions per Minute

A convenient chart for calculating the various power, force, torque, revolutions per minute, and velocities for gearing is shown in Fig. 10.82.

10.24 Additional Gear Data and References

When working with gears and gear systems, keep the following points in mind:

- Module is an *index* of metric gear tooth sizes and is measured in millimeters. Module is equal to the pitch diameter, in millimeters, divided by the number of teeth in the gear and is thus given in millimeters.
- Diametral pitch is an *index* of U.S. Customary gear tooth sizes but is a *ratio*. It is the ratio of the number of teeth in the gear per inch of pitch diameter. The smaller the number of the diametral pitch, the larger is the number of teeth.

Special stem pinions. Figure 10.83 shows a standard spur stem pinion which has been specially designed for a double-reduction compact gear box. This stem pinion has eight teeth, which are specially cut for proper mesh with standard involute spur gears of

14.5° pressure angle. The diameters on this special-purpose stem pinion marked *A* and *B* are the needle roller-bearing support surfaces. This gear was machined, case-hardened, and then abrasively finished by sand blasting with special abrasive material. The far end of this stem-pinion gear is machined square for the drive member to engage the gear in operation. The sand-blasted, satin finish on the bearing sections of this gear are of a fine enough surface texture that the needles in the bearings will quickly wear-in the bearing surfaces.

Gear wear and failure. Figure 10.84 shows a stem-pinion/spur gear set which failed in service due to improper heat treatment. The gear material was substantially softer than the needle rollers in the support bearings and galled and eroded after a short time in operation, causing the needles in the bearings to fracture. As soon as the needles fractured, the shaft was very quickly destroyed. This particular gear set was loaded very heavily in operation, but was rated for intermittent duty cycles. With the correct heat treatment, no problems were apparent after prolonged service.

P	D_r	R Min	D_s Min	D_s Tolerance *
1/4	0.130	0.0670	0.134	0.0055
3/8	0.200	0.1020	0.204	0.0055
1/2	0.306	0.1585	0.317	0.0060
1/2	0.312	0.1585	0.317	0.0060
5/8	0.400	0.2025	0.405	0.0060
3/4	0.469	0.2370	0.474	0.0065
1	0.625	0.3155	0.631	0.0070
1-1/4	0.750	0.3785	0.757	0.0070
1-1/2	0.875	0.4410	0.882	0.0075
1-3/4	1.000	0.5040	1.008	0.0080
2	1.125	0.5670	1.134	0.0085
2-1/4	1.406	0.7080	1.416	0.0090
2-1/2	1.562	0.7870	1.573	0.0095
3	1.875	0.9435	1.887	0.0105

Note: * Denotes plus tolerance only.

Figure 10.80 Seating curve data for ANSI roller chain (inches).

(Text continued on page 990.)

Diam. of Hole	St'd Keyway W	St'd Keyway d	Recom-mended Setscrew
5/16 to 7/16"	3/32"	3/64"	10–32
1/2 to 9/16	1/8	1/16	1/4–20
5/8 to 7/8	3/16	3/32	5/16–18
15/16 to 1-1/4	1/4	1/8	3/8–16
1- 5/16 to 1-3/8	5/16	5/32	7/16–14
1- 7/16 to 1-3/4	3/8	3/16	1/2–13
1-13/16 to 2-1/4	1/2	1/4	9/16–12
2- 5/16 to 2-3/4	5/8	5/16	5/8–11
2-13/16 to 3-1/4	3/4	3/8	3/4–10
3- 5/16 to 3-3/4	7/8	7/16	7/8–9
3-13/16 to 4-1/2	1	1/2	1–8
4- 9/16 to 5-1/2	1-1/4	7/16	1-1/8–7
5- 9/16 to 6-1/2	1-1/2	1/2	1-1/4–6

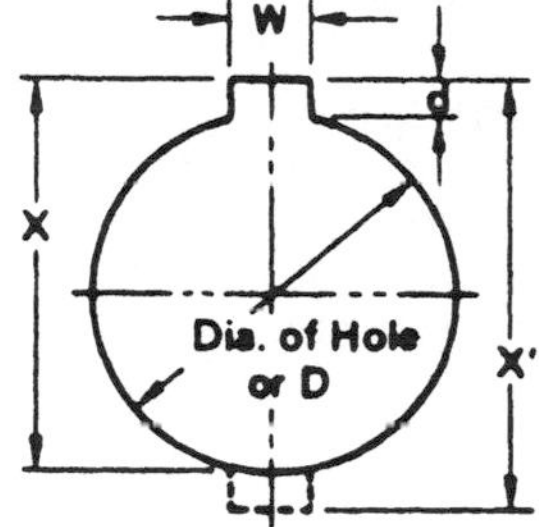

FORMULA:

$$X = \sqrt{(D/2)^2 - (W/2)^2} + d + D/2$$

$$X' = 2X - D$$

Figure 10.81 Standard keyways and set screws.

TO OBTAIN	HAVING	FORMULA
Velocity (V) Feet Per Minute	Pitch Diameter (D) of Gear or Sprocket — Inches & Rev. Per Min. (RPM)	$V = .2618 \times D \times RPM$
Rev. Per Min. (RPM)	Velocity (V) Ft. Per Min. & Pitch Diameter (D) of Gear or Sprocket — Inches	$RPM = \frac{V}{.2618 \times D}$
Pitch Diameter (D) of Gear or Sprocket — Inches	Velocity (V) Ft. Per Min. & Rev. Per Min. (RPM)	$D = \frac{V}{.2618 \times RPM}$
Torque (T) In. Lbs.	Force (W) Lbs. & Radius (R) Inches	$T = W \times R$
Horsepower (HP)	Force (W) Lbs. & Velocity (V) Ft. Per Min.	$HP = \frac{W \times V}{33000}$
Horsepower (HP)	Torque (T) In. Lbs. & Rev. Per Min. (RPM)	$HP = \frac{T \times RPM}{63025}$
Torque (T) In. Lbs.	Horsepower (HP) & Rev. Per Min. (RPM)	$T = \frac{63025 \times HP}{RPM}$
Force (W) Lbs.	Horsepower (HP) & Velocity (V) Ft. Per Min.	$W = \frac{33000 \times HP}{V}$
Rev. Per Min. (RPM)	Horsepower (HP) & Torque (T) In. Lbs.	$RPM = \frac{63025 \times HP}{T}$

Figure 10.82 Power, force, torque, rpm, and velocity equations for gears and sprockets.

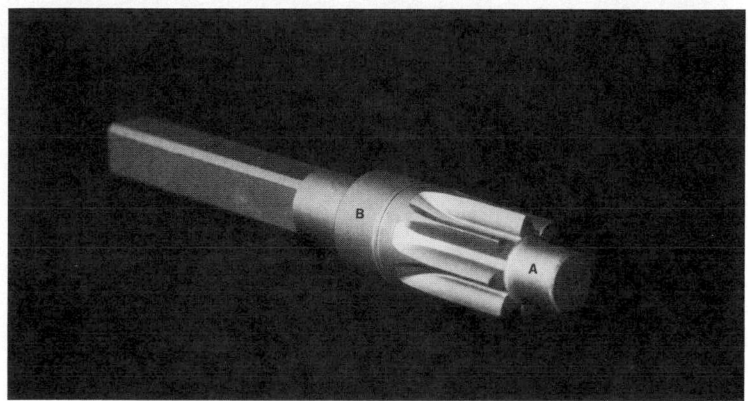

Figure 10.83 A specially machined spur stem pinion.

Figure 10.84 Example of gear failure due to improper heat treatment.

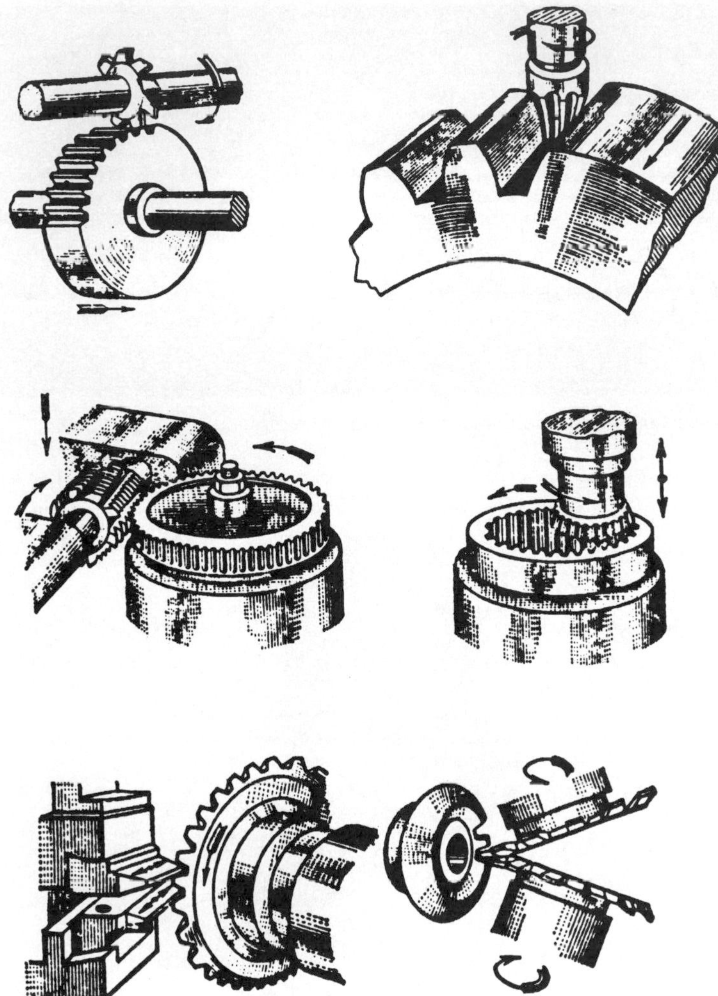

Figure 10.85 Details of methods of gear production. (*Above, left*) Milling a spur gear. (*Above, right*) End milling a spur gear. (*Center, left*) Hobbing a spur gear. (*Center, right*) Shaping an internal spur gear. (*Below, left*) Shaping a bevel gear. (*Below, right*) Milling a bevel gear on a special machine. Arrows indicate the directions of feed and cut.

TABLE 10.12 Spiral Bevel Gear Dimensions: No. M S006651

	Pinion	Gear
Number of teeth	16	49
Part number		
Module		5.000
Face width	38.00	38.00
Pressure angle	20D OM	
Shaft angle	90D OM	
Transverse contact ratio		1.192
Face contact ratio		2.006
Modified contact ratio		2.333
Outer cone distance		128.87
Mean cone distance		109.87
Pitch diameter	80.00	245.00
Circular pitch	15.71	
Working depth	8.28	
Whole depth	9.22	9.22
Clearance	0.94	0.94
Addendum	5.91	2.38
Dedendum	3.32	6.85
Outside diameter	91.23	246.48
Face angle junction diameter		
Theoretical cutter radius	3.751″	
Cutter radius	3.750″	
Calc. gear finish. pt. width		0.100″
Gear finishing point width		0.100″
Roughing point width	0.045″	0.080″
Outer slot width	0.071″	0.100″
Mean slot width	0.083″	0.100″
Inner slot width	0.073″	0.100″
Finishing cutter blade point	0.045″	0.065″
Stock allowance	0.026″	0.020″
Max. radius—cutter blades	0.043″	0.074″
Max. radius—mutilation	0.061″	0.076″
Max. radius—interference	0.045″	0.096″
Cutter edge radius	0.025″	0.025″
Calc. cutter number	3	9
Max. no. blades in cutter		11.295
Cutter blades required	Std depth	Std depth
Gear angular face—concave		26D 47M
Gear angular face—convex		29D 30M
Gear angular face—total		31D 52M

NOTE: All dimensions are in metric unless denoted otherwise. Angles are in degrees (D) and minutes (M).

Gear manufacturing processes. Figure 10.85 shows in detail the methods used to manufacture different types of gears. Some of these methods were shown in previous sections, but not as clearly as in this figure.

10.25 Gear Lubrication

All the major oil companies and lubrication specialty companies provide lubricants for gearing and other applications to meet a very broad range of operating conditions. General gear lubrication consists of a high-quality type of machine oil when there are no temperature extremes or other adverse ambient conditions. Many of the automotive greases and oils are suitable for a broad range of gearing applications.

For adverse temperatures, environmental extremes, and high-pressure applications, consult the lubrication specialty companies or the major oil companies to meet your particular requirements or specifications.

The science and technology of lubrication and its applications to various machinery and conditions are complex and should be referred to the lubrication specialists.

Gear summary sheets. Table 10.12 shows a typical gear summary sheet used for manufacturing the gears. This summary sheet is for a set of spiral bevel gears from the Dudley Engineering Company. This sheet was extracted from the *Handbook of Practical Gear Design* (McGraw-Hill, New York, 1984), by Darle W. Dudley.

Chapter

11

Antifriction Bearings

Antifriction bearings are among the most important mechanical elements. Most mechanical devices and machines contain antifriction bearings of one type or another. By providing reduced frictional drag on moving parts, antifriction bearings allow machines and mechanical devices to operate at their most efficient levels.

Many factors are taken into account in the selection of any particular type of bearing for any particular application. One type of bearing may be more suitable for a given application than another type. Among the factors that influence the selection of a bearing for a particular application are

- Available size
- Load-bearing characteristics
- Life of the bearing
- Permissible loads
- Efficiency
- Type of application
- Operating temperature
- Speed, linear or rotational
- Mounting
- Cost

Common bearing types include

- Ball bearings, radial and thrust
- Roller bearings, radial and thrust
- Needle roller bearings, radial and thrust
- Tapered roller bearings, radial and thrust
- Cylindrical roller bearings
- Plain bearings, sleeve and flanged, radial and thrust

Figure 11.1 shows sections through the major bearing types, which include ball, roller, tapered roller, needle, and cylindrical roller. Figure 11.2 shows the detailed construction of the widely used tapered roller bearing, which is shown in Fig. 11.1*c*. This bearing is made with a pressed-steel cage for the rollers or a pin-type cage. Figure 11.3 shows the detailed construction of the major types of bearings used throughout industry. Both radial and thrust types are shown.

Industry rolls on antifriction bearings that are made in sizes from near microscopic to over 100 in in diameter in order to carry loads of minute value to many tons. The simplest type of antifriction bearing is the plain sleeve or flanged type, with which we will begin our bearing section.

11.1 Plain Bearings: Sleeve and Flanged (Journal)

The plain bearing is available in either sleeve or flanged type. These types of bearings are usually made of sintered bronze with impregnated lubrication. Minute pores are produced in the bearing material during the sintering process, and these are impregnated with a high-quality, long-lasting lubricant, making the bearings self-lubricating. Plain bearings are also made of aluminum alloys, copper-lead alloys, babbitt alloys, and various types of thermoplastics and thermoset plastics such as acetal, polycarbonates, Teflons, nylons, and phenolic-impregnated cloth thermosets.

Most of the plain sleeve and flanged bearings are designed for a force fit into their receiving housing bore. The outside and inside diameters of these types of bearings are manufactured to close tolerances so that a force fit is easily accomplished using

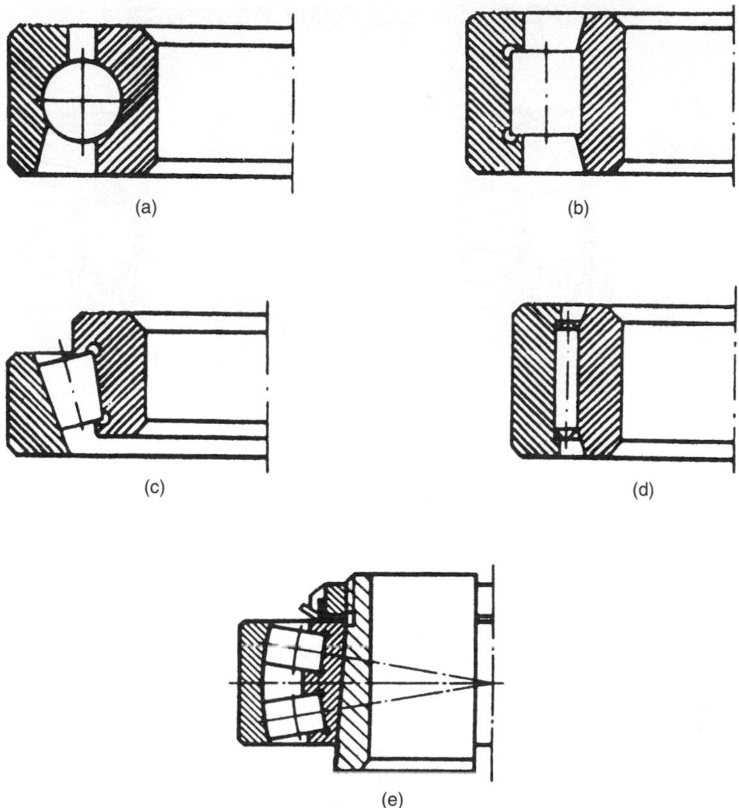

Figure 11.1 Sections through common bearings: (*a*) ball; (*b*) roller; (*c*) tapered roller; (*d*) needle; (*e*) spherical roller.

TYPE TS SINGLE-ROW BEARINGS

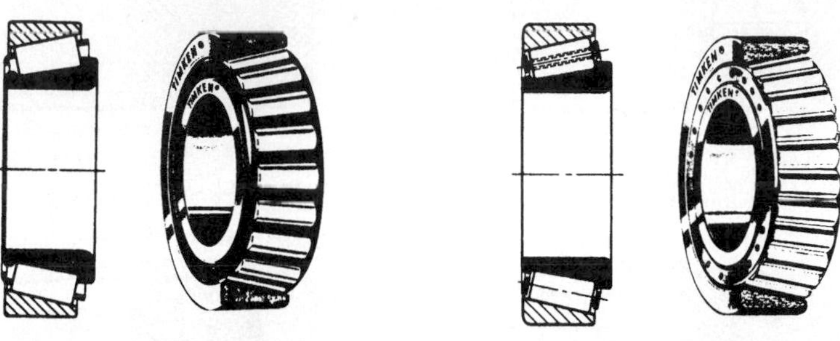

Figure 11.2 Detailed construction, tapered roller bearings. *(Source: The Timken Company.)*

the properly bored bearing mounting hole. It should be noted that if a bearing mounting hole is *overbored* and the bearing has a loose fit, the assembly can be saved by using a compound called Quick-Metal produced by Locktite Corporation. The Quick-Metal is applied over the outside diameter of the bearing and then inserted into the loose-fitting hole. The Quick-Metal will permanently bond the bearing in the hole after a setting time of approximately 20 min to 1 h. An otherwise ruined bearing assembly may thus be saved. This application may be limited to noncritical assemblies and in certain tooling practices (tool repairs) and maintenance procedures (see Fig. 11.5 for plain bearing press fits).

Plain bearing stock is available for manufacturing your own bearings to a particular set of dimensions. The following bearing rules should be kept in mind when designing a plain cylindrical bearing. The length of a plain cylindrical bearing should be from one to two times the shaft diameter, and the outside diameter should be approximately 25 percent larger than the shaft diameter. The bearing stock material must have adequate compressive strength for the application.

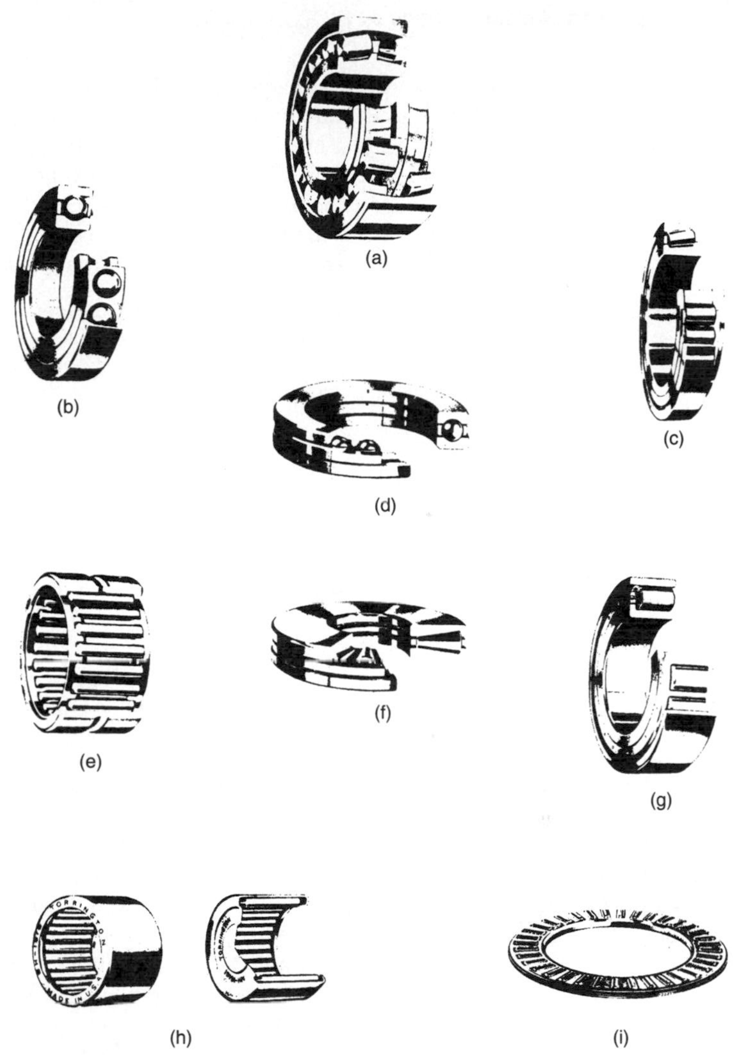

Figure 11.3 Detailed construction of common bearings: (*a*) spherical roller; (*b*) ball; (*c*) tapered roller; (*d*) ball thrust; (*e*) caged needle; (*f*) roller thrust; (*g*) caged roller; (*h*) drawn-cup needle, open and closed end; (*i*) needle thrust. *(Source: The Torrington Company.)*

11.1.1 Selection of plain bearings by *PV* calculations

Load and velocity value limits are established for plain bearings by the use of pressure-velocity (*PV*) calculations. *PV* represents a pressure and velocity factor and is a means of measuring the performance capabilities of plain bearings. *P* is expressed as a pressure, or pounds per square inch, on the projected area of a bearing. *V* is the velocity in feet per minute of the wear surface (surface feet per minute). *PV* is expressed by the following relational equations:

$$PV = \frac{W}{Ld} \times \frac{\pi dn}{12} = \frac{\pi Wn}{12L} = \frac{0.262Wn}{L}$$

$$P = \frac{W}{A}$$

$$V = \text{surface velocity of the shaft, ft/min}$$

$$= 0.262 \times \text{rpm} \times \text{shaft diameter}$$

where W = bearing load, lb
L = bearing length, in
d = inside diameter of bearing, in
n = shaft speed, rpm
A = projected bearing area = (bearing inside diameter × length, in^2)

Each bearing material has a specific maximum *PV* rating, as shown in Fig. 11.4. In addition, the bearing material also has a maximum pressure *P* and velocity *V* limitation. At no time can all maximum values be utilized. The selection of a plain bearing by *PV* calculation is a balance of the *P, V,* and *PV* values. The following example will illustrate the selection procedures.

When selecting a bearing, you must know the *PV, P,* and *V* values of the bearing material (see Fig. 11.4). (The bearing manufacturers' catalogs also list these values.) Note that

$$PV_m = P_m \times V_m$$

$$P_m = \frac{PV_m}{V_m}$$

$$V_m = \frac{PV_m}{P_m}$$

where PV_m = maximum PV value
P_m = maximum pressure, psi
V_m = maximum velocity, sfpm

Do not exceed the maximum values.

Example Select a plain bearing to satisfy the following conditions, using the previous equations and the values given in Fig. 11.4*a*. Known:

$$\text{Shaft diameter} = 0.625 \text{ in}$$

$$n = 500 \text{ rpm}$$

$$W_1 = \text{load on bearing } 1 = 60 \text{ lb}$$

$$W_2 = \text{load on bearing } 2 = 100 \text{ lb}$$

$$L = \text{length of bearing} = 1 \text{ in}$$

For bearing 1, therefore,

$$PV = \frac{0.262 \times W_1 \times n}{L} = \frac{0.262 \times 60 \times 500}{1} = 7860$$

Nonmetallic journal bearing "PV" values.

Material	PV limit unlub.	P Load limit psi	Max. speed, fpm V	Max. temp, °F
Acetal	3,000	2,000	600	200
Carbon-graphite	15,000	600	2,500	600
Nylon	3,000	2,000	600	200
Phenolic	15,000	6,000	2,500	200
Polycarb.	3,000	1,000	1,000	225
PTFE	1,000	500	50	500
Filled PTFE	10,000	2,500	1,000	500
PTFE fabric	25,000	60,000	150	500

Figure 11.4 (*a*) *PV* values table, plastics. *(Source: Machine Design, June 1984.)*

PV values of metallic plain bearings.

Material	PV value
Lead-base babbitt	35,000
Tin-base babbitt	40,000
Cadmium base	90,000
Copper-lead	90,000

Figure 11.4 (*b*) *PV* values table, metal alloys. *(Source: Boston Gear.)*

For bearing 2,

$$PV = \frac{0.262 \times W_2 \times n}{L} = \frac{0.262 \times 100 \times 500}{1} = 13{,}100$$

With a calculated *PV* for bearing 1 of 7860 and for bearing 2 of 13,100, it can be seen from Fig. 11.4*a* that carbon graphite, phenolic, or PTFE fabric could possibly be used for these bearings. You must now check the maximum *P* and maximum *V* values using the relational equations shown previously to see which bearing material will be adequate for the job. If the plastic bearing materials cannot handle the required loads and speeds, the selection of a metallic bearing will be necessary. *PV* values for some of the metallic bearing materials are shown in Fig. 11.4*b*.

The press-fit allowances for the plain metallic bearings are shown in Fig. 11.5.

11.1.2 Plain bearing wear-life calculations

The concept of *wear life* is not applied to sintered-bronze types of bearings because, under ideal conditions, the shaft rides on a film of lubricant and thus will give almost infinite life, provided the lubricating film is not disturbed, causing metal-to-metal contact. A shaft that runs in a metallic or nonmetallic plain bearing should have a surface finish between 4 and 16 rms. Any finish rougher than this will tear the lubricating film and cause metal-to-metal contact, with subsequent bearing wear of an undeterminable nature.

Wear rate is usually defined as the volumetric loss of bearing material over a definite unit of time. Once a wear-rate factor *K* has been established, it can be used by the designer, engineer, or tool-

Housing diameter, in	Press fit (interference), in
0.500	0.0005
1.000	0.0008
1.500	0.0010
2.000	0.0015
2.500	0.0020
3.000	0.0025

Figure 11.5 Press-fit allowances for plain bearings (metallic).

ing engineer to calculate wear rates of plain bearings accurately. As a relative measure of the performance of one material versus another at the same operating conditions, the K factors have proven to be very reliable. The following relational equations will prove useful for determining plain bearing life:

$$t = K\,(PVT)$$

$$= \text{wear in inches}$$

$$P = \frac{W}{A}$$

$$V = \text{velocity in feet per minute}$$

$$= 0.262 \times \text{rpm} \times \text{shaft diameter}$$

$$A = \text{projected bearing area} = (\text{bearing inside diameter} \times \text{length, in}^2)$$

$$T = \frac{t}{KPV}$$

$$= \text{running time in hours}$$

$$K = \text{wear factor}$$

$$W = \text{total load, lbs}$$

The K factors for common nonmetallic bearing materials are as follows:

Material	K factor
Acetal (Delrin or Celcon)	50×10^{-10}
Nylatron GS	35×10^{-10}
Teflon-filled acetal	17×10^{-10}
Teflon-filled nylon	13×10^{10}
Glass-filled Teflon	12×10^{-10}
Nylon	12×10^{-10}

You may proceed to calculate the wear life of nonmetallic bearings by using the preceding equations to calculate the PV value first and then proceeding as shown below. After the PV value is determined, transpose the simple equation

$$t = K(PVT)$$

such that

$$T = \frac{t}{K(PV)}$$

Remember that *PV* is a single-valued expression.

Note: A low viscosity lubricant applied initially or periodically during operation will extend bearing life by several times the calculated value. For glass-filled Teflon bearings, the shaft material should be hardened to approximately Rockwell C45 to C55. Brass and aluminum shafts will exhibit a high rate of wear using glass-filled bearings. Hardened steel, stainless steel, and chromium-plated steel will exhibit lower coefficients of dynamic friction with subsequent less wear.

11.1.3 Heat dissipation in plain bearings

It is often necessary to know the rate of heat dissipated by bearings in operation. The heat dissipation in plain bearings is expressed by the simple equation

$$R = pvf$$

where p = bearing pressure on projected area, psi
v = rubbing velocity, ft/min
f = coefficient of dynamic friction
R = rate of radiation of the projected bearing area, ft · lb/min/in^2

Note that the work equivalent foot pounds may be converted to calories or British thermal units using the conversions shown in Chap. 4, "U.S. Customary and Metric Measures and Conversions."

Values of dynamic coefficients of friction for various materials. See Fig. 11.6 for coefficients of dynamic friction for various materials.

11.1.4 Standard specifications for babbitt metal bearing materials

Table 11.1 lists the composition and physical properties of white metal bearing alloys (babbitt metal). Table 11.2 lists the chemical compositions of white metal bearing alloys shown in Table 11.1.

11.2 Rolling-Element Antifriction Bearings

Rolling-element antifriction bearings consist of ball, roller, needle, tapered roller, and cylindrical roller types of bearings. The standard specifying authority for antifriction bearings is the Anti-Friction Bearing Manufacturers Association (AFBMA). This association has consolidated its standards with those of the American National Standards Institute (ANSI). Some of the important AFBMA standards include

- ANSI/AFBMA 1-1990, Terminology for antifriction ball and roller bearings and parts
- ANSI/AFBMA 4-1984, Tolerance definitions and gaging practices for ball and roller bearings

Coefficients of friction-dynamic.

Pressure Lb/in^2	Cast iron / Wrought iron	Steel / Cast iron	Brass / Cast iron
125	0.17	0.17	0.16
225	0.29	0.33	0.22
300	0.33	0.34	0.21
400	0.36	0.35	0.21
500	0.37	0.36	0.22
700	0.43	Seized	0.23
785	Seized	—	0.23
825	—	—	0.27

Surfaces lightly lubricated, Rennie.

Figure 11.6 (*a*) Coefficients of dynamic friction, metals.

Coefficients of Dynamic Friction Glass-filled Teflon

Shaft Material	
Hardened Steel	0.15
Stainless Steel	0.15
Chromium Plated Steel	0.16
Cast Iron	0.19
Hard Anodized Aluminum	0.20
Monel	0.23
Cold Rolled Steel	0.25
* Brass	0.33
* Aluminium	0.35

* High rate of shaft wear

Figure 11.6 (*b*) Coefficients of dynamic friction, Teflons.

TABLE 11.1 Composition and Physical Properties[a] of White Metal Bearing Alloys

Alloy number[b]	Specified nominal composition of alloys, %: Tin	Antimony	Lead	Copper	Arsenic	Specific gravity[c]	Composition of alloys tested, %: Tin	Antimony	Lead	Copper	Yield point, psi[d] (MPa): 68°F (20°C)	212°F (100°C)
1	91.0	4.5		4.5		7.34	90.9	4.52	None	4.56	4400 (30.3)	2650 (18.3)
2	89.0	7.5		3.5		7.39	89.2	7.4	0.03	3.1	6100 (42.0)	3000 (20.6)
3	84.0	8.0		8.0		7.46	83.4	8.2	0.03	8.3	6600 (45.5)	3150 (21.7)
7	10.0	15.0	Remainder		0.45	9.73	10.0	14.5	75.0	0.11	3550 (24.5)	1600 (11.0)
8	5.0	15.0	Remainder		0.45	10.04	5.2	14.9	79.4	0.14	3400 (23.4)	1750 (12.1)
15	1.0	16.0	Remainder		1.0	10.05						

Alloy number[b]	Johnson's apparent elastic limit psi (MPa)[e]: 68°F (20°C)	212°F (100°C)	Ultimate strength in compression[f]: 68°F (20°C)	212°F (100°C)	Brinell hardness[g]: 68°F (20°C)	212°F (100°C)	Melting point, °F (°C)	Temperature of complete liquefaction, °F (°C)	Proper pouring temperature, °F (°C)
1	2450 (16.9)	1050 (7.2)	12 850 (88.6)	6950 (47.9)	17.0	8.0	433 (223)	700 (371)	825 (441)
2	3350 (23.1)	1100 (7.6)	14 900 (102.7)	8700 (60.0)	24.5	12.0	466 (241)	669 (354)	795 (424)
3	5350 (36.9)	1300 (9.0)	17 600 (121.3)	9900 (68.3)	27.0	14.5	464 (240)	792 (422)	915 (491)
7	2500 (17.2)	1350 (9.3)	15 650 (107.9)	6150 (42.4)	22.5	10.5	464 (240)	514 (268)	640 (338)
8	2650 (18.3)	1200 (8.3)	15 600 (107.6)	6150 (42.4)	20.0	9.5	459 (237)	522 (272)	645 (341)
15					21.0	13.0	479 (248)	538 (281)	662 (350)

[a] The compression test specimens were cylinders 1.5 in (33 mm) in length and 0.5 in (13 mm) in diameter, machined from chill castings 2 in (51 mm) in length and 0.75 in (19 mm) in diameter. The Brinell tests were made on the bottom of parallel machined specimens cast in a mold 2 in (51 mm) in diameter and 0.625 in (16 mm) deep at room temperature.

[b] Data not available on alloy numbers 11 and 13.

[c] The specific gravity multiplied by 0.0361 equals the density in pounds per cubic inch.

[d] The values for yield point were taken from stress-strain curves at a deformation of 0.125% of gage length.

[e] Johnson's apparent elastic limit is taken as the unit stress at the point where the slope of the tangent to the curve is two-thirds times its slope at the origin.

[f] The ultimate strength values were taken as the unit load necessary to produce a deformation of 25% of the length of the specimen.

[g] These values are the average Brinell number of three impressions on each alloy using a 10-mm ball and a 500-kg load applied for 30 s.

SOURCE: ASTM.

TABLE 11.2 Chemical Composition*,†

	Alloy number							
	Tin base				Lead base			
	1	2	3	11	7	8	13	15
Chemical composition, %	UNS—55191	UNS—55193	UNS—55189	UNS—55188	UNS—53581	UNS—53565	UNS—53346	UNS—53620
Tin	90.0–92.0	88.0–90.0	83.0–85.0	86.0–89.0	9.3–10.7	4.5–5.5	5.5–6.5	0.8–1.2
Antimony	4.0–5.0	7.0–8.0	7.5–8.5	6.0–7.5	14.0–16.0	14.0–16.0	9.5–10.5	14.5–17.5
Lead	0.35	0.35	0.35	0.50	Remainder‡	Remainder‡	Remainder‡	Remainder‡
Copper	4.0–5.0	3.0–4.0	7.5–8.5	5.0–6.5	0.50	0.50	0.50	0.6
Iron	0.08	0.08	0.08	0.08	0.10	0.10	0.10	0.10
Arsenic	0.10	0.10	0.10	0.10	0.30–0.60	0.30–0.60	0.25	0.8–1.4
Bismuth	0.08	0.08	0.08	0.08	0.10	0.10	0.10	0.10
Zinc	0.005	0.005	0.005	0.005	0.005	0.005	0.005	0.005
Aluminum	0.005	0.005	0.005	0.005	0.005	0.005	0.005	0.005
Cadmium	0.05	0.05	0.05	0.05	0.05	0.05	0.05	0.05
Total named elements, min	99.80	99.80	99.80	99.80				

* All values not given as ranges are maximum unless shown otherwise.

† Alloy Number 9 was discontinued in 1946 and numbers 4, 5, 6, 10, 11, 12, 16, and 19 were discontinued in 1959. A new number 11, similar to SAE Grade 11, was added in 1966.

‡ To be determined by difference.

SOURCE: ASTM.

- ANSI/AFBMA 7-1988, Shaft and housing fits for radial ball and roller bearings (except tapered roller bearings) conforming to basic boundary plans
- ANSI/AFBMA 9-1990, Load ratings and fatigue life for ball bearings
- ANSI/AFBMA 11-1990, Load ratings and fatigue life for roller bearings
- ANSI/AFBMA 12.1, Instrument ball bearings, metric design
- ANSI/AFBMA 12.2, Instrument ball bearings, inch design
- ANSI/AFBMA 16.1, Airframe ball, roller, and needle roller bearings, metric design
- ANSI/AFBMA 16.2, Airframe ball, roller, and needle roller bearings, inch design
- ANSI/AFBMA 18.1-1982, Needle roller bearings radial, metric design
- ANSI/AFBMA 18.2-1982, Needle roller bearings radial, inch design
- ANSI/AFBMA 21.1-1988, Thrust needle roller and cage assemblies and thrust washers, metric design
- ANSI/AFBMA 21.2-1988, Thrust needle roller and cage assemblies and thrust washers, inch design

Ball and roller bearing designs. In order to gain a knowledge of the ball and roller bearing types that are currently being manufactured, Figs. 11.7 through 11.15 depict the various design configurations.

11.2.1 Load ratings and fatigue life for ball and roller bearings

The load rating and fatigue life for ball and roller bearing designs may be calculated using the procedures outlined in ANSI/AFBMA Standard 9-1990 and ANSI/AFBMA Standard 11-1990. The calculations are intricate and involved, requiring the use of many tables produced by the AFBMA and are thus not shown in this *Handbook*. The calculations for tapered roller bearings are likewise intricate and involved, requiring the use of many tables, and these data are available from The Timken Company bearing catalog or the Torrington Company catalog. Other manufacturers' catalogs also contain the data and calculation procedures.

(*Text continued on page 1012.*)

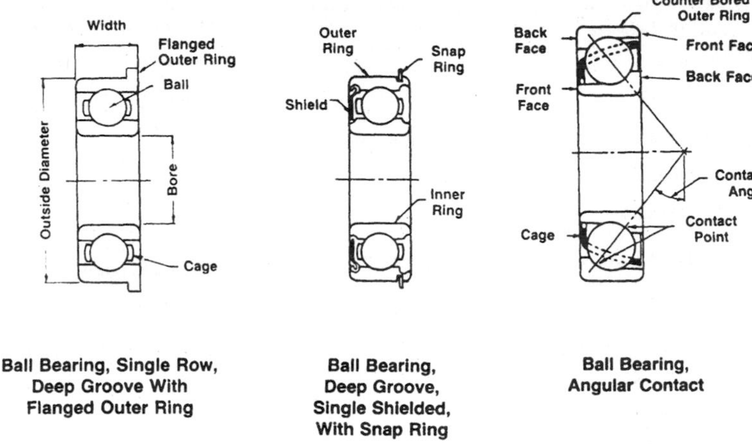

Ball Bearing, Single Row, Deep Groove With Flanged Outer Ring

Ball Bearing, Deep Groove, Single Shielded, With Snap Ring

Ball Bearing, Angular Contact

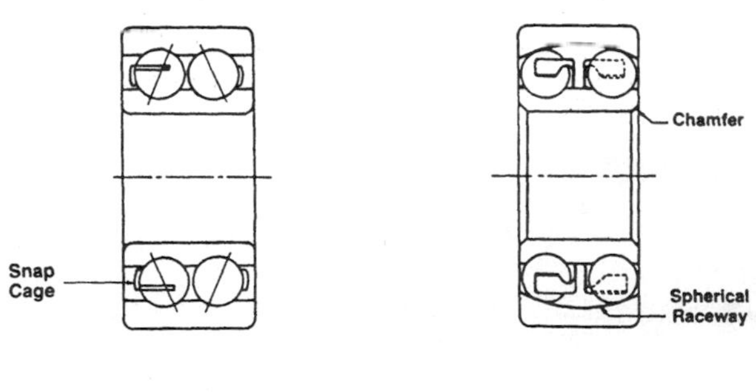

Ball Bearing Double Row, Deep Groove

Ball Bearing, Self Aligning, Double Row

Figure 11.7 *(Reprinted with permission, copyright 1990 by The Anti-Friction Bearing Manufacturers Association, Inc.)*

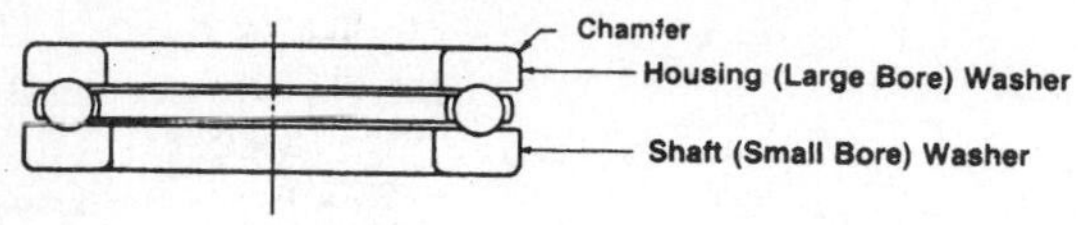

Ball Thrust Bearing

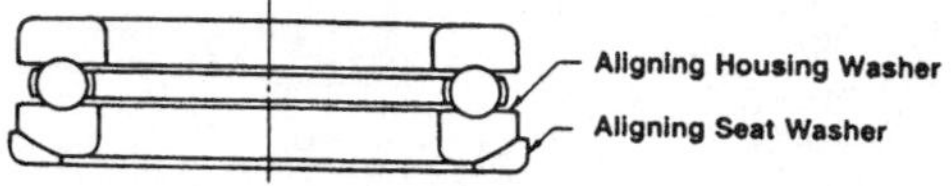

Ball Thrust Bearing With Aligning Washer

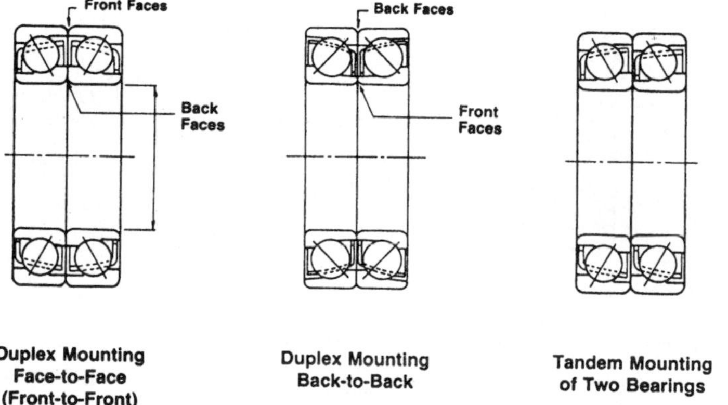

Duplex Mounting Face-to-Face (Front-to-Front)

Duplex Mounting Back-to-Back

Tandem Mounting of Two Bearings

Figure 11.8 *(Reprinted with permission, copyright 1990 by The Anti-Friction Bearing Manufacturers Association, Inc.)*

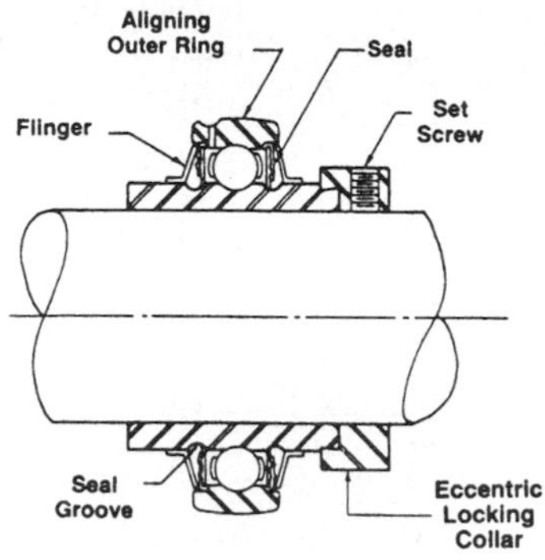

Extended Inner Ring Bearing, Eccentric Locking Collar

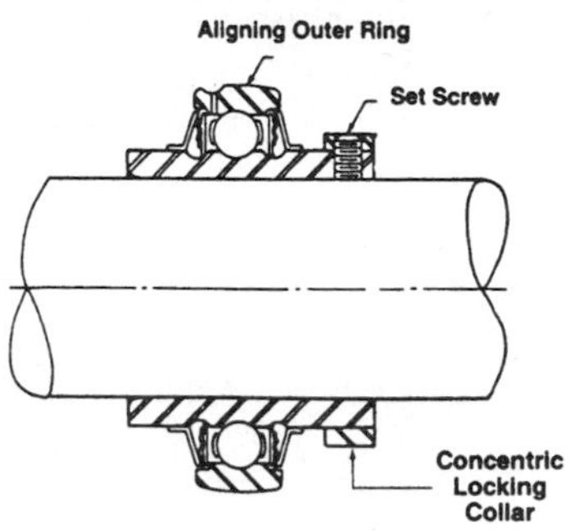

Extended Inner Ring Bearing, Concentric Locking Collar

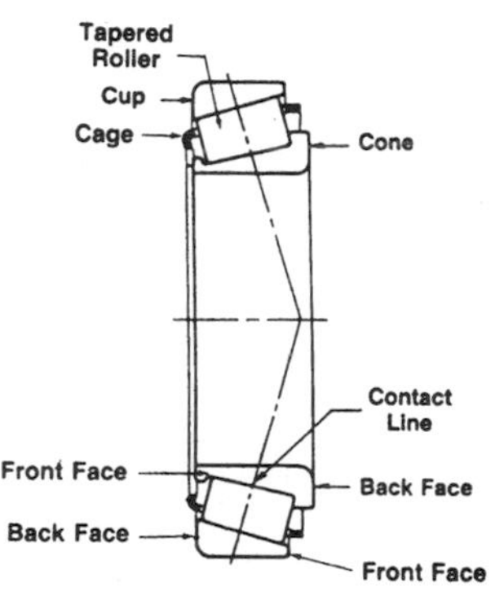

Tapered Roller Bearing, Radial

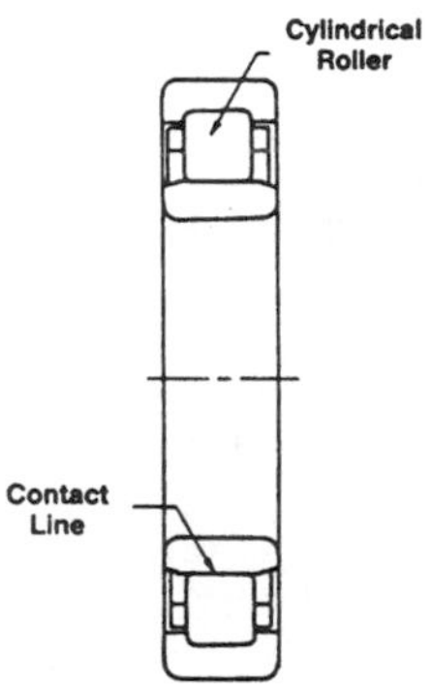

Cylindrical Roller Bearing, Radial

Figure 11.9 *(Reprinted with permission, copyright 1990 by The Anti-Friction Bearing Manufacturers Association, Inc.)*

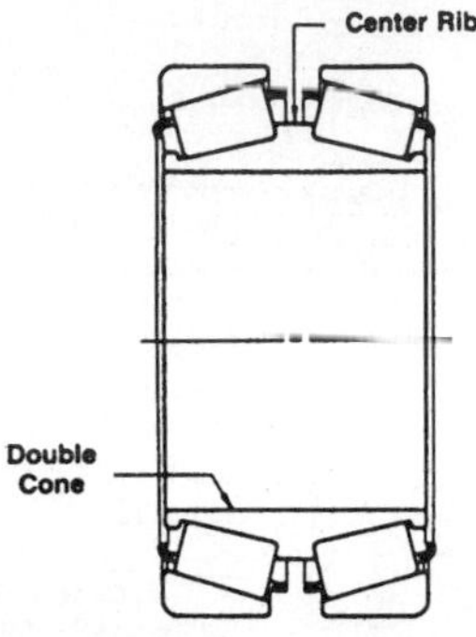

Tapered Roller Bearing
Double Row, Double Cone

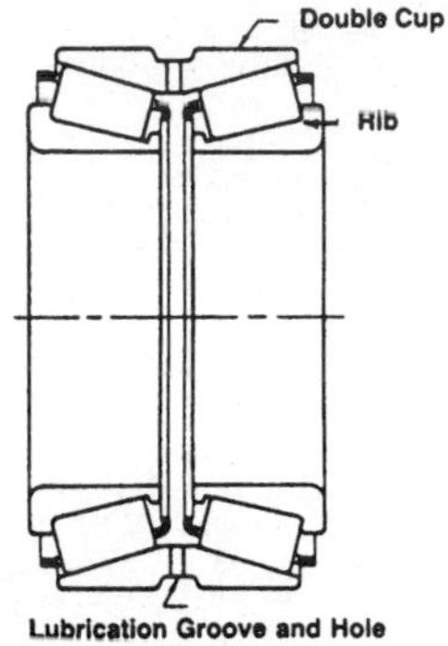

Tapered Roller Bearing
Double Row, Double Cup

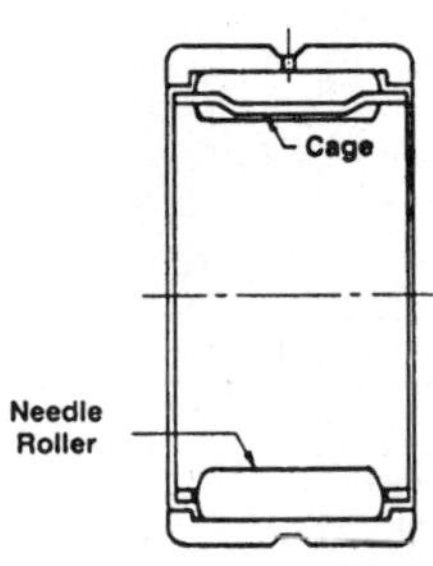

Needle Roller Bearing, With Cage,
Machined Ring, Without Inner Ring

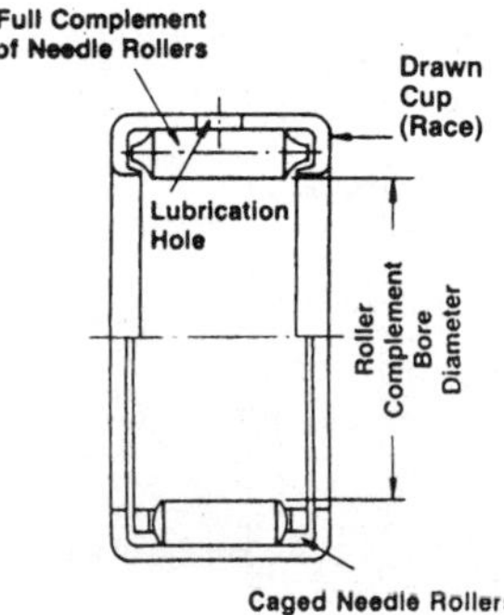

Needle Roller Bearing, Drawn Cup,
Without Inner Ring, Full Complement or
Caged Needle Rollers

Figure 11.10 *(Reprinted with permission, copyright 1990 by The Anti-Friction Bearing Manufacturers Association, Inc.)*

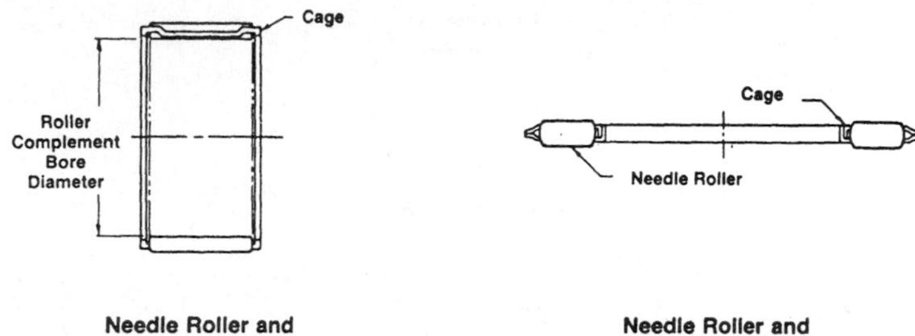

Needle Roller and Cage Assembly, Radial

Needle Roller and Cage Assembly, Thrust

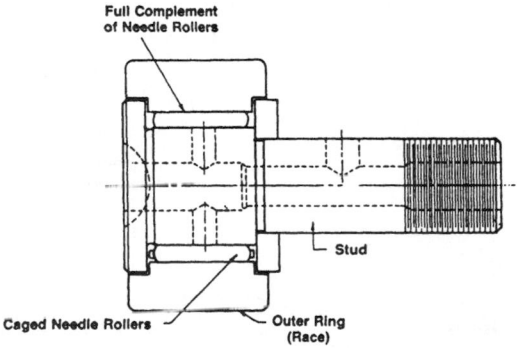

Full Complement of Needle Rollers

Stud

Caged Needle Rollers

Outer Ring (Race)

Needle Roller Bearing, Track Roller, Stud Type, Full Complement or With Cage

Figure 11.11 *(Reprinted with permission, copyright 1990 by The Anti-Friction Bearing Manufacturers Association, Inc.)*

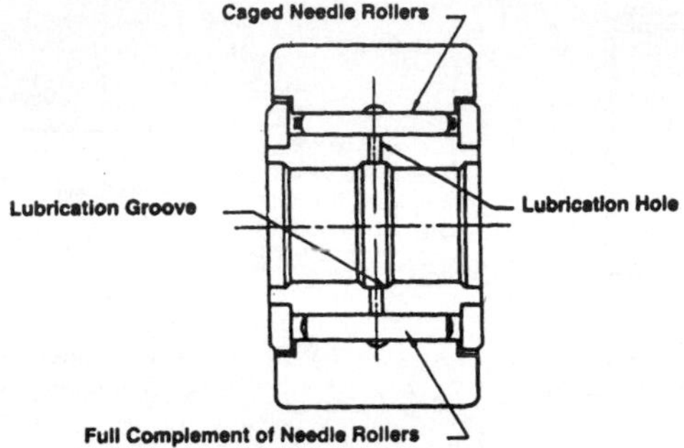

Needle Roller Bearing, Track Roller, Yoke Type, Full Complement or With Cage

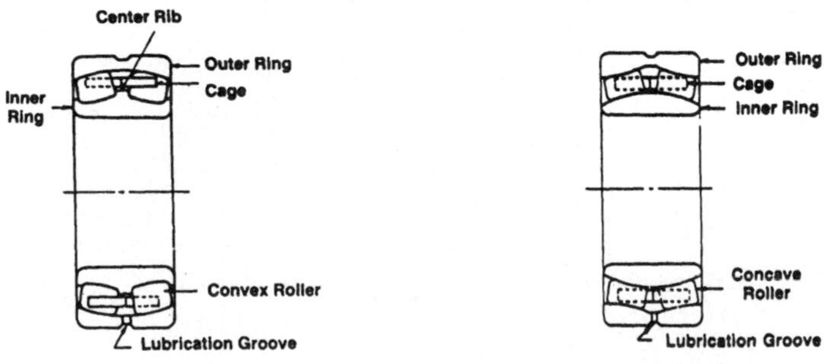

Spherical Roller Bearing Double Row, Convex Roller (Raceway of Outer Ring, Spherical)

Spherical Roller Bearing, Double Row, Concave Roller (Raceway of Inner Ring, Spherical)

Figure 11.12 *(Reprinted with permission, copyright 1990 by The Anti-Friction Bearing Manufacturers Association, Inc.)*

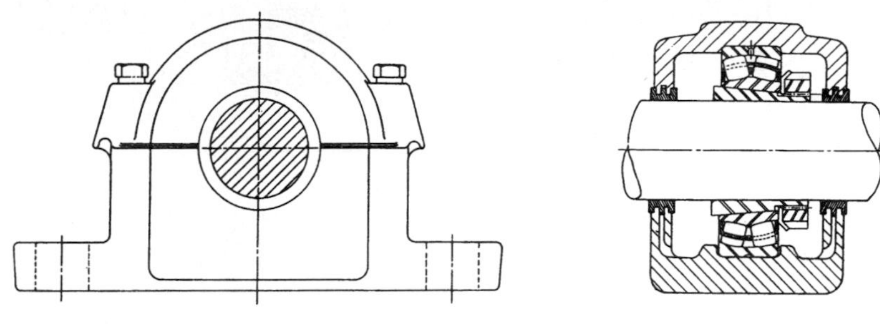

Pillow Block Assembly

Figure 11.13 *(Reprinted with permission, copyright 1990 by The Anti-Friction Bearing Manufacturers Association, Inc.)*

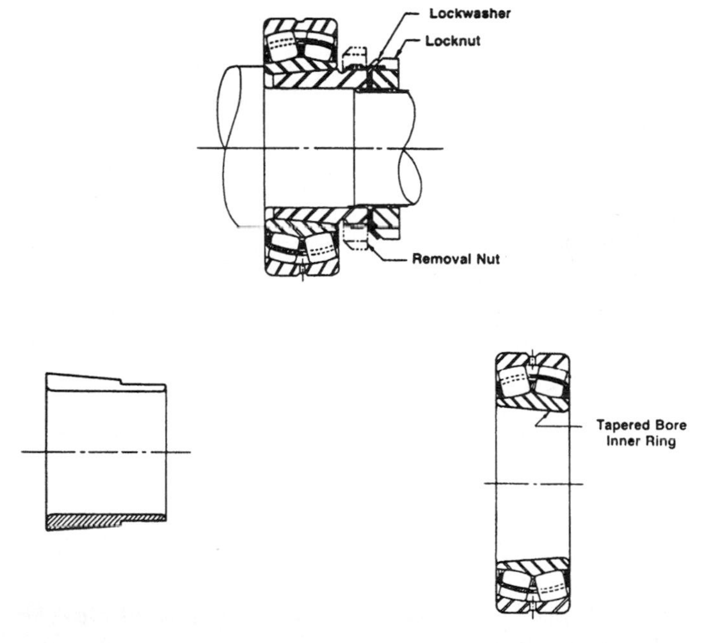

Adapter Sleeve

Tapered Bore Bearing

Figure 11.14 *(Reprinted with permission, copyright 1990 by The Anti-Friction Bearing Manufacturers Association, Inc.)*

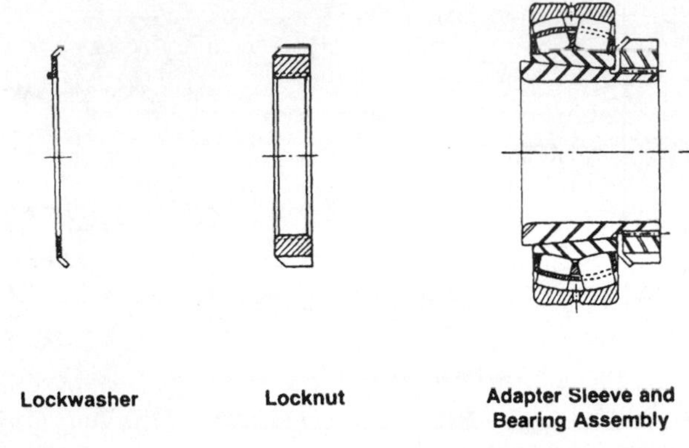

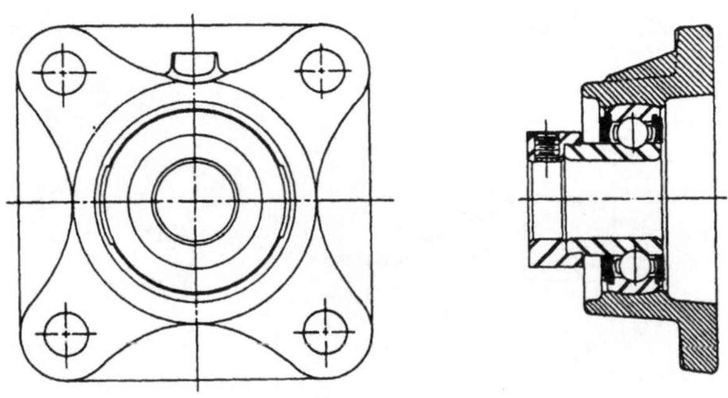

Figure 11.15 *(Reprinted with permission, copyright 1990 by The Anti-Friction Bearing Manufacturers Association, Inc.)*

Load and speed rules for bearings. The following general approximations apply to bearings:

- Doubling the bearing load reduces bearing life to one-tenth.
- Reducing the load by one-half increases bearing life approximately 10 times

- Doubling the bearing speed reduces bearing life to one-half.
- Reducing the bearing speed by one-half doubles bearing life.

11.3 Allowances for Fit Applicable to Antifriction Bearings

The fitting of a rolling-element bearing into its receiving housing or over its mounting shaft is a critical part of bearing applications and assembly. Figure 11.16 lists the different classes of fit and their respective dimensional limits. Figure 11.16 is applicable not only to bearing fits but also to all classes of machined part fits (cylindrical parts) from running fits to forced and driving fits. These data will prove useful to machinists, designers, and tool engineers in actual practice.

11.4 Selection of Bearings: Sources and Procedures

11.4.1 Bearing sources

All bearing manufacturers produce catalogs of their products, and many of these catalogs contain technical data and procedures necessary for the proper use and design of bearing systems. Because there are many bearing manufacturers who produce a very large array of bearing types and designs, a central source for bearing selection would be advantageous to those involved in the application of bearings. Fortunately, there is a central source for the selection and cross-referencing of all the bearings manufactured in the United States, both inch and metric series. The *Bearing Manual Cyclopedia* is the source for all bearing data, dimensions, and cross-references. This manual is produced as a two-volume set and is available from

Industrial Information Headquarters Company, Inc.
2601 W. 16th Street
Broadway, Illinois 60153
(708) 345-7944

Outside the United States, the manual may be obtained from

BHQ Export Services
3199 N. Shadeland Ave.
P.O. Box 26118
Indianapolis, Indiana 46226
(317) 545-2411

Class	Nominal Diameters	Up to 0.500"	0.5625-1"	1.0625-2"	2.0625-3"	3.0625-4"	4.0625-5"
	Tolerances in Standard Holes ♦						
A	High Limit	+0.00025	+0.0005	+0.00075	+0.0010	+0.0010	+0.0010
	Low Limit	-0.00025	-0.00025	-0.00025	-0.0005	-0.0005	-0.0005
	Tolerance	0.0005	0.00075	0.0010	0.0015	0.0015	0.0015
B	High Limit	+0.0005	+0.00075	+0.0010	+0.00125	+0.0015	+0.00175
	Low Limit	-0.0005	-0.0005	-0.0005	-0.00075	-0.00075	-0.00075
	Tolerance	0.0010	0.00125	0.0015	0.0020	0.00225	0.0025
	Allowances for Forced Fits						
F	High Limit	+0.0010	+0.0020	+0.0040	+0.0060	+0.0080	+0.0100
	Low Limit	+0.0005	+0.0015	+0.0030	+0.0045	+0.0060	+0.0080
	Tolerance	0.0005	0.0005	0.0010	0.0015	0.0020	0.0020
	Allowances for Driving Fits						
D	High Limit	+0.0005	+0.0010	+0.0015	+0.0025	+0.0030	+0.0035
	Low Limit	+0.00025	+0.00075	+0.0010	+0.0015	+0.0020	+0.0025
	Tolerance	0.00025	0.00025	0.0005	0.0010	0.0010	0.0010
	Allowances for Push Fits						
P	High Limit	-0.00025	-0.00025	-0.00025	-0.0005	-0.0005	-0.0005
	Low Limit	-0.00075	-0.00075	-0.00075	-0.0010	-0.0010	-0.0010
	Tolerance	0.0005	0.0005	0.0005	0.0005	0.0005	0.0005
	Allowances for Running Fits ■						
X	High Limit	-0.0010	-0.00125	-0.00175	-0.0020	-0.0025	-0.0030
	Low Limit	-0.0020	-0.00275	-0.0035	-0.00425	-0.0050	-0.00575
	Tolerance	0.0010	0.0015	0.00175	0.00225	0.0025	0.00275
Y	High Limit	-0.00075	-0.0010	-0.00125	-0.0015	-0.0020	-0.00225
	Low Limit	-0.00125	-0.0020	-0.0025	-0.0030	-0.0035	-0.0040
	Tolerance	0.0005	0.0010	0.00125	0.0015	0.0015	0.00175
Z	High Limit	-0.0005	-0.00075	-0.00075	-0.0010	-0.0010	-0.00125
	Low Limit	-0.00075	-0.00125	-0.0015	-0.0020	-0.00225	-0.0025
	Tolerance	0.00025	0.0005	0.00075	0.0010	0.00125	0.00125

Figure 11.16 (*a*) Table of allowances for different classes of fits of bearings and other cylindrical machined parts.

Class	High Limit	Low Limit
A	+ $(D)^{0.5}$ x 0.0006	- $(D)^{0.5}$ x 0.0003
B	+ $(D)^{0.5}$ x 0.0008	- $(D)^{0.5}$ x 0.0004
P	- $(D)^{0.5}$ x 0.0002	- $(D)^{0.5}$ x 0.0006
X	- $(D)^{0.5}$ x 0.00125	- $(D)^{0.5}$ x 0.0025
Y	- $(D)^{0.5}$ x 0.001	- $(D)^{0.5}$ x 0.0018
Z	- $(D)^{0.5}$ x 0.0005	- $(D)^{0.5}$ x 0.001

NOTE: ♦ Tolerance is provided for holes which ordinary standard reamers can produce, in two grades, classes A and B, the selection of which is a question for the user's decision and dependent upon the quality of the work required. Some prefer to use class A as working limits and class B as inspection limits.

■ Running fits, which are the most commonly required, are divided into three grades; class X, for engine and other work where easy fits are desired; class Y, for high speeds and good average machine work; and class Z, for fine tooling work.

Figure 11.16 (*b*) Equations for determining allowances.

Bearing Manual is a registered trademark of Industrial Information Headquarters Company, Inc.

Figures 11.17 and 11.18 are reproductions taken from the *Bearing Manual* for illustrative purposes to show the type of information contained in the manual.

11.4.2 Bearing loads in mechanical systems

The loads imposed on bearings used in gearing and belt-drive systems or other mechanical systems are calculated using the procedures shown in Sec. 10.15, "Forces in Gear Systems."

TAPERED ROLLER BEARINGS

Arranged by Bore Diameters

SINGLE ROW - STRAIGHT BORE

Type TS

Continued from the preceding page

DIMENSIONS					BOWER		TIMKEN		TYSON		Part Number
Cone Bore A	Cup O. D. B	Width C	Cone Length D	Cup Length E							
Inches	Inches	Inches	Inches	Inches	Cone	Cup	Cone	Cup	Cone	Cup	
1.0000	2.0470	0.5910	0.5614	0.5000	07100	07204	07100	07204	07100	07204	
1.0000	2.2400	0.7625	0.7810	0.6250	1780	1729	1780	1729	1780	1729	
* 1.0000	2.2400	0.7625	0.7810	0.6250	1780	1729X	1780	1729X	1780	1729X	
1.0000	2.2500	0.6875	0.6875	0.5313	15578	15520	15578	15520	15578	15520	
1.0000	2.2500	0.7650	0.7650	0.5800			M84548	M84510			
1.0000	2.3125	0.7500	0.7620	0.5937	1986	1932	1986	1932			
1.0000	2.3437	0.9200	0.9100	0.7200			M84249	M84210			
1.0000	2.3750	0.7812	0.6875	0.6250	15578	15523	15578	15523	15578	15523	
1.0000	2.3750	0.7813	0.7620	0.6250	1986	1931	1986	1931			
1.0000	2.4375	0.7500	0.8125	0.5625	15101	15243	15101	15243			
* 1.0000	2.4375	0.7500	0.8125	0.5625	15102	15243	15102	15243			
* 1.0000	2.4375	0.7500	0.8125	0.5625	15100	15243	15100	15243			
1.0000	2.4410	0.7500	0.8125	0.5625	15101	15245	15101	15245	15101	15245	
* 1.0000	2.4410	0.7500	0.8125	0.5625	15102	15245	15102	15245	15102	15245	
* 1.0000	2.4410	0.7500	0.8125	0.5625	15100	15245	15100	15245	15100	15245	
1.0000	2.4410	0.8125	0.8125	0.6250	15101	15244	15101	15244	15101	15244	
* 1.0000	2.4410	0.8125	0.8125	0.6250	15102	15244	15102	15244	15102	15244	
* 1.0000	2.4410	0.8125	0.8125	0.6250	15100	15244	15100	15244	15100	15244	
1.0000	2.5000	0.8125	0.8125	0.6250	15101	15250	15101	15250	15101	15250	
* 1.0000	2.5000	0.8125	0.8125	0.6250	15101	15250X	15101	15250X	15101	15250X	
* 1.0000	2.5000	0.8125	0.8125	0.6250	15102	15250	15102	15250	15102	15250	
* 1.0000	2.5000	0.8125	0.8125	0.6250	15102	15250X	15102	15250X	15102	15250X	
* 1.0000	2.5000	0.8125	0.8125	0.6250	15100	15250	15100	15250	15100	15250	
* 1.0000	2.5000	0.8125	0.8125	0.6250	15100	15250X	15100	15250X	15100	15250X	
1.0000	2.6150	0.9375	1.0013	0.7500	2687	2631	2687	2631			
1.0000	2.6875	0.8750	0.8750	0.6875			02473	02421			
1.0000	2.6875	0.8750	0.9375	0.6875			2473	2420			
1.0000	2.6875	0.8750	0.8750	0.6875	02473	02420	02473	02420			
1.0000	2.7450	0.7500	0.7450	0.7500			26100	26274			
1.0000	2.8336	1.0630	1.0000	0.8442			HM88630	HM88611			
1.0000	2.8345	0.7480	0.7450	0.6250			26100	26283			
1.0000	2.8360	1.1875	1.1810	0.9375			3189	3126			
1.0000	2.8438	1.0000	1.0000	0.7812			HM88630	HM88610			
1.0000	2.8593	1.1250	1.1810	0.8750			3189	3125			
1.0000	2.8593	1.1875	1.1810	0.9375			3189	3130			
* 1.0000	2.8593	1.1875	1.1810	0.9375	3189	3120	3189	3120			
1.0000	2.8750	1.0450	1.0000	0.8262			HM88630	HM88612			
1.0000	3.0000	0.7480	0.7450	0.6250			26100	26300			
1.0000	3.0000	1.1875	1.1810	0.9375			3189	3129			
1.0000	3.1496	0.8268	0.8820	0.7018			338	332			

* Differs from the preceding bearing number by cup or cone radius only.

Continued on the following page

Courtesy Bower

Courtesy Timken

Courtesy Tyson

Figure 11.17 Bearing manual sample sheet.

Inch
GROUND BEARINGS

RADIAL - SINGLE ROW

Continued from the preceding page

NO SHIELDS NS | SINGLE SHIELD SS | DOUBLE SHIELDED DS | SINGLE SEAL SC | DOUBLE SEALED DC

Courtesy Nice

OPEN .... | ONE SHIELD --7-- | TWO SHIELDS --77-- | ONE SEAL --9-- | TWO SEALS --99-- | SNAP RING GROOVE --4--

Courtesy Schatz

DIMENSIONS			Nice										Schatz***				
Bore	O.D.	Width	Open Type		Single Shield		Double Shield		Single Seal		Double Seal		Open Type	Single Shield	Double Shield	Single Seal	Double Seal
Inches	Inches	Inches	Old No.	New No.	Old No.	New No.	Old No.	New No.	Old No.	New No.	Old No.	New No.					
3/16	11/16	1/4	1601NS	1601NSTN	1601SS	1601SSTN	1601DS	1601DSTN					BR-01*	BR-701*	BR-7701*	BR-901*	BR-9901*
3/16	11/16	5/16							1601SC	1601SCTN	1601DC	1601DCTN					
1/4	11/16	1/4	1602NS	1602NSTN	1602SS	1602SSTN	1602DS	1602DSTN					BR-02*	BR-702*	BR-7702*	BR-902*	BR-9902*
1/4	11/16	5/16							1602SC	1602SCTN	1602DC	1602DCTN					
5/16	7/8	9/32	1603NS	1603NSTN	1603SS	1603SSTN	1603DS	1603DSTN					BR-03**	BR-703**	BR-7703**	BR-903**	BR-9903**
5/16	7/8	11/32							1603SC	1603SCTN	1603DC	1603DCTN					
5/16	29/32	9/32															
5/16	29/32	5/16	1605NS	1605NSTN	1605SS	1605SSTN	1605DS	1605DSTN	1605SC	1605SCTN	1605DC	1605DCTN	BR-05	BR-705	BR-7705	BR-905	BR-9905
3/8	7/8	9/32	1604NS	1604NSTN	1604SS	1604SSTN	1604DS	1604DSTN					BR-04**	BR-704**	BR-7704**	BR-904**	BR-9904**
3/8	7/8	11/32							1604SC	1604SCTN	1604DC	1604DCTN					
3/8	29/32	5/16	1606NS	1606NSTN	1606SS	1606SSTN	1606DS	1606DSTN	1606SC	1606SCTN	1606DC	1606DCTN	BR-06	BR-706	BR-7706	BR-906	BR-9906
3/8	29/32	19/32															
3/8	1- 1/8	3/8	1614NS	1614NSTN	1614SS	1614SSTN	1614DS	1614DSTN	1614SC	1614SCTN	1614DC	1614DCTN	BR-14	BR-714	BR-7714	BR-914	BR-9914
7/16	29/32	5/16	1607NS	1607NSTN	1607SS	1607SSTN	1607DS	1607DSTN	1607SC	1607SCTN	1607DC	1607DCTN	BR-07	BR-707	BR-7707	BR-907	BR-9907
7/16	1- 1/8	3/8	1615NS	1615NSTN	1615SS	1615SSTN	1615DS	1615DSTN	1615SC	1615SCTN	1615DC	1615DCTN	BR-15	BR-715	BR-7715	BR-915	BR-9915
7/16	1- 3/8	7/16	1620NS	1620NSTN	1620SS	1620SSTN	1620DS	1620DSTN	1620SC	1620SCTN	1620DC	1620DCTN	BR-20	BR-720	BR-7720	BR-920	BR-9920
1/2	1- 1/8	3/8	1616NS	1616NSTN	1616SS	1616SSTN	1616DS	1616DSTN	1616SC	1616SCTN	1616DC	1616DCTN	BR-16	BR-716	BR-7716	BR-916	BR-9916
1/2	1- 3/8	7/16	1621NS	1621NSTN	1621SS	1621SSTN	1621DS	1621DSTN	1621SC	1621SCTN	1621DC	1621DCTN	BR-21	BR-721	BR-7721	BR-921	BR-9921
9/16	1- 3/8	7/16	1622NS	1622NSTN	1622SS	1622SSTN	1622DS	1622DSTN	1622SC	1622SCTN	1622DC	1622DCTN	BR-22	BR-722	BR-7722	BR-922	BR-9922
5/8	1- 3/8	7/16	1623NS	1623NSTN	1623SS	1623SSTN	1623DS	1623DSTN	1623SC	1623SCTN	1623DC	1623DCTN	BR-23	BR-723	BR-7723	BR-923	BR-9923
5/8	1- 5/8	1/2	1628NS	1628NSTN	1628SS	1628SSTN	1628DS	1628DSTN	1628SC	1628SCTN	1628DS	1628DCTN	BR-28	BR-728	BR-7728	BR-928	BR-9928
5/8	1- 3/4	1/2	1633NS	1633NSTN	1633SS	1633SSTN	1633DS	1633DSTN	1633SC	1633SCTN	1633DS	1633DCTN	BR-33	BR-733	BR-7733	BR-923	BR-9933
11/16	1- 5/8	1/2											BR-34	BR-734	BR-7734	BR-934	BR-9934
3/4	1- 5/8	1/2	1630NS	1630NSTN	1630SS	1630SSTN	1630DS	1630DSTN	1630SC	1630SCTN	1630DS	1630DCTN	BR-30	BR-730	BR-7730	BR-930	BR-9930
3/4	1- 3/4	1/2	1635NS	1635NSTN	1635SS	1635SSTN	1635DS	1635DSTN	1535SC	1635SCTN	1635DS	1635DCTN	BR-35	BR-735	BR-7735	BR-935	BR-9935
3/4	2	9/16	1638NS	1638NSTN	1638SS	1638SSTN	1638DS	1638DSTN	1638SC	1638SCTN	1638DS	1638DCTN	BR-38	BR-738	BR-7738	BR-938	BR-9938
13/16	2	9/16											BR-39	NR-739	BR-7739	BR-939	BR-9939
7/8	2	9/16	1640NS	1640NSTN	1640SS	1640SSTN	1640DS	1640DSTN	1640SC	1640SCTN	1640DS	1640DCTN	BR-40	BR-740	BR-7740	BR-940	BR-9940
1	2	9/16	1641NS	1641NSTN	1641SS	1641SSTN	1641DS	1641DSTN	1641SC	1641SCTN	1641DS	1641DCTN	BR-41	BR-741	BR-7741	BR-941	BR-9941
1- 1/8	2- 1/2	5/8	1652NS	1652NSTN	1652SS	1652SSTN	1652DS	1652DSTN	1652SC	1652SCTN	1652DS	1652DCTN	BR-52	BR-752	BR-7752	BR-952	BR-9952
1- 1/4	2- 1/2	5/8	1654NS	1654NSTN	1654SS	1654SSTN	1654DS	1654DSTN	1654SC	1654SCTN	1654DS	1654DCTN	BR-54	BR-754	BR-7754	BR-954	BR-9954
1- 1/4	2- 9/16	11/16	1657NS	1657NSTN	1657SS	1657SSTN	1657DS	1657DSTN	1657SC	1657SCTN	1657DS	1657DCTN					
1- 5/16	2- 9/16	11/16	1658NS	1658NSTN	1658SS	1658SSTN	1658DS	1658DSTN	1658SC	1658SCTN	1658DS	1658DCTN					

* Also available in 5/16 inches width.
** Also available in 11/32 inches width.
*** Schatz also makes this series with snap ring.

Figure 11.18 Bearing manual sample sheet.

Chapter

12

Cams and Cam Development, Layout, and Design

Cams are mechanical components that convert rotary motion into a selective or controlled translating or oscillating motion or action by way of a cam follower that bears against the working surface of the cam profile or perimeter. As the cam rotates, the cam follower rises and falls according to the motions described by the displacement curve.

Cams can be used to translate power into motion, as in the cams on the camshaft of an internal combustion engine, or they can be used for selective motions, as in timing devices or generating functions. The operating/timing cycles of many machines are controlled by the action of cams.

There are basically two classes of cams: uniform-motion cams and accelerated-motion cams.

12.1 Cam Motions

The most important cam motions and displacement curves in common use are

- Uniform velocity motion, for low speeds
- Uniform acceleration, for moderate speeds

- Parabolic motion used in conjunction with uniform motion or uniform acceleration, low to moderate speeds
- Cycloidal, for high speeds

The design of a typical cam is initiated with a *displacement curve,* as shown in Fig. 12.1. Here, the y dimension corresponds to the cam rise or fall, and the x dimension corresponds either to degrees, radians, or time displacement. The slope lines of the rise and fall intervals should be terminated with a parabolic curve to prevent shock loads on the follower. The total length of the displacement (x dimension) on the displacement diagram represents one complete revolution of the cam. Standard graphic layout methods may be used to develop the displacement curves and simple cam profiles. The placement of the parabolic curves at the terminations of the rise and fall intervals on uniform-motion and uniform-acceleration cams is depicted in the detail view in Fig. 12.1. The graphic construction of the parabolic curves which begin and end the rise and fall intervals may be accomplished using the principles of geometric construction shown in Sec. 2.3 for parabolic curves.

The layout of the cam shown in Fig. 12.2 is a development of the displacement diagram shown in Fig. 12.1. In this cam, a dwell interval is followed by a uniform-motion/velocity rise, a short dwell period, a uniform fall, and then the remainder of the dwell to complete the cycle of one revolution.

The layout of a cam such as that shown in Fig. 12.2 is relatively simple. The rise and fall periods are developed by dividing the rise or fall into the same number of parts as the angular period of the rise and fall. The points of intersection of the rise/fall divisions with the angular divisions are then connected by a smooth curve, terminating in a small parabolic curve interval at the beginning and end of the rise/fall periods. Cams of this type have many uses in industry and are economical to manufacture because of their simple geometries.

12.2 Uniform-Motion Cam Layout

The cam shown in Fig. 12.3 is a uniform- or harmonic-motion cam, often called a *heart cam* because of its shape. The layout of this type of cam is simple, since the curve is a development of the intersection of the rise intervals with the angular displacement inter-

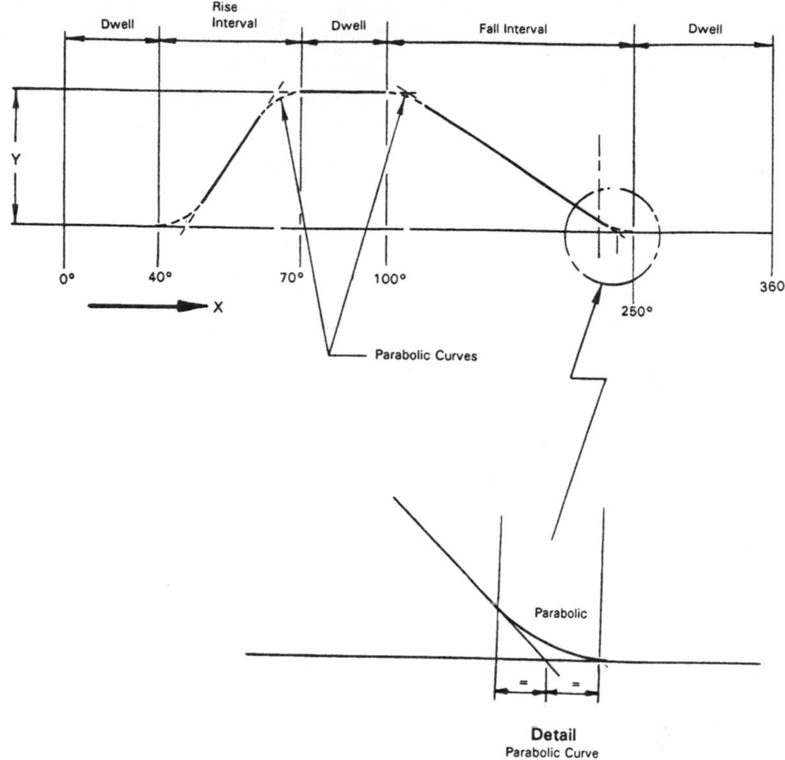

Figure 12.1 Cam displacement diagram (cam developed as in Fig. 12.2).

vals. The points of intersection are then connected by a smooth curve. See the spiral of Archimedes in Sec. 2.3.

12.3 Accelerated-Motion Cam Layout

The cam shown in Fig. 12.4 is a uniform acceleration cam. The layout of this type of cam is also simple. The rise interval is divided in increments of 1, 3, 5, 5, 3, 1, as shown in the figure. The angular rise interval is then divided into six equal angular sections as shown. The intersections of the projected rise intervals with the radial lines of the six equal angular intervals are then connected by

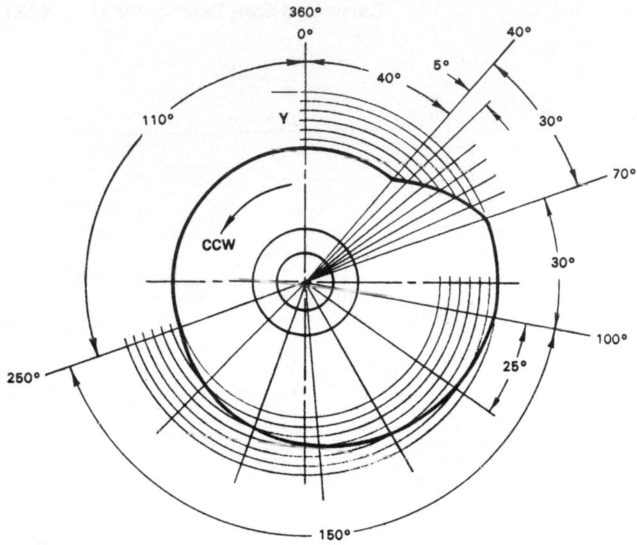

Figure 12.2 Development of a cam whose displacement diagram is shown in Fig. 12.1.

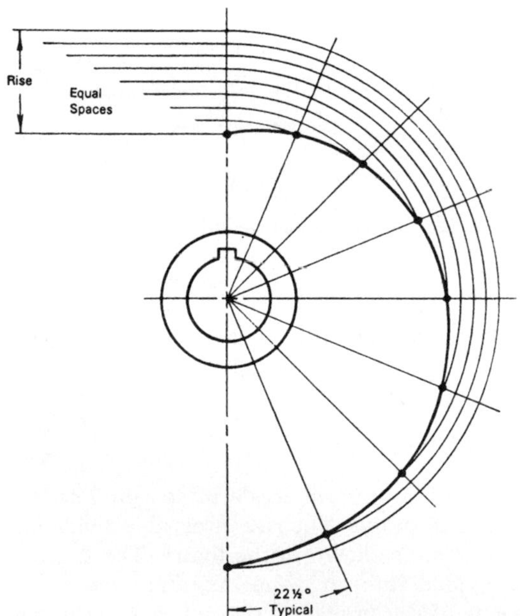

Figure 12.3 Uniform-motion cam layout (harmonic motion).

a smooth curve, completing the section of the cam described. The displacement diagram that is generated for the cam follower motion by the designer will determine the final configuration of the complete cam.

12.4 Cylindrical Cam Layout

A cylindrical cam is shown in Fig. 12.5 and is layed out in a similar manner to the cams in Figs. 12.3 and 12.4. A displacement diagram is made first, followed by the cam stretch-out view shown in Fig. 12.5. The points describing the curve that the follower rides in may be calculated mathematically for a precise motion of the follower. Four- and five-axis machining centers are used to cut the finished cams from a computer program generated in the engineering department and fed into the controller of the machining center.

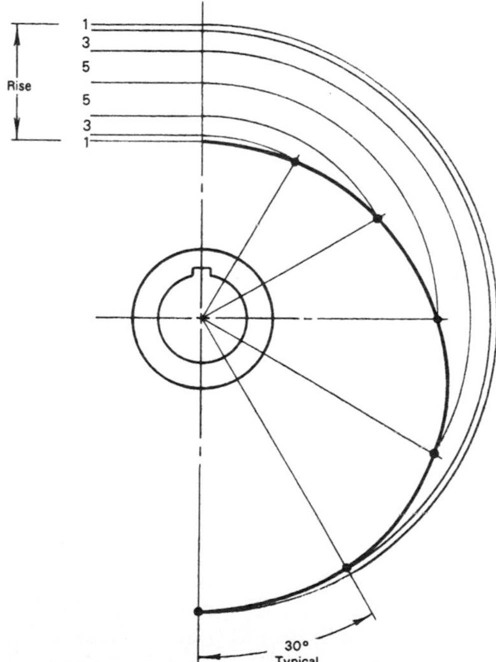

Figure 12.4 Uniform acceleration cam layout.

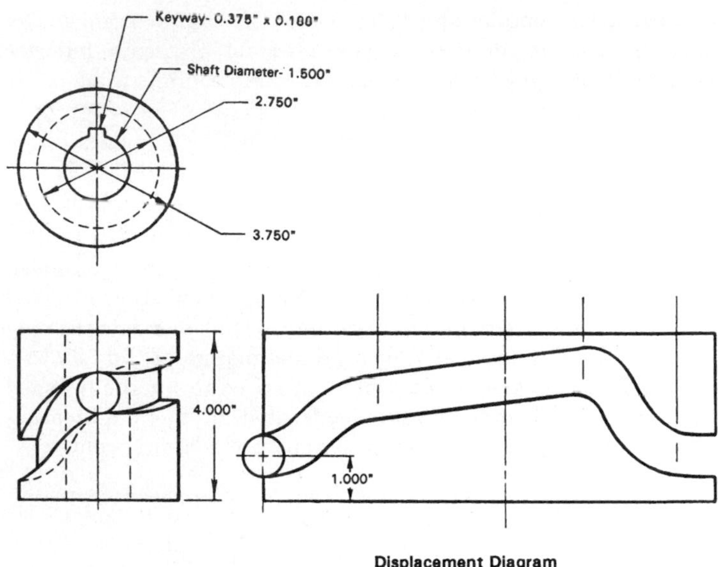

Figure 12.5 Development of a cylindrical cam.

Tracer cutting and incremental cutting are also used to manufacture cams but are seldom used when the manufacturing facility is equipped with four- and five-axis machining centers, which do the work faster and more accurately than ever before possible.

The design of cycloidal-motion cams is not discussed here because of their mathematical complexity and many special requirements. Cycloidal cams are also expensive to manufacture because of the design and programming functions required in the engineering department. The Bibliography lists handbooks covering cycloidal cam design.

12.5 Eccentric Cams

A cam that is required to actuate a roller limit switch in a simple application or to provide a simple rise function may be made from an eccentric shape, as shown in Fig. 12.6. The rise, diameter, and offset are calculated as shown in the figure. This type of cam is the most simple to design and is very economical to manufacture; it also has many practical applications. Materials used for this type of cam design can be steel, alloys or plastics, and compositions. Simple functions and light loads at low to moderate speeds are limiting factors for these types of cams.

Figure 12.6 presents the simple relationships of the cam variables as follows:

$$R = (x + r) - a$$

$$a = r - x$$

$$\text{Rise} = D - d$$

The eccentric cam may be designed using the relationships shown above.

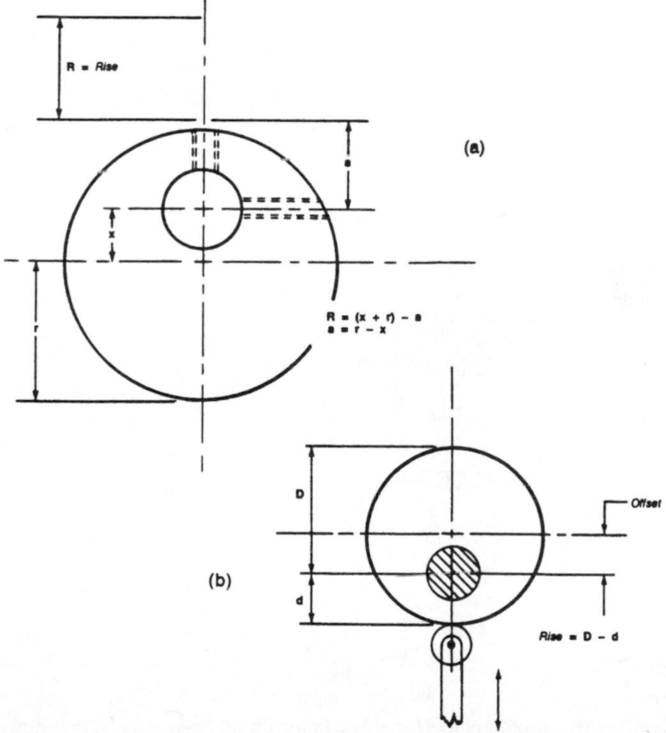

Figure 12.6 Eccentric cam geometry.

12.6 The Cam Follower

The most common types of cam follower systems are the radial translating, offset translating, and swinging roller followers, as depicted in Fig. 12.7. These cams are *open-track cams,* in which the follower must be held against the cam surface at all times, usually by a spring. A *closed-track cam* is one in which a roller follower travels in a slot or groove cut in the face of the cam. The cylindrical cam shown in Fig. 12.5 is a typical closed-track type of cam. The closed-track cam follower system is termed *positive* because the follower translates in the track without recourse to a spring holding the follower against the cam surface. The positive, closed-track cam has wide use on machines in which the breakage of a spring on the follower could cause damage to the machine. Note in Fig. 12.7*b* that where the cam follower is offset from the axis of the cam, the offset must be in a direction opposed to that of the cam's rotation.

On cam follower systems that use a spring to hold the follower against the working curve or surface of the cam, the spring must be designed properly in order to prevent *floating* of the spring during high-speed operation of the cam. The cyclic rate of the spring must

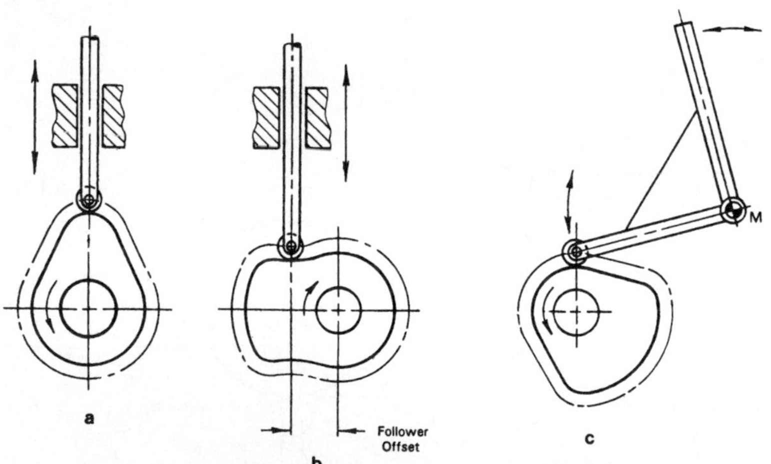

Figure 12.7 (*a*) In-line follower. (*b*) Offset follower. (*c*) Swinging-arm follower.

be kept below the natural frequency of the spring in order to prevent floating. Chapter 13 of this *Handbook* shows procedures for the design of high-pressure, high-cyclic-rate springs in order to prevent this phenomenon from occurring. When you know the cyclic rate of the spring used on the cam follower and its working stress and material, you can design the spring to have a natural frequency that is below the cyclic rate of operation. The placement of springs in *parallel* is often required to achieve the proper results. The valve springs on high-speed automotive engines is a good example of this practice, wherein the designer wants to control natural frequency and at the same time have a spring with a high spring rate in order to keep the engine valves tightly closed. The spring rate also must be high enough to prevent separation of the follower from the cam surface during acceleration, deceleration, and shock loads in operation. The cam follower spring is often preloaded to accomplish this.

12.7 Pressure Angle of the Cam Follower

The *pressure angle* ϕ (see Fig. 12.8) is generally made 30° or less for a reciprocating cam follower and 45° or less for an oscillating cam follower. These typical pressure angles also depend on the cam mechanism design and may be more or less than indicated above.

The pressure angle ϕ is the angle between a common *normal* to both the roller and the cam profile and the direction of the follower motion, with one leg of the angle passing through the axis of the follower roller axis. This pressure angle is found easily using graphic layout methods.

To avoid undercutting cams with a roller follower, the radius r of the roller must be less than C_r, which is the minimum radius of curvature along the cam profile.

Pressure-angle calculations. The pressure angle is an important factor in the design of cams. Variations in the pressure angle affect the transverse forces acting on the follower. The simple equations that define the maximum pressure angle α and the cam angle θ at α are as shown in Fig. 12.9, where α is maximum pressure angle of the cam (degrees), S is total lift for a given cam motion during cam rotation (inches), R is initial base radius of cam, center of cam to center of roller (inches), β is the cam rotation angle during which

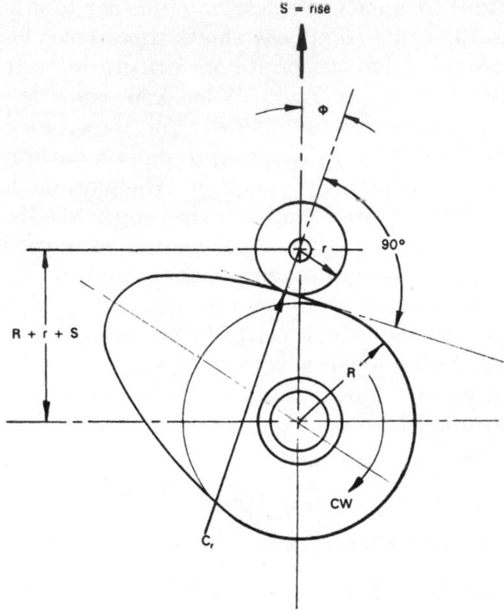

Figure 12.8 The pressure angle of the cam follower.

the total lift S occurs for a given cam motion (radians), and θ is the cam angle at pressure angle α.

For simple harmonic motion,

$$\alpha = \arctan \frac{\pi}{2\beta}\left[\frac{S/R}{\sqrt{1 + (S/R)}} \right]$$

$$\theta = \frac{\beta}{\pi} \arccos\left[\frac{S/R}{2 + (S/R)} \right]$$

For constant-velocity motion,

$$\alpha = \arctan \frac{1}{\beta}\left(\frac{S}{R}\right)$$

$$\theta = 0$$

For constant-acceleration motion,

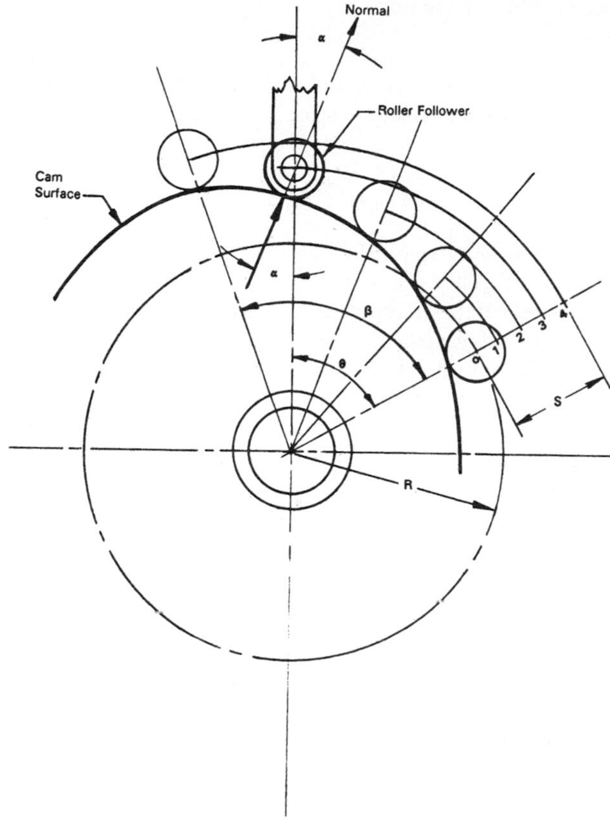

Figure 12.9 Diagram for pressure-angle calculations.

$$\alpha = \arctan \frac{2}{\beta}\left[\frac{S/R}{1 + (S/R)}\right]$$

$$\theta = \beta$$

For cycloidal motion,

$$\alpha = \arctan \frac{1}{2\beta}\left(\frac{S}{R}\right)$$

$$\theta = 0$$

12.8 Contact Stresses Between Follower and Cam

To calculate the approximate stress S_s developed between the roller and the cam surface, we can use the simple equation

$$S_s = C \frac{f_n}{w}\left(\frac{1}{r_f} + \frac{1}{R_c}\right)$$

where C = constant (2300 for steel to steel, 1900 for steel roller and cast iron cam)
S_s = calculated compressive stress, psi
f_n = normal load between follower and cam surface, lbf
w = width of cam and roller common contact surface, in
R_c = minimum radius of curvature of cam profile, in
r_f = radius of roller follower, in

The highest stress is developed at the minimum radius of curvature of the cam profile. The calculated stress S_s should be less than the maximum allowable stress of the weaker material of the cam or roller follower. The roller follower would normally be the harder material.

Cam or follower failure is usually due to fatigue when the surface endurance limit (permissible compressive stress) is exceeded. Some typical maximum allowable compressive stresses for various materials used for cams when the roller follower is hardened steel (Rockwell C45 to C55) include

Gray iron, cast (200 BHN)	55,000 psi
ASTM A48-48	
SAE 1020 steel (150 BHN)	80,000 psi
SAE 4150 steel HT (300 BHN)	180,000 psi
SAE 4340 steel HT (R_c 50)	220,000 psi

Note: BHN designates Brinnel hardness number; R_c is Rockwell C scale.

12.9 Cam Torque

As the follower bears against the cam, resisting torque develops during rise S and assisting torque develops during fall or return. The maximum torque developed during cam rise determines the cam drive requirements.

The instantaneous torque values T_i may be calculated using the equation

$$T_i = \frac{9.55vF_n \cos \alpha}{N}$$

where T_i = instantaneous torque, lb · in
v = velocity of follower, in/s
F_n = normal load, lb
α = maximum pressure angle, degrees
N = cam speed, rpm

The normal load F_n may be found graphically or calculated from the vector diagram shown in Fig. 12.10. Here, the horizontal or lateral pressure on the follower is $F_n \sin \alpha$, and the vertical component or axial load on the follower is $F_n \cos \alpha$.

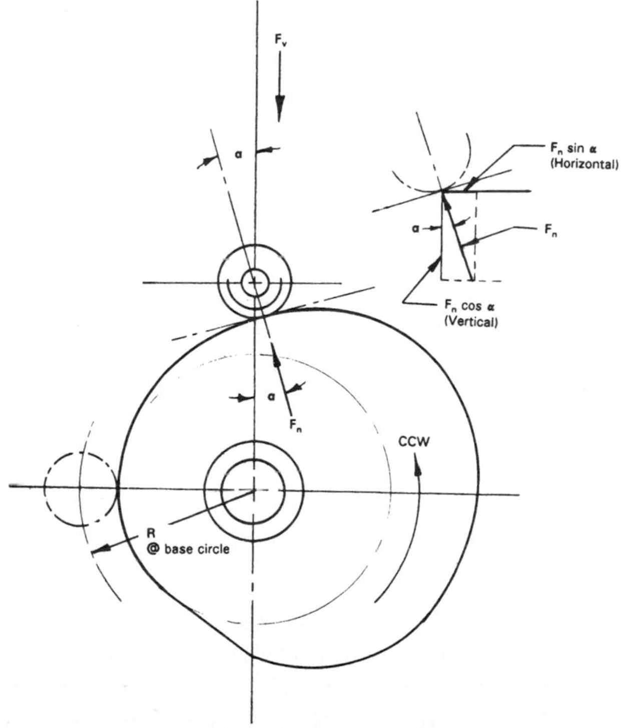

Figure 12.10 Normal load diagram and vectors.

When we know the vertical load (axial load) on the follower, we solve for F_n (the normal load) on the follower from

$$F_n \cos \alpha = F_v$$

where α = pressure angle, degrees
F_v = axial load on follower (from above equation), lb
F_n = normal load at the cam profile and follower, lb

Example Spring load on the follower is 80 lb, and the pressure angle α is 17.5°. Then,

$$F_v = F_n \cos \alpha$$

$$F_n = \frac{F_v}{\cos \alpha} = \frac{80}{\cos 17.5} = \frac{80}{0.954}$$

$$= 84 \text{ lb}$$

Knowing the normal force F_n allows us to calculate the pressure (stress) in pounds per square inch between the cam profile and roller on the follower (see Sec. 12.8).

12.10 Manufacturing Cams

The cam type and motion curve should be kept as simple as the application will allow in order to keep manufacturing costs low. Use the most economical material for each application. Plastic cams are indicated in low-speed, light-load systems and may be molded if the required quantity is large enough to justify the costs for tooling and molds. Cams are sometimes made of copper alloys such as high-strength aluminum bronze. Refer to the materials section of the *Handbook* (Chap. 5) for other materials which may be used for cam applications.

The cam profile may be cut on an EDM (electric discharge machine) using a computer program with high accuracy, and the cam thus produced can be used as the master cam for tracer or CNC-programmed milling of large numbers of cams. This may be the most accurate and cost-effective method of producing radial-face cams. The EDM machine is capable of accurately cutting hardened tool steels as thick as 2 in (see Fig. 1.4, which depicts a modern wire EDM machine).

12.11 Dynamic Analysis of Cams during Operation

With the advent of high-speed motion picture photography, it is now possible to analyze and measure the actions of high-speed cams in operation by way of a prototype of the cam system under study. Cameras with speeds of 1000 to 12,000 frames per second are available commercially for the study of high-speed mechanisms, allowing design corrections to be made which would be very difficult to accomplish mathematically. The solutions to many difficult engineering mechanics problems are thus available to the modern designer of mechanical systems with minimal recourse to advanced mathematical manipulations (which are, in most cases, approximations at best). The high-speed analyses are also accomplished with the additional use of oscillographs, accelerometers, and other transducers, including strain gages.

Figure 12.11 shows some typical low-speed, low-force, high-pressure, and economical cams which are used for the following applications. The cam in part *a* is used for roller limit-switch actuation in an electrical timing device. The cam in part *b* is used for general applications as a limit-switch actuator cam (see Fig. 12.6). Part *c* shows a pair of profile cams used in a clamping mechanism. These are made from 7075-T651 aluminum alloy which has been hard-coat anodized.

Various cam types or designs. The study of high-speed, high-load cams is mathematically complex and beyond the scope of this *Handbook,* although the cam systems shown in the beginning of this chapter are perfectly suitable for many low- and intermediate-speed applications. Graphic layout procedures and blending of the parabolic curves to the rise and fall intervals of simple cams are preferred methods of producing the simpler types of cam and follower systems shown in this chapter.

In advanced cam design, two classes of cams are generally recognized, namely, the trigonometric family and the polynomial family. Included in these systems are cams such as the polydyne cams used in high-speed automotive systems. The *desmodromic* system was used many years ago, it being a positive-action cam design wherein springs were not used to hold the follower against the cam profile, making it suitable for very high speed applications such as the cams in a racing engine.

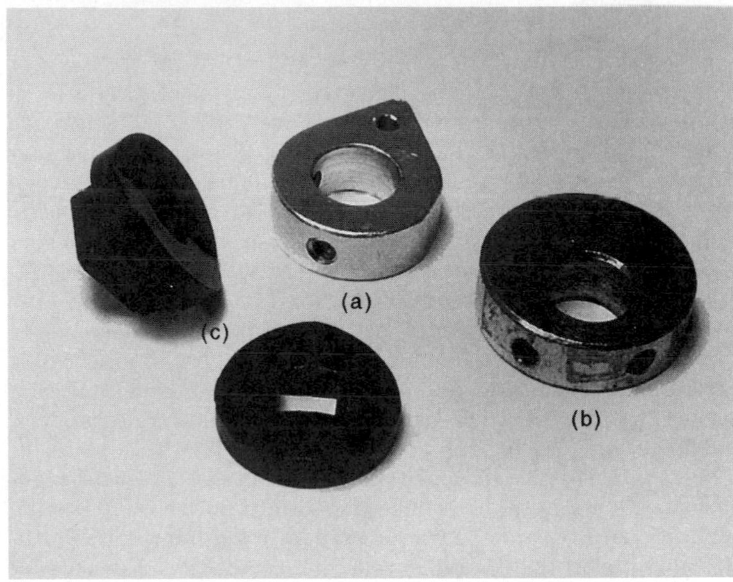

Figure 12.11 Typical cams: (*a*) quick-rise cam; (*b*) eccentric cam; (*c*) profile-cam set.

In conclusion, the more common types of cams include radial-plate cams, positive-action cams, face cams, and cylindrical cams. Cam followers take many forms, such as roller followers, flat-plate followers, roller-bearing followers, offset-disk followers, and chisel- or knife-point followers.

Chapter

13

Springs

Springs are among the most important and most often used mechanical components. Many mechanisms and assemblies would be virtually impossible to design and manufacture without the use of springs, in one form or another. There are many different types of springs and spring materials. We will cover all the most important and common types and forms which are designed and manufactured today. Figure 13.1 shows samples of typical springs.

Summary of spring types or forms described in this section

1. Compression springs, straight and conical
   a. Round wire
   b. Square wire
   c. Rectangular wire
2. Extension springs, straight
   a. Round wire
3. Torsion springs
   a. Round wire
   b. Square wire
4. Coil springs, spiral
5. Leaf springs
   a. Cantilever
   b. Both ends supported (beam)
6. Spring washers
   a. Curved
   b. Wave

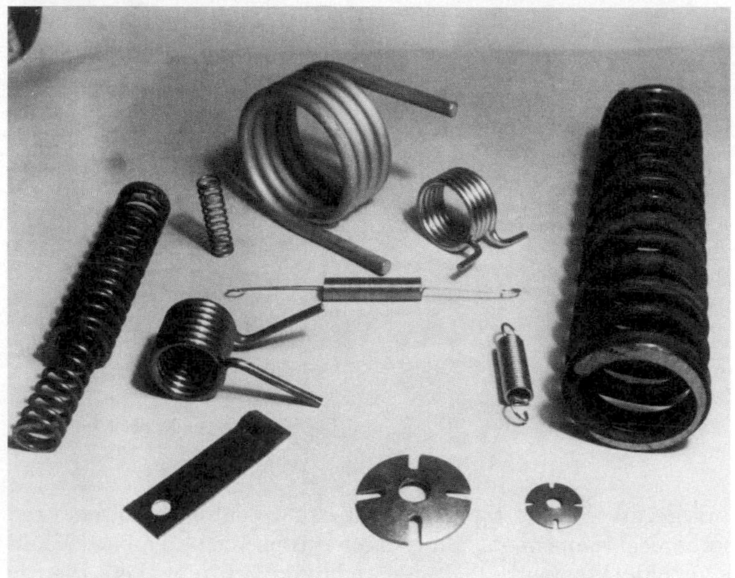

Figure 13.1 Samples of typical springs.

7. Hair springs, very light load
8. Torsion bars
9. Belleville washers (disk springs)

13.1 Introduction to Spring Design

It is important when designing springs to adhere to proper procedures and design considerations. Some of the important design considerations in spring work are outlined here.

Selection of material for spring construction

Space limitations. Do you have adequate space in the mechanism to use economical materials such as oil-tempered ASTM A-229 spring wire? If your space is limited by design and you need maximum energy per mass, you should look to materials such as music wire, ASTM A-228, chrome-vanadium, some stainless steels, or chrome-silicon steel wire.

Economy. Will economical materials such as ASTM A-229 wire suffice for the intended application?

Corrosion resistance. If the spring is used in a corrosive environment, you may select materials such as 17-7 PH stainless steel or the other stainless steels, i.e., 301, 302, 303, 304, etc.

Electrical conductivity. If you require the spring to carry an electric current, materials such as beryllium copper and phosphor bronze are available.

Temperature range. Whereas low temperatures induced by weather are seldom a consideration, high-temperature applications call for materials such as 301 and 302 stainless steel, nickel-chrome A-286, 17-7 PH, Inconel 600, and Inconel X750. Design stresses should be as low as possible for springs designed for use at high operating temperatures.

Shock loads, high endurance limit, and high strength. Materials such as music wire, chrome-vanadium, chrome-silicon, 17-7 stainless steel, and beryllium copper are indicated for these applications.

General spring design recommendations. Try to keep the ends of the spring, where possible, within such standard forms as closed loops, full loops to center, closed and ground, open loops, and so on.

Pitch. Keep the coil pitch constant unless you have a special requirement for a variable-pitch spring.

Keep the spring index *D*/*d* between 6.5 and 10 wherever possible. Stress problems occur when the index is too low, and entanglement and waste of material occur when the index is too high.

Do not electroplate the spring unless it is required by the design application. The spring will be subject to hydrogen embrittlement unless it is processed correctly after electroplating. Hydrogen embrittlement causes abrupt and unexpected spring failures. Plated springs must be baked at a specified temperature for a definite time interval immediately after electroplating to prevent hydrogen embrittlement. For cosmetic purposes and minimal corrosion protection, zinc electroplating is generally used, although other plating such as chromium, cadmium, tin, etc. is also used according to the application requirements. Die springs usually come from the die spring manufacturers with colored enamel paint finishes for identification purposes. Black oxide and blueing are also used for spring finishes.

Special processing either during or after manufacture. Shot peening improves surface qualities from the standpoint of reducing stress concentration points on the spring wire material. This process also can improve the endurance limit and maximum allowable stress on the spring. Subjecting the spring to a certain amount of permanent *set* during manufacture eliminates the set problem of high energy versus mass on springs that have been designed with stresses in excess of the recommended values. This practice is *not* recommended for springs that are used in critical applications.

Stress considerations. Design the spring to stay within the allowable stress limit when the spring is fully compressed, or "bottomed." This can be done when there is sufficient space available in the mechanism and economy is not a consideration. When space is not available, design the spring so that its maximum working stress at its maximum working deflection does not exceed 40 to 45 percent of its minimum yield strength for compression and extension springs and 75 percent for torsion springs. Remember that the minimum yield strength allowable is different for differing wire diameters, the higher yield strengths being indicated for smaller wire diameters. See the later subsections for tables indicating the minimum yield strengths for different wire sizes and different materials. Also see Chap. 5, "Materials and Their Uses."

13.1.1 Direction of winding on helical springs

Confusion sometimes exists as to what constitutes a right-hand or left-hand wound spring. Standard practice recognizes that the winding hand of helical springs is the same as standard right-hand screw thread and left-hand screw thread. A right-hand wound spring has its coils going in the same direction as a right-hand screw thread and the opposite for a left-hand spring. On a right-hand helical spring, the coil helix progresses away from your line of sight in a clockwise direction when viewed on end. This seems like a small problem, but it can be quite serious when designing torsion springs, where the direction of wind is critical to proper spring function. In a torsion spring, the coils must "close down" or tighten when the spring is deflected during normal operation, going back to its initial position when the load is removed. If a torsion spring is operated in the wrong direction, or "opened" as the load is applied, the working stresses become much higher and the spring could fail. The torsion spring coils also increase in diameter when operated in the wrong direction and likewise decrease in diameter when operated in the correct direction. See equations under torsion springs for calculations that show the final diameter of torsion springs when they are deflected during operation (see Sect. 13.3.2).

Also note that when two helical compression springs are placed one inside the other for a higher combined rate, the coil helixes must be wound opposite hand from each other. This prevents the coils from jambing or tangling during operation. Compression springs employed in this manner are said to be in *parallel,* with the final rate equal to the combined rate of the two springs added together. Springs that are employed one atop the other or in a straight line are said to be in *series,* with their final rate equal to 1 divided by the sum of the recriprocals of the separate spring rates.

Example Springs in parallel:

$$R_f = R_1 + R_2 + R_3 + \cdots + R_n$$

Springs in series:

$$\frac{1}{R_f} = \frac{1}{R_1} + \frac{1}{R_2} + \frac{1}{R_3} + \cdots + \frac{1}{R_n}$$

where R_f = final combined rate
$R_{1,2,3}$ = rate of each individual spring

In the following subsections you will find all the design equations, tables, and charts required to do the majority of spring work today. Special springs such as irregularly shaped flat springs and other nonstandard forms are calculated using the standard beam and column equations found in other chapters of this *Handbook,* or they must be analyzed using involved stress calculations or prototypes made and tested for proper function.

13.1.2 Spring design procedures

1. Determine what spring rate and deflection or spring travel are required for your particular application.
2. Determine the space limitations the spring is required to work in, and try to design the spring accordingly using a parallel arrangement, if required, or allow space in the mechanism for the spring according to its calculated design dimensions.

3. Make a preliminary selection of the spring material dictated by the application or economics.
4. Make preliminary calculations to determine wire size or other stock size, mean diameter, number of coils, length, and so forth.
5. Perform the working stress calculations with the Wahl stress correction factor applied to see if the working stress is *below* the *allowable* stress.

The *working stress* is calculated using the appropriate equation with the working load applied to the spring. The load on the spring is found by multiplying the spring rate times the deflection length of the spring. For example, if the spring rate was calculated to be 25 lbf/in and the spring is deflected 0.5 in, then the load on the spring is $25 \times 0.5 = 12.5$ lbf.

The *maximum allowable stress* is found by multiplying the minimum tensile strength allowable for the particular wire diameter or size used in your spring times the appropriate multiplier. See the tables in this chapter for minimum tensile strength allowables for different wire sizes and materials and the appropriate multipliers.

Example You are designing a compression spring using 0.130-in-diameter music wire, ASTM A-228. The allowable maximum stress for this wire size is

$$0.45 \times 258{,}000 = 116{,}100 \text{ psi} \qquad \text{(see wire tables)}$$

Note: A more conservatively designed spring would use a multiplier of 40 percent (0.40), while a spring that is not cycled frequently can use a multiplier of 50 percent (0.50), with the spring possibly taking a slight *set* during repeated operations or cycles. The multiplier for torsion springs is 75 percent (0.75) in all cases and is conservative.

If the working stress in the spring is *below* the maximum allowable stress, the spring is properly designed relative to its stress level during operation. Remember that the modulus of elasticity of spring materials diminishes as the working temperature rises. This factor causes a decline in the spring rate. Also, working stresses should be decreased as the operating temperature rises. The tables in this chapter show the maximum working temperature limits for different spring and spring wire materials. Only appropriate tests will determine to what extent these recommended limits may be altered.

13.2 Compression and Extension Springs, Helical and Conical

This section contains equations for calculating compression and extension springs. Note that all equations throughout this chapter may be transposed for solving the required variable when all variables are known except one. The nomenclature for all symbols contained in the compression and extension spring design equations is listed in subsection 13.2.1.

Round wire. Rate:

$$R, \text{lb/in} = \frac{Gd^4}{8ND^3} \quad \Big\} \text{ Transpose for } d, N, \text{ or } D$$

Torsional stress:

$$S, \text{total corrected stress, psi} = \frac{8K_a DP}{\pi d^3} \quad \Big\} \text{ Transpose for } D, P, \text{ or } d$$

Wahl curvature-stress correction factor:

$$K_a = \frac{4C - 1}{4C - 4} + \frac{0.615}{C} \qquad \text{where } C = \frac{D}{d}$$

Square wire. Rate:

$$R, \text{lb/in} = \frac{Gt^4}{5.6ND^3} \quad \Big\} \text{ Transpose for } t, N, \text{ or } D$$

Torsional stress:

$$S, \text{total corrected stress, psi} = \frac{2.4K_{a1} DP}{t^3} \quad \Big\} \text{ Transpose for } D, P, \text{ or } t$$

Wahl curvature-stress correction factor:

$$K_{a1} = 1 + \frac{1.2}{C} + \frac{0.56}{C^2} + \frac{0.5}{C^3} \qquad \text{where } C = \frac{D}{t}$$

Rectangular wire. Rate (see Fig. 13.2 for a table of factors K_1 and K_2):

$$R, \text{lb/in} = \frac{Gbt^3}{ND^3} K_2 \quad \Big\} \text{ Transpose for } b, t, N, \text{ or } D$$

TABLE FACTORS FOR SQUARE AND RECTANGULAR SECTIONS

b · t	1	1.2	1.5	2	2.5	3	5	10	∞
Factor K_1	0.416	0.438	0.462	0.492	0.516	0.534	0.582	0.624	0.666
Factor K_2	0.180	0.212	0.250	0.292	0.317	0.335	0.371	0.398	0.424

STRESS FACTOR β FOR RECTANGULAR WIRE (b and t as shown)

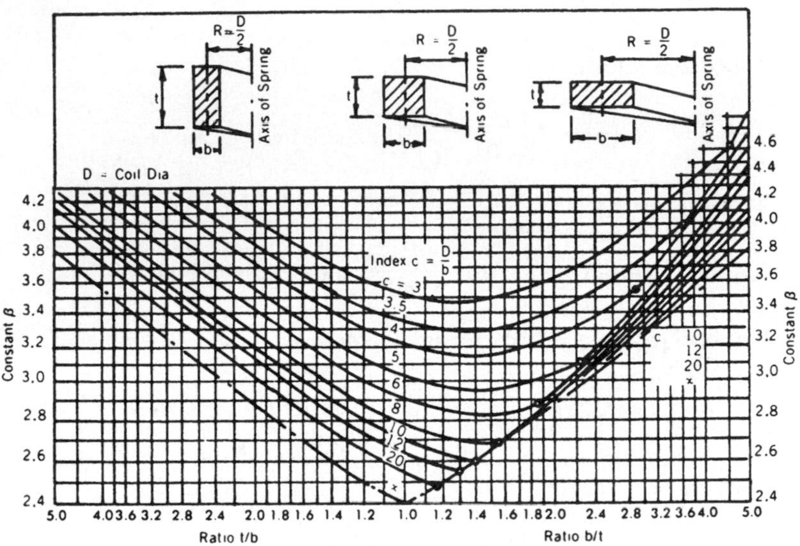

Figure 13.2 Factors and constants, square and rectangular wire.

Torsional stress, corrected:

$$S, \text{psi} = \frac{PD}{bt\sqrt{bt}}\beta \quad \Big\} \quad \text{Transpose for } b, t, P, \text{ or } D$$

Note: β is obtained from Fig. 13.2.

Solid height of compression springs. For round wire, see Fig. 13.3.

For square and rectangular wire. Due to distortion of the cross section of square and rectangular wire when the spring is formed, the compressed solid height can be determined from

Feature	Type of End: Open or Plain (not ground)	Open or Plain (with ends ground)	Squared or Closed (not ground)	Closed and Ground
	Formula			
Pitch (p)	$\frac{FL-d}{N}$	$\frac{FL}{TC}$	$\frac{FL-3d}{N}$	$\frac{FL-2d}{N}$
Solid Height (SH)	$(TC+1)d$	$TC \times d$	$(TC+1)d$	$TC \times d$
Number of Active Coils (N)	$N = TC$ or $\frac{FL-d}{p}$	$N = TC-1$ or $\frac{FL}{p}-1$	$N = TC-2$ or $\frac{FL-3d}{p}$	$N = TC-2$ or $\frac{FL-2d}{p}$
Total Coils (TC)	$\frac{FL-d}{p}$	$\frac{FL}{p}$	$\frac{FL-3d}{p}+2$	$\frac{FL-2d}{p}+2$
Free Length (FL)	$(p \times TC)+d$	$p \times TC$	$(p \times N)+3d$	$(p \times N)+2d$

d = wire dia.

Figure 13.3 Compression-spring features.

$$t' = 0.48t\left(\frac{\text{OD}}{D}+1\right)$$

where t' = new thickness of inner edge of section in the axial direction, after coiling
t = thickness of section before coiling
D = mean diameter of the spring

Active coils in compression springs. Style of ends may be selected as follows:

- Open ends, not ground: All coils are active.
- Open ends, ground: One coil is inactive.
- Closed ends, not ground: Two coils are inactive.
- Closed ends, ground: Two coils are inactive.

When using the compression spring equations, the variable N refers to the number of *active* coils in the spring being calculated.

Conical compression springs. Conical compression springs are calculated as follows (see Figs. 13.4 and 13.5):

1. If the spring is to have equal pitch (distance between coils), find the average geometric mean diameter from

$$D_{\text{m}} = \frac{D_1+D_2}{2}$$

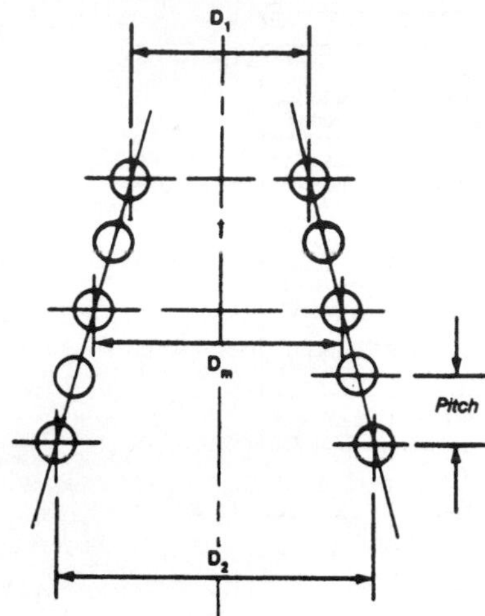

Figure 13.4 Conical compression spring.

Figure 13.5 Sample conical compression spring.

where D_1 = mean diameter of the top coil and D_2 = mean diameter of the bottom coil.

2. The spring rate may now be found from

$$R,\ \text{lb/in} = \frac{Gd^4}{8ND_m^3} \quad \Bigg\}\ \text{Transpose for } d, N, \text{ or } D_m$$

and the corrected stress from

$$S,\ \text{in psi} = \frac{8K_a D_m P}{\pi d^3} \quad \Bigg\}\ \text{Transpose for } d, P, \text{ or } D_m$$

where D_m = geometric mean diameter. Note that when the spring is deflected until the working bottom coil is bottomed, the original rate equation is no longer valid because the spring rate will change to a new value as a result of the loss of the bottom working coil. The new rate may be calculated by changing the variable N to one less coil and by calculating the new geometric mean diameter D_m.

Helical extension springs (close-wound). This type of spring is calculated using the same equations for the standard helical compression spring, namely, rate, stress, and Wahl stress-correction factor. One exception when working with helical extension springs is that this type of spring is sometimes wound by the spring manufacturer with an initial tension in the wire. This initial tension keeps the coils tightly closed together and creates a pretension in the spring. When designing the spring, you may specify the initial tension on the spring, in pounds. When you do specify the initial tension, you must calculate the torsional stress developed in the spring as a result of this initial tension.

First, calculate torsional stress S_i due to initial tension P_1 in

$$S_i = \frac{8DP_1}{\pi d^3}$$

where P_1 = initial tension, lb. Second, for the value of S_i calculated and the known spring index D/d, determine on the graph in Fig. 13.6 whether or not S_i appears in the preferred (shaded) area. If S_i falls in the shaded area, the spring can be produced readily. If S_i is above the shaded area, reduce it by increasing the wire size. If S_i is below the shaded area, select a smaller wire size. In either case, recalculate the stress and alter the number of coils, axial space, and initial tension as necessary.

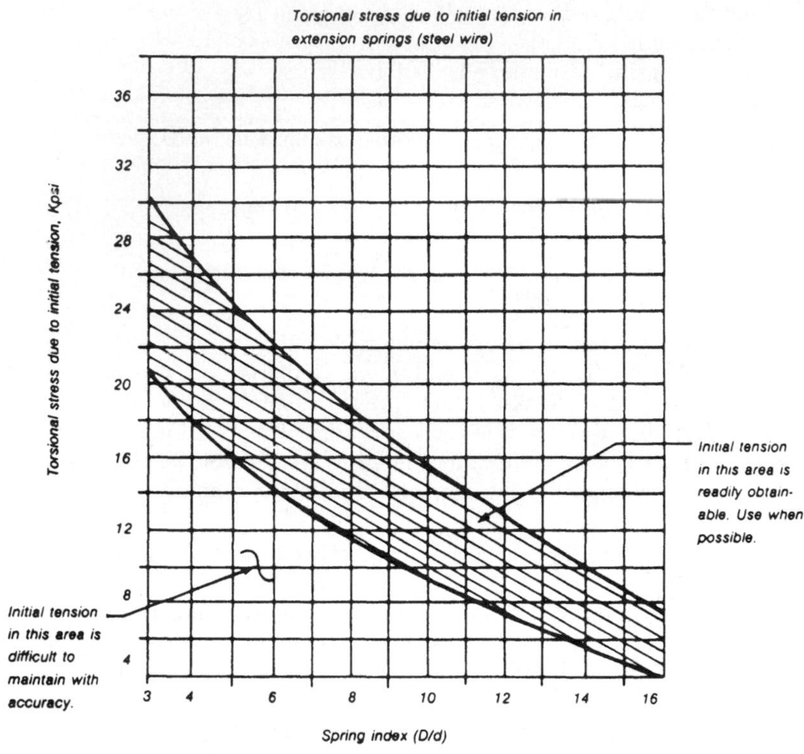

Figure 13.6 Graph for preferred initial tension for extension springs.

Spring energy content of compression and extension springs. The potential energy which may be stored in a deflected compression or extension spring is given by

$$P_e = \frac{Rs^2}{2}$$

Also:

$$P_e = \tfrac{1}{2} R(s_2^2 - s_1^2) \qquad \text{in moving from point } s_1 \text{ to } s_2$$

where R = rate of the spring, lb/in, lb/ft, N/m
s = distance spring is compressed or extended, in, m
P_e = potential energy, in · lb, ft · lb, J
s_1, s_2 = distances moved, in

Example A compression spring with a rate of 50 lb/in is compressed 4 in. What is the potential energy stored in the loaded spring?

$$P_e = \frac{50(4)^2}{2} = 400 \text{ in} \cdot \text{lb or } 33.33 \text{ ft} \cdot \text{lb}$$

Thus the spring will perform 33.33 ft · lb of work energy when released from its loaded position. Internal losses are negligible. This procedure is useful to mechanical designers and tool engineers who need to know the work a spring will produce in a mechanism or die set and the input energy required to load the spring.

Expansion of compression springs when deflected. A compression spring outside diameter will expand when the spring is compressed. This may pose a problem if the spring must work within a tube or cylinder and its outside diameter is close to the inside diameter of the containment. The following equation may be used to calculate the amount of expansion that takes place when the spring is compressed to solid height. For intermediate heights, use the percent of compression multiplied by the total expansion.

Total expansion = outside diameter (solid) – outside diameter

Expanded diameter is

$$\text{Outside diameter, solid} = \sqrt{D^2 + \frac{p^2 - d^2}{\pi^2}} + d$$

where p = pitch (distance between adjacent coil center lines), in

d = wire diameter, in

D = mean diameter of the spring, in

and outside diameter, solid = expanded diameter when compressed solid, in

13.2.1 Symbols for compression and extension springs

R = rate, pounds of load per inch of deflection
P = load, lb
F = deflection, in
D = mean coil diameter, OD – d
d = wire diameter, in
t = side of square wire or thickness of rectangular wire, in

b = width of rectangular wire, in
G = torsional modulus of elasticity, psi
N = number of active coils, determined by the types of ends on a compression spring; equal to *all* the coils of an extension spring
S = torsional stress, psi
OD = outside diameter of coils, in
ID = inside diameter, in
C = spring index, D/d
L = length of spring, in
H = solid height, in
K_a = Wahl stress-correction factor
K_1, K_2, β (see Fig. 13.2)

For preferred and special end designs for extension springs, see Fig. 13.7.

13.3 Torsion Springs

Refer to Fig. 13.8.

Round wire. Moment (torque) is

$$M\text{, lb} \cdot \text{in} = \frac{Ed^4T}{10.8ND} \quad \Big\} \quad \text{Transpose for } d, T, N, \text{ or } D$$

Tensile stress is

$$S\text{, psi} = \frac{32M}{\pi d^3} K \quad \Big\} \quad \text{Transpose for } M \text{ or } d$$

Square wire. Moment, (torque) is

$$M\text{, lb} \cdot \text{in} = \frac{Ed^4T}{6.6ND} \quad \Big\} \quad \text{Transpose for } t, T, N, \text{ or } D$$

Tensile stress is

$$S\text{, psi} = \frac{6M}{t^3} K_1 \quad \Big\} \quad \text{Transpose for } M \text{ or } t$$

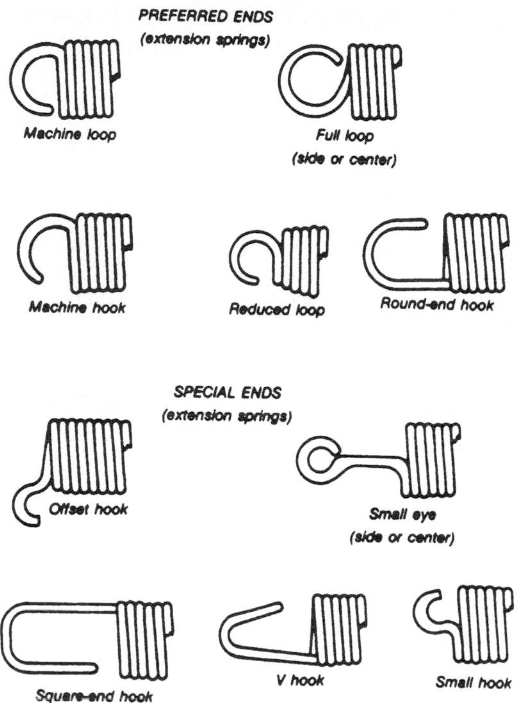

Figure 13.7 Preferred and special ends, extension springs.

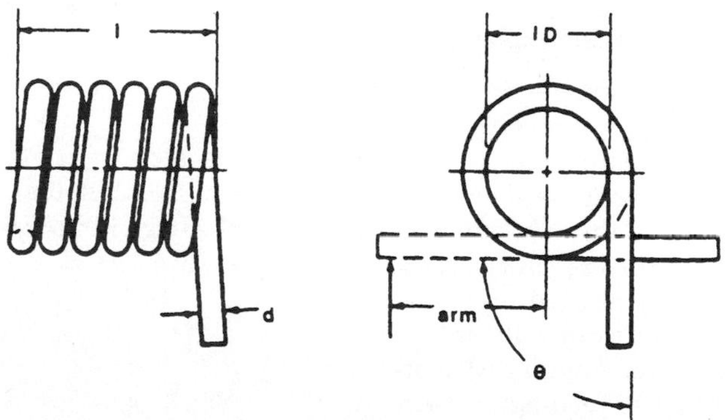

Figure 13.8 Torsion spring.

The stress-correction factor K or K_1 for torsion springs with round or square wire, respectively, is applied according to the spring index as follows:

$$\left.\begin{aligned}\text{When spring index} &= 6,\ K = 1.15\\ &= 8,\ K = 1.11\\ &= 10,\ K = 1.08\end{aligned}\right\}\ \text{for round wire}$$

$$\left.\begin{aligned}\text{When spring index} &= 6,\ K_1 = 1.13\\ &= 8,\ K_1 = 1.09\\ &= 10,\ K_1 = 1.07\end{aligned}\right\}\ \text{for square wire}$$

For spring indexes that fall between the values shown, interpolate the new correction factor value. Use standard interpolation procedures.

Rectangular wire. Moment (torque) is

$$M,\ \text{lb}\cdot\text{in} = \frac{Ebt^3T}{6.6ND}\quad\Big\}\ \text{Transpose for } b, t, T, N, \text{ or } D$$

Tensile stress is

$$S,\ \text{psi} = \frac{6M}{bt^2}\quad\Big\}\ \text{Transpose for } M, t, \text{ or } b$$

13.3.1 Symbols for torsion springs

D = mean coil diameter, in
d = diameter of round wire, in
N = total number of coils, i.e., 6 turns, 7.5 turns, etc.
E = torsional modulus of elesticity (see charts in this chapter)
T = revolutions through which the spring works (e.g., 90° arc = 90/360 = 0.25 revolutions, etc.)
S = bending stress, psi
M = moment or torque, lb · in
b = width of rectangular wire, in
t = thickness of rectangular wire, in
K, K_1 = stress-correction factor for round and square wire, respectively

13.3.2 Torsion spring reduction of diameter during deflection

When a torsion spring is operated in the correct direction (coils close down when load is applied), the springs inside diameter (ID) is reduced as a function of the number of degrees the spring is rotated in the closing direction and the number of coils. This may be calculated from the following equation:

$$\mathrm{ID_r} = \frac{360N(\mathrm{ID_f})}{360N + R^\circ}$$

where $\mathrm{ID_r}$ = inside diameter after deflection (closing), in
$\mathrm{ID_f}$ = inside diameter before deflection (free), in
N = number of coils
R° = number of degrees rotated in the closing direction

Note: When a spring is manufactured, great care must be taken to ensure that *no* marks or indentations are formed on the spring coils. Figure 13.9 shows a torsion spring with a deep manufacturing indent at the inside radius of one of the legs of the spring. When operated a few thousand times at a high stress level, the spring will break abruptly at the deformation mark. In order to avoid this type of problem, a generous bend radius should be allowed at the bend in the spring leg, as shown in Fig. 13.10. In Fig. 13.10, the spring on the right has a larger bend radius with no deformation marks present, and this spring will not fail in service. The larger bend radius makes it easier for the spring manufacturer to produce the spring without indents or deformations on the wire.

Figure 13.11 shows two torsion springs, one with four coils and the other with three coils. The spring on the left, which contains four coils, required a redesign due to tightness of operation in its assigned position in its assembly, where no more room could be allowed for the spring. The only recourse was to redesign the spring with fewer coils and a reduction in wire diameter so that the new spring would have the same rate as the spring with four coils. When alternate designs such as this are undertaken, the new spring must be rechecked to see if the working stresses are lower than the maximum allowable stress for the new wire diameter. All springs, both large and small, follow the same design rules, with similar results, provided that the proper procedures are used. See Fig. 13.11*b* for an example of small and very large torsion springs.

Figure 13.9 Manufacturing marks on a torsion spring.

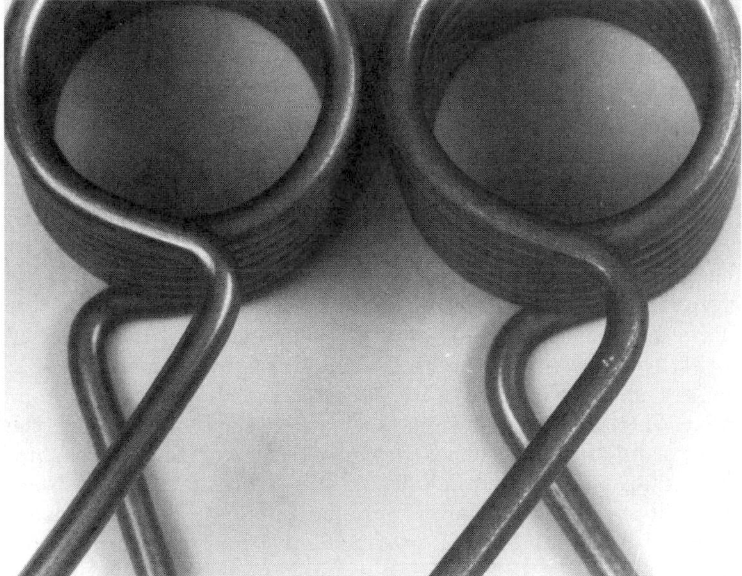

Figure 13.10 Radius of bend at legs of torsion springs.

Figure 13.11 (*a*) Torsion springs of same rates.

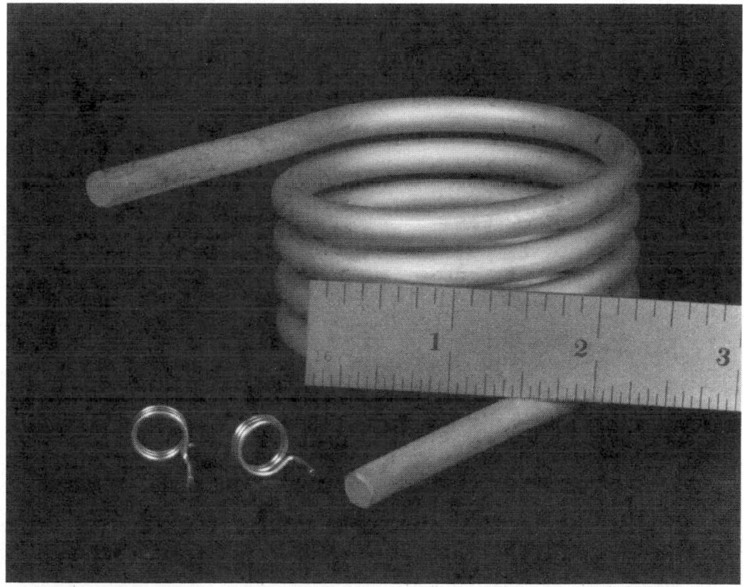

Figure 13.11 (*b*) Samples of large and small torsion springs.

13.4 Spiral Torsion Springs

For these coil springs, moment (torque) is calculated from

$$M, \text{lb} \cdot \text{in} = \frac{\pi E b t^3 \theta}{6L} \quad \Big\} \text{ Transpose for } b, t, \theta, \text{ or } L$$

Bending stress is

$$S, \text{psi} = \frac{6M}{bt^2} \quad \Big\} \text{ Transpose for } b, t, \text{ or } M$$

Space occupied by the spring is

$$OD_f = \frac{2L}{\pi\left(\dfrac{\sqrt{A^2 + 1.27Lt} - A}{2t} - \theta\right)}$$

This equation is based on concentric circles with a uniform space between coils and gives a close approximation of the minimum OD_f. See Fig. 13.12.

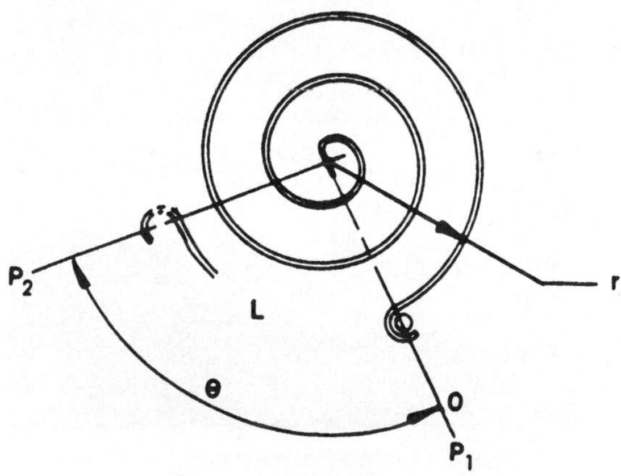

Figure 13.12 Spiral torsion spring.

13.4.1 Spring energy content (torsion, coil, or spiral springs)

In the case of a torsion or spiral spring, the potential energy P_e the spring will contain when deflected in the closing direction can be calculated from

$$P_e = \frac{1}{2} R\theta_r^2 \qquad \text{also} \quad M = R\theta_r$$

where M = resisting torque, lb · ft, N · m
R = spring rate, lb/rad, N/rad
θ_r = angle of deflection, rad

Remember that there are 2π radians in 360° and 1 radian = 0.01745 degrees.

Note: Units of elastic potential energy are the same as those for work and are expressed in foot pounds in the U.S. Customary system and in joules in the SI system. Although spring rates for most commercial springs are not strictly linear, they are close enough for most calculations where extreme accuracy is not required.

In a similar manner, the potential energy content of leaf and beam springs can be derived approximately by finding the apparent rate and the distance through which the spring moves.

13.4.2 Symbols for spiral torsion springs

E = bending modulus of elasticity, psi (e.g., 30×10^6 for most steels)
θ_r = angular deflection, rad (for energy equations)
θ = angular deflection, revolutions (e.g., 90° = 0.25 revolutions)
L = length of active spring material, in
M = moment or torque, lb · in
b = material width, in
t = material thickness, in
A = arbor diameter, in
OD_f = outside diameter in the free condition

13.5 Flat Springs

Cantilever spring. Load (see Fig. 13.13) is

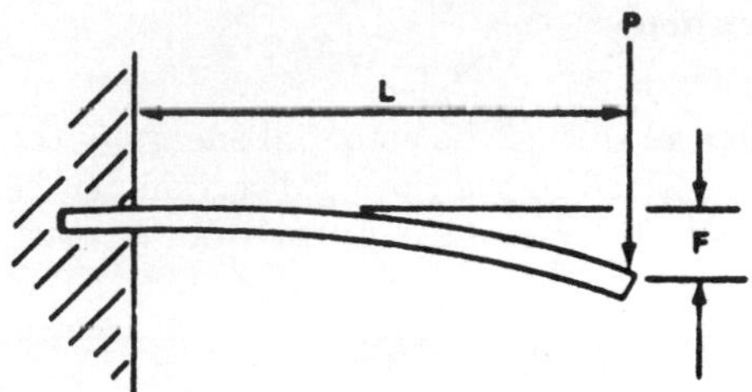

Figure 13.13 Flat spring, cantilever.

$$P, \text{lb} = \frac{EFbt^3}{4L^3} \quad \Bigg\} \text{ Transpose for } F, b, t, \text{ or } L$$

Stress is

$$S, \text{psi} = \frac{3EFt}{2L^2} = \frac{6PL}{bt^2} \quad \Bigg\} \text{ Transpose for } F, t, L, b, \text{ or } P$$

Simple beam springs. Load (see Fig. 13.14) is

$$P, \text{lb} = \frac{4EFbt^3}{L^3} \quad \Bigg\} \text{ Transpose for } F, b, t, \text{ or } L$$

Stress is

$$S, \text{psi} = \frac{6EFt}{L^2} = \frac{3PL}{2bt^2} \quad \Bigg\} \text{ Transpose for } F, b, t, L, \text{ or } P$$

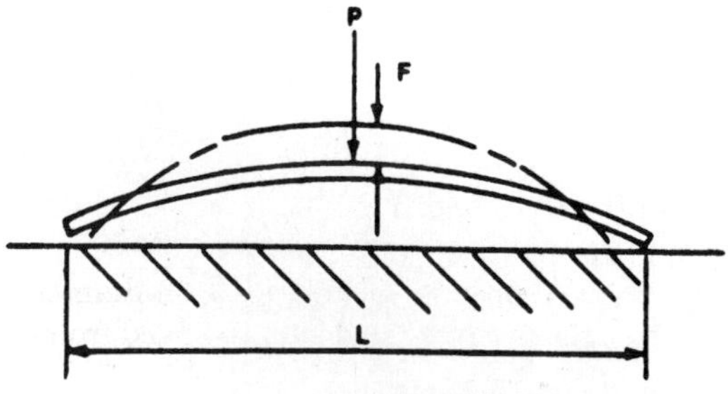

Figure 13.14 Flat spring, beam.

Symbols used in the preceding equations for leaf and beam springs are

P = load, lb
E = tension modulus of elasticity, psi
F = deflection, in (see figures)
t = thickness of material, in
b = width of material, in
S = design bending stress, psi
L = active spring length, in

13.6 Spring Washers (Curved and Wave)

Curved washers. Load (see Fig. 13.15*a*) is

$$P\text{, lb} = \frac{4EFt^3N^4(\text{OD} - \text{ID})}{(\text{OD})^3} \quad \Big\} \text{ Transpose for OD, ID, } F\text{, or } t$$

Stress is

$$S\text{, psi} = \frac{1.5P(\text{OD})}{t^2(\text{OD} - \text{ID})} \quad \Big\} \text{ Transpose for OD, ID, } P\text{, or } t$$

The preceding equations yield approximate results only. For exact loads, test the spring under an applied load and induced deflection.

Wave washers. Load (see Fig. 13.15*b*) is

$$P\text{, lb} = \frac{EFbt^3N^4}{2.4D^3}\left(\frac{\text{OD}}{\text{ID}}\right) \quad \Big\} \text{ Transpose for } F\text{, } b\text{, } t\text{, } N\text{, or } D$$

Stress is

$$S\text{, psi} = \frac{3\pi PD}{4bt^2N^2} \quad \Big\} \text{ Transpose for } P\text{, } D\text{, } b\text{, } t\text{, or } N$$

These equations also yield approximate results only.

For deflections between $0.25h$ and $0.75h$, the outside diameter increases and the new mean diameter D_1 can be calculated from

$$D_1 = \sqrt{D^2 + 0.458h^2N^2}$$

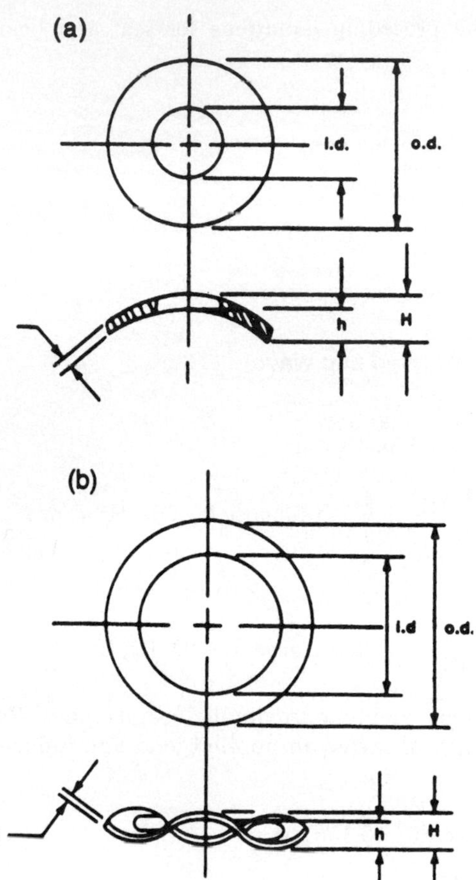

Figure 13.15 (*a*) Curved spring washer. (*b*) Wave washer.

Symbols for curved and wave washers are as follows:

P = load, lb
E = tensile modulus of elasticity, psi
F = deflection, in
t = material thickness, in
b = radial width of material, in
h = free height minus t, in
H = free overall height, in
N = number of waves
D = mean diameter, in = (OD + ID)/2
S = bending stress, psi

13.7 Belleville Washers (Disk Springs)

Equations for load P, stress at the convex inner edge S, and constants (M, C_1, and C_2) are given as

$$P\text{, lb} = \frac{4Ef}{M(1-\mu^2)(\text{OD})^2}\left[\left(h-\frac{f}{2}\right)(h-f)t+t^3\right]$$

$$S\text{, psi} = \frac{4Ef}{M(1-\mu^2)(\text{OD})^2}\left[C_1\left(h-\frac{f}{2}\right)+C_2t\right]$$

$$M = \frac{6}{\pi \ln a}\left[\frac{(a-1)^2}{a^2}\right] \qquad \text{constant } M$$

$$C_1 = \frac{6}{\pi \ln a}\left[\frac{(a-1)}{\ln a}-1\right] \qquad \text{constant } C_1$$

$$C_2 = \frac{6}{\pi \ln a}\left(\frac{a-1}{2}\right) \qquad \text{constant } C_2$$

Refer to Fig. 13.16, which diagrams a Belleville spring; Fig. 13.17, which displays a load/deflection chart; and Fig. 13.18, which gives the stress constants (M, C_1, and C_2).

Symbols used in these equations are

a = OD/ID
μ = Poissons' ratio (see Poisson ratio chart, Fig. 13.19)
f = deflection, in
h = inner height of washer, in
E = tensile modulus of elasticity, psi (Youngs' modulus)

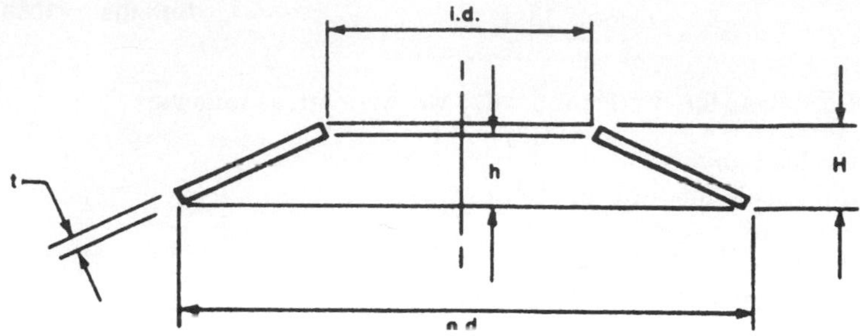

Figure 13.16 Belleville washer (disk spring).

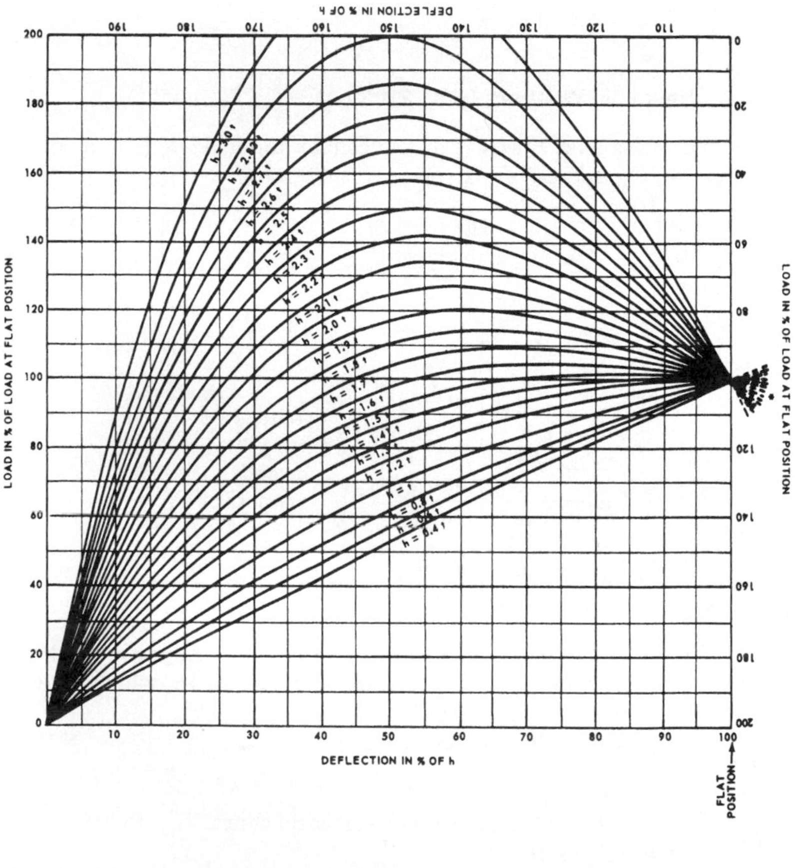

*Dotted lines indicate that the curves are symmetrical beyond the flat position.

Figure 13.17 Load/deflection characteristics for Belleville disk springs.

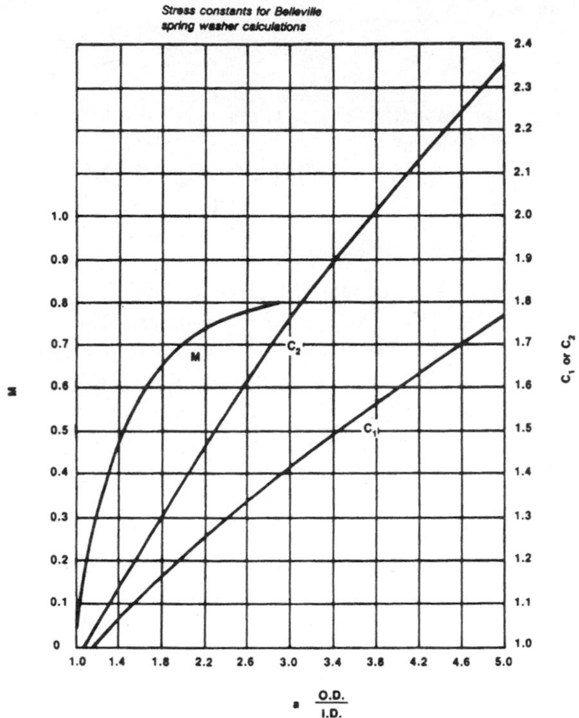

Figure 13.18 Stress constants, disk springs.

Material	Poisson's Ratio, μ
Music wire ASTM A228	0.30
Hard drawn ASTM A227	0.30
Oil tempered ASTM A229	0.30
AISI 1065 carbon steel	0.30
AISI 1075 carbon steel	0.30
AISI 1095 carbon steel	0.30
AISI 6150 vanadium steel	0.30
AISI 5160 chromium steel	0.30
Inconel 600	0.28
Inconel 718	0.28
Inconel X750	0.29
AISI 301/302 stainless steel	0.31
17-7 PH stainless steel	0.34
Carpenter 455 stainless steel	0.30
Phosphor-bronze ASTM B103 and B159	0.20
Beryllium-copper ASTM B194 and B197	0.33

Figure 13.19 Poisson's ratios for various materials.

P = load, lb
S = stress at the convex inner edge, psi
t = thickness of washer, in
M, C_1, C_2 = constants (see equations and chart in Fig. 13.18)

13.7.1 Simple Belleville washer applications

Parallel stacking. Refer to Fig. 13.20*a*. Placing Belleville washers in this configuration will double the load for a given deflection. Calculations for determining the exact load for a given deflection in this configuration are not accurate enough because of the additional variable of unknown coefficient of friction between the surfaces of the washers and the fact that the friction changes as the load is increased on the washers. The designer must perform load/deflection tests to arrive at a solution for this type of problem.

Series stacking. Refer to Fig. 13.20*b*. Placing Belleville washers in this configuration will equal the load for a given deflection of one washer. Load/deflection tests also must be done for this configuration to arrive at accurate loads for a given deflection.

Belleville washers may be stacked in various series and parallel arrangements to produce varying results.

A form of Belleville washer that is useful for many applications is the slotted-spring washer made with a radiused section. Note that the equations for Belleville washers apply *only* to those washers which have a conical section, as in Fig. 13.16. A washer with a radiused section will exhibit a different rate on deflection than will a standard Belleville washer of comparable dimensions. On critical applications of slotted-spring washers, a load cell may be used to find the load value for a given deflection, thus arriving at an accurate load figure. This also holds true for critical applications for standard Belleville washers, since the equations given in this chapter will predict the loads only to ±20 percent accuracy. A typical loading application of Belleville washers is shown in Fig. 13.21.

Example If it requires 200 lb to flatten one Belleville washer, flattening both as in Fig. 13.21 will produce a 200-lb clamping load or tension in the bolt. The reactions at R_1 and R_2 = 200 lb, and the clamp load is thus 200 lb. These Belleville washers are essentially in a *series* configuration, where the load is equal to that for the deflection of one washer. Flattening the two washers in this example will *not* double the load as is sometimes presumed. Load doubling occurs only when two Belleville washers are placed in a *parallel* configuration and deflected a given amount.

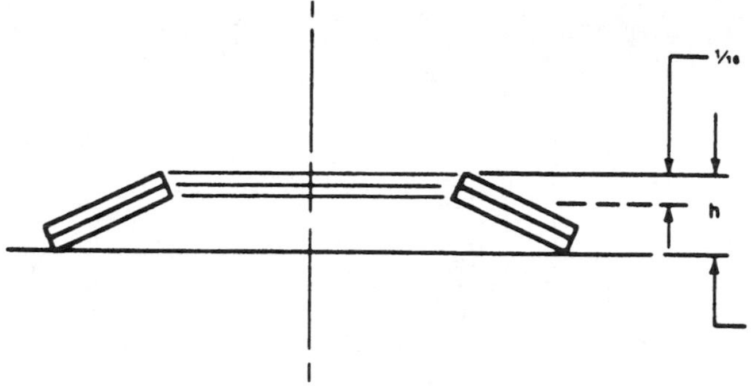

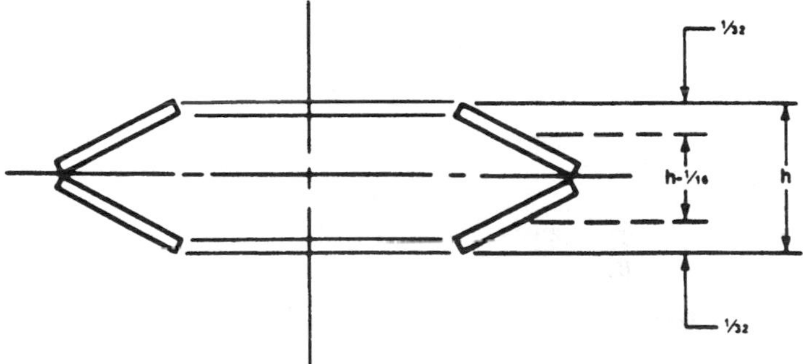

Figure 13.20 Disk springs: (*a*) in parallel; (*b*) in series.

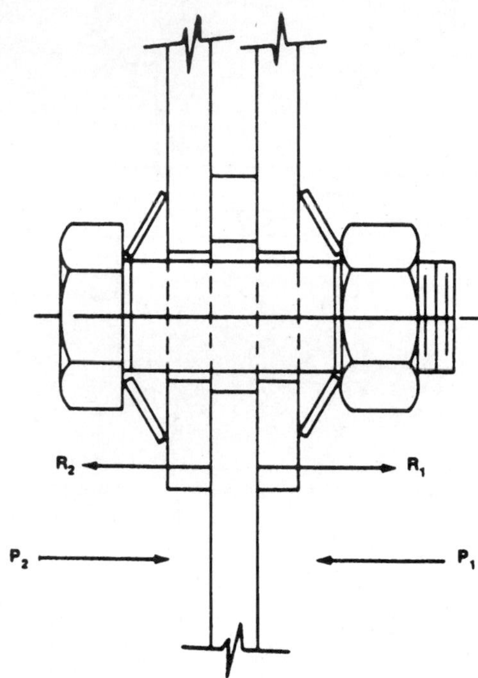

Figure 13.21 Disk spring bolted joint.

13.8 Hair Springs

These springs find application in clocks, meters, instruments, and gauges. Moment (torque) is

$$M\text{, lb}\cdot\text{in or oz}\cdot\text{in} = \frac{\pi b t^3 \theta}{6L} \quad \Big\} \quad \text{Transpose for } b, t, L, \text{ or } \theta$$

Stress is

$$S\text{, psi} = \frac{6M}{bt^2} \quad \Big\} \quad \text{Transpose for } b, t, \text{ or } M$$

These equations are for light loads *only*. The moment measure would normally be given in pound-inches when the load L is given in pounds and the spring dimensions are given in inches.

13.8 Torsion Bars

See Fig. 13.2 for a table of values for K_1 and K_2 as used here.

Round bar. Moment (torque) is

$$\text{M, lb}\cdot\text{in} = \frac{\pi^2 d^4 G\theta}{16L} \quad \Big\} \quad \text{Transpose for } d, L, \text{ or } \theta$$

Stress is

$$S, \text{psi} = \frac{16M}{\pi d^3} = \frac{\pi d G\theta}{L} \quad \Big\} \quad \text{Transpose for } d, M, L, \text{ or } \theta$$

Rectangular bar. Moment (torque) is

$$M, \text{lb}\cdot\text{in} = \frac{\pi^2 G b t^3 \theta}{2L} K_2 \quad \Big\} \quad \text{Transpose for } b, t, L, \text{ or } \theta$$

Stress is

$$S, \text{psi} = \frac{2M}{bt^3 K_1} \quad \Big\} \quad \text{Transpose for } b, t, \text{ or } M$$

13.8.1 Symbols for hair springs and torsion bars

M = moment or torque, lb · in
b = width of spring material, in
t = thickness of spring material, in
E = bending modulus of elasticity, psi (typically 30×10^6 for steel)
θ = angular deflection, revolutions (e.g., 90° = 90/360 = 0.25 revolutions)
G = torsional modulus of elasticity (typically 11.5×10^6 for steel)
S = bending stress, psi
L = active length of spring material, in
K_1, K_2 = constants derived from table factors in Fig. 13.2

13.9 Allowable Working Stresses in Springs

Maximum design stress allowables are derived by taking a percentage of the minimum tensile strength of a particular spring material. These minimum tensile strength values are shown in tables in the following sections and in Chap. 5, "Materials and Their Uses."

The stress allowables are as follows:

1. Extension springs, compression springs, and torsion bars.

Hard-drawn steel (ASTM A227)

Stainless steels (ASTM A313)

Allowable stress (torsional, G) = 40% of the minimum tensile strength for each particular wire size (see Figs. 13.22, 13.23a, and 13.23b).

Oil-tempered (ASTM A229)

Music wire (ASTM A228)

Chrome-vanadium (AISI 6150)

Chrome-silicon (AISI 9254)

17-7 PH stainless steel (AMS 5673B)

Beryllium copper (ASTM B197)

Allowable stress (torsional, G) = 45% of the minimum tensile strength for each particular wire size (see Figs. 13.22, 13.23a, and 13.23b).

2. Torsion springs, flat springs, and hair springs.

All materials

Allowable stress (bending, E) = 75% of the minimum tensile strength for each particular wire size or or gage (see Figs. 13.22, 13.23a, and 13.23b).

The listed values for stress allowables are for average design applications. For cyclic loading and repetition of loading and unloading, lower values (percentage) should be used initially. Life testing in critical applications is indicated and must be performed.

It should be noted that these values also may be increased in cases where permanent set is performed during spring manufacture and where only ocassional deflection of the spring is encountered. Also, higher values of permissible stress are sometimes used on statically loaded springs.

It also should be understood by the designer that allowable stress values for spring materials *cannot* be "generalized." The minimum tensile or torsional strength of each wire size or gage must be known precisely in order to calculate and design springs accurately without failures.

In highly stressed spring designs, the spring manufacturer should be consulted and its recommendations followed. Whenever possible in mechanism design, space for a moderately stressed spring should be allowed. This will avoid the problem of marginally designed springs, that is, springs that tend to be stressed close to or beyond the maximum allowable stress. This, of course, is not always possible, and adequate space for moderately stressed springs is not always available. Music wire and some of the other high-stress wire materials are commonly used when high stress is a factor in design and cannot be avoided.

13.10 Spring Materials and Properties

See Fig. 13.22 for physical properties of spring wire and strip that are used for spring design calculations.

13.11 Minimum Yield Strength for Spring-Wire Materials

See Fig. 13.23 for minimum yield strengths of spring-wire materials: ferrous, stainless steels, chrome-silicon/chrome-vanadium alloys, and copper-base alloys in various diameters.

13.12 Spring Design Using a Programmable Calculator and Computer Program

Because of the large number of calculations frequently required in initial spring design, it is advisable for the designer who deals with springs on a regular basis to use a programmable calculator. A typical programmable pocket electronic calculator is shown in Fig. 3.3. In this type of calculator, the spring design equations are placed into the calculator's permanent memory and are recalled as needed to perform very rapid spring design calculations. With this type of system, the calculator prompts the user to type in the unknown variables and then solves the spring design equation in less than 2 seconds. You may thus solve many complex equations in a few minutes, which allows you to arrive at the final spring dimensions in a short time with very little chance of error.

If in your design work you deal with many springs that are similar, you can easily construct a set of standard spring rate curves for various spring types. Figures 13.24 and 13.25 show two exam-

Material and specification	E 10^6 psi	G 10^6 psi	Design stress % min. yield	Cond. % IACS	Density lb/in^3	Max. oper. temp. °F	F.A.*	S.A.*
High-carbon wire								
Music								
ASTM A228	30	11.5	45	7	0.284	250	E	H
Hard-drawn								
ASTM A227	30	11.5	40	7	0.284	250	P	M
ASTM A679	30	11.5	45	7	0.284	250	P	M
Oil-tempered								
ASTM A229	30	11.5	45	7	0.284	300	P	M
Carbon valve								
ASTM A230	30	11.5	45	7	0.284	300	E	H
Alloy steel wire								
Chrome-vanadium								
ASTM A231	30	11.5	45	7	0.284	425	E	H
Chrome-silicon								
ASTM A401	30	11.5	45	5	0.284	475	F	H
Silicon-manganese								
AISI 9260	30	11.5	45	4.5	0.284	450	F	H
Stainless wire								
AISI 302/304								
ASTM A313	28	10	35	2	0.286	550	G	M
AISI 316								
ASTM A313	28	10	40	2	0.286	550	G	M
17-7 PH								
ASTM A313 (631)	29.5	11	45	2	0.286	650	G	H
Non-ferrous alloy wire								
Phosphor-bronze								
ASTM B159	15	6.25	40	18	0.320	200	G	M
Beryllium-copper								
ASTM B197	18.5	7	45	21	0.297	400	E	H
Monel 400								
AMS 7233	26	9.5	40	—	—	450	F	M
Monel K 500								
QQ-N-286	26	9.5	40	—	—	550	F	M
High temperature alloy wire								
Nickel-chrome								
ASTM A286	29	10.4	35	2	0.290	510	—	L
Inconel 600								
QQ-W-390	31	11	40	1.5	0.307	700	F	L
Inconel X750								
AMS 5698, 5699	31	12	40	1	0.298	1100	F	L

Figure 13.22 Physical properties for spring materials.

Material and specification	E 10^6 psi	G 10^6 psi	Design stress % min. yield	Cond. % IACS	Density lb/in^3	Max. oper. temp. °F	F.A.*	S.A.*
High carbon steel strip								
AISI 1065	30	11.5	75	7	0.284	200	F	M
AISI 1075	30	11.5	75	7	0.284	250	G	H
AISI 1095	30	11.5	75	7	0.284	250	E	H
Stainless steel strip								
AISI 301	28	10.5	75	2	0.286	300	G	M
AISI 302	28	10.5	75	2	0.286	550	G	M
AISI 316	28	10.5	75	2	0.286	550	G	M
17-7 PH ASTM A693	29	11	75	2	0.286	650	G	H
Non-ferrous alloy strip								
Phosphor-bronze ASTM B103	15	6.3	75	18	0.320	200	G	M
Beryllium-copper ASTM B194	18.5	7	75	21	0.297	400	E	H
Monel 400 AMS 4544	26	—	75	—	—	450	—	—
Monel K 500 QQ-N-286	26	—	75	—	—	550	—	—
High temperature alloy strip								
Nickel-chrome ASTM A286	29	10.4	75	2	0.290	510	—	L
Inconel 600 ASTM B168	31	11	40	1.5	0.307	700	F	L
Inconel X750 AMS 5542	31	12	40	1	0.298	1100	F	L

*Letter designations of the last two columns indicate: F.A. = fatigue applications, S.A. = strength applications, E = excellent, G = good, F = fair, L = low, H = high, M = medium, P = poor.

Figure 13.22 *(Continued)*

Ferrous

Wire Size In.	Music Wire	Hard Drawn	Oil Temp.	Wire Size In.	Music Wire	Hard Drawn	Oil Temp.	Wire Size In.	Music Wire	Hard Drawn	Oil Temp.
.008	399	307	315	.046	309	249		.094	274		
.009	393	305	313	.047	309	248	259	.095	274	219	
.010	387	303	311	.048	306	247		.099	274		
.011	382	301	309	.049	306	246		.100	271		
.012	377	299	307	.050	306	245		.101	271		
.013	373	297	305	.051	303	244		.102	270		
.014	369	295	303	.052	303	244		.105	270	216	225
.015	365	293	301	.053	303	243		.106	268		
.016	362	291	300	.054	303	243	253	.109	268		
.017	362	289	298	.055	300	242		.110	267		
.018	356	287	297	.056	300	241		.111	267		
.019	356	285	295	.057	300	240		.112	266		
.020	350	283	293	.058	300	240		.119	266		
.021	350	281		.059	296	239		.120	263	210	220
.022	345	280		.060	296	238		.123	263		
.023	345	278	289	.061	296	237		.124	261		
.024	341	277		.062	296	237	247	.129	261		
.025	341	275	286	.063	293	236		.130	258		
.026	337	274		.064	293	235		.135	258	206	215
.027	337	272		.065	293	235		.139	258		
.028	333	271	283	.066	290			.140	256		
.029	333	267		.067	290	234		.144	256		
.030	330	266		.069	290	233		.145	254		
.031	330	266	280	.070	289			.148	254	203	210
.032	327	265		.071	288			.149	253		
.033	327	264		.072	287	232	241	.150	253		
.034	324	262		.074	287	231		.151	251		
.035	324	261	274	.075	287			.160	251		
.036	321	260		.076	284	230		.161	249		
.037	321	258		.078	284	229		.162	249	200	205
.038	318	257		.079	284			.177	245	195	200
.039	318	256		.080	282	227	235	.192	241	192	195
.040	315	255		.083	282			.207	238	190	190
.041	315	255	266	.084	279			.225	235	186	188
.042	313	254		.085	279	225		.250	230	182	185
.043	313	252		.089	279			.3125		174	183
.044	313	251		.090	276	222		.375		167	180
.045	309	250		.091	276		230	.4375		165	175
				.092	276	220		.500		156	170
				.093	276						

Figure 13.23 (*a*) Minimum yield strengths for ferrous spring wire.

Stainless steels

Wire Size In.	Type 302	Type* 17-7 PH	Wire Size In.	Type 302	Type* 17-7 PH	Wire Size In.	Type 302	Type* 17-7 PH
.008	325	345	.033	276		.060	256	
.009	325		.034	275		.061	255	305
.010	320	345	.035	274		.062	255	297
.011	318	340	.036	273		.063	254	
.012	316		.037	272		.065	254	
.013	314		.038	271		.066	250	
.014	312		.039	270		.071	250	297
.015	310	340	.040	270		.072	250	292
.016	308	335	.041	269	320	.075	250	
.017	306		.042	268	310	.076	245	
.018	304		.043	267		.080	245	292
.019	302		.044	266		.092	240	279
.020	300	335	.045	264		.105	232	274
.021	298	330	.046	263		.120	225	272
.022	296		.047	262		.125		272
.023	294		.048	262		.131		260
.024	292		.049	261		.148	210	256
.025	290	330	.051	261	310	.162	205	256
.026	289	325	.052	260	305	.177	195	
.027	287		.055	260		.192		
.028	286		.056	259		.207	185	
.029	284		.057	258		.225	180	
.030	282	325	.058	258		.250	175	
.031	280	320	.059	257		.375	140	
.032	277							

*After aging

Chrome silicon/chrome vanadium

Wire Size In.	Chrome Silicon	Chrome Vanadium
.020		300
.032	300	290
.041	298	280
.054	292	270
.062	290	265
.080	285	255
.092	280	
.105		245
.120	275	
.135	270	235
.162	265	225
.177	260	
.192	260	220
.218	255	
.250	250	210
.312	245	203
.375	240	200
.437		195
.500		190

Copper-base alloys

Phosphor Bronze (Grade A)	
Wire Size Range—in.	
.007–.025	145
.026–.062	135
.063 and over	130
Beryllium Copper (Alloy 25 pretemp)	
.005–.040	180
.041 and over	170
Spring Brass all sizes	120

Nickel-base alloys

Inconel (Spring Temper)	
Wire Size Range—in.	
up to .057	185
.057–.114	175
.114–.318	170
Inconel X Spring Temper	After Aging
190	220

Figure 13.23 (*b*) Minimum yield strengths for various spring wire materials.

ples of spring rate curves that are used to approximate the variables of the spring which you wish to design, allowing you to arrive at a quick and accurate answer. You also may use the composite-type spring design charts, which are shown in some of the engineering handbooks, to approximate the initial dimensions of your spring. The programmable calculator is then used to finalize the spring dimensions and check the maximum working stress of the spring to make sure it is lower than the allowable stress for your spring's material and wire diameter or gauge.

In order to construct your own spring rate curves, you must run between 10 and 15 spring rate equations for a particular wire diameter, mean diameter, and number of coils. The curve is then drawn on graph paper, as shown in Figs. 13.24 and 13.25. You may then construct a series of these rate curves and keep them for reference when beginning initial spring design.

A spring design calculator similar to a circular slide rule was available at one time from the Spring Manufacturers Institute. This type of mechanical calculator was very useful in estimating spring values and is still used today by many spring manufacturers. Figure 13.26 shows the front and rear sides of this type of device.

Another alternative available to designers who design springs on a regular basis is to use some of the available computer programs, running on fast computers such as the 386SX and 486 machines in common use today in many engineering departments. A typical computer program for this type of engineering application is Mathcad 2.5. With this program, the spring design equations are entered and assigned a set of range variables, and the computer will perform as many as 50 complex calculations or more in less than a few seconds. The answers appear on the monitor screen in a descending chart. The entire monitor screen may then be printed out as a permanent record. Figure 13.27 shows a typical page of spring working-stress calculations which were run on a 386SX personal computer using Mathcad 2.5 and then printed on a laser printer. This process is a typical example of the power and productivity of the modern computer as used in an involved engineering procedure. These modern machines will accomplish work in a few seconds that at one time required many hours of laborious calculations using logarithms and a wooden pencil, not to mention the fact that many of these calculations involving logarithms were very error-prone.

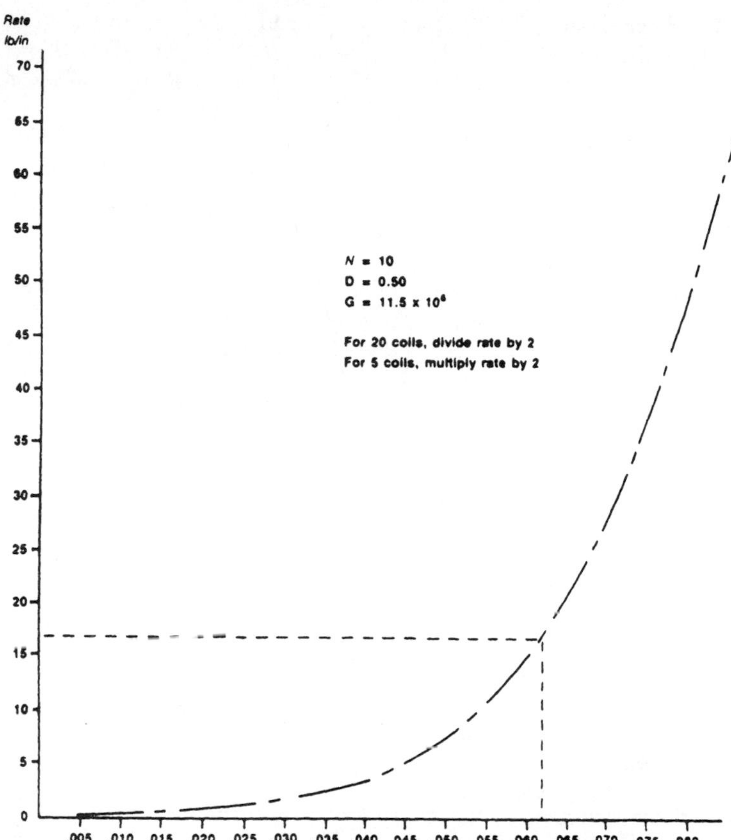

Figure 13.24 Spring rate curve.

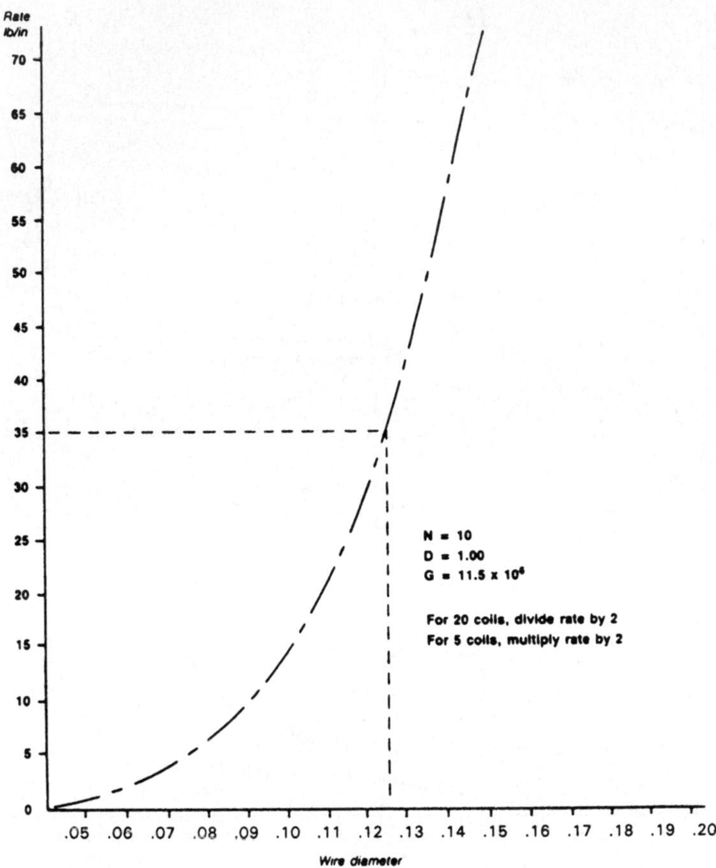

Figure 13.25 Spring rate curve.

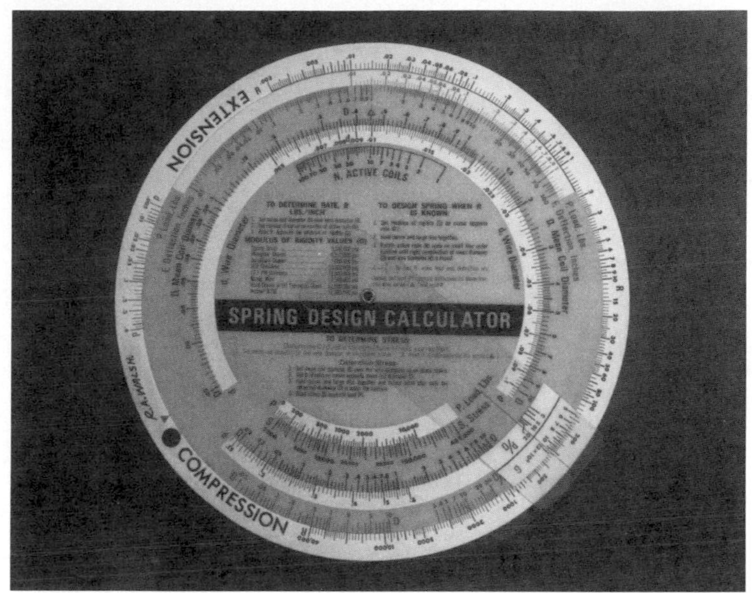

Figure 13.26 (a) Front side of spring design calculator.

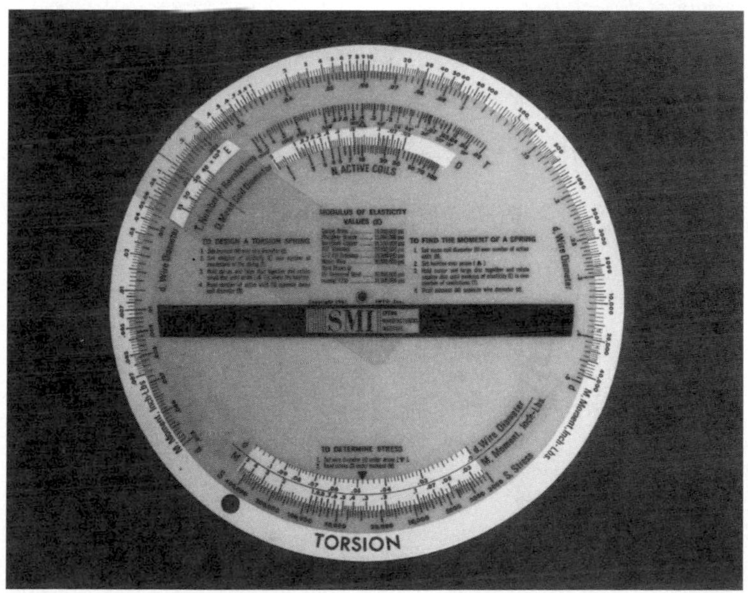

Figure 13.26 (b) Rear side of spring design calculator.

MATHCAD 2.5

Analysis of main power spring of interrupter switch

G := 11500000   d := 0.250   D := 1.700   N := 13 $\frac{D}{d} = 6.8$ INDEX

C := 6.8   P := 250,260 ..400   K := 1.220

$$\frac{4\cdot C - 1}{4\cdot C - 4} + \frac{0.615}{C} = 1.22$$

RATE = R

$$\frac{G\cdot d^4}{8\cdot N\cdot D^3} = 87.918$$

$$\frac{8\cdot K\cdot D\cdot P}{3.1416\cdot d^3} = \text{STRESS}$$

STRESS	LOAD lb-f
$8.45\cdot 10^4$	250
$8.788\cdot 10^4$	260
$9.126\cdot 10^4$	270
$9.464\cdot 10^4$	280
$9.802\cdot 10^4$	290
$1.014\cdot 10^5$	300
$1.048\cdot 10^5$	310
$1.082\cdot 10^5$	320
$1.115\cdot 10^5$	330
$1.149\cdot 10^5$	340
$1.183\cdot 10^5$	350 **
$1.217\cdot 10^5$	360
$1.251\cdot 10^5$	370
$1.284\cdot 10^5$	380
$1.318\cdot 10^5$	390
$1.352\cdot 10^5$	400

Minimum tensile strength of 0.250" dia. music wire, ASTM A-228 = 230,000 psi.

Allowable stress = .50 x 230,000 = 115,000 psi (.50 used due to intermittant spring duty cycle)

Spring is compressed 4", so: 4 x 88 = 352 lb-f

At 350 pounds load, the stress on this spring is: 118,300 psi.

The spring is stressed slightly above the allowable of 50% of tensile strength.

This spring has performed satisfactorily in over 50,000 mechanisms with only a very slight tendancy to take "permanent set". When the spring is properly heat treated by the spring manufacturer, no problems occurred. The operating temperature range of this spring is from -40 degrees F to 150 degrees F.

REFERENCE: Electromechanical Design Handbook, Chapter 7. TAB/McGraw-Hill Book Co. Bk #3102.

R. A. Walsh, Mgr.
R & D Department
POWERCON Corporation
Severn, Maryland 21061
March 25, 1991

Figure 13.27 Computer print-out of spring design problem using Mathcad program.

13.13 Spring Drawings and Forms

When a spring is to be manufactured, a formal spring drawing is usually submitted to the spring manufacturer. This type of drawing must describe the spring accurately, including all pertinent information required by the spring manufacturer to satisfy the listed engineering specifications shown on the drawing. In many instances where special features or conditions are required of the spring, the spring manufacturer should be consulted. The following data should be indicated on the drawing for each spring type.

Compression springs

1. Wire diameter
2. Wire material and specification (e.g., ASTM A-228 music wire, etc.)
3. Inside or outside diameters, whichever one is more important
4. Free length
5. Spring rate or load value at a specified deflection
6. Direction of coil wind, right-hand, left-hand, or optional
7. Type of end
8. Finish, if any, and applicable specification, if required
9. Number of active and total coils
10. Mean coil diameter

Extension springs

1. Wire diameter
2. Length inside the ends
3. Inside or outside diameter
4. Rate or loads at different deflections
5. Maximum extended length without permanent set
6. Loop positions, angular
7. Direction of coil wind, right-hand, left-hand, or optional
8. Type of end

9. Mean coil diameter
10. Number of coils
11. Body length
12. Initial tension (preload)
13. Type of material and specification number
14. Finish, if any, and applicable specification

Torsion springs

1. To work over______diameter shaft at a specified angular deflection
2. Inside diameter, minimum
3. Moment or torque at a specified angular deflection
4. Body length
5. Length of moment arm
6. Wire diameter
7. Mean coil diameter
8. Number of coils
9. Direction of coil wind, right-hand or left-hand
10. Type of material and specification number
11. Finish, if any, and applicable specification
12. Type of end
13. Close or open coils (coil spacing, if any, or tightly wound)

Examples of standard spring drawings are shown in Fig. 13.28.

13.14 Spring Tolerances

Charts providing tolerances on all spring wire and strip available commercially are shown in the various handbooks published by the Spring Manufacturers Institute (see Chap. 23, “Societies, Institutes, and Specification Authorities”). Tolerances on coil diameters, loads, free lengths, squareness, and solid height are also published by the institute. Tolerances on spring materials are also shown in Chap. 5, “Materials and Their Uses,” in this Handbook.

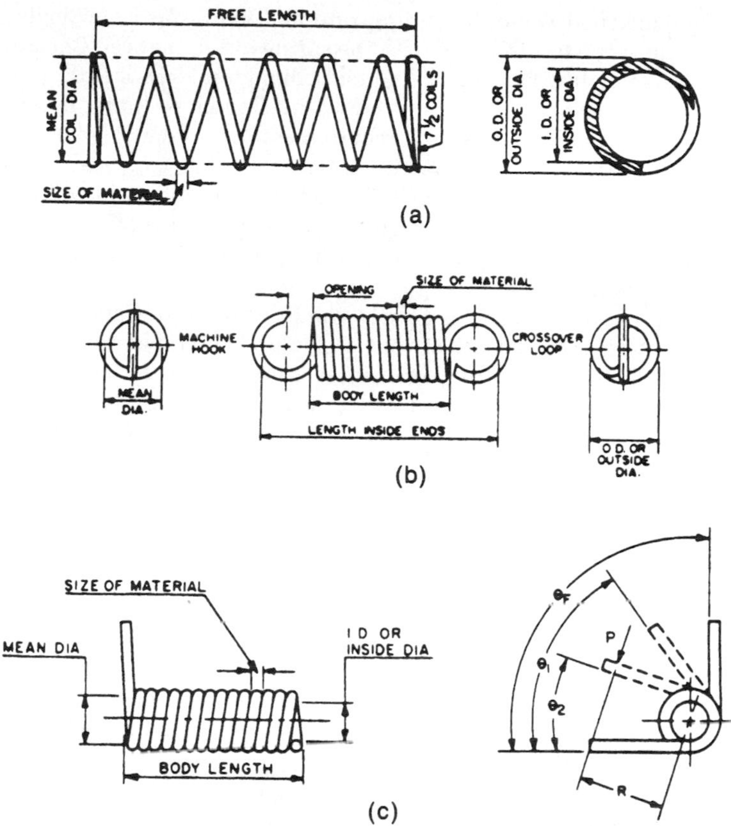

Figure 13.28 Spring drawing formats: (*a*) compression spring; (*b*) extension spring; (*c*) torsion spring.

Any specified value—including rate and load—for a particular spring also can be discussed with the spring manufacturer. Certain dimensions, such as a critical outside diameter, free length, and load at a specified deflection, may be held to close limits by the spring manufacturer, but such requirements will incur higher cost for the particular spring involved. Unless you have a critical application, the tolerance variations allowed on wire and strip will not affect your spring to a significant extent. Also, tolerances on many other spring features usually do not have a significant effect on a common-usage spring.

However, if you have a special condition or requirement, the allowed tolerances can affect your design and should be referred to the spring manufacturer. Tolerances that must be maintained must be shown on the formal spring drawing that is presented to the spring manufacturer. No one is in a better position than the spring manufacturer to know exactly what tolerances and limits can be maintained when manufacturing a spring. Assigning arbritrary tolerances to a spring usually incurs additional costs that are often unwarranted for the application.

13.15 Spring Material Analysis

Designers and manufacturers should be aware that *all* spring materials can be analyzed precisely for proper identification. There is a possibility of materials being substituted accidentally during manufacture. If this occurs with a highly stressed spring, the spring may fail in service. This can happen if hard-drawn or oil-tempered wire is accidentally used in place of music wire or other high-strength material. If you design a spring with a high stress level that has been functional but suddenly fails in service, have the spring analyzed at a materials and engineering laboratory before you attempt to redesign the spring.

Materials such as the stainless steels, beryllium copper, phosphor bronze, and chrome vanadium can be identified quickly by chemical analysis. Materials such as music wire (ASTM A-228), hard-drawn steel (ASTM A-227), and oil-tempered spring steel (ASTM A-229) *cannot* be identified chemically because their chemistries overlap as a result of the compositional tolerances of their constituent elements. However, these materials *can* be differentiated by microscopic analysis. Oil-tempered spring steel will show a definite martensitic structure under 100× to 400× magnification, while music wire will show a definite "cold-work" structure due to cold drawing during its manufacture. In this manner, it may be ascertained which type of steel was used to make the spring being analyzed. The microstructures for these listed steels differ and can be identified at the test laboratory using the *ASTM Book of Microstructures of Steels*. Figure 13.29 is a photomicrograph of a section of a spring made of oil-tempered spring steel, showing in detail the martensitic structure of this type of steel.

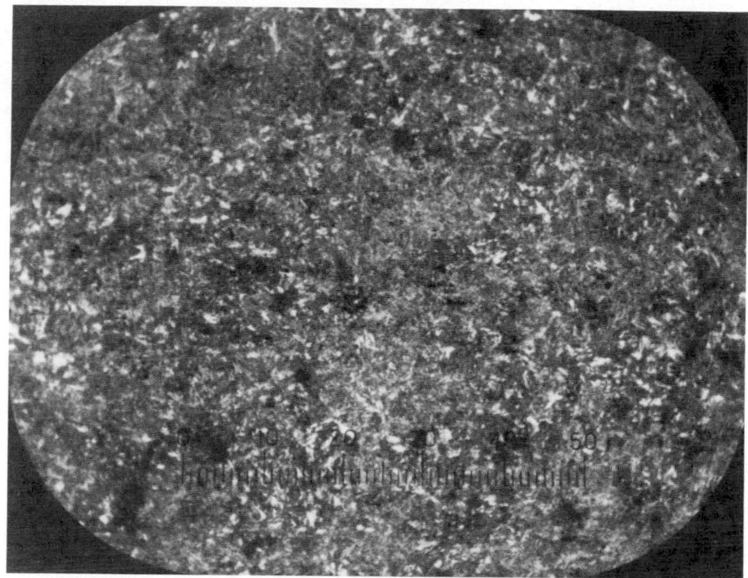

Figure 13.29 Photomicrograph of section of spring material.

The laboratory report shown in Fig. 13.30 was made as a consequence to the photomicrograph shown in Fig. 13.29. The spring sample analyzed was supposed to have been manufactured from ASTM A-228 music wire but was in fact manufactured accidentally from oil-tempered ASTM A-229 steel wire. The consequence of this mistake in materials selection during spring manufacture was the rejection of 5000 large compression springs, which were returned to the spring manufacturer because they were not capable of withstanding the working stresses without taking a permanent *set*. The springs, in effect, were unsuitable for the intended application and did not satisfy the spring specifications shown on the spring drawing.

DR. WM. B. D. PENNIMAN
1866-1938
DR. ARTHUR LEE BROWNE
1867-1958

EXECUTIVE STAFF
PHILIP M. AIDT
ALLEN W. THOMPSON
DANTE G. BERETTA
J. ADRIAN BUTT
DONALD W. SMITH

PENNIMAN & BROWNE, INC.
CHEMISTS-ENGINEERS-INSPECTORS
6252 FALLS ROAD
BALTIMORE, MARYLAND 21209

ESTABLISHED
1896

CABLE ADDRESS
"BALTEST"

TELEPHONE
825-4131
AREA CODE 301

ENGINEERING DIVISION

REPORT OF TEST

Attn: R. A. Walsh May 27, 1981

No. 811265

Sample of Compression Spring

Client

Marks or Other Data Verify material to be Music Wire (ASTM A 228) Service failures suggest possibility that material might be oil tempered (ASTM A 229)

The above indicated ASTM specifications were checked and found to have overlapping chemistries preventing the use of chemical analysis for identification.

The ASTM Handbook of Microstructures showed the difference between the hard drawn structure (ASTM A 228) and the oil tempered microstructure.

Samples were cut from the spring, mounted for examination in transverse and longitudinal directions, ground, polished, etched and examined at 100X to 400X magnification. The attached micrograph at 200X magnification clearly shows a martensitic, oil-tempered structure indicating an A229 material.

No hardness requirements are listed for these materials.

PENNIMAN & BROWNE, INC.

J. A. Butt

J. A. Butt

FORM 30 L/B

Figure 13.30 Material test laboratory report.

13.16 Heat Treatment and Electroplate Postbaking of Springs

13.16.1 Heat treatment of springs

When a helical compression, extension, or torsion spring is formed on the spring coiling machine during manufacture, residual stresses induced during the coiling operation must be relieved soon after the spring is completed. The normal heat-treatment procedures are as follows:

Music wire (ASTM A-228), oil-tempered (ASTM A-229) and hard-drawn (ASTM A-227 and A-679): Oven heated at 500°F for 30 to 40 min

Stainless steels, 17-7PH, types 301, 302, 304 (ASTM A-313): Oven heated at 600 to 650°F for 30 to 40 min

Inconel 600 and X750: Oven heated at 700 to 1200°F for as long as 4 h (Inconel X750)

13.16.2 Electroplating springs

Springs may be electroplated with a number of different metals, such as cadmium, chromium, zinc, copper, tin, and nickel. The most common and widely used metal for plating springs is bright zinc. The zinc plating federal specification is QQ-P-416 and includes:

Type 1: Bright zinc

Type 2: Bright zinc with chromate

Class 1 plating thickness: 0.2 mils (0.0002 in)

Class 2 plating thickness: 0.3 mils (0.0003 in)

Class 3 plating thickness: 0.5 mils (0.0005 in)

13.16.3 Postbaking electroplated springs

Immediately after the electroplating process is completed, the plated spring must be postbaked at a specified temperature for a specific time interval to prevent *hydrogen embrittlement,* which will invariably occur if the postbaking operation is not performed. The postbaking operation usually consists of oven heating the spring at 500°F for 3 h.

13.17 Dynamics of Helical Compression and Extension Springs

When a helical compression spring is rapidly loaded or unloaded, a surge wave is generated within the spring. This surge wave limits the rate at which the spring can release or absorb energy by limiting the impact velocity. The impact velocity is defined by

$$V \cong 10.1S\sqrt{\frac{g}{2\rho G}} \qquad \text{meters per second (approximately)}$$

$$V \cong S\sqrt{\frac{g}{2\rho G}} \qquad \text{inches per second (approximately)}$$

where S = maximum stress in the spring, psi, MPa
g = gravity constant, 386 in/sec^2, 9.8 m/s^2
ρ = density of spring material, g/cm^3, lb/in^3
G = shear modulus of elasticity, MPa, psi (G = 11,500,000 psi for steel)

When a compressed helical compression spring is released instantaneously and the stress is known, the maximum spring velocity is a function of the maximum stress S and the spring material. When the impact velocity is known, the maximum stress induced in the spring may be calculated approximately. High spring loading velocities limit spring performance and often cause *resonance;* e.g., valve springs in high-performance internal combustion engines may "float" or bounce due to this effect at high engine rpms.

Dynamic loading: Resonance (compression and extension springs). A spring will exhibit resonance when the cyclic loading/unloading rate is near the spring's natural frequency or a multiple of its natural frequency. Resonance can cause spring bounce or floating, resulting in lower loads than those calculated. The natural frequency should be a minimum of 13 times the operating frequency. If the operating frequency is 100 cycles per second (hertz), the design natural frequency should be 13 × 100 = 1300 cycles (Hz).

For helical compression springs with both ends fixed, the natural frequency is given by

$$n = \frac{1120d}{ND^2}\sqrt{\frac{Gg}{\rho}} \qquad \text{for SI units}$$

$$n = \frac{0.111d}{ND^2}\sqrt{\frac{Gg}{\rho}} \qquad \text{for U.S. Customary units}$$

Helical extension springs (resonance). With one end fixed, the natural frequency (hertz) of a helical extension spring is given by

$$n = \frac{560d}{ND^2}\sqrt{\frac{Gg}{\rho}} \qquad \text{for SI units}$$

$$n = \frac{0.056d}{ND^2}\sqrt{\frac{Gg}{\rho}} \qquad \text{for U.S. Customary units}$$

where n = natural frequency, Hz, or cycles per second
d = wire diameter, mm, in
D = mean diameter, mm, in
G = shear modulus, psi, MPa, (11,500,000 psi for steels)
g = acceleration of gravity, 386 in/s^2, 9.81 m/s^2
ρ = density of spring material, lb/in^3, g/cm^3
N = number of active coils in the spring (all coils are active in an extension spring and active coils in compression springs are determined by the type of end)

Note: To prevent resonance, energy-damping devices are sometimes used on springs when the natural frequency cannot be made more than 13 times the operating frequency.

Chapter 14

Power Transmission Systems

Power transmission components detailed in this chapter include

- V-belts, standard and narrow, single and multiple
- Flat belts
- Ribbed and timing belts
- Chains and sprockets
- Gears (see Chap. 10)
- Shafts and couplings
- Clutches
- Power screws and ratchet systems

14.1 Belts and Sheaves

The most common belts used today include

- Flat
- Classic V
- Narrow V
- Cogged V

- Variable speed
- Synchronous
- V-ribbed

Although flat belts are still used today, the classic V-belt is usually the first choice when a belt drive is designed, either single or multiple.

Sheaves and pulleys. The *sheave* is the grooved wheel in which the V-belt runs. For a flat belt, the wheel on which the belt runs is commonly called the *pulley* (see Fig. 14.1 for typical belt types).

14.1.1 Standard V-belts

The classic or conventional V-belt comes in standard sizes A, B, C, D, and E. V-belts are commonly used individually in sizes A and B, but multiple-belt drives in sizes A and B are also more economical than multiple-belt drives in sizes C, D, and E.

The *narrow* V-belt transfers the applied loads in the belt cords more directly to the sides of the sheave, producing better force distribution than the classic V-belts. For a given width, the narrow V-belts have higher power ratings than the classic types of V-belts. Narrow V-belts are standardized with the designations 3v, 5v, and 8v. Some of these are *cogged* to allow use over smaller-diameter sheaves.

V-ribbed belts are a combination of flat and V-belt designs offering high power capacity with tensioning requirements only 20 percent greater than V-belts. These belts are used in high-power automotive applications as well as in mass-produced consumer products. V-ribbed belts are available in sizes H, J, K, L, and M.

Synchronous belts are available in sizes XL, L, and H, as well as in dual-drive sections termed DXL, DL, and DH.

14.1.2 V-belt drive calculations

When power is transmitted by a V-belt, the belt is tight on one side and slack on the other side. The difference between these two tensions is the *effective pull* applied to the rim of the sheave. This pull produces work and may be represented by the equation

$$\text{hp} = \frac{(T_{\text{T}} - T_{\text{S}})d}{33{,}000t}$$

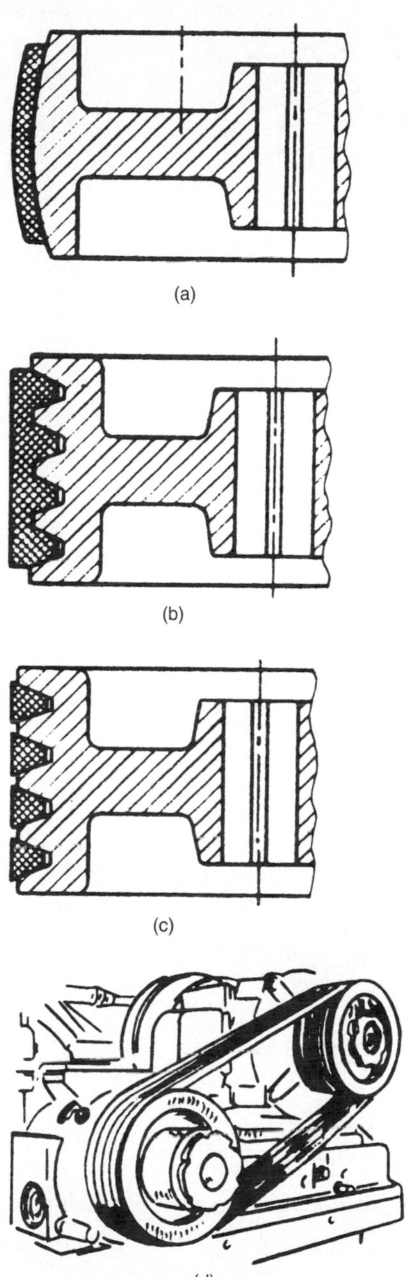

Figure 14.1 Belts: (*a*) flat; (*b*) V-ribbed; (*c*) multiple-V; (*d*) multiple-V belt motor drive.

where $T_T - T_S$ = effective pull, lb
T_T = tight side tension
T_S = slack side tension
hp = horsepower
d = distance moved, ft
t = time, min

Belt speed V is then calculated from

$$V = \frac{D(\text{rpm})}{3.82}$$

where V = belt speed, ft/min
D = sheave pitch diameter, in

Then,

$$\text{hp} = \frac{(T_T - T_S)V}{33{,}000}$$

The tension ratio R is

$$R = \frac{T_T}{T_S}$$

As the ratio increases, the percentage of belt slip increases. Using the *arc of contact* correction factor G from Fig. 14.2, you can calculate tight side and slack side tensions using the following simplified equations:

$$T_T = \frac{41{,}250\text{hp}}{GV}$$

$$T_S = \frac{33{,}000(1.25 - G)\text{hp}}{GV}$$

where G = arc of contact correction factor
V = belt speed (see previous equation for V), ft/min

The arc of contact A_c on the smaller sheave can be calculated from

$$A_c = \frac{(D - d)60°}{C}$$

Arc of contact correction factors for V-groove Belts.

$(D-d)/C$	Arc of contact, deg	Correction factor (G)
0.0	180	1.00
0.1	174	0.99
0.2	169	0.97
0.3	163	0.96
0.4	157	0.94
0.5	151	0.93
0.6	145	0.91
0.7	139	0.89
0.8	133	0.87
0.9	127	0.85
1.0	120	0.82
1.1	113	0.80
1.2	106	0.77
1.3	99	0.73
1.4	91	0.70
1.5	83	0.65

Figure 14.2 Correction-factor table.

where D = pitch diameter of larger sheave, in
d = pitch diameter of smaller sheave, in
C = center distance between sheaves, in

Speed ratio. Most belt drives provide speed reduction, and

$$\text{Speed ratio} = \frac{\text{faster sheave rpm}}{\text{slower sheave rpm}}$$

Belt drive ratio is always considered to be equal to or greater than 1, whether the drive is for speed-increasing or speed-reducing applications. As a general rule, for belt speeds over 5000 ft/min, the sheaves should be statically and dynamically balanced.

Belt length. For two-sheave drives,

$$L = 2C + 1.57(D + d) + \frac{(D - d)^2}{4C}$$

where D = pitch diameter of large sheave, in
d = pitch diameter of small sheave, in
L = length of belt, in
C = center distance of sheaves, in

Application of belt drives. The designer must select the belt size, number of belts, and sheave sizes in order to satisfy these stipulations:

- Correct shaft speed
- Proper center distance
- Acceptable belt life

The *horsepower-rating* method presumes an acceptable value for belt life in industrial applications. The *life-in-hours* of a belt drive can be considered to be from 200 to 2000 hours, depending on the application. What the designer should strive for in the belt-drive system is the maximum life probability weighed against the cost of the drive. Accurate life-in-hours for a belt-drive system is determined by testing with simulated operating conditions.

Belt-drive design procedures. For a V-belt drive, you must know the following factors:

- The horsepower requirement of the drive
- Speed of the *driver* machine
- Speed of the *driven* machine
- Center distance for the sheaves

Proceed as follows:

1. Find the design horsepower from

$$\text{Design horsepower} = \text{service factor} \times \text{hp required}$$

The service factor ranges from 1.0 to 1.8 and is approximated from the following chart:

Intermittent service (3–5 h/day)		Normal service (8–10 h/day)	Continuous duty (18–24 h/day)
Heavier duty ↓	1.0 ↓	1.3 ↓	1.3 ↓
	1.3	1.5	1.8

2. Select the proper V-belt (see Fig. 14.3).
3. Find the speed ratio.
4. Select the sheave diameters. Use one standard diameter for the larger sheave. Find the sheave rim speed from

$$R_s = 1/3.82 \times \text{pitch diameter of sheave} \times \text{rpm of sheave}$$

Keep rim speeds below 6500 ft/min for narrow V-belts and 6000 ft/min for classic V-belts (types A, B, C, D, and E)

5. Using a selected center distance, calculate the tentative belt length from

$$L_T = 1.57(D + d) + (\text{c.d.} \times 2)$$

where D = pitch diameter of larger sheave, in
d = pitch diameter of smaller sheave, in
c.d. = center distance of the sheaves

When you have selected the belt by choosing the closest standard belt length from the belt catalog, you may calculate the real center distance using the following equation:

$$C = 0.0625\left[b + \sqrt{b^2 - 32(D \quad d)^2}\right]$$

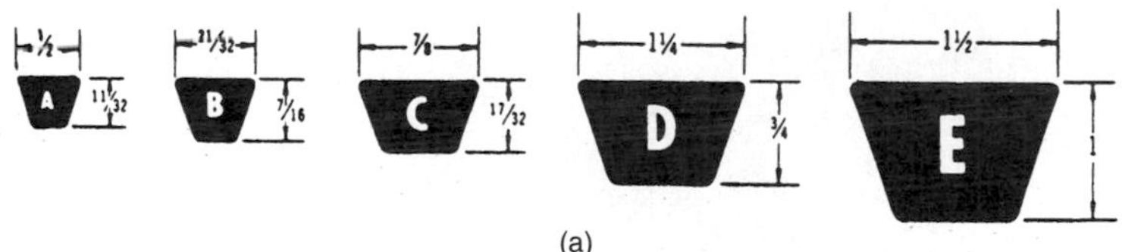

(a)

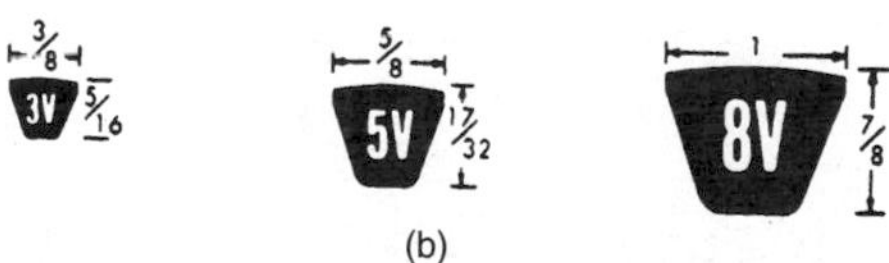

(b)

Figure 14.3 (*a*) Standard V-belts. (*b*) Narrow V-belts.

where $b = 4L - 6.28(D + d)$
L = V-belt pitch length, in
C = center distance of the sheaves, in
D = pitch diameter of larger sheave, in
d = pitch diameter of smaller sheave, in

Note that V-belt pitch lengths for drives with more than two sheaves are determined geometrically or by scaled layout.

6. Find the number of belts required. From manufacturers' tables, find the rated horsepower per belt. Divide the design horsepower by the horsepower per belt to obtain the number of belts. This figure is usually a fraction, so advance to the next highest whole number for the number of belts required.

Selection of belt type and size also can be determined with the use of Figs. 14.4 and 14.5 when the design horsepower and the speed of the faster sheave are known.

Timing belts. Timing belt sheaves must be in accurate alignment with both sheave shafts parallel. Avoid *preload* on timing belts. The belt should fit snugly but not be too tight. Provision for sheave-center distance adjustment should be made in the drive design.

Center distance for timing belts. The center distance for timing belts is given approximately by

$$C = \frac{P}{4}\left[\text{n.b.} - \frac{N_1 + N_2}{2} + \sqrt{\left(\text{n.b.} - \frac{N_1 + N_2}{2}\right) - 2\left(\frac{N_1 + N_2}{\pi}\right)^2}\,\right]$$

where C = center distance, in
P = belt pitch, in
n.b. = number of teeth in the belt
N_1 = number of grooves in larger sheave
N_2 = number of grooves in smaller sheave

V-belt drive shaft loads. The shaft loading used to calculate bearing loads on V-belt drives with 180° arc of contact is given as

$$P_B = 1.5(T_1 - T_2) = \frac{1.5 \times 63{,}025 \times \text{hp}}{\text{rpm} \times r}$$

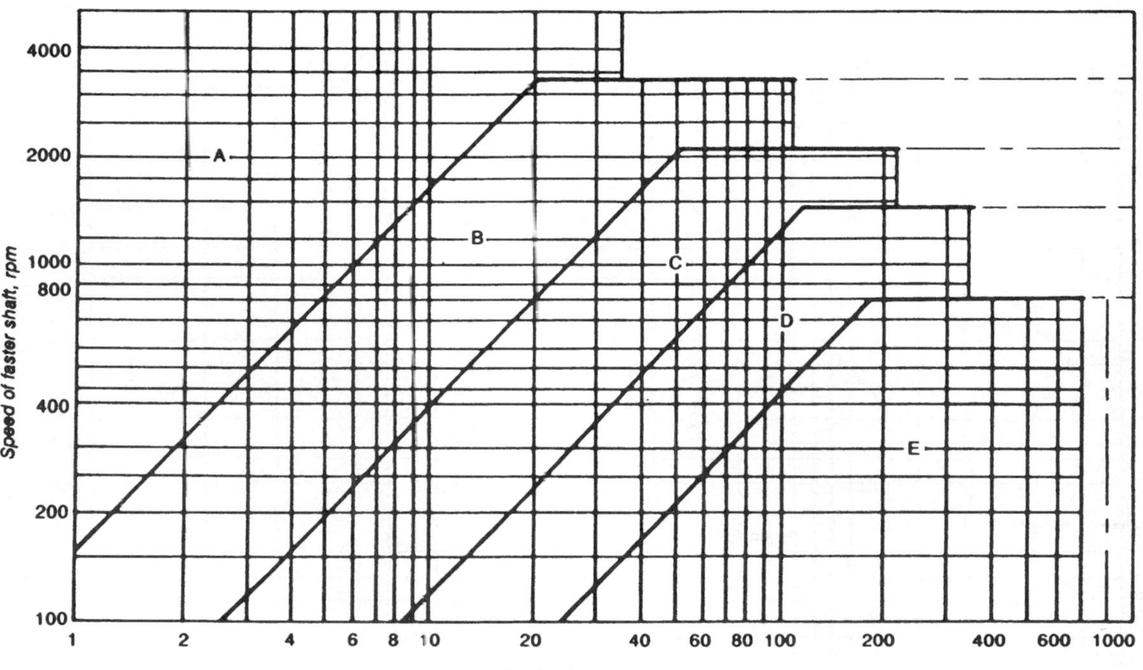

Figure 14.4 Standard V-belt selection chart.

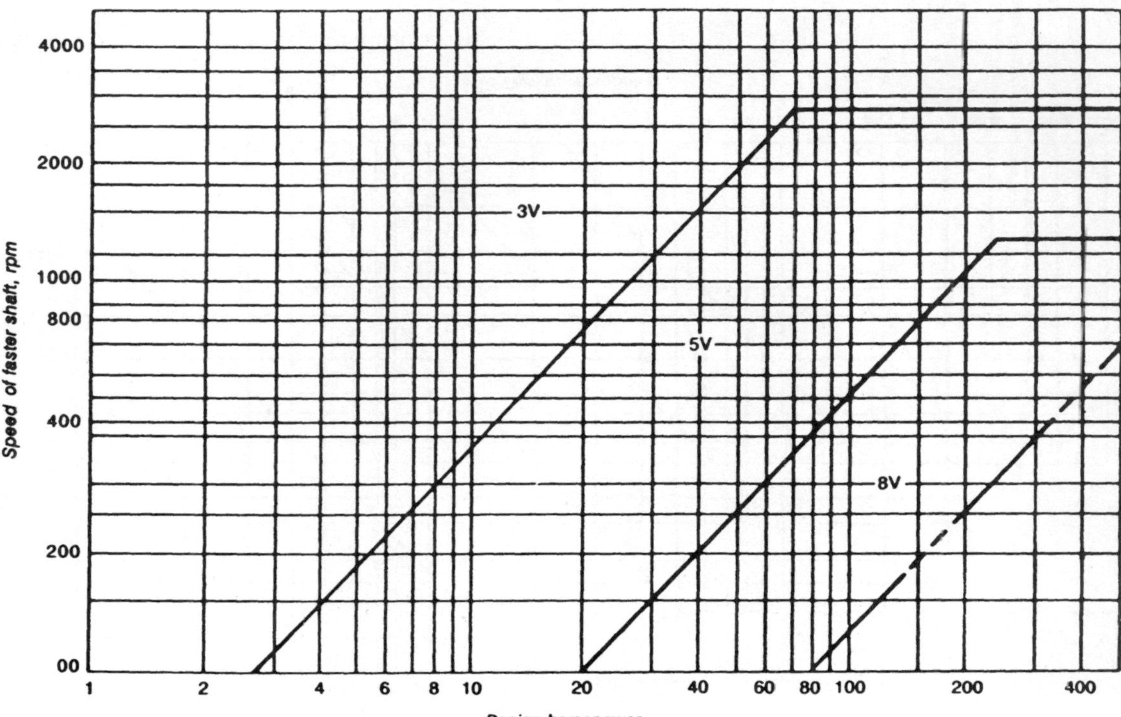

Figure 14.5 Narrow V-belt selection chart.

For belts with other than 180° arc of contact, use

$$P_B = \left(\frac{2.5 - A_c}{A_c}\right)(T_1 - T_2)$$

$$= \left(\frac{2.5 - A_c}{A_c}\right)\left(\frac{33{,}000 \times \text{hp}}{\text{fpm}}\right)$$

where P_B = belt pull, lb
A_c = arc of contact factor (see Fig. 14.2)
T_1 = tight side tension, lb
T_2 = slack side tension, lb
r = sheave pitch radius, in
hp = horsepower
rpm = revolutions per minute
fpm = feet per minute

Sheave diameters for electric motor V-belt drives. The minimum recommended sheave diameters for electric motor drives, in inches, are shown in Fig. 14.6.

Conclusion. After the design of a belt drive is completed, you should additionally provide an adjustable means in the belt drive to take up belt slack. One adjustable sheave should be provided, but this is not always possible. An idler sheave or pully is sometimes used for belt tensioning when other means of adjusting sheave centers are difficult or not possible. The use of an idler sheave or pulley is generally not recommended by the belt manufacturers. Idlers reduce the horsepower capacity of a belt-drive system and also cause premature belt wear. Use an idler *only* when it is unavoidable. Correct placement and size of an idler are important points in design. Refer to the belt manufacturers' catalogs for application data on idler placement.

Conventional V-belt drive-tensioning procedures

Step 1. With all belts in their proper grooves, adjust the centers to take up all slack until the belts are fairly taut.

Step 2. Start the drive and continue to adjust the tension until the belts have a slight bow on the slack side of the drive while operating under load.

Step 3. After a few days of operation the belts will "seat" themselves in the sheave grooves. It may then become necessary to read-

Minimum recommended sheave diameters for electric motors, in.

	Motor rpm					
Motor hp	575	695	870	1160	1750	3450
½	—	—	2¼	—	—	—
¾	—	—	2½	2¼	—	—
1	3	2½	2½	2½	2¼	—
1½	3	2½	2½	2½	2¼	2¼
2	3¾	3	3	2½	2½	2½
3	4½	3¾	3	3	2½	2½
5	4½	4½	3¾	3	3	2¼
7½	5¼	4½	4½	3¾	3	3
10	6	5¼	4½	4½	3¾	3
15	6¾	6	5¼	4½	4½	3¾
20	8¼	6¾	6	5¼	4½	4½
25	9	8¼	6¾	6	4½	4½
30	10	9	6¾	6¾	5¼	—
40	10	10	8¼	6¾	6	—
50	11	10	9	8¼	6¾	—
60	12	11	10	9	7½	—
75	14	13	10	10	9	—
100	18	15	13	13	10	—

Figure 14.6 Sheave diameters for electric motor drives.

just the belt tension until there is again a slight bow on the slack side under load.

Occasional readjustment may be necessary at periodic intervals as the belts and sheaves wear in service.

14.2 Chains and Sprockets

Roller chain normally is supplied in both riveted and detachable types. The detachable types are assembled with cotter pins and are generally supplied in sizes larger than 1-in pitch. See Fig. 14.7 for ANSI standard roller chain specifications and Fig. 14.8 for dimensions of the various chain sizes. Figure 14.9 gives the ultimate strength (in tension) of ANSI standard roller chain in carbon and stainless steels.

Roller chain is manufactured in single through six strands. Speed ratios for chain sprockets are calculated using the same equations shown for spur gears in Chap. 10. The overall diameter of the chain on the sprocket is determined from the sum of pitch diameter plus the F dimension for the given chain number shown in Fig. 14.8.

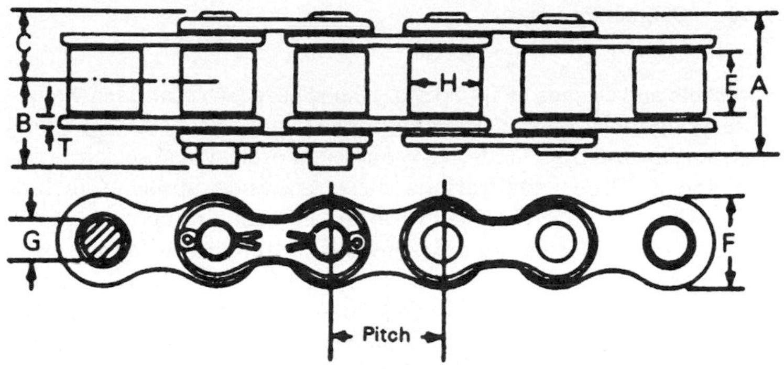

Figure 14.7 ANSI standard roller chain.

Chain number	Pitch	E	H	A	B	C	T	F	G	Weight/ ft, lb
25*	1/4	0.125	0.130	0.31	0.19	0.15	0.030	0.23	0.0905	0.104
35*	3/8	0.187	0.200	0.47	0.34	0.23	0.050	0.36	0.141	0.21
40	1/2	0.312	0.312	0.65	0.42	0.32	0.060	0.46	0.156	0.41
S41	1/2	0.250	0.306	0.51	0.37	0.26	0.050	0.39	0.141	0.28
S43	1/2	0.125	0.306	0.39	0.31	0.20	0.050	0.39	0.141	0.22
50	5/8	0.375	0.400	0.79	0.56	0.40	0.080	0.59	0.200	0.69
60	3/4	0.500	0.468	0.98	0.64	0.49	0.094	0.70	0.234	0.96
80	1	0.625	0.625	0.128	0.74	0.64	0.125	0.93	0.312	1.60
100	1 1/4	0.750	0.750	1.54	0.91	0.77	0.156	1.18	0.375	2.56
120	1 1/2	1.00	0.875	1.94	1.14	0.97	0.187	1.38	0.437	3.60
140	1 3/4	1.00	1.00	2.08	1.22	1.04	0.218	1.63	0.500	4.90
160	2	1.25	1.12	2.48	1.46	1.24	0.250	1.88	0.562	6.40
180	2 1/4	1.41	1.41	2.81	1.74	1.40	0.281	2.13	0.687	8.70
200	2 1/2	1.50	1.56	3.02	1.86	1.51	0.312	2.32	0.781	10.30
240	3	1.88	1.88	3.76	2.27	1.88	0.375	2.80	0.937	16.90

Figure 14.8 ANSI standard chain dimensions (see Fig. 14.7).

Chain number	Carbon steel (pounds)	Stainless steel (pounds)
25*	925	700
35*	2,100	1,700
40	3,700	3,000
S41	2,000	1,700
S43	1,700	—
50	6,100	4,700
60	8,500	6,750
80	14,500	12,000
100	24,000	18,750
120	34,000	27,500
140	46,000	—
160	58,000	—
180	80,000	—
200	95,000	—
240	130,000	—

*Rollerless

Figure 14.9 Ultimate strength of roller chain in tension.

Sprockets and classes of sprockets. There are two standard classes of sprockets for roller chain, commercial and precision. When very high speeds and high loads are required, a precision sprocket is recommended. Other applications for a precision sprocket include those which require fixed centers and critical timing or registration. A standard commercial sprocket is applicable for all other chain/sprocket uses.

Note that all chain made in the same chain number designation is *not* necessarily the same. All American-manufactured chain that meets the requirements of ANSI and ASTM specifications is a high-quality product that will meet the strength specifications shown in Fig. 14.9. Imported roller chain must be inspected carefully and tested *before* applying it to your product. Various imported roller chain has performed below American standard specifications in a similar manner to the counterfeit hardware (such as bolts and screws) that has been plaguing the industry for several years. See Chap. 6 for more information on counterfeit hardware.

Sprocket-to-shaft assembly. Sprockets should be assembled to shafts with keys and set screws. The set screw should be secured over the flat of the key and sized according to the following chart (see the shaft section for key sizes):

Shaft diameter/sprocket bore (range), in	Set screw size (diameter), in
0.5–0.875	0.25
0.937–1.75	0.375
1.812–2.25	0.50
2.312–3.25	0.625

Permanent assemblies may be made by welding the sprocket to the shaft if the design permits. Note that some of the smaller-sized sprockets are made using *powder-metal technology* and that this type of sprocket is *not* recommended for welding. Welding a powder-metal sprocket usually results in the sprocket breaking at the weld area. Brazing such sprockets to a shaft may be possible if the loads are not excessive. Figure 14.10 shows the two standard types of sprockets in common use.

Types of chains for chain drives. Commercial standard chain types include

- Roller, single- and multiple-strand
- Rollerless
- Double pitch
- Detachable link
- Silent, inverted-tooth
- Offset sidebar
- Bead

Allowable speed ratios. The speed ratio for roller chain or silent chain should not exceed 10:1 and for other types should not exceed 6:1. Use a double-reduction drive to overcome these limitations. Double-reduction ratios are calculated the same as those for spur gears (see Chap. 10).

Horsepower capacity. In the sample comparison chart shown in Fig. 14.11, horsepower ratings versus rotating speeds are shown for 15-tooth sprockets as a reference only. Actual capacities and ratings for different applications are calculated according to the preceding detailed procedures.

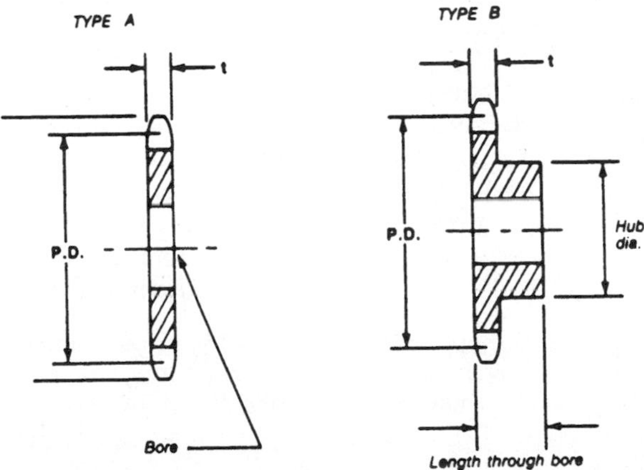

Figure 14.10 Types of sprockets.

Conveyor applications for roller chain. For conveyor applications, the chain pull W can be calculated from

$$W = \frac{2T}{D} \qquad W = \frac{33{,}000P}{V} \qquad \text{or} \qquad W = \frac{126{,}050P}{nD}$$

where W = chain pull, lb
T = torque, lb · in
D = sprocket pitch diameter, in
P = horsepower
V = chain velocity, ft/min
n = sprocket speed, rpm

When the chain pull is determined by one of the preceding equations, select the chain size required from the table in Fig. 14.12. When the center distance of the sprockets is known, the number of pitches required in the chain can be calculated by

$$\text{Chain length, pitches} = N_p = \left(\frac{2\text{ c.d.}}{P}\right) + \left(\frac{T_{DR} + T_{DN}}{2}\right)$$

where c.d. = center distance of sprockets, in
P = pitch of chain, in
T_{DR} = number of teeth in driver sprocket
T_{DN} = number of teeth in driven sprocket
N_p = number of pitches in chain length

The center distance between sprockets should be greater than half the sum of the outside diameters of the sprockets.

Slow-speed partial drive. Chains and sprockets are used in many applications where a high torque is transmitted at a partial revolution or small number of turns of the driving sprocket. In these types of cases, the minimum tensile strength of the chain, along with a factor of safety or multiplier, is used to determine the chain size. Thus you may calculate the maximum tensile load on the chain and multiply this figure by 2 or 3 and determine the chain size from this value.

Example For the sample application (see Fig. 14.13), let the reduction ratio be 1.5. Sprocket S_1 must rotate 1.5 times to revolve S_2 once. If the torque required at the driven sprocket S_2 is 2000 lb · in, the torque at sprocket S_1 will be

$$\frac{2000}{1.5} = 1333 \text{ lb} \cdot \text{ins}$$

rpm sprocket is	Roller chain	
	Single strand	Four strand
100	100	330
500	180	600
700	100	335
1,000	60	195
1,400	30	98
1,800	18	55
2,200	11	37
2,600	7	25
3,000	6	19
3,500	3.5	12.5
4,500	2	7
5,500	1.75	6.1
6,500	1.3	4.7
7,500	1.2	3.8
8,500	1	3.2
10,000	.75	2.4

Figure 14.11 Reference chart for maximum horsepower capacity.

	CHAIN NUMBERS								
Single Pitch	35*	40	50	60	80	100	120	140	160
Double Pitch		C2040	C2050	C2060	C2080	C2100	C2120		C2160
Velocity of Chain (FPM)	MAXIMUM WORKING LOAD OR CHAIN PULL (Lbs.)								
25	250	443	690	995	1770	2760	3990	5430	7100
50	243	432	675	970	1730	2690	3880	5290	6900
75	233	414	645	930	1660	2580	3720	5060	6630
100	220	391	610	880	1570	2440	3520	4800	6250
125	206	366	570	820	1460	2280	3290	4470	5850
150	190	338	528	760	1350	2110	3040	4140	5400
175	175	311	485	700	1240	1940	2800	3810	4970
200	160	284	444	640	1140	1770	2560	3480	4550
225	146	259	405	584	1040	1620	2340	3180	4150
250	133	236	368	530	940	1470	2120	2890	3770
275	120	214	333	480	855	1330	1920	2610	3310
300	110	195	305	440	780	1220	1760	2390	3120
	STANDARD PITCH BOSTON SPROCKETS TO OPERATE WITH ABOVE CHAIN								
Pitch	3/8″	1/2″	5/8″	3/4″	1″	1-1/4″	1-1/2″	1-3/4″	2″

* No. 35 Chain is a Rollerless Chain.

Figure 14.12 Chain load-rating chart.

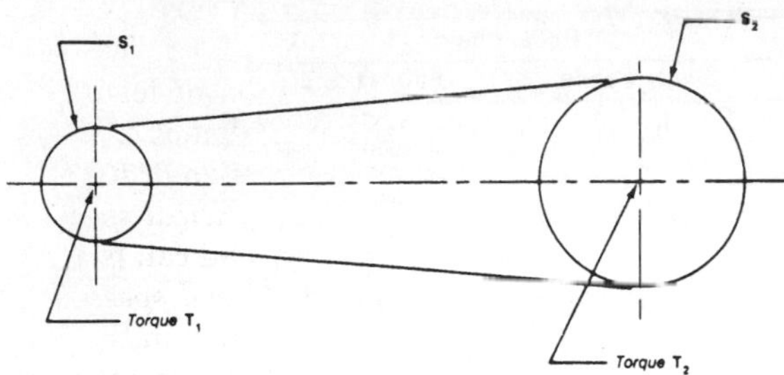

Figure 14.13 Sprocket and chain drive.

If you limit the tension in the chain to approximately 700 lb, you will need to calculate the pitch radius (p.r.) of sprocket S_2. Therefore,

$$T_2 = \text{p.r.} \times 700$$

$$2000 = \text{p.r.} \times 700$$

$$\text{p.r.} = \frac{2000}{700} = 2.86 \text{ in}$$

Thus the pitch diameter of sprocket $S_2 = 2 \times 2.86 = 5.72$ in. Now, select a sprocket for the appropriate chain size from Fig. 14.9. Multiplying 700 by 2.5, the safety factor, gives 1750 lb. S43 chain will suffice for this application. Select an S43 sprocket whose pitch diameter is close to 5.72 in, and then select the driver sprocket with the correct number of teeth to give the reduction ratio of 1.5:1. That is,

$$\frac{1.5}{1} = \frac{\text{no. of teeth in driven } S_2}{\text{no. of teeth in driver } S_1}$$

An S43 sprocket whose pitch diameter is close to 5.72 in is the 36-tooth sprocket whose pitch diameter is 5.737 in. Now, we may determine the number of teeth in the driver sprocket (S_1) from the preceding simple relation:

$$\frac{1.5}{1} = \frac{36}{x} \qquad 1.5x = 36 \qquad x = 24 \text{ teeth in } S_1$$

This then is the method of properly selecting a chain drive system for partial drive applications. A chain drive system selected using this conservative method will provide many hours of trouble-free service. Selection of the bearings for this type of system is detailed in other chapters of this *Handbook*.

14.3 Shafts and Shafting Materials

In operation, shafts are subject to different types of loads and stresses, such as angular deviation (torque displacement α), bending (linear deflection), bending stresses, and torsional stresses. Shafts are also subject to the condition known as *critical speed.* A shaft carrying a number of loads or a distributed load can have an infinite number of critical speeds, but the *first critical speed* is of importance in the design of shafts and will be detailed in this section. The selection and processing of shafting and shafting materials also will be detailed.

Torsion in shafts. The angle of torsional deflection α of a shaft subject to a torsional moment M_t is given as follows. For *any* cross section,

$$\alpha = \frac{180 M_t l}{\pi I_p G}$$

For a round cross-sectional shaft,

$$\alpha = \frac{583.6 M_t l}{D^4 G}$$

$$I_p \text{ for a round shaft} = \frac{\pi D^4}{32}$$

where D = diameter, in
l = length being twisted, in
I_p = polar moment of inertia of the section through the shaft, in^3
α = angle of torsional deflection, degrees
M_t = torsional moment, lb · in
G = torsional modulus of elasticity, psi (for mild carbon steel $G = 11.5 \times 10^6$ psi; see Chap. 5 for other materials)

The torsional modulus of elasticity is approximately 40 percent of the modulus of elasticity in tension (Youngs' modulus) for many metals.

The degree of torsional deflection permissible for line shafting is determined by the application. Shafts carrying gears should be particularly stiff, with a recommended angular deflection not to exceed 0.08° per foot of length. The angle of torsional deflection α for different shaft forms includes the following.

For square shafts

$$\alpha = \frac{343.7 M_t l}{h^4 G}$$

where h = length of the side of the square

For hollow round shafts or tubes

$$\alpha = \frac{583.6 M_t l}{(D^4 - d^4) G}$$

where D = outside diameter of shaft and d = inside diameter, in

Bending in shafts (linear deflection). The shaft shown in Fig. 14.14 is taken as a beam of uniform cross section loaded transversely with a concentrated load P. Here,

$$\Delta_x = \frac{Pa^2b^2}{3EIl} \qquad \text{(see beam equations, in the Index)}$$

If the load P on the gear is 400 lb, the shaft diameter d = 1.25 in, a = 10 in, b = 14 in, $E = 30 \times 10^6$ psi, I = moment of inertia (in^4), and Δ_x = deflection at point P (in), we may proceed as follows: Find the moment of inertia I of the shaft cross section (see properties of geometric sections, in the Index) from

$$I = \frac{\pi d^4}{64} = \frac{3.14(1.25)^4}{64} = \frac{7.666}{64} = 0.12 \text{ in}^4 \qquad \text{(moment of inertia)}$$

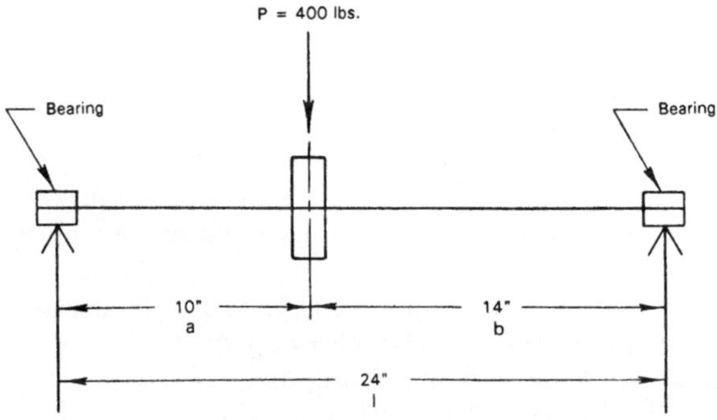

Figure 14.14 Loaded shaft.

From the preceding equation for bending of a uniform beam with a concentrated load,

$$\Delta_x = \frac{Pa^2b^2}{3EIl} = \frac{400(10)^2(14)^2}{3(30 \times 10^6)(0.12)(24)} = \frac{7{,}840{,}000}{2.592 \times 10^8} = 0.0302 \text{ in}$$

From this example, it can be seen that the deflection of the 1.25-in-diameter shaft will be 0.0302 in. For a gearing application, this deflection is unacceptable, and the shaft size would need to be increased in diameter or the support points moved closer together. Moving the support points or increasing the shaft size would require recalculation.

Bending stresses in shafts. To analyze the shaft system shown in Fig. 14.15, we begin by taking moments about R_1:

$$3000 \times 6 = R_2 \times 24$$

$$R_2 = \frac{3000 \times 6}{24} = 750\text{-lb reaction at } R_2$$

Taking moments about R_2,

$$R_1 \times 24 = 3000 \times 18$$

$$R_1 = \frac{3000 \times 18}{24} = 2250\text{-lb reaction at } R_1$$

The bending moment at a is

$$M_a = 750 \times 5 = 3750 \text{ lb} \cdot \text{in.}$$

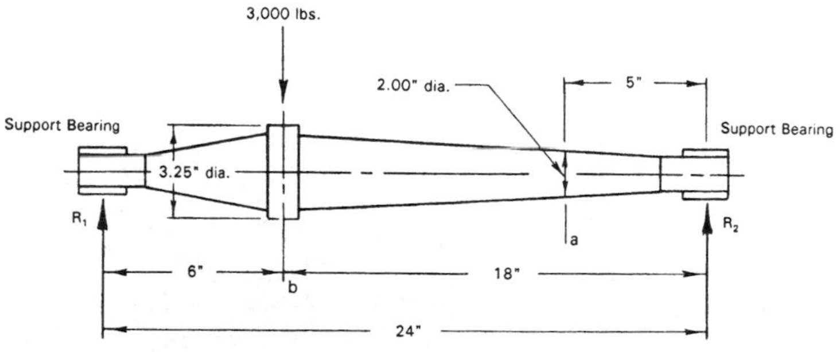

Figure 14.15 Shaft system.

The section modulus at a is

$$Z = 0.098d^3 = 0.098(2)^3 - 0.784 \text{ in}^3$$

The stress at point a is

$$S_a = \frac{M_a}{Z} = \frac{3{,}750}{0.784} = 4{,}783 \text{ psi}$$

Bending moment at b is

$$M_b = 2250 \times 6 = 13{,}500 \text{ lb} \cdot \text{in}$$

Section modulus at b is

$$Z = 0.098d^3 = 0.098(3.25)^3 = 3.364 \text{ in}^3$$

The stress at point b is

$$S_b = \frac{M_b}{Z} = \frac{13{,}500}{3.364} = 4013 \text{ psi}$$

Note that in this example,

$$S = \frac{M}{Z}$$

or

$$\text{Stress on the section at a given point} = \frac{\text{bending moment at the point}}{\text{section modulus of cross section at the point}}$$

Torsional stresses in shafts. Shaft torsional stress S_{ts} for a solid round shaft is given as

$$S_{ts} = \frac{\text{hp} \times 321{,}000}{\text{rpm} \times d^3}$$

Shaft diameter d_s for a solid shaft is given as

$$d_s = \sqrt[3]{\frac{\text{hp} \times 321{,}000}{\text{rpm} \times \text{allowable stress}}}$$

Shaft torsional stress S_{ts} for a tubular shaft is

$$S_{ts} = \frac{\text{hp} \times 321{,}000}{\text{rpm}(D^4 - d^4)}$$

where d = inside diameter. The outside diameter D when the inside diameter d is known is

$$D = \sqrt[3]{\frac{321{,}000 \times \text{hp}}{\text{rpm} \times S_a} + d^4}$$

where S_a = allowable stress

Torque, force, and horsepower relationships

$$F = \frac{M_t}{r} \qquad M_t = \frac{63{,}000 \times \text{hp}}{n} \qquad \text{hp} = \frac{M_t n}{63{,}000} \qquad n = \frac{63{,}000 \times \text{hp}}{M_t}$$

where hp = horsepower
n = rpm (revolutions per minute)
M_t = torque, lb · in
F = force, lb
r = radius, in

Critical speeds of shafts. The following equations for the critical speeds of rotating shafts are according to S. H. Weaver and apply to shafts with single concentrated loads and shafts carrying uniformly distributed loads with the shaft mounted horizontally or vertically. These equations apply to materials with a modulus of elasticity of 29×10^6, psi, which is normal for most steel shafting. A shaft carrying a number of loads or a distributed load can have an infinite number of critical speeds, but the *first critical speed* is of importance in designing shafts and is the speed obtained by using the equations given for the following shaft loading conditions.

Symbols for the following equations: d = diameter of shaft, in; W = load applied to shaft, lb; l = distance between centers of bearings, in; a and b = distances from bearings to load, in; N = critical speed, rpm; and N_1 = critical speed of shaft alone, rpm.

For single concentrated loads, use Figs. 14.16 through 14.21. For uniformly distributed loads, use Figs. 14.22 through 14.24.

$$N = 387{,}000\,\frac{d^2}{ab}\sqrt{\frac{l}{W}}\quad \text{(Fig. 14.16)}$$

$$N = 1{,}550{,}500\,\frac{d^2}{l\sqrt{Wl}}\quad \text{(Fig. 14.17)}$$

$$N = 387{,}000\,\frac{d^2}{ab}\sqrt{\frac{l}{Wab}}\quad \text{(Fig. 14.18)}$$

$$N = 3{,}100{,}850\,\frac{d^2}{l\sqrt{Wl}}\quad \text{(Fig. 14.19)}$$

$$N = 775{,}200\,\frac{d^2 l}{ab}\sqrt{\frac{l}{Wa(3l+b)}}\quad \text{(Fig. 14.20)}$$

$$N = 387{,}000\,\frac{d^2}{l\sqrt{Wl}}\quad \text{(Fig. 14.21)}$$

$$\left.\begin{aligned} N &= 2{,}232{,}500\,\frac{d^2}{l\sqrt{Wl}} \\ N_1 &= 4{,}760{,}000\,\frac{d}{l^2} \end{aligned}\right\}\quad \text{(Fig. 14.22)}$$

$$\left.\begin{aligned} N &= 4{,}979{,}250\,\frac{d^2}{l\sqrt{Wl}} \\ N_1 &= 10{,}616{,}740\,\frac{d}{l^2} \end{aligned}\right\}\quad \text{(Fig. 14.23)}$$

$$\left.\begin{aligned} N &= 795{,}200\,\frac{d^2}{l\sqrt{Wl}} \\ N_1 &= 1{,}695{,}500\,\frac{d}{l^2} \end{aligned}\right\}\quad \text{(Fig. 14.24)}$$

Shaft polar moment and polar section modulus. For shafting, polar moment of inertia I_p and polar section modulus Z_p are given in Fig. 14.25 for the illustrated shaft cross sections.

(Text continued on page 1116.)

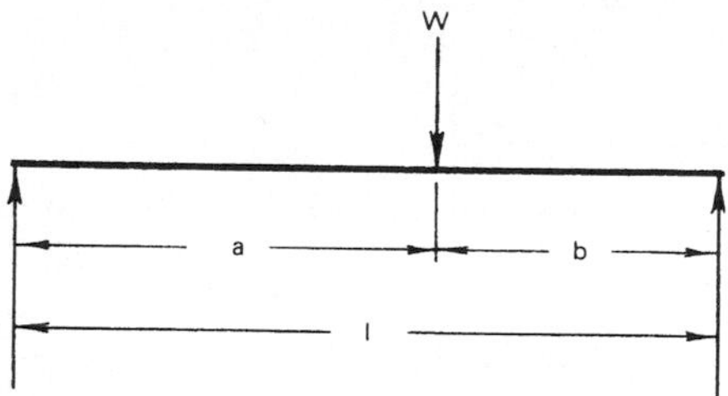

Figure 14.16 Single concentrated load.

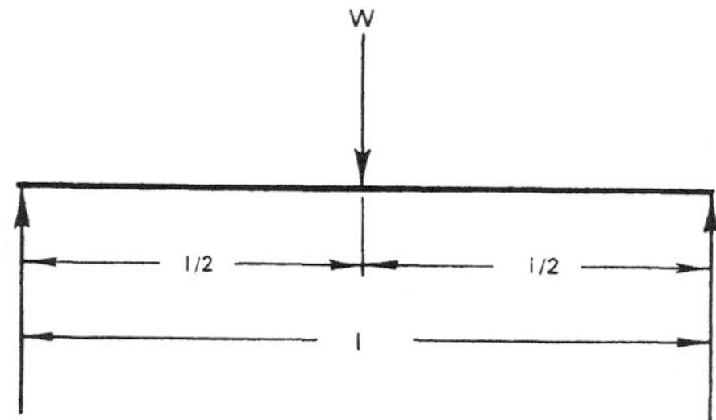

Figure 14.17 Single concentrated load at center.

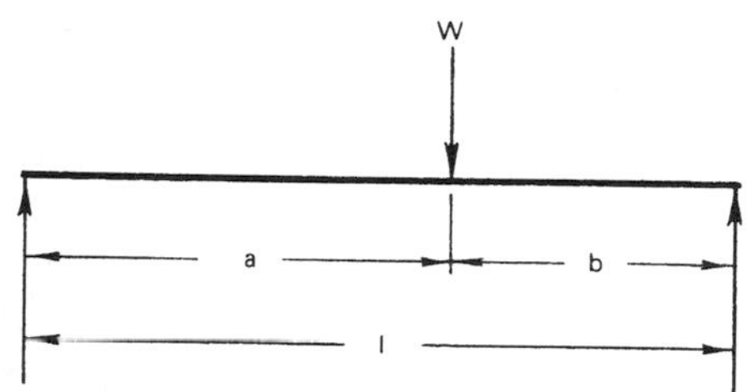

Figure 14.18 Single concentrated load, ends fixed.

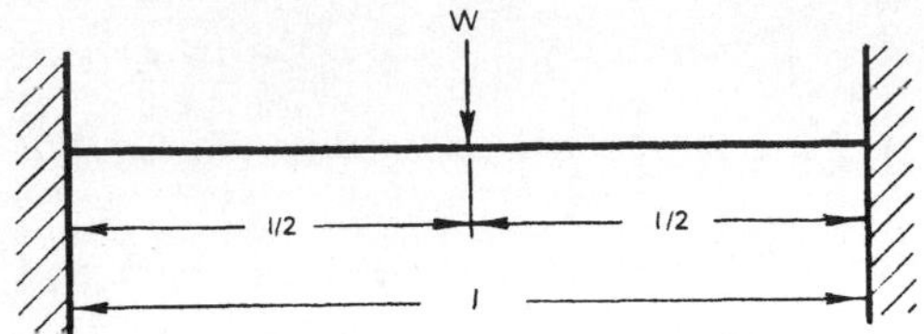

Figure 14.19 Single concentrated load at center, ends fixed.

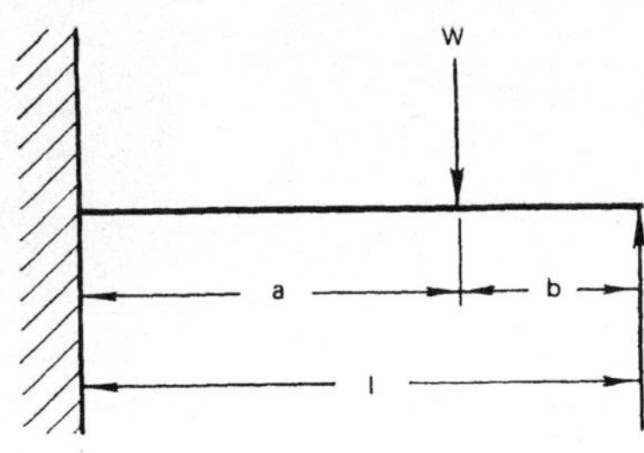

Figure 14.20 Cantilever load.

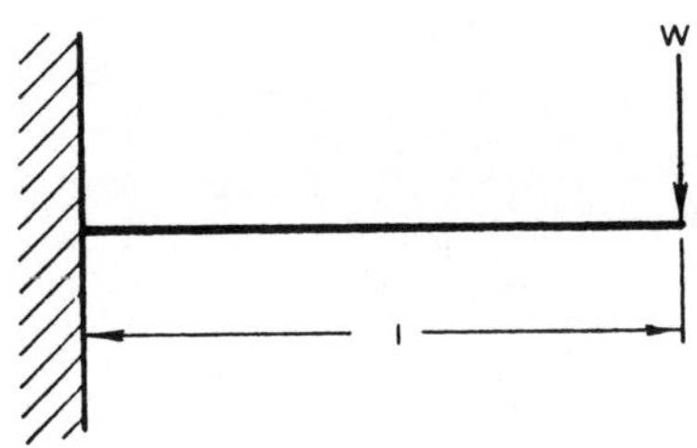

Figure 14.21 Cantilever load at end.

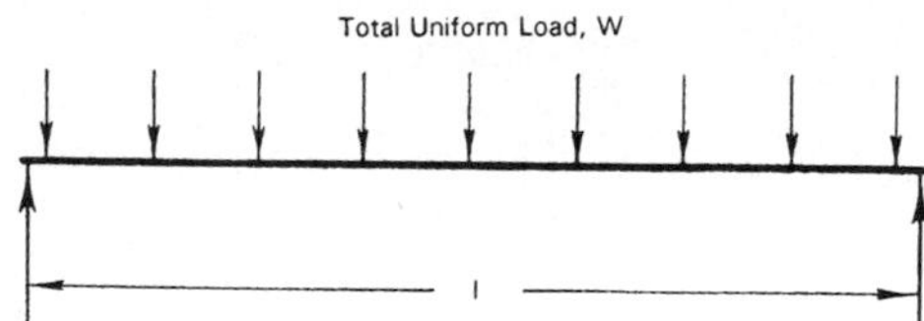

Figure 14.22 Uniform load.

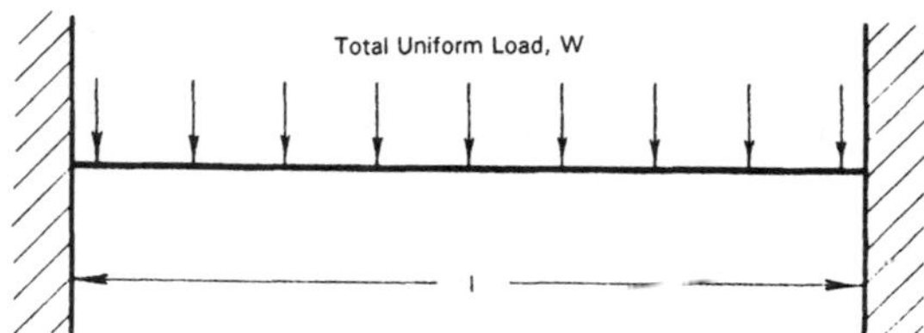

Figure 14.23 Uniform load, ends fixed.

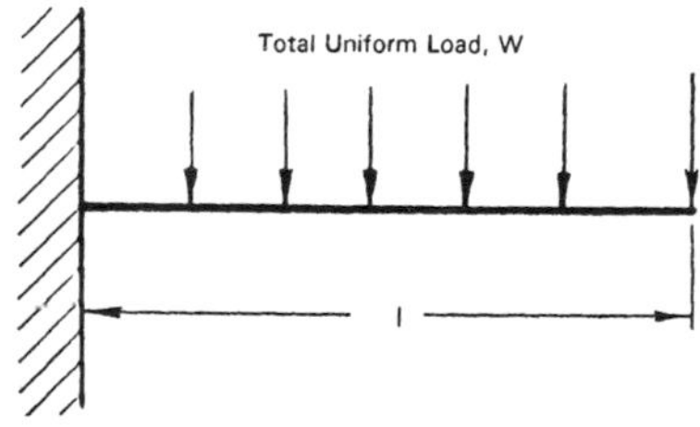

Figure 14.24 Uniform cantilever load.

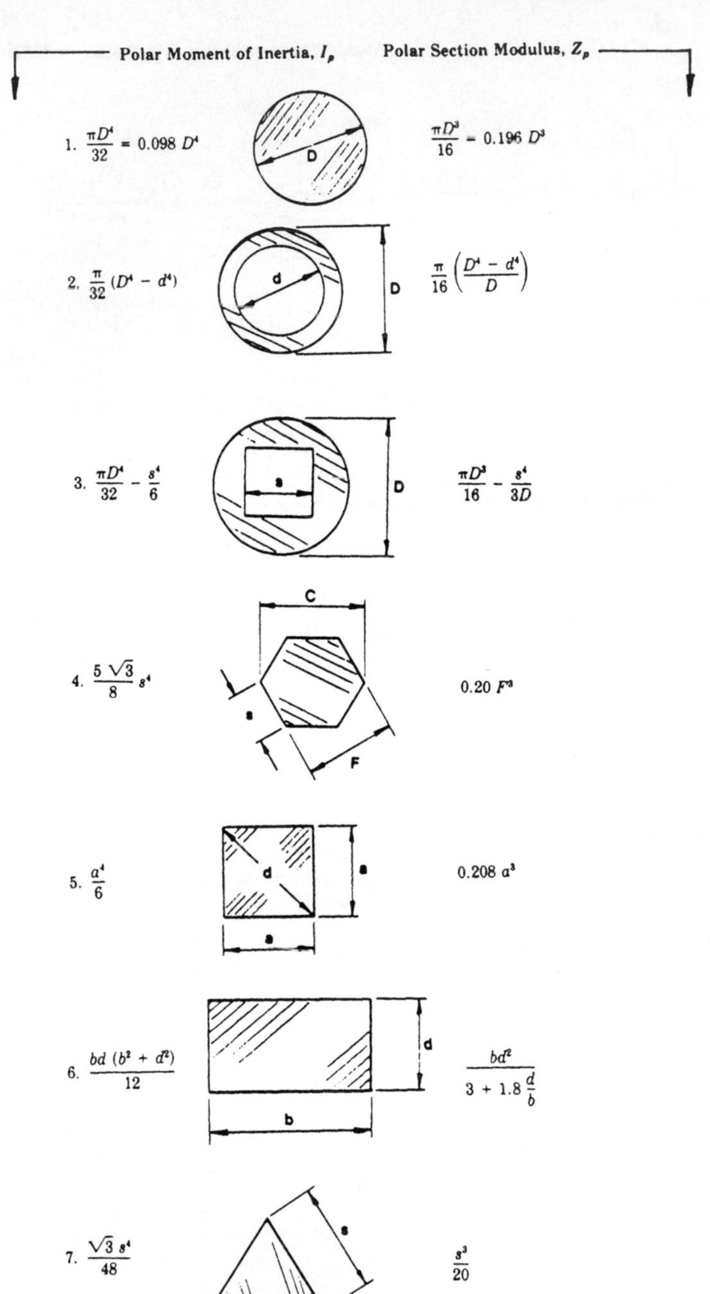

Polar Moment of Inertia, I_p
Polar Section Modulus, Z_p
1. $\frac{\pi D^4}{32} = 0.098\ D^4$
D
$\frac{\pi D^3}{16} = 0.196\ D^3$
2. $\frac{\pi}{32}(D^4 - d^4)$
d
D
$\frac{\pi}{16}\left(\frac{D^4 - d^4}{D}\right)$
3. $\frac{\pi D^4}{32} - \frac{s^4}{6}$
s
D
$\frac{\pi D^3}{16} - \frac{s^4}{3D}$
C
4. $\frac{5\sqrt{3}}{8}s^4$
s
F
$0.20\ F^3$
5. $\frac{a^4}{6}$
d
a
a
$0.208\ a^3$
6. $\frac{bd\,(b^2 + d^2)}{12}$
d
b
$\frac{bd^2}{3 + 1.8\frac{d}{b}}$
7. $\frac{\sqrt{3}\,s^4}{48}$
s
$\frac{s^3}{20}$

Figure 14.25 Polar moment of inertia and polar section modulus, various sections.

Diameter of hole, in	Standard Keyway W, in	Standard Keyway d, in	Setscrew size
5/16 to 7/16	3/32	3/64	#10–32
1/2 to 9/16	1/8	1/16	1/4–20
5/8 to 7/8	3/16	3/32	5/16–18
15/16 to 1 1/4	1/4	1/8	3/8–16
1 5/16 to 1 3/8	5/16	5/32	7/16–14
1 7/16 to 1 3/4	3/8	3/16	1/2–13
1 13/16 to 2 1/4	1/2	1/4	9/16–12
2 5/16 to 2 3/4	5/8	5/16	5/8–11
2 13/16 to 3 1/4	3/4	3/8	3/4–10
3 5/16 to 3 3/4	7/8	7/16	7/8–9
3 13/16 to 4 1/2	1	1/2	1–8
4 9/16 to 5 1/2	1 1/4	7/16	1 1/8–7
5 9/16 to 6 1/2	1 1/2	1/2	1 1/4–6

Figure 14.26 Standard keyways and set screws for shafts.

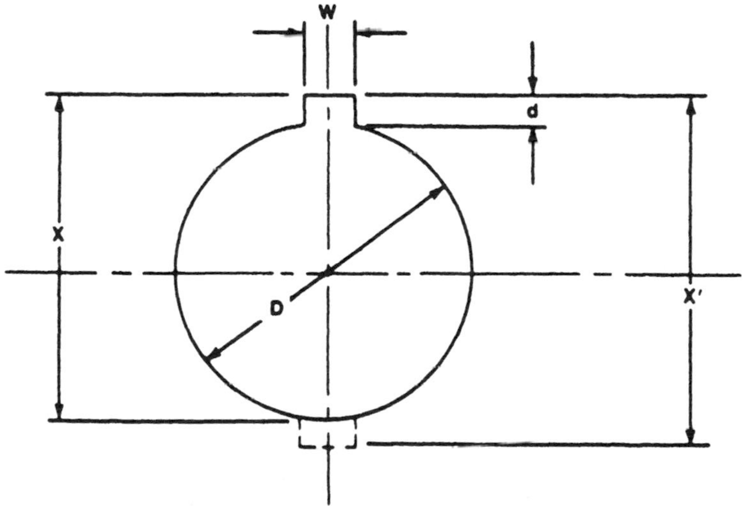

Figure 14.27 Keyways.

Standard keyways and set screws for shafts. Refer to Figs. 14.26 and 14.27. In Fig. 14.27, x and x' for the key slots are as follows:

$$x = \sqrt{\left(\frac{D}{2}\right)^2 - \left(\frac{W}{2}\right)^2} + d + \frac{D}{2}$$

$$x' = 2x - D$$

Keyway stress for nonmetallic gears. For phenolic laminated gears or pinions, the keyway stress S should not exceed 3000 psi, and

$$S = \frac{33{,}000 \times \text{hp}}{V \times A}$$

where S = unit stress, psi
hp = transmitted horsepower
V = surface speed of the shaft, ft/min
A = area of keyway (length × height), in^2

Shaft overhung loads. Refer to Fig. 14.28.

$$\text{Overhung load, lb} = \frac{(1.26 \times 10^5)\text{hp} \times F_c \times L_f}{\text{p.d.} \times \text{rpm}}$$

$$\text{Overhung load, N} = \frac{(1.91 \times 10^7)\text{kW} \times F_c \times L_f}{\text{p.d.} \times \text{rpm}}$$

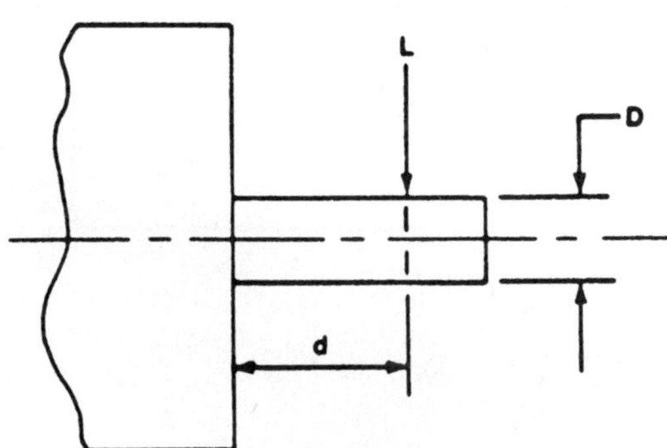

Figure 14.28 Overhung load.

where L_f = load location factor (for $d = D$, $L_f = 1$)
F_c = load connection factor (see chart below)
hp = horsepower
kW = kilowatts
rpm = revolutions per minute
p.d. = pitch diameter, in or mm

Values of F_c

Sprocket or timing belt	1.00
Machined pinion and gear	1.25
V-belt	1.50
V-ribbed belt	2.00
Flat belt	2.50

Shafting applications, materials, and heat treatment. Shafts fabricated from carbon and alloy steels may require case hardening or through hardening according to the application. Shafts that must fit standard-size bearings are normally purchased as "ground and polished shafting." This type of shafting always has a minimum tolerance on the basic diameter. Standard bearings are normally manufactured with a plus tolerance on their bore diameters. The condition of a minus tolerance on the shafting and a plus tolerance on the bearing bore ensures a clearance fit at assembly of the shaft into the bearing.

Note: If the shaft is plated, the plating thickness must be taken into consideration. Plating thicknesses on common shafting applications should not exceed 0.2 mil (0.0002 in). Also, the type of plating must be considered so that the bearing will not destroy the plating.

Some of the commonly used shafting stock materials are as follows:

Potomac & 1045 (UNS G10450)	Medium-carbon steel (direct hardening), flame and induction. Yield strength = 59,000 psi.
Cumsco & 1140 (UNS G11410)	Medium-carbon steel (direct hardening), flame and induction. Yield strength = 61,000 psi (good "as rolled" strength and toughness).
"Stressproof" & 1144 SRA-100	Medium-carbon steel (high manganese). Yield strength = 100,000 psi (does not require heat treatment).
1040 & 1042	Medium-carbon steel (direct hardening), flame and induction.

1144	Similar to 1141 except higher carbon and sulfur for improved machining and response to heat treatment. Used for induction hardening to Rockwell C55.
"Fatigue-proof"	High manganese, induction hardenable. Yield strength = 125,000 psi.

Note: For 1040, 1042, 1144, and "stress-proof" steels you may need tolerance specifications for shafting service when ordering.

Specialty steel shafting: E4130, E4140, and E4340 are aircraft alloy steels of high strength that are used for critical applications. See Chap. 5 for compositions and heat treatment procedures.

Hardness ranges: Shafting. The general hardness range for the previously listed carbon and alloy steel shafting is from Rockwell C40 through C58 depending on the specific steel, the hardness requirement of the application, and the ability of the heat treater to attain the required hardness with a minimum of distortion on the shaft. The shaft designer should consult the heat treater to arrive at a satisfactory solution. Small parts generally present no problems, but large parts and long shafts pose heat-treating problems. Flame and induction hardening of small areas or sections of long shafts running on far-spread bearings is a common practice. This method eliminates distortion caused by hardening the entire length of the shaft. The heat treater can eliminate distortion in shafts by "hanging" the shaft during the heat-treating process, but this practice is limited by the physical length of the shaft and the size of the heat treater's equipment.

Shafting materials such as "stress-proof" and "fatigue-proof" steels and 1144 SRA100 do not require heat treatment because they are severely "cold worked." Readily machinable with minimum distortion, these high-manganese steels attain yield strengths to 125,000 psi with a Brinell hardness range between 270 and 285 (Rockwell C30). Additional hardening may be attained through heat treatment (induction hardening). The type of antifriction bearing used in the shafting application will determine the extent of the hardening required. As stated previously, the hardness range for shafting may be from Rockwell C40 through C58. See hardness tables in Chap. 5.

14.4 Couplings

The common couplings used to connect driving machines such as electric motors and internal combustion engines or turbines to their drive shafts consist of the basic types listed here:

- Hooke's coupling (Cardan universal joint)
- Simple flanged couplings
- Sleeve couplings
- Flexible couplings

Hooke's coupling (Cardan universal joint). This common universal joint is used to connect two shafts whose axes are not in line but which intersect at a point. The typical universal joint is generally used at an angle α between 5° and 30° (see Fig. 14.29). The angular velocity of the driven shaft through a universal joint will not be the same as that of the *driving* shaft. That is, if the driving shaft has uniform motion, the *driven* shaft will *not*. The speed relationship is as follows:

$$\text{Minimum speed of driven shaft} = \text{driver shaft speed} \times \cos \alpha$$

$$\text{Maximum speed of driven shaft} = \text{driver shaft speed} \times \sec \alpha$$

Example If the driver shaft rotates at a constant speed of 250 rpm, and the shaft angle α is 23°, then the speed difference is 41.5 rpm.

This mechanical characteristic of the universal joint would be detrimental to many mechanisms and machine drives. The solution to this problem is to use two universal joints and an intermediate shaft. In this arrangement, two conditions must be met to achieve a constant speed ratio between the driver and the driven shafts:

1. The driver and driven shafts must be parallel.
2. The forks on the intermediate shaft must be arranged in the same plane as shown in Fig. 14.30. Figure 14.30*a* shows the *correct* connection of two typical universal joint systems, and Fig. 14.30*b* shows the *incorrect* connection.

Selection of a Cardan universal joint. The universal shaft torque can be calculated from

$$\text{Torque load, lb} \cdot \text{in} = \frac{63{,}025 \times \text{hp}}{\text{rpm}}$$

The equivalent *static load* equals the torque load times the speed angle factor. The universal joint is rated for static torque (lb-in).

After calculating the torque load of your application, check the universal joint factor from the manufacturer's catalog (e.g., Boston,

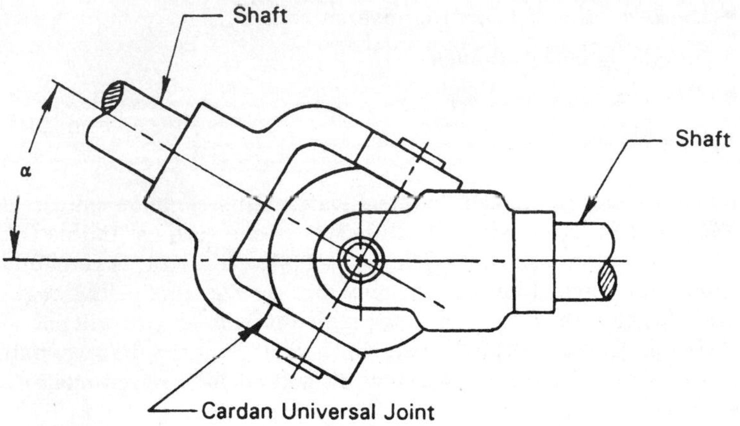

Figure 14.29 Universal (Cardan) joint.

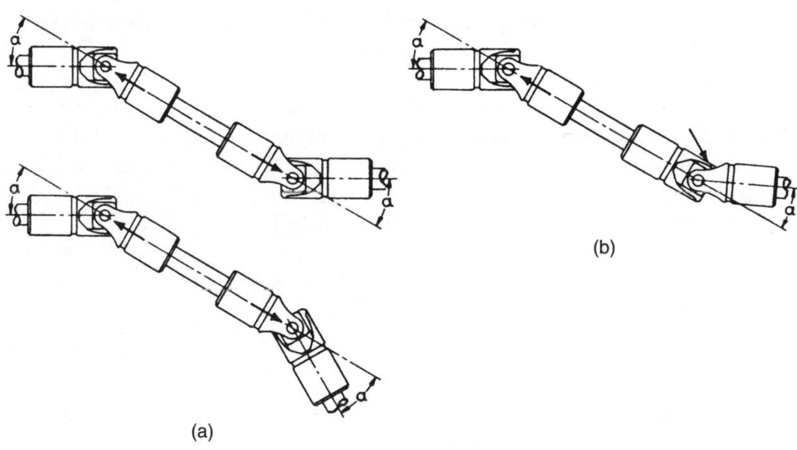

Figure 14.30 Universal joint connections: (*a*) correct; (*b*) incorrect.

etc.). Calculate the equivalent static load, and select a universal joint rated for this calculated load.

Sleeve couplings. Figure 14.31 shows a typical clamping-sleeve coupling which may be used to connect shafts of the same or different sizes according to the table shown in the figure. Larger sleeve couplings are available from different manufacturers.

Flanged and flexible couplings. Flange-type couplings are chosen for heavy machinery and high-torque loads. American shaft couplings are standardized to 10-in-diameter drive shafts, with flange diameters reaching 18 in.

Flexible couplings are generally used to connect electrical machinery. The flexible-insert coupling is popular for light- to medium-duty machinery and allows for shaft misalignment. The flexible-insert material may be rubber or various tough plastics such as urethane or acetal. Flexible couplings are applied using the manufacturer's installation instructions.

Types of flexible and flange couplings are shown in Fig. 14.32, while Fig. 14.33 shows the Falk type of flexible ribbon coupling. The Falk coupling is used in moderate- to heavy-load applications.

The basic factors a designer must evaluate when specifying a coupling are allowable shaft misalignment, torque rating, lubrication and maintenance, conditions of service, service life, and cost.

14.5 Clutches

The two types of clutches used commonly throughout industry are the *toothed* or *positive clutch* and the *friction clutch.* Positive clutches are connected by interlocking teeth of various forms, while friction clutches transmit power through frictional surfaces in the clutch. The positive-tooth clutch is normally spring "loaded," wherein the teeth disengage after a predetermined amount of torque is encountered. The friction clutch styles include disk, conical, and centrifugal shoe. Another form of friction clutch is the electromagnetic plate clutch, which has vast applications throughout industry.

Figure 14.34 shows some of the basic clutch types, such as one-way locking clutch, positive-toothed clutch, ball-detent clutch, and centrifugal-shoe clutch. Figure 14.35 shows a heavy-duty positive-toothed clutch, a cam clutch, and a typical friction-cone clutch. Figure 14.36 indicates the geometry of the friction-cone clutch, which is described in the following text. Figure 14.37 depicts a heavy-duty friction-disk clutch used to drive a pulley for flat belt power-

(Text continued on page 1128.)

DIMENSIONS			
BORE 'A' +002 -000	BORE 'B' +002 -000	O.D.	LENGTH
.250 .250	.1875 .250	5/8″	15/16″
.375 .375■	.250 .375■	7/8	1-3/8
.500 .500■	.375■ .500■	1-1/8	1-3/4
.625 .625 .625■	.375■ .500■ .625■	1-5/16	2
.750 .750 .750■	.500■ .625■ .750■	1-1/2	2-1/4
.875 .875 .875■	.625■ .750■ .875■	1-5/8	2-1/2
1.000 1.000 1.000 1.000■	.500■ .750■ .875■ 1.000■	1-3/4	3
1.125 1.125 1.125■	.875■ 1.000■ 1.125■	1-7/8	3-1/8
1.250 1.250 1.250 1.250■	.750■ 1.000■ 1.125■ 1.250■	2-1/16	3-1/4

STANDARD KEY WAYS

BORE	K'WAY
3/8″	3/32″
1/2	1/8
5/8	3/16
3/4	3/16
7/8	3/16
1	1/4
1-1/8	1/4
1-1/4	1/4

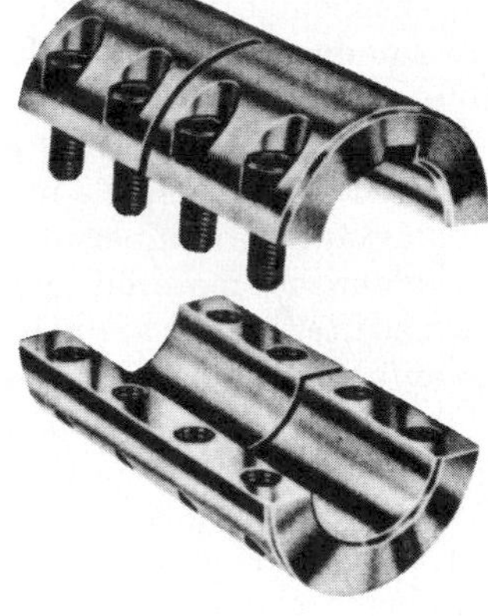

■ THESE BORES HAVE KEY WAYS

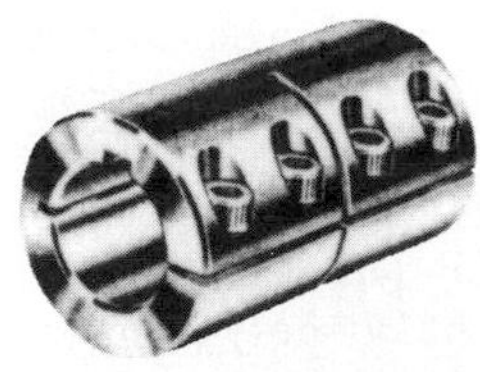

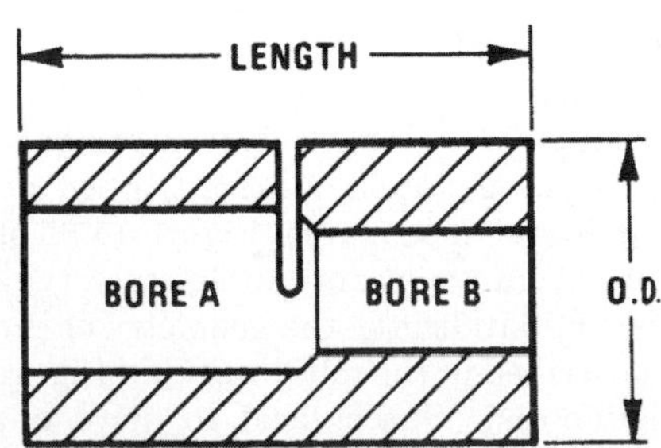

Figure 14.31 Typical clamping-sleeve coupling. *(Source: Ruland Company.)*

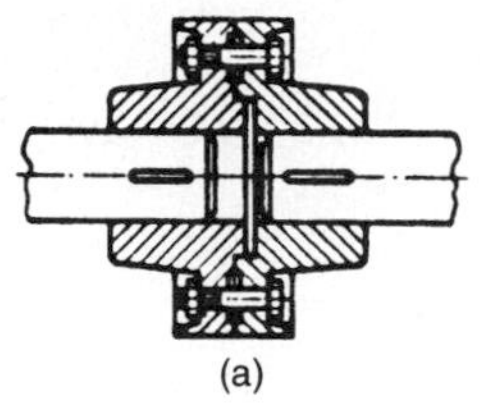
(a)

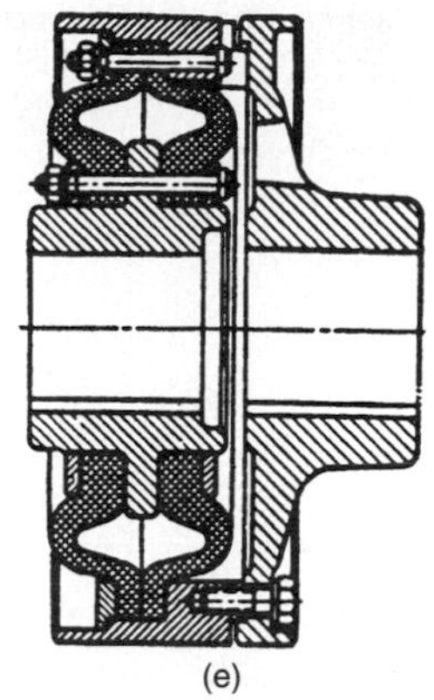
(e)

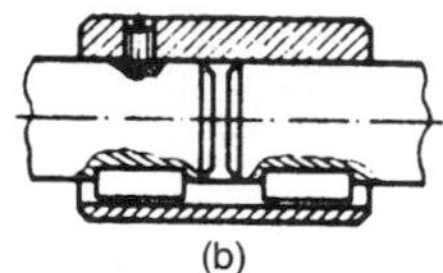
(b)

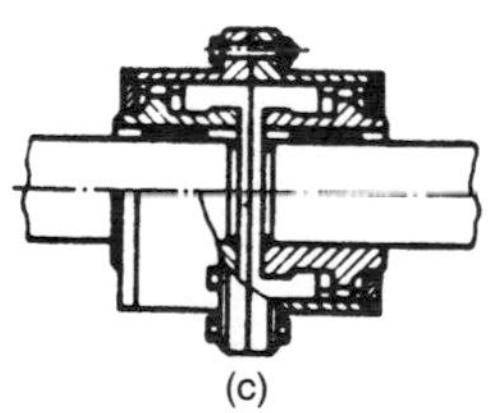
(c)

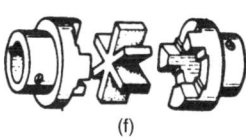

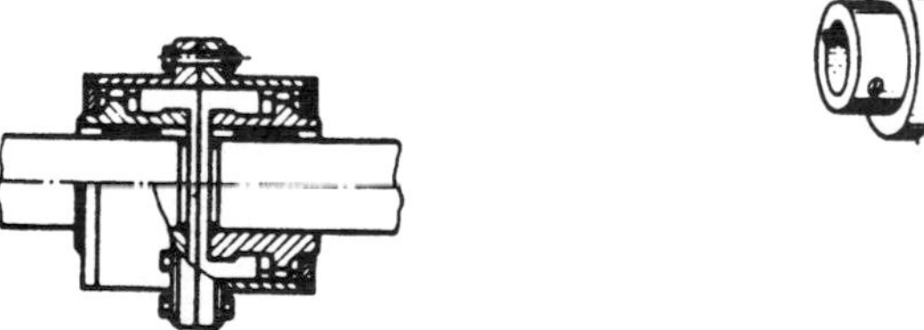
(f)

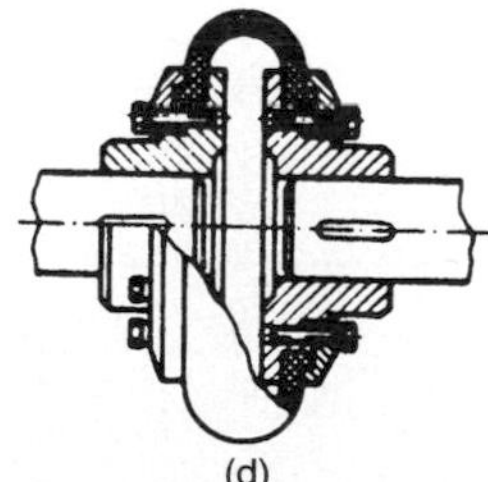
(d)

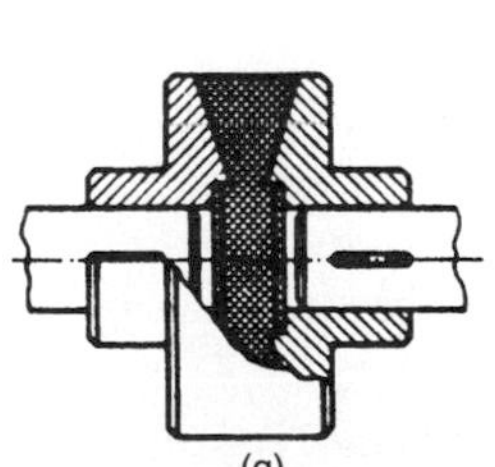
(g)

Figure 14.32 Types of flexible couplings.

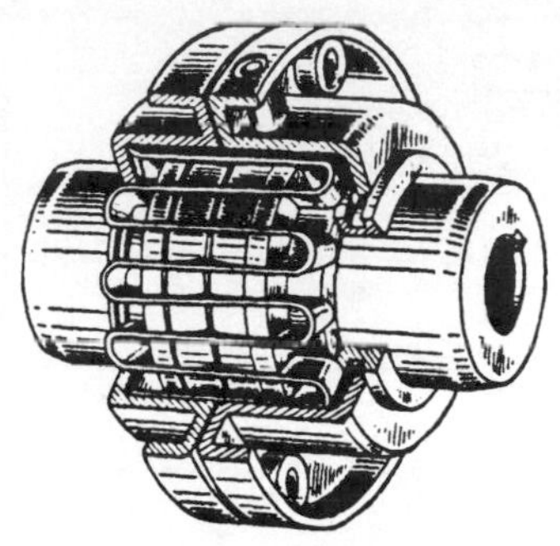

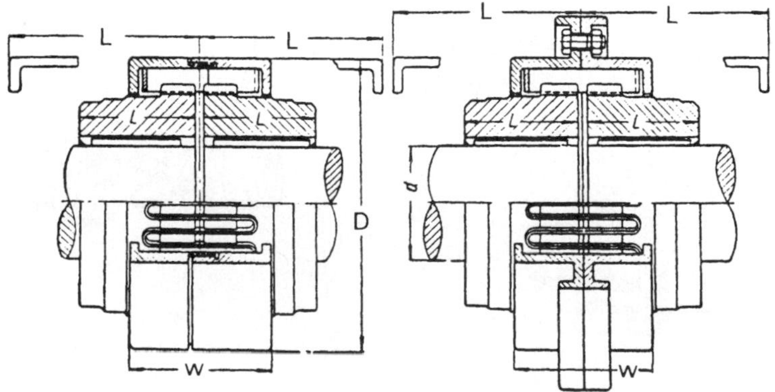

Figure 14.33 Falk-type flexible coupling.

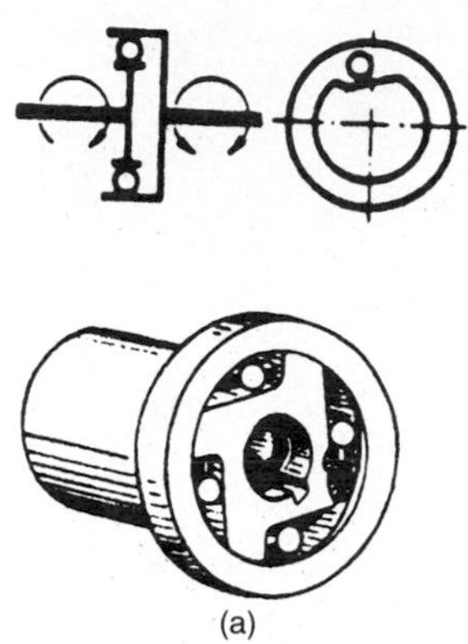
(a)

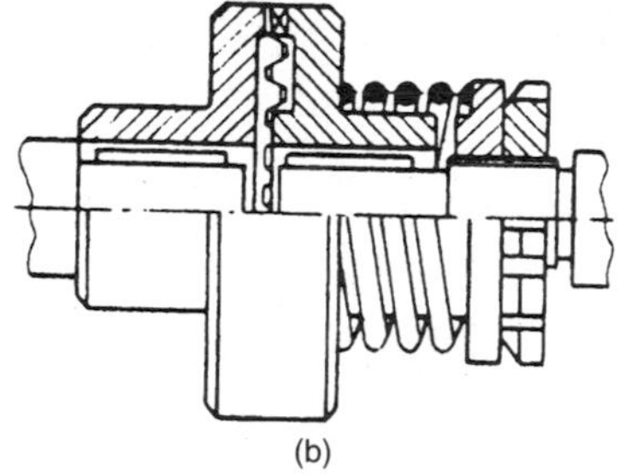
(b)

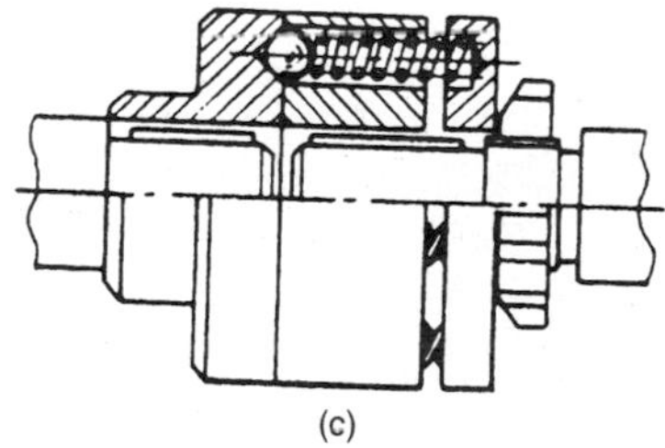
(c)

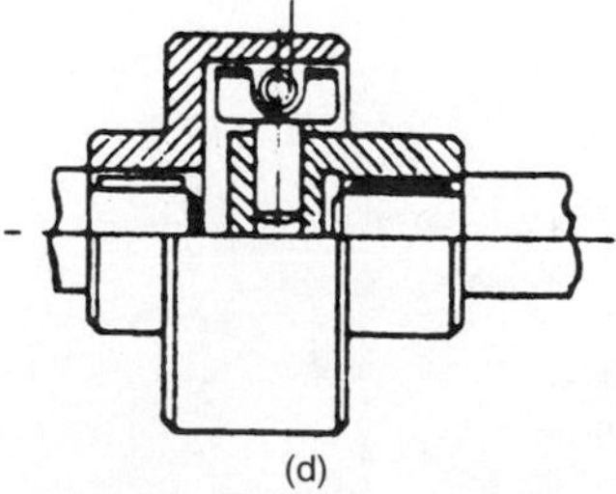
(d)

Figure 14.34 Types of clutches: (*a*) one-way locking clutch; (*b*) spring-detent clutch; (*c*) ball-detent clutch; (*d*) centrifugal friction clutch.

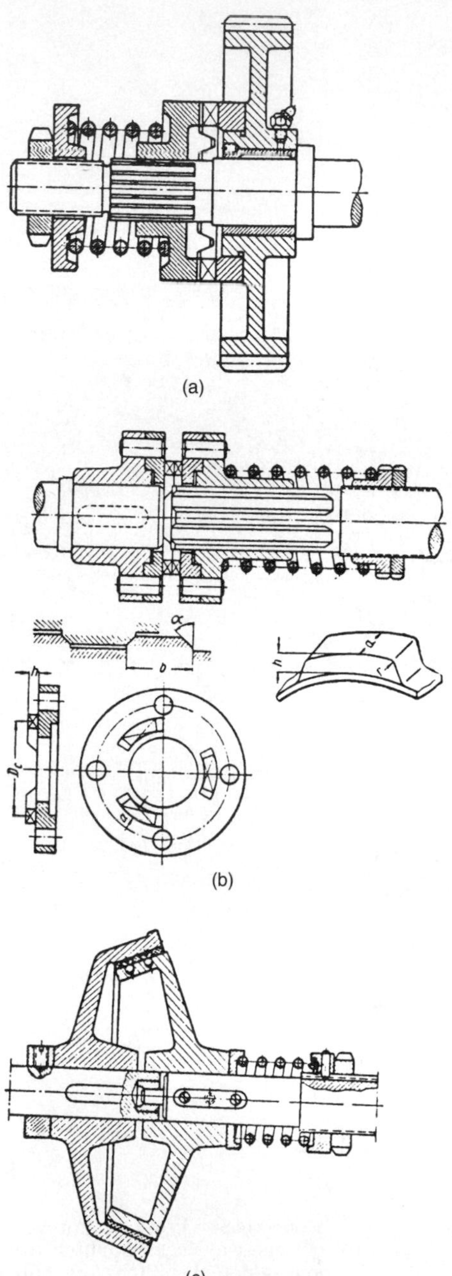

Figure 14.35 Heavy-duty clutches: (*a*) positive-tooth clutch; (*b*) cam clutch; (*c*) friction-cone clutch.

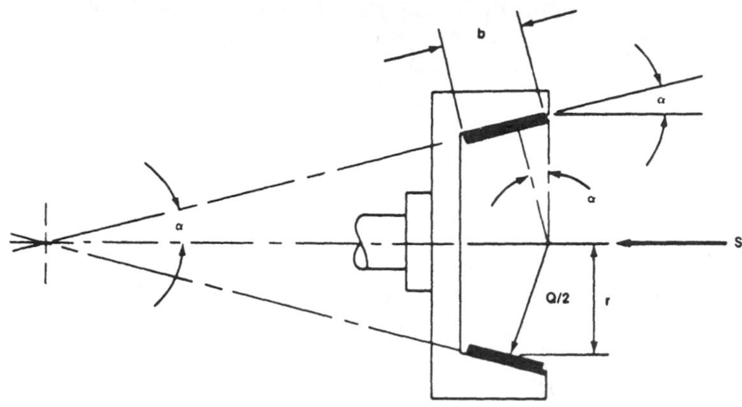

Figure 14.36 Geometry of the friction-cone clutch.

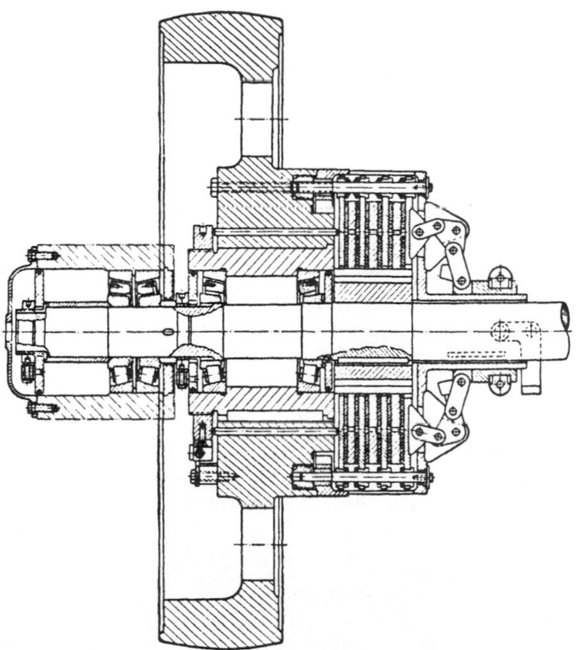

Figure 14.37 Heavy-duty friction-disk clutch.

transmission applications. All the aforementioned clutches are mechanical types. The application of friction-disk clutches is detailed in the text that follows.

Power transmitted by disk clutches. Referring to Fig. 14.37, we approximate

$$\text{hp} = \frac{\mu n R_m F S}{63{,}000}$$

where μ = coefficient of friction (static)
R_m = mean radius of engaged frictional surfaces, in
F = axial force holding the disks in contact, lb
n = number of frictional surfaces
and S = speed of drive shaft, rpm

Values for the coefficient of static friction μ are as follows:

Cork on metal, oiled	0.32
Cork on metal, dry	0.35
Metal on metal, dry	0.15
Disks, metal, oiled	0.10
Asbestos to steel, dry	0.45
Phenolic fiber to cast iron, dry	0.25
Cast iron on brass, dry	0.21

Slipping torque. Single-plate-clutch slipping torque T is given as

$$T,\ \text{lb} \cdot \text{in} = PR\mu n$$

$$T,\ \text{N} \cdot \text{m} = \frac{R\mu n}{1000}$$

And spring pressure or actuating force P is given as

$$P,\ \text{lb} = \frac{T}{R\mu n}$$

$$P,\ \text{N} = \frac{1000T}{R\mu n}$$

where T = torque capacity, lb·in or N·m
μ = coefficient of static friction
P = spring pressure or actuating force, lb or N
R = effective friction radius, in or mm
n = number of frictional surfaces

Proportions of disk linings. The average radius or effective frictional radius R is

$$R = \frac{d_o + d_i}{4}$$

where R = effective frictional radius, in or mm
d_o = outside diameter of disk lining, in or mm
d_i = inside diameter of disk lining, in or mm

Note: For any selected outside diameter, the torque capacity is maximized when $d_o/d_i = 1.73$ ratio.

Slipping torque capacities (plate clutches). The *slipping-torque capacity* of a friction-plate clutch is the amount of torque the clutch is capable of transmitting when the clutch is just in the process of slipping. In order to prevent slipping in service, a factor of safety or multiplier must be applied to the slipping-torque capacity of the clutch. This factor or multiplier should be kept from 1.40 to 1.60 above the maximum torque of the driving element or motor supplying torque through the clutch.

Example If you wish to transmit 2500 lb · in of torque through the clutch, the clutch should be designed so that its slipping-torque capacity is approximately $1.50 \times 2500 = 3750$ lb·in. Use the preceding equations to do the simple calculations.

Spring pressure or actuating force. The clutch spring pressure or actuating force should be applied so that the pressure on the clutch disk material is kept at 20 to 35 psi when the clutch is engaged (automotive-type clutches). For allowable pressures of other clutch materials, see the table in Fig. 14.38.

Cone clutches. Refer to Figs. 14.35*c* and 14.36. When the horsepower to be transmitted and the revolutions per minute of the shaft are given,

$$M_t = \frac{63{,}025\text{hp}}{n}$$

Clutch materials	Allowable Pressure	
	psi	MPa
Steel to steel	99	0.68
Steel to cork	*7.25 to 14.5	*0.05 to 0.10
Phenolic to steel or cast iron	99	0.68
Carbon-graphite to steel	297	2.05

*Low figure, wet; high figure, dry.

Figure 14.38 Allowable pressures on clutch materials.

$$P = \frac{M_t}{r}$$

$$S = \frac{\sin \alpha + \mu \cos \alpha}{\mu}$$

$$\rho = \frac{Q}{b2\pi r} \qquad \text{and} \qquad b = \frac{Q}{\rho 2\pi r}$$

Values of ρ are taken to be 7 to 10 psi for leather-equivalent to steel, 3 to 5 psi for cork to steel, and 50 to 60 psi for steel to steel.

In the equations, M_t = torque of shaft, lb·in; hp = horsepower; n = rpm of shaft; S = spring pressure or axial force, lb; r = mean radius of cone, in; μ = coefficient of static friction; Q = total force normal to conical surface, lb; b = width of cone section, in; P = tangential force at rim of cone, lb; α = half cone angle, degrees; and ρ = pressure normal to cone surface, psi. (For other types of clutches, see Figs. 14.34 and 14.35.)

Note: 1 Pa = 0.0001450337 psi and 0.68 MPa = $(0.68 \times 10^6) \times$ 0.0001450377 = 99 psi.

Electromagnetic clutches. The electromagnetic clutch has a vast number of applications in industry. These types of clutches are manufactured in many different sizes and torque ratings. Figure 14.39 shows an exploded view of a small electromagnetic clutch. These clutches also are available in different operating voltage ranges. Although the small clutch shown in Fig. 14.39 is rated for 280 lb·in of torque at 90 V dc, it may be used to disconnect a large load by placing the clutch between the drive motor and the output gearbox when the gearbox has a high reduction ratio. If the gearbox has a reduction ratio of 8:1, the clutch will drive a load whose torque value is $8 \times 280 = 2240$ lb·in.

The electromagnetic clutch catalogs show the sizes, ratings, and dimensions of the various clutches available. These catalogs also contain magnetic brakes which are similar to electromagnetic clutches, except that the design calculations required to select the proper size for a particular application are different. In the design of magnetic brakes, heat energy and dissipation factors are taken into consideration.

14.6 Power Screws

Power screws with square threads, acme threads, and V threads have many uses in a large number of mechanical applications. Power screws used to lift a load vertically are termed *jack-screws.* Figure 14.40 shows the basic types of thread forms used in power screws. In the figure, l = lead of the thread, C = half angle between V-thread faces (degrees), and r = mean radius of the thread.

Turning force (torque) and resulting loads on power or jack-screws may be calculated from the following equations. For motion in the direction of the load L, assisted by the load (i.e., lowering a raised jack or unclamping a load),

$$F = L\frac{2\pi\mu r - l}{2\pi r + \mu l}\left(\frac{r}{R}\right)$$

For motion opposite the load L (i.e., raising a jack or clamping a load),

$$F = L\frac{2\pi\mu r + l}{2\pi r - \mu l}\left(\frac{r}{R}\right)$$

where F = force at end of handle or lever arm
R = lever arm of F, in
r = pitch radius of screw (see screw thread sections of this *Handbook*), in
l = lead of thread = $1/n$ when n is the number of threads per inch, in
L = load, lb
μ = coefficient of friction (dynamic)

Figure 14.41 lists coefficients of dynamic friction at various pressures for various material combinations. Note that the values for

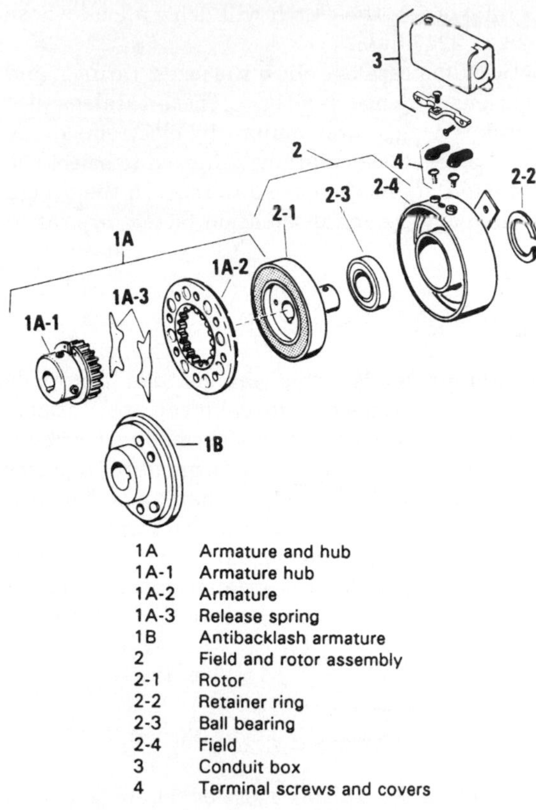

Figure 14.39 Electromagnetic clutch parts.

the coefficients of dynamic or static friction are general in nature due to the following:

- Surface condition (rms value)
- Temperature
- Pressure between faying surfaces
- Type of lubricant
- Surface hardness
- Metallic plating (if present)

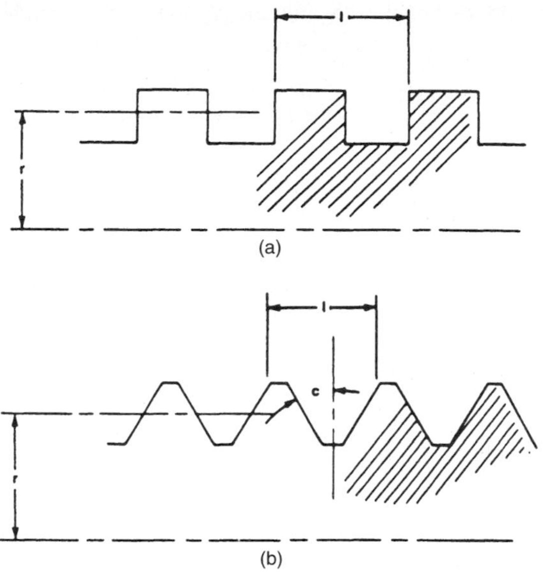

Figure 14.40 Power screw thread forms: (*a*) square; (*b*) Acme or V thread.

Pressure Lb/in^2	Cast iron / Wrought iron	Steel / Cast iron	Brass / Cast iron
125	0.17	0.17	0.16
225	0.29	0.33	0.22
300	0.33	0.34	0.21
400	0.36	0.35	0.21
500	0.37	0.36	0.22
700	0.43	Seized	0.23
785	Seized	—	0.23
825	—	—	0.27

Surfaces lightly lubricated, Rennie.

Figure 14.41 Coefficients of friction, dynamic.

Various tests may be conducted by the designer to arrive at more meaningful values for these coefficients for critical applications.

The preceding power screw equations are greatly simplified and will give approximate results with a minimum amount of calculation. The following equations are more precise, being written for the specific type of thread form indicated.

Power screw loads and efficiencies for square, V, and Acme threads. For square threads,

$$P = L\tan(b+a) = L\frac{l+2\pi rf}{2\pi r - lf} \qquad \text{(for motion opposed to load)}$$

$$\text{Efficiency } e = \frac{\tan b}{\tan(b+a)} \qquad \text{(for motion opposed to load)}$$

$$P = L\tan(b-a) = L\frac{l-2\pi rf}{2\pi r + lf} \qquad \text{(for motion assisted by load)}$$

$$\text{Efficiency } e = \frac{\tan(b-a)}{\tan b} \qquad \text{(for motion assisted by load)}$$

For V and Acme threads,

$$P = L\frac{l+2\pi rf\sec C}{2\pi r - lf\sec C} \qquad \text{(for motion opposed to load)}$$

$$\text{Efficiency } e = \frac{\tan b(1 - f\tan b\sec C)}{(\tan b + f\sec C)} \qquad \text{(for motion opposed to load)}$$

$$P = L\frac{l-2\pi rf\sec C}{2\pi r + lf\sec C} \qquad \text{(for motion assisted by load)}$$

$$\text{Efficiency } e = \frac{(\tan b - f\sec C)}{\tan b\,(1 + f\tan b\sec C)} \qquad \text{(for motion assisted by load)}$$

In the preceding equations for square, V, and Acme threads,

a = friction angle ($\tan a = f$), degrees
f = coefficient of friction, dynamic
l = lead or thread advance in one revolution, in
b = lead angle ($\tan b = l/2\pi r$), degrees
r = mean radius of thread = ½(root radius + outside radius), in
P = equivalent driving force at radius r from screw axis, lb
L = axial load, lb
e = efficiency
C = half angle between V and Acme thread faces, degrees

The coefficients of dynamic friction f have different values at different surface pressures (see Fig. 14.41).

Note: The screw equations shown in the preceding section may be used to calculate the tightening torque required on bolts when the clamp-load objective is specified or determined by the designer.

Figure 14.42 shows a typical application for a power screw. This power screw assembly is used on certain types of milling machines to control backlash when the table feed screw rotates.

Load capabilities of power screws. After the initial stages of power screw design shown in the preceding equations, the power screw system must be checked to see if it will carry the design load for the application. The following simple equations are used, together with the preceding equations, to finalize the design. Or you may wish to use the following equations to help establish the basic thread size and diameter before using the preceding equations. In any case, repeated calculations may be required before the final power screw system is completed.

Bending stress S_b at the thread mean root radius is given as

$$S_b \approx \frac{3Wh}{2\pi n r_m b^2}, \text{ psi} \qquad \text{and} \qquad S_{bf} = S_b \times \text{f.s.}$$

Mean transverse shear stress is given as

$$S_s = \frac{W}{2\pi n r_m b}, \text{ psi} \qquad \text{and} \qquad S_{sf} = S_s \times \text{f.s.}$$

where n = number of thread turns subject to load (thread engagement)
b = width of thread section at root, in
r_m = mean thread radius, in
W = load parallel to screw axis, lb
h = height of thread, in
f.s. = factor of safety—1.25 to 1.35.

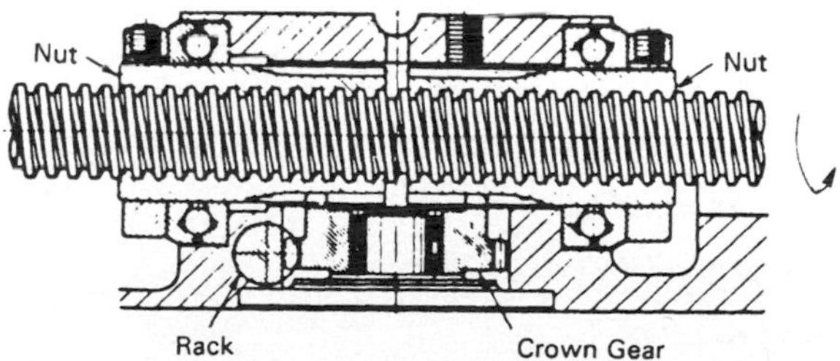

Figure 14.42 Application of a power screw.

Note: In these equations, multiply S_b and S_s by the factor of safety range of 1.25 to 1.35 to arrive at final stress levels, S_{bf} and S_{sf}.

Surface bearing pressure. The pressure P between surfaces of the screw and nut threads is a *critical* design factor in power screws and is given approximately by

$$P = \frac{W}{2\pi n r_m h}, \text{ psi} \qquad \text{(see Fig. 14.43)}$$

Since this simple equation gives an estimate of a pressure that is lower than the actual value, a factor of safety must be applied, such as

$$P_f = P \times \text{f.s.}$$

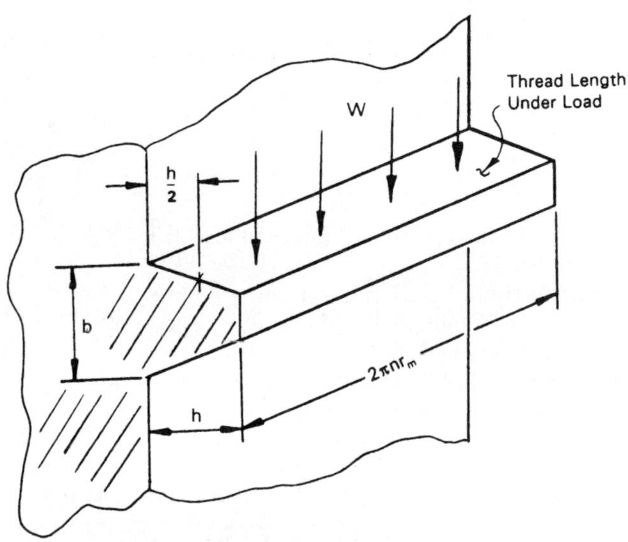

Figure 14.43 Power screw thread geometry.

where P_f = final pressure between surfaces, psi
P = approximate pressure from the equation shown
f.s. = 1.25 to 1.35 (factor of safety)

The allowable stresses (tensile and shear) for various materials are shown in Chap. 5, "Materials and Their Uses." As a rule-of-thumb practice, the shear stress of many metals and alloys is taken as 40 percent of the value of the maximum allowable tensile strengths. This rule is appropriate for most ferrous metals and alloys (irons and steels).

14.7 Ratchets and Ratchet Gearing

A *ratchet* is a form of gear in which the teeth are cut for one-way operation or to transmit intermittent motion. The ratchet wheel is used widely in machinery and many mechanisms. Ratchet-wheel teeth can be either on the perimeter of a disk or on the inner edge of a ring.

The *pawl,* which engages the ratchet teeth, is a beam member pivoted at one end, the other end being shaped to fit the ratchet-tooth flank.

Ratchet gear design. In the design of ratchet gearing, the teeth must be designed so that the pawl will remain in engagement under ratchet-wheel loading. In ratchet gear systems, the pawl will either push the ratchet wheel or the ratchet wheel will push on the pawl and/or the pawl will pull the ratchet wheel or the ratchet wheel will pull on the pawl. See Fig. 14.44 for the four variations of ratchet and pawl action. In the figure, F indicates the origin and direction of the force and R indicates the reaction direction.

Tooth geometry for case I in Fig. 14.44*a* is shown in Fig. 14.45. A line perpendicular to the face of the ratchet-wheel tooth must pass between the center of the ratchet wheel and the center of the pawl pivot point.

Tooth geometry for case II in Fig. 14.44*b* is shown in Fig. 14.46. A line perpendicular to the face of the ratchet-wheel tooth must fall outside the pivot center of the pawl and the ratchet wheel.

Spring loading the pawl is usually employed to maintain constant contact between the ratchet wheel and pawl (gravity or weight on the pawl is also sometimes used). The pawl should be pulled automatically in and kept in engagement with the ratchet wheel, independent of the spring or weight loading imposed on the pawl.

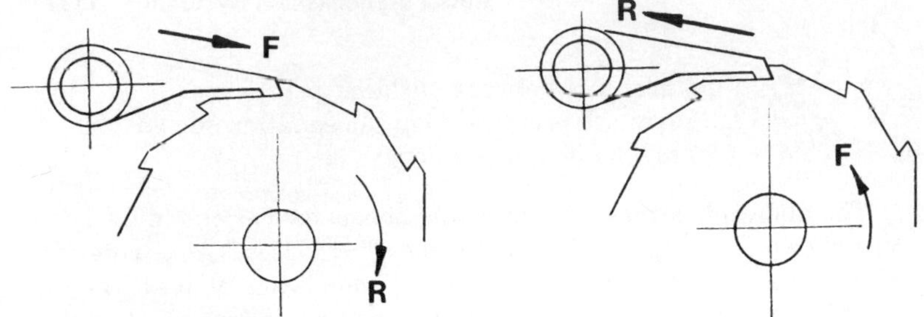

Figure 14.44 (*a*) Variation of ratchet and pawl action (F = force; R = reaction).

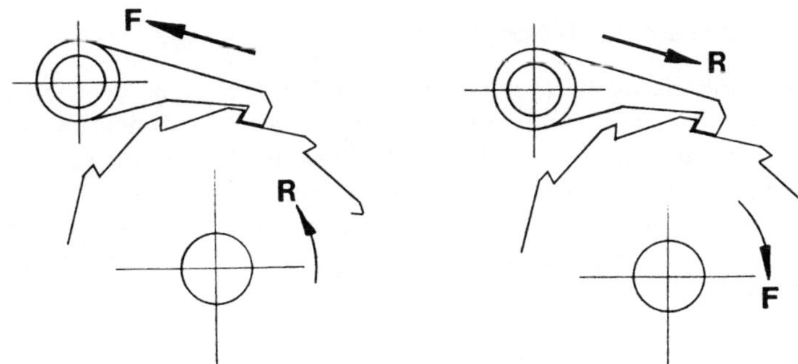

Figure 14.44 (*b*) Variation of ratchet and pawl action (F = force; R = reaction).

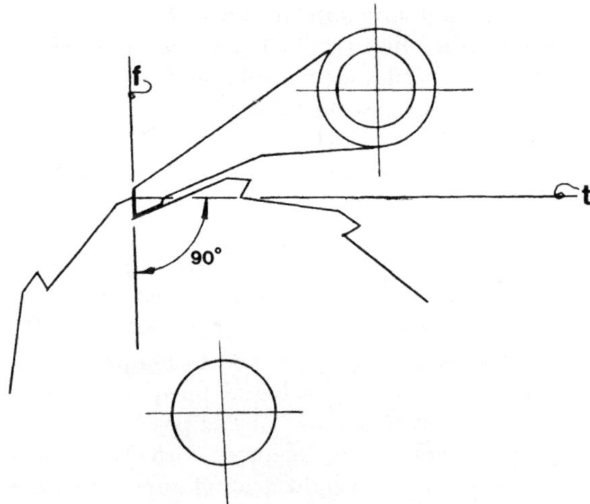

Figure 14.45 Tooth geometry for case I.

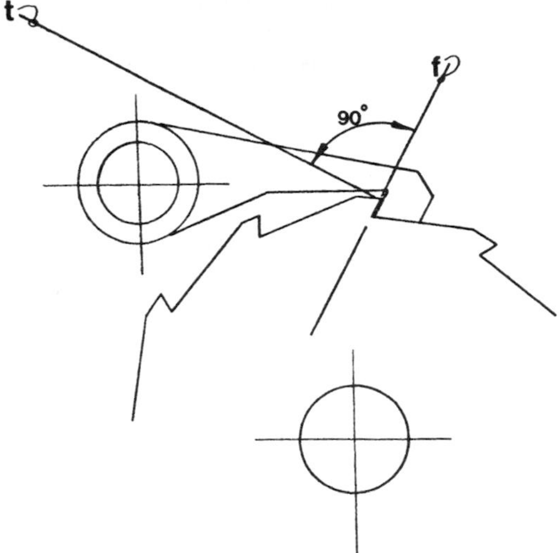

Figure 14.46 Tooth geometry for case II.

Methods for laying out ratchet gear systems

Type I: External-teeth ratchet wheels (see Fig. 14.47)

1. Determine the pitch, tooth size, and radius R to meet the strength and mechanical requirements of the ratchet gear system (see: "Calculating the Pitch and Face of Ratchet-Wheel Teeth," below).

2. Select the position points O, O_1, and A so that they all fall on a circle C with angle OAO_1 equal to 90°.

3. Determine angle ϕ through the relationship $\tan \phi = r/c =$ a value greater than the coefficient of static friction of the ratchet wheel and pawl material—0.25 is sufficient for standard low- to medium-carbon steel. Or $r/R = 0.25$, since the sine and tangent of angle ϕ are close for angles from 0 to 30°.

Note: The value c is determined by the required ratchet wheel geometry; therefore, you must solve for r, so

$$r = c \tan \phi \qquad \text{or} \qquad r = R \tan \phi$$

$$= c(0.25) \qquad\qquad = R(0.25)$$

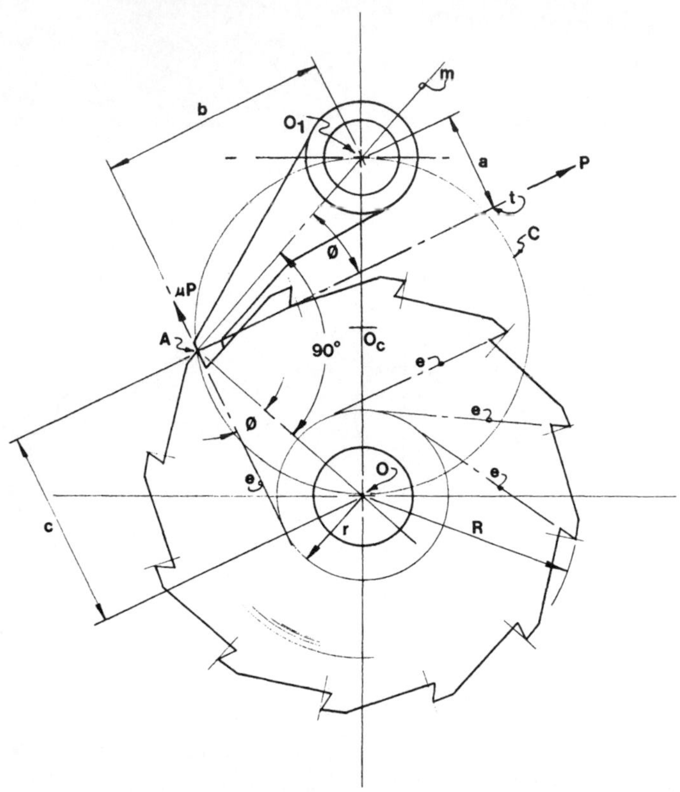

Figure 14.47 Ratchet wheel geometry, external teeth.

4. Angle ϕ is also equal to arctan (a/b), and to keep the pawl as small as practical, the center pivot point of the pawl O_1 may be moved along line t toward point A to satisfy space requirements.

5. The pawl is then self-engaging. This follows the principle stated earlier that a line perpendicular to the tooth face must fall *between* the centers of the ratchet wheel and pawl pivot points.

Type II: Internal-teeth ratchet wheels (see Fig. 14.48)

1. Determine the pitch, tooth size, and radii R and R_1 to meet the strength and mechanical requirements of the ratchet gear system. For simplicity, let points O and O_1 be on the same centerline.

2. Select r so that $f/g \geq 0.20$.

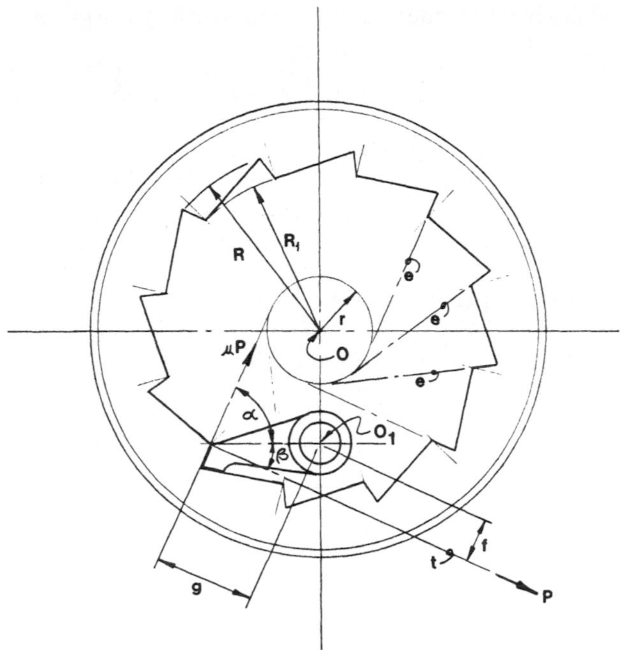

Figure 14.48 Ratchet wheel geometry, internal teeth.

3. A convenient angle for β is 30°, and $\tan \beta = f/g = 0.557$, which is greater than the coefficient of static friction for steel (0.15). This makes angle $\alpha = 60°$ because $\alpha + \beta = 90°$.

Note: Locations of tooth faces are generated by element lines *e*. For self-engagement of the pawl, note that a line *t* perpendicular to the tooth face must fall outside the pawl pivot point O_1.

Calculating the pitch and face of ratchet-wheel teeth. The following equation may be used in calculating the pitch or the length of the tooth face (thickness of ratchet wheel) and is applicable to most general ratchet-wheel designs. Note that selection of the values for S_s (safe stress, psi) may be made more or less conservatively, according to the requirements of the application. Low values for S_s are selected for applications involving safety conditions. Note also that the shock stress allowable levels (psi) are 10 times less than for normal loading applications, where a safety factor is not a consideration.

The general pitch design equation and transpositions are given as

$$P = \sqrt{\frac{\alpha m}{l S_s N}} \qquad P^2 = \frac{\alpha m}{l S_s N} \qquad N = \frac{\alpha m}{l S_s P^2} \qquad l = \frac{\alpha m}{N S_s P^2}$$

where P = circular pitch measured at the outside circumference, in
m = turning moment (torque) at ratchet-wheel shaft, lb · in
l = length of tooth face, thickness of ratchet-wheel, in
S_s = safe stress (steel C-1018; 4000 psi shock and 25,000 psi static)
N = number of teeth in ratchet wheel
α = coefficient: 50 for 12 teeth or less, 35 for 13 to 20 teeth, and 20 for more than 20 teeth

For other materials such as brass, bronze, stainless steel, zinc castings, etc., the S_s rating may be proportioned to the values given for C-1018 steel.

Chapter

15

Mechanisms and Linkages

The mechanisms and linkages discussed in this chapter have many applications for the product designer, tool engineer, and others involved in the design and manufacture of machinery, tooling, and mechanical devices and assemblies used in the industrial context. These mechanisms have been selected from a large assortment as the more important, most commonly used types for a wide variety of applications. A number of important mechanical linkages are shown in Sec. 15.2, together with the mathematical calculations that govern their operation.

15.1 Mechanisms

When you study the operating principles of these devices, you will be able to see the relationships they have with the basic simple machines such as the lever, wheel and axle, inclined plane or wedge, gear wheel, and so forth. There are six basic simple machines from which all machines and mechanisms may be constructed either singly or in combination, not including the Rolomite mechanism. The hydraulic cylinder and gear wheel are also considered members of the basic simple machines.

Shown in Fig. 9.49 in Chap. 9 of this *Handbook* are other mechanisms which are used for tool-clamping purposes. Also, Sect. 10.17 in Chap. 10 shows many of the basic gear devices that have a multitude of uses in machine and product design practice.

A number of practical mechanisms are shown in Figs. 15.1 through 15.43, together with explanations of their operation.

15.1.1 Space mechanisms

There are potentially hundreds of space mechanisms, but only a few important types have been developed to date. A listing of the classification of all the kinematically possible pairs (joints) is shown in Fig. 15.44. Many modern industrial products utilize space mechanisms of one type or another to perform functions and to operate in spaces that would be difficult using standard mechanisms. Figure 15.45 illustrates the nine most practical four-bar space mechanisms. These nine four-bar space mechanisms have superior practicability because they contain only those joints which have area contact and are self-connecting. All these mechanisms can produce rotary or sliding output motion from a rotary input, the most common mechanical requirement for which linkage mechanisms are designed.

The type letters of the kinematic pairs shown in Fig. 15.45 are used to identify the mechanism by ordering the letter symbols consecutively around the closed kinematic chain. The first letter identifies the pair or joint connecting the input link and the fixed link; the last letter identifies the output link. Thus a mechanism labeled R-S-C-R is a double-crank mechanism with a spherical pair or joint between the input crank and the coupler and a cylinder pair or joint between the coupler and the output link. The pair or joint designation letters are as follows (also see Fig. 15.44):

R = revolute joint, which permits rotation only
P = prism joint, which permits sliding motion only
H = helix or screw-type joint
C = cylinder joint, which permits both rotation and sliding (hence the two degrees of freedom)
S = sphere joint, which is the common ball joint permitting rotation in any direction (three degrees of freedom)

Figure 15.46 shows an R-S-S-R practicable space mechanism. This is one of the *maverick* space mechanisms and one of the easiest and more practical to implement. By varying the length of the internal links between the ball joints, various reciprocating outputs may be obtained. Mathematical analysis of space mechanisms is extremely complicated and beyond the scope of this *Handbook*.

(Text continued on page 1176.)

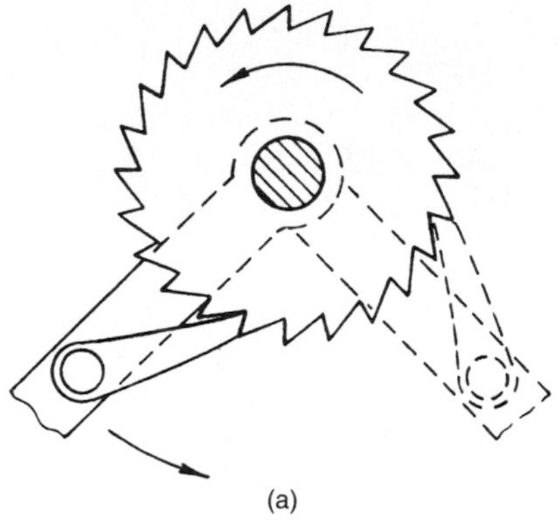

(a)

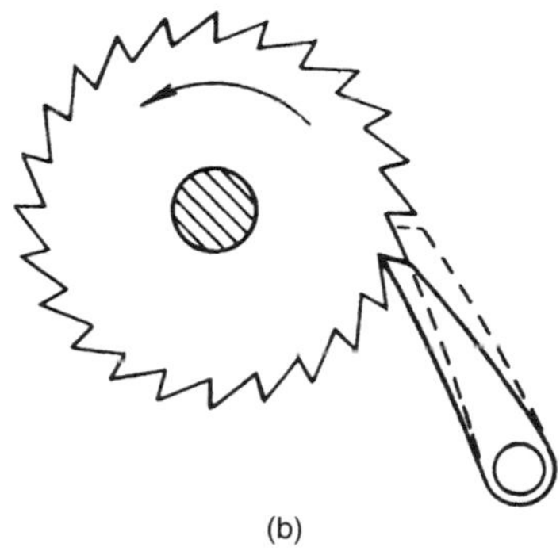

(b)

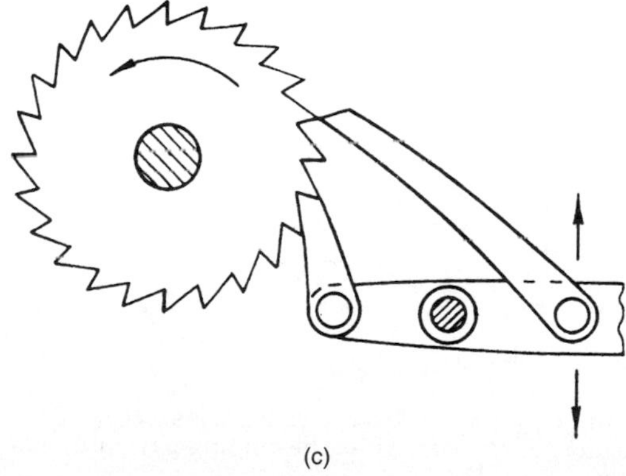

(c)

Figure 15.1 Ratchet systems: (*a*) standard pawl and lever; (*b*) staggered pawls; (*c*) double pawls.

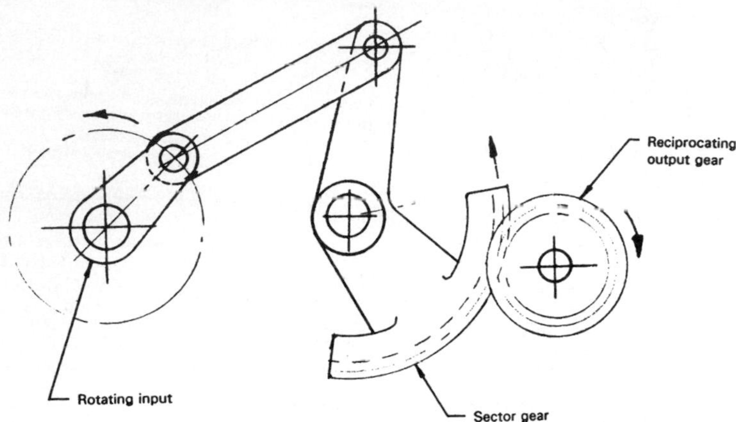

Figure 15.2 Rotation at input produces reciprocating output via sector gear.

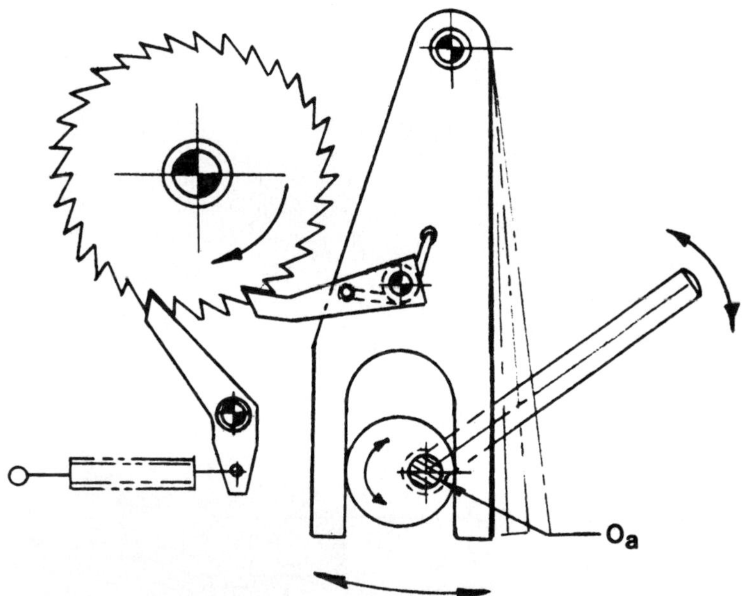

Figure 15.3 Rotation at point O_a, either by lever or continuous, actuates the ratchet wheel in one direction (clockwise), while the holding pawl prevents the ratchet from reversing.

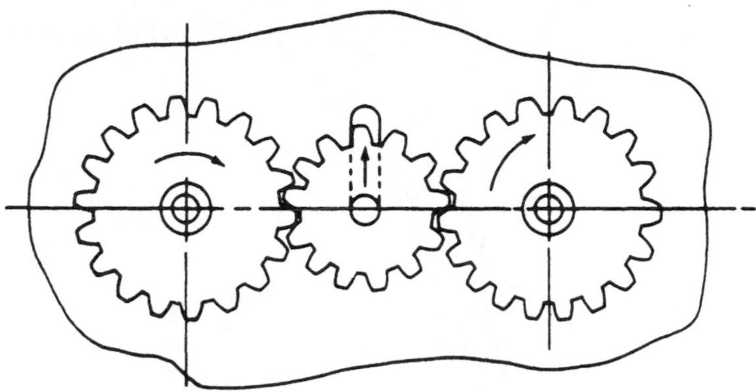

Figure 15.4 A one-way gear drive. Reversing rotation of larger gears causes small center gear to rise in slot, thus disconnecting the train.

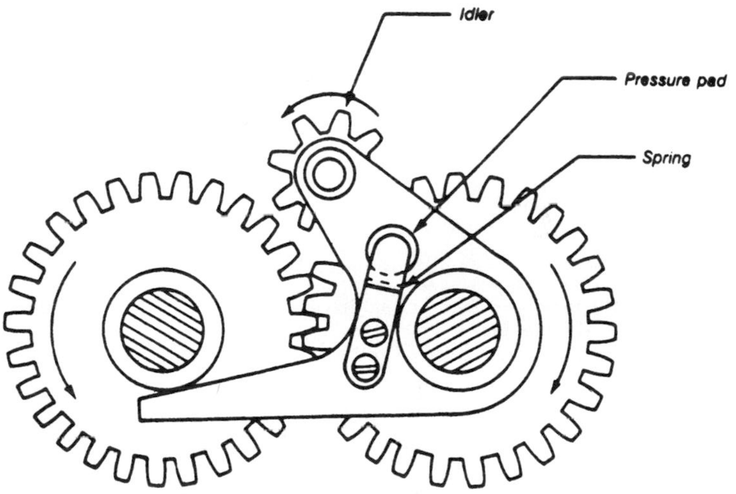

Figure 15.5 Spring-loaded friction pads load the right gear. The idler meshes with and locks the gears when motion is reversed.

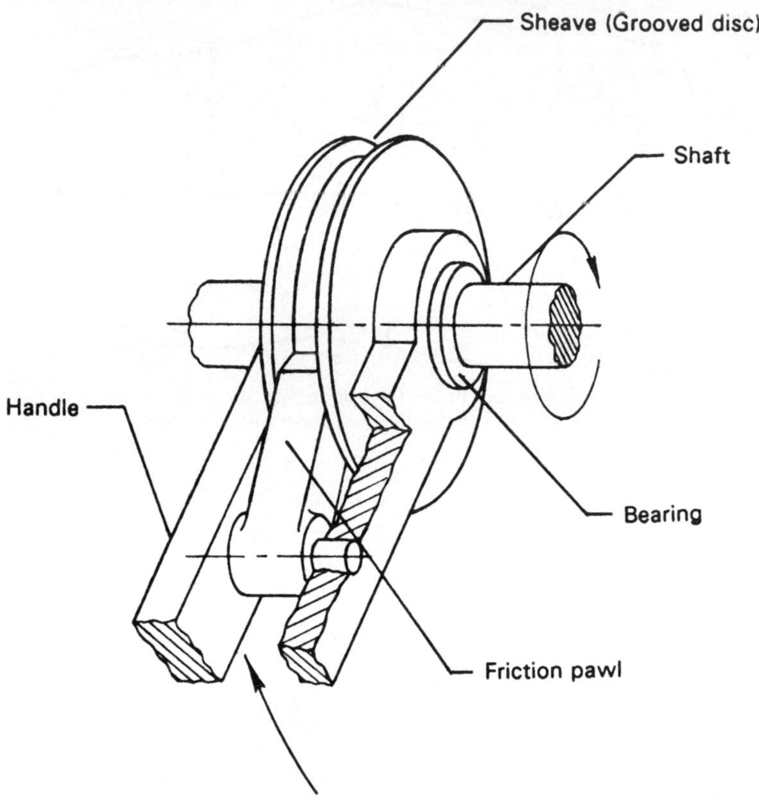

Figure 15.6 A one-way friction-action drive similar to a ratchet but allowing various drive increments.

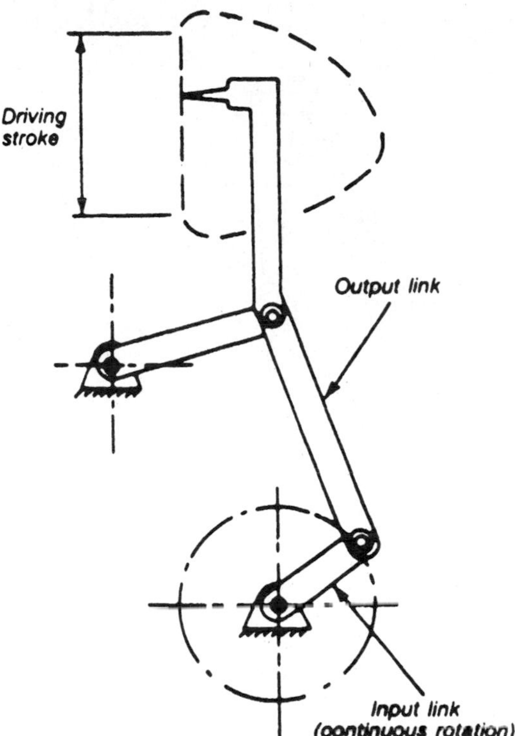

Figure 15.7 In this straight-line linkage, the point on the output link describes a figure D, a portion of which is straight-line motion. A very useful mechanism.

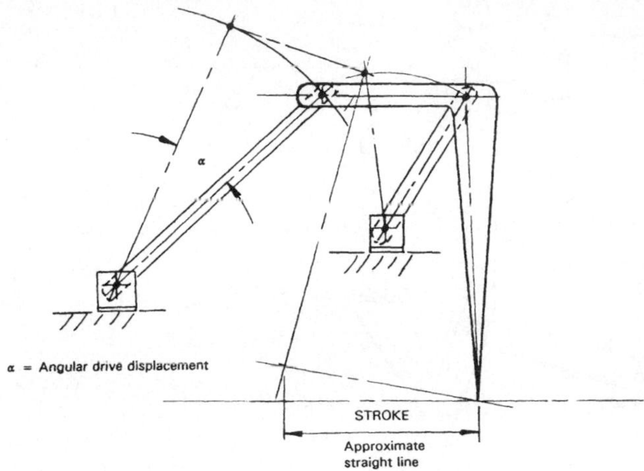

Figure 15.8 A four-bar linkage which produces an approximate straight-line motion. A small angular displacement (α) produces a long, almost-straight line.

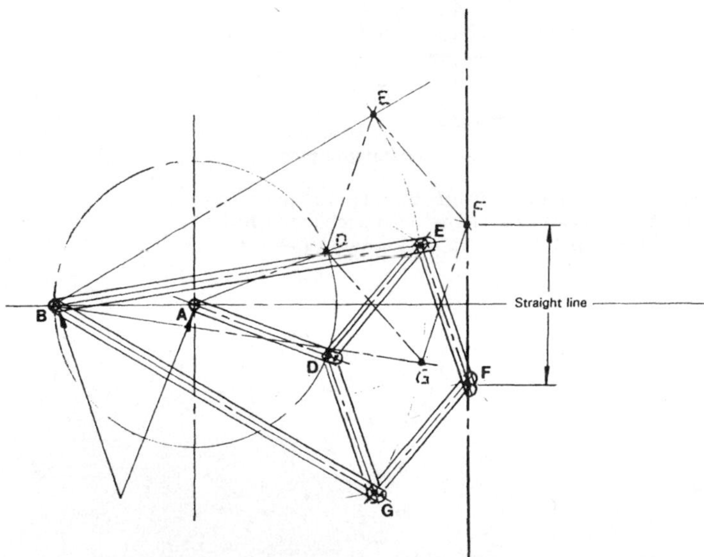

Figure 15.9 The Peaucellier cell for generating a straight line with a linkage. The requirements of this linkage are $AB = BC$, $AD = AE$, and CD, DF, FE, and EC must all be equal. The straight line is generated perpendicular to the line through points A and B.

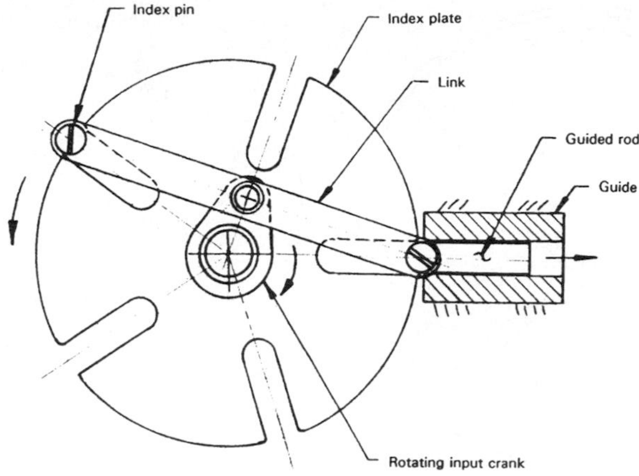

Figure 15.10 The rotating-input crank causes the index pin to move the index plate, and the guided rod locks the index plate between indexing dwell periods.

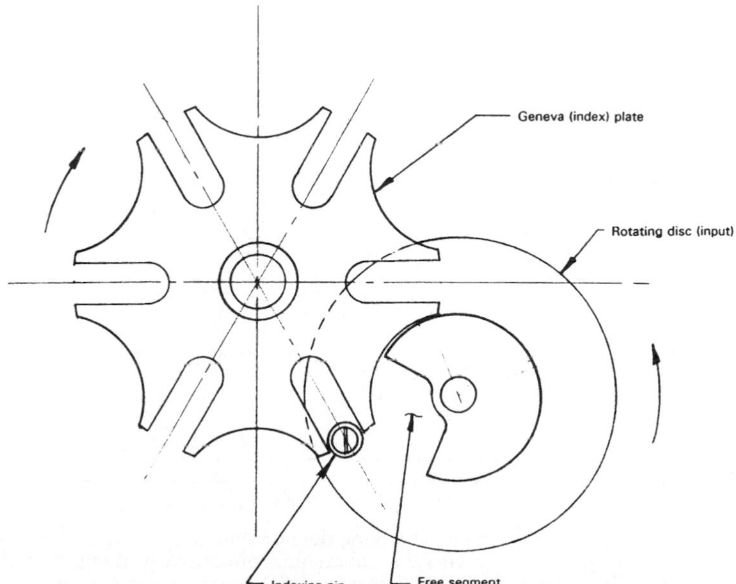

Figure 15.11 An indexing mechanism which is locked by the segment on the rotating-disk input during dwell periods.

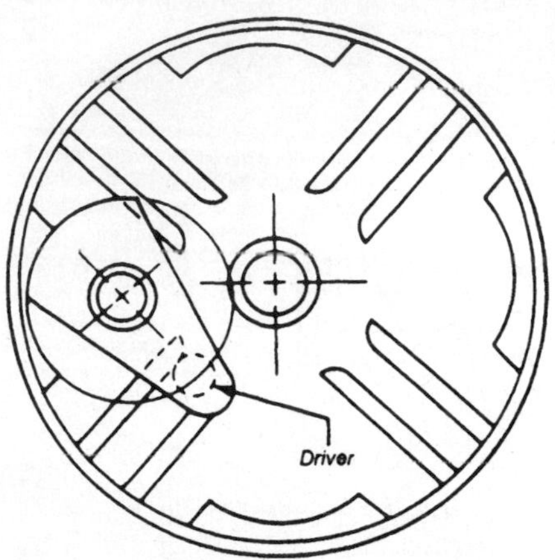

Figure 15.12 An internal Geneva mechanism. The driver and driven wheels rotate in the same direction. Duration of the dwell is more than 180° of driver rotation.

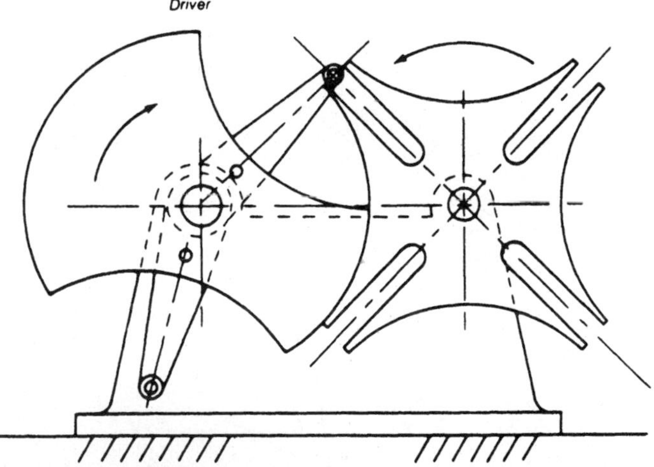

Figure 15.13 In this Geneva mechanism, the duration of dwell time is changed by arranging the driving rollers unsymmetrically about their axes. This does not affect the duration of the motion periods.

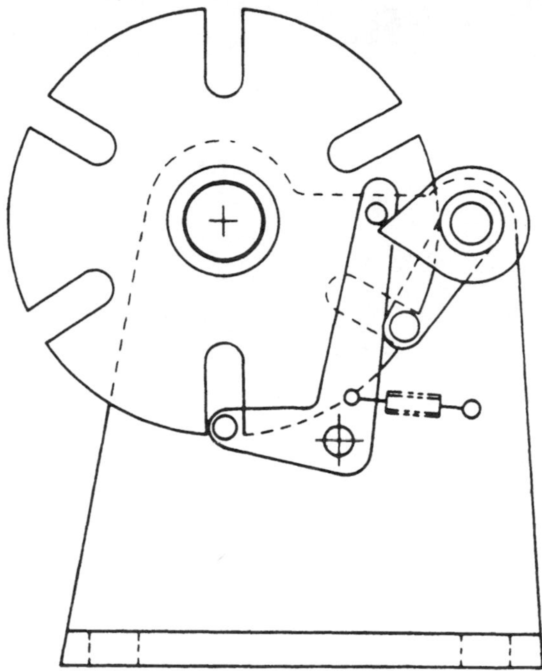

Figure 15.14 As with most Geneva drives, the driver follower on the input crank enters a slot and rapidly indexes the output. On this mechanism, the roller in the locking arm (shown leaving the slot) enters a slot to prevent the index plate from rotating when not indexing.

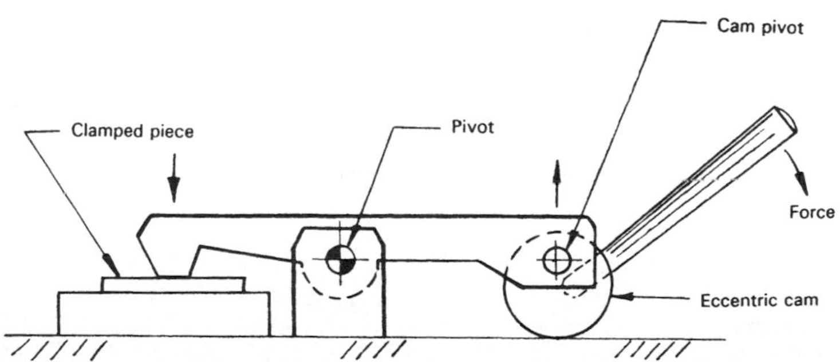

Figure 15.15 A simple eccentric cam-action clamp mechanism. (See Chap. 10 for various other clamp mechanisms.)

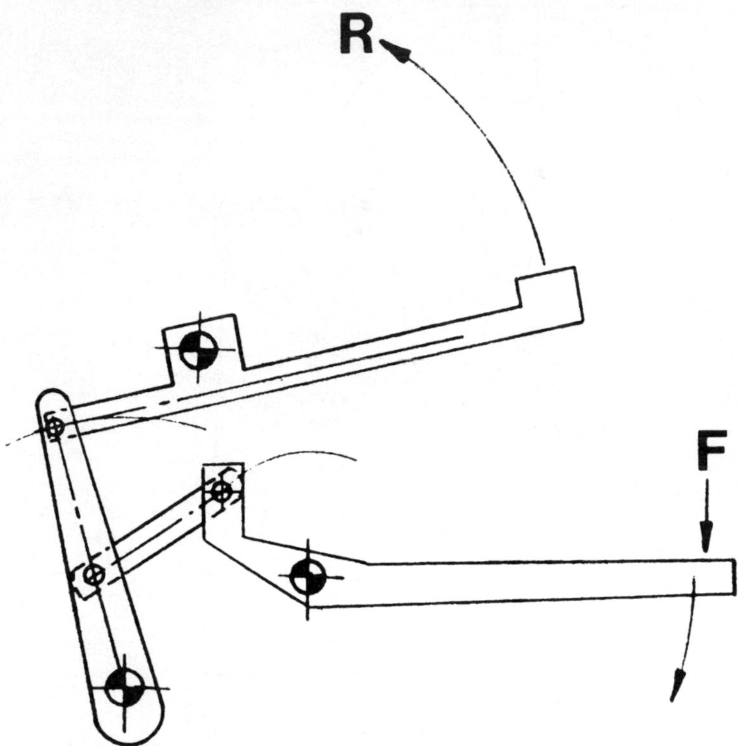

Figure 15.16 A linkage for producing a long travel at R with a small displacement at F.

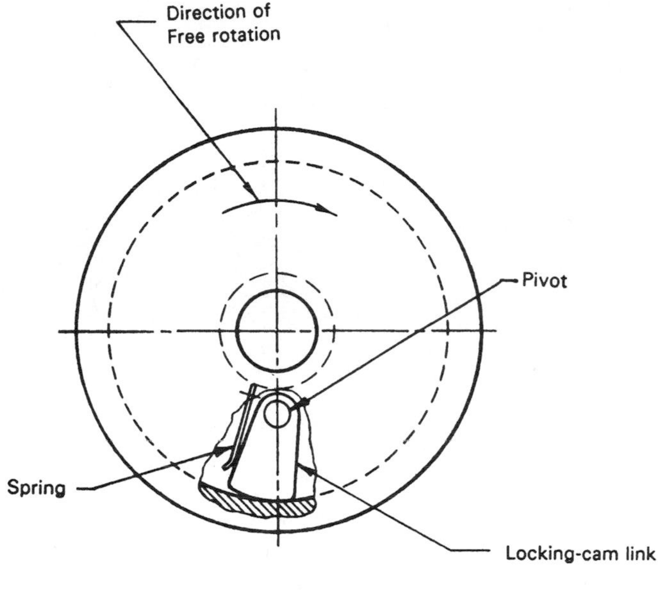

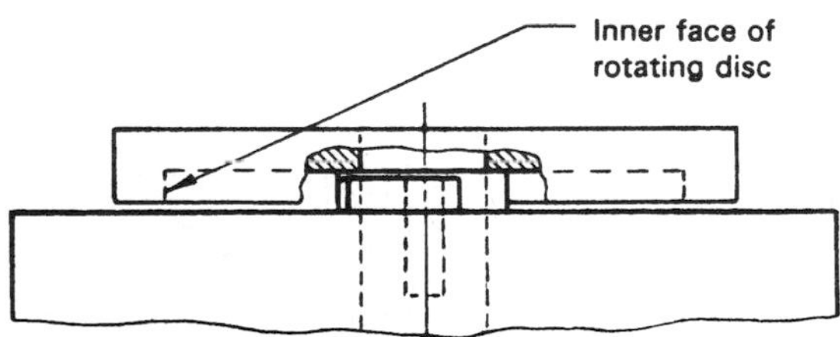

Figure 15.17 A one-way rotating mechanism. The locking cam prevents counterclockwise rotation.

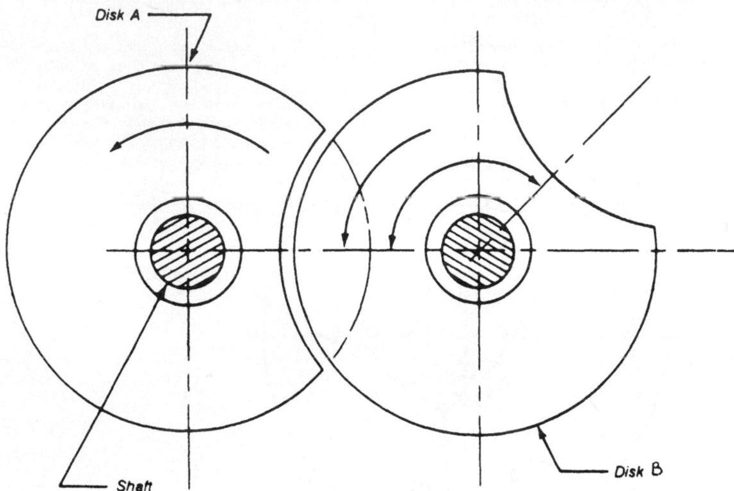

Figure 15.18 Interlocking-disk mechanism allows selective rotation of either shaft. As shown, disk *B* is free to rotate. Lining up the segment notches allows rotation of only one disk at a time.

Figure 15.19 For each revolution of the input disk, the ratchet advances one tooth.

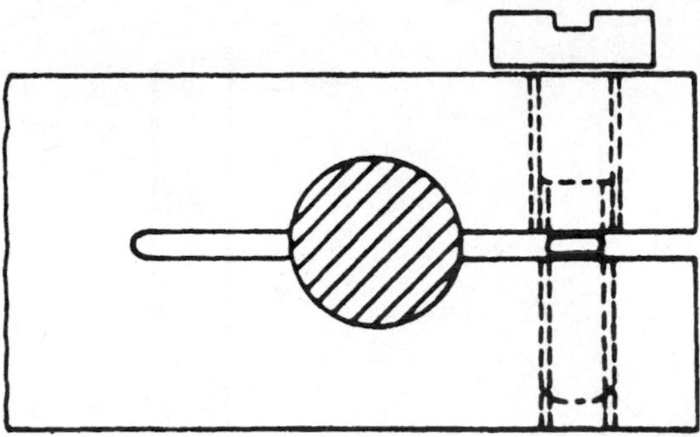

Figure 15.20 A locking-yoke clamp.

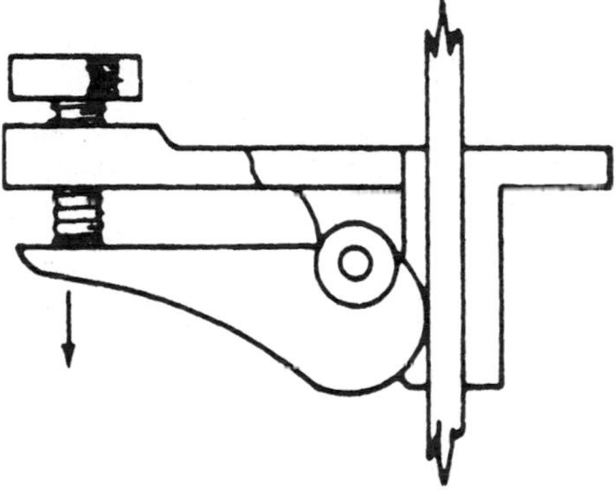

Figure 15.21 A locking cam, actuated by a pressure screw.

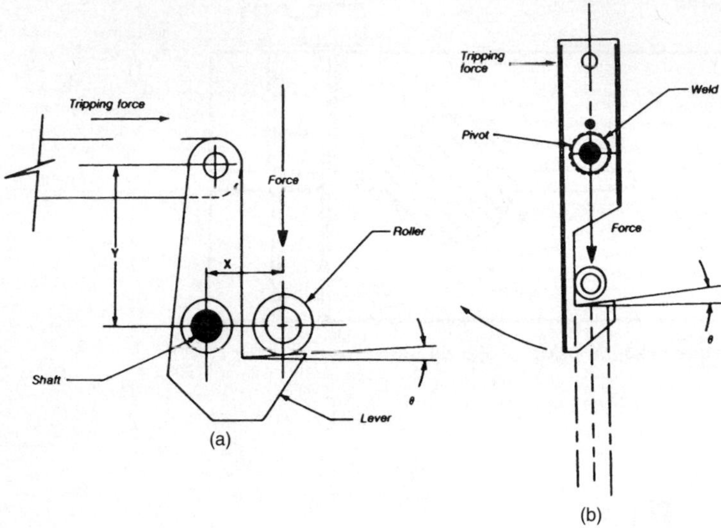

Figure 15.22 Two sear tripping mechanisms for controlling a large force with small tripping pressures. The ratio of X to Y on the lever arms determines the required tripping pressure.

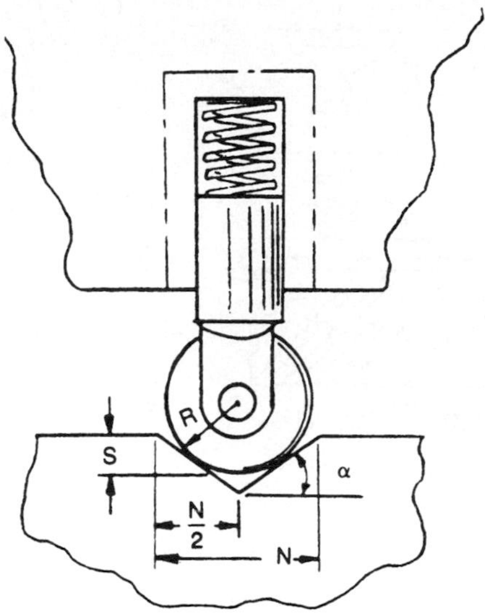

$$S\text{, rise} = \frac{N \tan \alpha}{2} - R\left(\frac{1 - \cos \alpha}{\cos \alpha}\right)$$

$$R\text{, radius} = \left(\frac{N \tan \alpha}{2} - S\right)\left(\frac{\cos \alpha}{1 - \cos \alpha}\right)$$

Figure 15.23 A roller-wheel detent, spring loaded. In this device, the rise and roller radius are determined by the indicated equations.

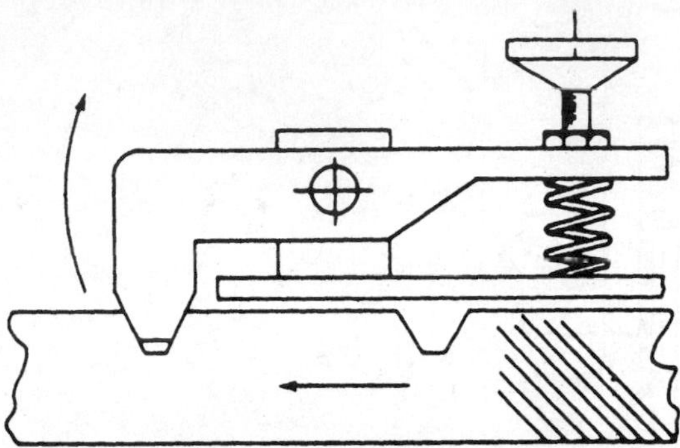

Figure 15.24 A spring-loaded detent with release lever.

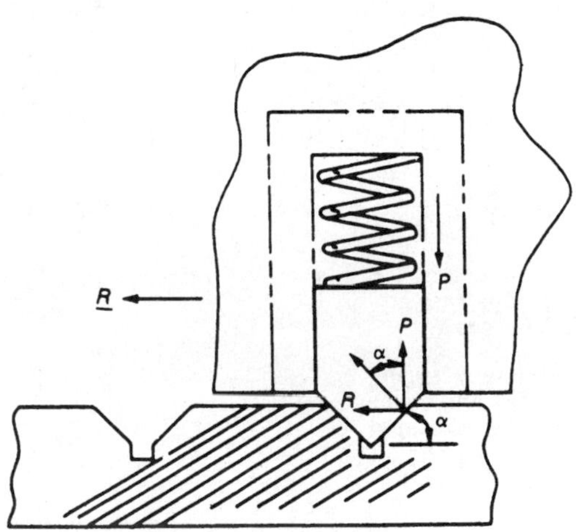

Holding power is $R = P \tan \alpha$;
for friction coefficient, F,
at contact surface
$R = P(\tan \alpha + F)$

Figure 15.25 A spring-loaded detent for positioning and holding. Holding power is calculated from the equation shown.

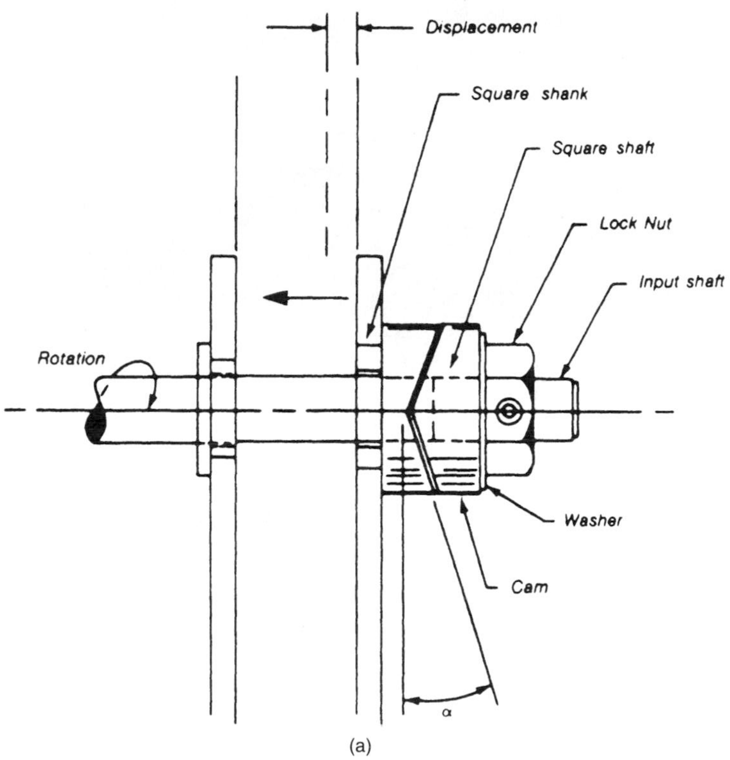

Figure 15.26 (*a*) A cam-actuated pressure clamping mechanism. Rotation of the input shaft displaces the profile cams and creates a clamping action. The clamping pressure of this mechanism is determined by the angle α in relation to the torque applied to the shaft.

(b)

Figure 15.26 (*b*) Clamping mechanism described in part *a*. Note the TIG welding on the central arm.

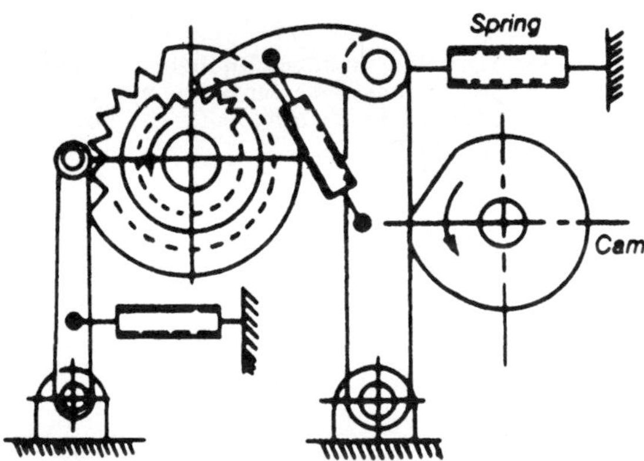

Figure 15.27 A cam-driven ratchet. The ratchet advance is determined by the vertical location of the cam on the pawl's lever arm.

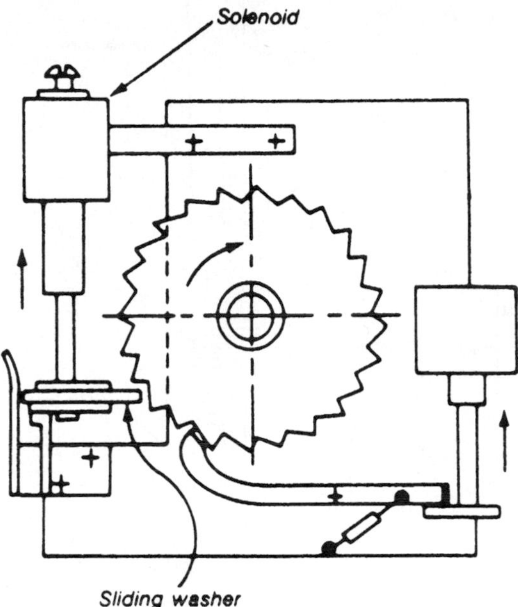

Figure 15.28 A solenoid-operated ratchet with solenoid resetting mechanism. The teeth are engaged by the sliding washer.

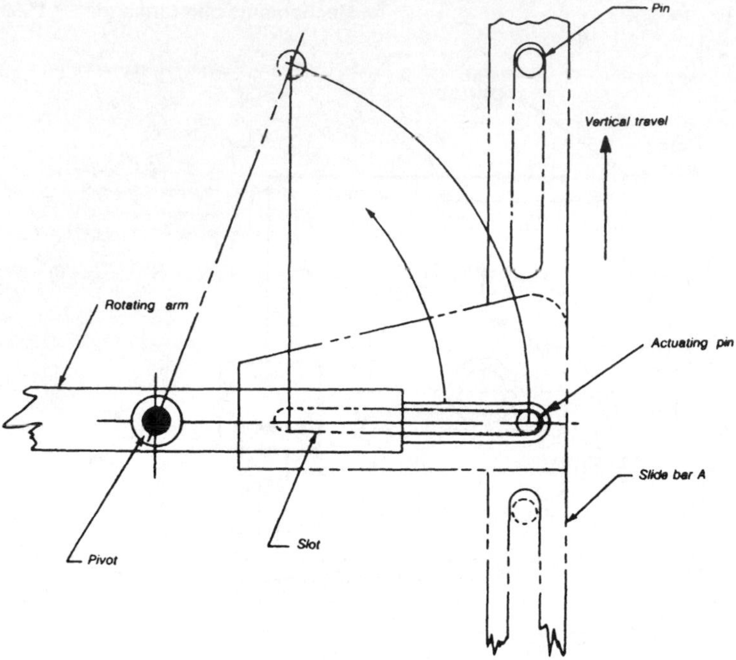

Pin

Vertical travel

Rotating arm

Actuating pin

Slide bar A

Slot

Pivot

Figure 15.29 Rotation translated into vertical travel of a slide bar (A). The actuating pin is attached to the end of the rotating arm.

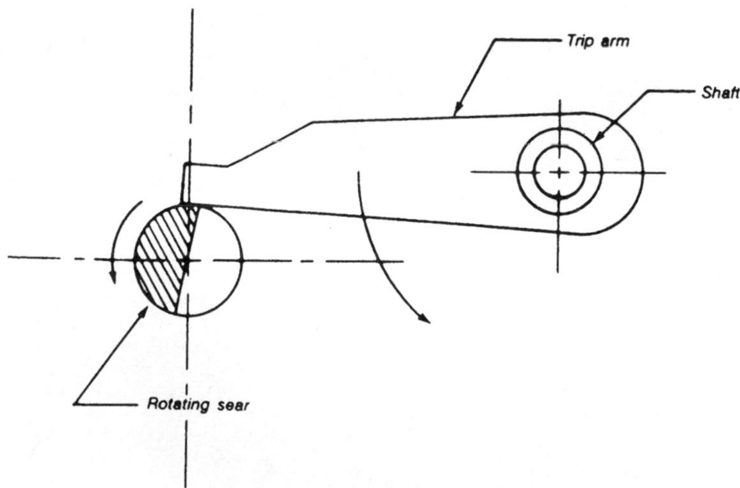

Figure 15.30 A rotating sear mechanism used to actuate a large force with a small turning movement of the sear shaft.

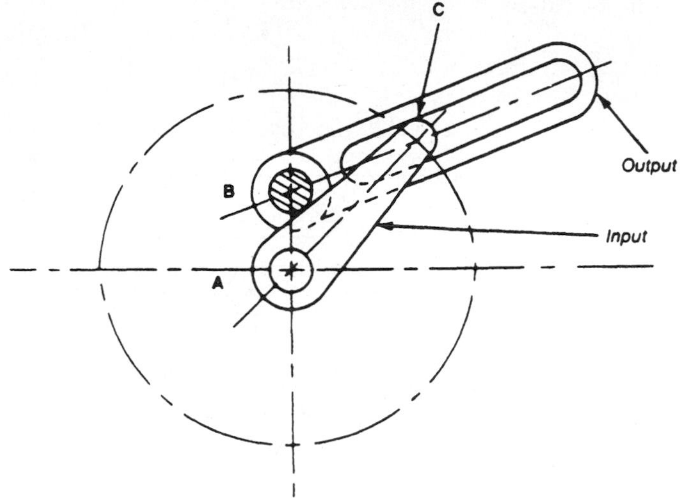

Figure 15.31 The Whitworth "quick return," a simple method for varying the output motion of shaft (B). The axes of shafts A and B are not collinear. The driving pin is at point C.

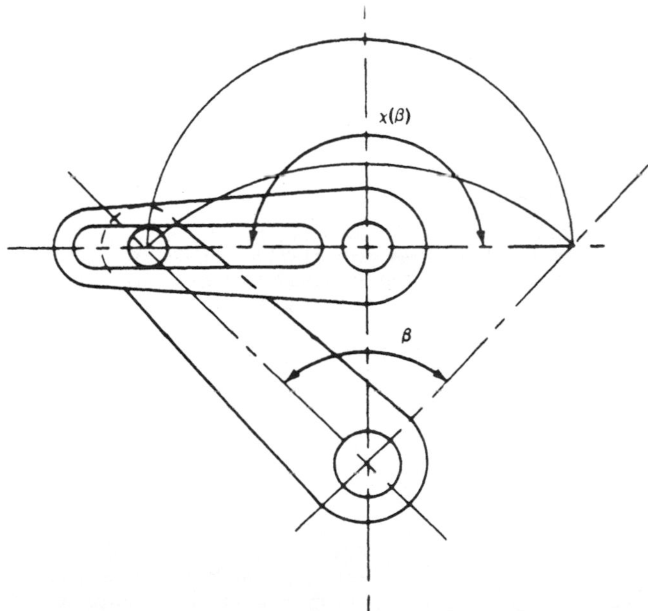

Figure 15.32 A mechanism for enlarging the oscillating motion of a shaft. Rotating the input link through angle β will cause the follower arm to rotate $x\beta$, according to the center distance between the two shafts.

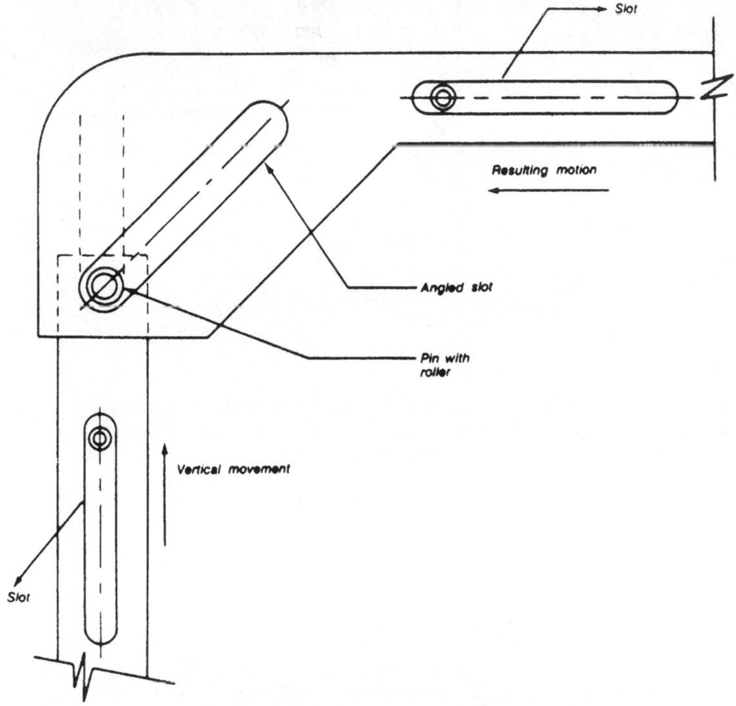

Figure 15.33 A sliding mechanism for changing the direction of the linearly moving bars. When bar *A* is moved vertically, bar *B* moves to the left, as indicated. The angled slot can be repositioned for varying movements.

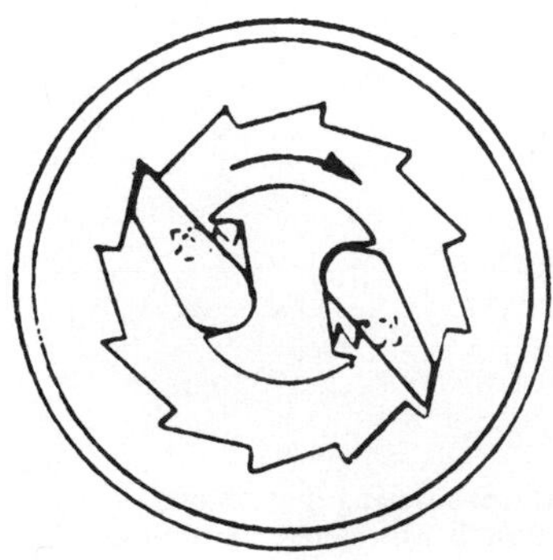

Figure 15.34 A one-way internal ratcheting drive that transmits rotary motion in one direction only.

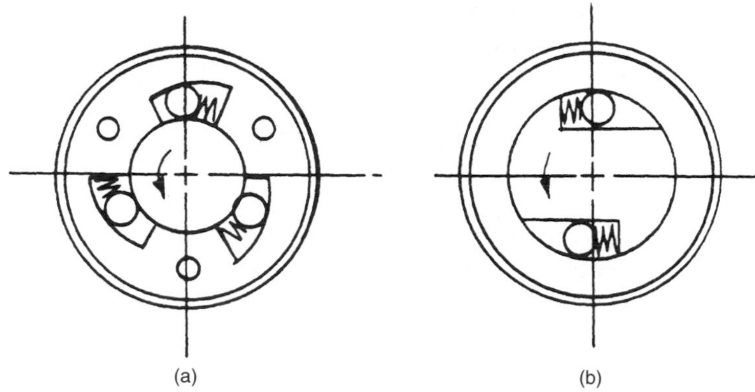

Figure 15.35 (*a*) A one-way ball-lock clutch. (*b*) Another variation of the one-way ball-lock clutch.

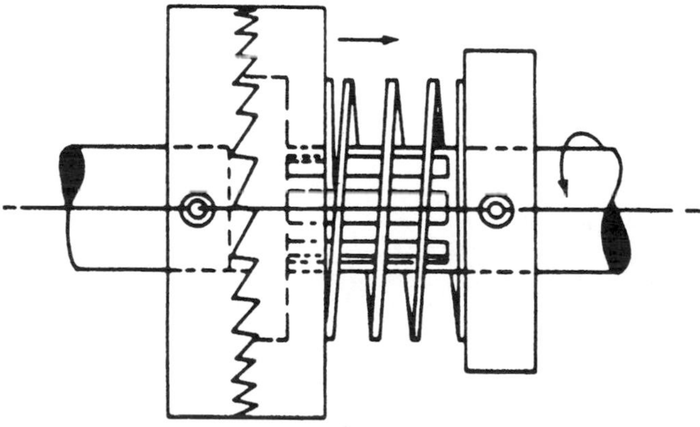

Figure 15.36 A one-way "ratcheting dog" clutch with spring-loaded engagement.

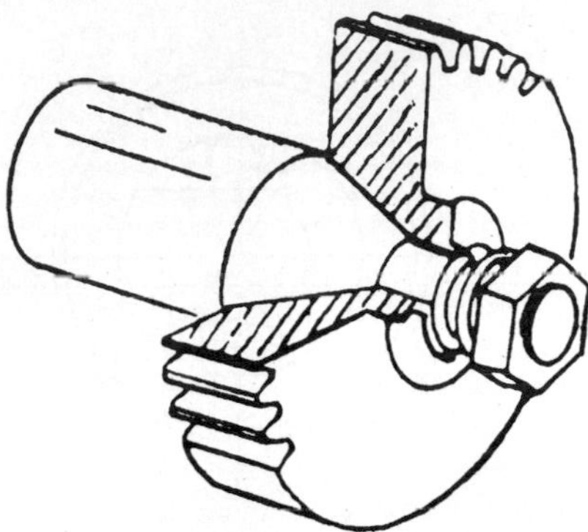

Figure 15.37 A friction-cone drive. The spring is put under pressure by tightening the nut, providing a means for allowing slippage in case of overload.

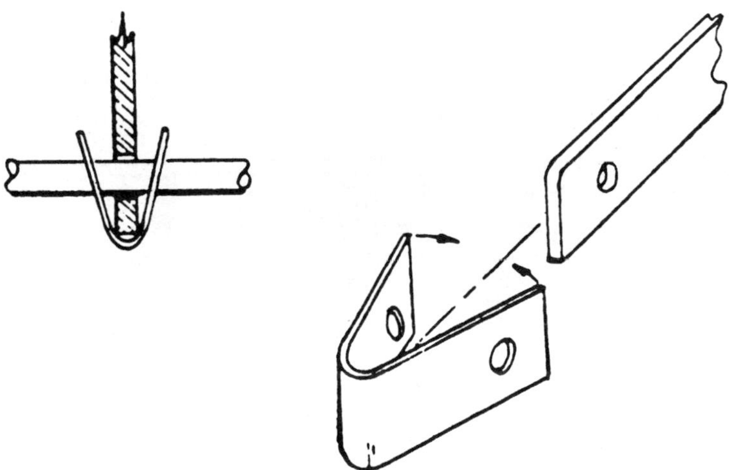

Figure 15.38 A spring clip locking a shaft in position, with means for quick release.

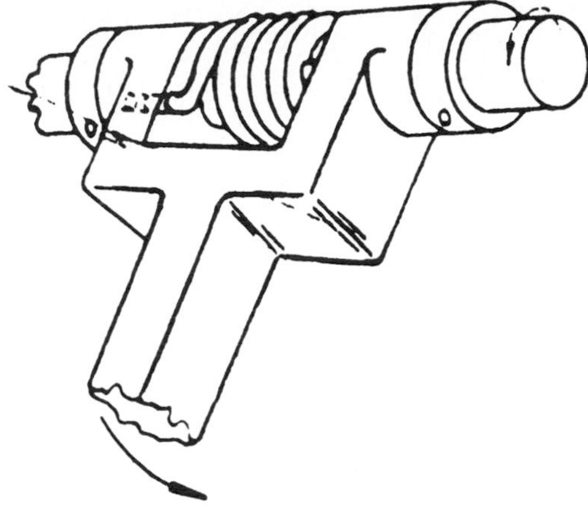

Figure 15.39 A one-way drive using the tightening action of a torsion spring to allow motion to be transmitted in one direction only.

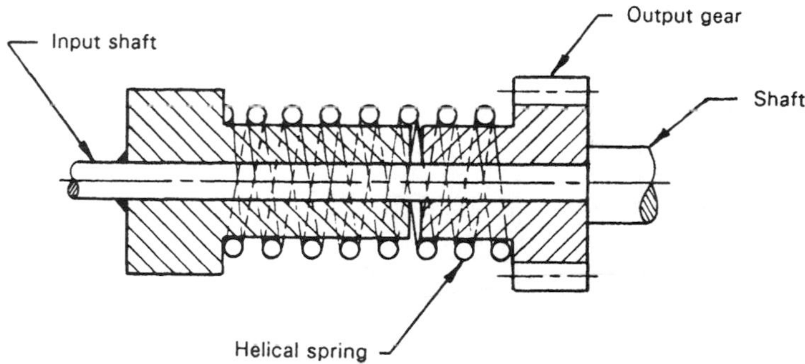

Figure 15.40 A one-way spring clutch drive. In one direction, the spring tightens and transmits rotary motion; in the other direction, the spring unwinds and disconnects the shafts.

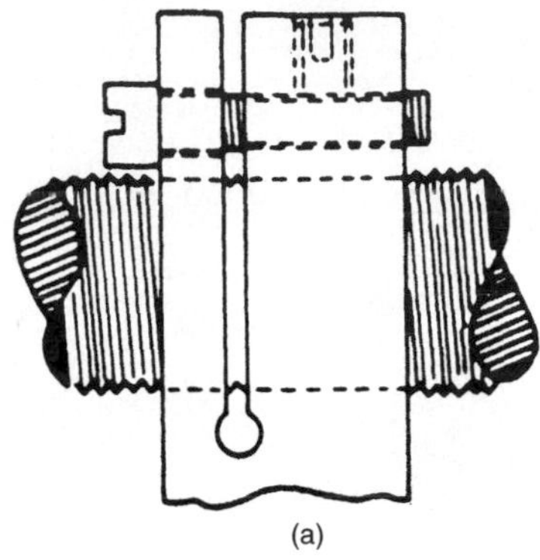

(a)

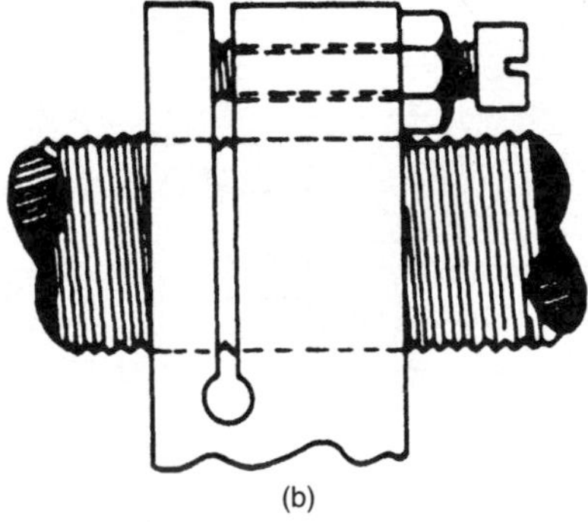

(b)

Figure 15.41 (*a*) A method of locking or preventing backlash on a threaded shaft. (*b*) Another method for controlling backlash.

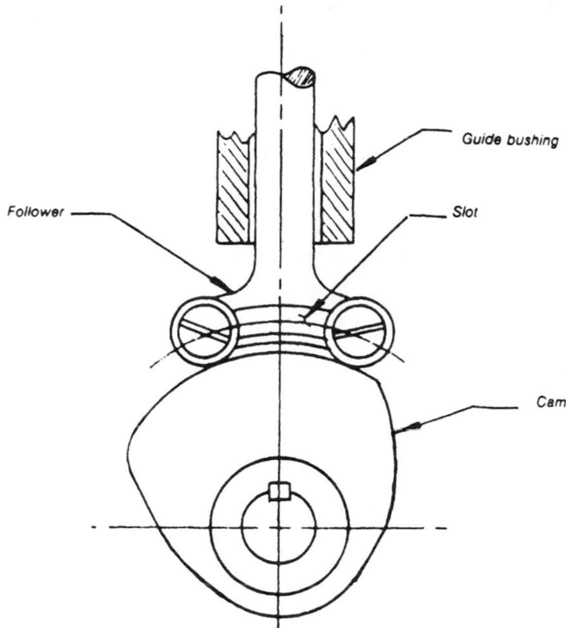

Figure 15.42 An adjustable-dwell cam.

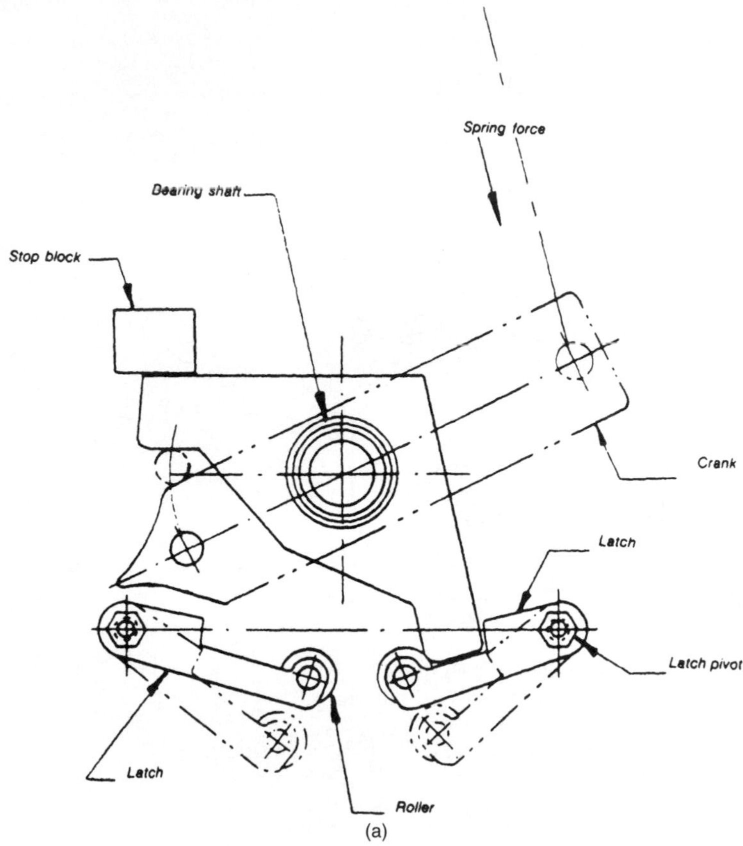

Figure 15.43 (*a*) A toggle-drive mechanism with automatic locking latches. In this compound mechanism, an input shaft rotates a spring-loaded crank until it passes top dead center. At this time, the crank tip unlocks the latch holding the A-shaped cam that is attached to the output shaft, driving the output shaft until the A cam strikes the stop block. At the end of its rotation, the A cam is again locked by the opposite latch. The latches are torsion spring loaded.

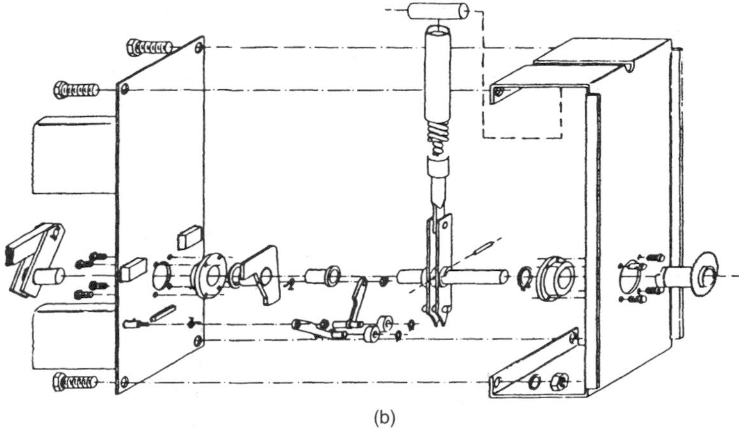

(b)

Figure 15.43 (*b*) Mechanism described in part *a*.

(c)

Figure 15.43 (*c*) Photograph of mechanism shown in parts *a* and *b*.

Degree of Freedom	Type Number ♦	Type of Joint	
		Symbol	Name
1	100	R	Revolute
	010	P	Prism
	001	H	Helix
2	200	T	Torus
	110	C	Cylinder
	101	T_H	Torus-Helix
	020	.....	.....
	011	.....	.....
3	300	S	Sphere
	210	S_S	Sprere-Slotted Cylinder
	201	S_{SH}	Sphere-Slotted Helix
	120	P_L	Plane
	021	.....	.....
	111	.....	.....
4	310	S_G	Sphere-Groove
	301	S_{GH}	Sphere-Grooved Helix
	220	C_P	Cylinder-Plane
	121	.....	.....
	211	.....	.....
5	320	S_P	Sphere-Plane
	221	.....	.....
	311	.....	.....

Note: ♦ Number of freedoms, given in the order of N_R, N_T, N_H.
R = revolution joint, which permits rotation only; P = prism joint, which permits sliding motion only; H = helix or screw type of joint; C = cylinder joint, which permits both rotation and sliding (hence, has two degrees of freedom); S = sphere joint, which is the common ball joint permitting rotation in any direction, (three degrees of freedom).

Figure 15.44 Classification of kinematic pairs, space mechanisms.

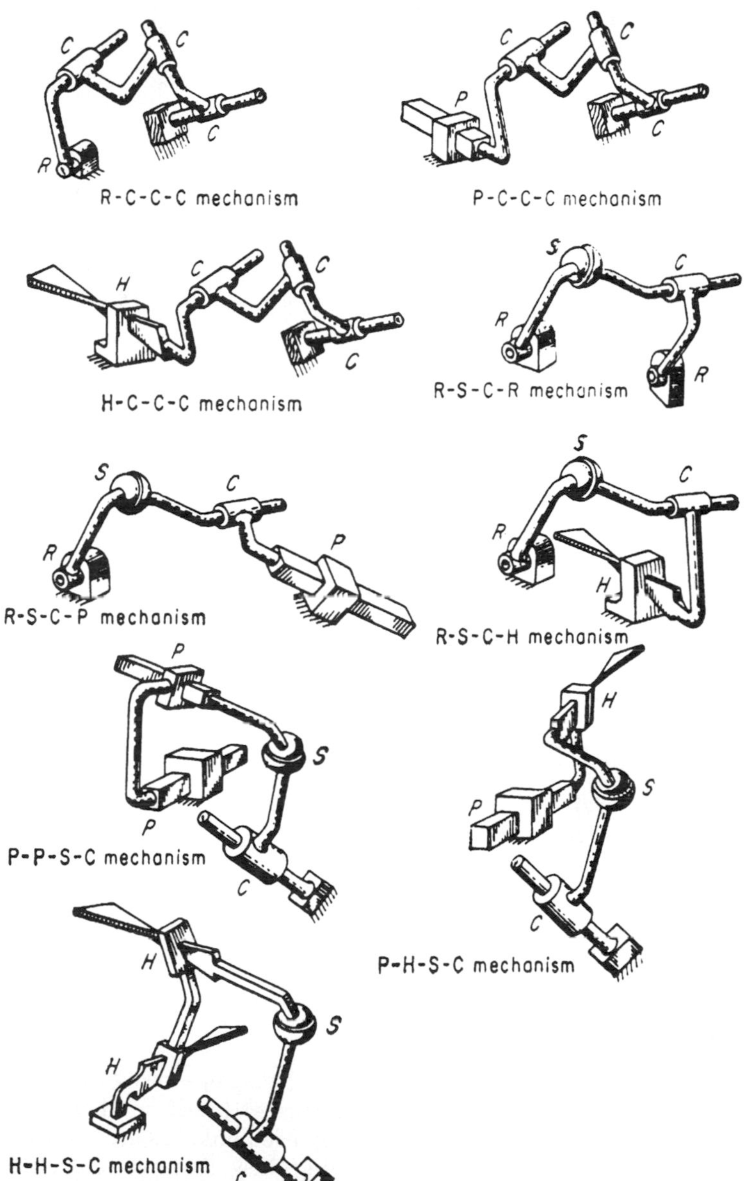

Figure 15.45 The nine most useful four-bar space mechanisms.

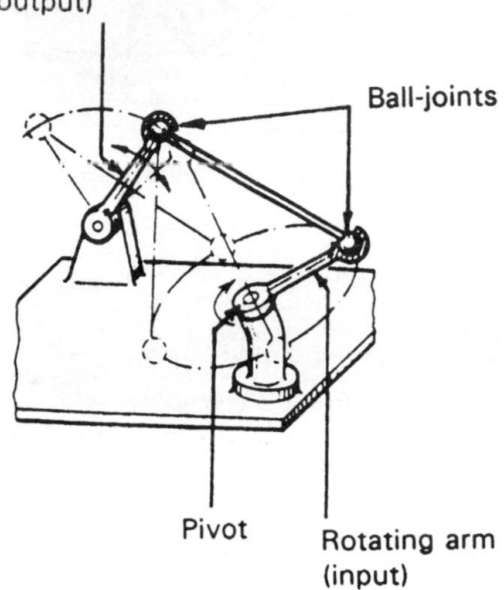

Figure 15.46 A typical R-S-S-R space mechanism/linkage.

Three space mechanisms are known which are classified as *maverick* space mechanisms, and they include

- The Bennet R-R-R-R
- The R-S-S-R
- The R-C-C-R

These maverick mechanisms do not follow the kinematic rules shown in Fig. 15.44. Moreover, there may be undiscovered maverick types which would prove to be practicable.

15.2 Linkages

Linkages are an important element of machine design and are therefore detailed in this section, together with their mathematical solutions. Some of the more commonly used linkages are shown in Figs. 15.47 through 15.52. By applying these linkages to applications containing the simple machines, a wide assortment of workable mechanisms may be produced.

15.2.1 Linkage analysis

Toggle-joint linkages. Figure 15.47 shows the well-known and often used toggle mechanism. The mathematical relationships are shown in the figure. The famous Luger pistol action is based on the toggle-joint mechanism.

Figure 15.48 shows the application of a double-toggle joint, wherein the mechanical advantage may be multiplied. This mechanism is used in rock-crushing machinery, where an enormous force is required to crush rocks.

The four-bar linkage. Figure 15.49 shows the very important four-bar linkage, which is used in countless mechanisms. The linkage looks simple, but it was not until the 1950's that a mathematician was able to find the mathematical relationship between this linkage and all its parts. The equational relationship of the four-bar linkage is known as the *Freudenstein relationship* and is shown in the figure. The geometry of the linkage may be ascertained with the use of trigonometry, but the velocity ratios of points p and p' and the actions are extremely complex and can only be solved using advanced mathematics.

The use of high-speed photography on a four-bar mechanism makes its analysis possible without recourse to advanced mathematical methods, provided that the mechanism can be photographed.

Simple linkages. In Fig. 15.50, the torque applied at point T is known, and we wish to find the force along link F. We proceed as follows: First, find the effective value of force F_1, which is

$$F_1 \times R = T$$

$$F_1 = \frac{T}{R}$$

Then

$$\sin \phi = \frac{F_1}{F}$$

$$F = \frac{F_1}{\sin \phi} \qquad \text{or} \qquad \frac{(T/R)}{\sin \phi}$$

Note: $T/R = F_1$ = torque at T divided by R (radius).

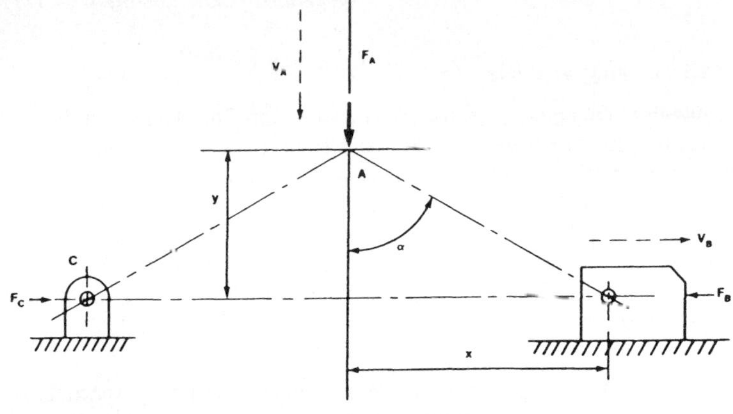

$$M_a = \frac{F_B}{F_A} = \frac{1}{2}\cdot\frac{x}{y} = \frac{1}{2}\tan\alpha = \frac{V_A}{V_B}.$$

As angle α approaches 90°, the links come into toggle, and the mechanical advantage and velocity ratio both approach infinity.

M_a = Mechanical advantage (ratio)
F_B = Force at point B
F_A = Force at point A
V_A = Velocity at point A
V_B = Velocity at point B
X = Horizontal displacement
Y = Vertical displacement

Figure 15.47 The standard "toggle" mechanism/linkage.

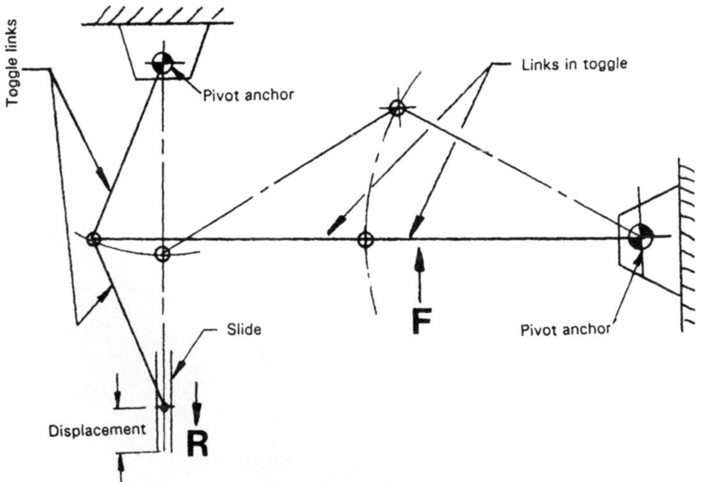

Figure 15.48 The double-toggle-joint linkage.

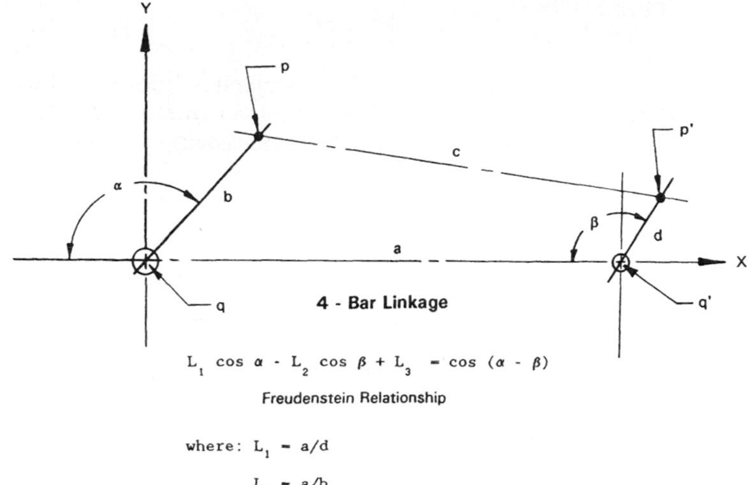

$$L_1 \cos \alpha - L_2 \cos \beta + L_3 = \cos (\alpha - \beta)$$

Freudenstein Relationship

where: $L_1 = a/d$

$L_2 = a/b$

and

$$L_3 = \frac{b^2 - c^2 + d^2 + a^2}{2\,bd}$$

Figure 15.49 The geometry of the four-bar linkage.

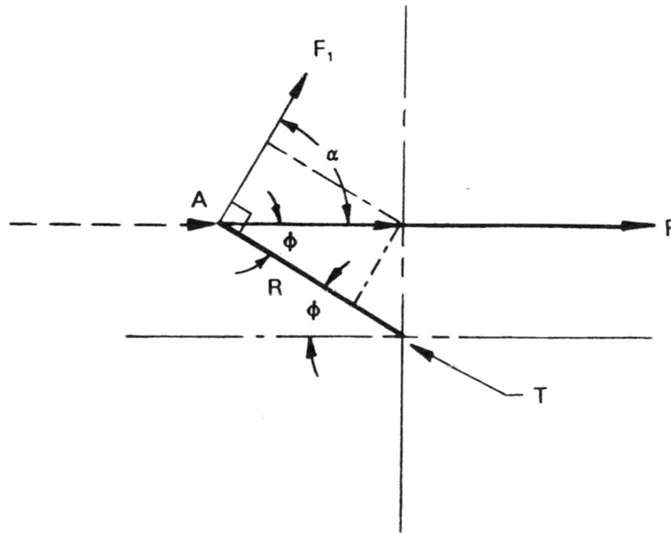

Figure 15.50 A simple linkage.

In Fig. 15.51, the force F acting at an angle θ is known, and we wish to find the torque at point T. First, we determine angle α from $\alpha = 90° - \theta$ and then proceed to find the vector component force F_1, which is

$$\cos \alpha = F_1/F \qquad \text{and} \qquad F_1 = F \cos \alpha$$

The torque at point T is $F \cos \alpha R$, which is F_1R. (Note: F_1 is at 90° to R.)

Crank linkage. In Fig. 15.52, a downward force F will produce a vector force F_1 in link AB. The instantaneous force at 90° to the radius arm R, which is P_n, will be

$$F_1 \qquad \text{or} \qquad P = \frac{F}{\cos \alpha}$$

and

$$P_n = F_1 \qquad \text{or} \qquad P \cos \lambda \qquad \text{or} \qquad P_n = \frac{F}{\cos \phi} \sin (\phi - \theta)$$

The resulting torque at T will be $T = P_nR$, where R is the arm BT.

The preceding case is typical of a piston acting through a connecting rod to a crankshaft. This particular linkage is used many times in machine design, and the applications are countless.

The preceding linkage solutions have their roots in engineering mechanics, further practical study of which may be made using the *Electromechanical Design Handbook* (McGraw-Hill, 1990).

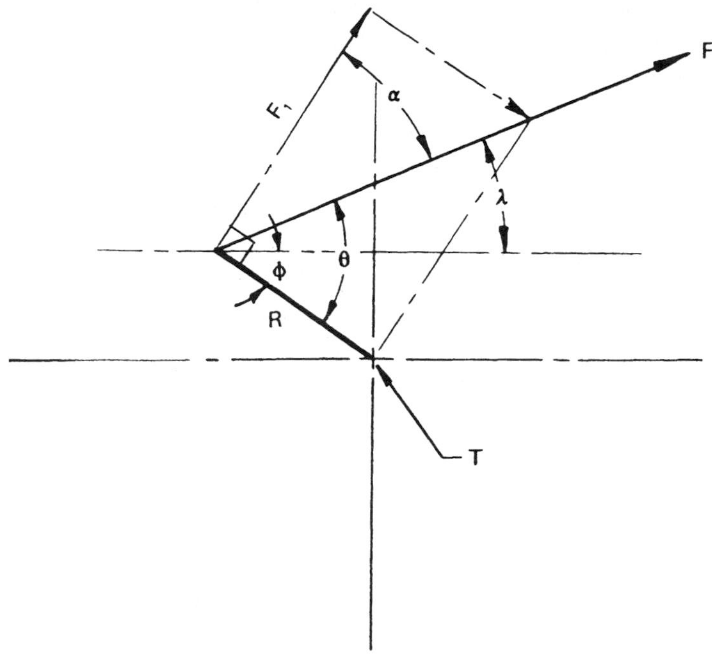

Figure 15.51 A simple linkage.

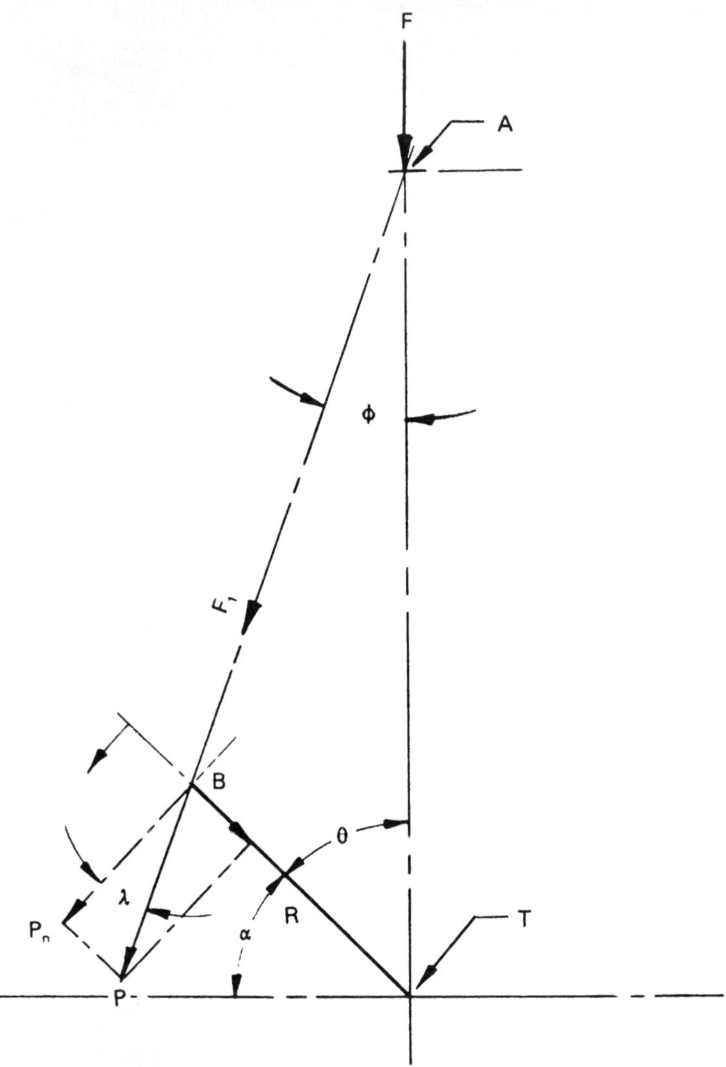

Figure 15.52 The well-known engine crank linkage.

Chapter

16

Sheet Metal Practices and Layout

The branch of metalworking known as *sheet metal* comprises a large and important element. Sheet metal parts are used in countless commercial and military products. Sheet metal parts are found on almost every product produced by the metalworking industries throughout the world.

Sheet metal gages run from under 0.001 in to 0.500 in. Hot-rolled steel products can run from ½ in thick to no. 18 gage (0.0478 in) and still be considered as "sheet." Cold-rolled steel sheets are generally available from stock in sizes from no. 10 gage (0.1345 in) down to no. 28 gage (0.0148 in). Other sheet thicknesses are available as special-order "mill-run" products when the order is large enough. Large manufacturers who use vast tonnages of steel products such as the automobile makers, switch-gear producers, and other sheet metal fabricators may order their steel to their own specifications (composition, gages, and physical properties).

The steel sheets are supplied in flat form or rolled into coils. Flat-form sheets are made to specific standard sizes unless ordered to special nonstandard dimensions.

16.1 Carbon and Low-Alloy Steel Sheets

Carbon steel sheets and coils are produced in the following grades or classes:

Hot rolled

- Low carbon (commercial quality)
- Pickled and oiled
- 0.40/0.50 carbon
- Abrasion resisting
- Hi-Form (A715), high strength/low alloy (grade 50, grade 80)
- A607 specification, high strength/low alloy (INX 45, INX 50, Ex-Ten 50)
- A606 specification, high strength/low alloy (Cor-Ten)

Note: The code numbers indicate the yield strength of the high-strength/low-alloy steels; i.e., INX 45 = 45,000 psi yield; grade 80 = 80,000 psi yield.

Cold rolled

- Low carbon (commercial quality)
- Special killed (drawing quality)
- Auto prototype (special killed drawing quality)
- Vitreous enameling
- Plating quality
- Stretcher leveled

The applications for the previously listed sheet steels are as follows:

Hot-rolled applications

Low carbon (commercial quality): Conforms to ASTM A569 and is used for tanks, barrels, farm implements, and other applications where surface quality is not critical or important.

Pickeled and oiled: Conforms to ASTM A569 and is used for automotive parts, switch gear, appliances, toys, and other applications where a better surface quality is required and paint and enamel adhere well. Carbon content is 10 percent maximum, and this material may be easily formed and welded same as low-carbon sheet (commercial quality).

0.40/0.50 carbon: Has 50 percent more yield strength and abrasion resistance than low-carbon sheets. May be heat-treated for more strength and hardness. Used for scrapers, blades, tools, and other applications requiring a strong, moderate-cost steel sheet.

Abrasion resistant: Medium carbon content and higher manganese greatly improve resistance to abrasion. Brinell hardness = 210 minimum. Uses include scrapers, liners, chutes, conveyors, and other applications requiring a strong, abrasion-resistant steel sheet. Formability is moderate.

A607 specification: Lowest-cost low-alloy steel sheet. Low carbon content ensures good formability. Excellent weldability. Typical uses include utility poles, transmission towers, automotive parts, truck trailers, and other applications requiring a low-cost, high-strength alloy steel sheet.

A606 specification: Five times more resistant to atmospheric corrosion than low-carbon steel. Excellent weldability and formability.

A715 specification: Fine-grained columbium bearing series of high-strength steel. Enhanced bending and forming properties. Tough and fatigue resistant, with excellent weldability using all welding processes. Yield-point levels range from 40,000 to 80,000 psi.

Cold-rolled applications

Low carbon (commercial quality): Produced with a high degree of gage accuracy, with uniform physical characteristics. Excellent surface for painting (enamel or lacquer). Good for stamping and moderate drawing applications. Improved welding and forming characteristics with uses such as household appliances, truck bodies, signs, panels, and many other applications.

Special killed (drawing quality): Used for severe forming and drawing applications. Freedom from age hardening and fluting. Conforms to ASTM A365 specification.

Auto prototype (special killed drawing quality): Used for prototype work and other deep drawing applications. Closely controlled gage thickness with better tolerances compared with commercial-quality grades.

Vitreous enameling: Cold rolled from commercially pure iron ingots for porcelain-enameled products. Textured surface and suitable for forming and moderate drawing applications and flatwork. Conforms to ASTM A424, grade A.

Plating quality: Two finishes are provided which are suitable for most plating applications: commercial bright and extra light matte.

Stretcher leveled: Uniform, high-quality matte sheets, further processed by stretching to provide superior flattness. Furnished resquared or not resquared. Resquared sheets have the stretching gripper marks removed. Used in the manufacture of table tops, cabinets, truck body panels, partitions, templates, and many other applications. Conforms to ASTM A336 specification.

Galvanized sheet and coil. The galvanic coating is zinc, and it is applied to standard steel sheets or coils in two basic methods: *hot-dipped galvanized* and *electrogalvanized.* The hot-dipped galvanized processes are known as Ti-Co galvanized, galvanized bonderized, galvannealed, galvannealed A, and hot-dipped galvanized. Galvanizing specifications are found in ASTM A526 and A527. Some of the hot-dipped sheets may have 1.25 oz zinc per square foot of surface area and others a lighter deposit.

Electrogalvanized sheets are cold-rolled steel sheets zinc coated by electrolytic deposition and conform to ASTM A591. These sheets should be painted if they are to be exposed to outdoor conditions. These sheets can be formed, rolled, or stamped without flaking, peeling, or cracking of the zinc coating. These galvanized sheets have the same gage thickness as cold-rolled sheets. Applications include cabinets, signs, light fixtures, and others where an excellent finish is required. Coating weight is typically 0.1 oz/ft^2, or each side is 0.00008 in thick. Trade names include Paint-Lok, Bethzin, Gripcoat, Lifecote 1, Weirzin Bonderized, and others.

Aluminized and long-terne sheets. Sheet steel is also aluminized and produced in long-terne sheets. Aluminized steel sheet is hot-dip coated on both sides with aluminum-silicon alloy by the continuous method. Strong and corrosion resistant, aluminized sheet is also inexpensive. The aluminum coating is typically 0.001 in thick on both sides or 0.40 oz/ft^2. Aluminized sheet conforms to ASTM A463 specification. Applications include dry kiln fan walls, dryers, incinerators, mufflers, and oven and space-heater components. Long-terne sheet is a soft steel coated with an 85 percent lead and 15 percent tin alloy for maximum ease in soldering. These long-terne sheets conform to ASTM A308 and are used for soldered tanks, automotive accessories, hood and radiator work, and many other stamped and formed products.

As can be seen from the preceding description of sheet steels that are commercially available, the selection of a particular steel for a particular sheet metal application is relatively easy. Not only are there a great number of different sheet metal stocks available, but special sheet steels may be ordered to your specifications when quantities are large enough to justify their production by the American steel makers.

16.2 Nonferrous Sheet Metal

The nonferrous sheet metals include aluminum and aluminum alloys, copper and copper alloys, magnesium alloys, titanium alloys, and other special alloys. See Chap. 5, "Materials and Their Uses," for data and specifications on the nonferrous as well as the ferrous materials which are specified by the American Society for Testing and Materials (ASTM) and the Society of Automotive Engineers (SAE). Supplier catalogs are also available from companies such as Ryerson, Vincent, Atlantic, Alcoa, Reynolds, Anaconda, Chase, and others, which may be selected from an industrial supplier master index such as the *Thomas Register of American Manufacturers.*

16.3 Machinery for Sheet Metal Fabrication

Some of the typical machinery found in a large manufacturing plant for processing and producing sheet metal parts includes

- Shears, hydraulic and squaring
- Press brakes
- Leaf brakes
- Roll-forming machines
- Automatic (CNC), multistation punch presses
- Single-die punch presses, strippit and unipunch setups
- Slitting machines
- Stretcher-bending machines
- Hydropresses (Marforming presses, Martin-Marietta Corp.)

- Pin routers
- Yoder hammers
- Spin forming machines
- Tumbling and deburring machines
- Sand-blasting equipment
- Explosive forming facilities
- Ironworkers (for structural shapes)

The designer and tool engineer should be familiar with all machinery used to manufacture parts in a factory. These specialists must know the limitations of the machinery that will produce the parts as designed and tooled. Coordination of design with the tooling and manufacturing departments within a company is essential to the quality and economics of the products that are manufactured. Our modern machinery has been designed and is constantly being improved to allow us to manufacture a quality product at an affordable price to the consumer. Medium- to large-sized companies can no longer afford to manufacture products whose quality standards do not meet the demands and requirements of the end user. (See the Introduction for an explanation of the term *quality* and what it means in the modern world marketplace.)

16.3.1 Modern sheet metal manufacturing machinery

The processing of sheet metal begins with the hydraulic shear, where the material is squared and cut to size for the next operation. Figure 16.1 shows a typical hydraulic shear with the capacity to do a 120-in cut in up to no. 7 gage steel sheet. These types of machines are the "workhorses" of the typical sheet metal department, since all operations on sheet metal parts start at the shear.

Figure 16.2 shows a Wiedemann Optishear, which shears and squares the sheet metal to a high degree of accuracy. Blanks which are used in blanking, punching, and forming dies are produced on this machine, as are other flat and accurate pieces which proceed to the next stage of manufacture.

The flat, sheared sheet metal parts may then be routed to the punch presses, where holes of various sizes and patterns are produced. Figure 16.3 shows a medium-sized CNC-controlled multistation turret punch press, which is both highly accurate and very high speed. (See Chap. 1, "Modern Metalworking Machinery and Measuring Devices," for other types of machinery used by the metalworking industry.)

After a sheet metal part is sheared and punched, it may require a press-brake operation to form flanges or produce hemmed edges. Figure 16.4 shows a small, digital-readout press brake which has a digital readout for the "back-gage" dimension. A larger press brake may be seen in Fig. 1.7. A small press brake such as that shown in Fig. 16.4 may be used for bending small sheet metal parts, flat bar stock, and copper and aluminum bus bars.

To quickly check a sheet metal gage, either ferrous or nonferrous, a tool similar to that shown in Fig. 16.5 is frequently used in the sheet metal department. The tool gage shown in the figure is for nonferrous metals such as stainless steel sheets and nonferrous wires.

16.4 Gaging Systems

To specify the thickness of different metal products such as steel sheets, wire, strip and tubing, music wire, and others, a host of gauging systems were developed over the course of many years. Shown in Fig. 16.6 are the common gaging systems used for commercial steel sheets, strip and tubing, and brass and steel wire. The steel sheets column in Fig. 16.6 lists the gages and equivalent thicknesses used by American steel sheet manufacturers and steel makers. This gaging system can be recognized immediately by its no. 11 gage equivalent of 0.1196 in, which is standard today for this very common and high-usage gage of sheet steel.

Figure 16.7 is a table of gaging systems that were used widely in the past, although some are still in use today, including the American or Brown and Sharpe system. The Brown and Sharpe system is also shown in Fig. 16.6, but there it is indicated in only four-place decimal equivalents.

16.4.1 Aluminum sheet metal standard thicknesses

Aluminum is used widely in the aerospace industry, and over the years, the gage thicknesses of aluminum sheets have developed on their own. Aluminum sheet is now generally available in the thicknesses shown in Fig. 16.8. The fact that the final weight of an aerospace vehicle is very critical to its performance has played an important role in the development of the standard aluminum sheet gages, wherein the strength-to-weight ratio is critical and a few thousandths of an inch extra on an aluminum sheet will mean more final weight of the aerospace vehicle. The gages or thicknesses of other metals and alloys, together with their stock tolerances, are shown in Chap. 5, "Materials and Their Uses."

16.5 Methods of Sheet Metal Fabrication

Many methods have been developed for working or fabricating sheet metal parts, including those employed to cut, punch, and form sheet metal parts.

16.5.1 Sheet metal cutting methods

Shearing: The sheet metal stock sheet is cut on a hydraulic-powered shear to its appropriate flat pattern or blank size.

Slitting: The sheet metal stock sheet is run through a slitting machine, where accurate widths are slit with slitting knives to various lengths. The edges are sharp and accurate, with excellent straightness along the edges.

Welding-process cutting: The sheet metal stock sheet may be oxyacetylene torch cut, oxyhydrogen cut, oxygen lance cut, plasma arc cut, arc cut, laser beam cut, or water jet cut. All these methods are used today to cut not only sheet metal but also bar stock, plates, structures and extruded shapes, and other materials, both metallic and nonmetallic.

16.5.2 Sheet metal punching methods

Turret punch press: The sheet metal stock sheet or blank is punched with various holes of different shapes by the punching dies contained on the punch press. Punch presses usually have a revolving turret which contains punches of different sizes and shapes, and these are interchangeable. The modern multistation punch presses are often CNC controlled and high speed.

Die punched: The sheet metal blank is placed in a punching die, where a pattern of holes is punched simultaneously with one stroke of the punching press. The high-tonnage brake press is often used to provide the power stroke required on the punching-die block.

Strippit punched: The sheet metal blank is punched, one hole at a time, on a strippit punch press. The punching dies may be changed quickly for punching different sizes or shapes of holes, such as round, square, rectangular, oval, or obround, or other special shapes for which the dies are designed.

16.5.3 Sheet metal forming methods

Press brake: This type of machine tool is found in every sheet metal department and is used to bend flanges, hems, and other special shapes. Figure 16.9 shows the various bending abilities of the press brake when equipped with the proper tooling.

Die bending, forming, and molding: Hard dies are produced for making bends and molds and for forming and drawing sheet metal parts. The forming or drawing dies may be all metal or a combination of metal and neoprene pads, which force the metal against the die block or male form. This process is widely used in the aerospace industry, where aluminum sheet matal parts are formed on hydropresses. (Marforming is a hydropressing process originated at the Martin Company, Middle River, Maryland.) Large lead-alloy form blocks are also used in the aircraft industry to form large, compound curved surfaces in sheet metal, generally aluminum alloys.

Yoder hammering: This is a specialized metal forming operation where a rapidly moving set of vertical forming hammers of various shapes is used to form special surfaces on sheet metal sections in a hammering process. This is a manual operation which requires operator skill and practice and is relatively rare today.

Spin forming: In this sheet metal forming process, a sheet metal disk is rotated in a special type of lathe tool while a special forming tool is pressed against the rotating disk of metal in a rotary swaging operation, thus forming or spin-drawing the part to the required shape. The process is limited to metal sections which are of a symmetrical rotated section of revolution, such as bell shapes, cones, parabolic sections, cylinders, etc.

Explosive forming: In this process of metal forming, a shaped charge of explosive is suspended above a sheet metal flat pattern, both of which are submerged under water. When the explosive charge is detonated, the shock waves from the explosion exert a hydrostatic pressure against the sheet metal, forcing it against a forming die block almost instantaneously. The sheet metal part conforms to the shape of the die block. Very complex sheet metal parts may be formed with this process. Some companies in the United States are devoted entirely to this specialized form of sheet metal fabrication. This process dates back to the 1950s, when it was used by the Martin Company, Middle River, Maryland, in their aircraft manufacturing facilities.

Stretcher bending: This process for sheet metal forming uses a machine known as a *stretcher bender,* wherein a sheet metal formed section such as an angle, channel, or Z section is pulled against a radiused die block to accurately form structural frame sections to a specified radius of curvature. The frame structures of rockets and aerospace vehicles, which have a single radius of curvature, are formed on the stretcher-bending machine. This is the only cost-effective method known for producing such sheet metal frame parts quickly and accurately on a relatively simple machine. In this operation, the straight frame section which was press-brake bent is held in a set of grippers at each end of the part. The part is stretched and pulled against the radiused die block simultaneously by the gripper arms, thus forming the part

Figure 16.1 The hydraulic shear used to cut sheet metal.

(Text continued on page 1200.)

Figure 16.2 A highly accurate squaring shear which is CNC controlled.

Figure 16.3 The Amada Pega high-speed, CNC-controlled multistation punch press.

Figure 16.4 A small press brake with digital back gage.

Figure 16.5 American standard wire gage-measuring tool.

Gauge no.	Brass (Brown & Sharpe)	Steel sheets*	Strip and Tubing	Steel wire ga.†
6-0	0.5800	—	—	0.4615
5-0	0.5165	—	0.500	0.4305
4-0	0.4600	—	0.454	0.3938
3-0	0.4096	—	0.425	0.3625
2-0	0.3648	—	0.380	0.3310
0	0.3249	—	0.340	0.3065
1	0.2893	—	0.300	0.2830
2	0.2576	—	0.284	0.2625
3	0.2294	0.2391	0.259	0.2437
4	0.2043	0.2242	0.238	0.2253
5	0.1819	0.2092	0.220	0.2070
6	0.1620	0.1943	0.203	0.1920
7	0.1443	0.1793	0.180	0.1770
8	0.1285	0.1644	0.165	0.1620
9	0.1144	0.1495	0.148	0.1483
10	0.1019	0.1345	0.134	0.1350
11	0.0907	0.1196	0.120	0.1205
12	0.0808	0.1046	0.109	0.1055
13	0.0720	0.0897	0.095	0.0915
14	0.0641	0.0747	0.083	0.0800
15	0.0571	0.0673	0.072	0.0720
16	0.0508	0.0598	0.065	0.0625
17	0.0453	0.0538	0.058	0.0540
18	0.0403	0.0478	0.049	0.0475
19	0.0359	0.0418	0.042	0.0410
20	0.0320	0.0359	0.035	0.0348
21	0.0285	0.0329	0.032	0.0317
22	0.0253	0.0299	0.028	0.0286
23	0.0226	0.0269	0.025	0.0258
24	0.0201	0.0239	0.022	0.0230
25	0.0179	0.0209	0.020	0.0204
26	0.0159	0.0179	0.018	0.0181
27	0.0142	0.0164	0.016	0.0173
28	0.0126	0.0149	0.014	0.0162
29	0.0113	0.0135	0.013	0.0150
30	0.0100	0.0120	0.012	0.0140
31	0.0089	0.0105	0.010	0.0132
32	0.0080	0.0097	0.009	0.0128
33	0.0071	0.0090	0.008	0.0118
34	0.0063	0.0082	0.007	0.0104
35	0.0056	0.0075	0.005	0.0095
36	0.0050	0.0067	0.004	0.0090
37	0.0045	0.0064	—	0.0085
38	0.0040	0.0060	—	0.0080

*Common commercial standard.
†Reference only.

Figure 16.6 Gaging decimals system table.

Number of wire gauge	American or Brown & Sharpe	Birmingham or Stubs' Iron wire	Washburn & Moen, Worcester, Mass.	W. & M. steel music wire	American S. & W. Co's. music wire gauge	Stubs' steel wire	U.S. Standard gauge for sheet and plate iron and steel	Number of wire gauge
00000000				0.0083				00000000
0000000				0.0087				0000000
000000				0.0095	0.004		0.46875	000000
00000				0.010	0.005		0.4375	00000
0000	0.460	0.454	0.3938	0.011	0.006		0.40625	0000
000	0.40964	0.425	0.3625	0.012	0.007		0.375	000
00	0.3648	0.380	0.3310	0.0133	0.008		0.34375	00
0	0.32486	0.340	0.3065	0.0144	0.009		0.3125	0
1	0.2893	0.300	0.2830	0.0156	0.010	0.227	0.28125	1
2	0.025763	0.284	0.2625	0.0166	0.011	0.219	0.265625	2
3	0.22942	0.259	0.2437	0.0178	0.012	0.212	0.250	3
4	0.20431	0.238	0.2253	0.0188	0.013	0.207	0.234375	4
5	0.18194	0.220	0.2070	0.0202	0.014	0.204	0.21875	5
6	0.16202	0.203	0.1920	0.0215	0.016	0.201	0.203125	6
7	0.14428	0.180	0.1770	0.023	0.018	0.199	0.1875	7
8	0.12849	0.165	0.1620	0.0243	0.020	0.197	0.171875	8
9	0.11443	0.148	0.1483	0.0256	0.022	0.194	0.15625	9
10	0.10189	0.134	0.1350	0.027	0.024	0.191	0.140625	10
11	0.090742	0.120	0.1205	0.0284	0.026	0.188	0.125	11
12	0.080808	0.109	0.1055	0.0296	0.029	0.185	0.109375	12
13	0.071961	0.095	0.0915	0.0314	0.031	0.182	0.09375	13
14	0.064084	0.083	0.0800	0.0326	0.033	0.180	0.078125	14

15	0.057068	0.072	0.0720	0.0345	0.035	0.178	0.0703125	15
16	0.05082	0.065	0.0625	0.036	0.037	0.175	0.0625	16
17	0.045257	0.058	0.0540	0.0377	0.039	0.172	0.05625	17
18	0.040303	0.049	0.0475	0.0395	0.041	0.168	0.050	18
19	0.03589	0.042	0.0410	0.0414	0.043	0.164	0.04375	19
20	0.031961	0.035	0.0348	0.0434	0.045	0.161	0.0375	20
21	0.028462	0.032	0.03175	0.046	0.047	0.157	0.034375	21
22	0.025347	0.028	0.0286	0.0483	0.049	0.155	0.03125	22
23	0.022571	0.025	0.0258	0.051	0.051	0.153	0.028125	23
24	0.0201	0.022	0.0230	0.055	0.055	0.151	0.025	24
25	0.0179	0.020	0.0204	0.0586	0.059	0.148	0.021875	25
26	0.01594	0.018	0.0181	0.0626	0.063	0.146	0.01875	26
27	0.014195	0.016	0.0173	0.0658	0.067	0.143	0.0171875	27
28	0.012641	0.014	0.0162	0.072	0.071	0.139	0.015625	28
29	0.011257	0.013	0.0150	0.076	0.075	0.134	0.0140625	29
30	0.010025	0.012	0.0140	0.080	0.080	0.127	0.0125	30
31	0.008928	0.010	0.0132		0.085	0.120	0.0109375	31
32	0.00795	0.009	0.0128		0.090	0.115	0.01015625	32
33	0.00708	0.008	0.0118		0.095	0.112	0.009375	33
34	0.006304	0.007	0.0104			0.110	0.00859375	34
35	0.005614	0.005	0.0095			0.108	0.0078125	35
36	0.005	0.004	0.0090			0.106	0.00703125	36
37	0.004453					0.103	0.006640625	37
38	0.003965					0.101	0.00625	38
39	0.003531					0.099		39
40	0.003144					0.097		40

Figure 16.7 Other gaging systems.

Standard thickness, in	Weight, lb/ft^2
0.010	0.141
0.016	0.226
0.020	0.282
0.025	0.353
0.032	0.452
0.040	0.564
0.050	0.706
0.063	0.889
0.071	1.002
0.080	1.129
0.090	1.270
0.100	1.411
0.125	1.764
0.160	2.258
0.190	2.681
0.250	3.528

Weight based on an average aluminum weight of 0.098 lb/in^3.

Figure 16.8 Standard aluminum sheet metal thicknesses and weights.

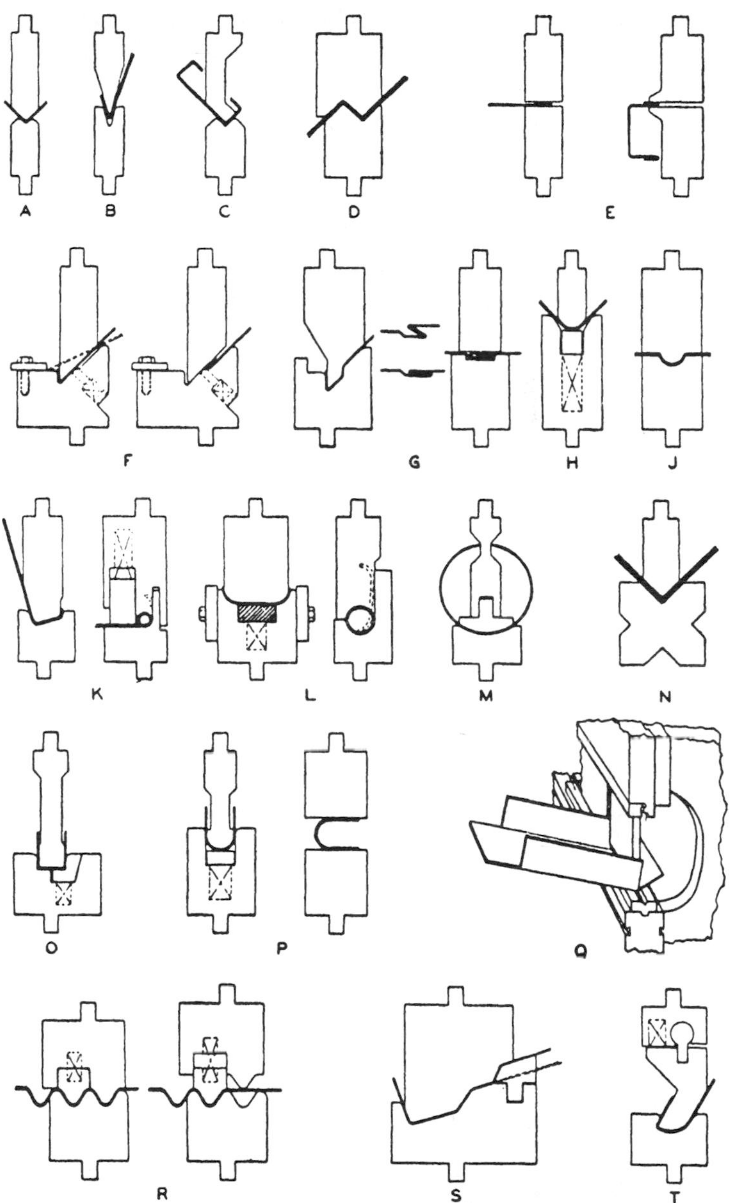

Figure 16.9 Press brake bending dies showing bending capabilities of the press brake.

to the specified radius. Allowance is made for "spring back" of the formed part by overbending and then allowing the metal to spring back or return to the correct form.

Roll forming: In the roll-forming process, a flat strip of sheet metal is fed into the roll-forming machine which has a series of rolling dies whose shape gradually changes as the metal is being fed past each stage of rolls, until the final roll-formed section is completed. The number of different cross sections of roll-formed sheet metal parts is limitless. The roll-formed part is usually made to a specific length or stock length or may be produced to any special length required. Figure 16.10 is a sample page of roll-formed sections taken from the Dahlstrom catalog of molded and rolled sections, Dahlstrom Manufacturing Corporation, Jamestown, New York.

A sample of sheet metal parts which have been press-brake bent and die formed may be seen in photographs shown in Chap. 9, "Tooling, Die Making, Molds, Jigs, and Fixtures."

16.6 Sheet Metal Flat Patterns

The correct determination of the flat-pattern dimensions of a sheet metal part which is formed or bent is of prime importance to sheet metal workers, designers, and design drafters. There are three methods for performing the calculations to determine flat patterns which are considered normal practice. The method chosen also can determine the accuracy of the results. The three common methods employed for doing the work include

- By bend deduction (B.D.) or setback
- By bend allowance (B.A.)
- By inside dimensions (IML), for sharply bent parts only

Other methods are also used for calculating the flat-pattern length of sheet metal parts. Some take into consideration the ductility of the material, and others are based on extensive experimental data for determining the bend allowances. The methods included in this section are accurate when the bend radius has been selected properly for each particular gage and condition of the material. When the proper bend radius is selected, there is no stretching of the *neutral axis* within the part (the neutral axis is generally accepted as being located 0.445 × material thickness inside the inside mold line (IML) (see Fig. 16.12).

Methods of determining flat patterns. Refer to Fig. 16.11.

Method 1: By bend deduction or setback

$$L = a + b - \text{setback}$$

Method 2: By bend allowance

$$L = a' + b' + c$$

where c = bend allowance or length along neutral axis.

Method 3: By inside dimensions or inside mold line (IML)

$$L = (a - T) + (b - T)$$

The calculation of bend allowance and bend deduction (setback) is keyed to Fig. 16.12 and is as follows:

$$\text{Bend allowance (B.A.)} = A(0.01745R + 0.00778T)$$

$$\text{Bend deduction (B.D.)} = \left(2 \tan \frac{1}{2}A\right)(R + T) - (\text{B.A.})$$

$$X = \left(\tan \frac{1}{2}A\right)(R + T)$$

$$Z = T\left(\tan \frac{1}{2}A\right)$$

$$Y = X - Z \qquad \text{or} \qquad R\left(\tan \frac{1}{2}A\right)$$

On "open" angles that are bent less than 90° (see Fig. 16.13),

$$X = \left(\tan \frac{1}{2}A\right)(R + T)$$

The method used to calculate the sheet metal flat pattern may be determined by designer option, company standards, order of accuracy, and method of manufacture. For soft steel (1010, etc.), the inside dimension method (method 3 described previously) is used whenever the material may be bent with a sharp or minimal inside bend radius (0.062 in or less). The inside bend method is accurate enough for all gages up to and including 0.375-in-thick stock where the tolerance of bent parts is ±0.032 in. On stock thicknesses from no. 7 gage to 0.375 in, 0.062 in is added to the sum of the inside bend dimensions and divided across the bend, 0.032 in going into each leg or flange inside dimension. The 0.062-in allowance is added for each 90° bend in the part. This method is popular in industries such as the electrical switch-gear industry, appliance industry, and others where great accuracy is not required.

For recommended bend radii on various materials and gages, see Sec. 9.5.2. Also, your company may have the recommended bend radii listed in the design manuals used in the design and tool engineering departments. All the aerospace companies and automobile makers have this information as part of the company design standards.

For very accurate flat-pattern dimensions intended for aerospace vehicles, automotive work, appliances, and other consumer products, the bend deduction or setback method is used in *lofting* procedures and standard sheet metal tooling drawings. The tooling department is usually responsible for generating the flat-pattern drawings of parts produced with stamping dies, punching dies, and drawing dies. The engineering department is usually responsible for generating the lofting drawings for flat patterns of regular and irregular shapes. In lofting, the part is drawn very accurately in flat pattern on flat metal sheets with specially prepared surfaces or directly onto heavy Mylar drafting film. The loft, or drawing, is then photographed, and the pattern is transferred to another metal sheet in full scale.

The part is then accurately cut out and becomes a master pattern. A stack of sheets can then be pin routed or tracer milled using the master template as a guide or jig. The cutout parts are then sent to the forming dies or the brakes for the final bending or forming operations. With modern CNC equipment, the part outline may be programmed and then automatically cut on the appropriate machine prior to the bending or forming operations.

When the sheet metal part is to be press-brake bent only on radiused bending dies, the bend allowance method can be used to calculate the flat pattern whenever accuracy and a specific inside bend radius are required. Bend deduction or setback also may be used in this case.

16.6.1 Setback or J chart for determining bend deductions

Figure 16.14*a* shows a form of bend deduction (B.D.) or setback chart known as a *J chart.* You may use this chart to determine bend deduction or setback when the angle of bend, material thickness, and inside bend radius are known. The chart in the figure shows a sample line running from the top to the bottom and drawn through the 3⁄16-in radius and the material thickness of 0.075 in. For a 90° bend, read across from the right to where the line intersects the closest curved line in the body of the chart. In this case, it can be seen that the line intersects the curve whose value is 0.18. This value is then the required setback or bend deduction for a bend of 90° in a part whose thickness is 0.075 in with an inside bend radius of 3⁄16 in. If we check this setback or bend deduction value using the appropriate equations shown previously, we can check the value given by the J chart.

Checking. Bend deduction (B.D.) or setback is given as

$$\text{Bend deduction or setback} = \left(2 \tan \frac{1}{2}A\right)(R + T) - (\text{B.A.})$$

We must first find the bend allowance from

$$\begin{aligned}\text{Bend allowance} &= A(0.01745R + 0.00778T) \\ &= 90(0.01745 \times 0.1875 + 0.00778 \times 0.075) \\ &= 90(0.003855) \\ &= 0.34695\end{aligned}$$

Now, substituting the bend allowance of 0.34695 into the bend deduction equation yields

$$\begin{aligned}\text{Bend deduction or setback} &= \left[2 \tan \frac{1}{2}(90)\right](0.1875 + 0.075) - 0.34695 \\ &= (2 \times 1)(0.2625) - 0.34695 \\ &= 0.525 - 0.34695 \\ &= 0.178 \quad \text{or} \quad 0.18, \text{ as shown in the chart (Fig. 16.14)}\end{aligned}$$

The J chart in Fig. 16.14 is thus an important tool for determining the bend deduction or setback of sheet metal flat patterns without recourse to tedious calculations. The accuracy of this chart has been shown to be of a high order. This chart as well as the equations were developed after extensive experimentation and practical working experience in the aerospace industry.

16.6.2 Bend radii for aluminum-alloy and steel sheet (average)

Figure 16.14*b* and *c* shows average bend radii for various aluminum alloys and steel sheets. For other bend radii in different materials and gages, see Sec. 9.5.2.

16.7 Sheet Metal Developments and Transitions

The layout of sheet metal as required in "development and transition" parts is an important phase of sheet metal design and practice. The methods included here will prove useful in many design and working applications. These methods have application in duct work, aerospace vehicles, automotive equipment, and other areas of product design and development requiring the use of transitions and developments.

When sheet metal is to be formed into a curved section, it may be layed out, or *developed,* with resonable accuracy by *triangulation* if it forms a simple curved surface without compound curves or curves in multiple directions. Sheet metal curved sections are found on many products, and if a straight edge can be placed flat against *elements* of the curved section, accurate layout or development is possible using the methods shown in this section.

On double-curved surfaces such as are found on automobile and truck bodies and aircraft, forming dies are created from a full-scale model in order to duplicate these compound curved surfaces in sheet metal. The full-scale models used in aerospace vehicle manufacturing facilities are commonly called *mock-ups,* and the models used to transfer the compound curved surfaces are made by tool makers in the tooling department.

16.7.1 Skin development

Skin development on aerospace vehicles or other applications may be accomplished by triangulation when the surface is not double curved. Figure 16.15 presents a side view of the nose section of a simple aircraft. If we wish to develop the outer skin or sheet metal between stations 20.00 and 50.00, the general procedure is as follows: The "master lines" of the curves at stations 20.00 and 50.00 must be determined. In actual practice, the curves are developed by the "master lines" engineering group of the company, or you may know or develop your own curves. The procedure for layout of the flat pattern is as follows (see Fig. 16.16):

1. Divide curve *A* into a number of equally spaced points. Use the spline lengths (arc distances), *not* chordal distances.
2. Lay an accurate triangle tangent to one point on curve *A,* and by parallel action, transfer the edge of the triangle back to curve *B* and mark a point where the edge of the triangle is tangent to curve *B* (e.g., point *b* on curve *A* back to point *h* on curve *B;* see Fig. 16.16). Then parallel transfer all points on curve *A* back to curve *B* and label all points for identification. Draw the element lines and diagonals on the frontal view, that is, 1*A,* 2*B,* 3*C,* etc.
3. Construct a true-length diagram as shown in Fig. 16.16(*A*), where all the element and diagonal true lengths can be found (elements are 1, 2, 3, 4, etc; diagonals are *A, B, C, D,* etc.). The true distance between the two curves is 30.00; that is, 50.00 – 20.00, from Fig. 16.15.
4. Transfer the element and diagonal true-length lines to the triangulation flat-pattern layout as shown in Fig. 16.16(*C*). The triangulated flat pattern is completed by transferring all elements and diagonals to the flat-pattern layout.

16.7.2 Canted-station skin development (bulkheads at an angle to axis)

When the planes of the curves *A* and *B* (Fig. 16.17) are *not* perpendicular to the axis of the curved section, layout procedures to determine the true lengths of the element and diagonal lines are as shown in Fig. 16.17. The remainder of the procedure is as explained in Sec. 16.7.1 to develop the triangulated flat pattern.

In aerospace terminology, the locations of points on the craft are determined by station, waterline, and buttline. These terms are defined as follows:

Station: The numbered locations from the front to the rear of the craft.

Waterline: The vertical locations from the lowest point to the highest point of the craft.

Buttline: The lateral locations from the centerline of the axis of the craft to the right and to the left of the axis of the craft. There are right buttlines and left buttlines.

With these three axes, any exact point on the craft may be described or dimensioned.

16.8 Developing Flat Patterns

Developing flat patterns can be done by bend deduction or setback. Figure 16.18 shows a type of sheet metal part that may be bent on a press brake. The flat-pattern part is bent on the brake, with the center of bend line (CBL) held on the bending die centerline. The machine's back gage is set by the operator in order to form the part. If you study the figure closely, you can see how the dimensions progress: The bend deduction is drawn in, and the next dimension is taken from the end of the first bend deduction. The next dimension is then measured, the bend deduction is drawn in for that bend, and then the next dimension is taken from the end of the second bend deduction, etc. Notice that the second bend deduction is larger because of the larger radius of the second bend (0.16*R*).

16.9 Stiffening Sheet Metal Parts

On many sheet metal parts that have large areas, stiffening can be achieved by creasing the metal in an X configuration by means of brake bending. On certain parts where great stiffness and rigidity are required, a method called *beading* is employed. The beading is carried out at the same time as the part is being hydropressed, Marformed, or hard-die formed. See Fig. 16.19*b* and Chap. 9, "Tooling, Die Making, Molds, Jigs, and Fixtures," for more data on beading sheet metal parts.

Another method for stiffening the edge of a long sheet metal part is to hem or "Dutch bend" the edge as shown in Fig. 16.19*a*. In aerospace and automotive sheet metal parts, flanged *lightening holes* are used as shown in Fig. 16.19*c*. The lightening hole not only makes the part lighter in weight but also more rigid. This method is used commonly in wing ribs, airframes, and gussets or brackets. The lightening hole need not be circular but can take any convenient shape as required by the application.

16.10 Sheet Metal Faying Surfaces

Faying surfaces are those where two sheet metal parts come into contact with each other, such as the joining of a flange with a web section or the joining of two flanges. All faying surfaces should be primer painted or finished in some manner to prevent corrosion. A standard finish for many applications is zinc-chromate primer.

Other finishes include zinc plating, nickel plating, cadmium plating, chrome plating, etc. Since cadmium plating and plating solutions are toxic, zinc plating is used in its place where the application allows this. New designs should specify zinc or nickel in place of cadmium unless there is a specific technical reason for using cadmium.

16.11 Design Points for Sheet Metal Parts

- Do not specify flanges that are too narrow for the type of bending operation. That is, do not design a part with a 0.375-in flange width unless you have the equipment or dies to produce such a short flange on the press brake or other type of machine. Bottoming dies can enable the bending of such a flange in very light gages up to no. 11 gage.
- Do not specify gages that are heavier than necessary for the function of the part. An exception to this rule is code specifications such as for electrical switch-gear equipment, where a minimum of no. 11 gage steel is specified for certain sections of the equipment, whether it is structurally required or not. The heavy gage limit in this application is for the prevention of the spread of fires between adjacent units if there is an electrical fault.
- Use proper edge distances for hardware components, keeping the flanges as narrow as practical with respect to their required rigidity or strength.
- Do not design a part that is impractical to bend on the type of machinery with which your operation is equipped.
- Keep brake-formed parts in a size range where the parts can be handled manually by the brake operators, unless your operation is equipped with automatic machinery or other special-handling equipment.
- When using hot-rolled steel sheets, use tolerances on your parts that are functionally related to the equipment used in your operation. That is, do not expect to hold dimensions to $\pm\frac{1}{64}$ in when

you are producing no. 11 gage hot-rolled sheet metal parts on a press brake. Normal shop tolerance on general sheet metal parts is usually ±1/32 in for parts under 3 ft in length in both directions. One of the reasons that hot-rolled steel sheet metal parts between nos. 16 and 7 gages need a generous tolerance is that the steel sheet metal thickness varies from sheet to sheet. This variation can reach ±½ a gage step on a batch of steel of the same gage. The variation of the gage causes the flanges to be bent to different outside dimensions even though the back-gage dimension is the same and is very apparent when more than two bends are made on the same part.

In high-speed, mass-production operations there is no remedy for this condition of variable thickness within the same gage of hot-rolled steel sheet material except a favorable tolerance spread on the dimensions of the parts. Some of the larger companies specify the gage-variation limits when they order steel sheet metal, but the mill order must be large in order to do this. These problems do not occur when using gage-accurate cold-rolled steel sheets.

16.12 Typical Transitions and Developments

The following transitions and developments are the most common types, and learning or using them for reference will prove helpful in many industrial applications. Using the principles shown will enable you to apply these to many different variations or geometric forms. The principles shown and described in Sec. 16.7 will prove helpful in trying to understand and put to practice the transitions and developments shown in this section. Construction of the true-length diagrams is of particular importance.

16.12.1 Development of a Truncated Right Pyramid

Refer to Fig. 16.20. Draw the projections of the pyramid that show (1) a normal view of the base or right section and (2) a normal view of the axis. Lay out the pattern for the pyramid and then superimpose the pattern on the truncation.

Since this is a portion of a right regular pyramid, the lateral edges are all of equal length. The lateral edges *OA* and *OD* are parallel to the frontal plane and consequently show in their true length on the front view. With the center at O_1, taken at any convenient place, and a radius $O_F A_F$, draw an arc that is the stretchout of the pattern. On it, step off the six equal sides of the hexagonal base obtained from the top view, and connect these points successively with each other and with the vertex O_1, thus forming the pattern for the pyramid.

The intersection of the cutting plane and lateral surfaces is developed by laying off the true length of the intercept of each lateral edge on the corresponding line of the development. The true length of each of these intercepts, such as *OH, OJ,* etc., is found by rotating it about the axis of the pyramid until it coincides with $O_F A_F$ as previously explained. The path of any point, such as *H,* will be projected on the front view as a horizontal line. To obtain the development of the entire surface of the truncated pyramid, attach the base; also find the true size of the cut face, and attach it on a common line.

16.12.2 To develop an oblique pyramid

Refer to Fig. 16.21. Since the lateral edges are unequal in length, the true length of each must be found separately by rotating it parallel to the frontal plane. With O_1 taken at any convenient place, lay off the seam line O_1A_1 equal to $O_F A_R$. With A_1 as center and radius O_1B_1 equal to $O_F B_R$, describe a second arc intersecting the first in vertex B_1. Connect the vertices O_1, A_1, and B_1, thus forming the pattern for the lateral surface *OAB*. Similarly, lay out the pattern for the remaining three lateral surfaces, joining them on their common edges. The stretchout is equal to the summation of the base edges. If the complete development is required, attach the base on a common line.

16.12.3 To develop a truncated right cylinder

Refer to Fig. 16.22. The development of a cylinder is similar to the development of a prism. Draw two projections of the cylinder:

1. A normal view of a right section
2. A normal view of the elements

In rolling the cylinder out on a tangent plane, the base or right section, being perpendicular to the axis, will develop into a straight line. For convenience in drawing, divide the normal view of the

(*Text continued on page 1221.*)

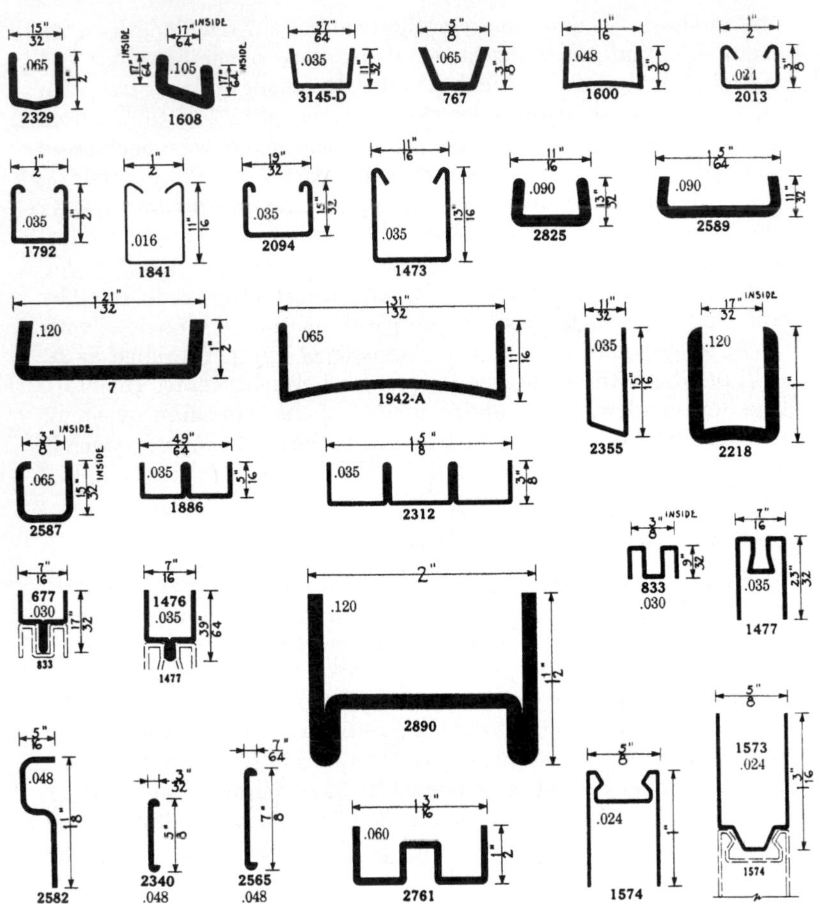

Figure 16.10 Samples of roll-formed sections of sheet metal.

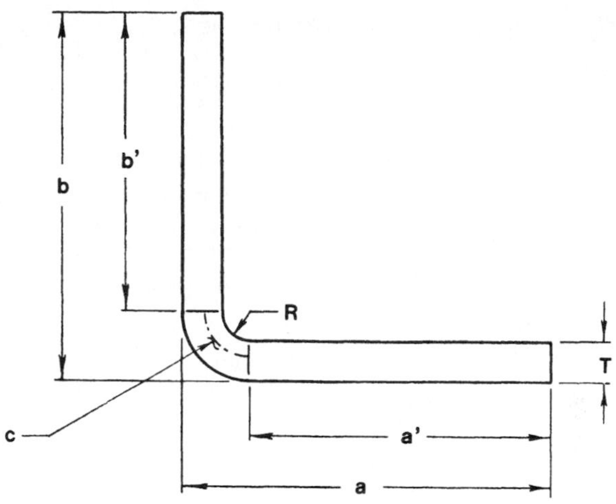

Figure 16.11 Sample of a bent sheet metal angle.

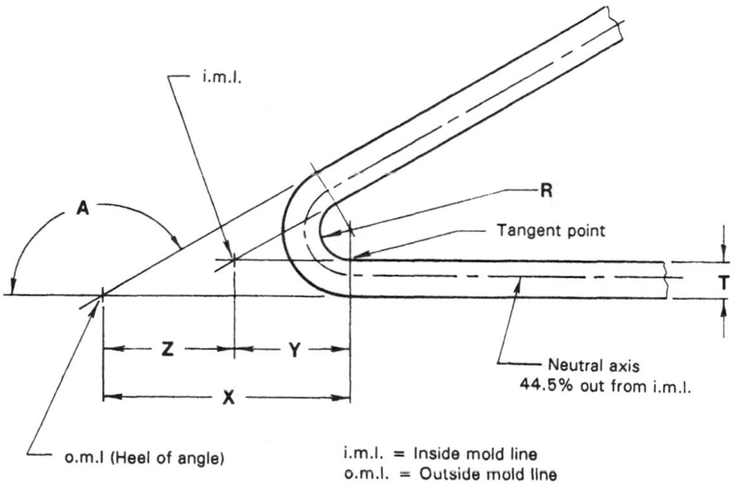

Figure 16.12 Geometry of a bend angle.

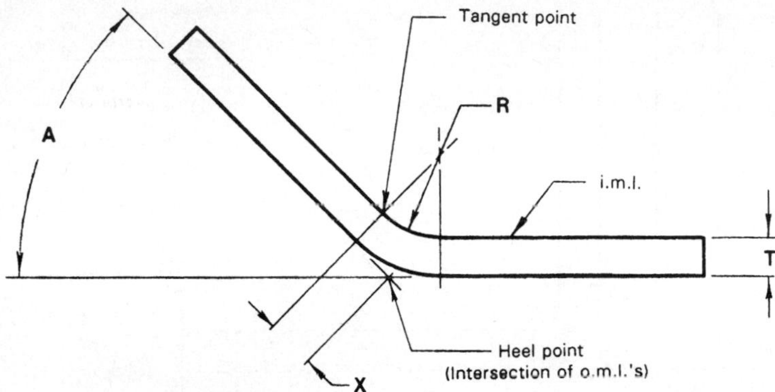

Figure 16.13 An open angle.

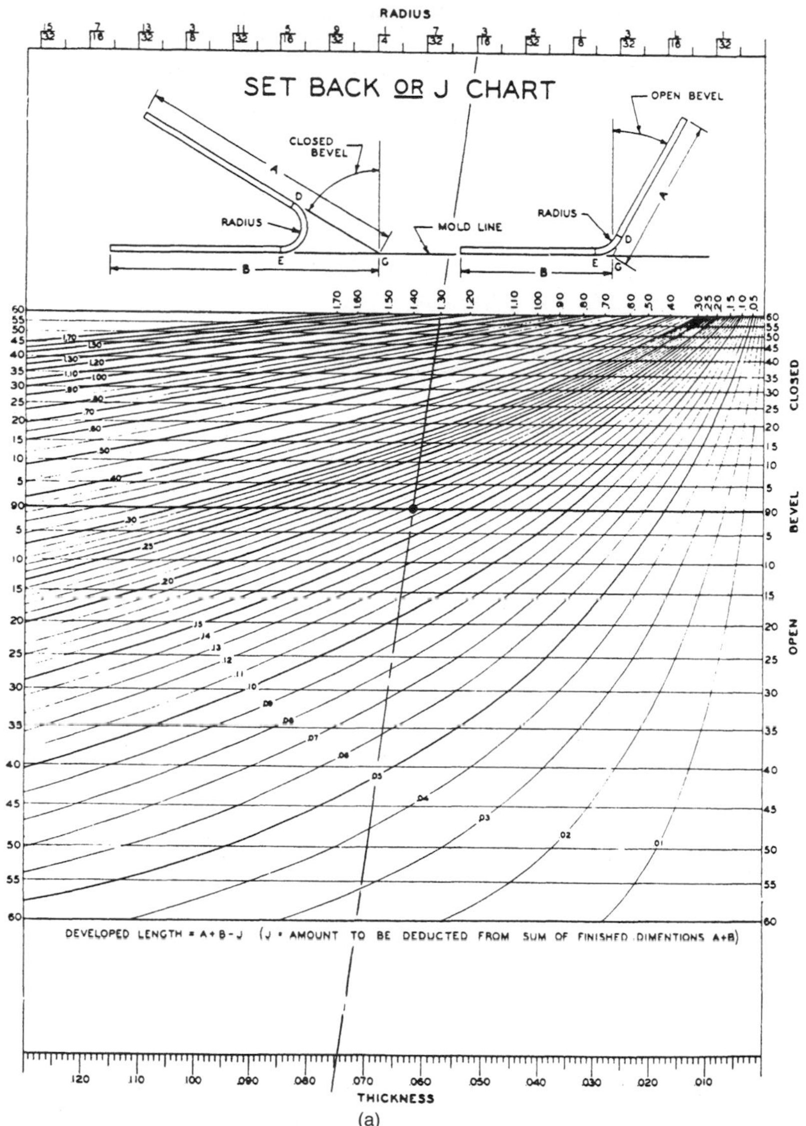

(a)

Figure 16.14 (*a*) Setback or J chart.

Sheet-metal bend radii for several steel designations.

Material Gauge	Steel designation	
	1020	302-303-304
0.010	1/32	1/32
0.020	1/32	1/32
0.030	1/32	1/32
0.040	1/32	1/32
0.050	1/32	1/32
0.060	1/32	1/16
0.070	1/32	1/16
0.080	1/32	1/16
0.090	1/16	1/16
0.120	1/16	1/8
0.190	1/8	1/4
0.250	1/8	1/4

(b)

Figure 16.14 (*b*) Bend radius table for sheet metal.

Bend radii for several aluminum alloy sheet-metal designations.

Material Gauge	Aluminum designation		
	6061-T6 5052-H36 1100-H18	5052-H22 3003-H14	2024-T3
0.010	1/16	1/32	1/16
0.020	1/16	1/32	1/16
0.030	1/16	1/32	1/8
0.040	1/8	1/32	1/4
0.050	1/8	1/32	1/4
0.060	1/8	1/32	1/4
0.070	1/4	1/16	1/4
0.080	1/4	1/32	3/8
0.090	3/8	1/8	3/8
0.120	3/8	1/8	1/2
0.190	3/4	1/4	3/4
0.250	1	1/2	1

(c)

Figure 16.14 (*c*) Bend radius table for aluminum sheet.

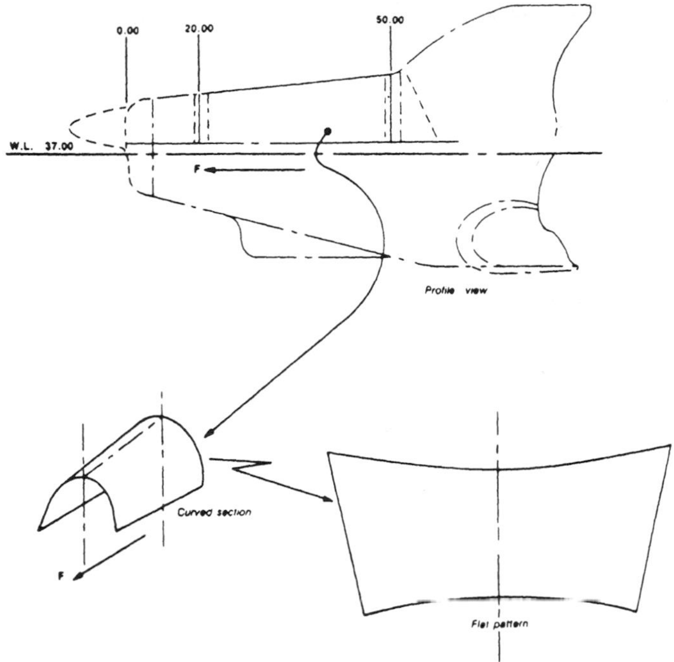

Figure 16.15 Section of "skin" on an aircraft developed in Fig. 16.16.

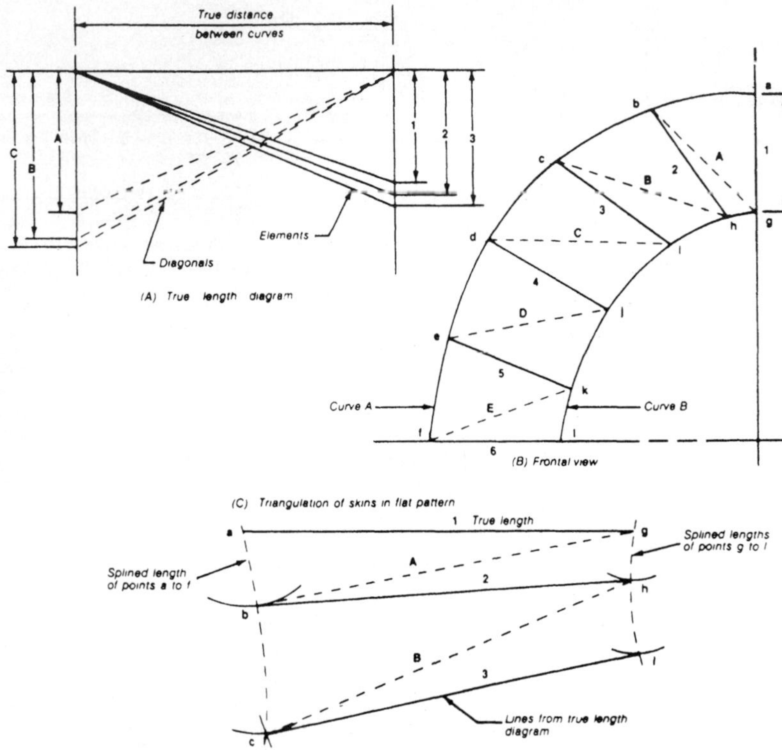

Figure 16.16 Layout of skin flat pattern.

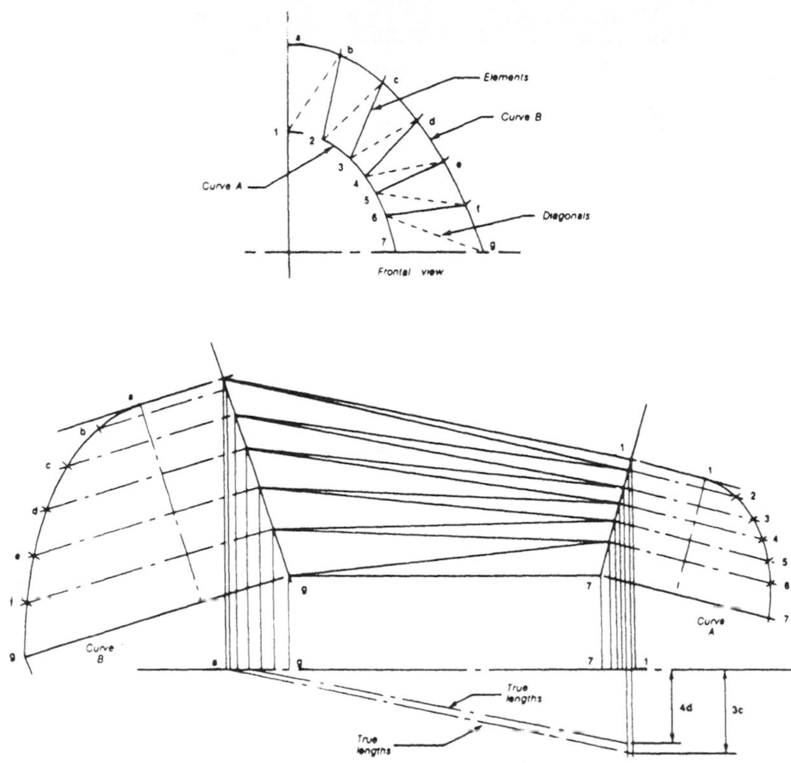

Figure 16.17 Layout of skin with canted bulkheads.

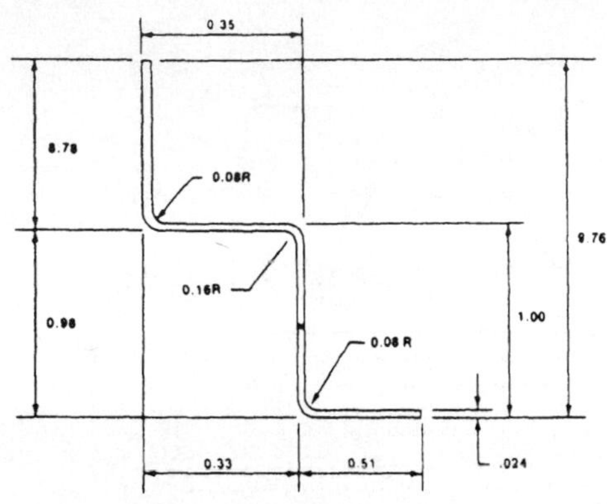

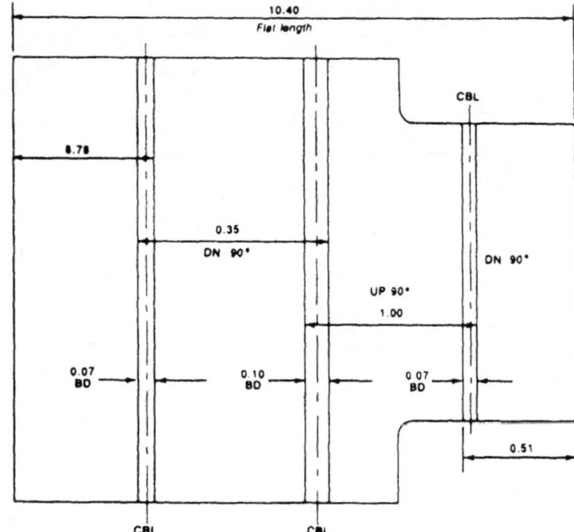

Figure 16.18 Layout of bent sheet metal by bend-deduction method.

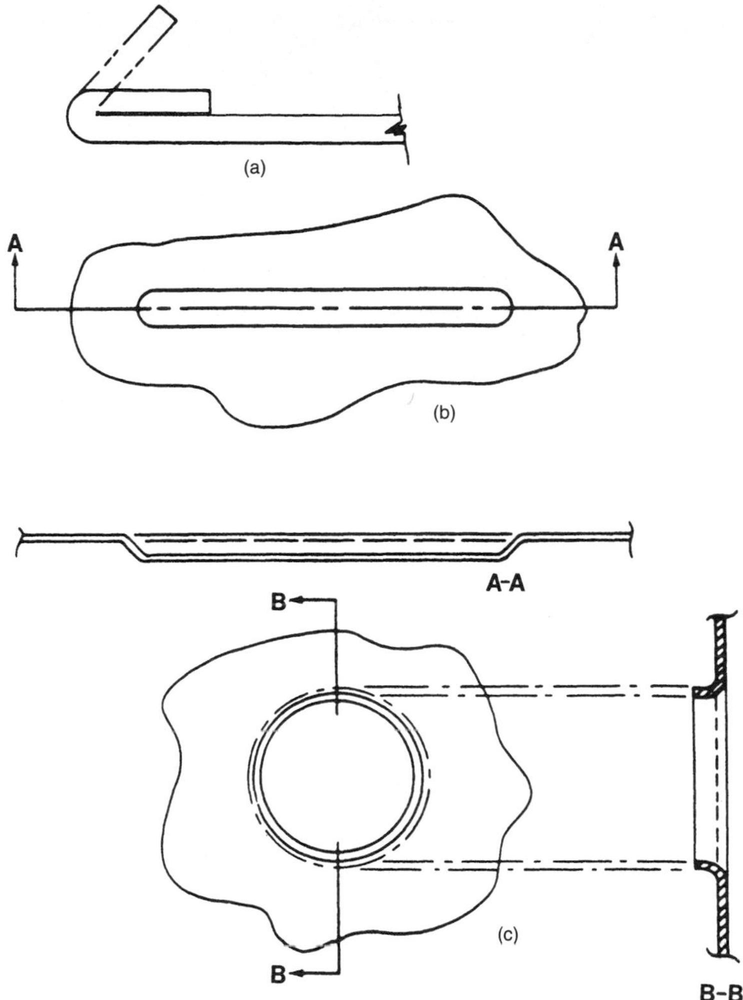

Figure 16.19 (*a*) A hemmed edge. (*b*) A stiffening bead. (*c*) A lightening hole.

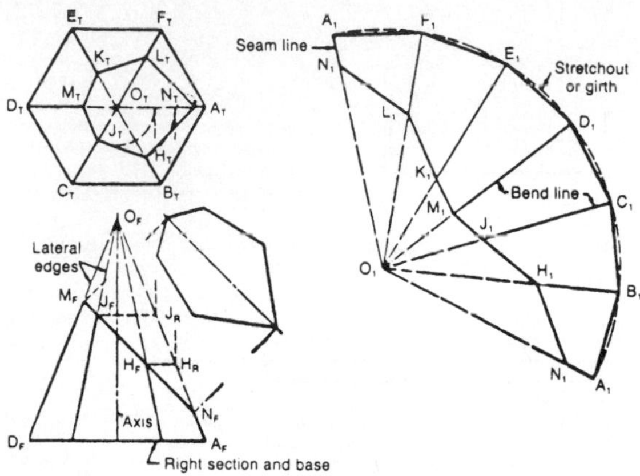

Figure 16.20 A truncated right pyramid.

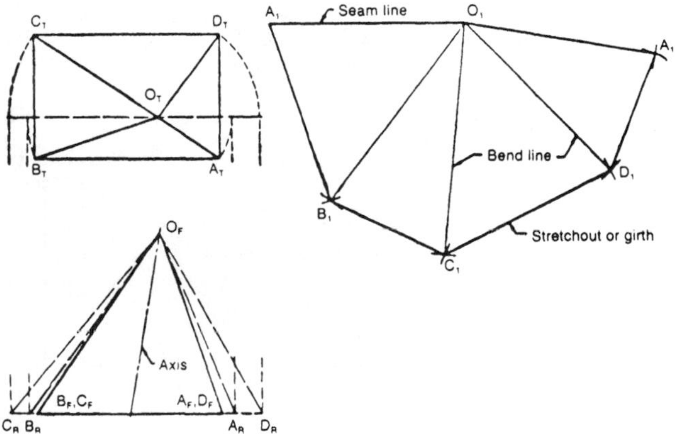

Figure 16.21 An oblique pyramid.

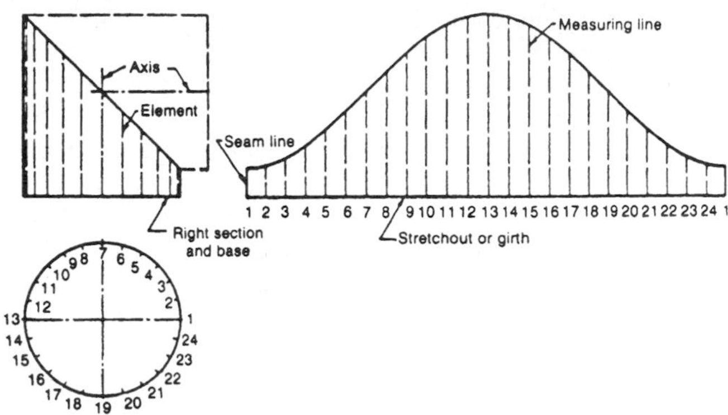

Figure 16.22 A truncated right cylinder.

base, shown here in the bottom view, into a number of equal parts by points that represent elements. These divisions should be spaced so that the chordal distances approximate the arc closely enough to make the stretchout practically equal to the periphery of the base or right section.

Project these elements to the front view. Draw the stretchout and measuring lines, the cylinder now being treated as a many-sided prism. Transfer the lengths of the elements in order, either by projection or by using dividers, and join the points thus found by a smooth curve. Sketch the curve in very lightly, freehand, before fitting the French curve or ship's curve to it. This development might be the pattern for one-half of a two-piece elbow.

Three-piece, four-piece, and five-piece elbows may be drawn similarly, as illustrated in Fig. 16.23. Since the base is symmetrical, only one-half of it need be drawn. In these cases, the intermediate pieces such as *B, C,* and *D* are developed on a stretchout line formed by laying off the perimeter of a right section. If the right section is taken through the middle of the piece, the stretchout line becomes the center of the development. Evidently, any elbow could be cut from a single sheet without waste if the seams were made alternately on the long and short sides.

16.12.4 To develop a truncated right circular cone

Refer to Fig. 16.24. Draw the projection of the cone that will show (1) a normal view of the base or right section and (2) a normal view of the axis. First, develop the surface of the complete cone and then superimpose the pattern for the truncation.

Divide the top view of the base into a sufficient number of equal parts that the sum of the resulting chordal distances will closely approximate the periphery of the base. Project these points to the front view, and draw front views of the elements through them. With center A_1 and a radius equal to the slant height $A_F I_F$, which is the true length of all the elements, draw an arc, which is the stretchout. Lay off on it the chordal divisions of the base, obtained from the top view. Connect these points 2, 3, 4, 5, etc. with A_1, thus forming the pattern for the cone.

Find the true length of each element from vertex to cutting plane by rotating it to coincide with the contour element A_1, and lay off this distance on the corresponding line of the development. Draw a smooth curve through these points. The pattern for the cut surface is obtained from the auxiliary view.

Triangulation. Nondevelopable surfaces are developed approximately by assuming them to be made of narrow sections of developable surfaces. The most common and best method for approximate development is *triangulation;* that is, the surface is assumed to be made up of a large number of triangular strips or plane triangles with very short bases. This method is used for all warped surfaces as well as for oblique cones. Oblique cones are single-curved surfaces that are capable of true theoretical development, but they can be developed much more easily and accurately by triangulation.

16.12.5 To develop an oblique cone

Refer to Fig. 16.25. An oblique cone differs from a cone of revolution in that the elements are all of different lengths. The development of a right circular cone is made up of a number of equal triangles meeting at the vertex whose sides are elements and whose bases are the chords of short arcs of the base of the cone. In the oblique cone, each triangle must be found separately.

Draw two views of the cone showing (1) a normal view of the base and (2) a normal view of the altitude. Divide the true size of the base, shown here in the top view, into a number of equal parts such that the sum of the chordal distances will closely approximate the length of the base curve. Project these points to the front view of the base. Through these points and the vertex, draw the elements in each view.

Since the cone is symmetrical about a frontal plane through the vertex, the elements are shown only on the front half of it. Also, only one-half of the development is drawn. With the seam on the shortest element, the element OC will be the centerline of the development and may be drawn directly at O_1C_1, since its true length is given by O_FC_F.

Find the true length of the elements by rotating them until they are parallel to the frontal plane or by constructing a *true-length diagram*. The true length of any element will be the hypotenuse of a triangle with one leg the length of the projected element, as seen in the top view, and the other leg equal to the altitude of the cone. Thus, to make the diagram, draw the leg OD coinciding with or parallel to O_FD_F. At D and perpendicular to OD, draw the other leg, and lay off on it the lengths $D1$, $D2$, etc. equal to D_T1_T, D_T2_T, etc., respectively. Distances from point O to points on the base of the diagram are the true lengths of the elements.

Construct the pattern for the front half of the cone as follows. With O_1 as the center and radius $O1$, draw an arc. With C_1 as center and the radius C_T1_T, draw a second arc intersecting the first at 1_1. Then O_11_1 will be the developed position of the element $O1$. With 1_1 as the center and radius 1_T2_T, draw an arc intersecting a second arc with O_1 as center and radius $O2$, thus locating 2_1. Continue this procedure until all the elements have been transferred to the development. Connect the points C_1, 1_1, 2_1, etc. with a smooth curve, the stretchout line, to complete the development.

16.12.6 Conical connection between two cylindrical pipes

Refer to Fig. 16.26. The method used in drawing the pattern is the application of the development of an oblique cone. One-half the elliptical base is shown in true size in an auxiliary view (here attached to the front view). Find the true size of the base from its major and minor axes; divide it into a number of equal parts so that the sum of these chordal distances closely approximates the periphery of the curve. Project these points to the front and top views. Draw the elements in each view through these points, and find the vertex O by extending the contour elements until they intersect.

The true length of each element is found by using the vertical distance between its ends as the vertical leg of the diagram and its horizontal projection as the other leg. As each true length from vertex to base is found, project the upper end of the intercept horizontally across from the front view to the true length of the corresponding element to find the true length of the intercept. The development is drawn by laying out each triangle in turn, from vertex to base, as in Sec. 16.12.5, starting on the centerline O_1C_1, and then measuring on each element its intercept length. Draw smooth curves through these points to complete the pattern.

16.12.7 To develop transition pieces

Refer to Figs. 16.27 and 16.28. Transitions are used to connect pipes or openings of different shapes or cross sections. Figure 16.27, showing a transition piece for connecting a round pipe and a rectangular pipe, is typical. These pieces are always developed by triangulation. The piece shown in Fig. 16.27 is, evidently, made up of four triangular planes whose bases are the sides of the rectangle and four parts of oblique cones whose common bases are arcs of the circle and whose vertices are at the corners of the rectangle. To develop the piece, make a true-length diagram as shown in Sec. 16.12.6. The true length of $O1$ being found, all the sides of triangle A will be known. Attach the developments of cones B and B^1, then those of triangle C and C^1, and so on.

Figure 16.28 is another transition piece joining a rectangle to a circular pipe whose axes are not parallel. By using a partial right-side view of the round opening, the divisions of the bases of the oblique cones can be found. (Since the object is symmetrical, only one-half the opening need be divided.) The true lengths of the elements are obtained as shown in Fig. 16.27.

16.12.8 Triangulation of warped surfaces

The approximate development of a warped surface is made by dividing it into a number of narrow quadrilaterals and then splitting each of these into two triangles by a diagonal line, which is assumed to be a straight line, although it is really a curve. Figure 16.29 shows a warped transition piece that connects on ovular (upper) pipe with a right-circular cylindrical pipe (lower). Find the true size of one-half the elliptical base by rotating it until horizontal about an axis through 1, when its true shape will be seen. The major axis is $1–7_R$, and the minor axis through 4_R will be equal to the diameter of the lower pipe.

Divide the semiellipse into a sufficient number of equal parts, and project these to the top and front views. Divide the top semicircle into the same number of equal parts, and connect similar points on each end, thus dividing the surface into approximate quadrilaterals. Cut each into two triangles by a diagonal. On true-length diagrams, find the lengths of the elements and the diagonals, and draw the development by constructing the true sizes of the triangles in regular order.

16.13 Sheet Metal Fabrication Practices

Figures 16.30 through 16.37 illustrate some of the methods used in sheet metal design and fabrication practices. A detailed description of the figures follows: Figure 16.30 shows the accepted methods of relieving the corner stresses and deformation that occur when sheet metal flanges meet at a 90° corner. Circular punch, oblong punch, and sawcuts are illustrated. Figure 16.31 shows that a sheet metal angle may be offset (joggled) to fit over another sheet metal part (common practice in the aerospace industries). Corners are formed and fastened by welding directly or with gusset plates.

In Fig. 16.32, a partially closed sheet metal part that would normally be roll formed is produced on a press brake using this sequence. The outer flanges are bent; then the center is bent to form a W section; finally, the section is completed with a flattening die. Figure 16.33 shows that a return flange on a sheet metal part is possible only when a "gooseneck" die is used in the operation. This forming operation is normally done in a press brake.

Figure 16.34*a* shows a sheet metal stake. Stakes are used as stops as well as for spring anchors. Figure 16.34*b* shows how an integral flange is produced in the web of a sheet metal part. The sheet metal must first be die punched prior to the bending operation.

The punch tap is an economical method for producing tapped holes in sheet metal parts. The hole is first punched and extruded by the same die and then tapped with the appropriate thread (Fig. 16.35). The maximum practical size of the punch-tapped hole is generally 0.375-16 in #11 gage sheet steel. Figure 16.36*a* shows the common "corner break" or stiffening notch which is formed in the heel section of a sheet metal angle. These simple metal deformation methods add a great amount of strength and stiffness to light-gage sheet metal parts. Figure 16.37 illustrates some of the common methods of applying gaskets to sheet metal doors and the sheet metal configurations required in these gasketing methods.

(Text continued on page 1238.)

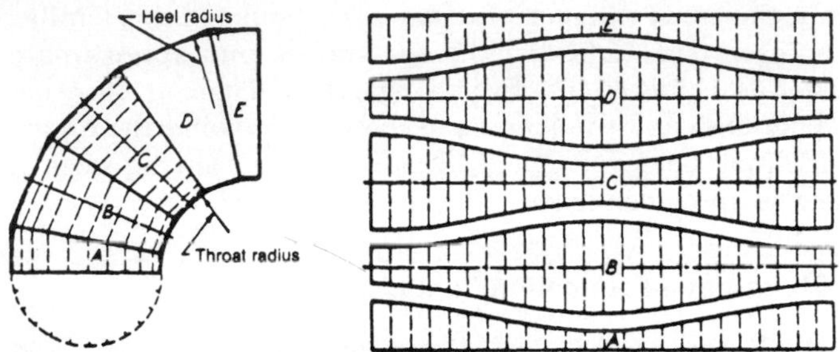

Figure 16.23 A five-piece elbow.

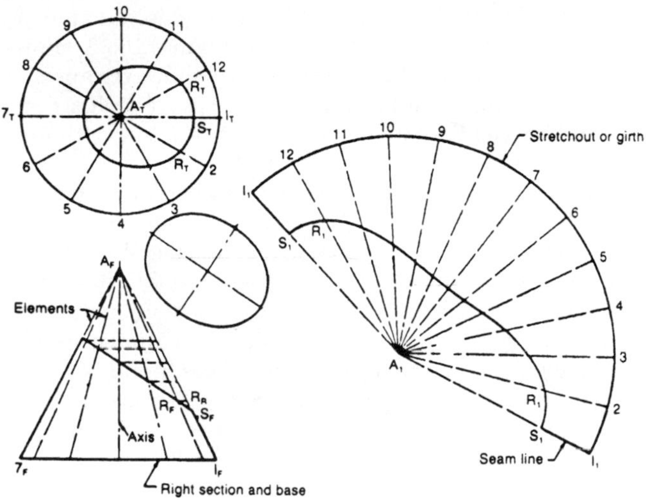

Figure 16.24 A truncated right circular cone.

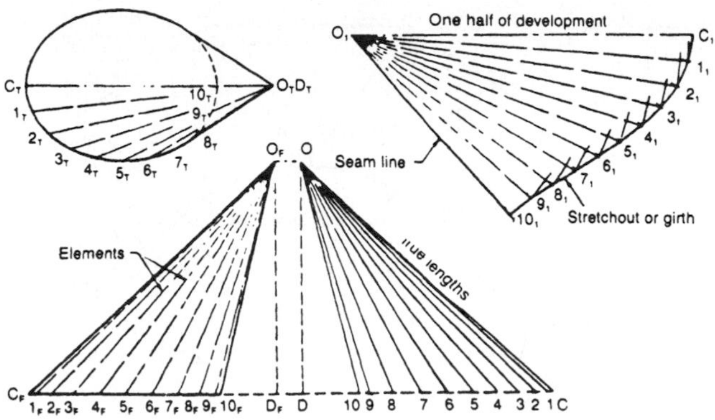

Figure 16.25 An oblique cone.

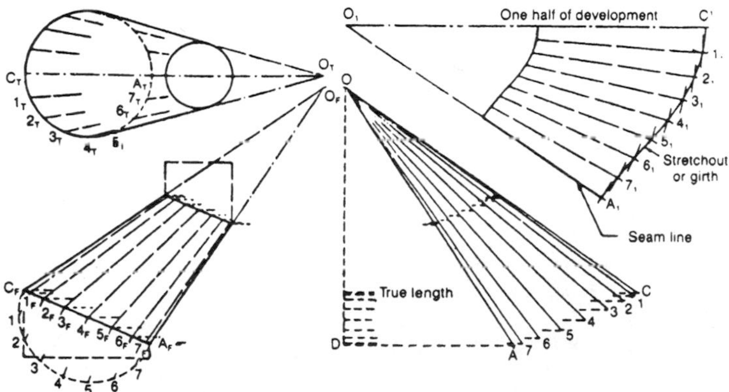

Figure 16.26 A conical connection between two cylinders.

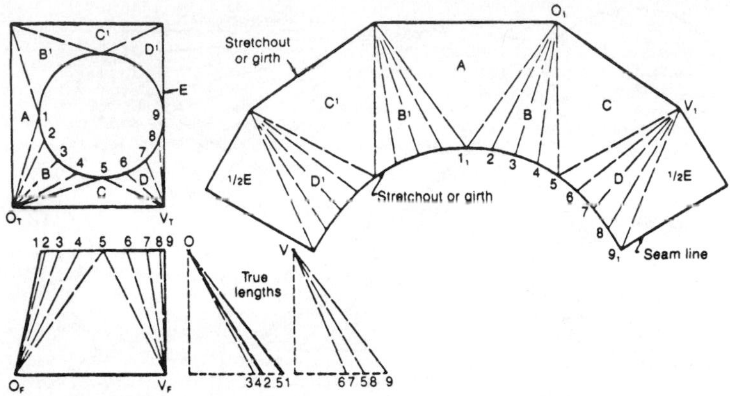

Figure 16.27 A transition piece.

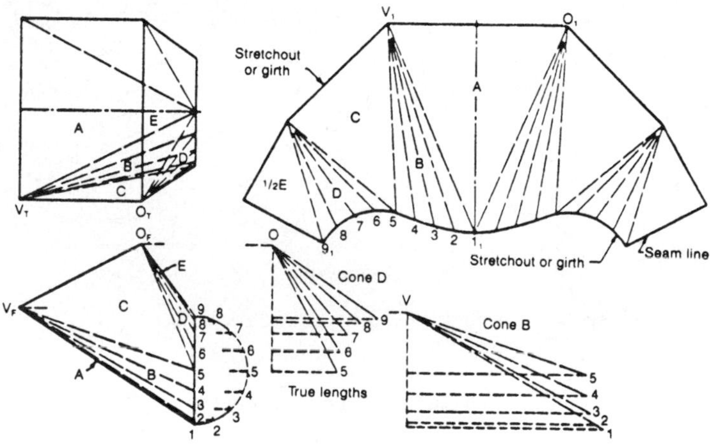

Figure 16.28 A transition piece.

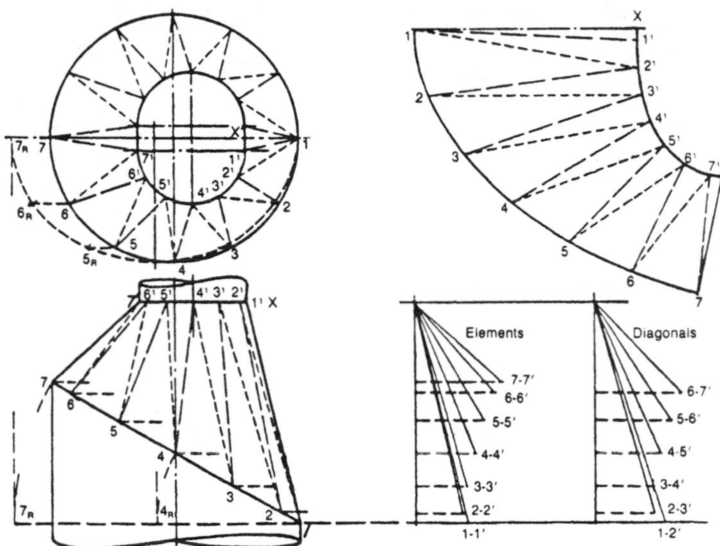

Figure 16.29 A warped transition piece.

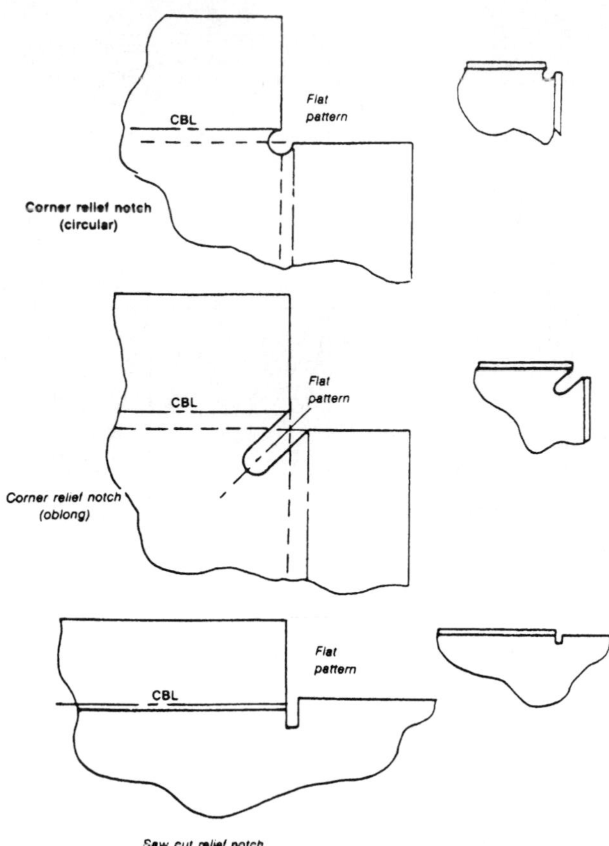

Figure 16.30 Sheet metal corners.

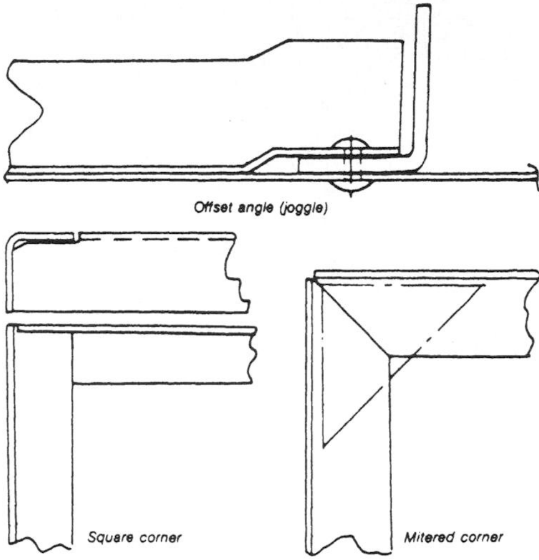

Figure 16.31 Sheet metal intersections.

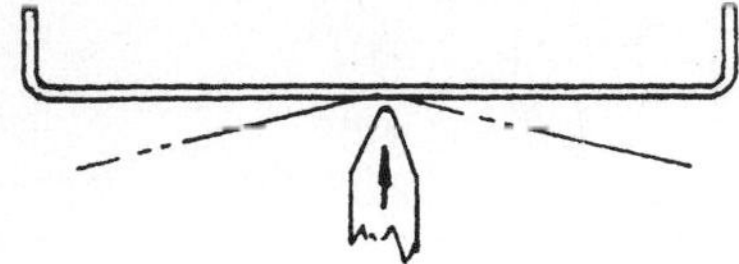

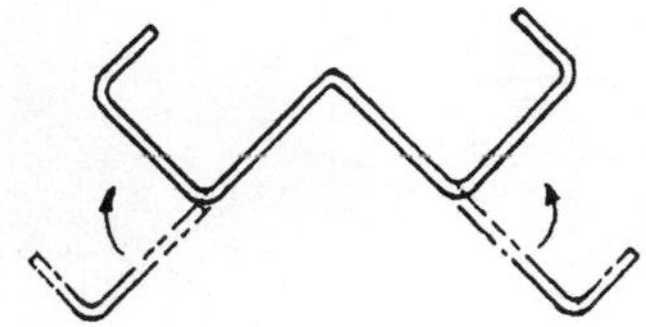

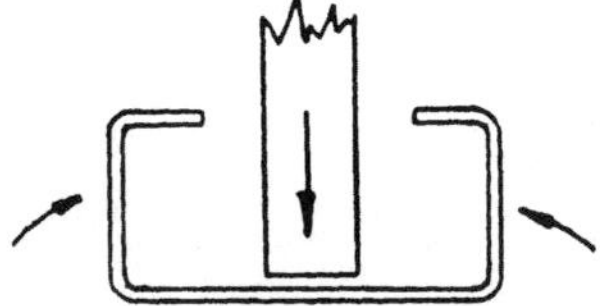

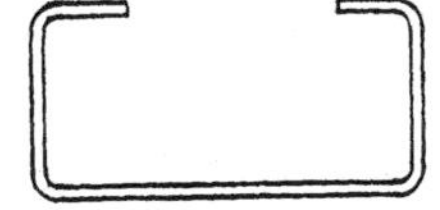

Figure 16.32 Press brake forming a partially closed section.

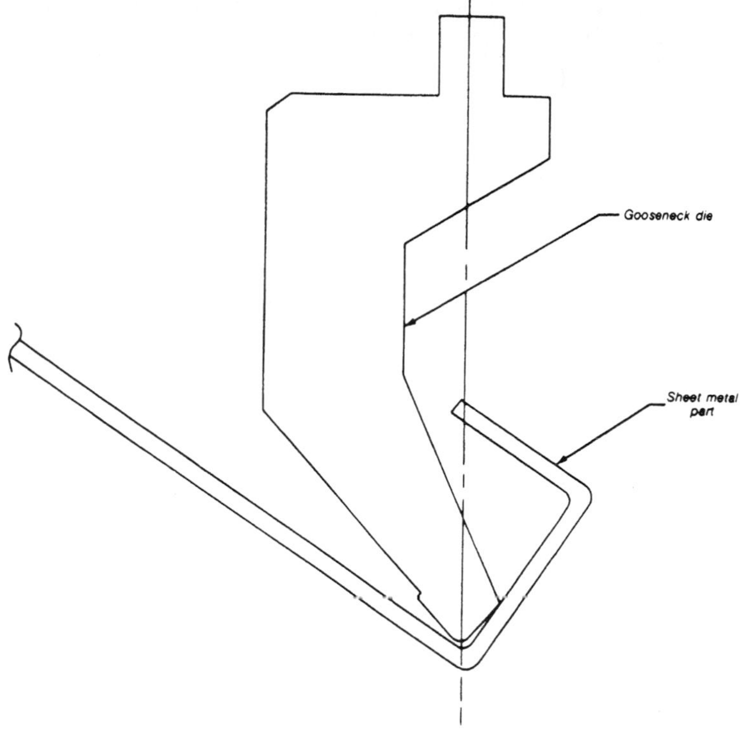

Figure 16.33 Return flange bending.

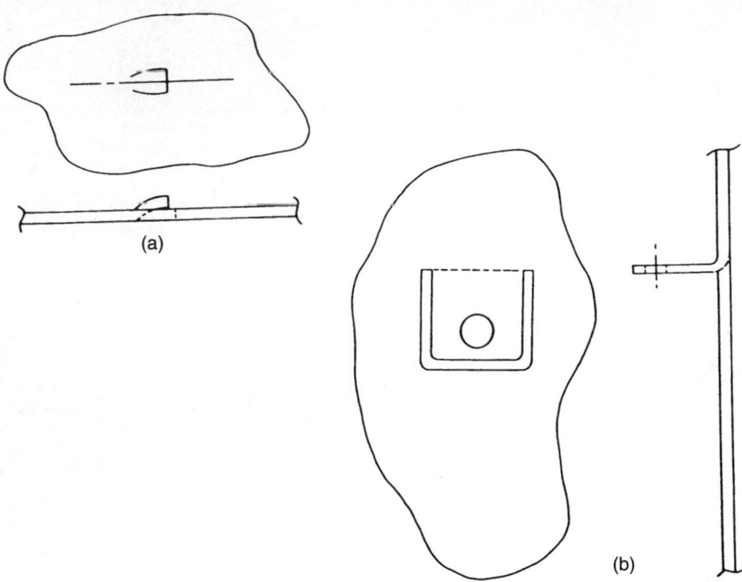

Figure 16.34 Stakes and integral flanges.

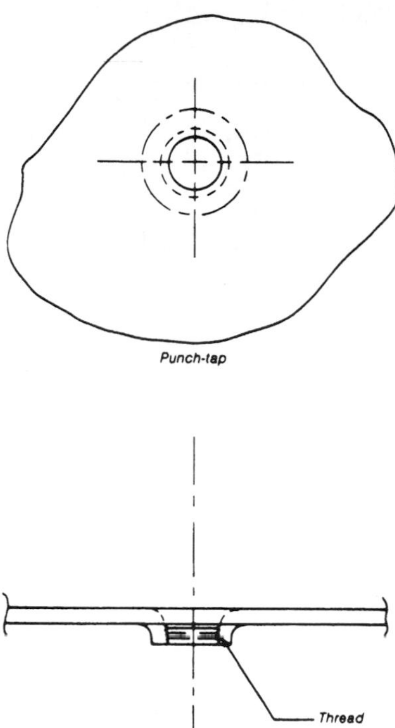

Figure 16.35 A punch-tapped hole.

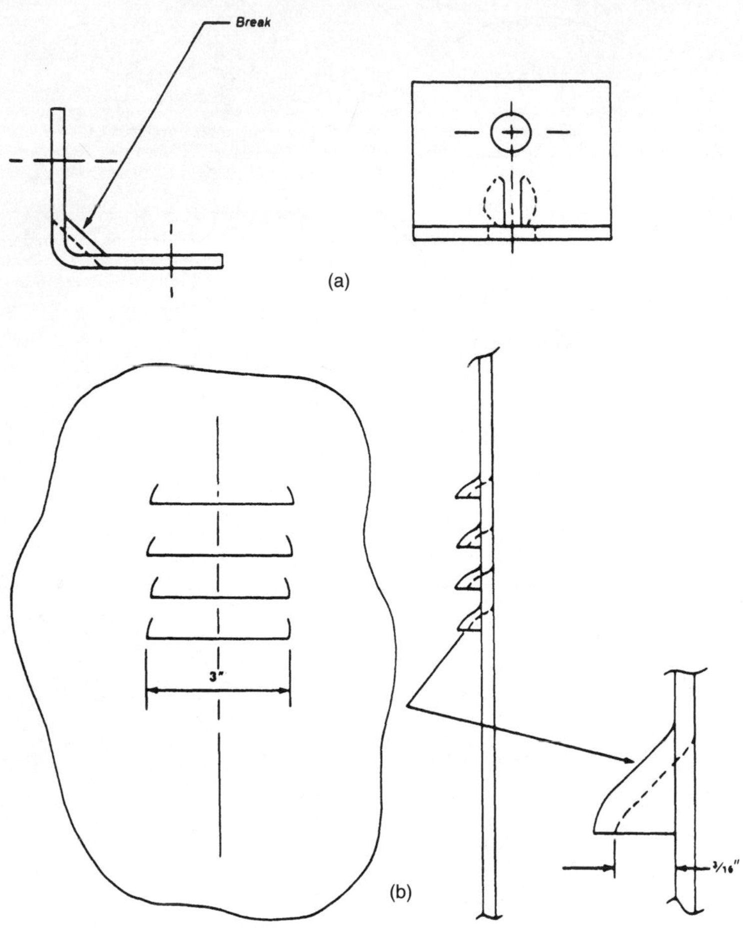

Figure 16.36 (*a*) Corner break. (*b*) Louvers (air vents).

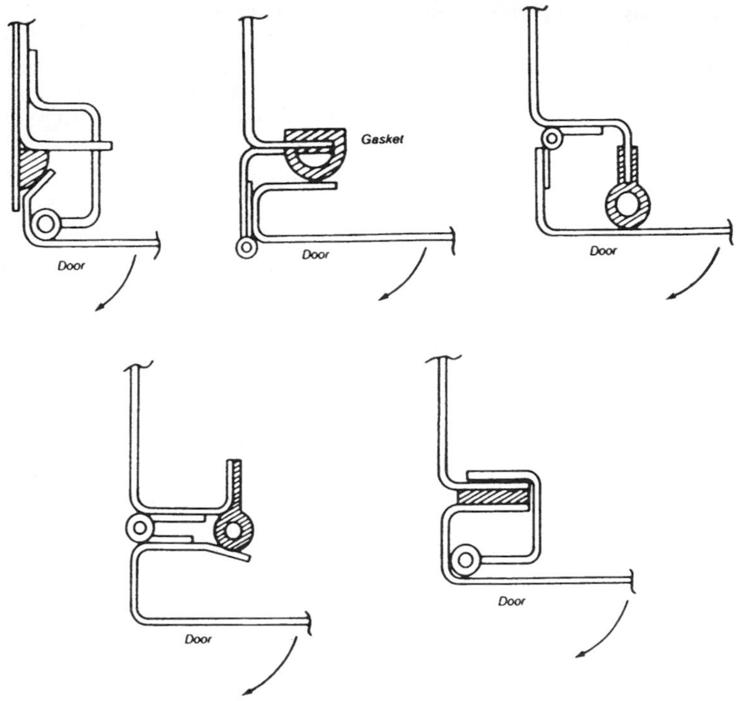

Figure 16.37 Methods of applying door gaskets.

16.14 Light-Gage Sheet Metal Structural Forms: Dimensions and Strengths

Tables 16.1 through 16.11 show the complete dimensions and properties of sheet metal structural shapes which have a wide range of uses in industrial applications. Light-gage cold-formed steel sheet metal shapes have a high strength-to-weight ratio and are used in countless applications. The tables were extracted from the *Light-Gage Cold-Formed Steel Design Manual,* which was produced by the American Iron and Steel Institute (AISI). The latest edition of this engineering design manual may be obtained from the AISI (see Chap. 23, "Societies, Associations, Institutes, and Specification Authorities," for the address).

In the tables, the properties about the *xx* and *yy* axes are most important from a design standpoint for calculating the simple strength capabilities of each particular shape. The following symbolism is defined in the tables:

$I_{x,y}$ = moment of inertia, in^4 (about the *xx* or *yy* axes)
$S_{x,y}$ = section modulus, in^3 (about the *xx* or *yy* axes)
$r_{x,y}$ = radius of gyration, in (about the *xx* or *yy* axes)
x = Location of centroid, in (center of gravity of the section)

The equations for calculating the deflection under a given load and the maximum stress imposed on the member for various conditions of loading may be found in other chapters of this *Handbook.* Also, column-bending calculations may be found herein (see Index).

16.15 The Effects of Cold Working Steel

It has long been known that any cold working, such as cold stretching, bending, twisting, etc., affects the mechanical properties of steel. Generally, such operations produce strain hardening; that is, they increase the yield strength and, to a lesser degree, the ultimate tensile strength of steels while decreasing the ductility. Cold working of one sort or another occurs in all cold-forming operations, such as roll forming or forming in press brakes. The properties of the cold-worked parts are thus different from the metal prior to the cold-forming operations. The effects of cold forming depend strongly on the details of the particular cold-forming process. The effects of cold forming are also much more evident in the bent corners than in the flat sections. Metallurgically different kinds of structural carbon steels react differently to the same cold-forming process. The actual effects of any cold-forming operation on sheet steels are, of course, of an extremely complex nature. Unusual or excessive cold working of structural sheet steel may render the formed section unsuitable for a particular application. In other words, the cold-worked section may be weakened by excessive cold-forming operations.

Bending and buckling of sheet metal sections used as columns and bracing or support beams may be calculated by referring to the chapters of this *Handbook* that cover engineering subjects (also see the Index).

An interesting aspect of the cold-working applications may be seen in Fig. 16.38. Here we see a copper bus bar which has been axially twisted into a 90° spiral bend. This practice is common in industry, where the direction of the flats on the bar must be changed in a limited amount of space. This copper bus bar was bent on a specially designed machine on which various sized bars may be bent axially to different angles. The machine used to bend this particular bar was designed by the author and has been in operation for 14 years with no maintenance required. The machine referred to will bend bars of cold-drawn ETP no. 110 copper from 0.125×1.00 in through 0.625×8 in, and a 90° bending operation requires approximately 15 seconds. The gripper jaws which hold the bar are spaced an appropriate distance (according to bar size) to allow an almost perfect spiral bend, unsupported.

Figure 16.39 shows a machine that is used to cut and notch structural steel shapes, such as angles, channels, and Zs or sheet metal roll-formed shapes efficiently and accurately. In structural welding work, the structural shapes often must be notched, mitered, or cut at an angle prior to the welding operation. This machine allows accurate notches to be made for corners and other structural intersections.

Figure 16.40 shows a lineup of electrical switch gear that is made almost entirely of sheet metal cold-formed parts. The common gauges of sheet steel used on this type of industrial equipment include no. 7 gage, no. 11 gage, no. 13 gage, and no. 16 gage. Most of the sheet steel used in this type of application is hot-rolled, pickled, and oiled, commercial quality.

The sheet metal flat-pattern calculation method for producing this type of large equipment consists mainly of the inside bend method, as outlined earlier, where the sheet metal is sharply bent on the press brake.

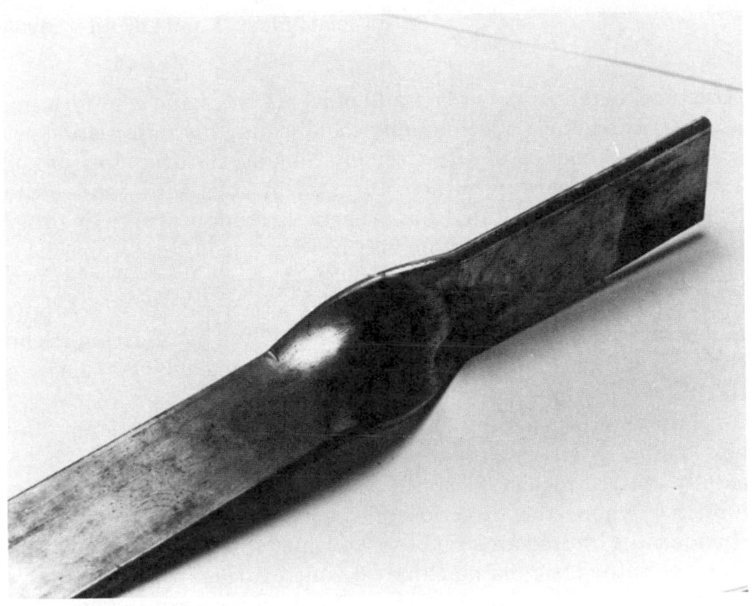

Figure 16.38 A copper bus bar with a 90° axial twist.

Figure 16.39 The Peddiworker structural shape cutter.

Figure 16.40 Electrical power distribution equipment which consists mainly of formed sheet steel.

TABLE 16.1 Channel or Zee with Stiffened Flanges

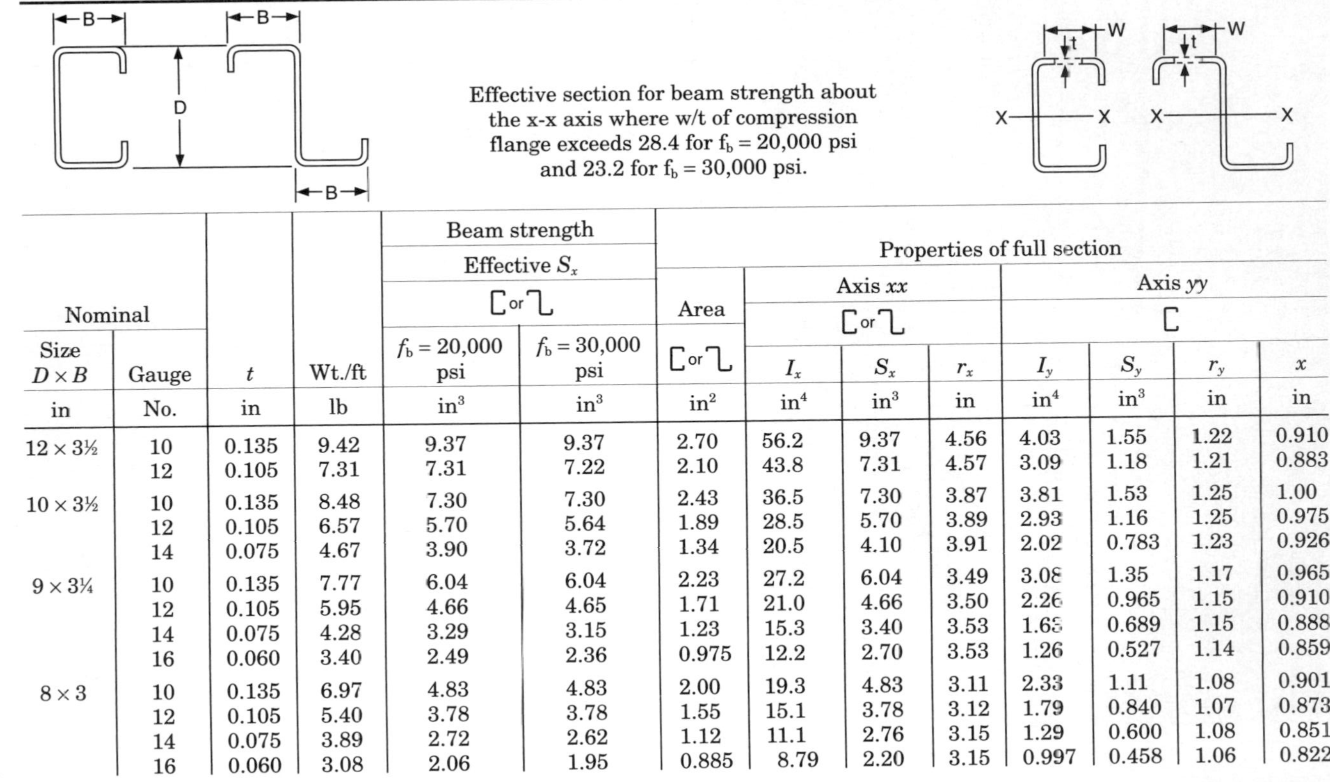

Effective section for beam strength about the x-x axis where w/t of compression flange exceeds 28.4 for $f_b = 20{,}000$ psi and 23.2 for $f_b = 30{,}000$ psi.

Nominal Size $D \times B$	Nominal Gauge	t	Wt./ft	Beam strength, Effective S_x (C or Z), $f_b = 20{,}000$ psi	Beam strength, Effective S_x (C or Z), $f_b = 30{,}000$ psi	Area (C or Z)	Axis xx (C or Z) I_x	Axis xx S_x	Axis xx r_x	Axis yy (C) I_y	Axis yy S_y	Axis yy r_y	Axis yy x
in	No.	in	lb	in^3	in^3	in^2	in^4	in^3	in	in^4	in^3	in	in
12 × 3½	10	0.135	9.42	9.37	9.37	2.70	56.2	9.37	4.56	4.03	1.55	1.22	0.910
	12	0.105	7.31	7.31	7.22	2.10	43.8	7.31	4.57	3.09	1.18	1.21	0.883
10 × 3½	10	0.135	8.48	7.30	7.30	2.43	36.5	7.30	3.87	3.81	1.53	1.25	1.00
	12	0.105	6.57	5.70	5.64	1.89	28.5	5.70	3.89	2.93	1.16	1.25	0.975
	14	0.075	4.67	3.90	3.72	1.34	20.5	4.10	3.91	2.02	0.783	1.23	0.926
9 × 3¼	10	0.135	7.77	6.04	6.04	2.23	27.2	6.04	3.49	3.08	1.35	1.17	0.965
	12	0.105	5.95	4.66	4.65	1.71	21.0	4.66	3.50	2.26	0.965	1.15	0.910
	14	0.075	4.28	3.29	3.15	1.23	15.3	3.40	3.53	1.63	0.689	1.15	0.888
	16	0.060	3.40	2.49	2.36	0.975	12.2	2.70	3.53	1.26	0.527	1.14	0.859
8 × 3	10	0.135	6.97	4.83	4.83	2.00	19.3	4.83	3.11	2.33	1.11	1.08	0.901
	12	0.105	5.40	3.78	3.78	1.55	15.1	3.78	3.12	1.79	0.840	1.07	0.873
	14	0.075	3.89	2.72	2.62	1.12	11.1	2.76	3.15	1.29	0.600	1.08	0.851
	16	0.060	3.08	2.06	1.95	0.885	8.79	2.20	3.15	0.997	0.458	1.06	0.822

7 × 2¾	10	0.135	6.17	3.75	3.75	1.77	13.1	3.75	2.72	1.71	0.893	0.982	0.837
	12	0.105	4.86	2.98	2.98	1.39	10.4	2.98	2.74	1.38	0.723	0.996	0.837
	14	0.075	3.50	2.18	2.11	1.00	7.66	2.19	2.76	1.00	0.517	0.999	0.815
	16	0.060	2.77	1.67	1.59	0.795	6.10	1.74	2.77	0.773	0.393	0.986	0.786
6 × 2½	10	0.135	5.37	2.81	2.81	1.54	8.42	2.81	2.34	1.21	0.700	0.885	0.774
	12	0.105	4.23	2.24	2.24	1.21	6.72	2.24	2.35	0.983	0.570	0.900	0.774
	14	0.075	3.10	1.68	1.65	0.891	5.04	1.68	2.38	0.756	0.440	0.921	0.780
	16	0.060	2.46	1.31	1.26	0.705	4.01	1.34	2.39	0.583	0.333	0.910	0.751
5 × 2	10	0.135	4.43	1.88	1.88	1.27	4.69	1.88	1.92	0.651	0.480	0.715	0.644
	12	0.105	3.50	1.51	1.51	1.00	3.76	1.51	1.94	0.534	0.394	0.729	0.643
	14	0.075	2.53	1.12	1.12	0.726	2.80	1.12	1.96	0.390	0.283	0.733	0.622
	16	0.060	2.00	0.890	0.881	0.573	2.23	0.891	1.97	0.298	0.212	0.721	0.594
	18	0.048	1.61	0.706	0.681	0.461	1.80	0.722	1.98	0.244	0.173	0.727	0.594
4 × 2	10	0.135	3.96	1.38	1.38	1.14	2.76	1.38	1.56	0.601	0.466	0.727	0.712
	12	0.105	3.14	1.11	1.11	0.900	2.22	1.11	1.57	0.493	0.383	0.740	0.712
	14	0.075	2.27	0.832	0.832	0.651	1.67	0.832	1.60	0.361	0.276	0.745	0.689
	16	0.060	1.79	0.665	0.655	0.513	1.33	0.665	1.61	0.277	0.206	0.735	0.660
	18	0.048	1.44	0.529	0.508	0.413	1.08	0.540	1.62	0.226	0.169	0.740	0.660
3½ × 2	10	0.135	3.73	1.15	1.15	1.07	2.01	1.15	1.37	0.571	0.458	0.730	0.753
	12	0.105	2.95	0.927	0.927	0.847	1.62	0.927	1.38	0.469	0.376	0.744	0.753
	14	0.075	2.14	0.699	0.699	0.613	1.22	0.699	1.41	0.344	0.271	0.750	0.729
	16	0.060	1.68	0.559	0.551	0.483	0.979	0.560	1.42	0.264	0.203	0.740	0.699
	18	0.048	1.36	0.444	0.426	0.389	0.795	0.455	1.43	0.216	0.166	0.745	0.699
3 × 1¾	12	0.105	2.59	0.679	0.679	0.742	1.02	0.679	1.17	0.319	0.300	0.655	0.689
	14	0.075	1.82	0.509	0.509	0.523	0.764	0.509	1.21	0.219	0.196	0.647	0.635
	16	0.060	1.47	0.416	0.416	0.423	0.624	0.416	1.22	0.181	0.162	0.654	0.635
	18	0.048	1.16	0.331	0.322	0.331	0.498	0.332	1.23	0.137	0.119	0.642	0.604

NOTE: The effective section moduli in bending about the *yy* axis have not been tabulated. When one of the webs acts as a compression flange, the section modulus should be calculated on the basis of its effective width as provided in Section 2.3 of the Design Specification. When the web acts as a tension flange, the section modulus of the full section is effective. For all of the sections listed in this table the moment of inertia I_x of the full section may be used in deflection calculations without appreciable error.

TABLE 16.1 Channel or Zee with Stiffened Flanges (*Continued*)

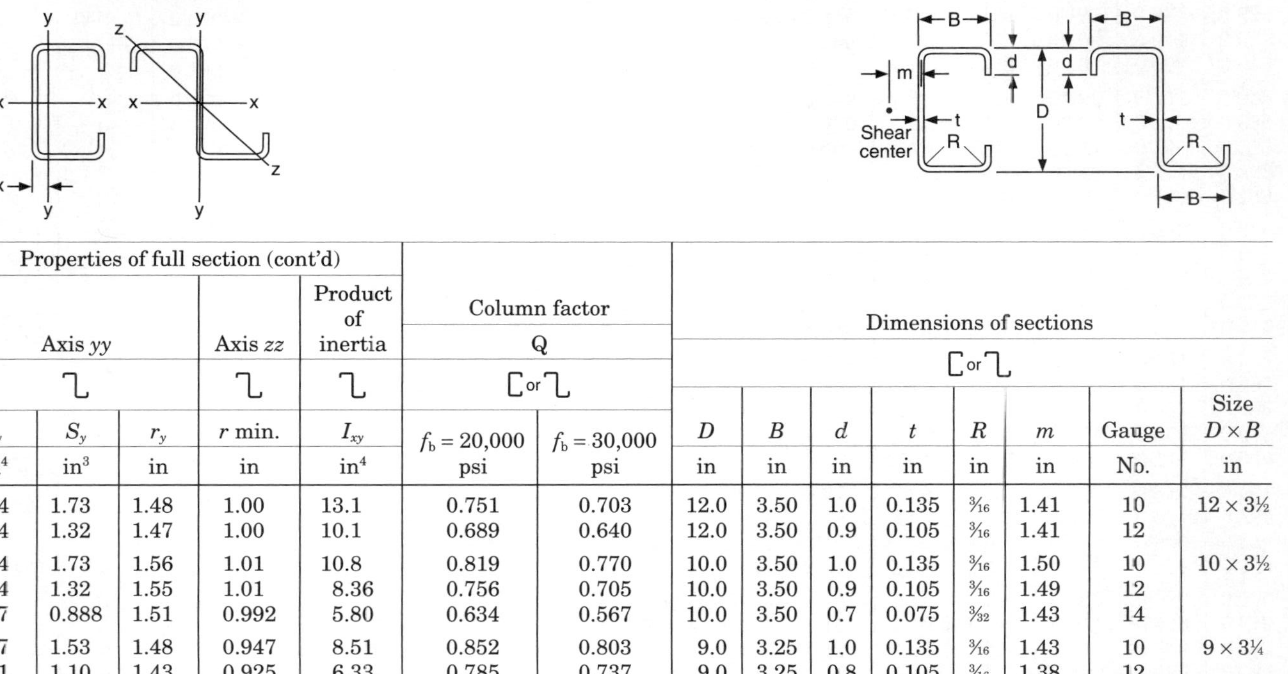

Properties of full section (cont'd)					Column factor		Dimensions of sections							
Axis *yy*			Axis *zz*	Product of inertia	Q		[or ⌐							
⌐			⌐	⌐	[or ⌐									
I_y	S_y	r_y	*r* min.	I_{xy}	$f_b = 20{,}000$	$f_b = 30{,}000$	*D*	*B*	*d*	*t*	*R*	*m*	Gauge	Size $D \times B$
in^4	in^3	in	in	in^4	psi	psi	in	in	in	in	in	in	No.	in
5.94	1.73	1.48	1.00	13.1	0.751	0.703	12.0	3.50	1.0	0.135	3⁄16	1.41	10	12 × 3½
4.54	1.32	1.47	1.00	10.1	0.689	0.640	12.0	3.50	0.9	0.105	3⁄16	1.41	12	
5.94	1.73	1.56	1.01	10.8	0.819	0.770	10.0	3.50	1.0	0.135	3⁄16	1.50	10	10 × 3½
4.54	1.32	1.55	1.01	8.36	0.756	0.705	10.0	3.50	0.9	0.105	3⁄16	1.49	12	
3.07	0.888	1.51	0.992	5.80	0.634	0.567	10.0	3.50	0.7	0.075	3⁄32	1.43	14	
4.87	1.53	1.48	0.947	8.51	0.852	0.803	9.0	3.25	1.0	0.135	3⁄16	1.43	10	9 × 3¼
3.51	1.10	1.43	0.925	6.33	0.785	0.737	9.0	3.25	0.8	0.105	3⁄16	1.38	12	

2.52	0.783	1.43	0.928	4.56	0.674	0.607	9.0	3.25	0.7	0.075	3⁄32	1.35	14	
1.93	0.599	1.41	0.916	3.55	0.590	0.522	9.0	3.25	0.6	0.060	3⁄32	1.32	16	
3.72	1.27	1.36	0.864	6.29	0.887	0.837	8.0	3.00	0.9	0.135	3⁄16	1.32	10	8 × 3
2.83	0.960	1.35	0.860	4.85	0.821	0.774	8.0	3.00	0.8	0.105	3⁄16	1.31	12	
2.03	0.685	1.35	0.863	3.50	0.719	0.653	8.0	3.00	0.7	0.075	3⁄32	1.27	14	
1.55	0.523	1.32	0.851	2.73	0.635	0.565	8.0	3.00	0.6	0.060	3⁄32	1.25	16	
2.76	1.03	1.25	0.782	4.49	0.924	0.876	7.0	2.75	0.8	0.135	3⁄16	1.22	10	7 × 2¾
2.24	0.830	1.27	0.793	3.61	0.861	0.814	7.0	2.75	0.8	0.105	3⁄16	1.24	12	
1.61	0.593	1.27	0.796	2.61	0.764	0.701	7.0	2.75	0.7	0.075	3⁄32	1.20	14	
1.23	0.451	1.24	0.785	2.03	0.686	0.615	7.0	2.75	0.6	0.060	3⁄32	1.18	16	
1.98	0.813	1.13	0.699	3.06	0.962	0.919	6.0	2.50	0.7	0.135	3⁄16	1.12	10	6 × 2½
1.62	0.660	1.15	0.710	2.48	0.905	0.858	6.0	2.50	0.7	0.105	3⁄16	1.14	12	
1.25	0.507	1.18	0.729	1.88	0.815	0.759	6.0	2.50	0.7	0.075	3⁄32	1.13	14	
0.950	0.385	1.16	0.718	1.46	0.744	0.674	6.0	2.50	0.6	0.060	3⁄32	1.11	16	
1.07	0.555	0.919	0.570	1.68	0.994	0.964	5.0	2.00	0.7	0.135	3⁄16	0.913	10	5 × 2
0.885	0.454	0.939	0.580	1.37	0.951	0.907	5.0	2.00	0.7	0.105	3⁄16	0.936	12	
0.638	0.325	0.938	0.583	0.998	0.858	0.811	5.0	2.00	0.6	0.075	3⁄32	0.900	14	
0.480	0.244	0.915	0.573	0.772	0.801	0.745	5.0	2.00	0.5	0.060	3⁄32	0.878	16	
0.393	0.199	0.924	0.577	0.629	0.737	0.670	5.0	2.00	0.5	0.048	3⁄32	0.890	18	
1.07	0.555	0.971	0.558	1.31	1.000	0.998	4.0	2.00	0.7	0.135	3⁄16	0.976	10	4 × 2
0.885	0.454	0.992	0.568	1.07	0.994	0.968	4.0	2.00	0.7	0.105	3⁄16	0.998	12	
0.638	0.325	0.990	0.571	0.786	0.926	0.885	4.0	2.00	0.6	0.075	3⁄32	0.954	14	
0.480	0.244	0.967	0.561	0.610	0.875	0.821	4.0	2.00	0.5	0.060	3⁄32	0.934	16	
0.393	0.199	0.976	0.565	0.498	0.810	0.738	4.0	2.00	0.5	0.048	3⁄32	0.942	18	
1.07	0.555	1.00	0.544	1.13	1.000	1.000	3.5	2.00	0.7	0.135	3⁄16	1.01	10	3½ × 2
0.885	0.454	1.02	0.553	0.923	1.000	0.991	3.5	2.00	0.7	0.105	3⁄16	1.03	12	
0.638	0.325	1.02	0.556	0.681	0.959	0.922	3.5	2.00	0.6	0.075	3⁄32	0.992	14	

TABLE 16.1 Channel or Zee with Stiffened Flanges (*Continued*)

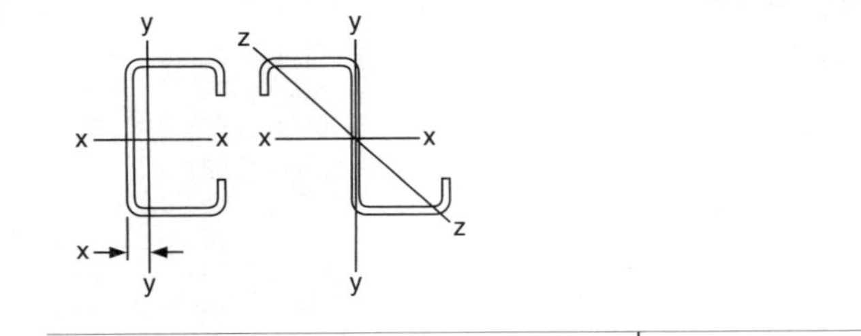

Properties of full section (cont'd)					Column factor		Dimensions of sections							
Axis *yy*			Axis *zz*	Product of inertia	Q									
Zee			Zee	Zee	Channel or Zee		Channel or Zee							
I_y	S_y	r_y	*r* min.	I_{xy}	$f_b = 20{,}000$	$f_b = 30{,}000$	*D*	*B*	*d*	*t*	*R*	*m*	Gauge	Size $D \times B$
in⁴	in³	in	in	in⁴	psi	psi	in	in	in	in	in	in	No.	in
0.480	0.244	0.997	0.547	0.529	0.914	0.861	3.5	2.00	0.5	0.060	3/32	0.966	16	
0.393	0.199	1.01	0.551	0.432	0.851	0.779	3.5	2.00	0.5	0.048	3/32	0.972	18	
0.619	0.365	0.913	0.488	0.610	1.000	1.000	3.0	1.75	0.7	0.105	3/16	0.932	12	3 × 1¾
0.406	0.239	0.881	0.477	0.430	0.985	0.954	3.0	1.75	0.5	0.075	3/32	0.860	14	
0.336	0.195	0.891	0.482	0.354	0.949	0.910	3.0	1.75	0.5	0.060	3/32	0.867	16	
0.248	0.144	0.865	0.471	0.272	0.900	0.840	3.0	1.75	0.4	0.048	3/32	0.841	18	

DIMENSIONS: Equipment and forming practices vary with different manufacturers, resulting in minor variations in some of these dimensions. These minor variations do not affect the published properties. Consult the manufacturer for actual weight per foot and actual dimensions.

TABLE 16.2 Channel or Zee with Unstiffened Flanges

Nominal				Properties of full section										
				Area	Axis xx			Axis yy						
				[or Z	[or Z			[				Z		
Size $D \times B$	Gauge	t	Wt./ft		I_x	S_x	r_x	I_y	S_y	r_y	x	I_y	S_y	r_y
in	No.	in	lb	in^2	in^4	in^3	in	in^4	in^3	in	in	in^4	in^3	in
8 × 2	10	0.135	5.38	1.55	12.9	3.24	2.89	0.465	0.293	0.548	0.383	0.621	0.327	0.634
	12	0.105	4.23	1.21	10.3	2.57	2.91	0.379	0.236	0.559	0.376	0.510	0.263	0.648
	14	0.075	3.08	0.884	7.66	1.91	2.94	0.294	0.178	0.577	0.373	0.396	0.199	0.669
	16	0.060	2.44	0.699	6.02	1.50	2.93	0.211	0.132	0.549	0.343	0.279	0.146	0.632
7 × 1½	10	0.135	4.39	1.26	7.54	2.15	2.45	0.170	0.148	0.368	0.260	0.214	0.161	0.413
	12	0.105	3.50	1.00	6.18	1.77	2.48	0.160	0.131	0.399	0.268	0.209	0.145	0.456
	14	0.075	2.53	0.725	4.54	1.30	2.50	0.113	0.0930	0.395	0.248	0.144	0.101	0.446
	16	0.060	1.99	0.572	3.54	1.01	2.49	0.077	0.0669	0.368	0.221	0.985	0.0730	0.415
6 × 1½	10	0.135	3.91	1.12	5.12	1.70	2.13	0.164	0.146	0.382	0.283	0.214	0.161	0.437
	12	0.105	3.13	0.898	4.22	1.40	2.17	0.155	0.130	0.415	0.293	0.209	0.145	0.482
	14	0.075	2.26	0.650	3.10	1.03	2.19	0.109	0.0918	0.410	0.272	0.144	0.101	0.471
	16	0.060	1.78	0.512	2.42	0.806	2.17	0.075	0.0660	0.383	0.243	0.0985	0.0730	0.439
	18	0.048	1.43	0.409	1.94	0.646	2.18	0.059	0.0519	0.378	0.234	0.0764	0.0572	0.432
5 × 1¼	12	0.105	2.58	0.741	2.38	0.953	1.79	0.087	0.0884	0.343	0.252	0.118	0.0991	0.398
	14	0.075	1.84	0.528	1.71	0.683	1.80	0.053	0.0563	0.316	0.214	0.0690	0.0620	0.362

TABLE 16.2 Channel or Zee with Unstiffened Flanges (*Continued*)

Nominal				Properties of full section											
				Area	Axis xx			Axis yy							
				[or ⌉	[or ⌉			[				⌉			
Size $D \times B$	Gauge	t	Wt./ft		I_x	S_x	r_x	I_y	S_y	r_y	x	I_y	S_y	r_y
in	No.	in	lb	in^2	in^4	in^3	in	in^4	in^3	in	in	in^4	in^3	in
	16	0.060	1.47	0.422	1.37	0.547	1.80	0.041	0.0439	0.311	0.202	0.0533	0.0485	0.355
	18	0.048	1.15	0.331	1.06	0.423	1.79	0.027	0.0307	0.284	0.176	0.0346	0.0337	0.323
4 × 1⅛	12	0.105	2.17	0.623	1.33	0.663	1.46	0.071	0.0779	0.337	0.265	0.0981	0.0878	0.397
	14	0.075	1.61	0.462	1.02	0.512	1.49	0.058	0.0611	0.355	0.262	0.0807	0.0689	0.418
	16	0.060	1.26	0.362	0.792	0.396	1.48	0.039	0.0430	0.327	0.230	0.0533	0.0485	0.384
	18	0.048	1.01	0.289	0.635	0.318	1.48	0.030	0.0337	0.322	0.220	0.0410	0.0378	0.377
3 × 1⅛	12	0.105	1.80	0.518	0.658	0.439	1.13	0.065	0.0750	0.354	0.303	0.0980	0.0877	0.435
	14	0.075	1.35	0.387	0.515	0.344	1.15	0.054	0.0590	0.372	0.306	0.0807	0.0688	0.457
	16	0.060	1.05	0.302	0.398	0.265	1.15	0.036	0.0416	0.344	0.270	0.0533	0.0485	0.420
	18	0.048	0.841	0.241	0.319	0.213	1.15	0.028	0.0326	0.339	0.259	0.0410	0.0373	0.412
2 × 1⅛	12	0.105	1.44	0.413	0.250	0.250	0.779	0.056	0.0702	0.369	0.374	0.0979	0.0876	0.487
	14	0.075	1.09	0.312	0.200	0.200	0.800	0.047	0.0556	0.387	0.370	0.0807	0.0688	0.509
	16	0.060	0.843	0.242	0.154	0.154	0.799	0.031	0.0392	0.360	0.330	0.0533	0.0484	0.469
	18	0.048	0.673	0.193	0.124	0.124	0.802	0.024	0.0308	0.356	0.318	0.0410	0.0378	0.461

NOTE: The effective section moduli in bending about the *yy* axis have not been tabulated. When one of the webs acts as a compression flange, the section modulus should be calculated on the basis of its effective width as provided in Section 2.3 of the Design Specification. When the web acts as a tension flange, the section modulus of the full section is effective.

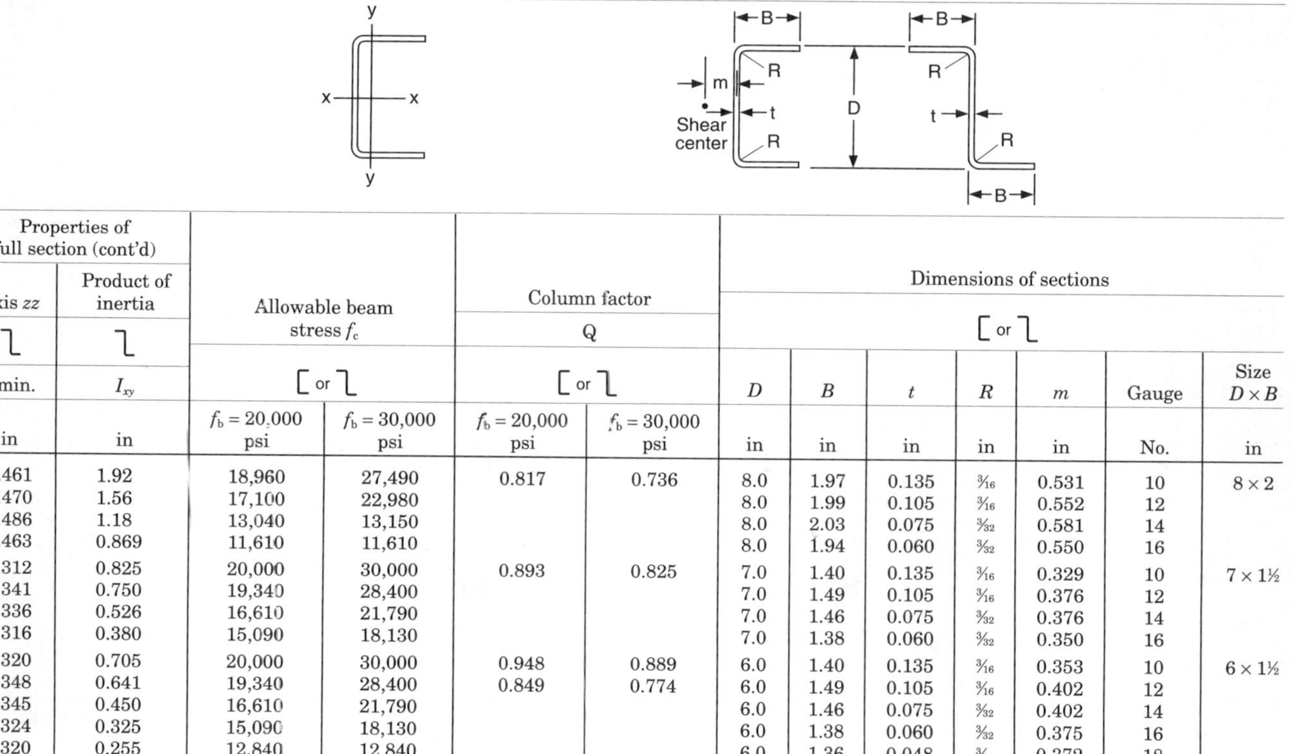

Properties of full section (cont'd)		Allowable beam stress f_c		Column factor Q		Dimensions of sections						
Axis zz	Product of inertia	[or ⅂		[or ⅂		[or ⅂						
r min.	I_{xy}	$f_b = 20,000$ psi	$f_b = 30,000$ psi	$f_b = 20,000$ psi	$f_b = 30,000$ psi	D	B	t	R	m	Gauge	Size $D \times B$
in	in					in	in	in	in	in	No.	in
0.461	1.92	18,960	27,490	0.817	0.736	8.0	1.97	0.135	3/16	0.531	10	8 × 2
0.470	1.56	17,100	22,980			8.0	1.99	0.105	3/16	0.552	12	
0.486	1.18	13,040	13,150			8.0	2.03	0.075	3/32	0.581	14	
0.463	0.869	11,610	11,610			8.0	1.94	0.060	3/32	0.550	16	
0.312	0.825	20,000	30,000	0.893	0.825	7.0	1.40	0.135	3/16	0.329	10	7 × 1½
0.341	0.750	19,340	28,400			7.0	1.49	0.105	3/16	0.376	12	
0.336	0.526	16,610	21,790			7.0	1.46	0.075	3/32	0.376	14	
0.316	0.380	15,090	18,130			7.0	1.38	0.060	3/32	0.350	16	
0.320	0.705	20,000	30,000	0.948	0.889	6.0	1.40	0.135	3/16	0.353	10	6 × 1½
0.348	0.641	19,340	28,400	0.849	0.774	6.0	1.49	0.105	3/16	0.402	12	
0.345	0.450	16,610	21,790			6.0	1.46	0.075	3/32	0.402	14	
0.324	0.325	15,090	18,130			6.0	1.38	0.060	3/32	0.375	16	
0.320	0.255	12,840	12,840			6.0	1.36	0.048	3/32	0.372	18	

TABLE 16.2 Channel or Zee with Unstiffened Flanges (*Continued*)

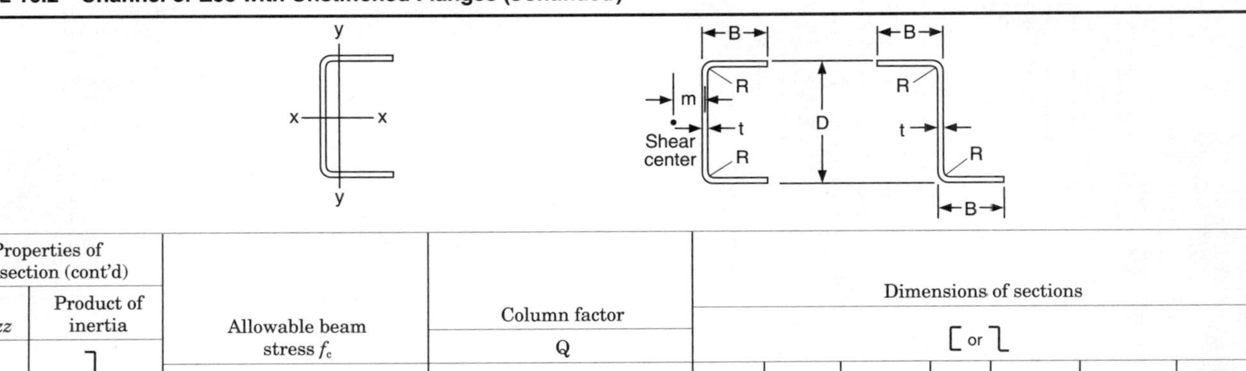

Properties of full section (cont'd)		Allowable beam stress f_c		Column factor Q		Dimensions of sections						
Axis zz	Product of inertia	[or ⅂		[or ⅂		[or ⅂						
r min.	I_{xy}					D	B	t	R	m	Gauge	Size D × B
in	in	f_b = 20,000 psi	f_b = 30,000 psi	f_b = 20,000 psi	f_b = 30,000 psi	in	in	in	in	in	No.	in
0.287	0.363	20,000	30,000	0.934	0.874	5.0	1.24	0.105	3/16	0.327	12	5 × 1¼
0.267	0.229	18,550	26,490			5.0	1.15	0.075	3/32	0.303	14	
0.263	0.180	17,050	22,870			5.0	1.13	0.060	3/32	0.301	16	
0.243	0.125	15,810	19,850			5.0	1.05	0.048	3/32	0.273	18	
0.274	0.256	20,000	30,000	0.991	0.953	4.0	1.17	0.105	3/16	0.327	12	4 × 1⅛
0.291	0.203	18,180	25,580	0.827	0.734	4.0	1.21	0.075	3/32	0.357	14	
0.271	0.143	17,050	22,870			4.0	1.13	0.060	3/32	0.330	16	
0.267	0.112	15,220	18,430			4.0	1.11	0.048	3/32	0.326	18	
0.276	0.191	20,000	30,000	1.000	1.000	3.0	1.17	0.105	3/16	0.362	12	3 × 1⅛
0.294	0.151	18,180	25,580	0.897	0.815	3.0	1.21	0.075	3/32	0.394	14	

0.275	0.107	17,050	22,870	0.808	0.694	3.0	1.13	0.060	3/32	0.365	16	
0.272	0.0836	15,220	18,430	0.687	0.538	3.0	1.11	0.048	3/32	0.361	18	
0.262	0.124	20,000	30,000	1.000	1.000	2.0	1.17	0.105	3/16	0.405	12	2 × 1⅛
0.280	0.0993	18,180	25,580	0.909	0.853	2.0	1.21	0.075	3/32	0.439	14	
0.266	0.0705	17,050	22,870	0.853	0.762	2.0	1.13	0.060	3/32	0.408	16	
0.264	0.0553	15,220	18,430	0.759	0.608	2.0	1.11	0.048	3/32	0.404	18	

DIMENSIONS: Equipment and forming practices vary with different manufacturers, resulting in minor variations in some of these dimensions. These minor variations do not affect the published properties. Consult the manufacturer for actual weight per foot and actual dimensions. Column form factors Q for members having webs with w/t ratios in excess of 60 are not shown. See limitations of Section 2.3.3(a) of the Specification applicable to element stiffened by simple lip.

TABLE 16.3 Equal Leg Angle with Unstiffened Legs

Nominal				Properties of full section							Beam strength $f_b = 20{,}000$ psi		
					Axis *xx* and Axis *yy*				Axis *zz*			*M* max.	*M* max.
												Comp. x–x tension	Comp. x–x tension
Size	Gauge	t	Wt./ft	Area	I	S	r	$x = y$	I	r	f_c		
in	No.	in	lb	in²	in⁴	in³	in	in	in⁴	in	psi	in · lb	in · lb
4 × 4	10	0.135	3.66	1.05	1.715	0.582	1.28	1.07	0.662	0.794	12,300	7,160	11,640
3 × 3	10	0.135	2.72	0.781	0.712	0.324	0.955	0.819	0.271	0.589	15,340	4,970	6,480
	12	0.105	2.16	0.620	0.586	0.262	0.972	0.817	0.224	0.601	12,600	3,300	5,240
2½ × 2½	10	0.135	2.25	0.646	0.407	0.223	0.793	0.694	0.153	0.487	17,080	3,310	4,460
	12	0.105	1.79	0.515	0.338	0.182	0.811	0.692	0.128	0.499	14,600	2,560	3,640
2 × 2	10	0.135	1.78	0.511	0.204	0.141	0.632	0.569	0.0756	0.385	18,830	2,650	2,820
	12	0.105	1.43	0.410	0.173	0.116	0.649	0.567	0.0643	0.396	16,830	1,950	2,320
	14	0.075	1.08	0.311	0.144	0.092	0.680	0.570	0.0555	0.423	12,590	1,160	1,840
	16	0.060	0.840	0.241	0.104	0.069	0.658	0.545	0.0404	0.409	11,040	760	1,380

NOTE: The allowable bending moments shown in this table apply only when the sections are adequately braced laterally. Where the vertical legs of the angles are in compression, *M* max is based on the values of f_c (see 3.2 of Design Specification) indicated: where the vertical legs of the angles are in tension, *M* max is based on f_b (tension) since the compression stress is always less than f_c for the sections listed. Because it is virtually impossible to load single angle struts concentrically, the design of any such strut should take the eccentricity into

Beam strength (cont'd)			Column factor		Dimensions of sections					
$f_b = 30{,}000$ psi			Q							
	M max. Comp. x–x tension	M max. Comp. x–x tension	$f_b = 20{,}000$	$f_b = 30{,}000$	B	t	R	Wt./ft	Gauge	Size
f_c psi	in · lb	in · lb	psi	psi	in	in	in	lb	No.	in
12300	7160	17460	0.542	0.361	4.01	0.135	3/16	3.66	10	4 × 4
18730	6070	9720	0.767	0.624	3.01	0.135	3/16	2.72	10	3 × 3
12600	3300	7860	0.587	0.391	3.05	0.105	3/16	2.16	12	
22950	5120	6690	0.854	0.764	2.51	0.135	3/16	2.25	10	2½ × 2½
16920	3080	5460	0.730	0.563	2.55	0.105	3/16	1.79	12	
27150	3830	4230	0.941	0.904	2.01	0.135	3/16	1.78	10	2 × 2
22330	2590	3480	0.842	0.745	2.05	0.105	3/16	1.43	12	
12590	1160	2760	0.586	0.390	2.14	0.075	3/32	1.08	14	
11040	760	2070	0.401	0.267	2.06	0.060	3/32	0.840	16	

DIMENSIONS: Equipment and forming practices vary with different manufacturers, resulting in minor variations in some of these dimensions. These minor variations do not affect the published properties. Consult the manufacturer for actual weight per foot and actual dimensions.

TABLE 16.4 Equal Leg Angle with Stiffened Legs

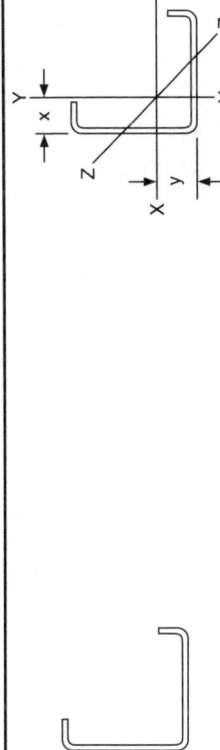

Nominal				Properties of full section						
					Axis xx and Axis yy				Axis zz	
Size	Gauge	t	Wt./ft	Area	I	S	r	$x = y$	I	r
in	No.	in	lb	in^2	in^4	in^3	in	in	in^4	in
4 × 4	10	0.135	4.46	1.28	2.62	0.962	1.43	1.29	1.25	0.988
3 × 3	10	0.135	3.34	0.957	1.08	0.536	1.06	0.993	0.531	0.745
	12	0.105	2.59	0.743	0.864	0.416	1.08	0.973	0.407	0.740
2½ × 2½	10	0.135	2.68	0.768	0.579	0.342	0.868	0.818	0.277	0.600
	12	0.105	2.15	0.617	0.494	0.286	0.895	0.824	0.236	0.618
2 × 2	10	0.135	2.21	0.633	0.306	0.233	0.695	0.695	0.159	0.501
	12	0.105	1.78	0.512	0.267	0.198	0.722	0.701	0.137	0.517
	14	0.075	1.33	0.381	0.222	0.154	0.763	0.693	0.107	0.530
	16	0.060	1.00	0.287	0.153	0.108	0.731	0.646	0.071	0.497

NOTE: The properties listed in this table apply only when the sections are adequately braced laterally. Unless lipped angle compression struts are checked for torsional buckling, these Q values apply only to situations where such torsional buckling is prevented, as for instance when two angles are connected back to back. Because it is virtually impossible to load single angle struts concentrically, the design of any such strut should take the eccentricity into account.

Column form factor		Dimensions of sections						
Q		B	d	t	R	Wt./ft	Gauge	Size
$f_b = 20{,}000$ psi	$f_b = 30{,}000$ psi	in	in	in	in	lb	No.	in
1.000	0.997	4.01	1.1	0.135	3/16	4.46	10	4 × 4
1.000	1.000	3.01	0.9	0.135	3/16	3.34	10	3 × 3
1.000	1.000	3.05	0.8	0.105	3/16	2.59	12	
1.000	1.000	2.51	0.7	0.135	3/16	2.68	10	2½ × 2½
1.000	1.000	2.55	0.7	0.105	3/16	2.15	12	
1.000	1.000	2.01	0.7	0.135	3/16	2.21	10	2 × 2
1.000	1.000	2.05	0.7	0.105	3/16	1.78	12	
1.000	1.000	2.14	0.6	0.075	3/32	1.33	14	
1.000	0.985	2.06	0.5	0.060	3/32	1.00	16	

DIMENSIONS: Equipment and forming practices vary with different manufacturers, resulting in minor variations in some of these dimensions. These minor variations do not affect the published properties. Consult the manufacturer for actual weight per foot and actual dimensions.

TABLE 16.5 Two Channels with Stiffened Flanges Back-to-Back

Effective section for beam strength about the xx axis where w/t of compression flange exceeds 28.4 for $f_b = 20{,}000$ psi and 23.2 for $f_b = 30{,}000$ psi

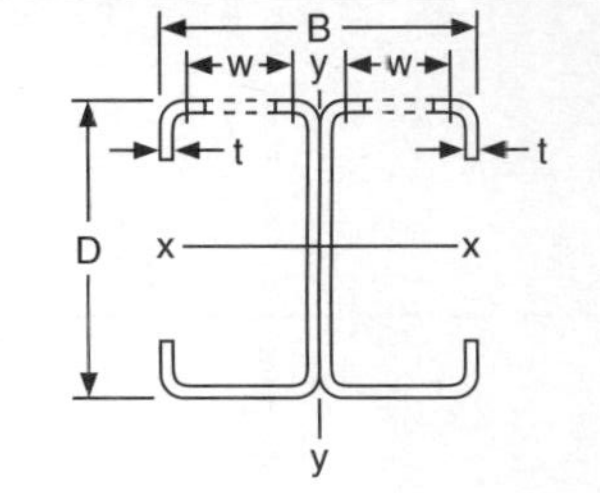

Nominal				Beam strength			Properties of full section			
				Effective				Axis xx		
				S_x		S_y				
Size $D \times B$	Gauge	t	Wt./ft	$f_b = 20{,}000$ psi	$f_b = 30{,}000$ psi	$f_b = 20{,}000$ $f_b = 30{,}000$	Area	I_x	S_x	r_x
in	No.	in	lb	in^3	in^3	in^3	in^2	in^4	in^3	in
12×7	10	0.135	18.8	18.7	18.7	3.58	5.40	112.0	18.7	4.56
	12	0.105	14.6	14.6	14.5	2.70	4.20	87.7	14.6	4.57
10×7	10	0.135	17.0	14.6	14.6	3.58	4.86	73.0	14.6	3.87
	12	0.105	13.1	11.4	11.3	2.70	3.78	57.0	11.4	3.89
	14	0.075	9.34	7.80	7.44	1.81	2.68	41.0	8.20	3.91
$9 \times 6\frac{1}{2}$	10	0.135	15.5	12.1	12.1	3.17	4.46	54.3	12.1	3.49
	12	0.105	11.9	9.32	9.30	2.26	3.42	41.9	9.32	3.50
	14	0.075	8.56	6.56	6.30	1.60	2.46	30.6	6.80	3.53
	16	0.060	6.80	4.95	4.72	1.22	1.95	24.3	5.40	3.53
8×6	10	0.135	13.9	9.66	9.66	2.63	4.00	38.6	9.66	3.11
	12	0.105	10.8	7.56	7.56	1.98	3.10	30.2	7.56	3.12

	14	0.075	7.78	5.42	5.24	1.40	2.24	22.1	5.52	3.15
	16	0.060	6.16	4.11	3.91	1.06	1.77	17.6	4.40	3.15
7 × 5½	10	0.135	12.3	7.50	7.50	2.14	3.54	26.2	7.50	2.72
	12	0.105	9.72	5.96	5.96	1.71	2.78	20.9	5.96	2.74
	14	0.075	7.00	4.35	4.22	1.21	2.00	15.3	4.38	2.76
	16	0.060	5.54	3.33	3.18	0.919	1.59	12.2	3.48	2.77
6 × 5	10	0.135	10.7	5.62	5.62	1.71	3.08	16.8	5.62	2.34
	12	0.105	8.46	4.48	4.48	1.37	2.42	13.4	4.48	2.35
	14	0.075	6.20	3.35	3.30	1.04	1.78	10.1	3.36	2.38
	16	0.060	4.92	2.61	2.51	0.785	1.41	8.02	2.68	2.39
5 × 4	10	0.135	8.86	3.76	3.76	1.18	2.54	9.38	3.76	1.92
	12	0.105	7.00	3.02	3.02	0.950	2.00	7.53	3.02	1.94
	14	0.075	5.06	2.24	2.24	0.671	1.45	5.60	2.24	1.96
	16	0.060	4.00	1.78	1.76	0.500	1.15	4.45	1.78	1.97
	18	0.048	3.22	1.41	1.36	0.406	0.922	3.61	1.44	1.98
4 × 4	10	0.135	7.92	2.76	2.76	1.18	2.28	5.51	2.76	1.56
	12	0.105	6.28	2.22	2.22	0.950	1.80	4.44	2.22	1.57
	14	0.075	4.54	1.66	1.66	0.670	1.30	3.33	1.66	1.60
	16	0.060	3.58	1.33	1.31	0.500	1.03	2.66	1.33	1.61
	18	0.048	2.88	1.06	1.02	0.406	0.826	2.16	1.08	1.62
3½ × 4	10	0.135	7.46	2.30	2.30	1.18	2.14	4.01	2.30	1.37
	12	0.105	5.90	1.85	1.85	0.950	1.69	3.24	1.85	1.38
	14	0.075	4.28	1.40	1.40	0.670	1.23	2.45	1.40	1.41
	16	0.060	3.36	1.12	1.10	0.500	0.966	1.96	1.12	1.42
	18	0.048	2.72	0.888	0.852	0.406	0.778	1.59	0.910	1.43
3 × 3½	12	0.105	5.18	1.36	1.36	0.767	1.48	2.04	1.36	1.17
	14	0.075	3.64	1.02	1.02	0.491	1.05	1.53	1.02	1.21
	16	0.060	2.94	0.832	0.832	0.402	0.846	1.25	0.832	1.22
	18	0.048	2.32	0.661	0.644	0.294	0.662	0.995	0.664	1.23

NOTE: The properties of this table apply only when the channels are adequately joined together. See Section 4 of Design Specification.

TABLE 16.5 Two Channels with Stiffened Flanges Back-to-Back (*Continued*)

Properties of full section (cont'd)			Column factor		Dimensions of sections							Nominal	
Axis yy			Q										
I_y	S_y	r_y	$f_b = 20{,}000$ psi	$f_b = 30{,}000$ psi	D	B	d	t	R	I_y	r_y	Gauge	Size $D \times B$
in⁴	in³	in			in	in	in	in	in	in⁴	in	No.	in
12.52	3.58	1.52	0.751	0.703	12.0	7.0	1.0	0.135	3/16	44.28	2.86	10	12 × 7
9.45	2.70	1.50	0.689	0.640	12.0	7.0	0.9	0.105	3/16	34.95	2.88	12	
12.52	3.58	1.60	0.819	0.770	10.0	7.0	1.0	0.135	3/16	38.00	2.80	10	10 × 7
9.45	2.70	1.58	0.756	0.705	10.0	7.0	0.9	0.105	3/16	29.96	2.81	12	
6.33	1.81	1.54	0.634	0.567	10.0	7.0	0.7	0.075	3/32	21.80	2.85	14	
10.31	3.17	1.52	0.852	0.803	9.0	6.5	1.0	0.135	3/16	29.45	2.57	10	9 × 6½
7.34	2.26	1.47	0.785	0.737	9.0	6.5	0.8	0.105	3/16	23.25	2.60	12	
5.19	1.60	1.45	0.674	0.607	9.0	6.5	0.7	0.075	3/32	16.98	2.62	14	
3.96	1.22	1.42	0.590	0.522	9.0	6.5	0.6	0.060	3/32	13.67	2.65	16	
7.90	2.63	1.41	0.887	0.837	8.0	6.0	0.9	0.135	3/16	22.28	2.36	10	8 × 6
5.94	1.98	1.38	0.821	0.774	8.0	6.0	0.8	0.105	3/16	17.60	2.38	12	
4.20	1.40	1.37	0.719	0.653	8.0	6.0	0.7	0.075	3/32	12.92	2.40	14	
3.19	1.06	1.34	0.635	0.565	8.0	6.0	0.6	0.060	3/32	10.39	2.42	16	

5.90	2.14	1.29	0.924	0.876	7.0	5.5	0.8	0.135	3⁄16	16.38	2.15	10	7 × 5½
4.72	1.71	1.30	0.861	0.814	7.0	5.5	0.8	0.105	3⁄16	12.93	2.16	12	
3.33	1.21	1.29	0.764	0.701	7.0	5.5	0.7	0.075	3⁄32	9.49	2.18	14	
2.53	0.919	1.26	0.686	0.615	7.0	5.5	0.6	0.060	3⁄32	7.68	2.20	16	
4.26	1.71	1.18	0.962	0.919	6.0	5.0	0.7	0.135	3⁄16	11.60	1.94	10	6 × 5
3.42	1.37	1.19	0.905	0.858	6.0	5.0	0.7	0.105	3⁄16	9.18	1.95	12	
2.60	1.04	1.21	0.815	0.759	6.0	5.0	0.7	0.075	3⁄32	6.78	1.95	14	
1.96	0.785	1.18	0.744	0.674	6.0	5.0	0.6	0.060	3⁄32	5.48	1.97	16	
2.36	1.18	0.962	0.994	0.964	5.0	4.0	0.7	0.135	3⁄16	5.97	1.53	10	5 × 4
1.90	0.950	0.973	0.951	0.907	5.0	4.0	0.7	0.105	3⁄16	4.75	1.54	12	
1.34	0.671	0.961	0.858	0.811	5.0	4.0	0.6	0.075	3⁄32	3.54	1.56	14	
1.00	0.500	0.934	0.801	0.745	5.0	4.0	0.5	0.060	3⁄32	2.86	1.58	16	
0.813	0.406	0.939	0.737	0.670	5.0	4.0	0.5	0.048	3⁄32	2.31	1.58	18	
2.35	1.18	1.02	1.000	0.998	4.0	4.0	0.7	0.135	3⁄16	4.98	1.48	10	4 × 4
1.90	0.950	1.03	0.994	0.968	4.0	4.0	0.7	0.105	3⁄16	3.97	1.49	12	
1.34	0.670	1.02	0.926	0.885	4.0	4.0	0.6	0.075	3⁄32	2.96	1.51	14	
1.00	0.500	0.987	0.875	0.821	4.0	4.0	0.5	0.060	3⁄32	2.40	1.53	16	
0.812	0.406	0.992	0.810	0.738	4.0	4.0	0.5	0.048	3⁄32	1.94	1.53	18	
2.35	1.18	1.05	1.000	1.000	3.5	4.0	0.7	0.135	3⁄16	4.47	1.45	10	3½ × 4
1.90	0.950	1.06	1.000	0.991	3.5	4.0	0.7	0.105	3⁄16	3.57	1.45	12	
1.34	0.670	1.05	0.959	0.922	3.5	4.0	0.6	0.075	3⁄32	2.67	1.48	14	
1.00	0.500	1.02	0.914	0.861	3.5	4.0	0.5	0.060	3⁄32	2.16	1.50	16	
0.812	0.406	1.02	0.851	0.779	3.5	4.0	0.5	0.048	3⁄32	1.75	1.50	18	
1.34	0.767	0.951	1.000	1.000	3.0	3.5	0.7	0.105	3⁄16	2.31	1.25	12	3 × 3½
0.860	0.491	0.906	0.985	0.954	3.0	3.5	0.5	0.075	3⁄32	1.74	1.29	14	
0.703	0.402	0.912	0.949	0.910	3.0	3.5	0.5	0.060	3⁄32	1.41	1.29	16	
0.515	0.294	0.881	0.900	0.840	3.0	3.5	0.4	0.048	3⁄32	1.14	1.31	18	

DIMENSIONS: Equipment and forming practices vary with different manufacturers, resulting in minor variations in some of these dimensions. These minor variations do not affect the published properties. Consult the manufacturer for actual weight per foot and actual dimensions.

TABLE 16.6 Two Channels with Unstiffened Flanges Back-to-Back

Nominal				Properties of full section							
					Axis *xx*			Axis *yy*			
Size $D \times B$	Gauge	t	Wt./ft	Area	I_x	S_x	r_x	I_y	S_y	r_y
in	No.	in	lb	in^2	in^4	in^3	in	in^4	in^3	in
8 × 4	10	0.135	10.8	3.10	25.8	6.48	2.89	1.38	0.704	0.669
	12	0.105	8.46	2.42	20.6	5.14	2.91	1.10	0.555	0.674
	14	0.075	6.16	1.77	15.3	3.82	2.94	0.834	0.411	0.687
	16	0.060	4.88	1.40	12.0	3.00	2.93	0.586	0.303	0.647
7 × 3	10	0.135	8.78	2.52	15.1	4.30	2.45	0.510	0.363	0.450
	12	0.105	7.00	2.00	12.4	3.54	2.48	0.464	0.313	0.481
	14	0.075	5.06	1.45	9.08	2.60	2.50	0.315	0.215	0.466
	16	0.060	3.98	1.14	7.08	2.02	2.49	0.211	0.152	0.429
6 × 3	10	0.135	7.82	2.24	10.2	3.40	2.13	0.509	0.362	0.476
	12	0.105	6.26	1.80	8.44	2.80	2.17	0.464	0.312	0.508
	14	0.075	4.52	1.30	6.20	2.06	2.19	0.315	0.215	0.492
	16	0.060	3.56	1.02	4.84	1.61	2.17	0.211	0.152	0.454
	18	0.048	2.86	0.818	3.88	1.29	2.18	0.162	0.119	0.445

5 × 2½	12	0.105	5.16	1.48	4.76	1.91	1.79	0.268	0.217	0.425
	14	0.075	3.68	1.06	3.42	1.37	1.80	0.154	0.134	0.382
	16	0.060	2.94	0.844	2.74	1.09	1.80	0.116	0.103	0.370
	18	0.048	2.30	0.662	2.12	0.846	1.79	0.074	0.071	0.335
4 × 2¼	12	0.105	4.34	1.25	2.66	1.33	1.46	0.229	0.195	0.429
	14	0.075	3.22	0.924	2.04	1.02	1.49	0.180	0.148	0.441
	16	0.060	2.52	0.724	1.58	0.792	1.48	0.116	0.103	0.400
	18	0.048	2.02	0.578	1.27	0.636	1.48	0.088	0.079	0.390
3 × 2¼	12	0.105	3.60	1.04	1.32	0.878	1.13	0.228	0.195	0.470
	14	0.075	2.70	0.774	1.03	0.688	1.15	0.180	0.148	0.481
	16	0.060	2.10	0.604	0.796	0.530	1.15	0.115	0.102	0.437
	18	0.048	1.68	0.482	0.638	0.426	1.15	0.088	0.079	0.427
2 × 2¼	12	0.105	2.88	0.826	0.500	0.500	0.779	0.227	0.194	0.525
	14	0.075	2.18	0.624	0.400	0.400	0.800	0.179	0.148	0.536
	16	0.060	1.69	0.484	0.308	0.308	0.799	0.115	0.102	0.488
	18	0.048	1.35	0.386	0.248	0.248	0.802	0.088	0.079	0.477

NOTE: The properties of this table apply only when the channels are adequately joined together. See Section 4 of Design Specification.

TABLE 16.6 Two Channels with Unstiffened Flanges Back-to-Back (*Continued*)

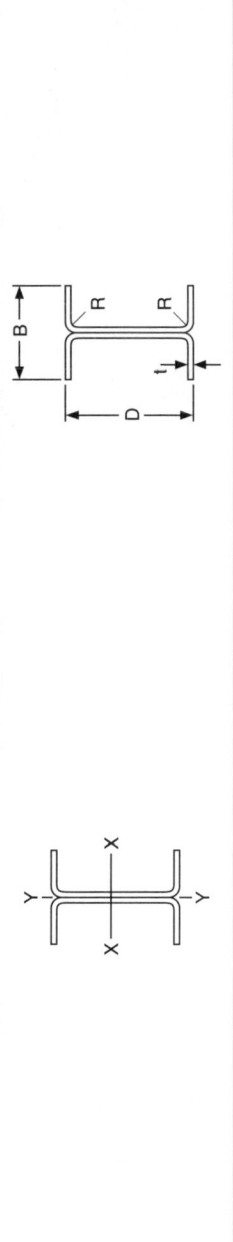

Allowable beam stress f_c, psi		Column factor Q		Dimensions of sections						
$f_b = 20{,}000$ psi	$f_b = 30{,}000$ psi	$f_b = 20{,}000$ psi	$f_b = 30{,}000$ psi	D in	B in	t in	R in	Wt./ft lb	Gauge No.	Size $D \times B$ in
18960	27490	0.817	0.736	8.0	3.934	0.135	3/16	10.8	10	8 × 4
17100	22980			8.0	3.972	0.105	3/16	8.46	12	
13040	13150			8.0	4.052	0.075	3/32	6.16	14	
11610	11610			8.0	3.882	0.060	3/32	4.88	16	
20000	30000	0.893	0.825	7.0	2.810	0.135	3/16	8.78	10	7 × 3
19340	28400			7.0	2.972	0.105	3/16	7.00	12	
16610	21790			7.0	2.928	0.075	3/32	5.06	14	
15090	18130			7.0	2.758	0.060	3/32	3.98	16	
20000	30000	0.948	0.889	6.0	2.810	0.135	3/16	7.82	10	6 × 3
19340	28400	0.849	0.774	6.0	2.972	0.105	3/16	6.26	12	
16610	21790			6.0	2.928	0.075	3/32	4.52	14	
15090	18130			6.0	2.758	0.060	3/32	3.56	16	
12840	12840			6.0	2.722	0.048	3/32	2.86	18	

20000	30000	0.934	0.874	5.0	2.472	0.105	3/16	5.16	12	5 × 2½
18550	26490			5.0	2.302	0.075	3/32	3.68	14	
17050	22870			5.0	2.258	0.060	3/32	2.94	16	
15810	19850			5.0	2.098	0.048	3/32	2.30	18	
20000	30000	0.991	0.953	4.0	2.346	0.105	3/16	4.34	12	4 × 2¼
18180	25580	0.827	0.734	4.0	2.428	0.075	3/32	3.22	14	
17050	22870			4.0	2.258	0.060	3/32	2.52	16	
15220	18430			4.0	2.222	0.048	3/32	2.02	18	
20000	30000	1.000	1.000	3.0	2.346	0.105	3/16	3.60	12	3 × 2¼
18180	25580	0.897	0.815	3.0	2.428	0.075	3/32	2.70	14	
17050	22870	0.808	0.694	3.0	2.258	0.060	3/32	2.10	16	
15220	18430	0.687	0.538	3.0	2.222	0.048	3/32	1.68	18	
20000	30000	1.000	1.000	2.0	2.346	0.105	3/16	2.88	12	2 × 2¼
18180	25580	0.909	0.853	2.0	2.428	0.075	3/32	2.18	14	
17050	22870	0.853	0.762	2.0	2.258	0.060	3/32	1.69	16	
15220	18430	0.759	0.608	2.0	2.222	0.048	3/32	1.35	18	

DIMENSIONS: Equipment and forming practices vary with different manufacturers, resulting in minor variations in some of these dimensions. These minor variations do not affect the published properties. Consult the manufacturer for actual weight per foot and actual dimensions. Column form factors Q for members having webs with w/t-ratios in excess of 60 are not shown. See limitations of Section 2.3.3(a) of the Specification applicable to element stiffened by simple lip.

TABLE 16.7 Two Equal-Leg Angles, Back-to-Back, Unstiffened Legs

Column properties					Dimensions				
Full theoretical outline			Q						
Area	r_x	r_y	$f_b = 20,000$ psi	$f_b = 30,000$ psi	B	Thickness t	Radius R	Weight per ft	Nominal size
in^2	in	in			in	in	in	lb	in
2.10	1.28	1.67	0.542	0.361	8.030	.135	3/16	7.32	4 × 4
1.56	0.955	1.26	0.767	0.624	6.030	.135	3/16	5.44	3 × 3
1.24	0.972	1.27	0.587	0.391	6.110	.105	3/16	4.32	
1.29	0.793	1.05	0.854	0.764	5.030	.135	3/16	4.50	2½ × 2½
1.03	0.811	1.07	0.730	0.563	5.110	.105	3/16	3.58	
1.02	0.632	0.850	0.941	0.904	4.030	.135	3/16	3.56	2 × 2
0.820	0.649	0.862	0.842	0.745	4.110	.105	3/16	2.86	
0.622	0.680	0.887	0.586	0.390	4.276	.075	3/32	2.16	
0.482	0.658	0.855	0.401	0.267	4.128	.060	3/32	1.68	

DIMENSIONS: Equipment and forming practices vary with different manufacturers, resulting in minor variations in some of these dimensions. These minor variations do not affect the published properties. Consult the manufacturer for actual weight per foot and actual dimensions.

Nominal (one angle)			Beam strength							Deflection	
			Section modulus based on full theoretical outline	f_b = 20,000 psi			f_b = 30,000 psi			Any grade of steel	
				M max.			M max.				
Size	Gauge	Thickness	S_z	f_c	Comp. (vertical legs up) tension	Comp. (vertical legs down) tension	f_c	Comp. (vertical legs up) tension	Comp. (vertical legs down) tension	y	I_x
in	No.	in	in³	psi	in • lb	in • lb	psi	in • lb	in • lb	in	in⁴
4 × 4	10	.135	1.164	12300	14320	23280	12300	14320	34920	1.069	3.430
3 × 3	10	.135	0.648	15340	9940	12960	18730	12140	19440	0.819	1.424
	12	.105	0.524	12600	6600	10480	12600	6600	15720	0.817	1.172
2½ × 2½	10	.135	0.446	17090	7620	8920	22950	10230	13380	0.694	0.814
	12	.105	0.364	14600	5310	7280	16920	6160	10920	0.692	0.676
2 × 2	10	.135	0.282	18830	5310	5640	27150	7660	8460	0.569	0.408
	12	.105	0.232	16830	3910	4640	22330	5180	6960	0.567	0.346
	14	.075	0.183	12590	2320	3680	12590	2320	5520	0.570	0.288
	16	.060	0.137	11040	1520	2760	11040	1520	4140	0.546	0.208

NOTE: The properties of this table may be used only when the angles are adequately joined and adequately braced laterally. Q is the column factor (Sec. 3.6.1, Design Specification). Where the vertical legs of the angles are in compression M_{max} is based on the values of f_c (Sec. 3.2 of Design Specification) indicated; where the vertical legs of the angles are in tension M_{max} is based on f_b (tension) since the compression stress is always less than f_c for the sections listed.

TABLE 16.8 Two Equal-Leg Angles, Back-to-Back, Stiffened Legs

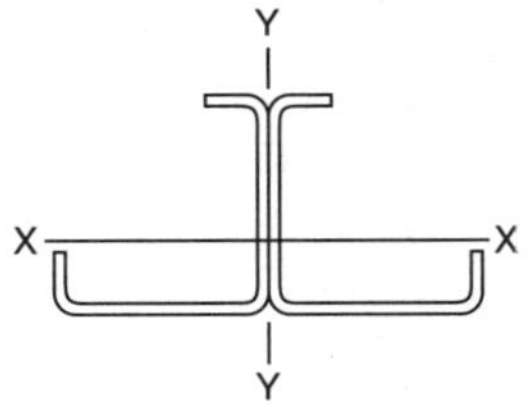

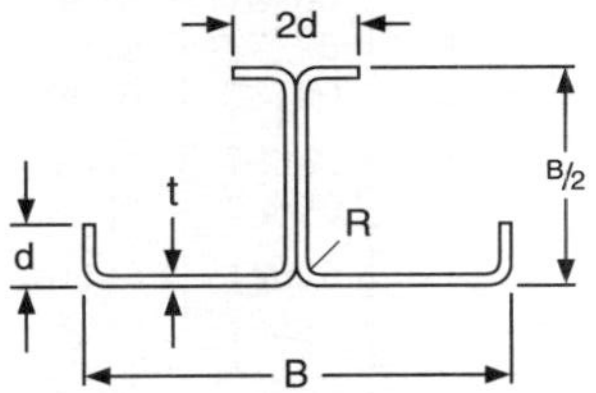

Column form factor		Dimensions of sections						
Q		B	d	t	R	Wt./ft	Gauge	Size
$f_b = 20{,}000$ psi	$f_b = 30{,}000$ psi	in	in	in	in	lb	No.	in
1.000	0.997	8.030	1.1	0.135	3/16	8.92	10	4 × 4
1.000	1.000	6.030	0.9	0.135	3/16	6.68	10	3 × 3
1.000	1.000	6.110	0.8	0.105	3/16	5.18	12	
1.000	1.000	5.030	0.7	0.135	3/16	5.36	10	2½ × 2½
1.000	1.000	5.110	0.7	0.105	3/16	4.30	12	
1.000	1.000	4.030	0.7	0.135	3/16	4.42	10	2 × 2
1.000	1.000	4.110	0.7	0.105	3/16	3.56	12	
1.000	1.000	4.276	0.6	0.075	3/32	2.66	14	
1.000	0.985	4.128	0.5	0.060	3/32	2.00	16	

DIMENSIONS: Equipment and forming practices vary with different manufacturers, resulting in minor variations in some of these dimensions. These minor variations do not affect the published properties. Consult the manufacturer for actual weight per foot and actual dimensions.

Nominal (one angle)					Properties of full section					
					Axis xx				Axis yy	
Size	Gauge	Thickness	Wt./ft	Area	I	S	r	y	I	r
in	No.	in	lb	in^2	in^4	in^3	in	in	in^4	in
4 × 4	10	0.135	8.92	2.56	5.23	1.92	1.43	1.29	9.51	1.93
3 × 3	10	0.135	6.68	1.91	2.16	1.07	1.06	0.993	4.05	1.46
	12	0.105	5.18	1.49	1.73	0.832	1.08	0.973	3.13	1.45
2½ × 2½	10	0.135	5.36	1.54	1.16	0.684	0.868	0.818	2.19	1.19
	12	0.105	4.30	1.23	0.989	0.572	0.895	0.824	1.83	1.22
2 × 2	10	0.135	4.42	1.27	0.612	0.466	0.695	0.695	1.22	0.981
	12	0.105	3.56	1.02	0.534	0.396	0.722	0.701	1.04	1.008
	14	0.075	2.66	0.762	0.444	0.308	0.763	0.693	0.810	1.031
	16	0.060	2.00	0.574	0.306	0.216	0.731	0.646	0.546	0.975

NOTE: The properties listed in this table may be used only when the angles are adequately joined and adequately braced laterally.

TABLE 16.9 Hat Sections

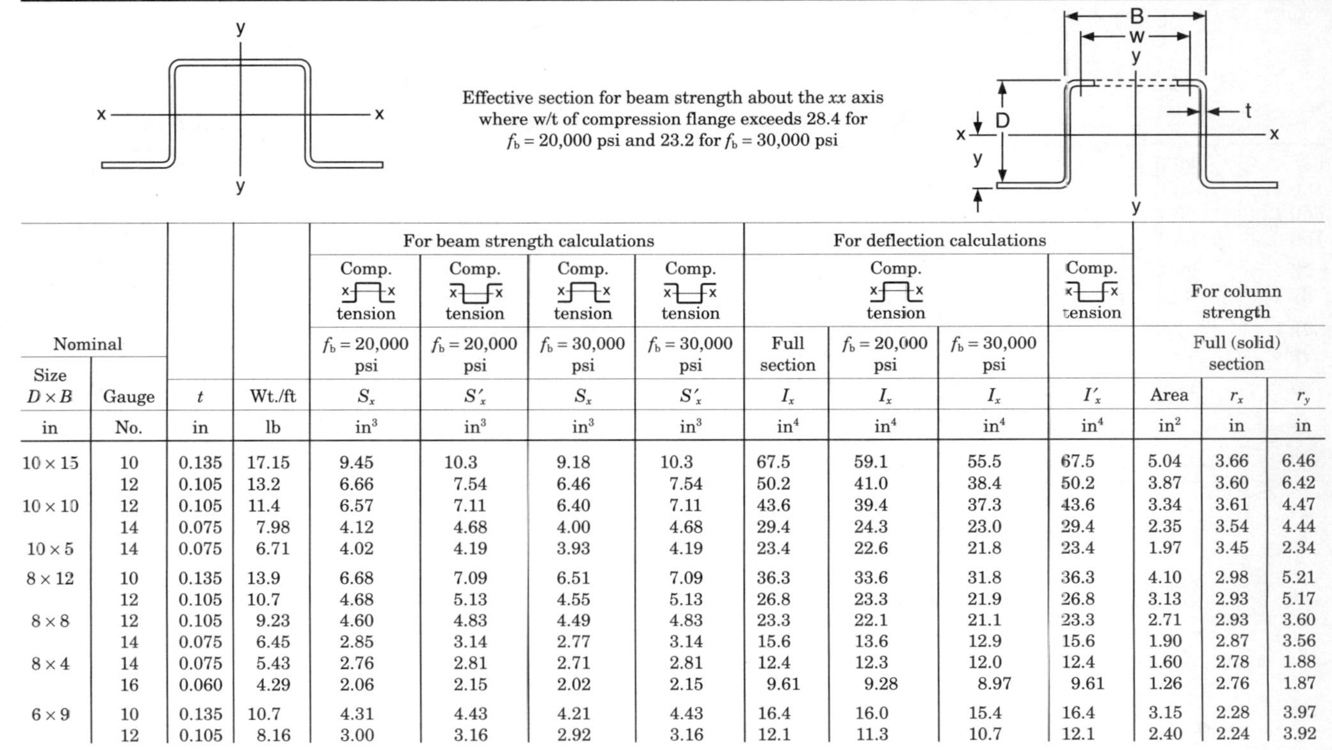

Effective section for beam strength about the *xx* axis where w/t of compression flange exceeds 28.4 for $f_b = 20{,}000$ psi and 23.2 for $f_b = 30{,}000$ psi

Nominal				For beam strength calculations				For deflection calculations				For column strength		
				Comp. tension	Comp. tension	Comp. tension	Comp. tension	Comp. tension			Comp. tension	Full (solid) section		
				$f_b = 20{,}000$ psi	$f_b = 20{,}000$ psi	$f_b = 30{,}000$ psi	$f_b = 30{,}000$ psi	Full section	$f_b = 20{,}000$ psi	$f_b = 30{,}000$ psi				
Size $D \times B$	Gauge	t	Wt./ft	S_x	S'_x	S_x	S'_x	I_x	I_x	I_x	I'_x	Area	r_x	r_y
in	No.	in	lb	in^3	in^3	in^3	in^3	in^4	in^4	in^4	in^4	in^2	in	in
10 × 15	10	0.135	17.15	9.45	10.3	9.18	10.3	67.5	59.1	55.5	67.5	5.04	3.66	6.46
	12	0.105	13.2	6.66	7.54	6.46	7.54	50.2	41.0	38.4	50.2	3.87	3.60	6.42
10 × 10	12	0.105	11.4	6.57	7.11	6.40	7.11	43.6	39.4	37.3	43.6	3.34	3.61	4.47
	14	0.075	7.98	4.12	4.68	4.00	4.68	29.4	24.3	23.0	29.4	2.35	3.54	4.44
10 × 5	14	0.075	6.71	4.02	4.19	3.93	4.19	23.4	22.6	21.8	23.4	1.97	3.45	2.34
8 × 12	10	0.135	13.9	6.68	7.09	6.51	7.09	36.3	33.6	31.8	36.3	4.10	2.98	5.21
	12	0.105	10.7	4.68	5.13	4.55	5.13	26.8	23.3	21.9	26.8	3.13	2.93	5.17
8 × 8	12	0.105	9.23	4.60	4.83	4.49	4.83	23.3	22.1	21.1	23.3	2.71	2.93	3.60
	14	0.075	6.45	2.85	3.14	2.77	3.14	15.6	13.6	12.9	15.6	1.90	2.87	3.56
8 × 4	14	0.075	5.43	2.76	2.81	2.71	2.81	12.4	12.3	12.0	12.4	1.60	2.78	1.88
	16	0.060	4.29	2.06	2.15	2.02	2.15	9.61	9.28	8.97	9.61	1.26	2.76	1.87
6 × 9	10	0.135	10.7	4.31	4.43	4.21	4.43	16.4	16.0	15.4	16.4	3.15	2.28	3.97
	12	0.105	8.16	3.00	3.16	2.92	3.16	12.1	11.3	10.7	12.1	2.40	2.24	3.92

6 × 6	12	0.105	7.09	2.92	2.98	2.87	2.98	10.4	10.3	10.0	10.4	2.08	2.24	2.74
	14	0.075	4.92	1.79	1.90	1.75	1.90	6.91	6.47	6.16	6.91	1.45	2.18	2.69
6 × 3	14	0.075	4.16	1.70	1.70	1.68	1.70	5.48	5.44	5.46	5.48	1.22	2.12	1.43
	16	0.060	3.27	1.27	1.29	1.25	1.29	4.23	4.21	4.13	4.23	0.963	2.10	1.42
	18	0.048	2.59	0.954	0.986	0.93	0.984	3.28	3.20	3.10	3.28	0.761	2.08	1.41
4 × 6	10	0.135	7.51	2.34	2.35	2.31	2.35	5.43	5.43	5.40	5.43	2.21	1.57	2.76
	12	0.105	5.66	1.62	1.65	1.59	1.65	3.96	3.94	3.83	3.96	1.66	1.54	2.69
4 × 4	12	0.105	4.94	1.55	1.55	1.54	1.55	3.39	3.39	3.39	3.39	1.45	1.53	1.91
	14	0.075	3.39	0.945	0.961	0.928	0.961	2.23	2.22	2.16	2.23	0.998	1.49	1.83
4 × 2	14	0.075	2.88	0.863	0.863	0.863	0.863	1.75	1.75	1.75	1.75	0.848	1.44	0.996
	16	0.060	2.25	0.639	0.643	0.641	0.643	1.34	1.34	1.34	1.34	0.663	1.42	0.972
	18	0.048	1.77	0.482	0.483	0.477	0.483	1.03	1.03	1.03	1.03	0.520	1.41	0.956
3 × 4½	10	0.135	5.90	1.51	1.51	1.52	1.52	2.47	2.47	2.46	2.47	1.736	1.19	2.19
	12	0.105	4.41	1.05	1.05	1.04	1.05	1.81	1.81	1.80	1.81	1.297	1.18	2.09
3 × 3	12	0.105	3.87	0.993	0.993	0.993	0.993	1.53	1.53	1.53	1.53	1.139	1.16	1.52
	14	0.075	2.63	0.603	0.604	0.597	0.604	1.01	1.01	1.00	1.01	0.773	1.14	1.41
3 × 1½	14	0.075	2.25	0.504	0.504	0.504	0.504	0.784	0.784	0.784	0.784	0.660	1.09	0.793
	16	0.060	1.74	0.400	0.400	0.400	0.400	0.599	0.599	0.599	0.599	0.513	1.08	0.760
	18	0.048	1.36	0.297	0.297	0.297	0.297	0.459	0.459	0.459	0.459	0.400	1.07	0.738
2 × 4	12	0.105	3.52	0.596	0.596	0.593	0.596	0.672	0.672	0.671	0.672	1.03	0.806	1.90
	14	0.075	2.37	0.350	0.353	0.345	0.353	0.433	0.432	0.423	0.433	0.698	0.787	1.77
2 × 2	14	0.075	1.86	0.321	0.321	0.321	0.321	0.329	0.329	0.329	0.329	0.548	0.774	1.01
	16	0.060	1.44	0.233	0.233	0.233	0.233	0.250	0.248	0.248	0.250	0.423	0.768	0.973
2 × 1	16	0.060	1.23	0.178	0.178	0.178	0.178	0.193	0.193	0.193	0.193	0.363	0.729	0.566
	18	0.048	0.953	0.142	0.142	0.142	0.142	0.147	0.147	0.147	0.147	0.280	0.725	0.532
1½ × 3	12	0.105	2.80	0.390	0.390	0.390	0.390	0.304	0.304	0.304	0.304	0.824	0.607	1.54
	14	0.075	1.86	0.230	0.230	0.228	0.230	0.198	0.198	0.198	0.198	0.548	0.602	1.39
1½ × 1½	14	0.075	1.48	0.187	0.187	0.187	0.187	0.148	0.148	0.148	0.148	0.435	0.583	0.832
	16	0.060	1.13	0.150	0.150	0.150	0.150	0.113	0.113	0.113	0.113	0.333	0.582	0.779
1½ × ¾	16	0.060	0.979	0.0993	0.0993	0.0993	0.0993	0.0856	0.0856	0.086	0.0856	0.288	0.545	0.484
	18	0.048	0.749	0.0795	0.0795	0.0795	0.0795	0.0657	0.0657	0.066	0.0657	0.220	0.546	0.442

NOTE: $S'x$ and $I'x$ in this table are properties of full (unreduced) section and are applicable as indicated. The effective section moduli in bending about the *yy* axis have not been tabulated. When one of the webs acts as a compression flange the section modulus should be calculated on the basis of its effective width as provided in Section 2.3 of the Design Specification. When the web acts as a tension flange the section modulus of the full section is effective.

TABLE 16.9 Hat Sections (*Continued*)

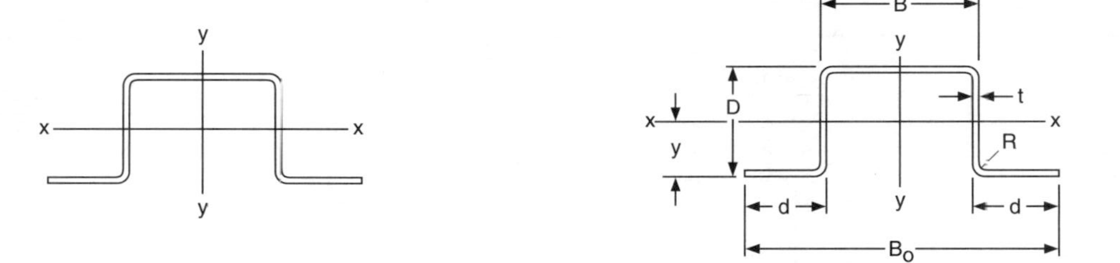

Column factor		Additional properties of full (unreduced) sections			Dimensions of sections								
Q		S_y	I_y	y	D	B	B_o	d	t	R	Wt./ft	Gauge	Size $D \times B$
$f_b = 20{,}000$ psi	$f_b = 30{,}000$ psi	in³	in⁴	in	in	in	in	in	in	in	lb	No.	in
		23.3	210.3	6.54	10.0	15.0	18.07	1.67	0.135	3/16	17.15	10	10 × 15
		18.3	159.5	6.65	10.0	15.0	17.47	1.34	0.105	3/16	13.2	12	
		10.7	66.77	6.14	10.0	10.0	12.47	1.34	0.105	3/16	11.4	12	10 × 10
		7.91	46.21	6.30	10.0	10.0	11.68	0.915	0.075	3/32	7.98	14	
		3.23	10.79	5.60	10.0	5.0	6.68	0.915	0.075	3/32	6.71	14	10 × 5
		14.8	111.2	5.12	8.0	12.0	15.07	1.67	0.135	3/16	13.9	10	8 × 12
		11.6	83.63	5.23	8.0	12.0	14.47	1.34	0.105	3/16	10.7	12	
		6.72	35.21	4.81	8.0	8.0	10.47	1.34	0.105	3/16	9.23	12	8 × 8
		4.97	24.07	4.97	8.0	8.0	9.68	0.915	0.075	3/32	6.45	14	
		1.99	5.66	4.40	8.0	4.0	5.68	0.915	0.075	3/32	5.43	14	8 × 4
		1.65	4.43	4.47	8.0	4.0	5.38	0.75	0.060	3/32	4.29	16	
0.859	0.781	8.24	49.74	3.71	6.0	9.0	12.07	1.67	0.135	3/16	10.7	10	6 × 9
0.751	0.671	6.42	36.84	3.82	6.0	9.0	11.47	1.34	0.105	3/16	8.16	12	
0.835	0.752	3.71	15.70	3.49	6.0	6.0	8.47	1.34	0.105	3/16	7.09	12	6 × 6
		2.73	10.48	3.64	6.0	6.0	7.68	0.915	0.075	3/32	4.92	14	
		1.07	2.51	3.21	6.0	3.0	4.68	0.915	0.075	3/32	4.16	14	6 × 3

		0.883	1.93	3.28	6.0	3.0	4.38	0.75	0.060	3/32	3.27	16	
		0.728	1.51	3.33	6.0	3.0	4.14	0.618	0.048	3/32	2.59	18	
0.974	0.942	3.72	16.86	2.31	4.0	6.0	9.07	1.67	0.135	3/16	7.51	10	4 × 6
0.924	0.861	2.84	12.05	2.41	4.0	6.0	8.47	1.34	0.105	3/16	5.66	12	
0.988	0.939	1.64	5.31	2.19	4.0	4.0	6.47	1.34	0.105	3/16	4.94	12	4 × 4
0.856	0.773	1.18	3.35	2.32	4.0	4.0	5.68	0.915	0.075	3/32	3.39	14	
0.887	0.822	0.457	0.842	2.03	4.0	2.0	3.68	0.915	0.075	3/32	2.88	14	4 × 2
		0.369	0.626	2.09	4.0	2.0	3.38	0.75	0.060	3/32	2.25	16	
		0.303	0.476	2.14	4.0	2.0	3.14	0.618	0.048	3/32	1.77	18	
1.000	0.990	2.19	8.28	1.63	3.0	4.5	7.57	1.67	0.135	3/16	5.90	10	3 × 4½
0.982	0.955	1.63	5.69	1.71	3.0	4.5	6.97	1.34	0.105	3/16	4.41	12	
1.000	1.000	0.956	2.62	1.54	3.0	3.0	5.47	1.34	0.105	3/16	3.87	12	3 × 3
0.969	0.907	0.659	1.54	1.67	3.0	3.0	4.68	0.915	0.075	3/32	2.63	14	
0.976	0.928	0.261	0.415	1.45	3.0	1.5	3.18	0.915	0.075	3/32	2.25	14	3 × 1½
0.915	0.853	0.205	0.296	1.50	3.0	1.5	2.88	0.75	0.060	3/32	1.74	16	
0.839	0.772	0.165	0.218	1.55	3.0	1.5	2.64	0.618	0.048	3/32	1.36	18	
0.994	0.971	1.15	3.72	1.13	2.0	4.0	6.47	1.34	0.105	3/16	3.52	12	2 × 4
0.931	0.892	0.772	2.19	1.22	2.0	4.0	5.68	0.915	0.075	3/32	2.37	14	
1.000	1.000	0.307	0.564	1.02	2.0	2.0	3.68	0.915	0.075	3/32	1.86	14	2 × 2
1.000	0.978	0.237	0.400	1.07	2.0	2.0	3.38	0.75	0.060	3/32	1.44	16	
1.000	0.982	0.0976	0.116	0.920	2.0	1.0	2.38	0.75	0.060	3/32	1.23	16	2 × 1
0.975	0.928	0.0743	0.0795	0.961	2.0	1.0	2.14	0.618	0.048	3/32	0.953	18	
1.000	1.000	0.715	1.96	0.778	1.5	3.0	5.47	1.34	0.105	3/16	2.80	12	1½ × 3
0.986	0.956	0.454	1.06	0.864	1.5	3.0	4.68	0.915	0.075	3/32	1.86	14	
1.000	1.000	0.189	0.301	0.709	1.5	1.5	3.18	0.915	0.075	3/32	1.48	14	1½ × 1½
1.000	1.000	0.141	0.202	0.750	1.5	1.5	2.88	0.75	0.060	3/32	1.13	16	
1.000	1.000	0.0633	0.0674	0.637	1.5	0.75	2.13	0.75	0.060	3/32	0.979	16	1½ × ¾
1.000	0.996	0.0455	0.0430	0.673	1.5	0.75	1.89	0.618	0.048	3/32	0.749	18	

DIMENSIONS: Equipment and forming practices vary with different manufacturers, resulting in minor variations in some of these dimensions. These minor variations do not affect the published properties. Consult the manufacturer for actual weight per foot and actual dimensions. Column form factors Q for members having webs with w/t-ratios in excess of 60 are not shown. See limitations of Section 2.3.3(a) of the Specification applicable to element stiffened by a simple lip.

TABLE 16.10 One-Flange Stiffener (Which Includes One 90° Corner): Properties and Dimensions

Stock Width of Blank Taken at $t/3$ Distance From Inner Surface.

Nominal Gauge	Thickness t	Depth d	Properties: xx Axis I_x	xx Axis y	yy Axis I_y	yy Axis x	Area	Dimensions: Max. flange B	Blank width	Thickness t	Radius R	Depth d	Nominal Gauge
No.	in	in	in^4	in	in^4	in	in^2	in	in	in	in	in	No.
10	0.135	1.0	0.01255	0.4737	0.000796	0.1005	0.14554	3.87	1.043	0.135	3/16	1.0	10
		0.9	0.00916	0.4250	0.000759	0.1039	0.13204	3.25	0.943	0.135	3/16	0.9	
		0.8	0.00643	0.3766	0.000719	0.1080	0.11854	2.81	0.843	0.135	3/16	0.8	
		0.7	0.00430	0.3286	0.000674	0.1133	0.10504	2.53	0.743	0.135	3/16	0.7	
		0.6	0.00269	0.2811	0.000621	0.1200	0.09154	2.37	0.643	0.135	3/16	0.6	
		0.5	0.00153	0.2346	0.000556	0.1291	0.07804	2.30	0.543	0.135	3/16	0.5	
		0.4	0.00076	0.1896	0.000474	0.1420	0.06454	2.27	0.443	0.135	3/16	0.4	
12	0.105	0.9	0.00735	0.4205	0.000475	0.0850	0.10337	4.28	0.957	0.105	3/16	0.9	12
		0.8	0.00518	0.3719	0.000453	0.0886	0.09287	3.34	0.857	0.105	3/16	0.8	
		0.7	0.00348	0.3237	0.000428	0.0932	0.08237	2.66	0.757	0.105	3/16	0.7	
		0.6	0.00219	0.2761	0.000398	0.0992	0.07187	2.22	0.657	0.105	3/16	0.6	
		0.5	0.00126	0.2292	0.000362	0.1072	0.06137	1.98	0.557	0.105	3/16	0.5	
		0.4	0.00064	0.1836	0.000314	0.1185	0.05087	1.88	0.457	0.105	3/16	0.4	

14	0.075	0.9	0.00493	0.4351	0.000081	0.0475	0.07031	6.79	0.918	0.075	3/32	0.9	14
		0.8	0.00348	0.3855	0.000076	0.0487	0.06281	4.94	0.818	0.075	3/32	0.8	
		0.7	0.00234	0.3361	0.000072	0.0502	0.05531	3.50	0.718	0.075	3/32	0.7	
		0.6	0.00148	0.2869	0.000067	0.0522	0.04781	2.46	0.618	0.075	3/32	0.6	
		0.5	0.00086	0.2379	0.000062	0.0549	0.04031	1.77	0.518	0.075	3/32	0.5	
		0.4	0.00044	0.1894	0.000055	0.0589	0.03281	1.40	0.418	0.075	3/32	0.4	
16	0.060	0.8	0.00283	0.3836	0.000048	0.0400	0.05044	7.50	0.825	0.060	3/32	0.8	16
		0.7	0.00191	0.3341	0.000045	0.0414	0.04444	5.19	0.725	0.060	3/32	0.7	
		0.6	0.00121	0.2848	0.000043	0.0432	0.03844	3.46	0.625	0.060	3/32	0.6	
		0.5	0.00071	0.2357	0.000040	0.0456	0.03244	2.23	0.525	0.060	3/32	0.5	
		0.4	0.00036	0.1871	0.000036	0.0492	0.02644	1.48	0.425	0.060	3/32	0.4	
18	0.048	0.7	0.00155	0.3325	0.000030	0.0344	0.03567	7.96	0.731	0.048	3/32	0.7	18
		0.6	0.00099	0.2831	0.000028	0.0360	0.03087	5.19	0.631	0.048	3/32	0.6	
		0.5	0.00058	0.2340	0.000026	0.0382	0.02607	3.20	0.531	0.048	3/32	0.5	
		0.4	0.00030	0.1853	0.000024	0.0414	0.02127	1.87	0.431	0.048	3/32	0.4	

TABLE 16.11 One 90° Corner: Properties and Dimensions

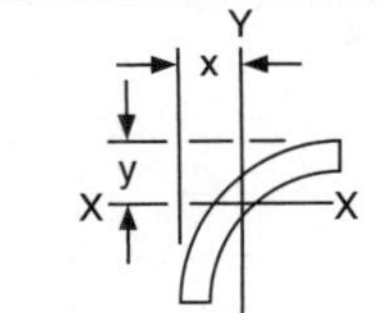

Stock Width of Blank Taken at $t/3$ Distance From Inner Surface.

Nominal	Thickness	Properties				Dimensions		Nominal
		Moment of inertia	Centroid coordinates			Thickness	Radius inside	
Gauge	t	$I_x = I_y$	$x = y$	Area	Blank width	t	R	Gauge
No.	in	in^4	in	in^2	in	in	in	No.
10	0.135	0.0003889	0.1564	0.05407	0.3652	0.135	0.1875	10
12	0.105	0.0002408	0.1373	0.03958	0.3495	0.105	0.1875	12
14	0.075	0.0000301	0.0829	0.01546	0.1865	0.075	0.0938	14
16	0.060	0.0000193	0.0734	0.01166	0.1787	0.060	0.0938	16
18	0.048	0.0000128	0.0658	0.00888	0.1724	0.048	0.0938	18
20	0.036	0.00000313	0.0464	0.00452	0.1170	0.036	0.0625	20

Chapter

17

Hardening and Tempering Steels and Nonferrous Alloys

The hardening and tempering of steels and nonferrous alloys are important aspects of metalworking. Carbon and alloy steels are relied on to perform a great number of services in the metalworking industries. Some of the nonferrous metals and alloys are also capable of being hardened above their normal condition either through heat treatment or cold working and find countless uses in product design and manufacturing.

17.1 Standard Steels and Steel Making Practices

Steel is the generic name for a large group of iron-carbon alloys. The basic materials used in steel making are iron ore, coke, and limestone. A blast furnace converts these materials into a product known as *pig iron,* which contains considerable amounts of carbon, manganese, sulfur, phosphorus, and silicon. Basic oxygen furnaces are also employed in steel making, as are other methods. Steel making's basic constituent, pig iron, is hard and brittle and unsuitable for processing into usable wrought iron or steel products. Steel making is the process of refining pig iron and iron and steel scrap by removing unwanted elements and adding the desirable elements in predetermined and controlled amounts. Most steel making processes cause a combination of carbon and oxygen to form a gas. When a steel is deoxidized strongly with a deoxidizing agent, no gas forms and the steel is called *killed steel*. The degree of deoxidation affects some of the properties of the steel, and the degree of gas evolution characterizes steels that are known as *semikilled, capped,* and *rimmed*. In addition to oxygen, fused steel contains small amounts of hydrogen and nitrogen. Special deoxidation practices, including vacuum treatment, may be used to control the amount of dissolved gases in the steel.

The carbon content of the common steel grades ranges from a few hundredths of 1 percent to 0.95 percent. All common steels contain manganese, sulfur, phosphorus, and silicon to some degree.

Wrought steels are the most common and widely used engineering materials. There is no other single material that offers such a broad range of practical applications as the various types and grades of steels.

The unified numbering system for steels is shown in Chap. 5, "Materials and Their Uses." This system classifies the various types of steels and provides identification numbers.

17.2 Constituents of Steel: Phases

When carbon steels are heated to various temperatures, changes take place in the structure, which are known as *phases*. Figure 17.1 is a diagram showing the relationship between temperature and the amount of carbon in the steel that affects the basic structure. The diagram is presented strictly for academic reasons and serves the purpose of describing the different states that the steel assumes when the temperature and carbon content are varied. The actions and reactions that occur during the heating and cooling of carbon and alloy steels are complex and form the basis for the controlled heat treatments that are performed on the various types of steels.

The diagram in Fig. 17.1 indicates the phase transformations that occur in steels with up to 6.67 percent carbon content, where the main form of the steel above 2066°F is called *cementite*. The other forms or states/phases are indicated by the various letters and combinations of letters shown below the figure. Some of the other forms that occur are shown below the letter designations, the most important of which is *martensite*. Martensite is the phase or form of carbon steel that is produced in the hardening process, which will be described in a later section.

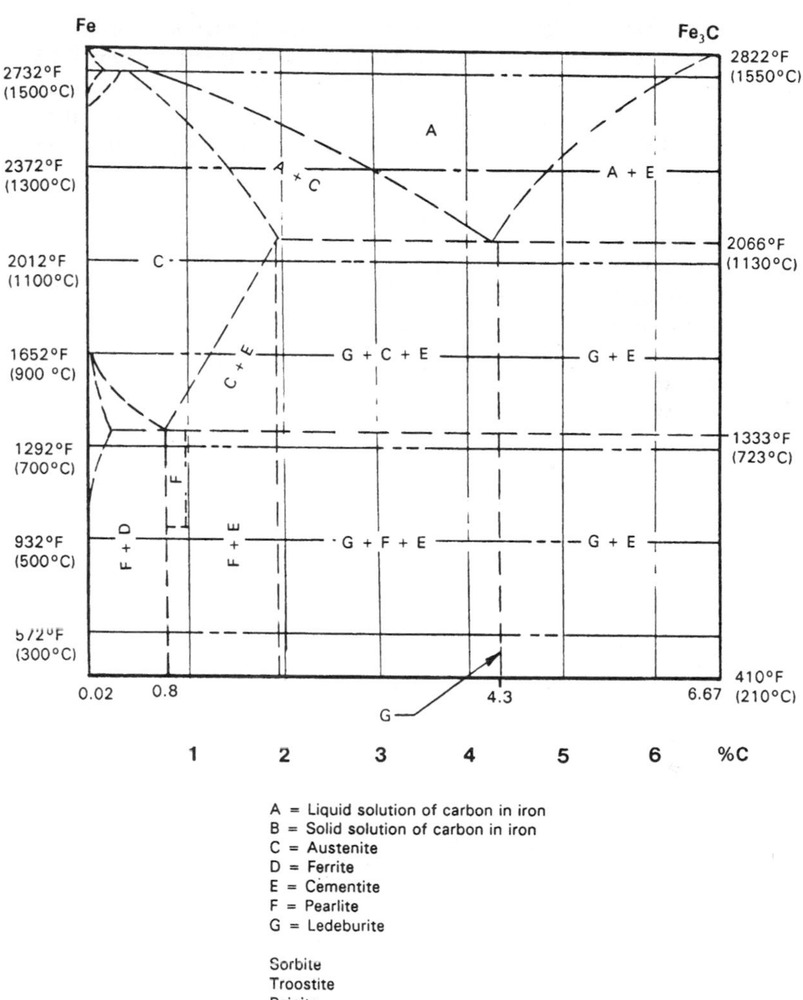

Figure 17.1 Iron, iron-carbide diagram.

Carbon steels with less than 0.85 percent carbon are called *hypoeutectoid,* and those with carbon contents greater than 0.85 percent are called *hypereutectoid.* In binary-alloy systems, a *eutectoid alloy* is a mechanical mixture of two phases that form simultaneously from a solid solution when it cools through the eutectoid temperature. Alloys leaner or richer in one of the constituents or metals undergo transformation from the solid solution phase over a range of temperatures beginning above and ending at the eutectoid temperature. The structure of such alloys will consist of primary particles of one of the stable phases in addition to the eutectoid, e.g., ferrite and pearlite in low-carbon steel.

17.3 Standard Definitions of Terms Pertaining to Heat Treatment of Metals

Many terms are associated with the heat treatment of metals, and the American Society for Testing and Materials (ASTM) has classified these terms in ASTM Standard E44-84. Figure 17.2 outlines the terms and definitions as described in ASTM Standard E44-84 and is reproduced with permission from the ASTM.

By studying the diagram shown in Fig. 17.1 and the definitions of terms shown in Fig. 17.2, you will gain an excellent insight into the practice of heat treatment of metals.

17.4 Heat Treatment of Steels

In fully annealed carbon steels, the percentage of carbon determines the structural constitution of the steel. Figure 17.1 shows the constitution or phases for varying carbon content versus temperature.

Effect of heating fully annealed carbon steels. When fully annealed carbon steels are heated above the *lower critical point,* which ranges between 1335 and 1355°F, depending on the carbon content, *austenite* is formed. If the temperature continues to rise, the steel structure will change completely to austenite. The temperature at which excess ferrite and cementite are completely dissolved in the austenite is called the *upper critical point.* This critical temperature varies with the carbon content of the steel. If the steel is slowly cooled to ambient temperature, the steel returns to its original condition.

Standard Definitions of Terms Relating to Heat Treatment of Metals ASTM E44-84

(Temperatures have been omitted from these definitions, which are not intended as specifications)

Ac_{cm}, Ac_1, Ac_3, Ac_4—See **transformation temperature.**

age hardening—hardening by aging, usually after rapid cooling or cold working. See **aging.**

aging—a change in the properties of certain metals and alloys that occurs at ambient or moderately elevated temperatures after hot working or a heat treatment (quench aging in ferrous alloys, natural or artificial aging in ferrous and nonferrous alloys) or after a cold-working operation (strain aging). The change in properties is often, but not always, due to a phase change (precipitation), but never involves a change in chemical composition of the metals or alloys. See also **age hardening, artificial aging, natural aging, overaging, precipitation hardening, precipitation heat treatment, progressive aging, quench aging,** and **strain aging.**

annealing—heating to and holding at a suitable temperature and then cooling at a suitable rate, for such purposes as reducing hardness, improving machinability, facilitating cold working, producing a desired microstructure, or obtaining desired mechanical, physical, or other properties. When applicable, the following more specific terms should be used:

black annealing
blue annealing
box annealing
bright annealing
flame annealing
full annealing
graphitizing
intermediate annealing
isothermal annealing
malleableizing
process annealing
quench annealing
recrystallization annealing
spheroidizing

Definitions of the above terms are given below in their alphabetic positions.

When applied to ferrous alloys, the term "annealing," without qualification, implies full annealing.

When applied to nonferrous alloys, the term "annealing" implies a heat treatment designed to soften a cold-worked structure by recrystallization or subsequent grain growth or to soften an age-hardened alloy by causing a nearly complete precipitation of the second phase in relatively coarse form.

Any process of annealing will usually reduce stresses but if the treatment is applied for the sole purpose of such relief it should be designated **stress relieving.**

Ar_{cm}, Ar_1, Ar_3, Ar_4—See **transformation temperature.**

artificial aging—aging above room temperature. See **aging** and **precipitation heat treatment.** Compare with **natural aging.**

austempering—quenching a ferrous alloy from a temperature above the transformation range in a medium having a rate of heat abstraction high enough to prevent the formation of high-temperature transformation products, and then holding the alloy, until transformation is complete, at a temperature below that of pearlite formation and above that of martensite formation.

austenitizing—forming austenite by heating a ferrous alloy into the transformation range (partial austenitizing) or above the transformation range (complete austenitizing).

baking—heating to a low temperature in order to remove gases.

black annealing—box annealing or pot annealing ferrous alloy sheet, strip, or wire. See **box annealing.**

blank carburizing—simulating the carburizing operation without introducing carbon. This is usually accomplished by using an inert material in place of the carburizing agent, or by applying a suitable protective coating to the ferrous alloy.

blank nitriding—simulating the nitriding operation without introducing nitrogen. This is usually accomplished by using an inert material in place of the nitriding agent, or by applying a suitable protective coating to the ferrous alloy.

blue annealing—heating hot-rolled ferrous sheet in an open furnace to a temperature within the transformation range and then cooling in air, in order to soften the metal. The formation of a bluish oxide on the surface is incidental.

bluing—subjecting the scale-free surface of a ferrous alloy to the action of air, steam or other agents at a suitable temperature, thus forming a thin blue film of oxide and improving the appearance and resistance to corrosion.

[1] These definitions are under the jurisdiction of ASTM Committee A-1 on Steel, Stainless Steel, and Related Alloys and are the direct responsibility of Subcommittee A1.92 on Terminology.

Current edition approved Oct. 26, 1984. Published December 1984. Originally published as E 44 – 42 T. Last previous edition E 44 – 83.

Figure 17.2 Standard terms relating to the heat treatment of metals *(Reprinted with permission from the Annual Book of ASTM Standards, copyright 1992, American Society for Testing and Materials.)*

NOTE—This term is ordinarily applied to sheet, strip, or finished parts. It is used also to denote the heating of springs after fabrication, in order to improve their properties.

box annealing—annealing a metal or alloy in a sealed container under conditions that minimize oxidation. In box annealing a ferrous alloy, the charge is usually heated slowly to a temperature below the transformation range, but sometimes above or within it, and is then cooled slowly; this process is also called "close annealing" or "pot annealing." See **black annealing.**

bright annealing—annealing in a protective medium to prevent discoloration of the bright surface.

burning (burnt, burned)—a term applied to metal which has been permanently damaged by having been heated to a temperature close to or within the melting range. This results in a structure exhibiting incipient melting or intergranular oxidation.

carbonitriding—a case hardening process in which a suitable ferrous material is heated above the lower transformation temperature in a gaseous atmosphere of such composition as to cause simultaneous absorption of carbon and nitrogen by the surface and, by diffusion, create a concentration gradient. The process is completed by cooling at a rate that produces the desired properties in the workpiece.

carbon potential—a measure of the ability of an environment containing active carbon to alter or maintain, under prescribed conditions, the carbon content of the steel.

NOTE—In any particular environment, the carbon level attained will depend on such factors as temperature, time, and steel composition.

carbon restoration—replacing the carbon lost in the surface layer from previous processing by carburizing this layer to substantially the original carbon level.

carburizing—a process in which an austenitized ferrous material is brought into contact with a carbonaceous atmosphere of sufficient carbon potential to cause absorption of carbon at the surface and by diffusion, create a concentration gradient.

case—*in a ferrous alloy,* the outer portion that has been made harder than the inner portion (see **core**) as a result of altered composition, or structure, or both, from treatments such as carburizing, nitriding, and induction hardening.

case hardening—a generic term covering several processes applicable to steel that change the chemical composition of the surface layer by absorption of carbon, nitrogen, or a mixture of the two and, by diffusion, create a concentration gradient. The processes commonly used are: **carburizing** and **quench hardening**; **cyaniding**; **nitriding**; and **carbonitriding.** The use of the applicable specific process name is preferred.

cementation—the introduction of one or more elements into the outer portion of a metal object by means of diffusion at high temperature.

close annealing—See **box annealing.**

cold treatment—exposing to subzero temperatures for the purpose of obtaining desired conditions or properties, such as dimensional or structural stability. When the treatment involves transformation of retained austenite, it is usually followed by a tempering treatment.

conditioning heat treatment—a preliminary heat treatment used to prepare a material for a desired reaction to a subsequent heat treatment. For the term to be meaningful, the exact treatment must be specified.

controlled cooling—cooling from an elevated temperature in a predetermined manner to avoid hardening, cracking, or internal damage or to produce a desired microstructure or mechanical properties.

core—(*1*) *case hardening*—interior portion of unaltered composition, or microstructure, or both, of a case-hardened steel article.

(*2*) *clad products*—the central portion of a multilayer composite metallic material.

critical cooling rate—the minimum rate of continuous cooling to prevent undesirable transformations. For steel, unless otherwise specified, it is the slowest rate at which austenite can be cooled from above critical temperature to prevent its transformation above the M_s temperature.

critical temperature range—synonymous with **transformation range.** The term is of historic significance only, and its use is discouraged.

cyaniding—introducing carbon and nitrogen into a solid ferrous alloy by holding above Ac_1 in contact with molten cyanide of suitable composition. The cyanided alloy is usually quench hardened.

cycle annealing—an annealing process employing a predetermined and closely controlled time-temperature cycle to produce specific properties or microstructure.

decarburization—the loss of carbon from the surface of a ferrous alloy as a result of heating in a medium that reacts with the carbon.

differential heating—heating that intentionally produces a temperature gradient within an object such that, after cooling, a desired stress distribution or variation in properties is present within the object.

diffusion coating—any process whereby a basis metal or alloy is either: (*1*) coated with another metal or alloy and heated to a sufficient temperature in a suitable environment, or (*2*) exposed to a gaseous or liquid medium containing the other metal or alloy, thus causing diffusion of the coating or of the other metal or alloy into the basis metal with resultant change in the composition and properties of its surface.

direct quenching—quenching carburized parts directly from the carburizing operation.

double aging—employment of two different aging treatments to control the type of precipitate formed from a supersaturated alloy matrix in order to obtain the desired properties. The first aging treatment, sometimes referred to as intermediate or stabilizing, is usually carried out at a higher temperature than the second.

double tempering—a treatment in which quench-hardened steel is given two complete tempering cycles at substantially the same temperature for the purpose of assuring completion of the tempering reaction and promoting stability of the resulting microstructure.

drawing—a misnomer for **tempering.**

ferritizing anneal—the process of producing a predominantly ferritic matrix in a ferrous alloy through an appropriate heat treatment.

flame annealing—annealing in which the heat is applied directly by a flame.

Figure 17.2 (*Continued*)

flame hardening—a surface hardening process in which only the surface layer of a suitable workpiece is heated by a suitably intense flame to above the upper transformation temperature and immediately quenched.

fog quenching—quenching in a mist.

full annealing—annealing a ferrous alloy by austenitizing and then cooling slowly through the transformation range. The austenitizing temperature for hypoeutectoid steel is usually above Ac_3 and for hypereutectoid steel usually between Ac_1 and Ac_{cm}.

gas cyaniding—a misnomer for **carbonitriding.**

grain growth—an increase in the grain size of a metal, usually as a result of heating at an elevated temperature.

grain size—the dimensions of the grains or crystals in a polycrystalline metal exclusive of twinned regions and subgrains when present. Grain size is usually estimated or measured on the cross section of an aggregate of grains. Common units are: (*1*) average diameter, (*2*) average area, (*3*) number of grains per linear unit, (*4*) number of grains per unit area, and (*5*) number of grains per unit volume. See Methods E 112, for Determining The Average Grain Size.[2]

(*1*) ASTM grain size number—a grain size designation bearing a relationship to average intercept distance at 100 diameters magnification according to the equation: G = ASTM Grain Size Number = $10.00 - 2 \log_2 \bar{L}$, where $\bar{L}$ is the average intercept distance in millimetres at 100 diameters magnification.

(*2*) average grain diameter—the mean diameter of an equiaxed grain section whose size is representative of all the grain sections in the aggregate being measured.

graphitizing—annealing a ferrous alloy in such a way that some or all of the carbon is precipitated as graphite.

hardenability—in a ferrous alloy, the property that determines the depth and distribution of hardness induced by quenching.

hardening—increasing the hardness by suitable treatment, usually involving heating and cooling. When applicable, the following more specific terms should be used: **age hardening, case hardening, flame hardening, induction hardening, precipitation hardening,** and **quench hardening.**

heat treatment—heating and cooling a solid metal or alloy in such a way as to obtain desired conditions or properties. Heating for the sole purpose of hot working is excluded from the meaning of this definition.

homogeneous carburizing—a process that converts a low-carbon ferrous alloy to one of substantially uniform and higher carbon content throughout the section, so that a specific response to hardening may be obtained.

homogenizing—holding at high temperature to eliminate or decrease chemical segregation by diffusion.

hot-cold working—mechanical deformation of austenitic and precipitation hardening alloys at a temperature just below the recrystallization range to increase the yield strength and hardness by either plastic deformation or precipitation hardening effects induced by plastic deformation, or both.

hot quenching—an imprecise term used to cover a variety of quenching procedures in which a quenching medium is maintained at a prescribed temperature above 160°F (71°C).

induction hardening—a surface hardening process in which only the surface layer of a suitable ferrous workpiece is heated by electrical induction to above the upper transformation temperature and immediately quenched.

induction heating—heating by electrical induction.

intermediate annealing—annealing wrought metals at one or more stages during manufacture and before final thermal treatment.

interrupted aging—aging at two or more temperatures, by steps, and cooling to room temperature after each step. See **aging** and compare with **progressive aging.**

interrupted quenching—quenching in which the metal object being quenched is removed from the quenching medium while the object is at a temperature substantially higher than that of the quenching medium. See also **time quenching.**

isothermal annealing—austenitizing a ferrous alloy and then cooling to and holding at a temperature at which austenite transforms to a relatively soft ferrite-carbide aggregate.

isothermal transformation—a change in phase at any constant temperature.

malleableizing—a process in which the ascast malleable-type (white) iron is thermally treated for the purpose of converting most or all of the carbon in Fe_3C to graphite (temper carbon) to produce a family of products with improved ductility.

maraging—a precipitation hardening treatment applied to a special group of iron-base alloys to precipitate one or more intermetallic compounds in a matrix of essentially carbon-free martensite.

NOTE—The first developed series of maraging steels contained, in addition to iron, more than 10 % nickel and one or more supplemental hardening elements. In this series, the aging is done at approximately 900°F (482°C).

martempering—quenching an austenitized ferrous alloy in a medium at a temperature in the upper part of the martensite range, or slightly above that range, and holding in the medium until the temperature throughout the alloy is substantially uniform. The alloy is then allowed to cool in air through the martensite range.

martensite range—the temperature interval between M_s and M_f.

M_f—See **transformation temperature.**

M_s—See **transformation temperature.**

natural aging—spontaneous aging of a super-saturated solid solution at room temperature. See **aging** and compare with **artificial aging.**

nitriding—introducing nitrogen into a solid ferrous alloy by holding at a suitable temperature (below Ac_1 for ferritic steels) in contact with a nitrogenous material, usually ammonia or molten cyanide of appropriate composition. Quenching is not required to produce a hard case.

normalizing—heating a ferrous alloy to a suitable temperature above the transformation range and then cooling in air to a temperature substantially below the transformation range.

Figure 17.2 *(Continued)*

overaging—aging under conditions of time and temperature greater than those required to obtain maximum change in a certain property, so that the property is altered in the direction of the initial value. See **aging.**

overheating—(*1*)*in ferrous alloys,* heating to an excessively high temperature such that the properties/structure undergo modification. The resulting structure is very coarse-grained. Unlike burning, it may be possible to restore the original properties/structure by further heat treatment or mechanical working, or a combination thereof.

(*2*) in aluminum alloys, overheating produces structures that show areas of resolidified eutectic or other evidence that indicates the metal has been heated within the melting range.

patenting—in wire making, a heat treatment applied to medium-carbon or high-carbon steel before the drawing of wire or between drafts. This process consists in heating to a temperature above the transformation range and then cooling to a temperature below Ae_1 in air or in a bath of molten lead or salt.

postheating—heating weldments immediately after welding, for tempering, for stress relieving, or for providing a controlled rate of cooling to prevent formation of a hard or brittle structure.

pot annealing—See **box annealing.**

precipitation hardening—hardening caused by the precipitation of a constituent from a supersaturated solid solution. See also **age hardening** and **aging.**

precipitation heat treatment—artificial aging in which a constituent precipitates from a supersaturated solid solution. See **artificial aging, interrupted aging,** and **progressive aging.**

preheating—heating before some further thermal or mechanical treatment. For tool steel, heating to an intermediate temperature immediately before final austenitizing. For some nonferrous alloys, heating to a high temperature for a long time in order to homogenize the structure before working.

process annealing—in the sheet and wire industries, heating a ferrous alloy to a temperature close to, but below, the lower limit of the transformation range and then cooling, in order to soften the alloy for further cold working.

progressive aging—aging by increasing the temperature in steps or continuously during the aging cycle. See **aging** and compare with **interrupted aging.**

pseudocarburizing—See **blank carburizing.**

pseudonitriding—See **blank nitriding.**

quench aging—aging induced by rapid cooling after **solution heat treatment.**

quench annealing—annealing an austenitic ferrous alloy by **solution heat treatment.**

quench hardening—hardening a ferrous alloy by austenitizing and then cooling rapidly enough so that some or all of the austenite transforms to martensite. The austenitizing temperature for hypoeutectoid steels is usually above Ac_3 and for hypereutectoid steels usually between Ac_1 and Ac_{cm}.

quenching—rapid cooling. When applicable, the following more specific terms should be used: **direct quenching, fog quenching, hot quenching, interrupted quenching, selective quenching, spray quenching,** and **time quenching.**

recrystallization—the formation of a new grain structure through nucleation and growth commonly produced by subjecting a metal, which may be strained, to suitable conditions of time and temperature.

recrystallization annealing—annealing cold-worked metal to produce a new grain structure without phase change.

recrystallization temperature—the approximate minimum temperature at which recrystallization of a cold worked metal occurs within a specified time.

secondary hardening—the hardening phenomenon that occurs during high-temperature tempering of certain steels containing one or more carbide-forming alloying elements. Up to an optimum combination of tempering time and temperature, the reaction results either in the retention of hardness or an actual increase in hardness.

selective heating—intentionally heating only certain portions of an object.

selective quenching—quenching only certain portions of an object.

shell hardening—a surface hardening process in which a suitable steel workpiece, when heated through and quench hardened, develops a martensitic layer or shell that closely follows the contour of the piece and surrounds a core of essentially pearlitic transformation product. This result is accomplished by a proper balance between section size, steel hardenability, and severity of quench.

slack quenching—the incomplete hardening of steel due to quenching from the austenitizing temperature at a rate slower than the *critical cooling rate* for the particular steel, resulting in the formation of one or more transformation products in addition to martensite.

snap temper—a precautionary interim stress-relieving treatment applied to high-hardenability steels immediately after quenching to prevent cracking because of delay in tempering them at the prescribed higher temperature.

soaking—prolonged holding at a selected temperature.

solution heat treatment—heating an alloy to a suitable temperature, holding at that temperature long enough to cause one or more constituents to enter into solid solution and then cooling rapidly enough to hold these constituents in solution.

spheroidizing—heating and cooling to produce a spheroidal or globular form of carbide in steel. Spheroidizing methods frequently used are:

(*1*) Prolonged holding at a temperature just below Ae_1.

(*2*) Heating and cooling alternately between temperatures that are just above and just below Ae_1.

(*3*) Heating to a temperature above Ae_1 or Ae_3 and then cooling very slowly in the furnace or holding at a temperature just below Ae_1.

(*4*) Cooling at a suitable rate from the minimum temperature at which all carbide is dissolved, to prevent the re-formation of a carbide network, and then reheating in accordance with method (*1*) or (*2*) above. (Applicable to hypereutectoid steel containing a carbide network.)

spinodal decomposition—mechanism of a phase separation from a solid solution into two homogeneous phases of different chemical composition, each having the same crystal structure as the parent metal.

spray quenching—quenching in a spray of liquid.

Figure 17.2 *(Continued)*

stabilizing treatment—any treatment intended to stabilize the structure of an alloy or the dimensions of a part.

(*1*) heating austenitic stainless steels that contain titanium, columbium, or tantalum to a suitable temperature below that of a full anneal in order to inactivate the maximum amount of carbon by precipitation as a carbide of titanium, columbium, or tantalum.

(*2*) transforming retained austenite in parts made from tool steel.

(*3*) precipitating a constituent from a non-ferrous solid solution to improve the workability, to decrease the tendency of certain alloys to age harden at room temperature, or to obtain dimensional stability.

strain aging—aging induced by cold working. See **aging.**

stress relieving—heating to a suitable temperature, holding long enough to reduce residual stresses and then cooling slowly enough to minimize the development of new residual stresses.

surface hardening—a generic term covering several processes applicable to a suitable ferrous alloy that produces by quench hardening only, a surface layer that is harder or more wear resistant than the core. There is no significant alteration of the chemical composition of the surface layer. The processes commonly used are induction hardening, flame hardening, and shell hardening. Use of the applicable specific process name is preferred.

temper brittleness—brittleness that results when certain steels are held within, or are cooled slowly through, a certain range of temperature below the transformation range. The brittleness is revealed by notched-bar impact tests at or below room temperature.

tempering—(*1*) reheating a quench hardened or normalized ferrous alloy to a temperature below the transformation range (Ac_1), and then cooling at any desired rate. (*2*) a term used in conjunction with a qualifying adjective to designate the relative properties of a particular metal or alloy induced by cold work or heat treatment, or both.

time quenching—interrupted quenching in which the duration of holding in the quenching medium is controlled.

transformation ranges or **transformation temperature ranges**—those ranges of temperature within which austenite forms during heating and transforms during cooling. The two ranges are distinct, sometimes overlapping but never coinciding. The limiting temperatures of the ranges depend on the composition of the alloy and on the rate of change of temperature, particularly during cooling. See **transformation temperature.**

transformation temperature—the temperature at which a change in phase occurs. The term is sometimes used to denote the limiting temperature of a transformation range. The following symbols are used for iron and steels:

Ac_{cm}—in hypereutectoid steel, the temperature at which the solution of cementite in austenite is completed during heating.

Ac_1—the temperature at which austenite begins to form during heating.

Ac_3—the temperature at which transformation of ferrite to austenite is completed during heating.

Ac_4—the temperature at which austenite transforms to delta ferrite during heating.

Ae_1, Ae_3, Ae_{cm}, Ae_4—the temperatures of phase changes at equilibrium.

Ar_{cm}—in hypereutectoid steel, the temperature at which precipitation of cementite starts during cooling.

Ar_1—the temperature at which transformation of austenite to ferrite or to ferrite plus cementite is completed during cooling.

Ar_3—the temperature at which austenite begins to transform to ferrite during cooling.

Ar_4—the temperature at which delta ferrite transforms to austenite during cooling.

M_s—the temperature at which transformation of austenite to martensite starts during cooling.

M_f—the temperature, during cooling, at which transformation of austenite to martensite is substantially completed.

NOTE—All these changes except the formation of martensite occur at lower temperatures during cooling than during heating, and depend on the rate of change of temperature.

Figure 17.2 (*Continued*)

Effect of rapid cooling or quenching carbon steels. Simply stated, when carbon steels are heated to a certain temperature, suddenly cooling the steel at the proper cooling rate causes the austenite to transform to *martensite,* which has very high hardness. Thus the operation of hardening steels consists of two steps. The first step is to heat the steel at least 100°F higher than its transformation point, and the second step is to cool the steel at some rate that is faster than the *critical rate.* (The *critical rate* is determined by or depends on the carbon content and alloying elements present in the steel.) The hardness of a martensitic steel depends on its carbon content and ranges from 460 Brinell at 0.20 percent carbon to 710 Brinell at 0.50 percent carbon. Ferrite has a hardness of approximately 90 Brinell, pearlite approximately 240 Brinell, and cementite approximately 550 Brinell.

The critical temperature points for hardening steel are also called the *decalescence point* and the *recalescence point*. These critical temperature points have a direct relation to the hardening of steel. Unless the hardening temperature passes the decalescence point, no hardening can take place, and unless the steel is cooled suddenly before its temperature reaches the recalescence point, no hardening can take place. These critical temperature points (decalescence and recalescence) vary for different types of steels and must be determined by tests. This variation in critical temperature points makes it necessary to heat different steels to different hardening temperatures together with the proper quench, or cooling rate.

The maximum temperature to which a steel is heated before quenching to harden is called the *hardening temperature*. The hardening temperatures for steels of various carbon contents may be summarized generally by the following:

Carbon content, %	Hardening temperature, °F
0.65–0.80	1450–1550
0.80–0.95	1410–1460
0.95–1.10	1390–1430
1.10 and over	1380–1420

Average hardening and tempering temperatures of steels. Generally, the average hardening temperature range for carbon and alloy steels is from 1375 to 1575°F. The average tempering range for steels is from 300 to 700°F.

17.4.1 Treatments for heat-treating grades of carbon steels

Figure 17.3 lists data for heat treating the common-usage heat-treating grades of carbon steels. The tempering temperatures are not shown, and tempering is not mandatory on many applications. When tempering is required, the tempering range varies from 250 to 450°F.

17.4.2 Heat treatments for directly hardenable grades of alloy steels

Figure 17.4 lists data for heat treating the common-usage directly hardenable grades of alloy steels. Tempering temperatures range from 250 to 350°F.

SAE Steel	Normalizing Temperature (°F)	Annealing Temperature (°F)	Hardening Temperature (°F)	Quenching Medium
1025 1030	.....	.....	1575-1650	Water or brine
1035	.....	.....	1525-1575	oil or water
1036	1600-1700	.....	1525-1575	oil or water
1038 1039* 1040	1600-1700	.....	1525-1575	oil or water
1041	1600-1700 and/or	1400-1500	1474-1550	oil
1042 1043* 1045* 1046* 1050*	1600-1700	.....	1475-1550	oil or water
1052 1055 1060 1065 1070 1074	1550-1650 and/or	1400-1500	1475-1550	oil
1078	.....	1400-1500	1450-1500	water or brine
1080 1090	1550-1650 and/or	1400-1500■	1450-1500	oil ♦
1095	....	1400-1500■ 1400-1500■	1450-1500 1500-1600	oil, water or brine oil
1137	1600-1700 and/or	1400-1500	1525-1575	oil or water
1140	1600-1700	.....	1500-1550	oil or water
1141 1144	1600-1700	1400-1500	1475-1550	oil
1146	1600-1700	.....	1475-1550	oil or water

NOTES: * = Commonly used on parts where induction hardening is employed. However, all steels from SAE 1030 up may have induction hardening applications. ♦ = May be water or brine quenched by special techniques such as partial immersion, or time-quenched; otherwise, they are subject to quench cracking. ■ = Spheroidal structures are often required on these high-carbon steels for machining purposes and should be cooled very slowly or be isothermally transformed to produce the desired structure.

Figure 17.3 Table of treatments for heat-treating grades of carbon steels.

SAE Steel	Normalizing Temperature (°F)	Annealing Temperature (°F)	Hardening Temperature (°F)	Quenching Medium
1330	1600-1700 and/or	1500-1600	1525-1575	water or oil
1335	1600-1700 and/or	1500-1600	1500-1550	oil
1340				
4037	.....	1525-1575	1500-1575	oil
4047	.....	1450-1550	1500-1575	oil
4130	1600-1700 and/or	1450-1550	1600-1650	water or oil
4137	1600-1700 and/or	1450-1550	1550-1600	oil
4140				
4145				
4150				
4340	1600-1700 & temper	1100-1225	1475-1525	oil
5130	1650-1750 and/or	1450-1550	1500-1550	water or caustic
5132				
5140				oil
5150				oil
50100	.....	1350-1450	1425-1475	water
51100	.....		1500-1600	oil
52100				
6150	1650-1750 and/or	1550-1650	1600-1650	oil
9260	.....	.....	1500-1650	oil
8630	1600-1700	1450-1550	1550-1650	water or oil
8637	1600-1700 and/or	1450-1550	1525-1575	oil
8640				
8645	1600-1700 and/or	1450-1550	1500-1550	oil
8650				

NOTE: Except as noted, the steel is to be tempered to the required hardness. The exceptions are gears made from steels 4037 and 5150; temper at 350 to 400°F.

Figure 17.4 Table of heat treatments for directly hardenable grades of alloy steels.

17.4.3 Heat treatment of tool steels

Tool steels are an important family of steels that have many applications throughout industry. The heat treatment and application of the different grades or classes of tool steels are covered in Sec. 9.1.2, "Heat Treatment of Tool Steels."

17.4.4 Heat treatment of gear materials

For heat treatment of gear materials, see Tables 10.1 through 10.9 (AGMA data on hardening gears).

17.4.5 Quenching baths and temperatures

The purpose of the quenching bath is to cool the heated steel at a rate that is faster than the critical cooling rate. To obtain different cooling rates, different quenching baths are used, including

- Water bath (70 to 100°F bath temperature)
- Water spray (ambient temperature)
- Brine solution (9% by weight or 0.75 lb sodium chloride per gallon of water)
- Caustic soda solution [5% solution by weight potassium hydroxide (lye)]
- Oil (ambient or 90 to 140°F)
- Oil over water
- Molten salt bath (nitrate salts) to 700°F
- Forced air

17.5 Tempering and Case Hardening Steels

Tempering. The purpose of *tempering* or *drawing* is to reduce the brittleness of hardened steel and to remove the internal stresses caused by the sudden cooling or quenching done in the hardening operation. In the tempering operation, the hardened steel is heated to a certain temperature and then quench cooled. Steel in the fully hardened condition consists mainly of martensite. When reheated to a temperature of approximately 300 to 750°F, a softer and tougher structure called *troostite* is formed. When the hardened steel is reheated to a temperature from 750 to 1290°F, a structure called *sorbite* is formed, which has less strength than troostite but which is much more ductile.

17.5.1 Tempering temperatures for steels

The color of the oxide coating on the reheated steel was used in the past as a means of determining the tempering temperature. Since this color may be affected by the composition of the steel, it is not considered as the most reliable method of determining the tempering temperature, although it served satisfactorily for many years. Today, the optical (infrared) pyrometer is used to determine the temperature to very accurate limits. Figure 17.5 shows the temperature of plain carbon steels by the surface color indicated.

Figure 17.6 shows the temperature of metals by the color of the radiation or glow of the metal. Metals below 900°F do not produce a radiated color, but only the color of the oxide coating, if present.

Degrees Fahrenheit	Degrees Celsius	Color of Steel
430	221.1	Very pale yellow
440	226.7	Light yellow
450	232.2	Pale straw-yellow
460	237.8	Straw-yellow
470	243.3	Deep straw-yellow
480	248.9	Dark-yellow
490	254.4	Yellow-brown
500	260.0	Brown-yellow
510	265.6	Spotted red-brown
520	271.1	Brown-purple
530	276.7	Light purple
540	282.2	Full purple
550	287.8	Dark purple
560	293.3	Full blue
570	298.9	Dark blue
640	337.8	Light blue

Figure 17.5 Tempering temperatures by color indication for plain carbon steels.

Temperature (°F)	Temperature (°C)	Color
932 - 1,022	500 - 550	Dull red
1,202 - 1,382	650 - 750	Dark red
1,562 - 1,742	850 - 950	Bright red
1,922 - 2,102	1,050 - 1,150	Yellowish red
2,282 - 2,462	1,250 - 1,350	Dull white
2,642 - 2,822	1,450 - 1,550	Bright white

Figure 17.6 Color scale for metal temperatures. Radiated color (glow).

This color scale may be used in an emergency situation, where a fair indication of hardening temperature may be made for hardening plain carbon steels, and Fig. 17.5 surface color equivalent temperatures may be used for tempering.

Additional data on hardening and tempering steels may be obtained from Chap. 5, "Materials and Their Uses." A good understanding of the hardening and tempering operations used today may be obtained by reviewing the heat-treatment terms and definitions in Sec. 17.3.

17.5.2 Case hardening carbon and alloy steels

The case-hardening operation is performed on steels when a tough outer layer is required on the part and through-hardening of the steel is not required. This process has applications on parts that must be hardened to prevent wear on the outer surfaces only, while the core remains at its normal condition. Case hardening of low-carbon steels is a two-step operation. First, the outer layer of the part is *carburized* by introducing carbon into the surface, and second, the outer carburized layer is heat treated to form a hard "case." Surface or case hardening processes include

- Carburization
- Cyanide hardening
- Nitriding
- Carbonitriding
- Induction hardening
- Flame hardening

Low-carbon steels containing 0.10 to 0.20 percent carbon are suitable for carburized case-hardening operations. Additional heat-treating data may be found in Chap. 5, "Materials and Their Uses."

Case-hardening depths

Light case	0.003 to 0.015 in
Medium case	0.015 to 0.040 in
Heavy case	0.040 to 0.250 in

Case depth measurements. A production method for determining the depth of the case-hardened layer consists of air cooling a test pin from the carburizing temperature, reheating to 1475°F, and quenching in oil. This treatment refines the effective case and leaves the core material coarse grained. Etching the fractured surface of the test pin in an aqueous solution of 7% concentrated nitric acid produces good contrast between the case-hardened layer and the core material. The test pin is made of the same material as the case-hardened parts being checked and consists of a cylindrical pin 0.500 in in diameter, 3.5 in long, with a 0.468-in-diameter groove (0.060 in wide), approximately 0.30 in in from the end of the pin. Test rings are usually 1.500 in outside diameter with a 0.75-in hole through the center of the ring and a thickness of 0.375 in.

Other methods of determining the case depth include

- Reading of case depth with a Brinell microscope
- Step grinding and reading the Rockwell hardness at different depths
- Bluing of the fractured surface
- Carbon-cut analysis
- The martensite-start method

Cyanide case-hardening precautions. Cyanide compounds are deadly poisons. Care should be taken so that even minute portions are not consumed accidentally. In storage, keep cyanide-containing salts separate from acids, because mixing these chemicals will produce deadly hydrocyanic gas. Do not add nitrate or nitrite salts to those containing cyanide because of the danger of explosion.

Surface hardness versus case depth. Figure 17.7 shows several different common steels and the case depth to be expected from the Brinell hardness reading taken on the surface of the case-hardened part.

17.5.3 Heat treatments for carburizing grades of carbon steels

Figure 17.8 shows the heat-treating process for carburizing grades of some of the common carbon steels.

17.5.4 Heat treatments for carburizing grades of alloy steels

Figure 17.9 shows the heat-treating process for some of the common carburizing grades of alloy steels.

Case Depth as Determined by Brinell Hardness - **Tabulated values are in inches and indicate case depths.**

Steel	SAE 1020		SAE 6118		SAE 1020		SAE 4617		SAE 8620		SAE 4820	
Quench Temp (°F)	1675	1500	1675	1500	1675	1500	1675	1500	1675	1500	1675	1500
Quench Medium	Oil	Oil	Oil	Oil	Water	Water	Oil	Oil	Oil	Oil	Oil	Oil
Brinell												
156	.....	0.000										
167	.....	0.010										
170	.....	0.014										
179	0.000	0.019										
187	0.007	0.024										
192	0.009	0.026	.....	.....	.....	0.000						
197	0.011	0.029	.....	.....	.....	0.003						
207	0.016	0.035	.....	.....	.....	0.005						
217	0.023	0.041	.....	.....	.....	0.009	.....	0.000				
229	0.030	0.049	.....	.....	0.000	0.013	.....	0.004				
241	0.035	0.069	.....	0.000	0.005	0.018	.....	0.009				
255	0.040	0.077	.....	0.003	0.008	0.023	.....	0.015				
269	0.046	.....	.....	0.007	0.015	0.027	0.000	0.021				
285	0.053	.....	.....	0.013	0.022	0.034	0.007	0.024	.....	0.000		
302	0.060	.....	.....	0.018	0.027	0.039	0.010	0.028	.....	0.005		
321	0.074	.....	0.000	0.023	0.034	0.046	0.013	0.032	0.000	0.009		
341	.....	.....	0.004	0.029	0.041	0.054	0.017	0.035	0.003	0.012	.....	0.000
363	.....	.....	0.009	0.036	0.048	0.062	0.021	0.039	0.005	0.016	0.000	0.004
387	.....	.....	0.014	0.043	0.056	.....	0.024	0.041	0.010	0.022	0.008	0.010
412	.....	.....	0.019	0.048	0.062	.....	0.030	0.045	0.016	0.027	0.012	0.015
444	.....	.....	0.026	0.060	.....	.....	0.033	0.048	0.022	0.035	0.024	0.022
460	.....	.....	0.030	.....	.....	.....	0.035	0.051	0.026	0.039	0.028	0.026
477	.....	.....	0.034	.....	.....	.....	0.037	0.054	0.030	0.043	0.033	0.030
495	.....	.....	0.038	.....	.....	.....	0.039	0.056	0.034	0.047	0.038	0.035
512	.....	.....	0.042	.....	.....	.....	0.043	0.058	0.037	0.050	0.043	0.039
532	.....	.....	0.046	.....	.....	.....	0.051	0.060	0.042	0.055	0.049	0.043
555	.....	.....	0.051	.....	.....	.....	0.064	.....	0.047	0.061	0.055	0.049
578	.....	.....	0.057	.....	.....	.....	.....	.....	0.051	0.066	0.063	0.054
600	.....	.....	0.062	.....	.....	.....	.....	.....	0.055	.....	.....	0.060
627	.....	.....	.....	.....	.....	.....	.....	.....	0.061	.....	.....	.....

Figure 17.7 Case-depth table.

SAE Steel	Normalizing Temperature (°F)	Carburizing Temperature (°F)	Cooling Method	Reheat Temp. (°F)	Cooling Medium	Second Reheat (°F)	Cooling medium	Temper (°F)
1010	.....	1650-1700	water/brine	.....	.....	.....	.....	250-400
1015	.....	1650-1700	oil or water	1400-1450	water/brine	.....	.....	250-400
1018	.....	1650-1700	cool slowly	1650-1700	oil/water	1400-1450	water/brine	250-400
1020	.....	1500-1650	air/oil	.....	.....	.....	.....	optional
1024	1650-1750	1650-1700	oil	.....	.....	.....	.....	250-400
1025	.....	1650-1700	water/brine	.....	.....	.....	.....	250-400
1026	.....	1500-1650	oil/water	.....	.....	.....	.....	optional
1027	.....	1350-1575	air/oil	.....	.....	.....	.....	optional
1030	.....	1500-1650	oil/water	.....	.....	.....	.....	optional
1117	.....	1650-1700	cool slowly	1650-1700	oil/water	1400-1450	water/brine	250-400
1118	.....	1500-1650	oil/water	.....	.....	.....	.....	optional

NOTE: Even when the tempering temperatures are shown, the tempering operation is not mandatory on many applications. Tempering is generally employed for a partial stress relief and improves resistance to cracking from grinding operations. Higher temperatures than those shown may be used where the hardness specification on the finished parts permits. For more extensive data on hardening these classes of steels, see Section 5 - Materials and Their Uses, (steel section).

Figure 17.8 Heat-treatment table for carburizing grades of common carbon steels (also see Chap. 5).

SAE Steel	Alternate Pretreatments Normalize■	+ Temper♦	Cycle Anneal	Carburizing Temperature (°F)	Cooling Method	Reheat Temp (°F)	Cooling Medium	Tempering Temp (°F)●
4023 4027 4028	Yes	.....	Yes	1650-1700	oil quench	.....	.....	250-350
4118	Yes	.....	.....	1650-1700	oil quench	.....	.....	250-350
4320	Yes	.....	Yes	1650-1700	oil quench	1425-1475	oil	250-350
4620				1650-1700	cool slowly	1475-1525	oil	250-350
4820	.....	.....	.....	1650-1700	oil quench	.....	.....	250-350
5120	Yes	.....	.....	1650-1700	cool slowly	1500-1550	oil	250-350
8615	Yes	.....	Yes	1650-1700	oil quench	1475-1525	oil	250-350
8617						1525-1575		
8620					cool slowly	1475-1525		
8622					cool slowly	1525-1575		
8720				1500-1650	oil quench	.....	.....	

NOTE: ■ Normalizing temperatures should be not less than 50°F higher than the carburizing temperature, followed by air cooling. ♦ After normalizing, reheat to temperature of 1000 to 1250°F and hold for approximately 4 hours. ● The tempering treatment is optional. For more extensive data on hardening these classes of steels, see Section 5 - Materials and Their Uses, (steel section).

Figure 17.9 Heat-treatment table for carburizing grades of common alloy steels (also see Chap. 5).

Note: Extensive data on hardening all types of steels is contained in Chap. 5, "Materials and Their Uses." Also, in Sec. 9.1.2, "Heat Treatment of Tool Steels," data are shown for hardening these classes of steels. Chap. 10, "Gearing," also contains data for hardening gear materials.

17.6 Heat Treatment of Aluminum Alloys

The heat treatment of aluminum alloys is a precision operation. The temperature/time cycles are critical and must be carried out by using the proper equipment and controls. The general types of heat treatments applied to aluminum and its alloys are

1. Preheating or homogenizing to reduce chemical segregation of cast structures and to improve their workability.
2. Annealing to soften strain-hardened (work-hardened) and heat-treated alloy structures, to relieve stresses, and to stabilize properties and dimensions.
3. Solution heat treatments to effect solid solution of alloying constituents and improve mechanical properties.
4. Precipitation heat treatments to provide hardening by precipitation of constituents from solid solution.

The temper designations for aluminum and its alloys are detailed in Figs. 5.3, 5.4, 5.5, and 5.6. Pertinent data for the heat-treatable alloys are also described in Chap. 5, "Materials and Their Uses."

17.6.1 Solution Heat Treatment of Aluminum Alloys

The solution heat treatment of aluminum alloys improves mechanical properties by developing the maximum practical concentration of the hardening constituents in solid solution. This requires heating the aluminum-alloy part to a temperature close to the eutectic temperature, holding it there long enough to effect the desired solution, and then quenching fast enough to retain the desired solid solution.

The usual quenching medium for aluminum alloys is water. In quenching some products, water below 100°F provides the required quench rate for optimal properties of the alloy being heat treated.

In other alloys or products, the water may be heated to temperatures above 100°F or even to the boiling point to control distortion and residual internal stresses. Hot oil is also used for some applications because it provides a quenching rate that improves resistance to stress corrosion. The water quench is either by total immersion or by spray.

The recommended conditions of temperature and time for heat treating some of the common aluminum alloys, produced by various methods, are given in Figs. 17.10 through 17.15.

17.6.2 Precipitation heat treatment of aluminum alloys

The rate of precipitation from the supersaturated solid solution existing immediately after quenching increases as the temperature of the metal is raised above room temperature. Precipitation occurs naturally at room temperature, providing useful degrees of precipitation hardening for some alloys. Precipitation heat treatment generally denotes treatment at an elevated temperature and is often called *artificial aging*. See Figs. 17.10 through 17.15 for the precipitation-hardening temperature/times for those alloys which may be precipitation hardened (artificially aged).

17.7 Heat Treating Beryllium-Copper Alloys

Beryllium-copper alloys are important metallic products which over recent years have found many applications in various industries, including the electrical, electronics, and mechanical industries. Beryllium-copper alloys have many desirable characteristics, including corrosion resistance, good electrical conductivity, good spring properties, good heat conductivity, and excellent stress fatigue resistance. Beryllium is also alloyed with nickel, called *beryllium-nickel alloys,* whose tensile strengths are quite high when the alloys are cold worked. Many products that formerly used spring-tempered phosphor-bronzes are now using the beryllium-copper alloys.

The element beryllium is toxic, as are its alloys. The OSHA safety regulations prescribe the conditions under which these alloys should be processed. The percentage of the population to which beryllium causes toxicity is small, but safeguards must be taken. The toxic effects of beryllium are seen as chronic pulmonary (lung) problems.

Alloy Designation	Temper	Solution Heat Treatment Metal Temperature (°F)	Precipitation Heat Treatment Metal Temp. (°F)	Time @ Temp. Hours
2014	T4, T6, T651	935	320	18
2024	T3, T4, T6	920	375	16
6061	T4, T6	985	320	18
7075	T6, T651	900	250	24
7178	T6, T651	875	250	24

Figure 17.10 Heat-treatment table for aluminum-alloy sheet and plate.

Alloy Designation	Temper	Solution Heat Treatment Metal Temperature (°F)	Precipitation Heat Treatment Metal Temp. (°F)	Time @ Temp. Hours
2014	T4, T6, T651	935	320	18
2024	T351	920	.....	.....
6061	T4, T6, T651	980	350	8
7075	T6, T651	870	250	24
7178	T6, T651	870	250	24

Figure 17.11 Heat-treatment table for extruded aluminum-alloy rod, bar, shapes, and tube.

Alloy Designation	Temper	Solution Heat Treatment Metal Temperature (°F)	Precipitation Heat Treatment Metal Temp. (°F)	Time @ Temp. Hours
2011	T3	975	.....	.....
2014	T4, T6, T651	935	320	18
2024	T3, T4,	920	.....	.....
	T6	920	375	16
6061	T4,	985	.....	.....
	T6, T651	985	320	18
7075	T6, T651	915	250	24
7178	T6, T651	900	250	24

Figure 17.12 Heat-treatment table for rolled or drawn aluminum-alloy wire, rod, bar, shapes, and tube.

Alloy Designation	Temper	Solution Heat Treatment Metal Temperature (°F) (Quench water temp.)		Precipitation Heat Treatment Metal Temp. (°F)	Time @ Temp. Hours
2014	T4	935	(140-160)	.....	.....
	T6	935	(140-160)	340	10
2024	T4	920	(Room)	.....	.....
	T6	920	(Room)	375	18
6061	T6	985	(Room)	350	8
7075	T6	880	(140-160)	250	24
7178	T6	870	(Room)	250	24

Figure 17.13 Heat-treatment table for aluminum-alloy forgings.

Alloy Designation	Temper	Solution Heat Treatment Metal Temp. (°F)	Time Hours	Precipitation Heat Treatment Metal Temp. (°F)	Time Hours
142	T61	960	6	450	2
220	T4	810	16	.....	.....
319	T6	940	10	310	4
355	T6	980	10	310	4
356	T6	1000	10	310	4
357	T6	1000	10	350	6
363	T6	940	10	310	4
A750	T5	.....	.....	430	8

NOTE: Many of these alloys are covered by ASTM B26. Solution heat treatment is followed by quenching in water at 150 to 212°F. A boiling water quench is recommended when minimum quenching stresses and distortion are required. Maintain steady furnace temperatures for the solution heat treatment process.

Figure 17.14 Heat-treatment table for sand- and plaster-cast aluminum alloys.

Alloy Designation	Temper	Solution Heat Treatment Metal Temp. (°F)	Time Hours	Precipitation Heat Treatment Metal Temp. (°F)	Time Hours
142	T61	960	6	400	4
319	T6	940	6	310	4
354	T61	980	8	310	10
355	T6	980	6	310	4
356	T6	1000	8	310	4
357	T6	1000	8	350	6
359	T61	1000	10	310	10
750/A750	T5	.....	.....	430	8

NOTE: Many of these alloys are covered by ASTM B108. The solution heat treatment is followed by quenching in water at 150 to 212°F. Boiling water is recommended when minimum quenching stresses and distortion are required. Maintain steady furnace temperatures for the solution heat treatment process.

Figure 17.15 Heat-treatment table for permanent-mold cast aluminum alloys.

In the heat treatment of beryllium-copper alloys, the product is furnace heated to a prescribed temperature and held at this temperature for a number of hours, followed by still-air cooling to room temperature. Figure 17.16 shows the popular and common beryllium-copper alloys and their heat-treatment procedures. Figure 17.17 defines the ASTM temper designations used in Fig. 17.16.

17.8 Cold Work Hardening of Metals and Alloys

Many metals and alloys obtain their physical properties through the process of work hardening. The work-hardening processes include drawing, rolling, stretching, and hammering. Materials such as phosphor-bronze acquire their spring characteristics through the action of cold rolling or drawing. The percentage of reduction of the cross-sectional area of the material determines the degree of "temper" in the material. Figure 17.17 listed the percentage of reduction that determines the temper designation for beryllium-copper alloys. The phosphor-bronze alloys also receive their temper designations from the percentage of reduction that takes place in the cold-rolling operation (quarter hard, half hard, full hard, spring, and extra spring).

Alloy Designation (UNS system)	Temper (*)	Heat Treatment Time/Temperature	Tensile Strength Kpsi
25	(TF00)	3 hrs @ 600 °F	140-175
(C17200)	(TH01)	2 hrs @ 600 °F	150-185
	(TH02)	2 hrs @ 600 °F	185-215
	(TH04)	2 hrs @ 600 °F	190-220
190	(TM00)	Mill	100-110
(C17200)	(TM01)	Mill	110-120
	(TM02)	Mill	120-135
	(TM04)	Mill	135-150
	(TM05)	Mill	150-160
	(TM06)	Mill	155-175
	(TM08)	Mill	175-190
290	(TM00)	Mill	100 minimum
(C17200)	(TM02)	Mill	120 minimum
	(TM04)	Mill	140 minimum
	(TM06)	Mill	155 minimum
	(TM08)	Mill	175 minimum
165	(TF00)	3 hrs @ 600 °F	150-180
(C17000)	(TH01)	2 hrs @ 600 °F	160-190
	(TH02)	2 hrs @ 600 °F	170-200
	(Th04)	2 hrs @ 600 °F	180-210
	(TM00)	Mill	100-110
	(TM01)	Mill	110-120
	(TM02)	Mill	120-135
	(TM04)	Mill	135-150
	(TM05)	Mill	150-160
	(TM06)	Mill	155-175
3 (C17510)	(TF00)	2-3 hrs @ 900 °F	100-130
and	(TH04)	2-3 hrs @ 900 °F	110-135
10 (C17500)			
174	(TH04)	Mill	110-130
(C17410)			

NOTE: (*) = ASTM alphanumeric code for product tempers. Mill = product normally heat treated at the mill. For heat treatment, the part must be fully annealed, then accurately held at the indicated temperatures for the times shown. Uniform heating of the parts within the furnace MUST be maintained for a successful heat treatment. Annealed strip which is "dead-soft" offers maximum deep drawing and die-forming capabilities.

Figure 17.16 Heat-treatment table for beryllium-copper alloys.

ASTM Designation	Description	Cold Rolled Thickness Reduction in Percent
TB00	Solution annealed	0
TD01	Quarter hard	11
TD02	Half-hard	21
TD03	Three-quarters hard	29
TD04	Hard	37
TF00	The suffix "T" added to temper designations indicates that the material has been age-hardened by the standard heat treatment.	
TH01		
TH02		
TH03		
TH04		
TM00	Mill hardened to specific property ranges, no further heat treatment required.	
TM01		
TM02		
TM04		
TM05		
TM06		
TM08		

NOTE: Temper designations are defined in the specification ASTM B601, "Standard practice for temper designations for copper and copper alloys".

Figure 17.17 ASTM temper designations (for Fig. 17.16).

Stainless steels such as AISI types 303, 304, and others may acquire very high tensile strengths and spring properties through the cold-rolling process. The 300 series stainless steels are termed *austenitic* and cannot be heat treated by using conventional heat-treating processes. The spring properties of these and many other metals and alloys are obtainable only through cold-working processes. The *martensitic* stainless steels (400 series) may be heat treated using conventional heat-treating methods. The 440 series stainless steels are popular martensitic stainless steels which may be hardened to a high degree by heating and quenching at specified temperatures and cooling rates (see Chap. 5, "Materials and Their Uses," for hardening procedures for all classes of steels).

Chapter

18

Castings, Moldings, Extrusions, and Powder-Metal Technology

18.1 Castings

The casting of metals and alloys is an important branch of the metalworking industry. Castings allow parts to be made at a rapid pace with controlled accuracy. Castings replace parts that would otherwise be difficult or impossible to machine and very costly to manufacture. However, castings cannot replace many types of machined parts because of material, configuration, and other physical considerations. There are many types or processes used in the casting or foundry industries to produce cast parts in different materials and for various dimensional accuracy requirements. The casting processes or methods that are in use today include

- Sand casting
- Shell casting
- Carbon dioxide casting
- Fluid sand casting
- Composite-mold casting
- Plaster-mold casting
- Slush casting

- Evaporative pattern casting (EPC)
- Die casting
- Permanent-mold casting
- Ceramic-mold casting
- Investment casting (lost-wax process)

The casting method or process chosen by the design engineer and the foundry is determined by the following factors

- Type of metal to be cast
- Size of part to be cast
- Required cast accuracy of the part
- Economics
- Required secondary operations such as machining, hardening, welding, and plating

18.1.1 Sand Casting

In the sand-casting process, a wooden, plastic, or metal pattern is packed in a special sand, which is dampened with water and then removed, leaving a hollow space having the part's shape. The pattern is purposely made larger than the size of the cast part to allow for shrinkage of the casting as it cools.

The mold consists of two steel frames, which are called the *cope* (top half) and the *drag* (bottom half). Figure 18.1 is an illustration of a typical sand-casting setup.

Sand cores may be placed in the cavity to produce holes in the part where required. Once the cope and drag are clamped together, the molten metal is poured into the "gate" of the mold. Vent holes placed appropriately in the mold allow hot gases to escape from the mold cavity during pouring. The pouring temperature of the metal is always made a few hundred degrees higher than the melting point so that the metal has good fluidity during the pour and does not cool prematurely, causing voids in the part.

Sand casting is the least expensive of all the casting processes on a part-to-part basis, but a need for secondary machining operations may indicate the use of one of the other casting processes. Figure 18.2 shows a sand-cast part made of a copper alloy. This part would be difficult to machine from solid stock.

Figure 18.3 shows another sand-cast part of intricate design. This part is made of 356-T6 aluminum alloy (heat treated). Note that at the center section of the part there is a sprocket for number 40 ANSI roller chain. The sprocket in this application does not need a high degree of accuracy, since the sprocket and chain action is only intermittent. A part of such design would be extremely difficult and costly to manufacture using the machining processes or methods.

Figure 18.4 shows some of the gating and venting methods employed in sand casting and similar casting processes. Figure 18.5 shows a typical combination casting/machining engineering drawing. This drawing provides enough information for the pattern maker, foundry, and machine shop to be able to produce the part.

18.1.2 Shell casting

This process entails forming a mold from a mixture of sand and a thermosetting-resin binder. The sand and thermoset mix are placed against a heated pattern, which causes the resin to bind the sand particles and form a strong shell. After the shell is cured and stripped from the pattern, cores may be set. The cope and drag are secured together and placed in a flask with added backup material. The mold is then ready for pouring the molten metal.

18.1.3 Carbon dioxide casting

The carbon dioxide process uses sodium silicate (water glass) binders instead of the clay binders employed in conventional sand casting. Treated with carbon dioxide gas, the sodium silicate/sand mixture is dried and strengthened.

Ready-for-use cores or molds can be made using this process in a few minutes, with no baking required. Excellent dimensional accuracy is obtained even while making cores rapidly. This process is used more often to make cores than to make molds.

18.1.4 Plaster-mold casting

This process is used when nonferrous metals must be cast more accurately than is possible with conventional sand casting. The four recognized plaster-mold processes are

- Conventional mold
- Match-plate pattern

- The Antioch method
- The foamed plaster method

Castings produced by the plaster-mold process have smoother surfaces, better accuracy, and finer detail than those made by conventional sand casting, but they are also more expensive.

18.1.5 Composite-mold casting

Composite-mold casting utilizes different sections of the mold and cores made by different methods so that the greatest advantage is obtained from each process in the appropriate section. This process is usually chosen for aluminum parts and is sometimes called *premium-quality casting* or *engineered casting*. The use of plaster-mold sections affords accuracy and stability wherever it is essential on the cast part. Composite molds are used for the following reasons:

- Decreased cost of mold material
- Increased casting accuracy
- Decreased amount of gassing
- Improved finish or surface
- Quicker processing time

18.1.6 Investment casting

In this casting process, an expendable pattern is coated with a refractory slurry that sets at ambient temperature. The expendable pattern (wax or plastic) is then melted out of the refractory shell. Ceramic cores are used as required.

There are two distinct processes or methods followed in investment casting: shell investment and solid investment. Investment casting is also known as the *lost-wax process* and *precision casting*. Cast parts can be produced in almost any pourable metal or alloy. The finished parts are dimensionally accurate and are generally used "as cast." The process is used for high-accuracy, mass-produced parts and for jewelry making.

The economics of this process must be weighed against the complexity of the part. Simple parts are generally not economical to produce with this process. The process is advantageous for applicable parts not in excess of 10 lb weight, although heavier parts are frequently investment cast.

18.1.7 Ceramic-mold casting

Ceramic-mold techniques are proprietary processes. They utilize permanent patterns and fine-grain zircon and calcined, high-alumina mullite slurries for molding.

As in other processes, the molds are constructed as a cope and a drag. Fine detail may be produced with high dimensional accuracy. The refractory mold allows the pouring of high-melting-point metals and alloys. The ferrous alloys and metals are more commonly cast with this process. Aluminum, beryllium-copper, titanium, ductile iron, carbon and low-alloy steels, and tool steels are cast using ceramic-mold processes.

Two of the proprietary processes for ceramic-mold casting are

- The Shaw method
- The Unicast method

18.1.8 Permanent-mold casting

In this process, a metal mold consisting of two or more parts produces the cast parts. Metal, sand, or plaster cores are also used, in which case the process is known as *semipermanent-mold casting.*

Intricate castings can be produced, but mold cost is high. Not all metals and alloys can be cast, and some shapes cannot be made because of the parting line or the difficulty of removing the part from the mold. Suitable casting metals include

- Aluminum alloys, up to 30 lb
- Magnesium alloys, up to 15 lb
- Copper alloys, up to 20 lb
- Zinc alloys, up to 20 lb
- Gray iron (hypereutectic), up to 30 lb

A variation of this process chills the cast metal rapidly, producing enhanced properties with regard to grain configuration and size. Surface qualities of permanent-mold castings are better than conventional sand castings, but the mold cost must always be evaluated with respect to quantity of parts produced and secondary operations required (machining) to produce a finished part. Many parts cast with this process can be used as-cast when close tolerances are not required. Figure 18.6 shows a relatively complex part which was cast by the permanent-mold chill-cast process in an aluminum-bronze high-strength alloy.

The types of metals that can be permanent-mold cast are limited to those whose melting points are not above the copper-base alloys. Pouring higher-temperature alloys causes permanent damage to the steel molds.

18.1.9 Die casting

Die castings are made by forcing molten metal under high pressure into permanent molds called *dies*. The advantages of die casting include

- Complex shapes possible
- Thin-walled sections possible
- High production rates
- High dimensional accuracy
- High volume of parts with little change in the dies
- Minimum surface preparation required for plating

The disadvantages of die casting include

- Casting size limited: 50 lb seldom exceeded
- Air entrapment and porosity difficulties in complex shapes
- Expensive machinery and dies
- Limited to metals having melting points no higher than copper-base alloys

Figure 18.7 shows some typical die-cast parts made of zinc alloy. The intricate designs shown are easily produced with the die-casting process.

18.1.10 Evaporative Pattern Casting (EPC)

Although this process was known and patents were issued as early as 1958, it has not developed until very recently. In this

(*Text continued on page 1312.*)

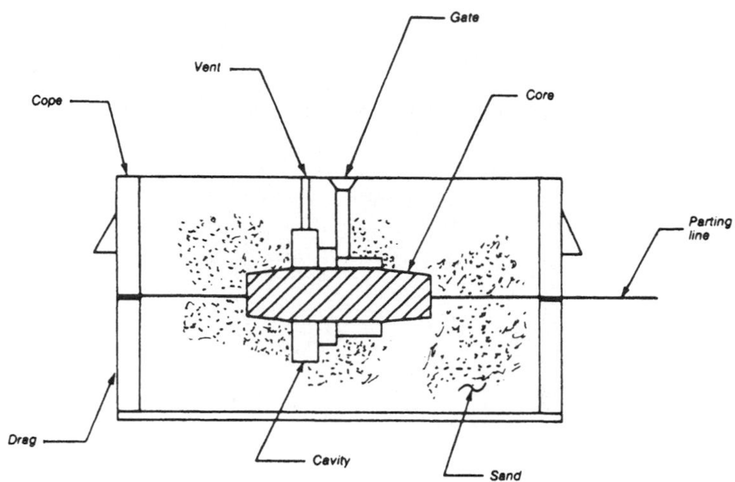

Figure 18.1 A typical sand-casting setup.

Figure 18.2 A typical sand-cast copper-alloy part prior to machining.

Figure 18.3 An intricate sand-cast aluminum-alloy part.

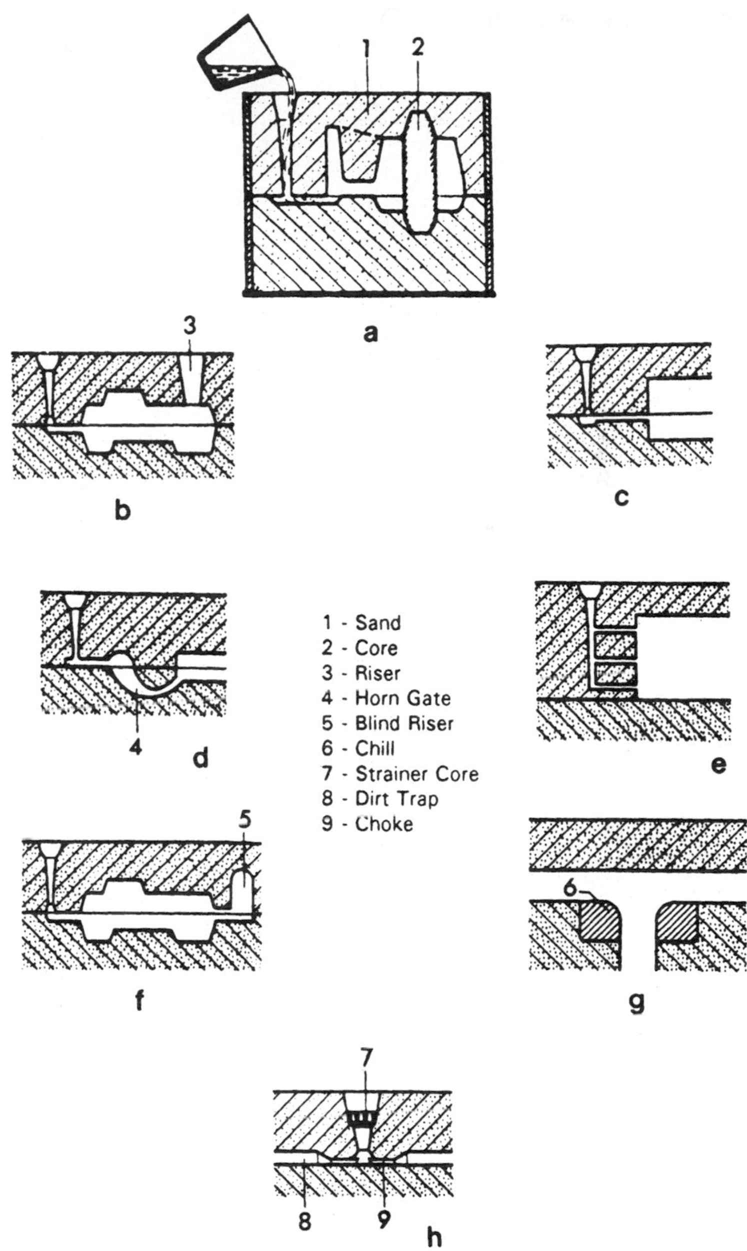

Figure 18.4 Gating, venting, and chills.

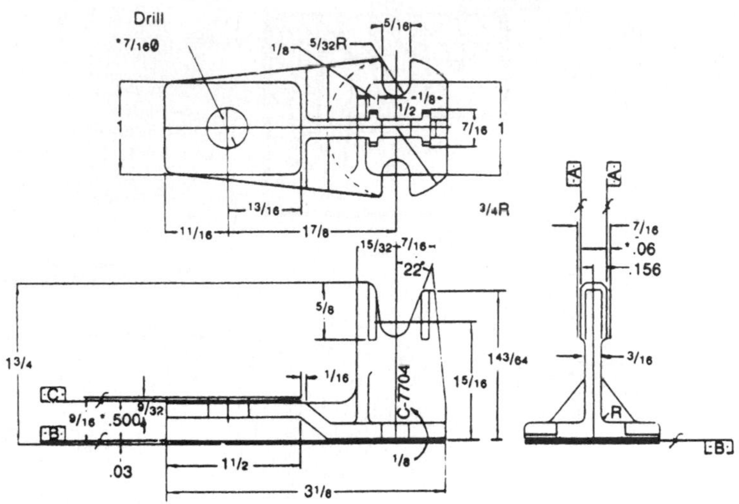

NOTES:

1- All dimensions in fractions for pattern. Tolerance = ± 1/64. (Use minimum draft angles)

2- -Indicates machined surface.
*-Indicates machining dimensions ± .005"

3- Surfaces -A- to be machined parallel to one another and perpendicular to surface -B-. Surface -C- to be parallel to surface -B-. Tolerance .003 total misalignment.

4- Δ material = CDA * 811000, 99.7& copper, 92% IACS conductivity.

5- Grind all flash lines and sharp edges from casting.

6- Fillet radii = 1/16".

7- All machined surfaces to be 63 RMS maximum.

8- Add part number on the casting as indicated.

Δ- Alternate material = chrome copper, CDA * 81500 sand cast Mil Spec MIL-C-19310, heat treated, conductivity = 82% IACS.

Casting & Machining Drawing Sample

Figure 18.5 Typical casting/machining drawing.

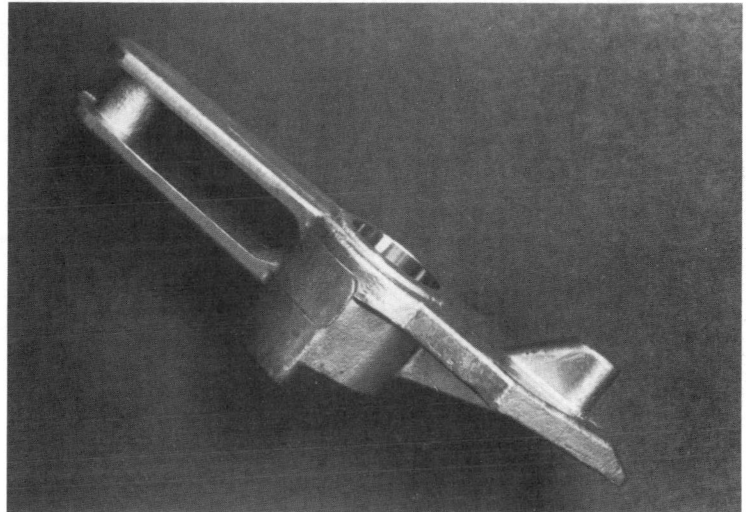

Figure 18.6 A permanent-mold, chill-cast copper-alloy part.

Figure 18.7 Typical die-cast zinc-alloy parts.

process, a plastic expendable pattern (usually styrofoam) is coated with a refractory slurry and cured. The composition of the coating is critical to the casting process, since it must allow outgassing of the vaporized styrofoam during the pouring of the molten metal. When the molten metal pours into the mold, the styrofoam vaporizes and gasses out of the mold and through the sand, leaving the molten metal in the void left by the styrofoam. The process allows the coated styrofoam pattern to be packed in sand as in conventional sand casting, except that a cope and drag are not needed because the pattern is not mechanically removed, but vaporizes.

This process permits the casting of any pourable metal or alloy. Complexity of parts is generally not a problem, and cores may be utilized as in the investment process. Complex shapes are devised by gluing sections of the styrofoam patterns together. Risers and gates form part of the pattern. The entire refractory coated assembly is packed in sand and then cast. This process is highly applicable to some of the automated systems and robotization.

18.1.11 Slush casting

This process is limited to hollow castings. Zinc- or lead-base alloys are generally utilized. Products made by this process include lamp bases and parts and consumer novelty items.

In this process, the molten metal is poured into a split bronze mold and allowed to set a specified time, after which the mold is inverted and the remaining liquid metal is poured out. Remaining is a thin shell that has hardened at the mold surface, thus producing a hollow cast shape.

18.2 Ferrous Metal Alloys Used in Casting

The general ferrous metals and alloys used to produce castings include white iron, gray iron, malleable iron (ferritic and pearlitic), carbon steels, alloy steels, and stainless steels.

18.2.1 Gray iron castings

Carbon content in this iron ranges from 2.8 to 4 percent. Gray iron is poured at the lowest casting temperature and has the best castability and least shrinkage of all the ferrous metal cast alloys.

Gray iron may be heat treated in softening for better machinability or hardening for wear resistance. Pouring temperatures range from 2500 to 2700°F. Gray iron castings may be repaired by welding (shielded metal arc or oxyacetylene gas).

18.2.2 Ductile iron castings

The composition and handling of ductile irons are very similar to those of gray irons. The difference between the two irons is that in ductile iron, solidified graphite is spherical, whereas it is in flake form in gray iron. The metallurgy of the two irons is similar. Pouring temperatures range from 2500 to 2700°F. Ductile iron, as the name implies, has high ductility with resulting high impact strength for shock load applications.

18.2.3 Malleable iron castings

This iron is produced from base metal having the following general composition:

Carbon	2 to 3 percent
Silicon	1 to 1.8 percent
Manganese	0.2 to 0.5 percent

There are traces of sulfur, phosphorus, boron, and aluminum, with the remainder being iron.

Pouring range is 2700 to 2900°F. Ferritic malleable iron and pearlitic malleable iron receive different heat treatments to induce their metallurgical differences. Ferritic malleable iron must have a carbon-free matrix, and pearlitic malleable iron must have a matrix containing a controlled amount of carbon in the combined form. Liquid-quenched and tempered malleable iron is made by two processes, both of which produce high-quality, high-strength cast irons.

Note that white cast iron is frequently formed on purpose at high-wear points of a casting by incorporating *chills* in the mold. A chill is an insert that causes rapid cooling of the cast iron, with the consequent formation of white iron at the points selected. White cast iron is brittle but extremely hard and wear resistant. Figure 18.4, illustration *g*, shows the position of chills in a sand casting mold (6).

18.2.4 Steel and alloy-steel castings

Green sand, dry sand, shell, investment, and ceramic molds are all used to produce steel and alloy-steel castings. Plaster molds cannot be used because the high pouring temperature of steels destroys plaster molds. Green sand is the most widely used method for producing steel castings. Pouring temperature of steels for casting commonly reach as high as 3200°F.

Large steel castings are commonly produced in dry sand molds and may range from 1 ton to over 100 tons in weight. Steel castings are welded for repairs and for joining two or more castings into a structural assembly.

18.3 Representative Casting Metals and Alloys

Shown in the following figures is a selection of data on commonly used engineering alloys for casting processes. These represent only a small sample of the materials that are available but include many favorite engineering alloys that have been proven by many design applications. Chapter 5, "Materials and Their Uses," also should be consulted for many other metallic alloys used throughout industry for a broad range of applications.

Representative casting metals and alloys. Figure 18.8 shows the physical properties of the common cast irons. Figure 18.9 shows the mechanical properties of cast structural steels. Figure 18.10 shows the designations and properties of cast stainless steels. Figure 18.11 shows the designations, types of processes, and physical properties of common cast aluminum alloys. Figure 18.12 shows the designations and mechanical properties of cast magnesium alloys. Figure 18.13 shows the Copper Development Association (CDA) designations and properties and application data for the common cast copper alloys.

18.4 ASTM Listed Cast Irons and Steels

The ASTM cast irons and steels shown in the following subsection have physical and chemical characteristics which make them suitable for the types of applications and services listed below:

- High-temperature applications
- Low-temperature applications
- Impact resistance
- Structural applications
- Pressure-vessel service

- High ductility
- Corrosion resistance

18.4.1 ASTM cast irons and cast steels

ASTM A159-83 (R1988), Standard specification for automotive gray iron castings. See Figs. 18.14 and 18.15 for compositional and mechanical properties. The grades of gray cast iron consist of the following:

G1800	Ferritic-pearlitic
G2500	Pearlitic-ferritic
G3000	Pearlitic
G3500	Pearlitic
G4000	Pearlitic

Figure 18.16 lists the typical applications for the automotive gray cast irons.

ASTM A 148/A 148M-89a, Standard specification for steel castings, high strength, for structural applications. Figure 18.17 lists the tensile strength properties.

ASTM A 297/A 297M-89, Standard specification for steel castings, iron-chromium, iron-chromium-nickel, heat resistant, for general applications. Figures 18.18 and 18.19 list the chemical and physical properties.

ASTM A 352/A 352M-89, Standard specification for steel castings, ferritic and martensitic, for pressure containing parts, suitable for low-temperature service. Table 18.1 lists the chemical, tensile, and impact properties.

ASTM A 436-84, Standard specification for austenitic gray iron castings. Figure 18.20 lists the chemical and mechanical requirements.

ASTM A 439-83, Standard specification for austenitic ductile iron castings. Figure 18.21 lists the chemical and mechanical properties.

ASTM A 487/A 487M-89a, Standard specification for steel castings suitable for pressure service. Tables 18.2, 18.3, and 18.4 list the heat-treatment, chemical, and mechanical requirements.

ASTM A 743/743M-89, Standard specification for castings, iron-chromium, iron-chromium-nickel, corrosion resistant, for general applications. Tables 18.5, 18.6, and 18.7 list the heat-treatment, chemical, and mechanical requirements.

(*Text continued on page 1337.*)

	Tensile Strength psi	Yield Strength psi	Elongation Elongation % in 2 in.	Impact Impact ft-lbs	Young's Modulus psi
Ductile iron ASTM A536-77Δ	90,000 / 150,000	60,000 / 125,000	15 / 40	2 / 10	22×10^6 / 25×10^6
Gray iron* ASTM A48-76	20,000 / 65,000	12,000 / 40,000	*	0.5 / 1.0	12×10^6 / 20×10^6
Malleable iron (ferritic)	50,000 / 55,000	30,000 / 35,000	70 / 90	10 / 18	25×10^6
Malleable iron (pearlitic)	60,000 / 100,000	40,000 / 90,000	20 / 35	1 / 10	26×10^6 / 28×10^6
White iron	20,000 / 50,000	—	3 / 10	—	—

*Gray iron is not generally used for impact applications.
ΔDuctile iron is also Austempered (ADI), which approximately doubles its strength.

Figure 18.8 Physical properties of cast irons.

Grade	Tensile Strength, psi	Yield Strength, psi	Elongation % in 2 in	Impact ft-lbs	Endurance Limit, psi
60,000	63,000	35,000	30	12	30,000
65,000	68,000	38,000	28	35	30,000
70,000	75,000	42,000	27	30	35,000

Modulus of elasticity, typical: 29×10^6 to 30×10^6.

Figure 18.9 Mechanical properties of cast steels.

Designation †	Tensile Strength, psi	Yield Strength, psi	Elongation % in 2 in	Impact Charpy	Young's Modulus, psi
CA-15	115,000	100,000	30	35	29×10^6
CC-50 *(HC)	70,000 / 110,000	65,000	18	45	29×10^6
CE-30 *(HE)	87,000 / 92,000	63,000	18	10	25×10^6
CH-20 *(HH)	80,000 / 88,000	50,000	38	15	28×10^6

Typical physical properties of cast alloy steels

Melting temperature	2,700° to 2,800°F
Thermal conductivity (B.t.u-ft/hr-ft^2-°F)	18 to 27
Density, lb/in^3	0.283 to 0.284
Electrical resistivity (micro-ohm cm)	227

ASTM and SAE specifications—cast alloy steels

General mechanical	A27, A148
Low temperature applications	A352, A757
Weldability	A216
Automotive applications	SAE J435

*Heat-resistant grades. †ACI (Alloy Casting Institute) designations.

Figure 18.10 Properties of cast stainless steels.

Alloy Designation	Type	Uses and Typical Strengths
UNS A02010 (ANSI 201.0)	S PM	Very high strength, high impact, High ductility, high cost US = 60 YS = 50 El = 5.0
UNS A02060 (ANSI 206.0)	S PM	High tensile and yield, structural parts, automotive and aerospace US = 40 YS = 24 El = 8.0
UNS A02080 (ANSI 208.0)	S PM	Manifolds, valve bodies, pressure-tightness appiciations US = 20 YS = 12 El = 1.5
UNS A02220 (ANSI 222.0)	S PM	Pistons and air-cooled cylinder heads US = 30/40
UNS A03190 (ANSI 319.0)	S	Low cost, general purpose alloy US = 31 YS = 20 El = 1.5
UNS A03540 (ANSI 354.0)	PM	High strength premium alloy US = 48 YS = 37 El = 3.0
UNS A03560 (ANSI 356.0)	S PM	For intricate work, good strength and ductility US = 33 YS = 22 El = 3.0
UNS A03600 (ANSI 360.0)	D	Very good casting and strength US = 44 YS = 25 El = 2.5
UNS A13600 (ANSI A360)	D	Excellent casting, corrosion resistance, thin walls, intricate parts US = 46 YS = 24 El = 3.5
UNS A03840 (ANSI 384.0)	D	General purpose alloy, thin sect. US = 48 YS = 24 El = 2.5
UNS A03900 (ANSI 390.0)	D	High wear resistance, cylinder heads, pistons, engine crankcases US = 41 YS = 35 El = 1.0

In the preceding table: *US* = ultimate strength, *YS* = yield strength in kpsi, *El* = elongation, % in 2 in, *S* = sand casting alloy, *PM* = permanent mold casting alloy, *D* = die casting alloy.

Figure 18.11 Aluminum casting alloys.

Designation	Temper	US	YS	Elongation % in 2 in
ΔM10100	F	20,000	—	—
(ASTM-AM 100A)	T4	34,000	—	6
SAE 502	T6	35,000	17,000	—
ΔM11630	F	26,000	11,000	4
(ASTM-AZ 63A)	T4	34,000	11,000	7
SAE 50	T6	34,000	16,000	3
*M11910	—	34,000	23,000	3
(ASTM-AZ 91A)				
SAE 501				
*M11912	—	34,000	23,000	3
(ASTM-AZ 91B)				
SAE 501A				
ΔM11920	F	23,000	11,000	—
(ASTM-AZ 92A)	T4	34,000	11,000	6
	T6	34,000	18,000	1
ΔM16630	T6	40,000	27,000	5
(ASTM-ZE 63A)				

*Automotive die-casting alloys
ΔSand castings alloys

Figure 18.12 Magnesium casting alloys.

Alloy No. C80100
Composition: 99.95% copper, 0.05 trace elements
Conductivity: 100% IACS
Tensile strength: 19,000 psi min. to 25,000 psi typical
Yield strength: 6,500 psi min. to 9,000 psi typical (0.2% offset)
Typical uses: Electrical and thermal conductors, corrosion resistance applications.
Similar alloys: C80300, C80500, C80700, C80900
All are difficult to cast, with low casting yields.

Alloy No. C81500 (chrome-copper)
Composition: 1% chromium, balance copper
Conductivity: 82% IACS
Tensile strength: 45,000 psi min. to 51,000 psi typical (heat treated)
Yield strength: 35,000 psi. to 40,000 psi typical (0.5% exten. under load)
Typical uses: Electrical and thermal conductors where high strength and hardness are required. A premium quality alloy.

Alloy No. C81700
Composition: 0.4% beryllium, 0.9 cobalt, 0.9 nickel, 1.0 silver
Conductivity: 48% IACS
Tensile strength: 85,000 psi min. to 92,000 psi typical
Yield strength: 62,000 psi min. to 68,000 psi typical (0.2% offset)
Typical uses: Electrical and thermal conductors where high strength and hardness are required.

Alloy No. C82400 (former name: 165C)
Composition: 1.7% beryllium, 0.25 cobalt, remainder copper
Conductivity: 25% IACS
Tensile strength: 145,000 psi min. to 150,000 psi typical (heat treated)
Yield strength: 135,000 psi min. to 140,000 psi typical (0.2% offset)
Typical uses: Molds, cams, bushings, gears, bearings
Similar alloys: C82800, C82700, C82600

Alloy No. C83600 (115, leaded red brass, composition bronze)
Composition: 85% copper, 5.0 lead, 5.0 tin, 5.0 zinc
Conductivity: 15% IACS
Tensile strength: 30,000 psi min. to 37,000 psi typical (as cast)
Yield strength: 14,000 psi min. to 17,000 psi typical (0.5% exten. under load)
Typical uses: Pipie fittings, pump castings, impellers, small gears
Similar alloys: C83800, C84200, C84400, C84500

Alloy No. C85200 (400, leaded yellow brass)
Composition: 72% copper, 3.0 lead, 1.0 tin, 24.0 zinc
Conductivity: 18% IACS
Tensile strength: 35,000 psi min. to 38,000 psi typical (as cast)
Yield strength: 12,000 psi min. to 13,000 psi typical (0.5% exten. under load)
Typical uses: Ferrules, valves, hardware, plumbing fittings
Similar alloys: C85300, C85400, C85500

Figure 18.13 CDA designations and properties of cast copper alloys.

Alloy No. C86100 (high-strength yellow brass, 90 kpsi manganese bronze)
Composition: 5.0 aluminum, 67.0 copper, 3.0 iron, 4.0 manganese, 21.0 zinc
Conductivity: 7.5% IACS
Tensile strength: 90,000 psi min. to 95,000 psi typical
Yield strength: 45,000 psi min. to 50,000 psi typical (0.2% offset)
Typical uses: Marine castings, gears, bushings, bearings
Similar alloys: C86200, C86300, C86400, C86500

Alloy No. C87800 (die-cast silicon brass)
Composition: 82.0 copper, 4.0 silicon, 14.0 zinc
Conductivity: 6.7% IACS
Tensile strength: 85,000 psi typical
Yield strength: 50,000 psi typical (0.2% offset)
Typical uses: High-strength die castings, lever arms, brackets, hex nuts, clamps
Similar alloys: C87900

Alloy No. C94400 (phosphor bronze, 312)
Composition: 81.0 copper, 11.0 lead, .35 phosphorus, 8.0 tin
Conductivity: 10% IACS
Tensile strength: 32,000 psi typical
Yield strength: 16,000 psi typical (0.5% exten. under load)
Typical uses: Bushings, bearings, electrical items

Alloy No. C95400 (aluminum-bronze 9C, 415)
Composition: 11.0 aluminum, 85.0 copper, 4.0 iron
Conductivity: 13% IACS
Tensile strength: 75,000 psi min. to 85,000 psi typical
Yield strength: 30,000 psi min. to 35,000 psi typical (0.5% exten. under load)
Typical uses: Bearings, worms, gears, bushings, valve guides
Similar alloys: C95200, C95300, C95500

Alloy No. C95700 (manganese aluminum bronze)
Composition: 8.0 aluminum, 75.0 copper, 3.0 iron, 12.0 manganese, 2.0 nickel
Conductivity: 3.1% IACS
Tensile strength: 90,000 psi min. to 95,000 psi typical
Yield strength: 40,000 psi min. to 45,000 psi typical (0.5% exten. under load)
Typical uses: Impellers, propellers, safety tools, valves, pump castings

Note: The preceding alloy numbers refer to the UNS numbering system for copper cast alloys. For a complete listing of copper cast alloys, refer to the CDA handbook of cast copper alloys available from the Copper Development Association. Refer to Chapter 15 of this handbook.

Figure 18.13 *(Continued)*

Typical Base Compositions, %

Grade	Carbon	Silicon	Manganese	Sulfur, max	Phosphorus, max	Approximate Carbon Equivalent
G1800	3.40–3.70	2.30–2.80	0.50–0.80	0.15	0.25	4.25–4.5
G2500	3.20–3.50	2.00–2.40	0.60–0.90	0.15	0.20	4.0–4.25
G3000	3.10–3.40	1.90–2.30	0.60–0.90	0.15	0.15	3.9–4.15
G3500	3.00–3.30	1.80–2.20	0.60–0.90	0.15	0.12	3.7–3.9
G4000	3.00–3.30	1.80–2.10	0.70–1.00	0.15	0.10	3.7–3.9 (usually alloyed)

Figure 18.14 Compositions of gray-iron castings. *(Reprinted with permission from the Annual Book of ASTM Standards, copyright 1992, American Society for Testing and Materials.)*

Mechanical Properties for Design Purposes

Grade	Hardness Range[A]	Tensile Strength, min, psi (kgf/mm^2)	Transverse Strength, min, lb (kg)[B]	Deflection, min, in. (mm)[B]
G1800	HB 143-187 5.0–4.4 BID	18 000 (14)	1720 (780)	0.14 (3.6)
G2500	HB 170-229 4.6–4.0 BID	25 000 (17.5)	2000 (910)	0.17 (4.3)
G3000	HB 187-241 4.4–3.9 BID	30 000 (21)	2200 (1000)	0.20 (5.1)
G3500	HB 207-255 4.2–3.8 BID	35 000 (24.5)	2450 (1090)	0.24 (6.1)
G4000	HB 217-269 4.1–3.7 BID	40 000 (28)	2600 (1180)	0.27 (6.9)

[A] Brinell impression diameter (BID) is the diameter in millimetres of the impression of a 10-mm ball at 3000-kg load.
[B] See Method A 438 for information concerning the B transverse test bar and the transverse test.

Figure 18.15 Mechanical properties of gray-iron castings. *(Reprinted with permission from the Annual Book of ASTM Standards, copyright 1992, American Society for Testing and Materials.)*

Grade	General Data
G1800	Miscellaneous soft iron castings (as cast or annealed) in which strength is not of primary consideration. Exhaust manifolds may be made of this grade of iron, alloyed or unalloyed. These may be annealed castings for exhaust manifolds in order to avoid growth and cracking due to heat.
G2500	Small cylinder blocks, cylinder heads, air cooled cylinders, pistons, clutch plates, oil pump bodies, transmission cases, gear boxes, clutch housings, and light-duty brake drums.
G3000	Automobile and diesel cylinder blocks, cylinder heads, flywheels, differential carries castings, pistons, medium-duty brake drums, and clutch plates.
G3500	Diesel engine blocks, truck and tractor cylinder blocks and heads, heavy flywheels, tractor transmission cases, and heavy gear boxes.
G4000	Diesel engine castings, liners, cylinders, and pistons.

Figure 18.16 Typical applications of gray iron for automotive castings. *(Reprinted with permission from the Annual Book of ASTM Standards, copyright 1992, American Society for Testing and Materials.)*

Tensile Requirements

Grade	Tensile strength min, ksi [MPa]	Yield point min, ksi [MPa]	Elongation in 2 in. or 50 mm, min, %[A]	Reduction of Area, min, %
80-40 [550-275]	80 [550]	40 [275]	18	30
80-50 [550-345]	80 [550]	50 [345]	22	35
90-60 [620-415]	90 [620]	60 [415]	20	40
105-85 [725-585]	105 [725]	85 [585]	17	35
115-95 [795-655]	115 [795]	95 [655]	14	30
130-115 [895-795]	130 [895]	115 [795]	11	25
135-125 [930-860]	135 [930]	125 [860]	9	22
150-135 [1035-930]	150 [1035]	135 [930]	7	18
160-145 [1105-1000]	160 [1105]	145 [1000]	6	12
165-150 [1140-1035]	165 [1140]	150 [1035]	5	20
165-150L [1140-1035L][B]	165 [1140]	150 [1035]	5	20
210-180 [1450-1240]	210 [1450]	180 [1240]	4	15
210-180L [1450-1240L][B]	210 [1450]	180 [1240]	4	15
260-210 [1795-1450]	260 [1795]	210 [1450]	3	6
260-210L [1795-1450L][B]	260 [1795]	210 [1450]	3	6

[A] When ICI test bars are used in tensile testing as provided for in this specification, the gage length to reduced section diameter ratio shall be 4 to 1.

[B] These grades must be charpy impact tested.

Figure 18.17 Tensile-strength properties of steel castings. *(Reprinted with permission from the Annual Book of ASTM Standards, copyright 1992, American Society for Testing and Materials.)*

Chemical Requirements

Grade	Type	Composition, %							
		Carbon	Manganese, max	Silicon, max	Phosphorus, max	Sulfur, max	Chromium	Nickel	Molybdenum, max[A]
HF	19 Chromium, 9 Nickel	0.20–0.40	2.00	2.00	0.04	0.04	18.0–23.0	8.0–12.0	0.50
HH	25 Chromium, 12 Nickel	0.20–0.50	2.00	2.00	0.04	0.04	24.0–28.0	11.0–14.0	0.50
HI	28 Chromium, 15 Nickel	0.20–0.50	2.00	2.00	0.04	0.04	26.0–30.0	14.0–18.0	0.50
HK	25 Chromium, 20 Nickel	0.20–0.60	2.00	2.00	0.04	0.04	24.0–28.0	18.0–22.0	0.50
HE	29 Chromium, 9 Nickel	0.20–0.50	2.00	2.00	0.04	0.04	26.0–30.0	8.0–11.0	0.50
HT	15 Chromium, 35 Nickel	0.35–0.75	2.00	2.50	0.04	0.04	15.0–19.0	33.0–37.0	0.50
HU	19 Chromium, 39 Nickel	0.35–0.75	2.00	2.50	0.04	0.04	17.0–21.0	37.0–41.0	0.50
HW	12 Chromium, 60 Nickel	0.35–0.75	2.00	2.50	0.04	0.04	10.0–14.0	58.0–62.0	0.50
HX	17 Chromium, 66 Nickel	0.35–0.75	2.00	2.50	0.04	0.04	15.0–19.0	64.0–68.0	0.50
HC	28 Chromium	0.50 max	1.00	2.00	0.04	0.04	26.0–30.0	4.00 max	0.50
HD	28 Chromium, 5 Nickel	0.50 max	1.50	2.00	0.04	0.04	26.0–30.0	4.0–7.0	0.50
HL	29 Chromium, 20 Nickel	0.20–0.60	2.00	2.00	0.04	0.04	28.0–32.0	18.0–22.0	0.50
HN	20 Chromium, 25 Nickel	0.20–0.50	2.00	2.00	0.04	0.04	19.0–23.0	23.0–27.0	0.50
HP	26 Chromium, 35 Nickel	0.35–0.75	2.00	2.50	0.04	0.04	24–28	33–37	0.50

[A] Castings having a specified molybdenum range agreed upon by the manufacturer and the purchaser may also be furnished under these specifications.

Figure 18.18 Compositions of steel, iron-chromium-nickel, and heat-resisting castings. *(Reprinted with permission from the Annual Book of ASTM Standards, copyright 1992, American Society for Testing and Materials.)*

Tensile Requirements

Grade	Type	Tensile Strength, min		Yield Point, min		Elongation in 2 in. [50 mm], min, %[A]
		ksi	[MPa]	ksi	[MPa]	
HF	19 Chromium, 9 Nickel	70	485	35	240	25
HH	25 Chromium, 12 Nickel	75	515	35	240	10
HI	28 Chromium, 15 Nickel	70	485	35	240	10
HK	25 Chromium, 20 Nickel	65	450	35	240	10
HE	29 Chromium, 9 Nickel	85	585	40	275	9
HT	15 Chromium, 35 Nickel	65	450	...	...	4
HU	19 Chromium, 39 Nickel	65	450	...	...	4
HW	12 Chromium, 60 Nickel	60	415	...	...	...
HX	17 Chromium, 66 Nickel	60	415	...	...	...
HC	28 Chromium	55	380	...	...	...
HD	28 Chromium, 5 Nickel	75	515	35	240	8
HL	29 Chromium, 20 Nickel	65	450	35	240	10
HN	20 Chromium, 25 Nickel	63	435	...	...	8
HP	26 Chromium, 35 Nickel	62.5	430	34	235	4.5

[A] When ICI test bars are used in tensile testing as provided for in this specification, the gage length to reduced section diameter ratio shall be 4 to 1.

Figure 18.19 Tensile strengths for steel, iron-chromium-nickel, and heat-resisting castings. *(Reprinted with permission from the Annual Book of ASTM Standards, copyright 1992, American Society for Testing and Materials.)*

Chemical Requirements

Element	Composition, %							
	Type 1	Type 1b	Type 2	Type 2b	Type 3	Type 4	Type 5	Type 6
Carbon, total, max	3.00	3.00	3.00	3.00	2.60	2.60	2.40	3.00
Silicon	1.00–2.80	1.00–2.80	1.00–2.80	1.00–2.80	1.00–2.00	5.00–6.00	1.00–2.00	1.50–2.50
Manganese	0.5–1.5	0.5–1.5	0.5–1.5	0.5–1.5	0.5–1.5	0.5–1.5	0.5–1.5	0.5–1.5
Nickel	13.50–17.50	13.50–17.50	18.00–22.00	18.00–22.00	28.00–32.00	29.00–32.00	34.00–36.00	18.00–22.00
Copper	5.50–7.50	5.50–7.50	0.50 max	0.50 max	0.50 max	0.50 max	0.50 max	3.50–5.50
Chromium	1.5–2.5	2.50–3.50	1.5–2.5	3.00–6.00[A]	2.50–3.50	4.50–5.50	0.10 max	1.00–2.00
Sulfur, max	0.12	0.12	0.12	0.12	0.12	0.12	0.12	0.12
Molybdenum, max	...	...	...	...	...	...	...	1.00

[A] Where some machining is required, the 3.00–4.00 % chromium range is recommended.

Mechanical Requirements

	Type 1	Type 1b	Type 2	Type 2b	Type 3	Type 4	Type 5	Type 6
Tensile strength, min, ksi (MPa)	25 (172)	30 (207)	25 (172)	30 (207)	25 (172)	25 (172)	20 (138)	25 (172)
Brinell hardness (3000 kg)	131 183	149 212	118 174	171 248	118 159	149 212	99 124	124 174

Figure 18.20 Chemical and mechanical requirements for austenitic gray-iron castings. *(Reprinted with permission from the Annual Book of ASTM Standards, copyright 1992, American Society for Testing and Materials.)*

TABLE 18.1 Chemical, Tensile, and Impact Requirements

Grade	Carbon steel	Carbon steel	Carbon-manganese steel	Carbon-molybdenum steel	2½% nickel steel	Nickel-chromium-molybdenum steel	3½% nickel steel	4½% nickel steel	9% nickel steel	12½% chromium, nickel-molybdenum steel
Element, % (max, except where range is given)	LCA	LCB[a]	LCC	LC1	LC2	LC2-1	LC3	LC4	LC9	CA6NM
Carbon	0.25[a]	0.30	0.25[a]	0.25	0.25	0.22	0.15	0.15	0.13	0.06
Silicon	0.60	0.60	0.60	0.60	0.60	0.50	0.60	0.60	0.45	1.00
Manganese	0.70[a]	1.00	1.20[a]	0.50–0.80	0.50–0.80	0.55–0.75	0.50–0.80	0.50–0.80	0.90	1.00
Phosphorus	0.04	0.04	0.04	0.04	0.04	0.04	0.04	0.04	0.04	0.04
Sulfur	0.045	0.045	0.045	0.045	0.045	0.045	0.045	0.045	0.045	0.03
Nickel	0.50[b]	0.50[b]	0.50[b]	—	2.00–3.00	2.50–3.50	3.00–4.00	4.00–5.00	8.50–10.0	3.5–4.5
Chromium	0.50[b]	0.50[b]	0.50[b]	—	—	1.35–1.85	—	—	0.50	11.5–14.0
Molybdenum	0.20[b]	0.20[b]	0.20[b]	0.45–0.65	—	0.30–0.60	—	—	0.20	0.4–1.0
Copper	0.30[b]	0.30[b]	0.30[b]	—	—	—	—	—	0.30	—
Vanadium	0.03[b]	0.03[b]	0.03[b]	—	—	—	—	—	0.03	—
Tensile Requirements:[c]										
Tensile strength, ksi (MPa)	60.0–85.0 (415–585)	65.0–90.0 (450–620)	70.0–95.0 (485–655)	65.0–90.0 (450–620)	70.0–95.0 (485–655)	105.0–130.0 (725–895)	70.0–95.0 (485–655)	70.0–95.0 (485–655)	85.0 (585)	110.0–135.0 (760–930)
Yield strength,[d] min, ksi (MPa)	30.0 (205)	35.0 (240)	40.0 (275)	35.0 (240)	40.0 (275)	80.0 (550)	40.0 (275)	40.0 (275)	75.0 (515)	80.0 (550)
Elongation in 2 in or 50 mm, min, %[e]	24	24	22	24	24	18	24	24	20	15
Reduction of area, min, %	35	35	35	35	35	30	35	35	30	35

Impact requirements Charpy V-notch[c,f]										
Energy value, ft · lbf (J), min value for two specimens and min avg of three specimens	13 (18)	13 (18)	15 (20)	13 (18)	15 (20)	30 (41)	15 (20)	15 (20)	20 (27)	20 (27)
Energy value, ft·lbf (J), min for single specimen	10 (14)	10 (14)	12 (16)	10 (14)	12 (16)	25 (34)	12 (16)	12 (16)	15 (20)	15 (20)
Testing temperature, °F (°C)	−25 (−32)	−50 (−46)	−50 (−46)	−75 (−59)	−100 (−73)	−100 (−73)	−150 (−101)	−175 (−115)	−320 (−196)	−100 (−73)

[a]For each reduction of 0.01% below the specified maximum carbon content, an increase of 0.04% manganese above the specified maximum will be permitted up to a maximum of 1.10% for LCA, 1.28% for LCB, and 1.40% for LCC.

[b]Specified Residual Elements—The total content of these elements is 1.00% maximum.

[c]See 1.2.

[d]Determine by either 0.2% offset method or 0.5% extension-under-load method.

[e]When ICI test bars are used in tensile testing as provided for in Specification A 703/A 703M, the gauge length to reduced section diameter ratio shall be 4 to 1.

[f]See Appendix X1.

Chemical Requirements

Element	Type								
	D-2[A]	D-2B	D-2C	D-3[A]	D-3A	D-4	D-5	D-5B	D-5S
	Composition, %								
Total carbon, max	3.00	3.00	2.90	2.60	2.60	2.60	2.40	2.40	2.30
Silicon	1.50–3.00	1.50–3.00	1.00–3.00	1.00–2.80	1.00–2.80	5.00–6.00	1.00–2.80	1.00–2.80	4.90–5.50
Manganese	0.70–1.25	0.70–1.25	1.80–2.40	1.00 max[B]	1.00 max[B]	1.00 max[B]	1.00 max[B]	1.00 max[B]	1.00 max
Phosphorus, max	0.08	0.08	0.08	0.08	0.08	0.08	0.08	0.08	0.08
Nickel	18.00–22.00	18.00–22.00	21.00–24.00	28.00–32.00	28.00–32.00	28.00–32.00	34.00–36.00	34.00–36.00	34.00–37.00
Chromium	1.75–2.75	2.75–4.00	0.50 max[B]	2.50–3.50	1.00–1.50	4.50–5.50	0.10 max	2.00–3.00	1.75–2.25

[A] Additions of 0.7 to 1.0 % of molybdenum will increase the mechanical properties above 800°F (425°C).

[B] Not intentionally added.

Mechanical Requirements

Element	Type								
	D-2	D-2B	D-2C	D-3	D-3A	D-4	D-5	D-5B	D-5S
	Properties								
Tensile strength, min, ksi (MPa)	58 (400)	58 (400)	58 (400)	55 (379)	55 (379)	60 (414)	55 (379)	55 (379)	65 (449)
Yield strength (0.2 percent offset), min, ksi (MPa)	30 (207)	30 (207)	28 (193)	30 (207)	30 (207)	. . .	30 (207)	30 (207)	30 (207)
Elongation in 2 in. or 50 mm, min, %	8.0	7.0	20.0	6.0	10.0	. . .	20.0	6.0	10
Brinell hardness (3000 kg)	139–202	148–211	121–171	139–202	131–193	202–273	131–185	139–193	131–193

Figure 18.21 Specifications for austenitic ductile iron castings. *(Reprinted with permission from the Annual Book of ASTM Standards, copyright 1992, American Society for Testing and Materials.)*

TABLE 18.2 Heat Treatment Requirements

Grade	Class	Austenitizing temperature, min, °F (°C)	Media*	Quenching cool below, °F (°C)	Tempering temperature, °F (°C)†
1	A	1600 (870)	A	450 (230)	1100 (595)
1	B	1600 (870)	L	500 (260)	1100 (595)
1	C	1600 (870)	A or L	500 (260)	1150 (620)
2	A	1600 (870)	A	450 (230)	1100 (595)
2	B	1600 (870)	L	500 (260)	1100 (595)
2	C	1600 (870)	A or L	500 (260)	1150 (620)
4	A	1600 (870)	A or L	500 (260)	1100 (595)
4	B	1600 (870)	L	500 (260)	1100 (595)
4	C	1600 (870)	A or L	500 (260)	1150 (620)
4	D	1600 (870)	L	500 (260)	1150 (620)
4	E	1600 (870)	L	500 (260)	1100 (595)
6	A	1550 (845)	A	500 (260)	1100 (595)
6	B	1550 (845)	L	500 (260)	1100 (595)
7	A	1650 (900)	L	600 (315)	1100 (595)
8	A	1750 (955)	A	500 (260)	1250 (675)
8	B	1750 (955)	L	500 (260)	1250 (675)
8	C	1750 (955)	L	500 (260)	1250 (675)
9	A	1600 (870)	A or L	500 (260)	1100 (595)
9	B	1600 (870)	L	500 (260)	1100 (595)
9	C	1600 (870)	A or L	500 (260)	1150 (620)
9	D	1600 (870)	L	500 (260)	1150 (620)
9	E	1600 (870)	L	500 (260)	1100 (595)
10	A	1550 (845)	A	500 (260)	1100 (595)
10	B	1550 (845)	L	500 (260)	1100 (595)
11	A	1650 (900)	A	600 (315)	1100 (595)
11	B	1650 (900)	L	600 (315)	1100 (595)
12	A	1750 (955)	A	600 (315)	1100 (595)
12	B	1750 (955)	L	400 (205)	1100 (595)
13	A	1550 (845)	A	500 (260)	1100 (595)
13	B	1550 (845)	L	500 (260)	1100 (595)
14	A	1550 (845)	L	500 (260)	1100 (595)
16	A	1600 (870)‡	A	600 (315)	1100 (595)
CA15	A	1750 (955)	A or L	400 (205)	900 (480)
CA15	B	1750 (955)	A or L	400 (205)	1100 (595)
CA15	C	1750 (955)	A or L	400 (205)	1150 (620)§
CA15	D	1750 (955)	A or L	400 (205)	1150 (260)§
CA15M	A	1750 (955)	A or L	400 (205)	1100 (595)
CA6NM	A	1850 (1010)	A or L	200 (95)	1050–1150 (565–620)
CA6NM	B	1850 (1010)	A or L	200 (95)	1225–1275 (665–690)§,¶ 1050–1150 (565–620)

* A = air, L = liquid.
† Minimum temperature unless range is specified.
‡ Double austenitize.
§ Double temper.
¶ Air cool to below 200°F (95°C) after first temper.
SOURCE: Reprinted with permission from the *Annual Book of ASTM Standards,* copyright 1992, American Society of Testing and Materials.

TABLE 18.3 Chemical Requirements (Maximum Percent Unless Range is Given)

Grade	1.	2.	4.	6.	7.	8.	9.	10.	11.	12.
Class type	ABC vanadium	ABC manganese-molybdenum	ABCDE nickel-chromium-molybdenum	AB manganese-nickel-chromium-molybdenum	A nickel-chromium-molybdenum vanadium*	ABC chromium-molybdenum	ABCDE chromium-molybdenum	AB nickel-chromium-molybdenum	AB nickel-chromium-molybdenum	AB nickel-chromium-molybdenum
Carbon	0.30	0.30	0.30	0.05–0.38	0.05–0.20	0.05–0.20	0.05–0.33	0.30	0.05–0.20	0.05–0.20
Manganese	1.00	1.00–1.40	1.00	1.30–1.70	0.60–1.00	0.50–0.90	0.60–1.00	0.50–1.00	0.50–0.80	0.40–0.70
Phosphorus	0.04	0.04	0.04	0.04	0.04	0.04	0.04	0.04	0.04	0.04
Sulfur	0.045	0.045	0.045	0.045	0.045	0.045	0.045	0.045	0.045	0.045
Silicon	0.80	0.80	0.80	0.80	0.80	0.80	0.80	0.80	0.60	0.60
Nickel	—	—	0.40–0.80	0.40–0.80	0.70–1.00	—	—	1.40–2.00	0.70–1.10	0.60–1.00
Chromium	—	—	0.40–0.80	0.40–0.80	0.40–0.80	2.00–2.75	0.75–1.10	0.55–0.90	0.50–0.80	0.50–0.90
Molybdenum	—	0.10–0.30	0.15–0.30	0.30–0.40	0.40–0.60	0.90–1.10	0.15–0.30	0.20–0.40	0.45–0.65	0.90–1.20
Vanadium	0.04–0.12	—	—	—	0.03–0.10	—	—	—	—	—
Boron	—	—	—	—	0.002–0.006	—	—	—	—	—
Copper	—	—	—	—	0.15–0.50	—	—	—	—	—
Residual elements:										
Copper	0.50	0.50	0.50	0.50	0.50	0.50	0.50	0.50	0.50	0.50
Nickel	0.50	0.50	—	—	—	—	0.50	—	—	—
Chromium	0.35	0.35	—	—	—	—	—	—	—	—
Mo + W	0.25	—	—	—	—	—	—	—	—	—
Tungsten	—	0.10	0.10	0.10	0.10	0.10	0.10	0.10	0.10	0.10
Vanadium	—	0.03	0.03	0.03	—	0.03	0.03	0.03	0.03	0.03
Total content of residual elements	1.00	1.00	0.60	0.60	0.60	0.60	1.00	0.60	0.50	0.50

Grade	13.	14.	16	CA15	CA15M	CA6NM
Class type	AB nickel-molybdenum	A nickel-molybdenum	A Low-carbon-manganese-nickel	ABCD martensitic chromium	A martensitic chromium	AB martensitic chromium nickel
Carbon	0.30	0.55	0.12†	0.15	0.15	0.06
Manganese	0.80–1.10	0.80–1.10	2.10†	1.00	1.00	1.00
Phosphorus	0.04	0.04	0.02	0.040	0.040	0.04
Sulfur	0.045	0.045	0.02	0.040	0.040	0.03
Silicon	0.60	0.60	0.50	1.50	0.65	1.00
Nickel	1.40–1.75	1.40–1.75	1.00–1.40	1.00	1.0	3.5–4.5
Chromium	—	—	—	11.5–14.0	11.5–14.0	11.5–14.0
Molybdenum	0.20–0.30	0.20–0.30	—	0.50	0.15–1.0	0.4–1.0
Boron	—	—	—	—	—	—
Copper	—	—	—	—	—	—
Residual elements						
Copper	0.50	0.50	0.20	0.50	0.50	0.50
Nickel	—	—	—	—	—	—
Chromium	0.40	0.40	0.20	—	—	—
Molybdenum	—	—	0.10	—	—	—
Tungsten	0.10	0.10	0.10	0.10	0.10	0.10
Vanadium	0.03	0.03	0.02	0.05	0.05	0.05
Total content of residual elements	0.75	0.75	0.50	0.50	0.50	0.50

* Proprietary steel composition.

† For each reduction of 0.01% below the specified maximum carbon content, an increase of 0.04% manganese above the specified maximum will be permitted up to a maximum of 2.30%.

SOURCE: Reprinted with permission from the *Annual Book of ASTM Standards*, copyright 1992, American Society of Testing and Materials.

TABLE 18.4 Required Mechanical Properties

Previous designation	Grade	Class	Tensile strength,* min, ksi (MPa)	Yield strength, min, ksi (MPa), at 0.2% offset	Elongation, 2 in (50 mm) or 4*d*, min, %	Reduction of area, min %	Hardness max, HRC	Max thickness, in (mm)
1N	1	A	85 (585)–110 (760)	55 (380)	22	40		
1Q	1	B	90 (620)–115 (795)	65 (450)	22	45		
	1	C	90 (620)	65 (450)	22	45	22 (235)	
2N	2	A	85 (585)–110 (760)	53 (365)	22	35		
2Q	2	B	90 (620)–115 (795)	65 (450)	22	40		
	2	C	90 (620)	65 (450)	22	40	22 (235)	
4N	4	A	90 (620)–115 (795)	60 (415)	18	40		
4Q	4	B	105 (725)–130 (895)	85 (585)	17	35		
	4	C	90 (620)	60 (415)	18	35	22 (235)	
	4	D	100 (690)	75 (515)	17	35	22 (235)	
4QA	4	E	115 (795)	95 (655)	15	35		
6N	6	A	115 (795)	80 (550)	18	30		
6Q	6	B	120 (825)	95 (655)	12	25		
7Q	7	A	115 (795)	100 (690)	15	30		2.5 (63.5)
8N	8	A	85 (585)–110 (760)	55 (380)	20	35		
8Q	8	B	105 (725)	85 (585)	17	30		
	8	C	100 (690)	75 (515)	17	35	22 (235)	
9N	9	A	90 (620)	60 (415)	18	35		
9Q	9	B	105 (725)	85 (585)	16	35		
	9	C	90 (620)	60 (415)	18	35	22 (235)	
	9	D	100 (690)	75 (515)	17	35	22 (235)	
	9	E	115 (795)	95 (655)	15	35		
10N	10	A	100 (690)	70 (485)	18	35		
10Q	10	B	125 (860)	100 (690)	15	35		
11N	11	A	70 (484)–95 (655)	40 (275)	20	35		
11Q	11	B	105 (725)–130 (895)	85 (585)	17	35		
12N	12	A	70 (485)–95 (655)	40 (275)	20	35		

12Q	12	B	105 (725)–130 (895)	85 (585)	17	35	
13N	13	A	90 (620)–115 (795)	60 (415)	18	35	
13Q	13	B	105 (725)–130 (895)	85 (585)	17	35	
14Q	14	A	120 (825)–145 (1000)	95 (655)	14	30	
16N	16	A	70 (485)–95 (655)	40 (275)	22	35	
CA15A	CA15	A	140 (965)–170 (1170)	110 (760)–130 (895)	10	25	
CA15	CA15	B	90 (620)–115 (795)	65 (450)	18	30	
	CA15	C	90 (620)	60 (415)	18	35	22 (235)
	CA15	D	100 (690)	75 (515)	17	35	22 (235)
CA15M	CA15M	A	90 (620)–115 (795)	65 (450)	18	30	
CA6NM	CA6NM	A	110 (760)–135 (930)	80 (515)	15	35	
CA6NM	CA6NM	B	100 (690)	75 (520)	17	35	23 (255)†

* Minimum ksi, unless range is given.

† Test Methods and Definitions A 370, Table 3a does not apply to CA6NM. The conversion given is based on CA6NM test coupons. (For example, see ASTM STP 756.)

SOURCE: Reprinted with permission from the *Annual Book of ASTM Standards,* copyright 1992, American Society of Testing and Materials.

TABLE 18.5 Heat Treatment Requirements

Grade	Heat treatment
CF-8, CG-8M, CG-12, CF-20, CF-8M CF-8C, CF-16F, CF-16Fa	Heat to 1900°F (1040°C) minimum, hold for sufficient time to heat casting to temperature, quench in water or rapid cool by other means so as to develop acceptable corrosion resistance.
CH-20, CE-30, CK-20	Heat to 2000°F (1093°C) minimum, hold for sufficient time to heat casting to temperature, quench in water or rapid cool by other means so as to develop acceptable corrosion resistance.
CA-15, CA-15M, CA-40, CA-40F	(1) Heat to 1750°F (955°C) minimum, air cool and temper at 1100°F (595°C) minimum, or (2) Anneal at 1450°F (790°C) minimum.
CB-30, CC-50	(1) Heat to 1450°F (790°C) minimum, and air cool, or (2) Heat to 1450°F (790°C) minimum, and furnace cool.
CF-3, CF-3M, CF-3MN	(1) Heat to 1900°F (1040°C) minimum, hold for sufficient time to heat casting to temperature, and cool rapidly so as to develop acceptable corrosion resistance, or (2) As cast if corrosion resistance is acceptable.
CN-3M	Heat to 2150°F (1175°C) minimum, hold for sufficient time to heat casting to temperature, quench in water or rapid cool by other means so as to develop acceptable corrosion resistance.
CN-7M, CG-6MMN	Heat to 2050°F (1120°C) minimum, hold for sufficient time to heat casting to temperature, quench in water or rapid cool by other means so as to develop acceptable corrosion resistance.
CN-7MS	Heat to 2100°F (1150°C) minimum, 2150°F (1180°C) maximum, hold for sufficient time (2 h minimum) to heat casting to temperature and quench in water to develop acceptable corrosion resistance.
CA-6NM	Heat to 1750°F (955°C) minimum, air cool to 200°F (95°C) or lower prior to any optional intermediate temper and prior to the final temper. The final temper shall be between 1050°F (565°C) and 1150°F (620°C).
CD-4MCu	Heat to 1900°F (1040°C) minimum, hold for sufficient time to heat casting uniformly to temperature, quench in water or rapid cool by other means to develop acceptable corrosion resistance.
CA-6N	Heat to 1900°F (1040°C), air cool, reheat to 1500°F (815°C), air cool, and age at 800°F (425°C), holding at each temperature sufficient time to heat casting uniformly to temperature.
CF10SMnN	Heat to 1950°F (1065°C) minimum, hold for sufficient time to heat casting to temperature, quench in water or rapid cool by other means so as to develop acceptable corrosion resistance.
CA-28MWV	(1) Heat to 1875–1925°F (1025–1050°C), quench in air or oil, and temper at 1150°F (620°C) minimum, or (2) Anneal at 1400°F (760°C) minimum.
CK-3MCuN	Heat to 2100°F (1150°C) minimum, hold for sufficient time to heat casting to temperature, quench in water or rapid cool by other means so as to develop acceptable corrosion resistance.

SOURCE: Reprinted with permission from the *Annual Book of ASTM Standards*, copyright 1992, American Society of Testing and Materials.

Brinell hardness measurements: For castings and other applications. Calculation of the Brinell hardness number (BHN) can be performed using the equation shown in Sect. 5.7 of this *Handbook*. Table 18.8 is a table of Brinell hardness numbers as determined by the diameter of the indentation of a 10-mm ball at applied loads of 500, 1500, and 3000 kgf (kilogram-force). The table may be used for determining the hardness of most metals and alloys.

18.5 Plastic Moldings

There are two classifications of plastics and their moldings, thermoplastics and thermoset plastics. Thermoplastics are basically the same chemically after molding as they were in the raw form. This means that once molded, they may be reused, in most cases, by chopping the parts into small pieces and remelting. Thermoset plastics, once molded, cannot be remolded or reprocessed because they have a one-way chemistry that alters their "as molded" characteristics from their raw constituents.

Types of thermoplastics include

- ABS (acrylonitrile-butadiene-styrene)
- Acetal (Delrin)
- Acrylic (Lucite, Plexiglas)
- Cellulosics (acetates)
- Fluoroplastics (PTFE, FEP, PFA, CTFE, ETFE, PVDF)
- Nylon
- Phenylene oxide
- Polycarbonate (Lexan)
- Polyester (Mylar)
- Polyethylene
- Polyimide
- Polyphenylene sulfide
- Polypropylene
- Polystyrene
- Polysulfone
- Polyurethane
- Polyvinyl chloride

Types of thermoset plastics include

- Alkyd
- Allyl (diallyl phthalate)
- Amino (urea, melamine)
- Epoxy (including cycloaliphatic)
- Phenolic
- Polyester
- Polyurethane
- Silicone

Polyesters and polyurethanes include thermosets that are also thermoplastics. Thermoset grades are usually filled with reinforcing materials such as glass, carbon, and mineral fibers for added strength. Thermoset plastics are usually more dimensionally stable and heat resistant and have better electrical properties than thermoplastics.

Complex molded shapes of the plastics are analyzed today using the advanced finite-element analysis (FEA) techniques available for the personal computer and engineering design stations. Figure 18.22 shows a typical intricate plastic part which must be dimensionally accurate as well as chemical resistant.

18.5.1 Prototypes of the plastics

Building a prototype plastic part is a compromise, since the part is usually machined from plastic blocks and slabs and will not duplicate the exact performance of the finished part, which is made in a mold. The closest duplicate to a plastic production part is made by molding a prototype in mild-steel molds made specifically for the prototype. This method is expensive but is the closest method to use if you wish to avoid expensive rework or changes to a finished production mold. This approach will give the most accurate test results prior to building the actual production mold.

18.5.2 Properties and characteristics of modern plastics

Widely used plastics are discussed in Chap. 5, "Materials and Their Uses." The applications of the modern plastics are given there as well as the trade names and families of all plastics manufactured today.

18.5.3 Design of molded plastic parts

Final selection of plastic type and part configuration or design should be reviewed and coordinated with the mold maker and plastic part manufacturer before the final design drawings are made. Mold makers and molded part manufacturers can alert the designer to the many problem areas that are prevalent on many preliminary designs for plastic parts.

Plastic part design handbooks are available from all the leading producers of plastic materials, such as DuPont, General Electric, Monsanto, etc. These manuals or handbooks cover detail design, appropriate calculation techniques, and complete chemical, physical, and electrical properties of the materials. The design handbooks may be secured by writing directly to the plastics sections of the large suppliers or their distributors.

18.5.4 Plastics molding machinery and molds

A great many machines are made for molding plastic parts, most of which are expensive and require specialized techniques for operation. Figures 18.23 and 18.24 show a typical group of machines required for producing parts made of cycloaliphatic epoxy. This class of thermoset plastic has gained wide recognition in the electric power distribution industry for parts that support or brace high-voltage current-carrying busses and parts of switching devices such as breakers and switches of all classes, up to 34.5 kV. Figure 18.23 shows the mixing and dispensing machine, and Fig. 18.24 shows the complete group of equipment, with the mold-clamping machine at the front of the photograph.

Because of the high injection pressures developed in this plastic molding process, the clamping machine must exert a high load on the mold to prevent it from opening during the injection process. In this process, the hot, molten plastic is injected under pressure into the mold, where it is held for the "curing" or setting time prior to being released from the mold. In the molding of cycloaliphatic epoxy after the proper cure, the plastic part is removed from the mold, placed in an oven set to a preselected temperature, and baked for a predetermined time interval. Cycloaliphatic epoxy is being used in the electrical industries as a substitute for wet-process porcelain, which for many years was one of the few materials available for this type of service. Glass and polyester-glass thermosets are also used in electrical applications, as are other electrical-grade epoxies.

(Text continued on page 1350.)

TABLE 18.6 Chemical Requirements

Grade	Type	Composition, %													
		Carbon, max	Manganese, max	Silicon, max	Phosphorus, max	Sulfur, max	Chromium	Nickel	Molybdenum	Columbium	Selenium	Copper	Tungsten, max	Vanadium, max	Nitrogen
CF-8	19 Chromium, 9 Nickel	0.08	1.50	2.00	0.04	0.04	18.0–21.0	8.0–11.0	—	—	—	—	—	—	—
CG-12	22 Chromium, 12 Nickel	0.12	1.50	2.00	0.04	0.04	20.0–23.0	10.0–13.0	—	—	—	—	—	—	—
CF-20	19 Chromium, 9 Nickel	0.20	1.50	2.00	0.04	0.04	18.0–21.0	8.0–11.0	—	—	—	—	—	—	—
CF-8M	19 Chromium, 10 Nickel, with molybdenum	0.08	1.50	2.00	0.04	0.04	18.0–21.0	9.0–12.0	2.0–3.0	—	—	—	—	—	—
CF-8C	19 Chromium, 10 Nickel, with columbium	0.08	1.50	2.00	0.04	0.04	18.0–21.0	9.0–12.0	—	*	—	—	—	—	—
CF-16F[†]	19 Chromium, 9 Nickel, free machining	0.16	1.50	2.00	0.04[†]	0.04[†]	18.0–21.0	9.0–12.0	†	—	†	—	—	—	—
CH-20[‡]	25 Chromium, 12 Nickel	0.20[‡]	1.50	2.00	0.04	0.04	22.0–26.0	12.0–15.0	—	—	—	—	—	—	—
CK-20	25 Chromium, 20 Nickel	0.20	2.00	2.00	0.04	0.04	23.0–27.0	19.0–22.0	—	—	—	—	—	—	—
CE-30	29 Chromium, 9 Nickel	0.30	1.50	2.00	0.04	0.04	26.0–30.0	8.0–11.0	—	—	—	—	—	—	—
CA-15	12 Chromium	0.15	1.00	1.50	0.04	0.04	11.5–14.0	1.00 max	0.50 max	—	—	—	—	—	—
CA-15M	12 Chromium	0.15	1.00	0.65	0.040	0.040	11.5–14.0	1.0 max	0.15–1.0	—	—	—	—	—	—
CB-30	20 Chromium	0.30	1.00	1.50	0.04	0.04	18.0–21.0	2.00 max	—	—	—	§	—	—	—
CC-50	28 Chromium	0.50	1.00	1.50	0.04	0.04	26.0–30.0	4.00 max	—	—	—	—	—	—	—

CA-40	12 Chromium	0.20–0.40	1.00	1.50	0.04	0.04	11.5–14.0	1.0 max	0.5 max	—	—	—	—	—	—
CA-40F	12 Chromium, free machining	0.20–0.40	1.00	1.50	0.04	0.20–0.40	11.5–14.0	1.0 max	0.5 max	—	—	—	—	—	—
CF-3	19 Chromium, 9 Nickel	0.03[§]	1.50	2.00	0.04	0.04	17.0–21.0	8.0–12.0	—	—	—	—	—	—	—
CF10SMnN	17 Chromium, 8.5 nickel with nitrogen	0.10	7.00–9.00	3.50–4.50	0.060	0.030	16.0–18.0	8.0–9.0	—	—	—	—	—	—	0.08–0.18
CF-3M	19 Chromium, 10 Nickel, with molybdenum	0.03[¶]	1.50	1.50	0.04	0.04	17.0–21.0	9.0–13.0	2.0–3.0	—	—	—	—	—	—
CF-3MN	19 Chromium, 10 Nickel, with molybdenum, and nitrogen	0.03	1.50	1.50	0.040	0.040	17.0–22.0	9.0–13.0	2.0–3.0	—	—	—	—	—	0.10–0.20
CG6MMN		0.06	4.00–6.00	1.00	0.04	0.03	20.5–23.5	11.5–13.5	1.50–3.00	0.10–0.30	—	—	—	0.10–0.30	0.20–0.40
CG-8M	19 Chromium, 11 Nickel, with molybdenum	0.08	1.50	1.50	0.04	0.04	18.0–21.0	9.0–13.0	3.0–4.0	—	—	—	—	—	—
CN-3M		0.03	2.0	1.0	0.03	0.03	20.0–22.0	23.0–27.0	4.5–5.5	—	—	—	—	—	—
CN-7M	20 Chromium, 29 Nickel, with copper and molybdenum	0.07	1.50	1.50	0.04	0.04	19.0–22.0	27.5–30.5	2.0–3.0	—	—	3.0–4.0	—	—	—
CN-7MS	19 Chromium, 24 Nickel, with copper and molybdenum	0.07	1.00	2.50–3.50	0.04	0.03	18.0–20.0	22.0–25.0	2.5–3.0	—	—	1.5–2.0	—		
CA-6NM	12 Chromium, 4 Nickel	0.06	1.00	1.00	0.04	0.03	11.5–14.0	3.5–4.5	0.40–1.0	—	—	—	—	—	—
CD-4MCu		0.04	1.00	1.00	0.04	0.04	24.5–26.5	4.75–6.00	1.75–2.25	—	—	2.75–3.25	—	—	—
CA6N	11 Chromium, 7 Nickel	0.06	0.50	1.00	0.02	0.02	10.5–12.5	6.0–8.0	—	—	—	—	—	—	—

TABLE 18.6 Chemical Requirements (*Continued*)

Grade	Type	Composition, %													
		Carbon, max	Manganese, max	Silicon, max	Phosphorus, max	Sulfur, max	Chromium	Nickel	Molybdenum	Columbium	Selenium	Copper	Tungsten, max	Vanadium, max	Nitrogen
CA-28MWV	12 Chromium, with molybdenum, tungsten and vanadium	0.20–0.28	0.50–1.00	1.0	0.030	0.030	11.0–12.5	0.50–1.00	0.90–1.25	—	—	—	0.90–1.25	0.20–0.30	—
CK-3MCuN	20 Chromium 18 Nickel, with copper and molybdenum	0.025	1.20	1.00	0.045	0.010	19.5–20.5	17.5–19.5	6.0–7.0	—	—	0.50–1.00	—	—	0.180–0.240

* Grade CF-8C shall have a columbium content of not less than eight times the carbon content and not more than 1.0%. If a columbium-plus-tantalum alloy in the approximate Cb:Ta ratio of 3:1 is used for stabilizing this grade, the total columbium-plus-tantalum content shall not be less than nine times the carbon content and shall not exceed 1.1%.

† For free-machining properties the composition of grade CF-16F may contain suitable combinations of selenium, phosphorus, and molybdenum (grade CF-16F) or of sulfur and molybdenum (grade CF-16Fa) as follows:

Selenium, phosphorus and molybdenum:

Selenium, %	0.20–0.35
Phosphorus, max, %	0.17
Molybdenum, max, %	1.50

Sulfur and molybdenum:

Sulfur, %	0.20–0.40
Molybdenum, %	0.40–0.80

Other combinations of elements for free-machining properties may be agreed upon between the manufacturer and the purchaser.

‡ For the more severe general corrosive conditions, and when so specified, the carbon content shall not exceed 0.10%. This low-carbon grade shall be designated as Grade CH-10.

§ For grade CB-30 a copper content of 0.90 to 1.20% is optional.

¶ For purposes of determining conformance with this specification, the observed or calculated value for carbon content shall be rounded to the nearest 0.01% in accordance with the rounding method of Practice E 29.

SOURCE: Reprinted with permission from the *Annual Book of ASTM Standards,* copyright 1992, American Society of Testing and Materials.

TABLE 18.7 Preheat and Tensile Requirements

Minimum Preheat Temperatures

Grade	Minimum preheat temperatures °F	Minimum preheat temperatures °C
CA-15, CA-15M CA-40, CA-28MWV	400	[205]
Others	50	[10]

Tensile Requirements

Grade	Type	Tensile strength, min ksi	Tensile strength, min MPa	Yield strength, min ksi	Yield strength, min MPa	Elongation in 2 in (50 mm), min, %*	Reduction of area, min, %
CF-8	19 Chromium, 9 Nickel	70†	485†	30†	205†	35	—
CG-12	22 Chromium, 12 Nickel	70	485	28	195	35	—
CF-20	19 Chromium, 9 Nickel	70	485	30	205	30	—
CF-8M	19 Chromium, 10 Nickel, with molybdenum	70	485	30	205	30	—
CF-8C	19 Chromium, 10 Nickel with columbium	70	485	30	205	30	—
CF-16 and CF-16Fa	19 Chromium, 9 Nickel, free machining	70	485	30	205	25	—
CH-20 and CH-10	25 Chromium, 12 Nickel	70	485	30	205	30	—
CK-20	25 Chromium, 20 Nickel	65	450	28	195	30	—
CE-30	29 Chromium, 9 Nickel	80	550	40	275	10	—
CA-15 and CA-15M	12 Chromium	90	620	65	450	18	30
CB-30	20 Chromium	65	450	30	205	—	—
CC-50	28 Chromium	55	380	—	—	—	—

TABLE 18.7 Preheat and Tensile Requirements (*Continued*)

Grade	Type	Tensile Requirements: Tensile strength, min, ksi	Tensile strength, min, MPa	Yield strength, min, ksi	Yield strength, min, MPa	Elongation in 2 in (50 mm), min, %*	Reduction of area, min, %
CA-40	12 Chromium	100	690	70	485	15	25
CA-40F	12 Chromium, free machining	100	690	70	485	12	—
CF-3	19 Chromium, 9 nickel	70	485	30	205	35	—
CF10SMnN	17 Chromium, 8.5 nickel with nitrogen 9 Nickel	85	585	42	290	30	—
CF-3M	19 Chromium, 10 Nickel, with molybdenum	70	485	30	205	30	—
CF-3MN	19 Chromium, 10 Nickel, with molybdenum, and nitrogen	75	515	37	255	35	—
CG6MMN	Chromium-nickel-manganese-molybdenum	85	585	42	290	30	—
CG-8M	19 Chromium, 11 Nickel, with molybdenum	75	520	35	240	25	—
CN-3M		63	435	25	170	30	—
CN-7M	20 Chromium, 29 Nickel, with copper and molybdenum	62	425	25	170	35	—
CN-7MS	19 Chromium, 24 Nickel, with copper and molybdenum	70	485	30	205	35	—
CA-6NM	12 Chromium, 4 nickel	110	755	80	550	15	35
CD-4MCu		100	690	70	485	16	
CA-6N	11 Chromium, 7 nickel	140	965	135	930	15	50
CA-28MWV‡	12 Chromium, with molybdenum, tungsten, and vanadium	140	965	110	760	10	24
CK-3MCuN	20 Chromium 18 Nickel, with copper and molybdenum	80	550	38	260	35	—

* When ICI test bars are used in tensile testing as provided for in this specification, the gage length to reduced section diameter ratio shall be 4:1.

† For low ferrite or nonmagnetic castings of this grade, the following values shall apply; tensile strength, min, 65 ksi (450 MPa); yield point, min, 28 ksi (195 MPa).

‡ These mechanical properties apply only when heat treatment (1) has been used.

SOURCE: Reprinted with permission from the *Annual Book of ASTM Standards,* copyright 1992, American Society of Testing and Materials.

TABLE 18.8 Brinell Hardness Numbers*

(Ball 10 mm in Diameter, Applied Loads of 500, 1500, and 3000 kgf)

	Brinell hardness number				Brinell hardness number				Brinell hardness number				Brinell hardness number		
Diameter of indentation, mm	500-kgf load	1500-kgf load	3000-kgf load	Diameter of indentation, mm	500-kgf load	1500-kgf load	3000-kgf load	Diameter of indentation, mm	500-kgf load	1500-kgf load	3000-kgf load	Diameter of indentation, mm	500-kgf load	1500-kgf load	3000-kgf load
2.00	158	473	945	2.60	92.6	278	555	3.20	60.5	182	363	3.80	42.4	127	255
2.01	156	468	936	2.61	91.8	276	551	3.21	60.1	180	361	3.81	42.2	127	253
2.02	154	463	926	2.62	91.1	273	547	3.22	59.8	179	359	3.82	42.0	126	252
2.03	153	459	917	2.63	90.4	271	543	3.23	59.4	178	356	3.83	41.7	125	250
2.04	151	454	908	2.64	89.7	269	538	3.24	59.0	177	354	3.84	41.5	125	249
2.05	150	450	899	2.65	89.0	267	534	3.25	58.6	176	352	3.85	41.3	124	248
2.06	148	445	890	2.66	88.4	265	530	3.26	58.3	175	350	3.86	41.1	123	246
2.07	147	441	882	2.67	87.7	263	526	3.27	57.9	174	347	3.87	40.9	123	245
2.08	146	437	873	2.68	87.0	261	522	3.28	57.5	173	345	3.88	40.6	122	244
2.09	144	432	865	2.69	86.4	259	518	3.29	57.2	172	343	3.89	40.4	121	242
2.10	143	428	856	2.70	85.7	257	514	3.30	56.8	170	341	3.90	40.2	121	241
2.11	141	424	848	2.71	85.1	255	510	3.31	56.5	169	339	3.91	40.0	120	240
2.12	140	420	840	2.72	84.4	253	507	3.32	56.1	168	337	3.92	39.8	119	239
2.13	139	416	832	2.73	83.8	251	503	3.33	55.8	167	335	3.93	39.6	119	237
2.14	137	412	824	2.74	83.2	250	499	3.34	55.4	166	333	3.94	39.4	118	236
2.15	136	408	817	2.75	82.6	248	495	3.35	55.1	165	331	3.95	39.1	117	235
2.16	135	404	809	2.76	81.9	246	492	3.36	54.8	164	329	3.96	38.9	117	234
2.17	134	401	802	2.77	81.3	244	488	3.37	54.4	163	326	3.97	38.7	116	232
2.18	132	397	794	2.78	80.8	242	485	3.38	54.1	162	325	3.98	38.5	116	231
2.19	131	393	787	2.79	80.2	240	481	3.39	53.8	161	323	3.99	38.3	115	230
2.20	130	390	780	2.80	79.6	239	477	3.40	53.4	160	321	4.00	38.1	114	229
2.21	129	386	772	2.81	79.0	237	474	3.41	53.1	159	319	4.01	37.9	114	228

TABLE 18.8 Brinell Hardness Numbers* (*Continued*)

Diameter of indentation, mm	Brinell hardness number 500-kgf load	1500-kgf load	3000-kgf load	Diameter of indentation, mm	Brinell hardness number 500-kgf load	1500-kgf load	3000-kgf load	Diameter of indentation, mm	Brinell hardness number 500-kgf load	1500-kgf load	3000-kgf load	Diameter of indentation, mm	Brinell hardness number 500-kgf load	1500-kgf load	3000-kgf load
2.22	128	383	765	2.82	78.4	235	471	3.42	52.8	158	317	4.02	37.7	113	226
2.23	126	379	758	2.83	77.9	234	467	3.43	52.5	157	315	4.03	37.5	113	225
2.24	125	376	752	2.84	77.3	232	464	344	52.2	156	313	4.04	37.3	112	224
2.25	124	372	745	2.85	76.8	230	461	3.45	51.8	156	311	4.05	37.1	111	223
2.26	123	369	738	2.86	76.2	229	457	3.46	51.5	155	309	4.06	37.0	111	222
2.27	122	366	732	2.87	75.7	227	454	3.47	51.2	154	307	4.07	36.8	110	221
2.28	121	363	725	2.88	75.1	225	451	3.48	50.9	153	306	4.08	36.6	110	219
2.29	120	359	719	2.89	74.6	224	448	3.49	50.6	152	304	4.09	36.4	109	218
2.30	119	356	712	2.90	74.1	222	444	3.50	50.3	151	302	4.10	36.2	109	217
2.31	118	353	706	2.91	73.6	221	441	3.51	50.0	150	300	4.11	36.0	108	216
2.32	117	350	700	2.92	73.0	219	438	3.52	49.7	149	298	4.12	35.8	108	215
2.33	116	347	694	2.93	72.5	218	435	3.53	49.4	148	297	4.13	35.7	107	214
2.34	115	344	688	2.94	72.0	216	432	3.54	49.2	147	295	4.14	35.5	106	213
2.35	114	341	682	2.95	71.5	215	429	3.55	48.9	147	293	4.15	35.3	105	212
2.36	113	338	676	2.96	71.0	213	426	3.56	48.6	146	292	4.16	35.1	105	211
2.37	112	335	670	2.97	70.5	212	423	3.57	48.3	145	290	4.17	34.9	105	210
2.38	111	332	665	2.98	70.1	210	420	3.58	48.0	144	288	4.18	34.8	104	209
2.39	110	330	659	2.99	69.6	209	417	3.59	47.7	143	286	4.19	34.6	104	208
2.40	109	327	653	3.00	69.1	207	415	3.60	47.5	142	285	4.20	34.4	103	207
2.41	108	324	648	3.01	68.6	206	412	3.61	47.2	142	283	4.21	34.2	103	205
2.42	107	322	643	3.02	68.2	205	409	3.62	46.9	141	282	4.22	34.1	102	204
2.43	106	319	637	3.03	67.7	203	406	3.63	46.7	140	280	4.23	33.9	102	203
2.44	105	316	632	3.04	67.3	202	404	3.64	46.4	139	278	4.24	33.7	101	202

2.45	104	313	627	3.05	66.8	200	401	3.65	46.1	138	277	4.25	33.6	101	201
2.46	104	311	621	3.06	66.4	199	398	3.66	45.9	138	275	4.26	33.4	100	200
2.47	103	308	616	3.07	65.9	198	395	3.67	45.6	137	274	4.27	33.2	99.7	199
2.48	102	306	611	3.08	65.5	196	393	3.68	45.4	136	272	4.28	33.1	99.2	198
2.49	101	303	606	3.09	65.0	195	390	3.69	45.1	135	271	4.29	32.9	98.8	198
2.50	100	301	601	3.10	64.6	194	388	3.70	44.9	135	269	4.30	32.8	98.3	197
2.51	99.4	298	597	3.11	64.2	193	385	3.71	44.6	134	268	4.31	32.6	97.8	196
2.52	98.6	296	592	3.12	63.8	191	383	3.72	44.4	133	266	4.32	32.4	97.3	195
2.53	97.8	294	587	3.13	63.3	190	380	3.73	44.1	132	265	4.33	32.3	96.8	194
2.54	97.1	291	582	3.14	62.9	189	378	3.74	43.9	132	263	4.34	32.1	96.4	193
2.55	96.3	289	578	3.15	62.5	188	375	3.75	43.6	131	262	4.35	32.0	95.9	192
2.56	95.5	287	573	3.16	62.1	186	373	3.76	43.4	130	260	4.36	31.8	95.5	191
2.57	94.8	284	569	3.17	61.7	185	370	3.77	43.1	129	259	4.37	31.7	95.0	190
2.58	94.0	282	564	3.18	61.3	184	368	3.78	42.9	129	257	4.38	31.5	94.5	189
2.59	93.3	280	560	3.19	60.9	183	366	3.79	42.7	128	256	4.39	31.4	94.1	188
4.40	31.2	93.6	187	5.05	23.3	69.8	140	5.70	17.8	53.5	107	6.35	14.0	42.0	84.0
4.41	31.1	93.2	186	5.06	23.2	69.5	139	5.71	17.8	53.3	107	6.36	13.9	41.8	83.7
4.42	30.9	92.7	185	5.07	23.1	69.2	138	5.72	17.7	53.1	106	6.37	13.9	41.7	83.4
4.43	30.8	92.3	185	5.08	23.0	68.9	138	5.73	17.6	52.9	106	6.38	13.8	41.5	83.1
4.44	30.6	91.8	184	5.09	22.9	68.6	137	5.74	17.6	52.7	105	6.39	13.8	41.4	82.8
4.45	30.5	91.4	183	5.10	22.8	68.3	137	5.75	17.5	52.5	105	6.40	13.7	41.2	82.5
4.46	30.3	91.0	182	5.11	22.7	68.0	136	5.76	17.4	52.3	105	6.41	13.7	41.1	82.2
4.47	30.2	90.5	181	5.12	22.6	67.7	135	5.77	17.4	52.1	104	6.42	13.6	40.9	81.9
4.48	30.0	90.1	180	5.13	22.5	67.4	135	5.78	17.3	51.9	104	6.43	13.6	40.8	81.6
4.49	29.9	89.7	179	5.14	22.4	67.1	134	5.79	17.2	51.7	103	6.44	13.5	40.6	81.3
4.50	29.8	89.3	179	5.15	22.3	66.9	134	5.80	17.2	51.5	103	6.45	13.5	40.5	81.0
4.51	29.6	88.8	178	5.16	22.2	66.6	133	5.81	17.1	51.3	103	6.46	13.4	40.4	80.7
4.52	29.5	88.4	177	5.17	22.1	66.3	133	5.82	17.0	51.1	102	6.47	13.4	40.2	80.4
4.53	29.3	88.0	176	5.18	22.0	66.0	132	5.83	17.0	50.9	102	6.48	13.4	40.1	80.1
4.54	29.2	87.6	175	5.19	21.9	65.8	132	5.84	16.9	50.7	101	6.49	13.3	39.9	79.8
4.55	29.1	87.2	174	5.20	21.8	65.5	131	5.85	16.8	50.5	101	6.50	13.3	39.8	79.6
4.56	28.9	86.8	174	5.21	21.7	65.2	130	5.86	16.8	50.3	101	6.51	13.2	39.6	79.3
4.57	28.8	86.4	173	5.22	21.6	64.9	130	5.87	16.7	50.2	100	6.52	13.2	39.5	79.0
4.58	28.7	86.0	172	5.23	21.6	64.7	129	5.88	16.7	50.0	99.9	6.53	13.1	39.4	78.7
4.59	28.5	85.6	171	5.24	21.5	64.4	129	5.89	16.6	49.8	99.5	6.54	13.1	39.2	78.4

TABLE 18.8 Brinell Hardness Numbers* (*Continued*)

Diameter of indentation, mm	Brinell hardness number: 500-kgf load	1500-kgf load	3000-kgf load	Diameter of indentation, mm	Brinell hardness number: 500-kgf load	1500-kgf load	3000-kgf load	Diameter of indentation, mm	Brinell hardness number: 500-kgf load	1500-kgf load	3000-kgf load	Diameter of indentation, mm	Brinell hardness number: 500-kgf load	1500-kgf load	3000-kgf load
4.60	28.4	85.4	170	5.25	21.4	64.1	128	5.90	16.5	49.6	99.2	6.55	13.0	39.1	78.2
4.61	28.3	84.8	170	5.26	21.3	63.9	128	5.91	16.5	49.4	98.8	6.56	13.0	38.9	78.0
4.62	28.1	84.4	169	5.27	21.2	63.6	127	5.92	16.4	49.2	98.4	6.57	12.9	38.8	77.6
4.63	28.0	84.0	168	5.28	21.1	63.3	127	5.93	16.3	49.0	98.0	6.58	12.9	38.7	77.3
4.64	27.9	83.6	167	5.29	21.0	63.1	126	5.94	16.3	48.8	97.7	6.59	12.8	38.5	77.1
4.65	27.8	83.3	167	5.30	20.9	62.8	126	5.95	16.2	48.7	97.3	6.60	12.8	38.4	76.8
4.66	27.6	82.9	166	5.31	20.9	62.6	125	5.96	16.2	48.5	96.9	6.61	12.8	38.3	76.5
4.67	27.5	82.5	165	5.32	20.8	62.3	125	5.97	16.1	48.3	96.6	6.62	12.7	38.1	76.2
4.68	27.4	82.1	164	5.33	20.7	62.1	124	5.98	16.0	48.1	96.2	6.63	12.7	38.0	76.0
4.69	27.3	81.8	164	5.34	20.6	61.8	124	5.99	16.0	47.9	95.9	6.64	12.6	37.9	75.7
4.70	27.1	81.4	163	5.35	20.5	61.5	123	6.00	15.9	47.7	95.5	6.65	12.6	37.7	75.4
4.71	27.0	81.0	162	5.36	20.4	61.3	123	6.01	15.9	47.6	95.1	6.66	12.5	37.6	75.2
4.72	26.9	80.7	161	5.37	20.3	61.0	122	6.02	15.8	47.4	94.8	6.67	12.5	37.5	74.9
4.73	26.8	80.3	161	5.38	20.3	60.8	122	6.03	15.7	47.2	94.4	6.68	12.4	37.3	74.7
4.74	26.6	79.9	160	5.39	20.2	60.6	121	6.04	15.7	47.0	94.1	6.69	12.4	37.2	74.4
4.75	26.5	79.6	159	5.40	20.1	60.3	121	6.05	15.6	46.8	93.7	6.70	12.4	37.1	74.1
4.76	26.4	79.2	158	5.41	20.0	60.1	120	6.06	15.6	46.7	93.4	6.71	12.3	36.9	73.9
4.77	26.3	78.9	158	5.42	19.9	59.8	120	6.07	15.5	46.5	93.0	6.72	12.3	36.8	73.6
4.78	26.2	78.5	157	5.43	19.9	59.6	119	6.08	15.4	46.3	92.7	6.73	12.2	36.7	73.4
4.79	26.1	78.2	156	5.44	19.8	59.3	119	6.09	15.4	46.2	92.3	6.74	12.2	36.6	73.1
4.80	25.9	77.8	156	5.45	19.7	59.1	118	6.10	15.3	46.0	92.0	6.75	12.1	36.4	72.8
4.81	25.8	77.5	155	5.46	19.6	58.9	118	6.11	15.3	45.8	91.7	6.76	12.1	36.3	72.6
4.82	25.7	77.1	154	5.47	19.5	58.6	117	6.12	15.2	45.7	91.3	6.77	12.1	36.2	72.3

4.83	25.6	76.8	154	5.48	19.5	58.4	117	6.13	15.2	45.5	91.0	6.78	12.0	36.0	72.1
4.84	25.5	76.4	153	5.49	19.4	58.2	116	6.14	15.1	45.3	90.6	6.79	12.0	35.9	71.8
4.85	25.4	76.1	152	5.50	19.3	57.9	116	6.15	15.1	45.2	90.3	6.80	11.9	35.8	71.6
4.86	25.3	75.8	152	5.51	19.2	57.7	115	6.16	15.0	45.0	90.0	6.81	11.9	35.7	71.3
4.87	25.1	75.4	151	5.52	19.2	57.5	115	6.17	14.9	44.8	89.6	6.82	11.8	35.5	71.1
4.88	25.0	75.1	150	5.53	19.1	57.2	114	6.18	14.9	44.7	89.3	6.83	11.8	35.4	70.8
4.89	24.9	74.8	150	5.54	19.0	57.0	114	6.19	14.8	44.5	89.0	6.84	11.8	35.3	70.6
4.90	24.8	74.4	149	5.55	18.9	56.8	114	6.20	14.7	44.3	88.7	6.86	11.7	35.2	70.4
4.91	24.7	74.1	148	5.56	18.9	56.6	113	6.21	14.7	44.2	88.3	6.86	11.7	35.1	70.1
4.92	24.6	73.8	148	5.57	18.8	56.3	113	6.22	14.7	44.0	88.0	6.87	11.6	34.9	69.9
4.93	24.5	73.5	147	5.58	18.7	56.1	112	6.23	14.6	43.8	87.7	6.88	11.6	34.8	69.6
4.94	24.4	73.2	146	5.59	18.6	55.9	112	6.24	14.6	43.7	87.4	6.89	11.6	34.7	69.4
4.95	24.3	72.8	146	5.60	18.6	55.7	111	6.25	14.5	43.5	87.1	6.90	11.5	34.6	69.2
4.96	24.2	72.5	145	5.61	18.5	55.5	111	6.26	14.5	43.4	86.7	6.91	11.5	34.5	68.9
4.97	24.1	72.2	144	5.62	18.4	55.2	110	6.27	14.4	43.2	86.4	6.92	11.4	34.3	68.7
4.98	24.0	71.9	144	5.63	18.3	55.0	110	6.28	14.4	43.1	86.1	6.93	11.4	34.2	68.4
4.99	23.9	71.6	143	5.64	18.3	54.8	110	6.29	14.3	42.9	85.8	6.94	11.4	34.1	68.2
5.00	23.8	71.3	143	5.65	18.2	54.6	109	6.30	14.2	42.7	85.5	6.95	11.3	34.0	68.0
5.01	23.7	71.0	142	5.66	18.1	54.4	109	6.31	14.2	42.6	85.2	6.96	11.3	33.9	67.7
5.02	23.6	70.7	141	5.67	18.1	54.2	108	6.32	14.1	42.4	84.9	6.97	11.3	33.8	67.5
5.03	23.5	70.4	141	5.68	18.0	54.0	108	6.33	14.1	42.3	84.6	6.98	11.2	33.6	67.3
5.04	23.4	70.1	140	5.69	17.9	53.7	107	6.34	14.0	42.1	84.3	6.99	11.2	33.5	67.0

* Prepared by the Engineering Mechanics Section, Institute for Standards Technology.

The tonnage and size of the clamping machine for injection molding plastics are determined by the volume of plastic to be injected at one time (a single "shot"). A machine that handles parts up to 20 in^3 would be considered of moderate size, while a machine required to injection mold parts with a volume of 60 in^3 would be considered large. Clamping machines are made in sizes up to hundreds of tons clamping capacity, and these machines are usually found at the larger plastic molding manufacturers.

18.6 Extrusions

An extruded shape is one in which the material being extruded is pushed, under high pressure and high temperature, through a set of extrusion dies that have the shape of a cross section of the part. Extrusion is similar to drawing, except that in drawing, the drawn part is pulled out of or through the dies or series of dies of progressive sizes. The material is cold worked more effectively when it is drawn rather than extruded.

Aluminum alloys are particularly well suited for the extrusion processes. Very large, high-tonnage extrusion presses are required for the extrusion of aluminum and its alloys. Generally, two classes or grades of aluminum extrusions are widely available, these being structural aluminum and architectural aluminum shapes. These two classes of extrusions are available in the following alloys and tempers:

Class	Shape	Alloy, temper, and specification
Structural	Angles	6061-T6, ASTM B308
	Channels	6061-T6, ASTM B308
	Tees	6061-T6, ASTM B308
	Zees	6061-T6, ASTM B308
	H beams and I beams	6061-T6, ASTM B308
	Wide-flange beams	6061-T6, ASTM B308
Architectural	Angles	6063-T52, ASTM B221
	Channels	6063-T52, ASTM B221
	Tees	6063-T52, ASTM B221
	Zees	6063-T52, ASTM B221

Aluminum alloy extrusions are also available in the following standard shapes:

- Round rod
- Square bar
- Rectangular bar
- Hexagonal bar
- Round tube
- Square tube
- Rectangular tube

The alloy designations of the above-listed shapes may be one of the following:

- 2011
- 2017
- 2024
- 6061
- 6063

An aluminum-alloy extrusion may be designed to any practical shape that the extrusion dies may accommodate and are usually limited to the designers' imagination and ingenuity and the size of the part. Some of the standard extruded shapes which are available from various sources nationwide are shown in Fig. 18.25. The temper designations and lengths available are also shown in the figure.

A table of distances across flats for squares, hexagons, and octagons is given in Fig. 18.26. This will prove useful and time saving when these dimensions need to be known and you do not wish to calculate them by using the figures shown in Secs. 2.3 and 2.4 in this *Handbook.*

Plastic extrusions. A great many plastic-extruded shapes are available from the plastic manufacturers, whose catalogs may be obtained through such trade magazines as *The American Machinist, Machine Design, Product Design and Development, Modern Machine Shop,* and others. If you work with or need plastic-extruded shapes, keep a series of these catalogs in your reference files. The plastic-extruded shapes not only make the design job easier, but they also enhance the appearance of the final product and facilitate assembly in many cases.

18.7 Powder-Metal Technology

Powder-metal parts are made by compressing a highly purified metallic powder in a set of dies under extremely high pressure and then fusing the particles in an oven under controlled high temperature. This compression process compacts the powder metal until the part is approximately 90 percent the density of the solid metal or alloy. The density of the part can be controlled to an extent that the open pores in the powder-metal part, after fusion, may be impregnated with lubricants or filler resins and binders. The well-known sintered-bronze journal bearings with impregnated lubrication are prime examples of powder-metal technology.

Powder-metal parts may be made of aluminum alloys, copper alloys, steels, and stainless steels. Other metals and alloys also can be used in powder-metal processing.

The modern powder-metal part may be impregnated with resins and binders, which make possible the application of electroplated finishes such as copper, zinc, nickel, and chromium. If the part is made of one of the corrosion-resistant stainless steels, the plating process may be eliminated.

Parts may be produced using powder metal that normally would be difficult to machine. An example of powder-metal parts is shown in Fig. 18.27. Here are shown a group of metal parts, most of which would be difficult to make using other processes. The parts shown could be made using the investment casting process or machining techniques but would be costly and time-consuming to produce. Figure 18.28 is a closer view of the three small three-pointed parts, which shows a minute hole in the center of the parts. Each division on the scale shown in Fig. 18.28 is equal to 0.020 in ($\frac{1}{50}$th of an inch). One of the parts shown in Fig. 18.28 had secondary machining operations performed on it (threading). All the parts shown in both figures are easy and economical to produce using powder-metal technology.

Design of powder-metal parts

The design and manufacturing of powder-metal parts is not difficult if the basic rules of powder-metal part design are followed and if the powder-metal part manufacturer is consulted during the design stages. The part manufacturer will advise you if the part can be produced as designed and what remedial actions to take or design changes are needed to produce the part. The manufacturer also will advise you of the availability of the different metals and alloys for producing the part.

Basic rules for powder-metal part design

- Keep the outline elements of the part on lines parallel to the part axis or in the direction of compression of the male die.
- Do not design parts with reverse angles along the axis (the part cannot be extracted from the dies if this occurs).
- Keep wall sections or webs as thick as possible.
- Single tapered holes in the part are possible when the direction of taper allows extraction from the dies after compression of the powder metal.
- Limit the size or volume of the part to that which may be produced with available machinery.

Figure 18.22 Typical intricate plastic-cast parts.

(Text continued on page 1359.)

Figure 18.23 Mixing and dispensing sections of epoxy casting equipment.

Figure 18.24 Complete assembly of epoxy casting machinery: (*far left*) oven; (*center*) die-clamping machine; (*far right*) dispensing section; (*center*) background process control panel (CNC).

STANDARD ANGLES ①

ANGLES—UNEQUAL LEGS, EXTRUDED
Alloy 6061-T6 • Length—25 ft

Dimensions, in.			Est wt per ft, lb
A	B	t	
N 1-1/4	3/4	3/32	.21
N 1-1/4	1	1/8	.31
N 1-1/2	3/4	1/8	.31
1-1/2	3/4	N 3/16	.46
N 1-1/2	1	5/32	.43
1-1/2	1	N 1/4	.66
1-1/2	1-1/4	1/8	.38
1-1/2	1-1/4	3/16	.57
1-1/2	1-1/4	1/4	.74
1-3/4	1-1/4	1/8	.42
1-3/4	1-1/4	3/16	.62
1-3/4	1-1/4	1/4	.81
2	1-1/2	1/8	.50
2	1-1/2	3/16	.73
2	1-1/2	1/4	.96
2	1-1/2	3/8	1.38
N 2-1/2	1-1/2	3/16	.85
2-1/2	1-1/2	1/4	1.11
2-1/2	1-1/2	N 5/16	1.36
2-1/2	2	1/8	.65
2-1/2	2	3/16	.96
2-1/2	2	1/4	1.26

Dimensions, in.			Est wt per ft, lb
A	B	t	
2-1/2	2	5/16	1.55
2-1/2	2	3/8	1.83
3	2	3/16	1.07
3	2	1/4	1.40
3	2	5/16	1.73
3	2	3/8	2.05
3	2	N 7/16	2.35
3	2-1/2	1/4	1.54
3	2-1/2	5/16	1.90
3	2-1/2	3/8	2.25
3-1/2	2-1/2	1/4	1.68
3-1/2	2-1/2	5/16	2.08
3-1/2	2-1/2	3/8	2.47
3-1/2	2-1/2	N 1/2	3.23
3-1/2	3	1/4	1.84
3-1/2	3	5/16	2.28
3-1/2	3	N 3/8	2.70
4	3	1/4	1.99
4	3	5/16	2.46
4	3	3/8	2.93

Dimensions, in.			Est wt per ft, lb
A	B	t	
4	3	1/2	3.83
4	3	5/8	4.69
N 4	3-1/2	3/8	3.13
4	3-1/2	N 1/2	4.10
5	3	3/8	3.35
5	3	1/2	4.40
5	3-1/2	5/16	3.01
5	3-1/2	3/8	3.58
5	3-1/2	N 7/16	4.15
5	3-1/2	1/2	4.70
5	3-1/2	5/8	5.79
6	3-1/2	5/16	3.39
6	3-1/2	N 3/8	4.04
6	3-1/2	1/2	5.31
6	4	3/8	4.24
6	4	N 7/16	4.91
6	4	1/2	5.58
6	4	5/8	6.88
6	4	3/4	8.48
N 8	6	5/8	9.84
8	6	N 11/16	10.76
8	6	3/4	11.68

① Angle sections listed as "standard" are approximations of American Standard sections. For elements of sections and detailed dimensions, consult *Alcoa Structural Handbook*.
N Not stocked at plant.

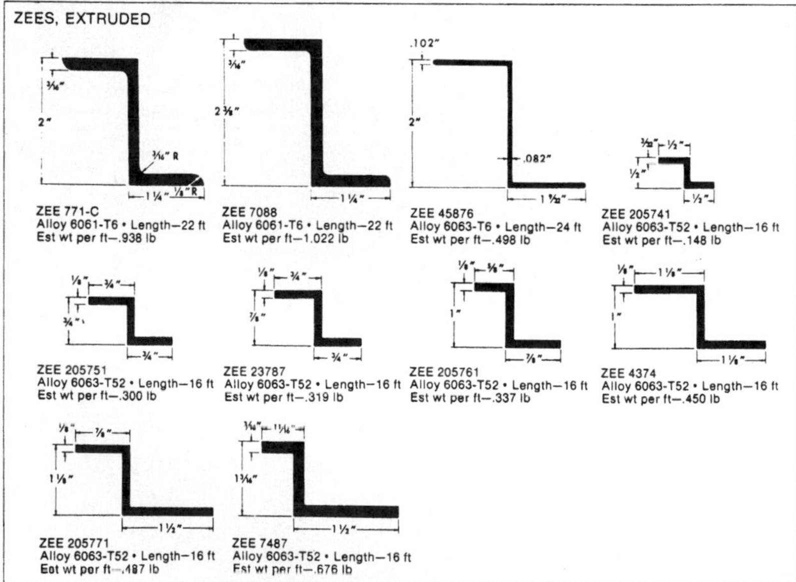

Figure 18.25 Samples of standard aluminum extruded shapes.

DISTANCES ACROSS CORNERS OF SQUARES, HEXAGONS & OCTAGONS

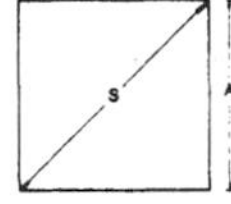

S=1.414A

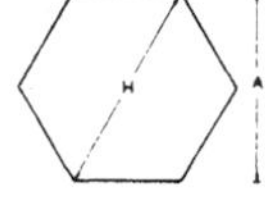

H=1.155A

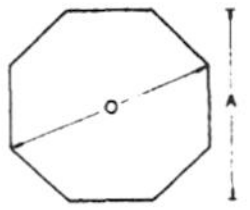

O=1.082A

A Size in Inches	Distance Across Corners in Inches S Square	H Hexagon	O Octagon
1/8	.177	.144	.135
3/16	.265	.217	.203
1/4	.354	.289	.271
5/16	.442	.361	.338
3/8	.530	.433	.406
7/16	.619	.505	.474
1/2	.707	.577	.541
9/16	.795	.650	.609
5/8	.884	.722	.677
11/16	.972	.794	.744
3/4	1.061	.866	.812
13/16	1.149	.938	.879
7/8	1.237	1.010	.947
15/16	1.326	1.083	1.015
1	1.414	1.155	1.082
1 1/16	1.503	1.227	1.150
1 1/8	1.591	1.299	1.218
1 3/16	1.679	1.371	1.285
1 1/4	1.768	1.443	1.353
1 5/16	1.856	1.516	1.421
1 3/8	1.945	1.588	1.488
1 7/16	2.033	1.660	1.556
1 1/2	2.121	1.732	1.624
1 9/16	2.210	1.804	1.691
1 5/8	2.298	1.876	1.759
1 11/16	2.386	1.949	1.827
1 3/4	2.475	2.021	1.894
1 13/16	2.563	2.093	1.962
1 7/8	2.652	2.165	2.031
1 15/16	2.740	2.237	2.097
2	2.828	2.309	2.165
2 1/16	2.917	2.382	2.232
2 1/8	3.005	2.454	2.300
2 3/16	3.094	2.526	2.368
2 1/4	3.182	2.598	2.435
2 5/16	3.270	2.670	2.503
2 3/8	3.359	2.742	2.571
2 7/16	3.447	2.815	2.638
2 1/2	3.536	2.887	2.706
2 9/16	3.624	2.959	2.774
2 5/8	3.712	3.031	2.841
2 11/16	3.801	3.103	2.909
2 3/4	3.889	3.175	2.977
2 13/16	3.977	3.248	3.044
2 7/8	4.066	3.320	3.112
2 15/16	4.154	3.392	3.180
3	4.243	3.464	3.247
3 1/8	4.419	3.608	3.383
3 1/4	4.596	3.753	3.518
3 3/8	4.773	3.897	3.653
3 1/2	4.950	4.041	3.788
3 5/8	5.126	4.186	3.924
3 3/4	5.303	4.330	4.059
3 7/8	5.480	4.474	4.194
4	5.657	4.619	4.330
4 1/4	6.010	4.907	4.600
4 1/2	6.364	5.196	4.871
4 3/4	6.717	5.485	5.141
5	7.071	5.774	5.412
5 1/4	7.425	6.062	5.683
5 1/2	7.778	6.351	5.953
5 3/4	8.132	6.640	6.224
6	8.485	6.928	6.494

Figure 18.26 Dimensions of squares, hexagons, and octagons.

Figure 18.27 Samples of powder-metal parts.

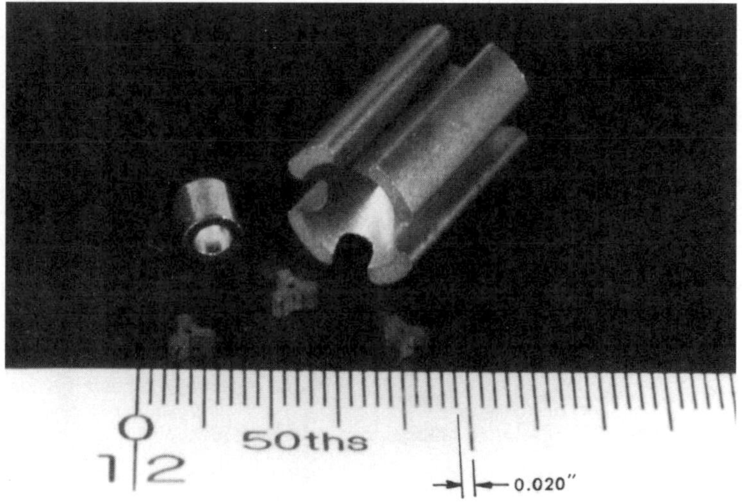

Figure 18.28 Close-up view of powder-metal parts. Note scale.

- Do not specify electroplated finishes unless necessary (the part may be produced in a corrosion-resistant alloy if necessary).
- Holes in the part may be controlled to close tolerances.
- Check with the part manufacturer to ascertain if the part can sustain the imposed stress loads anticipated.
- The outline accuracy of parts can be closely controlled.

Some of the powder-metal part producers can provide design manuals or brochures to the design engineer which outline in more detail the design procedures for powder-metal parts.

Chapters 9 and 10 show photographs of parts that are prime candidates for powder-metal technology. Some of these parts are machined and some are die stamped, and in many instances the part would have been more economical to produce in powder metal. Stamping dies are usually much more expensive than the dies required for producing the same part in powder metal. Secondary operations such as deburring and electroplating could have been eliminated using corrosion-resistant powder metal to produce the parts.

Small-part design always should be reviewed to see if the design requirements can be met using powder-metal technology. Powder-metal technology is much further advanced today than in the past, where it was mainly used to produce journal bearings with impregnated lubrication.

Chapter

19

Plating Practices and Finishes for Metals

Commercial products and equipment in all classifications require finishes of one type or other. These finishes range from basic oxide coatings to the various paints and plastics to electrodeposited metals such as copper, chromium, nickel, etc.

The finish or plating used on any particular part should contribute to the engineering qualities of the final product and not merely to its cosmetic appeal. The desired finish could include weather protection, resistance to corrosive chemicals, heat resistance, electrical conductivity, wear resistance, and improved lubrication qualities.

It is the design engineer's responsibility to specify the finish characteristics and specifications on a part or assembly. Designers should be aware of the types of finishes and plating processes that are commercially available and how to specify them on the design and detail part drawings. Arbitrary selection of a finish or plating and its thickness range can lead to many design problems relating to corrosion, cost, and dimensional interference.

This chapter will familiarize the designer, engineer, and other personnel in the metalworking industries with the common finishing processes, procedures for specifying thicknesses of platings, and the appropriate industrial standard specifications that control these finishes.

19.1 Finishes

The finishing processes and methods in common use for engineering applications are as follows:

Mechanical finishing

- Sanding or grinding
- Brushing (scratch and satin)
- Sandblasting
- Shot peening and tumbling (metal or ceramic ball)
- Burnishing
- Mechanical powder plating
- Polishing

Chemical finishing

- Etching
- Bonderite
- Alodine
- Iridite
- Phosphatizing
- Passivating (stainless steels)
- Black oxide
- Blueing
- Teflon coating
- Other plastic coatings

Electrolytic oxides

- Sulfuric acid anodize (Alumilite, Alcoa process)
- Chromic acid anodize (aerospace and other applications)
- Martin hardcoat anodize (Martin Marietta process)
- Electropolishing

Note: Anodizing may be performed on aluminum, magnesium, titanium, and zinc.

Electroplating

- Copper plate
- Cadmium plate
- Chromium plate (bright, hard, and black)
- Nickel plate (bright, black, and chromium-nickel)
- Gold plate
- Silver plate
- Tin plate (tin-cadmium, tin-lead, and tin-nickel)
- Indium plate
- Rhodium plate
- Palladium plate
- Zinc plate (nickel-zinc, zinc with chromate)
- Lead plate

The base metals and their alloys that are commonly electroplated are iron, steel, stainless steel (more commonly passivated), aluminum, copper, brass, bronze, titanium, and magnesium.

Hot-dip plating

- Hot-dip tin
- Hot-dip zinc
- Hot-dip aluminum
- Hot-dip lead

19.2 Corrosion of Metals: Principles

The design engineer has four choices when planning for corrosion resistance of a metal part:

1. Use a corrosion-resistant alloy steel.
2. Use a nonferrous, noncorroding metal alloy.
3. Use plated steel or anodized alloys.
4. Use a chemically coated, painted, or plastic-coated metal part (ferrous or nonferrous).

The third choice is usually the most economical, although it may not be the best choice. Plated-steel parts are the most common and suffice for most applications, although the choice of a more expensive alloy may be mandatory as a result of required antimagnetic properties, low electrical resistivity, restrictions on the weight of the part (such as in aerospace vehicles), and other considerations.

Basic principles of corrosion of metals and metallic alloys. All metals and alloys have a specific relative electrical potential. When metals of different electrical potentials, such as steel and copper, are in contact in the presence of moisture (electrolyte), a low-energy electric current flows from the metal having the higher potential to the one having the lower potential. This is called *galvanic action.* One result is that corrosion of the metal having the higher potential (steel in our example) is accelerated.

The mechanism is an anode reaction, a cathode reaction, the conduction of electrons through the metal from anode to cathode, and the conduction of ions through the electrolyte solution. Corrosion occurs in the anode area, while the cathode area is protected.

It is important to know from which of two metals current will flow. Figure 19.1 shows the galvanic or electromotive series for common engineering materials that gives potential differences (in volts) with respect to the hydrogen electrode. The chart in Fig. 19.1 will immediately show the difference in potential for these materials. The greater the potential difference, the greater is the galvanic action or the faster will the corrosion progress. By convention, the anode is considered positive and the cathode negative. Gold is the most noble metal, and magnesium one of the least noble metals.

If you study Fig. 19.1 closely, you will see why the different electrochemical batteries were derived. The potential differences between nickel, cadmium, zinc, iron, lead, and silver are such that electrochemical battery systems were able to evolve around these elements when used with the proper electrolytic solutions.

Corrosion has been estimated as causing over $125 billion in damages per year in the United States alone. Corrosion is at work 24 hours a day, 365 days a year and is a never-ending problem. Authorities on corrosion problems believe that much of this damage and loss can be prevented if design engineers pay closer attention to potential corrosion problems during the design process. Thinking about corrosion problems while selecting the design materials is the first step a product designer should undertake.

For example, the selection of high-strength steels to go into an environment containing sulfides or raw hydrogen is a grave design mistake. The high-strength steels will fail in these environments, although the authorities are not quite sure why this takes place, except that hydrogen embrittlement will occur (Source: J. Kruger, professor of materials science and engineering, Johns Hopkins University).

The use of dissimilar metals is another often-cited cause of corrosion problems. The welding of stainless steels which are not low in carbon content is another cause of stress-induced corrosion. Austenitic stainless steels with high nickel content and low carbon are recommended for welding applications (AISI 304, AISI 304L, AISI 316, and others).

One of the best books for design engineers to use as a reference for corrosion problems is *Design and Corrosion Control,* by V. R. Pludek (Macmillan, 1977).

Electrochemical equivalents for various metals. The electrochemical equivalents and other related data for the various plating metals and alloys are shown in Fig. 19.2. If you study the data for chromium, you will see why this metal is a difficult metal to plate, since it takes much electrical energy for thin coatings. Cadmium, on the other hand, is an easy metal to plate, but it is a toxic element, as are its salts.

Electroplating practice. The table in Fig. 19.3 lists the common plating metals and alloys and their possible baths, uses, and plating requirements. Procedures for actually performing different plating operations will be shown in a later section. Many of the plating processes and procedures are proprietary, their procedures being closely guarded trade secrets. Platings such as bright chromium, black chromium, gold, nickel-chromium, and others use proprietary procedures which are not published in any book. Plating has been called a "black art," and you will understand why when you try to obtain information on the exact processes and procedures used in some of the industrial plating practices. Plating procedures are difficult and must be closely controlled to exacting standards if the finished article is to be of high quality.

Galvanic/Electromotive Series - (for common engineering materials)

Engineering Material	Potential
Magnesium & magnesium alloys	-2.37v
Aluminum (1100 series)	-1.66
Zinc	-0.76
Chromium	-0.74
Type 304 stainless steel (active)	------
Type 316 stainless steel (active)	------
Steel, iron, cast iron	-0.41
Aluminum (2024)	------
Cadmium	-0.40
Nickel	-0.23
Tin	-0.14
Lead	-0.13
Copper	+0.34
Silver solder	------
Nickel (passive)	------
Chromium-iron (passive)	------
Type 304 & 316 Stainless steel (passive)	------
Silver	+0.80
Titanium	------
Platinum	+1.20
Gold	+1.50

Figure 19.1 Galvanic/electromotive series.

Electrochemical Equivalents and Related Data - Based on 100% Current Efficiency

Metal	mg/coulomb	gm/amp hr	oz/amp hr	Specific Gravity	oz/sq ft for 0.001 in	amp hr to deposit 0.001"/sq ft ♦	Symbol
Cadmium	0.58	2.10	0.074	8.64	0.72	9.73	Cd
Chromium	0.09	0.32	0.011	7.10	0.59	51.8	Cr
Copper	0.33	1.19	0.042	8.92	0.74	17.7	Cu
Gold	0.68	2.45	0.087	19.3	1.61	18.6	Au
Iron	0.29	1.04	0.037	7.90	0.66	17.9	Fe
Lead	1.07	3.87	0.136	11.3	0.94	6.91	Pb
Nickel	0.30	1.10	0.039	8.90	0.74	19.0	Ni
Palladium	0.28	0.10	0.035	12.0	0.10	28.6	Pd
Platinum	0.51	1.82	0.065	21.4	1.78	27.6	Pt
Rhodium	0.27	0.10	0.034	12.5	1.04	30.8	Rh
Silver	1.12	4.02	0.142	10.5	0.88	6.20	Ag
Tin	0.31	1.11	0.039	7.30	0.61	15.6	Sn
Zinc	0.34	1.22	0.43	7.10	0.59	13.7	Zn

NOTE: ♦ Equals specific gravity x 0.08323

Figure 19.2 Electrochemical equivalents and related data.

Electroplating Practice - Average operating conditions

Plating Metal	Typical Uses	Plating Solution Type	Plating Bath Temp. °F	Current Density Amps/ft²	Volts DC	Throwing Power	Time to Deposit 0.001"
Cadmium	Protection	Cyanide	70-95	15-45	1-4	Good	20 min.
Chromium	Decorative, Engineering (Hard), Cylinder liners	Chromic acid	120	200-250	6-8	Poor	2 hours
Copper	Electroforming,	Acid	75-120	15-40	1-2	Fair	35 min
	Undercoat	Cyanide	75-100	5-15	1.5-3	Good	90 min
	Step-off for casehardening	Rochelle	140-160	20-60	2-3	Good	45 min
Gold	Decorative, Electronics, PC boards	Cyanide	120-160	5-15	2-6	Good	......
		Proprietary	......	......	......	......	......
Indium	Bearing surfaces	Cyanide	70-75	10-150	......	Good	......
		Sulfate	70-75	20	......	Poor	......
		Fluoborate	70-90	50-100	......	Good	......
Iron	Electroforming,	Chloride	190	60	......	......	20 min
	Repair	Sulfate	70-75	20	......	......	1 hour
Lead	Protection Bearing surfaces	Fluoborate	70-75	10-80	0.5	Good	40 min
Nickel	Protection, Decorative, Base coat for chromium	Sulfate-chloride Sulfamate Fluoborate	75-100	Varies	0.5-3	Fair	30 min
Rhodium	Decorative, Optical	Sulfate Phosphate	110-120	10-80	2.5-5	......	......
Silver	Protective, Decorative, Electrical contacts	Cyanide	80	5-15	1	Good	......
Tin	Protective,	Sulfate	70-75	40	1-3	Fair	15 min

	Food & dairy,	Fluoborate	75-100	50	......	Good	10 min
	Bearings,	Stannate	150-190	40	4-8	Excellent	30 min
Zinc	Protective	Sulfate	75-100	15-400	......	Fair	10 min
		Cyanide	100	10-50	......	Good	40 min
			Alloys				
Brass	Rubber bonding, Decorative	Cyanide	75-100	3-10	2-3	Good	......
Bronze	Decorative, Base for chromium, Stop-off for steel	Cyanide-stannate	155	20-100	3-6	Excellent	30 min
Lead-tin	Bearings Solderability, Electrotyping	Fluoborate	70-75	60	1-2	Good	......
Tin-zinc	Solderability	Cyanide-stannate	150	10-75	4-5	Excellent	30 min
Tin-nickel	Printed circuits	Chloride-fluoride	150	25	1-2	Excellent	30 min

Figure 19.3 Electroplating practices table.

19.3 Electroplating Data and Specifications

19.3.1 Electroplating and oxide layer thickness ranges

Many plating thickness specifications call for plating thicknesses in micrometers (μm), but others may be specified in mils (0.001 in = 1 mil)

$$1\ \mu\text{m} = 0.00004\ \text{in} \quad \text{or} \quad \frac{4}{100}\ \text{mils (0.04 mil)}$$

$$25.4\ \mu\text{m} = 0.001\ \text{in} = 1\ \text{mil}$$

$$5\ \mu\text{m} = 0.0002\ \text{in} = 0.2\ \text{mil} = \frac{2}{10}\ \text{mil}$$

Both measurement units are given in the following listings, which summarize in outline form thickness specifications for various platings and coatings on a number of base-metal types.

19.3.2 Anodic coating thickness (anodized parts)

Aluminum

ASTM B 580-79

Type A hard coat	2.0 mil (50 μm)
B architectural	0.7 mil (18 μm)
D auto exterior	0.3 mil (8 μm)
E interior, a	0.2 mil (5 μm)
F interior, b	0.1 mil (3 μm)
G chromic acid	0.04 mil (1 μm)

Mil-A-8625C

Chromic acid	0.05–0.3 mil (1.3–8 μm)
Sulfuric acid	0.1–1.0 mil (3–30 μm)
Hard coat	0.5–4.5 mil (13–114 μm)

Magnesium

AMS 2478B

Acid, full coat	0.9–1.6 mil (23–41 μm)

Mil-M-45202C

Light HAE	0.1–0.3 mil (3–8 μm)
Heavy HAE	1.3–1.7 mil (33–43 μm)

19.3.3 Electroplating thicknesses and specifications

Cadmium plate

Range: 0.2 to 1.0 mil (5–25 μm)

Specification reference: ASTM A 165-80

Note: Cadmium metal is toxic, as are its salts. Use may be restricted.

Chromium plate

Range: 0.01 to 6.0 mil (0.3–150 μm)

Decorative: 0.01 mil (0.3 μm)

Engineering: 2 mil (50 μm)

Specify hard chrome on the drawing for corrosion resistance.

Heavy chrome plating (4–6 mil) range will have porosity.

Specification reference: Fed QQ-C-320B

Copper plate

Range: 0.1 to 5 mil (3–125 μm)

Specification reference: Mil-C-14550A

Used as a base for other platings.

Gold plate

Range: 0.02 to 1.5 mil (0.5–38 μm) in eight thickness classes

Specification reference: Mil-G-45204B

Nickel plate

Range: 0.2 to 7.9 mil (5–200 μm) engineering coatings

Specification reference: ASTM B 689-81 (may be soft or hard deposited within other specifications)

Nickel with chromium plate on steel

Range: 0.4 to 1.6 mil nickel; 0.01 mil chromium

Kinds of coatings include bright, dull, and layered.

Specification reference: ASTM B 456-79

Also covers nickel with chromium on copper and copper alloys.

Rhodium plate

Range: 0.008 to 0.25 mil (0.2–6.4 μm) engineering coatings

Specification reference: ASTM B 634-78

Palladium plate

Range: 0.05 to 0.2 mil (1.3–5 μm)

Specification reference: ASTM B 679-80

Silver plate

Range: 0.04 to 1.6 mil (1–40 μm)

Types include mat finish, bright finish, tarnish resistant (chromate-treated)

Specification reference: ASTM B 700-81

Note: Silver plating of electric current–carrying parts such as switch blades, breaker contacts, and other sliding parts is generally given as 0.2 mil (5 μm), except where industry specifications may call for 3 mil (76 μm). The 3-mil coating is more effective on surfaces subject to heavy friction, such as sliding electrical contacts.

Tin plate

Range: 0.2 to 1.2 mil (5–30 μm)

Specification reference: ASTM B 545-72

Note: On electrical switch gear and other industrial equipment, 3-mil thickness is usually specified for service at paper mills and other environments where hydrogen sulfide in the atmosphere corrodes silver and other platings.

Zinc plating on steel

Range: 0.2 to 1 mil (5–25 μm) service conditions 1 through 4

The standard general thickness on most parts is 0.2 mil (0.0002 in). For severe service, the plating thickness should be 13 to 15 μm or 0.00057 in, or 6/10 mil (0.0006 in). Hot-dip coatings of 1 mil (0.001 in) are given to parts that are subject to extremely severe service.

Specification reference: ASTM B 633-78

Note: Bright zinc plating on steel parts (usually sheet metal and machined parts) is often given a yellow chromate conversion coating after the zinc plate. This process imparts a gold, iridescent appearance. Many commercial parts are given this treatment for corrosion resistance in lieu of painting. Conversion coatings are also available for the following metals: silver, copper and its alloys, tin, aluminum, magnesium, zinc-base die-casting alloys, and electroplated chromium.

During the conversion process, a complex chromium metal gel forms on the part surface, which contains hexavalent and trivalent chromium. When the soft gel coating dries, it becomes hard and somewhat abrasion resistant. This then forms what is the preferred plating and coating for many engineering applications.

19.3.4 Plating metals: Characteristics and properties

Copper

Melting point: 1083°C (1981°F)

Specific gravity: 8.96 at 20°C

Reddish colored, malleable, and ductile metal. Excellent conductor of heat and electric current. Good corrosion resistance. Used as a plating base on irons and steels, and for other plating metals such as chromium, tin, and nickel.

Cadmium

Melting point: 320.9°C (609.6°F)

Specific gravity: 8.65 at 20°C

Soft, bluish white metal, similar to zinc in appearance. Cadmium is toxic, as are its compounds. Being replaced by zinc in many plating applications due to its toxic nature. Used to plate mechanical fasteners, etc. but should not be specified unless required by special application.

Chromium

Melting point: 1890°C (3434°F)

Specific gravity: 7.19 at 20°C

Steel-gray, lustrous, and very hard metal. On a scale of 1 to 10, it would be 9, with only diamond at 10. Hexavalent chromium compounds are toxic. Excellent corrosion resistance for many applications. Attacked by hydrochloric acid, in which it dissolves. Heavily plated deposits become porous on the outer layers. Used to plate hand tools, surgical instruments, decorative trim, cutting tools and drills, and wear-resistant surfaces.

Nickel

Melting point: 1453°C (2647°F)

Specific gravity: 8.90 at 20°C

Nickel is hard, malleable, ductile, slightly ferromagnetic, and a fair conductor of heat and electric current. Silvery-white–colored metal that will take a high polish. Excellent corrosion resistance. Used to plate handguns, hand tools, decorative trim, and corrosion-resistant containers.

Gold

Melting point: 1063°C (1945°F)

Specific gravity: 19.32 at 20°C

Yellow, soft metal which is extremely malleable and ductile. Excellent conductor of heat and electric current. Excellent corrosion resistance. The metal alloys are measured in karats, 24 karat being pure gold. 18 karat = $^{18}/_{24}$ = 0.75 or 75 percent pure gold; 14 karat = $^{14}/_{24}$ = 0.583 or 58.3 percent pure gold, etc. Used to plate electrical contacts, printed circuits, watches, and other jewelry.

Silver

Melting point: 960.8°C (1761.4°F)

Specific gravity: 10.50 at 20°C

Brilliant white, lustrous metal. Harder than gold but still very malleable and ductile. Highest thermal and electrical conductivity of all metals. Stable in normal air, but tarnishes when exposed to ozone, hydrogen sulfide, and air containing sulfur. Used to plate electrical contacts, conducting surfaces such as bus bars, eating utensiles, and jewelry.

Silver was at one time used to plate printed circuit boards, but it exhibited a detrimental property known as *silver migration.* Thin whiskers of silver would form on printed circuit board conductor foil in the presence of an electric current and short out the circuits on the printed circuit board by bridging the spaces between the conductor patterns. This property of silver was not discovered until some time after the printed circuit boards were put into service on many military and commercial products. The result was many millions of dollars in damage, which could only be corrected by replacing all the defective printed circuit boards using gold- or tin-plated conductor foil.

Tin

Melting point: 231.9°C (449.4°F)

Specific gravity: (white tin) 7.31, (gray tin) 5.75 at 20°C

Silvery-white metal which is malleable and slightly ductile. Resists seawater and tap water but is attacked by strong acids, alkalies, and acid salts. Used to plate electrical contacts, bus bars, and corrosion-resistant containers and tubing.

Indium

Melting point: 156.6°C (313.9°F)

Specific gravity: 7.31 at 20°C

Very soft, silvery-white metal. May be alloyed to produce very low melting point alloys. The metal is toxic.

Rhodium

Melting point: 1966°C (3570°F)

Specific gravity: 12.41 at 20°C

Silvery-white metal with low electrical resistance. Highly resistant to corrosion. Plated rhodium is extremely hard. The base metal is also ductile. Used to plate electrical contacts.

Palladium

Melting point: 1552°C (2825.6°F)

Specific gravity: 12.02 at 20°C

Steel-white metal which is soft and ductile when annealed. Very hard when cold worked. Does not tarnish in air. Uses include engineering plating and plating of electrical contacts.

Zinc

Melting point: 419.4°C (786.9°F)

Specific gravity: 7.13 at 20°C

Bluish white lustrous, brittle metal. Fair conductor of electricity. Will burn in air at a red heat, producing clouds of white zinc oxide. Good corrosion resistance and used widely to plate irons and steels.

19.3.5 Summary of plating and finishing

Figure 19.4 lists most of the presently available and widely used plating processes and protective finishes, excluding paints and plastic coatings. These finishes have a wide range of uses in aerospace, commercial aircraft, automobiles, consumer products, and other industrial applications. The name of the finish, its applications, and its final appearance are all listed in the figure. For further information concerning the latest military specifications and American standard specifications for these finishes, consult the plating companies or finishers.

The effective corrosion resistance of selective platings and finishes is shown in Fig. 19.5. The thicknesses or ranges are shown in inches. As can be seen from the data in Fig. 19.5, hard chromium is one of the best engineering finishes for metal products, although it is expensive compared with the other common platings.

19.4 Plating Baths and Procedures

This section discusses the chemical compositions of various plating baths, the plating voltages, current densities, and other requirements for plating the following metals:

- Cadmium
- Chromium (bright, decorative and hard, for engineering applications)
- Copper
- Gold
- Nickel
- Rhodium
- Silver
- Tin
- Zinc
- Woods nickel strike
- Silver strike

19.4.1 Cadmium plating

Figure 19.6 shows the composition of the bath and operating conditions for cadmium plating. Cadmium metal has a toxic effect that is similar to that of mercury. Mercury is highly toxic and has contributed to a large extent to pollution to the environment, especially in the water systems worldwide, where mercurous and cadmium solutions are disposed of on a regular basis. Zinc plating should be used to replace cadmium-plated parts, except where the specifications limit the choice to cadmium. The fumes of fusing cadmium are toxic, as are those of mercury. Grave physical damage is caused by the ingestion of either metal (elements).

Note: The key numbers for the materials of construction for cadmium plating include 3, 8, 12, 13, and 14. See Fig. 19.17, which shows the key numbers and the respective materials.

19.4.2 Copper plating

Figure 19.7 shows the composition of the bath and operating conditions for one of the popular and easy to use methods of applying copper plating to base metals. Both copper and nickel are used for "strikes" that are required before a plating metal is applied to a base metal such as iron or steel and other metals. Copper plating is

Summary of Plating and Finishing Types and Applications

Finish	Application	Appearance
Brass	Used on high strength fasteners where a decorative finish is required	Gold iridescent
Cadmium	General purpose plating. High degree of corrosion resistance especially in salt atmospheres. Soft finish not for threaded applications requiring frequent tightening cycles. Cadmium is toxic. Zinc recommended as replacement.	Silver-gray
Cadmium and clear chromate	Suited for applications for hand contact. Corrosion resistant	Clear
Cadmium and black chromate	Recommended where black color is desired. Note: chromate can be applied in red, green, blue or other color as suits the application.	Black or color
Cadmium and bronze chromate	Normally used in military applications for identification of plating type.	Gold iridescent
Cadmium and yellow iridescent chromate	Similar to bronze	Yellow iridescent
Cadmium and olive drab chromate	Good for paint bonding applications.	Dull olive
Cadmium and phosphate	Similar to cadmium and olive drab chromate	Black
Copper	Used on Allen threaded products. Also for high heat applications.	Copper-matte
Chromium, decorative	Decorative and corrosion applications. Plating is usually very thin.	Bright or satin
Chromium, hard	A most durable plating which is extremely hard. Expensive. Engineering aplications. Cutting tools and drills.	Satin
Lead	For soldering applications.	Matte
Nickel	Decorative appearance, excellent wear and corrosion resistance.	Matte or bright
Silver	Electrical properties, utensiles, appearance.	Matte or bright
Tin	Anti-seize properties, corrosion resistance, non-toxic.	Grayish-white
Zinc	Popular plating for many applications; hardware, steel sheets, machined parts.	Bluish-white
Zinc and clear chromate	Similar to cadmium and clear chromate. Corrosion resistance, economical.	Clear
Zinc and black chromate	Similar to cadmium and black chromate. Where black color is desired.	Black

Zinc and bronze chromate	Similar to cadmium and bronze chromate. Color applications.	Gold iridescent
Zinc and yellow iridescent chromate	Similar to cadmium and yellow iridescent chromate. Color applications. Popular engineering finish. Economical and attractive for industrial applications.	
Zinc and olive drab chromate	Similar to cadmium and olive drab chromate. Good paint adhesion properties.	Dull olive
Zinc and phosphate	Similar to cadmium and phosphate. Black for color applications.	Black
Anodic	Finishes for aluminum, magnesium, and titanium. Many types and thicknesses available.	Many colors
Black oxide	For threaded fasteners such as set-screws. Only mildly corrosion and rust resistant. Normally applied to irons and steels. Often oiled.	Black
Iron phosphate	For hardware which is severely handled. Decorative gray finish.	Oily gray-black (oil fin
Manganese phosphate	For thread lubrication applications. For frictional contact applications. Supplied oiled or waxed for additional protection	Gray-black (oil finish)
Black nitrate	For stainless steel fasteners which require uniform black finish.	Dull or luster black
Passivation	For stainless steel fasteners and parts to prevent corrosion. Acid treatment.	Bright or matte
Zinc phosphate	For exposed fasteners requiring good paint adhesion properties. Dry or lubricated.	Dull gray (oil coating)
Teflon coating	Corrosion resistant and high lubricity. For non-galling anti-seizing applications. Used for bearings. New processes incorporate anodizing with teflon impregnation.	Gray to black

Figure 19.4 Summary of plating and finishing.

Effective Corrosion Resistance of Selective Platings - Minimum thicknesses are given in inches

Plating or Surface Treatment	Specification	Type	Class	Minimum Thickness	Salt Spray Test (minimum hours) White Corrosion	Rust
Anodize	Mil-C-5541A	.....	.....	.....	168	.....
	Mil-A-8625B	I, II	.....	.....	240	.....
Cadmium and Chromate	AMS-2400L1	.....	.....	0.0002-0.0003	100	.....
	AMS-2400L2	.....	.....	0.0002-0.0004	100	.....
	AMS-2400L3	.....	.....	0.0003-0.0005	150	.....
Cadmium and Chromate	QQ-P-416a	II	1	0.0005	96	.....
	QQ-P-416a	II	2	0.0003	96	.....
	QQ-P-416a	II	3	0.0002	96	.....
	Mil-C-8837	II	1	0.0005	96	.....
	Mil-C-8837	II	2	0.0003	96	.....
	Mil-C-8837	II	3	0.0002	96	.....
Chromium, hard	Mil-C-11436	.....	.....	0.0012	.....	100
Lead	Mil-L-13808	I, II	3	0.00025	.....	24
	Mil-L-13808	I, II	2	0.0005	.....	48
Manganese Phosphate, dry	Mil-P-16232C	M	3	0.0002	.....	1.5
Manganese Phosphate, oil	Mil-P-16232C	M	2	0.0002	.....	24
Tin	Mil-T-10727A	I	.....	0.0002	.....	24
Zinc	Mil-Z-325a	I	2	0.0005	.....	96
	Mil-Z-325a	I	3	0.0002	.....	36
Zinc Phosphate, dry	Mil-P-16232C	Z	3	0.0002	.....	2
	Mil-P-16232C	Z	2	0.0002	.....	48
Zinc and Chromate	QQ-Z-325a	II	2	0.0005	96	.....
	AMS-2402E	.....	.....	0.0002-0.0003	100	.....
	QQ-Z-325a	II	3	0.0002	96	.....
	AMS-2402E	.....	.....	0.0003-0.0005	150	.....
Zinc and Phosphate	QQ-Z-325a	III	2	0.0005	.....	96
	QQ-Z-325a	III	3	0.0002	.....	36

Figure 19.5 Corrosion resistance of platings.

Plating Bath Composition and Operating Conditions for Cadmium

Composition	g/L	oz/gal
Cadmium fluoborate	240.0	32.2
Fluoboric acid		to pH, (see pH below)
Boric acid	22.5	3.0
Ammonium fluoborate	60.0	8.0
Licorice	1.0	0.134
Cadmium present	95.0	12.6
pH, calorimetric		3.0-3.5
Conditions:		
Temperature		70-100°F (20-38°C)
Current density		30-60 amp/ft^2 (3-6 amp/dm^2)
Agitation, cathode		Preferred
Cathode efficiency, %		100
Ratio of anode to cathode area		2:1
Anode material		Cadmium
Volts		4-6
(barrel)		6-12

Filtration: as required

Uses: Rust preventive coating
Application: Over all ferrous base metals. Freedom from hydrogen embrittlement.
Note: Excess free acid can reduce efficiency and cause hydrogen embrittlement. Contamination with copper, lead or zinc can effect color and corrosion resistance of the deposited plating.

Figure 19.6 Cadmium plating.

Plating Bath Composition and Operating Conditions for Copper

Composition	g/L	oz/gal
Copper sulfate	200-250	28-34
Sulfuric acid	30-75	4-10
Copper content	40-50	5.2-6.6
Sulfuric acid	30-75	4-10
Conditions:		
Temperature:		70-120°F (21-49°C)
Current density:		20-100 amp/ft^2 (2-10 amp/dm^2)
Agitation:		Preferred
Cathode efficiency, %		95-100
Ratio of anode to cathode area		1:1
Anode material		Copper
Volts		> 6 or higher for some applications

Filtration: continuous, especially for heavy coatings.

Uses: Heavy copper deposits to any required thickness.
Application: To all ferrous metals over copper strike. Under nickel and chromium deposits for protective coatings. For electroforming-electrotypes, printing rolls for textiles and rotogravure and other applications.
Note: check the acid content for most problems.

Figure 19.7 Copper plating.

most frequently applied over irons and steels prior to the final plating, which may be cadmium, nickel, chromium, tin, or another metal. Copper sulfate is poisonous and is also used to pressure-treat lumber and to provide a fungus-resistant coating to many articles, plus a great variety of other commercial applications.

Note: The key numbers for the materials of construction for copper plating include 5, 8, 13, 14, and 15. See Fig. 19.17, which shows the key numbers and the respective materials.

19.4.3 Chromium plating

Figure 19.8 shows the composition of the bath and operating conditions for chromium plating. Chromium plating may be applied directly over steel tools when proper procedures are followed. This application of chromium plating had been used to coat cutting tools and drills. The present technology coats cutting tools and drills with titanium nitride and titanium carbide, which are harder and more wear resistant than chromium. Chromium is a very hard metal with the hardness of sapphire, but the newer titanium coatings are found more often on modern cutting tools and drills. Chromium plating enhances the appearance and corrosion resistance of many articles, but by modern standards, it is considered an expensive electroplating process. Many applications still require chromium plate when the engineering specifications so direct. Chromium plating is difficult due to the high current densities required and the poor "throwing" power of chromium. The shape and area of the anode in chrome plating is important, as are its relative position to the cathode or article being plated.

Note: The key numbers for the materials of construction for chromium plating include 1, 5, 9, 10, 14, and 15. See Fig. 19.17, which shows the key numbers and the respective materials.

19.4.4 Gold plating

Figure 19.9 shows the composition of the baths and operating conditions for two types of gold plating. Gold plating has many industrial applications, including printed circuits, high-quality relay points, integrated circuit applications, and general electrical contact plating, where a high-conductivity, corrosion-resistant coating is required. The applications in jewelry are numerous but are not detailed in this section.

Note: The key numbers for the materials of construction for gold plating include 3, 9, and 14. See Fig. 19.17, which shows the key numbers and the respective materials.

19.4.5 Nickel plating

Nickel is a lustrous, highly corrosion resistant metal with countless applications in industry. The metal is used in alloying steels and beryllium-copper (beryllium-nickel) alloys, as well as in the construction of nickel-cadmium electrochemical cells for batteries. Figure 19.10 shows the composition of the baths and operating conditions for three types of nickel plating. Nickel plating is used in "nickel strikes" as a preplating deposit applied subsequent to the plating of other metals. A popular nickel strike called *Woods nickel strike* is shown in Fig. 19.15.

Note: The key numbers for the materials of construction for nickel plating include 3, 4, 5, 8, 13, 14, and 15. See Fig. 19.17, which shows the key numbers and the respective materials.

19.4.6 Rhodium plating

Figure 19.11 shows the composition of the baths and operating conditions for three types of rhodium plating. Rhodium is a highly corrosion resistant metal with a high luster used in special corrosion-resistant applications. See preceding sections for a description of this metal and its various applications.

Note: Thc key numbers for the materials of construction for rhodium plating include 8, 9, 12, 13, and 14. See Fig. 19.17, which shows the key numbers and the respective materials.

19.4.7 Silver plating

Figure 19.12 shows the composition of the baths and operating conditions for two types of silver plating. Silver plating should receive a "silver strike" prior to the finished plating being applied. Silver strike plating solutions are shown in Fig. 19.16.

Note: The key numbers for the materials of construction for silver plating include 1, 2, 3, 9, 10, 13, and 14. See Fig. 19.17, which shows the key numbers and the respective materials.

19.4.8 Tin plating

Figure 19.13 shows the composition of the baths and operating conditions for three types of tin plating. Tin plating has many applications in industry, including corrosion-resistant finishes, electrical conductivity, and solderability.

Note: The key numbers for the materials of construction for tin plating include 1, 2, 3, 13, and 14. See Fig. 19.17, which shows the key numbers and the respective materials.

19.4.9 Zinc plating

Figure 19.14 shows the composition of the baths and operating conditions for two types of zinc plating for rack and barrel applications. Zinc is the most widely used of all plating metals because of its good corrosion resistance, quick and easy application, and low cost.

Note: The key numbers for the materials of construction for zinc plating include 14 [linings of polyvinyl chloride (PVC) or polypropylene].

19.4.10 Woods nickel strike solution

Figure 19.15 shows the composition of the striking bath and operating conditions for Woods nickel strike. This nickel strike can be applied on many base metals prior to other plating operations.

Note: The key numbers for the materials of construction for woods nickel strike include 3, 4, 8, 12, 13, 14, and 15. See Fig. 19.17, which shows the key numbers and the respective materials.

19.4.11 Silver strike solutions

Figure 19.16 shows the composition of the baths and operating conditions for three silver strike solutions. These strikes should be applied prior to the finished silver plating processes shown in Fig. 19.12.

Note: The key numbers for the materials of construction for silver strikes include the following: For baths 1 and 2, use 1, 2, 3, 9, 10, 13, and 14; for bath 3, use 8, 9, 10, 12, 13, 14, and 15. See Fig. 19.17, which shows the key numbers and the respective materials.

19.4.12 Materials of construction for electroplating processes

See Fig. 19.17 for the materials of construction for the previously listed plating processes. The key numbers are referenced to the respective applicable materials.

Precautionary note. The materials and chemicals used in the electroplating processes are almost all toxic to some extent, with some of the compounds being extremely poisonous (such as the cyanides). Extreme caution should be followed when handling these materials and chemicals. Also, some of the fumes created in the plating processes are also toxic to a high degree. The proper equipment and ventilation must be used with the electroplating processes. As an example, the fumes from the chromium plating processes which use chromic acid are not only toxic but also are corrosive. Any plating process that uses the cyanide compounds should be watched closely and handled with extreme caution, paying particular attention to proper venting of the fumes.

Because of the very high current densities used with some of the plating processes, the electrodes (anode and cathode) must be

(Text continued on page 1392.)

Plating Bath Composition and Operating Conditions for Chromium

Composition	g/L	oz/gal
Chromic acid	398	53.0
Sulfuric acid (concentrated)	4.0	0.53
Ratio CrO_3/H_2SO_4	100:1	

Conditions:	
Temperature:	110-120°F (43-49°C)
Current density	0.7-1.5 amp/in² (10-22
amp/dm²)Cathode efficiency, %	13-18
Anode material	Pure lead
Ratio of anode to cathode area	2:1 or more (variable)
Volts	6-12

Agitation: Not normally used.
Filtration: Uncommon.
Note: Trivalent chromium is usually required for normal operation of the bath (about 1% of the chromic acid content)

Uses: Bright decorative deposits 0.01 to 0.03 mil. Hard deposits are 0.1 mil and heavier.
Applications: Decorative coating over copper and/or nickel protective coatings on all base metals. Industrial or hard coating over ferrous base metals for tools and dies, cutting tools and drills. Piston rings and cylinder liners.
Note: Problems ocurr with improper trivalent chromium levels, contamination with iron, copper or nickel. Avoid contamination or problems will ocurr. Current densities must be maintained because of the poor throwing power of chromium plating baths.

Figure 19.8 Chromium plating.

Plating Bath Composition and Operating Conditions for Gold

Composition	Matte		Bright	
	g/L	oz/gal	g/L	oz/gal
Gold as cyanide	2-12	0.25-1.5	4-16	0.5-2
Potassium cyanide	15-45	2-6	15-90	2-12
Potassium carbonate	0-45	0-6	0-30	0-4
Potassium phosphate	0-45	0-6	0-45	0-6
Potassium hydroxide	10-30	1.3-4	10-30	1.3-4
Brighteners	0	0	0.1-10	0.01-1

Conditions:		
Temperature:	120-160°F (50-70°C)	60-75°F (15-25°C)
pH:	11-13	9-13
Current density	1-5 amp/ft² (0.1-0.5 amp/dm²)	3-15 amp/ft² (0.3-1.5 amp/dm²)
Agitation	Moderate	Rapid
Anodes	Platinum, stainless steel, gold	

Uses: Plating for corrosion prevention and electrical conductivity. Decorative.
Applications: Jewelry, printed circuit boards, integrated circuits, electrical contacts, relays.
Note: Problems with contamination. Gold solution baths are extremely sensitive to contamination, either organic or metallic. Nickel is used as the barrier or base layer (see nickel strike baths, Figure 19-10).

Figure 19.9 Gold plating.

Plating Bath Composition and Operating Conditions for Nickel - Also nickel strikes

Composition	Watts Type g/L	Watts Type oz/gal	High Chloride g/L	High Chloride oz/gal	All Chloride g/L	All Chloride oz/gal
Nickel sulfate	300	40	240	32	.....	.....
Nickel chloride	45	6	90	12	240	32
Boric acid	30-38	4-5	30-38	4-5	30	4
Nickel content	77.0	10.3	75	10	75	10
pH range (electrometric)	2.0-2.5		2.0-2.5		0.9-1.1	
Hydrogen peroxide to give free oxygen, ppm (Engineering applications)	5-10		5-10		5-10	

Conditions:			
Temperature:	130°F (55°C)	130°F (55°C)	130°F (55°C)
Current density:	10-60 amp/ft^2 (1-6 amp/dm^2)	10-60 amp/ft^2 (1-6 amp/dm^2)	50-100 amp/ft^2
Agitation:	Cathode		
Ratio of anode to cathode	1:1	1:1	1:1
Filtration:	Continuous		
Volts:	6-12	6-12	6-12
Anode material	Nickel, bagged, cast or rolled, depolarized or carbon type.		

Uses: Bath 1 and 2 (dull nickel 0.1-2.0 mil). For bright nickel proprietary brighteners are required. Bath 3 for hard, dull nickel, any thickness.
Applications: For decorative and protective coatings, copper and/or nickel-chromium, on most base metals use baths 1 or 2. For a nickel strike, especially over steel, copper and copper alloys prior to silver palting, use baths 1 or 3 (sometimes less concentrated).

Figure 19.10 Nickel plating.

Plating Bath Composition and Operating Conditions for Rhodium

Composition	Bath 1 g/L	Bath 2 g/L	Bath 3 g/L
Rhodium metal ♦	2	2	10-20
Sulfuric acid, pure, % vol	2.0	.....	2.5
Phosphoric acid, 85%, % vol	.....	2.0	.....

Conditions:			
Temperature:	104-113°F	104-113°F	122°F
Current density:	10-100 amp/ft^2	10-100 amp/ft^2	10-20 amp/ft^2
Agitation:	As required for all baths		
Cathode efficiency:	80%	80%	85%
Ratio of area anode to cathode:	1:1	1:1	1:1
Anode material:	Platinum for all baths		
Volts:	6	6	6

Note: nickel undercoat required, except for gold and platinum group.
Uses: Thin, bright decorative and corrosion resistant coating applications.
Decorative thickness: 0.001-0.006 mil; Scratch and corrosion resistance: 0.06 to over 1.0 mils.

Note: ♦ Metal is added in form of concentrate, as required.

Figure 19.11 Rhodium plating.

Plating Bath Composition and Operating Conditions for Silver

Composition	Bath 1		Bath 2	
	g/L	oz/gal	g/L	oz/gal
Silver cyanide	36	4.8	105	14.0
Cyanide potassium	60	8.0	113	15.0
Carbonate, potassium	45	6.0	15-115	2-15
Potassium hydroxide	.....	.....	30	4.0
Carbon disulfide	0.00075	0.0001		
Silver content	28.7	3.5 (Troy)	84	10.2 (Troy)
Free potassium cyanide	43	5.7	62	8.2

Conditions:	Bath 1	Bath 2
Temperature	75-90°F (24-32°C)	110-130°F (43-55°C)
Current density	5-15 amp/ft^2 (0.5-1.5 amp/dm^2)	60-150 amp/ft^2 (6-15 amp/dm^2)
Agitation	Cathode	Cathode and solution
Cathode efficiency	100%	100%
Ratio of anode to cathode area	1:1	2:1-4:1
Anode material	Silver	Silver
Volts	< 6	< 6
Filtration	As required	Continuous through paper

Uses: Bath 1 for bright silver deposits following silver strike, 0.1-1.3 mil. Bath 2 for heavy silver deposits after silver strike, up to 60 mil.

Applications: Bath 1 decorative and protective. Bath 2 for engineering applications

Problems: Avoid problems by closely controlling current densities, cleanliness of solution and prestrike quality. Avoid organic contamination. Proprietary solutions for full bright processing are available from the plating suppliers.

Figure 19.12 Silver plating.

Plating Bath Composition and Operating Conditions for Tin

Composition	Bath 1		Bath 2		Bath 3	
	g/L	oz/gal	g/L	oz/gal	g/L	oz/gal
Sodium stannate	90	12	80	10.6	140	19
Sodium hydroxide	7.5	1	.....	.....	15	2
Potassium hydroxide	.....	.....	30	4.0	.....	.....
Hydrogen peroxide, 100 vol	As required (0.07)					
Tin content	38	5.0	29	3.8	60	8.0

Conditions:	Bath 1	Bath 2	Bath 3
Temperature	140°F (60°C)	185°F (85°C)	200°F (95°C)
Current density	10-25 amp/ft^2 (1-2.5 a/dm^2)	40 amp/ft^2 (4 amp/dm^2)	55 amp/ft^2 (5.5 amp/dm^2)
Agitation, cathode & solution	Optional	Prefered	Not required
Cathode efficiency	60-90%	80-100%	90%
Ratio of anode to cathode area	1:1	1:1	1:1
Anode material	Tin	Tin	Tin
Filtration:	As required..		
Volts	6	6	6

Uses: Average tin coating thickness 0.03-0.3 mil. For protective coatings 1.0-3.0 mil.
Applications: Baths 2 and 3 are ffor electro tin plate. Bath 1 is used for plating all base metals for ease of soldering, protective coatings or good throwing power.

Figure 19.13 Tin plating.

Plating Bath Composition and Operating Conditions for Zinc

Composition	Rack g/L	Rack oz/gal	Barrel g/L	Barrel oz/gal
Ammoniated Solutions:				
Zinc chloride	75-95	10-12.5	35-65	4.5-8.5
Ammonium chloride	90-120	12-16	112-225	15-30
Sodium chloride	45-68	6-9	.....	.....
Boric acid or ammonium acetate	19-26	2.5-3.5	19-26	2.5-3.5
pH	4.4-5.6		4.4-5.6	
Temperature	60-110°F (15-45°C)		60-110°F (15-45°C)	
Conditions:				
Anode material	High purity zinc. Anode current density: 5-30 amp/ft²			
Cathode current density	2-60 amp/ft²			
Potassium solutions:				
Zinc chloride	75-85	10-11.3	50-85	6.7-11.3
Potassium chloride	200-270	27-36	180-270	24-36
Boric acid or Potassium acetate	7.5-12	1.0-1.6	7.5-12	1.0-1.6
pH	4.4-5.6		4.4-5.6	
Temperature	60-110°F (15-45°C)		60-110°F (15-45°C)	
Conditions:	Same as above baths			

Uses and applications: General corrosion resistant coating 0.2 to 3.0 mils for irons and steels. Bright zinc produced with these solutions. A yellow chromate coating is often applied over the deposited zinc plate.

Figure 19.14 Zinc plating.

Plating Bath Composition and Operating Conditions - Woods nickel strike

Composition	g/L	oz/gal
Nickel chloride	180	24
Hydrochloric acid (commercial)	10 to 12% by volume............	
Conditions:		
Temperature	100°F (35°C)	
Current density	20-100 amp/ft² (2-10 amp/dm²)	
Anodes	Nickel	

Uses and applications: This is a widely used strike which is effective on stainless steels, nickel, high-alloy steels and carburized and hardened steels. Time of strike: 30 seconds to 2 minutes. Nickel content will climb in this bath and should be maintained at 45-60 g/L (6-8 oz/gal), by decanting part of the solution and replacing it with hydrochloric acid.

Figure 19.15 Wood's nickel strike.

Plating Bath Composition and Operating Conditions for Silver Striking

Composition	Bath 1		Bath 2		Bath 3	
	g/L	oz/gal	g/L	oz/gal	g/L	oz/gal
Silver cyanide	1.7	0.23	7	0.9	.....	.....
Potassium cyanide	75	10	75	10		
Copper cyanide	15	2	.....	.....	.....	.....
Nickel chloride	.....	.....	.....	.....	240	32
Hydrochloric acid Specific gravity 1.18					10.0%/volume	
Silver content	1.6	0.2	6	0.7		
Copper	10.5	1.4	.....	.....	.....	.....
Nickel	.....	.....	.....	.....	60	8
Free cyanide, KCN	53	7	71	9.5	.....	.....

Conditions:	Bath 1	Bath 2	Bath 3
Temperature	75°F (24°C)	75°F (24°C)	75°F (24°C)
Current density	30 amp/ft^2 (3 amp/dm^2)	30 amp/ft^2 (3 amp/dm^2)	150 amp/ft^2 (15 amp/dm^2)
Time	0.33 min.	1 min	1-2 min
Anode material	Steel	Steel	Nickel, bagged
Volts	< 6	< 6	6
Filtration	As required	As required	Constant

Uses: Bath 1, first strike on steel; bath 2, second strike on steel or silver strike over nickel or other base metal; bath 3, first strike on steel or other base metal

Applications: Strikes 1, 2 and 3 for regular silver plating. Strike 3 for engineering applications.

Figure 19.16 Silver strike.

Materials of Construction for Plating Applications

Key	Material	Uses
1	Steel, low carbon	Tanks, filters, pumps, pipe, fittings and heating coils
2	Cast iron	Pumps, filters, valves and fittings
3	Stainless steel (316)	Tanks, pumps and filters
4	High silicon cast iron	Pumps, pipe, fittings and heat exchangers
5	Lead (6% antimony alloy)	Tank linings, pipe
6	Copper	Heating coils
7	Nickel	Heating coils
8	Carbon (Karbate)	Heaters and heat exchangers, pumps and air diffusers
9	Glass (Pyrex or tempered)	Tanks, heat exchangers and pumps
10	Chemical stoneware	Tanks, tower concentrators and tower packing
11	"Haveg"	Tanks and pipes
12	Hard rubber	Pipe, fittings and pumps
13	Rubber (Approved types)	Tank linings and hose
14	Plastics (Approved types)	Tank linings, hose, pipe, fittings, barrels, heating coils
15	Acid resistant brick	Tank linings
16	Wood	Tanks

Note: Plastic tanks or liners can influence the current distribution patterns within the plating tanks. Tests must be run to determine the proper plastic for each particular application. Polyurethane, polyethylene, polystyrene, polypropylene, ABS (Acrylonitrile-Butadene-Styrene), acetals, acrylics, nylons and polyvinyl chlorides may be usable for many applications.

Figure 19.17 Materials of construction for plating applications.

guarded against short-circuits. The operating voltages are low, but the power involved can be very high due to the large electric currents required in certain processes (chromium plating).

19.5 Coloring Processes for Metals and Alloys

This section lists some of the coloring processes used to color metals and alloys. Coloring of metals may be for appearance as well as for additional protection against corrosion and rusting. These processes have evolved over a span of many years and are widely used in the metal finishing industries. Most of the processes involve the use of chemical action together with the application of heat.

It should be noted that the finished appearance of the metal being colored is affected to a great extent by how well the bare metal itself is finished and polished. For example, in the blueing process for handguns and rifles, the base metal is finished very carefully and is highly polished prior to blueing. If the metal parts are not finished and highly polished, the blueing process will not hide the defects in the base metal.

19.5.1 Coloring metals (ferrous and nonferrous)

Black oxide. Irons and steels may be given a black finish or black oxide finish by either of two processes:

1. Heat the ferrous metal part to approximately 500 to 700°F and plunge it into a container of good-quality machine oil. Reheat and plunge the part into the oil a number of times until the desired depth of black is obtained. Use precautions on hardened and tempered parts.
2. A thin black oxide coating also may be applied to iron and steel parts by immersing the parts in a boiling solution of sodium hydroxide and mixtures of nitrates and nitrites (sodium nitrate, potassium nitrate, etc.).

Blueing irons and steels. Many ferrous metal parts receive a blueing operation to enhance their appearance and also as a rust-preventive coating. Handguns, rifles, and shotguns normally receive a blueing operation unless chromium or satin nickel are specified. The following blueing process imparts a fine blue to blue-black finish: Clean the metal with a potassium bichromate–sulfuric acid solution, and then wash with ammonium hydroxide solution and wipe dry with a clean, lint-free cloth. Apply ammonium polysulfide until the desired depth of bluing is obtained. The finish may be made nearly black by repeating the process of applying the ammonium polysulfide. A light machine oil or silicone cloth wipe will then additionally provide the surface with excellent corrosion and rust resistance.

Phosphatizing irons and steels. Three types of phosphate coatings (conversion coatings) are given to ferrous metals: zinc phosphate, iron phosphate, and manganese phosphate. Zinc phosphate coatings vary in color from light to dark gray; iron phosphate, dark gray; and manganese phosphate, dark gray, becoming black with service. The phosphate coatings are used for paint bases, for an aid in cold working the metal, and for rust prevention.

The phosphatizing solution contains approximately 3 to 5 percent phosphoric acid by volume. The part to be phosphatized is first thoroughly chemically cleaned and dipped into a solution of 2 percent by volume hydrochloric acid for approximately 15 s and then water rinsed and dried. The part is then immersed in the phosphatizing bath for the time required to impart the desired coating. Zinc plates and zinc parts are also phosphatized in the same manner. Stainless steels and certain alloy steels cannot be phosphatized.

Passivation of copper and copper alloys. A passivation coating may be applied to copper and its alloys, which imparts a blue-green color or patina. This coating is corrosion-resistant. The passivation solution may be made using the following solution composition:

1. 6 lb ammonium sulfate
2. 3 oz copper sulfate
3. 1.4 fluid oz. technical ammonia (sp. gr. = 0.09)
4. 6.5 gal water

Apply the solution with a spray to the chemically cleaned copper or copper-alloy parts in six applications, drying between applications. The patina appears after approximately 6 h and continues as the part weathers.

Copper and copper-alloy blackening (alloys with more than 85 percent copper). To color copper and its alloys black, use the following procedure: Make a solution consisting of 4 oz arsenious oxide, 8 fluid oz hydrochloric acid (sp. gr. = 1.16), and 1 gal water. Then

1. Heat the solution to 175 to 200°F
2. Immerse the copper or copper-alloy parts until a uniform black color is obtained.
3. Brush the parts while wet, dry the parts, and apply a protective clear finish such as polyurethane varnish.

Coloring brasses. Brass may be given a green color with the following procedure: Mix a solution containing 1 oz ferric nitrate, 6 oz sodium thiosulfate, and 1 gal water. Then

1. Heat the solution to 160 to 180°F.
2. Immerse the brass parts in the solution until the desired color is obtained.
3. Dry and coat with a clear protective finish such as clear lacquer or polyurethane varnish.

19.6 Etching Metals

The solutions used to etch various metals are often called *mordants,* and some of the solutions used in the etching processes are as follows.

19.6.1 Etching irons, steels, and zinc plate

Nitric acid solution. A popular solution for etching irons, steels, and zinc plates consists of a solution of 2 oz 50% nitric acid mixed into 15 oz water. This is a 1/16 solution. Always pour the acid into the water; never pour water into the acid. Pouring water into acid may cause a mixing reaction which could cause the acid to splash from the mixing container. The solution is relatively slow acting unless used with a splash-type etching machine. For hand etching, a stronger solution can be used, but the etching cut becomes rough at the edges of the etching action. Solutions as strong as 1/8 can be used: 1 part concentrated nitric acid to 7 parts water by volume.

19.6.2 Etching copper and copper alloys

Ferric chloride is often used to etch copper and its alloys. A 40°Bé solution of ferric chloride used at 75 to 80°F etches copper cleanly and not too rapidly so as to produce a rough etched edge. A 40°Bé solution is made by mixing 20 oz ferric chloride (anhydrous) with water to make a final volume of 1 liter (1000 ml). The specific gravity of this solution can be from 1.37 to 1.38. The designation Bé (Baumé) is pronounced "bow-may" and is defined with respect to specific gravity by the following equation:

$$\text{Specific gravity} = \frac{145}{145 - {}^\circ\text{Bé}}$$

With this equation, you may determine the degrees Baumé if you know what specific gravity you want or have or you may determine the specific gravity required of the solution if you know the degrees Baumé you wish to produce.

Note: The reaction of ferric chloride produces a great amount of heat when it is dissolved in water. The water temperature should be between 50 and 75°F prior to mixing the ferric chloride solution.

Solutions of ferric chloride as low as 30°Bé are used for fast etching of copper and its alloys, while the 40 to 42°Bé solutions are used for etching intaglio printing plates or photogravure work. These solutions also have been used to etch stainless steels. The ferric chloride bath should be contained in a glass, plastic, or wooden tank, since the solution is highly corrosive. Do not dispose of these solutions directly into standard drainage systems. The solutions should be diluted in water and neutralized with a base chemical such as sodium bicarbonate. Do not allow the solutions to come into contact with the skin; rubber gloves should be worn at all times during use of these solutions.

Printed circuit boards for electronic applications have been produced using ferric chloride solutions for many years. Using the lower °Bé solutions produces a fast and accurate etching action, or cut, and the ferric chloride is economical and long lasting. Perchlorate chemicals are also used for etching printed circuit boards.

Frank Short's etching solution. The Frank Short etching solution has been used by printing plate makers and other metalworkers for years and is a slow-acting but very accurate etchant (mordant). The solution may be made as follows:

- 88 parts by volume of distilled water
- 2 parts by volume potassium chloride
- 10 parts by volume of hydrochloric acid (concentrated)

This is a two-part mixture and must be made by mixing two solutions and then pouring the two solutions together.

Solution 1: Mix 1 oz potassium chloride into 10 oz water at 190 to 200°F

Solution 2: Mix 5 oz hydrochloric acid into 34 oz distilled water

Then pour solution 1 into solution 2 in a well-ventilated area. *Caution:* Chlorine gas is evolved when the two solutions are mixed.

Allow the solution to set for 30 min to 1 h before using. Store in a glass bottle with a rubber or glass stopper.

The part to be etched is lowered into a shallow glass pan or tank so that the solution covers the part to be etched by approximately ½ in. The etching action may be observed directly, since the etching solution is clear and transparent.

Copper and its alloys, irons and steels, and chromium-plated parts may be etched with this solution. Use adequate ventilation because chlorine gas in small amounts is evolved during the etching action. This solution is often used to check the etching mask for holes prior to fast etching in ferric chloride solutions. A copper part will begin to show a frosting effect in a few seconds after immersion in the solution. Holes in the etching mask may then be seen and repaired prior to the final etching.

As a final note, titanium heaters are used in etching baths for ferric chloride solutions.

19.6.3 Etching aluminum and aluminum alloys

Most aluminum alloys can be etched using sodium hydroxide solutions of varying strengths. Sodium hydroxide is commonly called *caustic soda* or *lye* and is a low-cost chemical. Sodium hydroxide is very corrosive or caustic and is poisonous. When aluminums are etched using sodium hydroxide solutions, one of the reaction products is hydrogen gas, which is highly explosive when mixed with normal air. Proper venting must be employed when using this process for etching aluminum alloys.

The etching action is relatively rapid, especially if the sodium hydroxide solution is above 1/16 (1 part sodium hydroxide to 15 parts water). Strong solutions produce a violent foaming reaction and substantial amounts of hydrogen gas.

Conversion formulas for chemical solutions. Figure 19.18 shows the conversion formulas for solutions having concentrations expressed in various ways.

19.7 Anodizing

Anodizing is a process of oxidation produced in an electrolytic bath. Aluminum and its alloys are most commonly anodized, although the anodizing process may be performed on magnesium, zinc, and titanium. This section will cover the anodize coatings and processes for aluminum and its alloys only. The anodic coating, being aluminum oxide, is extremely hard and abrasive, especially aluminum *hardcoat* anodized surfaces. The classifications for aluminum and aluminum-alloy anodic coatings are as follows:

Classifications

Type I: Chromic acid anodizing, conventional coatings produced from chromic acid baths. Shall not be applied to alloys containing over 5 percent copper, over 7 percent silicon, or when alloying elements exceed 7.5 percent.

Type IB: Chromic acid anodizing, low-voltage process, 20 V. Heat-treatable alloys, such as T4, T6, etc., should be tempered prior to anodizing.

Type II: Sulfuric acid anodizing, conventional coatings produced from sulfuric acid baths. Heat-treatable alloys, such as T4, T6, etc., should be tempered prior to anodizing.

Type III: Hard anodic coatings (hardcoat). Shall not be applied to alloys containing over 5 percent copper or over 8 percent silicon unless agreed on by the supplier. Heat-treatable alloys, such as T4, T6, etc., should be tempered.

Classes

Class 1: Nondyed, natural, including dichromate sealing

Class 2: Dyed

Standard specifications for anodized aluminum and aluminum alloys

ASTM B 244, Thickness of anodic coatings, measurement of

ANSI/ASTM B 137, Weight of coatings on anodized aluminum, measurement of

ASTM B 117, Method of salt spray (fog) testing

Sealing anodized aluminum and aluminum alloys. All types of anodizing must be sealed using any of the following methods after the electrolytic anodized coating is applied:

- Immersion in an aqueous solution of 5% sodium dichromate (15 min at 90 to 100°C)

- Immersion in deionized water (15 min at 100°C)
- Immersion in an aqueous solution of nickel or cobalt acetate (100°C for 15 min)
- Teflon impregnation processes (for sealing and lubricity)

Anodic coating design data

Radii of curvature on anodized parts

Nominal coating thickness, in	Radius of curvature (outside/inside), in
0.001	approx. 0.032
0.002	approx. 0.062
0.003	approx. 0.093
0.004	approx. 0.125

Thickness ranges of anodic coatings on aluminum and aluminum alloys

Coating type	Thickness range, in
I and IB	0.00002 to 0.0003
II	0.00007 to 0.0010
III	0.0005 to 0.0045

Minimum thickness (typical) of anodic coatings on aluminum and alloys. See Fig. 19.19 for minimum typical anodic coating thicknesses on various aluminum alloys per type.

Maximum thicknesses of anodic coatings on various aluminum alloys. See Fig. 19.20 for maximum attainable thicknesses of anodic coatings on selected aluminum alloys.

Design notes for anodized parts

1. A 2-mil hardcoat anodic coating (0.002 in) will penetrate the part 0.001 in and protrude from the part 0.001 in. A 1.000-in-diameter part which is anodized 2 mils (0.002 in) will have a finished diameter of 1.002 in. Half the coating is inside the part and half is on the outside.
2. Avoid blind holes in parts.

3. Avoid hollow weldments (drill 0.250-in-diameter weep holes in the part).
4. Avoid steel inserts.
5. Avoid sharp corners (see radii chart preceding).
6. Avoid heavy to thin cross sections on the part.
7. Allow for the anodic coating in your design tolerances on the part.

Anodic coating specifications

Name	Hardcoat anodize	Chromic anodize	Sulfuric anodize
Army/Navy	Mil-A-8625, Ty-3	Mil-A-8625, Ty-1	Mil-A-8625, Ty-2
G.E.	AMS-2468D	AMS-2470H	AMS-2471D
Boeing	Code-302	Code-300	Code-301
IBM	41-207	41-204	41-203
Grumman	G-9031	9030B	G-9032

Hardcoat anodize processes

- Martin
- Alumilite
- Alpha
- Mae
- Sanford
- Boeing
- Scionic
- Hardas
- Imperv-X

Hardcoat/Teflon processes

- Amphodize
- Hardtef
- Analon
- Tufram

- Polylube
- Lukon
- Nituf
- Kalon
- Ptfe
- Smoothcoat
- Sanfordize
- Hardlube

Hardcoat anodize physical data

Hardness	65 to 70 Rockwell C scale (harder than hard chrome)
Color	Dark gray to black
Dielectric strength	800 V/mil
Machining	Grinding, lapping, polishing, and honing
Sealing	Dichromate, nickel, or cobalt acetate, hot water or Teflon impregnation
Resistivity	10^8 to 10^{12} Ω·cm

Note: Parts which have been anodized cannot be reanodized, nor can the anodic coating be made thicker.

19.8 Paint Finishing

Paints are the most used of all finishes for metal products. The types and different varieties and colors available are limitless. Paint technology improves and changes constantly. Attesting to the quality and long-lasting ability of modern paints for metals are automotive vehicles and aircraft. Modern industrial paints not only must withstand the weather and corrosive elements, but many are chemically protected from the harmful effects of ultraviolet radiation from the sun.

Common industrial paints include

- Enamels (baked and air drying)
- Lacquers
- Epoxies (one- and two-part systems)

- Varnishes (glyptols, polyurethanes, and special chemical resistant)
- Latex/water-based

Pigments such as zinc and titanium oxide, carbon black, zinc chromate, Prussian blue, cobalt blue, and many others can be added to the paint for coloring and to improve durability.

Products that are built to customer or military specifications frequently have the type of finish listed in the specifications, together with the method of base metal preparation, such as phosphatizing, zinc chromate primer, zinc primer, etc. The color and the required minimum dry-film paint thickness are also frequently set out in the equipment specifications.

Some of the high-quality equipment manufacturers in the United States apply multiple coatings to their products, producing a finish that is not only attractive but also long-lasting and durable. Large equipment, primarily made of sheet steel, as emphasized in the switch-gear manufacturing industry, will often be multiple-coated. Some of the manufacturers use a phosphatizing process on the bare metal, followed by a zinc-based primer, which is then epoxy coated and finally given a high-quality polyurethane paint finish. Equipment of this caliber can be expected to withstand outdoor weathering for many years without finish problems.

When equipment is improperly base metal–prepared and then given a few coats of low-quality finish, corrosion usually begins soon after the equipment is exposed to the elements. Finish problems on large, fabricated metal equipment and structures are often a serious defect, and it becomes difficult to prevent further corrosion, even though repainting is undertaken. If the base metal preparation and primers are not selected or applied correctly, corrosion problems will always be prevalent.

Specific design questions and requirements for the paint finish must be directed to the proper paint manufacturer if high-quality results are to be expected. High-quality paints and correct base metal preparation techniques are expensive and require the proper equipment and facilities. There are many government regulations in force today which stipulate the procedures to be followed for environmental protection relative to the use of paint finishes. These regulations are formulated and enforced by the Environmental Protection Agency (EPA) and the Occupational Safety and Health Administration (OSHA). Chapter 22, "Safety Practices in Industry," lists the OSHA standards which help protect workers from industrial hazards caused by many substances and improper manufacturing practices, including paint ingredients and by-products.

19.8.1 Estimating paint-film thickness and coverage

Estimating the quantity of materials for a painting project is not as simple as one might expect. The surface-area coverage of any particular paint is usually listed on the paint container. But this coverage is for average wet-film area and does not take into consideration the dry-film thickness required on the product.

To determine the coverage for a 1-mil (0.001-in) dry-film thickness for a paint containing less than 100 percent solids, multiply the percentage of nonvolatile solids by 1604 and divide by 100. The percentage of nonvolatile solids is found on the paint container label or from the paint manufacturer's literature. The wet-film thickness required for a specific dry-film thickness is found by dividing the desired dry-film thickness by the percentage of solids by volume of the coating to be used. (Wet-film thickness is measured during application by a wet-film thickness gauge.)

A fast and accurate estimate of wet-film thickness required to obtain a specified dry-film thickness and theoretical coverage in square feet of area per gallon can be made using the nomograph shown in Fig. 19.21. To use the nomograph, connect the dry-film thickness on scale D with the percentage of solids on scale S and read the wet-film thickness required on scale T together with the square feet of coverage per gallon.

CONVERSION FORMULAE FOR SOLUTIONS HAVING CONCENTRATIONS EXPRESSED IN VARIOUS WAYS

A = Weight per cent of solute
B = Molecular weight of solvent
E = Molecular weight of solute
F = Grams of solute per liter of solution
G = Molality
M = Molarity
N = Mole fraction
R = Density of solution grams per cc

Concentration of solute—SOUGHT	Concentration of solute—GIVEN				
	A	B	G	M	F
A	—	$\frac{100N \times E}{N \times E + (1 - N)B}$	$\frac{100G \times E}{1000 + G \times E}$	$\frac{M \times E}{10R}$	$\frac{F}{10R}$
B	$\frac{\frac{A}{E}}{\frac{A}{E} + \frac{100 - A}{B}}$	—	$\frac{B \times G}{B \times G + 1000}$	$\frac{B \times M}{M(B - E) + 1000R}$	$\frac{B \times F}{F(B - E) + 1000R \times E}$
G	$\frac{1000A}{E(100 - A)}$	$\frac{100N}{B - N \times B}$	—	$\frac{1000M}{1000R - (M \times E)}$	$\frac{1000F}{E(1000R - F)}$
M	$\frac{10R \times A}{E}$	$\frac{10R \times N}{N \times E + (1 - N)B}$	$\frac{1000R \times G}{1000 + E \times G}$	—	$\frac{F}{E}$
F	10AR	$\frac{10R \times N \times E}{N \times E + (1 - N)B}$	$\frac{1000R \times G \times E}{1000 + G \times E}$	$M \times E$	—

Figure 19.18 Solution conversion equations. *(Source: Handbook of Chemistry and Physics, 50th ed., Chemical Rubber Publishing Company.)*

Minimum Typical Anodic Coating Thicknesses for Various Aluminum Alloys

Alloy Designation	Thickness of Coating, inches	
	Type I and IB	Type II
1100	0.000029	0.000093
2024-T4	......	0.000125
2024-T6	0.000044	......
3003	0.000035	0.000103
5052	0.000033	0.000098
5056	0.000021	......
6061-T6	0.000034	0.000099
7075-T6	0.000040	......
Alclad 2014-T6	0.000045	......
Alclad 7075-T6	0.000041	......
295-T6	......	0.000107
350-T6	......	0.000102
514	......	0.000086

Note: Anodic coating types I, IB and II are normally applied as thin coats, while type III (Hardcoat) is normally applied as the thicker coatings. See table of anodic thicknesses following.

Figure 19.19 Anodic coating thickness.

Maximum Anodic Coating Thicknesses on Various Aluminum Alloys

Alloy Designation	Anodic Coating Thickness - inches	Color
380	0.0006	Gray
360	0.001	Gray
319	0.0014	Gray
1100	0.0017	Bronze
2011	0.0021	Light gray
2014	0.0025	Gray
2019	0.0028	Bronze
6262	0.0031	Black
6061	0.0035	Black
2024	0.0040	Bronze
2017	0.0045	Bronze
6063	0.0050	Black
5052	0.0053	Black
2618	0.0055	Gray
2219	0.0058	Gray
218	0.0062	Gray
7079	0.0065	Dark gray
355	0.0075	Gray
7075	0.0082	Bronze
Almag 35	0.0100	Gray
356	0.0120	Light gray

Note: All above coatings may be dyed black. Coatings over 0.003 inches thick tend to chip and become milky in color and should be used only in the salvage of parts.
Source: Anodic, Inc., Stevenson, CT 06491.

Figure 19.20 Minimum anodic coating thickness.

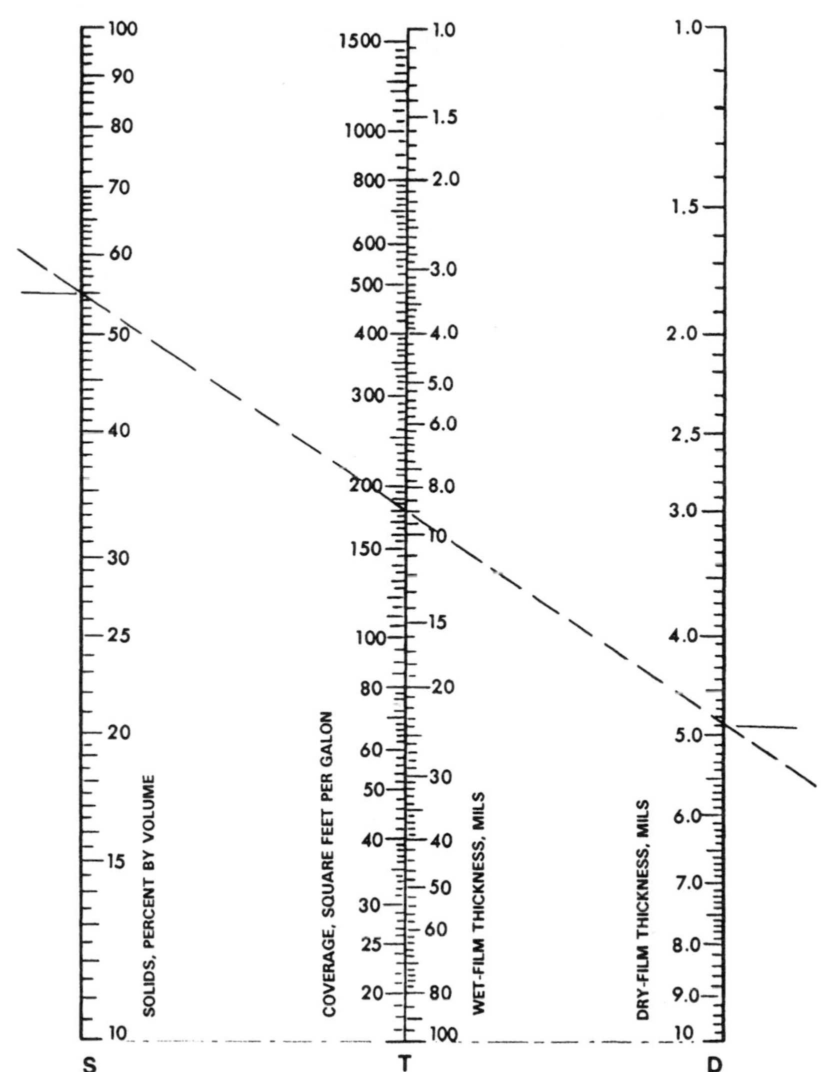

Figure 19.21 Wet-film to dry-film paint finish nomograph.

Chapter

20

Practical Pneumatics, Hydraulics, Air Handling, and Heat

20.1 Pneumatics

Pneumatics is the study of air and gases and the relationship between volume, pressure, and temperature of the air or gas. To begin the discussion, let us define the normal condition of atmospheric air as follows. At the reference conditions shown, the weight of atmospheric air is as follows:

Temperature = 32°F (0°C)

Atmospheric pressure = 29.92 inches mercury, by barometer (14.7 psi at sea level); 760 mmHg.

Weight = 0.08073 lb/ft^3; and 1 pound of air occupies 12.387 ft^3 at the listed temperature and pressure.

Then the weight of 1 ft^3 of air at any other pressure and temperature is

$$W = \frac{1.327 \times P_b}{T}$$

where W = weight, lb/ft^3
P_b = barometric pressure, in Hg
T = absolute temperature °R (Rankine) absolute 0 in Rankine = −459.69°F

20.1.1 Pressure, volume, and temperature of air

The relationship between pressure, volume, and temperature (variables) may be expressed as

$$\frac{PV}{T} = 53.33$$

where P = absolute pressure, lb/ft^2
V = volume in ft^3 of 1 lb air at the given temperature and pressure
T = absolute temperature, °R

20.1.2 Adiabatic and isothermal compression or expansion of air

Adiabatic compression or expansion of air takes place without the transmission of heat to or from the air during the compression or expansion. The relations between P, V, and T is given by the following series of equations:

$$\frac{P_2}{P_1} = \left(\frac{V_1}{V_2}\right)^{1.41} \quad \frac{P_2}{P_1} = \left(\frac{T_2}{T_1}\right)^{3.46}$$

$$\frac{V_2}{V_1} = \left(\frac{P_1}{P_2}\right)^{0.71} \quad \frac{V_2}{V_1} = \left(\frac{T_1}{T_2}\right)^{2.46}$$

$$\frac{T_2}{T_1} = (\frac{V_1}{V_2})^{0.41} \quad \frac{T_2}{T_1} = \left(\frac{P_2}{P_1}\right)^{0.29}$$

These equations are valid for both the U.S. Customary and SI systems. Use the appropriate units, as found in the conversion section.

The standard method of rearranging the equations for the unknown variable is illustrated by the following:

$$\frac{V_2}{V_1} = \left(\frac{P_1}{P_2}\right)^{0.71}$$

$$V_2(P_2)^{0.71} = V_1(P_1)^{0.71}$$

$$P_2 = \sqrt[0.71]{\frac{V_1(P_1)^{0.71}}{V_2}}$$

Isothermal compression or expansion takes place when a gas is compressed or expanded in conjunction with the addition or transmission of sufficient heat energy to maintain a constant temperature. Then, by Boyle's law for gases,

$$P_1V_1 = P_2V_2 = RT$$

where P_1 = initial absolute pressure, lb/ft^2
P_2 = absolute pressure after compression, lb/ft^2
V_1 = initial volume, ft^3
V_2 = volume of air after compression, ft^3
R = 53.33 (universal gas constant)
T = absolute temperature maintained during isothermal compression or expansion, °R

$PV = RT$ is known as the equation of state per mole (mol) for air or gases and holds true for any given gas (atmospheric air included). The *mole* is defined as the gram-molecule. Then, for 1 g, this equation becomes

$$PV = \frac{RT}{m}$$

where m = the molecular weight of the gas (or air). For G grams, this becomes

$$PV = \frac{GRT}{m}$$

where G = grams of gas or air.

20.1.3 Work or energy required in compressing air

Compressing air adiabatically,

$$E = 3.46P_1V_1 \left[(\frac{P_2}{P_1})^{0.29} - 1 \right]$$

Compressing air isothermally,

$$E = P_1V_1 \ln \frac{V_1}{V_2}$$

where P_1 = initial absolute pressure, lb/ft^2
P_2 = absolute pressure after compression, lb/ft^2
V_1 = initial volume, ft^3
V_2 = volume of air after compression, ft^3
E = energy, ft·lb

Energy requirements for isothermal compression are considerably less than those for adiabatic compression. In practice, the actual energy requirements fall between the power required for each of the two methods.

20.1.4 Horsepower requirements for air compression

For adiabatic compression,

$$\text{hp} = \frac{144nPVe}{33{,}000\,(e-1)}\left[\left(\frac{P_2}{P}\right)^{(e-1)/ne} - 1\right]$$

where P = atmospheric pressure, lb/in^2
P_2 = absolute final pressure, lb/in^2
n = number of stages of compression
V = volume of air compressed per minute, ft^3
e = 1.41 (constant for adiabatic compression)

For isothermal compression,

$$\text{hp} = \frac{144PV}{33{,}000}\left(\ln \frac{P_2}{P}\right)$$

20.1.5 Airflow in pipes

Airflow in pipes is expressed as

$$v = \sqrt{\frac{25{,}000\ \text{i.d.}P_1}{L}}$$

which, transposed, is

$$P_1 = \frac{Lv^2}{25{,}000(\text{i.d.})}$$

where v = air velocity, ft/s
P_1 = pressure loss due to flow, oz/in^2
i.d. = inside diameter of pipe, in
L = length of pipe, ft

The discharged air is therefore

$$D = vA$$

where v = air velocity, ft/s (other symbols defined below). Thus

$$\text{hp} = \frac{v_1 P}{550}$$

where D = discharged air, ft^3/s
A = area of pipe, ft^2
P = pressure, lb/ft^2
v_1 = volume of air moved in pipe, ft^3/s
hp = horsepower requirement to move the air

20.1.6 Compressed airflow in pipes

When the pressure difference at the ends of the pipe is small, the volume of flow is then

$$V = 58\sqrt{\frac{P(\text{i.d.})^5}{WL}}$$

where V = volume of air, ft^3/min
P = pressure difference, lb/in^2
i.d. = inside diameter of the pipe, in
L = length of pipe, ft
W = weight of entering air, lb/ft^3

20.1.7 Stresses in pressurized cylinders

The stress in the wall material of cylindrical containers may be calculated from the following equations. The ends of pressurized cylinders are normally made hemispherical or curved so that the stress is equal to or less than the stress in the cylindrical wall. The internal gas pressure or hydraulic pressure is equal per unit area inside of a pressurized container. If the container is pressurized to 125 psi, every 1 in^2 of internal surface has 125 lbf exerted on it.

The following equations are used for low-pressure, high-pressure, and very high pressure cylinders. For low-pressure, thin-walled cylinders (see Fig. 20.1),

$$S = \frac{\text{i.d.}P}{2t} \quad \Big\} \quad \text{Transpose for } t \text{ or } P$$

For high-pressure, thick-walled cylinders (see Fig. 20.2),

$$S = \frac{\text{o.d.}P}{2\text{T}} \quad \Big\} \quad \text{Transpose for } t \text{ or } P$$

For very high pressure cylinders, Lame's equation applies (see Fig. 20.3):

$$S = P\,\frac{R^2 + r^2}{R^2 - r^2} \qquad P = S\,\frac{R^2 - r^2}{R^2 + r^2}$$

$$R = r\sqrt{\frac{S+P}{S-P}} \qquad r = R\sqrt{\frac{S-P}{S+P}}$$

where P = pressure, lb/in^2
t = wall thickness, in
i.d. = inside diameter of cylinder, in
o.d. = outside diameter of cylinder, in
S = stress, lb/in^2
R = outside radius, in
r = inside radius, in

20.1.8 Gas constants

Figure 20.4 lists the gas constants which are of value in calculating the various requirements encountered in basic pneumatic design procedures using the preceding pneumatics equations.

20.2 Basic Hydraulics

The power required to drive a hydraulic pump is

$$\text{hp} = \frac{PG_{\text{pm}}}{1714E}$$

where hp = horsepower requirement
P = pressure of fluid, psi

G_{pm} = gallons per minute to be pumped
E = efficiency (e.g., 0.85 = 85 percent, etc.)

The accuracy for any positive-displacement pump is ±5 percent. Note regarding gauge and absolute pressures:

- psig = lb/in^2 gage
- psia = lb/in^2 absolute
- psia = psig + atmospheric pressure (atmospheric pressure is taken as 14.7 lb/in^2 (psi) at sea level; barometric pressure at 29.92 inches of mercury.

20.2.1 Fluid-flow, pressure, and volume equivalents

For fluid-flow equivalents, see Fig. 20.5. For pressure equivalents, see Fig. 20.6. For volume equivalents, see Fig. 20.7.

20.2.2 Basic fluid power equations

The following simple equations will be of use in calculating some of the basic requirements for hydraulics problems.

Torque

$$T = \frac{5252\text{hp}}{\text{rpm}}$$

Hydraulic horsepower

$$\text{hp} = \frac{PG_{pm}}{1714}$$

Velocity of oil flow in pipes

$$v = \frac{0.3208G_{pm}}{A}$$

Hydraulic-cylinder piston speed

$$S_p = \frac{C_m}{A}$$

Thrust force of a cylinder

$$T_f = A_1 P$$

Displacement and torque of a hydraulic motor

$$T = \frac{DP_d}{24\pi}$$

$$D = \frac{24\pi T}{P_d}$$

where hp = horsepower
rpm = revolutions per minute
T = torque, lb·ft
P = gauge pressure, psig
G_{pm} = oil flow, gal/min
v = oil velocity, ft/s
A = inside pipe area, in^2
S_p = piston travel speed, in/min
C_m = oil flow into cylinder, in^3/min
A_1 = piston area, in^2
D = displacement, in^3/revolution
P_d = pressure difference across motor, psi

Some approximate equivalents in hydraulics may be summarized as

- For every unit horsepower of drive, the equivalent of 1 gal/min at 1500 psi can be obtained.
- Pump idling requirement is equal to approximately 5 percent of the pump's rated horsepower.
- Hydraulic oil volume is reduced approximately 0.5 percent for every 1000 psi of fluid pressure in the system.

20.2.3 Hydraulic and air-line sizes and thread connections

Figure 20.8 shows the common hydraulic and air-line sizes available and the pipe thread sizes in common use for hydraulics and pneumatic applications.

20.3 Air-Handling Data

The Air Movement and Control Association (AMCA) establishes standards and tests and certifies the performance of air-moving devices and equipment in the United States and is a nationally rec-

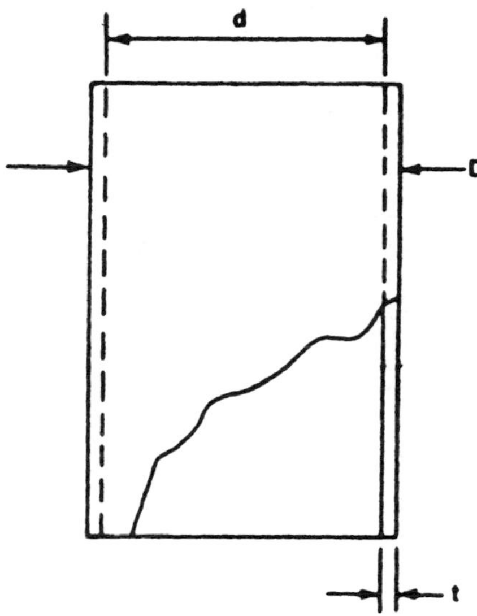

Figure 20.1 Thin-walled cylinder.

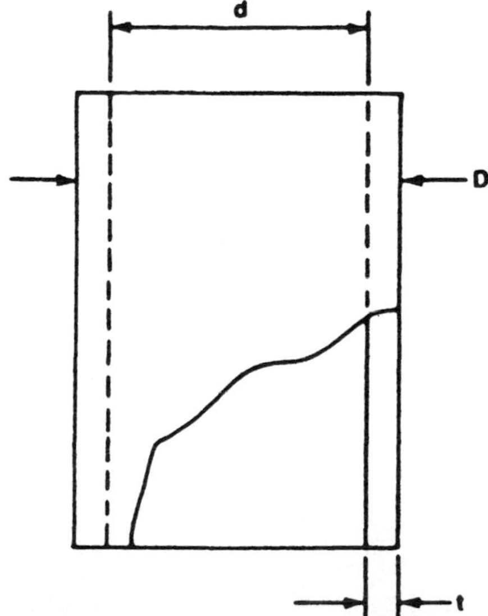

Figure 20.2 Thick-walled cylinder.

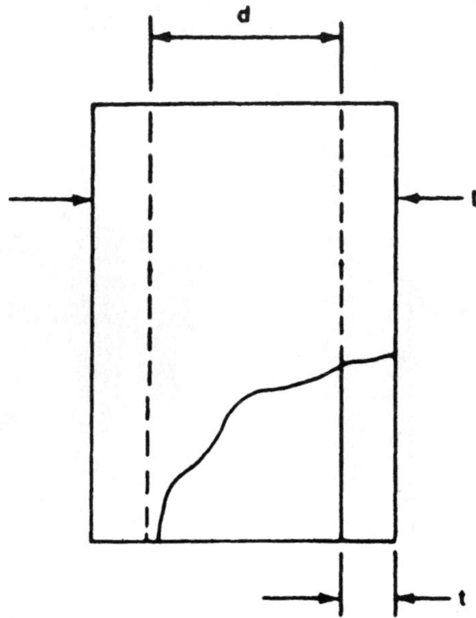

Figure 20.3 Very thick walled cylinder.

Gas Constants - Molecular Weight, Density, Specific Gravity and Weight in Lbs/ft³

Name of Gas	Molecular Weight	Density or Specific Gravity *	Weight: lb/ft³
Air (Normal)	......	1.000 *	0.08073
Ammonia	......	0.592 *	0.04779
Argon	39.948	1.784 g/l	0.11137
Carbon dioxide	44.010	1.977 g/l	0.12342
Carbon monoxide	......	0.967 *	0.07807
Chlorine	......	2.423 *	0.19561
Ethylene	......	0.967 *	0.07807
Acetylene (Ethyne)	......	0.920 *	0.07427
Helium	4.0026	0.1785 g/l	0.01114
Hydrogen	2.0159	0.0899 g/l	0.00561
Hydrogen Sulfide	34.080	1.539 g/l	0.09608
Krypton	83.800	3.736 g/l	0.23323
Natural gas (av.)	......	0.47-0.48 *	0.038-0.039
Nitrous oxide	......	1.527 *	0.12327
Nitrogen	......	0.971 *	0.07838
Oxygen	31.9988	1.429 g/l	0.08921
Ozone	47.9982	2.144 g/l	0.13385
Radon	222.000	9.730 g/l	0.60742
Sulfur dioxide	64.060	2.927 g/l	0.18273
Sulfur hexafluoride	146.05	6.602 g/l	0.41215
Xenon	131.30	5.887 g/l	0.36751

Note: * Specific gravity is in respect to air (1.000) at 32°F, 29.92" of mercury.
1 gram per liter (g/l) = 0.062428 lb/ft³. 1 pound of air occupies 12.387 ft³ at 32°F, 29.92" of mercury.

Figure 20.4 Gas constants.

gal/hr	gal/min	ft²/hr	ft²/min	L/hr	L/min	cm³/min
1	0.01667	0.1337	2.228×10^{-3}	3.7848	0.06308	63.08
60	1	8.022	0.1337	227.1	3.7848	3,784.8
7.48	0.1247	1	0.01667	28.32	0.472	472
448.8	7.48	60	1	0.47195	28.32	28.32×10^{-3}
0.26418	4.403×10^{3}	0.03531	5.886×10^{-4}	1	0.01667	16.67
15.8502	264.18×10^{3}	2.11887	0.03531	60	1	1,000
4.403×10^{-6}	264.2×10^{6}	0.5886×10^{-6}	35.3145×10^{6}	16.67×10^{-6}	0.001	1

Figure 20.5 Fluid-flow equivalents.

atmos	bar	kPa/cm²	psi	in Hg	microns Hg	torr (mmHg)
1	1.01325	1.0332	14.696	29.921	760×10^{3}	760
0.98692	1	1.01971	14.504	29.53	750.06×10^{3}	750.06
0.96784	0.98067	1	14.223	28.959	735.56×10^{3}	735.56
0.06805	0.06895	0.07031	1	2.036	51.72×10^{3}	51.72
0.03342	0.03364	0.03453	0.49116	1	2.54×10^{3}	25.4
1.3158×10^{-6}	1.3332×10^{-6}	1.3595×10^{-6}	19.337×10^{-6}	39.37×10^{-6}	1	1×10^{-3}
1.3158×10^{-3}	1.3332×10^{-3}	1.3595×10^{-3}	19.337×10^{-3}	39.37×10^{-3}	1×10^{3}	1

Figure 20.6 Pressure equivalents.

m^3	ft^3	gal	L	qt	in^3	cm^3 (ml)
1	35.31	264.2	1,000	1,056.8	61.023×10^3	1×10^6
28.317×10^{-3}	1	7.4805	28.317	29.92	1,728	28.317×10^3
3.785×10^{-3}	0.1337	1	3.785	4	231	3,785
1×10^{-3}	0.03531	0.2642	1	1.057	61.023	1,000
9.463×10^{-4}	0.03342	0.25	0.9463	1	57.75	946.25
1.639×10^{-5}	5.787×10^{-4}	43.29×10^{-4}	0.01639	0.01732	1	16.387
1×10^{-6}	35.31×10^{-6}	2.642×10^{-4}	1×10^{-3}	10.568×10^{-4}	0.06102	1

Figure 20.7 Volume equivalents.

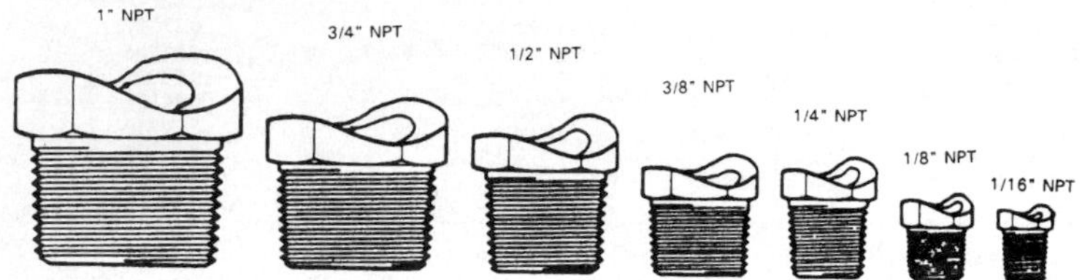

Pipe thread size NPT

Tubing O.D. size (inches)

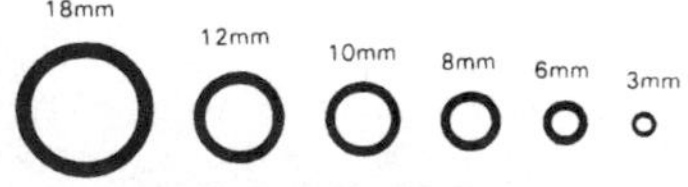

Metric tubing sizes

Figure 20.8 Hydraulic and air-line sizes and pipe thread.

ognized authority. The basics of air-moving or air-handling practice is detailed to a limited extent in this section. Air movement in shops and factory areas is an important aspect of manufacturing procedures because it may materially affect manufacturing efficiencies.

20.3.1 Basic laws for air-moving equipment

Air-moving terminology

cfm (cubic feet per minute) A measure of volume flow rate or air-moving capability of an air-moving device. Volume of air moved past a fixed point per minute.

dB (decibel) A measure of the sound intensity produced by air-moving equipment. dB (A) Sound level reading on the A-weighted scale of a sound meter. The A weighting adjusts the response of the meter to that of the human ear.

sone An internationally recognized unit of sound intensity (loudness). One sone is equivalent to the sound made by an average refrigerator in a kitchen. A device that is rated at 6 sones sounds twice as loud as one operating at a level of 3 sones. Sones are thus a linear quantity, unlike the decibel, which is rated on a logarithmic scale.

Sound power level or sound pressure level The acoustic power radiating from a sound source, expressed in decibels (dB).

SP (static pressure) A measure of the resistance to movement of forced air through a system or installation caused by ductwork, inlets, louvers, etc. SP is measured in inches of water gage (W.G.) or water column; the height in inches to which the pressure will lift a column of water. For any given system, the static pressure varies as the square of the flow rate.

Air-moving equations

Performance ratio

$$\text{Ratio} = \frac{\text{CFM new}}{\text{CFM existing}}$$

$$\text{rpm new} = \frac{\text{CFM new}}{\text{CFM existing}} \times \text{rpm existing}$$

Static pressure

$$\text{SP new} = \left(\frac{\text{CFM new}}{\text{CFM existing}}\right)^2 \times \text{SP existing}$$

Horsepower

$$\text{hp new} = \left(\frac{\text{CFM new}}{\text{CFM existing}}\right)^3 \times \text{hp existing}$$

A typical calculation using the preceding equations is as follows:

Existing conditions: 7000 cfm, 1500 rpm, 0.75 SP, 1-hp motor

Desired result: We now wish to move 10,000 cfm.

$$\text{Ratio} = \frac{10{,}000}{7{,}000} = 1.429$$

Then the new rpm is

$$\text{rpm} = 1.429 \times 1500 = 2144 \text{ rpm}$$

Then the new SP is

$$\text{New SP} = \left(\frac{10{,}000}{7{,}000}\right)^2 \times 0.75 = 2.042 \times 0.75 = 1.53 \text{ SP}$$

Then the new horsepower required is

$$\text{New hp} = \left(\frac{10{,}000}{7{,}000}\right)^3 \times 1.0 = (1.429)^3 \times 1.0 = 2.92 \text{ or } 3 \text{ hp}$$

The preceding is an illustration of the use of the equations.

Air-change recommendations for various industrial areas. Figure 20.9 lists the industry-recommended air changes for various types of industrial work areas. To determine the required fan capacity to meet these recommendations, calculate the volume of the area to be ventilated in cubic feet and divide by the rate of air change shown in Fig. 20.9. The result will be the required cfm, corresponding to fan ratings.

Example Your foundry area contains 800,000 ft^3. The recommended air-change rate is 2 to 8 min per air change (take 5 as average). Then,

$$\text{cfm required} = \frac{800{,}000}{5} = 160{,}000 \text{ cfm}$$

Check the fan ratings in cfm in the fan catalogs, and select one or more fans to do the job.

20.4 Transmission of Heat

The total heat transmission through containment or building surfaces can be calculated from

$$H = AU(t_o - t_i)$$

where H = sensible heat, Btu/h
A = area of transmitting surface, ft^2
U = coefficient of heat transmission of the transmitting surface
t_o = outside temperature, °F
t_i = inside temperature, °F

This equation can be used for calculating heat loss from a space or heat gain to a space. Coefficients of heat transmission and heat loss from personnel are shown in Fig. 20.10. Figure 20.11 shows heat transmission diagrammatically with respect to the preceding equation.

20.4.1 Ventilation

Infiltration air or air-change requirements were shown in Fig. 20.9.

Sensible heat of ventilation or infiltration. This quantity may be estimated from

$$H_s = 1.07V(t_o - t_i)$$

where H_s = sensible heat, Btu/h
V = ft^3/min of ventilation or infiltration air
t_o = outside temperature, °F
t_i = inside temperature, °F

Only infiltration air contributes to the internal heat load. Ventilation air, conditioned before entering the space, adds to the load of the conditioning or cooling equipment only.

Air quantity. The air quantity required to absorb a specific sensible-heat quantity is determined by

$$V = \frac{H_s}{60} \times \frac{56}{t_a - t_d}$$

where V = quantity of air, ft³/min
H_s = sensible heat, Btu/h
t_a = space temperature, °F
t_d = delivery temperature of air into space, °F

Note: 1 Btu will raise 4.16 lb of air 1°F or 56 ft³ of air 1°F.

20.5 Specific Heat (Thermal Capacity)

Specific heat is defined as the ratio of the heat required to raise the temperature of a unit weight of a substance 1° to the heat required to raise the temperature of a unit weight of pure water 1° at a specified temperature. The units of measurement are calories per gram per degrees Celsius (cal/g/°C) in the SI metric system and British thermal unit per pound per degrees Fahrenheit (Btu/lb/°F) in the U.S. Customary system.

$$\text{Btu or calories} = Wct$$

where W = weight of substance, lb or g
c = specific heat of substance
t = temperature rise, °F or °C

The specific heats for common materials are shown in Fig. 20.12.

Air Changes Recommended for Various Industrial Areas - Minutes per change

Ventilated Area	Minutes per Change
Assembly halls	5-10
Boiler rooms	2-3
Engine rooms	3-5
Factories	5-10
Foundries	4-8
Mills	6-8
Offices	6-12 (smoking areas require higher range > 8)
Electroplating rooms	3-5
Rest rooms	6-10
Toilets	4-6
Transformer rooms	2-5
Warehouses	5-10
Painting facilities (spray)	5-10 or more

Figure 20.9 Air-change requirements.

Single window	1.13
Double window	0.50
12-in brick wall	0.35
10-in concrete wall	0.61
4-in concrete slab roof	0.70
Wood siding, ¾-in drywall w/3-in insulation	0.07

(a)

Design Condition: 1 man	Total Heat Loss, B.t.u/hr
At rest	400
Light work	600
Moderate work	800

(b)

Figure 20.10 *(a)* Coefficients of heat transmission. *(b)* Heat loss from personnel.

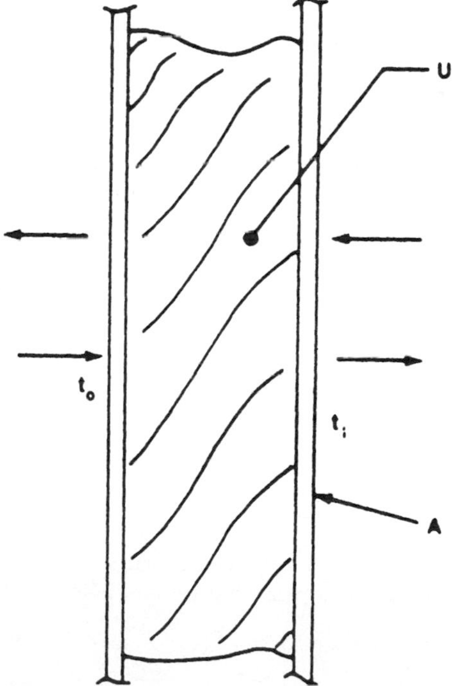

Figure 20.11 Diagram of heat transmission.

Substance	Specific Heat
Alcohol,	
Ethyl	0.548
Methyl	0.601
Aluminum	0.214
Benzene	0.400
Brass	0.094
Chromic acid (25%)	0.825
Copper	0.094
Ferric chloride (50%)	0.750
Glass, common	0.199
Graphite	0.201
Iron, cast	0.130
Iron, wrought	0.110
Lead	0.031
Mercury	0.033
Nickel	0.109
Platinum	0.032
Silver	0.056
Solder (60 Pb, 40 Sn)	0.047
Steel, low carbon	0.116
Sulfuric acid (50%)	0.915
Tin	0.056
Water (30°C)	0.997
Zinc	0.095

Values apply between 32 to 212°F, except as noted.

Figure 20.12 Specific heats of common materials.

20.6 Temperatures of Mixtures and Heat Requirements

When two volumes of liquids at different temperatures are mixed together, the final temperature of the mixture may be calculated from

$$T_{\mathrm{m}} = \frac{cwt + C_1 w_1 t_1}{cw + c_1 w_1}$$

where w, w_1 = weight of two substances, lb or g
t, t_1 = temperatures of the two substances, °F or °C
c, c_1 = specific heat of the two substances
T_{m} = final temperature of the mixture, °F or °C

20.6.1 Heat required to raise the temperature of materials

You may calculate the amount of heat required to raise the temperature of a material from an initial starting temperature from the following equation:

$$\text{Btus or calories} = ms(t_2 - t_1)$$

where m = mass of the substance, lb or g
s = specific heat of the substance
t_2 = final temperature of the substance, °F or °C
t_1 = initial temperature of the substance, °F or °C

20.6.2 Heat equivalents

1 horsepower = 2,546 Btu/h

1 horsepower = 42.5 Btu/min

1 ft·lb = 0.00129 Btu

1 Btu = 778 ft·lb

1 hp·h = 2,546 Btu

1 food calorie = 1,000 g·cal or 1 kg·cal

1 g·cal = 0.00397 Btu

1 g·cal = 41,855,000 erg (obsolete)

20.7 Heat Losses

System heat losses occur in three ways: conduction, convection, and radiation. Problems involving the addition or subtraction of heat from a system may be calculated for conduction, convection, and radiation using the following equations.

Conduction

$$Q_{L1},\ \text{Btu} = \frac{KA(T_2 - T_1)t_e}{L}$$

$$Q_{L1},\ \text{W·h} = \frac{KA(T_2 - T_1)t_e}{3.412L}$$

Convection

$$Q_{L2},\ \text{Btu} = 3.412A_1F_{vs}C_Ft_e$$

$$Q_{L2},\ \text{W·h} = A_1F_{vs}C_Ft_e$$

Radiation

$$Q_{L3}, \text{Btu} = 3.412AF_{bb}et_e$$

$$Q_{L3}, \text{W·h} = AF_{bb}et_e$$

where Q_{L1} = conduction heat losses, Btu or W·h
K = thermal conductivity, Btu·in/ft^2 · °F ·h
A = heat-transfer surface area, ft^2
L = thickness of material, in
T_2, T_1 = temperatures across material (T_2 is the higher temperature)
t_e = exposure time, h
Q_{L2} = surface heat losses, Btu or W·h
A_1 = surface area, in^2
F_{vs} = vertical surface convection loss factor (see Fig. 20.13)
C_F = surface orientation factor, whose typical values are:
Horizontal top 1.29
Vertical 1.00
Horizontal bottom 0.63
Q_{L3} = radiation heat losses, Btu or W·h
F_{bb} = black body radiation-loss factor, W/in^2 (see Fig. 20.14)
e = emissivity correction factor of the material (also termed emissivity coefficient; see Fig. 20.15)

Example To calculate the radiation heat losses (see Fig. 20.14). At 600°F, black-body losses are 4 W/in^2. Copper, with a medium oxide surface (e = 0.40), would thus radiate 4 × 0.04 = 0.16 W/in^2 of surface area at 600°F.

Specific heat and emissivity values are listed for common materials in Fig. 20.15. Note that heater ratings are expressed in units of power (watts). Energy is expressed in watthours (W·h) or British thermal units (Btu). Power is the rate at which energy is being used (Btu/h or W). Power and energy are thus related by the expression

$$\text{Power, W or Btu/h} = \frac{\text{energy, W·h or Btu}}{\text{time, h}}$$

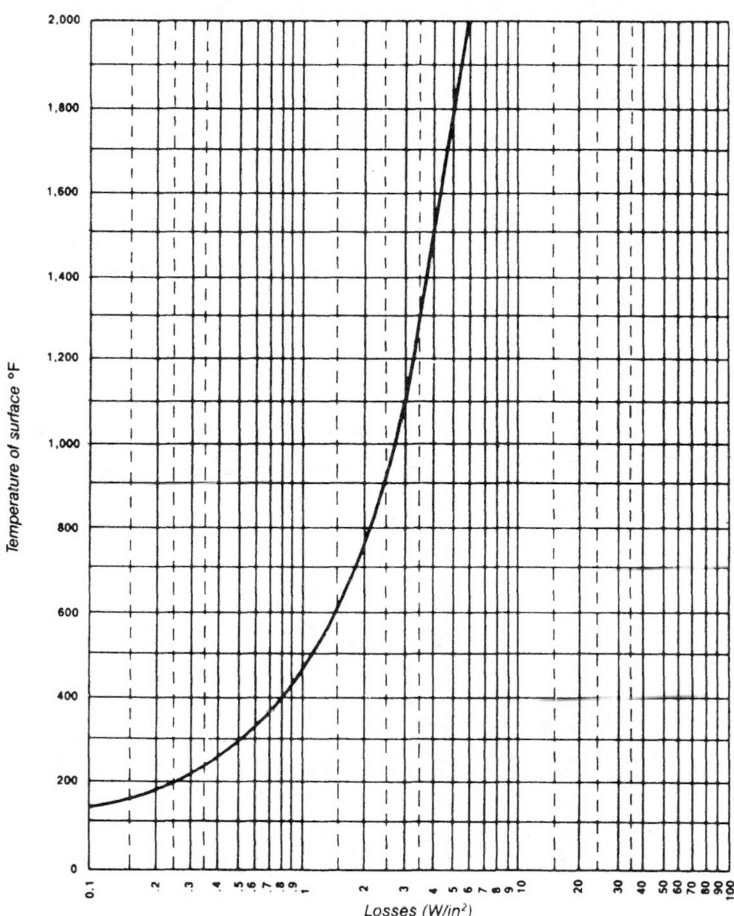

Figure 20.13 Convection-loss factors.

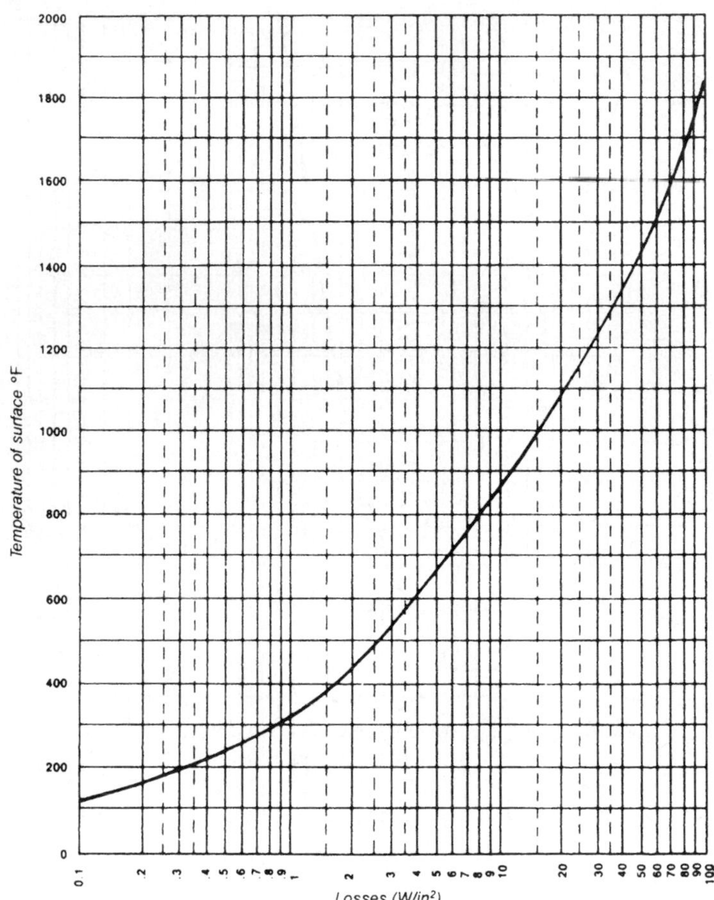

Figure 20.14 Black body radiation-loss factors.

Material	Specific Heat B.t.u/lb-°F	Emissivity		
		Polished	Med. Oxide	Heavy Oxide
Aluminum	0.24	0.09	0.11	0.22
Copper	0.10	0.04	0.40	0.65
Cast iron	0.12	—	0.80	0.85
Steel	0.12	0.10	0.75	0.85
S/S 304 and 430	0.11	0.17	0.57	0.85
Carbon	0.20			
Glass	0.20		(0.90 for most nonmetallics)	
Plastic	0.2 to 0.5			
Rubber	0.40			

Figure 20.15 Specific heats and emissivity correction factors.

20.7.1 Fan requirements for enclosed equipment

The basic equation for calculating the fan requirement in cubic feet per minute (cfm) for cooling an enclosure containing a heat-generating source is

$$\text{cfm} = \frac{3{,}160(kW_e)}{\Delta T}$$

where cfm = rating of fan or fans required in ft^3/min
kW_e = heat dissipated in the enclosure by a power source, kW
ΔT = difference in temperature of exhaust air from temperature of incoming or ambient air = $\Delta T = (t_f - t_a)$
t_f = allowable exit air temperature, °F
t_a = incoming air temperature, °F

Chapter

21

Engineering Design Data

The data and information contained in this chapter will prove useful in design engineering, tool engineering, sheet metal design practices, maintenance, and various branches of metalworking and processing.

21.1 Electric Motors

Electric motors are used, as we all know, in countless applications. They are available in a very broad range of sizes, types, and voltage and horsepower ratings. The modern standard types of electric motors are more efficient than the motors of 40 years ago in that they convert the input electrical energy into more useful work output with higher efficiency. Following are some of the procedures you can use to select the size, type, and rating of an electric motor for your particular application.

21.1.1 Electric motor definitions

Some of the common definitions for electric motor applications may be summarized as follows:

Ambient temperature The temperature of the air space surrounding the motor.

Efficiency The ratio of output power divided by the input power.

Thus, if an electric motor is rated at 5 horsepower and its rating is 220 V, 15 A, its efficiency may be calculated as follows. The relations between input, output, and efficiency for electric motors are expressed by the following equations:

$$\text{hp} = \text{horsepower}$$

$$\eta = \text{efficiency}$$

$$I = \text{line current, A}$$

$$V = \text{line voltage, V}$$

$$\text{p.f.} = \text{power factor}$$

For dc motors,

$$\text{hp} = \frac{\eta IV}{746}$$

For single-phase ac motors,

$$\text{hp} = \frac{\eta IV(\text{p.f.})}{746}$$

For three-phase ac motors,

$$\text{hp} = \frac{\sqrt{3}\,\eta IV(\text{p.f.})}{746} \qquad \eta = \frac{\text{hp}(746)}{\sqrt{3}\,IV(\text{p.f.})} \qquad \text{(transposed for efficiency)}$$

To solve the preceding equations for efficiency (η) or any other variable, transpose the equations.

Enclosures and housing types

- DP – dripproof
- TE = totally enclosed, i.e., no ventilation openings but not airtight
- TEFC = totally enclosed, fan-cooled
- TENV = totally enclosed, nonventilated
- TEAO = totally enclosed, air-over, i.e., airflow from driven device provides cooling for the motor.
- EX PRF = explosion-proof, i.e., a totally enclosed motor designed to withstand an internal explosion of specified gases and vapors and not allow the internal flame or explosion to escape.

Full-load amps Line current drawn by a motor when operating at rated load and voltage. Shown on the motor nameplate.

Frame Refers to the NEMA system of standardized motor mounting dimensions. (See later figures and tables of NEMA motor dimensions and mounts.)

Bearings: Sleeve and ball-bearing or needle-roller bearing types.

- Sleeve type—Used where low noise level is important.
- Ball type—Used where higher load capacity is required.
- Needle-roller type—Used where low noise and higher load capacity is required.
- Shields and seals—For preventing dirt from entering bearings and for sealing the lubricant in the motor gear box.

21.1.2 Selection of electric motor size and type

The proper application of an electric motor depends on the selection of a motor that meets the kinetic energy requirements of the driven machine without the motor overheating and without exceeding the torque rating of the motor.

Electric motor selection governing factors

- Speed
- Horsepower
- Inertial requirements
- Torque

Speed. Variation in speed, from no load to full load, is greatest with motors having series field windings and is absent with synchronous motors.

Horsepower. The peak horsepower determines the maximum torque required by the driven machine, and the motor maximum running torque must be in excess of this value.

Torque. Starting torque requirements can vary from 5 percent of full load to over 25 percent of full load depending on the driven machine requirements. The motor torque supplied to the driven machine must be well above that required by the driven machine at all points up to full speed. The greater the excess torque, the greater is the motor acceleration.

Time required t in seconds for acceleration from rest to full load speed is given by

$$t = \frac{WR^2 N_f}{308 T_a}$$

where WR^2 = inertia of rotating parts, lb·ft^2
W = weight, lb
R = radius of gyration of rotating part, ft
N_f = full load speed, rpm
308 = constant converting minutes to seconds, weight into mass, and radius into circumference
T_a = torque, average lb·ft available for acceleration

Note: If acceleration time t is greater than 20 s, special motors or starters may be required to prevent motor overheating.

Running torque T_r is given by

$$T_r = \frac{5250(\text{hp})}{N_r} \qquad \text{pounds-feet (lb·ft)}$$

where hp = horsepower supplied to the driven machine
N_r = running speed, rpm
5250 = constant converting hp to ft·lb/min and work per revolution into torque, lb·ft

Transposing for horsepower gives

$$T_r = \frac{5250(\text{hp})}{N_r} \qquad T_r N_r = 5250(\text{hp}) \qquad \text{hp} = \frac{T_r N_r}{5250}$$

Power. The term *Motor load* refers to the horsepower required to drive a machine. When the load is cyclic, a horsepower versus time curve for the driven machine is useful. Peak and rms horsepower can be determined from the curve, and rms horsepower indicates the required continuous motor rating. Peak-load horsepower is not always an indication of the required motor rating except when peak load is maintained for a period of time, in which case the motor horsepower rating should not be less than the peak-load horsepower.

Intermittent duty. The root-mean-square (rms) method is the usual technique for determining motor size (hp) for duty-cycle loads in which the motor is loaded for a time period and then idles for a time period. Then,

$$\text{RMS load (Hp)} = \text{peak load (Hp)}\ \sqrt{(t_p)}$$

where t_p = on-time cycle period (percent of cycle period, e.g., 35 percent = 0.35).

Motor curves. Different curves are available from the motor manufacturers, including

- Locked-rotor torque curves
- Motor speed-torque curves

Motor performance is determined from these curves. The designer needs to determine the following criteria:

1. Will the motor start under load?
2. Will the motor temperature rise to unacceptable levels during operation?
3. Can the motor attain running speed?

21.1.3 NEMA motor frame size tables (dimensions and mounting)

Figure 21.1 shows the dimensional indications for NEMA frame rated electric motors, and Fig. 21.2 shows the tabulated dimensional data in reference to Fig. 21.1. Figure 21.3 shows the NEMA C and J face motor mount dimensions, and Fig. 21.4 shows the tabulated dimensions in reference to Fig. 21.3.

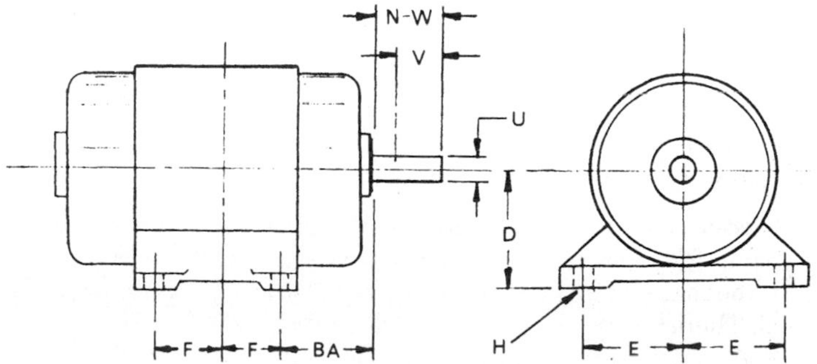

Figure 21.1 NEMA standard electric motor dimensions (see Fig. 21.2).

NEMA Frame	D ♦	2E	2F	BA	H	N-W	U	V ■	Key Wide	Key Thick	Key Long
42	2.625	3.500	1.688	2.063	0.281 slot	1.125	0.375	.....	.....	0.328 flat	.....
48	3.000	4.250	2.750	2.500	0.344 slot	1.500	0.500	.....	.....	0.453 flat	
56	3.500	4.875	3.000	2.750	0.344 slot	1.875*	0.625*	.....	0.188*	0.188*	1.375*
56H	3.500	4.875	3 & 5	2.750	0.344 slot	1.875*	0.625*	.....	0.188*	0.188*	1.375*
56HZ	3.500	4.875	3 & 5	2.750	0.344 slot	2.250	0.875	2.000	0.188	0.188	1.375
66	4.125	5.875	5.000	3.125	0.406 slot	2.250	0.750	.....	0.188	0.188	1.875
143T	3.500	5.500	4.000	2.250	0.344 dia.	2.250	0.875	2.000	0.188	0.188	1.375
145T	3.500	5.500	5.000	2.250	0.344 dia.	2.250	0.875	2.000	0.188	0.188	1.375
182	4.500	7.500	4.500	2.750	0.406 dia.	2.250	0.875	2.000	0.188	0.188	1.375
184	4.500	7.500	5.500	2.750	0.406 dia.	2.250	0.875	2.000	0.188	0.188	1.375
182T	4.500	7.500	4.500	2.750	0.406 dia.	2.750	1.125	2.500	0.250	0.250	1.750
184T	4.500	7.500	5.500	2.750	0.406 dia.	2.750	1.125	2.500	0.250	0.250	1.750
203#	5.000	8.000	5.500	3.125	0.406 dia.	2.250	0.750	2.000	0.188	0.188	1.375
204#	5.000	8.000	6.500	3.125	0.406 dia.	2.250	0.750	2.000	0.188	0.188	1.375
213	5.250	8.500	5.500	3.500	0.406 dia.	3.000	1.125	2.750	0.250	0.250	.....
215	5.250	8.500	7.000	3.500	0.406 dia.	3.000	1.125	2.750	0.250	0.250	.....
213T	5.250	8.500	5.500	3.500	0.406 dia.	3.375	1.375	3.125	0.312	0.312	2.375
215T	5.250	8.500	7.000	3.500	0.406 dia.	3.375	1.375	3.125	0.312	0.312	2.375
224#	5.500	9.000	6.750	3.500	0.406 dia	3.000	1.000	2.750	0.250	0.250	2.000
225#	5.500	9.000	7.500	3.500	0.406 dia.	3.000	1.000	2.750	0.250	0.250	2.000
254#	6.250	10.000	8.250	4.250	0.656 dia.	3.375	1.125	3.125	0.250	0.250	2.375
254U	6.250	10.000	8.250	4.250	0.531 dia.	3.750	1.375	3.500	0.312	0.312	2.750
256U	6.250	10.000	10.000	4.250	0.531 dia.	3.750	1.375	3.500	0.312	0.312	2.750
254T	6.250	10.000	8.250	4.250	0.531 dia.	4.000	1.625	3.750	0.375	0.375	2.875
256T	6.250	10.000	10.000	4.250	0.531 dia.	4.000	1.625	3.750	0.375	0.375	2.875
284#	7.000	11.000	9.500	4.750	0.656 dia.	3.750	1.250	3.500	0.250	0.250	2.750
284U	7.000	11.000	9.500	4.750	0.531 dia.	4.875	1.625	4.625	0.375	0.375	3.750
286U	7.000	11.000	11.000	4.750	0.531 dia.	4.875	1.625	4.625	0.375	0.375	3.750

284T	7.000	11.000	9.500	4.750	0.531 dia.	4.625	1.875	4.375	0.500	0.500	3.250
284TS	7.000	11.000	9.500	4.750	0.531 dia.	3.250 ●	1.625 ●	3.000 ●	0.375	0.375	1.875 ●
286T	7.000	11.000	11.000	4.750	0.531 dia.	4.625	1.875	4.375	0.500	0.500	3.250
324#	8.000	12.500	10.500	5.250	0.656 dia.	4.875	1.625	4.625	0.375	0.375	3.750
326#	8.000	12.500	12.000	5.250	0.656 dia.	4.875	1.625	4.625	0.375	0.375	3.750
324U	8.000	12.500	10.500	5.250	0.656 dia.	5.625	1.875	5.375	0.500	0.500	4.250
326U	8.000	12.500	12.000	5.250	0.656 dia.	5.625	1.875	5.375	0.500	0.500	4.250
324T	8.000	12.500	10.500	5.250	0.656 dia.	5.250	2.125	5.000	0.500	0.500	3.875
326T	8.000	12.500	12.000	5.250	0.656 dia.	5.250	2.125	5.000	0.500	0.500	3.875
326TS	8.000	12.500	12.000	5.250	0.656 dia.	3.750 ●	1.875 ●	3.500 ●	0.500	0.500	2.000 ●
364#	9.000	14.000	11.250	5.875	0.656 dia.	5.625	1.875	5.375	0.500	0.500	4.250
364S#	9.000	14.000	11.250	5.875	0.656 dia.	3.250	1.625	3.000	0.375	0.375	1.875
364T	9.000	14.000	11.250	5.875	0.656 dia.	5.875	2.375	5.625	0.625	0.625	4.250
365#	9.000	14.000	12.250	5.875	0.656 dia.	5.625	1.875	5.375	0.500	0.500	4.250
365T	9.000	14.000	12.250	5.875	0.656 dia.	5.875	2.375	5.375	0.625	0.625	4.250
364U	9.000	14.000	11.250	5.875	0.656 dia.	6.375	2.125	6.125	0.500	0.500	5.000
365U	9.000	14.000	12.250	5.875	0.656 dia.	6.375	2.125	6.125	0.500	0.500	5.000
404T	10.000	16.000	12.250	6.625	0.812 dia.	7.250	2.875	7.000	0.750	0.750	5.625
405T	10.000	16.000	13.750	6.625	0.812 dia.	7.250	2.875	7.000	0.750	0.750	5.625
444T	11.000	18.000	14.500	7.500	0.812 dia	8.500	3.375	8.250	0.875	0.875	6.938
445T	11.000	18.000	16.500	7.500	0.812 dia.	8.500	3.375	8.250	0.875	0.875	6.938

NOTES: ♦ Dimension D will never be greater than the above values on rigid mount motors, but it may be less, so that shims up to 0.063" thick may be required for coupled or geared machines. ● Standard short shaft for direct-drive applications. # Discontinued NEMA frames. * Certain NEMA 56Z frame motors have 0.500" diameter x 1.500" long shaft with 0.045" flat. ■ Dimension V is shaft length available for coupling, pinion or pulley hub; this is a minimum value.

NEMA letter designations following frame numbers:

H - Has 2F dimension larger than same frame without H suffix.
T, U - Integral horsepower motor dimensions set by NEMA in 1953 and 1964
Z - Non-standard shaft (N-W & U dimensions)

Figure 21.2 Motor dimensions for NEMA frames (inches).

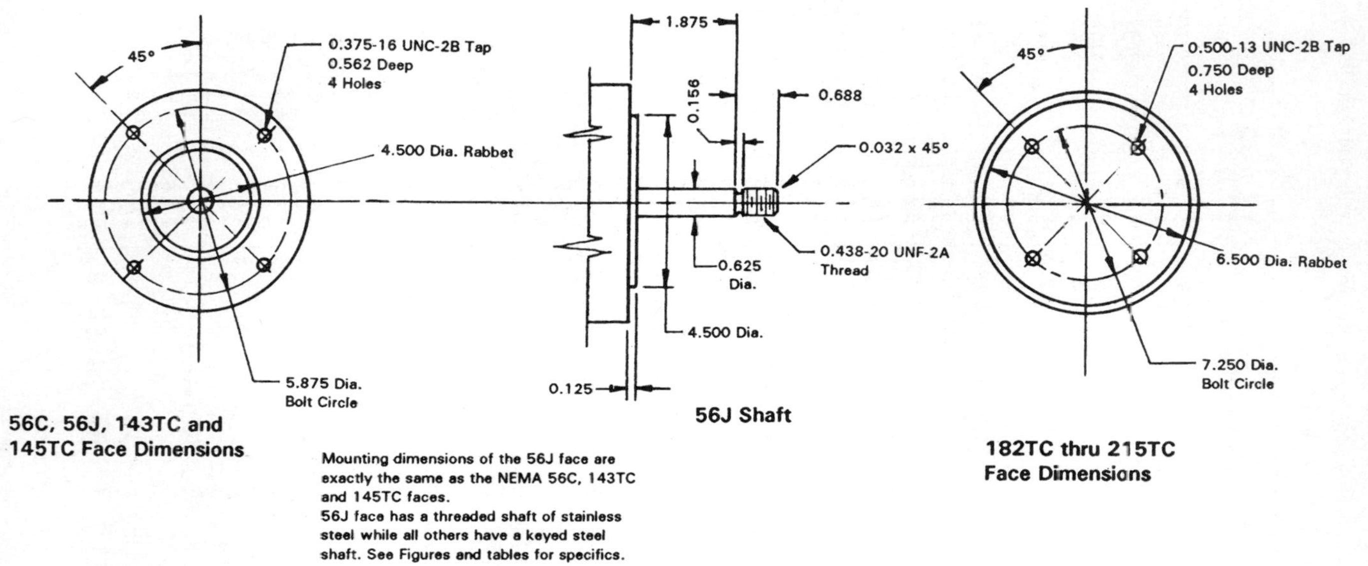

Figure 21.3 C- and J-face motor mounts.

NEMA Face	Shaft Diameter (U)	Shaft Long (N-W)	Rabbet Diameter	Bolt Circle Diameter
42C	0.375	1.125	3.000	3.750
48C	0.500	1.500	3.000	3.750
56C	0.625	1.875	4.500	5.875
56J	0.625	2.438	4.500	5.875
143TC & 145TC	0.875	2.250	4.500	5.875
182TC & 184TC	1.125	2.750	8.500	7.250
213TC & 215TC	1.375	3.375	8.500	7.250
254TC & 256TC	1.625	4.000	8.500	7.250
284TC & 286TC	1.875	4.625	10.500	9.000

Figure 21.4 NEMA C- and J-face mount dimensions (inches).

21.1.4 Types of electric motors

dc motors

- Permanent magnet
- Series wound
- Shunt wound
- Compound wound

ac motors

I. Single-phase class
  A. Induction
    1. Squirrel cage
      a. Split phase
      b. Capacitor start
      c. Permanent split capacitor
      d. Shaded pole
      e. Two-valve capacitor
    2. Wound rotor
      a. Repulsion
      b. Repulsion start
      c. Repulsion induction
  B. Synchronous
    1. Shaded pole
    2. Hysteresis
    3. Reluctance
    4. Permanent magnet

II. Polyphase class
   A. Induction
      1. Wound rotor
      2. Squirrel cage
   B. Synchronous
III. Universal motors
   A. ac/dc wound rotor

Selection of electric motors: General

ac motors. For light loads and where power is not applied until motor reaches top speed (belt-drive fans and blowers, table saws, and drill presses), use split-phase motors. For heavy loads (conveyors, compressors, and other heavy starting loads), use capacitor start motors or three-phase motors. For high-energy, low-weight applications, use universal motors (ac and dc)

dc motors. For high starting torque, use dc series wound motors or traction motors.

21.2 Properties of Materials

The properties of materials listed in this section are not contained in other sections of this *Handbook.* These data are useful in product design engineering and tool design.

21.2.1 Coefficients of linear expansion of common materials

Figure 21.5 lists the coefficients of linear expansion for commonly used materials, in both U.S. Customary and SI units.

21.2.2 Common and formal names of chemicals

Figure 21.6 lists common chemical names and their formal chemical names and formulas.

Note: Chapter 5, "Materials and Their Uses," lists many materials and other physical properties such as density, specific gravity, resistivity, etc.

Metal, alloy, or other material	Linear expansion	
	in per 1°F	in per 1°C
Aluminum, wrought	0.0000128	0.0000231
Brass	0.0000104	0.0000188
Bronze	0.0000101	0.0000181
Copper	0.0000093	0.0000168
Cast iron, gray	0.0000059	0.0000106
Wrought iron	0.0000067	0.0000120
Lead	0.0000159	0.0000286
Magnesium alloy	0.0000160	0.0000290
Nickel	0.0000070	0.0000126
Cast steel	0.0000061	0.0000110
Hard steel	0.0000073	0.0000132
Medium steel	0.0000067	0.0000120
Soft steel	0.0000061	0.0000110
Stainless steel	0.0000099	0.0000178
Zinc, rolled	0.0000173	0.0000263
Concrete	0.0000079	0.0000143
Granite	0.0000047	0.0000084
Marble	0.0000056	0.0000100
Plaster	0.0000092	0.0000166
Slate	0.0000058	0.0000104
Fir	0.0000021	0.0000037
Maple	0.0000036	0.0000064
Oak	0.0000027	0.0000049
Pine	0.0000030	0.0000054
Plate glass	0.0000050	0.0000089
Hard rubber	0.0000044	0.0000080
Porcelain	0.0000009	0.0000016
Silver	0.0000104	0.0000188
Tin	0.0000148	0.0000269
Tungsten	0.0000024	0.0000043

Figure 21.5 Coefficients of linear expansion for common materials. (*Source: Electromechanical Design Handbook, R. A. Walsh.*)

Common name	Formal name	Formula
Alum	Potassium aluminum sulfate	$K_2Al_2(SO_4)_4 \cdot 24H_2O$
Alundum	Fused alumina	Al_2O_3
Analine	Phenyl amine	—
Antichlor	Sodium thiosulfate	$Na_2S_2O_3 \cdot 5H_2O$
Antimony black	Antimony trisulfide	Sb_2S_3
Aqua fortis	Nitric acid	HNO_3
Aqua regia	Nitric and hydrochloric acid	$HNO_3 + 3HCl$
Bakelite	Resin from phenol and formaldehyde	—
Baking soda	Sodium bicarbonate	$NaHCO_3$
Barium white	Barium sulfate	$BaSO_4$
Bauxite	Hydrated alumina	$Al_2O_3 \cdot 2H_2O$
Benzine	Gasoline	—
Blue vitriol	Copper sulfate	$CuSO_4 \cdot 5H_2O$
Borax	Sodium tetraborate	$Na_2B_4O_7 \cdot 10H_2O$
Burnt lime	Calcium oxide	CaO
Calcite	Calcium carbonate	$CaCO_3$
Carbolic acid	Phenol	C_6H_5OH
Carbonic acid	Carbon dioxide	CO_2
Carborundum	Silicon carbide	SiC
Chalk	Calcium carbonate	$CaCO_3$
China clay	Aluminum silicate	$Al_2O_3 \cdot 2SiO_2 \cdot 2H_2O$
Chrome alum	Potassium chromium sulfate	$K_2Cr_2(SO_4)_4 \cdot 24H_2O$
Common salt	Sodium chloride	$NaCl$
Corundum	Aluminum oxide	Al_2O_3
Emery powder	Aluminum oxide	Al_2O_3
Epsom salts	Magnesium sulfate	$MgSO_4 \cdot 7H_2O$
Formalin	40% solution of formaldehyde and water	
Glycerin	Glycerol	—
Gypsum	Calcium sulfate	$CaSO_4 \cdot 2H_2O$
Kaolin	Aluminum silicate	$Al_2O_3 \cdot 2SiO_4 \cdot 2H_2O$
Lime	Calcium oxide	CaO
Methanol	Methyl alcohol	CH_3OH
Muriatic acid	Hydrochloric acid	HCl
Oil of vitriol	Sulfuric acid	H_2SO_4
Red lead	Lead tetroxide	Pb_3O_4
Rouge	Ferric oxide	Fe_2O_3
Sal ammoniac	Ammonium chloride	NH_4Cl
Silica	Silicon dioxide	SiO_2
Soda (washing)	Sodium carbonate	$Na_2CO_3 \cdot 10H_2O$
Sugar of lead	Lead acetate	—
Talc	Hydrated magnesium silicate	$Mg_3Si_4O_{11} \cdot H_2O$
Toluol	Toluene	$C_6H_6CH_3$
White lead	Lead carbonate	$2PbCO_3 + Pb(OH)$
Whiting	Calcium carbonate	$CaCO_3$
Zinc white	Zinc oxide	ZnO

Figure 21.6 Common and formal names of chemicals, with formulas.

21.3 Corrosion of Metals

Corrosion of metals is an important subject to those involved in the design and manufacturing of metallic products. The processes of corrosion do an estimated $125 billion damage in the United States every year. Corrosion takes place every hour of each day, every day of the year, and is a never-ending problem. The processes of corrosion can and do make products of all classes fail; some failures causing serious damage and even deaths. The product designer should always think of corrosion in the early stages of product design and development.

The processes of corrosive action are in many cases extremely complicated, and the actual causes, in certain cases, not fully understood by the materials scientists. Some corrosive actions are a long, slow process, while others can occur unexpectedly, at any time, with unpredictability.

The basic, well-known types of corrosion processes are summarized as follows:

1. *Direct chemical attack.* Corrosion by direct chemical attack occurs when the base material is soluble in the corroding substance or chemical.
2. *Corrosion by electrochemical action.* This type of corrosion occurs when metals of different electrical potentials come into contact in the presence of an electrolyte. Electrochemical corrosion is practically limited to metals. The different forms of electrochemical corrosion are as follows:
   - Galvanic corrosion
   - Stress corrosion—hydrogen embrittlement, stress embrittlement, stress corrosion cracking, hydrogen-assisted stress corrosion
   - Corrosion fatigue
   - Fretting
   - Crevice corrosion
   - Erosion corrosion
   - Pitting and cavitation

In galvanic corrosion, the presence of water in the atmosphere is enough to initiate the corrosive action. Minute electric currents flow from particles of high electropotential (cathodes –) through the electrolyte to the particles of lower electropotential (anodes +).

At the point that the electric current leaves the anode and enters the electrolyte, corrosion forms. The higher the electropotential between two dissimilar metals, the faster and more active is the corrosion. Figure 21.7 is a table of galvanic series of different groups of metals and alloys. From this series, it is easy to see which metals and alloys will cause the most galvanic corrosion problems, and this should be taken into consideration when performing the initial design criteria or selection of materials.

Galvanic action depends on the presence of an electrolyte, and the better its conductivity, the faster the corrosion takes place. Corrosion will normally appear on the anodic material immediately at the point that it contacts the cathodic material. The smaller the contact area of the anode in relation to the cathode, the faster and more severely the anode corrodes. Thus galvanic corrosion is greatest in areas of high current density.

Combatting Galvanic Corrosion

1. Introduce a barrier between dissimilar metals.
2. Avoid use of dissimilar metals (see Fig. 21.7) if possible.
3. Provide drainage.
4. The fastener should be the cathode (–).
5. Use metallic coatings (electroplating).
6. Use organic inhibitor compounds (Bitumastics, etc.).

Combatting stress corrosion. This is the least understood corrosion-related phenomenon and the most dangerous. All stress-corrosion failures occur only when the material is stressed in *tension.* It can occur in a few minutes, hours, months, or even years and is totally unpredictable. Service failures for these types of corrosion processes are serious, costly, and sometimes catastrophic. To avoid these types of corrosion failures, the following precautions should be used:

1. Do not use materials that are particularly susceptible to stress-corrosion failure (high-carbon, high-strength steels, certain brasses and nonferrous alloys).
2. Take note of the gases which may be present in the application. Atmospheres containing hydrogen and hydrogen sulfide are dangerous to high-strength, high-carbon steel fasteners. Atmospheres containing corrosive compounds are also potentially dangerous.

+ Corroded End (Anodic or least noble)
Magnesium Magnesium alloys Zinc Aluminum 1100 Cadmium Aluminum 2024-T4 Steel or iron Cast iron Chromium-iron (active) Ni-resist cast iron AISI 304 stainless steel (active) AISI 316 stainless steel (active) Lead-tin solders Lead Tin Nickel (active) Inconel alloys (active) Hastelloy alloy C (active) Brasses Copper Bronzes Copper-nickel alloys Monel alloy Silver solder Nickel (passive) Inconel alloys (passive) Chromium-iron (passive) AISI 304 stainless steel (passive) AISI 316 stainless steel (passive) Hastelloy alloy C (passive) Silver Titanium Graphite Gold Platinum
(-) Protected End (Cathodic or most noble)

Figure 21.7 Galvanic series of metals and alloys.

3. See Chap. 13, "Springs," Sec. 13.16 for hydrogen embrittlement prevention.
4. Use ferrous alloys with generous amounts of alloying chromium content.
5. Keep Rockwell hardness below C35 for steel fasteners or you will be required to use specially processed and heat-treated steel fasteners for high-strength applications.

21.4 Properties of Geometric Sections

Figure 21.8 shows the standard geometric sections and their properties. Symbols for these geometric sections are as follows:

A = area, in^2
c = distance to the neutral axis, in
I = moment of inertia of the section, in^4
S = elastic section modulus, in^3
r = governing radius of gyration, in
Z = plastic section modulus, in^3

21.5 Beam Equations

Figure 21.9 shows the two most important calculations for beams, namely, bending moments and deflections under load. These equations are useful for structural as well as machine-element design because they are applicable to both disciplines. Bending moment and deflection equations are shown for 15 often used configurations.

21.6 Properties of Structural Shapes (for Structures and Sheet Metal)

Figure 21.10 shows the most important common structural and sheet metal sections or shapes and the equations for calculating area, moment of inertia, section modulus, neutral axis, and radius of gyration. Areas are measured in square units, neutral axis in length units, moments of inertia in length units to the fourth power, section modulus in length units cubed, and radius of gyration in length units. Both U.S. Customary and SI units are applicable for these equations. The beam equations shown in Sec. 21.5 are also applicable with U.S. Customary or SI units.

(Text continued on page 1464.)

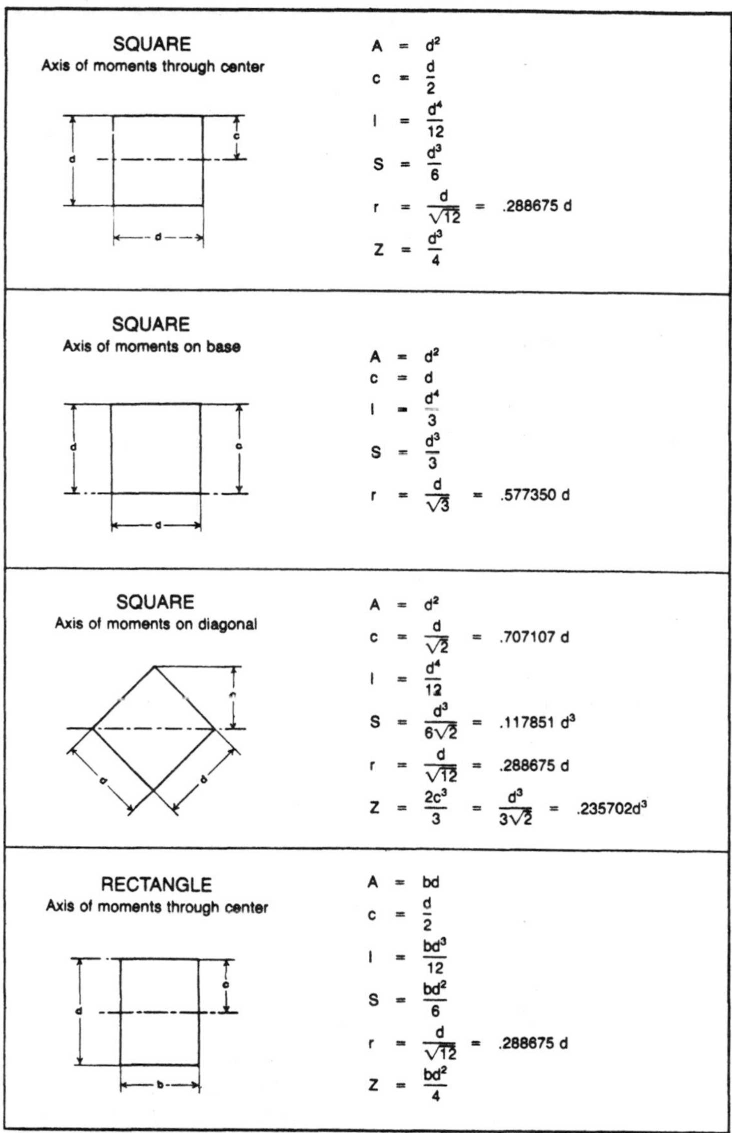

Figure 21.8 Properties of geometric sections. (*Source: American Institute of Steel Construction.*)

RECTANGLE
Axis of moments on base

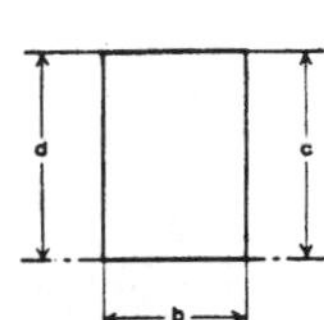

$$A = bd$$
$$c = d$$
$$I = \frac{bd^3}{3}$$
$$S = \frac{bd^2}{3}$$
$$r = \frac{d}{\sqrt{3}} = .577350\ d$$

RECTANGLE
Axis of moments on diagonal

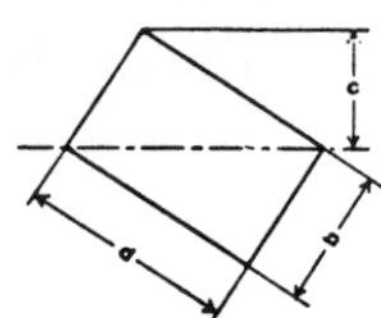

$$A = bd$$
$$c = \frac{bd}{\sqrt{b^2 + d^2}}$$
$$I = \frac{b^3d^3}{6\,(b^2 + d^2)}$$
$$S = \frac{b^2d^2}{6\sqrt{(b^2 + d^2)}}$$
$$r = \frac{bd}{\sqrt{6\,(b^2 + d^2)}}$$

RECTANGLE
Axis of moments any line through center of gravity

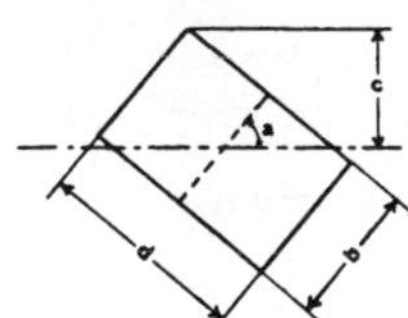

$$A = bd$$
$$c = \frac{b \sin a + d \cos a}{2}$$
$$I = \frac{bd\,(b^2 \sin^2 a + d^2 \cos^2 a)}{12}$$
$$S = \frac{bd\,(b^2 \sin^2 a + d^2 \cos^2 a)}{6\,(b \sin a + d \cos a)}$$
$$r = \sqrt{\frac{b^2 \sin^2 a + d^2 \cos^2 a}{12}}$$

HOLLOW RECTANGLE
Axis of moments through center

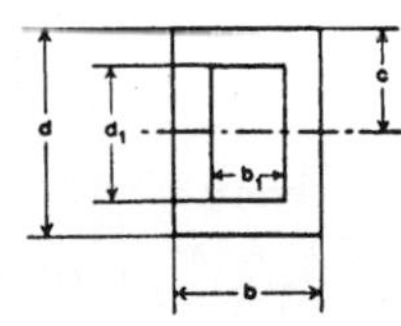

$$A = bd - b_1d_1$$
$$c = \frac{d}{2}$$
$$I = \frac{bd^3 - b_1d_1^3}{12}$$
$$S = \frac{bd^3 - b_1d_1^3}{6d}$$
$$r = \sqrt{\frac{bd^3 - b_1d_1^3}{12A}}$$
$$Z = \frac{bd^2}{4} - \frac{b_1d_1^2}{4}$$

Figure 21.8 *(Continued)*

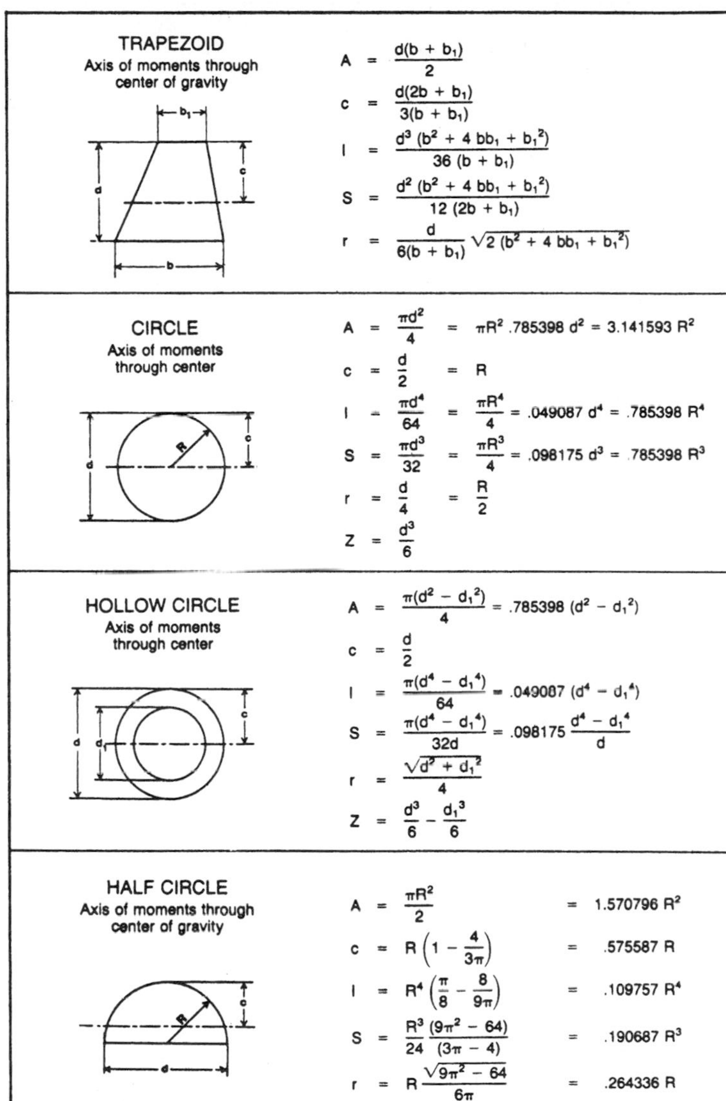

TRAPEZOID
Axis of moments through center of gravity

$$A = \frac{d(b + b_1)}{2}$$
$$c = \frac{d(2b + b_1)}{3(b + b_1)}$$
$$I = \frac{d^3 (b^2 + 4\,bb_1 + b_1^2)}{36\,(b + b_1)}$$
$$S = \frac{d^2 (b^2 + 4\,bb_1 + b_1^2)}{12\,(2b + b_1)}$$
$$r = \frac{d}{6(b + b_1)} \sqrt{2\,(b^2 + 4\,bb_1 + b_1^2)}$$

CIRCLE
Axis of moments through center

$$A = \frac{\pi d^2}{4} = \pi R^2\ .785398\ d^2 = 3.141593\ R^2$$
$$c = \frac{d}{2} = R$$
$$I = \frac{\pi d^4}{64} = \frac{\pi R^4}{4} = .049087\ d^4 = .785398\ R^4$$
$$S = \frac{\pi d^3}{32} = \frac{\pi R^3}{4} = .098175\ d^3 = .785398\ R^3$$
$$r = \frac{d}{4} = \frac{R}{2}$$
$$Z = \frac{d^3}{6}$$

HOLLOW CIRCLE
Axis of moments through center

$$A = \frac{\pi(d^2 - d_1^2)}{4} = .785398\ (d^2 - d_1^2)$$
$$c = \frac{d}{2}$$
$$I = \frac{\pi(d^4 - d_1^4)}{64} = .049087\ (d^4 - d_1^4)$$
$$S = \frac{\pi(d^4 - d_1^4)}{32d} = .098175\ \frac{d^4 - d_1^4}{d}$$
$$r = \frac{\sqrt{d^2 + d_1^2}}{4}$$
$$Z = \frac{d^3}{6} - \frac{d_1^3}{6}$$

HALF CIRCLE
Axis of moments through center of gravity

$$A = \frac{\pi R^2}{2} = 1.570796\ R^2$$
$$c = R\left(1 - \frac{4}{3\pi}\right) = .575587\ R$$
$$I = R^4\left(\frac{\pi}{8} - \frac{8}{9\pi}\right) = .109757\ R^4$$
$$S = \frac{R^3}{24}\frac{(9\pi^2 - 64)}{(3\pi - 4)} = .190687\ R^3$$
$$r = R\frac{\sqrt{9\pi^2 - 64}}{6\pi} = .264336\ R$$

Figure 21.8 *(Continued)*

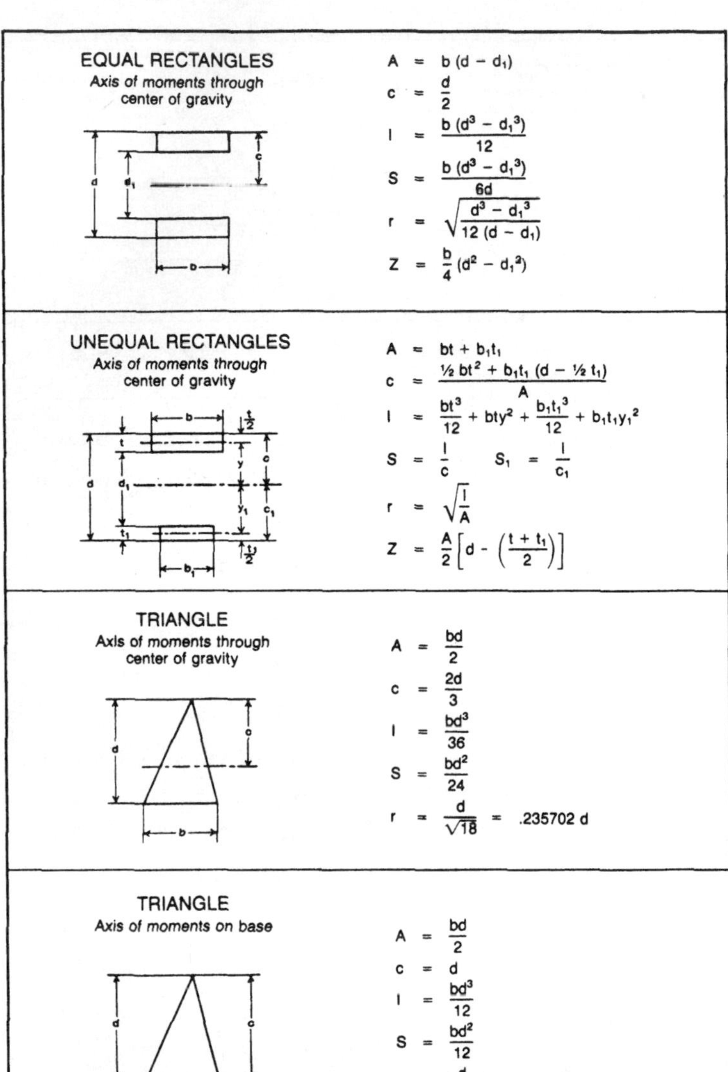

EQUAL RECTANGLES
Axis of moments through center of gravity
$A = b(d - d_1)$
$c = \frac{d}{2}$
$I = \frac{b(d^3 - d_1^3)}{12}$
$S = \frac{b(d^3 - d_1^3)}{6d}$
$r = \sqrt{\frac{d^3 - d_1^3}{12(d - d_1)}}$
$Z = \frac{b}{4}(d^2 - d_1^2)$
UNEQUAL RECTANGLES
Axis of moments through center of gravity
$A = bt + b_1t_1$
$c = \frac{\frac{1}{2}bt^2 + b_1t_1(d - \frac{1}{2}t_1)}{A}$
$I = \frac{bt^3}{12} + bty^2 + \frac{b_1t_1^3}{12} + b_1t_1y_1^2$
$S = \frac{I}{c} \quad S_1 = \frac{I}{c_1}$
$r = \sqrt{\frac{I}{A}}$
$Z = \frac{A}{2}\left[d - \left(\frac{t + t_1}{2}\right)\right]$
TRIANGLE
Axis of moments through center of gravity
$A = \frac{bd}{2}$
$c = \frac{2d}{3}$
$I = \frac{bd^3}{36}$
$S = \frac{bd^2}{24}$
$r = \frac{d}{\sqrt{18}} = .235702\ d$
TRIANGLE
Axis of moments on base
$A = \frac{bd}{2}$
$c = d$
$I = \frac{bd^3}{12}$
$S = \frac{bd^2}{12}$
$r = \frac{d}{\sqrt{6}} = .408248\ d$

Figure 21.8 *(Continued)*

*HALF ELLIPSE

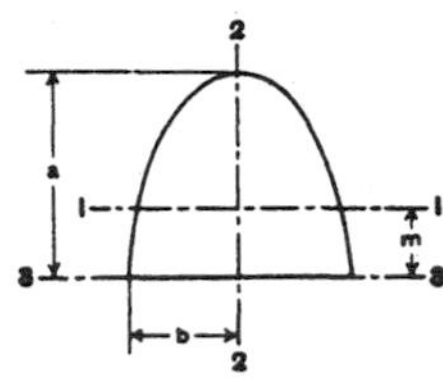

$$A = \frac{1}{2}\pi ab$$

$$m = \frac{4a}{3\pi}$$

$$I_1 = a^3b\left(\frac{\pi}{8} - \frac{8}{9\pi}\right)$$

$$I_2 = \frac{1}{8}\pi ab^3$$

$$I_3 = \frac{1}{8}\pi a^3b$$

*QUARTER ELLIPSE

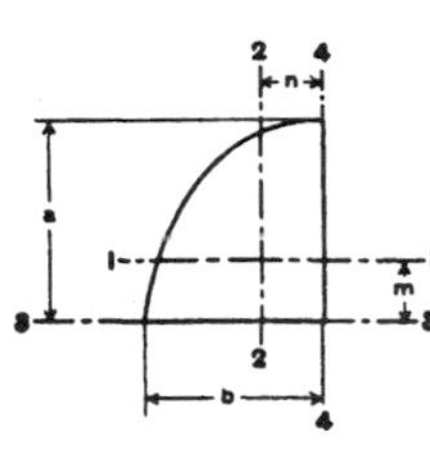

$$A = \frac{1}{4}\pi ab$$

$$m = \frac{4a}{3\pi}$$

$$n = \frac{4b}{3\pi}$$

$$I_1 = a^3b\left(\frac{\pi}{16} - \frac{4}{9\pi}\right)$$

$$I_2 = ab^3\left(\frac{\pi}{16} - \frac{4}{9\pi}\right)$$

$$I_3 = \frac{1}{16}\pi a^3b$$

$$I_4 = \frac{1}{16}\pi ab^3$$

*ELLIPTIC COMPLEMENT

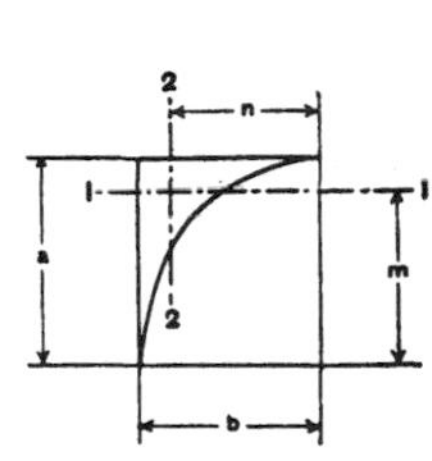

$$A = ab\left(1 - \frac{\pi}{4}\right)$$

$$m = \frac{a}{6\left(1 - \frac{\pi}{4}\right)}$$

$$n = \frac{b}{6\left(1 - \frac{\pi}{4}\right)}$$

$$I_1 = a^3b\left(\frac{1}{3} - \frac{\pi}{16} - \frac{1}{36\left(1 - \frac{\pi}{4}\right)}\right)$$

$$I_2 = ab^3\left(\frac{1}{3} - \frac{\pi}{16} - \frac{1}{36\left(1 - \frac{\pi}{4}\right)}\right)$$

*To obtain properties of half circle, quarter circle and circular complement substitute a = b = R.

Figure 21.8 *(Continued)*

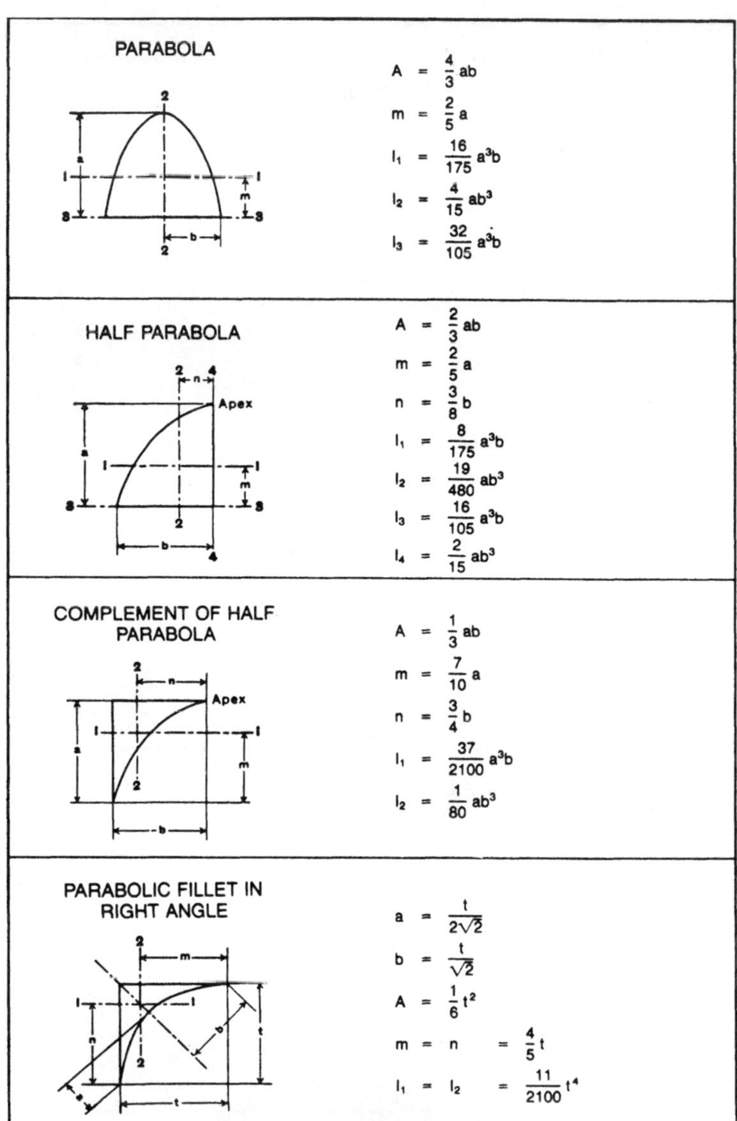
PARABOLA
$A = \frac{4}{3} ab$
$m = \frac{2}{5} a$
$I_1 = \frac{16}{175} a^3 b$
$I_2 = \frac{4}{15} ab^3$
$I_3 = \frac{32}{105} a^3 b$
HALF PARABOLA
Apex
$A = \frac{2}{3} ab$
$m = \frac{2}{5} a$
$n = \frac{3}{8} b$
$I_1 = \frac{8}{175} a^3 b$
$I_2 = \frac{19}{480} ab^3$
$I_3 = \frac{16}{105} a^3 b$
$I_4 = \frac{2}{15} ab^3$
COMPLEMENT OF HALF PARABOLA
Apex
$A = \frac{1}{3} ab$
$m = \frac{7}{10} a$
$n = \frac{3}{4} b$
$I_1 = \frac{37}{2100} a^3 b$
$I_2 = \frac{1}{80} ab^3$
PARABOLIC FILLET IN RIGHT ANGLE
$a = \frac{t}{2\sqrt{2}}$
$b = \frac{t}{\sqrt{2}}$
$A = \frac{1}{6} t^2$
$m = n = \frac{4}{5} t$
$I_1 = I_2 = \frac{11}{2100} t^4$

Figure 21.8 *(Continued)*

REGULAR POLYGON

Axis of moments through center

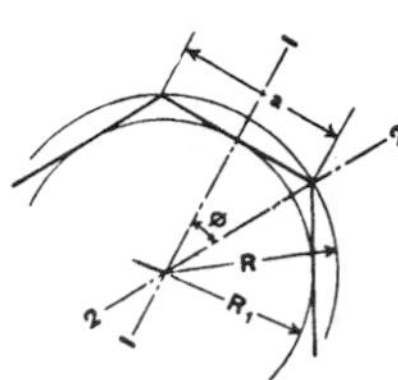

$$n = \text{Number of sides}$$

$$\phi = \frac{180°}{n}$$

$$a = 2\sqrt{R^2 - R_1^2}$$

$$R = \frac{a}{2 \sin \phi}$$

$$R_1 = \frac{a}{2 \tan \phi}$$

$$A = \frac{1}{4} na^2 \cot \phi = \frac{1}{2} nR^2 \sin 2\phi = nR_1^2 \tan \phi$$

$$I_1 = I_2 = \frac{A(6R^2 - a^2)}{24} = \frac{A(12R_1^2 + a^2)}{48}$$

$$r_1 = r_2 = \sqrt{\frac{6R^2 - a^2}{24}} = \sqrt{\frac{12R_1^2 + a^2}{48}}$$

ANGLE

Axis of moments through center of gravity

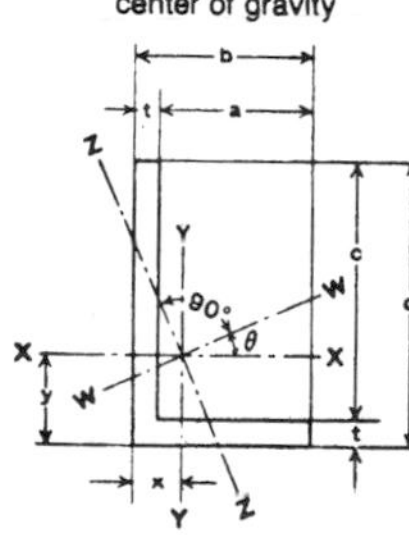

Z-Z is axis of minimum I

$$\tan 2\theta = \frac{2K}{I_Y - I_X}$$

$$A = t(b + c) \quad x = \frac{b^2 + ct}{2(b + c)} \quad y = \frac{d^2 + at}{2(b + c)}$$

K = Product of Inertia about X-X & Y-Y

$$= \mp \frac{abcdt}{4(b + c)}$$

$$I_X = \frac{1}{3}[t(d - y)^3 + by^3 - a(y - t)^3]$$

$$I_Y = \frac{1}{3}[t(b - x)^3 + dx^3 - c(x - t)^3]$$

$$I_Z = I_X \sin^2\theta + I_Y \cos^2\theta + K \sin 2\theta$$

$$I_W = I_X \cos^2\theta + I_Y \sin^2\theta - K \sin 2\theta$$

K is negative when heel of angle, with respect to c. g., is in 1st or 3rd quadrant, positive when in 2nd or 4th quadrant.

BEAMS AND CHANNELS

Transverse force oblique through center of gravity

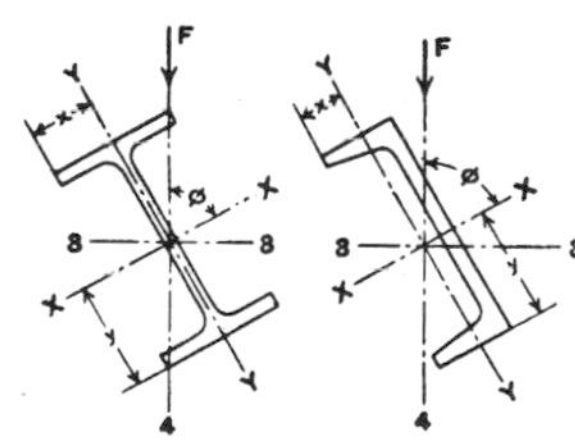

$$I_3 = I_X \sin^2\phi + I_Y \cos^2\phi$$

$$I_4 = I_X \cos^2\phi + I_y \sin^2\phi$$

$$f_b = M\left(\frac{y}{I_X} \sin\phi + \frac{x}{I_Y} \cos\phi\right)$$

where Mj is bending moment due to force F.

Figure 21.8 *(Continued)*

BENDING MOMENTS AND DEFLECTIONS OF BEAMS

1. CANTILEVER BEAM

Concentrated Load at Free End

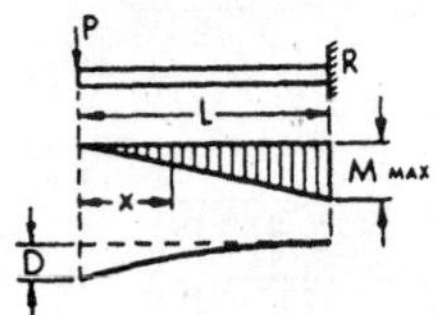

Reaction, $R = P$

Moment at any point: $M = Px$

Maximum moment, $M_{max} = PL$

Maximum deflection, $D = \dfrac{PL^3}{3\,EI}$

2. CANTILEVER BEAM

Uniform Load, w per unit of length, total load W

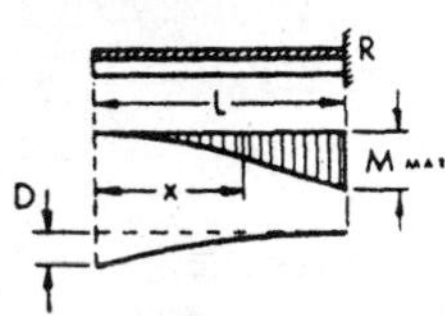

Reaction, $R = wL = W$

Moment at any point: $M = \dfrac{wx^2}{2} = \dfrac{Wx^2}{2L}$

Maximum moment, $M_{max} = \dfrac{wL^2}{2} = \dfrac{WL}{2}$

Maximum deflection, $D = \dfrac{wL^4}{8\,EI} = \dfrac{WL^3}{8\,EI}$

3. SIMPLE BEAM

Concentrated Load at Center

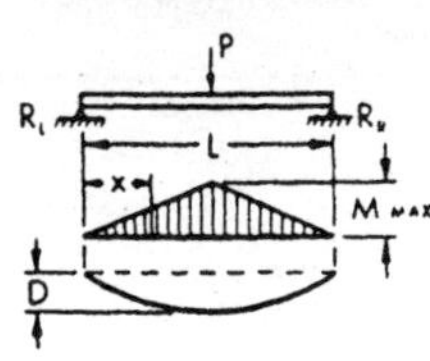

Reactions: $R_L = R_R = \dfrac{P}{2}$

Moment at any point:

$$x \leq \frac{L}{2},\ M = \frac{Px}{2}$$

$$x \geq \frac{L}{2},\ M = \frac{P(L-x)}{2}$$

Maximum moment, at center, $M_{max} = \dfrac{PL}{4}$

Maximum deflection, $D = \dfrac{PL^3}{48\,EI}$

Figure 21.9 Beam equations.

4. SIMPLE BEAM

Concentrated Load at any point

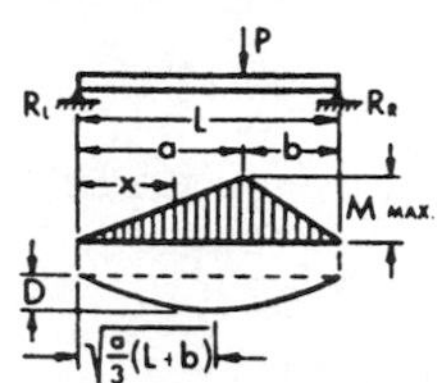

Reactions: $R_L = \frac{Pb}{L}$, $R_R = \frac{Pa}{L}$

Moment at any point:

$$x \leq a,\ M = R_{LX} = \frac{Pbx}{L}$$

$$x \geq a,\ M = R_R\,(L - x) = \frac{Pa(L - x)}{L}$$

Maximum moment, at $x = a$, $M_{max} = \frac{Pab}{L}$

Maximum deflection, $D = \frac{Pab(L + b)\sqrt{3a(L + b)}}{27\ EIL}$

5. SIMPLE BEAM

Two equal, concentrated loads, symmetrically placed

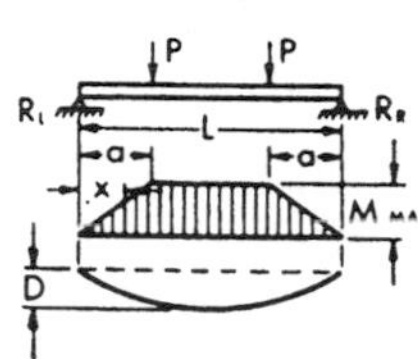

Reactions: $R_L = R_R = P$

Moment at any point:

$$x \leq a,\ M = R_{LX} = Px$$

$$a \leq x \leq (L - a),\ M = Pa$$

$$x \geq (L - a),\ M = P(L - x)$$

Maximum moment, $M_{max} = Pa$

Maximum deflection, $D = \frac{Pa}{24\ EI}(3L^2 - 4a^2)$

6. SIMPLE BEAM

Uniform Load, w per unit of length, total load W

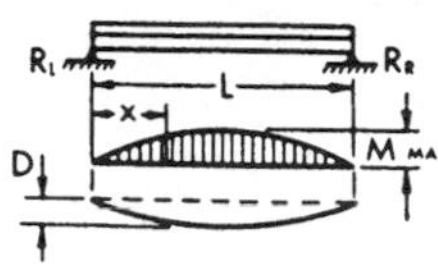

Reactions: $R_L = R_R = \frac{wL}{2} = \frac{W}{2}$

Moment at any point:

$$M = \frac{wx(L - x)}{2} = \frac{Wx(L - x)}{2L}$$

Maximum moment, at center, $M_{max} = \frac{wL^2}{8} = \frac{WL}{8}$

Maximum deflection, $D = \frac{5wL^4}{384\ EI} = \frac{5WL^3}{384\ EI}$

Figure 21.9 *(Continued)*

7. SIMPLE BEAM

Uniform Load, w per unit of length, on part of span

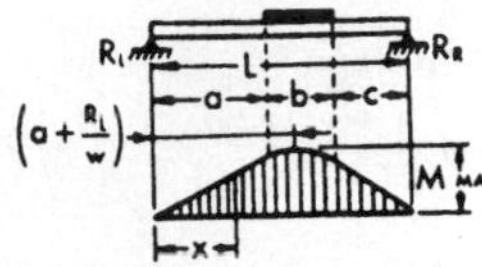

Reactions: $R_L = \frac{bw(2c+b)}{2L}$, $R_R = \frac{bw(2a+b)}{2L}$

Moment at any point:

$$x \leqq a,\ M = R_{LX} = \frac{bwx(2c+b)}{2L}$$

$$a \leqq x \leqq (a+b),\ M = R_{LX} - \frac{(x-a)^2 w}{2}$$

$$x \geqq (a+b),\ M = R_R\,(L-x)$$

Maximum moment, $M_{max} = R_L\left(a + \frac{R_L}{2w}\right)$

8. BEAM FIXED AT ONE END, SIMPLE SUPPORT AT OTHER

Concentrated Load at any point

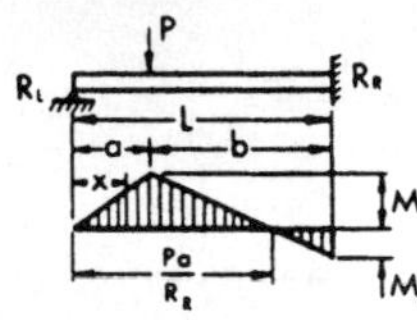

Reactions: $R_L = \frac{Pb^2}{2L^3}(2L+a)$, $R_R = P - R_L$

Moment at any point:

$$x \leqq a,\ M = R_{LX} = \frac{Pb^2x}{2L^3}(2L+a)$$

$$x \geqq a,\ M = R_{LX} - P(x-a)$$

Moment at $x = L$, $M_2 = \frac{-Pab}{2L^2}(L+a)$

Moment at $x = a$, $M_1 = \frac{Pab^2}{2L^3}(2L+a)$

9. BEAM FIXED AT ONE END, SIMPLE SUPPORT AT OTHER

Uniform Load, w per unit of length, total load W

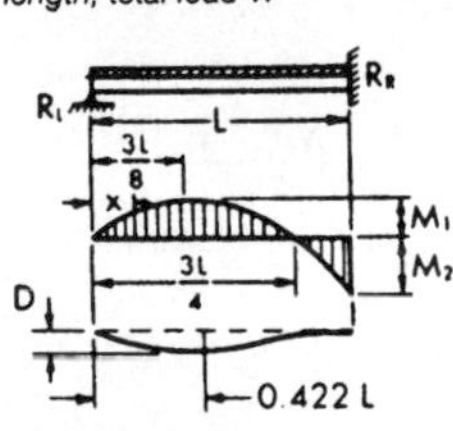

Reactions: $R_L = \frac{3wL}{8}$, $R_R = \frac{5wL}{8}$

Moment at any point:

$$x \leqq L,\ M = wx\left(\frac{3L}{8} - \frac{x}{2}\right)$$

Moment at $x = \frac{3L}{8}$, $M_1 = \frac{9wL^2}{128}$

Maximum moment, $x = L$, $M_2 = \frac{-wL^2}{8}$

Maximum deflection, $D = 0.00542\frac{wL^4}{EI} = 0.00542\frac{WL^3}{EI}$

Figure 21.9 *(Continued)*

10. BEAM FIXED AT BOTH ENDS

Concentrated Load at center

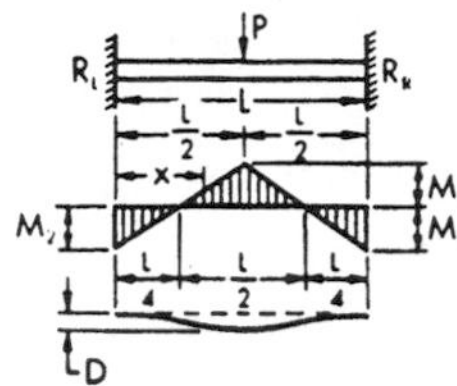

Reactions: $R_L = R_R = \frac{P}{2}$

Moment at any point:

$$x \leq \frac{L}{2},\ M = \frac{-P}{2}\left(\frac{L}{4} - x\right)$$

$$x \geq \frac{L}{2},\ M = \frac{P}{2}\left(\frac{3L}{4} - x\right)$$

Maximum moment:

$x = 0$ and $x = L$, $M_2 = \frac{-PL}{8}$

$x = \frac{L}{2}$, $M_1 = \frac{PL}{8}$

Maximum deflection, $D = \frac{PL^3}{192\ EI}$

11. BEAM FIXED AT BOTH ENDS

Concentrated Load at any point

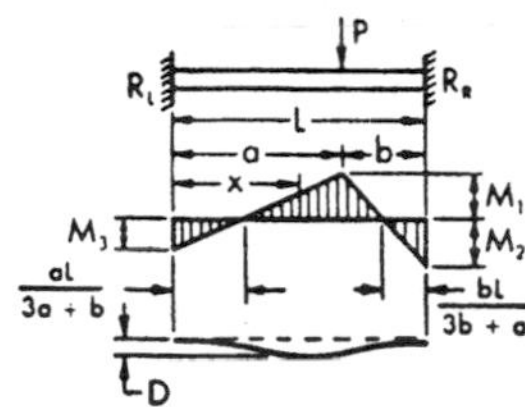

Reactions: $R_L = \frac{Pb^2}{L^3}(L + 2a)$, $R_R = \frac{Pa^2}{L^3}(L + 2b)$

Moment at any point:

$$x \leq a,\ M = \frac{-Pab^2}{L^2} + R_{Lx}$$

$$x \geq a,\ M = \frac{-Pa^2b}{L^2} + R_R(L - x)$$

Moment at $x = 0$, $M_3 = \frac{-Pab^2}{L^2}$

Moment at $x = a$, $M_1 = \frac{2Pa^2b^2}{L^3}$

Maximum moment, $a \geq b$, $M_2 = \frac{-Pa^2b}{L^2}$

Maximum deflection, $a \geq b$, $D = \frac{2Pa^3b^2}{3\ EI\ (3a + b)^2}$

12. BEAM FIXED AT BOTH ENDS

Uniform Load, w per unit of length, total load W

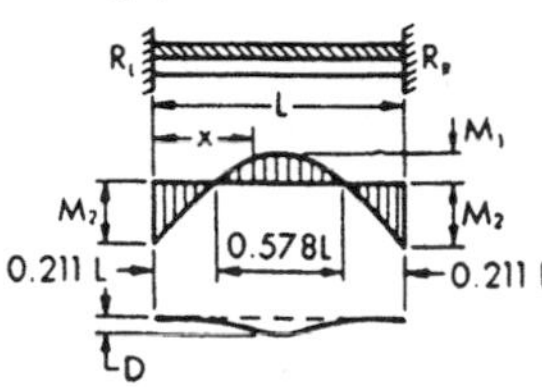

Reactions: $R_L = R_R = \frac{wL}{2} = \frac{W}{2}$

Moment at any point:

$$x \leq L,\ M = \frac{-wL^2}{12} - \frac{wx^2}{2} + \frac{wLx}{2}$$

Maximum moment, $x = 0$ and $x = L$, $M_2 = \frac{-wL^2}{12} = \frac{-WL}{12}$

Moment at $x = \frac{L}{2}$, $M_1 = \frac{wL^2}{24} = \frac{WL}{24}$

Maximum deflection, $D = \frac{wL^4}{384\ EI} = \frac{WL^3}{384\ EI}$

Figure 21.9 *(Continued)*

13. BEAM

Constant Moment, M, applied at ends

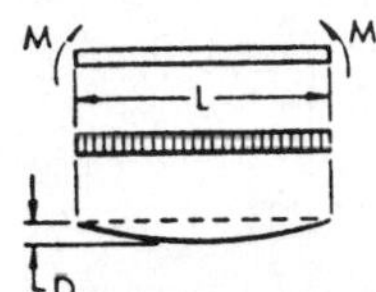

Moment at any point $= M$

Maximum deflection, $D = \dfrac{ML^2}{8\,EI}$

14. SIMPLE BEAM

Moment applied at one end

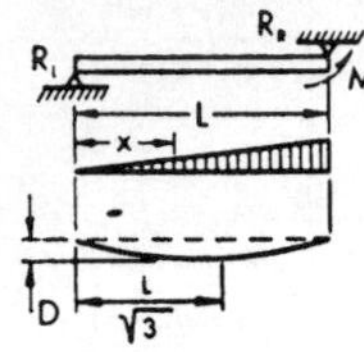

Reactions: $R_L = -R_R = \dfrac{M}{L}$

Moment at any point $= R_{LX}$

Maximum moment $= M$

Maximum deflection, $D = 0.0642\,\dfrac{ML^2}{8\,EI}$

15. CONTINUOUS BEAM, TWO EQUAL SPANS

Concentrated Load, P, at any point

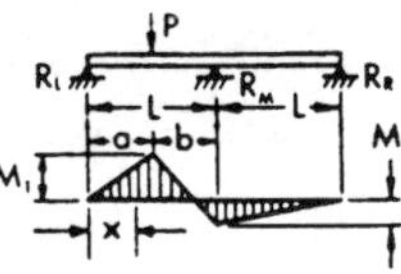

Reactions:

$$R_L = \frac{Pb}{4L^3}[4L^2 - a(L + a)]$$

$$R_M = \frac{Pa}{2L^3}(3L^2 - a^2)$$

$$R_R = \frac{Pa}{4L^3}(L^2 - a^2)$$

Moment at any point:

$x \leqq a,\ M = R_{LX}$
$a \leqq x \leqq L,\ M = R_{LX} - P(x - a)$
$x \geqq L,\ M = -R_R\,(2L - x)$

Moment at $x = L$, $M_2 = -R_RL$

Maximum moment, $M_1 = R_La$

Figure 21.9 *(Continued)*

Area, Neutral Axis, Moment of Inertia, Section Modulus & Radius of Gyration

SECTION	Area	Neutral Axis	Moment of Inertia	Section Modulus	Radius of Gyration
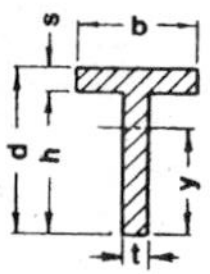	$bs + ht$	$d - \frac{d^2t + s^2(b - t)}{2(bs + ht)}$	$\frac{1}{3}\left[ty^3 + b(d - y)^3 - (b - t)(d - y - s)^2\right]$	$\frac{I}{y}$	$\sqrt{\frac{I}{3(bs + ht)}}$ $\frac{\left[ty^3 + b(d - y)^3 - \right.}{\left.(b - t)(d - y - s)^3\right]}$
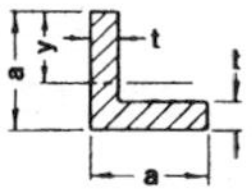	$t(2a - t)$	$a - \frac{a^2 + at - t^2}{2(2a - t)}$	$\frac{1}{3}\left[ty^3 + a(a - y)^3 - (a - t)(a - y - t)^3\right]$	$\frac{I}{y}$	$\sqrt{\frac{I}{A}}$
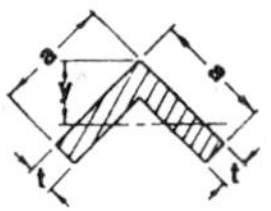	$t(2a - t)$	$\frac{a^2 + at - t^2}{2(2a - t)\cos 45}$	$\frac{1}{3}\left[2x^4 - 2(x - t)^4 + t\left[a - (2x - 0.5t)^3\right]\right]$ $x = \frac{a^2 + at - t^2}{2(2a - t)}$	$\frac{I}{y}$	$\sqrt{\frac{I}{A}}$
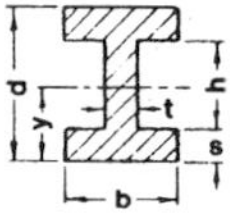	$bd - h(b - t)$	$\frac{d}{2}$	$\frac{bd^3 - h^3(b - t)}{12}$	$\frac{bd^3 - h^3(b - t)}{6d}$	$\sqrt{\frac{bd^3 - h^3(b - t)}{12[bd - h(b - t)]}}$

Figure 21.10 Properties of structural sections.

SECTION	Area	Neutral Axis	Moment of Inertia	Section Modulus	Radius of Gyration
	$bd - h(b - t)$	$\frac{b}{2}$	$\frac{2sb^3 + ht^3}{12}$	$\frac{2sb^3 + ht^3}{6b}$	$\sqrt{\frac{2sb^3 - h^3(b - t)}{12[bd - h(b - t)]}}$
	$bd - h(b - t)$	$\frac{d}{2}$	$\frac{bd^3 - h^3(b - t)}{12}$	$\frac{bd^3 - h^3(b - t)}{6d}$	$\sqrt{\frac{bd^3 - h^3(b - t)}{12[bd - h(b - t)]}}$
	$bd - h(b - t)$	$b - \frac{2b^2s + ht^2}{2bd - 2h(b - t)}$	$\frac{2sb^3 + ht^3}{3} - A(b - y)^2$	$\frac{I}{y}$	$\sqrt{\frac{I}{A}}$
	$t(a + b - t)$	$b - \frac{t(2d + a) + d^2}{2(d + a)}$	$\frac{1}{3}\Big[ty^3 + a(b - y)^3 - (a - t)(b - y - t)^3\Big]$	$\frac{I}{y}$	$\sqrt{\frac{I}{3t(a + b - t)}}$ $\Big[ty^3 + a(b - y)^3 -$ $(a - t)(b - y - t)^3\Big]$

Figure 21.10 *(Continued)*

SECTION	Area	Neutral Axis	Moment of Inertia	Section Modulus	Radius of Gyration
	$t(a + b - t)$	$a - \frac{t(2c + b) + c^2}{2(d + a)}$	$\frac{1}{3}\left[ty^3 + b(a - y)^3 - (b - t)(a - y - t)^3\right]$	$\frac{I}{y}$	$\sqrt{\frac{I}{3t(a + b - t)}}$ $\left[ty^3 + b(a - y)^3 - (b - t)(a - y - t)^3\right]$
	$t\left[b + 2(a - t)\right]$	$\frac{b}{2}$	$\frac{ab^3 - c(b - 2t)^3}{12}$	$\frac{ab^3 - c(b - 2t)^3}{6b}$	$\sqrt{\frac{ab^3 - c(b - 2t)^3}{12t[b + 2(a - t)]}}$
	$t\left[b + 2(a - t)\right]$	$\frac{2a - t}{2}$	$\frac{b(a + c)^3 - 2c^3d - 6a^2cd}{12}$	$\frac{b(a + c)^3 - 2c^3d - 6a^2cd}{6(2a - t)}$	$\sqrt{\frac{b(a + c)^3 - 2c^3d - 6a^2cd}{12t[b + 2(a - t)]}}$

Figure 21.10 *(Continued)*

21.7 U.S. Customary and SI Units of Measurement

The basic units of measurement and their symbols are shown in Figs. 21.11 and 21.12 for the U.S. Customary and SI systems. A more detailed listing of all measurements and conversions is given in Chap. 4, "U.S. Customary and SI (Metric) Measures and Conversions." The data shown here and in Chap. 6 will enable you to convert and interpret all U.S. Customary and SI units.

21.8 Interpolation and Extrapolation

Interpolation is the mathematical process for finding an incremental value between minimum and maximum given values. *Extrapolation* is the process for finding a value beyond minimum and maximum given values.

21.8.1 Interpolation: Linear

The interpolation process allows intermediate values to be found within a linear numerical interval of values.

Example Linear interpolation between values of a numerical interval.

Amperes	Inches
20	0.158 in
(24)	x
30	0.198 in
(38)	x_1
40	0.278 in

In the example we are given values of current (amperes) and the corresponding values of the width of the copper foil on a printed circuit board required to carry the given current. If we wish to know what the foil width must be to carry 24 or 38 A, we procede to set up a proportional relationship to find the unknown values of x and x_1.

The process is easily explained with the following diagram:

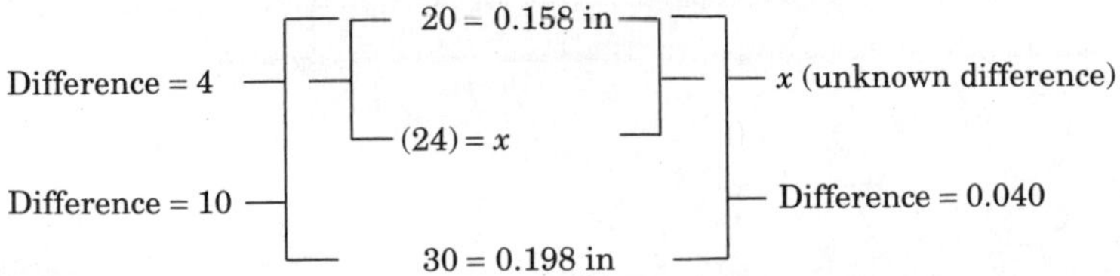

20 = 0.158 in

Difference = 4 — x (unknown difference)

(24) = x

Difference = 10 — Difference = 0.040

30 = 0.198 in

LINEAR MEASURE

Inches	Feet	Yards	Rods	Furlongs	Miles
1.0 =	.08333 =	.02778 =	.0050505 =	.00012626 =	.00001578
12.0 =	1.0 =	.33333 =	.0606061 =	.00151515 =	.00018939
36.0 =	3.0 =	1.0 =	.1818182 =	.00454545 =	.00056818
198.0 =	16.5 =	5.5 =	1.0 =	.025 =	.003125
7920.0 =	660.0 =	220.0 =	40.0 =	1.0 =	.125
63360.0 =	5280.0 =	1760.0 =	320.0 =	8.0 =	1.0

SQUARE AND LAND MEASURE

Sq. In.	Sq. Ft	Sq. Yds.	Sq. Rods	Acres	Sq. Miles
1.0 =	.006944 =	.000772			
144.0 =	1.0 =	.111111			
1296.0 =	9.0 =	1.0 =	.03306 =	.000207	
39204.0 =	272.25 =	30.25 =	1.0 =	.00625 =	.0000098
	43560.0 =	4840.0 =	160.0 =	1.0 =	.0015625
		3097600.0 =	102400.0 =	640.0 =	1.0

AVOIRDUPOIS WEIGHTS

Grains	Drams	Ounces	Pounds	Tons
1.0 =	.03657 =	.002286 =	.000143 =	.0000000714
27.34375 =	1.0 =	.0625 =	.003906 =	.00000195
437.5 =	16.0 =	1.0 =	.0625 =	.00003125
7000.0 =	256.0 =	10.0 =	1.0 =	.0005
14000000.0 =	512000.0 =	32000.0 =	2000.0 =	1.0

DRY MEASURE

Pints	Quarts	Pecks	Cubic Feet	Bushels
1.0 =	.5 =	.0625 =	.01945 =	.01563
2.0 =	1.0 =	.125 =	.03891 =	.03125
16.0 =	8.0 =	1.0 =	.31112 =	.25
51.42627 =	25.71314 =	3.21414 =	1.0 =	.80354
64.0 =	32.0 =	4.0 =	1.2445 =	1.0

LIQUID MEASURE

Gills	Pints	Quarts	U.S. Gallons	Cubic Feet
1.0 =	.25 =	.125 =	.03125 =	.00418
4.0 =	1.0 =	.5 =	.125 =	.01671
8.0 =	2.0 =	1.0 =	.250 =	.03342
32.0 =	8.0 =	4.0 =	1.0 =	.13378
			7.48052 =	1.0

Figure 21.11 Weights and measures, U.S. Customary system.

WEIGHTS AND MEASURES
International System of Units (SI)[a]
(Metric practice)

BASE UNITS

Quantity	Unit	Symbol
Length	Metre	m
Mass	Kilogram	kg
Time	Second	s
Electric current	Ampere	A
Thermodynamic temperature	Kelvin	K
Amount of substance	Mole	mol
Luminous intensity	Candela	cd

SUPPLEMENTARY UNITS

Quantity	Unit	Symbol
Plane angle	Radian	rad
Solid angle	Steradian	sr

DERIVED UNITS (WITH SPECIAL NAMES)

Quantity	Unit	Symbol	Formula
Force	Newton	N	$kg\text{-}m/s^2$
Pressure, stress	Pascal	Pa	N/m^2
Energy, work, quantity of heat	Joule	J	N-m
Power	Watt	W	J/s

DERIVED UNITS (WITHOUT SPECIAL NAMES)

Quantity	Unit	Formula
Area	Square metre	m^2
Volume	Cubic metre	m^3
Velocity	Metre per second	m/s
Acceleration	Metre per second squared	m/s^2
Specific volume	Cubic metre per kilogram	m^3/kg
Density	Kilogram per cubic metre	kg/m^3

SI PREFIXES

Multiplication Factor	Prefix	Symbol
1 000 000 000 000 000 000 $= 10^{18}$	exa	E
1 000 000 000 000 000 $= 10^{15}$	peta	P
1 000 000 000 000 $= 10^{12}$	tera	T
1 000 000 000 $= 10^{9}$	giga	G
1 000 000 $= 10^{6}$	mega	M
1 000 $= 10^{3}$	kilo	k
100 $= 10^{2}$	hecto[b]	h
10 $= 10^{1}$	deka[b]	da
0.1 $= 10^{-1}$	deci[b]	d
0.01 $= 10^{-2}$	centi[b]	c
0.001 $= 10^{-3}$	milli	m
0.000 001 $= 10^{-6}$	micro	μ
0.000 000 001 $= 10^{-9}$	nano	n
0.000 000 000 001 $= 10^{-12}$	pico	p
0.000 000 000 000 001 $= 10^{-15}$	femto	f
0.000 000 000 000 000 001 $= 10^{-18}$	atto	a

[a]Refer to ASTM E380-79 for more complete information on SI.
[b]Use is not recommended.

Figure 21.12 Weights and measures, SI system.

Then, by proportion,

$$\frac{4}{10} = \frac{x}{0.040} \qquad 10x = 0.16 \qquad x = 0.016$$

x is the difference which must be added to 0.158. So, at 24 A, the foil width is (0.158 + 0.016) = 0.174 in. As can be seen, the value 0.174 is located proportionally between the values 0.158 and 0.198.

The interpolation process, by proportion, is accurate for all linear intervals, allowing us to find any corresponding foil width for any current (between linear intervals).

Find the value of the foil width required to carry 38 A of current.

21.8.2 Extrapolation: Linear

The extrapolation process allows unknown values to be found either preceding or following a linear numerical interval.

Example Linear extrapolation beyond given values of a numerical interval

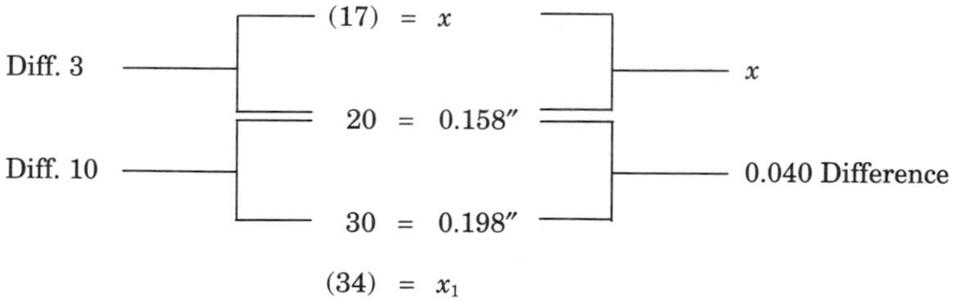

	(17) = x	
Diff. 3		x
	20 = 0.158″	
Diff. 10		0.040 Difference
	30 = 0.198″	
	(34) = x_1	

Thus $$\frac{3}{10} = \frac{x}{0.040} \qquad 10x = 0.120 \qquad x = 0.012$$

Then 0.012 is the value to be deducted from 0.158. Then, at 17 A, the foil width is (0.158 − 0.012) = 0.146 in.

Find the foil width for a current of 34 A.

21.9 Identification of Plastics

In design engineering practice, it is often desirable to know the type of plastic from which a manufactured article is made. This is appro-

Plastic Material	No Flame	Burns but extinguishes on removal of flame			Continues to burn after removal of flame				
	■ Odor	Odor	Color of flame	Drips	Odor	Color of flame	Drips	Burn Speed	Remarks
ABS	.....	Acrid	Yellow, blue edges	No	Acrid	Yellow, blue edges	Yes	Slow	Black smoke, soot in air
Acetals	.....	.....	.....	.....	Formaldehyde	Blue, no smoke	Yes	Slow	....
Acrylics	.....	.....	.....	.....	Fruity	Blue, yellow tip	No (cast) Yes (molded)	Slow	Flame may spurt if rubber molded.
Cellulosics (Acetate)	.....	Vinegar	Yellow with sparks	No	Vinegar	Yellow	Yes	Slow	Flame may spark
Fluocarbons									
FEP	Burnt hair (Faint)	.....	.....	.....	.....	.....	.....	.....	Deforms, no combustion but drips.
PTFE	"	.....	.....	.....	.....	.....	.....	.....	Deforms but does not drip.
CTFE	Acetic acid	.....	.....	.....	.....	.....	.....	.....	Deforms, no combustion but drips.
PVF	Acidic	.....	.....	.....	.....	.....	.....	.....	Deforms.
Nylons Type 6 & 6/6	.....	Burnt wool	Blue, yellow tip	Yes	.....	.....	.....	.....	6/6 more rigid
Polycarbonates	.....	Faint sweet (aromatic)	Orange	Yes	.....	.....	.....	.....	Black smoke with soot.
Polyethylenes	.....	.....	.....	.....	Paraffin	Blue, yellow tip	Yes	Slow	Floats in water.
Polyimides	♦	.....	.....	.....	.....	.....	.....	.....	Chars, material rigid.
Polypropylenes	.....	Acrid	Yellow	No	Sweet	Blue, yellow tip	Yes	Slow	Floats in water. More difficult to scratch than polyethylene.
Polystyrenes	.....	.....	.....	.....	Illuminating gas	Yellow	Yes	Rapid	Black smoke with soot in air.
Polysulfones	.....	♦	Orange	Yes	.....	.....	.....	.....	Black smoke.
Polyurethanes	.....	.....	.....	.....	♦	Yellow	No	Slow	Black smoke.

Vinyls: Flex - rigid	.....	Hydrochloric Acid	Yellow with green spurts.	No	.....	.....	.....	.....	Chars, melts.
Polyblends:									
ABS/Polycarbonate	.....	.....	.....	.....	♦	Yellow, blue edges	No	.....	Black smoke, soot in air.
ABS-PVC	.....	Acrid	Yellow, blue edges	No	.....	.....	.....	.....	Black smoke, soot in air.
PVC/Acrylic	.....	Fruity	Blue, yellow tip	No	.....	.....	.....	.....	.....
Melamines	Formaldehyde and fish.	.....	.....	.....	.....	.....	.....	.....	.....
Phenolics	Formaldehyde and phenol	Phenol and wood/paper	Yellow	No	.....	.....	.....	.....	May crack.
Polyesters	.....	Hydrochloric Acid	Yellow	No	♦	Yellow, blue edges	No	Slow	Cracks and breaks.
Silicones	♦	.....	.....	.....	.....	.....	.....	.....	Deforms.
Ureas	Formaldehyde	.....	.....	.....	.....	.....	.....	.....	.....

NOTES: ♦ = Nondescript. ■ = Freshly cut or filed to bring out odor.
Source: Laird Plastics, West Palm Beach, Florida.

Figure 21.13 Identification of plastics: simple test procedures.

priate when you know the performance value of an article which is made of an unknown plastic compound and you wish to design a similar part. The article may be analyzed at a materials laboratory to determine its composition and possible class or type of plastic, but this is expensive, may require rigorous analysis, and is not always appropriate. The table in Fig. 21.13 will allow you to identify many basic types of plastics through the simple tests shown.

Data on plastic materials are shown in Chap. 5, "Materials and Their Uses." Plastics are of importance in modern metalworking practices because plastics now replace metals and alloys in a vast number of applications. When a metal can be replaced with a plastic material, the benefits usually include such factors as lower cost, more design flexibility, corrosion resistance, insulation value, impact resistance, and lighter weight.

21.10 Standard Sizes of Engineering Drawings

The recommended trimmed sheet sizes for engineering drawings, based on ANSI Y14.1-1980, are shown in Fig. 21.14. Both the U.S. Customary and SI size standard sizes are shown. Use of the standard 8.5×11 in size and multiples thereof permits filing of small tracings and folded Xerox black and white prints in commercial standard letter files. The metric (SI) standard sizes are based on the width-to-length ratio of 1 to $(2)^{1/2}$ or 1 to 1.414.

Drawing Size, Inches		Drawing Size, Metric (SI)	
Designation	Size, inches	Designation	Size, mm
A	8.5 x 11	A0	841 x 1149
B	11 x 17	A1	594 x 841
C	17 x 22	A2	420 x 594
D	22 x 34	A3	297 x 420
E	34 x 44	A4	210 x 297
F	28 x 40	.....	.....

Figure 21.14 Standard engineering drawing sizes, American and metric (SI).

Chapter

22

Safety Practices in Industry

The metalworking industries in the United States and throughout the world perform their functions and manufacturing practices under a variety of conditions, some of which are hazardous and which may pose health problems to the metalworker. In order to protect the people involved in all classes of industrial manufacturing processes and situations, the Occupational Safety and Health Administration (OSHA) was created by the United States government.

OSHA is responsible for generating and administering the rules and regulations which were designed to protect American workers from industrial and manufacturing practices and materials which have proven to be safety and health hazards. For example, for many years workers handled and processed asbestos without the slightest idea or knowledge that this material was dangerous to their health and in many instances caused fatal health problems. Likewise, processes for mercury and cadmium metals can pose serious health and environmental problems, as can the indiscriminate handling and disposal of toxic waste products.

In order to help protect the environment, the Environmental Protection Agency (EPA) was established. This agency generates and administers the rules and regulations designed to help protect the environment from poisonous and otherwise harmful chemicals and materials used throughout industry. It should be noted that many of the heavy metals and their compounds are toxic. Also, many organic, carbon-based materials and chemicals are also toxic, some to an extreme extent. Many materials and compounds are also nonbiodegradable, which means that they will remain in the environment indefinitely as waste products.

Bearing the preceding in mind, we can readily see why these regulating agencies and administrations are necessary in the modern industrial world. Following (Sec. 22.1.2) is a reference listing of the OSHA standards for use in any of the categories which are currently under regulation. The standard which you are interested in checking may be obtained directly from OSHA or your company risk manager. All manufacturing installations are required to keep the OSHA and EPA regulating standards on their premises and make them available to any employee interested in obtaining information from these regulatory standards.

If you have doubts pertaining to the possible hazards of the materials, substances, and processes which you use or come into contact with during your job duties, check the applicable OSHA or EPA standards. Modern American industrial employees are no longer required to forfeit their health or lives because of their job requirements, which may be in violation of the OSHA and EPA regulatory standards.

22.1 Typical Industrial Hazards

The following list of safety and health hazards is only a minute example of the conditions and materials and substances that a metalworking employee could be subjected to.

- Welding over cadmium-plated parts (highly toxic fumes from the cadmium)
- Case-hardening steel parts with cyanide compounds without proper ventilation and equipment
- Fumes from the electroplating processes
- Grinding and machining beryllium alloys (beryllium-copper, beryllium-nickel)
- Machining and grinding magnesium
- Machining plastics with fiberglass fillers without ventilation and evacuation equipment

- Skin contact with plating solutions
- Fumes from the metal-etching processes
- Foot and hand injuries when handling large sheet metal parts
- Injuries on machine tools not equipped with guards and shields
- Injuries on stamping dies due to inadequate or missing shields
- Ultraviolet radiation burns and eye injuries from welding processes
- Paint fumes in nondesignated painting areas

22.1.1 Safety practices when operating machine tools

Many grave injuries occur in the operation of machine tools, especially during manual operations. The following list of precautions will help to prevent injury to machine tool operators, machinists, and tool and die makers.

- Wear the proper eye protection.
- Know exactly what to expect your machine to do *before* you turn on the power switch.
- Do not wear neckties or any loose clothing while operating a machine tool; the sleeves of long-sleeve shirts also must be rolled-up past the elbow.
- Do not wear rings, watches, neck chains, or wrist bracelets while operating machine tools.
- Do not wear gloves while operating machine tools.
- Know instinctively where the power switch is located on your machine tool so that it may be quickly switched off in an emergency.
- Keep your work area clear of obstructions.
- Other machining precautions are described in Chap. 7, "Machining: Machine Tools and Practices."

22.1.2 OSHA standards, by category

See Fig. 22.1.

(Text continued on page 1479.)

PART 1910

OCCUPATIONAL SAFETY AND HEALTH STANDARDS

SUBPART A—GENERAL

1910.1 Purpose and scope.
1910.2 Definitions.
1910.3 Petitions for the issuance, amendment, or repeal of a standard.
1910.4 Amendments to this part.
1910.5 Applicability of standards.
1910.6 Incorporation by reference.
1910.7 Definition and requirements for a nationally recognized testing laboratory.

SUBPART B—ADOPTION AND EXTENSION OF ESTABLISHED FEDERAL STANDARDS

1910.11 Scope and purpose.
1910.12 Construction work.
1910.13 Ship repairing.
1910.14 Shipbuilding.
1910.15 Shipbreaking.
1910.16 Longshoring.
1910.17 Effective dates.
1910.18 Changes in established Federal standards.
1910.19 Special provisions for air contaminants.

SUBPART C—GENERAL SAFETY AND HEALTH PROVISIONS

1910.20 Access to employee exposure and medical records.

SUBPART D—WALKING—WORKING SURFACES

1910.21 Definitions.
1910.22 General requirements.
1910.23 Guarding floor and wall openings and holes.
1910.24 Fixed industrial stairs.
1910.25 Portable wood ladders.
1910.26 Portable metal ladders.
1910.27 Fixed ladders.
1910.28 Safety requirements for scaffolding.
1910.29 Manually propelled mobile ladder stands and scaffolds (towers).
1910.30 Other working surfaces.
1910.31 Sources of standards.
1910.32 Standards organizations.

SUBPART E—MEANS OF EGRESS

1910.35 Definitions.
1910.36 General requirements.
1910.37 Means of egress, general.
1910.38 Specific means of egress requirements by occupancy. [Reserved]

1

Figure 22.1 Table of OSHA standards.

1910.39 Sources of standards.
1910.40 Standards organizations.

SUBPART F—POWERED PLATFORMS, MANLIFTS AND VEHICLE-MOUNTED WORK PLATFORMS

1910.66 Power platforms for building maintenance.
1910.67 Vehicle-mounted elevating and rotating work platforms.
1910.68 Manlifts.
1910.69 Sources of standards.
1910.70 Standards organizations.

SUBPART G—OCCUPATIONAL HEALTH AND ENVIRONMENTAL CONTROL

1910.94 Ventilation.
1910.95 Occupational noise exposure.
1910.96 Ionizing radiation.
1910.97 Nonionizing radiation.
1910.98 Additional delay in effective date.
1910.99 Sources of standards.
1910.100 Standards organizations.

SUBPART H—HAZARDOUS MATERIALS

1910.101 Compressed gases (general requirements).
1910.102 Acetylene.
1910.103 Hydrogen.
1910.104 Oxygen.
1910.105 Nitrous oxide.
1910.106 Flammable and combustible liquids.
1910.107 Spray finishing using flammable and combustible materials.
1910.108 Dip tanks containing flammable or combustible liquids.
1910.109 Explosives and blasting agents.
1910.110 Storage and handling of liquified petroleum gases.
1910.111 Storage and handling of anhydrous ammonia.
1910.112 [Reserved]
1910.113 [Reserved]
1910.114 Effective dates.
1910.115 Sources of standards.
1910.116 Standards organizations.
1910.120 Hazardous Waste Operations and Emergency Response

SUBPART I—PERSONAL PROTECTIVE EQUIPMENT

1910.132 General requirements.
1910.133 Eye and face protection.
1910.134 Respiratory protection.
1910.135 Occupational head protection.
1910.136 Occupational foot protection.
1910.137 Electrical protective devices.
1910.138 Effective dates.
1910.139 Sources of standards.
1910.140 Standards organizations.

2

Figure 22.1 *(Continued)*

SUBPART J—GENERAL ENVIRONMENTAL CONTROLS

1910.141 Sanitation.
1910.142 Temporary labor camps.
1910.143 Nonwater carriage disposal systems.
1910.144 Safety color code for marking physical hazards.
1910.145 Specificatons for accident prevention signs and tags.
1910.146 [Reserved]
1910.147 Sources of standards.
1910.148 Standards organizations.
1910.149 Effective dates.

SUBPART K—MEDICAL AND FIRST AID

1910.151 Medical services and first aid.
1910.152 [Reserved]
1910.153 Sources of standards.

SUBPART L—FIRE PROTECTION

1910.155 Scope, application and definitions applicable to this part.
1910.156 Fire brigades.

PORTABLE FIRE SUPPRESSION EQUIPMENT

1910.157 Portable fire extinguishers.
1910.158 Standpipe and hose systems.

FIXED FIRE SUPPRESSION EQUIPMENT

1910.159 Automatic sprinkler systems
1910.160 Fixed extinguishing systems, general.
1910.161 Fixed extinguishing systems, dry chemical.
1910.162 Fixed extinguishing systems, gaseous agent.
1910.163 Fixed extinguishing systems, water, spray and foam.

OTHER FIRE PROTECTION SYSTEMS

1910.164 Fire detection systems
1910.165 Employee alarm systems
Appendices A–E

SUBPART M—COMPRESSED GAS AND COMPRESSED AIR EQUIPMENT

1910.166 Reserved
1910.167 Reserved
1910.168 Reserved

1910.169 Air receivers.
1910.170 Sources of standards.
1910.171 Standards organizations.

SUBPART N—MATERIALS HANDLING AND STORAGE

1910.176 Handling materials—general.
1910.177 Servicing multi-piece and single piece rim wheels.
1910.178 Powered industrial trucks.

3

Figure 22.1 (*Continued*)

1910.179 Overhead and gantry cranes.
1910.180 Crawler, locomotive, and truck cranes.
1910.181 Derricks.
1910.182 Effective dates.
1910.183 Helicopters.
1910.184 Slings.
1910.189 Sources of standards.
1910.190 Standards organizations.

SUBPART O—MACHINERY AND MACHINE GUARDING

1910.211 Definitions.
1910.212 General requirements for all machines.
1910.213 Woodworking machinery requirements.
1910.214 Cooperage machinery.
1910.215 Abrasive wheel machinery.
1910.216 Mills and calenders in the rubber and plastics industries.
1910.217 Mechanical power presses.
1910.218 Forging machines.
1910.219 Mechanical power-transmission apparatus.
1910.220 Effective dates.
1910.221 Sources of standards.
1910.222 Standards organizations.

SUBPART P—HAND AND PORTABLE POWERED TOOLS AND OTHER HAND-HELD EQUIPMENT

1910.241 Definitions.
1910.242 Hand and portable powered tools and equipment, general.
1910.243 Guarding of portable powered tools.
1910.244 Other portable tools and equipment.
1910.245 Effective dates.
1910.246 Sources of standards.
1910.247 Standards organizations.

SUBPART Q—WELDING, CUTTING AND BRAZING

1910.251 Definitions.
1910.252 General requirements.
1910.253 Oxygen-fuel gas welding and cutting.
1910.254 Arc welding and cutting.
1910.255 Resistance welding.
1910.256 Sources of standards.
1910.257 Standards organizations.

SUBPART R—SPECIAL INDUSTRIES

1910.261 Pulp, paper, and paperboard mills.
1910.262 Textiles.
1910.263 Bakery equipment.
1910.264 Laundry machinery and operations.
1910.265 Sawmills.
1910.266 Pulpwood logging.
1910.267 Agricultural operations.
1910.268 Telecommunications.
1910.272 Grain handling facilities.
1910.274 Sources of standards.
1910.275 Standards organizations.

SUBPART S—ELECTRICAL

1910.301 Introduction
1910.302 Electric utilization systems

4

Figure 22.1 *(Continued)*

1910.303	General requirements
1910.304	Wiring design and protection
1910.305	Wiring methods, components, and equipment for general use
1910.306	Specific purpose equipment and installations
1910.307	Hazardous (classified) locations
1910.308	Special systems
1910.309	
1910.330	[Reserved] Safety-Related Work practices
1910.331	
360	[Reserved] Safety-Related Maintenance Requirements
1910.361	
380	[Reserved] Safety Requirements for Special Equipment
1910.381	
398	[Reserved] Definitions
1910.399	Definitions applicable to this subpart
	Appendices A–C

Subpart T—Commercial Diving Operations

1910.401	Scope and application.
1910.401	Definitions.
1910.410	Qualifications of dive team.
1910.411	Medical requirements.
1910.420	Safe practice manual.
1910.421	Pre-dive procedures.
1910.422	Procedures during dive.
1910.423	Post-dive procedures.
1910.424	SCUBA diving
1910.425	Surface-supplied air diving.
1910.426	Mixed-gas diving.
1910.427	Liveboating.
1910.430	Equipment.
1910.440	Recordkeeping requirements.
1910.441	Effective date.
	Appendix A
	Subpart U–Y [Reserved]

SUBPART Z—TOXIC AND HAZARDOUS SUBSTANCES

1910.1000	Air Contaminants.
1910.1001	Asbestos tremolite, anthophyllite, and actinolite
1910.1002	Coal tar pitch volatiles; interpretation of term.
1910.1003	4-Nitrobiphenyl.
1910.1004	alpha-Naphthylamine.
1910.1005	4, 4'-Methylene bis(2-chloroaniline).
1910.1006	Methyl chloromethyl ether
1910.1007	3, 3'-Dichlorobenzine (and its salts)
1910.1008	bis-Chloromethyl ether.
1910.1009	beta-Naphthylamine.
1910.1010	Benzidine.
1910.1011	4-Aminodiphenyl.
1910.1012	Ethyleneimine.
1910.1013	beta-Propiolactone.
1910.1014	2-Acetylaminofluorene.
1910.1015	4-Dimethylaminoazobenzine.

5

Figure 22.1 *(Continued)*

1910.1016	N-Nitrosodimethylamine.
1910.1017	Vinyl Chloride.
1910.1018	Inorganic arsenic.
1910.1025	Lead.
1910.1028	Benzene.
1910.1029	Coke Oven Emissions
1910.1043	Cotton dust.
1910.1044	1,2 - dibromo - 3 - chloropropane.
1910.1045	Acrylonitrile.
1910.1047	Ethylene Oxide
1910.1048	Formaldehyde
1910.1011	Asbestos
1910.1200	Hazard communication.
1910.1450	Occupational Exposure to Hazardous Chemicals in Laboratories.

AUTHORITY: The provisions of this Part 1910 issued under secs. 6(a), 8(g), 84 Stat. 1593, 1598; 29 U.S.C. 655, 657.

6

Figure 22.1 *(Continued)*

22.2 Product Liability

Safety in product design should be of prime importance to all product designers. There have been over 500 awards of more than a million dollars granted in the United States since 1962 arising from product-liability lawsuits brought against manufacturers. It is of prime importance for a product designer or design group never to sacrifice safety for profit. Some of the criteria to consider and make note of during the design stages of a product are

1. All possible hazards in using or misusing the product
2. The environment in which the product is used
3. The typical user of the product and the typical nonuser
4. All instructions and warnings that are to be presented with the product

Nearly all products can be dangerous to one degree or another if misapplied. This leaves the product designer with much to consider when designing a product. Some of the strongest safeguards available to designers and manufacturers against product liability lawsuits are

1. The use of prototypes and fully functional models to demonstrate a product's characteristics. Also important are quality-control tests of random-production-run samples of the product.

2. Accurate records of qualitative test results, including high-speed film records and laboratory test equipment readings.
3. The application of warning labels and the supplying of accurate instructions with the product in the form of instruction books and product brochures. Warning labels must attract the attention of the user, be clear and understandable, and finally, convey the nature and extent of the probable harm resulting from misuse or failure to follow the warnings and instructions issued with the product.

Following the safeguards listed above, the product designer and manufacturer will be in a strong position if a product-liability lawsuit is brought against the manufacturer in relation to one of its products.

Chapter

23

Societies, Associations, Institutes, and Specification Authorities

Following is a listing of recognized specification authorities, societies, and institutes from which the design engineer can obtain specifications and standards covering many areas of engineering design and manufacturing.

Many of the standards are revised periodically by these authorities to keep pace with changing technology. It is therefore suggested that copies of the American standards which you require to perform your job function be obtained directly from the standards organizations which generate them. In this way, you are assured that you will be using the most recent standard and its revisions. Updates to the standards listings are distributed periodically to those on the organization mailing lists, or annual standards listing manuals may be ordered directly from the standard organizations.

Many of the standards organizations publish handbooks and manuals related to their particular fields which are technically excellent. Indexes to the standards are also available for pinpointing your area of interest in the form of annual standards catalogs.

23.1 Standards Organizations and Acronyms

AAR
Association of American Railroads
59 East Van Buren Street
Chicago, Ill. 60605

ACA
American Chain Association
1000 Vermont Ave., N.W.
Washington, D.C. 20005

AEMS
American Engineering Model Society
Box 2066
Aiken, S.C. 29801

AFBMA
Anti-Friction Bearing Manufacturers Association
2341 Jefferson Davis Highway, Suite 1015
Arlington, Va. 22202

AGMA
American Gear Manufacturers Association
1901 N. Fort Meyer Drive, Suite 1000
Arlington, Va. 22209

AISC
American Institute of Steel Construction
400 N. Michigan Ave.
Chicago, Ill. 60611

AISI
American Iron and Steel Institute
1000 16th Street, NW
Washington, D.C. 20006

The Aluminum Association
818 Connecticut Ave., NW
Washington, D.C. 20006

AMS (Aeronautical Materials Specifications)
Society of Automotive Engineers, Inc.
400 Commonwealth Drive
Warrendale, Pa. 15096

ANSI
American National Standards Institute, Inc.
11 West 42nd Street
New York, N.Y. 10036

API
American Petroleum Institute
300 Corrigan Tower Bldg.
Dallas, Texas 75201

ASLE
American Society of Lubrication Engineers
838 Busse Highway
Park Ridge, Ill. 60068

ASM
American Society for Metals
Metals Park, Ohio 44073

ASME
American Society of Mechanical Engineers
345 East 47th Street
New York, N.Y. 10017

ASMMA
American Supply and Machinery Manufacturers Association
1230 Keith Bldg.
Cleveland, Ohio 44115

ASTM
American Society for Testing and Materials
1916 Race Street
Philadelphia, Pa. 19103

AWS
American Welding Society
550 NW Lejeune Road
PO Box 351040
Miami, Fla. 33135

BSA
Bearing Specialists Association
221 N LaSalle St., Suite 2026
Chicago, Ill. 60601

CDA
Copper Development Association, Inc.
405 Lexington Ave.
New York, N.Y. 10017

EEI
Edison Electric Institute
750 Third Ave.
New York, N.Y. 10017

Federal Specifications
U.S. Navy Supply Depot
5801 Tabor Ave.
Philadelphia, Pa. 19120

FEMA
Farm Equipment Manufacturers Association
230 S. Bemiston, Suite 809
St. Louis, Mo. 63105

IEEE
Institute of Electrical and Electronics Engineers
345 E. 47th Street
New York, N.Y. 10017

IFI
Industrial Fasteners Institute
1505 E. Ohio Bldg.
1717 E. 9th Street
Cleveland, Ohio 44114

IIE
Institute of Industrial Engineers
25 Technology Park
Atlanta, Norcross, Ga. 30092

Ingot Number
Brass and Bronze Ingot Institute
33 N. LaSalle St., Room 3500
Chicago, Ill. 60602

ISA
Instrument Society of America
PO Box 12277
Research Triangle Park, N.C. 27709

Military Specifications
U.S. Naval Supply Depot
5801 Tabor Ave.
Philadelphia, Pa. 19120

MPTA
Mechanical Power Transmission Association
3451 W. Church St.
Evanston, Ill. 60203

NASC
National Aerospace Standards Committee
1321 Fourteenth St.
Washington, D.C. 20005

NBS
National Bureau of Standards
Washington, D.C. 20234

NEMA
National Electrical Manufacturers Association
2101 L Street NW, Suite 300
Washington, D.C. 20037

NFPA (National Electrical Code)
National Fire Protection Association
Batterymarch Park
Quincy, Mass. 02269

NIBA
National Industrial Belting Association
1900 Arch Street
Philadelphia, Pa. 19103

NLGI
National Lubricating Grease Institute
4635 Wyandotte St.
Kansas City, Mo. 64112

NSC
National Safety Council
444 N. Michigan Ave.
Chicago, Ill. 60611

RIA
Robot Institute of America
PO Box 1366
Dearborn, Mich. 48121

RMA
Rubber Manufacturers Association
1901 Pennsylvania Ave., NW
Washington, D.C. 20006

SAE
Society of Automotive Engineers
400 Commonwealth Drive
Warrendale, Pa. 15096

SME
Society of Manufacturing Engineers
One SME Drive
PO Box 930
Dearborn, Mich. 48128

SMI
Spring Manufacturers Institute
380 W. Palatine Road
Wheeling, Ill. 60090

TWI
The Welding Institute
PO Box 5268
Hilton Head Island, S.C. 29928

UL
Underwriters Laboratories, Inc.
333T Pfingsten Road
Northbrook, Ill. 60062

23.2 Approval Associations and Their Trademarks

See Secs. 8.2 and 8.3 for approval associations and their trademarks.

Bibliography

The Aluminum Association. 1979. *Aluminum Data and Standards,* 6th ed., Washington, D.C.: The association.
Aluminum Company of America. 1960. *Alcoa Structural Handbook.* Pittsburgh, Pa.: Alcoa.
American Institute of Steel Construction. 1991. *Manual of Steel Construction,* 9th ed., Chicago, Ill.: AISC.
American Iron and Steel Institute. 1962. *Light Gage Cold-Formed Steel Design Manual.* New York: AISI.
American Society for Metals. 1961. *Metals Handbook,* Vol. 1: *Properties and Selection of Metals,* 8th ed. Metals Park, Ohio: ASM.
American Society for Metals. 1967. *Metals Handbook,* Vol. 3: *Machining,* 8th ed. Metals Park, Ohio: ASM.
American Society for Metals. 1969. *Metals Handbook,* Vol. 4: *Forming,* 8th ed. Metals Park, Ohio: ASM.
American Society for Testing and Materials. 1992. *Annual Book of ASTM Standards.* Philadelphia, Pa.: ASTM.
American Welding Society. 1991. *Welding Handbook,* 8th ed., Vol. 2. Miami, Fla.: AWS.
Chironis, N. P. 1965. *Mechanisms, Linkages, and Mechanical Controls.* New York: McGraw-Hill.
Copper Development Association. 1964. *Standard Handbook: Copper and Copper Alloys,* CDA pub. no. 101, 5th ed. New York: CDA.
Dallas, D. B. 1976. *Tool and Manufacturing Engineers Handbook,* 3d ed. New York: McGraw-Hill (Society of Manufacturing Engineers).
Dudley, D. W. 1962. *Gear Handbook.* New York: McGraw-Hill.
Dudley, D. W. 1984. *Handbook of Practical Gear Design.* New York: McGraw-Hill.
Durney, L. J. 1984. *Electroplating Engineering Handbook,* 4th ed. New York: Van Nostrand Reinhold.
Eves, H. 1969. *History of Mathematics,* 3d ed. New York: Holt, Reinhart & Winston.
French, T. E., and Vierck, C. J. 1953. *Engineering Drawing,* 8th ed. New York: McGraw-Hill.
Gerolde, S. 1979. *Universal Conversion Factors.* Tulsa, Okla.: Petroleum Publishing Co.
Hall, A. S., Holowenko, A. R., and Laughlin, H. G. 1961. *Machine Design: Theory and Problems.* New York: McGraw-Hill (Shaum's Outline Series).
Hicks, T. G. 1972. *Standard Handbook of Engineering Calculations.* New York: McGraw-Hill.
Industrial Fasteners Institute. 1983. *Metric Fastener Standards,* 2d ed. Cleveland, Ohio: IFI.

Industrial Fasteners Institute. 1988. *Fastener Standards,* 6th ed. Cleveland, Ohio: IFI.

Industrial Information Headquarters, Inc. 1991. *Bearing Manual Cyclopedia,* Vols. 1 and 2. Broadview, Ill.: IIH.

Jones, F. D., and Horton, H. L. 1988. *Machinery's Handbook,* 23d ed. New York: Industrial Press.

LeGrand, R. 1983. *The New American Machinist's Handbook.* New York: McGraw-Hill.

Middlemiss, R. R. 1952. *College Algebra.* New York: McGraw-Hill.

Parmley, R. O. 1977. *Standard Handbook of Fastening and Joining.* New York: McGraw-Hill.

Salmon, S. C. 1992. *Modern Grinding Process Technology.* New York: McGraw-Hill.

Selby, S. M., Weast, R. C., Shankland, R. S., and Hodgman, C. D. 1962. *Handbook of Mathematical Tables.* Cleveland, Ohio: Chemical Rubber Publishing Company.

Shigley, J. E., and Mischke, C. R. 1986. *Standard Handbook of Machine Design.* New York: McGraw-Hill.

Society of Automotive Engineers. 1992. *SAE Handbook,* Vol. 1: *Materials.* Warrendale, Pa.: SAE.

Walsh, R. A. 1990. *Electromechanical Design Handbook.* Blue Ridge Summit, Pa.: TAB Professional and Reference Books, Division of McGraw-Hill.

Wilson, F. W., and Harvey, P. D. 1965. *Die Design Handbook,* 2d ed. New York: McGraw-Hill (Society of Manufacturing Engineers).

Index

Index note: An *f.* after a page number refers to a figure; and *t.* to a table.